ORACLE®

Oracle Press™

Oracle Database 10g: The Complete Reference

Kevin Loney

Tata McGraw-Hill Publishing Company Limited

NEW DELHI

McGraw-Hill Offices

New Delhi New York St Louis San Francisco Auckland Bogotá Caracas
Kuala Lumpur Lisbon London Madrid Mexico City Milan Montreal
San Juan Santiago Singapore Sydney Tokyo Toronto

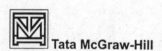

Tata McGraw-Hill

Oracle Database 10g: The Complete Reference

Copyright © 2004 by The McGraw-Hill Companies, Inc.,
All rights reserved. No part of this publication may be reproduced or distributed
in any form or by any means, or stored in a database or retrieval system, without
the prior written permission of the publisher

Tata McGraw-Hill Edition 2004

Third reprint 2006
RQCQCRZKDZDDX

Reprinted in India by arrangement with The McGraw-Hill Companies,
Inc., New York

Sales territories: India, Pakistan, Nepal, Bangladesh, Sri Lanka and Bhutan

ISBN 0-07-059425-2

Published by Tata McGraw-Hill Publishing Company Limited,
7 West Patel Nagar, New Delhi 110 008, and printed at
Pashupati Printers Pvt. Ltd., Delhi 110 095

To my parents, and to Sue, Emily, Rachel, and Jane.

About the Author

Kevin Loney is a senior technical management consultant with TUSC (http://www.tusc.com), an Oracle-focused consultancy headquartered in Chicago. He was selected as *ORACLE Magazine*'s Consultant of the Year in 2002. He is an expert in the design, development, administration, tuning, security, and recovery of Oracle-based applications. An Oracle DBA and developer since 1987, he is the primary author of 15 books for Oracle DBAs and developers. He is a frequent and highly-rated presenter at local and international Oracle user groups.

About the Technical Reviewers

Pete Sharman has 16 years' IT experience designing, implementing, and managing the performance of Oracle solutions. As a solo consultant and team leader, Pete has provided administrative and technical leadership to leading Internet-based businesses as well as several Fortune 100 and Fortune 500 companies. He has also completed world-class benchmarks and implementation reviews of the Oracle RDBMS, and performed high-impact performance tuning. A proven technical leader, Pete has acquired expert-level skills in Oracle Parallel Server and Real Application Clusters database design, administration, backup and recovery, operations planning and management, performance management, system management, and security and management of complex data centers.

Currently, Pete is performing the role of Oracle9*i* and Oracle 10*g* Database Global Consulting Lead, acting as an interface between Oracle Development and North America Sales and Consulting. Pete has also passed all the Oracle DBA Certifications (Oracle7, Oracle8, Oracle8*i*, and Oracle9*i*) and was one of the first 20 people in the world to qualify as an Oracle9*i* Certified Master.

Bob Bryla is an Oracle 8, 8*i*, 9*i*, and 10*g* Certified Professional with more than 15 years of experience in database design, database application development, training, and database administration, and he is the tech editor and author of several Oracle Press and Sybex Oracle DBA books. He is an Internet database analyst and Oracle DBA at Lands' End, Inc., in Dodgeville, Wisconsin.

Contents

PART I
Critical Database Concepts

PART II

SQL and SQL*Plus

PART III

Beyond the Basics

PART IV
PL/SQL

PART V
Object-Relational Databases

PART VI
Java in Oracle

PART VII

Clustered Oracle—The Grid

PART VIII

Hitchhiker's Guides

Acknowledgments

This book is dedicated to my family. Thank you for your patience, support, and love. This book is the product of many hands, and countless hours from many people. My thanks go out to all those who helped, whether through their comments, feedback, edits, or suggestions. For additional information about the book, see the publisher's site (http://www.osborne.com) and my site (http://www.kevinloney.com). Additional articles and presentations can be found on the company site at http://www.tusc.com.

- To the contributors and reviewers at TUSC, including Chris Ostrowski, Brad Brown, and Shaun O'Brien.

- To the management, including Rich Niemiec, Joe Trezzo, Brad Brown, and others for their dedication to the Oracle user community and their commitment to establishing and following best practices.

- To my peers at TUSC, including Bill Callahan, Patrick Callahan, Tony Catalano, Holly Clawson, Judy Corley, Mike Killough, Randy Swanson, Bob Taylor, Bob Yingst, and many others for their insights and contributions.

Thanks to my colleagues and friends, including Eyal Aronoff, Steve Bobrowski, Rachel Carmichael, Steven Feuerstein, Mike McDonnell, Vinny Smith, Susan St. Claire, and Marlene Theriault. This book has benefited from the knowledge they have shared, and I have benefited from their friendship and guidance.

Thanks to the folks at McGraw-Hill/Osborne who guided this product through its stages: Scott Rogers, Athena Honore, Lisa McClain, Patty Mon, Bart Reed, Margaret Berson, Bill McManus, and the others at Osborne with whom I never directly worked. Thanks to the reviewers, including Pete Sharman and Bob Bryla (who also contributed material). Thanks also to the Oracle component of Oracle Press. This book would not have been possible without the earlier excellent work of George Koch and Robert Muller.

Thanks to the writers and friends along the way: Jerry Gross, Jan Riess, Robert Meissner, Marie Paretti, Br. Declan Kane, CFX, Br. William Griffin, CFX, Chris O'Neill, Cheryl Bittner, Bill Fleming, and the FSOUG board.

Special thanks to Sue, Emily, Rachel, Jane, and the rest of the home team. As always, this has been a joint effort.

—Kevin Loney

Introduction

Oracle documentation is thoroughgoing and voluminous, currently spanning multiple CDs. *Oracle Database 10g: The Complete Reference* is the first entity that has gathered all the major Oracle definitions, commands, functions, features, and products together in a single, massive core reference—one volume that every Oracle user and developer can keep handy on his or her desk.

The audience for this book will usually fall into one of three categories:

- **An Oracle end user** Oracle can easily be used for simple operations such as entering data and running standard reports. But such an approach would ignore its great power; it would be like buying a high-performance racing car and then pulling it around with a horse. With the introduction provided in the first two sections of this book, even an end user with little or no data processing background can become a proficient Oracle user—generating ad hoc, English-language reports, guiding developers in the creation of new features and functions, and improving the speed and accuracy of the real work done in a business. The language of the book is simple, clear English without data processing jargon, and with few assumptions about previous knowledge of computers or databases. It will help beginners to become experts with an easy-to-follow format and numerous real examples.

- **A developer who is new to Oracle** With as many volumes of documentation as Oracle provides, finding a key command or concept can be a time-consuming effort. This book attempts to provide a more organized and efficient manner of learning the essentials of the product. The format coaches a developer new to Oracle quickly through the basic concepts, covers areas of common difficulty, examines misunderstandings of the product and relational development, and sets clear guidelines for effective application building.

- **An experienced Oracle developer** As with any product of great breadth and sophistication, there are important issues about which little, if anything, has been published. Knowledge comes through long experience, but is often not transferred to others. This book delves deeply into many such subject areas (including new features such as the flashback options, Data Pump, and many others). The text also reveals many common misconceptions and suggests rigorous guidelines for application development and designing for performance issues.

In Chapter 1, you will see a roadmap to the organization of this book. Briefly, the first part of the book focuses on installing Oracle, upgrading from prior versions of Oracle, and reviewing new features introduced with the latest version. The following sections provide guidance on the technologies you use to exploit Oracle's capabilities—SQL, PL/SQL, dynamic SQL, object-relational features, Java, and more. The chapters progress from basic information on SQL to detailed examples of complex programs.

The final two parts of the book contain the "hitchhiker's guides"—guided tours of the data dictionary, optimizer, tuning case studies, the application server, database administration, and XML—and the Alphabetical Reference. The Alphabetical Reference contains the syntax and description of all functions and commands supported by Oracle Database 10*g*. The reference is intended for use by both developers and users of Oracle but assumes some familiarity with the products.

PART
I

Critical Database
Concepts

CHAPTER
1

Oracle Database 10g
Architecture Options

racle Database 10*g* is a significant upgrade from prior releases of Oracle. New features give developers, database administrators, and end users greater control over the storage, processing, and retrieval of their data. In this chapter, you will see highlights of the Oracle Database 10*g* architecture. You will see detailed discussions of new features such as regular expression support, flashback version queries, and Data Pump in later chapters. The goal of this chapter is to present a high-level overview of the capabilities you can feature in your Oracle applications and provide an introduction to the chapters that describe them.

This book is divided into nine major sections.

In Part I, "Critical Database Concepts," you will see an overview of Oracle Database 10*g*'s options, how to install the Oracle software, how to create or upgrade a database, and advice on planning your application implementation. These chapters establish the common vocabulary that both end users and developers can use to coherently and intelligently share concepts and ensure the success of any development effort. This introductory chapter and Chapter 4 are intended for both developers and end users of Oracle; Chapters 2 and 3 are intended for database administrators.

Part II, "SQL and SQL*Plus," teaches the theory and techniques of relational database systems and applications, including SQL (Structured Query Language) and SQL*Plus. The section begins with relatively few assumptions about data-processing knowledge on the part of the reader and then advances, step by step, through some very deep issues and complex techniques. The method very consciously uses clear, conversational English, with unique and interesting examples, and strictly avoids the use of undefined terms or jargon. This section is aimed primarily at developers and end users who are new to Oracle or need a quick review of certain Oracle features. It moves step by step through the basic capabilities of SQL and Oracle's interactive query facility, SQL*Plus. When you've completed this section, you should have a thorough understanding of all SQL keywords, functions, and operators. Within an Oracle database, you should be able to produce complex queries, create tables, and insert, update, and delete data.

Part III, "Beyond the Basics," covers advanced options, including virtual private databases, Data Pump, replication, text indexing, external tables, and the use of the flashback options for developers and database administrators. Most of the features described in this section will not be directly used by end users, but the applications they use can be based on these features.

Part IV, "PL/SQL," provides coverage of PL/SQL. The topics include a review of PL/SQL structures, plus triggers, stored procedures, and packages. Both standard and native dynamic PL/SQL is covered.

Part V, "Object-Relational Databases," provides extensive coverage of object-oriented features such as abstract datatypes, methods, object views, object tables, nested tables, varying arrays, and large objects.

Part VI, "Java in Oracle," provides coverage of the Java features in the Oracle database. This section includes an overview of Java syntax as well as chapters on JDBC and Java stored procedures.

Part VII, "Clustered Oracle—The Grid," provides an overview of the Real Application Cluster and grid architecture available in Oracle Database 10*g*.

Part VIII contains several "hitchhiker's" guides—to the data dictionary, the database optimizer, Oracle Application Server, database administration, and Oracle's XML implementation. These guides provide an overview of areas that developers may need to use in their application development and administration.

Part IX, the "Alphabetical Reference," is a reference for the Oracle server—a book unto itself. Reading the introductory pages to this reference will make its use much more effective and understandable. This section contains references for most major Oracle commands, keywords, products, features, and functions, with extensive cross-referencing of topics. The reference is

intended for use by both developers and users of Oracle but assumes some familiarity with the products. To make the most productive use of any of the entries, it's worthwhile to read the introductory pages of the reference. These pages explain in greater detail what is and is not included and how to read the entries.

The CD that accompanies this book contains a special electronic edition of *Oracle Database 10g: The Complete Reference*. Now, with this electronic version, you can easily store all the valuable information contained in the book on your PC while the print version of the book remains in your office or home. The CD also contains the table-creation statements and row insertions for all the tables used in this book. For anyone learning Oracle, having these tables available on your own Oracle ID, or on a practice ID, will make trying or expanding on the examples very easy.

Databases and Instances

An Oracle database is a collection of data in one or more files. The database contains physical and logical structures. In the course of developing an application, you create structures such as tables and indexes to store rows and speed their retrieval. You can create synonyms for the object names, view objects in different databases (across database links), and you can restrict access to the objects. You can even use *external tables* to access files outside the database as if the rows in the files were rows in tables. In this book, you will see how to create these objects and develop applications based on them.

An Oracle *instance* comprises a memory area called the *System Global Area (SGA)* and the background processes that interact between the SGA and the database files on disk. In an Oracle Real Application Cluster (RAC), more than one instance will use the same database (see Chapter 40). The instances generally are on separate servers connected by a high-speed interconnect.

Inside the Database

Within the Oracle database, the basic structure is a table. Oracle Database 10*g* supports many types of tables, including the following:

- **Relational tables** Using the Oracle-supplied datatypes (see "Datatypes" in the Alphabetical Reference), you can create tables to store the rows inserted and manipulated by your applications. Tables have column definitions, and you can add or drop columns as the application requirements change. Tables are created via the **create table** command.

- **Object-relational tables** To take advantage of features such as type inheritance, you can use Oracle's object-relational capabilities. You can define your own datatypes and then use them as the basis for column definitions, object tables, nested tables, varying arrays, and more. See Part V of this book.

- **Index-organized tables** You can create a table that stores its data within an index structure, allowing the data to be sorted within the table. See Chapter 17.

- **External tables** Data stored in flat files may be treated as a table that users can query directly and join to other tables in queries. You can use external tables to access large volumes of data without ever loading them into your database. See Chapter 26. Note that Oracle also supports BFILE datatypes, a pointer to an external binary file. Before creating a BFILE or an external table, you must create a directory alias within Oracle

(via the **create directory** command) pointing to the physical location of the file. See Chapter 35 for details on BFILEs and other large object datatypes.

- **Partitioned tables** You can divide a table into multiple partitions, which allows you to separately manage each part of the table. You can add new partitions to a table, split existing partitions, and administer a partition apart from the other partitions of the table. Partitioning may simplify or improve the performance of maintenance activities and user queries. You can partition tables on ranges of values, on lists of values, on hashes of column values, or on combinations of those options. See Chapter 17.

- **Materialized views** A materialized view is a replica of data retrieved by a query. User queries may be redirected to the materialized views to avoid large tables during execution—the optimizer will rewrite the queries automatically. You can establish and manage refresh schedules to keep the data in the materialized views fresh enough for the business needs. See Chapter 24.

- **Temporary tables** You can use the **create global temporary table** command to create a table in which multiple users can insert rows. Each user sees only his or her rows in the table. See Chapter 14.

- **Clustered tables** If two tables are commonly queried together, you can physically store them together via a structure called a *cluster.* See Chapter 17.

- **Dropped tables** As of Oracle Database 10*g,* you can quickly recover dropped tables via the **flashback table to before drop** command. You can flash back multiple tables at once or flash back the entire database to a prior point in time. Oracle supports *flashback queries,* which return earlier versions of rows from an existing table.

To support access to tables, you can use views that perform joins and aggregations, limit the rows returned, or alter the columns displayed. Views may be read-only or updatable, and they can reference local or remote tables. Remote tables can be accessed via database links. You can use synonyms to mask the physical location of the tables. See Chapter 23 for details on database links, and Chapter 17 for details on views and synonyms.

To tune the accesses to these tables, Oracle supports many types of indexes, including the following:

- **B*-tree indexes** A B*-tree index is the standard type of index available in Oracle, and it's very useful for selecting rows that meet an equivalence criteria or a range criteria. Indexes are created via the **create index** command.

- **Bitmap indexes** For columns that have few unique values, a bitmap index may be able to improve query performance. Bitmap indexes should only be used when the data is batch loaded (as in many data warehousing or reporting applications).

- **Reverse key indexes** If there are I/O contention issues during the inserts of sequential values, Oracle can dynamically reverse the indexed values prior to storing them.

- **Function-based indexes** Instead of indexing a column, such as Name, you can index a function-based column, such as **UPPER**(Name). The function-based index gives the Oracle optimizer additional options when selecting an execution path.

■ **Partitioned indexes** You can partition indexes to support partitioned tables or to simplify the index management. Index partitions can be local to table partitions or may globally apply to all rows in the table.

■ **Text indexes** You can index text values to support enhanced searching capabilities, such as expanding word stems or searching for phrases. Text indexes are sets of tables and indexes maintained by Oracle to support complex text-searching requirements. Oracle Database 10*g* offers enhancements to text indexes that simplify their administration and maintenance.

See Chapters 17 and 43 for further details on the index types listed here (excluding text indexes). For text indexes, see Chapter 25.

Storing the Data

All of these logical structures in the database must be stored somewhere in the database. Oracle maintains a data dictionary (see Chapter 42) that records *metadata* about each object—the object owner, a definition, related privileges, and so on. For objects that require physical storage space of their own, Oracle will allocate space within a *tablespace*.

Tablespaces

A tablespace consists of one or more datafiles; a datafile can be a part of one and only one tablespace. Oracle Database 10*g* creates at least two tablespaces for each database—SYSTEM and SYSAUX—to support its internal management needs. You can use Oracle managed files (OMF) to simplify the creation and maintenance of datafiles.

As of Oracle Database 10*g*, you can create a special kind of tablespace, called a *bigfile* tablespace, that can be many thousands of terabytes in size. Along with OMF, the management of bigfiles makes tablespace management completely transparent to the DBA; the DBA can manage the tablespace as a unit without worrying about the size and structure of the underlying datafiles.

If a tablespace is designated as a *temporary* tablespace, the tablespace itself is permanent; only the segments saved in the tablespace are temporary. Oracle uses temporary tablespaces to support sorting operations such as index creations and join processing. Temporary segments should not be stored in the same tablespaces as permanent objects.

Tablespaces can be either *dictionary managed* or *locally managed*. In a dictionary-managed tablespace, space management is recorded in the data dictionary. In a locally managed tablespace (the default in Oracle Database 10*g*), Oracle maintains a bitmap in each datafile of the tablespace to track space availability. Only quotas are managed in the data dictionary, dramatically reducing the contention for data dictionary tables.

Automated Storage Management

Automatic storage management (ASM), available as of Oracle Database 10*g*, automates the layout of datafiles and other operating system–level files used by the database, by distributing them across all available disks. When new disks are added to the ASM instance, the database files are automatically redistributed across all disks in the defined disk group for optimal performance. The multiplexing features of an ASM instance minimize the possibility of data loss and are generally more effective than a manual scheme that places critical files and backups on different physical drives. See Chapter 46.

Automatic Undo Management

To support your transactions, Oracle can dynamically create and manage *undo segments,* which help maintain prior images of the changed blocks and rows. Users who have previously queried the rows you are changing will still see the rows as they existed when their queries began. Automatic Undo Management (AUM) allows Oracle to manage the undo segments directly with no database administrator intervention required. The use of AUM also simplifies the use of flashback queries. As of Oracle Database 10*g,* you can execute *flashback version queries* to see the different versions of a row as it changed during a specified time interval. See Chapter 27 for further details on the use of undo segments, flashback queries, and flashback version queries.

Dropped Data

The *recycle bin* concept introduced with Oracle Database 10*g* impacts the space requirements for your tablespaces and datafiles. In Oracle Database 10*g,* the default behavior for the drop of a table is for the table to retain its space allocation; you can see its space usage via the RECYCLEBIN data dictionary view. If you create and drop a table twice, there will be two copies of the table in the recycle bin. Although this architecture greatly simplifies recoveries of accidentally dropped tables, it may considerably increase the space used in your database. Use the **purge** command to remove old entries from your recycle bin. See the Alphabetical Reference for the syntax of the **purge** command.

Guarding the Data

You can fully control the access to your data. You can grant other users privileges to perform specific functions (such as **select**, **insert**, and so on) on your objects. You can pass along the right to execute further grants. You can grant privileges to roles, which are then granted to users, grouping privileges into manageable sets.

Oracle supports a very detailed level of privileges; you can control which rows are accessible and, during auditing, which rows trigger audit events to be recorded. When you use the Virtual Private Database (VPD) option, users' queries of tables are always limited regardless of the method by which they access the tables. As of Oracle Database 10*g,* VPD has been further enhanced to include column masking for columns containing sensitive data. See Chapter 19 for details on the implementation of VPD.

In addition to securing access to the data, you can audit activities in the database. Auditable events include privileged actions (such as creating users), changes to data structures, and access of specific rows and tables.

Programmatic Structures

Oracle supports a wide array of programmatic access methods. The SQL language, described in detail throughout this book, is key to any application development effort. Other access methods include the following:

- **PL/SQL** As described in Part IV of this book, PL/SQL is a critical component of most application implementations. You can use PL/SQL to create stored procedures and functions, and you can call your functions within queries. Procedures and functions can be collected into packages. You can also create triggers, telling the database what steps to take when different events occur within the database. Triggers may occur during database events (such as database startup), changes to structures (such as attempts to drop

tables), or changes to rows. In each case, you will use PL/SQL to control the behavior of the database or application when the triggering event occurs.

- **Dynamic SQL** You can generate SQL at run time and pass it to procedures that execute it via dynamic SQL. See Chapter 32.

- **SQL*Plus** As shown throughout this book, SQL*Plus provides a simple interface to the Oracle database. SQL*Plus can support rudimentary reporting requirements, but it is better known for its support of scripting. It provides a consistent interface for retrieving data from the data dictionary and creating database objects.

- **Java and JDBC** As shown in Part VI of this book, Oracle's support for Java and JDBC allow you to use Java in place of PL/SQL for many operations. You can even write Java-based stored procedures. Oracle's Java offerings have been expanded and enhanced with each new release.

- **XML** As described in Chapter 47, you can use Oracle's XML interfaces and XML types to support inserting and retrieving data via XML.

- **Object-oriented SQL and PL/SQL** You can use Oracle to create and access object-oriented structures, including user-defined datatypes, methods, large objects (LOBs), object tables, and nested tables. See Part V.

- **Data Pump** Data Pump Import and Data Pump Export, both introduced in Oracle Database 10*g*, greatly enhance the manageability and performance of the earlier Import and Export utilities. You can use Data Pump to quickly extract data and move it to different databases while altering the schema and changing the rows. See Chapter 22 for details on the use of Data Pump.

- **SQL*Loader** You can use SQL*Loader to quickly load flat files into Oracle tables. A single flat file can be loaded into multiple tables during the same load, and loads can be parallelized. See Chapter 21.

- **External programs and procedures** You can embed SQL within external programs, or you can create procedural libraries that are later linked to Oracle. See Chapter 31.

- **UTL_MAIL** A package introduced in Oracle Database 10*g*, UTL_MAIL allows a PL/SQL application developer to send e-mails without having to know how to use the underlying SMTP protocol stack.

Choosing Architectures and Options

Oracle provides a full array of tools for developing applications based on Oracle Database 10*g*. Although this book does not cover each of the possible tools and their uses, see Chapter 45 for a detailed overview of the Oracle Application Server and its capabilities. You can use Oracle Application Server as the middle tier for three-tier applications that access Oracle Database 10*g*.

Many of the features introduced with Oracle Database 10*g* will be available to you regardless of the application architecture you select. These features include database administration features such as automatic storage management, automatic tuning, and automatic resizing of the memory areas in the SGA. See Chapter 46 for descriptions of the primary tasks performed by database administrators.

If you have previously implemented applications in earlier versions of Oracle, you should review your database to identify areas where new features will benefit your application. For example, if you have previously implemented materialized views, you may be able to take advantage of new features that expand the possibilities for incremental ("fast") refreshes of the materialized views. Oracle provides a set of procedures that help you manage your materialized view refresh schedule. For example, you can execute a procedure that will generate a description of your refresh possibilities and the configuration issues (if any) that prevent you from using the fastest options possible. You can use another Oracle-provided procedure to generate recommendations for tuning materialized view structures based on a provided set of sample queries.

Some of the new features may contain small changes that can have dramatic impact on your application or your coding approach. For example, regular expression searches are available as of Oracle Database 10g. If you are not performing complex string searches, you may decide not to change an existing application to use the new search functions. However, the regular expression search functionality includes the ability to perform case-insensitive searches—potentially eliminating the need for other function calls or function-based indexes. You should evaluate your previous architecture decisions in light of the new features available.

In the next several chapters, you will see how to install Oracle Database 10g and how to upgrade to Oracle Database 10g from prior releases. Following those chapters, you will see an overview of application planning, followed by many chapters on the use of SQL, PL/SQL, Java, object-oriented features, and XML to get the most out of your Oracle database. Your application architecture may change over time as the business process changes. During those changes you should be sure to review the latest features to determine how your application can best exploit them for functionality and performance.

CHAPTER
2

Installing Oracle
Database 10g and
Creating a Database

s Oracle's installation software becomes easier to use with each release, it is very tempting to open the box of CDs and start the installation right away. Although this is fine if you're going to experiment with some new database features, a lot more planning is required to perform a successful installation without rework or even reinstallation a month from now. Although the complete details of an Oracle Database 10*g* installation are beyond the scope of this book, you will see the basics of an Oracle install using the Oracle Universal Installer (OUI), along with a basic template for doing a manual install of the database using the **create database** command. In any case, a thorough review of the installation guide for your specific platform is another key to a successful Oracle database deployment.

NOTE
Although this chapter is intended for beginning database administrators, the planning process should include end users, application developers, and system administrators, so the workload and space requirements will be as accurate as possible.

The following issues should be addressed or resolved before you start the installation:

- Decide on the local database name, and which domain will contain this database. These names are set in the initialization parameters DB_NAME and DB_DOMAIN.

- For the first project to use the database, estimate the number of tables and indexes as well as their size, to plan for disk space estimates beyond what is required for the Oracle SYSTEM tablespace and the associated Oracle software and tools.

- Plan the locations of the physical datafiles on the server's disk to maximize performance and recoverability. In general, the more physical disks, the better. If a RAID or Network Attached Storage area will be used for the datafiles, consider Oracle Managed Files to manage the placement of the datafiles. As of Oracle Database 10*g*, you can use automatic storage management (ASM) to simplify your storage management. See Chapter 46 for details on ASM.

- Review and understand the basic initialization parameters.

- Select the database character set, along with an alternate character set. Although it's easy to let the character sets default on install, you may need to consider where the users of the database are located and their language requirements. Character sets can be changed after installation only if the new character set is a superset of the existing character set.

- Decide on the best default database block size. The default block size defined by DB_ BLOCK_SIZE cannot be changed later without reinstalling the database. Note that Oracle can support multiple block sizes within a single database.

- Plan to store non-SYSTEM user objects in non-SYSTEM tablespaces. Make sure that all nonadministrative users are assigned a non-SYSTEM tablespace as their default tablespace.

- Plan to implement Automatic Undo Management to ease administration of transaction undo information.

- Plan a backup and recovery strategy. Decide how the database needs to be backed up, and how often. Plan to use more than one method to back up the database.

Familiarity with a couple of key Web sites is a must. Oracle Technology Network (OTN), at http://otn.oracle.com, has a wealth of information, including white papers, free tools, sample code, and the online version of *Oracle Magazine*. There is no charge for using OTN, other than registering on the site.

Purchasing a license for Oracle database software is a good start, but an Oracle support contract with Web support may be the key to a successful installation and deployment. Using Oracle's Metalink (http://metalink.oracle.com) means you might never have to leave the friendly confines of your Web browser to keep your database up and running. Through Metalink, you can submit a support request, search through other support requests, download patches, download white papers, and search the bug database.

Overview of Licensing and Installation Options

A successful initial software installation is the first step. Regardless of the software and hardware platform on which you're installing Oracle, the types of installations you can perform are the same. Although these may change with product releases, they generally include the following:

- **Enterprise Edition** This is the most feature rich and extensible version of the Oracle database. It includes features such as Flashback Database and allows you to add additional pieces of licensed functionality, such as Oracle Spatial, Oracle OLAP, Oracle Label Security, and Oracle Data Mining.

- **Standard Edition** This edition provides a good subset of the features of the Enterprise Edition, generally including the features that a small business will need.

- **Personal Edition** This edition allows for development of applications that will run on either the Standard or Enterprise Edition. This edition cannot be used in a production environment.

As of Oracle Database 10*g*, licensing for the Oracle database is only by named user or CPU, and there is no longer a concurrent user licensing option. Therefore, the DBA should use the initialization parameter LICENSE_MAX_USERS to specify the maximum number of users that can be created in the database. As a result, LICENSE_MAX_SESSIONS and LICENSE_SESSIONS_WARNING are deprecated in Oracle Database 10*g*.

In addition, the Oracle Management Server (the back end for an Oracle Enterprise Manager, or OEM, client) can be installed during a server- or client-side installation. However, it is recommended that this installation be performed after a basic database installation has been completed.

Using OUI to Install the Oracle Software

Use the *Oracle Universal Installer (OUI)* to install and manage all Oracle components for both the server-side and client-side components. You can also deinstall any Oracle products from the initial OUI screens.

During the server installation, you will choose the version of Oracle Database 10*g* from the list in the previous section: Enterprise Edition, Standard Edition, or one of the other options available for your platform.

It is strongly recommended that you create a starter database when prompted during the install. Creating the starter database is a good way to make sure the server environment is set up correctly, as well as to review any new features of Oracle Database 10*g*. The starter database may also be a good candidate as a repository for either OEM or Recovery Manager.

The exact flow of the installation process may change depending on your operating environment and Oracle version.

NOTE
For UNIX environments, you will need to set a proper value for the DISPLAY environment variable and enable xhost prior to starting OUI via the runInstaller script.

For the major steps related to database creation, figures of screen contents will be shown in the next section of this chapter.

NOTE
The following steps are based on a custom installation. Standard installations may not prompt you for all the steps described here.

In general, the steps will be as follows:

1. An opening screen, choose to install products or deinstall previously installed products.

2. Specify source file locations for the products you want to install and the home directory into which the Oracle software will be installed. The installer should present you with default values. In general, the default values for the software source files should be correct, whereas the others may have to be changed.

3. Select a product to install. Your options here will include the database and the client. If you received a client or companion CD with the installation media, you should install that as well because it will include important files and software libraries. If you select the "database" option, OUI will install a preconfigured starter database, product options, management tools, networking services, and basic client software for the Oracle database server. If you select the "client" option, OUI will install enterprise management tools, networking services, utilities, development tools, precompilers, and basic client software. For your first installation, you should use the "database" option to create the starter database.

4. Choose installation type—Enterprise Edition, Personal Edition, or Custom.

5. If you chose the "database" option in step 3, you will now be prompted to confirm the creation of the starter database.

6. You will be prompted to choose among standard database configurations (general purpose, transaction processing, or data warehouse).

7. For the starter database, choose the database configuration options. These options include the global database name, the instance name, the character set, and whether or not to include sample schemas.

8. Specify a single password to use for all preloaded schemas in the starter database, or specify separate passwords for all accounts.

9. Specify the database storage option to use. If you are using file system files, specify the directories to use. Other options include automatic storage management and raw devices.

10. You will be prompted to finalize the selection of management and services options prior to accepting the configuration and beginning the installation.

During the software installation, the *Database Configuration Assistant (DBCA)* takes over and prompts you for the parameters necessary to size and configure your database (starting at step 6 in this list). The installation steps in the next session assume that you have already completed the software installation and created a starter database; we will create and configure a second database on the same server with DBCA.

NOTE
As of Oracle 10g, DBCA can configure nodes in a Real Application Clusters environment.

Using DBCA to Create a Database

In UNIX, you can start DBCA by executing the dbca file located in the $ORACLE_HOME/bin directory. You must configure your DISPLAY environment variable and xhost settings prior to starting DBCA.

In Windows, DBCA is located under the Configuration and Migration Tools submenu under the Oracle programs menu.

In the subsections that follow, you will receive tips and guidance for most of the screens during the creation of the database.

DBCA Options

After an initial welcome screen, you are presented with a choice of four options:

- **Create a Database** This one is fairly straightforward; you are creating a new database from scratch, using a template as a starting point.

- **Configure Database Options in a Database** Some of the system parameters for an existing database installation can be changed, such as changing from a dedicated server mode to shared server.

- **Delete a Database** This one is also straightforward—and very dangerous! It will shut down the database and delete all the datafiles and control files associated with the database. You will need the SYS or SYSTEM password to proceed with this option.

- **Manage Templates** This option allows you to add, modify, or delete templates. During a DBCA session, once all database parameters have been gathered, you have the option to save your settings as a template. In many cases, the predefined templates that Oracle provides are not quite perfect for your environment, and it is a time-saver to be able to save your database options for selection as a template in a future DBCA session.

Selecting a Database Template

In Figure 2-1, you are presented with the list of templates available. If you have created your own templates in previous DBCA sessions, they will appear on this screen also.

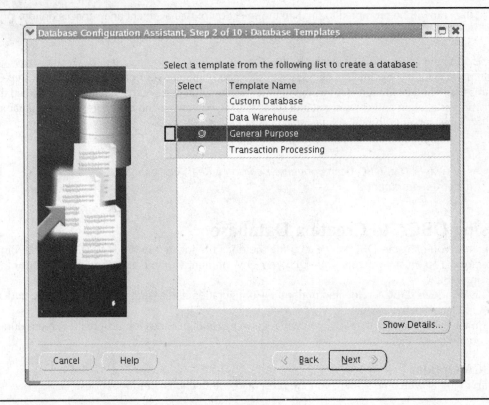

FIGURE 2-1. *Database template selection screen*

The template choices are as follows:

- **Custom Database** Use this option if you have performed many installations and know ahead of time the values for all the options you need in the database. This option is good if you are creating a new template from scratch or have very specific requirements for the configuration of your database.

- **Data Warehouse** This template is for database environments where users are performing numerous, complex queries that join many large tables for reporting, forecasting, and analytics.

- **General Purpose** If you are not sure of the intended use of your database yet, or if you need to host users with both analytical and transaction-processing requirements, choose this template.

- **Transaction Processing** In 24×7 environments where the number of users is high, the transactions are heavy but short, and the bulk of the activity is creating and updating, use this template.

In this installation, we are choosing the General Purpose template. It combines the features of both a data warehouse and an OLTP environment into a single database; use this option if you

must use this database for both environments. Ideally, however, any database you create should be configured and tuned for the types of users and transactions on the database.

Database Identification

In the next step of DBCA, you will identify the name of the instance along with the global database name.

> **NOTE**
> *If the global database name needs to be changed in the future, you must use the **alter database** command to change it, in addition to changing it in the initialization parameter file. The global database name is stored in the data dictionary when the database is created.*

Unless you have an existing domain, use the default domain name .world. Check with your system administrator to see if a specific global database name should be used.

Database Credentials

Figure 2-2 shows the setting of the initial passwords for the SYS and SYSTEM user accounts. After the installation, be sure to create at least one account with DBA privileges to use instead of SYS or SYSTEM for day-to-day administrative tasks.

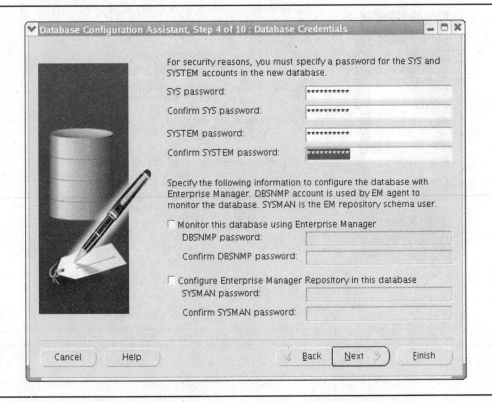

FIGURE 2-2. *Database Credentials screen*

On this screen, you can also set up this instance to be included as a managed node in an existing OEM environment, or you can specify this instance as the OEM Repository. If you specify this node as the OEM Repository, it is strongly recommended that this node be used only for that purpose.

Storage Options

The database can use a number of different methods for storing datafiles, control files, and redo log files. If you have the resources to dedicate another database instance for managing disk space, choose ASM. If you are in a Real Application Clusters environment and you don't have a cluster file system available (such as OCFS), choose Raw Devices. Figure 2-3 shows these options on the Storage Options screen.

File Locations

The next screen, shown in Figure 2-4, is where you select the locations for datafiles, control files, and redo log files, as well as the archiving and backup and recovery locations.

New to Oracle Database 10*g* is the concept of a Flash Recovery Area. This is a dedicated location on disk, separate from the location of the database's operational files, containing the

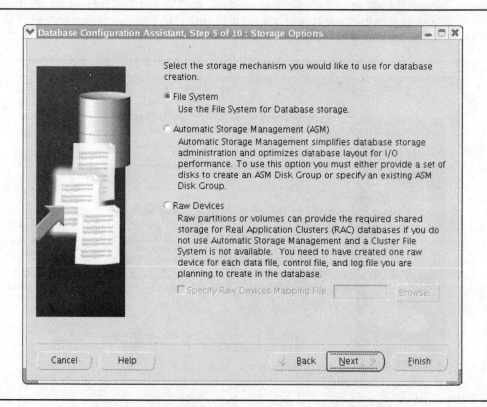

FIGURE 2-3. *Storage Options screen*

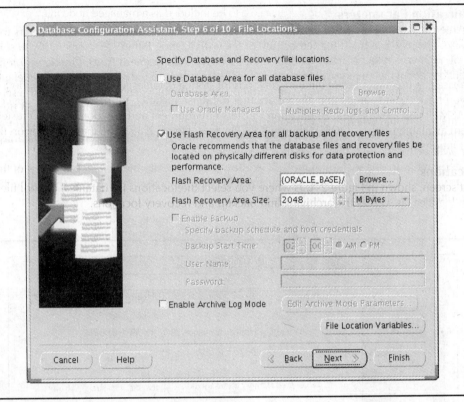

FIGURE 2-4. *File Locations screen*

backup files from RMAN (Recovery Manager). It is highly recommended that you use a Flash
Recovery Area so that RMAN can more easily manage backup and recovery operations. Be sure
that the Flash Recovery Area is large enough to hold at least two copies of all datafiles, incremental
backups, control files, SPFILEs, and archived redo log files that are still on disk.

You can also enable ARCHIVELOG mode, as well as specify the location or locations for the
archived redo log files. It is recommended that you leave archiving off until the database is installed,
because enabling it will increase the database creation time. The parameters for ARCHIVELOG mode
can easily be changed in init.ora or the SPFILE immediately after the database is up and running.

Database Components

In the next step of the DBCA session, you are asked about installing sample schemas. In non-
production databases, it is highly recommended that you install the sample schemas; many tutorials
and study guides rely on the sample schemas being in the database. They are also useful in that the
samples demonstrate nearly all datatypes and constructs available in the database, ranging from
bitmapped indexes to clustered tables and object types.

Initialization Parameters

The screen shown in Figure 2-5 allows the DBA to adjust the key initialization parameters for the database. Figure 2-5 shows the Memory tab of the Initialization Parameters screen. If you select Typical, or if you select Custom with Shared Memory Management Auto, Oracle will make assumptions about the memory it can use for the SGA and background processes. Even by defaulting many of the parameters in a Typical configuration, you can still specify how much of the server's physical memory should be used for Oracle, depending on how much memory is used by the operating system and whether any other applications are going to be running on this server along with Oracle. The value for Java Pool must be at least the size of one granule in the database, either 4MB or 16MB, but at least 20MB is recommended.

Later screens in this section of the DBCA allow you to specify the default block size of the database, the total number of processes that will be simultaneously connecting, the connection mode to use, and the character set for the database.

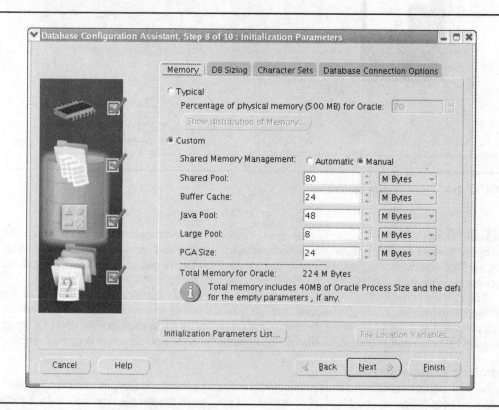

FIGURE 2-5. *Initialization Parameters screen's Memory tab*

Database Storage

On the DBCA Database Storage screen, you can review and revise the locations of the control files, datafiles, and redo log files, as well as multiplex the control files and create redo log file groups. The names and locations of the control files on this screen determine the value of CONTROL_FILES in the initialization parameter file.

Creation Options

In Figure 2-6, we are ready to create the database. In addition, we can use the information we provided in the previous screens and save it to a template. If in doubt, save it as a template; the storage required to save only a template is minimal, and it can easily be deleted later by rerunning DBCA.

Before the database is created, an HTML summary of your template is presented, and you have the option to save this report as an HTML file for documentation purposes.

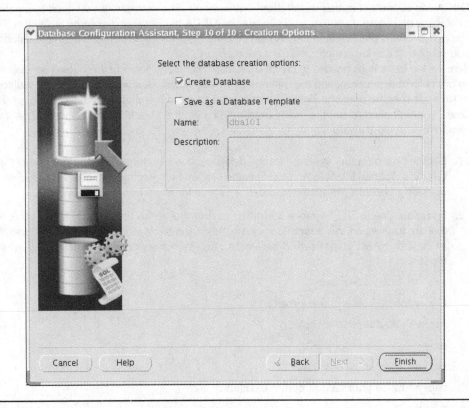

FIGURE 2-6. *Database and template creation options*

Completing the Installation

After you click OK on the Summary screen, DBCA performs the tasks needed to create the database and start the instance. A standard set of scripts is run when the database first starts; this includes the scripts that create the sample schemas, plus any custom scripts you may have specified earlier. The standard set of scripts will vary depending on the options you've selected via the DBCA.

Once the initialization and creation scripts have completed, a summary screen is presented, giving the location of the log file for this installation. It is recommended that you review this log file to ensure that there were no unexpected errors during the install. You should also save this log file with the other documentation for this database; it can also be useful for future installations as a baseline.

The Oracle database you just created is up and running. You have the option to unlock other accounts created during this install and to assign passwords to them.

Manually Creating a Database

The DBCA can support complex installation requirements. For example, if you need to create the same database on different servers, you can use the DBCA to create and execute templates.

You can manually create a database instead of using DBCA. Oracle provides a sample database-creation script that can be customized for a manual install.

Here are the basic steps needed to create a database manually. Some of these steps are operating system or platform dependent, and the differences will be noted. Be sure to review the Installation Guide for your specific platform before attempting a manual installation. For example, under Windows, you will need to run the utility **oradim** to create the Oracle background process and to set the relevant registry values.

1. Decide on a directory structure for the database; it is recommended that you comply with Oracle's Optimal Flexible Architecture standards when placing your files on disk. See your operating system's Installation Guide for Oracle for more information on OFA.

2. Select an Oracle SID (instance identifier) to distinguish this instance from any other ones that are running on this server. Frequently, this is the same as the database name specified in the DB_NAME initialization parameter. In a Windows command prompt, you will type this:

   ```
   set ORACLE_SID=rjbdb
   ```

 Under UNIX, you will use either

   ```
   export ORACLE_SID=rjbdb
   ```

 or

   ```
   setenv ORACLE_SID=rjbdb
   ```

 depending on your default command shell.

3. Establish an authentication method for connecting privileged users to the database. Use the **orapwd** command-line utility to create a password file if you want Oracle to authenticate the privileged users; you will set the initialization parameter REMOTE_LOGIN_PASSWORDFILE to EXCLUSIVE. If you are using operating system authentication, there is no need for a password file; therefore, set REMOTE_LOGIN_PASSWORDFILE to NONE.

4. Create an initialization parameter file and place it in the default location for your platform, at least initially for the install. Under UNIX, the default location is $ORACLE_HOME/dbs; under Windows, it is $ORACLE_HOME\database. Here is a sample initialization file:

```
# Cache and I/O
DB_BLOCK_SIZE=4096
DB_CACHE_SIZE=20971520

# Cursors and Library Cache
CURSOR_SHARING=SIMILAR
OPEN_CURSORS=300

# Diagnostics and Statistics
BACKGROUND_DUMP_DEST=/u01/oracle10g/admin/rjbdb/bdump
CORE_DUMP_DEST=/u01/oracle10g/admin/rjbdb/cdump
TIMED_STATISTICS=TRUE
USER_DUMP_DEST=/u01/oracle10g/admin/rjbdb/udump

# Control File Configuration
CONTROL_FILES=("/u01/oracle10g/prod/rjbdb/control01.ctl",
                "/u02/oracle10g/prod/rjbdb/control02.ctl",
                "/u03/oracle10g/prod/rjbdb/control03.ctl")

# Archive
LOG_ARCHIVE_DEST_1='LOCATION=/u06/oracle10g/oradata/rjbdb/archive'
# New log archive format. If compatibility 10.0 and up,
# this is enforced.
LOG_ARCHIVE_FORMAT=%t_%s_%r.dbf
# The following parameter is deprecated in 10iR1
# LOG_ARCHIVE_START=TRUE

# Shared Server
# Starts shared server if set > 0.
SHARED_SERVERS=2
# Uncomment and use first DISPATCHERS parameter
# below when your listener is
# configured for SSL
# (listener.ora and sqlnet.ora)
# DISPATCHERS = "(PROTOCOL=TCPS)(SER=MODOSE)",
#                "(PROTOCOL=TCPS)(PRE=oracle.aurora.server.SGiopServer)"
DISPATCHERS="(PROTOCOL=TCP)(SER=MODOSE)",
            "(PROTOCOL=TCP)(PRE=oracle.aurora.server.SGiopServer)",
            (PROTOCOL=TCP)

# Miscellaneous
COMPATIBLE=10.0.0
DB_NAME=rjbdb
```

```
# Distributed, Replication and Snapshot
DB_DOMAIN=rjbdba.com
REMOTE_LOGIN_PASSWORDFILE=EXCLUSIVE

# Network Registration
INSTANCE_NAME=rjbdb

# Pools
JAVA_POOL_SIZE=31457280
LARGE_POOL_SIZE=1048576
SHARED_POOL_SIZE=52428800

# Processes and Sessions
PROCESSES=150

# Redo Log and Recovery
FAST_START_MTTR_TARGET=300

# Resource Manager
RESOURCE_MANAGER_PLAN=SYSTEM_PLAN

# Sort, Hash Joins, Bitmap Indexes
SORT_AREA_SIZE=524288

# Automatic Undo Management
UNDO_MANAGEMENT=AUTO
UNDO_TABLESPACE=undotbs
```

5. Connect to the instance using SQL*Plus:

```
sqlplus /nolog
connect SYS/password as sysdba
```

Note that although the instance itself exists, there is not much we can do with it because we have not created the database yet.

6. Create a server parameter file (SPFILE). If the initialization file is in the default location, the following command will create the SPFILE:

```
create spfile from pfile;
```

7. Start the instance using the following command:

```
startup nomount
```

Note that because we do not have a database created yet, this is the only option we can use with the **startup** command.

8. Issue the **create database** command. Here is an example (note that we are specifying passwords for the SYS and SYSTEM accounts):

```
CREATE DATABASE rjbdb
  USER SYS IDENTIFIED BY paris703
```

```
USER SYSTEM IDENTIFIED BY tyler12
LOGFILE GROUP 1 ('/u02/oracle10g/oradata/rjbdb/redo01.log') SIZE 100M,
        GROUP 2 ('/u04/oracle10g/oradata/rjbdb/redo02.log') SIZE 100M,
        GROUP 3 ('/u06/oracle10g/oradata/rjbdb/redo03.log') SIZE 100M
MAXLOGFILES 6
MAXLOGMEMBERS 5
MAXLOGHISTORY 1
MAXDATAFILES 100
MAXINSTANCES 1
CHARACTER SET US7ASCII
NATIONAL CHARACTER SET AL16UTF16
DATAFILE '/u01/oracle10g/oradata/rjbdb/system01.dbf' SIZE 325M REUSE
EXTENT MANAGEMENT LOCAL
SYSAUX DATAFILE '/u01/oracle10g/oradata/rjbdb/sysaux01.dbf'
    SIZE 325M REUSE
DEFAULT TABLESPACE tbs_1
DEFAULT TEMPORARY TABLESPACE tempts1
    TEMPFILE '/u01/oracle10g/oradata/rjbdb/temp01.dbf'
    SIZE 20M REUSE
UNDO TABLESPACE undotbs
    DATAFILE '/u02/oracle10g/oradata/rjbdb/undotbs01.dbf'
    SIZE 200M REUSE AUTOEXTEND ON MAXSIZE UNLIMITED;
```

Several things are worth noting in this example. We are explicitly setting the passwords for SYS and SYSTEM; if we didn't specify them here, they will default to "change_on_install" and "manager," respectively.

The redo log file groups have only one member each; once our database is in production, we should multiplex them. Because we specified an undo tablespace with the UNDO_TABLESPACE parameter in the initialization parameter file, we need to create that tablespace here; otherwise, the instance will not start.

After the **create database** command completes successfully, the database is mounted and opened for use.

9. Create additional tablespaces for users, indexes, and applications.

10. Build data dictionary views with the supplied scripts catalog.sql and catproc.sql. The script catalog.sql creates views against the data dictionary tables, dynamic performance views, and public synonyms for most of the views. The group PUBLIC is granted read-only access to the views. The script catproc.sql sets up PL/SQL.

11. Back up the database using either a cold backup or Recovery Manager. In case of a database failure in the early stages of deployment, you have a complete and running database to fall back on, and most likely you will not have to re-create the database from scratch.

You have now installed the Oracle software, created the starter database, and optionally created a second database. In the next chapter, you will see how to upgrade to Oracle Database 10*g* from prior releases of Oracle.

CHAPTER
3

Upgrading to
Oracle Database 10g

f you have previously installed an earlier version of the Oracle database server, you can upgrade your database to Oracle Database 10g. Multiple upgrade paths are supported; the right choice for you will depend on factors such as your current Oracle software version and your database size. In this chapter, you will see descriptions of these methods along with guidelines for their use.

If you have not used a version of Oracle prior to Oracle Database 10g, you can skip this chapter for now. However, you will likely need to refer to it when you upgrade from Oracle Database 10g to a later version or when you migrate data from a different database into your database.

Prior to beginning the upgrade, you should read the Oracle Database 10g Installation Guide for your operating system. A successful installation is dependent on a properly configured environment—including operating system patch levels and system parameter settings. Plan to get the installation and upgrade right the first time, rather than attempting to restart a partially successful installation.

This chapter assumes that your installation of the Oracle Database 10g software (see Chapter 2) completed successfully and that you have an Oracle database that uses an earlier version of the Oracle software. To upgrade that database, you have four options:

■ *Use the Database Upgrade Assistant to guide and perform the upgrade in place.* The old database will become an Oracle 10g database during this process.

■ *Perform a manual upgrade of the database.* The old database will become an Oracle 10g database during this process.

■ *Use the Export and Import utilities to move data from an earlier version of Oracle to the Oracle 10g database.* Two separate databases will be used—the old database as the source for the export, and the new database as the target for the import.

■ *Copy data from an earlier version of Oracle to an Oracle 10g database.* Two separate databases will be used—the old database as the source for the copy, and the new database as the target for the copy.

Upgrading a database in place—via either the Database Upgrade Assistant or the manual upgrade path—is called a *direct upgrade*. Because a direct upgrade does not involve creating a second database for the one being upgraded, it may complete faster and require less disk space than an indirect upgrade.

NOTE
Direct upgrade of the database to version 10 is only supported if your present database is using one of these releases of Oracle: 8.0.6, 8.1.7, 9.0.1, or 9.2. If you are using any other release, you will have to first upgrade the database to one of those releases, or you will need to use a different upgrade option. Oracle 8.0.6 is only supported for some versions (generally 64-bit), so be sure to check the online certification matrixes at Oracle's Metalink site.

NOTE
Plan your upgrades carefully; you may need to allow time for multiple incremental upgrades (such as from 8.1.6 to 8.1.7) prior to upgrading to Oracle Database 10g.

Choosing an Upgrade Method

As described in the previous section, two direct upgrade paths and two indirect upgrade paths are available. In this section, you will see a more detailed description of the options, followed by usage descriptions.

In general, the direct upgrade paths will perform the upgrade the fastest because they upgrade the database in place. The other methods involve copying data, either to an Export dump file on the file system or across a database link. For very large databases, the time required to completely re-create the database via the indirect methods may exclude them as viable options.

The first direct method relies on the *Database Upgrade Assistant (DBUA)*. DBUA is an interactive tool that guides you through the upgrade process. DBUA evaluates your present database configuration and recommends modifications that can be implemented during the upgrade process. These recommendations may include the sizing of files and the specifications for the new SYSAUX tablespace. After you accept the recommendations, DBUA performs the upgrade in the background while a progress panel is displayed. DBUA is very similar in approach to Database Configuration Assistant (DBCA). As discussed in Chapter 2, DBCA is a graphical interface to the steps and parameters required to make the upgrade a success.

The second direct method is called a *manual upgrade*. Whereas DBUA runs scripts in the background, the manual upgrade path involves database administrators' running the scripts themselves. The manual upgrade approach gives you a great deal of control, but it also adds to the level of risk in the upgrade because you must perform the steps in the proper order.

You can use Export and Import as an indirect method for upgrading a database. In this method, you export the data from the old version of the database and then import it into a database that uses the new version of the Oracle software. This process may require disk space for multiple copies of the data—in the source database, in the Export dump file, and in the target database. In exchange for these costs, this method gives you great flexibility in choosing which data will be migrated. You can select specific tablespaces, schemas, tables, and rows to be exported.

In the Export/Import method, the original database is not upgraded; its data is extracted and moved, and the database can then either be deleted or be run in parallel with the new database until testing of the new database has been completed. In the process of performing the export/import, you are selecting and reinserting each row of the database. If the database is very large, the import process may take a long time, impacting your ability to provide the upgraded database to your users in a timely fashion. See Chapters 22 and 46 for details on the Export and Import utilities.

NOTE
Depending on the version of the source database, you will need to use a specific version of the Export and Import utilities. See "Export and Import Versions to Use" later in this chapter.

In the data-copying method, you issue a series of **create table as select** or **insert as select** commands that cross database links (see Chapter 23) to retrieve the source data. The tables are created in the Oracle 10*g* database based on queries of data from a separate source database. This method allows you to bring over data incrementally and to limit the rows and columns migrated. However, you will need to be careful that the copied data maintains all the necessary relationships among tables. As with the Export/Import method, this method may require a significant amount of time for large databases.

Selecting the proper upgrade method requires you to evaluate the technical expertise of your team, the data that is to be migrated, and the allowable downtime for the database during the migration. In general, using DBUA will be the method of choice for very large databases, whereas smaller databases may use an indirect method.

Before Upgrading

Prior to beginning the migration, you should back up the existing database and database software. If the migration fails for some reason and you are unable to revert the database or software to its earlier version, you will be able to restore your backup and re-create your database.

You should develop and test scripts that will allow you to evaluate the performance and functionality of the database following the upgrade. This evaluation may include the performance of specific database operations or the overall performance of the database under a significant user load.

Prior to executing the upgrade process on a production database, you should attempt the upgrade on a test database so that any missing components (such as operating system patches) can be identified and the time required for the upgrade can be measured.

Prior to performing a direct upgrade, you should analyze the data dictionary tables. During the upgrade process to Oracle Database 10*g*, the data dictionary will be analyzed if it has not been analyzed already, so performing this step in advance will aid the performance of the upgrade.

Using the Database Upgrade Assistant

You can start the Database Upgrade Assistant (DBUA) via the

```
dbua
```

command (in UNIX environments) or by selecting "Database Upgrade Assistant" from the Oracle Configuration and Migration Tools menu option (in Windows environments).

When started, DBUA will display a Welcome screen. At the next screen, select the database you want to upgrade from the list of available databases. You can upgrade only one database at a time.

After you make your selection, the upgrade process begins. DBUA will perform preupgrade checks (such as for obsolete initialization parameters or files that are too small). DBUA will then create the SYSAUX tablespace, a standard tablespace in all Oracle 10*g* databases. You can override Oracle's defaults for the location and size parameters for the datafiles used by the SYSAUX tablespace.

DBUA will then prompt you to recompile invalid PL/SQL objects (see Part IV of this book) following the upgrade. If you do not recompile these objects after the upgrade, the first user of these objects will be forced to wait while Oracle performs a run-time recompilation.

DBUA will then prompt you to back up the database as part of the upgrade process. If you have already backed up the database prior to starting DBUA, you may elect to skip this step. If you choose to have DBUA back up the database, it will shut down the database and perform an offline backup of the datafiles to the directory location you specify. DBUA will also create a batch file in that directory to automate the restoration of those files to their earlier locations.

The next step is to choose whether or not to enable Oracle Enterprise Manager (OEM) to manage the database. If you enable the Oracle Management Agent, the upgraded database will automatically be available via OEM.

You will then be asked to finalize the security configuration for the upgraded database. As with the database-creation process, you can specify passwords for each privileged account or you can set a single password to apply to all the OEM user accounts.

Finally, you will be prompted for details on the flash recovery area location (see Chapter 28), the archive log setting (see Chapter 46), and the network configuration. A final summary screen displays your choices for the upgrade, and the upgrade starts when you accept them. After the upgrade has completed, DBUA will display the Checking Upgrade Results screen, showing the steps performed, the related log files, and the status. The section of the screen titled Password Management allows you to manage the passwords and the locked/unlocked status of accounts in the upgraded database.

If you are not satisfied with the upgrade results, you can choose the Restore option. If you used DBUA to perform the backup, the restoration will be performed automatically; otherwise, you will need to perform the restoration manually.

When you exit DBUA after successfully upgrading the database, DBUA removes the old database's entry in the network listener configuration file, inserts an entry for the upgraded database, and reloads the file.

Performing a Manual Direct Upgrade

In a manual upgrade, you must perform the steps that DBUA performs. The result will be a direct upgrade of the database in which you are responsible for (and control) each step in the upgrade process.

You should use the Pre-Upgrade Information Tool to analyze the database prior to its upgrade. This tool is provided in a SQL script that is installed with the Oracle Database 10*g* software; you will need to run it against the database to be upgraded. The file, named utlu101i.sql, is located in the /rdbms/admin subdirectory under the Oracle Database 10*g* software home directory. You should run that file in the database to be upgraded as a SYSDBA-privileged user, spooling the results to a log file. The results will show potential problems that should be addressed prior to the upgrade.

If there are no issues to resolve prior to the upgrade, you should shut down the database and perform an offline backup before continuing with the upgrade process.

Once you have a backup you can restore if needed, you are ready to proceed with the upgrade process. The process is detailed and script-based, so you should consult with the Oracle installation and upgrade documentation for your environment and version. The steps are as follows:

1. Copy configuration files (init.ora, spfile.ora, password file) from their old location to the new Oracle software home directory. By default, the configuration files are found in the /dbs subdirectory on UNIX platforms and in the /database directory on Windows platforms.

2. Remove obsolete and deprecated initialization parameters from the configuration files. Update the COMPATIBLE parameter for Oracle 10. Make sure your SHARED_POOL_SIZE parameter is set to at least 96MB for 32-bit platforms and at least 144MB for 64-bit platforms. Set PGA_AGGREGATE_TARGET to at least 24MB, LARGE_POOL_SIZE to at least 8MB, and JAVA_POOL_SIZE to at least 48MB. For Windows parameters, set BACKGROUND_DUMP_DEST to \oradata*database_name* under the Oracle base software directory, and set USER_DUMP_DEST to \oradata*database_name*\archive under the Oracle base software directory. Use full pathnames in the parameter files.

3. If you are upgrading a cluster database, set the CLUSTER_DATABASE initialization parameter to FALSE. After the upgrade, you must set this initialization parameter back to TRUE.

4. Shut down the instance.

5. If you are using Windows, stop the service associated with the instance and delete the Oracle service at the command prompt. For Oracle 8.0, use the command ORADIM80 –DELETE –SID *instance_name*. For Oracle8.1 and higher, use ORADIM –DELETE –SID *instance_name*. Then create the new Oracle Database 10*g* service using ORADIM, as shown here:

```
C:\> ORADIM -NEW -SID SID -INTPWD PASSWORD -MAXUSERS USERS
    -STARTMODE AUTO -PFILE ORACLE_HOME\DATABASE\INITSID.ORA
```

Here's a list of the variables for this command:

Variable	Description
SID	The name of the SID (instance identifier) of the database you are upgrading.
PASSWORD	The password for the new release 10.1 database instance. This is the password for the user connected with SYSDBA privileges. If you do not specify INTPWD, operating system authentication is used and no password is required.
USERS	The maximum number of users who can be granted SYSDBA and SYSOPER privileges.
ORACLE_HOME	The release 10.1 Oracle home directory. Ensure that you specify the full pathname with the -PFILE option, including the drive letter of the Oracle home directory.

6. If your operating system is UNIX, make sure that the following environment variables point to the new release 10.1 directories: ORACLE_HOME, PATH, ORA_NLS33, and LD_LIBRARY_PATH.

7. Log into the system as the owner of the Oracle Database 10*g* software.

8. Change your directory to the /rdbms/admin subdirectory under the Oracle software home directory.

9. Connect to SQL*Plus as a user with SYSDBA privileges.

10. Issue the **startup upgrade** command.

11. Use the **spool** command to log the results of the following steps.

12. Create a SYSAUX tablespace via the **create tablespace** command. You should allocate SYSAUX between 500MB and 5GB of disk space, depending on the number of user objects. SYSAUX must be created with the following clauses: **online**, **permanent**, **read write**, **extent management local**, and **segment space management auto**. Here's an example:

```
create tablespace SYSAUX
  datafile '/u01/oradata/db1/sysaux01.dbf'
  size 500m reuse
  extent management local
  segment space management auto
  online;
```

13. Run the script for the old release. For example, if you are upgrading from Release 8.0.6, run only the u0800060.sql script and then move on to the next step in the upgrade process.

Upgrading From:	Run Script:
8.0.6	u0800060.sql
8.1.7	u0801070.sql
9.0.1	u0900010.sql
9.2	u0902000.sql

14. Stop spooling (via **spool off**) and review the spool file for errors. Resolve any problems identified there.

15. Run the utlu101s.sql file, with TEXT as the input parameter:

```
@utlu101s TEXT
```

Oracle will then display the status of the upgrade. The upgrade elements should all be listed with a status of "Normal successful completion."

16. Shut down and restart the instance.

17. Run the utlrp.sql script to recompile invalid packages. You can then verify that all packages and classes are valid:

```
select distinct Object_Name from DBA_OBJECTS
  where Status = 'INVALID';
```

18. Exit SQL*Plus.

19. Shut down the database and perform an offline backup of the database; then restart the database. The upgrade is complete.

NOTE
After the upgrade, you should never start your Oracle 10g database with the software from an earlier release.

Using Export and Import

Export and Import provide you with an indirect method for the upgrade. You can create an Oracle 10g database alongside your existing database and use Export and Import to move data from the old database to the new database. When the movement of the data is complete, you will need to point your applications to connect to the new database instead of the old database. You will also need to update any configuration files, version-specific scripts, and the networking configuration files (tnsnames.ora and listener.ora) to point to the new database.

Export and Import Versions to Use

When you create an Export dump file via the Export utility, that file can be imported into all later releases of Oracle. Export dump files are not backward compatible, so if you ever need to revert to an earlier version of Oracle, you will need to carefully select the version of Export and Import used. The following table shows the versions of the Export and Import executables you should use when going between versions of Oracle.

Export From:	Import To:	Use Export Utility For:	Use Import Utility For:
Release 9.2	Release 10.1	Release 9.2	Release 10.1
Release 8.1.7	Release 10.1	Release 8.1.7	Release 10.1
Release 8.0.6	Release 10.1	Release 8.0.6	Release 10.1
Release 7.3.4	Release 10.1	Release 7.3.4	Release 10.1
Release 10.1	Release 8.0.6	Release 8.0.6	Release 8.0.6
Release 10.1	Release 8.1.7	Release 8.1.7	Release 8.1.7
Release 10.1	Release 9.0.1	Release 9.0.1	Release 9.0.1
Release 10.1	Release 9.2	Release 9.2	Release 9.2
Release 10.1	Release 10.1	Release 10.1	Release 10.1

Note that when you are exporting in order to downgrade your database release, you should use the older version of the Export utility to minimize compatibility problems. You may still encounter compatibility problems if the newer version of the database uses new features (such as new datatypes) that the old version will not support.

Performing the Upgrade

Export the data from the source database using the version of the Export utility specified in the prior section. Perform a consistent export, or perform the export when the database is not available for updates during and after the export.

NOTE
If you have little free space available, you may back up and delete the existing database at this point and then install Oracle Database 10g software and create a target database for the import. If at all possible, maintain the source and target databases concurrently during the upgrade. The only benefit of having only one database on the server at a time is that they can share the same database name.

Install the Oracle Database 10g software and create the target database. In the target database, precreate the users and tablespaces needed to store the source data. If the source and target databases will coexist on the server, you need to be careful not to overwrite datafiles from one database with datafiles from the other. The Import utility will attempt to execute the **create tablespace** commands found in the Export dump file, and those commands will include the datafile names from the source database. By default, those commands will fail if the files already exist (although this can be overridden via Import's DESTROY parameter). Precreate the tablespaces with the proper datafile names to avoid this problem.

NOTE
You can export specific tablespaces, users, tables, and rows.

Once the database has been prepared, use Import or Data Pump Import (see Chapter 22) to load the data from the Export dump file into the target database. Review the log file for information about objects that did not import successfully.

Using the Data-Copying Method

The data-copying method requires that the source database and target database coexist. This method is most appropriate when the tables to be migrated are fairly small and few in number. As with the Export/Import method, you must guard against transactions occurring in the source database during and after the extraction of the data. In this method, the data is extracted via queries across database links.

Create the target database using the Oracle Database 10g software and then precreate the tablespaces, users, and tables to be populated with data from the source database. Create database links (see Chapter 23) in the target database that access accounts in the source database. Use the **insert as select** command to move data from the source database to the target.

The data-copying method allows you to bring over just the rows and columns you need; your queries limit the data migrated. You will need to be careful with the relationships between the tables in the source database so you can re-create them properly in the target database. If you have a long application outage available for performing the upgrade and you need to modify the data structures during the migration, the data-copying method may be appropriate for your needs. Note that this method requires that the data be stored in multiple places at once, thus impacting your storage needs.

To improve the performance of this method, you may consider the following options:

- Disable all indexes and constraints until all the data has been loaded.
- Run multiple data-copying jobs in parallel.
- Use the parallel query option to enhance the performance of individual queries and inserts.
- Use the APPEND hint to enhance the performance of inserts.

See Chapter 43 for additional advice on performance tuning.

After Upgrading

Following the upgrade, you should double-check the configuration and parameter files related to the database, particularly if the instance name changed in the migration process. These files include

- The tnsnames.ora file
- The listener.ora file
- Programs that may have hard-coded instance names in them

NOTE
You will need to manually reload the modified listener.ora file if you are not using DBUA to perform the upgrade.

You should review your database initialization parameters to make sure deprecated and obsolete parameters have been removed; these should have been identified during the migration process. Be sure to recompile any programs you have written that rely on the database software libraries.

Once the upgrade has completed, perform the functional and performance tests identified before the upgrade began. If there are issues with the database functionality, attempt to identify any parameter settings or missing objects that may be impacting the test results. If the problem cannot be resolved, you may need to revert to the prior release.

CHAPTER
4

Planning Oracle
Applications—
Approaches, Risks,
and Standards

or an Oracle application to be built and used rapidly and effectively, users and developers must share a common language and a deep and common understanding of both the business application and the Oracle tools. In the preceding chapters you have seen the overall Oracle product descriptions and the installation/upgrade steps involved. Now that the software is installed, you have the opportunity to build applications that build on the shared business and data understanding among your technical and business area staff members.

Historically, the systems analyst studied the business requirements and built an application to meet those needs. The user was involved only in describing the business and, perhaps, in reviewing the functionality of the application after it was completed.

With the new tools and approaches available, and especially with Oracle, applications can be built that more closely match the needs and work habits of the business—but only if a common understanding exists.

This book is aimed specifically at fostering this understanding, and at providing the means for both user and developer to exploit Oracle's full potential. The end user will know details about the business that the developer will not comprehend. The developer will understand internal functions and features of Oracle and the computer environment that will be too technically complex for the end user. But these areas of exclusive expertise will be minor compared with what both end users and developers can share in using Oracle. There is a remarkable opportunity here.

It is no secret that "business" people and "systems" people have been in conflict for decades. Reasons for this include differences in knowledge, culture, professional interests, and goals, and the alienation that simple physical separation between groups can often produce. To be fair, this syndrome is not peculiar to data processing. The same thing occurs between people in accounting, personnel, or senior management, as members of each group gather apart from other groups on a separate floor or in a separate building or city. Relations between the individuals from one group and another become formalized, strained, and abnormal. Artificial barriers and procedures that stem from this isolationism become established, and these also contribute to the syndrome.

This is all very well, you say, and may be interesting to sociologists, but what does it have to do with Oracle?

Because Oracle isn't cloaked in arcane language that only systems professionals can comprehend, it fundamentally changes the nature of the relationship between business and systems people. Anybody can understand it. Anybody can use it. Information that previously was trapped in computer systems until someone in systems created a new report and released it now is accessible, instantly, to a business person, simply by typing an English query. This changes the rules of the game.

Where Oracle is used, it has radically improved the understanding between the two camps, has increased their knowledge of one another, and has even begun to normalize relations between them. This has also produced superior applications and end results.

Since its first release, Oracle has been based on the easily understood relational model (explained shortly), so nonprogrammers can readily understand what Oracle does and how it does it. This makes it approachable and unimposing.

Some individuals neither accept nor understand this yet, nor do they realize just how vital it is that the dated and artificial barriers between "users" and "systems" continue to fall. But the advent of cooperative development will profoundly affect applications and their usefulness.

However, many application developers have fallen into an easy trap with Oracle: carrying forward unhelpful methods from previous-generation system designs. There is a lot to unlearn.

Many of the techniques (and limitations) that were indispensable to a previous generation of systems are not only unnecessary in designing with Oracle, they are positively counterproductive. In the process of explaining Oracle, the burden of these old habits and approaches must be lifted. Refreshing new possibilities are available.

Throughout this book, the intent will be to explain Oracle in a way that is clear and simple, in terms that both users and developers can understand and share. Outdated or inappropriate design and management techniques will be exposed and replaced.

The Cooperative Approach

The Oracle database is an *object-relational database management system.* A relational database is an extremely simple way of thinking about and managing the data used in a business. It is nothing more than a collection of tables of data. We all encounter tables every day—weather reports, stock charts, sports scores, and so on. These are all tables, with column headings and rows of information simply presented. Even so, the relational approach can be sophisticated and powerful enough for even the most complex of businesses. An object-relational database supports all the features of a relational database while also supporting object-oriented concepts and features. You can use Oracle as a relational database management system (RDBMS) or take advantage of its object-oriented features.

Unfortunately, the very people who can benefit most from a relational database—the business users—usually understand it the least. Application developers, who must build systems that these users need to do their jobs, often find relational concepts difficult to explain in simple terms. A common language is needed to make this cooperative approach work.

The first two parts of this book explain, in readily understandable terms, just what a relational database is and how to use it effectively in business. It may seem that this discussion is for the benefit of "users" only. An experienced relational application designer may be inclined to skip these early chapters and simply use the book as a primary source Oracle reference. Although much of this material may seem like elementary review, it is an opportunity for an application designer to acquire a clear, consistent, and workable terminology with which to talk to users about their needs and how these needs might be quickly met. If you are an application designer, this discussion may also help you unlearn some unnecessary and probably unconscious design habits. Many of these habits will be uncovered in the course of introducing the relational approach. It is important to realize that even Oracle's power can be diminished considerably by design methods appropriate only to nonrelational development.

If you are an end user, understanding the basic ideas behind object-relational databases will help you express your needs cogently to application developers and comprehend how those needs can be met. An average person working in a business role can go from beginner to expert in short order. With Oracle, you'll have the power to get and use information, have hands-on control over reports and data, and possess a clear-eyed understanding of what the application does and how it does it. Oracle gives you, the user, the ability to control an application or query facility expertly and *know* whether you are getting all the available flexibility and power.

You also will be able to unburden programmers of their least favorite task: writing new reports. In large organizations, as much as 95 percent of all programming backlog is composed of new report requests. Because you can write your own reports, in minutes instead of months, you will be delighted to have the responsibility.

Everyone Has "Data"

A library keeps lists of members, books, and fines. The owner of a baseball-card collection keeps track of players' names, dates, averages, and card values. In any business, certain pieces of information about customers, products, prices, financial status, and so on must be saved. These pieces of information are called *data.*

Information philosophers like to say that data is just data until it is organized in a meaningful way, at which point it becomes "information." If this is true, then Oracle is also a means of easily turning data into information. Oracle will sort through and manipulate data to reveal pieces of knowledge hidden there—such as totals, buying trends, or other relationships—that are as yet undiscovered. You will learn how to make these discoveries. The main point here is that you have data, and you do three basic things with it: acquire it, store it, and retrieve it.

Once you've achieved the basics, you can make computations with data, move it from one place to another, or modify it. This is called *processing,* and, fundamentally, it involves the same three steps that affect how information is organized.

You could do all this with a cigar box, pencil, and paper, but as the volume of data increases, your tools tend to change. You may use a file cabinet, calculators, pencils, and paper. Although at some point it makes sense to make the leap to computers, your tasks remain the same.

A *relational database management system* (*RDBMS*) such as Oracle gives you a way of doing these tasks in an understandable and reasonably uncomplicated way. Oracle basically does three things:

- ■ Lets you put data into it
- ■ Keeps the data
- ■ Lets you get the data out and work with it

Figure 4-1 shows how simple this process is.

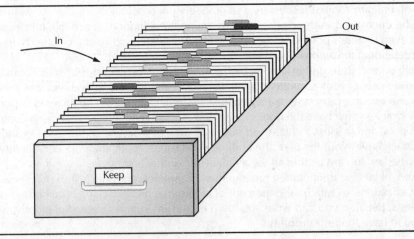

FIGURE 4-1. *What Oracle does with data*

Oracle supports this in/keep/out approach and provides clever tools that allow you considerable sophistication in how the data is captured, edited, modified, and put in; how you keep it securely; and how you get it out to manipulate and report on it.

The Familiar Language of Oracle

The information stored in Oracle is kept in tables—much like the weather table from a daily newspaper, shown in Figure 4-2.

This table has four columns: City, Temperature, Humidity, and Condition. It also has a row for each city from Athens to Sydney. Last, it has a table name: WEATHER.

These are the three major characteristics of most tables you'll see in print: *columns, rows,* and a *name.* The same is true in a relational database. Anyone can understand the words and the ideas they represent, because the words used to describe the parts of a table in an Oracle database are the same words used in everyday conversation. The words have no special, unusual, or esoteric meanings. What you see is what you get.

Tables of Information

Oracle stores information in tables, an example of which is shown in Figure 4-3. Each of these tables has one or more columns. The column headings—such as City, Temperature, Humidity, and Condition in Figure 4-3—describe the kind of information kept in the column. The information is stored row after row (city after city). Each unique set of data, such as the temperature, humidity, and condition for the city of Manchester, gets its own row.

Oracle avoids specialized, academic terminology in order to make the product more approachable. In research papers on relational theory, a column may be called an "attribute," a row may be called a "tuple" (rhymes with "couple"), and a table may be called an "entity." For an end user, however, these terms are confusing. More than anything, they are an unnecessary renaming of things for which there are already commonly understood names in our shared everyday language. Oracle takes advantage of this shared language, and developers can too. It is imperative to recognize the wall of mistrust and misunderstanding that the use of unnecessary technical jargon produces. Like Oracle, this book will stick with "tables," "columns," and "rows."

```
                          WEATHER

    City          Temperature    Humidity    Condition
      Athens.......        97          89      Sunny
      Chicago......        66          88      Rain
      Lima.........        45          79      Rain
      Manchester...        66          98      Fog
      Paris........        81          62      Cloudy
      Sparta.......        74          63      Cloudy
      Sydney.......        69          99      Sunny
```

FIGURE 4-2. *A weather table from a newspaper*

FIGURE 4-3. *A WEATHER table from Oracle*

Structured Query Language

Oracle was the first company to release a product that used the English-based *Structured Query Language,* or *SQL.* This language allows end users to extract information themselves, without using a systems group for every little report.

Oracle's query language has structure, just as English or any other language has structure. It has rules of grammar and syntax, but they are basically the normal rules of careful English speech and can be readily understood.

SQL, pronounced either "sequel" or "S-Q-L," is an astonishingly capable tool, as you will see. Using it does not require any programming experience.

Here's an example of how you might use SQL. If someone asked you to select from the preceding WEATHER table the city where the humidity is 89, you would quickly respond "Athens." If you were asked to select cities where the temperature is 66, you would respond "Chicago and Manchester."

Oracle is able to answer these same questions nearly as easily as you are, and in response to simple queries very much like the ones you were just asked. The keywords used in a query to Oracle are **select**, **from**, **where**, and **order by**. They are clues to Oracle to help it understand your request and respond with the correct answer.

A Simple Oracle Query

If Oracle had the example WEATHER table in its database, your first query (with a semicolon to tell Oracle to execute the command) would be simply this:

```
select City from WEATHER where Humidity = 89 ;
```

Oracle would respond as follows:

```
City
----------
ATHENS
```

Your second query would be this:

```
select City from WEATHER where Temperature = 66 ;
```

For this query, Oracle would respond with the following:

```
City
-----------
MANCHESTER
CHICAGO
```

As you can see, each of these queries uses the keywords **select**, **from**, and **where**. What about **order by**? Suppose you wanted to see all the cities listed in order by temperature. You'd simply type this:

```
select City, Temperature from WEATHER
  order by Temperature ;
```

and Oracle would instantly respond with this:

```
City          Temperature
-----------   -----------
LIMA              45
MANCHESTER        66
CHICAGO           66
SYDNEY            69
SPARTA            74
PARIS            81
ATHENS           97
```

Oracle has quickly reordered your table by temperature. (This table lists lowest temperatures first; in a later chapter, you'll learn how to specify whether you want low numbers or high numbers first.)

There are many other questions you can ask with Oracle's query facility, but these examples show how easy it is to obtain the information you need from an Oracle database in the form that will be most useful to you. You can build complicated requests from simple pieces of information, but the method used to do this will always be understandable. For instance, you can combine the **where** and **order by** keywords, both simple by themselves, to tell Oracle to select those cities where the temperature is greater than 80, and show them in order by increasing temperature. You would type this:

```
select City, Temperature from WEATHER
  where Temperature > 80
  order by Temperature ;
```

and Oracle would instantly respond with this:

```
City          Temperature
-----------   -----------
PARIS            81
ATHENS           97
```

Or, to be even more specific, you could request cities where the temperature is greater than 80 and the humidity is less than 70:

```
select City, Temperature, Humidity from WEATHER
  where Temperature > 80
    and Humidity < 70
  order by Temperature ;
```

and Oracle would respond with this:

```
City         Temperature Humidity
-----------  ----------- --------
PARIS                 81       62
```

Why It Is Called "Relational"

Notice that the WEATHER table lists cities from several countries, and some countries have more than one city listed. Suppose you need to know in which country a particular city is located. You could create a separate LOCATION table of cities and their countries, as shown in Figure 4-4.

For any city in the WEATHER table, you can simply look at the LOCATION table, find the name in the City column, look over to the Country column in the same row, and see the country's name.

These are two completely separate and independent tables. Each contains its own information in columns and rows. The tables have one significant thing in common: the City column. For each city name in the WEATHER table, there is an identical city name in the LOCATION table.

For instance, what are the current temperature, humidity, and condition in an Australian city? Look at the two tables, figure it out, and then resume reading this.

```
                                             LOCATION

                                   City          Country
                   WEATHER         -----------   --------
                                   ATHENS        GREECE
                                   CHICAGO       UNITED STATES
City         Temperature Humidity  Condition  CONAKRY    GUINEA
-----------  ----------- --------  ---------  LIMA       PERU
ATHENS                97       89  SUNNY      MADRAS     INDIA
CHICAGO               66       88  RAIN       MADRID     SPAIN
LIMA                  45       79  RAIN       MANCHESTER ENGLAND
MANCHESTER            66       98  FOG        MOSCOW     RUSSIA
PARIS                 81       62  CLOUDY     PARIS      FRANCE
SPARTA                74       63  CLOUDY     ROME       ITALY
SYDNEY                69       99  SUNNY      SHENYANG   CHINA
                                              SPARTA     GREECE
                                              SYDNEY     AUSTRALIA
                                              TOKYO      JAPAN
```

FIGURE 4-4. *WEATHER and LOCATION tables*

WEATHER						LOCATION	
City	Temperature	Humidity	Condition			City	Country
---------	-----------	--------	---------			----------	-------
						ATHENS	GREECE
						CHICAGO	UNITED STATES
ATHENS	97	89	SUNNY			CONAKRY	GUINEA
CHICAGO	66	88	RAIN			LIMA	PERU
LIMA	45	79	RAIN			MADRAS	INDIA
MANCHESTER	66	98	FOG			MADRID	SPAIN
PARIS	81	62	CLOUDY			MANCHESTER	ENGLAND
SPARTA	74	63	CLOUDY			MOSCOW	RUSSIA
SYDNEY	69	99	SUNNY			PARIS	FRANCE
						ROME	ITALY
						SHENYANG	CHINA
						SPARTA	GREECE
	Relationship					SYDNEY	AUSTRALIA
						TOKYO	JAPAN

FIGURE 4-5. *The relationship between the WEATHER and LOCATION tables*

How did you solve it? You found just one AUSTRALIA entry, under the Country column, in the LOCATION table. Next to it, in the City column of the same row, was the name of the city, SYDNEY. You took this name, SYDNEY, and then looked for it in the City column of the WEATHER table. When you found it, you moved across the row and found the Temperature, Humidity, and Condition: 69, 99, and SUNNY.

Even though the tables are independent, you can easily see that they are related. The city name in one table is *related* to the city name in the other (see Figure 4-5, above). This relationship is the basis for the name *relational* database.

This is the basic idea of a relational database (sometimes called a *relational model*). Data is stored in tables. Tables have columns, rows, and names. Tables can be related to each other if each has a column with a common type of information.

That's it. It's as simple as it seems.

Some Common, Everyday Examples

Once you understand the basic idea of relational databases, you'll begin to see tables, rows, and columns everywhere. Not that you didn't see them before, but you probably didn't think about them in quite the same way. Many of the tables you are accustomed to seeing could be stored in Oracle. They could be used to quickly answer questions that would take you quite some time to answer using nearly any other method.

A typical stock market report in the paper might look like the one in Figure 4-6. This is a small portion of a dense, alphabetical listing that fills several narrow columns on several pages in a newspaper. Which stock traded the most shares? Which had the biggest percentage change in its price, either positively or negatively? The answers to these questions can be obtained through simple English queries in Oracle, which can find the answers much faster than you could by searching the columns on the newspaper page.

Company	Close Yesterday	Close Today	Shares Traded
Ad Specialty	31.75	31.75	18,333,876
Apple Cannery	33.75	36.50	25,787,229
AT Space	46.75	48.00	11,398,323
August Enterprises	15.00	15.00	12,221,711
Brandon Ellipsis	32.75	33.50	25,789,769
General Entropy	64.25	66.00	7,598,562
Geneva Rocketry	22.75	27.25	22,533,944
Hayward Antiseptic	104.25	106.00	3,358,561
IDK	95.00	95.25	9,443,523
India Cosmetics	30.75	30.75	8,134,878
Isaiah James Storage	13.25	13.75	22,112,171
KDK Airlines	80.00	85.25	7,481,566
Kentgen Biophysics	18.25	19.50	6,636,863
LaVay Cosmetics	21.50	22.00	3,341,542
Local Development	26.75	27.25	2,596,934
Maxtide	8.25	8.00	2,836,893
MBK Communications	43.25	41.00	10,022,980
Memory Graphics	15.50	14.25	4,557,992
Micro Token	77.00	76.50	25,205,667
Nancy Lee Features	13.50	14.25	14,222,692
Northern Boreal	26.75	28.00	1,348,323
Ockham Systems	21.50	22.00	7,052,990
Oscar Coal Drayage	87.00	88.50	25,798,992
Robert James Apparel	23.25	24.00	19,032,481
Soup Sensations	16.25	16.75	22,574,879
Wonder Labs	5.00	5.00	2,553,712

FIGURE 4-6. *A stock market table*

Figure 4-7 is an index to a newspaper. What's in section F? If you read the paper from front to back, in what order would you read the articles? The answers to these questions are obtainable via simple English queries in Oracle. You will learn how to do all these queries, and even build the tables to store the information, in the course of using this reference.

Throughout this book, the examples use data and objects encountered frequently in business and everyday life. Similar data to use for your exercises should be as easy to find as your nearest bookshelf. You will learn how to enter and retrieve data in the pages ahead, using examples based on these everyday data sources.

As with any new technology or new venture, it's sensible to think through not only the benefits and opportunities that are presented, but also the costs and risks. Combine a relational database with a series of powerful and easy-to-use tools, as Oracle does, and the possibility of being seduced into disaster by its simplicity becomes real. Add in object-oriented and web capabilities, and the dangers increase. The following sections discuss some of the dangers that both developers and users need to consider.

Feature	Section	Page
Births	F	7
Bridge	B	2
Business	E	1
Classified	F	8
Comics	C	4
Doctor's In	F	6
Editorials	A	12
Modern Life	B	1
Movies	B	4
National News	A	1
Obituaries	F	6
Sports	D	1
Television	B	7
Weather	C	2

FIGURE 4-7. *A table based on sections of a newspaper*

What Are the Risks?

The primary risk in developing relational database applications is that it *is* as easy as they say. Understanding tables, columns, and rows isn't difficult. The relationship between two tables is conceptually simple. Even *normalization,* the process of analyzing the inherent or "normal" relationships between the various elements of a company's data, is fairly easy to learn.

Unfortunately, this often produces instant "experts," full of confidence but with little experience in building real, production-quality applications. For a tiny marketing database, or a home inventory application, this doesn't matter very much. The mistakes made will reveal themselves in time, the lessons will be learned, and the errors will be avoided the next time around. In an important application, however, this is a sure formula for disaster. This lack of experience is usually behind the press's stories of major project failures.

Older development methods are generally slower, primarily because the tasks of the older methods—coding, submitting a job for compilation, linking, and testing—result in a slower pace. The cycle, particularly on a mainframe, is often so tedious that programmers spend a good deal of time "desk-checking" in order to avoid going through the delay of another full cycle because of an error in the code.

Fourth-generation tools seduce developers into rushing into production. Changes can be made and implemented so quickly that testing is given short shrift. The elimination of virtually all desk-checking compounds the problem. When the negative incentive (the long cycle) that encouraged desk-checking disappeared, desk-checking went with it. The attitude of many seems to be, "If the application isn't quite right, we can fix it quickly. If the data gets corrupted, we can patch it with a quick update. If it's not fast enough, we can tune it on the fly. Let's get it in ahead of schedule and show the stuff we're made of."

The testing cycle in an important Oracle project should be longer and more thorough than in a traditional project. This is true even if proper project controls are in place, and even if seasoned project managers are guiding the project, because there will be less desk-checking and an inherent overconfidence. This testing must check the correctness of data-entry screens and reports, of data loads and updates, of data integrity and concurrence, and particularly of transaction and storage volumes during peak loads.

Because it really is as easy as they say, application development with Oracle's tools can be breathtakingly rapid. But this automatically reduces the amount of testing done as a normal part of development, and the planned testing and quality assurance must be consciously lengthened to compensate. This is not usually foreseen by those new to either Oracle or fourth-generation tools, but you must budget for it in your project plan.

The Importance of the New Vision

Many of us look forward to the day when we can simply type a "natural" language query in English, and have the answer back, on our screen, in seconds.

We are closer to this goal than most of us realize. The limiting factor is no longer technology, but rather the rigor of thought in our application designs. Oracle can straightforwardly build English-based systems that are easily understood and exploited by unsophisticated users. The potential is there, already available in Oracle's database and tools, but only a few have understood and used it.

Clarity and understandability should be the hallmarks of any Oracle application. Applications can operate in English, be understood readily by end users who have no programming background, and provide information based on a simple English query.

How? First of all, a major goal of the design effort must be to make the application easy to understand and simple to use. If you err, it must always be in this direction, even if it means consuming more CPU or disk space. The limitation of this approach is that you could make an application exceptionally easy to use by creating overly complex programs that are nearly impossible to maintain or enhance. This would be an equally bad mistake. However, all things being equal, an end-user orientation should never be sacrificed for clever coding.

Changing Environments

Consider that the cost to run a computer, expressed as the cost per million instructions per second (MIPS), has historically declined at the rate of 20 percent per year. Labor costs, on the other hand, have risen steadily. This means that any work that can be shifted from human laborers to machines may represent a cost savings.

Have we factored this incredible shift into our application designs? The answer is "somewhat," but terribly unevenly. The real progress has been in *environments,* such as the visionary work first done at Xerox Palo Alto Research Center (PARC), and then on the Macintosh, and now in web-based browsers and other graphical icon-based systems. These environments are much easier to learn and understand than the older, character-based environments, and people who use them can produce in minutes what previously took days. The improvement in some cases has been so huge that we've entirely lost sight of how hard some tasks used to be.

Unfortunately, this concept of an accommodating and friendly environment hasn't been grasped by many application developers. Even when they work in these environments, they continue old habits that are just no longer appropriate.

Codes, Abbreviations, and Naming Standards

The problem of old programming habits is most pronounced in codes, abbreviations, and naming standards, which are almost completely ignored when the needs of end users are considered. When these three issues are thought about at all, usually only the needs and conventions of the systems groups are considered. This may seem like a dry and uninteresting problem to be forced to think through, but it can make the difference between great success and grudging acceptance, between an order-of-magnitude leap in productivity and a marginal gain, between interested, effective users and bored, harried users who make continual demands on the developers.

Here's what happened. Business records used to be kept in ledgers and journals. Each event or transaction was written down, line by line, in English. As we developed applications, codes were added to replace data values (such as "01" for "Accounts Receivable," "02" for "Accounts Payable," and so on). Key-entry clerks would actually have to know or look up most of these codes and type them in at the appropriately labeled fields on their screens. This is an extreme example, but literally thousands of applications take exactly this approach and are every bit as difficult to learn or understand.

This problem has been most pronounced in large, conventional mainframe systems development. As relational databases are introduced into these groups, they are used simply as replacements for older input/output methods such as Virtual Storage Access Method (VSAM) and Information Management System (IMS). The power and features of the relational database are virtually wasted when used in such a fashion.

Why Are Codes Used Instead of English?

Why use codes at all? Two primary justifications are usually offered:

- ■ A category has so many items in it that all of them can't reasonably be represented or remembered in English.

- ■ To save space in the computer.

The second point is an anachronism. Memory and permanent storage were once so expensive and CPUs so slow (with less power than a modern hand-held calculator) that programmers had to cram every piece of information into the smallest possible space. Numbers, character for character, take half of the computer storage space of letters, and codes reduce the demands on the machine even more.

Because machines were expensive, developers had to use codes for *everything* to make *anything* work at all. It was a technical solution to an economic problem. For users, who had to learn all sorts of meaningless codes, the demands were terrible. Machines were too slow and too expensive to accommodate the humans, so the humans were trained to accommodate the machines. It was a necessary evil.

This economic justification for codes vanished years ago. Computers are now fast enough and cheap enough to accommodate the way people work, and use words that people understand. It's high time that they did so. Yet, without really thinking through the justifications, developers and designers continue to use codes.

The first point—that of too many items per category—is more substantive, but much less so than it first appears. One idea is that it takes less effort (and is therefore less expensive) for someone to key in the numeric codes than actual text string values such as book titles. This justification is

untrue in Oracle. Not only is it more costly to train people to know the correct customer, product, transaction, and other codes, and more expensive because of the cost of mistakes (which are high with code-based systems), but using codes also means not using Oracle fully; Oracle is able to take the first few characters of a title and fill in the rest of the name itself. It can do the same thing with product names, transactions (a "b" will automatically fill in with "buy," an "s" with "sell"), and so on, throughout an application. It does this with very robust pattern-matching capabilities.

The Benefit of User Feedback

There is an immediate additional benefit: Key-entry errors drop almost to zero because the users get immediate feedback, in English, of the business information they're entering. Digits don't get transposed; codes don't get remembered incorrectly; and, in financial applications, money rarely is lost in accounts due to entry errors, with significant savings.

Applications also become much more comprehensible. Screens and reports are transformed from arcane arrays of numbers and codes into a readable and understandable format. The change of application design from code-oriented to English-oriented has a profound and invigorating effect on a company and its employees. For users who have been burdened by code manuals, an English-based application produces a tremendous psychological release.

How to Reduce the Confusion

Another version of the "too many items per category" justification is that the number of products, customers, or transaction types is just too great to differentiate each by name, or there are too many items in a category that are identical or very similar (customers named "John Smith," for instance). A category can contain too many entries to make the options easy to remember or differentiate, but more often this is evidence of an incomplete job of categorizing information: Too many dissimilar things are crammed into too broad a category. Developing an application with a strong English-based (or French, German, Spanish, and so on) orientation, as opposed to code-based, requires time spent with users and developers—taking apart the information about the business, understanding its natural relationships and categories, and then carefully constructing a database and naming scheme that simply and accurately reflect these discoveries.

There are three basic steps to doing this:

1. Normalize the data.

2. Choose English names for the tables and columns.

3. Choose English words for the data.

Each of these steps will be explained in order. The goal is to design an application in which the data is sensibly organized, is stored in tables and columns whose names are familiar to the user, and is described in familiar terms, not codes.

Normalization

Relations between countries, or between departments in a company, or between users and developers, are usually the product of particular historical circumstances, which may define current relations even though the circumstances have long since passed. The result of this can be abnormal relations, or, in current parlance, *dysfunctional* relations. History and circumstance

often have the same effect on data—on how it is collected, organized, and reported. And data, too, can become abnormal and dysfunctional.

Normalization is the process of putting things right, making them normal. The origin of the term is *norma,* the Latin word for a carpenter's square that's used for ensuring a right angle. In geometry, when a line is at a right angle to another line, it is said to be "normal" to it. In a relational database, the term also has a specific mathematical meaning having to do with separating elements of data (such as names, addresses, or skills) into *affinity groups,* and defining the normal, or "right," relationships between them.

The basic concepts of normalization are being introduced here so that users can contribute to the design of an application they will be using, or better understand one that has already been built. It would be a mistake, however, to think that this process is really only applicable to designing a database or a computer application. Normalization results in deep insights into the information used in a business and how the various elements of that information are related to each other. This will prove educational in areas apart from databases and computers.

The Logical Model

An early step in the analysis process is the building of a *logical model,* which is simply a normalized diagram of the data used by the business. Knowing why and how the data gets broken apart and segregated is essential to understanding the model, and the model is essential to building an application that will support the business for a long time, without requiring extraordinary support.

Normalization is usually discussed in terms of *form*: First, Second, and Third Normal Form are the most common, with Third representing the most highly normalized state. There are Fourth and Fifth normalization levels defined as well, but they are beyond the scope of this discussion.

Consider a bookshelf: For each book, you can store information about it—the title, publisher, authors, and multiple categories or descriptive terms for the book. Assume that this book-level data became the table design in Oracle. The table might be called BOOKSHELF, and the columns might be Title, Publisher, Author1, Author2, Author3, and Category1, Category2, Category3. The users of this table already have a problem: In the BOOKSHELF table, users are limited to listing just three authors or categories for a single book.

What happens when the list of acceptable categories changes? Someone has to go through every row in the BOOKSHELF table and correct all the old values. And what if one of the authors changes his or her name? Again, all the related records must be changed. What will you do when a fourth author contributes to a book?

These are not really computer or technical issues, even though they became apparent because you were designing a database. They are much more basic issues of how to sensibly and logically organize the information of a business. They are the issues that normalization addresses. This is done with a step-by-step reorganization of the elements of the data into affinity groups, by eliminating dysfunctional relationships and by ensuring normal relationships.

Normalizing the Data

Step one of the reorganization is to put the data into First Normal Form. This is done by moving data into separate tables, where the data in each table is of a similar type, and giving each table a *primary key*—a unique label or identifier. This eliminates repeating groups of data, such as the authors on the bookshelf.

Instead of having only three authors allowed per book, each author's data is placed in a separate table, with a row per name and description. This eliminates the need for a variable number of authors in the BOOKSHELF table and is a better design than limiting the BOOKSHELF table to just three authors.

Next, you define the primary key to each table: What will uniquely identify and allow you to extract one row of information? For simplicity's sake, assume the titles and authors' names are unique, so AuthorName is the primary key to the AUTHOR table.

You now have split BOOKSHELF into two tables: AUTHOR, with columns AuthorName (the primary key) and Comments, and BOOKSHELF, with a primary key of Title, and with columns Publisher, Category1, Category2, Category3, Rating, and RatingDescription. A third table, BOOKSHELF_AUTHOR, provides the associations: Multiple authors can be listed for a single book and an author can write multiple books—known as a *many-to-many* relationship. Figure 4-8 shows these relationships and primary keys.

The next step in the normalization process, Second Normal Form, entails taking out data that's only dependent on a part of the key. If there are attributes that do not depend on the entire key, those attributes should be moved to a new table. In this case, RatingDescription is not really dependent on Title—it's based on the Rating column value, so it should be moved to a separate table.

The final step, Third Normal Form, means getting rid of anything in the tables that doesn't depend solely on the primary key. In this example, the categories are interrelated; you would not list a title as both Fiction and Nonfiction, and you would have different subcategories under the Adult category than you would have under the Children category. Category information is therefore moved to a separate table. Figure 4-9 shows the tables in Third Normal Form.

Anytime the data is in Third Normal Form, it is already automatically in Second and First Normal Form. The whole process can therefore actually be accomplished less tediously than by going from form to form. Simply arrange the data so that the columns in each table, other than the primary key, are dependent only on the *whole primary key.* Third Normal Form is sometimes described as "the key, the whole key, and nothing but the key."

Navigating Through the Data

The bookshelf database is now in Third Normal Form. Figure 4-10 shows a sample of what these tables might contain. It's easy to see how these tables are related. You navigate from one to the other to pull out information on a particular author, based on the keys to each table. The primary key in each table is able to uniquely identify a single row. Choose Stephen Jay Gould, for instance, and you can readily discover his record in the AUTHOR table, because AuthorName is the primary key.

FIGURE 4-8. *The BOOKSHELF, AUTHOR, and BOOKSHELF_AUTHOR tables*

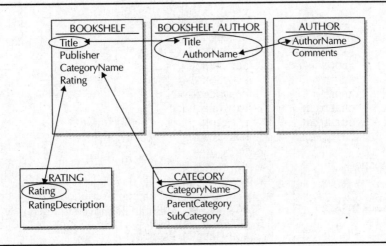

FIGURE 4-9. *BOOKSHELF and related tables*

```
AUTHOR
AuthorName              Comments
--------------------    -------------------------------------------

DIETRICH BONHOEFFER     GERMAN THEOLOGIAN, KILLED IN A WAR CAMP
ROBERT BRETALL          KIERKEGAARD ANTHOLOGIST
ALEXANDRA DAY           AUTHOR OF PICTURE BOOKS FOR CHILDREN
STEPHEN JAY GOULD       SCIENCE COLUMNIST, HARVARD PROFESSOR
SOREN KIERKEGAARD       DANISH PHILOSOPHER AND THEOLOGIAN
HARPER LEE              AMERICAN NOVELIST, PUBLISHED ONLY ONE NOVEL
LUCY MAUD MONTGOMERY    CANADIAN NOVELIST
JOHN ALLEN PAULOS       MATHEMATICS PROFESSOR
J. RODALE               ORGANIC GARDENING EXPERT

RATING
Rating      RatingDescription
----------  ------------------
1           ENTERTAINMENT
2           BACKGROUND INFORMATION
3           RECOMMENDED
4           STRONGLY RECOMMENDED
5           REQUIRED READING
```

FIGURE 4-10. *Sample data from the BOOKSHELF tables*

```
CATEGORY
CategoryName    ParentCategory    SubCategory
-------------   --------------    ------------
ADULTREF        ADULT             REFERENCE
ADULTFIC        ADULT             FICTION
ADULTNF         ADULT             NONFICTION
CHILDRENPIC     CHILDREN          PICTURE BOOK
CHILDRENFIC     CHILDREN          FICTION
CHILDRENNF      CHILDREN          NONFICTION

BOOKSHELF_AUTHOR
Title                             AuthorName
------------------------------    ----------------------
TO KILL A MOCKINGBIRD             HARPER LEE
WONDERFUL LIFE                    STEPHEN JAY GOULD
INNUMERACY                        JOHN ALLEN PAULOS
KIERKEGAARD ANTHOLOGY             ROBERT BRETALL
KIERKEGAARD ANTHOLOGY             SOREN KIERKEGAARD
ANNE OF GREEN GABLES              LUCY MAUD MONTGOMERY
GOOD DOG, CARL                    ALEXANDRA DAY
LETTERS AND PAPERS FROM PRISON    DIETRICH BONHOEFFER

BOOKSHELF
Title                             Publisher              CategoryName  Rating
------------------------------    ---------------------  ------------  ------
TO KILL A MOCKINGBIRD             HARPERCOLLINS          ADULTFIC      5
WONDERFUL LIFE                    W.W.NORTON & CO.       ADULTNF       5
INNUMERACY                        VINTAGE BOOKS          ADULTNF       4
KIERKEGAARD ANTHOLOGY             PRINCETON UNIV PR      ADULTREF      3
ANNE OF GREEN GABLES              GRAMMERCY              CHILDRENFIC   3
GOOD DOG, CARL                    LITTLE SIMON           CHILDRENPIC   1
LETTERS AND PAPERS FROM PRISON    SCRIBNER               ADULTNF       4
```

FIGURE 4-10. *Sample data from the BOOKSHELF tables* (continued)

Look up Harper Lee in the AuthorName column of the BOOKSHELF_AUTHOR table and you'll see that she has published one novel, whose title is *To Kill A Mockingbird.* You can then check the publisher, category, and rating for that book in the BOOKSHELF table. You can check the RATING table for a description of the rating.

When you looked up *To Kill A Mockingbird* in the BOOKSHELF table, you were searching by the primary key for the table. To find the author of that book, you could reverse your earlier search path, looking through BOOKSHELF_AUTHOR for the records that have that value in the Title column—the column Title is a foreign key in the BOOKSHELF_AUTHOR table. When the primary key for BOOKSHELF appears in another table, as it does in the BOOKSHELF_AUTHOR table, it is called a *foreign key* to that table.

These tables also show real-world characteristics: There are ratings and categories that are not yet used by books on the bookshelf. Because the data is organized logically, you can keep a record of potential categories, ratings, and authors even if none of the current books use those values.

This is a sensible and logical way to organize information, even if the "tables" are written in a ledger book or on scraps of paper kept in cigar boxes. Of course, there is still some work to do to turn this into a real database. For instance, AuthorName probably ought to be broken into FirstName and LastName, and you might want to find a way to show which author is the primary author, or if one is an editor rather than an author.

This whole process is called normalization. It really isn't any trickier than this. Although some other issues are involved in a good design, the basics of analyzing the "normal" relationships among the various elements of data are just as simple and straightforward as they've just been explained. It makes sense regardless of whether or not a relational database or a computer is involved at all.

One caution needs to be raised, however. Normalization is a part of the process of analysis. It is not design. Design of a database application includes many other considerations, and it is a fundamental mistake to believe that the normalized tables of the logical model are the "design" for the actual database. This fundamental confusion of analysis and design contributes to the stories in the press about the failure of major relational applications. These issues are addressed for developers more fully later in this chapter.

English Names for Tables and Columns

Once the relationships between the various elements of the data in an application are understood and the data elements are segregated appropriately, considerable thought must be devoted to choosing names for the tables and columns into which the data will be placed. This is an area given too little attention, even by those who should know better. Table and column names are often developed without consulting end users and without rigorous review. Both of these failings have serious consequences when it comes to actually using an application.

For example, consider the tables shown in Figure 4-10. The table and column names are virtually all self-explanatory. An end user, even one new to relational ideas and SQL, would have little difficulty understanding or even replicating a query such as this:

```
select Title, Publisher
   from BOOKSHELF
 order by Publisher;
```

Users understand this because the words are all familiar. There are no obscure or ill-defined terms. When tables with many more columns in them must be defined, naming the columns can be more difficult, but a few consistently enforced rules will help immensely. Consider some of the difficulties commonly caused by a lack of naming conventions. What if you had chosen these names instead?

BOOKSHELF	B_A	AUTHS	CATEGORIES
title	title	anam	cat
pub	anam	comms	p_cat
cat			s_cat
rat			

The naming techniques in this table, as bizarre as they look, are unfortunately very common. They represent tables and columns named by following the conventions (and lack of conventions) used by several well-known vendors and developers.

Here are a few of the more obvious difficulties in the list of names:

- *Abbreviations are used without good reason.* This makes remembering the "spelling" of a table or column name virtually impossible. The names may as well be codes, because the users will have to look them up.

- *Abbreviations are inconsistent.*

- *The purpose or meaning of a column or table is not apparent from the name.* In addition to abbreviations making the spelling of names difficult to remember, they obscure the nature of the data that the column or table contains. What is P_cat? Comms?

- *Undescores are used inconsistently.* Sometimes they are used to separate words in a name, but other times they are not. How will anyone remember which name does or doesn't have an underscore?

- *Use of plurals is inconsistent.* Is it CATEGORY or CATEGORIES? Comm or Comms?

- *Rules apparently used have immediate limitations.* If the first letter of the table name is to be used for a name column, as in Anam for a table whose table name starts with *A*, what happens when a second table beginning with the letter *A* becomes necessary? Does the name column in that table also get called Anam? If so, why isn't the column in both simply called Name?

These are only a few of the most obvious difficulties. Users subjected to poor naming of tables and columns will not be able to simply type English queries. The queries won't have the intuitive and familiar "feel" that the BOOKSHELF table query has, and this will harm the acceptance and usefulness of the application significantly.

Programmers used to be required to create names that were a maximum of six to eight characters in length. As a result, names unavoidably were confused mixes of letters, numbers, and cryptic abbreviations. Like so many other restrictions forced on users by older technology, this one is just no longer applicable. Oracle allows table and column names up to 30 characters long. This gives designers plenty of room to create full, unambiguous, and descriptive names.

The difficulties outlined here imply solutions, such as avoiding abbreviations and plurals, and either eliminating underscores or using them consistently. These quick rules of thumb will go a long way in solving the naming confusion so prevalent today. At the same time, naming conventions need to be simple, easily understood, and easily remembered. In a sense, what is called for is a normalization of names. In much the same way that data is analyzed logically, segregated by purpose, and thereby normalized, the same sort of logical attention needs to be given to naming standards. The job of building an application is improperly done without it.

English Words for the Data

Having raised the important issue of naming conventions for tables and columns, the next step is to look at the data itself. After all, when the data from the tables is printed on a report, how self-evident the data is will determine how understandable the report is. In the BOOKSHELF example, Rating is a code value, and Category is a concatenation of multiple values. Is this an improvement? If you asked another person about a book, would you want to hear that it was rated a 4 in AdultNF? Why should a machine be permitted to be less clear?

Additionally, keeping the information in English makes writing and understanding queries much simpler. The query should be as English-like as possible:

```
select Title, AuthorName
   from BOOKSHELF_AUTHOR;
```

Capitalization in Names and Data

Oracle makes it slightly easier to remember table and column names by ignoring whether you type in capital letters, small letters, or a mixture of the two. It stores table and column names in its internal data dictionary in uppercase. When you type a query, it instantly converts the table and column names to uppercase, and then checks for them in the dictionary. Some other relational systems are case sensitive. If users type a column name as "Ability," but the database thinks it is "ability" or "ABILITY" (depending on what it was told when the table was created), it will not understand the query.

> **NOTE**
> *You can force Oracle to create tables and columns with mixed-case names, but doing so will make querying and working with the data difficult. Use the default uppercase behavior.*

The ability to create case-sensitive table names is promoted as a benefit because it allows programmers to create many tables with, for instance, similar names. They can make a worker table, a Worker table, a wORker table, and so on. These will all be separate tables. How is anyone, including the programmer, supposed to remember the differences? This is a drawback, not a benefit, and Oracle was wise not to fall into this trap.

A similar case can be made for data stored in a database. There are ways to find information from the database regardless of whether the data is in uppercase or lowercase, but these methods impose an unnecessary burden. With few exceptions, such as legal text or form-letter paragraphs, it is much easier to store data in the database in uppercase. It makes queries easier and provides a more consistent appearance on reports. When and if some of this data needs to be put into lowercase, or mixed uppercase and lowercase (such as the name and address on a letter), then the Oracle functions that perform the conversion can be invoked. It will be less trouble overall, and less confusing, to store and report data in uppercase. You can interact with Oracle in ways that

make queries case insensitive, but it is generally simpler to develop applications with consistent case choices for your data.

Looking back over this chapter, you'll see that this practice was not followed. Rather, it was delayed until the subject could be introduced and put in its proper context. From here on, with the exception of one or two tables and a few isolated instances, data in the database will be in uppercase.

Normalizing Names

Several query tools have come on the market whose purpose is to let you make queries using common English words instead of odd conglomerations. These products work by building a logical map between the common English words and the hard-to-remember, non-English column names, table names, and codes. The mapping takes careful thought, but once completed, it makes the user's interaction with the application easy. But why not put the care in at the beginning? Why create a need for yet another layer, another product, and more work, when much of the confusion can be avoided simply by naming things better the first time around?

For performance reasons, it may be that some of an application's data must still be stored in a coded fashion within the computer's database. These codes should not be exposed to users, during either data entry or retrieval, and Oracle allows them to be easily hidden.

The instant that data entry requires codes, key-entry errors increase. When reports contain codes instead of English, errors of interpretation begin. And when users need to create new or ad hoc reports, their ability to do so quickly and accurately is severely impaired both by codes and by not being able to remember strange column and table names.

Oracle gives users the power to see and work with English throughout the entire application. It is a waste of Oracle's power to ignore this opportunity, and it will without question produce a less understandable and less productive application. Developers should seize the opportunity. Users should demand it. Both will benefit immeasurably.

Good Design Has a Human Touch

At this point, if you are new to Oracle you may want to go right into working with Oracle and the SQL language. That is covered in the next chapter; the remainder of this chapter focuses on performance, naming, and design considerations. You can refer back to this section later when you are ready to design and implement an application.

This section looks at a method of approaching a development project that takes into account the real business tasks your end users have to accomplish. This distinguishes this method from the more common data orientation of many developers and development methodologies. Data normalization and CASE (Computer Aided Software Engineering) technologies have become so much the center of attention with relational application development that a focus on the data and the issues of referential integrity, keys, normalization, and table diagrams has become almost an obsession. These issues are so often confused with design—and even believed to *be* design—that the reminder that they are analysis is often met with surprise.

Normalization is analysis, not design. And it is only a part of the analysis necessary to understand a business and build a useful application. The goal of application development, after all, is to help the business run more successfully by improving the speed and efficiency with which business tasks are done and by making the environment in which people work as meaningful and supportive as possible. Give people control over their information, and intuitive, straightforward access to it,

and they will respond gratefully and productively. Assign the control to a remote group, cloud the information in codes and user-hostile interfaces, and they will be unhappy and unproductive.

The methods outlined in this section are not intended to be a rigorous elucidation of the process, and the tools you use and are familiar with for data structures or flows are probably sufficient for the task. The purpose here is to disclose an approach that is effective in creating responsive, appropriate, and accommodating applications.

Understanding the Application Tasks

One of the often-neglected steps in building software is understanding the end user's job—the tasks that computer automation is intended to support. Occasionally, this is because the application itself is quite specialized; more often, it is because the approach to design tends to be data oriented. Frequently, these are the major questions asked in the analysis:

- ■ What data should be captured?

- ■ How should the data be processed?

- ■ How should the data be reported?

These questions expand into a series of subquestions, and they include issues such as input forms, codes, screen layouts, computations, postings, corrections, audit trails, retention, storage volumes, processing cycles, report formatting, distribution, and maintenance. These are all vitally important areas. One difficulty, however, is that they all focus solely on data.

People *use* data, but they *do* tasks. One might argue that although this may be true of professional workers, key-entry clerks really only transfer data from an input form to a keyboard; their tasks are very data oriented. This is a fair portrayal of these jobs today. But is this a consequence of the real job that needs to get done, or is it a symptom of the design of the computer application? Using humans as input devices, particularly for data that is voluminous, consistent in format (as on forms), and in a limited range of variability, is an expensive and antiquated, not to mention dehumanizing, method of capturing data. Like the use of codes to accommodate machine limitations, it's an idea whose time has passed.

This may sound like so much philosophy, but it has practical import in the way application design is done. People use data, but they do tasks. And they don't do tasks through to completion one at a time. They do several tasks that are subsets of or in intersection with each other, and they do them all at once, in parallel.

When designers allow this idea to direct the analysis and creation of an application, rather than focusing on the data orientation that has been historically dominant, the very nature of the effort changes significantly. Why have windowing environments been so successful? Because they allow a user to jump quickly among small tasks, keeping them all active without having to shut down and exit one in order to begin another. The windowing environment comes closer to mapping the way people really think and work than the old "one thing at a time" approach ever did. This lesson should not be lost. It should be built upon.

Understanding the application tasks means going far beyond identifying the data elements, normalizing them, and creating screens, processing programs, and reports. It means really understanding what the users do and what their tasks are, and designing the application to be responsive to those tasks, not just to capture the data associated with them. In fact, when the orientation is toward the data, the resulting design will inevitably *distort* the users' tasks rather than support them.

How do you design an application that is responsive to tasks rather than data? The biggest hurdle is simply understanding that focusing on tasks is necessary. This allows you to approach the analysis of the business from a fresh perspective.

The first step in the analysis process is to understand the tasks. For which tasks do the members of this group really need to use computers? What is the real service or product produced? This seems like a fundamental and even simplistic first question, but you'll find that a surprising number of business people are quite unclear about the answer. An amazing number of businesses, from healthcare to banking, from shipping to manufacturing, used to think they were in the data processing business. After all, they input data, process it, and report it, don't they? This delusion is yet another symptom of the data orientation our systems designs have had that has led dozens of companies to attempt to market their imagined "real" product, data processing, with disastrous consequences for most of them.

Hence the importance of learning about a business application: You have to keep an open mind, and may often have to challenge pet notions about what the business is in order to learn what it really is. This is a healthy, if sometimes difficult, process.

And, just as it is essential that business people become literate users of SQL and understand the basics of the relational model, so it is important that application designers really understand the service or product being delivered, and the tasks *necessary* to make that happen. A project team that includes end users who have been introduced to the essentials of SQL and the relational approach, such as by reading this book, and designers who are sensitive to end users' needs and understand the value of a task-oriented, readable application environment, will turn out extraordinarily good systems. The members of such a project team check, support, and enhance each other's efforts.

One approach to this process is to develop two converging documents: a task document and a data document. It is in the process of preparing the task document that the deep understanding of the application comes about. The data document will help implement the vision and ensure that the details and rules are all accounted for, but the task document defines the vision of what the business is.

Outline of Tasks

The task document is a joint effort of the business users and the application designers. It lists the tasks associated with the business from the top down. It begins with a basic description of the business. This should be a simple declarative sentence of three to ten words, in the active voice, without commas and with a minimum of adjectives:

We sell insurance.

It should not be:

Amalgamated Diversified is a leading international supplier of financial resources, training, information processing, transaction capture and distribution, communications, customer support, and industry direction in the field of shared risk funding for health care maintenance, property preservation, and automobile liability.

There is a tremendous temptation to cram every little detail about a business and its dreams about itself into this first sentence. Don't do it. The effort of trimming the descriptive excesses down to a simple sentence focuses the mind wonderfully. If you can't get the business down to ten words, you haven't understood it yet.

But, as an application designer, creating this sentence isn't your task alone; it is a joint effort with the business user, and it initiates the task documentation process. It provides you with the opportunity to begin serious questioning about what the business does and how it does it. This is a valuable process for the business itself, quite independent of the fact that an application is being built. You will encounter numerous tasks and subtasks, procedures, and rules that will prove to be meaningless or of marginal use. Typically, these are artifacts of either a previous problem, long since solved, or of information or reporting requests from managers long since departed.

Some wags have suggested that the way to deal with too many reports being created, whether manually or by computer, is to simply stop producing them and see if anyone notices. This is a humorous notion, but the seed of truth it contains needs to be a part of the task documentation process. In fact, it proved quite useful in Y2K remediation efforts—many programs and reports didn't have to be fixed, simply because they were no longer used!

Your approach to the joint effort of documenting tasks allows you to ask skeptical questions and look at (and reevaluate the usefulness of) what may be mere artifacts. Be aware, however, that you need to proceed with the frank acknowledgment that you, as a designer, cannot understand the business as thoroughly as the user does. There is an important line between seizing the opportunity of an application development project to rationalize what tasks are done and why, and possibly offending the users by presuming to understand the "real" business better than they do.

Ask the user to describe a task in detail and explain to you the reason for each step. If the reason is a weak one, such as "We've always done it this way," or "I think they use this upstairs for something," red flags should go up. Say that you don't understand, and ask again for an explanation. If the response is still unsatisfactory, put the task and your question on a separate list for resolution. Some of these will be answered simply by someone who knows the subject better, others will require talking to senior management, and many tasks will end up eliminated because they are no longer needed. One of the evidences of a good analysis process is the improvement of existing procedures, independent of, and generally long before, the implementation of a new computer application.

General Format of the Task Document
This is the general format for the task document:

- Summary sentence describing the business (three to ten words)

- Summary sentences describing and numbering the major tasks of the business (short sentences, short words)

- Additional levels of task detail, as needed, within each of the major tasks

By all means, follow the summary sentence for every level with a short, descriptive paragraph, if you want, but don't use this as an excuse to avoid the effort of making the summary sentence clear and crisp. Major tasks are typically numbered 1.0, 2.0, 3.0, and so on, and are sometimes referred to as *zero-level tasks*. The levels below each of these are numbered using additional dots, as in 3.1 and 3.1.14. Each major task is taken down to the level where it is a collection of *atomic tasks*—tasks for which no subtask is meaningful in itself and that, once started, is either taken to completion or dropped entirely. Atomic tasks are never left half-finished.

Writing a check is an atomic task; filling in the dollar amount is not. Answering the telephone as a customer service representative is not an atomic task; answering the phone and fulfilling the customer's request is atomic. Atomic tasks must be meaningful and must complete an action.

The level at which a task is atomic will vary by task. The task represented by 3.1.14 may be atomic yet still have several additional sublevels. The task 3.2 may be atomic, or 3.1.16.4 may be. What is important is not the numbering scheme (which is nothing more than a method for outlining a hierarchy of tasks) but the decomposition to the atomic level. The atomic tasks are the fundamental building blocks of the business. Two tasks can still be atomic if one occasionally depends upon the other, but only if each can and does get completed independently. If two tasks always depend upon each other, they are not atomic. The real atomic task includes them both.

In most businesses, you will quickly discover that many tasks do not fit neatly into just one of the major (zero-level) tasks, but seem to span two or more, and work in a network or "dotted line" fashion. This is nearly always evidence of improper definition of the major tasks or incomplete atomization of the lower tasks. The goal is to turn each task into a conceptual "object," with a well-defined idea of what it does (its goal in life) and what resources (data, computation, thinking, paper, pencil, and so on) it uses to accomplish its goal.

Insights Resulting from the Task Document

Several insights come out of the task document. First, because the task document is task oriented rather than data oriented, it is likely to substantially change the way user screens are designed. It will affect what data is captured, how it is presented, how help is implemented, and how users switch from one task to another. The task orientation will help ensure that the most common kinds of jumping between tasks will not require inordinate effort from the user.

Second, the categorization of major tasks will change as conflicts are discovered; this will affect how both the designers and the business users understand the business.

Third, even the summary sentence itself will probably change. Rationalizing a business into atomic task "objects" forces a clearing out of artifacts, misconceptions, and unneeded dependencies that have long weighed down the business unnecessarily.

This is not a painless process, but the benefits in terms of the business's self-understanding, the cleanup of procedures, and the automation of the tasks will usually far exceed the emotional costs and time spent. It helps immensely if there is general understanding going into the project that uncomfortable questions will be asked, incorrect assumptions will be corrected, and step-by-step adjustments will be made to the task document until it is completed.

Understanding the Data

In conjunction with the decomposition and description of the tasks, the resources required at each step are described in the task document, especially in terms of the data required. This is done on a task-by-task basis, and the data requirements are then included in the data document. This is a conceptually different approach from the classical view of the data. You will not simply take the forms and screens currently used by each task and record the elements they contain. The flaw in this "piece of paper in a cigar box" approach lies in our tendency (even though we don't like to admit it) to accept anything printed on paper as necessary or true.

In looking at each task, you should determine what data is necessary to do the task, rather than what data elements are on the form you use to do the task. By requiring that the definition of the data needed come from the task rather than from any existing forms or screens, you force an examination of the true purpose of the task and the real data requirements. If the person doing the task doesn't know the use to which data is put, the element goes on the list for resolution. An amazing amount of garbage is eliminated by this process.

Once the current data elements have been identified, they must be carefully scrutinized. Numeric and letter codes are always suspect. They disguise real information behind counterintuitive, meaningless symbols. There are times and tasks for which codes are handy, easily remembered, or made necessary by sheer volume. But, in your final design, these cases should be rare and obvious. If they are not, you've lost your way.

In the scrutiny of existing data elements, codes should be set aside for special attention. In each case, ask yourself whether the element should be a code. Its continued use as a code should be viewed suspiciously. There must be good arguments and compelling reasons for perpetuating the disguise. The process for converting codes back into English is fairly simple, but it's a joint effort. The codes are first listed by data element, along with their meanings. These are then examined by users and designers, and short English versions of the meanings are proposed, discussed, and tentatively approved.

In this same discussion, designers and end users should decide on names for the data elements. These will become column names in the database, and will be regularly used in English queries, so the names should be descriptive (avoiding abbreviations, other than those common to the business) and singular. Because of the intimate relationship between the column name and the data it contains, the two should be specified simultaneously. A thoughtful choice of a column name will vastly simplify determining its new English contents.

Data elements that are not codes also must be rigorously examined. By this point, you have good reason to believe that all the data elements you've identified are necessary to the business tasks, but they are not necessarily well organized. What appears to be one data element in the existing task may in fact be several elements mixed together that require separation. Names, addresses, and phone numbers are very common examples of this, but every application has a wealth of others.

First and last names were mixed together, for example, in the AUTHOR table. The AuthorName column held both first and last names, even though the tables were in Third Normal Form. This would be an extremely burdensome way to actually implement an application, in spite of the fact that the normalization rules were technically met. To make the application practical and prepare it for English queries, the AuthorName column needs to be decomposed into at least two new columns, LastName and FirstName. This same categorization process is regularly needed in rationalizing other data elements, and it's often quite independent of normalization.

The degree of decomposition depends on how the particular data elements are likely to be used. It is possible to go much too far and decompose categories that, though made up of separable pieces, provide no additional value in their new state. Decomposition is application dependent on an element-by-element basis. Once decomposition has been done, these new elements, which will become columns, need to be thoughtfully named, and the data they will contain needs to be scrutinized. Text data that will fall into a definable number of values should be reviewed for naming. These column names and values, like those of the codes, are tentative.

The Atomic Data Models

Now the process of normalization begins, and with it the drawing of the atomic data models. There are many good texts on the subject and a wide variety of analysis and design tools that can speed the process, so this book doesn't suggest any particular method, because recommending one method may hinder rather than help.

Each atomic transaction should be modeled, and it should be labeled with the task number to which it applies. Included in the model are table names, primary and foreign keys, and major

columns. Each normalized relationship should have a descriptive name, and estimated row counts and transaction rates should appear with each table. Accompanying each model is an additional sheet with all the columns and datatypes, their ranges of value, and the tentative names for the tables, columns, and named values in the columns.

The Atomic Business Model

This data document is now combined with the task document. The combined document is a business model. It's reviewed jointly by the application designers and end users for accuracy and completeness.

The Business Model

At this point, both the application designers and the end users should possess a clear vision of the business, its tasks, and its data. Once the business model is corrected and approved, the process of synthesizing the tasks and data models into an overall business model begins. This part of the process sorts common data elements between tasks, completes final, large-scale normalization, and resolves consistent, definitive names for all the parts.

This can be quite a large drawing for major applications, with supporting documentation that includes the tasks, the data models (with corrected element names, based on the full model), and a list of all the full-scale tables and their column names, datatypes, and contents. A final check of the effort is made by tracing the data access paths of each transaction in the full business model to determine that all the data the transaction requires is available for selection or insertion, and that no tasks insert data with elements missing that are essential to the model's referential integrity.

With the exception of the effort spent to properly name the various tables, columns, and common values, virtually everything to this point has been analysis, not design. The aim has been to promote understanding of the business and its components.

Data Entry

Screen design does not proceed from the business model. It is not focused on tables, but rather on tasks, so screens are created that support the task orientation and the need to jump between subtasks when necessary. In practical terms, this will often map readily to a primary table used by the task, and to other tables that can be queried for values or updated as the primary table is accessed.

But there will also be occasions when there simply is no main table, but instead a variety of related tables, all of which will supply or receive data to support the task. These screens will look and act quite differently from the typical table-oriented screens developed in many applications, but they will significantly amplify the effectiveness of their users and their contribution to the business. And that's the whole purpose of this approach.

The interaction between the user and the machine is critical; the input and query screens should consistently be task oriented and descriptive, in English. The use of icons and graphical interfaces plays an important role as well. Screens must reflect the way work is actually done and be built to respond in the language in which business is conducted.

Query and Reporting

If anything sets apart the relational approach, and SQL, from more traditional application environments, it is the ability for end users to easily learn and execute ad hoc queries. These are those reports and one-time queries that are outside of the basic set usually developed and delivered along with the application code.

With Oracle's SQL*Plus utility, a command line utility for creating and querying database objects, end users are given unprecedented control over their own data. Both the users and developers benefit from this ability: the users because they can build reports, analyze information, modify their queries, and reexecute them, all in a matter of minutes, and the developers because they are relieved of the undesirable requirement of creating new reports.

Users are granted the power to look into their data, analyze it, and respond with a speed and thoroughness unimaginable just a few years ago. This leap in productivity is greatly extended if the tables, columns, and data values are carefully crafted in English; it is greatly foreshortened if bad naming conventions and meaningless codes and abbreviations are permitted to infect the design. The time spent in the design process to name the objects consistently and descriptively will pay off quickly for the users, and therefore for the business.

Some people, typically those who have not built major relational applications, fear that turning query facilities over to end users will cripple the machine on which the facilities are used. The fear is that users will write inefficient queries that will consume overwhelming numbers of CPU cycles, slowing the machine and every other user. Experience shows that this generally is not true. Users quickly learn which kinds of queries run fast, and which do not. Further, most business intelligence and reporting tools available today can estimate the amount of time a query will take, and restrict access—by user, time of day, or both—to queries that would consume a disproportionate amount of resources. In practice, the demands users make on a machine only occasionally get out of hand, but the benefits they derive far exceed the cost of the processing. Virtually any time you can move effort from a person to a machine, you save money.

The real goal of design is to clarify and satisfy the needs of the business and business users. If there is a bias, it must always be toward making the application easier to understand and use, particularly at the expense of CPU or disk, but less so if the cost is an internal complexity so great that maintenance and change become difficult and slow.

Toward Object Name Normalization

The basic approach to naming is to choose meaningful, memorable, and descriptive readable names, avoiding abbreviations and codes, and using underscores either consistently or not at all. In a large application, table, column, and data names will often be multiword, as in the case of ReversedSuspenseAccount or Last_GL_Close_Date. The goal of thoughtful naming methods is ease of use: The names must be easily remembered and must follow rules that are easily explained and applied. In the pages ahead, a somewhat more rigorous approach to naming is presented, with the ultimate goal of developing a formal process of object name normalization.

Level-Name Integrity

In a relational database system, the hierarchy of objects ranges from the database, to the table owners, to the tables, to the columns, to the data values. In very large systems, there may even be multiple databases, and these may be distributed within locations. For the sake of brevity, the higher levels will be ignored for now, but what is said will apply to them as well.

Each level in this hierarchy is defined within the level above it, and each level should be given names appropriate to its own level and should not incorporate names from outside its own level. For example, a table cannot have two columns called Name, and the account named George cannot own two tables named AUTHOR.

There is no requirement that each of George's tables have a name that is unique throughout the entire database. Other owners may have AUTHOR tables as well. Even if George is granted

access to them, there is no confusion, because he can identify each table uniquely by prefixing its owner's name to the table name, as in Dietrich.AUTHOR. It would not be logically consistent to incorporate George's owner name into the name of each of his tables, as in GEOAUTHOR, GEOBOOKSHELF, and so on. This confuses and complicates the table name by placing part of its parent's name in its own, in effect a violation of *level-name integrity.*

Brevity should never be favored over clarity. Including pieces of table names in column names is a bad technique, because it violates the logical idea of levels and the level-name integrity that this requires. It is also confusing, requiring users to look up column names virtually every time they want to write a query. Object names must be unique within their parent, but no incorporation of names from outside an object's own level should be permitted.

The support for abstract datatypes in Oracle strengthens your ability to create consistent names for attributes. If you create a datatype called ADDRESS_TY, it will have the same attributes each time it is used. Each of the attributes will have a consistent name, datatype, and length, making their implementation more consistent across the enterprise. However, using abstract datatypes in this manner requires that you do both of the following:

- Properly define the datatypes at the start so that you can avoid the need to modify the datatype later.

- Support the syntax requirements of abstract datatypes.

Foreign Keys

The one area of difficulty with using brief column names is the occasional appearance of a foreign key in a table in which another column has the same name that the foreign key column has in its home table. One possible long-term solution is to allow the use of the full foreign key name, including the table name of its home table, as a column name in the local table (such as BOOKSHELF.Title as a column name).

The practical need to solve the same-name column problem requires one of the following actions:

- Invent a name that incorporates the source table of the foreign key in its name without using the dot (using an underscore, for instance).

- Invent a name that incorporates an abbreviation of the source table of the foreign key in its name.

- Invent a name different from its name in its source table.

- Change the name of the conflicting column.

None of these is particularly attractive, but if you come across the same-name dilemma, you'll need to take one of these actions.

Singular Names

One area of great inconsistency and confusion is the question of whether objects should have singular or plural names. Should it be the AUTHOR table or the AUTHORS table? Should it be the Name column or the Names column?

There are two helpful ways to think about this issue. First, consider some columns common to nearly every database: Name, Address, City, State, and Zip. Other than the first column, does it ever occur to anyone to make these names plural? It is nearly self-evident when considering these names that they describe the contents of a single row, a record. Even though relational databases are "set oriented," clearly the fundamental unit of a set is a row, and it is the content of that row that is well-described by singular column names. When designing a data-entry screen to capture a person's name and address, should it look like this?

```
Names: _____

Addresses: _____

Cities: _____ States __ Zips _____-____
```

Or will you make these column names singular on the screen because you're capturing *one* name and address at a time, but tell the users that when they write queries they must all be converted to plural? It is simply more intuitive and straightforward to restrict column names to singular.

If all objects are named consistently, neither you nor a user has to try to remember the rules for what is plural and what isn't. The benefit of this should be obvious. Suppose we decide that all objects will henceforth be plural. We now have "s" or "es" on the end of virtually every object, perhaps even on the end of each word in a long multiword object name. Of what possible benefit is it to key all these extra letters all the time? Is it easier to use? Is it easier to understand? Is it easier to remember? Obviously, it is none of these.

Therefore, the best solution is this: All object names are always singular. The sole exception to this rule is any widely accepted term already commonly used in the business, such as "sales."

Brevity

As mentioned earlier, clarity should never be sacrificed for brevity, but given two equally meaningful, memorable, and descriptive names, always choose the shorter. During application development, propose alternative column and table names such as these to a group of users and developers and get their input on choosing the clearest name. How do you build lists of alternatives? Use a thesaurus and a dictionary. On a project team dedicated to developing superior, productive applications, every team member should be given a thesaurus and a dictionary as basic equipment, and then should be reminded over and over again of the importance of careful object naming.

Object Name Thesaurus

Ultimately, relational databases should include an object name thesaurus, just as they include a data dictionary. This thesaurus should enforce the company's naming standards and ensure consistency of name choice and abbreviation (where used).

Such standards may require the use of underscores in object naming to make the parsing of the name into component parts a straightforward task. This also helps enforce the consistent use of underscores, rather than the scattered, inconsistent usage within an application that underscores frequently receive now.

If you work directly with a government agency or large firm, that organization may already have object-naming standards. The object-naming standards of large organizations have over the

years radiated into the rest of the commercial marketplace, and they may form the basis for the naming standards used at your company. For example, those standards may provide the direction to choose between "Corporation" and "Firm." If they do not, you should develop your naming standards to be consistent, both with those base standards and with the guidelines put forth in this chapter.

Intelligent Keys and Column Values

Intelligent keys are so named because they contain nontrivial combinations of information. The term is misleading in the extreme because it implies something positive or worthwhile. A more meaningful term might be *overloaded* keys. General ledger and product codes often fall into this category and contain all the difficulties associated with other codes, and more. Further, the difficulties found in overloaded keys also apply to non-key columns that are packed with more than one piece of meaningful data.

Typical of an overloaded key or column value is this description: "The first character is the region code. The next four characters are the catalog number. The final digit is the cost center code, unless this is an imported part, in which case an *I* is tagged onto the end of the number, or unless it is a high-volume item, such as screws, in which case only three digits are used for catalog number, and the region code is HD."

Eliminating overloaded key and column values is essential in good relational design. The dependencies built on pieces of these keys (usually foreign keys into other tables) are all at risk if the structure is maintained. Unfortunately, many application areas have overloaded keys that have been used for years and are deeply embedded in the company's tasks. Some of them were created during earlier efforts at automation, using databases that could not support multiple key columns for composite keys. Others came about through historical accretion, by forcing a short code, usually numeric, to mean more and to cover more cases than it was ever intended to at the beginning. Eliminating the existing overloaded keys may have practical ramifications that make it impossible to do immediately. This makes building a new, relational application more difficult.

The solution to this problem is to create a new set of keys, both primary and foreign, that properly normalizes the data; then, make sure that people can access tables only through these new keys. The overloaded key is then kept as an additional, and unique, table column. Access to it is still possible using historical methods (matching the overloaded key in a query, for instance), but the newly structured keys are promoted as the preferred method of access. Over time, with proper training, users will gravitate to the new keys. Eventually, the overloaded keys (and other overloaded column values) can simply be **NULL**ed out or dropped from the table.

Failing to eliminate overloaded keys and values makes extracting information from the database, validating the values, ensuring data integrity, and modifying the structure all extremely difficult and costly.

The Commandments

All the major issues in designing for productivity have now been discussed. It probably is worthwhile to sum these up in a single place—thus "The Commandments" (or perhaps "The Suggestions"). Their presentation does not assume that you need to be told what to do, but rather that you are capable of making rational judgments and can benefit from the experience of others facing the same challenges. The purpose here is not to describe the development cycle, which you probably

understand better than you want to, but rather to bias that development with an orientation that will radically change how the application will look, feel, and be used. Careful attention to these ideas can dramatically improve the productivity and happiness of an application's users.

The ten commandments of humane design:

1. Include users. Put them on the project team and teach them the relational model and SQL.

2. Name tables, columns, keys, and data jointly with the users. Develop an application thesaurus to ensure name consistency.

3. Use English words that are meaningful, memorable, descriptive, short, and singular. Use underscores consistently or not at all.

4. Don't mix levels in naming.

5. Avoid codes and abbreviations.

6. Use meaningful keys where possible.

7. Decompose overloaded keys.

8. Analyze and design from the tasks, not just the data. Remember that normalization is not design.

9. Move tasks from users to the machine. It is profitable to spend cycles and storage to gain ease of use.

10. Don't be seduced by development speed. Take time and care in analyses, design, testing, and tuning.

There's a reason why this chapter precedes the ones on the commands and functions—if you have a poor design, your application will suffer no matter what commands you use. Plan for functionality, plan for performance, plan for recoverability, plan for security, and plan for availability. Plan for success.

PART
II

SQL and SQL*Plus

CHAPTER
5

The Basic Parts of
Speech in SQL

ith the Structured Query Language (SQL), you tell Oracle which information you want it to **select**, **insert**, **update**, or **delete**. In fact, these four verbs are the primary words you will use to give Oracle instructions. As of Oracle9*i*, you can use an additional command, **merge**, to perform **insert**s and **update**s with a single command. As of Oracle Database 10*g*, the **merge** command capabilities have been extended to include greater control over the **insert**s, **update**s, and even **delete**s performed within a single statement. Also as of Oracle Database 10*g*, these basic commands are further enhanced to support flashback version queries and other features.

In Part I, you saw what is meant by "relational," how tables are organized into columns and rows, and how to instruct Oracle to select certain columns from a table and show you the information in them, row by row. In this and the following chapters, you will learn how to do this more completely for the different datatypes supported by Oracle. In this part, you will learn how to interact with SQL*Plus, a powerful Oracle product that can take your instructions for Oracle, check them for correctness, submit them to Oracle, and then modify or reformat the response Oracle gives, based on orders or directions you've set in place.

It may be a little confusing at first to understand the difference between what SQL*Plus is doing and what Oracle is doing, especially because the error messages that Oracle produces are simply passed on to you by SQL*Plus, but you will see as you work through this book where the differences lie. As you get started, just think of SQL*Plus as a coworker—an assistant who follows your instructions and helps you do your work more quickly. You interact with this coworker by typing on your keyboard.

You may follow the examples in this and subsequent chapters by typing the commands shown. Your Oracle and SQL*Plus programs should respond just as they do in these examples. However, you do need to make certain that the tables used in this book have been loaded into your copy of Oracle.

You can understand what is described in this book without actually typing it in yourself; for example, you can use the commands shown with your own tables. It will probably be clearer and easier, though, if you have the same tables loaded into Oracle as the ones used here and practice using the same queries.

The CD contains instructions on loading the tables. Assuming that you have loaded the demo tables into an Oracle database, you can connect to SQL*Plus and begin working by typing this:

```
sqlplus
```

(If you want to run SQL*Plus from your desktop client machine, select the SQL Plus program option from the Application Development menu option under the Oracle software menu option.) This starts SQL*Plus. (Note that you don't type the * that is in the middle of the official product name, and the asterisk doesn't appear in the program name, either. Because Oracle is careful to guard who can access the data it stores, it requires that you enter an ID and password to connect to it. Oracle will display a copyright message and then ask for your username and password. Log into your database using the account and password you created to hold the sample tables (such as practice/practice). If you provide a valid username and password, SQL*Plus will announce that you're connected to Oracle and then will display this prompt:

```
SQL>
```

You are now in SQL*Plus, and it awaits your instructions. If the command fails, there are several potential reasons: Oracle is not in your path, you are not authorized to use SQL*Plus, or Oracle hasn't been installed properly on your computer. If you get the message

```
ERROR: ORA-1017: invalid username/password; logon denied
```

either you've entered the username or password incorrectly or your username has not yet been set up properly on your copy of Oracle. After three unsuccessful attempts to enter a username and password that Oracle recognizes, SQL*Plus will terminate the attempt to log on, showing this message:

```
unable to CONNECT to ORACLE after 3 attempts, exiting SQL*Plus
```

If you get this message, contact your company's database administrator. Assuming everything is in order, and the SQL> prompt has appeared, you may now begin working with SQL*Plus. When you want to quit working and leave SQL*Plus, type this:

```
quit
```

Style

First, some comments on style. SQL*Plus doesn't care whether the SQL commands you type are in uppercase or lowercase. For example, the command

```
SeLeCt feaTURE, section, PAGE FROM newsPaPeR;
```

will produce exactly the same result as this one:

```
select Feature, Section, Page from NEWSPAPER;
```

Case matters only when SQL*Plus or Oracle is checking an alphanumeric value for equality. If you tell Oracle to find a row where Section = 'f', and Section is really equal to 'F', Oracle won't find it (because *f* and *F* are not identical). Aside from this usage, case is completely irrelevant. (Incidentally, 'F', as used here, is called a *literal*, meaning that you want Section to be tested literally against the letter *F*, not a column *named* F. The single quote marks enclosing the letter tell Oracle that this is a literal and not a column name.)

As a matter of style, this book follows certain conventions about case to make the text easier to read:

- **select**, **from**, **where**, **order by**, **having**, and **group by** will always be lowercase and boldface in the body of the text.

- SQL*Plus commands also will be lowercase and boldface (for example, **column**, **set**, **save**, **ttitle**, and so on).

- **IN**, **BETWEEN**, **UPPER**, and other SQL operators and functions will be uppercase and boldface.

- Column names will be mixed uppercase and lowercase without boldface (for example, Feature, EastWest, Longitude, and so on).

- Table names will be uppercase without boldface (for example, NEWSPAPER, WEATHER, LOCATION, and so on).

You may want to follow similar conventions in creating your own queries, or your company already may have standards it would like you to use. You may even choose to invent your own. Regardless, the goal of any such standards should always be to make your work simple to read and understand.

Creating the NEWSPAPER Table

The examples in this book are based on the tables created by the scripts located on the CD. Each table is created via the **create table** command, which specifies the names of the columns in the table, as well as the characteristics of those columns. Here is the **create table** command for the NEWSPAPER table, which is used in many of the examples in this chapter:

```
create table NEWSPAPER (
Feature       VARCHAR2(15) not null,
Section       CHAR(1),
Page          NUMBER
);
```

In later chapters in this book, you'll see how to interpret all the clauses of this command. For now, you can read it as, "Create a table called NEWSPAPER. It will have three columns, named Feature (a variable-length character column), Section (a fixed-length character column), and Page (a numeric column). The values in the Feature column can be up to 15 characters long, and every row must have a value for Feature. Section values will all be one character long."

In later chapters, you'll see how to extend this simple command to add constraints, indexes, and storage clauses. For now, the NEWSPAPER table will be kept simple so that the examples can focus on SQL.

Using SQL to Select Data from Tables

Figure 5-1 shows a table of features from a local newspaper. If this were an Oracle table, rather than just paper and ink on the front of the local paper, SQL*Plus would display it for you if you typed this:

```
select Feature, Section, Page from NEWSPAPER;

FEATURE          S     PAGE
--------------- - ----------
National News    A       1
Sports           D       1
Editorials       A      12
Business         E       1
Weather          C       2
```

```
Television      B       7
Births          F       7
Classified      F       8
Modern Life     B       1
Comics          C       4
Movies          B       4
Bridge          B       2
Obituaries      F       6
Doctor Is In    F       6

14 rows selected.
```

NOTE
*Depending on your configuration, the listing may have a page break in it. If that happens, use the **set pagesize** command to increase the size of each displayed page of results. See the Alphabetical Reference for details on this command.*

What's different between the table you created and the one shown in the output in Figure 5-1? Both tables have the same information, but the format differs and the order of rows may be different.

Feature	Section	Page
Births	F	7
Bridge	B	2
Business	E	1
Classified	F	8
Comics	C	4
Doctor Is In	F	6
Editorials	A	12
Modern Life	B	1
Movies	B	4
National News	A	1
Obituaries	F	6
Sports	D	1
Television	B	7
Weather	C	2

FIGURE 5-1. *A NEWSPAPER table*

For example, the column headings differ slightly. In fact, they even differ slightly from the columns you just asked for in the **select** statement.

Notice that the column named Section shows up as just the letter *S*. Also, although you used uppercase and lowercase letters to type the column headings in the command

```
select Feature, Section, Page from NEWSPAPER;
```

the column headings came back with all the letters in uppercase.

These changes are the result of the assumptions SQL*Plus makes about how information should be presented. You can change these assumptions, and you probably will, but until you give SQL*Plus different orders, this is how it changes what you input:

- It changes all the column headings to uppercase.

- It allows columns to be only as wide as a column is defined to be in Oracle.

- It squeezes out any spaces if the column heading is a function. (This will be demonstrated in Chapter 7.)

The first point is obvious. The column names you used were shifted to uppercase. The second point is not obvious. How *are* the columns defined? To find out, ask Oracle. Simply tell SQL*Plus to **describe** the table, as shown here:

```
describe NEWSPAPER
```

Name	Null?	Type
FEATURE	NOT NULL	VARCHAR2(15)
SECTION		CHAR(1)
PAGE		NUMBER

This display is a descriptive table that lists the columns and their definitions for the NEWSPAPER table; the **describe** command works for any table. Note that the details in this description match the **create table** command given earlier in this chapter.

The first column tells the names of the columns in the table being described.

The second column (Null?) is really a rule about the column named to its left. When the NEWSPAPER table was created, the **NOT NULL** rule instructed Oracle not to allow any user to add a new row to the table if he or she left the Feature column empty (**NULL** means empty). Of course, in a table such as NEWSPAPER, it probably would have been worthwhile to use the same rule for all three columns. What good is it to know the title of a feature without also knowing what section it's in and what page it's on? But, for the sake of this example, only Feature was created with the rule that it could not be **NULL**.

Because Section and Page have nothing in the Null? column, they are allowed to be empty in any row of the NEWSPAPER table.

The third column (Type) tells the basic nature of the individual columns. Feature is a VARCHAR2 (variable-length character) column that can be up to 15 characters (letters, numbers, symbols, or spaces) long.

Section is a character column as well, but it is only one character long. The creator of the table knew that newspaper sections in the local paper are only a single letter, so the column was defined

to be only as wide as it needed to be. It was defined using the CHAR datatype, which is used for fixed-length character strings. When SQL*Plus went to display the results of your query

```
select Feature, Section, Page from NEWSPAPER;
```

it knew from Oracle that Section was a maximum of only one character. It assumed that you did not want to use up more space than this, so it displayed a column just one character wide and used as much of the column name as it could—in this case, just the letter *S*.

The third column in the NEWSPAPER table is Page, which is simply a number. Notice that the Page column shows up as ten spaces wide, even though no pages use more than two digits— numbers usually are not defined as having a maximum width, so SQL*Plus assumes a maximum just to get started.

You also may have noticed that the heading for the only column composed solely of numbers, Page, was *right-justified*—that is, it sits over on the right side of the column, whereas the headings for columns that contain characters sit over on the left. This is standard alignment for column headings in SQL*Plus. As with other column features, you'll see in Chapter 6 how to change alignment as needed.

Finally, SQL*Plus tells you how many rows it found in Oracle's NEWSPAPER table. (Notice the "14 rows selected" notation at the bottom of the display.) This is called *feedback*. You can make SQL*Plus stop giving feedback by setting the **feedback** option, as shown here:

```
set feedback off
```

Alternatively, you can set a minimum number of rows for **feedback** to work:

```
set feedback 25
```

This last example tells Oracle that you don't want to know how many rows have been displayed until there have been at least 25. Unless you tell SQL*Plus differently, **feedback** is set to 6.

The **set** command is a SQL*Plus command, which means that it is an instruction telling SQL*Plus how to act. There are many SQL*Plus options, such as **feedback**, that you can set. Several of these will be shown and used in this chapter and in the chapters to follow. For a complete list, look up **set** in the Alphabetical Reference section of this book.

The **set** command has a counterpart named **show** that allows you to see what instructions you've given to SQL*Plus. For instance, you can check the setting of **feedback** by typing

```
show feedback
```

SQL*Plus will respond with the following:

```
FEEDBACK ON for 25 or more rows
```

The width used to display numbers also is changed by the **set** command. You check it by typing

```
show numwidth
```

SQL*Plus will reply as shown here:

```
numwidth 9
```

Because 9 is a wide width for displaying page numbers that never contain more than two digits, shrink the display by typing

```
set numwidth 5
```

However, this means that all number columns will be five digits wide. If you anticipate having numbers with more than five digits, you must use a number higher than 5. Individual columns in the display also can be set independently. This will be covered in Chapter 6.

select, from, where, and order by

You will use four primary keywords in SQL when selecting information from an Oracle table: **select**, **from**, **where**, and **order by**. You will use **select** and **from** in every Oracle query you do.

The **select** keyword tells Oracle which columns you want, and **from** tells Oracle the name(s) of the table(s) those columns are in. The NEWSPAPER table example showed how these keywords are used. In the first line that you entered, a comma follows each column name except the last. You'll notice that a correctly typed SQL query reads pretty much like an English sentence. A query in SQL*Plus usually ends with a semicolon (sometimes called the *SQL terminator*). The **where** keyword tells Oracle what qualifiers you'd like to put on the information it is selecting. For example, if you input

```
select Feature, Section, Page from NEWSPAPER
  where Section = 'F';

FEATURE          S  PAGE
---------------  -  -----
Births           F     7
Classified       F     8
Obituaries       F     6
Doctor Is In     F     6
```

Oracle checks each row in the NEWSPAPER table before sending the row back to you. It skips over those without the single letter *F* in their Section column. It returns those where the Section entry is 'F', and SQL*Plus displays them to you.

To tell Oracle that you want the information it returns sorted in the order you specify, use **order by**. You can be as elaborate as you like about the order you request. Consider these examples:

```
select Feature, Section, Page from NEWSPAPER
  where Section = 'F'
  order by Feature;

FEATURE          S  PAGE
---------------  -  -----
Births           F     7
Classified       F     8
Doctor Is In     F     6
Obituaries       F     6
```

They are nearly reversed when ordered by page, as shown here:

```
select Feature, Section, Page from NEWSPAPER
  where Section = 'F'
  order by Page;

FEATURE          S  PAGE
---------------  -  -----
Obituaries       F    6
Doctor Is In     F    6
Births           F    7
Classified       F    8
```

In the next example, Oracle first puts the features in order by page (see the previous listing to observe the order they are in when they are ordered only by page). It then puts them in further order by feature, listing Doctor Is In ahead of Obituaries.

```
select Feature, Section, Page from NEWSPAPER
  where Section = 'F'
  order by Page, Feature;

FEATURE          S  PAGE
---------------  -  -----
Doctor Is In     F    6
Obituaries       F    6
Births           F    7
Classified       F    8
```

Using **order by** also can reverse the normal order, like this:

```
select Feature, Section, Page from NEWSPAPER
  where Section = 'F'
  order by Page desc, Feature;

FEATURE          S  PAGE
---------------  -  -----
Classified       F    8
Births           F    7
Doctor Is In     F    6
Obituaries       F    6
```

The **desc** keyword stands for *descending*. Because it followed the word Page in the **order by** line, it put the page numbers in descending order. It would have the same effect on the Feature column if it followed the word Feature in the **order by** line.

Notice that each of these keywords—**select**, **from**, **where**, and **order by**—has its own way of structuring the words that follow it. The groups of words including these keywords are often called *clauses*, as shown in Figure 5-2.

```
Select Feature, Section, Page          <--select clause
    from NEWSPAPER                     <--from clause
    where Section = 'F'                <--where clause
```

FIGURE 5-2. *Clauses*

Logic and Value

Just as the **order by** clause can have several parts, so can the **where** clause, but with a significantly greater degree of sophistication. You control the extent to which you use **where** through the careful use of logical instructions to Oracle on what you expect it to return to you. These instructions are expressed using mathematical symbols called *logical operators*. These are explained shortly, and they also are listed in the Alphabetical Reference section of this book.

The following is a simple example in which the values in the Page column are tested to see if any equals 6. Every row where this is true is returned to you. Any row in which Page is not equal to 6 is skipped (in other words, those rows for which Page = 6 is false).

```
select Feature, Section, Page
   from NEWSPAPER
 where Page = 6;

FEATURE         S PAGE
--------------- - -----
Obituaries      F     6
Doctor Is In    F     6
```

The equal sign is called a *logical operator,* because it operates by making a logical test that compares the values on either side of it—in this case, the value of Page and the value 6—to see if they are equal.

In this example, no quotes are placed around the value being checked because the column the value is compared to (the Page column) is defined as a NUMBER datatype. Number values do not require quotes around them during comparisons.

Single-Value Tests

You can use one of several logical operators to test against a single value, as shown in the upcoming sidebar "Logical Tests Against a Single Value." Take a few examples from any of the expressions listed in this sidebar. They all work similarly and can be combined at will, although they must follow certain rules about how they'll act together.

Logical Tests Against a Single Value

All these operators work with letters or numbers, and with columns or literals.

Equal, Greater Than, Less Than, Not Equal

Page=	6	Page is equal to 6.
Page>	6	Page is greater than 6.
Page>=	6	Page is greater than or equal to 6.
Page<	6	Page is less than 6.
Page<=	6	Page is less than or equal to 6.
Page!=	6	Page is not equal to 6.
Page^=	6	Page is not equal to 6.
Page<>	6	Page is not equal to 6.

Because some keyboards lack an exclamation mark (!) or a caret (^), Oracle allows three ways of typing the not equal operator. The final alternative, <>, qualifies as a not equal operator because it permits only numbers less than 6 (in this example) or greater than 6, but not 6 itself.

LIKE

Feature LIKE 'Mo%'	Feature begins with the letters *Mo*.
Feature LIKE '_ _ l%'	Feature has an *l* in the third position.
Feature LIKE '%o%o%'	Feature has two *o*'s in it.

LIKE performs pattern matching. An underline character (_) represents exactly one character. A percent sign (%) represents any number of characters, including zero characters.

IS NULL, IS NOT NULL

Precipitation IS NULL	Precipitation is unknown.
Precipitation IS NOT NULL	Precipitation is known.

NULL tests to see if data exists in a column for a row. If the column is completely empty, it is said to be "null." The word **IS** must be used with **NULL** and **NOT NULL**; equal, greater-than, and less-than signs do not work with **NULL** and **NOT NULL.**

Equal, Greater Than, Less Than, Not Equal

Logical tests can compare values, both for equality and for relative value. Here, a simple test is made for all sections equal to 'B':

```
select Feature, Section, Page
   from NEWSPAPER
  where Section = 'B';

FEATURE           S  PAGE
---------------   -  -----
Television        B    7
Modern Life       B    1
Movies            B    4
Bridge            B    2
```

The following is the test for all pages greater than 4:

```
select Feature, Section, Page
   from NEWSPAPER
  where Page > 4;

FEATURE           S  PAGE
---------------   -  -----
Editorials        A   12
Television        B    7
Births            F    7
Classified        F    8
Obituaries        F    6
Doctor Is In      F    6
```

The following is the test for sections greater than 'B' (this means later in the alphabet than the letter *B*):

```
select Feature, Section, Page
   from NEWSPAPER
  where Section > 'B';

FEATURE           S  PAGE
---------------   -  -----
Sports            D    1
Business          E    1
Weather           C    2
Births            F    7
Classified        F    8
Comics            C    4
Obituaries        F    6
Doctor Is In      F    6
```

Just as a test can be made for greater than, so can a test be made for less than, as shown here (all page numbers less than 8):

```
select Feature, Section, Page
   from NEWSPAPER
  where Page < 8;

FEATURE          S    PAGE
---------------  -  ----------
National News    A         1
Sports           D         1
Business         E         1
Weather          C         2
Television       B         7
Births           F         7
Modern Life      B         1
Comics           C         4
Movies           B         4
Bridge           B         2
Obituaries       F         6
Doctor Is In     F         6
```

The opposite of the test for equality is the not equal test, as given here:

```
select Feature, Section, Page
   from NEWSPAPER
  where Page <> 1;

FEATURE          S    PAGE
---------------  -  ----------
Editorials       A        12
Weather          C         2
Television       B         7
Births           F         7
Classified       F         8
Comics           C         4
Movies           B         4
Bridge           B         2
Obituaries       F         6
Doctor Is In     F         6
```

NOTE

*Be careful when using the greater-than and less-than operators against
numbers that are stored in character datatype columns. All values in
VARCHAR2 and CHAR columns will be treated as characters during
comparisons. Therefore, numbers that are stored in those types of
columns will be compared as if they were character strings, not numbers.
If the column's datatype is NUMBER, then 12 is greater than 9. If it is
a character column, then 9 is greater than 12, because the character
'9' is greater than the character '1'.*

LIKE

One of the most powerful features of SQL is a marvelous pattern-matching operator called **LIKE**, which is able to search through the rows of a database column for values that look like a pattern you describe. It uses two special characters to denote which kind of matching to do: a percent sign, called a *wildcard,* and an underline, called a *position marker.* To look for all the features that begin with the letters *Mo,* use the following:

```
select Feature, Section, Page from NEWSPAPER
  where Feature LIKE 'Mo%';

FEATURE          S     PAGE
---------------  -  ----------
Modern Life      B        1
Movies           B        4
```

The percent sign (%) means anything is acceptable here: one character, a hundred characters, or no characters. If the first letters are *Mo,* **LIKE** will find the feature. If the query had used 'MO%' as its search condition instead, then no rows would have been returned, due to Oracle's case-sensitivity in data values.

If you want to find those features that have the letter *i* in the third position of their titles, and you don't care which two characters precede the *i* or what set of characters follows, using two underlines (_ _) specifies that any character in those two positions is acceptable. Position three must have a lowercase *i,* and the percent sign after that says anything is okay.

```
select Feature, Section, Page from NEWSPAPER
  where Feature LIKE '__i%';

FEATURE          S     PAGE
---------------  -  ----------
Editorials       A       12
Bridge           B        2
Obituaries       F        6
```

Multiple percent signs also can be used. To find those words with two lowercase *o*'s anywhere in the Feature title, three percent signs are used, as shown here:

```
select Feature, Section, Page from NEWSPAPER
  where Feature LIKE '%o%o%';

FEATURE          S     PAGE
---------------  -  ----------
Doctor Is In     F        6
```

For the sake of comparison, the following is the same query, but it is looking for two *i*'s:

```
select Feature, Section, Page from NEWSPAPER
   where Feature LIKE '%i%i%';

FEATURE         S     PAGE
-------------- - ----------
Editorials      A       12
Television       B        7
Classified       F        8
Obituaries       F        6
```

This pattern-matching feature can play an important role in making an application friendlier by simplifying searches for names, products, addresses, and other partially remembered items. In Chapter 8, you will see how to use advanced regular expression searches available as of Oracle Database 10g.

NULL and NOT NULL

The NEWSPAPER table has no columns in it that are **NULL**, even though the **describe** you did on it showed that they are allowed. The following query on the COMFORT table contains, among other data, the precipitation for San Francisco, California, and Keene, New Hampshire, for four sample dates during 2003:

```
select City, SampleDate, Precipitation
   from COMFORT;

CITY           SAMPLEDAT PRECIPITATION
-------------- --------- -------------
SAN FRANCISCO 21-MAR-03            .5
SAN FRANCISCO 22-JUN-03            .1
SAN FRANCISCO 23-SEP-03            .1
SAN FRANCISCO 22-DEC-03           2.3
KEENE          21-MAR-03           4.4
KEENE          22-JUN-03           1.3
KEENE          23-SEP-03
KEENE          22-DEC-03           3.9
```

You can find out the city and dates on which precipitation was not measured with this query:

```
select City, SampleDate, Precipitation
   from COMFORT
   where Precipitation IS NULL;

CITY           SAMPLEDAT PRECIPITATION
-------------- --------- -------------
KEENE          23-SEP-03
```

IS NULL essentially instructs Oracle to identify columns in which the data is missing. You don't know for that day whether the value should be 0, 1, or 5 inches. Because it is unknown, the value

in the column is not set to 0; it stays empty. By using **NOT**, you also can find those cities and dates for which data exists, with this query:

```
select City, SampleDate, Precipitation
  from COMFORT
 where Precipitation IS NOT NULL;

CITY            SAMPLEDAT PRECIPITATION
--------------  --------- -------------
SAN FRANCISCO   21-MAR-03            .5
SAN FRANCISCO   22-JUN-03            .1
SAN FRANCISCO   23-SEP-03            .1
SAN FRANCISCO   22-DEC-03           2.3
KEENE           21-MAR-03           4.4
KEENE           22-JUN-03           1.3
KEENE           22-DEC-03           3.9
```

Oracle lets you use the relational operators (=, !=, and so on) with **NULL**, but this kind of comparison will not return meaningful results. Use **IS** or **IS NOT** for comparing values to **NULL**.

Simple Tests Against a List of Values

If there are logical operators that test against a single value, are there others that will test against many values, such as a list? The sidebar "Logical Tests Against a List of Values" shows just such a group of operators.

Logical Tests Against a List of Values

Logical tests with numbers:

Page IN (1,2,3)	Page is in the list (1,2,3)
Page NOT IN (1,2,3)	Page is not in the list (1,2,3)
Page BETWEEN 6 AND 10	Page is equal to 6, 10, or anything in between
Page NOT BETWEEN 6 AND 10	Page is below 6 or above 10

With letters (or characters):

Section IN ('A','C','F')	Section is in the list ('A','C','F')
Section NOT IN ('A','C','F')	Section is not in the list ('A','C','F')
Section BETWEEN 'B' AND 'D'	Section is equal to 'B', 'D', or anything in between (alphabetically)
Section NOT BETWEEN 'B' AND 'D'	Section is below 'B' or above 'D' (alphabetically)

Here are a few examples of how these logical operators are used:

```
select Feature, Section, Page
   from NEWSPAPER
  where Section IN ('A','B','F');

FEATURE            S       PAGE
--------------- - ----------
National News      A          1
Editorials         A         12
Television         B          7
Births             F          7
Classified         F          8
Modern Life        B          1
Movies             B          4
Bridge             B          2
Obituaries         F          6
Doctor Is In       F          6

select Feature, Section, Page
   from NEWSPAPER
  where Section NOT IN ('A','B','F');

FEATURE            S       PAGE
--------------- - ----------
Sports             D          1
Business           E          1
Weather            C          2
Comics             C          4

select Feature, Section, Page
   from NEWSPAPER
  where Page BETWEEN 7 and 10;

FEATURE            S       PAGE
--------------- - ----------
Television         B          7
Births             F          7
Classified         F          8
```

These logical tests also can be combined, as in this case:

```
select Feature, Section, Page
   from NEWSPAPER
  where Section = 'F'
    AND Page > 7;

FEATURE            S       PAGE
--------------- - ----------
Classified         F          8
```

The **AND** command has been used to combine two logical expressions and requires any row Oracle examines to pass *both* tests; both Section = 'F' and Page > 7 must be true for a row to be returned to you. Alternatively, **OR** can be used, which will return rows to you if *either* logical expression turns out to be true:

```
select Feature, Section, Page
   from NEWSPAPER
 where Section = 'F'
    OR Page > 7;

FEATURE          S  PAGE
--------------   -  -----
Editorials       A    12
Births           F     7
Classified       F     8
Obituaries       F     6
Doctor Is In     F     6
```

There are some sections here that qualify even though they are not equal to 'F' because their page is greater than 7, and there are others whose page is less than or equal to 7 but whose section is equal to 'F'.

Finally, choose those features in Section F between pages 7 and 10 with this query:

```
select Feature, Section, Page
   from NEWSPAPER
 where Section = 'F'
    and Page BETWEEN 7 AND 10;

FEATURE          S  PAGE
--------------   -  -----
Births           F     7
Classified       F     8
```

There are a few additional *many-value operators* whose use is more complex; they will be covered in Chapter 9. They also can be found, along with those just discussed, in the Alphabetical Reference section of this book.

Combining Logic

Both **AND** and **OR** follow the commonsense meanings of the words. They can be combined in a virtually unlimited number of ways, but you must use care, because **AND**s and **OR**s get convoluted very easily.

Suppose you want to find the features in the paper that the editors tend to bury, those that are placed somewhere past page 2 of section A or B. You might try this:

```
select Feature, Section, Page
   from NEWSPAPER
 where Section = 'A'
    or Section = 'B'
   and Page > 2;
```

```
FEATURE           S  PAGE
--------------    -  -----
National News     A    1
Editorials        A   12
Television        B    7
Movies            B    4
```

Note that the result you got back from Oracle is not what you wanted. Somehow, page 1 of section A was included. Why is this happening? Is there a way to get Oracle to answer the question correctly? Although both **AND** and **OR** are logical connectors, **AND** is stronger. It binds the logical expressions on either side of it more strongly than **OR** does (technically, **AND** is said to have *higher precedence*), which means the **where** clause

```
where Section = 'A'
    or Section = 'B'
  and Page > 2;
```

is interpreted to read, "where Section = 'A', or where Section = 'B' *and* Page > 2." If you look at the failed example just given, you'll see how this interpretation affected the result. The **AND** is always acted on first.

You can break this bonding by using parentheses that enclose those expressions you want to be interpreted together. Parentheses override the normal precedence:

```
select Feature, Section, Page
  from NEWSPAPER
 where Page > 2
   and ( Section = 'A' or Section = 'B' );
```

```
FEATURE           S  PAGE
--------------    -  ----
Editorials        A   12
Television        B    7
Movies            B    4
```

The result is exactly what you wanted in the first place. Note that although you can type this with the sections listed first, the result is identical because the parentheses tell Oracle what to interpret together. Compare this to the different results caused by changing the order in the first example, where parentheses were not used.

Another Use for where: Subqueries

What if the logical operators in the previous sidebars, "Logical Tests Against a Single Value" and "Logical Tests Against a List of Values," could be used not just with a single literal value (such as 'F') or a typed list of values (such as 4,2,7 or 'A','C','F'), but with values brought back by an Oracle query? In fact, this is a powerful feature of SQL.

Imagine that you are the author of the "Doctor Is In" feature, and each newspaper that publishes your column sends along a copy of the table of contents that includes your piece. Of course, each editor rates your importance a little differently, and places you in a section he or she deems suited to your feature. Without knowing ahead of time where your feature is, or with what other features

you are placed, how could you write a query to find out where a particular local paper places you?
You might do this:

```
select Section from NEWSPAPER
  where Feature = 'Doctor Is In';

S
-
F
```

The result is 'F'. Knowing this, you could do this query:

```
select FEATURE from NEWSPAPER
  where Section = 'F';

FEATURE
---------------
Births
Classified
Obituaries
Doctor Is In
```

You're in there with births, deaths, and classified ads. Could the two separate queries have
been combined into one? Yes, as shown here:

```
select FEATURE from NEWSPAPER
  where Section = (select Section from NEWSPAPER
                     where Feature = 'Doctor Is In');

FEATURE
---------------
Births
Classified
Obituaries
Doctor Is In
```

Single Values from a Subquery

In effect, the **select** in parentheses (called a *subquery*) brought back a single value, F. The main
query then treated this value as if it were a literal 'F', as was used in the previous query. Remember
that the equal sign is a single-value test. It can't work with lists, so if your subquery returned more
than one row, you'd get an error message like this:

```
select * from NEWSPAPER
  where Section = (select Section from NEWSPAPER
                     where Page = 1);
where Section = (select Section from NEWSPAPER
                 *
ERROR at line 2:
ORA-01427:  single-row subquery returns more than one row
```

All the logical operators that test single values can work with subqueries, as long as the subquery returns a single row. For instance, you can ask for all the features in the paper where the section is *less than* (that is, earlier in the alphabet) the section that carries your column. The asterisk in this **select** shows a shorthand way to request all the columns in a table without listing them individually. They will be displayed in the order in which they were created in the table.

```
select * from NEWSPAPER
  where Section < (select Section from NEWSPAPER
                     where Feature = 'Doctor Is In');

FEATURE          S  PAGE
---------------  -  -----
National News    A    1
Sports           D    1
Editorials       A    12
Business         E    1
Weather          C    2
Television       B    7
Modern Life      B    1
Comics           C    4
Movies           B    4
Bridge           B    2

10 rows selected.
```

Ten other features rank ahead of your medical advice in this local paper.

Lists of Values from a Subquery

Just as the single-value logical operators can be used on a subquery, so can the many-value operators. If a subquery returns one or more rows, the value in the column for each row will be stacked up in a list. For example, suppose you want to know the cities and countries where it is cloudy. You could have a table of complete weather information for all cities, and a LOCATION table for all cities and their countries, as shown here:

```
select City, Country from LOCATION;

CITY                         COUNTRY
---------------------------  ---------------------------
ATHENS                       GREECE
CHICAGO                      UNITED STATES
CONAKRY                      GUINEA
LIMA                         PERU
MADRAS                       INDIA
MANCHESTER                   ENGLAND
MOSCOW                       RUSSIA
PARIS                        FRANCE
SHENYANG                     CHINA
ROME                         ITALY
TOKYO                        JAPAN
```

```
SYDNEY                   AUSTRALIA
SPARTA                   GREECE
MADRID                   SPAIN

select City, Condition from WEATHER;

CITY          CONDITION
-----------   -----------
LIMA          RAIN
PARIS         CLOUDY
MANCHESTER    FOG
ATHENS        SUNNY
CHICAGO       RAIN
SYDNEY        SUNNY
SPARTA        CLOUDY
```

First, you'd discover which cities were cloudy:

```
select City from WEATHER
  where Condition = 'CLOUDY';

CITY
-----------
PARIS
SPARTA
```

Then, you would build a list including those cities and use it to query the LOCATION table:

```
select City, Country from LOCATION
  where City IN ('PARIS', 'SPARTA');

CITY                      COUNTRY
-------------------------   -------------------------
PARIS                     FRANCE
SPARTA                    GREECE
```

The same task can be accomplished by a subquery, where the **select** in parentheses builds a list of cities that are tested by the **IN** operator, as shown here:

```
select City, Country from LOCATION
  where City IN (select City from WEATHER
                 where Condition = 'CLOUDY');

CITY                      COUNTRY
-------------------------   -------------------------
PARIS                     FRANCE
SPARTA                    GREECE
```

The other many-value operators work similarly. The fundamental task is to build a subquery that produces a list that can be logically tested. The following are some relevant points:

■ The subquery must either have only one column or compare its selected columns to multiple columns in parentheses in the main query (covered in Chapter 13).

■ The subquery must be enclosed in parentheses.

■ Subqueries that produce only one row can be used with *either* single- or many-value operators.

■ Subqueries that produce more than one row can be used *only* with many-value operators.

Combining Tables

If you've normalized your data, you'll probably need to combine two or more tables to get all the information you want.

Suppose you are the oracle at Delphi. The Athenians come to ask about the forces of nature that might affect the expected attack by the Spartans, as well as the direction from which they are likely to appear:

```
select City, Condition, Temperature from WEATHER;

CITY          CONDITION    TEMPERATURE
-----------   -----------  -----------
LIMA          RAIN                  45
PARIS         CLOUDY                81
MANCHESTER    FOG                   66
ATHENS        SUNNY                 97
CHICAGO       RAIN                  66
SYDNEY        SUNNY                 69
SPARTA        CLOUDY                74
```

You realize your geography is rusty, so you query the LOCATION table:

```
select City, Longitude, EastWest, Latitude, NorthSouth
   from LOCATION;

CITY                   LONGITUDE E LATITUDE N
--------------------   --------- - -------- -
ATHENS                     23.43 E    37.58 N
CHICAGO                    87.38 W    41.53 N
CONAKRY                    13.43 W     9.31 N
LIMA                       77.03 W    12.03 S
MADRAS                     80.17 E    13.05 N
MANCHESTER                  2.15 W    53.3  N
MOSCOW                     37.35 E    55.45 N
PARIS                       2.2  E    48.52 N
SHENYANG                  123.27 E    41.48 N
ROME                       12.29 E    41.54 N
TOKYO                     139.46 E    35.42 N
SYDNEY                    151.13 E    33.52 S
SPARTA                     22.27 E    37.05 N
MADRID                      3.41 W    40.24 N
```

This is much more than you need, and it doesn't have any weather information. Yet these two tables, WEATHER and LOCATION, have a column in common: City. You can therefore put the information from the two tables together by joining them. You merely use the **where** clause to tell Oracle what the two tables have in common:

```
select WEATHER.City, Condition, Temperature, Latitude,
       NorthSouth, Longitude, EastWest
  from WEATHER, LOCATION
 where WEATHER.City = LOCATION.City;
```

```
CITY          CONDITION   TEMPERATURE LATITUDE N LONGITUDE E
-----------   ----------- ----------- -------- - --------- -
ATHENS        SUNNY                97    37.58 N     23.43 E
CHICAGO       RAIN                 66    41.53 N     87.38 W
LIMA          RAIN                 45    12.03 S     77.03 W
MANCHESTER    FOG                  66     53.3 N      2.15 W
PARIS         CLOUDY               81    48.52 N      2.2 E
SYDNEY        SUNNY                69    33.52 S    151.13 E
SPARTA        CLOUDY               74    37.05 N     22.27 E
```

Notice that the only rows in this combined table are those where the same city is in *both* tables. The **where** clause is still executing your logic, as it did earlier in the case of the NEWSPAPER table. The logic you gave described the relationship between the two tables. It says, "Select those rows in the WEATHER table and the LOCATION table where the cities are equal." If a city is only in one table, it would have nothing to be equal to in the other table. The notation used in the **select** statement is TABLE.ColumnName—in this case, WEATHER.City.

The **select** clause has chosen those columns from the two tables that you'd like to see displayed; any columns in either table that you did not ask for are simply ignored. If the first line had simply said

```
select City, Condition, Temperature, Latitude
```

then Oracle would not have known to which city you were referring. Oracle would tell you that the column name City was ambiguous. The correct wording in the **select** clause is WEATHER.City or LOCATION.City. In this example, it won't make a bit of difference which of these alternatives is used, but you will encounter cases where the choice of identically named columns from two or more tables will contain very different data.

The **where** clause also requires the names of the tables to accompany the identical column name by which the tables are combined: "where weather dot city equals location dot city" (that is, where the City column in the WEATHER table equals the City column in the LOCATION table).

Consider that the combination of the two tables looks like a single table with seven columns and seven rows. Everything that you excluded is gone. There is no Humidity column here, even though it is a part of the WEATHER table. There is no Country column here, even though it is a part of the LOCATION table. And of the 14 cities in the LOCATION table, only those that are in the WEATHER table are included in this table. Your **where** clause didn't allow the others to be selected.

A table that is built from columns in one or more tables is sometimes called a *projection table,* or a *result table.*

Creating a View

There is even more here than meets the eye. Not only does this look like a new table, but you can give it a name and treat it like one. This is called "creating a view." A *view* provides a way of hiding the logic that created the joined table just displayed. It works this way:

```
create view INVASION AS
select WEATHER.City, Condition, Temperature, Latitude,
       NorthSouth, Longitude, EastWest
  from WEATHER, LOCATION
 where WEATHER.City = LOCATION.City;

View created.
```

Now you can act as if INVASION were a real table with its own rows and columns. You can even ask Oracle to describe it to you:

```
describe INVASION
```

Name	Null?	Type
CITY		VARCHAR2(11)
CONDITION		VARCHAR2(9)
TEMPERATURE		NUMBER
LATITUDE		NUMBER
NORTHSOUTH		CHAR(1)
LONGITUDE		NUMBER
EASTWEST		CHAR(1)

You can query it, too (note that you will not have to specify which table the City columns were from, because that logic is hidden inside the view):

```
select City, Condition, Temperature, Latitude, NorthSouth,
       Longitude, EastWest
  from INVASION;
```

CITY	CONDITION	TEMPERATURE	LATITUDE	N	LONGITUDE	E
ATHENS	SUNNY	97	37.58	N	23.43	E
CHICAGO	RAIN	66	41.53	N	87.38	W
LIMA	RAIN	45	12.03	S	77.03	W
MANCHESTER	FOG	66	53.3	N	2.15	W
PARIS	CLOUDY	81	48.52	N	2.2	E
SYDNEY	SUNNY	69	33.52	S	151.13	E
SPARTA	CLOUDY	74	37.05	N	22.27	E

There will be some Oracle functions you won't be able to use on a view that you can use on a plain table, but they are few and mostly involve modifying rows and indexing tables, which will be discussed in later chapters. For the most part, a view behaves and can be manipulated just like any other table.

NOTE
Views do not contain any data. Tables contain data. Although you can create "materialized views" that contain data, they are truly tables, not views.

Suppose now you realize that you don't really need information about Chicago or other cities outside of Greece, so you change the query. Will the following work?

```
select City, Condition, Temperature, Latitude, NorthSouth,
       Longitude, EastWest
  from INVASION
 where Country = 'GREECE';
```

SQL*Plus passes back this message from Oracle:

```
where Country = 'GREECE'
         *
ERROR at line 4:
ORA-00904: "COUNTRY": invalid identifier
```

Why? Because even though Country is a real column in one of the tables behind the view called INVASION, it was not in the **select** clause when the view was created. It is as if it does not exist. So, you must go back to the **create view** statement and include only the country of Greece there:

```
create or replace view INVASION as
select WEATHER.City, Condition, Temperature, Latitude,
       NorthSouth, Longitude, EastWest
  from WEATHER, LOCATION
 where WEATHER.City = LOCATION.City
   and Country = 'GREECE';

View created.
```

Using the **create or replace view** command allows you to create a new version of a view without first dropping the old one. This command will make it easier to administer users' privileges to access the view, as will be described in Chapter 18.

The logic of the **where** clause has now been expanded to include both joining two tables, and a single-value test on a column in one of those tables. Now, query Oracle. You'll get this response:

```
select City, Condition, Temperature, Latitude, NorthSouth,
       Longitude, EastWest
  from INVASION;

CITY        CONDITION   TEMPERATURE LATITUDE N LONGITUDE E
----------- ----------- ----------- -------- - --------- -
ATHENS      SUNNY                97    37.58 N     23.43 E
SPARTA      CLOUDY               74    37.05 N     22.27 E
```

This allows you to warn the Athenians that the Spartans are likely to appear from the southwest but will be overheated and tired from their march. With a little trigonometry, you could even make Oracle calculate how far they will have marched.

Expanding the View

The power of views to hide or even modify data can be used for a variety of useful purposes. Very complex reports can be built up by the creation of a series of simple views, and specific individuals or groups can be restricted to seeing only certain pieces of the whole table.

In fact, any qualifications you can put into a query can become part of a view. You could, for instance, let supervisors looking at a payroll table see only their own salaries and those of the people working for them, or you could restrict operating divisions in a company to seeing only their own financial results, even though the table actually contains results for all divisions. Most importantly, views are *not* snapshots of the data at a certain point in the past. They are dynamic and always reflect the data in the underlying tables. The instant data in a table is changed, any views created with that table change as well.

For example, you may create a view that restricts values based on column values. As shown here, a query that restricts the LOCATION table on the Country column could be used to limit the rows that are visible via the view:

```
create or replace view PERU_LOCATIONS as
select * from LOCATION
 where Country = 'PERU';
```

A user querying PERU_LOCATIONS would not be able to see any rows from any country other than Peru.

The queries used to define views may also reference *pseudo-columns*. A pseudo-column is a "column" that returns a value when it is selected, but is not an actual column in a table. The User pseudo-column, when selected, will always return the Oracle username that executed the query. So, if a column in the table contains usernames, those values can be compared against the User pseudo-column to restrict its rows, as shown in the following listing. In this example, the NAME table is queried. If the value of its Name column is the same as the name of the user entering the query, then rows will be returned.

```
create or replace view RESTRICTED_NAMES as
select * from NAME
 where Name = User;
```

This type of view is very useful when users require access to selected rows in a table. It prevents them from seeing any rows that do not match their Oracle username.

Views are powerful tools. There will be more to come on the subject of views in Chapter 17.

The **where** clause can be used to join two tables based on a common column. The resulting set of data can be turned into a view (with its own name), which can be treated as if it were a regular table itself. The power of a view is in its ability to limit or change the way data is seen by a user, even though the underlying tables themselves are not affected.

CHAPTER

6

Basic SQL*Plus
Reports and
Commands

QL*Plus is usually thought of as a tool to manipulate data and perform ad hoc queries against the database; it can also function as an interactive report writer. It uses SQL to get information from the Oracle database, and it lets you create reports by giving you easy control over titles, column headings, subtotals and totals, reformatting of numbers and text, and much more. It also can be used to change the database through the **insert**, **update**, **merge**, and **delete** commands in SQL. SQL*Plus can even be used as a code generator, where a series of commands in SQL*Plus can dynamically build a program and then execute it.

In most production applications, more-advanced report writers are used—such as Web-based parameter-driven reports. SQL*Plus is most commonly used for simple queries and printed reports. Getting SQL*Plus to format information in reports according to your tastes and needs requires only a handful of *commands*—keywords that instruct SQL*Plus how to behave. These are listed in Table 6-1. Detailed explanations, examples, and additional features of each of these commands are given in the Alphabetical Reference section of this book.

In this chapter, you will see a basic report that was written using SQL*Plus, along with an explanation of the features used to create it. If building a report seems a bit daunting at first, don't worry. Once you try the steps, you'll find them simple to understand, and they will soon become familiar.

You can write SQL*Plus reports while working interactively with SQL*Plus—that is, you can type commands about page headings, column titles, formatting, breaks, totals, and so on, and then execute a SQL query, and SQL*Plus will immediately produce the report formatted to your specifications. For quick answers to simple questions that aren't likely to recur, this is a fine approach. More common, however, are complex reports that need to be produced periodically and that you'll want to print rather than just view on the screen. Unfortunately, when you quit SQL*Plus, it promptly forgets every instruction you've given it. If you were restricted to using SQL*Plus only in this interactive way, then running the same report at a later time would require typing everything all over again.

The alternative is very straightforward. You simply type the commands, line by line, into a file. SQL*Plus can then read this file as if it were a script, and execute your commands just as if you were typing them. In effect, you create a report program, but you do it without a programmer or a compiler. You create this file using any of the popular editor programs available, or even (given certain restrictions) a word processor.

The editor is not a part of Oracle. Editors come in hundreds of varieties, and every company or person seems to have a favorite. Oracle realized this and decided to let you choose which editor program to use, rather than packaging a program with Oracle and forcing you to use it. When you're ready to use your editor program, you suspend SQL*Plus, jump over to the editor program, create or change your SQL*Plus report program (also called a *start file*), and then jump back to SQL*Plus, right at the spot you left, and run the report (see Figure 6-1).

SQL*Plus also has a built-in editor of its own, sometimes called the *command line editor*, that allows you to quickly modify a SQL query without leaving SQL*Plus. The editor's use will be covered later in this chapter.

Command	Definition
remark	Tells SQL*Plus that the words to follow are to be treated as comments, not instructions.
set headsep	The heading separator identifies the single character that tells SQL*Plus to split a title into two or more lines.
ttitle	Sets the top title for each page of a report.
btitle	Sets the bottom title for each page of a report.
column	Gives SQL*Plus a variety of instructions on the heading, format, and treatment of a column.
break on	Tells SQL*Plus where to put spaces between sections of a report, or where to break for subtotals and totals.
compute sum	Makes SQL*Plus calculate subtotals.
set linesize	Sets the maximum number of characters allowed on any line of the report.
set pagesize	Sets the maximum number of lines per page.
set newpage	Sets the number of blank lines between pages.
spool	Moves a report you would normally see displayed on the screen into a file, so you can print it.
/* */	Marks the beginning and ending of a comment within a SQL entry. Similar to **remark**.
--	Marks the beginning of an inline comment within a SQL entry. Treats everything from the mark to the end of the line as a comment. Similar to **remark**.
set pause	Makes the screen display stop between pages of display.
save	Saves the SQL query you're creating into the file of your choice.
host	Sends any command to the host operating system.
start or **@**	Tells SQL*Plus to follow (execute) the instructions you've saved in a file.
edit	Pops you out of SQL*Plus and into an editor of your choice.
define _editor	Tells SQL*Plus the name of the editor of your choice.
exit or **quit**	Terminates SQL*Plus.

TABLE 6-1. *Basic SQL*Plus Commands*

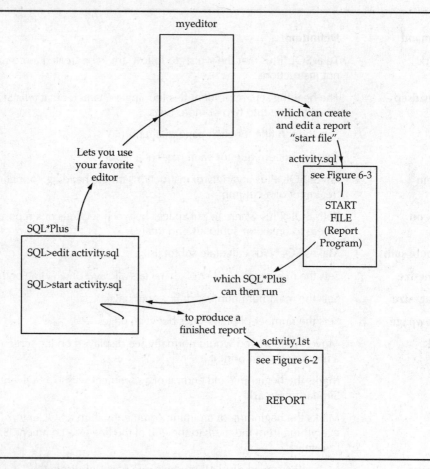

FIGURE 6-1. *Report-creation process*

Building a Simple Report

Figure 6-2 provides a quick-and-easy report showing the dates books were checked out and returned during a three-month time period.

⓵ **remark**

The first line of Figure 6-3, at Circle 1, is documentation about the start file itself. Documentation lines begin with

```
rem
```

which stands for **remark**. SQL*Plus ignores anything on a line that begins with **rem**, thus allowing you to add comments, documentation, and explanations to any start file you create. It is always a good idea to place remarks at the top of a start file, giving the filename, its creator and date of creation, the name of anyone who has modified it, the date of modification, what was modified, and an explanation of the purpose of the file. This will prove invaluable later on, as you develop more complex reports or when dozens of reports begin to accumulate.

```
Thu Apr 04                                                    page 1
                     Checkout Log for 1/1/02-3/31/02

                                                            Days
NAME                  TITLE                 CHECKOUTD RETURNEDD   Out
-------------------- -------------------- --------- --------- -------
DORAH TALBOT         EITHER/OR            02-JAN-02 10-JAN-02    8.00
                     POLAR EXPRESS        01-FEB-02 15-FEB-02   14.00
                     GOOD DOG, CARL       01-FEB-02 15-FEB-02   14.00
                     MY LEDGER            15-FEB-02 03-MAR-02   16.00
*******************                                           -------
avg                                                            13.00

EMILY TALBOT         ANNE OF GREEN GABLES 02-JAN-02 20-JAN-02   18.00
                     MIDNIGHT MAGIC       20-JAN-02 03-FEB-02   14.00
                     HARRY POTTER AND THE 03-FEB-02 14-FEB-02   11.00
                     GOBLET OF FIRE
*******************                                           -------
avg                                                            14.33

FRED FULLER          JOHN ADAMS           01-FEB-02 01-MAR-02   28.00
                     TRUMAN               01-MAR-02 20-MAR-02   19.00
*******************                                           -------
avg                                                            23.50

GERHARDT KENTGEN     WONDERFUL LIFE       02-JAN-02 02-FEB-02   31.00
                     MIDNIGHT MAGIC       05-FEB-02 10-FEB-02    5.00
                     THE MISMEASURE OF    13-FEB-02 05-MAR-02   20.00
                     MAN
*******************                                           -------
avg                                                            18.67

JED HOPKINS          INNUMERACY           01-JAN-02 22-JAN-02   21.00
                     TO KILL A            15-FEB-02 01-MAR-02   14.00
                     MOCKINGBIRD
*******************                                           -------
avg                                                            17.50

PAT LAVAY            THE SHIPPING NEWS    02-JAN-02 12-JAN-02   10.00
                     THE MISMEASURE OF    12-JAN-02 12-FEB-02   31.00
                     MAN
*******************                                           -------
avg                                                            20.50

ROLAND BRANDT        THE SHIPPING NEWS    12-JAN-02 12-MAR-02   59.00
                     THE DISCOVERERS      12-JAN-02 01-MAR-02   48.00
                     WEST WITH THE NIGHT  12-JAN-02 01-MAR-02   48.00
*******************                                           -------
avg                                                            51.67

                                                             -------
avg                                                            22.58

                         from the Bookshelf
```

FIGURE 6-2. *Bookshelf checkout report output*

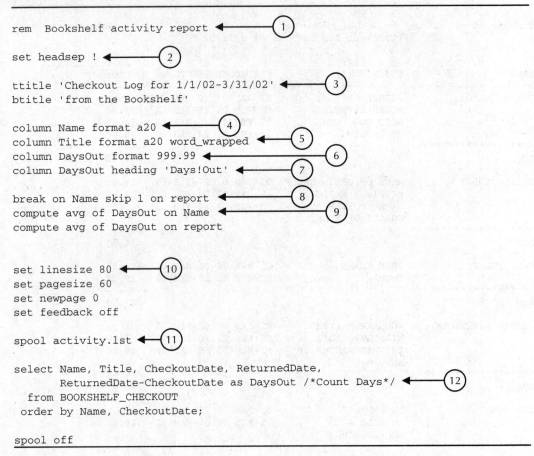

```
rem  Bookshelf activity report                    (1)

set headsep !                          (2)

ttitle 'Checkout Log for 1/1/02-3/31/02'              (3)
btitle 'from the Bookshelf'

column Name format a20                  (4)
column Title format a20 word_wrapped          (5)
column DaysOut format 999.99                 (6)
column DaysOut heading 'Days!Out'           (7)

break on Name skip 1 on report           (8)
compute avg of DaysOut on Name            (9)
compute avg of DaysOut on report

set linesize 80                (10)
set pagesize 60
set newpage 0
set feedback off

spool activity.lst           (11)

select Name, Title, CheckoutDate, ReturnedDate,
       ReturnedDate-CheckoutDate as DaysOut /*Count Days*/   (12)
  from BOOKSHELF_CHECKOUT
 order by Name, CheckoutDate;

spool off
```

FIGURE 6-3. *The activity.sql file*

SQL*Plus and SQL

The **select** statement toward the bottom of Figure 6-3, beginning with the word "select" and ending with the semicolon (;), is Structured Query Language—the language you use to talk to the Oracle database. Every other command on the page is a SQL*Plus command, used to format the results of a SQL query into a report.

The SQL*Plus **start** command causes SQL*Plus to read the file activity.sql and execute the instructions you've placed in it. Reviewing this start file will show you the basic SQL*Plus instructions you can use to produce reports or change the way SQL*Plus interacts with you. Depending on your experience, this may seem formidable or elementary. It is made up of a series of simple instructions to SQL*Plus.

Figure 6-3 shows the SQL*Plus start file that produced this report (in this case, named activity.sql). To run this report program in SQL*Plus, type the following:

```
start activity.sql
```

② set headsep

The punctuation that follows **set headsep** (for **head**ing **sep**arator) at Circle 2 in Figure 6-3 tells SQL*Plus how you will indicate where you want to break a page title or a column heading that runs longer than one line. When you first activate SQL*Plus, the default **headsep** character is the vertical bar (|), but if you want to use vertical bars in your titles, you may find it simpler to use a different **headsep** character.

 `set headsep !`

CAUTION
Choosing a character that may otherwise appear in a title or column heading will cause unexpected splitting.

③ ttitle and btitle

The line

 `ttitle 'Checkout Log for 1/1/02-3/31/02'`

at Circle 3 in Figure 6-3 instructs SQL*Plus to put this "top **title**" at the top of each page of the report. The title you choose must be enclosed in single quotation marks. The line

`btitle 'from the Bookshelf'`

works similarly to **ttitle**, except that it goes at the **b**ottom of each page (as the **b** indicates), and it also must be in single quotation marks. Because single quotes are used to enclose the entire title, an apostrophe (the same character on your keyboard) would trick SQL*Plus into believing the title had ended.

NOTE
*Put two single quotation marks right next to each other when you want to print an apostrophe or a single quotation mark. Because both SQL and SQL*Plus rely on single quotation marks to enclose strings of characters, this technique is used throughout SQL and SQL*Plus whenever an apostrophe needs to be printed or displayed.*

When using **ttitle** this way, SQL*Plus will always center the title you choose based on the **linesize** you set (**linesize** will be discussed later in the chapter), and it will always place the weekday, month, and the day of the month on which the report was run in the upper-left corner and the page number in the upper-right corner.

You can use the **repheader** and **repfooter** commands to create headers and footers for reports. See the Alphabetical Reference section of this book for descriptions of **repheader** and **repfooter**.

column

column allows you to change the heading and format of any column in a **select** statement. Look at the report shown earlier in Figure 6-2. The fifth column, Days Out, is not a column in the database, and it's called DaysOut in the query shown in Figure 6-3. The line

```
column DaysOut heading 'Days!Out'
```

relabels the column and gives it a new heading. This heading breaks into two lines because it has the **headsep** character (!) embedded in it. The line

```
column Name format a20
```

(4) at Circle 4 sets the width for the Name column's display at 20. The *a* tells SQL*Plus that this is an alphabetic column, as opposed to a numeric column. The width can be set to virtually any value, irrespective of how the column is defined in the database.

(5) The Name column is defined as 25 characters wide, so it's possible that some names will have more than 20 characters. If you did nothing else in defining this column on the report, any name more than 20 characters long would wrap onto the next line. Looking at Figure 6-2 again, you can see that four of the titles have wrapped; the Title column is defined as VARCHAR2(100) but is formatted as a20 (see Circle 5).

Instead of using the **word_wrapped** format, you could choose **truncated**, eliminating the display of any characters that exceed the specified format length for the column.

(6) Circle 6 in Figure 6-3 shows an example of formatting a number:

```
column DaysOut format 999.99
```

This defines a column with room for five digits and a decimal point. If you count the spaces in the report for the DaysOut column, you'll see seven spaces. Just looking at the **column** command might lead you to believe the column would be six spaces wide, but this would leave no room for a minus sign if the number were negative, so an extra space on the left is always provided for numbers.

(7) Circle 7 in Figure 6-3 refers to a column that didn't appear in the table when we had SQL*Plus describe it:

```
column DaysOut heading 'Days!Out'
```

What is DaysOut? Look at the **select** statement at the bottom of Figure 6-3. DaysOut appears in the following line:

```
ReturnedDate-CheckoutDate as DaysOut /*Count Days*/
```

This tells SQL to perform date arithmetic—count the number of days between two dates—and give the computation a simpler column name. As a consequence, SQL*Plus sees a column named DaysOut, and all its formatting and other commands will act as if it were a real column in the table. The **column** command for DaysOut is an example. "DaysOut" is referred to as a *column alias*—another name to use when referring to a column.

⑧ **break on**

Look at Circle 8 in Figure 6-3. Note on the report in Figure 6-2 how the checkout records for each name are grouped together. This effect was produced by the line

```
break on Name skip 1 on report
```

as well as by the line

```
order by Name, CheckoutDate;
```

in the **select** statement near the end of the start file.

SQL*Plus looks at each row as it is brought back from Oracle and keeps track of the value in Name. For the first four rows, this value is DORAH TALBOT, so SQL*Plus displays the rows it has gotten. On the fifth row, Name changes to EMILY TALBOT. SQL*Plus remembers your break instructions, which tell it that when Name changes, it should break away from the normal display of row after row, and skip one line. You'll notice one line between the Name sections on the report. Unless the names were collected together because of the **order by** clause, it wouldn't make sense for **break on** to skip one line every time Name changed. This is why the **break on** command and the **order by** clause must be coordinated.

You also may notice that the name DORAH TALBOT is only printed on the first line of its section, as are the rest of the names. This is done to eliminate the duplicate printing of each of these names for every row in each section, which is visually unattractive. If you want, you can force SQL*Plus to duplicate the name on each row of its section by altering the **break on** command to read

```
break on Name duplicate skip 1
```

The report output in Figure 6-2 shows an average for DaysOut for the entire report. To be able to get a grand total for a report, add an additional break using the **break on report** command. Be careful when adding breaks because they all need to be created by a single command; entering two consecutive **break on** commands will cause the first command's instructions to be replaced by the second command. See Circle 8 for the **break on** command used for the report:

```
break on Name skip 1 on report
```

⑨ **compute avg**

The averages calculated for each section on the report were produced by the **compute avg** command at Circle 9. This command always works in conjunction with the **break on** command, and the totals computed will always be for the section specified by **break on**. It is probably wise to consider these two related commands as a single unit:

```
break on Name skip 1 on report
compute avg of DaysOut on Name
compute avg of DaysOut on report
```

In other words, this tells SQL*Plus to compute the average of the DaysOut for each Name. SQL*Plus will do this first for DORAH TALBOT, then for each successive name. Every time SQL*Plus sees a new name, it calculates and prints an average for the previous DaysOut values. **compute avg**

also puts a row of asterisks below the column that **break on** is using, and it prints "avg" underneath. For reports with many columns that need to be added, a separate **compute avg** (or **compute sum** if you're calculating sums) statement is used for each calculation. It also is possible to have several different kinds of breaks on a large report (for Name, Title, and dates, for example), along with coordinated **compute avg** commands.

You can use a **break on** command without a **compute sum** command, such as for organizing your report into sections where no totals are needed (addresses with a **break on** City would be an example), but the reverse is not true.

> **NOTE**
> *Every **compute avg** command must have a **break on** command to guide it, and the **on** portion of both commands must match (such as **on Name** in the preceding example: **break on Name skip 1 on report** and **compute avg of DaysOut on Name**).*

The following are the basic rules:

- Every **break on** must have a related **order by**.
- Every **compute avg** must have a related **break on**.

This makes sense, of course, but it's easy to forget one of the pieces. In addition to **compute avg**, you can also use **compute sum**, **compute count**, **compute max**, or any other of Oracle's grouping functions on the set of records.

⑩ set linesize

The four commands at Circle 10 in Figure 6-3 control the gross dimensions of your report. The command **set linesize** governs the maximum number of characters that will appear on a single line. For letter-size paper, this number is usually around 70 or 80, unless your printer uses a very compressed (narrow) character font.

If you put more columns of information in your SQL query than will fit into the **linesize** you've allotted, SQL*Plus will wrap the additional columns down onto the next line and stack columns under each other. You actually can use this to very good effect when a lot of data needs to be presented.

SQL*Plus also uses **linesize** to determine where to center the **ttitle**, and where to place the date and page number. Both the date and page number appear on the top line, and the distance between the first letter of the date and the last digit of the page number will always equal the **linesize** you set.

set pagesize

The **set pagesize** command sets the total number of lines SQL*Plus will place on each page, including the **ttitle**, **btitle**, **column** headings, and any blank lines it prints. On letter- and computer-size paper, this is usually 66 (six lines per inch times 11 inches [U.S.]). **set pagesize** is coordinated with **set newpage**.

As of Oracle Database 10g, the default **pagesize** is 14; in prior versions, it is 24.

set newpage

A better name for **set newpage** might have been "set blank lines," because what it really does is print blank lines before the top line (date, page number) of each page in your report. This is useful both for adjusting the position of reports coming out on single pages on a laser printer and for skipping over the perforations between the pages of continuous-form computer paper.

NOTE

*set pagesize does not set the size of the body of the report (the number of printed lines from the date down to the **btitle**); instead, it sets the total length of the page, measured in lines.*

Therefore, if you type

```
set pagesize 66
set newpage 9
```

SQL*Plus produces a report starting with nine blank lines, followed by 57 lines of information (counting from the date down to the **btitle**). If you increase the size of **newpage**, SQL*Plus puts fewer rows of information on each page, but produces more pages altogether.

That's understandable, you say, but what has been done at Circle 10 on Figure 6-3?

```
set pagesize 60
set newpage 0
```

This is a strange size for a report page. Is SQL*Plus to put zero blank lines between pages? No. Instead, the 0 after **newpage** switches on a special property: **set newpage 0** produces a *top-of-form character* (usually a hex 13) just before the date on each page. Most modern printers respond to this by moving immediately to the top of the next page, where the printing of the report will begin. The combination of **set pagesize 60** and **set newpage 0** produces a report whose body of information is exactly 60 lines long and which has a top-of-form character at the beginning of each page. This is a cleaner and simpler way to control page printing than jockeying around with blank lines and lines per page. You can also use the **set newpage none** command, which will result in no blank lines and no form feeds between report pages.

(11) spool

In the early days of computers, most file storage was done on spools of either magnetic wire or tape. Writing information into a file and spooling a file were virtually synonymous. The term has survived, and *spooling* now generally refers to any process of moving information from one place to another. In SQL*Plus,

```
spool activity.lst
```

tells SQL to take all the output from SQL*Plus and write it to the file named activity.lst. Once you've told SQL*Plus to spool, it continues to do so until you tell it to stop, which you do by inputting the following:

```
spool off
```

This means, for instance, that you could type

```
spool work.fil
```

and then type a SQL query, such as

```
select Feature, Section, Page from NEWSPAPER
 where Section = 'F';
```

```
FEATURE         S  PAGE
--------------- -  ----
Births          F     7
Classified      F     8
Obituaries      F     6
Doctor Is In    F     6
```

or a series of SQL*Plus commands, such as

```
set pagesize 60
column Section heading 'My Favorites'
```

or anything else. Whatever prompts SQL*Plus produces, whatever error messages you get, whatever appears on the computer screen while spooling—it all ends up in the file work.fil. Spooling doesn't discriminate. It records everything that happens from the instant you use the **spool** command until you use **spool off**, which brings us back to the report at Circle 11 of Figure 6-3:

```
spool activity.lst
```

This phrase is carefully placed as the command just before the **select** statement, and **spool off** immediately follows. Had **spool activity.lst** appeared any earlier, the SQL*Plus commands you were issuing would have ended up on the first page of your report file. Instead, they go into the file activity.lst, which is what you see in Figure 6-2: the results of the SQL query, formatted according to your instructions, and nothing more. You are now free to print the file, confident that a clean report will show up on your printer.

This set of commands will print the SQL query on the first page of the output, followed by the data starting on the second page. To not show the SQL query with the output, you can also change the order of commands: Type in the SQL query but without the concluding semicolon. Press ENTER twice, and the command will still be in SQL*Plus's buffer, unexecuted. You can then start spooling and execute the command:

```
 (SQL command typed here)

spool activity.lst
/
spool off
```

As of Oracle Database 10g, you can append data to existing spool files. The default is (as in prior versions) to create a new output file. You can now use the **append** or **replace** option of the

spool command to either append data to an existing file that matches the name you give, or replace that existing file with your new output, respectively.

(12) **/* */**

Circle 12 of Figure 6-3 shows how a comment can be embedded in a SQL statement. This is different in method and use from the **remark** statement discussed earlier. **remark** (or **rem**) must appear at the beginning of a line, and it works only for the single line on which it appears. Furthermore, a multiple-line SQL statement is not permitted to have a **remark** within it. For example, the following is wrong:

```
select Feature, Section, Page
rem this is just a comment
  from NEWSPAPER
 where Section = 'F';
```

This will not work, and you'll get an error message. However, you can embed remarks in SQL following the method shown at Circle 12, or like this:

```
select Feature, Section, Page
 /* this is just a comment */
  from NEWSPAPER
 where Section = 'F';
```

The secret lies in knowing that **/*** tells SQL*Plus a comment has begun. Everything it sees from that point forward, even if it continues for many words and lines, is regarded as a comment, until SQL*Plus sees ***/**, which tells it that the comment has ended. You can also use the characters – – to begin a comment. The end of the line ends the comment. This kind of comment works just like a single-line version of **/* */**, except that you use – – (two dashes) instead.

Some Clarification on Column Headings

It's possible that the difference between the renaming that occurs in

```
ReturnedDate-CheckoutDate as DaysOut
```

and the new heading given the column Item in

```
column DaysOut heading 'Days!Out'
```

is not quite clear, particularly if you look at this command:

```
compute avg of DaysOut on Name
```

SQL*Plus commands are aware only of columns that actually appear in the **select** statement. Every **column** command refers to a column in the **select** statement. Both **break on** and **compute** refer only to columns in the **select** statement. The only reason a **column** command or a **compute** command is aware of the column DaysOut is that it got its name in the **select** statement itself. The renaming of "ReturnedDate-CheckoutDate" to "DaysOut" is something done by SQL, *not* by SQL*Plus.

Other Features

It's not terribly difficult to look at a start file and the report it produces and see how all the formatting and computation was accomplished. It's possible to begin by creating the start file, typing into it each of the commands you expect to need, and then running it in SQL*Plus to see if it is correct. But when you're creating reports for the first time, it is often much simpler to experiment interactively with SQL*Plus, adjusting column formats, the SQL query, the titles, and the totals, until what you really want begins to take shape.

Command Line Editor

When you type a SQL statement, SQL*Plus remembers each line as you enter it, storing it in what is called the *SQL buffer* (a fancy name for a computer scratchpad where your SQL statements are kept). Suppose you've entered this query:

```
select Featuer, Section, Page
   from NEWSPAPER
 where Section = 'F';
```

SQL*Plus responds with the following:

```
select Featuer, Section, Page
       *
ERROR at line 1:
ORA-00904: "FEATUER": invalid identifier
```

You now realize you've misspelled "Feature." You do not have to retype the entire query. The command line editor is already present and waiting for instructions. First, ask it to list your query:

```
list
```

SQL*Plus immediately responds with this:

```
1    select Featuer, Section, Page
2    from NEWSPAPER
3*   where Section = 'F'
```

Notice that SQL*Plus shows all three lines and numbers them. It also places an asterisk next to line 3, which means it is the line your editing commands are able to affect. But you want to change line 1, so you type, and SQL*Plus lists, the following:

```
list 1

  1* select Featuer, Section, Page
```

Line 1 is displayed and is now the current line. You can change it by typing this:

```
change /Featuer/Feature

  1* select Feature, Section, Page
```

You can check the whole query again with this:

```
list
```

```
1   select Feature, Section, Page
2      from NEWSPAPER
3*  where Section = 'F'
```

If you believe this is correct, enter a single slash after the prompt. This slash has nothing to do with the **change** command or the editor. Instead, it tells SQL*Plus to execute the SQL in the buffer:

```
/
```

```
FEATURE          S  PAGE
---------------  -  ----
Births           F     7
Classified       F     8
Obituaries       F     6
Doctor Is In     F     6
```

The **change** command requires that you mark the start and end of the text to be changed with a slash (/) or some other character. The line

```
change $Featuer$Feature
```

would have worked just as well. SQL*Plus looks at the first character after the word "change" and assumes that is the character you've chosen to use to mark the start and end of the incorrect text (these markers are usually called *delimiters*). You can also delete the current line, as shown here:

```
list
```

```
1   select Feature, Section, Page
2      from NEWSPAPER
3*  where Section = 'F'
```

```
del
```

```
list
```

```
1   select Feature, Section, Page
2      from NEWSPAPER
```

del will delete just what is on the current line. You can pass the **del** command a range of line numbers, to delete multiple lines at once, by specifying the first and last line numbers for the range of lines to delete. To delete lines 3 through 7, use **del 3 7**. Note this has a space before the number of the first line to delete (3) and another space before the number of the last line to delete (7). If you leave out the space between the 3 and the 7, SQL*Plus will try to delete line 37. To delete from line 2 to the end of the buffer, use **del 2 LAST**. You can use the same kind of syntax with the **list** command; for example, **list 3 7** will list the lines 3 through 7. See the entries for the **del** and **list** commands in the Alphabetical Reference for the full syntax options.

The word "delete" (spelled out) will erase all the lines and put the word "delete" as line 1. This will only cause problems, so avoid typing the whole word "delete." If your goal is to clear out the **select** statement completely, type this:

```
clear buffer
```

If you'd like to append something to the current line, you can use the **append** command:

```
list 1

    1* select Feature, Section, Page

append  "WhereItIs"

    1* select Feature, Section, Page "WhereItIs"
```

append places its text right up against the end of the current line, with no spaces in between. To put a space in, as was done here, type *two* spaces between the word **append** and the text.

You may also **input** a whole new line after the current line, as shown here:

```
list

    1  select Feature, Section, Page "WhereItIs"
    2*    from NEWSPAPER

input where Section = 'A'

list

    1  select Feature, Section, Page "WhereItIs"
    2     from NEWSPAPER
    3* where Section = 'A'
```

Then you can set the column heading for the WhereItIs column:

```
column WhereItIs heading "Where It Is"
```

And then you can run the query:

```
/

FEATURE         S Where It Is
--------------- - -----------
National News   A           1
Editorials      A          12
```

To review, the command line editor can **list** the SQL statement you've typed, **change** or **del**ete the current line (marked by the asterisk), **append** something onto the end of the current line, or **input** an entire line after the current line. Once your corrections are made, the SQL statement will execute if you type a slash at the SQL> prompt. Each of these commands can be abbreviated to its own first letter, except **del**, which must be exactly the three letters **del**.

The command line editor can edit only your SQL statement. It cannot edit SQL*Plus commands. If you've typed **column Name format a18**, for instance, and want to change it to **column Name format a20**, you must retype the whole thing (this is in the SQL*Plus interactive mode—if you've got the commands in a file, you obviously can change them with your own editor). Also note that in interactive mode, once you've started to type a SQL statement, you must complete it before you can enter any additional SQL*Plus commands, such as **column** formats or **ttitle**. As soon as SQL*Plus sees the word **select**, it assumes everything to follow is part of the **select** statement until it sees *either* a semicolon (;) at the end of the last SQL statement line *or* a slash (/) at the beginning of the line after the last SQL statement line.

Either of these is correct:

```
select * from LEDGER;

select * from LEDGER
/
```

This, however, is not:

```
select * from LEDGER/
```

set pause

During the development of a new report or when using SQL*Plus for quick queries of the database, it's usually helpful to set the **linesize** at 79 or 80, the **pagesize** at 24 (the default in Oracle Database 10*g* is 14), and **newpage** at 1. You accompany this with two related commands, as shown here:

```
set pause 'More. . .'
set pause on
```

The effect of this combination is to produce exactly one full screen of information for each page of the report that is produced, and to pause at each page for viewing ("More. . ." will appear in the lower-left corner) until you press ENTER. After the various column headings and titles are worked out, the **pagesize** can be readjusted for a page of paper, and the pause eliminated with this:

```
set pause off
```

save

If the changes you want to make to your SQL statement are extensive, or if you simply want to work in your own editor, save the SQL you've created so far, in interactive mode, by writing the SQL to a file, like this:

```
save fred.sql
```

SQL*Plus responds with

```
Created file fred.sql
```

Your SQL (but not any **column**, **ttitle**, or other SQL*Plus commands) is now in a file named fred.sql (or a name of your choice), which you can edit using your own editor.

If the file already exists, you must use the **replace** option (abbreviated **rep**) of the **save** command to save the new query in a file with that name. For this example, the syntax would be

```
save fred.sql rep
```

Alternatively, you could append to the fred.sql file with the command **save fred.sql app**.

store

You can use the **store** command to save your current SQL*Plus environment settings to a file. The following will create a file called my_settings.sql and will store the settings in that file:

```
store set my_settings.sql create
```

If the my_settings.sql file already exists, you can use the **replace** option instead of **create**, replacing the old file with the new settings. You could also use the **append** option to append the new settings to an existing file.

Editing

Everyone has a favorite editor. Word processing programs can be used with SQL*Plus, but only if you save the files created in them in ASCII format (see your word processor manual for details on how to do this). Editors are just programs themselves. They are normally invoked simply by typing their name at the operating system prompt. On UNIX, it usually looks something like this:

```
> vi fred.sql
```

In this example, vi is your editor's name, and fred.sql represents the file you want to edit (the start file described previously was used here only as an example—you would enter the real name of whatever file you want to edit). Other kinds of computers won't necessarily have the > prompt, but they will have something equivalent. If you can invoke an editor this way on your computer, it is nearly certain you can do the same from within SQL*Plus, *except* that you don't type the name of your editor, but rather the word **edit**:

```
SQL> edit fred.sql
```

You should first tell SQL*Plus your editor's name. You do this while in SQL*Plus by *defining* the editor, like this:

```
define _editor = "vi"
```

(That's an underscore before the *e* in editor.) SQL*Plus will then remember the name of your editor (until you **quit** SQL*Plus) and allow you to use it anytime you want. See the sidebar "Using login.sql to Define the Editor" for directions on making this happen automatically.

host

In the unlikely event that none of the editing commands described in the preceding section work, but you do have an editor you'd like to use, you can invoke it by typing this:

```
host vi fred.sql
```

host tells SQL*Plus that this is a command to simply hand back to the operating system for execution. It's the equivalent of typing **vi fred.sql** at the operating system prompt. Incidentally, this same **host** command can be used to execute almost any operating system command from within SQL*Plus, including **dir**, **copy**, **move**, **erase**, **cls**, and others.

Using login.sql to Define the Editor

If you'd like SQL*Plus to define your editor automatically, put the **define _editor** command in a file named login.sql. This is a special filename that SQL*Plus always looks for whenever it starts up. If it finds login.sql, it executes any commands in the file as if you had entered them by hand. It looks first at the directory you are in when you type **SQLPLUS**. If it doesn't find login.sql there, it then looks in the home directory for Oracle. If it doesn't find login.sql there, it stops looking.

You can put virtually any command in login.sql that you can use in SQL*Plus, including both SQL*Plus commands and SQL statements; all of them will be executed before SQL*Plus gives you the SQL prompt. This can be a convenient way to set up your own individual SQL*Plus environment, with all the basic layouts the way you prefer them. Here's an example of a typical login.sql file:

```
prompt Login.sql loaded.
set feedback off
set sqlprompt 'What now, boss? '
set sqlnumber off
set numwidth 5
set pagesize 24
set linesize 79
define _editor="vi"
```

As of Oracle Database 10g, Oracle provides three new predefined environment variables: _DATE, _PRIVILEGE ('AS SYSDBA', 'AS SYSOPER', or blank), and _USER (same value as **show user** returns).

Another file, named glogin.sql, is used to establish default SQL*Plus settings for all users of a database. This file, usually stored in the administrative directory for SQL*Plus, is useful in enforcing column and environment settings for multiple users.

The meaning of each of these commands can be found in the Alphabetical Reference section of this book.

Adding SQL*Plus Commands

Once you've saved a SQL statement into a file, such as fred.sql, you can add to the file any SQL*Plus commands you want. Essentially, you can build this file in a similar fashion to activity.sql in Figure 6-3. When you've finished working on it, you can exit your editor and be returned to SQL*Plus.

start

Once you are back in SQL*Plus, test your editing work by executing the file you've just edited:

```
start fred.sql
```

All the SQL*Plus and SQL commands in that file will execute, line by line, just as if you'd entered each one of them by hand. If you've included a **spool** and a **spool off** command in the file, you can use your editor to view the results of your work. This is just what was shown in Figure 6-2—the product of starting activity.sql and spooling its results into activity.lst.

To develop a report, use steps like these, in cycles:

1. Use SQL*Plus to build a SQL query interactively. When it appears close to being satisfactory, save it under a name such as test.sql. (The extension .sql is usually reserved for start files, scripts that will execute to produce a report.)

2. Edit the file test.sql using a favorite editor. Add **column**, **break**, **compute**, **set**, and **spool** commands to the file. You usually spool to a file with the extension .lst, such as test.lst. Exit the editor.

3. Back in SQL*Plus, the file test.sql is **start**ed. Its results fly past on the screen, but also go into the file test.lst. The editor examines this file.

4. Incorporate any necessary changes into test.sql and run it again.

5. Continue this process until the report is correct and polished.

Checking the SQL*Plus Environment

You saw earlier that the command line editor can't change SQL*Plus commands, because it can affect only SQL statements—those lines stored in the SQL buffer. You also saw that you can **save** SQL statements and **store** environment settings into files, where they can be modified using your own editor.

If you'd like to check how a particular column is defined, type

```
column DaysOut
```

without anything following the column name. SQL*Plus will then list all the instructions you've given about that column, as shown here:

```
COLUMN   DaysOut ON
HEADING  'Days!Out' headsep '!'
FORMAT   999.99
```

If you type just the word **column**, without any column name following it, then *all* the columns will be listed. You will see all the columns Oracle sets up by default, plus the ones that you've defined:

```
COLUMN    Title ON
FORMAT    a20
word_wrap

COLUMN    DaysOut ON
HEADING   'Days!Out' headsep '!'
FORMAT    999.99

COLUMN    Name ON
FORMAT    a20
```

ttitle, **btitle**, **break**, and **compute** are displayed simply by typing their names, with nothing following. SQL*Plus answers back immediately with the current definitions. The first line in each of the next examples is what you type; the following lines show SQL*Plus's replies:

```
ttitle
ttitle ON and is the following 31 characters:
Checkout Log for 1/1/02-3/31/02

btitle
btitle ON and is the following 18 characters:
from the Bookshelf

break
break on report nodup
          on Name skip 1 nodup

compute
COMPUTE avg LABEL 'avg' OF DaysOut ON Name
COMPUTE avg LABEL 'avg' OF DaysOut ON report
```

Looking at those settings (also called *parameters*) that follow the **set** command requires the use of the word **show**:

```
show headsep
headsep "!" (hex 21)

show linesize
linesize 80

show pagesize
pagesize 60

show newpage
newpage 0
```

See the Alphabetical Reference section of this book under **set** and **show** for a complete list of parameters.

The **ttitle** and **btitle** settings can be disabled by using the **btitle off** and **ttitle off** commands. The following listing shows these commands (note that SQL*Plus does not reply to the commands):

```
ttitle off

btitle off
```

The settings for columns, breaks, and computes can be disabled via the **clear columns**, **clear breaks**, and **clear computes** commands. The first line in each example in the following listing is what you type; the lines that follow show how SQL*Plus replies:

```
clear columns
columns cleared

clear breaks
breaks cleared

clear computes
computes cleared
```

Building Blocks

This has been a fairly dense chapter, particularly if SQL*Plus is new to you; yet on reflection, you'll probably agree that what was introduced here is not really difficult. If Figure 6-3 looked daunting when you began the chapter, look at it again now. Is there any line on it that you don't understand, or don't have a sense for what is being done and why? You could, if you wanted, simply copy this file (activity.sql) into another file with a different name and then begin to modify it to suit your own tastes and to query against your own tables. The structure of any reports you produce will, after all, be very similar.

There is a lot going on in activity.sql, but it is made up of simple building blocks. This will be the approach used throughout the book. Oracle provides building blocks, and lots of them, but each separate block is understandable and useful.

In the previous chapters, you learned how to select data out of the database, choosing certain columns and ignoring others, choosing certain rows based on logical restrictions you set up, and combining two tables to give you information not available from either one on its own.

In this chapter, you learned how to give orders that SQL*Plus can follow in formatting and producing the pages and headings of polished reports.

In the next several chapters, you'll change and format your data, row by row. Your expertise and confidence should grow chapter by chapter. By the end of Part II of this book, you should be able to produce very sophisticated reports in short order, to the considerable benefit of your company and yourself.

CHAPTER

7

Getting Text
Information and
Changing It

his chapter introduces *string functions,* which are software tools that allow you to manipulate a string of letters or other characters. To quickly reference individual functions, look them up by name in the Alphabetical Reference section of this book. This chapter focuses on the manipulation of text strings; to perform word searches (including word stem expansions and fuzzy matches), you should use Oracle Text, as described in Chapter 25.

Functions in Oracle work in one of two ways. Some functions create new objects from old ones; they produce a result that is a modification of the original information, such as turning lowercase characters into uppercase. Other functions produce a result that tells you something about the information, such as how many characters are in a word or sentence.

NOTE
If you are using PL/SQL, you can create your own functions with the **create function** *statement. See Part IV for details.*

Datatypes

Just as people can be classified into different types based on certain characteristics (shy, outgoing, smart, silly, and so forth), different kinds of data can be classified into *datatypes* based on certain characteristics.

Datatypes in Oracle include NUMBER, CHAR (short for CHARACTER), DATE, VARCHAR2, LONG, RAW, LONG RAW, BLOB, CLOB, and BFILE. The first several are probably obvious. The rest are special datatypes that you'll encounter later. A full explanation of each of these can be found by name or under "Datatypes" in the Alphabetical Reference section of this book. Each datatype is covered in detail in the chapters ahead. As with people, some of the "types" overlap, and some are fairly rare.

If the information is of the character (VARCHAR2 or CHAR) type—a mixture of letters, punctuation marks, numbers, and spaces (also called *alphanumeric*)—you'll need string functions to modify or inform you about it. Oracle's SQL provides quite a few such tools.

What Is a String?

A *string* is a simple concept: a bunch of things in a line, such as houses, popcorn, pearls, numbers, or characters in a sentence.

Strings are frequently encountered in managing information. Names are strings of characters, as in Juan L'Heureaux. Phone numbers are strings of numbers, dashes, and sometimes parentheses, as in (415) 555-2676. Even a pure number, such as 5443702, can be considered as either a number or a string of characters.

NOTE
Datatypes that are restricted to pure numbers (plus a decimal point and minus sign, if needed) are called NUMBER, and they are not usually referred to as strings. A number can be used in certain ways that a string cannot, and vice versa.

Strings that can include any mixture of letters, numbers, spaces, and other symbols (such as punctuation marks and special characters) are called *character strings,* or just *character* for short.

There are two string datatypes in Oracle. CHAR strings are always a fixed length. If you set a value to a string with a length less than that of a CHAR column, Oracle automatically pads the string with blanks. When you compare CHAR strings, Oracle compares the strings by padding them out to equal lengths with blanks. This means that if you compare "character" with "character" in CHAR columns, Oracle considers the strings to be the same. The VARCHAR2 datatype is a variable-length string. The VARCHAR datatype is synonymous with VARCHAR2, but this may change in future versions of Oracle, so you should avoid using VARCHAR. Use CHAR for fixed-length character string fields and VARCHAR2 for all other character string fields.

The simple Oracle string functions, explained in this chapter, are shown in Table 7-1.

Function Name	Use
I I	Glues or concatenates two strings together. The I symbol is called a *vertical bar* or *pipe.*
ASCII	Returns the decimal representation in the database character set of the first character of the string.
CHR	Returns the character having the binary equivalent to the string in either the database character set or the national character set.
CONCAT	Concatenates two strings together (same as I I).
INITCAP	Initial capital. Capitalizes the first letter of a word or series of words.
INSTR	Finds the location of a character in a string.
LENGTH	Tells the length of a string.
LOWER	Converts every letter in a string to lowercase.
LPAD	Left pad. Makes a string a certain length by adding a certain set of characters to the left.
LTRIM	Left trim. Trims all the occurrences of any one of a set of characters off the left side of a string.
NLS_INITCAP	Initcap based on the National Language Support (NLS) value.
NLS_LOWER	Lower based on the NLS value.
NLS_UPPER	Upper based on the NLS value.
NLSSORT	Sort based on the national language selected.
REGEXP_INSTR, REGEXP_REPLACE, and REGEXP_SUBSTR	INSTR, REPLACE, and SUBSTR for regular expressions.

TABLE 7-1. *Oracle String Functions*

Function Name	Use
RPAD	Right pad. Makes a string a certain length by adding a certain set of characters to the right.
RTRIM	Right trim. Trims all the occurrences of any one of a set of characters off the right side of a string.
SOUNDEX	Finds words that sound like the example specified.
SUBSTR	Substring. Clips out a piece of a string.
TREAT	Changes the declared type of an expression.
TRIM	Trims all occurrences of any one of a set of characters off either or both sides of a string.
UPPER	Converts every letter in a string into uppercase.

TABLE 7-1. *Oracle String Functions* (continued)

Notation

Functions are shown with this kind of notation throughout the book:

```
FUNCTION(string [,option])
```

The function itself will be in uppercase. The thing it affects (usually a string) will be shown in lowercase italics. Any time the word *string* appears, it represents either a literal string of characters or the name of a character column in a table. When you actually use a string function, any literal must be in single quotes; any column name must appear without single quotes.

Every function has only one pair of parentheses. The value that function works on, as well as additional information you can pass to the function, goes between the parentheses.

Some functions have *options,* parts that are not always required that you can use to make the function work as you want. Options are always shown in square brackets: []. See the discussion on **LPAD** and **RPAD** in the following section for an example of how options are used.

A simple example of how the **LOWER** function is printed follows:

```
LOWER(string)
```

The word "LOWER" with the two parentheses is the function itself, so it is shown here in uppercase; *string* stands for the actual string of characters to be converted to lowercase, and it's shown in lowercase italics. Therefore,

```
LOWER('CAMP DOUGLAS')
```

would produce

```
camp douglas
```

The string 'CAMP DOUGLAS' is a literal, meaning that it is literally the string of characters that the function **LOWER** is to work on. Oracle uses single quotation marks to denote the beginning and end of any literal string. The string in **LOWER** also could have been the name of a column from a table, in which case the function would have operated on the contents of the column for every row brought back by a **select** statement. For example,

```
select City, LOWER(City), LOWER('City') from WEATHER;
```

would produce this result:

```
CITY            LOWER(CITY) LOWE
--------------  ----------- ----
LIMA            lima        city
PARIS           paris       city
MANCHESTER      manchester  city
ATHENS          athens      city
CHICAGO         chicago     city
SYDNEY          sydney      city
SPARTA          sparta      city
```

At the top of the second column, in the **LOWER** function, CITY is not inside single quotation marks. This tells Oracle that it is a column name, not a literal.

In the third column's **LOWER** function, 'CITY' is inside single quotation marks. This means you literally want the function **LOWER** to work on the word "CITY" (that is, the string of letters C-I-T-Y), not the column by the same name.

Concatenation (| |)

The following notation tells Oracle to *concatenate*, or stick together, two strings:

```
string || string
```

The strings, of course, can be either column names or literals. Here's an example:

```
select City||Country from LOCATION;
```

```
CITY || COUNTRY
-------------------------------------------------
ATHENSGREECE
CHICAGOUNITED STATES
CONAKRYGUINEA
LIMAPERU
MADRASINDIA
MANCHESTERENGLAND
MOSCOWRUSSIA
PARISFRANCE
SHENYANGCHINA
ROMEITALY
TOKYOJAPAN
```

```
SYDNEYAUSTRALIA
SPARTAGREECE
MADRIDSPAIN
```

Here, the cities vary in width from 4 to 12 characters. The countries push right up against them. This is just how the concatenate function is supposed to work: It glues columns or strings together with no spaces in between.

This isn't very easy to read, of course. To make this a little more readable, you could list cities and countries with a comma and a space between them. You'd simply concatenate the City and Country columns with a literal string of a comma and a space, like this:

```
select City ||', '||Country from LOCATION;

CITY ||','||COUNTRY
-------------------------------------------------------
ATHENS, GREECE
CHICAGO, UNITED STATES
CONAKRY, GUINEA
LIMA, PERU
MADRAS, INDIA
MANCHESTER, ENGLAND
MOSCOW, RUSSIA
PARIS, FRANCE
SHENYANG, CHINA
ROME, ITALY
TOKYO, JAPAN
SYDNEY, AUSTRALIA
SPARTA, GREECE
MADRID, SPAIN
```

Notice the column title. See Chapter 6 for a review of column titles.

You could also use the **CONCAT** function to concatenate strings. For example, the query

```
select CONCAT(City, Country) from LOCATION;
```

is equivalent to

```
select City||Country from LOCATION;
```

How to Cut and Paste Strings

In this section, you learn about a series of functions that often confuse users: **LPAD**, **RPAD**, **LTRIM**, **RTRIM**, **TRIM**, **LENGTH**, **SUBSTR**, and **INSTR**. These all serve a common purpose: they allow you to *cut* and *paste*.

Each of these functions does some part of cutting and pasting. For example, **LENGTH** tells you how many characters are in a string. **SUBSTR** lets you clip out and use a *substring*—a portion of a string—starting at one position in the string and continuing for a given length. **INSTR** lets you find the location of a group of characters within another string. **LPAD** and **RPAD** allow you to easily concatenate spaces or other characters on the left or right side of a string. **LTRIM** and **RTRIM** clip

characters off the ends of strings, and **TRIM** can clip characters from both ends at once. Most interesting is that all of these functions can be used in combination with each other, as you'll soon see.

RPAD and LPAD

RPAD and **LPAD** are very similar functions. **RPAD** allows you to "pad" the right side of a column with any set of characters. The character set can be almost anything: spaces, periods, commas, letters or numbers, caret signs (^), or even exclamation marks (!). **LPAD** does the same thing as **RPAD**, but to the left side.

Here are the formats for **RPAD** and **LPAD**:

```
RPAD(string,length [,'set'])

LPAD(string,length [,'set'])
```

Here, *string* is the name of a CHAR or VARCHAR2 column from the database (or a literal string), *length* is the total number of characters long that the result should be (in other words, its width), and *set* is the set of characters that do the padding. The set must be enclosed in single quotation marks. The square brackets mean that the set (and the comma that precedes it) is optional. If you leave this off, the function will automatically pad with spaces. This is sometimes called the *default*; that is, if you don't tell the function which set of characters to use, it will use spaces by default.

Many users produce tables with dots to help guide the eye from one side of the page to the other. Here's how **RPAD** does this. In this example, the values are padded to a length of 35:

```
select RPAD(City,35,'.'), Temperature from WEATHER;

RPAD(CITY,35,'.')                    TEMPERATURE
----------------------------------- -----------
LIMA...............................          45
PARIS..............................          81
MANCHESTER.........................          66
ATHENS.............................          97
CHICAGO............................          66
SYDNEY.............................          69
SPARTA.............................          74
```

Notice what happened here. **RPAD** took each city, from Lima through Sparta, and concatenated dots on the right of it, adding just enough for each city so that the result (City plus dots) is exactly 35 characters long. The concatenate function (||) could not have done this. It would have added the same number of dots to every city, leaving a ragged edge on the right.

LPAD does the same sort of thing, but on the left. Suppose you want to reformat cities and temperatures so that the cities are right-justified (that is, they all align at the right). For this example, the padded length is 11:

```
select LPAD(City,11), Temperature from WEATHER;

LPAD(CITY,1 TEMPERATURE
----------- -----------
       LIMA          45
```

```
        PARIS          81
   MANCHESTER          66
       ATHENS          97
      CHICAGO          66
       SYDNEY          69
       SPARTA          74
```

LTRIM, RTRIM, and TRIM

LTRIM and **RTRIM** are like hedge trimmers. They trim off unwanted characters from the left and right ends of strings. For example, suppose you have a MAGAZINE table with a column in it that contains the titles of magazine articles, but the titles were entered by different people. Some people always put the titles in quotes, whereas others simply entered the words; some used periods, others didn't; some started titles with "The," whereas others did not. How do you trim these?

```
select Title from MAGAZINE;

TITLE
------------------------------------
THE BARBERS WHO SHAVE THEMSELVES.
"HUNTING THOREAU IN NEW HAMPSHIRE"
THE ETHNIC NEIGHBORHOOD
RELATIONAL DESIGN AND ENTHALPY
"INTERCONTINENTAL RELATIONS."
```

Here are the formats for **RTRIM** and **LTRIM**:

```
RTRIM(string [,'set'])

LTRIM(string [,'set'])
```

Here, *string* is the name of the column from the database (or a literal string), and *set* is the collection of characters you want to trim off. If no set of characters is specified, the functions trim off spaces.

You can trim off more than one character at a time; to do so, simply make a list (a string) of the characters you want removed. First, let's get rid of the quotes and periods on the right, as shown here:

Set of characters being trimmed

The preceding produces this:

```
RTRIM(TITLE,'."')
------------------------------------
THE BARBERS WHO SHAVE THEMSELVES
"HUNTING THOREAU IN NEW HAMPSHIRE
```

```
THE ETHNIC NEIGHBORHOOD
RELATIONAL DESIGN AND ENTHALPY
"INTERCONTINENTAL RELATIONS
```

RTRIM removed both the double quotation marks and the periods from the right side of each of these titles. The *set* of characters you want to remove can be as long as you want. Oracle will check and recheck the right side of each title until every character in your string has been removed— that is, until it runs into the first character in the string that is *not* in your set.

Combining Two Functions

Now what? You can use the **LTRIM** function to get rid of the quotes on the left. The Title column is buried in the middle of the **RTRIM** function. In this section, you learn how to combine functions.

You know that when you ran the **select** statement

```
select Title from MAGAZINE;
```

the result you got back was the content of the Title column, as shown next:

```
THE BARBERS WHO SHAVE THEMSELVES.
"HUNTING THOREAU IN NEW HAMPSHIRE"
THE ETHNIC NEIGHBORHOOD
RELATIONAL DESIGN AND ENTHALPY
"INTERCONTINENTAL RELATIONS."
```

Remember that the purpose of

```
RTRIM(Title,'."')
```

is to take each of these strings and remove the quotes on the right side, effectively producing a result that is a *new* column whose contents are shown here:

```
THE BARBERS WHO SHAVE THEMSELVES
"HUNTING THOREAU IN NEW HAMPSHIRE
THE ETHNIC NEIGHBORHOOD
RELATIONAL DESIGN AND ENTHALPY
"INTERCONTINENTAL RELATIONS
```

Therefore, if you pretend that **RTRIM(Title,'."')** is simply a column name itself, you can substitute it for *string* in the following:

```
LTRIM(string,'set')
```

So you simply type your **select** statement to look like this:

```
select LTRIM(RTRIM(Title,'."'),'"') from MAGAZINE;
```

Taking this apart for clarity, you see the following:

Is this how you want it? And what is the result of this combined function?

```
LTRIM(RTRIM(TITLE,'."'),'"')
-----------------------------------
THE BARBERS WHO SHAVE THEMSELVES
HUNTING THOREAU IN NEW HAMPSHIRE
THE ETHNIC NEIGHBORHOOD
RELATIONAL DESIGN AND ENTHALPY
INTERCONTINENTAL RELATIONS
```

Your titles are now cleaned up.

Looking at a combination of functions the first (or the thousandth) time can be confusing, even for an experienced query user. It's difficult to assess which commas and parentheses go with which functions, particularly when a query you've written isn't working correctly; discovering where a comma is missing, or which parenthesis isn't properly matched with another, can be a real adventure.

One simple solution to this is to break functions onto separate lines, at least until they're all working the way you want. SQLPLUS doesn't care at all where you break a SQL statement, as long as it's not in the middle of a word or a literal string. To better visualize how this **RTRIM** and **LTRIM** combination works, you could type it like this:

```
select LTRIM(
               RTRIM(Title,'."')
                             ,'"')
   from MAGAZINE;
```

This makes what you are trying to do obvious, and it will work even if it is typed on four separate lines with lots of spaces. SQLPLUS simply ignores extra spaces.

Suppose now you decide to trim off THE from the front of two of the titles, as well as the space that follows it (and, of course, the double quote you removed before). You might do this:

```
select LTRIM(RTRIM(Title,'."'),'"THE ')
   from MAGAZINE;
```

which produces the following:

```
LTRIM(RTRIM(TITLE,'."'),'"THE')
-----------------------------------
BARBERS WHO SHAVE THEMSELVES
```

```
UNTING THOREAU IN NEW HAMPSHIRE
NIC NEIGHBORHOOD
RELATIONAL DESIGN AND ENTHALPY
INTERCONTINENTAL RELATIONS
```

What happened? The second and third row got trimmed more than expected. Why? Because **LTRIM** was busy looking for and trimming off anything that was a double quote, a *T*, an *H*, an *E*, or a space. It was not looking for the word THE. It was looking for the letters in it, and **LTRIM** didn't quit the first time it saw any of the letters it was looking for. It quit when it saw a character that wasn't in its set.

What it trimmed: What is left behind:

```
THE                       BARBERS WHO SHAVE THEMSELVES
"H                        UNTING THOREAU IN NEW HAMPSHIRE
THE ETH                   NIC NEIGHBORHHOOD
                          RELATIONAL DESIGN AND ENTHALPY
"                         INTERCONTINENTAL RELATIONS
```

In the set '"THE'

NOT in the set '"THE'

In other words, all of the following and many other combinations of the letters will have the same effect when used as the set of an **LTRIM** or **RTRIM**:

```
'"THE'
'HET"'
'E"TH'
'H"TE'
'ET"H'
```

The order of the letters of the set has no effect on how the function works. Note, however, that the *case* of the letters is important. Oracle will check the case of both the letters in the set and in the string. It will remove only those with an exact match.

LTRIM and **RTRIM** are designed to remove any characters in a set from the left or right of a string. They're not intended to remove words. To do that requires clever use of **INSTR**, **SUBSTR**, and even **DECODE**, which you will learn about in Chapter 16.

The previous example makes one point clear: It's better to make certain that data gets cleaned up or edited before it is stored in the database. It would have been a lot less trouble if the individuals typing these magazine article titles had simply avoided the use of quotes, periods, and the word THE.

Using the TRIM Function

The preceding example showed how to combine two functions—a useful skill when dealing with string manipulation. If you are trimming the exact same data from both the beginning and the end of the string, you can use the **TRIM** function in place of an **LTRIM/RTRIM** combination.

TRIM uses a unique syntax. The following example shows the use of the **TRIM** function with its associated **from** clause within the function. In this example, the double quotes are removed from the beginning and the end of the magazine article titles. Because the double quote is a character string, it is placed inside two single quotes:

```
select TRIM('"' from Title) from MAGAZINE;

TRIM('"'FROMTITLE)
-----------------------------------
THE BARBERS WHO SHAVE THEMSELVES.
HUNTING THOREAU IN NEW HAMPSHIRE
THE ETHNIC NEIGHBORHOOD
RELATIONAL DESIGN AND ENTHALPY
INTERCONTINENTAL RELATIONS.
```

The quotes have been removed from the beginning and ending of the strings. If you just want to trim one end of the strings, you could use the **leading** or **trailing** clause, as shown in the following listing:

```
select TRIM(leading '"' from Title) from MAGAZINE;
select TRIM(trailing '"' from Title) from MAGAZINE;
```

Using **leading** makes **TRIM** act like **LTRIM**; **trailing** makes it act like **RTRIM**. The most powerful use of **TRIM** is its ability to act on both ends of the string at once, thus simplifying the code you have to write—provided the same characters are being removed from both ends of the string.

Adding One More Function

Suppose that you decide to **RPAD** your trimmed-up titles with dashes and carets, perhaps also asking for a magazine name and page number. Your query would look like this:

```
select Name, RPAD(LTRIM(RTRIM(Title,'"'),'."'),47,'-^'), Page
   from MAGAZINE;

NAME              RPAD(LTRIM(RTRIM(TITLE,'"'),'."'),47,'-^')  PAGE
----------------  -------------------------------------------  -----
BERTRAND MONTHLY  THE BARBERS WHO SHAVE THEMSELVES-^-^-^-^-^    70
LIVE FREE OR DIE  HUNTING THOREAU IN NEW HAMPSHIRE-^-^-^-^-^   320
PSYCHOLOGICA      THE ETHNIC NEIGHBORHOOD-^-^-^-^-^-^-^-^-^-^  246
FADED ISSUES      RELATIONAL DESIGN AND ENTHALPY-^-^-^-^-^-^   279
ENTROPY WIT       INTERCONTINENTAL RELATIONS-^-^-^-^-^-^-^-^    20
```

Each function has parentheses that enclose the column it is going to affect, so the real trick in understanding combined functions in **select** statements is to read from the outside to the inside on both the left and right, watching (and even counting) the pairs of parentheses.

LOWER, UPPER, and INITCAP

These three related and very simple functions often are used together. **LOWER** takes any string or column and converts any letters in it to lowercase. **UPPER** does the opposite, converting any letters

to uppercase. **INITCAP** takes the initial letter of every word in a string or column and converts just those letters to uppercase.

Here are the formats for these functions:

```
LOWER(string)
UPPER(string)
INITCAP(string)
```

Returning to the WEATHER table, recall that each city is stored in uppercase letters, like this:

```
LIMA
PARIS
ATHENS
CHICAGO
MANCHESTER
SYDNEY
SPARTA
```

Therefore,

```
select City, UPPER(City), LOWER(City), INITCAP(LOWER(City))
   from WEATHER;
```

produces this:

```
City         UPPER(CITY) LOWER(CITY) INITCAP(LOW
-----------  ----------- ----------- -----------
LIMA         LIMA        lima        Lima
PARIS        PARIS       paris       Paris
MANCHESTER   MANCHESTER  manchester  Manchester
ATHENS       ATHENS      athens      Athens
CHICAGO      CHICAGO     chicago     Chicago
SYDNEY       SYDNEY      sydney      Sydney
SPARTA       SPARTA      sparta      Sparta
```

Look carefully at what is produced in each column, and at the functions that produced it in the SQL statement. The fourth column shows how you can apply **INITCAP** to **LOWER(City)** and have it appear with normal capitalization, even though it is stored as uppercase.

Another example is the Name column as stored in a MAGAZINE table:

```
NAME
----------------
BERTRAND MONTHLY
LIVE FREE OR DIE
PSYCHOLOGICA
FADED ISSUES
ENTROPY WIT
```

This is then retrieved with the combined **INITCAP** and **LOWER** functions, as shown here:

```
select INITCAP(LOWER(Name)) from MAGAZINE;

INITCAP(LOWER(NA
----------------
Bertrand Monthly
Live Free Or Die
Psychologica
Faded Issues
Entropy Wit
```

And here it's applied to the Name, cleaned-up Title, and Page columns (note that you'll also rename the columns):

```
select INITCAP(LOWER(Name)) AS Name,
       INITCAP(LOWER(RTRIM(LTRIM(Title,'"'),'."'))) AS Title,
       Page
  from Magazine;

NAME             TITLE                                    PAGE
---------------- ---------------------------------------- -----
Bertrand Monthly The Barbers Who Shave Themselves            70
Live Free Or Die Hunting Thoreau In New Hampshire           320
Psychologica     The Ethnic Neighborhood                    246
Faded Issues     Relational Design And Enthalpy             279
Entropy Wit      Intercontinental Relations                  20
```

LENGTH

This one is easy. **LENGTH** tells you how long a string is—how many characters it has in it, including letters, spaces, and anything else. Here is the format for **LENGTH**:

```
LENGTH(string)
```

And here's an example:

```
select Name, LENGTH(Name) from MAGAZINE;

NAME             LENGTH(NAME)
---------------- ------------
BERTRAND MONTHLY           16
LIVE FREE OR DIE           16
PSYCHOLOGICA               12
FADED ISSUES               12
ENTROPY WIT                11
```

This isn't normally useful by itself, but it can be used as part of another function, for calculating how much space you'll need on a report, or as part of a **where** or an **order by** clause.

NOTE
You cannot perform functions such as **LENGTH** *on a column that uses
a LONG datatype.*

SUBSTR

You can use the **SUBSTR** function to clip out a piece of a string. Here is the format for **SUBSTR**:

```
SUBSTR(string,start [,count])
```

This tells SQL to clip out a subsection of *string*, beginning at position *start* and continuing for *count* characters. If you don't specify *count*, **SUBSTR** will clip beginning at *start* and continuing to the end of the string. For example,

```
select SUBSTR(Name,6,4) from MAGAZINE;
```

gives you this:

```
SUBS
----
AND
FREE
OLOG
 ISS
PY W
```

You can see how the function works. It clipped out the piece of the magazine name starting in position 6 (counting from the left) and including a total of four characters.

A more practical use might be in separating out phone numbers from a personal address book. For example, assume that you have an ADDRESS table that contains, among other things, last names, first names, and phone numbers, as shown here:

```
select LastName, FirstName, Phone from ADDRESS;
```

LASTNAME	FIRSTNAME	PHONE
BAILEY	WILLIAM	213-555-0223
ADAMS	JACK	415-555-7530
SEP	FELICIA	214-555-8383
DE MEDICI	LEFTY	312-555-1166
DEMIURGE	FRANK	707-555-8900
CASEY	WILLIS	312-555-1414
ZACK	JACK	415-555-6842
YARROW	MARY	415-555-2178
WERSCHKY	ARNY	415-555-7387
BRANT	GLEN	415-555-7512
EDGAR	THEODORE	415-555-6252
HARDIN	HUGGY	617-555-0125
HILD	PHIL	603-555-2242

```
LOEBEL                   FRANK                      202-555-1414
MOORE                    MARY                       718-555-1638
SZEP                     FELICIA                    214-555-8383
ZIMMERMAN                FRED                       503-555-7491
```

Suppose you want just those phone numbers in the 415 area code. One solution would be to have a separate column called AreaCode. Thoughtful planning about tables and columns will eliminate a good deal of fooling around later with reformatting. However, in this instance, area codes and phone numbers are combined in a single column, so a way must be found to separate out the numbers in the 415 area code.

```
select LastName, FirstName, Phone from ADDRESS
  where Phone like '415-%';

LASTNAME                 FIRSTNAME                  PHONE
------------------------ -------------------------- ------------
ADAMS                    JACK                       415-555-7530
ZACK                     JACK                       415-555-6842
YARROW                   MARY                       415-555-2178
WERSCHKY                 ARNY                       415-555-7387
BRANT                    GLEN                       415-555-7512
EDGAR                    THEODORE                   415-555-6252
```

Next, because you do not want to dial your own area code when calling friends in the 415 area code, you can eliminate this from the result by using another **SUBSTR**:

```
select LastName, FirstName, SUBSTR(Phone,5) from ADDRESS
  where Phone like '415-%';

LASTNAME                 FIRSTNAME                  SUBSTR(P
------------------------ -------------------------- --------
ADAMS                    JACK                       555-7530
ZACK                     JACK                       555-6842
YARROW                   MARY                       555-2178
WERSCHKY                 ARNY                       555-7387
BRANT                    GLEN                       555-7512
EDGAR                    THEODORE                   555-6252
```

Notice that the default version of **SUBSTR** was used here. **SUBSTR(Phone,5)** tells SQL to clip out the substring of the phone number, starting at position 5 and going to the end of the string. Doing this eliminates the area code.

Of course,

```
SUBSTR(Phone,5)
```

has exactly the same effect as the following:

```
SUBSTR(Phone,5,8)
```

You can combine this with the concatenation and column-renaming techniques discussed in Chapter 6 to produce a quick listing of local friends' phone numbers, as shown here:

```
select LastName ||', '||FirstName AS Name,
       SUBSTR(Phone,5) AS Phone
  from ADDRESS
 where Phone like '415-%';
```

```
NAME                                                 PHONE
----------------------------------------------------  --------
ADAMS, JACK                                          555-7530
ZACK, JACK                                           555-6842
YARROW, MARY                                         555-2178
WERSCHKY, ARNY                                       555-7387
BRANT, GLEN                                          555-7512
EDGAR, THEODORE                                      555-6252
```

To produce a dotted line following the name, add the **RPAD** function:

```
select RPAD(LastName ||', '||FirstName,25,'.') AS Name,
       SUBSTR(Phone,5) AS Phone
  from ADDRESS
 where Phone like '415-%';
```

```
NAME                     PHONE
-----------------------  --------
ADAMS, JACK............. 555-7530
ZACK, JACK.............. 555-6842
YARROW, MARY............ 555-2178
WERSCHKY, ARNY.......... 555-7387
BRANT, GLEN............. 555-7512
EDGAR, THEODORE......... 555-6252
```

The use of negative numbers in the **SUBSTR** function also works. Normally, the position value you specify for the starting position is relative to the *start* of the string. When you use a negative number for the position value, it is relative to the *end* of the string. For example,

```
SUBSTR(Phone,-4)
```

would use the fourth position from the end of the Phone column's value as its starting point. Because no length parameter is specified in this example, the remainder of the string will be returned.

NOTE
*Use this feature only for VARCHAR2 datatype columns. Do not use it with columns that use the CHAR datatype. CHAR columns are fixed-length columns, so their values are padded with spaces to extend them to the full length of the column. Using a negative number for the **SUBSTR** position value in a CHAR column will determine the starting position relative to the end of the column, not the end of the string.*

The following example shows the result of a negative number in the **SUBSTR** function when it is used on a VARCHAR2 column:

```
select SUBSTR(Phone,-4)
  from ADDRESS
 where Phone like '415-5%';

SUBS
----
7530
6842
2178
7387
7512
6252
```

The *count* value of the **SUBSTR** function must always be positive or unspecified. Using a negative *count* will return a **NULL** result.

INSTR

The **INSTR** function allows for simple or sophisticated searching through a string for a set of characters, not unlike **LTRIM** and **RTRIM**, except that **INSTR** doesn't clip anything off. It simply tells you where in the string it found what you were searching for. This is similar to the **LIKE** logical operator described in Chapter 5, except that **LIKE** can only be used in a **where** or **having** clause, and **INSTR** can be used anywhere except in the **from** clause. Of course, **LIKE** can be used for complex pattern searches that would be quite difficult, if even possible, using **INSTR**. Here is the format for **INSTR**:

```
INSTR(string,set [,start [,occurrence ] ])
```

INSTR searches in the string for a certain set of characters. It has two options, one within the other. The first option is the default: It will look for the set starting at position 1. If you specify the location to *start*, it will skip over all the characters up to that point and begin its search there.

The second option is *occurrence*. A set of characters may occur more than once in a string, and you may really be interested only in whether something occurs more than once. By default, **INSTR** will look for the first *occurrence* of the set. By adding the option *occurrence* and making it equal to 3, for example, you can force **INSTR** to skip over the first two occurrences of the set and give the location of the third.

Some examples will make all this simpler to grasp. Recall the table of magazine articles. Here is a list of their authors:

```
select Author from MAGAZINE;

AUTHOR
------------------------
BONHOEFFER, DIETRICH
CHESTERTON, G.K.
RUTH, GEORGE HERMAN
WHITEHEAD, ALFRED
CROOKES, WILLIAM
```

To find the location of the first occurrence of the letter *O,* **INSTR** is used without its options and with *set* as 'O' (note the single quotation marks, since this is a literal), as shown in the following listing:

```
select Author, INSTR(Author,'O') from MAGAZINE;

AUTHOR                    INSTR(AUTHOR,'O')
------------------------  -----------------
BONHOEFFER, DIETRICH                      2
CHESTERTON, G.K.                          9
RUTH, GEORGE HERMAN                       9
WHITEHEAD, ALFRED                         0
CROOKES, WILLIAM                          3
```

This is, of course, the same as the following:

```
select Author, INSTR(Author,'O',1,1) from MAGAZINE;
```

If **INSTR** had looked for the second occurrence of the letter *O,* it would have found

```
select Author, INSTR(Author,'O',1,2) from MAGAZINE;

AUTHOR                    INSTR(AUTHOR,'O',1,2)
------------------------  ---------------------
BONHOEFFER, DIETRICH                          5
CHESTERTON, G.K.                              0
RUTH, GEORGE HERMAN                           0
WHITEHEAD, ALFRED                             0
CROOKES, WILLIAM                              4
```

INSTR found the second *O* in Bonhoeffer's name, at position 5, and in Crookes' name, at position 4. Chesterton has only one *O,* so for him, Ruth, and Whitehead, the result is zero, meaning no success—no second *O* was found.

To tell **INSTR** to look for the second occurrence, you also must tell it where to start looking (in this case, position 1). The default value of *start* is 1, which means that's what it uses if you don't specify anything, but the *occurrence* option requires a *start,* so you have to specify both.

If *set* is not just one character but several, **INSTR** gives the location of the first letter of the set, as shown here:

```
select Author, INSTR(Author,'WILLIAM') from MAGAZINE;

AUTHOR                    INSTR(AUTHOR,'WILLIAM')
------------------------  -----------------------
BONHOEFFER, DIETRICH                            0
CHESTERTON, G.K.                                0
RUTH, GEORGE HERMAN                             0
WHITEHEAD, ALFRED                               0
CROOKES, WILLIAM                               10
```

This has many useful applications, such as in the MAGAZINE table, for instance:

```
select Author, INSTR(Author,',') from MAGAZINE;

AUTHOR                   INSTR(AUTHOR,',')
------------------------ -----------------
BONHOEFFER, DIETRICH                    11
CHESTERTON, G.K.                        11
RUTH, GEORGE HERMAN                      5
WHITEHEAD, ALFRED                       10
CROOKES, WILLIAM                         8
```

Here, **INSTR** searched the strings of author names for a comma and then reported back the position in each string where it found one.

Suppose you want to reformat the names of the authors from the formal "last name/comma/ first name" approach, and present them as they are normally spoken, as shown here:

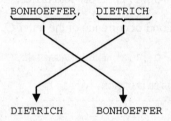

To do this using **INSTR** and **SUBSTR**, find the location of the comma, and use this location to tell **SUBSTR** where to clip. Taking this step by step, you must first find the comma as we did in the preceding listing.

Two **SUBSTR**s will be needed—one that clips out the author's last name up to the position before the comma, and one that clips out the author's first name from two positions after the comma through to the end.

First, look at the one that clips from position 1 to just before the comma:

```
select Author, SUBSTR(Author,1,INSTR(Author,',')-1)
   from MAGAZINE;

AUTHOR                   SUBSTR(AUTHOR,1,INSTR(AUT
------------------------ -------------------------
BONHOEFFER, DIETRICH     BONHOEFFER
CHESTERTON, G.K.         CHESTERTON
RUTH, GEORGE HERMAN      RUTH
WHITEHEAD, ALFRED        WHITEHEAD
CROOKES, WILLIAM         CROOKES
```

Next, look at the one that clips from two positions past the comma to the end of the string:

```
select Author, SUBSTR(Author,INSTR(Author,',')+2) from MAGAZINE;
```

```
AUTHOR                    SUBSTR(AUTHOR,INSTR(AUTHO
------------------------  -------------------------
BONHOEFFER, DIETRICH      DIETRICH
CHESTERTON, G.K.          G.K.
RUTH, GEORGE HERMAN       GEORGE HERMAN
WHITEHEAD, ALFRED         ALFRED
CROOKES, WILLIAM          WILLIAM
```

Look at the combination of these two, with the concatenate function putting a space between them, and a quick renaming of the column to ByFirstName:

```
column ByFirstName heading "By First Name"

select Author, SUBSTR(Author,INSTR(Author,',')+2)
               ||' '||
               SUBSTR(Author,1,INSTR(Author,',')-1)
            AS ByFirstName
  from MAGAZINE;

AUTHOR                    By First Name
------------------------  ------------------------
BONHOEFFER, DIETRICH      DIETRICH BONHOEFFER
CHESTERTON, G.K.          G.K. CHESTERTON
RUTH, GEORGE HERMAN       GEORGE HERMAN RUTH
WHITEHEAD, ALFRED         ALFRED WHITEHEAD
CROOKES, WILLIAM          WILLIAM CROOKES
```

It is daunting to look at a SQL statement like this one, but it was built using simple logic, and it can be broken down the same way. Bonhoeffer can provide the example. The first part looks like this:

```
SUBSTR(Author,INSTR(Author,',')+2)
```

This tells SQL to get the **SUBSTR** of Author starting two positions to the right of the comma and going to the end. This will clip out DIETRICH—the author's first name.

The beginning of the author's first name is found by locating the comma at the end of his last name (**INSTR** does this) and then sliding over two steps to the right (where his first name begins).

The following illustration shows how the **INSTR** function (plus 2) serves as the start for the **SUBSTR** function:

Here is the second part of the combined statement:

```
||' '||
```

This, of course, simply tells SQL to concatenate a space in the middle.
 Here is the third part of the combined statement:

```
SUBSTR(Author,1,INSTR(Author,',')-1)
```

This tells SQL to clip out the portion of the author's name starting at position 1 and ending one position before the comma, which results in the author's last name:

The fourth part simply assigns a column alias:

```
AS ByFirstName
```

It was only possible to accomplish this transposition because each Author record in the MAGAZINE table followed the same formatting conventions. In each record, the last name was always the first word in the string and was immediately followed by a comma. This allowed you to use the **INSTR** function to search for the comma. Once the comma's position was known, you could determine which part of the string was the last name, and the rest of the string was treated as the first name.

This is not often the case. Names are difficult to force into standard formats. Last names may include prefixes (such as *von* in von Hagel) or suffixes (such as Jr., Sr., and III). Using the previous example's SQL, the name Richards, Jr., Bob would have been transformed into Jr., Bob Richards.

Because of the lack of a standard formatting for names, many applications store the first and last names separately. Titles (such as MD) are usually stored in yet another column. A second option when storing such data is to force it into a single format and use **SUBSTR** and **INSTR** to manipulate that data when needed.

ASCII and CHR

The **ASCII** and **CHR** functions are seldom used during ad hoc queries. **CHR** converts numeric values to their ASCII character string equivalents:

```
select CHR(70)||CHR(83)||CHR(79)||CHR(85)||CHR(71)
    as ChrValues
  from DUAL;
```

```
CHRVA
-----
FSOUG
```

Oracle translated **CHR(70)** to an *F*, **CHR(83)** to an *S*, and so on, based on the database's character set.

The **ASCII** function performs the reverse operation—but if you pass it a string, only the first character of the string will be acted upon:

```
select ASCII('FSOUG') from DUAL;

ASCII('FSOUG')
--------------
            70
```

To see each ASCII value, you will need to evaluate each of the letters via separate executions of the **ASCII** function.

Using order by and where with String Functions

String functions can be used in a **where** clause, as shown here:

```
select City
   from WEATHER
 where LENGTH(City) < 7;

CITY
-----------
LIMA
PARIS
ATHENS
SYDNEY
SPARTA
```

They can also be used in an **order by** clause, as shown here:

```
select City
   from WEATHER
 order by LENGTH(City);

CITY
-----------
LIMA
PARIS
ATHENS
SYDNEY
SPARTA
CHICAGO
MANCHESTER
```

These are simple examples; much more complex clauses could be used. For example, you could find all the authors with more than one *O* in their names by using **INSTR** in the **where** clause:

```
select Author from MAGAZINE
  where INSTR(Author,'O',1,2) > 0;

AUTHOR
------------------------
BONHOEFFER, DIETRICH
CROOKES, WILLIAM
```

This works by finding a second occurrence of the letter *O* in the author names. The > **0** is a logical technique: Recall that functions generally produce two different kinds of results—one that creates new objects, and the other that tells you something about existing objects.

The **INSTR** function tells something about a string, specifically the position of the set it has been asked to find. Here, it is asked to locate the second *O* in the Author string. Its result will be a number that's greater than zero for those names with at least two *O*'s, and zero for those with one or less (when **INSTR** doesn't find something, its result is a zero). So, a simple test for a result greater than zero checks for the success of the **INSTR** search for a second *O*.

The **where** clause using **INSTR** produces the same result as this:

```
where Author LIKE '%O%O%'
```

Remember that the percent sign (%) is a wildcard, meaning it takes the place of anything, so the **like** clause here tells SQL to look for two *O*'s with anything before, between, or after them. This is probably easier to understand than the previous example of **INSTR**.

There are often several ways to produce the same result in Oracle. Some will be easier to understand, some will work more quickly, some will be more appropriate in certain situations, and some simply will be a matter of personal style.

SOUNDEX

One string function is used almost exclusively in a **where** clause: **SOUNDEX**. It has the unusual ability to find words that sound like other words, virtually regardless of how either is spelled. This is especially useful when you're not certain how a word or name is really spelled. Here is the format for **SOUNDEX**:

```
SOUNDEX(string)
```

And here are a few of examples of its use:

```
select City, Temperature, Condition from WEATHER
  where SOUNDEX(City) = SOUNDEX('menncestr');

CITY        TEMPERATURE CONDITION
----------- ----------- ---------
MANCHESTER           66 FOG
```

```
select Author from MAGAZINE
  where SOUNDEX(Author) = SOUNDEX('Banheffer');
```

```
AUTHOR
------------------------
BONHOEFFER, DIETRICH
```

SOUNDEX compares the sound of the entry in the selected column with the sound of the word in single quotation marks, and it looks for a close match. **SOUNDEX** makes certain assumptions about how letters and combinations of letters are usually pronounced in English, and the two words being compared must begin with the same letter. **SOUNDEX** will not always find the word you're searching for or have misspelled, but it can help.

It is not necessary that one of the two **SOUNDEX**s in the **where** clause have a literal in it. **SOUNDEX** could be used to compare the data in two columns to find those that sound alike.

One useful purpose for this function is cleaning up mailing lists. Many lists have duplicate entries with slight differences in the spelling or format of the customers' names. By using **SOUNDEX** to list all the names that sound alike, many of these duplicates can be discovered and eliminated.

Let's apply this to the ADDRESS table:

```
select LastName, FirstName, Phone
  from ADDRESS;
```

LASTNAME	FIRSTNAME	PHONE
BAILEY	WILLIAM	213-555-0223
ADAMS	JACK	415-555-7530
SEP	FELICIA	214-555-8383
DE MEDICI	LEFTY	312-555-1166
DEMIURGE	FRANK	707-555-8900
CASEY	WILLIS	312-555-1414
ZACK	JACK	415-555-6842
YARROW	MARY	415-555-2178
WERSCHKY	ARNY	415-555-7387
BRANT	GLEN	415-555-7512
EDGAR	THEODORE	415-555-6252
HARDIN	HUGGY	617-555-0125
HILD	PHIL	603-555-2242
LOEBEL	FRANK	202-555-1414
MOORE	MARY	718-555-1638
SZEP	FELICIA	214-555-8383
ZIMMERMAN	FRED	503-555-7491

To find duplicates, you must force Oracle to compare each last name in the table to all the others in the same table.

Join the ADDRESS table to itself by creating an alias for the table, calling it first **a** and then **b**. Now it is as if there are two tables, a and b, with the common column LastName.

In the **where** clause, eliminate any row in which the last name in the result set from table **a** matches the last name in the result set from table **b**. This prevents a last name from matching to itself.

Those that sound alike are then selected:

```
select a.LastName, a.FirstName, a.Phone
  from ADDRESS a, ADDRESS b
 where a.LastName != b.LastName
   and SOUNDEX(a.LastName) = SOUNDEX(b.LastName);

LASTNAME                 FIRSTNAME                 PHONE
------------------------ ------------------------  ------------
SZEP                     FELICIA                   214-555-8383
SEP                      FELICIA                   214-555-8383
```

You can also perform **SOUNDEX** searches on individual words within a text entry. For examples of this and other complex text searches, see Chapter 25.

National Language Support

Oracle doesn't have to use English characters; it can represent data in any language through its implementation of *National Language Support*. By using characters made up of longer pieces of information than ordinary characters, Oracle can represent Japanese and other such strings. See **NLSSORT**, **NLS_INITCAP**, **NLS_LOWER**, and **NLS_UPPER** in the Alphabetical Reference section of this book. In addition to the **SUBSTR** function, Oracle supports **SUBSTRB** (using bytes instead of characters), **SUBSTRC** (using Unicode complete characters), **SUBSTR2** (using UCS2 codepoints), and **SUBSTR4** (using UCS4 codepoints).

Regular Expression Support

As of Oracle Database 10g, the string functions **INSTR**, **REPLACE**, and **SUBSTR** have been extended to support regular expressions. Chapter 8 is devoted to the coverage of these advanced text-search features.

Review

Data comes in several types, primarily DATE, NUMBER, and character. Character data is basically a string of letters, numbers, or other symbols, and is often called a *character string,* or just a *string*. These strings can be changed or described by string functions. Oracle features two types of character datatypes: variable-length strings (the VARCHAR2 datatype) and fixed-length strings (the CHAR datatype). Values in CHAR columns are padded with spaces to the full column length if they are shorter than the defined length of the column.

Functions such as **RPAD**, **LPAD**, **LTRIM**, **RTRIM**, **TRIM**, **LOWER**, **UPPER**, **INITCAP**, and **SUBSTR** actually change the contents of a string before displaying it to you.

Functions such as **LENGTH**, **INSTR**, and **SOUNDEX** describe the characteristics of a string, such as how long it is, where in it a certain character is located, or what it sounds like.

All these functions can be used alone or in combination to select and present information from an Oracle database. This is a straightforward process, built up from simple logical steps that can be combined to accomplish very sophisticated tasks.

CHAPTER
8

Searching for
Regular Expressions

A
s of Oracle Database 10g, the **SUBSTR**, **INSTR**, **LIKE** and **REPLACE** functions have been enhanced and extended to support searches for regular expressions. Regular expressions support a wide array of standardized controls and checks—for example, matching values a specific number of times, searches for punctuation characters, or searches for digits. You can use these new functions to perform advanced searches against strings. The new functions are named **REGEXP_SUBSTR**, **REGEXP_INSTR**, **REGEXP_LIKE**, and **REGEXP_REPLACE**.

Users who have previously used the UNIX **grep** command to search for regular expressions in text files may already be familiar with the concepts and search techniques involved.

Search Strings

Let's start with an example. Phone numbers in the ADDRESS table are in the format 123-456-7890. To select all the exchanges (the middle set of numbers), you can **select** for any string within the phone number that starts and ends with a hyphen (-) character.

Within the **REGEXP_SUBSTR** function, we need to tell Oracle where to start the string. In this case, we are looking for '-'. The regular expression to search for begins thus:

```
select REGEXP_SUBSTR('123-456-7890', '-
```

We now need to tell Oracle to continue until it finds another '-' character in the string. To do this, use the '[^' operator, a bracket expression that says that the acceptable values match any character except for the expressions represented in the list. The command now looks like this:

```
select REGEXP_SUBSTR('123-456-7890', '-[^-]+' )
       "REGEXP_SUBSTR"
  from DUAL;

REGE
----
-456
```

This command tells Oracle to look for '-', followed by one or more characters that are not '-', followed by '-'. Note that if you add an extra '-' at the end of the regular expression, you get the trailing '-' as part of the returned string:

```
select REGEXP_SUBSTR('123-456-7890', '-[^-]+-' )
       "REGEXP_SUBSTR"
  from DUAL;

REGEX
-----
-456-
```

Most users (and developers) are not going to be comfortable typing in strings such as

```
'-[^-]+'
```

without training and practice. But as you use the **REGEXP_** functions, you can quickly see how much more functionality they give you. Consider that to generate the same result as the preceding using only **SUBSTR** and **INSTR**, and assuming that the length of the string between the '-' characters is not known, you would need to execute this query:

```
select SUBSTR('123-456-7890',
              INSTR('123-456-7890', '-',1,1),
              INSTR('123-456-7890', '-',1,2)-
              INSTR('123-456-7890', '-',1,1))
   from DUAL;
```

By comparison, the **REGEXP_SUBSTR** function is much more concise. As you will see in the examples later in this chapter, the regular expression searches enable you to encode complex search patterns within a single function call.

Table 8-1 shows the regular expression operators and their descriptions. Understanding the operators involved is critical for effective use of the regular expression search capabilities.

Let's apply some of these operators and character classes, starting with a simple search. First, select all the strings in the sample string that contain a colon:

```
select REGEXP_SUBSTR
       ('MY LEDGER: Debits, Credits, and Invoices 1940',
        ':' )    "REGEXP_SUBSTR"
   from DUAL;

R
-
:
```

Now, replace that search with a search for a punctuation character, using the [:punct:] character class:

```
select REGEXP_SUBSTR
       ('MY LEDGER: Debits, Credits, and Invoices 1940',
        '[:punct:]' )   "REGEXP_SUBSTR"
   from DUAL;

R
-
:
```

Operator	Description
\ [a]	The backslash character can have four different meanings, depending on the context. It can stand for itself, quote the next character, introduce an operator, or do nothing.
*	Matches zero or more occurrences.
+	Matches one or more occurrences.
?	Matches zero or one occurrence.
\|	Alternation operator for specifying alternative matches.
^ [b]	Matches the beginning-of-line character.
$ [b]	Matches the end-of-line character.
. [c]	Matches any character in the supported character set except **NULL**.
[] [d]	Bracket expression for specifying a matching list that should match any one of the expressions represented in the list. A nonmatching list expression begins with a caret (^) and specifies a list that matches any character except for the expressions represented in the list.
()	Grouping expression, treated as a single subexpression.
{m}	Matches exactly m times.
{m,}	Matches at least m times.
{m,n}	Matches at least m times but no more than n times.
\n [e]	The backreference expression (n is a digit between 1 and 9) matches the nth subexpression enclosed between parentheses and preceding \n.
[..] [f]	Specifies one collation element and can be a multicharacter element (for example, [.ch.] in Spanish).
[: :] [g]	Specifies character classes (for example, [:alpha:]). It matches any character within the character class.
[==] [h]	Specifies equivalence classes. For example, [=a=] matches all characters having base letter 'a'.

Notes on the POSIX operators and Oracle enhancements:

a. The backslash operator can be used to make the character following it normal if it is an operator. For example, '*' is interpreted as the asterisk string literal.

b. The characters '^' and '$' are the POSIX anchoring operators. By default, they match only the beginning or end of an entire string. Oracle lets you specify '^' and '$' to match the start or end of any line anywhere within the source string. This, in turn, lets you treat the source string as multiple lines.

c. In the POSIX standard, the "match any character" operator (.) is defined to match any English character except **NULL** and the newline character. In the Oracle implementation, the '.' operator can match any character in the database character set, including the newline character.

TABLE 8-1. *Regular Expression Operators*

d. In the POSIX standard, a range in a regular expression includes all collation elements between the start and end points of the range in the linguistic definition of the current locale. Therefore, ranges in regular expressions are linguistic ranges rather than byte values ranges, and the semantics of the range expression are independent of character set. Oracle implements this independence by interpreting range expressions according to the linguistic definition determined by the NLS_SORT initialization parameter.

e. The backreference expression '*n*' matches the same string of characters as was matched by the *n*th subexpression. The character *n* must be a digit from 1 to 9, designating the *n*th subexpression, numbered from left to right. The expression is invalid if the source string contains fewer than *n* subexpressions preceding the *n*. For example, the regular expression ^(.*)\1$ matches a line consisting of two adjacent appearances of the same string. Oracle supports the backreference expression in the regular expression pattern and the replacement string of the **REGEXP_REPLACE** function.

f. A collating element is a unit of collation and is equal to one character in most cases, but may comprise two or more characters in some languages. Historically, regular expression syntax does not support ranges containing multicharacter collation elements, such as the range 'a' through 'ch'. The POSIX standard introduces the collation element delimiter '[..]', which lets you delimit multicharacter collection elements such as '[a-[.ch.]]'. The collation elements supported by Oracle are determined by the setting of the NLS_SORT initialization parameter. The collation element is valid only inside the bracketed expression.

g. In English regular expressions, range expressions often indicate a character class. For example, '[a-z]' indicates any lowercase character. This convention is not useful in multilingual environments where the first and last character of a given character class may not be the same in all languages. The POSIX standard introduces the portable character class syntax '[::]'.

In addition to the operators, Oracle supports the following character classes based on character class definitions in NLS classification data:

Character Class Syntax	Meaning
[:alnum:]	All alphanumeric characters
[:alpha:]	All alphabetic characters
[:blank:]	All blank space characters
[:cntrl:]	All control characters (nonprinting)
[:digit:]	All numeric digits
[:graph:]	All [:punct:], [:upper:], [:lower:], and [:digit:] characters
[:lower:]	All lowercase alphabetic characters
[:print:]	All printable characters
[:punct:]	All punctuation characters
[:space:]	All space characters (nonprinting)
[:upper:]	All uppercase alphabetic characters
[:xdigit:]	All valid hexadecimal characters

This character class syntax lets you make better use of NLS character definitions to write flexible regular expressions. These character classes are valid only inside the bracketed expression.

h. Oracle supports the equivalence classes through the POSIX '[==]' syntax. A base letter and all of its accented versions constitute an equivalence class. For example, the equivalence class '[=a=]' matches ä and â. The equivalence classes are valid only inside the bracketed expression.

Note this restriction on equivalence classes: Composed and decomposed versions of the same equivalence class do not match. For example, 'ä' does not match 'a' followed by umlaut.

TABLE 8-1. *Regular Expression Operators* (continued)

Beginning from that point in the string, search from there to the next comma encountered:

```
select REGEXP_SUBSTR
       ('MY LEDGER: Debits, Credits, and Invoices 1940',
        '[:punct:][^,]+,' )   "REGEXP_SUBSTR"
   from DUAL;

REGEXP_SU
---------
: Debits,
```

You can use the [:digit:] character class to find the numbers in the string:

```
select REGEXP_SUBSTR
       ('MY LEDGER: Debits, Credits, and Invoices 1940',
        '[[:digit:]]+' )   "REGEXP_SUBSTR"
   from DUAL;

REGE
----
1940
```

As shown in this example, you can use the character classes to consolidate searches for multiple values. When you're working with search strings—particularly if you do not have prior experience with regular expressions—begin with the simplest version possible and then increase in complexity.

REGEXP_SUBSTR

The **REGEXP_SUBSTR** function, as shown in the preceding examples, uses regular expressions to specify the beginning and ending points of the returned string. The syntax for **REGEXP_SUBSTR** is shown in the following listing. **REGEXP_SUBSTR** returns the string as VARCHAR2 or CLOB data in the same character set as the *source_string*.

```
REGEXP_SUBSTR(source_string, pattern
              [, position
                [, occurrence
                  [, match_parameter ]
                ]
              ]
              )
```

The examples thus far in this chapter have focused on the *pattern* variable—the regular expression. The regular expression can contain up to 512 bytes. As shown in the syntax, you can also specify parameters related to the *position, occurrence,* and *match_parameter* conditions.

The *position* variable tells **REGEXP_SUBSTR** where to start searching within the *source_string*. The default *position* value is 1 (the first character). The *occurrence* variable is an integer indicating which occurrence of *pattern* in *source_string* Oracle should search for. The default *occurrence* value is 1. The *position* and *occurrence* variables are not available in the standard **SUBSTR** function—

they allow you to combine the capabilities of **SUBSTR** with **INSTR** while also supporting regular expression searches. These represent significant extensions to the standard **SUBSTR** functionality.

You can use the *match_parameter* variable to further customize the search. *match_parameter* is a text literal that lets you change the default matching behavior of the function. Its possible values are as follows:

- **'i'** Used for case-insensitive matching.

- **'c'** Used for case-sensitive matching.

- **'n'** Allows the period (.), which is a wildcard (see Table 8-1), to match the newline character. If you omit this parameter, the period does not match the newline character.

- **'m'** Treats the source string as multiple lines. Oracle interprets ^ and $ as the start and end, respectively, of any line anywhere in the source string, rather than only at the start or end of the entire source string. If you omit this parameter, Oracle treats the source string as a single line.

If you specify multiple contradictory values for *match_parameter,* Oracle uses the last value. For example, if you specify 'ic', Oracle will use case-sensitive matching. If you specify a character other than those shown here, Oracle will return an error.

If you omit *match_parameter*, the following happen:

- The default case sensitivity is determined by the value of the NLS_SORT parameter.

- A period (.) does not match the newline character.

- The source string is treated as a single line.

Here is the **REGEXP_SUBSTR** search performed with case-insensitive matching:

```
select REGEXP_SUBSTR
       ('MY LEDGER: Debits, Credits, and Invoices 1940',
        'my' ,1,1, 'i')    "REGEXP_SUBSTR"
   from DUAL;

RE
--
MY
```

Now, change that to perform a case-sensitive search:

```
select REGEXP_SUBSTR
       ('MY LEDGER: Debits, Credits, and Invoices 1940',
        'my' ,1,1,'c')    "REGEXP_SUBSTR"
   from DUAL;

RE
--
```

Nothing is returned due to the case mismatch. By default, searches are case sensitive.

You can use the *pattern* and *occurrence* parameters the same as you use them in **INSTR**. In the following example, the second digit is returned:

```
select REGEXP_SUBSTR
        ('MY LEDGER: Debits, Credits, and Invoices 1940',
         '[[:digit:]]' ,1,2)   "REGEXP_SUBSTR"
   from DUAL;

R
-
9
```

Writing the same query using **SUBSTR** and **INSTR** (and assuming the two digits may not be consecutive) would be much more complex.

REGEXP_INSTR

The **REGEXP_INSTR** function uses regular expressions to return the beginning or ending point of the search pattern. The syntax for **REGEXP_INSTR** is shown in the following listing. **REGEXP_INSTR** returns an integer indicating the position of the beginning or ending of the search pattern, or a 0 if no match is found.

```
REGEXP_INSTR (source_string, pattern
             [, position
               [, occurrence
                 [, return_option
                   [, match_parameter ]
                 ]
               ]
             ]
             )
```

The **REGEXP_SUBSTR** function, shown in the preceding section, performs some of the capabilities normally associated with **INSTR**. **REGEXP_INSTR** adds a unique feature that makes it an important addition to your SQL toolset. Like **REGEXP_SUBSTR**, it has the variables *pattern, position* (starting position), *occurrence,* and *match_parameter;* see the prior section for a description of those variables. The new capability introduced here, *return_option,* allows you to tell Oracle what to return in relation to the occurrence of the pattern:

■ If *return_option* is 0, Oracle returns the position of the first character of the occurrence. This is the default, and it's the same as the behavior of **INSTR**.

■ If *return_option* is 1, Oracle returns the position of the character following the occurrence.

For example, the following query returns the location of the first digit found in the string:

```
select REGEXP_INSTR
        ('MY LEDGER: Debits, Credits, and Invoices 1940',
```

```
              '[[:digit:]]')    "REGEXP_INSTR"
    from DUAL;

REGEXP_INSTR
------------
          42
```

What is the next position after that string?

```
select REGEXP_INSTR
        ('MY LEDGER: Debits, Credits, and Invoices 1940',
        '[[:digit:]]',1,1,1)    "REGEXP_INSTR"
    from DUAL;

REGEXP_INSTR
------------
          43
```

Even for searches that do not have complex patterns, you may decide to use **REGEXP_INSTR** in place of **INSTR** in order to simplify the math and logic involved in your queries that combine **INSTR** and **SUBSTR** capabilities. Be sure to carefully consider the case-sensitivity settings you specify via the *match_parameter* setting.

REGEXP_LIKE

In addition to the regular expression functions shown in previous listings, you can use the **REGEXP_LIKE** function. **REGEXP_LIKE** supports the use of regular expressions within **where** clauses. For example, which phone numbers start with '415'?

```
select LastName
   from ADDRESS
 where REGEXP_LIKE (Phone,'415+');

LASTNAME
----------------------------
ADAMS
ZACK
YARROW
WERSCHKY
BRANT
EDGAR
```

The format for **REGEXP_LIKE** is

```
REGEXP_LIKE(source_string, pattern
            [match_parameter ]
        )
```

Within the pattern, you can use all the search features shown earlier in this chapter—including the character class definitions—as part of a **REGEXP_LIKE** search. This capability makes it simple to perform very complex searches.

For example, how can you tell if a column value contains a numeric digit?

```
select LastName
   from ADDRESS
 where REGEXP_LIKE (Phone, '[[:digit:]]');
```

If a **TO_NUMBER** function fails because a punctuation mark is found in the value, you can display the rows that caused it to fail:

```
select LastName
   from ADDRESS
 where REGEXP_LIKE (Phone, '[[:punct:]]');
```

REPLACE and REGEXP_REPLACE

The **REPLACE** function replaces one value in a string with another. For example, you can replace each occurrence of a letter with a matching number. The format for **REPLACE** is

```
REPLACE ( char, search_string [,replace_string])
```

If you do not specify a value for the *replace_string* variable, the *search_string* value, when found, is removed. The input can be any of the character datatypes—CHAR, VARCHAR2, NCHAR, NVARCHAR2, CLOB, or NCLOB. Here's an example:

```
REPLACE('GEORGE', 'GE', 'EG') = EGOREG
REPLACE('GEORGE', 'GE', NULL) = OR
```

If the length of the search string is nonzero, you can tell how many times a string was found in the search string. First, you calculate the original string length:

```
LENGTH('GEORGE')
```

Then you calculate the length of the string after the search string values are removed:

```
LENGTH(REPLACE('GEORGE', 'GE', NULL))
```

Then you divide the difference by the length of the search string to find out how many occurrences of the search string were replaced:

```
select LENGTH('GEORGE')
       - LENGTH(REPLACE('GEORGE', 'GE', NULL))
       /
       LENGTH('GE')  AS Counter
from DUAL;
```

```
COUNTER
-------
      2
```

The **REGEXP_REPLACE** function extends the capabilities of the **REPLACE** function in several ways. It supports the use of regular expressions in the search pattern, and it also supports the variables described earlier in this chapter—*position, occurrence,* and *match_parameter.* You can thus choose to replace only certain matched values, or make the matching case insensitive. The syntax for the **REGEXP_REPLACE** function is shown in the following listing:

```
REGEXP_REPLACE(source_string, pattern
               [, replace_string
                  [, position
                     [, occurrence
                        [, match_parameter ]
                     ]
                  ]
               ]
            )
```

With the exception of *replace_string,* all these variables have been described in the earlier parts of this chapter. The *replace_string* variable tells Oracle what to use to replace the part of the *source_string* that matched the *pattern.* The *occurrence* variable is a nonnegative integer that specifies the occurrence of the operation: If it is 0, all occurrences of the match are replaced; if you specify a positive integer, Oracle replaces the *n*th occurrence.

Let's consider the Phone column of the ADDRESS table. First, we will look for numbers that are in the format ###-###-####. In that format, there are three digits followed by another set of three digits and then a set of four digits, separated by '-' characters. We can find the rows that match that criteria by looking for those sets of digits within a **REGEXP_SUBSTR** function call:

```
select REGEXP_SUBSTR (Phone,
        '([[:digit:]]{3})-([[:digit:]]{3})-([[:digit:]]{4})'
        ) "REGEXP_SUBSTR"
   from ADDRESS;

REGEXP_SUBST
------------
213-555-0223
415-555-7530
214-555-8383
312-555-1166
707-555-8900
312-555-1414
415-555-6842
415-555-2178
415-555-7387
415-555-7512
415-555-6252
```

```
617-555-0125
603-555-2242
202-555-1414
718-555-1638
214-555-8383
503-555-7491
```

Now, use **REGEXP_REPLACE** to put parentheses around the first three digits while leaving out the first '-' character found. To do this, we will refer to that first set of data as \1, the second as \2, and the third as \3.

```
select REGEXP_REPLACE (Phone,
       '([[:digit:]]{3})-([[:digit:]]{3})-([[:digit:]]{4})'
       , '(\1) \2-\3'
       ) "REGEXP_REPLACE"
  from ADDRESS;

REGEXP_REPLACE
-----------------------------------------
(213) 555-0223
(415) 555-7530
(214) 555-8383
(312) 555-1166
(707) 555-8900
(312) 555-1414
(415) 555-6842
(415) 555-2178
(415) 555-7387
(415) 555-7512
(415) 555-6252
(617) 555-0125
(603) 555-2242
(202) 555-1414
(718) 555-1638
(214) 555-8383
(503) 555-7491
```

The output shows the result of the **REGEXP_REPLACE** function call—the area codes are enclosed within parentheses and the first '-' has been eliminated.

To show how the *occurrence* variable works, the following **REGEXP_REPLACE** function call replaces with a period the second '5' found in a phone number:

```
select REGEXP_REPLACE (Phone,
       '5', '.',
       1, 2
       ) "REGEXP_REPLACE"
  from ADDRESS;
```

```
REGEXP_REPLACE
-----------------------------------------
213-5.5-0223
415-.55-7530
214-5.5-8383
312-5.5-1166
707-5.5-8900
312-5.5-1414
415-.55-6842
415-.55-2178
415-.55-7387
415-.55-7512
415-.55-6252
617-5.5-0125
603-5.5-2242
202-5.5-1414
718-5.5-1638
214-5.5-8383
503-.55-7491
```

You can modify that query further to exclude the first three digits as possible matches (set the starting position to 4) and replace the fourth occurrence instead:

```
select REGEXP_REPLACE (Phone,
        '5', '.',
        4, 4
        ) "REGEXP_REPLACE"
   from ADDRESS;
```

```
REGEXP_REPLACE
-----------------------------------------
213-555-0223
415-555-7.30
214-555-8383
312-555-1166
707-555-8900
312-555-1414
415-555-6842
415-555-2178
415-555-7387
415-555-7.12
415-555-62.2
617-555-012.
603-555-2242
202-555-1414
718-555-1638
214-555-8383
503-555-7491
```

You can limit the rows returned by using **REGEXP_INSTR** in a **where** clause. In this case, only those rows that have at least four instances of '5' in them (beginning at the fourth character) will be displayed. Because this search pattern is not complex, you could use **INSTR** here instead:

```
select REGEXP_REPLACE (Phone,
       '5', '.',
       4, 4
       ) "REGEXP_REPLACE"
  from ADDRESS
 where REGEXP_INSTR(Phone, '5',4,4) > 0;

REGEXP_REPLACE
-----------------------------------------
415-555-7.30
415-555-7.12
415-555-62.2
617-555-012.
```

You can use the ability to search for alternate values to combine multiple search criteria in a single query. The following replaces *either* a 5 or a 2; occurrences of both '5' and '2' count toward the *occurrence* count:

```
select REGEXP_REPLACE (Phone,
       '(5|2)', '.',
       4, 4
       ) "REGEXP_REPLACE"
  from ADDRESS
 where REGEXP_INSTR(Phone, '(5|2)',4,4) > 0;

REGEXP_REPLACE
-----------------------------------------
213-555-0.23
415-555-7.30
415-555-684.
415-555-.178
415-555-7.12
415-555-6.52
617-555-01.5
603-555-.242
```

The '|' character shown in this example is an alternation operator, so matches of either of the values specified will return a row. See Table 8-1 for additional operators supported within your regular expressions.

Your use of the **REGEXP_SUBSTR**, **REGEXP_INSTR**, **REGEXP_LIKE**, and **REGEXP_REPLACE** functions is limited only by your ability to develop regular expressions that reflect your needs. As shown in the examples in this chapter, you can use these functions to modify the display of existing data, to find complex patterns, and to return strings within patterns.

CHAPTER
9

Playing the Numbers

irtually everything we do, particularly in business, is measured, explained, and often guided by numbers. Although Oracle cannot correct our obsession with numbers and the illusion of control they often give us, it will facilitate capable and thorough analysis of the information in a database. Good mathematical analysis of familiar numbers will often show trends and facts that were initially not apparent.

The Three Classes of Number Functions

Oracle functions deal with three classes of numbers: single values, groups of values, and lists of values. As with string functions (discussed in Chapters 7 and 8), some of these functions change the values they are applied to, whereas others merely report information about the values. The classes are distinguished as detailed in the following paragraphs.

A *single value* is one number, such as these:

- A literal number, such as 544.3702

- A variable in SQL*Plus or PL/SQL

- One number from one column and one row of the database

Oracle single-value functions usually change these values through a calculation.

A *group of values* is all the numbers in one column from a series of rows, such as the closing stock price for all the rows of stocks in the stock market table from Chapter 4. Oracle group-value functions tell you something about the whole group, such as average stock price, but not about the individual members of the group.

A *list of values* is a series of numbers that can include the following:

- Literal numbers, such as 1, 7.3, 22, and 86

- Variables in SQL*Plus or PL/SQL

- Columns, such as OpeningPrice, ClosingPrice, Bid, and Ask

Oracle list functions choose one member of a list of values.

Table 9-1 shows these functions by class. Some functions fit into more than one class. Other functions fall somewhere between string and number functions, or are used to convert data from one to the other. These are covered in Chapter 11.

Notation

Functions will be shown with this kind of notation:

```
FUNCTION(value [,option])
```

The function itself will be uppercase. Values and options will be shown in lowercase italics. Whenever the word *value* appears this way, it represents one of the following: a literal number, the name of a number column in a table, the result of a calculation, or a variable. Because Oracle does not allow numbers to be used as column names, a literal number should not appear in single quotation marks (as a literal string would be in a string function). Column names also must not have single quotation marks.

Function	Definition
Single-Value Functions	
value1 + *value2*	Addition.
value1 − *value2*	Subtraction.
value1 * *value2*	Multiplication.
value1 / *value2*	Division.
ABS(*value*)	Absolute value.
ACOS(*value*)	Arc cosine of *value*, in radians.
ASIN(*value*)	Arc sine of *value*, in radians.
ATAN(*value*)	Arc tangent of *value*, in radians.
ATAN2 (*value1, value2*)	ATAN2 returns the arc tangent of two values. Input values are unbounded; outputs are expressed in radians.
BITAND (*value1, value2*)	Bitwise AND of *value1* and *value2*, both of which must resolve to nonnegative integers. Returns an integer.
CEIL(*value*)	Numeric ceiling (the smallest integer larger than or equal to *value*).
COS(*value*)	Cosine of *value*.
COSH(*value*)	Hyperbolic cosine of *value*.
EXP(*value*)	e raised to *value* exponent.
FLOOR(*value*)	Largest integer smaller than or equal to *value*.
LN(*value*)	Natural logarithm of *value*.
LOG(*value*)	Base 10 logarithm of *value*.
MOD(*value, divisor*)	Modulus. The remainder left after dividing a value by a divisor.
NANVL(*value1,value2*)	For BINARY_FLOAT and BINARY_DOUBLE numbers, this function returns *value2* if *value1* is not a number.
NVL(*value, substitute*)	Substitute for *value* if *value* is **NULL**.
NVL2(*expr1 , expr2 , expr3*)	If *expr1* is not **NULL**, then *expr2* is returned; otherwise, *expr3* is returned.
POWER(*value, exponent*)	*value* raised to an *exponent* power.
REMAINDER(*value1,value2*)	Remainder of *value1* divided by *value2*.
ROUND(*value, precision*)	Rounding of *value* to *precision*.
SIGN(*value*)	1 if *value* is positive; −1 if *value* is negative; 0 if *value* is zero.

TABLE 9-1. *Number Functions*

SIN(*value*)	Sine of *value*.
SINH(*value*)	Hyperbolic sine of *value*.
SQRT(*value*)	Square root of *value*.
TAN(*value*)	Tangent of *value*.
TANH(*value*)	Hyperbolic tangent of *value*.
TRUNC(*value, precision*)	*value* truncated to *precision*.
VSIZE(*value*)	Storage size of *value* in Oracle.

Aggregate Functions

AVG(*value*)	Average of *value* for a group of rows.
CORR(*value1, value2*)	Coefficient of correlation of a set of number pairs. CORR_K and CORR_S support nonparametric or rank correlation.
COUNT(*value*)	Count of rows for a table, or of non-**NULL** values for a column.
COVAR_POP(*value1, value2*)	Population covariance of a set of number pairs.
COVAR_SAMP(*value1, value2*)	Sample covariance of a set of number pairs.
CUME_DIST(*value*)	Cumulative distribution of a *value* in a group of values.
DENSE_RANK(*value*)	Rank of a row in an ordered group of rows.
FIRST(*value*)	Analytic function performed on the row ranking first in a set.
GROUP_ID(*value*)	Distinguishes duplicate groups resulting from a GROUP BY specification.
GROUPING(*expression*)	Used in conjunction with the ROLLUP and CUBE functions to detect **NULL**s.
GROUPING_ID	Returns a number corresponding to the GROUPING bit vector associated with a row.
LAST(*value*)	Analytic function performed on the row ranking last in a set.
MAX(*value*)	Maximum of all values for group of rows.
MEDIAN (*expr*)	Returns the median value for a group of rows, ignoring **NULL**s.
MIN(*value*)	Minimum of all values for group of rows.
PERCENTILE_CONT(*value*)	Calculates the percentile ranking of a *value* in a set, assuming a continuous linear model.
PERCENTILE_DISC(*value*)	Calculates the percentile ranking of a *value* in a set, assuming a discrete distribution model.
PERCENT_RANK(*value*)	Calculates the percentile ranking of a *value* in a set.

TABLE 9-1. *Number Functions* (continued)

RANK(*value*)	Calculates the rank of a *value* in a group of values.
REGR functions	These functions perform linear regression analysis on a group of values.
STATS_BINOMIAL_TEST	Tests the difference between a sample proportion and a given proportion.
STATS_CROSSTAB	Analyzes two nominal values.
STATS_F_TEST	Tests whether two variables are significantly different.
STATS_KS_TEST	Tests whether two variables are from the same population.
STATS_MODE	Returns the value that occurs with the greatest frequency in a group.
STATS_MW_TEST	Tests two independent samples against a null hypothesis.
STATS_ONE_WAY_ANOVA	A one-way analysis of variance.
STATS_T_TEST_* functions	These functions measure the significance of a difference of means.
STATS_WSR_TEST	Determines whether the differences between samples are significantly different from zero.
STDDEV(*value*)	Standard deviation of all values for a group of rows.
STDDEV_POP(*value*)	Population standard deviation.
STDDEV_SAMP(*value*)	Sample standard deviation.
SUM(*value*)	Sum of all values for a group of rows.
VAR_POP(*value*)	Population variance.
VAR_SAMP(*value*)	Sample variance.
VARIANCE(*value*)	Variance of all values for a group of rows.
WIDTH_ BUCKET(*expr,min,max,num*)	Constructs equal-width histograms.
List Functions	
COALESCE(*value1, value2, ...*)	Returns the first non-**NULL** value in the expression list.
GREATEST(*value1, value2, ...*)	Greatest value of a list.
LEAST(*value1, value2, ...*)	Least value of a list.

TABLE 9-1. *Number Functions* (continued)

Every function has only one pair of parentheses. The value that function works on, as well as additional information you can pass to the function, goes between the parentheses.

Some functions have *options*—parts that are not required to make the function work but that can give you more control if you choose to use them. Options are always shown in square brackets: []. The necessary parts of a function always come before the optional parts.

Single-Value Functions

Most single-value functions are pretty straightforward. This section gives short examples of the major functions, and it shows both the results of the functions and how they correspond to columns, rows, and lists. After the examples, you'll see how to combine these functions. The syntax for all the functions is found in the Alphabetical Reference of this book.

A table named MATH was created to show the calculation effects of the many math functions. It has only four rows and four columns, as shown here:

```
select Name, Above, Below, Empty from MATH;

NAME            ABOVE    BELOW EMPTY
------------- ------- ------- -----
WHOLE NUMBER       11     -22
LOW DECIMAL     33.33  -44.44
MID DECIMAL      55.5   -55.5
HIGH DECIMAL   66.666 -77.777
```

This table is useful because it has values with a variety of characteristics, which are spelled out by the names of the rows. WHOLE NUMBER contains no decimal parts. LOW DECIMAL has decimals that are less than .5, MID DECIMAL has decimals equal to .5, and HIGH DECIMAL has decimals greater than .5. This range is particularly important when using the **ROUND** and **TRUNC** (truncate) functions, and in understanding how they affect the value of a number.

To the right of the Name column are three other columns: Above, which contains only numbers above zero (positive numbers); Below, which contains only numbers below zero; and Empty, which is **NULL**.

NOTE
In Oracle, a number column may have no value in it at all. When it is
NULL*, it is not zero; it is simply empty. This has important implications*
in making computations, as you will see.

Not all the rows in this MATH table are needed to demonstrate how most math functions work, so the examples primarily use the last row, HIGH DECIMAL. In addition, the SQL*Plus **column** command has been used to explicitly show the precision of the calculation so that the results of functions that affect a number's precision can be clearly seen. To review the SQL and SQL*Plus commands that produced the results that follow, see the script that accompanies the **create table** commands for the sample tables.

Addition (+), Subtraction (–), Multiplication (*), and Division (/)

The following query shows each of the four basic arithmetic functions, using Above and Below:

```
select Name, Above, Below, Empty,
       Above + Below  AS Plus,
       Above - Below  AS Subtr,
       Above * Below  AS Times,
       Above / Below  AS Divided
  from MATH
 where Name = 'HIGH DECIMAL';
```

```
NAME            ABOVE   BELOW EMPTY    PLUS   SUBTR     TIMES    DIVIDED
-----------     ------  ------- -----  ------- ------- ---------- ----------
HIGH DECIMAL 66.666 -77.777        -11.111 144.443 -5185.0815 -.85714286
```

NULL

In the following example, the same four arithmetic operations are now done again, except instead of using Above and Below, Above and Empty are used. Note that any arithmetic operation that includes a **NULL** value has **NULL** as a result. The calculated columns (columns whose values are the result of a calculation) Plus, Subtr, Times, and Divided are all empty.

```
select Name, Above, Below, Empty,
       Above + Empty  AS Plus,
       Above - Empty  AS Subtr,
       Above * Empty  AS Times,
       Above / Empty  AS Divided
  from MATH
 where Name = 'HIGH DECIMAL';
```

```
NAME            ABOVE    BELOW  EMPTY   PLUS    SUBTR   TIMES   DIVIDED
-----------     ------  -------- ------ ------- -------- ------- ---------
HIGH DECIMAL  66.666   -77.777
```

What you see here is evidence that a **NULL** value cannot be used in a calculation. **NULL** isn't the same as zero; think of **NULL** as a value that is unknown. For example, suppose you have a table with the names of your friends and their ages, but the Age column for PAT SMITH is empty, because you don't know it. What's the difference in your ages? It's clearly not your age minus zero. Your age minus an unknown age is also unknown, or **NULL**. You can't fill in an answer because you don't have an answer. Because you can't make the computation, the answer is **NULL**.

This is also the reason you cannot use **NULL** with an equal sign in a **where** clause (see Chapter 5). It makes no sense to say *x* is unknown and *y* is unknown, therefore *x* and *y* are equal. If Mrs. Wilkins's and Mr. Adams's ages are unknown, it doesn't mean they're the same age.

There also will be instances where **NULL** means a value is irrelevant, such as an apartment number for a house. In some cases, the apartment number might be **NULL** because it is unknown (even though it really exists), while in other cases it is **NULL** because there simply isn't one. **NULL**s will be explored in more detail later in this chapter, under "NULLs in Group-Value Functions."

NVL: NULL-Value Substitution

The preceding section states the general case about **NULL**s—that **NULL** represents an unknown or irrelevant value. In particular cases, however, although a value is unknown, you may be able

to make a reasonable guess. If you're a package carrier, for instance, and 30 percent of the shippers who call you for pickups can't tell you the weight or volume of their packages, will you declare it completely impossible to estimate how many cargo planes you'll need tonight? Of course not. You know from experience the average weight and volume of your packages, so you'd plug in these numbers for those customers who didn't supply you with the information. Here's the information as supplied by your clients:

```
select Client, Weight from SHIPPING;

CLIENT          WEIGHT
-------------   ------
JOHNSON TOOL        59
DAGG SOFTWARE       27
TULLY ANDOVER
```

This is what the **NULL**-value substitution (**NVL**) function does:

```
select Client, NVL(Weight,43) from SHIPPING;

CLIENT          NVL(WEIGHT,43)
-------------   --------------
JOHNSON TOOL               59
DAGG SOFTWARE              27
TULLY ANDOVER             43
```

Here, you know that the average package weight is 43 pounds, so you use the **NVL** function to plug in 43 anytime a client's package has an unknown weight—that is, where the value in the column is **NULL**. In this case, TULLY ANDOVER didn't know the weight of their package when they called it in, but you can still total these package weights and have a fair estimate.

Here is the format for **NVL**:

```
NVL(value,substitute)
```

If *value* is **NULL**, this function is equal to *substitute*. If *value* is not **NULL**, this function is equal to *value*. Note that *substitute* can be a literal number, another column, or a computation. If you really were a package carrier with this problem, you could even have a table join in your **select** statement where *substitute* was from a view that actually averaged the weight of all non-**NULL** packages.

NVL is not restricted to numbers. It can be used with CHAR, VARCHAR2, DATE, and other datatypes as well, but *value* and *substitute* must be the same datatype. Also, **NVL** is really useful only in cases where the data is unknown, not where it's irrelevant.

A companion function, **NVL2**, is slightly more complex. Its format is

```
NVL2 ( expr1 , expr2 , expr3 )
```

In **NVL2**, *expr1* can never be returned; either *expr2* or *expr3* will be returned. If *expr1* is not **NULL**, **NVL2** returns *expr2*. If *expr1* is **NULL**, **NVL2** returns *expr3*. The argument *expr1* can have

any datatype. The arguments *expr2* and *expr3* can have any datatypes except LONG. As of Oracle Database 10*g*, you can use the **NANVL** function for the BINARY_FLOAT and BINARY_DOUBLE datatypes. **NANVL** takes two variables, and returns the second if the first is not a number.

ABS: Absolute Value

Absolute value is the measure of the magnitude of something. For instance, in a temperature change or a stock index change, the magnitude of the change has meaning in itself, regardless of the direction of the change (which is important in its own right). Absolute value is always a positive number.

Here is the format for **ABS**:

```
ABS(value)
```

Note these examples:

```
ABS(146) = 146
ABS(-30) =  30
```

CEIL

CEIL (for *ceiling*) simply produces the smallest integer (or whole number) that is greater than or equal to a specific value. Pay special attention to its effect on negative numbers.

The following shows the format for **CEIL** and some examples:

```
CEIL(value)

CEIL(2)    =  2
CEIL(1.3)  =  2
CEIL(-2)   = -2
CEIL(-2.3) = -2
```

FLOOR

FLOOR is the intuitive opposite of **CEIL**. Here is the format for **FLOOR** and some examples:

```
FLOOR(value)

FLOOR(2)    =  2
FLOOR(1.3)  =  1
FLOOR(-2)   = -2
FLOOR(-2.3) = -3
```

MOD

MOD (*modulus*) is an odd little function primarily used in data processing for esoteric tasks such as "check digits," which help ensure the accurate transmission of a string of numbers. **MOD** divides a value by a divisor and tells you the remainder. For example, **MOD(23,6) = 5** means divide 23 by 6. The answer is 3 with 5 left over, so 5 is the result of the modulus.

Here is the format for **MOD**:

```
MOD(value,divisor)
```

Both *value* and *divisor* can be any real number. The value of **MOD** is zero if *divisor* is zero or negative. Note the following examples:

```
MOD(100,10)    =   0
MOD(22,23)     =  22
MOD(10,3)      =   1
MOD(-30.23,7)  =  -2.23
MOD(4.1,.3)    =   .2
```

The second example shows what **MOD** does whenever the divisor is larger than the dividend (the number being divided). It produces the dividend as a result. Also note this important case where *value* is an integer:

```
MOD(value,1)   =  0
```

The preceding is a good test to see if a number is an integer.

You can use the **REMAINDER** function in the same way:

```
REMAINDER(-30.23,7) = -2.23
```

POWER

POWER simply provides the ability to raise a value to a given positive exponent, as shown here:

```
POWER(value,exponent)
```

```
POWER(3,2)        =      9
POWER(3,3)        =     27
POWER(-77.777,2)  = 6049.26173
POWER(3,1.086)    =    3.29726371
POWER(64,.5)      =      8
```

The *exponent* can be any real number.

SQRT: Square Root

Oracle has a separate square root function that gives results equivalent to **POWER**(*value*,.5):

```
SQRT(value)
```

```
SQRT(64)     = 8
SQRT(66.666) = 8.16492498
SQRT(4)      = 2
```

The square root of a negative number is an imaginary number. Oracle doesn't support imaginary numbers, so it returns an error if you attempt to find the square root of a negative number.

EXP, LN, and LOG

The **EXP, LN,** and **LOG** functions are rarely used in business calculations but are quite common in scientific and technical work. **EXP** is e (2.71828183…) raised to the specified power; **LN** is the "natural," or base e, logarithm of a value. The first two functions are reciprocals of one another; **LN(EXP(i))** = $value$. The **LOG** function takes a base and a positive value. **LN**($value$) is the same as **LOG**(2.71828183,$value$).

```
EXP(value)

EXP(3)          =  20.0855369
EXP(5)          = 148.413159

LN(value)

LN(3)           = 1.09861229
LN(20.0855369)  = 3

LOG(value)

LOG(EXP(1),3)   = 1.09861229
LOG(10,100)     = 2
```

ROUND and TRUNC

ROUND and **TRUNC** are two related single-value functions. **TRUNC** truncates, or chops off, digits of precision from a number; **ROUND** rounds numbers to a given number of digits of precision.

Here are the formats for **ROUND** and **TRUNC**:

```
ROUND(value,precision)
TRUNC(value,precision)
```

There are some properties worth paying close attention to here. First, look at this simple example of a **select** from the MATH table. Two digits of precision are called for (counting toward the right from the decimal point).

```
select Name, Above, Below,
       ROUND(Above,2),
       ROUND(Below,2),
       TRUNC(Above,2),
       TRUNC(Below,2)
  from MATH;
```

NAME	ABOVE	BELOW	ROUND (ABOVE,2)	ROUND (BELOW,2)	TRUNC (ABOVE,2)	TRUNC (BELOW,2)
WHOLE NUMBER	11	-22	11	-22	11	-22
LOW DECIMAL	33.33	-44.44	33.33	-44.44	33.33	-44.44
MID DECIMAL	55.5	-55.5	55.5	-55.5	55.5	-55.5
HIGH DECIMAL	66.666	-77.777	66.67	-77.78	66.66	-77.77

Only the bottom row is affected, because only it has three digits beyond the decimal point. Both the positive and negative numbers in the bottom row were rounded or truncated: 66.666 was rounded to a higher number (66.67), but –77.777 was rounded to a lower (more negative) number (–77.78). When rounding is done to zero digits, this is the result:

```
select Name, Above, Below,
       ROUND(Above,0),
       ROUND(Below,0),
       TRUNC(Above,0),
       TRUNC(Below,0)
  from MATH;
```

NAME	ABOVE	BELOW	ROUND (ABOVE,0)	ROUND (BELOW,0)	TRUNC (ABOVE,0)	TRUNC (BELOW,0)
WHOLE NUMBER	11	-22	11	-22	11	-22
LOW DECIMAL	33.33	-44.44	33	-44	33	-44
MID DECIMAL	55.5	-55.5	56	-56	55	-55
HIGH DECIMAL	66.666	-77.777	67	-78	66	-77

Note that the decimal value of .5 was rounded up when 55.5 went to 56. This follows the most common American rounding convention (some rounding conventions round up only if a number is larger than .5). Compare these results with **CEIL** and **FLOOR**. They have significant differences:

```
ROUND(55.5)  = 56      ROUND(-55.5)  = -56
TRUNC(55.5)  = 55      TRUNC(-55.5)  = -55
CEIL(55.5)   = 56      CEIL(-55.5)   = -55
FLOOR(55.5)  = 55      FLOOR(-55.5)  = -56
```

Finally, note that both **ROUND** and **TRUNC** can work with negative precision, moving to the left of the decimal point:

```
select Name, Above, Below,
       ROUND(Above,-1),
       ROUND(Below,-1),
       TRUNC(Above,-1),
       TRUNC(Below,-1)
  from MATH;
```

NAME	ABOVE	BELOW	ROUND (ABOVE,-1)	ROUND (BELOW,-1)	TRUNC (ABOVE,-1)	TRUNC (BELOW,-1)
WHOLE NUMBER	11	-22	10	-20	10	-20
LOW DECIMAL	33.33	-44.44	30	-40	30	-40
MID DECIMAL	55.5	-55.5	60	-60	50	-50
HIGH DECIMAL	66.666	-77.777	70	-80	60	-70

Rounding with a negative number can be useful when producing such things as economic reports, where populations or dollar sums need to be rounded up to the millions, billions, or trillions.

SIGN

SIGN is the flip side of absolute value. Whereas **ABS** tells you the magnitude of a value but not its sign, **SIGN** tells you the sign of a value but not its magnitude.

Here is the format for **SIGN**:

```
SIGN(value)
```

```
Examples: SIGN(146) =  1  Compare to: ABS(146) = 146
          SIGN(-30) = -1              ABS(-30) =  30
```

The **SIGN** of 0 is 0:

```
SIGN(0)=0
```

The **SIGN** function is often used in conjunction with the **DECODE** function. **DECODE** will be described in Chapter 16.

SIN, SINH, COS, COSH, TAN, TANH, ACOS, ATAN, ATAN2, and ASIN

The trigonometric functions sine, cosine, and tangent are scientific and technical functions not used much in business. **SIN**, **COS**, and **TAN** give you the standard trigonometric function values for an angle expressed in radians (degrees multiplied by *pi* divided by 180). **SINH**, **COSH**, and **TANH** give you the hyperbolic functions for an angle.

```
SIN(value)
```

```
SIN(30*3.141592655/180) = .5
```

```
COSH(value)
```

```
COSH(0)                 = 1
```

The **ASIN**, **ACOS**, and **ATAN** functions return the arc sine, arc cosine, and arc tangent values (in radians) of the values provided. **ATAN2** returns the arc tangent of two values. Input values are unbounded; outputs are expressed in radians.

Aggregate Functions

Aggregate or "group-value" functions are those statistical functions such as **SUM**, **AVG**, **COUNT**, and the like that tell you something about a group of values taken as a whole: the average age of all the friends in the table, for instance, or the oldest member of the group, or the youngest, or the number of members in the group, and more. Even when one of these functions is supplying information about a single row—such as the oldest person—it is still information that is defined by the row's relation to the group.

You can use a wide array of advanced statistical functions against your data—including regression testing and sampling. In the following discussions, you will see descriptions of the

most commonly used group-value functions; for the others (all are listed in Table 9-1), see the Alphabetical Reference.

NULLs in Group-Value Functions

Group-value functions treat **NULL** values differently than single-value functions do. Group functions ignore **NULL** values and calculate a result in spite of them.

Take **AVG** as an example. Suppose you have a list of 100 friends and their ages. If you picked 20 of them at random and averaged their ages, how different would the result be than if you picked a different list of 20, also at random, and averaged it, or if you averaged all 100? In fact, the averages of these three groups would be very close. What this means is that **AVG** is somewhat insensitive to missing records, even when the missing data represents a high percentage of the total number of records available.

NOTE
AVG is not immune to missing data, and there can be cases where it will be significantly off (such as when missing data is not randomly distributed), but these cases will be less common.

The relative insensitivity of **AVG** to missing data needs to be contrasted with, for instance, **SUM**. How close to correct is the **SUM** of the ages of only 20 friends to the **SUM** of all 100 friends? Not close at all. So if you had a table of friends, but only 20 out of 100 supplied their age, and 80 out of 100 had **NULL** for their age, which one would be a more reliable statistic about the whole group and less sensitive to the absence of data—the **AVG** age of those 20 friends, or the **SUM** of them? Note that this is an entirely different issue than whether it is possible to estimate the sum of all 100 based on only 20 (in fact, it is precisely the **AVG** of the 20, times 100). The point is, if you don't know how many rows are **NULL**, you can use the following to provide a fairly reasonable result:

```
select AVG(Age) from BIRTHDAY;
```

You cannot get a reasonable result from this, however:

```
select SUM(Age) from BIRTHDAY;
```

This same test of whether or not results are reasonable defines how the other group functions respond to **NULL**s. **STDDEV** and **VARIANCE** are measures of central tendency; they, too, are relatively insensitive to missing data. (These will be shown in "STDDEV and VARIANCE," later in this chapter.)

MAX and **MIN** measure the extremes of your data. They can fluctuate wildly while **AVG** stays relatively constant: If you add a 100-year-old man to a group of 99 people who are 50 years old, the average age only goes up to 50.5—but the maximum age has doubled. Add a newborn baby, and the average goes back to 50, but the minimum age is now 0. It's clear that missing or unknown **NULL** values can profoundly affect **MAX**, **MIN**, and **SUM**, so be cautious when using them, particularly if a significant percentage of the data is **NULL**.

Is it possible to create functions that also take into account how sparse the data is and how many values are **NULL**, compared to how many have real values, and make good guesses about

MAX, **MIN**, and **SUM**? Yes, but such functions would be statistical projections, which must make explicit their assumptions about a particular set of data. This is not an appropriate task for a general-purpose group function. Some statisticians would argue that these functions should return **NULL** if they encounter any **NULL**s because returning any value can be misleading. Oracle returns something rather than nothing, but leaves it up to you to decide whether the result is reasonable.

 COUNT is a special case. It can go either way with **NULL** values, but it always returns a number; it will never evaluate to **NULL**. The format and usage for **COUNT** will be shown shortly, but to simply contrast it with the other group functions, it will count all the non-**NULL** rows of a column, or it will count all the rows. In other words, if asked to count the ages of 100 friends, **COUNT** will return a value of 20 (because only 20 of the 100 gave their age). If asked to count the rows in the table of friends without specifying a column, it will return 100. An example of these differences is given in "DISTINCT in Group Functions," later in this chapter.

Examples of Single- and Group-Value Functions

Neither the group-value functions nor the single-value functions are particularly difficult to understand, but a practical overview of how each function works is helpful in fleshing out some of the options and consequences of their use.

 The COMFORT table in these examples contains basic temperature data, by city, at noon and midnight on each of four sample days in one year: the equinoxes (about March 21 and September 23) and the solstices (about June 22 and December 22). You ought to be able to characterize cities based on their temperatures on these days in one year.

 For the sake of these examples, this table has only eight rows: the data from the four dates in 2003 for San Francisco, California and Keene, New Hampshire. You can use Oracle's number functions to analyze these cities, their average temperature, the volatility of the temperature, and so on, for 2003. With more years and data on more cities, an analysis of temperature patterns and variability throughout the century could be made.

 The table looks like this:

```
describe COMFORT
```

Name	Null?	Type
CITY	NOT NULL	VARCHAR2(13)
SAMPLEDATE	NOT NULL	DATE
NOON		NUMBER(3,1)
MIDNIGHT		NUMBER(3,1)
PRECIPITATION		NUMBER

It contains this temperature data:

```
select City, SampleDate, Noon, Midnight from COMFORT;
```

CITY	SAMPLEDAT	NOON	MIDNIGHT
SAN FRANCISCO	21-MAR-03	62.5	42.3
SAN FRANCISCO	22-JUN-03	51.1	71.9
SAN FRANCISCO	23-SEP-03		61.5
SAN FRANCISCO	22-DEC-03	52.6	39.8

```
KEENE          21-MAR-03 39.9       -1.2
KEENE          22-JUN-03 85.1       66.7
KEENE          23-SEP-03 99.8       82.6
KEENE          22-DEC-03 -7.2       -1.2
```

AVG, COUNT, MAX, MIN, and SUM

Due to a power failure, the noon temperature in San Francisco on September 23 did not get recorded. The consequences of this can be seen in the following query:

```
select AVG(Noon), COUNT(Noon), MAX(Noon), MIN(Noon), SUM(Noon)
  from COMFORT
 where City = 'SAN FRANCISCO';

AVG(NOON) COUNT(NOON) MAX(NOON) MIN(NOON) SUM(NOON)
--------- ----------- --------- --------- ---------
     55.4           3      62.5      51.1     166.2
```

AVG(Noon) is the average of the three temperatures that are known. **COUNT**(Noon) is the count of how many rows there are in the Noon column that are not **NULL**. **MAX** and **MIN** are self-evident. **SUM**(Noon) is the sum of only three dates because of the **NULL** for September 23. Note that

```
SUM(NOON)
---------
    166.2
```

is by no coincidence exactly three times **AVG**(Noon).

Combining Group-Value and Single-Value Functions

Suppose you would like to know how much the temperature changes in the course of a day. This is a measure of *volatility*. Your first attempt to answer the question might be to subtract the temperature at midnight from the temperature at noon:

```
select City, SampleDate, Noon-Midnight
  from COMFORT
 where City = 'KEENE';

CITY          SAMPLEDAT NOON-MIDNIGHT
------------- --------- -------------
KEENE         21-MAR-03          41.1
KEENE         22-JUN-03          18.4
KEENE         23-SEP-03          17.2
KEENE         22-DEC-03            -6
```

With only four rows to consider in this table, you can quickly convert (or ignore) the pesky minus sign. Volatility in temperature is really a magnitude—which means it asks by how much the temperature changed. It doesn't include a sign, so –6 isn't really correct. If this goes uncorrected

and is included in a further calculation, such as the average change in a year, the answer you get will be absolutely wrong, as shown here:

```
select AVG(Noon-Midnight)
   from COMFORT
 where City = 'KEENE';

AVG(NOON-MIDNIGHT)
------------------
            17.675
```

The correct answer requires an absolute value, as shown next.

```
select AVG(ABS(Noon-Midnight))
   from COMFORT
 where City = 'KEENE';

AVG(ABS(NOON-MIDNIGHT))
-----------------------
                 20.675
```

Combining functions this way follows the same technique given in Chapter 7 in the section on string functions. An entire function such as

```
ABS(Noon-Midnight)
```

is simply plugged into another function as its value, like this:

```
AVG(value)
```

which produces

```
AVG(ABS(Noon-Midnight))
```

This shows both single-value and group-value functions at work. You see that you can place single-value functions inside group-value functions. The single-value functions will calculate a result for every row, and the group-value functions will view that result as if it were the actual value for the row. Single-value functions can be combined (*nested* inside each other) almost without limit. Group-value functions can contain single-value functions in place of their value. They can, in fact, contain many single-value functions in place of their value.

What about combining group functions? First of all, it doesn't make any sense to nest them this way:

```
select SUM(AVG(Noon)) from COMFORT;
```

The preceding will produce this error:

```
ERROR at line 1:
ORA-00978: nested group function without GROUP BY
```

Besides, if it actually worked, it would produce exactly the same result as

```
AVG(Noon)
```

because the result of **AVG**(Noon) is just a single value. The **SUM** of a single value is just the single value, so it is not meaningful to nest group functions. The exception to this rule is in the use of **group by** in the **select** statement, the absence of which is why Oracle produced the error message here. This is covered in Chapter 12.

It *can* be meaningful to add, subtract, multiply, or divide the results of two or more group functions. For example,

```
select MAX(Noon) - MIN(Noon)
   from COMFORT
 where City = 'SAN FRANCISCO';

MAX(NOON)-MIN(NOON)
-------------------
               11.4
```

gives the range of the temperatures in a year. In fact, a quick comparison of San Francisco and Keene could be done with just a bit more effort:

```
select City, AVG(Noon), MAX(Noon), MIN(Noon),
        MAX(Noon) - MIN(Noon) AS Swing
   from COMFORT
 group by City;

CITY          AVG(NOON) MAX(NOON) MIN(NOON) SWING
------------- --------- --------- --------- -----
KEENE              54.4      99.8      -7.2   107
SAN FRANCISCO      55.4      62.5      51.1  11.4
```

This query is a good example of discovering information in your data: The average temperatures in the two cities are nearly identical, but the huge temperature swing in Keene, compared to San Francisco, says a lot about the yearly temperature volatility of the two cities, and the relative effort required to dress (or to heat and cool a home) in one city compared to the other. The **group by** clause will be explained in detail in Chapter 12. Briefly, in this example it forced the group functions to work not on the total table, but on the subgroups of temperatures by city.

STDDEV and VARIANCE

Standard deviation and variance have their common statistical meanings, and they use the same format as all group functions:

```
select MAX(Noon), AVG(Noon), MIN(Noon), STDDEV(Noon),
        VARIANCE(Noon)
   from COMFORT
 where City = 'KEENE';
```

```
MAX(NOON) AVG(NOON) MIN(NOON) STDDEV(NOON) VARIANCE(NOON)
--------- --------- --------- ------------ --------------
     99.8      54.4      -7.2   48.3337701    2336.15333
```

See the Alphabetical Reference for the syntax for the statistical functions listed in Table 9-1.

DISTINCT in Group Functions

All group-value functions have a **DISTINCT** versus **ALL** option. **COUNT** provides a good example of how this works.

Here is the format for **COUNT** (note that | means "or"):

```
COUNT([DISTINCT | ALL] value)
```

Here is an example:

```
select COUNT(DISTINCT City), COUNT(City), COUNT(*)
  from COMFORT;

COUNT(DISTINCTCITY) COUNT(CITY) COUNT(*)
------------------- ----------- --------
                  2           8        8
```

This query shows a couple of interesting results. First, **DISTINCT** forces **COUNT** to count only the number of unique city names. If asked to count the **DISTINCT** midnight temperatures, it would return 7, because two of the eight temperatures were the same. When **COUNT** is used on City but not forced to look at **DISTINCT** cities, it finds 8.

This also shows that **COUNT** can work on a character column. It's not making a computation on the values in the column, as **SUM** or **AVG** must; it is merely counting how many rows have a value in the specified column.

COUNT has another unique property: *value* can be an asterisk, meaning that **COUNT** tells you how many rows are in the table, regardless of whether any specific columns are **NULL**. It will count a row even if all its fields are **NULL**.

The other group functions do not share **COUNT**'s ability to use an asterisk, nor its ability to use a character column for *value* (although **MAX** and **MIN** can). They do all share its use of **DISTINCT**, which forces each of them to operate only on unique values. A table with values such as

```
select FirstName, Age from BIRTHDAY;

FIRSTNAME        AGE
--------------- ----
GEORGE            42
ROBERT            52
NANCY             42
VICTORIA          42
FRANK             42
```

would produce this result:

```
select AVG(DISTINCT Age) AS Average,
       SUM(DISTINCT Age) AS Total
  from BIRTHDAY;

AVERAGE  TOTAL
-------  ------
     47      94
```

which, if you wanted to know the average age of your friends, is not the right answer. The use of **DISTINCT** other than in **COUNT** is likely to be extremely rare, except perhaps in some statistical calculations. **MAX** and **MIN** produce the same result with or without **DISTINCT**.

The alternative option to **DISTINCT** is **ALL**, which is the default. **ALL** tells SQL to check every row, even if the value is a duplicate of the value in another row. You do not need to type **ALL**; if you don't type **DISTINCT**, **ALL** is used automatically.

List Functions

Unlike the group-value functions, which work on a group of rows, the list functions work on a group of columns, either actual or calculated values, within a single row. In other words, list functions compare the values of each of several columns and pick either the greatest or least of the list. Consider the COMFORT table, shown here:

```
select City, SampleDate, Noon, Midnight from COMFORT;

CITY           SAMPLEDAT NOON MIDNIGHT
-------------  --------- ---- --------
SAN FRANCISCO  21-MAR-03 62.5     42.3
SAN FRANCISCO  22-JUN-03 51.1     71.9
SAN FRANCISCO  23-SEP-03          61.5
SAN FRANCISCO  22-DEC-03 52.6     39.8
KEENE          21-MAR-03 39.9     -1.2
KEENE          22-JUN-03 85.1     66.7
KEENE          23-SEP-03 99.8     82.6
KEENE          22-DEC-03 -7.2     -1.2
```

Now compare this query result with the following one. Note especially June and September in San Francisco, and December in Keene:

```
select City, SampleDate, GREATEST(Midnight,Noon) AS High,
       LEAST(Midnight,Noon) AS Low
  from COMFORT;

CITY           SAMPLEDAT HIGH  LOW
-------------  --------- ----  ----
SAN FRANCISCO  21-MAR-03 62.5  42.3
SAN FRANCISCO  22-JUN-03 71.9  51.1
```

```
SAN FRANCISCO 23-SEP-03
SAN FRANCISCO 22-DEC-03  52.6  39.8
KEENE        21-MAR-03  39.9  -1.2
KEENE        22-JUN-03  85.1  66.7
KEENE        23-SEP-03  99.8  82.6
KEENE        22-DEC-03  -1.2  -7.2
```

September in San Francisco has a **NULL** result because **GREATEST** and **LEAST** couldn't legitimately compare an actual midnight temperature with an unknown noon temperature. In the other two instances, the midnight temperature was actually higher than the noon temperature.

Here are the formats for **GREATEST** and **LEAST**:

```
GREATEST(value1,value2,value3. . .)
LEAST(value1,value2,value3. . .)
```

Both **GREATEST** and **LEAST** can be used with many values, and the values can be columns, literal numbers, calculations, or combinations of other columns. **GREATEST** and **LEAST** can also be used with character columns. For example, they can choose the names that fall last (**GREATEST**) or first (**LEAST**) in alphabetical order:

```
GREATEST('Bob','George','Andrew','Isaiah') = Isaiah
   LEAST('Bob','George','Andrew','Isaiah') = Andrew
```

You can use the **COALESCE** function to evaluate multiple values for non-**NULL** values. Given a string of values, **COALESCE** will return the first non-**NULL** value encountered; if all are **NULL**, then a **NULL** result will be returned.

In the COMFORT table, there is a **NULL** value for Noon for one of the San Francisco measurements. The following query returns

```
select COALESCE(Noon, Midnight) from COMFORT
  where City = 'SAN FRANCISCO';

COALESCE(NOON,MIDNIGHT)
-----------------------
                   62.5
                   51.1
                   61.5
                   52.6
```

In the first two records of the output, the value displayed is the Noon value. In the third record, Noon is **NULL**, so Midnight is returned instead. Oracle's **DECODE** and **CASE** functions provide similar functionality, as described in Chapter 16.

Finding Rows with MAX or MIN

Which city had the highest temperature ever recorded, and on what date? The answer is easy with just eight rows to look at, but what if you have data from every city in the country and for

every day of every year for the last 50 years? Assume for now that the highest temperature for the year occurred closer to noon than midnight. The following won't work:

```
select City, SampleDate, MAX(Noon)
   from COMFORT;
```

Oracle flags the City column and gives this error message:

```
select City, SampleDate, MAX(Noon)
       *
ERROR at line 1:
ORA-00937: not a single-group group function
```

This error message is a bit opaque. It means that Oracle has detected a flaw in the logic of the question. Asking for columns means you want individual rows to appear; asking for **MAX**, a group function, means you want a group result for all rows. These are two different kinds of requests. The first asks for a set of rows, but the second requests just one computed row, so there is a conflict. Here is how to construct the query:

```
select City, SampleDate, Noon
   from COMFORT
  where Noon = (select MAX(Noon) from COMFORT);

CITY          SAMPLEDAT  NOON
------------  ---------- -----
KEENE         23-SEP-03  99.8
```

This only produces one row. You might think, therefore, that the combination of a request for the City and SampleDate columns, along with the **MAX** of Noon, is not so contradictory as was just implied. But what if you'd asked for the minimum temperature instead?

```
select City, SampleDate, Midnight
   from COMFORT
  where Midnight = (select MIN(Midnight) from COMFORT);

CITY          SAMPLEDAT MIDNIGHT
------------  --------- --------
KEENE         21-MAR-03    -1.2
KEENE         22-DEC-03    -1.2
```

Two rows! More than one satisfied the **MIN** request, so there is a conflict in trying to combine a regular column request with a group function.

It is also possible to use two subqueries, each with a group-value function in it (or two subqueries, where one does and the other doesn't have a group function). Suppose you want to know the highest and lowest noon temperatures for the year:

```
select City, SampleDate, Noon
   from COMFORT
  where Noon = (select MAX(Noon) from COMFORT)
```

```
or Noon = (select MIN(Noon) from COMFORT);
```

```
CITY            SAMPLEDAT NOON
--------------- --------- -----
KEENE           23-SEP-03  99.8
KEENE           22-DEC-03  -7.2
```

Precedence and Parentheses

When more than one arithmetic or logical operator is used in a single calculation, which one is executed first, and does it matter what order they are in? Consider the following query of the DUAL table (a one-column, one-row table provided by Oracle):

```
select 2/2/4 from DUAL;
```

```
2/2/4
-----
  .25
```

When parentheses are introduced, although the numbers and the operation (division) stay the same, the answer changes considerably:

```
select 2/(2/4) from DUAL;
```

```
2/(2/4)
-------
      4
```

The reason for this is *precedence*. Precedence defines the order in which mathematical computations are made, not just in Oracle but in mathematics in general. The rules are simple: Operations within parentheses have the highest precedence, then multiplication and division, then addition and subtraction. When an equation is computed, any calculations inside parentheses are made first. Multiplication and division are next. Finally, any addition and subtraction are completed. When operations of equal precedence are to be performed, they are executed from left to right. Here are a few examples:

```
2*4/2*3 = 12            (the same as ( (2*4)/2 )*3)
(2*4)/(2*3) = 1.333
4-2*5 = -6              (the same as 4 - (2*5))
(4-2)*5 = 10
```

AND and **OR** also obey precedence rules, with **AND** having the higher precedence. Observe the effect of the **AND** as well as the left-to-right order in these two queries:

```
select * from NEWSPAPER
  where Section = 'B' AND Page = 1 OR Page = 2;
```

```
FEATURE         S PAGE
--------------- - -----
Weather         C    2
```

```
Modern Life      B      1
Bridge           B      2

3 rows selected.

select * from NEWSPAPER
 where Page = 1 OR Page = 2 AND Section = 'B';

FEATURE          S  PAGE
--------------- - -----
National News    A      1
Sports           D      1
Business         E      1
Modern Life      B      1
Bridge           B      2

5 rows selected.
```

If what you really want is page 1 or 2 in Section B, then parentheses are needed to overcome the precedence of the **AND**. Parentheses override any other operations.

```
select * from NEWSPAPER
 where Section = 'B' AND (Page = 1 OR Page = 2);

FEATURE          S  PAGE
--------------- - -----
Modern Life      B      1
Bridge           B      2

2 rows selected.
```

The truth is that even experienced programmers and mathematicians have trouble remembering what will execute first when they write a query or an equation. It is always wise to make explicit the order you want Oracle to follow. Use parentheses whenever there could be the slightest risk of confusion.

Review

Single-value functions work on values in a row-by-row fashion. List functions compare columns and choose just one, again in a row-by-row fashion. Single-value functions almost always change the value of the column they are applied to. This doesn't mean, of course, that they have modified the database from which the value was drawn, but they do make a calculation with that value, and the result is different from the original value.

List functions don't change values in this way, but rather they simply choose (or report) the **GREATEST** or **LEAST** of a series of values in a row. Both single-value and list functions will not produce a result if they encounter a value that is **NULL**.

Both single-value and list functions can be used anywhere an expression can be used, such as in the **select** and **where** clauses.

The group-value functions tell something about a whole group of numbers—all of the rows in a set. The group-value functions tell you the average of those numbers, or the largest of them, or how many there are, or the standard deviation of the values, and so on. Group functions ignore **NULL** values, and this fact must be kept firmly in mind when reporting about groups of values; otherwise, there is considerable risk of misunderstanding the data.

Group-value functions also can report information on subgroups within a table, or they can be used to create a summary view of information from one or more tables. Chapter 12 gives details on these additional features.

Finally, mathematical and logical precedence affect the order in which queries are evaluated, and this can have a dramatic effect on query results. Get into the habit of using parentheses to make the order you want both explicit and easy to understand.

CHAPTER
10

Dates: Then, Now, and the Difference

ne of Oracle's strengths is its ability to store and calculate dates, and the number of seconds, minutes, hours, days, months, and years between dates. In addition to basic date functions, Oracle supports a wide array of time zone–conversion functions. It also has the ability to format dates in virtually any manner you can conceive of, from the simple 01-MAY-04, to May 1st in the 778th Year of the Reign of Louis IX. You probably won't use many of these date-formatting and -computing functions, but the most basic ones will prove to be very important.

Date Arithmetic

DATE is an Oracle datatype, just as VARCHAR2 and NUMBER are, and it has its own unique properties. The DATE datatype is stored in a special internal Oracle format that includes not just the month, day, and year, but also the hour, minute, and second. The benefit of all this detail should be obvious. If you have, for instance, a customer help desk, for each call that is logged in, Oracle can automatically store the date and time of the call in a single DATE column. You can format the DATE column on a report to show just the date, or the date and the hour, or the century, date, hour, and minute, or the date, hour, minute, and second. You can use the TIMESTAMP datatype to store fractional seconds. See the "Using the TIMESTAMP Datatypes" section later in this chapter for details.

SQL*Plus and SQL recognize columns that are of the DATE datatype, and they understand that instructions to do arithmetic with them call for *date arithmetic,* not regular math. Adding 1 to a date, for instance, will give you another *date*—the next day. Subtracting one date from another will give you a *number*—the count of days between the two dates.

However, because Oracle dates can include hours, minutes, and seconds, doing date arithmetic can prove to be tricky because Oracle could tell you, for example, that the difference between today and tomorrow is .516 days! (This will be explained later in this chapter.)

SYSDATE, CURRENT_DATE, and SYSTIMESTAMP

Oracle taps into the computer's operating system for the current date and time. It makes these available to you through a special function called **SYSDATE**. Think of **SYSDATE** as a function whose result is always the current date and time, and it can be used anywhere any other Oracle function can be used. You also can regard it as a hidden column or pseudo-column that is in every table. Here, **SYSDATE** shows today's date:

```
select SysDate from DUAL;

SYSDATE
---------
23-MAR-04
```

NOTE
DUAL is a small but useful Oracle table created for testing functions or doing quick calculations. Later in this chapter, the sidebar "The DUAL Table for Quick Tests and Calculations" describes DUAL.

A second function, **CURRENT_DATE**, reports the system date in the session's time zone (you can set the time zone within your local session, which may differ from the database's time zone).

```
select Current_Date from DUAL;

CURRENT_D
---------
23-MAR-04
```

Another function, **SYSTIMESTAMP**, reports the system date in the TIMESTAMP datatype format:

```
select SysTimeStamp from DUAL;

SYSTIMESTAMP
---------------------------------------------
23-MAR-04 04.49.31.718000 PM -05:00
```

See the "Using the TIMESTAMP Datatypes" section later in this chapter for details on the TIMESTAMP datatype and the time zone format and functions. The following sections focus on the use of the DATE datatype, because DATE will satisfy most date-processing requirements.

The Difference Between Two Dates

HOLIDAY is a table of some secular holidays in the United States during 2004:

```
select Holiday, ActualDate, CelebratedDate from HOLIDAY;

HOLIDAY                   ACTUALDAT CELEBRATE
------------------------- --------- ---------
NEW YEARS DAY             01-JAN-04 01-JAN-04
MARTIN LUTHER KING, JR.   15-JAN-04 19-JAN-04
LINCOLNS BIRTHDAY         12-FEB-04 16-FEB-04
WASHINGTONS BIRTHDAY      22-FEB-04 16-FEB-04
FAST DAY, NEW HAMPSHIRE   22-FEB-04 22-FEB-04
MEMORIAL DAY              30-MAY-04 31-MAY-04
INDEPENDENCE DAY          04-JUL-04 04-JUL-04
LABOR DAY                 06-SEP-04 06-SEP-04
COLUMBUS DAY              12-OCT-04 11-OCT-04
THANKSGIVING             25-NOV-04 25-NOV-04
```

Which holidays are not celebrated on the actual date of their anniversary during 2004? This can be easily answered by subtracting CelebratedDate from ActualDate. If the answer is not zero, there is a difference between the two dates:

```
select Holiday, ActualDate, CelebratedDate
  from Holiday
 where CelebratedDate - ActualDate != 0;

HOLIDAY                   ACTUALDAT CELEBRATE
------------------------- --------- ---------
MARTIN LUTHER KING, JR.   15-JAN-04 19-JAN-04
```

```
LINCOLNS BIRTHDAY          12-FEB-04 16-FEB-04
WASHINGTONS BIRTHDAY       22-FEB-04 16-FEB-04
MEMORIAL DAY               30-MAY-04 31-MAY-04
COLUMBUS DAY               12-OCT-04 11-OCT-04
```

The DUAL Table for Quick Tests and Calculations

DUAL is a tiny table Oracle provides with only one row and one column in it:

```
describe DUAL

Name                           Null?       Type
------------------------------ ----------- -------------
DUMMY                                      VARCHAR(1)
```

Because Oracle's many functions work on both columns and literals, using DUAL lets you see some functioning using just literals. In these examples, the **select** statement doesn't care which columns are in the table, and a single row is sufficient to demonstrate a point. For example, suppose you want to quickly calculate **POWER**(4,3)—that is, four "cubed":

```
select POWER(4,3) from DUAL;

POWER(4,3)
----------
        64
```

The actual column in DUAL is irrelevant. This means that you can experiment with date formatting and arithmetic using the DUAL table and the date functions in order to understand how they work. Then, those functions can be applied to actual dates in real tables.

Date Functions

The major functions performed on DATE datatype columns are as follows:

- **ADD_MONTHS**(*date,count*) Adds *count* **months** to *date*.

- **CURRENT_DATE** Returns the **current date** in the session's time zone.

- **CURRENT_TIMESTAMP** Returns the **current timestamp** with the active time zone information.

- **DBTIMEZONE** Returns the current **database time zone**, in UTC format.

- **EXTRACT**(*timeunit FROM datetime*) **Extract**s a portion of a date from a date value—such as extracting the month value from a DATE column's values.

■ **FROM_TZ**(*timestamp*) Converts a timestamp value to a timestamp with a time zone value.

■ **GREATEST**(*date1,date2,date3,…*) Picks the latest date from a list of dates.

■ **LEAST**(*date1,date2,date3,…*) Picks the earliest date from a list of dates.

■ **LAST_DAY**(*date*) Gives the date of the **last day** of the month that *date* is in.

■ **LOCALTIMESTAMP** Returns the **local timestamp** in the active time zone, with no time zone information shown.

■ **MONTHS_BETWEEN**(*date2,date1*) Gives *date2* minus *date1* in **months** (can be fractional months).

■ **NEW_TIME**(*date,'this','other'*) Gives the *date* (and time) in *this* time zone. *this* will be replaced by a three-letter abbreviation for the current time zone. *other* will be replaced by a three-letter abbreviation for the other time zone for which you'd like to know the time and date. The time zones are as follows:

AST/ADT	Atlantic standard/daylight time
BST/BDT	Bering standard/daylight time
CST/CDT	Central standard/daylight time
EST/EDT	Eastern standard/daylight time
GMT	Greenwich mean time
HST/HDT	Alaska-Hawaii standard/daylight time
MST/MDT	Mountain standard/daylight time
NST	Newfoundland standard time
PST/PDT	Pacific standard/daylight time
YST/YDT	Yukon standard/daylight time

■ **NEXT_DAY**(*date,'day'*) Gives the date of the **next day** after *date*, where *'day'* is 'Monday', 'Tuesday', and so on.

■ **NUMTODSINTERVAL**(*'value','dateunit'*) Converts *value* to an INTERVAL DAY TO SECOND literal, where *'dateunit'* is 'DAY', 'HOUR', 'MINUTE', or 'SECOND'.

■ **NUMTOYMINTERVAL**(*'value','dateunit'*) Converts *value* to an INTERVAL YEAR TO MONTH literal, where *'dateunit'* is 'YEAR' or 'MONTH'.

■ **ROUND**(*date,'format'*) Without *format* specified, this function **round**s a *date* to 12 A.M. (midnight, the beginning of that day) if the time of *date* is before noon; otherwise, it **round**s up to the next day. For the use of *format* for rounding, see **ROUND** in the Alphabetical Reference.

- **SESSIONTIMEZONE** Returns the value of the current **session**'s **time zone**.

- **SYS_EXTRACT_UTC** Extracts the Coordinated Universal Time (UTC) from the current date.

- **SYSTIMESTAMP** Returns the system date, including fractional seconds and the time zone of the database.

- **SYSDATE** Returns the current date and time.

- **TO_CHAR**(*date*,'*format*') Reformats *date* according to *format*. (See the sidebar "Date Formats" later in this chapter.)

- **TO_DATE**(*string*,'*format*') Converts a *string* in a given *format* into an Oracle date. Will also accept a *number* instead of a *string*, with certain limits. *format* is restricted.

- **TO_DSINTERVAL**('*value*') Converts the *value* of a CHAR, VARCHAR2, NCHAR, or NVARCHAR2 datatype to an INTERVAL DAY TO SECOND type.

- **TO_TIMESTAMP**('*value*') Converts the *value* of a CHAR, VARCHAR2, NCHAR, or NVARCHAR2 datatype to a value of the TIMESTAMP datatype.

- **TO_TIMESTAMP_TZ**('*value*') Converts the *value* of a CHAR, VARCHAR2, NCHAR, or NVARCHAR2 datatype to a value of the TIMESTAMP WITH TIME ZONE datatype.

- **TO_YMINTERVAL**('*value*') Converts the *value* of a CHAR, VARCHAR2, NCHAR, or NVARCHAR2 datatype to a value of the INTERVAL YEAR TO MONTH datatype.

- **TRUNC**(*date*,'*format*') Without *format* specified, this function sets a *date* to 12 A.M. (midnight, the beginning of that day). For the use of *format* for truncating, see **TRUNC** in the Alphabetical Reference.

- **TZ_OFFSET**('*value*') Returns the time zone offset corresponding to the *value* entered based on the date the statement is executed.

Adding Months

If February 22 is "Fast Day" in New Hampshire, perhaps six months later could be celebrated as "Feast Day." If so, what would the date be? Simply use the **ADD_MONTHS** function, adding a *count* of six months, as shown here:

```
column FeastDay heading "Feast Day"

select ADD_MONTHS(CelebratedDate,6) AS FeastDay
  from HOLIDAY
 where Holiday like 'FAST%';
```

```
Feast Day
---------
22-AUG-04
```

Subtracting Months

If picnic area reservations have to be made at least six months before Columbus Day, what's the last day you can make them? Take the CelebratedDate for Columbus Day and use **ADD_MONTHS**, adding a *negative count* of six months (this is the same as subtracting months). This will tell you the date six months before Columbus Day. Then subtract one day.

```
column LastDay heading "Last Day"

select ADD_MONTHS(CelebratedDate,-6) - 1 AS LastDay
   from HOLIDAY
 where Holiday = 'COLUMBUS DAY';

Last Day
---------
10-APR-04
```

GREATEST and LEAST

Which comes first for each of the holidays that were moved to fall on Mondays, the actual or the celebrated date? The **LEAST** function chooses the earliest date from a list of dates, whether columns or literals; **GREATEST**, on the other hand, chooses the latest date. These **GREATEST** and **LEAST** functions are exactly the same ones used with numbers and character strings:

```
select Holiday, LEAST(ActualDate, CelebratedDate) AS First,
       ActualDate, CelebratedDate
   from HOLIDAY
 where ActualDate - CelebratedDate != 0;

HOLIDAY                    FIRST     ACTUALDAT CELEBRATE
------------------------- --------- --------- ---------
MARTIN LUTHER KING, JR.   15-JAN-04 15-JAN-04 19-JAN-04
LINCOLNS BIRTHDAY         12-FEB-04 12-FEB-04 16-FEB-04
WASHINGTONS BIRTHDAY      16-FEB-04 22-FEB-04 16-FEB-04
MEMORIAL DAY              30-MAY-04 30-MAY-04 31-MAY-04
COLUMBUS DAY             11-OCT-04 12-OCT-04 11-OCT-04
```

Here, **LEAST** worked just fine, because it operated on DATE columns from a table. What about literals?

```
select LEAST('20-JAN-04','20-DEC-04') from DUAL;

LEAST('20
---------
20-DEC-04
```

A Warning about GREATEST and LEAST

Unlike many other Oracle functions and logical operators, the **GREATEST** and **LEAST** functions will not evaluate literal strings that are in date format as dates. The dates are treated as strings:

```
select Holiday, CelebratedDate
  from HOLIDAY
 where CelebratedDate =  LEAST('19-JAN-04', '06-SEP-04');

HOLIDAY                  CELEBRATE
------------------------ ---------
LABOR DAY                02-SEP-02
```

In order for **LEAST** and **GREATEST** to work properly, the function **TO_DATE** must be applied to the literal strings:

```
select Holiday, CelebratedDate
  from HOLIDAY
 where CelebratedDate = LEAST( TO_DATE('19-JAN-04'),
                               TO_DATE('06-SEP-04') );

HOLIDAY                  CELEBRATE
------------------------ ---------
MARTIN LUTHER KING, JR.  04-JAN-04
```

This is quite wrong, almost as if you'd said **GREATEST** instead of **LEAST**. December 20, 2004 is not earlier than January 20, 2004. Why did this happen? Because **LEAST** treated these literals as *strings*.

It did not know to treat them as dates. The **TO_DATE** function converts these literals into an internal DATE format Oracle can use for its date-oriented functions:

```
select LEAST( TO_DATE('20-JAN-04'), TO_DATE('20-DEC-04') )
  from DUAL;

LEAST(TO_
---------
20-JAN-04
```

NEXT_DAY

NEXT_DAY computes the date of the next named day of the week (that is, Sunday, Monday, Tuesday, Wednesday, Thursday, Friday, or Saturday) after the given date. For example, suppose payday is always the first Friday after the 15th of the month. The table PAYDAY contains only the pay cycle dates, each one being the 15th of the month, with one row for each month of the year:

```
select CycleDate from PAYDAY;

CYCLEDATE
---------
15-JAN-04
15-FEB-04
15-MAR-04
15-APR-04
15-MAY-04
15-JUN-04
15-JUL-04
15-AUG-04
15-SEP-04
15-OCT-04
15-NOV-04
15-DEC-04
```

What will be the actual payment dates?

```
column Payday heading "Pay Day"

select NEXT_DAY(CycleDate,'FRIDAY') AS Payday
  from PAYDAY;

Pay Day
---------
16-JAN-04
20-FEB-04
19-MAR-04
16-APR-04
21-MAY-04
18-JUN-04
16-JUL-04
20-AUG-04
17-SEP-04
22-OCT-04
19-NOV-04
17-DEC-04
```

This is nearly correct, except for October, because **NEXT_DAY** is the date of the *next* Friday after the cycle date. Because October 15, 2004, is a Friday, this (wrongly) gives the following Friday instead. The correct version is as follows:

```
column Payday heading "Pay Day"

select NEXT_DAY(CycleDate-1,'FRIDAY') AS PayDay
  from PAYDAY;
```

NEXT_DAY is really a "greater than" kind of function. It asks for the next date *greater than* the given date that falls on a specific day of the week. To catch those cycle dates that are already on Friday, subtract one from the cycle date. This makes every cycle date appear one day earlier to **NEXT_DAY**. The paydays are then always the correct Friday.

LAST_DAY

LAST_DAY produces the date of the last day of the month. Suppose that commissions and bonuses are always paid on the last day of the month. What are those dates in 2004?

```
column EndMonth heading "End Month"

select LAST_DAY(CycleDate) AS EndMonth
  from PAYDAY;

End Month
---------
31-JAN-04
29-FEB-04
31-MAR-04
30-APR-04
31-MAY-04
30-JUN-04
31-JUL-04
31-AUG-04
30-SEP-04
31-OCT-04
30-NOV-04
31-DEC-04
```

MONTHS_BETWEEN Two Dates

You recently came across a file containing the birthdates of a group of friends. You load the information into a table called BIRTHDAY and display it:

```
select FirstName, LastName, BirthDate from BIRTHDAY;

FIRSTNAME        LASTNAME         BIRTHDATE
---------------  ---------------  ---------
GEORGE           SAND             12-MAY-46
ROBERT           JAMES            23-AUG-37
NANCY            LEE              02-FEB-47
VICTORIA         LYNN             20-MAY-49
FRANK            PILOT            11-NOV-42
```

To calculate each person's age, compute the months between today's date and their birth dates, and divide by 12 to get the years. The division will print the age with a decimal component. Because most people over the age of 7 don't report their age using portions of years, apply a **FLOOR** function to the computation.

```
select FirstName, LastName, Birthdate,
       FLOOR(
             MONTHS_BETWEEN(SysDate,Birthdate)/12
             ) AS Age
  from BIRTHDAY;
```

```
FIRSTNAME        LASTNAME          BIRTHDATE    AGE
---------------  ----------------  ---------  -------
GEORGE           SAND              12-MAY-46     57
ROBERT           JAMES             23-AUG-37     66
NANCY            LEE               02-FEB-47     57
VICTORIA         LYNN              20-MAY-49     54
FRANK            PILOT             11-NOV-42     61
```

Combining Date Functions

You are hired on March 23, 2004, at a great new job, with a starting salary that is lower than you had hoped, but with a promise of a review the first of the month after six months have passed. If the current date is March 23, 2004, when is your review date?

```
select SysDate AS Today,
       LAST_DAY(ADD_MONTHS(SysDate,6)) + 1 Review
  from DUAL;

TODAY      REVIEW
---------  ---------
23-MAR-04  01-OCT-04
```

ADD_MONTHS takes the SysDate and adds six months to it. **LAST_DAY** takes this result and figures the last day of that month. You then add 1 to the date to get the first day of the next month. How many days until that review? You simply subtract today's date from it. Note the use of parentheses to ensure the proper order of the calculation:

```
select (LAST_DAY(ADD_MONTHS(SysDate,6))+ 1)-SysDate  Wait
  from DUAL;

  WAIT
-----
   192
```

ROUND and TRUNC in Date Calculations

Assume that this is today's SysDate:

```
SYSDATE
---------
23-MAR-04
```

In the beginning of the chapter, it was noted that Oracle could subtract one date from another, such as tomorrow minus today, and come up with an answer other than a whole number. Let's look at it:

```
select TO_DATE('24-MAR-04') - SysDate from DUAL;
```

```
TO_DATE('24-MAR-04')-SYSDATE
----------------------------
                        .516
```

The reason for the fractional number of days between today and tomorrow is that Oracle keeps hours, minutes, and seconds with its dates, and SysDate is always current, up to the second. It is obviously less than a full day until tomorrow.

To simplify some of the difficulties you might encounter using fractions of days, Oracle makes a couple of assumptions about dates:

- A date entered as a literal, such as '24-MAR-04', is given a default time of 12 A.M. (midnight) at the beginning of that day.

- A date entered through SQL*Plus, unless a time is specifically assigned to it, is set to 12 A.M. (midnight) at the beginning of that day.

- SysDate always includes both the date and the time, unless you intentionally round it off. Using the **ROUND** function on any date sets it to 12 A.M. for that day if the time is before exactly noon, and to 12 A.M. the next day if it is after noon. The **TRUNC** function acts similarly, except that it sets the time to 12 A.M. for any time up to and including one second before midnight.

To get the rounded number of days between today and tomorrow, use this:

```
select TO_DATE('25-MAR-04') - ROUND(SysDate) from DUAL;

TO_DATE('25-MAR-04')-ROUND(SYSDATE)
-----------------------------------
                                  1
```

If the current time is after noon, the rounded difference will be 0 days.

ROUND, without a '*format*' (see the earlier sidebar, "Date Functions"), always rounds a date to 12 A.M. of the closest day. If dates that you will be working with contain times other than noon, either use **ROUND** or accept possible fractional results in your calculations. **TRUNC** works similarly, but it sets the time to 12 A.M. of the current day.

TO_DATE and TO_CHAR Formatting

TO_DATE and **TO_CHAR** are alike insofar as they both have powerful formatting capabilities. They are opposite insofar as **TO_DATE** converts a character string or a number into an Oracle date, whereas **TO_CHAR** converts an Oracle date into a character string. The formats for these two functions are as follows:

```
TO_CHAR(date[,'format'[,'NLSparameters']])

TO_DATE(string[,'format'[,'NLSparameters']])
```

date must be a column defined as a DATE datatype in Oracle. It cannot be a string, even if it is in the most common date format of DD-MON-YY. The only way to use a string where *date* appears in the **TO_CHAR** function is to enclose it within a **TO_DATE** function.

string is a literal string, a literal number, or a database column containing a string or a number. In every case but one, the format of *string* must correspond to that described by *format*. Only if a string is in the default format can *format* be left out. The default starts out as 'DD-MON-YY', but you can change this with

```
alter session set NLS_DATE_FORMAT = "DD/MON/YYYY";
```

for a given SQL session or with the NLS_DATE_FORMAT init.ora parameter.

format is a collection of many options that can be combined in virtually an infinite number of ways. The sidebar "Date Formats" lists these options with explanations. Once you understand the basic method of using the options, putting them into practice is simple.

NLSparameters is a string that sets the NLS_DATE_LANGUAGE option to a specific language, as opposed to using the language for the current SQL session. You shouldn't need to use this option often. Oracle will return day and month names in the language set for the session with **alter session**.

> **NOTE**
> *In many cases, you can use the **EXTRACT** function in place of **TO_CHAR**. See the "Using the EXTRACT Function" section later in this chapter for examples.*

TO_CHAR will be used as an example of how the options work. Defining a column format for the **TO_CHAR** function results is the first task, because without it, **TO_CHAR** will produce a column in SQL*Plus nearly 100 characters wide. By renaming the column (so its heading is intelligible) and setting its format to 30 characters, a practical display is produced:

```
column Formatted format a30 word_wrapped
select BirthDate,
       TO_CHAR(BirthDate,'MM/DD/YY') AS Formatted
  from BIRTHDAY
 where FirstName = 'VICTORIA';

BIRTHDATE FORMATTED
--------- ------------------------------
20-MAY-49 05/20/49
```

BirthDate shows the default Oracle date format: DD-MON-YY (day of the month, dash, three-letter abbreviation for the month, dash, the last two digits of the year). The **TO_CHAR** function in the **select** statement is nearly self-evident. MM, DD, and YY in the **TO_CHAR** statement are key symbols to Oracle in formatting the date. The slashes (/) are just punctuation, and Oracle will accept a wide variety of punctuation.

```
select BirthDate, TO_CHAR(BirthDate,'YYMM>DD') Formatted
  from BIRTHDAY
 where FirstName = 'VICTORIA';

BIRTHDATE FORMATTED
--------- ------------------------------
20-MAY-49 4905>20
```

Date Formats

Date format models are used in conversion functions. Here are the data model components:

/, - : . ;	Punctuation to be incorporated in display for **TO_CHAR** or ignored in format for **TO_DATE**.
A.D. or AD	AD indicator, with or without periods.
A.M. or AM	Displays A.M. or P.M., depending upon time of day, with or without periods.
B.C. or BC	Same as A.D. or AD.
CC	Century (for example, 21 for 2004).
SCC	Century, with BC dates prefixed with -.
D	Number of days in a week: 1 to 7.
DAY	The day fully spelled out, padded to nine characters.
DD	Number of days in a month: 1 to 31.
DDD	Number of days in a year (since Jan 1): 1 to 366.
DL	The date in local long format; in the U.S. format this is equivalent to 'fmDay, Month dd, yyyy'.
DS	The date in local short format; in the U.S. format this is equivalent to 'MM/DD/RRRR'.
DY	Three-letter abbreviation of a day (for example, FRI).
E	Abbreviated era name (Japanese Imperial, ROC Official, and Thai Buddha calendars).
EE	Full era name version of the E format.
FF [1..9]	Fractional seconds. The number following FF specifies the number of digits in the fractional seconds portion displayed.
FM	Suppresses leading and trailing blanks. Without FM, all months and days are displayed at the same width.
FX	Specifies the exact format matching for the character argument and the date format model.
HH	Hour of the day (always 1 to 12).
HH12	Same as HH.
HH24	Hour of the day, 24-hour clock (values 0 to 23).

I	One-digit year from ISO standard.
IW	Weeks in the year from ISO standard (1 to 53).
IY	Two-digit year from ISO standard.
IYY	Three-digit year from ISO standard.
IYYY	Four-digit year from ISO standard.
J	"Julian" (days since December 31, 4712 B.C.).
MI	Minutes of the hour (values 0 to 59).
MM	Number of the month (for example, 12).
MON	Three-letter abbreviation of the month (for example, AUG).
MONTH	The month fully spelled out (for example, AUGUST).
P.M.	Same effect as A.M.
Q	Quarter of the year (1 to 4).
RM	Roman numeral month.
RR	Last two digits of the year relative to the current date.
RRRR	Rounded year, accepting either two- or four-digit input.
SS	Seconds of the minute (for example, 43).
SSSSS	Seconds since midnight, always 0 to 86399 (for example, 43000).
TS	Short time format, for use with DL or DS.
TZD	Daylight savings time information.
TZH	Time zone hour.
TZM	Time zone minute.
TZR	Time zone region.
W	Number of weeks in a month, where Week 1 starts on the first day of the month.
WW	Number of weeks in a year, where Week 1 starts on the first day of the year.
X	Local radix character.
YEAR or SYEAR	The year spelled out; 'S' marks B.C. dates with a leading minus sign.
YYYY or SYYYY	Full four-digit year; 'S' marks B.C. dates with a leading minus sign.
Y,YYY	Year, with a comma.

Y	Last one digit of a year.
YY	Last two digits of a year.
YYY	Last three digits of a year.

Date formats that work only with **TO_CHAR**, but not **TO_DATE**, include the following:

"string"	*string* is incorporated in the display for **TO_CHAR**.
TH	Suffix to a number. For example, ddTH or DDTH produces 24th or 24TH, respectively. Capitalization comes from the case of the number—DD—not from the case of TH. Works with any number in a date: YYYY, DD, MM, HH, MI, SS, and so on.
SP	Suffix to a number that forces the number to be spelled out. For example, DDSP, DdSP, or ddSP produces THREE, Three, or three, respectively. Capitalization comes from the case of the number—DD—not from the case of SP. Works with any number in a date: YYYY, DD, MM, HH, MI, SS, and so on.
SPTH	Suffix combination of TH and SP that forces a number to be both spelled out and given an ordinal suffix. For example, Ddspth produces Third. Capitalization comes from the case of the number—DD—not from the case of SP. Works with any number in a date: YYYY, DD, MM, HH, MI, SS, and so on.
THSP	Same as SPTH.

In addition to standard punctuation, Oracle allows you to insert text into the *format*. This is done by enclosing the desired text in *double* quotation marks:

```
select BirthDate,
       TO_CHAR(BirthDate,'Month, DDth "in, um,"
             YyyY') AS Formatted
  from BIRTHDAY ;

BIRTHDATE FORMATTED
--------- ----------------------------
12-MAY-46 May       , 12TH   in, um,
          1946
23-AUG-37 August    , 23RD   in, um,
          1937
02-FEB-47 February  , 02ND   in, um,
          1947
```

```
20-MAY-49 May       , 20TH   in, um,
          1949
11-NOV-42 November , 11TH    in, um,
          1942
```

Several consequences of the *format* are worth observing here. The full word "Month" told Oracle to use the full name of the month in the display. Because it was typed with the first letter in uppercase and the remainder in lowercase, each month in the result was formatted the same way. The options for month are as follows:

Format	Result
Month	August
Month	August
Mon	Aug
Mon	Aug

The day of the month is produced by the DD in the *format*. A suffix of **th** on DD tells Oracle to use *ordinal* suffixes, such as "TH", "RD", and "ND" with the number. In this instance, the suffixes are also case sensitive, but their case is set by the DD, not the **th**:

Format	Result
DDth or DDTH	11TH
Ddth or DdTH	11Th
Ddth or ddTH	11th

This same approach holds true for all numbers in the *format*, including century, year, quarter, month, week, day of the month (DD), Julian day, hours, minutes, and seconds.

The words between double quotation marks are simply inserted where they are found. Spaces between any of these format requests are reproduced in the result (look at the three spaces before the word "in" in the preceding example). YyyY is included simply to show that case is irrelevant unless a suffix such as Th is being used. For simplicity's sake, consider this format request:

```
select BirthDate, TO_CHAR(BirthDate,'Month, ddth, YyyY')
       AS Formatted
  from BIRTHDAY;

BIRTHDATE FORMATTED
--------- ------------------------------
12-MAY-46 May       , 12th, 1946
23-AUG-37 August    , 23rd, 1937
02-FEB-47 February , 02nd, 1947
20-MAY-49 May       , 20th, 1949
11-NOV-42 November , 11th, 1942
```

This is a reasonably normal format. The days are all aligned, which makes comparing the rows easy. This is the default alignment, and Oracle accomplishes it by padding the month names on the right with spaces up to a width of nine spaces. There will be circumstances when it is more important for a date to be formatted normally, such as at the top of a letter. The spaces between the month and the comma would look odd. To eliminate the spaces, **fm** is used as a prefix for the words "month" and "day":

Format	Result
Month, ddth	August , 20th
fmMonth, ddth	August, 20th
Day, ddth	Monday , 20th
fmDay, ddth	Monday, 20th

This is illustrated in the following example:

```
select BirthDate, TO_CHAR(BirthDate,'fmMonth, ddth, YyyY')
       AS Formatted
   from BIRTHDAY;

BIRTHDATE FORMATTED
--------- ------------------------------
12-MAY-46 May, 12th, 1946
23-AUG-37 August, 23rd, 1937
02-FEB-47 February, 2nd, 1947
20-MAY-49 May, 20th, 1949
11-NOV-42 November, 11th, 1942
```

By combining all these format controls and adding hours and minutes, you can produce a birth announcement:

```
select FirstName, Birthdate, TO_CHAR(BirthDate,
'"Baby Girl on" fmMonth ddth, YYYY, "at" HH:MI "in the Morning"')
       AS Formatted
   from BIRTHDAY
 where FirstName = 'VICTORIA';

FIRSTNAME       BIRTHDATE FORMATTED
--------------- --------- ------------------------------
VICTORIA        20-MAY-49 Baby Girl on May 20th, 1949,
                          at 3:27 in the Morning
```

Suppose that after looking at this, you decide you'd rather spell out the date. Do this with the **sp** control:

```
select FirstName, Birthdate, TO_CHAR(BirthDate,
'"Baby Girl on the" Ddsp "of" fmMonth, YYYY, "at" HH:MI')
       AS Formatted
```

```
   from BIRTHDAY
 where FirstName = 'VICTORIA';

FIRSTNAME        BIRTHDATE FORMATTED
---------------  --------- ------------------------------
VICTORIA         20-MAY-49 Baby Girl on the Twenty of
                           May, 1949, at 3:27
```

Well, 20 was spelled out, but it still doesn't look right. Add the **th** suffix to **sp**:

```
select FirstName, Birthdate, TO_CHAR(BirthDate,
'"Baby Girl on the" Ddspth "of" fmMonth, YYYY, "at" HH:MI')
        AS Formatted
   from BIRTHDAY
 where FirstName = 'VICTORIA';

FIRSTNAME        BIRTHDATE FORMATTED
---------------  --------- ------------------------------
VICTORIA         20-MAY-49 Baby Girl on the Twentieth of
                           May, 1949, at 3:27
```

But was it 3:27 A.M. or 3:27 P.M.? These could be added inside double quotation marks, but then the result would always say "A.M." or "P.M.", regardless of the actual time of the day (because double quotation marks enclose a literal). Instead, Oracle lets you add *either* "A.M." or "P.M." after the time, but not in double quotation marks. Oracle then interprets this as a request to display whether it is A.M. or P.M. Note how the **select** has this formatting control entered as P.M., but the result shows A.M., because the birth occurred in the morning:

```
select FirstName, Birthdate, TO_CHAR(BirthDate,
'"Baby Girl on the" Ddspth "of" fmMonth, YYYY, "at" HH:MI P.M.')
        AS Formatted
   from BIRTHDAY
 where FirstName = 'VICTORIA';

FIRSTNAME        BIRTHDATE FORMATTED
---------------  --------- ------------------------------
VICTORIA         20-MAY-49 Baby Girl on the Twentieth of
                           May, 1949, at 3:27 A.M.
```

Consult the sidebar "Date Formats," earlier in the chapter, for a list of all the possible date options. How would you construct a date format for the 778th Year of the Reign of Louis IX? Use date arithmetic to alter the year from A.D. to A.L. (Louis's reign began in 1226, so subtract 1,226 years from the current year) and then simply format the result using **TO_CHAR**.

The Most Common TO_CHAR Error

Always check the date formats when using the **TO_CHAR** function. The most common error is to interchange the 'MM' (Month) format and the 'MI' (Minutes) format when formatting the time portion of a date.

For example, to view the current time, use the **TO_CHAR** function to query the time portion of SysDate:

```
select TO_CHAR(SysDate,'HH:MI:SS') Now
  from DUAL;

NOW
--------
05:11:48
```

This example is correct because it uses 'MI' to show the minutes. However, users often select 'MM' instead—partly because they are also selecting two other pairs of double letters, 'HH' and 'SS'. Selecting 'MM' will return the month, not the minutes:

```
select TO_CHAR(SysDate,'HH:MM:SS') NowWrong
  from DUAL;

NOWWRONG
--------
05:03:48
```

This time is incorrect, because the month was selected in the minutes place. Because Oracle is so flexible and has so many different supported date formats, it does not prevent you from making this error.

NEW_TIME: Switching Time Zones

The **NEW_TIME** function tells you the time and date of a date column or literal date in other time zones. Here is the format for **NEW_TIME**:

```
NEW_TIME(date,'this','other')
```

date is the date (and time) in *this* time zone. *this* will be replaced by a three-letter abbreviation for the current time zone. *other* will be replaced by a three-letter abbreviation of the other time zone for which you'd like to know the time and date. The time zone options are given in the sidebar "Date Functions," earlier in this chapter. To compare just the date, without showing the time, of Victoria's birth between Eastern standard time and Hawaiian standard time, use this:

```
select Birthdate, NEW_TIME(Birthdate,'EST','HST')
  from BIRTHDAY
 where FirstName = 'VICTORIA';

BIRTHDATE NEW_TIME(
--------- ---------
20-MAY-49 19-MAY-49
```

But how could Victoria have been born on two different days? Because every date stored in Oracle also contains a time, it is simple enough using **TO_CHAR** and **NEW_TIME** to discover both the date and the time differences between the two zones. This will answer the question:

```
select TO_CHAR(Birthdate,'fmMonth Ddth, YYYY "at" HH:MI AM') AS Birth,
       TO_CHAR(NEW_TIME(Birthdate,'EST','HST'),
       'fmMonth ddth, YYYY "at" HH:MI AM') AS Birth
  from BIRTHDAY
 where FirstName = 'VICTORIA';

BIRTH                            BIRTH
-----------------------------    -----------------------------
May 20th, 1949 at 3:27 AM        May 19th, 1949 at 10:27 PM
```

TO_DATE Calculations

TO_DATE follows the same formatting conventions as **TO_CHAR**, with some restrictions. The purpose of **TO_DATE** is to turn a literal string, such as MAY 20, 1949, into an Oracle date format. This allows the date to be used in date calculations.

Here is the format for **TO_DATE**:

```
TO_DATE(string[,'format'])
```

To put the string 22-MAR-04 into Oracle date format, use this:

```
select TO_DATE('22-MAR-04','DD-MON-YY') from DUAL;

TO_DATE('
---------
22-MAR-04
```

Note, however, that the 22-MAR-04 format is already in the default format in which Oracle displays and accepts dates. When a literal string has a date in this format, the *format* in **TO_DATE** can be left out, with exactly the same result:

```
select TO_DATE('22-MAR-04') from DUAL;

TO_DATE('
---------
22-MAR-04
```

Note that the punctuation is ignored. Even if your default date format is 22/MAR/04, the query will still work, but it will return data in the format 22/MAR/04.

But what century is the date in? Is it 1902 or 2002? If you do not specify the full four-digit value for the year, then you are relying on the database to default to the proper century value.

If the string is in a familiar format, but not the default Oracle format of DD-MON-YY, **TO_DATE** fails:

```
select TO_DATE('03/22/04') from DUAL;

select TO_DATE('03/22/04') from DUAL;
                *
ERROR at line 1:
ORA-01843: not a valid month
```

When the format matches the literal string, the string is successfully converted to a date and is then displayed in the default date format:

```
select TO_DATE('03/22/04','MM/DD/YY') from DUAL;

TO_DATE('
---------
22-MAR-04
```

Suppose you need to know the day of the week of March 22. The **TO_CHAR** function will not work, even with the literal string in the proper format, because **TO_CHAR** requires a date (see its format at the very beginning of the "TO_DATE and TO_CHAR Formatting" section):

```
select TO_CHAR('22-FEB-02','Day') from DUAL;

ERROR at line 1:
ORA-01722: invalid number
```

The message is somewhat misleading, but the point is that the query fails. You could use the **EXTRACT** function, but this query will also work if you first convert the string to a date. Do this by combining the two functions **TO_CHAR** and **TO_DATE**:

```
select TO_CHAR( TO_DATE('22-MAR-04'), 'Day') from DUAL;

TO_CHAR(T
---------
Monday
```

TO_DATE can also accept numbers, without single quotation marks, instead of strings, as long as they are formatted consistently. Here is an example:

```
select TO_DATE(11051946,'MMDDYYYY') from DUAL;

TO_DATE(1
---------
05-NOV-46
```

The punctuation in the *format* is ignored, but the number must follow the order of the format controls. The number itself must not have punctuation.

How complex can the format control be in **TO_DATE**? Suppose you simply reversed the **TO_CHAR select** statement shown earlier, put its result into the **string** portion of **TO_DATE**, and kept its format the same as **TO_CHAR**:

```
select TO_DATE('Baby Girl on the Twentieth of May, 1949,
       at 3:27 A.M.',
       '"Baby Girl on the" Ddspth "of" fmMonth, YYYY,
       "at" HH:MI P.M.')
       AS Formatted
   from BIRTHDAY
```

```
where FirstName = 'VICTORIA';

ERROR at line 1:
ORA-01858: a non-numeric character was found
 where a numeric was expected
```

This failed. As it turns out, only a limited number of the format controls can be used. Here are the restrictions on *format* that govern **TO_DATE**:

- No literal strings are allowed, such as "Baby Girl on the".
- Days cannot be spelled out. They must be numbers.
- Punctuation is permitted.
- **fm** is not necessary. If used, it is ignored.
- If Month is used, the month in the string must be spelled out. If Mon is used, the month must be a three-letter abbreviation. Uppercase and lowercase are ignored.

Dates in where Clauses

Early in this chapter, you saw an example of date arithmetic used in a **where** clause:

```
select Holiday, ActualDate, CelebratedDate
  from Holiday
 where CelebratedDate - ActualDate != 0;

HOLIDAY                  ACTUALDAT CELEBRATE
------------------------ --------- ---------
MARTIN LUTHER KING, JR.  15-JAN-04 19-JAN-04
LINCOLNS BIRTHDAY        12-FEB-04 16-FEB-04
WASHINGTONS BIRTHDAY     22-FEB-04 16-FEB-04
MEMORIAL DAY             30-MAY-04 31-MAY-04
COLUMBUS DAY             12-OCT-04 11-OCT-04
```

Dates can be used with other Oracle logical operators as well, with some warnings and restrictions. The **BETWEEN** operator will do date arithmetic if the column preceding it is a date, even if the test dates are literal strings:

```
select Holiday, CelebratedDate
  from HOLIDAY
 where CelebratedDate BETWEEN
       '01-JAN-04' and '22-FEB-04';

HOLIDAY                  CELEBRATE
------------------------ ---------
NEW YEARS DAY            01-JAN-04
MARTIN LUTHER KING, JR.  19-JAN-04
LINCOLNS BIRTHDAY        16-FEB-04
```

```
WASHINGTONS BIRTHDAY        16-FEB-04
FAST DAY, NEW HAMPSHIRE     22-FEB-04
```

The logical operator **IN** works as well with literal strings:

```
select Holiday, CelebratedDate
   from HOLIDAY
 where CelebratedDate IN ('01-JAN-04', '22-FEB-04');

HOLIDAY                     CELEBRATE
------------------------    ---------
NEW YEARS DAY               01-JAN-04
FAST DAY, NEW HAMPSHIRE     22-FEB-04
```

If you cannot rely on 2000 being the default century value, you can use the **TO_DATE** function to specify the century values for the dates within the **IN** operator:

```
select Holiday, CelebratedDate
   from HOLIDAY
 where CelebratedDate IN
        (TO_DATE('01-JAN-2004','DD-MON-YYYY'),
         TO_DATE('22-FEB-2004','DD-MON-YYYY'));

HOLIDAY                     CELEBRATE
------------------------    ---------
NEW YEARS DAY               01-JAN-04
FAST DAY, NEW HAMPSHIRE     22-FEB-04
```

LEAST and **GREATEST** do not work, because they assume the literal strings are *strings,* not *dates.* Refer to the sidebar "A Warning about GREATEST and LEAST," earlier in this chapter, for an explanation of **LEAST** and **GREATEST**.

Dealing with Multiple Centuries

If your applications use only two-digit values for years, you may encounter problems related to the year 2000. If you only specify two digits of a year (such as '98' for '1998'), you are relying on the database to specify the century value (the '19') when the record is inserted. If you are putting in dates prior to the year 2000 (for example, birth dates), you may encounter problems with the century values assigned to your data.

In Oracle, all date values have century values. If you only specify the last two digits of the year value, Oracle will, by default, use the current century as the century value when it inserts a record. For example, the following listing shows an **insert** into the BIRTHDAY table:

```
insert into BIRTHDAY
(FirstName, LastName, BirthDate)
values
('ALICIA', 'ANN', '21-NOV-39');
```

In the preceding example, no century value is specified for the BirthDate column, and no age is specified. If you use the **TO_CHAR** function on the BirthDate column, you can see the full birth date Oracle inserted—it defaulted to the current century:

```
select TO_CHAR(BirthDate,'DD-MON-YYYY') AS Bday
   from BIRTHDAY
 where FirstName = 'ALICIA'
   and LastName = 'ANN';

BDAY
-----------
21-NOV-2039
```

For dates that can properly default to the current century, using the default does not present a problem. Alicia's BirthDate value is 21-NOV-2039—wrong by 100 years! Wherever you insert date values, you should specify the full four-digit year value.

Using the EXTRACT Function

You can use the **EXTRACT** function in place of the **TO_CHAR** function when you are selecting portions of date values—such as just the month or day from a date. The **EXTRACT** function's syntax is

```
EXTRACT
( { { YEAR
    | MONTH
    | DAY
    | HOUR
    | MINUTE
    | SECOND
    }
  | { TIMEZONE_HOUR
    | TIMEZONE_MINUTE
    }
  | { TIMEZONE_REGION
    | TIMEZONE_ABBR
    }
  }
  FROM { datetime_value_expression | interval_value_expression }
)
```

For instance, to extract the month in which Victoria was born, you could execute the following:

```
select BirthDate,
       EXTRACT(Month from BirthDate) AS Month
   from BIRTHDAY
 where FirstName = 'VICTORIA';
```

```
BIRTHDATE       MONTH
---------     ----------
20-MAY-49          5
```

For more complex extractions, you will need to use **TO_CHAR**, but **EXTRACT** can support many common date value queries.

Using the TIMESTAMP Datatypes

The DATE datatype stores the date and time to the second; TIMESTAMP datatypes store the date to the billionth of a second.

The base datatype for timestamp values is called TIMESTAMP. Like DATE, it stores the year, month, day, hour, minute, and second. It also includes a *fractional_seconds_precision* setting that determines the number of digits in the fractional part of the seconds field. By default, the precision is 6; valid values are 0 to 9.

In the following example, a table is created with the TIMESTAMP datatype, and it's populated via the **SYSTIMESTAMP** function:

```
create table X1
(tscol  TIMESTAMP(5));

insert into X1 values (SYSTIMESTAMP);
```

Now select that value from the table:

```
select * from X1;

TSCOL
---------------------------------
23-MAR-04 05.27.32.71800 PM
```

The output shows the second the row was inserted, down to five places after the decimal.

The **SYSTIMESTAMP** function returns data in the form of the TIMESTAMP (*fractional_seconds_precision*) WITH TIME ZONE datatype. The exact same row, inserted into a column that is defined with the TIMESTAMP(5) WITH TIME ZONE datatype, returns the data in the following format:

```
create table X2
(tscol  TIMESTAMP(5) WITH TIME ZONE);

insert into X2 values (SYSTIMESTAMP);

select * from X2;

TSCOL
---------------------------------
23-MAR-04 05.29.11.64000 PM -05:00
```

In this output, the time zone is displayed as an offset of Coordinated Universal Time (UTC). The database is presently set to a time zone that is five hours prior to UTC.

Oracle also supports the TIMESTAMP (*fractional_seconds_ precision*) WITH LOCAL TIME ZONE datatype, which is similar to TIMESTAMP WITH TIME ZONE. It differs in that the data is normalized to the database time zone when it is stored in the database, and during retrievals the users see data in the session time zone.

In addition to the TIMESTAMP datatypes, Oracle also supports two interval datatypes: INTERVAL YEAR (*year_precision*) TO MONTH and INTERVAL DAY (*day_precision*) TO SECOND (*fractional_seconds_precision*). INTERVAL YEAR TO MONTH stores a period of time in years and months, where the precision is the number of digits in the YEAR field (ranging from 0 to 9, with the default being 2). The INTERVAL DAY TO SECOND datatype stores a period of time in days, hours, minutes, and seconds; the precision for the day and seconds accepts values from 0 to 9. The INTERVAL datatypes are mostly used during statistical analysis and data mining.

CHAPTER
11

Conversion and Transformation Functions

his chapter looks at functions that convert, or *transform,* one datatype into another. Four major datatypes and their associated functions have been covered thus far:

- CHAR (fixed-length character strings) and VARCHAR2 (variable-length character strings) include any letter of the alphabet, any number, and any of the symbols on the keyboard. Character literals must be enclosed in single quotation marks:

 `'Sault Ste. Marie!'`

- NUMBER includes just the digits 0 through 9, a decimal point, and a minus sign, if necessary. NUMBER literals are not enclosed in quotation marks:

 `-246.320`

- DATE is a special type that includes information about the date, time, and time zone. It has a default format of DD-MON-YY, but can be displayed in many ways using the **TO_CHAR** function, as you saw in Chapter 10. DATE literals must be enclosed in single quotation marks:

 `'26-AUG-81'`

Each of these datatypes has a group of functions designed especially to manipulate data of its own type, as shown in Chapters 7, 8, 9, and 10. String functions are used with character columns or literals, arithmetic functions are used with NUMBER columns or literals, and DATE functions are used with DATE columns or literals. Most group and miscellaneous functions work with any of these types. Some of these functions change the object they affect (whether CHAR, VARCHAR2, NUMBER, or DATE), whereas others report information about the object.

In one sense, most of the functions studied so far have been *transformation functions,* meaning they changed their objects. However, the functions covered in this chapter change their objects in an unusual way: They transform them from one datatype into another, or they make a profound transformation of the data in them. Table 11-1 describes these functions.

Function Name	Definition
ASCIISTR	Translates a string in any character set and returns an ASCII string in the database character set.
BIN_TO_NUM	Converts a binary value to its numerical equivalent.
CAST	Casts one built-in or collection type to another; commonly used with nested tables and varying arrays.
CHARTOROWID	Changes a character string to act like an internal Oracle row identifier, or RowID.

TABLE 11-1. *Conversion Functions*

Function Name	Definition
COMPOSE	Translates a string in any datatype to a Unicode string in its fully normalized form in the same character set as the input.
CONVERT	Converts a character string from one national language character set to another.
DECODE	Decodes a CHAR, VARCHAR2, or NUMBER into any of several different character strings or NUMBERs, based on value. This is a very powerful *if-then-else* function. Chapter 16 is devoted to DECODE.
DECOMPOSE	Translates a string in any datatype to a Unicode string after canonical decomposition in the same character set as the input.
HEXTORAW	Changes a character string of hexadecimal numbers into binary.
NUMTODSINTERVAL	Converts a number to an INTERVAL DAY TO SECOND literal.
NUMTOYMINTERVAL	Converts a number to an INTERVAL YEAR TO MONTH literal.
RAWTOHEX	Changes a string of binary numbers to a character string of hex numbers.
RAWTONHEX	Converts raw to an NVARCHAR2 character value containing its hexadecimal equivalent.
ROWIDTOCHAR	Changes an internal Oracle row identifier, or RowID, to a character string.
ROWIDTONCHAR	Converts a RowID value to an NVARCHAR2 datatype.
SCN_TO_TIMESTAMP	Converts a system change number to an approximate timestamp.
TIMESTAMP_TO_SCN	Converts a timestamp to an approximate system change number.
TO_BINARY_DOUBLE	Returns a double-precision floating-point number.
TO_BINARY_FLOAT	Returns a single-precision floating-point number.
TO_CHAR	Converts a NUMBER or DATE to a character string.
TO_CLOB	Converts NCLOB values in a LOB column or other character strings to CLOB values.
TO_DATE	Converts a NUMBER, CHAR, or VARCHAR2 to a DATE (an Oracle datatype).
TO_DSINTERVAL	Converts a character string of the datatype CHAR, VARCHAR2, NCHAR, or NVARCHAR2 to an INTERVAL DAY TO SECOND type.
TO_LOB	Converts a LONG to a LOB as part of an **insert as select**.
TO_MULTI_BYTE	Converts the single-byte characters in a character string to multibyte characters.
TO_NCHAR	Converts a character string, NUMBER, or DATE from the database character set to the national character set.
TO_NCLOB	Converts CLOB values in a LOB column or other character strings to NCLOB values.
TO_NUMBER	Converts a CHAR or VARCHAR2 to a number.
TO_SINGLE_BYTE	Converts the multibyte characters in a CHAR or VARCHAR2 to single bytes.

TABLE 11-1. *Conversion Functions* (continued)

Function Name	Definition
TO_TIMESTAMP	Converts a character string to a value of the TIMESTAMP datatype.
TO_TIMESTAMP_TZ	Converts a character string to a value of the TIMESTAMP WITH TIME ZONE datatype.
TO_YMINTERVAL	Converts a character string of the datatype CHAR, VARCHAR2, NCHAR, or NVARCHAR2 to an INTERVAL YEAR TO MONTH type.
TRANSLATE	Translates characters in a string into different characters.
UNISTR	Converts a string into Unicode in the database Unicode character set.

TABLE 11-1. *Conversion Functions* (continued)

Elementary Conversion Functions

Although Table 11-1 lists many conversion functions, the most commonly used are the following three, whose purpose is to convert one datatype into another:

- **TO_CHAR** Transforms a DATE or NUMBER into a character string.

- **TO_DATE** Transforms a NUMBER, CHAR, or VARCHAR2 into a DATE. For working with timestamps, you can use **TO_TIMESTAMP** or **TO_TIMESTAMP_TZ**.

- **TO_NUMBER** Transforms a CHAR or VARCHAR2 into a NUMBER.

Why are these transformations important? **TO_DATE** is obviously necessary to accomplish date arithmetic. **TO_CHAR** allows you to manipulate a number as if it were a string, using string functions. **TO_NUMBER** allows you to use a string that happens to contain only numbers as if it were a number; by using it, you can add, subtract, multiply, divide, and so on.

This means that if you stored a nine-digit ZIP code as a number, you could transform it into a string and then use **SUBSTR** and concatenation to add a dash (such as when printing addresses on envelopes):

```
select SUBSTR(TO_CHAR(948033515),1,5)||'-'||
       SUBSTR(TO_CHAR(948033515),6)  AS Zip
  from DUAL;

ZIP
-----------------------------------------
94803-3515
```

Here, the **TO_CHAR** function transforms the pure number 948033515 (notice that it has no single quotation marks around it, as a CHAR or VARCHAR2 string must) into a character string. **SUBSTR** then clips out positions 1 to 5 of this string, producing 94803. A dash is concatenated on the right end of this string, and then another **TO_CHAR** creates another string, which another **SUBSTR** clips out from position 6 to the end. The second string, 3515, is concatenated after the dash. The whole rebuilt string is relabeled Zip, and Oracle displays it: 94803-3515. This **TO_CHAR** function lets you use string-manipulation functions on numbers (and dates) as if they were actually strings. Handy? Yes. But watch this:

```
select SUBSTR(948033515,1,5)||'-'||
       SUBSTR(948033515,6) AS Zip
  from DUAL;

ZIP
-------------------------------------------
94803-3515
```

This shouldn't work, because 948033515 is a NUMBER, not a character string. Yet, the string function **SUBSTR** clearly worked anyway. Would it work with an actual NUMBER database column? Here's a table with Zip as a NUMBER:

```
describe ADDRESS
```

Name	Null?	Type
LASTNAME		VARCHAR2(25)
FIRSTNAME		VARCHAR2(25)
STREET		VARCHAR2(50)
CITY		VARCHAR2(25)
STATE		CHAR(2)
ZIP		NUMBER
PHONE		VARCHAR2(12)
EXT		VARCHAR2(5)

Select just the ZIP code for all the Marys in the table:

```
select SUBSTR(Zip,1,5)||'-'||
       SUBSTR(Zip,6)  AS Zip
  from ADDRESS
 where FirstName = 'MARY';

ZIP
-------------------------------------------
94941-4302
60126-2460
```

SUBSTR works here just as well as it does with strings, even though Zip is a NUMBER column from the ADDRESS table. Will other string functions also work?

```
select Zip, RTRIM(Zip,20)
  from ADDRESS
 where FirstName = 'MARY';

       ZIP RTRIM(ZIP,20)
---------- -------------------------------------
 949414302 9494143
 601262460 60126246
```

The column on the left demonstrates that Zip is a NUMBER; it is even right-justified, as numbers are by default. But the **RTRIM** column is left-justified, just as strings are, and it has removed zeros

and twos from the right side of the ZIP codes. Something else is peculiar here. Recall from Chapter 7 the format for **RTRIM**, shown here:

```
RTRIM(string [,'set'])
```

The *set* to be removed from the string is enclosed within single quotation marks, yet in this next example, there are no quotation marks:

```
RTRIM(Zip,20)
```

So what is going on?

Automatic Conversion of Datatypes

Oracle is automatically converting these numbers, both Zip and 20, into strings, almost as if they both had **TO_CHAR** functions in front of them. In fact, with a few clear exceptions, Oracle will automatically transform any datatype into any other datatype, based on the function that is going to affect it. If it's a string function, Oracle will convert a NUMBER or a DATE instantly into a string, and the string function will work. If it's a DATE function and the column or literal is a string in the format DD-MON-YY, Oracle will convert it into a DATE. If the function is arithmetic and the column or literal is a character string, Oracle will convert it into a NUMBER and do the calculation.

Will this always work? No. For Oracle to automatically convert one datatype into another, the first datatype must already "look" like the datatype it is being converted to. The basic guidelines are as follows:

- Any NUMBER or DATE can be converted to a character string. Any string function can be used on a NUMBER or DATE column. Literal NUMBERs do not have to be enclosed in single quotation marks when used in a string function; literal DATEs do.

- A CHAR or VARCHAR2 value will be converted to a NUMBER if it contains only NUMBERs, a decimal point, or a minus sign on the left.

- A CHAR or VARCHAR2 value will be converted to a DATE only if it is in the default date format (usually DD-MON-YY). This is true for all functions except **GREATEST** and **LEAST**, which will treat the value as a string, and it's true for **BETWEEN** only if the column to the left after the word **BETWEEN** is a DATE. Otherwise, **TO_DATE** must be used, with the proper format.

These guidelines may be confusing, so favor the use of **TO_DATE** and other conversion functions to make sure the values are treated properly. The following examples should help to clarify the guidelines. The following are the effects of several randomly chosen string functions on NUMBERs and DATEs:

```
select INITCAP(LOWER(SysDate)) from DUAL;

INITCAP(LOWER(SYSDATE))
-----------------------
22-Mar-04
```

Note that the **INITCAP** function put the first letter of "mar" into uppercase even though "mar" was buried in the middle of the string "22-mar-04." This is a feature of **INITCAP** that is not confined to dates, although it is illustrated here for the first time. It works because the following works:

```
select INITCAP('this-is_a.test,of:punctuation;for+initcap')
   from DUAL;

INITCAP('THIS-IS_A.TEST,OF:PUNCTUATION;FO
-----------------------------------------
This-Is_A.Test,Of:Punctuation;For+Initcap
```

INITCAP puts the first letter of every word into uppercase. It determines the beginning of a word based on its being preceded by any character other than a letter. You can also cut and paste dates using string functions, just as if they were strings:

```
select SUBSTR(SysDate,4,3) from DUAL;

SUB
---
MAR
```

NOTE
*You can also use the **TO_CHAR** or **EXTRACT** function to return the month value from a date.*

Here, a DATE is left-padded with 9s for a total length of 20:

```
select LPAD(SysDate,20,'9') from DUAL;

LPAD(SYSDATE,20,'9')
--------------------
9999999999922-MAR-04
```

LPAD, or any other string function, also can be used on NUMBERs, whether literal (as shown here) or as a column:

```
select LPAD(9,20,0) from DUAL;

LPAD(9,20,0)
--------------------
00000000000000000009
```

These examples show how string functions treat both NUMBERs and DATEs as if they were character strings. The result of the function (what you see displayed) is itself a character string.

In this next example, a string (note the single quotation marks) is treated as a NUMBER by the NUMBER function **FLOOR**:

```
select FLOOR('-323.78') from DUAL;

FLOOR('-323.78')
----------------
            -324
```

Here, two literal character strings are converted to DATEs for the DATE function **MONTHS_BETWEEN**. This works only because the literal strings are in the default date format DD-MON-YY:

```
select MONTHS_BETWEEN('16-MAY-04','01-NOV-04') from DUAL;

MONTHS_BETWEEN('16-MAY-02','01-NOV-02')
---------------------------------------
                             -5.516129
```

One of the guidelines says that a DATE will not be converted to a NUMBER. Yet, here is an example of addition and subtraction with a DATE. Does this violate the guideline?

```
select SysDate, SysDate + 1, SysDate - 1 from DUAL;

SYSDATE     SYSDATE+1 SYSDATE-1
---------   --------- ---------
22-MAR-04 23-MAR-04 21-MAR-04
```

It does not, because the addition and subtraction is date arithmetic, not regular arithmetic. Date arithmetic (covered in Chapter 10) works only with addition and subtraction, and only with DATEs. Most functions will automatically convert a character string in default date format into a DATE. An exception is this attempt at date addition with a literal:

```
select '22-MAR-04' + 1 from DUAL;

ERROR: ORA-01722: invalid number
```

Date arithmetic, even with actual DATE datatypes, works only with addition and subtraction. Any other arithmetic function attempted with a date will fail. Dates are not converted to numbers, as this attempt to divide a date by 2 illustrates:

```
select SysDate / 2 from DUAL;
           *
ERROR at line 1:
ORA-00932: inconsistent datatypes: expected NUMBER got DATE
```

Finally, a NUMBER will never be automatically converted to a DATE, because a pure number cannot be in the default format for a DATE, which is DD-MON-YY:

```
select NEXT_DAY(032602,'FRIDAY') from DUAL;
                  *
ERROR at line 1:
ORA-00932: inconsistent data types: expected DATE got NUMBER
```

To use a NUMBER in a DATE function, **TO_DATE** is required.

A Warning About Automatic Conversion

The issue of whether it is a good practice to allow SQL to do automatic conversion of datatypes has arguments on either side. On one hand, this practice considerably simplifies and reduces the functions necessary to make a **select** statement work. On the other hand, if your assumption about what will be in the column is wrong (for example, you assume a particular character column will always have a number in it, meaning you can use it in a calculation), then, at some point, a query will stop working, Oracle will produce an error, and time will have to be spent trying to find the problem. Further, another person reading your **select** statement may be confused by what appear to be inappropriate functions at work on characters or numbers. Using **TO_NUMBER** makes it clear that a numeric value is always expected, even if the column uses the VARCHAR2 datatype.

A simple rule of thumb might be that it is best to use functions where the risk is low, such as string-manipulation functions on numbers, rather than arithmetic functions on strings. For your benefit and that of others using your work, always put a note near the **select** statement signaling the use of automatic type conversion.

Specialized Conversion Functions

As shown earlier in Table 11-1, Oracle includes several specialized conversion functions. If you expect to use SQL*Plus and Oracle simply to produce reports, you probably won't ever need any of these functions. On the other hand, if you plan to use SQL*Plus to **update** the database, if you expect to build Oracle applications, or if you are using National Language Support, this information will eventually prove valuable. The functions can be found, by name, in the Alphabetical Reference section of this book.

NOTE
*The **CAST** function is used with nested tables and varying arrays; see Chapter 34 for details. The **DECODE** function is covered in Chapter 16.*

The conversion functions generally take a single value as input and return a single converted value as output. For example, the **BIN_TO_NUM** function converts binary values to decimal numeric values. Its input value is a list of the digits of a binary value, separated by commas and treated as a single input string:

```
select BIN_TO_NUM(1,1,0,1) from DUAL;

BIN_TO_NUM(1,1,0,1)
-------------------
                 13
```

```
select BIN_TO_NUM(1,1,1,0) from DUAL;

BIN_TO_NUM(1,1,1,0)
-------------------
                 14
```

When working with flashback operations (see Chapters 27 and 28), you can convert system change numbers (SCNs) to timestamp values via the **SCN_TO_TIMESTAMP** function; **TIMESTAMP_TO_SCN** returns the SCN for a particular timestamp.

As of Oracle Database 10g, you can use the **TO_BINARY_DOUBLE** and **TO_BINARY_FLOAT** functions to convert values into double- and single-precision floating-point numbers, respectively.

Transformation Functions

Although in one sense any function that changes its object could be called a transformation function, there are two unusual functions that you can use in many interesting ways to control your output based on your input, instead of simply transforming it. These functions are **TRANSLATE** and **DECODE**.

TRANSLATE

TRANSLATE is a simple function that does an orderly character-by-character substitution in a string. This is the format for **TRANSLATE**:

```
TRANSLATE(string,if,then)
```

TRANSLATE looks at each character in *string* and then checks *if* to see whether that character is there. If it is, it notes the position in *if* where it found the character and then looks at the same position in *then*. **TRANSLATE** substitutes whichever character it finds there for the character in *string*. Normally, the function is written on a single line, like this:

```
select TRANSLATE(7671234,234567890,'BCDEFGHIJ')
   from DUAL;

TRANSLA
-------
GFG1BCD
```

But it might be easier to understand if it's simply broken onto two lines (SQL doesn't care, of course):

```
select TRANSLATE(7671234,234567890,
                         'BCDEFGHIJ')
   from DUAL;

TRANSLA
-------
GFG1BCD
```

When **TRANSLATE** sees a 7 in *string,* it looks for a 7 in *if* and translates it to the character in the same position in *then* (in this case, an uppercase *G*). If the character is not in *if,* it is not translated (observe what **TRANSLATE** did with the 1).

TRANSLATE is technically a string function, but, as you can see, it will do automatic data conversion and work with a mix of strings and numbers. The following is an example of a very simple code cipher, where every letter in the alphabet is shifted one position. Many years ago, spies used such character-substitution methods to encode messages before sending them. The recipient simply reversed the process. Do you remember the smooth-talking computer, HAL, in the movie *2001: A Space Odyssey*? If you **TRANSLATE** HAL's name with a one-character shift in the alphabet, you get this:

```
select TRANSLATE('HAL','ABCDEFGHIJKLMNOPQRSTUVWXYZ',
                  'BCDEFGHIJKLMNOPQRSTUVWXYZA') AS Who
   from DUAL;

WHO
---
IBM
```

See the discussion of the **REGEXP_REPLACE** function in Chapter 8 for details on the string manipulation possible with regular expressions in Oracle Database 10*g.*

DECODE

If **TRANSLATE** is a character-by-character substitution, **DECODE** can be considered a value-by-value substitution. For every value it sees in a field, **DECODE** checks for a match in a series of *if-then* tests. **DECODE** is an incredibly powerful function, with a broad range of areas where it can be useful. Chapter 16 is devoted entirely to the advanced use of **DECODE** and **CASE**.

This is the format for **DECODE**:

```
DECODE(value,if1,then1,if2,then2,if3,then3,. . . ,else)
```

Only three *if-then* combinations are illustrated here, but there is no practical limit. To see how this function works, recall the NEWSPAPER table you saw in earlier chapters:

```
select * from NEWSPAPER;

FEATURE         S    PAGE
--------------- -  ----------
National News   A        1
Sports          D        1
Editorials      A       12
Business        E        1
Weather         C        2
Television      B        7
Births          F        7
Classified      F        8
Modern Life     B        1
Comics          C        4
```

```
Movies           B        4
Bridge           B        2
Obituaries       F        6
Doctor Is In     F        6
```

In the next example, the page number is decoded. If the page number is 1, then the words "Front Page" are substituted. If the page number is anything else, the words "Turn to" are concatenated with the page number. This illustrates that *else* can be a function, a literal, or another column.

```
select Feature, Section,
       DECODE(Page,'1','Front Page','Turn to '||Page)
  from NEWSPAPER;

FEATURE           S DECODE(PAGE,'1','FRONTPAGE','TURNTO'||PAGE)
---------------   - ----------------------------------------------
National News     A Front Page
Sports            D Front Page
Editorials        A Turn to 12
Business          E Front Page
Weather           C Turn to 2
Television        B Turn to 7
Births            F Turn to 7
Classified        F Turn to 8
Modern Life       B Front Page
Comics            C Turn to 4
Movies            B Turn to 4
Bridge            B Turn to 2
Obituaries        F Turn to 6
Doctor Is In      F Turn to 6
```

There are some restrictions on the datatypes in the list of *if* and *then* clauses, which will be covered in Chapter 16.

Review

Most functions in Oracle, although they are intended for a specific datatype such as CHAR, VARCHAR2, NUMBER, or DATE, will actually work with other datatypes as well. They do this by performing an automatic type conversion. With a few logical exceptions, and the hope of future compatibility, they will do this as long as the data to be converted "looks" like the datatype required by the function.

Character functions will convert any NUMBER or DATE. NUMBER functions will convert a CHAR or VARCHAR2 if it contains the digits 0 through 9, a decimal point, or a minus sign on the left. NUMBER functions will not convert DATEs. DATE functions will convert character strings if they are in the format DD-MON-YY. However, they will not convert NUMBERs.

Two functions, **TRANSLATE** and **DECODE**, will fundamentally change the data they act on. **TRANSLATE** will do a character substitution according to any pattern you specify, and **DECODE** will do a value substitution for any pattern you specify.

CHAPTER
12

Grouping Things
Together

p to this point, you've seen how SQL can **select** rows of information from database tables, how the **where** clause can limit the number of rows being returned to only those that meet certain rules that you define, and how the rows returned can be sorted in ascending or descending sequence using **order by**. You've also seen how the values in columns can be modified by character, NUMBER, and DATE functions, and how group functions can tell you something about the whole set of rows.

Beyond the group functions you've seen, there are also two group clauses: **having** and **group by**. These are parallel to the **where** and **order by** clauses, except that they act on groups, not on individual rows. These clauses can provide very powerful insights into your data.

The Use of group by and having

If you want to generate a count of titles on the bookshelf, categorized by the type of book, you would write a query like this:

```
select CategoryName, COUNT(*)
   from BOOKSHELF
 group by CategoryName;
```

and Oracle would respond with the following:

```
CATEGORYNAME             COUNT(*)
-------------------- ----------
ADULTFIC                        6
ADULTNF                        10
ADULTREF                        6
CHILDRENFIC                     5
CHILDRENNF                      1
CHILDRENPIC                     3
```

Notice the mix of a column name, CategoryName, and the group function **COUNT** in the **select** clause. This mix is possible only because CategoryName is referenced in the **group by** clause. If it were not there, the opaque message first encountered in Chapter 9 would have resulted in this:

```
select CategoryName, COUNT(*) from BOOKSHELF;

select CategoryName, COUNT(*) from BOOKSHELF
       *
ERROR at line 1:
ORA-00937: not a single-group group function
```

This result occurs because the group functions, such as **SUM** and **COUNT**, are designed to tell you something about a group of rows, not the individual rows of the table. The error is avoided by using CategoryName in the **group by** clause, which forces the **COUNT** function to count all the rows grouped within each CategoryName.

The **having** clause works very much like a **where** clause, except that its logic is only related to the results of group functions, as opposed to columns or expressions for individual rows, which can still be selected by a **where** clause. Here, the rows in the previous example are further restricted to just those where there are more than five books in a category:

```
select CategoryName, COUNT(*)
   from BOOKSHELF
 group by CategoryName
having COUNT(*) > 5;

CATEGORYNAME            COUNT(*)
--------------------  ----------
ADULTFIC                     6
ADULTNF                     10
ADULTREF                     6
```

To determine the average rating by category, you can use the **AVG** function, as shown in the following listing:

```
select CategoryName, COUNT(*), AVG(Rating)
   from BOOKSHELF
 group by CategoryName;

CATEGORYNAME            COUNT(*) AVG(RATING)
--------------------  ---------- -----------
ADULTFIC                     6  3.66666667
ADULTNF                     10         4.2
ADULTREF                     6  3.16666667
CHILDRENFIC                  5         2.8
CHILDRENNF                   1           3
CHILDRENPIC                  3           1
```

Rating is a character column, defined as a VARCHAR2, but it contains numeric values, so Oracle can perform numeric functions on it (see Chapter 11). What is the overall average rating?

```
select AVG(Rating) from BOOKSHELF;

AVG(RATING)
-----------
 3.32258065
```

In this case, there is no **group by** clause because the entire set of rows in the BOOKSHELF table is treated as the group. Now you can use this result as part of a larger query: What categories have average ratings that are greater than the average rating of all books?

```
select CategoryName, COUNT(*), AVG(Rating)
   from BOOKSHELF
 group by CategoryName
having AVG(Rating) >
      (select AVG(Rating) from BOOKSHELF);

CATEGORYNAME            COUNT(*) AVG(RATING)
--------------------  ---------- -----------
ADULTFIC                     6  3.66666667
ADULTNF                     10         4.2
```

Looking back at the earlier listings, this result is correct—only two of the groups have average rating values greater than the overall average.

Although the results are sorted by the CategoryName column, the purpose of **group by** is not to produce a desired sequence but rather to collect "like" things together. The order they appear in is a byproduct of how **group by** works; **group by** is not meant to be used to change the sorting order.

Adding an order by

The solution for creating an alternative order for display is the addition of an **order by** clause following the **having** clause. For example, you could add the following:

```
order by CategoryName desc
```

This would reverse the order of the list:

```
select CategoryName, COUNT(*)
   from BOOKSHELF
 group by CategoryName
 order by CategoryName desc;
```

```
CATEGORYNAME           COUNT(*)
-------------------- ----------
CHILDRENPIC                   3
CHILDRENNF                    1
CHILDRENFIC                   5
ADULTREF                      6
ADULTNF                      10
ADULTFIC                      6
```

Or, you could use this instead:

```
order by COUNT(*) desc
```

Here's the result:

```
CATEGORYNAME           COUNT(*)
-------------------- ----------
ADULTNF                      10
ADULTFIC                      6
ADULTREF                      6
CHILDRENFIC                   5
CHILDRENPIC                   3
CHILDRENNF                    1
```

Although you can use the column alias as part of the **order by** clause, you can't use it as part of the **having** clause. Giving **COUNT**(*) an alias of "Counter" and attempting to use **having Counter > 1** as a clause in this query will result in an "invalid column name" error:

```
select CategoryName, COUNT(*) as Counter
   from BOOKSHELF
```

```
  group by CategoryName
having Counter > 1
 order by COUNT(*) desc;
```

```
having Counter > 1
       *
ERROR at line 4:
ORA-00904: "COUNTER": invalid identifier
```

Order of Execution

The previous query has quite a collection of competing clauses! Here are the rules Oracle uses to execute each of them, and the order in which execution takes place:

1. Choose rows based on the **where** clause.

2. Group those rows together based on the **group by** clause.

3. Calculate the results of the group functions for each group.

4. Choose and eliminate groups based on the **having** clause.

5. Order the groups based on the results of the group functions in the **order by** clause. The **order by** clause must use either a group function or a column specified in the **group by** clause.

The order of execution is important because it has a direct impact on the performance of your queries. In general, the more records that can be eliminated via **where** clauses, the faster the query will execute. This performance benefit is due to the reduction in the number of rows that must be processed during the **group by** operation.

If a query is written to use a **having** clause to eliminate groups, you should check to see if the **having** condition can be rewritten as a **where** clause. In many cases, this rewrite won't be possible. It is usually only available when the **having** clause is used to eliminate groups based on the grouping columns.

For example, suppose you have this query:

```
select CategoryName, COUNT(*), AVG(Rating)
   from BOOKSHELF
 where Rating > 1
 group by CategoryName
having CategoryName like 'A%'
 order by COUNT(*) desc;
```

```
CATEGORYNAME          COUNT(*) AVG(RATING)
-------------------- ---------- -----------
ADULTNF                    10          4.2
ADULTFIC                    6   3.66666667
ADULTREF                    6   3.16666667
```

The order of execution would be as follows:

1. Eliminate rows based on

   ```
   where Rating > 1
   ```

2. Group the remaining rows based on

   ```
   group by CategoryName
   ```

3. For each CategoryName, calculate the

   ```
   COUNT(*)
   ```

4. Eliminate groups based on

   ```
   having CategoryName like 'A%'
   ```

5. Order the remaining groups.

This query will run faster if the *groups* eliminated in Step 4 can be eliminated as *rows* in Step 1. If they are eliminated at Step 1, fewer rows will be grouped (Step 2), fewer calculations will be performed (Step 3), and no groups will be eliminated (Step 4). Thus, each of these steps in the execution will run faster.

Because the **having** condition in this example is not based on a calculated column, it is easily changed into a **where** condition:

```
select CategoryName, COUNT(*), AVG(Rating)
  from BOOKSHELF
 where Rating > 1
   and CategoryName like 'A%'
 group by CategoryName
 order by COUNT(*) desc;
```

In the modified version, fewer rows will be grouped, resulting in a performance savings. As the number of rows in your tables increases, the performance savings from early row elimination can grow dramatically.

This may seem like a trivial tuning example because the table has few rows in it. But even such a small query can have a significant impact in a production application. There are many examples of production applications whose performance is severely impacted by high volumes of executions of seemingly small queries. When those small queries are executed thousands or millions of times per day, they become the most resource-intensive queries in the database. When planning the SQL access paths for your application, tune even the small queries.

Views of Groups

In Chapter 5, a view called INVASION, which joined together the WEATHER and LOCATION tables, was created for the oracle at Delphi. This view appeared to be a table in its own right, with columns and rows, but each of its rows contained columns that actually came from two separate tables.

The same process of creating a view can be used with groups. The difference is that each row will contain information about a group of rows—a kind of subtotal table. For example, consider this group query:

```
select CategoryName, COUNT(*)
   from BOOKSHELF
 group by CategoryName;
```

You can create a view based on this query, and you can then query the view:

```
create or replace view CATEGORY_COUNT as
select CategoryName, COUNT(*) AS Counter
   from BOOKSHELF
 group by CategoryName;

desc CATEGORY_COUNT
```

```
Name                                    Null?    Type
--------------------------------------  -------- -----------
CATEGORYNAME                                     VARCHAR2(20)
COUNTER                                          NUMBER
```

```
select * from CATEGORY_COUNT;
```

```
CATEGORYNAME          COUNTER
-------------------- ----------
ADULTFIC                    6
ADULTNF                    10
ADULTREF                    6
CHILDRENFIC                 5
CHILDRENNF                  1
CHILDRENPIC                 3
```

NOTE
*Because the **COUNT**(*) column is a function, you have to give it a
column alias (in this case, Counter) when using the query as the basis
for a view.*

Renaming Columns with Aliases

Notice the name Counter in the **select** clause. The **AS Counter** clause *renames* the column it
follows. The new names are called *aliases,* because they are used to disguise the real names of
the underlying columns (which are complicated because they have functions).

When you query the view, you can (and must) now use the new column names:

```
select CategoryName, Counter from CATEGORY_COUNT;
```

"Counter" is referred to as a *column alias*—another name to use when referring to a column. In the
description of the view, and in the query, there is no evidence of the grouping function performed—
just the Counter column name. It is as if the view CATEGORY_COUNT were a real table with rows
of monthly sums. Why?

Oracle automatically takes a single word, without quotes, and uses it to rename the column the word follows. When it does this, Oracle forces the word—the alias—into uppercase, regardless of how it was typed. You can see evidence of this by comparing the column names in the **create view** and the **describe** commands. When creating a view, *never* put double quotes around your column aliases. Always leave aliases in **create view** statements without quotes. This will cause them to be stored in uppercase, which is required for Oracle to find them. See the sidebar "Aliases in View Creation" for a warning on aliases.

You now have Category counts collected in a view. A total for the entire bookshelf could also be created, using BOOKCOUNT as both the view name and the column alias for **COUNT**(*):

```
create or replace view BOOKCOUNT as
select COUNT(*) BOOKCOUNT
   from BOOKSHELF;

View created.
```

If you query the view, you'll discover it has only one record:

```
select BOOKCOUNT
   from BOOKCOUNT;

BOOKCOUNT
---------
       31
```

As new rows are added and committed to the BOOKSHELF table, the BOOKCOUNT and CATEGORY_COUNT views will reflect the changes to the counts.

The Power of Views of Groups

Now you'll see the real power of a relational database. You've created a view with the count by Category and a second view displaying the count for the entire table. These views can now be *joined* together, just as the tables were in Chapter 5, to reveal information never before apparent. For instance, what percentage of the books are in each category?

Aliases in View Creation

Internally, Oracle works with all column and table names in uppercase. This is how they are stored in its data dictionary, and this is how it always expects them to be. When aliases are typed to create a view, they should always be naked—without quotation marks around them. Putting double quotation marks around an alias can force the column name stored internally by Oracle to be in mixed case. If you do this, Oracle will not be able to find the column when you execute a **select** unless you enclose the column name within quotes during all your queries.

Never use double quotation marks in creating aliases for a view.

```
select CategoryName, Counter, (Counter/BookCount)*100 as Percent
   from CATEGORY_COUNT, BOOKCOUNT
 order by CategoryName;
```

```
CATEGORYNAME              COUNTER    PERCENT
--------------------   ----------  ----------
ADULTFIC                       6  19.3548387
ADULTNF                       10  32.2580645
ADULTREF                       6  19.3548387
CHILDRENFIC                    5  16.1290323
CHILDRENNF                     1  3.22580645
CHILDRENPIC                    3  9.67741935
```

In this query, two views are listed in the **from** clause, but they are not joined in a **where** clause. Why not? In this particular case, no **where** clause is necessary, because one of the views, BOOKCOUNT, will only return one row (as shown in the previous listing). The one row in BOOKCOUNT is joined to each row in CATEGORY_COUNT, yielding one row of output for each row in CATEGORY_COUNT. The same results could have been obtained by directly joining the BOOKSHELF *table* with the BOOKCOUNT *view*, but as you can see, the query is more complicated and difficult to understand—and as the number of groups expands, the query will grow even more cumbersome:

```
select CategoryName, COUNT(*),
    (COUNT(*)/MAX(BookCount))*100 as Percent
  from BOOKSHELF, BOOKCOUNT
 group by CategoryName
 order by CategoryName;
```

Notice the percentage calculation:

```
   (COUNT(*)/MAX(BookCount))*100 as Percent
```

Because this result is part of a grouping function, each of the values must be grouped. Therefore, an initial attempt such as this would fail because BookCount is not grouped:

```
   (COUNT(*)/BookCount)*100 as Percent
```

Because there is only one row in the BOOKCOUNT view, you can perform a **MAX** function on it to return that single row, grouped by itself.

To create queries that compare one grouping of rows with another grouping of rows, at least one of the groupings must be a view or an "inline view" created in the **from** clause of the query. Beyond this technical restriction, however, it is just simpler and easier to understand doing the queries with views. Compare the last two examples, and the difference in clarity is apparent. Views hide complexity.

To use the inline view method, put the view's text within the **from** clause and give its columns aliases there:

```
select CategoryName, Counter, (Counter/BookCount)*100 as Percent
   from CATEGORY_COUNT,
        (select COUNT(*) as BookCount from BOOKSHELF)
 order by CategoryName;
```

In this example, the BOOKCOUNT view has been removed from the **from** clause and replaced by its base query. In that query, the BookCount alias is given to the result of a **COUNT**(*) performed against the BOOKSHELF table. In the main query, that BookCount alias is then used as part of a calculation. Using this coding method, there is no need to create the BOOKCOUNT view. Be careful when working with multiple grouping levels within the same query—creating views commonly helps to simplify the creation and maintenance of the code.

Using order by in Views

From a strictly theoretical perspective, there is no reason to have an **order by** clause stored in a view—you can issue an **order by** clause when you query the view. Oracle supports the **order by** clause within views, as shown here:

```
create view BOOKSHELF_SORTED
as select * from BOOKSHELF
order by Title;
```

Having the data sorted in the view may simplify your application development. For example, if your code steps through a set of records, having those records presorted may make your processing and error checking simpler. In your application development, you will know that the data will always be returned to you in an ordered fashion. The following query selects the Title values, using the RowNum pseudo-column to limit the output to nine records:

```
select Title from BOOKSHELF_SORTED
  where Rownum < 10;

TITLE
---------------------------------------
ANNE OF GREEN GABLES
BOX SOCIALS
CHARLOTTE'S WEB
COMPLETE POEMS OF JOHN KEATS
EITHER/OR
EMMA WHO SAVED MY LIFE
GOOD DOG, CARL
GOSPEL
HARRY POTTER AND THE GOBLET OF FIRE
```

The BOOKSHELF_SORTED view is doing more work than just querying from the BOOKSHELF table—it is performing a sorting operation to return the rows in a particular order. If you do not need the rows returned in that order, you are asking the database to do work that does not benefit your application.

The views also give you more power to use the many character, NUMBER, and DATE datatypes at will, without worrying about things such as months appearing in alphabetical order.

Logic in the having Clause

In the **having** clause, the choice of the group function and the column on which it operates might bear no relation to the columns or group functions in the **select** clause:

```
select CategoryName, COUNT(*),
     (COUNT(*)/MAX(BookCount))*100 as Percent
   from BOOKSHELF, BOOKCOUNT
  group by CategoryName
having Avg(Rating) > 4
  order by CategoryName;

CATEGORYNAME            COUNT(*)     PERCENT
-------------------- ---------- ----------
ADULTNF                       10 32.2580645
```

Here, the **having** clause selected only those categories (the **group by** collected all the rows into groups by CategoryName) with an average rating greater than 4. All other groups are eliminated. For the group that met that criterion, the percentage of the total count was calculated.

The **having** clause is very effective for determining which rows in a table have duplicate values in specific columns. For example, if you are trying to establish a new unique index on a column (or set of columns) in a table, and the index creation fails due to uniqueness problems with the data, you can easily determine which rows caused the problem.

First, select the columns you want to be unique, followed by a **COUNT**(*) column. Group by the columns you want to be unique, and use the **having** clause to return only those groups having **COUNT(*)>1**. The only records returned will be duplicates. The following query shows this check being performed for the AuthorName column of the AUTHOR table:

```
select AuthorName, COUNT(*)
   from AUTHOR
  group by AuthorName
having COUNT(*)>1
  order by AuthorName;

no rows selected
```

Which books have more than one author? Select the titles from BOOKSHELF_AUTHOR for which the group (by Title) has more than one member:

```
column Title format a40

select Title, COUNT(*)
from BOOKSHELF_AUTHOR
group by Title
having COUNT(*)>1;

TITLE                                      COUNT(*)
---------------------------------------- ----------
COMPLETE POEMS OF JOHN KEATS                      2
JOURNALS OF LEWIS AND CLARK                       4
KIERKEGAARD ANTHOLOGY                             2
RUNAWAY BUNNY                                     2
```

Who are those ten authors? You could create a view based on this query, or try it as an inline view:

```
column Title format a40
column AuthorName format a30

select Title, AuthorName
from BOOKSHELF_AUTHOR,
   (select Title as GroupedTitle, COUNT(*) as TitleCounter
      from BOOKSHELF_AUTHOR
    group by Title
    having COUNT(*) > 1)
where Title = GroupedTitle
order by Title, AuthorName;
```

```
TITLE                                      AUTHORNAME
----------------------------------------   ---------------------
COMPLETE POEMS OF JOHN KEATS               JOHN BARNARD
COMPLETE POEMS OF JOHN KEATS               JOHN KEATS
JOURNALS OF LEWIS AND CLARK                BERNARD DE VOTO
JOURNALS OF LEWIS AND CLARK                MERIWETHER LEWIS
JOURNALS OF LEWIS AND CLARK                STEPHEN AMBROSE
JOURNALS OF LEWIS AND CLARK                WILLIAM CLARK
KIERKEGAARD ANTHOLOGY                      ROBERT BRETALL
KIERKEGAARD ANTHOLOGY                      SOREN KIERKEGAARD
RUNAWAY BUNNY                              CLEMENT HURD
RUNAWAY BUNNY                              MARGARET WISE BROWN
```

This query may look complicated (and using a view would make it simpler to read), but it is based on the concepts covered in this chapter: An inline view performs a **group by** function and uses a **having** clause to return only those titles with multiple authors. Those titles are then used as the basis of a query against the BOOKSHELF_AUTHOR table. In a single query, the BOOKSHELF_AUTHOR table is queried for grouped data and individual row data.

Using order by with Columns and Group Functions

The **order by** clause is executed after the **where**, **group by**, and **having** clauses. It can employ group functions, or columns from the **group by**, or a combination. If it uses a group function, that function operates on the groups, and then the **order by** sorts the *results* of the function in order. If the **order by** uses a column from the **group by**, it sorts the rows that are returned based on that column. Group functions and single columns (so long as the column is in the **group by**) can be combined in the **order by**.

In the **order by** clause, you can specify a group function and the column it affects even though they have nothing at all to do with the group functions or columns in the **select**, **group by**, or **having** clause. On the other hand, if you specify a column in the **order by** clause that is not part of a group function, it must be in the **group by** clause. Let's take the last example and modify the **order by** clause:

```
order by TitleCounter desc, Title, AuthorName
```

The titles and authors will now be ordered based on the number of authors (with the greatest number first), then by Title and AuthorName:

```
TITLE                             AUTHORNAME
--------------------------------- ----------------------
JOURNALS OF LEWIS AND CLARK       BERNARD DE VOTO
JOURNALS OF LEWIS AND CLARK       MERIWETHER LEWIS
JOURNALS OF LEWIS AND CLARK       STEPHEN AMBROSE
JOURNALS OF LEWIS AND CLARK       WILLIAM CLARK
COMPLETE POEMS OF JOHN KEATS      JOHN BARNARD
COMPLETE POEMS OF JOHN KEATS      JOHN KEATS
KIERKEGAARD ANTHOLOGY             ROBERT BRETALL
KIERKEGAARD ANTHOLOGY             SOREN KIERKEGAARD
RUNAWAY BUNNY                     CLEMENT HURD
RUNAWAY BUNNY                     MARGARET WISE BROWN
```

Join Columns

As explained in Chapters 4 and 5, joining two tables together requires that they have a relationship defined by a common column. This is also true in joining views, or tables and views. The only exception is when one of the tables or views has just a single row, as the BOOKCOUNT table does. In this case, SQL joins the single row to every row in the other table or view, and no reference to the joining columns needs to be made in the **where** clause of the query.

Any attempt to join two tables that both have more than one row without specifying the joined columns in the **where** clause will produce what's known as a *Cartesian product,* usually a giant result where every row in one table is joined with every row in the other table. A small 80-row table joined to a small 100-row table in this way would produce 8,000 rows in your display, and few of them would be at all meaningful.

More Grouping Possibilities

In addition to the operations shown in this chapter, you can perform complex groupings of rows—creating crosstab reports, following hierarchies within the data, and more. Those groupings, and the related functions and clauses (such as **connect by**, **ROLLUP**, **GROUPING**, and **CUBE**), are described in Chapter 14.

As you work with groupings within your application-development environment, you will generally find that using views makes the writing of complex queries simpler. You can use views to represent logical groupings of rows that are helpful to end users writing reports, while leaving the underlying table structures unchanged. This benefits the users—the data is presented in a format they understand—while allowing you to preserve the integrity of your database design.

CHAPTER
13

When One
Query Depends
upon Another

his chapter and Chapter 14 introduce concepts that are more difficult than we've previously seen. Although many of these concepts are rarely used in the normal course of running queries or producing reports, there will be occasions that call for the techniques taught in these chapters. If they seem too challenging as you study them, read on anyway. The odds are good that by the time you need these methods, you'll be able to use them.

Advanced Subqueries

You've encountered *subqueries*—those **select** statements that are part of a **where** clause in a preceding **select** statement—in earlier chapters. Subqueries also can be used in **insert**, **update**, and **delete** statements. This use will be covered in Chapter 15.

Often, a subquery will provide an alternative approach to a query. For example, suppose you want to know what categories of books have been checked out. The following three-way join provides this information:

```
select distinct C.ParentCategory, C.SubCategory
   from CATEGORY C, BOOKSHELF B, BOOKSHELF_CHECKOUT BC
 where C.CategoryName = B.CategoryName
   and B.Title = BC.Title;

PARENTCA SUBCATEGORY
-------- --------------------
ADULT    FICTION
ADULT    NONFICTION
ADULT    REFERENCE
CHILDREN FICTION
CHILDREN PICTURE BOOK
```

Three tables are joined in the same way that two tables are. The common columns are set equal to each other in the **where** clause, as shown in the preceding listing. To join three tables together, you must join two of them to a third. In this example, the CATEGORY table is joined to the BOOKSHELF table, and the result of that join is joined to the BOOKSHELF_CHECKOUT table. The **distinct** clause tells Oracle to return only the distinct combinations of ParentCategory and SubCategory.

NOTE
Not every table is joined to every other table. In fact, the number of links between the tables is usually one less than the number of tables being joined.

Once the tables are joined, as shown in the first two lines of the **where** clause, you can determine the count of checkouts by parent category and subcategory.

Correlated Subqueries

Is there another way to perform multitable joins? Recall that a **where** clause can contain a subquery **select**. Subquery **select**s can be nested—that is, a **where** clause in a subquery also can contain a **where** clause with a subquery, which can contain a **where** clause with a subquery—on down for more levels than you are ever likely to need. The following shows three **select**s, each connected to another through a **where** clause:

```
select distinct C.ParentCategory, C.SubCategory
   from CATEGORY C
 where CategoryName in
       (select CategoryName from BOOKSHELF
          where Title in
                   (select Title from BOOKSHELF_CHECKOUT)
       );

PARENTCA SUBCATEGORY
-------- --------------------
ADULT    FICTION
ADULT    NONFICTION
ADULT    REFERENCE
CHILDREN FICTION
CHILDREN PICTURE BOOK
```

This query selects any categories containing books that have been checked out. It does this simply by requesting a book whose title is in the BOOKSHELF table and whose checkout record is in the BOOKSHELF_CHECKOUT table. In a subquery, Oracle assumes the columns to be from the first **select** statement, the one that contains the subquery in its **where** clause. This is called a *nested* subquery, because for every CategoryName in the main (outer) query, the CategoryName may be correlated in the second **where** clause.

Said differently, a subquery may refer to a column in a table used in its main query (the query that has the subquery in its **where** clause). Consider the following query:

```
select Title from BOOKSHELF_AUTHOR
  where Title in
       (select Title from BOOKSHELF
          where AuthorName = 'STEPHEN JAY GOULD');

TITLE
-----------------------------------------------------
WONDERFUL LIFE
THE MISMEASURE OF MAN
```

Why does this query work? Taken on its own, the subquery would fail:

```
select Title from BOOKSHELF
   where AuthorName = 'STEPHEN JAY GOULD';
```

```
where AuthorName = 'STEPHEN JAY GOULD'
      *
ERROR at line 2:
ORA-00904: "AUTHORNAME": invalid identifier
```

When executed as a subquery, it is correlated to the parent query—you can reference columns of the first **select** in the subquery. You'll see additional examples of correlated subqueries in this chapter and the chapters that follow.

Coordinating Logical Tests

If a reader is looking for more books in a particular category, what authors should he or she read? Suppose that Fred Fuller, who has checked out two biographies, asks for recommendations. Who else should you recommend?

```
select distinct AuthorName from BOOKSHELF_AUTHOR
  where Title in
    (select Title from BOOKSHELF
      where CategoryName in
        (select distinct CategoryName from BOOKSHELF
          where Title in
            (select Title
               from BOOKSHELF_CHECKOUT bc
             where BC.Name = 'FRED FULLER')));
```

This may look a bit daunting at first, but it's easy to follow if you talk through the code. Start at the innermost query: Get a list of the titles that Fred Fuller has checked out. For those titles, go to the BOOKSHELF table and get a list of the distinct CategoryName values those books are assigned to. Now go to BOOKSHELF a second time and get all the titles in those categories. For those titles, go to the BOOKSHELF_AUTHOR table and generate the list of authors. Here are the results:

```
AUTHORNAME
--------------------
BERNARD DE VOTO
BERYL MARKHAM
DANIEL BOORSTIN
DAVID MCCULLOUGH
DIETRICH BONHOEFFER
G. B. TALBOT
JOHN ALLEN PAULOS
MERIWETHER LEWIS
STEPHEN AMBROSE
STEPHEN JAY GOULD
WILLIAM CLARK
```

Fred is asking for recommendations for new authors, so let's exclude the ones he's already read. To see who Fred has read, simply query the BOOKSHELF_CHECKOUT and BOOKSHELF_AUTHOR tables:

```
select distinct AuthorName
   from BOOKSHELF_AUTHOR ba, BOOKSHELF_CHECKOUT bc
 where ba.Title = bc.Title
   and bc.Name = 'FRED FULLER';
```

```
AUTHORNAME
-----------------------
DAVID MCCULLOUGH
```

Now let's exclude that author from the list we're going to provide. We'll do that by adding an extra **and** clause to the query:

```
select distinct AuthorName from BOOKSHELF_AUTHOR
 where Title in
    (select Title from BOOKSHELF
      where CategoryName in
         (select distinct CategoryName from BOOKSHELF
             where Title in
                (select Title
                    from BOOKSHELF_CHECKOUT bc
                    where BC.Name = 'FRED FULLER')))
     and AuthorName not in
       (select AuthorName
           from BOOKSHELF_AUTHOR ba, BOOKSHELF_CHECKOUT bc
          where ba.Title = bc.Title
            and bc.Name = 'FRED FULLER');
```

```
AUTHORNAME
--------------------
BERNARD DE VOTO
BERYL MARKHAM
DANIEL BOORSTIN
DIETRICH BONHOEFFER
G. B. TALBOT
JOHN ALLEN PAULOS
MERIWETHER LEWIS
STEPHEN AMBROSE
STEPHEN JAY GOULD
WILLIAM CLARK
```

This **and** is a part of the main query, even though it follows the subquery. Also note that some of the tables are queried at multiple points within the script; each of those queries is treated as a separate access of the table.

Using EXISTS and Its Correlated Subquery

EXISTS is a test for existence. It is placed the way **IN** might be placed with a subquery, but it differs in that it is a logical test for the return of rows from a query, not for the rows themselves.

How many authors have written more than one book on the bookshelf?

```
select AuthorName, COUNT(*)
  from BOOKSHELF_AUTHOR
 group by AuthorName
having COUNT(*) > 1;

AUTHORNAME                         COUNT(*)
-----------------------------  ----------
DAVID MCCULLOUGH                          2
DIETRICH BONHOEFFER                       2
E. B. WHITE                               2
SOREN KIERKEGAARD                         2
STEPHEN JAY GOULD                         2
W. P. KINSELLA                            2
WILTON BARNHARDT                          2
```

Attempting to find both AuthorName and Title fails, however, because the **group by** made necessary by the **COUNT**(*) is on the primary key of the BOOKSHELF_AUTHOR table (AuthorName, Title). Because each primary key, by definition, uniquely identifies only one row, the count of titles for that one row can never be greater than 1, so the **having** clause always tests false—it doesn't find any rows:

```
select AuthorName, Title, COUNT(*)
  from BOOKSHELF_AUTHOR
 group by AuthorName, Title
having COUNT(*) > 1;

no rows selected.
```

EXISTS provides a solution. The following subquery asks, for each AuthorName selected in the outer query, whether an AuthorName exists in the BOOKSHELF_AUTHOR table with a count of Titles greater than one. If the answer for a given name is yes, the **EXISTS** test is true, and the outer query **select**s an AuthorName and Title. The author names are correlated by the "BA" alias given to the first BOOKSHELF_AUTHOR table.

```
column AuthorName format a25
column Title format a30

select AuthorName, Title
  from BOOKSHELF_AUTHOR BA
 where EXISTS
        (select *
           from BOOKSHELF_AUTHOR  BA2
          where BA.AuthorName = BA2.AuthorName
          group by BA2.AuthorName
         having COUNT(BA2.Title) > 1)
order by AuthorName, Title;
```

```
AUTHORNAME                 TITLE
------------------------   ------------------------------------
DAVID MCCULLOUGH           JOHN ADAMS
DAVID MCCULLOUGH           TRUMAN
DIETRICH BONHOEFFER        LETTERS AND PAPERS FROM PRISON
DIETRICH BONHOEFFER        THE COST OF DISCIPLESHIP
E. B. WHITE                CHARLOTTE'S WEB
E. B. WHITE                TRUMPET OF THE SWAN
SOREN KIERKEGAARD          EITHER/OR
SOREN KIERKEGAARD          KIERKEGAARD ANTHOLOGY
STEPHEN JAY GOULD          THE MISMEASURE OF MAN
STEPHEN JAY GOULD          WONDERFUL LIFE
W. P. KINSELLA             BOX SOCIALS
W. P. KINSELLA             SHOELESS JOE
WILTON BARNHARDT           EMMA WHO SAVED MY LIFE
WILTON BARNHARDT           GOSPEL
```

The two queries are correlated—note that the subquery references the BA.AuthorName column even though that column is in the outer query, not the subquery. Within the subquery, the BA2 alias is not required but helps make the code easier to maintain.

This same query could have been built using **IN** and a test on the column name. No correlated subquery is necessary here:

```
select AuthorName, Title
   from BOOKSHELF_AUTHOR BA
  where AuthorName in
        (select AuthorName
           from BOOKSHELF_AUTHOR
          group by AuthorName
         having COUNT(Title) > 1)
 order by AuthorName, Title;
```

Outer Joins

The syntax for outer joins has changed considerably in Oracle9*i*. In the following examples, you will see both the Oracle9*i* syntax and the pre-Oracle9*i* syntax. The pre-Oracle9*i* syntax is still supported in Oracle9*i*, but its use should be discontinued. New development should use the new syntax. The new syntax complies with ANSI SQL standards, whereas the old syntax does not. The old syntax is discussed here because many third-party tools continue to use it.

Pre-Oracle9*i* Syntax for Outer Joins

What books were checked out during the time period tracked in the BOOKSHELF_CHECKOUT table?

```
column Title format a40

select distinct Title
   from BOOKSHELF_CHECKOUT;
```

```
TITLE
-------------------------------------------
ANNE OF GREEN GABLES
EITHER/OR
GOOD DOG, CARL
HARRY POTTER AND THE GOBLET OF FIRE
INNUMERACY
JOHN ADAMS
MIDNIGHT MAGIC
MY LEDGER
POLAR EXPRESS
THE DISCOVERERS
THE MISMEASURE OF MAN
THE SHIPPING NEWS
TO KILL A MOCKINGBIRD
TRUMAN
WEST WITH THE NIGHT
WONDERFUL LIFE
```

That's a correct report, but it doesn't show the 0 counts—the books that were not checked out. If you need to see the inventory of all books along with the checkout list, you'll need to join BOOKSHELF_CHECKOUT to BOOKSHELF:

```
select distinct B.Title
   from BOOKSHELF_CHECKOUT BC, BOOKSHELF B
where BC.Title = B.Title;
```

But that query will return the exact same records—the only rows in BOOKSHELF that can meet the join criteria are those that have been checked out. To list the rest of the books, you'll need to use an *outer join*—telling Oracle to return a row even if the join does not produce a match. Pre-Oracle9*i*, the syntax for an outer join uses (+) on the side of the join that will be returning additional rows. In this case, that's BOOKSHELF_CHECKOUT. The following query shows the maximum number of days each book was checked out:

```
select B.Title, MAX(BC.ReturnedDate - BC.CheckoutDate)
        "Most Days Out"
  from BOOKSHELF_CHECKOUT BC, BOOKSHELF B
 where BC.Title (+) = B.Title
 group by B.Title;
```

```
TITLE                                         Most Days Out
-------------------------------------------   -------------
ANNE OF GREEN GABLES                                    18
BOX SOCIALS
CHARLOTTE'S WEB
COMPLETE POEMS OF JOHN KEATS
EITHER/OR                                               8
EMMA WHO SAVED MY LIFE
GOOD DOG, CARL                                          14
```

```
GOSPEL
HARRY POTTER AND THE GOBLET OF FIRE            11
INNUMERACY                                     21
JOHN ADAMS                                     28
JOURNALS OF LEWIS AND CLARK
KIERKEGAARD ANTHOLOGY
LETTERS AND PAPERS FROM PRISON
MIDNIGHT MAGIC                                 14
MY LEDGER                                      16
POLAR EXPRESS                                  14
PREACHING TO HEAD AND HEART
RUNAWAY BUNNY
SHOELESS JOE
THE COST OF DISCIPLESHIP
THE DISCOVERERS                                48
THE GOOD BOOK
THE MISMEASURE OF MAN                          31
THE SHIPPING NEWS                              59
TO KILL A MOCKINGBIRD                          14
TRUMAN                                         19
TRUMPET OF THE SWAN
UNDER THE EYE OF THE CLOCK
WEST WITH THE NIGHT                            48
WONDERFUL LIFE                                 31
```

All the titles in BOOKSHELF are returned, even those that do not meet the join criteria. If you display the BOOKSHELF_CHECKOUT.Title values instead, you will see that those values are **NULL**. Think of (+), which must immediately follow the join column of the shorter table, as saying "add an extra (**NULL**) row of BC.Title anytime there's no match for B.Title."

Current Syntax for Outer Joins

You can use the ANSI SQL standard syntax for outer joins. In the **from** clause, you can tell Oracle to perform a **left**, **right**, or **full outer** join. Let's start with the example from the last section:

```
select B.Title, MAX(BC.ReturnedDate - BC.CheckoutDate)
       "Most Days Out"
  from BOOKSHELF_CHECKOUT BC, BOOKSHELF B
 where BC.Title (+) = B.Title
 group by B.Title;
```

In this case, the BOOKSHELF_CHECKOUT table is having rows returned from it during the join, even if no matches are found. This can be rewritten as follows:

```
select B.Title, MAX(BC.ReturnedDate - BC.CheckoutDate)
       "Most Days Out"
  from BOOKSHELF_CHECKOUT BC right outer join BOOKSHELF B
    on BC.Title = B.Title
 group by B.Title;
```

Note the use of the **on** clause as part of the outer join syntax. Note that

```
from BOOKSHELF_CHECKOUT BC right outer join BOOKSHELF B
```

is equivalent to

```
from BOOKSHELF B left outer join BOOKSHELF_CHECKOUT BC
```

You can replace the **on** clause with a **using** clause along with the name of the column the tables have in common—do not qualify the column name with a table name or table alias.

```
select Title, MAX(BC.ReturnedDate - BC.CheckoutDate)
       "Most Days Out"
  from BOOKSHELF_CHECKOUT BC right outer join BOOKSHELF B
 using (Title)
 group by Title;
```

Note that you cannot specify a table alias for the columns listed in the **using** clause—even in the **group by** and **select** clauses.

As with the old syntax, the side used as the driving table for the outer join makes a difference; doing a **left outer join** will not return all the titles.

```
select B.Title, MAX(BC.ReturnedDate - BC.CheckoutDate)
       "Most Days Out"
  from BOOKSHELF_CHECKOUT BC left outer join BOOKSHELF B
    on BC.Title = B.Title
 group by B.Title;
```

TITLE	Most Days Out
ANNE OF GREEN GABLES	18
EITHER/OR	8
GOOD DOG, CARL	14
HARRY POTTER AND THE GOBLET OF FIRE	11
INNUMERACY	21
JOHN ADAMS	28
MIDNIGHT MAGIC	14
MY LEDGER	16
POLAR EXPRESS	14
THE DISCOVERERS	48
THE MISMEASURE OF MAN	31
THE SHIPPING NEWS	59
TO KILL A MOCKINGBIRD	14
TRUMAN	19
WEST WITH THE NIGHT	48
WONDERFUL LIFE	31

```
16 rows selected.
```

A third option, **full outer join**, returns all rows from both tables. Rows that do not satisfy the **on** condition return **NULL** values. In this example, there are no rows to satisfy this condition, so the query returns the same 31 rows as the **right outer join**.

```
select B.Title, MAX(BC.ReturnedDate - BC.CheckoutDate)
       "Most Days Out"
  from BOOKSHELF_CHECKOUT BC full outer join BOOKSHELF B
    on BC.Title = B.Title
 group by B.Title;
```

Prior to Oracle9*i*, you can generate the **full outer join** results by performing two separate outer joins—using each table as the outer table—and using a **union** operation to combine the results in a single query.

Replacing NOT IN with an Outer Join

The various logical tests that can be done in a **where** clause all have their separate performance measures. A **NOT IN** test may force a full read of the table in the subquery **select**. For example, what books were not checked out? You could write a query like this:

```
select Title
  from BOOKSHELF
 where Title not in
       (select Title from BOOKSHELF_CHECKOUT)
 order by Title;

TITLE
----------------------------------------
BOX SOCIALS
CHARLOTTE'S WEB
COMPLETE POEMS OF JOHN KEATS
EMMA WHO SAVED MY LIFE
GOSPEL
JOURNALS OF LEWIS AND CLARK
KIERKEGAARD ANTHOLOGY
LETTERS AND PAPERS FROM PRISON
PREACHING TO HEAD AND HEART
RUNAWAY BUNNY
SHOELESS JOE
THE COST OF DISCIPLESHIP
THE GOOD BOOK
TRUMPET OF THE SWAN
UNDER THE EYE OF THE CLOCK
```

This is typically the way such a query would be written, even though experienced Oracle users know it may be slow—you may be forcing Oracle to perform a time-intensive full table scan on the BOOKSHELF_CHECKOUT table. The optimizer may internally transform that **NOT IN** to one of the following functionally identical approaches. The following query uses an outer

join and produces the same result. The difference is that this one will be efficient because the
optimizer can take advantage of indexes on the join columns:

```
select distinct B.Title
   from BOOKSHELF_CHECKOUT BC right outer join BOOKSHELF B
     on BC.Title = B.Title
 where BC.Title is NULL
 order by B.Title;

TITLE
----------------------------------------
BOX SOCIALS
CHARLOTTE'S WEB
COMPLETE POEMS OF JOHN KEATS
EMMA WHO SAVED MY LIFE
GOSPEL
JOURNALS OF LEWIS AND CLARK
KIERKEGAARD ANTHOLOGY
LETTERS AND PAPERS FROM PRISON
PREACHING TO HEAD AND HEART
RUNAWAY BUNNY
SHOELESS JOE
THE COST OF DISCIPLESHIP
THE GOOD BOOK
TRUMPET OF THE SWAN
UNDER THE EYE OF THE CLOCK
```

Why does it work and give the same results as the **NOT IN**? The outer join between the two
tables ensures that all rows are available for the test, including those titles for whom no checkout
records are listed in the BOOKSHELF_CHECKOUT table. The line

```
where BC.Title is NULL
```

produces only those titles that don't appear in the BOOKSHELF_CHECKOUT table (and are
therefore returned as **NULL** titles by Oracle). The logic here is obscure, but it works. The best
way to use this technique is simply to follow the model.

Replacing NOT IN with NOT EXISTS

A more common way of performing this type of query requires using the **NOT EXISTS** clause.
NOT EXISTS is typically used to determine which values in one table do not have matching
values in another table. In usage, it is identical to the **EXISTS** clause; in the following example,
you'll see the difference in the query logic and the records returned.

 NOT EXISTS allows you to use a correlated subquery to eliminate from a table all records
that may successfully be joined to another table. For this example, that means you can eliminate
from the BOOKSHELF table all titles that are present in the Title column of the BOOKSHELF_
CHECKOUT table. The following query shows how this is done:

```
select B.Title
   from BOOKSHELF B
```

```
where not exists
      (select 'x' from BOOKSHELF_CHECKOUT BC
       where BC.Title = B.Title)
order by B.Title;

TITLE
----------------------------------------
BOX SOCIALS
CHARLOTTE'S WEB
COMPLETE POEMS OF JOHN KEATS
EMMA WHO SAVED MY LIFE
GOSPEL
JOURNALS OF LEWIS AND CLARK
KIERKEGAARD ANTHOLOGY
LETTERS AND PAPERS FROM PRISON
PREACHING TO HEAD AND HEART
RUNAWAY BUNNY
SHOELESS JOE
THE COST OF DISCIPLESHIP
THE GOOD BOOK
TRUMPET OF THE SWAN
UNDER THE EYE OF THE CLOCK
```

This query shows the books that have not been checked out, as previously shown via the **NOT IN** and outer join methods. How does this query work?

For each record in the BOOKSHELF table, the **NOT EXISTS** subquery is checked. If the join of that record to the BOOKSHELF_CHECKOUT table returns a row, then the results of the subquery **EXIST**. **NOT EXISTS** tells the query to reverse that return code; therefore, any row in BOOKSHELF that can be successfully joined to BOOKSHELF_CHECKOUT will not be returned by the outer query. The only rows left are the BOOKSHELF rows that do not have a matching row in BOOKSHELF_ CHECKOUT.

NOT EXISTS is a very efficient way to perform this type of query, especially when multiple columns are used for the join. Because it uses a join, **NOT EXISTS** is frequently able to use available indexes, whereas **NOT IN** may not be able to use those indexes. The ability to use indexes for this type of query can have a dramatic impact on the query's performance.

Natural and Inner Joins

You can use the **natural** keyword to indicate that a join should be performed based on all columns that have the same name in the two tables being joined. For example, what titles in BOOK_ORDER match those already in BOOKSHELF?

```
select Title
   from BOOK_ORDER natural join BOOKSHELF;

TITLE
----------------------------------------
SHOELESS JOE
GOSPEL
```

The natural join returned the results as if you had typed in the following:

```
select BO.Title
   from BOOK_ORDER BO, BOOKSHELF
  where BO.Title = BOOKSHELF.Title
    and BO.Publisher = BOOKSHELF.Publisher
    and BO.CategoryName = BOOKSHELF.CategoryName;
```

The join was performed based on the columns the two tables had in common.

Support for inner join syntax was introduced in Oracle9*i*. Inner joins are the default—they return the rows the two tables have in common, and are the alternative to outer joins. Note that they support the **on** and **using** clauses, so you can specify your join criteria as shown in the following listing:

```
select BO.Title
   from BOOK_ORDER BO inner join BOOKSHELF B
     on BO.Title = B.Title;

TITLE
-----------------------------------------
GOSPEL
SHOELESS JOE
```

UNION, INTERSECT, and MINUS

Sometimes you need to combine information of a similar type from more than one table. A classic example of this is merging two or more mailing lists prior to a mailing campaign. Depending on the purpose of a particular mailing, you might want to send letters to any of these combinations of people:

- Everyone in both lists (while avoiding sending two letters to someone who happens to be in both lists)

- Only those people who are in both lists

- Those people in only one of the lists

These three combinations of lists are known in Oracle as **UNION**, **INTERSECT**, and **MINUS**. In the following examples, you will see how to use these three clauses to manage the results of multiple queries. The examples will compare the books on hand (BOOKSHELF) with those on order (BOOK_ORDER).

To see all the books, **UNION** the two tables. To reduce the size of the output, only the BOOKSHELF entries from the first half of the alphabet are selected. The following **select** returns 14 rows:

```
select Title from BOOKSHELF
  where Title < 'M%';
```

And this **select** returns six rows:

```
select Title from BOOK_ORDER;
```

If we **UNION** them together, how many rows are returned?

```
select Title from BOOKSHELF
  where Title < 'M%'
union
select Title from BOOK_ORDER;

TITLE
----------------------------------------
ANNE OF GREEN GABLES
BOX SOCIALS
CHARLOTTE'S WEB
COMPLETE POEMS OF JOHN KEATS
EITHER/OR
EMMA WHO SAVED MY LIFE
GALILEO'S DAUGHTER
GOOD DOG, CARL
GOSPEL
HARRY POTTER AND THE GOBLET OF FIRE
INNUMERACY
JOHN ADAMS
JOURNALS OF LEWIS AND CLARK
KIERKEGAARD ANTHOLOGY
LETTERS AND PAPERS FROM PRISON
LONGITUDE
ONCE REMOVED
SHOELESS JOE
SOMETHING SO STRONG

19 rows selected.
```

Where did the extra record go? The problem is that one of the Title values in BOOK_ORDER is already in the BOOKSHELF table. To show the duplicates, use **UNION ALL** instead of **UNION**:

```
select Title from BOOKSHELF
  where Title < 'M%'
union all
select Title from BOOK_ORDER
  order by Title;

TITLE
----------------------------------------
ANNE OF GREEN GABLES
BOX SOCIALS
CHARLOTTE'S WEB
COMPLETE POEMS OF JOHN KEATS
EITHER/OR
EMMA WHO SAVED MY LIFE
```

```
GALILEO'S DAUGHTER
GOOD DOG, CARL
GOSPEL
GOSPEL
HARRY POTTER AND THE GOBLET OF FIRE
INNUMERACY
JOHN ADAMS
JOURNALS OF LEWIS AND CLARK
KIERKEGAARD ANTHOLOGY
LETTERS AND PAPERS FROM PRISON
LONGITUDE
ONCE REMOVED
SHOELESS JOE
SOMETHING SO STRONG

20 rows selected.
```

The duplicate title is now listed twice.

In the following, the two lists of books are intersected. This list contains only those names that are in *both* underlying tables (note that the restriction on Title < 'M%' has been eliminated for this example):

```
select Title from BOOKSHELF
intersect
select Title from BOOK_ORDER
 order by Title;

TITLE
----------------------------------------
GOSPEL
SHOELESS JOE
```

Next, the list of new books (in BOOK_ORDER but not already in BOOKSHELF) is generated, via the **MINUS** operator:

```
select Title from BOOK_ORDER
minus
select Title from BOOKSHELF
 order by Title;

TITLE
----------------------------------------
GALILEO'S DAUGHTER
LONGITUDE
ONCE REMOVED
SOMETHING SO STRONG
```

You could have also used **MINUS** to show which books had not been checked out:

```
select Title from BOOKSHELF
 minus
```

```
select Title from BOOKSHELF_CHECKOUT;

TITLE
------------------------------
BOX SOCIALS
CHARLOTTE'S WEB
COMPLETE POEMS OF JOHN KEATS
EMMA WHO SAVED MY LIFE
GOSPEL
JOURNALS OF LEWIS AND CLARK
KIERKEGAARD ANTHOLOGY
LETTERS AND PAPERS FROM PRISON
PREACHING TO HEAD AND HEART
RUNAWAY BUNNY
SHOELESS JOE
THE COST OF DISCIPLESHIP
THE GOOD BOOK
TRUMPET OF THE SWAN
UNDER THE EYE OF THE CLOCK

15 rows selected.
```

You've just learned the basics of **UNION**, **INTERSECT**, and **MINUS**. Now let's go into detail. In combining two tables, Oracle does not concern itself with column names on either side of the combination operator—that is, Oracle will require that each **select** statement be valid and have valid columns for its own table(s), but the column names in the first **select** statement do not have to be the same as those in the second. Oracle does have these stipulations:

■ The **select** statements must have the same number of columns. If the two tables being queried have differing numbers of columns selected, you can select strings in place of columns to make the two queries' column lists match.

■ The corresponding columns in the **select** statements must be the same datatype (they needn't be the same length).

When ordering the output, Oracle uses the column names from the first **select** statement in giving the query results. Consequently, only column names from the first **select** statement can be used in the **order by**.

You can use combination operators with two or more tables, but when you do, precedence becomes an issue, especially if **INTERSECT** and **MINUS** appear. Use parentheses to force the order you want.

IN Subqueries

Combination operators can be used in subqueries, but you must be careful with precedence. A query of the form

```
select ColA from TABLE_A
  where ColA in
```

```
(select Col1 from TABLE_1)
 union
(select Col2 from TABLE_2);
```

is poorly written and ambiguous. Which will be performed first, the **union** of the two queries as part of a single **where** clause, or the **in** clause based on the query of TABLE_1, followed by a **union** of that result with TABLE_2? Use parentheses to clarify your meaning and enforce the proper precedence of operations. The **in** clause is always given a higher precedence than **union**, unless you use parentheses to alter the way the query is executed. If you want the **union** to have higher precedence, use parentheses:

```
select ColA from TABLE_A
 where ColA in
(select Col1 from TABLE_1
 union
 select Col2 from TABLE_2);
```

Restrictions on UNION, INTERSECT, and MINUS

Queries that use **UNION**, **INTERSECT**, or **MINUS** in their **where** clause must have the same number and type of columns in their **select** list. Note that the equivalent **IN** construction does not have that limitation.

The use of combination operators in place of **IN**, **AND**, and **OR** is a matter of personal style. Most SQL users regard **IN**, **AND**, and **OR** as being clearer and easier to understand than combination operators.

CHAPTER
14

Some Complex
Possibilities

his chapter continues the study of the more complex Oracle functions and features. Of particular interest here is the creation of simple and group queries that can be turned into views, the use of totals in calculations, and the creation of reports showing tree structure. Like the techniques covered in Chapter 13, these techniques are not essential for most reporting needs. If they look overly difficult, don't be frightened off. If you are new to Oracle and the use of its query facilities, it is enough to know that these capabilities exist and you can turn to them if needed.

Complex Groupings

Views can build upon each other. In Chapter 12, you saw the concept of creating a view of a grouping of rows from a table. As shown in Chapter 12, you can easily join views to other views and tables to produce additional views to simplify the tasks of querying and reporting.

As your groupings grow more complex, you will find that views are invaluable to your coding efforts; they simplify the representation of data at different grouping levels within your application. They also make it easier to use the more advanced analytic functions available.

Consider the CATEGORY_COUNT view, first encountered in Chapter 12:

```
create or replace view CATEGORY_COUNT as
select CategoryName, COUNT(*) as Counter
  from BOOKSHELF
 group by CategoryName;

select * from CATEGORY_COUNT;

CATEGORYNAME            COUNTER
-------------------- ----------
ADULTFIC                      6
ADULTNF                      10
ADULTREF                      6
CHILDRENFIC                   5
CHILDRENNF                    1
CHILDRENPIC                   3
```

Let's order the results by their Counter column values, with the highest first:

```
select * from CATEGORY_COUNT
 order by Counter desc;

CATEGORYNAME            COUNTER
-------------------- ----------
ADULTNF                      10
ADULTFIC                      6
ADULTREF                      6
CHILDRENFIC                   5
CHILDRENPIC                   3
CHILDRENNF                    1
```

The output shows the ranking of the categories; the ADULTNF category ranks first in terms of the number of books. Without displaying this list, you could determine where a different Counter value would be in the rankings. To do this, we'll use the **RANK** function. As shown in the following listing, the **RANK** function takes a value as its input and has additional clauses—the **within group** and **order by** clauses—that tell Oracle how to do the ranking. Where would a Counter value of 3 rank?

```
select RANK(3) within group
(order by Counter desc)
  from CATEGORY_COUNT;

RANK(3)WITHINGROUP(ORDERBYCOUNTERDESC)
---------------------------------------
                                      5
```

A Counter value of 3 would be the fifth-highest Counter value. How about a Counter value of 8?

```
select RANK(8) within group
(order by Counter desc)
  from CATEGORY_COUNT;

RANK(8)WITHINGROUP(ORDERBYCOUNTERDESC)
---------------------------------------
                                      2
```

Adding those five books to the category would move it up to second place. From a percentile perspective, what would the ranking for that category be?

```
select PERCENT_RANK(8) within group
(order by Counter desc)
  from CATEGORY_COUNT;

PERCENT_RANK(8)WITHINGROUP(ORDERBYCOUNTERDESC)
----------------------------------------------
                                    .166666667
```

As expected, it would be in the top one-sixth of the categories.

With this technique of using both summary views and analytic functions, you can create views and reports that include weighted average, effective yield, percentage of total, percentage of subtotal, and many similar calculations. There is no effective limit to how many views can be built on top of each other, although even the most complex calculations seldom require more than three or four levels of views built upon views. Note that you can also create inline views in the **from** clause, as shown in Chapter 12.

Using Temporary Tables

You can create a table that exists solely for your session or whose data persists for the duration of your transaction. You can use temporary tables to support specialized rollups or specific application-processing requirements.

To create a temporary table, use the **create global temporary table** command. When you create a temporary table, you can specify whether it should last for the duration of your session (via the **on commit preserve rows** clause) or whether its rows should be deleted when the transaction completes (via the **on commit delete rows** clause).

Unlike a permanent table, a temporary table does not automatically allocate space when it is created. Space will be dynamically allocated for the table as rows are inserted:

```
create global temporary table YEAR_ROLLUP (
    Year    NUMBER(4),
    Month   VARCHAR2(9),
    Counter NUMBER)
on commit preserve rows;
```

You can see the duration of your data in YEAR_ROLLUP by querying the Duration column of USER_TABLES for this table. In this case, the value of Duration is SYS$SESSION. If **on commit delete rows** had been specified instead, the Duration value would be SYS$TRANSACTION.

Now that the YEAR_ROLLUP table exists, you can populate it, such as via an **insert as select** command with a complex query. You can then query the YEAR_ROLLUP table as part of a join with other tables. You may find this method simpler to implement than the methods shown earlier.

Using ROLLUP, GROUPING, and CUBE

How can you perform grouping operations, such as totals, within a single SQL statement rather than via SQL*Plus commands? You can use the **ROLLUP** and **CUBE** functions to enhance the grouping actions performed within your queries. Let's see how this enables us to manage the data related to book returns. The book loaner program has become more popular, so the loan time is now limited to 14 days, with a $0.20 fee per extra day. The following report shows the late charges by person:

```
set headsep !
column Name format a20
column Title format a20 word_wrapped
column DaysOut format 999.99 heading 'Days!Out'
column DaysLate format 999.99 heading 'Days!Late'

break on Name skip 1 on report
compute sum of LateFee on Name
set linesize 80
set pagesize 60
set newpage 0

select Name, Title, ReturnedDate,
       ReturnedDate-CheckoutDate as DaysOut /*Count days*/,
       ReturnedDate-CheckoutDate -14  DaysLate,
       (ReturnedDate-CheckoutDate -14)*0.20  LateFee
  from BOOKSHELF_CHECKOUT
 where ReturnedDate-CheckoutDate > 14
 order by Name, CheckoutDate;
```

NAME	TITLE	RETURNEDD	Days Out	Days Late	LATEFEE
--------------------	--------------------	---------	-------	-------	----------
DORAH TALBOT	MY LEDGER	03-MAR-02	16.00	2.00	.4
*******************					----------
sum					.4
EMILY TALBOT	ANNE OF GREEN GABLES	20-JAN-02	18.00	4.00	.8
*******************					----------
sum					.8
FRED FULLER	JOHN ADAMS	01-MAR-02	28.00	14.00	2.8
	TRUMAN	20-MAR-02	19.00	5.00	1
*******************					----------
sum					3.8
GERHARDT KENTGEN	WONDERFUL LIFE	02-FEB-02	31.00	17.00	3.4
	THE MISMEASURE OF MAN	05-MAR-02	20.00	6.00	1.2
*******************					----------
sum					4.6
JED HOPKINS	INNUMERACY	22-JAN-02	21.00	7.00	1.4
*******************					----------
sum					1.4
PAT LAVAY	THE MISMEASURE OF MAN	12-FEB-02	31.00	17.00	3.4
*******************					----------
sum					3.4
ROLAND BRANDT	THE SHIPPING NEWS	12-MAR-02	59.00	45.00	9
	THE DISCOVERERS	01-MAR-02	48.00	34.00	6.8
	WEST WITH THE NIGHT	01-MAR-02	48.00	34.00	6.8
*******************					----------
sum					22.6

We can eliminate the DaysOut display and focus on the late fees, showing the fees due on each of the return dates:

```
clear compute
clear break
select ReturnedDate, Name,
       SUM((ReturnedDate-CheckoutDate -14)*0.20)   LateFee
  from BOOKSHELF_CHECKOUT
 where ReturnedDate-CheckoutDate > 14
 group by ReturnedDate, Name
 order by ReturnedDate, Name;
```

```
RETURNEDD NAME                      LATEFEE
--------- -------------------- ----------
20-JAN-02 EMILY TALBOT                 .8
22-JAN-02 JED HOPKINS                 1.4
02-FEB-02 GERHARDT KENTGEN            3.4
12-FEB-02 PAT LAVAY                   3.4
01-MAR-02 FRED FULLER                 2.8
01-MAR-02 ROLAND BRANDT              13.6
03-MAR-02 DORAH TALBOT                 .4
05-MAR-02 GERHARDT KENTGEN            1.2
12-MAR-02 ROLAND BRANDT                 9
20-MAR-02 FRED FULLER                   1
```

Then we can modify it further to group the late fees by month:

```
select TO_CHAR(ReturnedDate,'MONTH'), Name,
       SUM((ReturnedDate-CheckoutDate -14)*0.20)  LateFee
  from BOOKSHELF_CHECKOUT
 where ReturnedDate-CheckoutDate > 14
 group by TO_CHAR(ReturnedDate,'MONTH'), Name;
```

```
TO_CHAR(R NAME                      LATEFEE
--------- -------------------- ----------
FEBRUARY  PAT LAVAY                   3.4
FEBRUARY  GERHARDT KENTGEN            3.4
JANUARY   JED HOPKINS                 1.4
JANUARY   EMILY TALBOT                 .8
MARCH     FRED FULLER                 3.8
MARCH     DORAH TALBOT                 .4
MARCH     ROLAND BRANDT              22.6
MARCH     GERHARDT KENTGEN            1.2
```

Instead of simply grouping by Month and Name, you can use the **ROLLUP** function to generate subtotals and totals. In the following example, the **group by** clause is modified to include a **ROLLUP** function call. Notice the additional rows generated at the end of the result set and after each month:

```
select TO_CHAR(ReturnedDate,'MONTH'), Name,
       SUM((ReturnedDate-CheckoutDate -14)*0.20)  LateFee
  from BOOKSHELF_CHECKOUT
 where ReturnedDate-CheckoutDate > 14
 group by ROLLUP(TO_CHAR(ReturnedDate,'MONTH'), Name);
```

```
TO_CHAR(R NAME                      LATEFEE
--------- -------------------- ----------
FEBRUARY  PAT LAVAY                   3.4
FEBRUARY  GERHARDT KENTGEN            3.4
FEBRUARY                              6.8
JANUARY   JED HOPKINS                 1.4
JANUARY   EMILY TALBOT                 .8
JANUARY                               2.2
```

```
MARCH       FRED FULLER              3.8
MARCH       DORAH TALBOT              .4
MARCH       ROLAND BRANDT           22.6
MARCH       GERHARDT KENTGEN         1.2
MARCH                                 28
                                      37
```

For each month, Oracle has calculated the total late fee, and shows it with a **NULL** name value. The output shows two separate charges of $3.40 in February, and a monthly total of $6.80. For the quarter, the total of the late charges is $37.00. You could have calculated these via SQL*Plus commands (see Chapter 6), but this method allows you to generate these sums via a single SQL command regardless of the tool used to query the database.

Let's refine the appearance of the report. You can use the **GROUPING** function to determine whether the row is a total or subtotal (generated by **ROLLUP**) or corresponds to a **NULL** value in the database. In the **select** clause, the Name column will be selected as follows:

```
select DECODE(GROUPING(Name),1, 'All names',Name),
```

The **GROUPING** function will return a value of 1 if the column's value is generated by a **ROLLUP** action. This query uses **DECODE** (discussed at length in Chapter 16) to evaluate the result of the **GROUPING** function. If the **GROUPING** output is 1, the value was generated by the **ROLLUP** function, and Oracle will print the phrase 'All names'; otherwise, it will print the value of the Name column. We will apply similar logic to the Date column. The full query is shown in the following listing, along with its output:

```
select DECODE(GROUPING(TO_CHAR(ReturnedDate,'MONTH')),1,
         'All months',TO_CHAR(ReturnedDate,'MONTH')),
       DECODE(GROUPING(Name),1, 'All names',Name),
       SUM((ReturnedDate-CheckoutDate -14)*0.20)   LateFee
  from BOOKSHELF_CHECKOUT
 where ReturnedDate-CheckoutDate > 14
 group by ROLLUP(TO_CHAR(ReturnedDate, 'MONTH'), Name);

DECODE(GRO DECODE(GROUPING(NAME),1,'    LATEFEE
---------- -------------------------- ----------
FEBRUARY   PAT LAVAY                      3.4
FEBRUARY   GERHARDT KENTGEN               3.4
FEBRUARY   All names                      6.8
JANUARY    JED HOPKINS                    1.4
JANUARY    EMILY TALBOT                    .8
JANUARY    All names                      2.2
MARCH      FRED FULLER                    3.8
MARCH      DORAH TALBOT                    .4
MARCH      ROLAND BRANDT                 22.6
MARCH      GERHARDT KENTGEN               1.2
MARCH      All names                       28
All months All names                       37
```

You can use the **CUBE** function to generate subtotals for all combinations of the values in the **group by** clause. The following query uses the **CUBE** function to generate this information:

```
select DECODE(GROUPING(TO_CHAR(ReturnedDate,'MONTH')),1,
         'All months',TO_CHAR(ReturnedDate,'MONTH')),
       DECODE(GROUPING(Name),1, 'All names',Name),
       SUM((ReturnedDate-CheckoutDate -14)*0.20)  LateFee
  from BOOKSHELF_CHECKOUT
 where ReturnedDate-CheckoutDate > 14
 group by CUBE(TO_CHAR(ReturnedDate,'MONTH'), Name);
```

```
DECODE(GRO DECODE(GROUPING(NAME),1,'     LATEFEE
---------- -------------------------- ----------
All months All names                         37
All months PAT LAVAY                        3.4
All months FRED FULLER                      3.8
All months JED HOPKINS                      1.4
All months DORAH TALBOT                      .4
All months EMILY TALBOT                      .8
All months ROLAND BRANDT                   22.6
All months GERHARDT KENTGEN                 4.6
FEBRUARY   All names                        6.8
FEBRUARY   PAT LAVAY                        3.4
FEBRUARY   GERHARDT KENTGEN                 3.4
JANUARY    All names                        2.2
JANUARY    JED HOPKINS                      1.4
JANUARY    EMILY TALBOT                      .8
MARCH      All names                         28
MARCH      FRED FULLER                      3.8
MARCH      DORAH TALBOT                      .4
MARCH      ROLAND BRANDT                   22.6
MARCH      GERHARDT KENTGEN                 1.2
```

The **CUBE** function provided the summaries generated by the **ROLLUP** option, plus it shows the sums by Name for the 'All months' category. Being able to perform these summaries in standard SQL greatly enhances your ability to pick the best reporting tool for your users.

Family Trees and connect by

One of Oracle's more interesting but little used or understood facilities is its **connect by** clause. Put simply, this method is used to report, in order, the branches of a *family tree*. Such trees are encountered often—the genealogy of human families, livestock, horses; corporate management, company divisions, manufacturing; literature, ideas, evolution, scientific research, theory, and even views built upon views.

The **connect by** clause provides a means to report on all of the family members in any of these many trees. It lets you exclude branches or individual members of a family tree, and allows you to travel through the tree either up or down, reporting on the family members encountered during the trip.

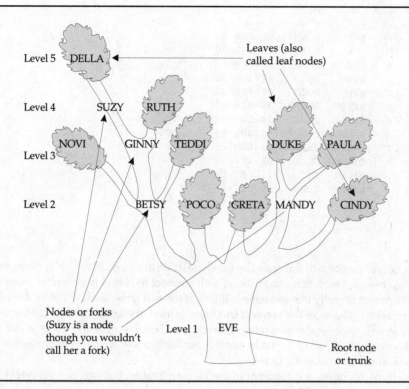

FIGURE 14-1. *Eve's descendants*

The earliest ancestor in the tree is technically called the *root node.* In everyday English, this would be called the *trunk.* Extending from the trunk are branches, which have other branches, which have still other branches. The forks where one or more branches split away from a larger branch are called *nodes,* and the very end of a branch is called a *leaf,* or a *leaf node.* Figure 14-1 (above) shows a picture of such a tree.

The following is a table of cows and bulls born between January 1900 and October 1908. As each offspring is born, it is entered as a row in the table, along with its sex, parents (the cow and bull), and birth date. If you compare the cows and offspring in this table with Figure 14-1, you'll find they correspond. EVE has no recorded cow or bull parent because she was born on a different farm, and ADAM and BANDIT are bulls brought in for breeding, again with no parents in the table.

```
column Cow format a6
column Bull format a6
column Offspring format a10
column Sex format a3

select * from BREEDING
 order by Birthdate;
```

```
OFFSPRING  SEX COW     BULL    BIRTHDATE
---------- --- ------- ------- ---------
BETSY       F  EVE     ADAM    02-JAN-00
POCO        M  EVE     ADAM    15-JUL-00
GRETA       F  EVE     BANDIT  12-MAR-01
MANDY       F  EVE     POCO    22-AUG-02
CINDY       F  EVE     POCO    09-FEB-03
NOVI        F  BETSY   ADAM    30-MAR-03
GINNY       F  BETSY   BANDIT  04-DEC-03
DUKE        M  MANDY   BANDIT  24-JUL-04
TEDDI       F  BETSY   BANDIT  12-AUG-05
SUZY        F  GINNY   DUKE    03-APR-06
PAULA       F  MANDY   POCO    21-DEC-06
RUTH        F  GINNY   DUKE    25-DEC-06
DELLA       F  SUZY    BANDIT  11-OCT-08
EVE         F
ADAM        M
BANDIT      M
```

Next, a query is written to illustrate the family relationships visually. This is done using **LPAD** and a special column, Level, that comes along with **connect by**. Level is a number, from 1 for EVE to 5 for DELLA, that is really the *generation*. If EVE is the first generation of cattle, then DELLA is the fifth generation. Whenever the **connect by** clause is used, the Level column can be used in the **select** statement to discover the generation of each row. Level is a *pseudo-column* like SysDate and User. It's not really a part of the table, but it is available under specific circumstances. The next listing shows an example of using Level.

The results of this query are apparent in the following table, but why did the **select** statement produce this? How does it work?

```
column Offspring format a30
select Cow, Bull, LPAD(' ',6*(Level-1))||Offspring AS Offspring,
       Sex, Birthdate
  from BREEDING
 start with Offspring = 'EVE'
 connect by Cow = PRIOR Offspring;
```

```
COW     BULL    OFFSPRING                               SEX BIRTHDATE
------- ------- ------------------------------          --- ---------
                EVE                                      F
EVE     ADAM       BETSY                                 F  02-JAN-00
BETSY   ADAM          NOVI                               F  30-MAR-03
BETSY   BANDIT        GINNY                              F  04-DEC-03
GINNY   DUKE             SUZY                            F  03-APR-06
SUZY    BANDIT              DELLA                        F  11-OCT-08
GINNY   DUKE             RUTH                            F  25-DEC-06
BETSY   BANDIT        TEDDI                              F  12-AUG-05
EVE     ADAM       POCO                                  M  15-JUL-00
EVE     BANDIT     GRETA                                 F  12-MAR-01
EVE     POCO       MANDY                                 F  22-AUG-02
MANDY   BANDIT        DUKE                               M  24-JUL-04
MANDY   POCO          PAULA                              F  21-DEC-06
EVE     POCO       CINDY                                 F  09-FEB-03
```

Note that this is really Figure 14-1 turned clockwise onto its side. EVE isn't centered, but she is the root node (trunk) of this tree. Her children are BETSY, POCO, GRETA, MANDY, and CINDY. BETSY's children are NOVI, GINNY, and TEDDI. GINNY's children are SUZY and RUTH. And SUZY's child is DELLA. MANDY also has two children, DUKE and PAULA.

This tree started with EVE as the first "offspring." If the SQL statement had said **start with** MANDY, only MANDY, DUKE, and PAULA would have been selected. **start with** defines the beginning of that portion of the tree that will be displayed, and it includes only branches stretching out from the individual that **start with** specifies. **start with** acts just as its name implies.

The **LPAD** in the **select** statement is probably somewhat confusing. Recall from Chapter 7 the format for **LPAD**:

```
LPAD(string,length [,'set'])
```

That is, take the specified *string* and left-pad it for the specified *length* with the specified *set* of characters. If no set is specified, left-pad the string with blanks.

Compare this syntax to the **LPAD** in the **select** statement shown earlier:

```
LPAD(' ',6*(Level-1))
```

In this case, the *string* is a single character (a space, indicated by the literal space enclosed in single quotation marks). Also, 6*(Level–1) is the *length*, and because the *set* is not specified, spaces will be used. In other words, this tells SQL to take this string of one space and left-pad it to the number of spaces determined by 6*(Level–1), a calculation made by first subtracting 1 from the Level and then multiplying this result by 6. For EVE, the Level is 1, so 6*(1–1), or 0 spaces, is used. For BETSY, the Level (her generation) is 2, so an **LPAD** of 6 is used. Thus, for each generation after the first, six additional spaces will be concatenated to the left of the Offspring column. The effect is obvious in the result just shown. The name of each Offspring is indented by left-padding with the number of spaces corresponding to its Level or generation.

Why is this done, instead of simply applying the **LPAD** directly to Offspring? For two reasons. First, a direct **LPAD** on Offspring would cause the names of the offspring to be right-justified. The names at each level would end up having their last letters lined up vertically. Second, if Level–1 is equal to 0, as it is for EVE, the resulting **LPAD** of EVE will be 0 characters wide, causing EVE to vanish:

```
select Cow, Bull, LPAD(Offspring,6*(Level-1),' ') AS Offspring,
       Sex, Birthdate   from BREEDING
  start with Offspring = 'EVE'
connect by Cow = PRIOR Offspring;

COW    BULL    OFFSPRING                              SEX BIRTHDATE
------ ------  -------------------------------------  --- ---------
                                                       F
EVE    ADAM    BETSY                                   F   02-JAN-00
BETSY  ADAM            NOVI                            F   30-MAR-03
BETSY  BANDIT          GINNY                           F   04-DEC-03
```

```
GINNY    DUKE                 SUZY                   F   03-APR-06
SUZY     BANDIT                         DELLA        F   11-OCT-08
GINNY    DUKE                 RUTH                   F   25-DEC-06
BETSY    BANDIT       TEDDI                          F   12-AUG-05
EVE      ADAM     POCO                               M   15-JUL-00
EVE      BANDIT   GRETA                              F   12-MAR-01
EVE      POCO     MANDY                              F   22-AUG-02
MANDY    BANDIT       DUKE                           M   24-JUL-04
MANDY    POCO         PAULA                          F   21-DEC-06
EVE      POCO     CINDY                              F   09-FEB-03
```

Therefore, to get the proper spacing for each level, to ensure that EVE appears, and to make the names line up vertically on the left, the **LPAD** should be used with the concatenation function, and not directly on the Offspring column.

Now, how does **connect by** work? Look again at Figure 14-1. Starting with NOVI and traveling downward, which cows are the offspring prior to NOVI? The first is BETSY, and the offspring just prior to BETSY is EVE. Even though it is not instantly readable, the clause

```
connect by Cow = PRIOR Offspring
```

tells SQL to find the next row in which the value in the Cow column is equal to the value in the Offspring column in the prior row. Look at the table and you'll see that this is true.

Excluding Individuals and Branches

There are two methods of excluding cows from a report. One uses the normal **where** clause technique, and the other uses the **connect by** clause itself. The difference is that the exclusion using the **connect by** clause will exclude not just the cow mentioned, but all of its children as well. If you use **connect by** to exclude BETSY, then NOVI, GINNY, TEDDI, SUZY, RUTH, and DELLA all vanish. The **connect by** clause really tracks the tree structure. If BETSY had never been born, none of her offspring would have been either. In this example, the **and** clause modifies the **connect by** clause:

```
select Cow, Bull, LPAD(' ',6*(Level-1))||Offspring AS Offspring,
       Sex, Birthdate
  from BREEDING
 start with Offspring = 'EVE'
connect by Cow = PRIOR Offspring
       and Offspring != 'BETSY';

COW    BULL    OFFSPRING                              SEX BIRTHDATE
------ ------  -------------------------------        --- ---------
                EVE                                    F
EVE    ADAM      POCO                                  M   15-JUL-00
EVE    BANDIT    GRETA                                 F   12-MAR-01
EVE    POCO      MANDY                                 F   22-AUG-02
MANDY  BANDIT       DUKE                               M   24-JUL-04
MANDY  POCO         PAULA                              F   21-DEC-06
EVE    POCO      CINDY                                 F   09-FEB-03
```

The **where** clause removes only the cow or cows it mentions. If BETSY dies, she is removed from the chart, but her offspring are not. In fact, notice that BETSY is still there under the Cow column as the mother of her children, NOVI, GINNY, and TEDDI:

```
select Cow, Bull, LPAD(' ',6*(Level-1))||Offspring AS Offspring,
       Sex, Birthdate
  from BREEDING
 where Offspring != 'BETSY'
 start with Offspring = 'EVE'
connect by Cow = PRIOR Offspring;
```

COW	BULL	OFFSPRING			SEX	BIRTHDATE	
		EVE			F		
BETSY	ADAM		NOVI		F	30-MAR-03	
BETSY	BANDIT		GINNY		F	04-DEC-03	
GINNY	DUKE			SUZY	F	03-APR-06	
SUZY	BANDIT				DELLA	F	11-OCT-08
GINNY	DUKE			RUTH	F	25-DEC-06	
BETSY	BANDIT		TEDDI		F	12-AUG-05	
EVE	ADAM	POCO			M	15-JUL-00	
EVE	BANDIT	GRETA			F	12-MAR-01	
EVE	POCO	MANDY			F	22-AUG-02	
MANDY	BANDIT		DUKE		M	24-JUL-04	
MANDY	POCO		PAULA		F	21-DEC-06	
EVE	POCO	CINDY			F	09-FEB-03	

The order in which the family tree is displayed when using **connect by** is basically level by level, left to right, as shown in Figure 14-1, starting with the lowest level, Level 1. For example, you may want to alter this order to collect the cows and their offspring by birth date:

```
select Cow, Bull, LPAD(' ',6*(Level-1))||Offspring AS Offspring,
       Sex, Birthdate   from BREEDING
 start with Offspring = 'EVE'
connect by Cow = PRIOR Offspring
 order by Cow, Birthdate;
```

COW	BULL	OFFSPRING		SEX	BIRTHDATE
BETSY	ADAM		NOVI	F	30-MAR-03
BETSY	BANDIT		GINNY	F	04-DEC-03
BETSY	BANDIT		TEDDI	F	12-AUG-05
EVE	ADAM	BETSY		F	02-JAN-00
EVE	ADAM	POCO		M	15-JUL-00
EVE	BANDIT	GRETA		F	12-MAR-01
EVE	POCO	MANDY		F	22-AUG-02
EVE	POCO	CINDY		F	09-FEB-03
GINNY	DUKE		SUZY	F	03-APR-06
GINNY	DUKE		RUTH	F	25-DEC-06
MANDY	BANDIT		DUKE	M	24-JUL-04

```
MANDY   POCO                    PAULA                  F   21-DEC-06
SUZY    BANDIT                              DELLA      F   11-OCT-08
                EVE                                    F
```

The generations are still obvious in the display, but siblings are more closely grouped with each other. Another way to look at the same family tree is by Birthdate, as follows:

```
select Cow, Bull, LPAD(' ',6*(Level-1))||Offspring AS Offspring,
       Sex, Birthdate
  from BREEDING
 start with Offspring = 'EVE'
connect by Cow = PRIOR Offspring
 order by Birthdate;

COW     BULL    OFFSPRING                       SEX BIRTHDATE
------  ------  ------------------------------  --- ---------
EVE     ADAM        BETSY                        F   02-JAN-00
EVE     ADAM        POCO                         M   15-JUL-00
EVE     BANDIT      GRETA                        F   12-MAR-01
EVE     POCO        MANDY                        F   22-AUG-02
EVE     POCO        CINDY                        F   09-FEB-03
BETSY   ADAM              NOVI                   F   30-MAR-03
BETSY   BANDIT            GINNY                  F   04-DEC-03
MANDY   BANDIT            DUKE                   M   24-JUL-04
BETSY   BANDIT            TEDDI                  F   12-AUG-05
GINNY   DUKE                    SUZY            F   03-APR-06
MANDY   POCO              PAULA                  F   21-DEC-06
GINNY   DUKE                    RUTH            F   25-DEC-06
SUZY    BANDIT                        DELLA      F   11-OCT-08
                EVE                              F
```

Now, the order of the rows no longer shows generations, as in a tree, but the indenting still preserves this information. You can't tell what offspring belong to which parents without looking at the Cow and Bull columns, though. Not knowing Eve's birth date clearly disrupts the display of the family tree.

Traveling Toward the Roots

Thus far, the direction of travel in reporting on the family tree has been from parents toward children. Is it possible to start with a child, and move backward to parent, grandparent, great-grandparent, and so on? To do so, the word **prior** is simply moved to the other side of the equal sign. In the following examples, the Offspring is set equal to the prior Cow value; in the earlier examples, the Cow was set equal to the prior Offspring value. The following traces DELLA's ancestry:

```
select Cow, Bull, LPAD(' ',6*(Level-1))||Offspring AS Offspring,
       Sex, Birthdate
  from BREEDING
 start with Offspring = 'DELLA'
connect by Offspring = PRIOR Cow;
```

```
COW      BULL    OFFSPRING                                SEX BIRTHDATE
------   ------  -------------------------------          --- ---------
SUZY     BANDIT  DELLA                                     F   11-OCT-08
GINNY    DUKE            SUZY                              F   03-APR-06
BETSY    BANDIT               GINNY                        F   04-DEC-03
EVE      ADAM                      BETSY                    F   02-JAN-00
                                        EVE                F
```

This shows DELLA's own roots, but it's a bit confusing if compared to the previous displays. It looks as if DELLA is the ancestor, and EVE the great-great-granddaughter. Adding an **order by** for Birthdate helps, but EVE is still further to the right:

```
select Cow, Bull, LPAD(' ',6*(Level-1))||Offspring AS Offspring,
       Sex, Birthdate
  from BREEDING
 start with Offspring = 'DELLA'
connect by Offspring = PRIOR Cow
 order by Birthdate;
```

```
COW      BULL    OFFSPRING                                SEX BIRTHDATE
------   ------  -------------------------------          --- ---------
EVE      ADAM                      BETSY                    F   02-JAN-00
BETSY    BANDIT               GINNY                        F   04-DEC-03
GINNY    DUKE            SUZY                              F   03-APR-06
SUZY     BANDIT  DELLA                                     F   11-OCT-08
                                        EVE                F
```

The solution is simply to change the calculation in the **LPAD**:

```
select Cow, Bull, LPAD(' ',6*(5-Level))||Offspring Offspring,
       Sex, Birthdate
  from BREEDING
 start with Offspring = 'DELLA'
connect by Offspring = PRIOR Cow
 order by Birthdate;
```

```
COW      BULL    OFFSPRING                                SEX BIRTHDATE
------   ------  -------------------------------          --- ---------
EVE      ADAM            BETSY                             F   02-JAN-00
BETSY    BANDIT               GINNY                        F   04-DEC-03
GINNY    DUKE                      SUZY                     F   03-APR-06
SUZY     BANDIT                          DELLA             F   11-OCT-08
                 EVE                                       F
```

Finally, look how different this report is when the **connect by** tracks the parentage of the bull. Here are ADAM's offspring:

```
select Cow, Bull, LPAD(' ',6*(Level-1))||Offspring AS Offspring,
       Sex, Birthdate
  from BREEDING
```

```
start with Offspring = 'ADAM'
connect by PRIOR Offspring = Bull;
```

```
COW      BULL    OFFSPRING                         SEX BIRTHDATE
------   ------  --------------------------------  --- ---------
                 ADAM                               M
EVE      ADAM            BETSY                       F   02-JAN-00
EVE      ADAM            POCO                        M   15-JUL-00
EVE      POCO                    MANDY               F   22-AUG-02
EVE      POCO                    CINDY               F   09-FEB-03
MANDY    POCO                    PAULA               F   21-DEC-06
BETSY    ADAM            NOVI                        F   30-MAR-03
```

ADAM and BANDIT were the original bulls at the initiation of the herd. To create a single tree that reports both ADAM's and BANDIT's offspring, you would have to invent a "father" for the two of them, which would be the root of the tree. One of the advantages that these alternative trees have over the type of tree shown earlier is that many inheritance groups—from families to projects to divisions within companies—can be accurately portrayed in more than one way:

```
select Cow, Bull, LPAD(' ',6*(Level-1))||Offspring AS Offspring,
       Sex, Birthdate
  from BREEDING
  start with Offspring = 'BANDIT'
connect by PRIOR Offspring = Bull;
```

```
COW      BULL    OFFSPRING                         SEX BIRTHDATE
------   ------  --------------------------------  --- ---------
                 BANDIT                             M
EVE      BANDIT          GRETA                       F   12-MAR-01
BETSY    BANDIT          GINNY                       F   04-DEC-03
MANDY    BANDIT          DUKE                        M   24-JUL-04
GINNY    DUKE                    SUZY                F   03-APR-06
GINNY    DUKE                    RUTH                F   25-DEC-06
BETSY    BANDIT          TEDDI                       F   12-AUG-05
SUZY     BANDIT          DELLA                       F   11-OCT-08
```

The Basic Rules

Using **connect by** and **start with** to create tree like reports is not difficult, but certain basic rules must be followed:

- The order of the clauses when using **connect by** is as follows:

 1. select

 2. from

 3. where

 4. start with

5. **connect by**

6. **order by**

■ **prior** forces reporting to be from the root out toward the leaves (if the **prior** column is the parent) or from a leaf toward the root (if the **prior** column is the child).

■ A **where** clause eliminates individuals from the tree, but not their descendants (or ancestors, if **prior** is on the right side of the equal sign).

■ A qualification in the **connect by** (particularly a not equal) eliminates both an individual and all of its descendants (or ancestors, depending on how you trace the tree).

■ **connect by** cannot be used with a table join in the **where** clause.

This particular set of commands is one that few people are likely to remember correctly. However, with a basic understanding of trees and inheritance, you should be able to construct a proper **select** statement to report on a tree just by referring to this chapter for correct syntax.

CHAPTER
15

Changing Data:
insert, update,
merge, and delete

ntil now, virtually everything you've learned about Oracle, SQL, and SQL*Plus has related to selecting data from tables in the database. This chapter shows how to *change* the data in a table—how to insert new rows, update the values of columns in rows, and delete rows entirely. Although these topics have not been covered explicitly, nearly everything you already know about SQL, including datatypes, calculations, string formatting, **where** clauses, and the like, can be used here, so there really isn't much new to learn. Oracle gives you a transparent, distributed database capability that inserts, updates, and deletes data in remote databases as well (see Chapter 23). As you'll see in this chapter, Oracle allows you to combine these commands via multitable inserts and the **merge** command (to perform inserts and updates in a single command).

insert

The SQL command **insert** lets you place a row of information directly into a table (or indirectly, through a view). The COMFORT table tracks temperatures at noon and midnight as well as daily precipitation, city by city, for four sample dates throughout the year:

```
describe COMFORT
```

Name	Null?	Type
CITY	NOT NULL	VARCHAR2(13)
SAMPLEDATE	NOT NULL	DATE
NOON		NUMBER(3,1)
MIDNIGHT		NUMBER(3,1)
PRECIPITATION		NUMBER

To add a new row to this table, use this:

```
insert into COMFORT
values ('WALPOLE', '21-MAR-03',
        56.7, 43.8, 0);
```

```
1 row created.
```

The word **values** must precede the list of data to be inserted. A character string must be in single quotation marks. Numbers can stand by themselves. Each field is separated by commas, and the fields must be in the same order as the columns are when the table is described.

A date must be in single quotation marks and in the default Oracle date format. To insert a date not in your default format, use the **TO_DATE** function, with a formatting mask, as shown in the following example:

```
insert into COMFORT
values ('WALPOLE', TO_DATE('06/22/2003','MM/DD/YYYY'),
        56.7, 43.8, 0);
```

```
1 row created.
```

Inserting a Time

Inserting dates without time values will produce a default time of midnight, the very beginning of the day. If you want to insert a date with a time other than midnight, simply use the **TO_DATE** function and include a time:

```
insert into COMFORT
values ('WALPOLE', TO_DATE('06/22/2003 1:35',
        'MM/DD/YYYY HH24:MI'), 56.7, 43.8, 0);
```

```
1 row created.
```

> **NOTE**
> *To store fractional seconds, you can use the TIMESTAMP and*
> *TIMESTAMP WITH TIME ZONE datatypes, as described in Chapter 10.*

Columns also can be inserted out of the order in which they appear when described, if you first (before the word **values**) list the order the data is in. This doesn't change the fundamental order of the columns in the table. It simply allows you to list the data fields in a different order. (See Part V for information on inserting data into user-defined datatypes.)

You also can "insert" a **NULL**. This simply means the column will be left empty for this row, as shown in the following example:

```
insert into COMFORT
        (SampleDate,  Precipitation, City, Noon, Midnight)
values ('23-SEP-03', NULL,
        'WALPOLE', 86.3, 72.1);
```

```
1 row created.
```

insert with select

You also can insert information that has been selected from a table. Here, a mix of columns selected from the COMFORT table, together with literal values for SampleDate (22-DEC-03) and City (WALPOLE), are inserted. Note the **where** clause in the **select** statement, which will retrieve only one row. Had the **select** retrieved five rows, five new ones would have been inserted; if ten rows had been retrieved, then ten new rows would have been inserted, and so on.

```
insert into COMFORT
        (SampleDate, Precipitation, City, Noon, Midnight)
select '22-DEC-03', Precipitation,
        'WALPOLE', Noon, Midnight
  from COMFORT
 where City = 'KEENE'
   and SampleDate = '22-DEC-03';
```

```
1 row created.
```

NOTE
*You cannot use the **insert into...select from** syntax with LONG datatypes unless you are using the **TO_LOB** function to insert the LONG data into a LOB column.*

Of course, you don't need to simply insert the value in a selected column. You can modify the column using any of the appropriate string, date, or number functions within the **select** statement. The results of those functions are what will be inserted. You can attempt to **insert** a value in a column that exceeds its width (for character datatypes) or its magnitude (for number datatypes). You have to fit the value within the constraints you defined on your columns. These attempts will produce a "value too large for column" or "mismatched datatype" error message. If you now query the COMFORT table for the city of Walpole, the results will be the records you inserted:

```
select * from COMFORT
 where City = 'WALPOLE';

CITY            SAMPLEDAT     NOON     MIDNIGHT  PRECIPITATION
-----------     ---------   ----------  ----------  -------------
WALPOLE         21-MAR-03     56.7       43.8              0
WALPOLE         22-JUN-03     56.7       43.8              0
WALPOLE         22-JUN-03     56.7       43.8              0
WALPOLE         23-SEP-03     86.3       72.1
WALPOLE         22-DEC-03     -7.2       -1.2            3.9

5 rows selected.
```

Two records are shown for '22-JUN-03' because one of them has a time component. Use the **TO_CHAR** function to see the time:

```
select City, SampleDate,
       TO_CHAR(SampleDate,'HH24:MI:SS') AS TimeofDay, Noon
  from COMFORT
 where City = 'WALPOLE';

CITY            SAMPLEDAT  TIMEOFDA     NOON
-----------     ---------  --------  ----------
WALPOLE         21-MAR-03  00:00:00      56.7
WALPOLE         22-JUN-03  00:00:00      56.7
WALPOLE         22-JUN-03  01:35:00      56.7
WALPOLE         23-SEP-03  00:00:00      86.3
WALPOLE         22-DEC-03  00:00:00      -7.2
```

Using the APPEND Hint to Improve insert Performance

As you will see in Chapter 43, Oracle uses an optimizer to determine the most efficient way to perform each SQL command. For **insert** statements, Oracle tries to insert each new record into an existing block of data already allocated to the table. This execution plan optimizes the use of space required to store the data. However, it may not provide adequate performance for an **insert** with a **select** command that inserts multiple rows. You can amend the execution plan by using the

APPEND hint to improve the performance of large inserts. The APPEND hint will tell the database to find the last block into which the table's data has ever been inserted. The new records will be inserted starting in the next block following the last previously used block. Furthermore, the inserted data is written directly to the datafiles, bypassing the data block buffer cache. As a result, there is much less space management work for the database to do during the **insert**. Therefore, the **insert** may complete faster when the APPEND hint is used.

You specify the APPEND hint within the **insert** command. A hint looks like a comment—it starts with /* and ends with */. The only difference is that the starting set of characters includes a plus sign (+) before the name of the hint. The following example shows an **insert** command whose data is appended to the table:

```
insert /*+ APPEND */ into BOOKSHELF (Title)
select Title from BOOK_ORDER
 where Title not in (select Title from BOOKSHELF);
```

The records from the BOOK_ORDER table will be inserted into the BOOKSHELF table. Instead of attempting to reuse space within the BOOKSHELF table, the new records will be placed at the end of the table's physical storage space.

Because the new records will not attempt to reuse available space that the table has already used, the space requirements for the BOOKSHELF table may increase. In general, you should use the APPEND hint only when inserting large volumes of data into tables with little reusable space. The point at which appended records will be inserted is called the table's *high-water mark*—and the only way to reset the high-water mark is to **truncate** the table. Because **truncate** will delete all records and cannot be rolled back, you should make sure you have a backup of the table's data prior to performing the **truncate**. See **truncate** in the Alphabetical Reference for further details.

rollback, commit, and autocommit

When you insert, update, or delete data from the database, you can reverse, or *roll back,* the work you've done. This can be very important when an error is discovered. The process of committing or rolling back work is controlled by two SQL*Plus commands: **commit** and **rollback**. Additionally, SQL*Plus has the facility to automatically commit your work without your explicitly telling it to do so. This is controlled by the **autocommit** feature of **set**. Like other **set** features, you can **show** it, like this:

```
show autocommit
```

```
autocommit OFF
```

OFF is the default, and in almost all cases it's the preferred mode. You can also specify a number for the **autocommit** value; this value will determine the number of commands after which Oracle will issue a **commit**. Having **autocommit off** means **insert**, **update**, and **delete** operations are not made final until you **commit** them:

```
commit;
```

```
commit complete
```

Until you **commit**, only you can see how your work affects the tables. Anyone else with access to these tables will continue to get the old information. You will see *new* information whenever you **select** from the table. Your work is, in effect, in a "staging" area, which you interact with until you **commit**. You can perform quite a large number of **insert**, **update**, and **delete** operations and still undo the work (return the tables to the way they used to be) by issuing this command:

```
rollback;
```

```
rollback complete
```

However, the message "rollback complete" can be misleading. It means only that Oracle has rolled back any work that hasn't been committed. If you **commit** a series of transactions, either explicitly with the word **commit** or implicitly by another action, the "rollback complete" message won't really mean anything.

Using savepoints

You can use *savepoints* to roll back portions of your current set of transactions. Consider the following commands:

```
insert into COMFORT
values ('WALPOLE', '22-APR-03',50.1, 24.8, 0);

savepoint A;

insert into COMFORT
values ('WALPOLE', '27-MAY-03',63.7, 33.8, 0);

savepoint B;

insert into COMFORT
values ('WALPOLE', '07-AUG-03',83.0, 43.8, 0);
```

Now, select the data from COMFORT for Walpole:

```
select * from COMFORT
 where City = 'WALPOLE';
```

CITY	SAMPLEDAT	NOON	MIDNIGHT	PRECIPITATION
WALPOLE	21-MAR-03	56.7	43.8	0
WALPOLE	22-JUN-03	56.7	43.8	0
WALPOLE	22-JUN-03	56.7	43.8	0
WALPOLE	23-SEP-03	86.3	72.1	
WALPOLE	22-DEC-03	-7.2	-1.2	3.9
WALPOLE	22-APR-03	50.1	24.8	0
WALPOLE	27-MAY-03	63.7	33.8	0
WALPOLE	07-AUG-03	83	43.8	0

The output shows the five former records plus the three new rows we've added. Now roll back just the last insert:

```
rollback to savepoint B;
```

If you now query COMFORT, you'll see that the last **insert** has been rolled back, but the others are still there:

```
select * from COMFORT
  where City = 'WALPOLE';
```

CITY	SAMPLEDAT	NOON	MIDNIGHT	PRECIPITATION
WALPOLE	21-MAR-03	56.7	43.8	0
WALPOLE	22-JUN-03	56.7	43.8	0
WALPOLE	22-JUN-03	56.7	43.8	0
WALPOLE	23-SEP-03	86.3	72.1	
WALPOLE	22-DEC-03	-7.2	-1.2	3.9
WALPOLE	22-APR-03	50.1	24.8	0
WALPOLE	27-MAY-03	63.7	33.8	0

The last two records are still not committed; you need to execute a **commit** command or another command to force a commit to occur. You can still roll back the second insert (to savepoint A) or roll back all the inserts (via a **rollback** command).

Implicit commit

The actions that will force a **commit** to occur, even without your instructing it to, are **quit**, **exit** (the equivalent of **quit**), and any Data Definition Language (DDL) command. Using any of these commands forces a **commit**.

Auto rollback

If you've completed a series of **insert**, **update**, or **delete** operations but have not yet explicitly or implicitly committed them, and you experience serious difficulties, such as a computer failure, Oracle will automatically roll back any uncommitted work. If the machine or database goes down, Oracle does the rollback as cleanup work the next time the database is brought back up.

Multitable Inserts

You can perform multiple inserts in a single command. You can perform all the inserts unconditionally or you can specify conditions—using a **when** clause to tell Oracle how to manage the multiple inserts. If you specify **all**, then all the **when** clauses will be evaluated; specifying **first** tells Oracle to skip subsequent **when** clauses after it finds one that is true for the row being evaluated. You can also use an **else** clause to tell Oracle what to do if none of the **when** clauses evaluates to true.

To illustrate this functionality, let's create a new table with a slightly different structure than COMFORT:

```
drop table COMFORT_TEST;
create table COMFORT_TEST (
City          VARCHAR2(13) NOT NULL,
SampleDate    DATE NOT NULL,
```

```
Measure          VARCHAR2(10),
Value            NUMBER(3,1)
);
```

COMFORT_TEST will have multiple records for each record in COMFORT—its Measure column will have values such as 'Midnight', 'Noon', and 'Precip', allowing us to store a greater number of measures for each city on each sample date.

Now populate COMFORT_TEST with data from COMFORT, unconditionally:

```
insert ALL
        into COMFORT_TEST (City, SampleDate, Measure, Value)
      values (City, SampleDate, 'NOON', Noon)
        into COMFORT_TEST (City, SampleDate, Measure, Value)
      values (City, SampleDate, 'MIDNIGHT', Midnight)
        into COMFORT_TEST (City, SampleDate, Measure, Value)
      values (City, SampleDate, 'PRECIP', Precipitation)
select City, SampleDate, Noon, Midnight, Precipitation
  from COMFORT
 where City = 'KEENE';

12 rows created.
```

This query tells Oracle to insert multiple rows for each row returned from the COMFORT table. The query of COMFORT returns four rows. The first **into** clause inserts the Noon value, along with a text string of 'NOON' in the Measure column. The second **into** clause inserts the Midnight value, and the third inserts the Precipitation value, as shown in the query of COMFORT_TEST following the **insert**:

```
select * from COMFORT_TEST;

CITY            SAMPLEDAT MEASURE        VALUE
--------------- --------- ---------- ----------
KEENE           21-MAR-03 NOON            39.9
KEENE           22-JUN-03 NOON            85.1
KEENE           23-SEP-03 NOON            99.8
KEENE           22-DEC-03 NOON            -7.2
KEENE           21-MAR-03 MIDNIGHT        -1.2
KEENE           22-JUN-03 MIDNIGHT        66.7
KEENE           23-SEP-03 MIDNIGHT        82.6
KEENE           22-DEC-03 MIDNIGHT        -1.2
KEENE           21-MAR-03 PRECIP           4.4
KEENE           22-JUN-03 PRECIP           1.3
KEENE           23-SEP-03 PRECIP
KEENE           22-DEC-03 PRECIP           3.9

12 rows selected.
```

What if you had used the **first** keyword instead of the **all** keyword? Unless you use **when** clauses, you can't use the **first** keyword. The following example shows the use of the **when** clause to restrict

which **insert**s are performed within the multi-**insert** command. For this example, the **all** keyword is used:

```
delete from COMFORT_TEST;
commit;

insert ALL
        when Noon > 80 then
            into COMFORT_TEST (City, SampleDate, Measure, Value)
        values (City, SampleDate, 'NOON', Noon)
        when Midnight > 70 then
            into COMFORT_TEST (City, SampleDate, Measure, Value)
        values (City, SampleDate, 'MIDNIGHT', Midnight)
        when Precipitation is not null then
            into COMFORT_TEST (City, SampleDate, Measure, Value)
        values (City, SampleDate, 'PRECIP', Precipitation)
select City, SampleDate, Noon, Midnight, Precipitation
   from COMFORT
 where City = 'KEENE';

6 rows created.
```

What six rows were inserted? The two Noon values met this condition:

```
        when Noon > 80 then
```

The one Midnight value met this condition:

```
        when Midnight > 70 then
```

And the three Precipitation values met this condition:

```
        when Precipitation is not null then
```

You can see the results in COMFORT_TEST:

```
select * from COMFORT_TEST;

CITY            SAMPLEDAT MEASURE         VALUE
--------------- --------- ---------- ----------
KEENE           22-JUN-03 NOON            85.1
KEENE           23-SEP-03 NOON            99.8
KEENE           23-SEP-03 MIDNIGHT        82.6
KEENE           21-MAR-03 PRECIP           4.4
KEENE           22-JUN-03 PRECIP           1.3
KEENE           22-DEC-03 PRECIP           3.9
```

What if you had used **first** instead?

```
delete from COMFORT_TEST;
commit;
```

```
insert FIRST
       when Noon > 80 then
          into COMFORT_TEST (City, SampleDate, Measure, Value)
       values (City, SampleDate, 'NOON', Noon)
       when Midnight > 70 then
          into COMFORT_TEST (City, SampleDate, Measure, Value)
       values (City, SampleDate, 'MIDNIGHT', Midnight)
       when Precipitation is not null then
          into COMFORT_TEST (City, SampleDate, Measure, Value)
       values (City, SampleDate, 'PRECIP', Precipitation)
select City, SampleDate, Noon, Midnight, Precipitation
  from COMFORT
 where City = 'KEENE';

4 rows created.
```

In this case, four rows are inserted:

```
select * from COMFORT_TEST;

CITY          SAMPLEDAT MEASURE         VALUE
------------- --------- ----------   ----------
KEENE         21-MAR-03 PRECIP            4.4
KEENE         22-DEC-03 PRECIP            3.9
KEENE         22-JUN-03 NOON             85.1
KEENE         23-SEP-03 NOON             99.8
```

What happened to the MIDNIGHT value? Only one record passed the MIDNIGHT **when** clause:

```
       when Midnight > 70 then
```

This record also passed the NOON **when** clause:

```
       when Noon > 80 then
```

Therefore, its Noon value (99.8) was inserted. Because the **first** keyword was used, and the condition that was evaluated first (Noon) was true, Oracle did not check the rest of the conditions for that row. The same process happened to the PRECIP measures—the other non-**NULL** Precipitation value was on the same record as the Noon reading of 85.1.

What if none of the conditions had been met? To show that option, let's create a third table, COMFORT2, with the same structure as COMFORT:

```
create table COMFORT2 (
City           VARCHAR2(13) NOT NULL,
SampleDate     DATE NOT NULL,
Noon           NUMBER(3,1),
Midnight       NUMBER(3,1),
Precipitation NUMBER
);
```

Now, we'll execute an **insert** for all cities (using the **first** clause) along with an **else** clause specifying that any rows that fail the conditions will be placed into the COMFORT2 table. For this example, the **when** conditions are changed to limit the number of rows that pass the conditions:

```
delete from COMFORT_TEST;
delete from COMFORT2;
commit;

insert FIRST
       when Noon > 80 then
          into COMFORT_TEST (City, SampleDate, Measure, Value)
       values (City, SampleDate, 'NOON', Noon)
       when Midnight > 100 then
          into COMFORT_TEST (City, SampleDate, Measure, Value)
       values (City, SampleDate, 'MIDNIGHT', Midnight)
       when Precipitation > 100 then
          into COMFORT_TEST (City, SampleDate, Measure, Value)
       values (City, SampleDate, 'PRECIP', Precipitation)
    else
          into COMFORT2
select City, SampleDate, Noon, Midnight, Precipitation
  from COMFORT
where City = 'KEENE';

4 rows created.
```

The feedback tells you how many rows were created, but not which table they were created in. The total reported is for all inserts combined. In this case, two records were inserted into COMFORT_TEST and two were inserted into COMFORT2 because of the **else** condition:

```
select * from COMFORT_TEST;

CITY          SAMPLEDAT MEASURE         VALUE
------------- --------- ---------- ----------
KEENE         22-JUN-03 NOON            85.1
KEENE         23-SEP-03 NOON            99.8

select * from COMFORT2;

CITY          SAMPLEDAT      NOON   MIDNIGHT PRECIPITATION
------------- --------- ---------- ---------- -------------
KEENE         21-MAR-03       39.9       -1.2           4.4
KEENE         22-DEC-03       -7.2       -1.2           3.9
```

delete

Removing a row or rows from a table requires the **delete** command, as seen in the examples in the last section. The **where** clause is essential to removing only the rows you intend. **delete** without

a **where** clause will empty the table completely. The following command deletes the Walpole entries from the COMFORT table:

```
delete from COMFORT where City = 'WALPOLE';
```

Of course, a **where** clause in a **delete**, just as in an **update** or a **select** that is part of an **insert**, can contain as much logic as any **select** statement, and may include subqueries, unions, intersects, and so on. You can always roll back a bad **insert**, **update**, or **delete**, but you really should experiment with **select** before actually making the change to the database, to make sure you are doing the right thing.

Now that you've just deleted the rows where City = 'WALPOLE', you can test the effect of that **delete** with a simple query:

```
select * from COMFORT
 where City = 'WALPOLE';
```

```
no rows selected
```

Now roll back the **delete** and run the same query:

```
rollback;
Rollback complete
```

```
select * from COMFORT
 where City = 'WALPOLE';
```

CITY	SAMPLEDAT	NOON	MIDNIGHT	PRECIPITATION
WALPOLE	21-MAR-03	56.7	43.8	0
WALPOLE	22-JUN-03	56.7	43.8	0
WALPOLE	22-JUN-03	56.7	43.8	0
WALPOLE	23-SEP-03	86.3	72.1	
WALPOLE	22-DEC-03	-7.2	-1.2	3.9
WALPOLE	22-APR-03	50.1	24.8	0
WALPOLE	27-MAY-03	63.7	33.8	0

```
7 rows selected.
```

This illustrates that recovery is possible, so long as a **commit** hasn't occurred. If the changes have been committed, you may be able to use flashback queries (see Chapter 27) to retrieve the data.

An additional command for deleting records, **truncate**, does not behave the same as **delete**. Whereas **delete** allows you to commit or roll back the deletion, **truncate** automatically deletes all records from the table. The action of the **truncate** command cannot be rolled back or committed; the truncated records are unrecoverable. You cannot perform a flashback query to see data that has been truncated. See the **truncate** command in the Alphabetical Reference for further details.

update

update requires setting specific values for each column you want to change, and specifying which row or rows you want to affect by using a carefully constructed **where** clause:

```
update COMFORT set Precipitation = .5, Midnight = 73.1
  where City = 'KEENE'
    and SampleDate = '22-DEC-03';

1 row updated.
```

Here is the effect, shown in the 22-DEC-03 record:

```
select * from COMFORT
  where City = 'KEENE';

CITY            SAMPLEDAT    NOON   MIDNIGHT PRECIPITATION
-------------   ---------   ------- -------- -------------
KEENE           21-MAR-03    39.9     -1.2        4.4
KEENE           22-JUN-03    85.1     66.7        1.3
KEENE           23-SEP-03    99.8     82.6
KEENE           22-DEC-03    -7.2     73.1         .5

4 rows selected.
```

What if you later discover that the thermometer used in Keene consistently reports its temperatures too high by one degree? You also can do calculations, string functions, and almost any other legitimate function in setting a value for the **update** (just as you can for an **insert**, or in the **where** clause of a **delete**). Here, each temperature in Keene is decreased by one degree:

```
update COMFORT set Midnight = Midnight - 1, Noon = Noon - 1
  where City = 'KEENE';

4 rows updated.
```

Here is the effect of the **update**:

```
select * from COMFORT
  where City = 'KEENE';

CITY            SAMPLEDAT    NOON   MIDNIGHT PRECIPITATION
-------------   ---------   ------- -------- -------------
KEENE           21-MAR-03    38.9     -2.2        4.4
KEENE           22-JUN-03    84.1     65.7        1.3
KEENE           23-SEP-03    98.8     81.6
KEENE           22-DEC-03    -8.2     72.1         .5
```

> **NOTE**
> *If your **update** violates the column definitions or constraints, it will
> fail. In this case, setting Noon or Midnight to values of 100 or greater
> will violate the numeric scale of the columns.*

As with **delete**, the **where** clause is critical. Without one, every row in the table will be updated. With an improperly constructed **where** clause, the wrong rows will be updated, often in ways that are hard to discover or fix, especially if your work has been committed. Always **set feedback on** when doing **update**s, and look at the feedback to be sure the number of rows updated is what you expected it to be. Query the rows after you **update** to see if the expected change took place.

update with Embedded select

It is possible to set values in an **update** by embedding a **select** statement right in the middle of it. Note that this **select** has its own **where** clause, picking out the temperature for the city of Manchester from the WEATHER table, and the **update** has its own **where** clause to affect just the city of Keene on a certain day:

```
update COMFORT set Midnight =
       (select Temperature
          from WEATHER
         where City = 'MANCHESTER')
 where City = 'KEENE'
   and SampleDate = '22-DEC-03';

1 row updated.
```

Here is the effect of the **update**:

```
select * from COMFORT
 where City = 'KEENE';
```

CITY	SAMPLEDAT	NOON	MIDNIGHT	PRECIPITATION
KEENE	21-MAR-03	38.9	-2.2	4.4
KEENE	22-JUN-03	84.1	65.7	1.3
KEENE	23-SEP-03	98.8	81.6	
KEENE	22-DEC-03	-8.2	66	.5

```
4 rows selected.
```

When using a subquery with an **update**, you must be certain that the subquery will return no more than one record for each of the records to be updated; otherwise, the **update** will fail. See Chapter 13 for details on correlated queries.

You also can use an embedded **select** to **update** multiple columns at once. The columns must be in parentheses and separated by a comma, as shown here:

```
update COMFORT set (Noon, Midnight) =
       (select Humidity, Temperature
```

```
        from WEATHER
         where City = 'MANCHESTER')
 where City = 'KEENE'
   and SampleDate = '22-DEC-03';
```

1 row updated.

Here is the effect:

```
select * from COMFORT
  where City = 'KEENE';
```

```
CITY          SAMPLEDAT     NOON   MIDNIGHT PRECIPITATION
-------------  ---------  ----------  ---------- -------------
KEENE         21-MAR-03     38.9        -2.2           4.4
KEENE         22-JUN-03     84.1        65.7           1.3
KEENE         23-SEP-03     98.8        81.6
KEENE         22-DEC-03       98          66            .5
```

4 rows selected.

update with NULL

You also can update a table and set a column equal to **NULL**. This is the sole instance of using the equal sign with **NULL**, instead of the word "is." For example,

```
update COMFORT set Noon = NULL
 where City = 'KEENE'
   and SampleDate = '22-DEC-03';
```

1 row updated.

will set the noon temperature to **NULL** for Keene on December 22, 2003.

NOTE
*The primary issues with **insert**, **update**, and **delete** are careful construction of **where** clauses to affect (or **insert**) only the rows you really want, and the normal use of SQL functions within these **insert**, **update**, and **delete** operations. It is extremely important that you exercise caution about committing work before you are certain it is correct. These commands extend the power of Oracle well beyond simple queries, and they allow direct manipulation of data.*

Using the merge Command

You can use the **merge** command to perform **insert** and **update** operations into a single table in a single command. Based on the conditions you specify, Oracle will take the source data—either a table, view, or query—and update existing values if the conditions are met. If the conditions are not met, the row will be inserted.

For example, we can change the rows in the COMFORT2 table created earlier in this chapter:

```
delete from COMFORT2;

insert into COMFORT2
values ('KEENE', '21-MAR-03',55, -2.2, 4.4);
insert into COMFORT2
values ('KEENE', '22-DEC-03',55, 66, 0.5);
 insert into COMFORT2
values ('KEENE', '16-MAY-03', 55, 55, 1);
commit;
```

The data in COMFORT2 should now look like this:

```
select * from COMFORT2;

CITY          SAMPLEDAT     NOON   MIDNIGHT PRECIPITATION
------------- --------- ---------- ---------- -------------
KEENE         21-MAR-03         55       -2.2           4.4
KEENE         22-DEC-03         55         66            .5
KEENE         16-MAY-03         55         55             1
```

The Keene data in COMFORT is

```
select * from COMFORT where City = 'KEENE';

CITY          SAMPLEDAT     NOON   MIDNIGHT PRECIPITATION
------------- --------- ---------- ---------- -------------
KEENE         21-MAR-03       38.9       -2.2           4.4
KEENE         22-JUN-03       84.1       65.7           1.3
KEENE         23-SEP-03       98.8       81.6
KEENE         22-DEC-03                    66            .5
```

With COMFORT2 as the data source, we can now perform a **merge** on the COMFORT table. For the rows that match (the '21-MAR-03' and '22-DEC-03' entries), we'll update the Noon values in COMFORT. The rows that exist only in COMFORT2 (the '16-MAY-03' row) will be inserted into COMFORT. The following listing shows the command to use:

```
merge into COMFORT    C1
using (select City, SampleDate, Noon, Midnight,
             Precipitation from COMFORT2)   C2
   on (C1.City = C2.City and C1.SampleDate=C2.SampleDate)
 when matched then
      update set Noon = C2.Noon
 when not matched then
      insert (C1.City, C1.SampleDate, C1.Noon,
             C1.Midnight, C1.Precipitation)
      values (C2.City, C2.SampleDate, C2.Noon,
             C2.Midnight, C2.Precipitation);

3 rows merged.
```

The output tells you the number of rows processed from the source table, but does not tell you how many rows were inserted or updated. You can see the changes by querying COMFORT (note the Noon=55 records):

```
select * from COMFORT where City = 'KEENE';

CITY          SAMPLEDAT     NOON   MIDNIGHT PRECIPITATION
------------- ----------- -------- -------- -------------
KEENE         16-MAY-03        55       55             1
KEENE         21-MAR-03        55     -2.2           4.4
KEENE         22-JUN-03      84.1     65.7           1.3
KEENE         23-SEP-03      98.8     81.6
KEENE         22-DEC-03        55       66            .5
```

Take a look at the command to see how this was accomplished. In the first line, the target table is named and given an alias of C1:

```
merge into COMFORT    C1
```

In the next two lines, the **using** clause provides the source data for the **merge**, and the source is given the alias C2:

```
using (select City, SampleDate, Noon, Midnight,
              Precipitation from COMFORT2)   C2
```

The condition for the merge is then specified in the **on** clause. If the source data's City and SampleDate values match those in the target table, the data will be updated. The **when matched then** clause, followed by an **update** command, tells Oracle what columns to update in the source table:

```
    on (C1.City = C2.City and C1.SampleDate=C2.SampleDate)
 when matched then
      update set Noon = C2.Noon
```

If there is no match, the row should be inserted, as specified in the **when not matched** clause:

```
when not matched then
        insert (C1.City, C1.SampleDate, C1.Noon,
                C1.Midnight, C1.Precipitation)
        values (C2.City, C2.SampleDate, C2.Noon,
                C2.Midnight, C2.Precipitation);
```

You can use the **merge** command to simplify operations in which many rows are inserted and updated from a single source. As with all **update** operations, you should be very careful to use the appropriate **where** clauses in the **using** clause of your **merge** commands.

NOTE
*You cannot update a column that is referenced in the **on** condition clause.*

In the **merge** command, you can specify either an **update** clause, an **insert** clause, or both.

To insert all the source rows into the table, you can use a *constant filter predicate* in the **on** clause condition. An example of a constant filter predicate is **on (0=1)**. Oracle recognizes such a predicate and makes an unconditional insert of all source rows into the table. No join is performed during the **merge** command if a constant filter predicate is provided.

As of Oracle Database 10*g*, you can include a **delete** clause within the **update** portion of the **merge** command. The **delete** clause (with its own **where** clause) can delete rows in the destination table that are updated by the **merge**. The **delete…where** clause evaluates the updated value, not the original value in the destination table. If a row of the destination table meets the **delete…where** condition but is not included in the set of rows acted on by the **merge** (as defined by the **on** condition), then it is not deleted. Here's an example:

```
merge into COMFORT    C1
using (select City, SampleDate, Noon, Midnight,
            Precipitation from COMFORT2)   C2
   on (C1.City = C2.City and C1.SampleDate=C2.SampleDate)
 when matched then
       update set Noon = C2.Noon
       delete where ( Precipitation is null )
 when not matched then
       insert (C1.City, C1.SampleDate, C1.Noon,
             C1.Midnight, C1.Precipitation)
       values (C2.City, C2.SampleDate, C2.Noon,
             C2.Midnight, C2.Precipitation);
```

Clearly, these commands can become very complex very quickly. In this example, we are performing a conditional **update** and a conditional **delete** on the rows that are updated, along with a conditional **insert** of other rows. You can incorporate very complex business logic into a single command, substantially enhancing the capability of the standard **insert**, **update**, and **delete** commands.

CHAPTER
16

DECODE and CASE:
if, then, and
else in SQL

he **DECODE** function is without doubt one of the most powerful in Oracle's SQL. It is one of several extensions Oracle added to the standard SQL language. This chapter will explore a number of ways that **DECODE** can be used, including the generation of "crosstab" reports. You can also use the **CASE** function and the **COALESCE** function to execute complex logical tests within your SQL statements. This is an advanced and often difficult chapter. Most of what is illustrated here is unnecessary for the vast majority of reporting; don't be concerned if it seems beyond your needs. Its real value is more for sophisticated reporting and programming.

if, then, else

In programming and logic, a common construction of a problem is in the pattern *if, then, else*. For example, *if* this day is a Saturday, *then* Adah will play at home; *if* this day is a Sunday, *then* Adah will go to her grandparents' home; *if* this day is a holiday, *then* Adah will go over to Aunt Dora's; *else* Adah will go to school. In each case, "this day" was tested, and if it was one of a list of certain days, then a certain result followed, or else (if it was none of those days) another result followed. **DECODE** follows this kind of logic. Chapter 11 provided an introduction that demonstrated the basic structure and usage of **DECODE**.

Here is **DECODE**'s format:

```
DECODE(value,if1,then1,if2,then2,if3,then3,. . . ,else)
```

Here, *value* represents any column in a table (regardless of datatype) or any result of a computation, such as one date minus another, a **SUBSTR** of a character column, one number times another, and so on. *value* is tested for each row. If *value* equals *if1*, then the result of the **DECODE** is *then1*; if *value* equals *if2*, then the result of the **DECODE** is *then2*. This continues for virtually as many *if-then* pairs as you can construct. If *value* equals none of the *ifs*, then the result of the **DECODE** is *else*. Each of the *ifs* and *thens* as well as the *else* also can be a column or the result of a function or computation. You can have up to 255 elements within the parentheses.

Let's consider the checkout history for the bookshelf, as recorded in the BOOKSHELF_CHECKOUT table:

```
column Name format a16
column Title format a24 word_wrapped
set pagesize 60

select * from BOOKSHELF_CHECKOUT;

NAME             TITLE                    CHECKOUTD RETURNEDD
---------------- ------------------------ --------- ---------
JED HOPKINS      INNUMERACY               01-JAN-02 22-JAN-02
GERHARDT KENTGEN WONDERFUL LIFE           02-JAN-02 02-FEB-02
DORAH TALBOT     EITHER/OR                02-JAN-02 10-JAN-02
EMILY TALBOT     ANNE OF GREEN GABLES     02-JAN-02 20-JAN-02
PAT LAVAY        THE SHIPPING NEWS        02-JAN-02 12-JAN-02
ROLAND BRANDT    THE SHIPPING NEWS        12-JAN-02 12-MAR-02
```

```
ROLAND BRANDT      THE DISCOVERERS            12-JAN-02 01-MAR-02
ROLAND BRANDT      WEST WITH THE NIGHT        12-JAN-02 01-MAR-02
EMILY TALBOT       MIDNIGHT MAGIC             20-JAN-02 03-FEB-02
EMILY TALBOT       HARRY POTTER AND THE       03-FEB-02 14-FEB-02
                   GOBLET OF FIRE
PAT LAVAY          THE MISMEASURE OF MAN      12-JAN-02 12-FEB-02
DORAH TALBOT       POLAR EXPRESS              01-FEB-02 15-FEB-02
DORAH TALBOT       GOOD DOG, CARL             01-FEB-02 15-FEB-02
GERHARDT KENTGEN   THE MISMEASURE OF MAN      13-FEB-02 05-MAR-02
FRED FULLER        JOHN ADAMS                 01-FEB-02 01-MAR-02
FRED FULLER        TRUMAN                     01-MAR-02 20-MAR-02
JED HOPKINS        TO KILL A MOCKINGBIRD      15-FEB-02 01-MAR-02
DORAH TALBOT       MY LEDGER                  15-FEB-02 03-MAR-02
GERHARDT KENTGEN   MIDNIGHT MAGIC             05-FEB-02 10-FEB-02
```

NOTE
Your output may contain an extra blank line due to word wrapping.
Extra blank lines are not shown here for readability.

As you look through the checkout list, you realize that some of the books were checked out for a rather long time. You can order this list by the number of days checked out, to highlight the readers who keep books for the longest time:

```
select Name, Title, ReturnedDate-CheckOutDate DaysOut
   from BOOKSHELF_CHECKOUT
 order by DaysOut desc;
```

```
NAME               TITLE                      DAYSOUT
---------------    ----------------------     ----------
ROLAND BRANDT      THE SHIPPING NEWS              59
ROLAND BRANDT      THE DISCOVERERS               48
ROLAND BRANDT      WEST WITH THE NIGHT           48
GERHARDT KENTGEN   WONDERFUL LIFE                31
PAT LAVAY          THE MISMEASURE OF MAN         31
FRED FULLER        JOHN ADAMS                    28
JED HOPKINS        INNUMERACY                    21
GERHARDT KENTGEN   THE MISMEASURE OF MAN         20
FRED FULLER        TRUMAN                        19
EMILY TALBOT       ANNE OF GREEN GABLES          18
DORAH TALBOT       MY LEDGER                     16
EMILY TALBOT       MIDNIGHT MAGIC                14
DORAH TALBOT       POLAR EXPRESS                 14
DORAH TALBOT       GOOD DOG, CARL                14
JED HOPKINS        TO KILL A MOCKINGBIRD         14
EMILY TALBOT       HARRY POTTER AND THE          11
                   GOBLET OF FIRE
PAT LAVAY          THE SHIPPING NEWS             10
DORAH TALBOT       EITHER/OR                      8
GERHARDT KENTGEN   MIDNIGHT MAGIC                 5
```

But is it specific readers who are the issue, or is it that there are certain categories of books that take longer to read? Multiple variables are involved, and looking at them in isolation may lead to incorrect decisions. What is the average number of days out for the books in each category?

```
select B.CategoryName,
       MIN(BC.ReturnedDate-BC.CheckOutDate) MinOut,
       MAX(BC.ReturnedDate-BC.CheckOutDate) MaxOut,
       AVG(BC.ReturnedDate-BC.CheckOutDate) AvgOut
  from BOOKSHELF_CHECKOUT BC, BOOKSHELF B
 where BC.Title = B.Title
 group by B.CategoryName;

CATEGORYNAME             MINOUT     MAXOUT     AVGOUT
--------------------     ------     ------     ------
ADULTFIC                     10         59 27.6666667
ADULTNF                      16         48 29.1111111
ADULTREF                      8          8          8
CHILDRENFIC                   5         18         12
CHILDRENPIC                  14         14         14
```

This is more useful, but it doesn't factor in the impact of the different people checking out books in these categories. To accomplish that, you could use an additional level of grouping, but the results will be easier to use if you create a *crosstab* report. The following listing generates a report that shows the minimum, maximum, and average days out by person, by category. This query uses the **DECODE** function to perform the calculations. Three borrowers are used for the purposes of this example.

```
column CategoryName format a11

select B.CategoryName,
       MAX(DECODE(BC.Name, 'FRED FULLER',
                  BC.ReturnedDate-BC.CheckOutDate,NULL)) MaxFF,
       AVG(DECODE(BC.Name, 'FRED FULLER',
                  BC.ReturnedDate-BC.CheckOutDate,NULL)) AvgFF,
       MAX(DECODE(BC.Name, 'DORAH TALBOT',
                  BC.ReturnedDate-BC.CheckOutDate,NULL)) MaxDT,
       AVG(DECODE(BC.Name, 'DORAH TALBOT',
                  BC.ReturnedDate-BC.CheckOutDate,NULL)) AvgDT,
       MAX(DECODE(BC.Name, 'GERHARDT KENTGEN',
                  BC.ReturnedDate-BC.CheckOutDate,NULL)) MaxGK,
       AVG(DECODE(BC.Name, 'GERHARDT KENTGEN',
                  BC.ReturnedDate-BC.CheckOutDate,NULL)) AvgGK
  from BOOKSHELF_CHECKOUT BC, BOOKSHELF B
 where BC.Title = B.Title
 group by B.CategoryName;
```

CATEGORYNAM	MAXFF	AVGFF	MAXDT	AVGDT	MAXGK	AVGGK
ADULTFIC						
ADULTNF	28	23.5	16	16	31	25.5
ADULTREF			8	8		
CHILDRENFIC					5	5
CHILDRENPIC			14	14		

The output now shows the borrowers across the top—Fred Fuller's maximum checkout time is the MaxFF column, Dorah Talbot's is the MaxDT column, and Gerhardt Kentgen's is the MaxGK column. The output shows that the AdultNF category has the longest average checkout time for each of the borrowers shown, and that in Gerhardt Kentgen's case it is significantly longer than the average checkout time in the other category he checked out.

How was this report generated? In the query, the grouping is by CategoryName. The MaxFF column query is shown here:

```
select B.CategoryName,
       MAX(DECODE(BC.Name, 'FRED FULLER',
              BC.ReturnedDate-BC.CheckOutDate,NULL)) MaxFF,
```

DECODE is performing an *if-then* check on the data: If the BC.Name column value in a row is 'FRED FULLER', then calculate the difference between the ReturnedDate and CheckOutDate; else, return a **NULL**. That list of values is then evaluated and the maximum value is returned. A similar set of operations returns the average checkout time for Fred Fuller:

```
       AVG(DECODE(BC.Name, 'FRED FULLER',
              BC.ReturnedDate-BC.CheckOutDate,NULL)) AvgFF,
```

Replacing Values via DECODE

In the last example, **DECODE** was used to return values conditionally, depending on the name of the person who checked out a book. You can also use **DECODE** to replace values in a list. For example, selecting the category names from BOOKSHELF yields the following:

```
select distinct CategoryName from BOOKSHELF;
```

```
CATEGORYNAM
-----------
ADULTFIC
ADULTNF
ADULTREF
CHILDRENFIC
CHILDRENNF
CHILDRENPIC
```

To replace these names, you could join BOOKSHELF to CATEGORY and select ParentCategory and SubCategory from the CATEGORY table. If the list of categories is static, you could avoid the join to the CATEGORY table and perform the replacement via a **DECODE** function, as shown in the following listing (note how **DECODE** supports multiple *if-then* combinations within a single call).

```
select distinct
        DECODE(CategoryName,'ADULTFIC','Adult Fiction',
                            'ADULTNF','Adult Nonfiction',
                            'ADULTREF','Adult Reference',
                            'CHILDRENFIC','Children Fiction',
                            'CHILDRENNF','Children Nonfiction',
                            'CHILDRENPIC','Children Picturebook',
                            CategoryName)
    from BOOKSHELF;

DECODE(CATEGORYNAME,
--------------------
Adult Fiction
Adult Nonfiction
Adult Reference
Children Fiction
Children Nonfiction
Children Picturebook
```

In this case, the data is static; for volatile data, hard-coding the translations into the application code would not be an acceptable programming practice. The technique shown here is useful for transaction-processing systems in which you are trying to minimize the number of database calls performed. In this example, there is no database access required to change 'ADULTNF' to 'Adult Nonfiction'; the change occurs within the **DECODE** function call. Note that if any other categories are found, the *else* condition in the **DECODE** function returns the original CategoryName column value.

DECODE Within DECODE

You can place **DECODE** function calls within other **DECODE** function calls. Let's say you want to charge late fees, with different late-fee rates for different categories of books. Adult category books may be kept later, but the penalty for late days will be higher.

Start with a basic flat rate charge of $0.20 per day for books checked out for more than 14 days:

```
column Name format a16
column Title format a20 word_wrapped
column DaysOut format 999.99 heading 'Days Out'
column DaysLate format 999.99 heading 'Days Late'
set pagesize 60
break on Name

select Name, Title, ReturnedDate,
       ReturnedDate-CheckoutDate as DaysOut /*Count days*/,
       ReturnedDate-CheckoutDate -14  DaysLate,
       (ReturnedDate-CheckoutDate -14)*0.20  LateFee
  from BOOKSHELF_CHECKOUT
where ReturnedDate-CheckoutDate > 14
 order by Name, CheckoutDate;
```

NAME	TITLE	RETURNEDD	Days Out	Days Late	LATEFEE
DORAH TALBOT	MY LEDGER	03-MAR-02	16.00	2.00	.4
EMILY TALBOT	ANNE OF GREEN GABLES	20-JAN-02	18.00	4.00	.8
FRED FULLER	JOHN ADAMS	01-MAR-02	28.00	14.00	2.8
	TRUMAN	20-MAR-02	19.00	5.00	1
GERHARDT KENTGEN	WONDERFUL LIFE	02-FEB-02	31.00	17.00	3.4
	THE MISMEASURE OF MAN	05-MAR-02	20.00	6.00	1.2
JED HOPKINS	INNUMERACY	22-JAN-02	21.00	7.00	1.4
PAT LAVAY	THE MISMEASURE OF MAN	12-FEB-02	31.00	17.00	3.4
ROLAND BRANDT	THE SHIPPING NEWS	12-MAR-02	59.00	45.00	9
	THE DISCOVERERS	01-MAR-02	48.00	34.00	6.8
	WEST WITH THE NIGHT	01-MAR-02	48.00	34.00	6.8

For books in the Adult categories, increase the allowed days late to 21 days. This won't change the number of days out, but it will change the DaysLate column calculation. Because CategoryName is not a column in BOOKSHELF_CHECKOUT, this modification also requires the addition of the BOOKSHELF table to the **from** clause:

```
select BC.Name, BC.Title, BC.ReturnedDate,
       BC.ReturnedDate-BC.CheckoutDate as DaysOut /*Count days*/,
       DECODE(SUBSTR(CategoryName,1,5), 'ADULT',
           BC.ReturnedDate-BC.CheckoutDate -21,
           BC.ReturnedDate-BC.CheckoutDate -14 ) DaysLate,
       DECODE(SUBSTR(CategoryName,1,5), 'ADULT',
          (BC.ReturnedDate-BC.CheckoutDate -21)*0.30,
          (BC.ReturnedDate-BC.CheckoutDate -14)*0.20 ) LateFee
  from BOOKSHELF_CHECKOUT BC, BOOKSHELF B
 where BC.Title = B.Title
   and BC.ReturnedDate-BC.CheckoutDate >
       DECODE(SUBSTR(CategoryName,1,5), 'ADULT',21,14)
 order by BC.Name, BC.CheckoutDate;
```

NAME	TITLE	RETURNEDD	Days Out	Days Late	LATEFEE
EMILY TALBOT	ANNE OF GREEN GABLES	20-JAN-02	18.00	4.00	.8
FRED FULLER	JOHN ADAMS	01-MAR-02	28.00	7.00	2.1
GERHARDT KENTGEN	WONDERFUL LIFE	02-FEB-02	31.00	10.00	3
PAT LAVAY	THE MISMEASURE OF MAN	12-FEB-02	31.00	10.00	3
ROLAND BRANDY	THE DISCOVERERS	01-MAR-02	48.00	27.00	8.1
	THE SHIPPING NEWS	12-MAR-02	59.00	38.00	11.4
	WEST WITH THE NIGHT	01-MAR-02	48.00	27.00	8.1

In the **select** clause, the query logic for the DaysLate column is

```
DECODE(SUBSTR(CategoryName,1,5), 'ADULT',
        BC.ReturnedDate-BC.CheckoutDate -21,
        BC.ReturnedDate-BC.CheckoutDate -14 ) DaysLate
```

In **DECODE**'s *if-then-else* format, this says, "If the first five characters of the CategoryName column match the string 'ADULT', then subtract 21 from the number of days late; otherwise, subtract 14 days." The LateFee calculation uses similar logic. The **where** clause uses **DECODE** to determine the limiting value for the rows returned—for ADULT category books, allow 21 days; otherwise, allow 14:

```
and BC.ReturnedDate-BC.CheckoutDate >
      DECODE(SUBSTR(CategoryName,1,5), 'ADULT',21,14)
```

Now add an additional rule: For Adult fiction category books, the late fee will be double the late fee for other Adult books. From the last query, the calculation for LateFee is

```
DECODE(SUBSTR(CategoryName,1,5), 'ADULT',
      (BC.ReturnedDate-BC.CheckoutDate -21)*0.30,
      (BC.ReturnedDate-BC.CheckoutDate -14)*0.20 ) LateFee
```

The new rule requires an additional category check within the **DECODE** function already performed. The new LateFee calculation is shown here:

```
DECODE(SUBSTR(CategoryName,1,5), 'ADULT',
      DECODE(SUBSTR(CategoryName,6,3),'FIC',
      (BC.ReturnedDate-BC.CheckoutDate -21)*0.60,
      (BC.ReturnedDate-BC.CheckoutDate -21)*0.30),
      (BC.ReturnedDate-BC.CheckoutDate -14)*0.20 ) LateFee
```

Reading through the preceding listing, the first **DECODE** function tells Oracle that if the first five letters of the CategoryName are 'ADULT', then perform the second **DECODE** function. The second **DECODE** tells Oracle that if letters 6, 7, and 8 of the CategoryName are 'FIC', then the late fee is $0.60 per day after the twenty-first day; otherwise, it is $0.30 per day after the twenty-first day. At that point, the inner **DECODE** function completes. For the first **DECODE** function, the **else** clause (for non-ADULT category books) then specifies the late-fee calculation. The query and result are shown in the following listing; you can see the impact by comparing the LateFee column for 'THE SHIPPING NEWS' in this report and the last report:

```
select BC.Name, BC.Title, BC.ReturnedDate,
       BC.ReturnedDate-BC.CheckoutDate as DaysOut /*Count days*/,
       DECODE(SUBSTR(CategoryName,1,5), 'ADULT',
          BC.ReturnedDate-BC.CheckoutDate -21,
          BC.ReturnedDate-BC.CheckoutDate -14 ) DaysLate,
       DECODE(SUBSTR(CategoryName,1,5), 'ADULT',
          DECODE(SUBSTR(CategoryName,6,3),'FIC',
          (BC.ReturnedDate-BC.CheckoutDate -21)*0.60,
          (BC.ReturnedDate-BC.CheckoutDate -21)*0.30),
          (BC.ReturnedDate-BC.CheckoutDate -14)*0.20 ) LateFee
  from BOOKSHELF_CHECKOUT BC, BOOKSHELF B
 where BC.Title = B.Title
   and BC.ReturnedDate-BC.CheckoutDate >
       DECODE(SUBSTR(CategoryName,1,5), 'ADULT',21,14)
 order by BC.Name, BC.CheckoutDate;
```

NAME	TITLE	RETURNEDD	Days Out	Days Late	LATEFEE
EMILY TALBOT	ANNE OF GREEN GABLES	20-JAN-02	18.00	4.00	.8
FRED FULLER	JOHN ADAMS	01-MAR-02	28.00	7.00	2.1
GERHARDT KENTGEN	WONDERFUL LIFE	02-FEB-02	31.00	10.00	3
PAT LAVAY	THE MISMEASURE OF MAN	12-FEB-02	31.00	10.00	3
ROLAND BRANDT	THE DISCOVERERS	01-MAR-02	48.00	27.00	8.1
	THE SHIPPING NEWS	12-MAR-02	59.00	38.00	22.8
	WEST WITH THE NIGHT	01-MAR-02	48.00	27.00	8.1

You can nest **DECODE**s within other **DECODE**s to support complex logic within your data processing. For example, you may choose to print one column if it has a non-**NULL** value, and a second column if the first is **NULL**. With **DECODE**, that is a simple function call:

```
DECODE(Column1, NULL, Column2, Column1)
```

If Column1 is **NULL**, Column2 will be returned; otherwise, Column1's non-**NULL** value will be returned. You could also use **NVL** or the **COALESCE** and **NULLIF** functions to perform similar logic.

COALESCE will return the first non-**NULL** value encountered in a list of values. The preceding **DECODE** example could be rewritten as

```
COALESCE(Column1, Column2)
```

NOTE
*COALESCE can take more than two arguments, but **NVL** cannot.*

Because **COALESCE**'s name does not clearly convey its usage, be sure to provide comments within your code to explain the logical tests performed.

Greater Than and Less Than in DECODE

DECODE supports logic checks, but how do you do numeric comparisons in this format? The simplest solution is often to use the **SIGN** function. **SIGN** returns a 1 if the number is positive, 0 if the number is 0, and –1 if the number is negative. Because **SIGN** operates on numbers, you can evaluate any function that returns a number, including date arithmetic.

Let's modify the LateFee business rule again. Using the same base calculation, we'll modify the outcome so that we will not collect late fees that are less than or equal to $4.00. Here is the original LateFee calculation:

```
DECODE(SUBSTR(CategoryName,1,5), 'ADULT',
    DECODE(SUBSTR(CategoryName,6,3),'FIC',
    (BC.ReturnedDate-BC.CheckoutDate -21)*0.60,
    (BC.ReturnedDate-BC.CheckoutDate -21)*0.30),
    (BC.ReturnedDate-BC.CheckoutDate -14)*0.20 ) LateFee
```

If that value is less than 4, we will return a 0; otherwise, we will return the calculated value. To implement this requirement, subtract 4 from the LateFee value; if the result is positive (its **SIGN** value is 1), return that result; otherwise, return a 0.

```
DECODE(SIGN(
        DECODE(SUBSTR(CategoryName,1,5), 'ADULT',
            DECODE(SUBSTR(CategoryName,6,3),'FIC',
            (BC.ReturnedDate-BC.CheckoutDate -21)*0.60,
            (BC.ReturnedDate-BC.CheckoutDate -21)*0.30),
            (BC.ReturnedDate-BC.CheckoutDate -14)*0.20 ) -4),
        1,
        DECODE(SUBSTR(CategoryName,1,5), 'ADULT',
            DECODE(SUBSTR(CategoryName,6,3),'FIC',
            (BC.ReturnedDate-BC.CheckoutDate -21)*0.60,
            (BC.ReturnedDate-BC.CheckoutDate -21)*0.30),
            (BC.ReturnedDate-BC.CheckoutDate -14)*0.20 ),
        0) LateFee
```

Building from a simple foundation, this series of **DECODE** function calls allows you to perform very complex logic on the LateFee calculations. The first **DECODE** evaluates the **SIGN** of the next **DECODE** function result when 4 is subtracted from it. If that number is positive, the calculated late fee is returned; otherwise, a 0 is returned. The following listing shows this calculation and the output that results:

```
select BC.Name, BC.Title, BC.ReturnedDate,
        BC.ReturnedDate-BC.CheckoutDate as DaysOut /*Count days*/,
        DECODE(SUBSTR(CategoryName,1,5), 'ADULT',
            BC.ReturnedDate-BC.CheckoutDate -21,
            BC.ReturnedDate-BC.CheckoutDate -14 ) DaysLate,
DECODE(SIGN(
        DECODE(SUBSTR(CategoryName,1,5), 'ADULT',
            DECODE(SUBSTR(CategoryName,6,3),'FIC',
            (BC.ReturnedDate-BC.CheckoutDate -21)*0.60,
            (BC.ReturnedDate-BC.CheckoutDate -21)*0.30),
            (BC.ReturnedDate-BC.CheckoutDate -14)*0.20 ) -4),
        1,
        DECODE(SUBSTR(CategoryName,1,5), 'ADULT',
            DECODE(SUBSTR(CategoryName,6,3),'FIC',
            (BC.ReturnedDate-BC.CheckoutDate -21)*0.60,
            (BC.ReturnedDate-BC.CheckoutDate -21)*0.30),
            (BC.ReturnedDate-BC.CheckoutDate -14)*0.20 ),
        0) LateFee
   from BOOKSHELF_CHECKOUT BC, BOOKSHELF B
  where BC.Title = B.Title
    and BC.ReturnedDate-BC.CheckoutDate >
        DECODE(SUBSTR(CategoryName,1,5), 'ADULT',21,14)
  order by BC.Name, BC.CheckoutDate;
```

NAME	TITLE	RETURNEDD	Days Out	Days Late	LATEFEE
EMILY TALBOT	ANNE OF GREEN GABLES	20-JAN-02	18.00	4.00	0
FRED FULLER	JOHN ADAMS	01-MAR-02	28.00	7.00	0
GERHARDT KENTGEN	WONDERFUL LIFE	02-FEB-02	31.00	10.00	0
PAT LAVAY	THE MISMEASURE OF MAN	12-FEB-02	31.00	10.00	0
ROLAND BRANDT	THE DISCOVERERS	01-MAR-02	48.00	27.00	8.1
	THE SHIPPING NEWS	12-MAR-02	59.00	38.00	22.8
	WEST WITH THE NIGHT	01-MAR-02	48.00	27.00	8.1

You can eliminate the display of the first four rows (with $0 late fees) by making a similar modification to the **where** clause.

Using CASE

You can use the **CASE** function in place of **DECODE**. The **CASE** function uses the keywords **when**, **then**, **else**, and **end** to indicate the logic path followed. In general, SQL using the **CASE** function is wordier than the equivalent **DECODE** but may be easier to read and maintain.

Consider this simple **DECODE** example from earlier in this chapter:

```
select distinct
        DECODE(CategoryName,'ADULTFIC','Adult Fiction',
                            'ADULTNF','Adult Nonfiction',
                            'ADULTREF','Adult Reference',
                            'CHILDRENFIC','Children Fiction',
                            'CHILDRENNF','Children Nonfiction',
                            'CHILDRENPIC','Children Picturebook',
                            CategoryName)
    from BOOKSHELF;
```

The equivalent **CASE** function is

```
select distinct
        CASE CategoryName
            when  'ADULTFIC' then 'Adult Fiction'
            when  'ADULTNF' then 'Adult Nonfiction'
            when  'ADULTREF' then 'Adult Reference'
            when  'CHILDRENFIC' then 'Children Fiction'
            when  'CHILDRENNF' then 'Children Nonfiction'
            when  'CHILDRENPIC' then 'Children Picturebook'
            else CategoryName
        end
    from BOOKSHELF;

CASECATEGORYNAMEWHEN
--------------------
Adult Fiction
Adult Nonfiction
Adult Reference
```

```
Children Fiction
Children Nonfiction
Children Picturebook
```

CASE evaluates the first **when** clause and returns a match if the limiting condition is met. As with **DECODE**, you can nest **CASE** function calls. How would you perform the LateFee column calculations using **CASE**?

The **DECODE** function began by calculating a higher rate for ADULT category books:

```
DECODE(SUBSTR(CategoryName,1,5), 'ADULT',
    (BC.ReturnedDate-BC.CheckoutDate -21)*0.30,
    (BC.ReturnedDate-BC.CheckoutDate -14)*0.20 ) LateFee
```

The **CASE** equivalent is

```
CASE SUBSTR(CategoryName,1,5)
    when 'ADULT' then (BC.ReturnedDate-BC.CheckoutDate -21)*0.30
    else (BC.ReturnedDate-BC.CheckoutDate -14)*0.20
end
```

The second rule (ADULTFIC books have doubled late fees) requires a nested **CASE** command:

```
CASE SUBSTR(CategoryName,1,5)
    when 'ADULT' then
        CASE SUBSTR(CategoryName,6,3)
            when 'FIC' then (BC.ReturnedDate-BC.CheckoutDate -21)*0.60
            else (BC.ReturnedDate-BC.CheckoutDate -21)*0.30
            end
    else (BC.ReturnedDate-BC.CheckoutDate -14)*0.20
end
```

This is more complex, but the logic is very easy to follow and will usually be simpler to maintain than the equivalent **DECODE** clause. Now consider the final condition: If the calculated late fee is less than or equal to $4, return a 0. Because we are using the **CASE** function, we do not need to use a **SIGN** function—we can just use a "<" comparison as part of the command processing. The following example shows how to add this check: An additional **CASE** function is added, and the inner **CASE** function call is enclosed in parentheses. The result is compared to $4:

```
CASE when
    (CASE SUBSTR(CategoryName,1,5)
        when 'ADULT' then
            CASE SUBSTR(CategoryName,6,3)
                when 'FIC' then (BC.ReturnedDate-BC.CheckoutDate -21)*0.60
                else (BC.ReturnedDate-BC.CheckoutDate -21)*0.30
                end
        else (BC.ReturnedDate-BC.CheckoutDate -14)*0.20
    end)
    < 4 then 0
```

The **else** clause for this **CASE** function call is the same as the inner **CASE** execution—it calculates the late fee:

```
else
    CASE SUBSTR(CategoryName,1,5)
      when 'ADULT' then
          CASE SUBSTR(CategoryName,6,3)
              when 'FIC' then (BC.ReturnedDate-BC.CheckoutDate -21)*0.60
              else (BC.ReturnedDate-BC.CheckoutDate -21)*0.30
              end
      else (BC.ReturnedDate-BC.CheckoutDate -14)*0.20
    end
end
```

The full query is shown in the following listing, along with its output:

```
column LateFee format 999.99

select BC.Name, BC.Title, BC.ReturnedDate,
       BC.ReturnedDate-BC.CheckoutDate as DaysOut /*Count days*/,
       DECODE(SUBSTR(CategoryName,1,5), 'ADULT',
           BC.ReturnedDate-BC.CheckoutDate -21,
           BC.ReturnedDate-BC.CheckoutDate -14 ) DaysLate,
CASE when
   (CASE SUBSTR(CategoryName,1,5)
      when 'ADULT' then
          CASE SUBSTR(CategoryName,6,3)
              when 'FIC' then (BC.ReturnedDate-BC.CheckoutDate -21)*0.60
              else (BC.ReturnedDate-BC.CheckoutDate -21)*0.30
              end
      else (BC.ReturnedDate-BC.CheckoutDate -14)*0.20
   end)
   < 4 then 0 else
   CASE SUBSTR(CategoryName,1,5)
      when 'ADULT' then
          CASE SUBSTR(CategoryName,6,3)
              when 'FIC' then (BC.ReturnedDate-BC.CheckoutDate -21)*0.60
              else (BC.ReturnedDate-BC.CheckoutDate -21)*0.30
              end
      else (BC.ReturnedDate-BC.CheckoutDate -14)*0.20
   end
end  AS LateFee
  from BOOKSHELF_CHECKOUT BC, BOOKSHELF B
 where BC.Title = B.Title
   and BC.ReturnedDate-BC.CheckoutDate >
       DECODE(SUBSTR(CategoryName,1,5), 'ADULT',21,14)
 order by BC.Name, BC.CheckoutDate;
```

NAME	TITLE	RETURNEDD	Days Out	Days Late	LATEFEE
EMILY TALBOT	ANNE OF GREEN GABLES	20-JAN-02	18.00	4.00	.00
FRED FULLER	JOHN ADAMS	01-MAR-02	28.00	7.00	.00
GERHARDT KENTGEN	WONDERFUL LIFE	02-FEB-02	31.00	10.00	.00
PAT LAVAY	THE MISMEASURE OF MAN	12-FEB-02	31.00	10.00	.00
ROLAND BRANDT	THE DISCOVERERS	01-MAR-02	48.00	27.00	8.10
	THE SHIPPING NEWS	12-MAR-02	59.00	38.00	22.80
	WEST WITH THE NIGHT	01-MAR-02	48.00	27.00	8.10

Comparing the **CASE** version to the **DECODE** version earlier in this chapter, you can see that the **CASE** command is six lines longer, but it's simpler to read and maintain. **CASE** offers a powerful alternative to **DECODE**—and both **CASE** and **DECODE** provide solid solutions when you need to perform logic within your queries.

CHAPTER
17

Creating and Managing
Tables, Views, Indexes,
Clusters, and Sequences

ntil now, the emphasis of this book has been on using tables. This chapter looks at creating, dropping, and changing tables, creating views, and using options such as index-organized and partitioned tables. You've seen numerous **create table** commands to this point; this chapter will reinforce those examples and show how to use the latest options. You will also see the commands for creating and managing views, indexes, clusters, and sequences.

Creating a Table

Consider the TROUBLE table. This is similar to the COMFORT table discussed earlier in the book, but it is used to track cities with unusual weather patterns.

```
describe TROUBLE

Name                             Null?     Type
-------------------------------- --------  ------------
CITY                             NOT NULL  VARCHAR2(13)
SAMPLEDATE                       NOT NULL  DATE
NOON                                       NUMBER(3,1)
MIDNIGHT                                   NUMBER(3,1)
PRECIPITATION                              NUMBER
```

The columns in the TROUBLE table represent three major datatypes in Oracle—VARCHAR2, DATE, and NUMBER. Here is the SQL that created this Oracle table:

```
create table TROUBLE (
City          VARCHAR2(13) NOT NULL,
SampleDate    DATE NOT NULL,
Noon          NUMBER(3,1),
Midnight      NUMBER(3,1),
Precipitation NUMBER
);
```

These are the basic elements of this command:

- The words **create table**

- The name of the table

- An opening parenthesis

- Column definitions

- A closing parenthesis

- A SQL terminator

The individual column definitions are separated by commas. There is no comma after the last column definition. The table and column names must start with a letter of the alphabet, but may include letters, numbers, and underscores. Names may be 1 to 30 characters in length, must be

unique within the table, and cannot be an Oracle reserved word (see "Reserved Words" in the Alphabetical Reference of this book).

If the names are not within double quotes, case does not matter in naming a table. There are no options for DATE datatypes. Varying-length character datatypes must have their maximum length specified. NUMBERs may be either high precision (up to 38 digits) or specified precision, based on the maximum number of digits and the number of places allowed to the right of the decimal (an Amount field for U.S. currency, for instance, would have only two decimal places).

NOTE
Do not enclose table and column names within double quotes; otherwise, case will matter. This can be disastrous for your users or developers.

See Part V of this book for additional **create table** options for object-relational features.

Character Width and NUMBER Precision
Specifying the maximum length for character (CHAR and VARCHAR2) columns and the precision for NUMBER columns has consequences that must be considered during the design of the table. Improper decisions can be corrected later, using the **alter table** command, but the process can be difficult.

Deciding on a Proper Width
A character column that is not wide enough for the data you want to put in it will cause an **insert** to fail and result in an error message:

```
ERROR at line 1:
ORA-12899: value too large for column "PRACTICE"."TROUBLE"."CITY"
(actual: 16, maximum: 13)
```

The maximum width for CHAR (fixed-length) columns is 2,000 characters. VARCHAR2 (varying-length character) columns can have up to 4,000 characters. In assigning width to a column, allot enough space to allow for all future possibilities. A CHAR(15) for a city name, for instance, is just going to get you in trouble later on. You'll have to either alter the table or truncate or distort the names of some cities.

NOTE
*There is no penalty in Oracle for defining a wide VARCHAR2 column. Oracle is clever enough not to store blank spaces at the end of VARCHAR2 columns. The city name SAN FRANCISCO, for example, will be stored in 13 spaces, even if you've defined the column as VARCHAR2(50). And if a column has nothing in it (**NULL**), Oracle will store nothing in the column, not even a blank space (it does store a couple of bytes of internal database control information, but this is unaffected by the size you specify for the column). The only effect that choosing a higher number will have is in the default SQL*Plus column formatting. SQL*Plus will create a default heading the same width as the VARCHAR2 definition.*

Choosing NUMBER Precision

A NUMBER column with incorrect precision will have one of two consequences. Oracle will either reject the attempt to **insert** the row of data, or will drop some of the data's precision. Here are four rows of data about to be entered into Oracle:

```
insert into TROUBLE values
    ('PLEASANT LAKE','21-MAR-03',
    39.99,  -1.31, 3.6);

insert into TROUBLE values
    ('PLEASANT LAKE','22-JUN-03',
    101.44,  86.2, 1.63);

insert into TROUBLE values
    ('PLEASANT LAKE','23-SEP-03',
    92.85,  79.6, 1.00003);

insert into TROUBLE values
    ('PLEASANT LAKE','22-DEC-03',
    -17.445, -10.4, 2.4);
```

These are the results of this attempt:

```
insert into TROUBLE values
    ('PLEASANT LAKE','21-MAR-03',
    39.99,  -1.31, 3.6);

1 row created.

insert into TROUBLE values
    ('PLEASANT LAKE','22-JUN-03',
    101.44,  86.2, 1.63);
    *
ERROR at line 3:
ORA-01438: value larger than specified precision allows for this column

insert into TROUBLE values
    ('PLEASANT LAKE','23-SEP-03',
    92.85,  79.6, 1.00003);

1 row created.

insert into TROUBLE values
    ('PLEASANT LAKE','22-DEC-03',
    -17.445, -10.4, 2.4);

1 row created.
```

The first, third, and fourth rows were inserted, but the second **insert** failed because 101.44 exceeded the precision set in the **create table** statement, where Noon was defined as NUMBER(3,1).

The 3 here indicates the maximum number of digits Oracle will store. The 1 means that one of those three digits is reserved for a position to the right of the decimal point. Therefore, 12.3 would be a legitimate number, but 123.4 would not be.

Note that the error here is caused by the 101, not the .44, because NUMBER(3,1) leaves only two positions available to the left of the decimal point. The .44 will not cause the "value larger than specified precision" error. It would simply be rounded to one decimal place. This will be demonstrated shortly, but first, let's look at the results of a query of the four rows we've attempted to **insert**:

```
select * from TROUBLE;

CITY          SAMPLEDAT    NOON MIDNIGHT PRECIPITATION
------------- --------- -------- -------- -------------
PLEASANT LAKE 21-MAR-03       40     -1.3           3.6
PLEASANT LAKE 23-SEP-03     92.9     79.6       1.00003
PLEASANT LAKE 22-DEC-03    -17.4    -10.4           2.4
```

The three rows were successfully inserted; only the problematic row is missing. Oracle never inserted the single row for the **insert** statement that failed.

Rounding During Insertion

Suppose you correct the **create table** statement and increase the number of digits available for Noon and Midnight, as shown here:

```
drop table TROUBLE;
create table TROUBLE (
City          VARCHAR2(13) NOT NULL,
SampleDate    DATE NOT NULL,
Noon          NUMBER(4,1),
Midnight      NUMBER(4,1),
Precipitation NUMBER
);
```

Now the four **insert** statements will all be successful. A query now will reveal this:

```
insert into TROUBLE values
    ('PLEASANT LAKE','21-MAR-03',
    39.99,  -1.31, 3.6);

insert into TROUBLE values
    ('PLEASANT LAKE','22-JUN-03',
    101.44,   86.2, 1.63);

insert into TROUBLE values
    ('PLEASANT LAKE','23-SEP-03',
    92.85,  79.6, 1.00003);

insert into TROUBLE values
    ('PLEASANT LAKE','22-DEC-03',
    -17.445, -10.4, 2.4);
```

```
select * from TROUBLE;

CITY          SAMPLEDAT   NOON MIDNIGHT PRECIPITATION
------------- --------- ------ -------- -------------
PLEASANT LAKE 21-MAR-03     40     -1.3           3.6
PLEASANT LAKE 22-JUN-03  101.4     86.2          1.63
PLEASANT LAKE 23-SEP-03   92.9     79.6       1.00003
PLEASANT LAKE 22-DEC-03  -17.4    -10.4           2.4
```

Look at the first **insert** statement. The value for Noon is 39.99. In the query, it is rounded to 40. Midnight in the **insert** is –1.31. In the query it is –1.3. Oracle rounds the number based on the digit just to the right of the allowed precision. Table 17-1 shows the effects of precision in several examples. See Chapter 9 for examples of the **ROUND** function.

Value in insert Statement	Actual Value in Table
For precision of NUMBER(4,1)	
123.4	123.4
123.44	123.4
123.45	123.5
123.445	123.4
1234.5	**insert** fails
For precision of NUMBER(4)	
123.4	123
123.44	123
123.45	123
123.445	123
1234.5	1235
12345	**insert** fails
For precision of NUMBER(4,-1)	
123.4	120
123.44	120
123.45	120
123.445	120
125	130

TABLE 17-1. *Effect of Precision on inserts*

Value in insert Statement	Actual Value in Table
1234.5	1230
12345	**insert** fails
For precision of NUMBER	
123.4	123.4
123.44	123.44
123.45	123.45
123.445	123.445
125	125
1234.5	1234.5
12345.6789012345678	12345.6789012345678

TABLE 17-1. *Effect of Precision on inserts* (continued)

Constraints in create table

You can use the **create table** statement to enforce several different kinds of constraints on a table: candidate keys, primary keys, foreign keys, and check conditions. A **constraint** clause can constrain a single column or group of columns in a table. The point of these constraints is to get Oracle to do most of the work in maintaining the integrity of your database. The more constraints you add to a table definition, the less work you have to do in applications to maintain the data. On the other hand, the more constraints there are in a table, the longer it takes to update the data.

You can specify constraints in one of two ways: as part of the column definition (known as a *column* constraint) or at the end of the **create table** statement (known as a *table* constraint). Clauses that constrain several columns must be table constraints.

The Candidate Key

A *candidate key* is a combination of one or more columns, the values of which uniquely identify each row of a table. The following listing shows the creation of a UNIQUE constraint for the TROUBLE table:

```
drop table TROUBLE;

create table TROUBLE (
City            VARCHAR2(13) NOT NULL,
SampleDate      DATE NOT NULL,
Noon            NUMBER(4,1),
Midnight        NUMBER(4,1),
Precipitation NUMBER,
constraint TROUBLE_UQ UNIQUE (City, SampleDate)
);
```

The key of this table is the combination of City and SampleDate. Notice that both columns are also declared to be **NOT NULL**. This feature requires you to specify values for certain columns in order for rows to be inserted. Clearly, temperature and precipitation information is not useful without knowing where or when it was collected. This technique is common for columns that are the primary key of a table, but it's also useful if certain columns are critical for the row of data to be meaningful. If **NOT NULL** isn't specified, the column can have **NULL** values.

When you create a UNIQUE constraint, Oracle will create a unique index to enforce the uniqueness of the values.

The Primary Key

The *primary key* of a table is one of the candidate keys that you give some special characteristics. You can have only one primary key, and a primary key column cannot contain **NULL**s.

The following **create table** statement has the same effect as the previous one, except that you can have several UNIQUE constraints but only one PRIMARY KEY constraint:

```
drop table TROUBLE;
create table TROUBLE (
City            VARCHAR2(13),
SampleDate      DATE,
Noon            NUMBER(4,1),
Midnight        NUMBER(4,1),
Precipitation NUMBER,
constraint TROUBLE_PK PRIMARY KEY (City, SampleDate)
);
```

For single-column primary or candidate keys, you can define the key on the column with a column constraint instead of a table constraint:

```
create table AUTHOR
(AuthorName  VARCHAR2(50) primary key,
Comments     VARCHAR2(100));
```

In this case, the AuthorName column is the primary key, and Oracle will generate a name for the PRIMARY KEY constraint. This is not recommended if you want to enforce a common naming standard for keys, as discussed later in "Naming Constraints."

Designating Index Tablespaces

UNIQUE and PRIMARY KEY constraints create indexes. Unless you tell Oracle differently, those indexes will be placed in your default tablespace (tablespaces are described fully in Chapter 20). To specify a different tablespace, use the **using index tablespace** clause of the **create table** command, as shown in the following listing:

```
create table AUTHOR2
(AuthorName  VARCHAR2(50),
Comments     VARCHAR2(100),
constraint AUTHOR_PK primary key (AuthorName)
            using index tablespace USERS);
```

The index associated with the AUTHOR_PK primary key constraint will be placed in the USERS tablespace. See Chapter 20 for details on the management of tablespaces.

NOTE
In most default installations, the USERS tablespace is created and is the default tablespace.

The Foreign Key

A *foreign key* is a combination of columns with values based on the primary key values from another table. A foreign key constraint, also known as a *referential integrity constraint,* specifies that the values of the foreign key correspond to actual values of the primary key in the other table. In the BOOKSHELF table, for example, the CategoryName column refers to values for the CategoryName column in the CATEGORY table:

```
create table BOOKSHELF
(Title          VARCHAR2(100) primary key,
Publisher       VARCHAR2(20),
CategoryName VARCHAR2(20),
Rating          VARCHAR2(2),
constraint CATFK foreign key (CategoryName)
references CATEGORY(CategoryName));
```

You can refer to a primary or unique key, even in the same table. However, you can't refer to a table in a remote database in the **references** clause. You can use the table form (which is used earlier to create a PRIMARY KEY on the TROUBLE table) instead of the column form to specify foreign keys with multiple columns.

Sometimes you may want to delete these dependent rows when you delete the row they depend on. In the case of BOOKSHELF and CATEGORY, if you delete a CategoryName from CATEGORY, you may want to make the matching BOOKSHELF CategoryName column values **NULL**. In another case, you might want to delete the whole row. The clause **on delete cascade** added to the **references** clause tells Oracle to delete the dependent row when you delete the corresponding row in the parent table. This action automatically maintains referential integrity. For more information on the clauses **on delete cascade** and **references**, consult "Integrity Constraint" in the Alphabetical Reference of this book.

The CHECK Constraint

Many columns must have values that are within a certain range or that satisfy certain conditions. With a *CHECK constraint,* you can specify an expression that must always be true for every row in the table. For example, the RATING table stores the valid ratings; to limit the available values beyond the limits enforced by the column definition, you can use a CHECK constraint, as shown in the following listing:

```
create table RATING_WITH_CHECK
(Rating  VARCHAR2(2) CHECK (Rating <= 9),
RatingDescription VARCHAR2(50));
```

A column-level CHECK constraint can't refer to values in other rows; it can't use the pseudo-columns such as SysDate, User, CurrVal, NextVal, Level, and RowNum. You can use the table constraint form (as opposed to the column constraint form) to refer to multiple columns in a CHECK constraint.

Naming Constraints

You can name your constraints. If you use an effective naming scheme for your constraint names, you will be better able to identify and manage the constraints. The name of a constraint should identify the table it acts upon and the type of constraint it represents. For example, the primary key on the TROUBLE table could be named TROUBLE_PK.

You can specify a name for a constraint when you create the constraint. If you do not specify a name for the constraint, Oracle will generate a name. Most of Oracle's generated constraint names are of the form SYS_C###### (for example, SYS_C000145). Because the system-generated constraint name does not tell you anything about the table or the constraint, you should name your constraints.

In the following example, the PRIMARY KEY constraint is created, and named, as part of the **create table** command for the TROUBLE table (notice the **constraint** clause):

```
create table TROUBLE (
City            VARCHAR2(13),
SampleDate      DATE,
Noon            NUMBER(4,1),
Midnight        NUMBER(4,1),
Precipitation NUMBER,
constraint TROUBLE_PK PRIMARY KEY (City, SampleDate)
);
```

The **constraint** clause of the **create table** command names the constraint (in this case, TROUBLE_PK). You may use this constraint name later when enabling or disabling constraints.

Dropping Tables

Dropping tables is very simple. You use the words **drop table** and the table name, as shown here:

```
drop table TROUBLE;
```

You drop a table only when you no longer need it. In Oracle, the **truncate** command lets you remove all the rows in the table and reclaim the space for other uses without removing the table definition from the database.

As of Oracle Database 10g, dropped tables retain their space—they are accessed via the "recycle bin." To drop a table and remove it from the recycle bin at the same time, use the **purge** clause of the **drop table** command:

```
drop table TROUBLE purge;
```

If the table has already been dropped, you can purge it from the recycle bin:

```
purge table TROUBLE;
```

You can purge all contents of your recycle bin:

```
purge recyclebin;
```

Truncating is also very simple:

```
truncate table TROUBLE;
```

```
Table truncated.
```

Truncating can't be rolled back. If there are triggers that delete rows that depend on rows in the table, truncating does not execute those triggers. You should be *sure* you really want to **truncate** before doing it. You can choose to release the table's storage (via the **drop storage** clause, the default) or to retain it (via **reuse storage**).

Altering Tables

Table definitions can be altered in several ways: by adding a column to an existing table, by changing a column's definition, or by dropping a column. DBAs commonly alter tables in other ways to manage space and memory usage. Adding a column is straightforward, and this process is similar to creating a table. Suppose you decide to add two new columns to the TROUBLE table: Condition, which you believe should be **NOT NULL**, and Wind, for the wind speed. The first attempt starts by creating the table and populating it with a few records:

```
drop table TROUBLE;

create table TROUBLE (
City          VARCHAR2(13),
SampleDate    DATE,
Noon          NUMBER(4,1),
Midnight      NUMBER(4,1),
Precipitation NUMBER);

insert into TROUBLE values
   ('PLEASANT LAKE','21-MAR-03',
    39.99,  -1.31, 3.6);

insert into TROUBLE values
   ('PLEASANT LAKE','22-JUN-03',
    101.44,  86.2, 1.63);

insert into TROUBLE values
   ('PLEASANT LAKE','23-SEP-03',
    92.85,  79.6, 1.00003);

insert into TROUBLE values
   ('PLEASANT LAKE','22-DEC-03',
    -17.445, -10.4, 2.4);
```

The first attempt at adding the new columns looks like this:

```
alter table TROUBLE add (
Condition     VARCHAR2(9) NOT NULL,
Wind          NUMBER(3)
);

alter table TROUBLE add (
            *
ERROR at line 1: ORA-01758: table must be empty to add
mandatory (NOT NULL) column
```

You get an error message because you cannot add a column defined as **NOT NULL**—when you try to add it, the column won't have anything in it. Each row in the table would have a new empty column defined as **NOT NULL**.

The **alter table** command's **add** clause will work with a **NOT NULL** column if the table is empty, but usually it is impractical to empty a table of all its rows just to add a **NOT NULL** column.

The alternative is to first alter the table by adding the column without the **NOT NULL** restriction:

```
alter table TROUBLE add (
Condition     VARCHAR2(9),
Wind          NUMBER(3)
);

Table altered.
```

Then, you fill the column with data for every row (either with legitimate data or a placeholder until legitimate data can be obtained):

```
update TROUBLE set Condition = 'SUNNY';
```

Finally, you alter the table again and modify the column definition to **NOT NULL**:

```
alter table TROUBLE modify (
Condition     VARCHAR2(9) NOT NULL,
City          VARCHAR2(17)
);

Table altered.
```

Note that the City column was also modified to enlarge it to 17 characters (just to show how this is done). When the table is described, it shows this:

```
describe TROUBLE
```

Name	Null?	Type
CITY		VARCHAR2(17)

```
SAMPLEDATE                           DATE
NOON                                 NUMBER(4,1)
MIDNIGHT                             NUMBER(4,1)
PRECIPITATION                        NUMBER
CONDITION                   NOT NULL VARCHAR2(9)
WIND                                 NUMBER(3)
```

The table contains the following:

```
select * from TROUBLE;

CITY              SAMPLEDAT    NOON MIDNIGHT PRECIPITATION CONDITION WIND
---------------   --------- ------- -------- ------------- --------- ----
PLEASANT LAKE     21-MAR-03      40     -1.3           3.6 SUNNY
PLEASANT LAKE     22-JUN-03   101.4     86.2          1.63 SUNNY
PLEASANT LAKE     23-SEP-03    92.9     79.6       1.00003 SUNNY
PLEASANT LAKE     22-DEC-03   -17.4    -10.4           2.4 SUNNY
```

Here, you see the effect of the changes. City is now 17 characters wide instead of 13. Condition has been added to the table as **NOT NULL** and is SUNNY (temporarily). Wind has been added and is **NULL**.

To make a **NOT NULL** column nullable, use the **alter table** command with the **NULL** clause, as follows:

```
alter table TROUBLE modify
(Condition NULL);
```

The Rules for Adding or Modifying a Column

These are the rules for adding a column to a table:

- You may add a column at any time if **NOT NULL** isn't specified.

- You may add a **NOT NULL** column in three steps:

 1. Add the column without **NOT NULL** specified.

 2. Fill that column with data for every row.

 3. Modify the column to be **NOT NULL**.

NOTE
*If you use the **default** clause when adding a column, Oracle will update each row with that default value when it adds the column; these updates fire any AFTER UPDATE triggers defined on the table (see Chapter 30).*

These are the rules for modifying a column:

■ You can increase a character column's width at any time.

■ You can increase the number of digits in a NUMBER column at any time.

■ You can increase or decrease the number of decimal places in a NUMBER column at any time.

In addition, if a column is **NULL** for every row of the table, you can make any of these changes:

■ You can change the column's datatype.

■ You can decrease a character column's width.

■ You can decrease the number of digits in a NUMBER column.

You can only change the datatype of a column if the column is empty (**NULL**) in all rows of the table.

Exceptions for LONG-LOB Column Changes

There is one notable exception to the restrictions on datatype changes. Oracle supports the changing of LONG datatype columns to the LOB datatype, even if there is data already in the LONG column. The following listing illustrates this functionality:

```
create table LONGTEST
(Col1    NUMBER,
Longcol  LONG);

Table created.

insert into LONGTEST values (1,'This is a LONG value');

1 row created.

alter table LONGTEST modify (Longcol CLOB);

Table altered.

desc LONGTEST

Name                                             Null?    Type
------------------------------------------------ -------- --------
COL1                                                      NUMBER
LONGCOL                                                   CLOB

select Longcol from LONGTEST;

LONGCOL
--------------------------------------
This is a LONG value
```

Dropping a Column

You can drop a column from a table. Dropping a column is more complicated than adding or modifying a column because of the additional work that Oracle has to do. Just removing the column from the list of columns in the table—so it doesn't show up when you **select** * from the table—is easy. It's recovering the space that was actually taken up by the column values that is more complex, and potentially very time-consuming for the database. For this reason, you can drop a column immediately or you can mark it as "unused," to be dropped at a later time. If the column is dropped immediately, the action may impact performance. If the column is marked as unused, there will be no impact on performance. The column can actually be dropped at a later time when the database is less heavily used.

To drop a column, use either the **set unused** clause or the **drop** clause of the **alter table** command. You cannot drop a pseudo-column, a column of a nested table, or a partition key column.

In the following example, column Wind is dropped from the TROUBLE table:

```
alter table TROUBLE drop column Wind;
```

Alternatively, you can mark the Wind column as unused:

```
alter table TROUBLE set unused column Wind;
```

Marking a column as "unused" does not release the space previously used by the column, until you drop the unused columns:

```
alter table TROUBLE drop unused columns;
```

You can query USER_UNUSED_COL_TABS, ALL_UNUSED_COL_TABS, and DBA_UNUSED_ COL_TABS to see all tables with columns marked as unused.

NOTE
Once you have marked a column as "unused," you cannot access that column.

You can drop multiple columns in a single command, as shown in the following listing:

```
alter table TROUBLE drop (Condition, Wind);
```

NOTE
*When dropping multiple columns, you should not use the **column** keyword of the **alter table** command; it causes a syntax error. The multiple column names must be enclosed in parentheses, as shown in the preceding listing.*

If the dropped columns are part of primary keys or unique constraints, you will need to also use the **cascade constraints** clause as part of your **alter table** command. If you drop a column that belongs to a primary key, Oracle will drop both the column and the primary key index.

Creating a Table from a Table

Oracle lets you create a new table on-the-fly, based on a **select** statement on an existing table:

```
create table RAIN_TABLE as
select City, Precipitation
   from TROUBLE;

Table created.
```

> **NOTE**
> The **create table ... as select ...** command will not work if one of the
> selected columns uses the LONG datatype.

When the new table is described, it reveals that it has "inherited" its column definitions from the TROUBLE table. A table created in this fashion can include all columns, using an asterisk if you like, or a subset of columns from another table. It also can include "invented" columns, which are the product of functions or the combination of other columns, just as in a view. The character column definitions will adjust to the size necessary to contain the data in the invented columns. NUMBER columns that had specified precision in the source table but undergo computation in inventing a new column, will simply be NUMBER columns, with no specified precision, in the new table. When the table RAIN is described, it shows its column definitions:

```
describe RAIN_TABLE
```

Name	Null?	Type
CITY		VARCHAR2(17)
PRECIPITATION		NUMBER

When RAIN_TABLE is queried, it contains just the columns and data selected from the TROUBLE table as it existed when RAIN_TABLE was created:

```
select * from RAIN_TABLE;
```

CITY	PRECIPITATION
PLEASANT LAKE	3.6
PLEASANT LAKE	1.63
PLEASANT LAKE	1.00003
PLEASANT LAKE	2.4

> **NOTE**
> If one of the columns in the query is generated via a formula, you
> must specify a column alias that Oracle will use as the column name
> during the table creation.

You also can use this technique to create a table with column definitions like those of the source table, but with no rows in it, by building a **where** clause that will select no rows from the old table:

```
create table RAIN_EMPTY as
select City, Precipitation
  from TROUBLE
 where 1=2;

Table created.
```

Querying this table will show there is nothing in it:

```
select * from RAIN_EMPTY;

no rows selected.
```

You can create a table based on a query without generating *redo log entries* (chronological records of database actions used during database recoveries). Avoiding the generation of these entries is accomplished by using the **nologging** keyword in the **create table** command. When the redo log entries are circumvented in this way, the performance of the **create table** command will improve because less work is being done; the larger the table, the greater the impact. However, because the new table's creation is not being written to the *redo log files* (which record the redo log entries), the table will not be re-created if, following a database failure, those redo log files are used to recover the database. Therefore, you should consider performing a backup of the database soon after using the **nologging** option if you want to be able to recover the new table.

The following example shows how to use the **nologging** keyword during table creations based on queries (by default, table creations based on queries generate redo log entries):

```
create table RAIN_NOLOG
nologging
as
select * from TROUBLE;

Table created.
```

Note that you can specify **nologging** at the partition level and at the LOB level. The use of **nologging** will improve the performance of the operations that load the data in the table.

Creating an Index-Organized Table

An *index-organized table* keeps its data sorted according to the primary key column values for the table. An index-organized table stores its data as if the entire table was stored in an index. Indexes serve two main purposes:

- ■ **To enforce uniqueness** When a PRIMARY KEY or UNIQUE constraint is created, Oracle creates an index to enforce the uniqueness of the indexed columns.

- ■ **To improve performance** When a query can use an index, the performance of the query may dramatically improve. See Chapter 43 for details on the conditions under which a query may use an index.

An index-organized table allows you to store its entire data in an index. A normal index only stores the indexed columns; an index-organized table stores all its columns in the index.

To create an index-organized table, use the **organization index** clause of the **create table** command, as shown in the following example:

```
create table TROUBLE_IOT (
City            VARCHAR2(13),
SampleDate      DATE,
Noon            NUMBER(4,1),
Midnight        NUMBER(4,1),
Precipitation NUMBER,
constraint TROUBLE_IOT_PK PRIMARY KEY (City, SampleDate))
organization index;
```

To create TROUBLE as an index-organized table, you must create a PRIMARY KEY constraint on it.

An index-organized table is appropriate if you will always be accessing the TROUBLE data by the City and SampleDate columns (in the **where** clauses of your queries). To minimize the amount of active management of the index required, you should use an index-organized table only if the table's data is very static. If the table's data changes frequently, you should use a regular table with indexes as appropriate.

In general, an index-organized table is most effective when the primary key constitutes a large part of the table's columns. If the table contains many frequently accessed columns that are not part of the primary key, the index-organized table will need to repeatedly access its overflow area. Despite this drawback, you may choose to use index-organized tables to take advantage of a key feature that is not available with standard tables: the ability to use the **move online** option of the **alter table** command. You can use that option to move a table from one tablespace to another while it is being accessed by **insert**, **update**, and **delete** operations. You cannot use the **move online** option for partitioned index-organized tables. Partitioning is described in the next section.

Using Partitioned Tables

You can divide the rows of a single table into multiple parts. Dividing a table's data in this manner is called *partitioning* the table; the table that is partitioned is called a *partitioned table,* and the parts are called *partitions.*

Partitioning is useful for very large tables. By splitting a large table's rows across multiple smaller partitions, you accomplish several important goals:

- The performance of queries against the tables may improve because Oracle may have to search only one partition (one part of the table) instead of the entire table to resolve a query.

- The table may be easier to manage. Because the partitioned table's data is stored in multiple parts, it may be easier to load and delete data in the partitions than in the large table.

- Backup and recovery operations may perform better. Because the partitions are smaller than the partitioned table, you may have more options for backing up and recovering the partitions than you would have for a single large table.

The Oracle optimizer will know that the table has been partitioned; as shown later in this section, you can also specify the partition to use as part of the **from** clause of your queries.

Creating a Partitioned Table

To create a partitioned table, you specify how to set up the partitions of the table's data as part of the **create table** command. Typically, tables are partitioned by ranges of values (known as *range partitioning*).

Consider the BOOKSHELF table:

```
create table BOOKSHELF
(Title        VARCHAR2(100) primary key,
Publisher     VARCHAR2(20),
CategoryName VARCHAR2(20),
Rating        VARCHAR2(2),
constraint CATFK foreign key (CategoryName)
references CATEGORY(CategoryName));
```

If you will be storing a large number of records in the BOOKSHELF table, you may want to separate the rows across multiple partitions. To partition the table's records, use the **partition by range** clause of the **create table** command, as shown next. The ranges will determine the values stored in each partition.

```
create table BOOKSHELF_RANGE_PART
(Title        VARCHAR2(100) primary key,
Publisher     VARCHAR2(20),
CategoryName VARCHAR2(20),
Rating        VARCHAR2(2),
constraint CATFK2 foreign key (CategoryName)
references CATEGORY(CategoryName)
)
partition by range (CategoryName)
  (partition PART1   values less than ('B')
     tablespace PART1_TS,
   partition PART2   values less than (MAXVALUE)
     tablespace PART2_TS);
```

The BOOKSHELF table will be partitioned based on the values in the CategoryName column:

```
partition by range (CategoryName)
```

For any Category values less than 'B' (the ADULT categories), the records will be stored in the partition named PART1. The PART1 partition will be stored in the PART1_TS tablespace (see Chapter 20 for details on tablespaces). Any other categories will be stored in the PART2 partition. Note that in the PART2 partition definition, the range clause is

```
partition PART2   values less than (MAXVALUE)
```

You do not need to specify a maximum value for the last partition; the **maxvalue** keyword tells Oracle to use the partition to store any data that could not be stored in the earlier partitions.

You can create multiple partitions, each with its own upper value defined. For each partition, you only specify the maximum value for the range. The minimum value for the range is implicitly determined by Oracle from the definition of the preceding partition.

In addition to range partitions, Oracle supports *hash partitions*. A hash partition determines the physical placement of data by performing a hash function on the values of the partition key. In *range partitioning,* consecutive values of the partition key are usually stored in the same partition. In *hash partitioning,* consecutive values of the partition key are not generally stored in the same partition. Hash partitioning distributes a set of records over a greater set of partitions than range partitioning does, potentially decreasing the likelihood for I/O contention.

To create a hash partition, use the **partition by hash** clause in place of the **partition by range** clause, as shown in the following listing:

```
create table BOOKSHELF_HASH_PART
(Title        VARCHAR2(100) primary key,
Publisher     VARCHAR2(20),
CategoryName VARCHAR2(20),
Rating        VARCHAR2(2),
constraint CATFK_HASH foreign key (CategoryName)
references CATEGORY(CategoryName)
)
partition by hash (CategoryName)
partitions 10;
```

You can name each partition and specify its tablespace, just as you would for range partitioning, as shown here:

```
create table BOOKSHELF_HASH_PART
(Title        VARCHAR2(100) primary key,
Publisher     VARCHAR2(20),
CategoryName VARCHAR2(20),
Rating        VARCHAR2(2),
constraint CATFK_HASH foreign key (CategoryName)
references CATEGORY(CategoryName)
)
partition by hash (CategoryName)
partitions 2
store in (PART1_TS, PART2_TS);
```

Following the **partition by hash (CategoryName)** line, you have two choices for format:

- As shown in the preceding listing, you can specify the number of partitions and the tablespaces to use:

    ```
    partitions 2
    store in (PART1_TS, PART2_TS);
    ```

 This method will create partitions with system-generated names in the format SYS_P*nnn*. The number of tablespaces specified in the **store in** clause does not have to equal the

number of partitions. If more partitions than tablespaces are specified, the partitions will be assigned to the tablespaces in a round-robin fashion.

- You can specify named partitions:

```
partition by hash (CategoryName)
(partition PART1 tablespace PART1_TS,
 partition PART2 tablespace PART2_TS);
```

In this method, each partition is given a name and a tablespace, with the option of using an additional **lob** or **varray** storage clause (see Chapters 34 and 35). This method gives you more control over the location of the partitions, with the added benefit of letting you specify meaningful names for the partitions.

List Partitioning

You can use *list partitions* in place of range and hash partitioning. In list partitioning, you tell Oracle all the possible values and designate the partitions into which the corresponding rows should be inserted. The following example shows the BOOKSHELF entries list-partitioned by CategoryName:

```
create table BOOKSHELF_LIST_PART
(Title       VARCHAR2(100) primary key,
Publisher    VARCHAR2(20),
CategoryName VARCHAR2(20),
Rating       VARCHAR2(2),
constraint CATFK4 foreign key (CategoryName)
references CATEGORY(CategoryName)
)
partition by list (CategoryName)
  (partition PART1   values ('ADULTFIC', 'ADULTNF', 'ADULTREF')
      tablespace PART1_TS,
   partition PART2   values
      ('CHILDRENFIC', 'CHILDRENNF', 'CHILDRENPIC')
      tablespace PART2_TS);
```

Creating Subpartitions

You can create *subpartitions*—that is, partitions of partitions. You can use subpartitions to combine the two types of partitions: range partitions and hash partitions. You can use hash partitions in combination with range partitions, creating hash partitions of the range partitions. For very large tables, this composite partitioning may be an effective way of separating the data into manageable and tunable divisions.

The following example range-partitions the BOOKSHELF table by the Title column, and it hash-partitions the Title partitions by CategoryName values:

```
create table BOOKSHELF_RANGE_HASH_PART
(Title       VARCHAR2(100) primary key,
Publisher    VARCHAR2(20),
CategoryName VARCHAR2(20),
Rating       VARCHAR2(2),
```

```
constraint CATFK3 foreign key (CategoryName)
references CATEGORY(CategoryName)
)
partition by range (Title)
subpartition by hash (CategoryName)
subpartitions 6
 (partition PART1   values less than ('M')
     tablespace PART1_TS,
  partition PART2   values less than (MAXVALUE)
     tablespace PART2_TS);
```

The BOOKSHELF table will be range-partitioned into two partitions, using the Title value ranges specified for the named partitions. Each of those partitions will be hash-partitioned on the CategoryName column.

Indexing Partitions

When you create a partitioned table, you should create an index on the table. The index may be partitioned according to the same range values that were used to partition the table. In the following listing, the **create index** command for the BOOKSHELF_LIST_PART (list-partitioned) table is shown. The index partitions are placed in the PART1_NDX_TS and PART2_NDX_TS tablespaces.

```
create index BOOKSHELF__LIST_CATEGORY
    on BOOKSHELF_LIST_PART(CategoryName)
      local
      (partition PART1
        tablespace PART1_NDX_TS,
       partition PART2
        tablespace PART2_NDX_TS);
```

Notice the **local** keyword. In this **create index** command, no ranges are specified. Instead, the **local** keyword tells Oracle to create a separate index for each partition of the BOOKSHELF_LIST_ PART table. Two partitions were created on BOOKSHELF_LIST_PART. This index will create two separate index partitions—one for each table partition. Because there is one index per partition, the index partitions are "local" to the partitions.

You can also create "global" indexes. A global index may contain values from multiple partitions.

```
create index BOOKSHELF_LIST_CATEGORY_G
on BOOKSHELF_LIST_PART(Publisher)
 global;
```

The **global** clause in this **create index** command allows you to create a nonpartitioned index (as shown here) or to specify ranges for the index values that are different from the ranges for the table partitions. Local indexes may be easier to manage than global indexes; however, global indexes may perform uniqueness checks faster than local (partitioned) indexes perform them.

NOTE
You cannot create global indexes for hash partitions or subpartitions.

Managing Partitioned Tables

You can use the **alter table** command to **add**, **drop**, **exchange**, **move**, **modify**, **rename**, **split**, and **truncate** partitions. These **alter table** command options allow you to alter the existing partition structure, as may be required after a partitioned table has been used heavily. For example, the distribution of the CategoryName values within the partitioned table may have changed, or the maximum value may have increased. See the "ALTER TABLE" entry in the Alphabetical Reference for information on these options.

During an **insert** into the partitioned table, Oracle uses the partitions' definitions to determine which partition the record should be inserted into. Thus, you can use a partitioned table as if it were a single table, and rely on Oracle to manage the internal separation of the data.

Creating a View

Since you've already seen the techniques for creating a view in prior chapters, they will not be reviewed extensively here. However, this section gives several additional points about views that will prove useful.

If a view is based on a single underlying table, you can **insert**, **update**, or **delete** rows in the view. This will actually **insert**, **update**, or **delete** rows in the underlying table. There are restrictions on your ability to do this, although the restrictions are quite sensible:

- You cannot **insert** if the underlying table has any **NOT NULL** columns that don't appear in the view.

- You cannot **insert** or **update** if any one of the view's columns referenced in the **insert** or **update** contains functions or calculations.

- You cannot **insert**, **update**, or **delete** if the view contains **group by**, **distinct**, or a reference to the pseudo-column RowNum.

You can **insert** into a view based on multiple tables if Oracle can determine the proper rows to insert. In a multitable view, Oracle determines which of the tables are *key-preserved*. If a view contains enough columns from a table to identify the primary key for that table, the key is preserved and Oracle may be able to insert rows into the table via the view.

Stability of a View

Remember that the results of querying a view are built instantly from a table (or tables) when you execute the query. Until that moment, the view has no data of its own, as a table does. It is merely a description (a SQL statement) of what information to pull out of other tables and how to organize it. As a consequence, if a table is dropped, the validity of a view is destroyed. Attempting to query a view where the underlying table has been dropped will produce an error message about the view.

NOTE
The sole exception to this rule is the use of materialized views. In fact, a materialized view is actually a table that stores data one would normally query via a view. Materialized views are described in detail in Chapter 24.

In the following sequence, a view is created on an existing table, the table is dropped, and the view then is queried.

First, the view is created:

```
create view RAIN_VIEW as
select City, Precipitation
  from TROUBLE;
```

```
View created.
```

The underlying table is dropped:

```
drop table TROUBLE;
```

```
Table dropped.
```

The view is queried:

```
select * from RAIN_VIEW;
           *
ERROR at line 1:
ORA-04063: view "PRACTICE.RAIN_VIEW" has errors
```

Similarly, a view is created using the asterisk in the view creation:

```
create or replace view RAIN_VIEW as
select * from TROUBLE;
```

```
View created.
```

But then the underlying table is altered:

```
alter table TROUBLE add (
Warning        VARCHAR2(20)
);
```

```
Table altered.
```

Despite the change to the view's base table, the view is still valid, but the Warning column is not visible through it. After altering the table, replace the view to enable the Warning column to be seen. To re-create a view while keeping in place all the privileges that have been granted for it, use the **create or replace view** command, as shown in the following listing. This command

will replace the view text of an existing view with the new view text, while the old grants on the view will not be affected.

```
create or replace view RAIN_VIEW as
select * from TROUBLE;
```

Using order by in Views

You can use an **order by** in a **create view** statement, as shown in the following listing based on the re-created TROUBLE table (note that queries against this view may incur a performance penalty because of the additional sort activity they perform):

```
create view TROUBLE_SORTED
     as select * from TROUBLE
 order by City, SampleDate;

View created.

select * from TROUBLE_SORTED;

CITY          SAMPLEDAT     NOON     MIDNIGHT PRECIPITATION
------------- --------- ---------- ---------- -------------
PLEASANT LAKE 21-MAR-03         40       -1.3           3.6
PLEASANT LAKE 22-JUN-03      101.4       86.2          1.63
PLEASANT LAKE 23-SEP-03       92.9       79.6       1.00003
PLEASANT LAKE 22-DEC-03      -17.4      -10.4           2.4
```

Creating a Read-Only View

You can use the **with read only** clause of the **create view** command to prevent users from manipulating records via the view. Consider the RAIN_VIEW view created in the previous section:

```
create or replace view RAIN_VIEW as
select * from TROUBLE;
```

If a user has the ability to **delete** records from the TROUBLE table, the user could **delete** the TROUBLE records via the RAIN_VIEW view:

```
delete from RAIN;
```

The user could also **insert** or **update** the records in the TROUBLE table by performing those operations against the RAIN_VIEW view. If the view is based on a join of multiple tables, the user's ability to **update** the view's records is limited; a view's base tables cannot be updated unless only one table is involved in the **update** and the updated table's full primary key is included in the view's columns.

To prevent modifications to the base tables via a view, you can use the **with read only** clause of the **create view** command. If you use the **with read only** clause when creating a view, users

will *only* be able to **select** records from the view. Users will be unable to manipulate the records obtained from the view even if the view is based on a single table:

```
create or replace view RAIN_READ_ONLY as
select * from TROUBLE
  with read only;
```

You can also use INSTEAD OF triggers to manage the data-manipulation commands executed against views. See Chapter 33 for details on INSTEAD OF triggers.

Indexes

An *index* is a simple concept. It is typically a listing of *keywords* accompanied by the *location* of information on a subject. To find information on indexes, for instance, you look up the word "indexes" in the index at the back of this book. It will give the number of the page you are reading now. The word "indexes" is the key, and the page numbers given point you to the location of discussions about indexes in this book.

Although you could find the information on indexes simply by reading through this book until you encountered the page with the information on it, this would be slow and time-consuming. Because the index at the back of the book is in alphabetical order, you can quickly go to the appropriate spot in the index (without reading every entry) where "index" is found. If the word is not common, this is quicker than reading through the book from front to back. These same principles apply to Oracle indexes. For example, if you are searching for a particular book, you can query with a limiting condition on the Title column:

```
select * from BOOKSHELF
  where Publisher = 'SCHOLASTIC';
```

If BOOKSHELF does not have an index on the Publisher column, Oracle has to read every row in the table until it finds all publishers that match the **where** clause of your query. If the table is small, that may not cause a performance problem. As the table grows in size, the time required to return all the matching rows to the user may impact the performance of the application and the business process it supports.

To speed the data retrieval, you can create an index on the Publisher column. Then, when you execute the same query, Oracle first looks in the index, which is sorted, thus finding the publisher named 'SCHOLASTIC' very quickly (Oracle doesn't read every entry, but jumps directly within close vicinity of the name, much as you would in looking through the index of a book). The index entry then gives Oracle the exact location in the table (and on disk) of the row(s) for that publisher. The standard type of index in Oracle is called a B*-tree index, matching column values to their related RowIDs.

Indexing an important column (one that's likely to appear in a **where** clause) will generally speed up Oracle's response to a query. Indexing will likewise speed up queries where two tables are joined, if the columns that are related (by the **where** clause) are indexed. These are the basics of indexing; the rest of this section shows a number of additional features and issues related to indexing that will affect how quickly it works. For the impact of indexes on the optimization of your queries, see Chapter 43.

Creating an Index

You create an index via the **create index** command. When you designate a primary key or a unique column during table creation or maintenance, Oracle will automatically create a unique index to support that constraint. The full command syntax for **create index** is shown in the Alphabetical Reference. Its most commonly used format is as follows:

```
create [bitmap | unique] index index
on table(column [,column]. . .) [reverse];
```

index must be a unique name and follow the naming conventions of Oracle columns. *table* is simply the name of the table on which the index will be established, and *column* is the name of the column being indexed.

Bitmap indexes allow you to create useful indexes on columns with very few distinct values; see "Creating a Bitmap Index," later in this chapter. The **reverse** keyword tells Oracle to reverse the bytes of the indexed value, which may improve the I/O distribution during the insert of many sequential data values.

You can establish a single index on multiple columns by listing the columns one after the other, separated by commas. For the following examples, the BOOKSHELF_AUTHOR table was created without a primary key:

```
create table BOOKSHELF_AUTHOR
(Title        VARCHAR2(100),
AuthorName   VARCHAR2(50),
constraint TitleFK Foreign key (Title) references BOOKSHELF(Title),
constraint AuthorNameFK Foreign key (AuthorName)
references AUTHOR(AuthorName));
```

Enforcing Uniqueness

Recall from Part I that a set of tables is said to be in Third Normal Form if all the columns in each table's rows are dependent only on the primary key. In the BOOKSHELF_AUTHOR table, the primary key is the combination of the columns Title and AuthorName. In other tables, a primary key might be an employee ID, a client ID, an account number, or, in a bank, a combination of branch number and account number.

In each of these cases, the uniqueness of the primary key is critical. A bank with duplicate account numbers, or a billing system with duplicate client IDs, would wreak havoc as transactions were posted to accounts belonging to different people but having the same primary key (this is why names usually are not commonly used as primary keys—there are too many duplicates). To avoid this danger, have your database help prevent the creation of duplicate primary keys. Oracle offers two facilities that help:

■ You can guarantee the uniqueness of a key through either indexing or constraints.

■ You can use the sequence generators (discussed later in this chapter).

Creating a Unique Index

You can create a unique index on the combination of Title and AuthorName in the BOOKSHELF_ AUTHOR table in one of three ways: by creating a primary key constraint, by creating a unique constraint, or by creating a unique index. If you create a constraint, you will be able to create foreign keys that refer to it. If you create the unique index first, you will still be able to create a primary key on the table—Oracle will use the existing index as the primary key index.

The following listing shows the **create index** command for this multicolumn index:

```
create unique index BA$TITLE_AUTHOR
    on BOOKSHELF_AUTHOR(Title, AuthorName);
```

The primary key method is shown here:

```
alter table BOOKSHELF_AUTHOR
    add constraint BA_PK primary key (Title, AuthorName);
```

To create a unique constraint, just replace the **primary key** clause with **unique**. When you attempt to create a unique index on a table that already has data in it, the command will fail if any duplicates exist. If the **create unique index** statement succeeds, any future attempt to **insert** (or **update**) a row that would create a duplicate key will fail and result in this error message:

```
ERROR at line 1:
ORA-00001: unique constraint (BOOKSHELF_AUTHOR.BA_PK) violated
```

When you create an index, it requires storage space. See "Placing an Index in the Database," later in this chapter, for details concerning the location of the created indexes.

Creating a Bitmap Index

To help tune queries that use nonselective columns in their limiting conditions, you can use *bitmap indexes*. Bitmap indexes should only be used if the data is infrequently updated, because they add to the cost of all data-manipulation transactions against the tables they index.

> **NOTE**
> *Bitmap indexes should not be used for tables involved in online transaction-processing applications due to the internal mechanisms Oracle uses to maintain them. Restrict their usage to tables involved in batch transactions.*

Bitmap indexes are appropriate when nonselective columns are used as limiting conditions in a query. For example, if there are very few distinct Rating values in a very large BOOKSHELF table, you would not usually create a traditional B*-tree index on Rating, even if it is commonly used in **where** clauses. However, Rating may be able to take advantage of a bitmap index.

Internally, a bitmap index maps the distinct values for the columns to each record. For this example, assume there are five Rating values (1, 2, 3, 4, and 5) in a very large BOOKSHELF table. Because there are five Rating values, there are five separate bitmap entries for the Rating bitmap index. If the first five rows in the table have a Rating value of 1, and the next five have a Rating value of 2, then the Rating bitmap entries would resemble those shown in the following listing:

Rating bitmaps:

```
1:  1 1 1 1 1 0 0 0 0 0
2:  0 0 0 0 0 1 1 1 1 1
3:  0 0 0 0 0 0 0 0 0 0
4:  0 0 0 0 0 0 0 0 0 0
5:  0 0 0 0 0 0 0 0 0 0
```

In the preceding listing, each column of 0's and 1's represents a row in the BOOKSHELF table. Because ten rows are considered, ten bitmap values are shown. Reading the bitmap for Rating, the first five records have a Rating value of 1 (the '1' values), and the next five do not (the '0' values). There is a separate bitmap entry for each possible value.

The Oracle optimizer can dynamically convert bitmap index entries to RowIDs during query processing. This conversion capability allows the optimizer to use indexes on columns that have many distinct values (via B*-tree indexes) and on those that have few distinct values (via bitmap indexes).

To create a bitmap index, use the **bitmap** clause of the **create index** command, as shown in the following listing. You should indicate its nature as a bitmap index within the index name so that it will be easy to detect during tuning operations.

```
create bitmap index BOOKSHELF$BITMAP_RATING
    on BOOKSHELF(Rating);
```

If you choose to use bitmap indexes, you will need to weigh the performance benefit during queries against the performance cost during data-manipulation commands. The more bitmap indexes there are on a table, the greater the cost will be during each transaction. You should not use bitmap indexes on a column that frequently has new values added to it. Each addition of a new value to the Rating column will require that a corresponding new bitmap be created.

When to Create an Index

Indexes are most useful on larger tables, on columns that are likely to appear in **where** clauses either as a simple equality, such as

```
where AuthorName = 'STEPHEN JAY GOULD'
    and Rating = '5'
```

or in joins, such as this:

```
where BOOKSHELF.Title = BOOKSHELF_AUTHOR.Title
```

In addition to supporting **where** clauses and joins, indexes also support **order by** clauses and the **MAX** and **MIN** functions. In some circumstances, Oracle may choose to scan an index instead of performing a full scan on the table. See Chapter 43 for details on the usage of indexes by the optimizer.

Variety in Indexed Columns

Traditional (B*-tree) indexes are most useful on columns with a significant amount of variety in their data. For instance, a column that indicates whether a company is a current client with a Y or N value would be a poor choice for a traditional index, and could actually slow down a query;

a bitmap index would be a much better choice for that example. A telephone number column would be a good candidate for a B*-tree index. An area code column would be marginal, depending on the distribution of unique area code values in the table.

In a multicolumn index, put the column likely to be accessed most often first. You can use the optimizer's skip-scan feature to use multicolumn indexes even if the leading column is not mentioned in the query. See Chapter 43 for examples of index usage.

Small tables may be better left unindexed, except to enforce uniqueness in the primary key. A small table is one that takes so few database blocks that Oracle can read all its data with one physical read; beyond that, indexing will nearly always be productive. The number of blocks read during a physical read is set via the DB_FILE_MULTIBLOCK_READ_COUNT initialization parameter.

Bitmap indexes present a viable indexing alternative for columns that have very few distinct values. Bitmap indexes are commonly used for "flag" columns that are restricted to values such as Y and N. Bitmap indexes are particularly effective when multiple bitmap indexes are used in a query; the optimizer can quickly evaluate the bitmaps and determine which rows meet all the criteria for which bitmap indexes are available.

How Many Indexes to Use on a Table

You can create many indexes on a single table, with many columns in each index. The tradeoff for indexing too many columns is the lessened speed of inserting new rows: Every index also must have a new entry made in it when an **insert** is done. If your table will be used primarily for queries, the only cost of indexing as many columns as you can (that have variety and will be used in **where** clauses, of course) is the extra disk space used. Strictly from a data-loading performance perspective, it is better to have a small number of indexes with many columns than to have many indexes with a small number of columns in each.

Except in cluster indexes (discussed later in this chapter), columns that are **NULL** will not appear in an index. Indexes based on more than one column will have an entry if any of the columns are not **NULL**. If all indexed columns are **NULL** for a given row, no entry will appear for this row in the index.

Placing an Index in the Database

You can specify where the index to a table is placed by assigning it to a specific tablespace. As will be described in detail in Chapter 20, a *tablespace* is a logical division of the database, corresponding to one or more datafiles. Datafiles provide the physical storage for the database—sections of disk where tables and indexes are stored. Databases have several tablespaces, each with its own name. To enhance availability and management options, an index for a table should be placed in a tablespace that is on a physically separate disk drive from its corresponding table.

To specify the tablespace in which to locate an index, the normal **create index** statement is simply followed by the word **tablespace** and the tablespace name, as shown here:

```
create unique index BA$TITLE_AUTHOR
    on BOOKSHELF_AUTHOR(Title, AuthorName)
tablespace BA_INDEXES;
```

In this example, BA_INDEXES is the name given to a tablespace previously created by the database administrator. The use of the **tablespace** option in a **create index** statement lets you physically separate your tables from their associated indexes.

When you create a primary key or unique constraint, Oracle will automatically create an index to enforce uniqueness. Unless you specify otherwise, that index will be created in the same tablespace as the table that the constraint modifies, and it will use the default storage parameters for that tablespace. Because that storage location is typically undesirable, you should take advantage of the **using index** clause when creating primary key and unique constraints.

The **using index** clause allows you to specify the storage parameters and tablespace location for an index created by a constraint. In the following example, a primary key is created on the BOOKSHELF_AUTHOR table and is placed in the BA_INDEXES tablespace. This example assumes that there is not an existing index on the specified columns.

```
alter table BOOKSHELF_AUTHOR
    add constraint BA_PK primary key (Title, AuthorName)
using index tablespace BA_INDEXES;
```

See "Integrity Constraint" in the Alphabetical Reference for further options for the **using index** clause, and see **create index** in the Alphabetical Reference for performance-related index-creation options.

Rebuilding an Index

Oracle provides a *fast index rebuild* capability that allows you to re-create an index without having to drop the existing index. The currently available index is used as the data source for the index, instead of the table's being used as the data source. During the index rebuild, you can change its **storage** parameters and **tablespace** assignment.

In the following example, the BA_PK index is rebuilt (via the **rebuild** clause). Its storage parameters are changed to use an initial extent size of 8MB and a next extent size of 4MB, in the BA_INDEXES tablespace.

```
alter index BA_PK rebuild
storage (initial 8M next 4M pctincrease 0)
tablespace BA_INDEXES;
```

NOTE
When the BA_PK index is rebuilt, there must be enough space for both the old index and the new index to exist simultaneously. After the new index has been created, the old index will be dropped.

When you create an index that is based on previously indexed columns, Oracle may be able to use the existing indexes as data sources for the new index. The Oracle optimizer may use parts of existing composite indexes as needed for queries, so you may not need to create many indexes to support the most common queries.

You can rebuild indexes while they are being accessed via the **rebuild online** clause of the **alter index** command.

Function-Based Indexes

You can create *function-based indexes*. Any query that performs a function on a column generally does not use that column's index. Therefore, this query could not use an index on the Title column:

```
select * from BOOKSHELF
  where UPPER(Title) = 'MY LEDGER';
```

However, this query could because it does not perform the **UPPER** function on the Title column:

```
select * from BOOKSHELF
  where Title = 'MY LEDGER';
```

You can create indexes that allow function-based accesses to be supported by index accesses. Instead of creating an index on the column Title, you can create an index on the column expression UPPER(Title), as shown in the following listing:

```
create index BOOKSHELF$UPPER_TITLE on
BOOKSHELF(UPPER(Title));
```

Although function-based indexes can be useful, be sure to consider the following questions when creating them:

- Can you restrict the functions that will be used on the column? If so, can you restrict all functions from being performed on the column?

- Do you have adequate storage space for the additional indexes?

- When you drop the table, will you be dropping more indexes (and therefore more extents) than before? How will that impact the time required to drop the table?

Function-based indexes are useful, but you should implement them sparingly. The more indexes you create on a table, the longer all **insert**, **update**, and **delete** operations will take.

Clusters

Clustering is a method of storing tables that are intimately related and often joined together into the same area on disk. For example, instead of the BOOKSHELF table being in one section of the disk and the BOOKSHELF_AUTHOR table being somewhere else, their rows could be interleaved together in a single area, called a *cluster*. The *cluster key* is the column or columns by which the tables are usually joined in a query (for example, Title for the BOOKSHELF and BOOKSHELF_ AUTHOR tables). To cluster tables, you must own the tables you are going to cluster together.

The following is the basic format of the **create cluster** command:

```
create cluster cluster
(column datatype [,column datatype]. . .) [other options];
```

The *cluster* name follows the table-naming conventions, and *column datatype* is the name and datatype you will use as the cluster key. The *column* name may be the same as one of the columns of a table you will put in this cluster, or it may be any other valid name. Here's an example:

```
create cluster BOOKandAUTHOR (Col1 VARCHAR2(100));

Cluster created.
```

This creates a cluster (a space is set aside, as it would be for a table) with nothing in it. The use of Col1 for the cluster key is irrelevant; you'll never use it again. However, its definition should match the primary key of the table to be added. Next, tables are created to be included in this cluster:

```
create table BOOKSHELF
(Title         VARCHAR2(100) primary key,
Publisher      VARCHAR2(20),
CategoryName VARCHAR2(20),
Rating         VARCHAR2(2),
constraint CATFK foreign key (CategoryName)
references CATEGORY(CategoryName)
)
cluster BOOKandAUTHOR (Title);
```

Prior to inserting rows into BOOKSHELF, you must create a cluster index:

```
create index BOOKandAUTHORndx
on cluster BOOKandAUTHOR;
```

Recall that the presence of a **cluster** clause here precludes the use of a **tablespace** or **storage** clause. Note how this structure differs from a standard **create table** statement:

```
create table BOOKSHELF
(Title         VARCHAR2(100) primary key,
Publisher      VARCHAR2(20),
CategoryName VARCHAR2(20),
Rating         VARCHAR2(2),
constraint CATFK foreign key (CategoryName)
references CATEGORY(CategoryName)
);
```

In the first **create table** statement, the cluster **BOOKandAUTHOR (Title)** clause *follows* the closing parenthesis of the list of columns being created in the table. **BOOKandAUTHOR** is the name of the cluster previously created. Title is the column in this table that will be stored in the cluster key Col1. It is possible to have multiple cluster keys in the **create cluster** statement, and to have multiple columns stored in those keys in the **create table** statement. Notice that nowhere does either statement say explicitly that the Title column goes into the Col1 cluster key. The match-up is done by position only: Col1 and Title were both the first objects mentioned in their respective cluster statements. Multiple columns and cluster keys are matched first to first, second to second, third to third, and so on. Now a second table is added to the cluster:

```
create table BOOKSHELF_AUTHOR
(Title         VARCHAR2(100),
AuthorName   VARCHAR2(50),
constraint TitleFK Foreign key (Title) references BOOKSHELF(Title),
```

```
constraint AuthorNameFK Foreign key (AuthorName)
references AUTHOR(AuthorName)
)
cluster BOOKandAUTHOR (Title);
```

When these two tables are clustered, each unique title is actually stored only once, in the cluster key. To each title are attached the columns from both of these tables.

The data from both of these tables is actually stored in a single location, almost as if the cluster were a big table containing data drawn from both of the tables that make it up.

An additional cluster option, a *hash cluster,* uses the cluster column values to determine the physical location in which the row is stored. See the entry for the **create cluster** command in the Alphabetical Reference.

Sequences

You can assign unique numbers, such as customer IDs, to columns in your database by using a sequence; you don't need to create a special table and code to keep track of the unique numbers in use. This is done by using the **create sequence** command, as shown here:

```
create sequence CustomerID increment by 1 start with 1000;
```

This will create a sequence that can be accessed during **insert** and **update** commands (also **select**, although this is rare). Typically, the unique sequence value is created with a statement like the following:

```
insert into CUSTOMER_DEMO  /*pseudocode example */
       (Name, Contact, ID)
values
       ('COLE CONSTRUCTION','VERONICA',CustomerID.NextVal);
```

The NextVal attached to CustomerID tells Oracle you want the next available sequence number from the CustomerID sequence. This is guaranteed to be unique; Oracle will not give it to anyone else. To use the same number more than once (such as in a series of **insert**s into related tables), CurrVal is used instead of NextVal, *after the first use.* That is, using NextVal ensures that the sequence table gets incremented and that you get a unique number, so you have to use NextVal first. Once you've used NextVal, that number is stored in CurrVal for your use anywhere, until you use NextVal again, at which point both NextVal and CurrVal change to the new sequence number.

If you use both NextVal and CurrVal in a single SQL statement, both will contain the value retrieved by NextVal. Neither of these can be used in subqueries, as columns in the **select** clause of a view, with **DISTINCT, UNION, INTERSECT,** or **MINUS,** or in the **order by, group by,** or **having** clause of a **select** statement.

You can also cache sequence values in memory for faster access, and you can make the sequence cycle back to its starting value once a maximum value is reached. See **create sequence** in the Alphabetical Reference.

CHAPTER
18

Basic Oracle Security

nformation is vital to success, but when damaged or in the wrong hands, it can threaten success. Oracle provides extensive security features to safeguard your information from both unauthorized viewing and intentional or inadvertent damage. This security is provided by granting or revoking privileges on a person-by-person and privilege-by-privilege basis, and is in addition to (and independent of) any security your computer system already has. Oracle uses the **create user**, **create role**, and **grant** commands to control data access.

In this chapter, you will see the basic security features available in Oracle. See Chapter 19 for coverage of advanced Oracle security features such as virtual private databases.

Users, Roles, and Privileges

Every Oracle user has a name and password and owns any tables, views, and other resources that he or she creates. An Oracle *role* is a set of *privileges* (or the type of access that each user needs, depending on his or her status and responsibilities). You can grant or bestow specific privileges to roles and then assign roles to the appropriate users. A user can also grant privileges directly to other users.

Database system privileges let you execute specific sets of commands. The CREATE TABLE privilege, for example, lets you create tables. The privilege GRANT ANY PRIVILEGE allows you to grant any system privilege.

Database object privileges give you the ability to perform some operation on various objects. The DELETE privilege, for example, lets you delete rows from tables and views. The SELECT privilege allows you to query with a **select** from tables, views, sequences, and snapshots (materialized views).

See "Privilege" in the Alphabetical Reference at the end of this book for a complete list of system and object privileges.

Creating a User

The Oracle system comes with many users already created, including SYSTEM and SYS. The SYS user owns the core internal tables Oracle uses to manage the database; SYSTEM owns additional tables and views. You can log onto the SYSTEM user to create other users because SYSTEM has that privilege.

When installing Oracle, you (or a system administrator) first create a user for yourself. This is the simplest format for the **create user** command:

```
create user user identified
        {by password | externally | globally as 'extnm'};
```

Many other account characteristics can be set via this command; see the **create user** command in the Alphabetical Reference for details.

To connect your computer system's userid and password into Oracle's security so that only one logon is required for host-based users, use **externally** instead of giving a password. A system administrator (who has a great many privileges) may want the extra security of having a separate password. Let's call the system administrator Dora in the following examples:

```
create user Dora identified by avocado;
```

Dora's account now exists and is secured by a password.

You also can set up the user with specific tablespaces and *quotas* (limits) for space and resource usage. See **create user** in the Alphabetical Reference and Chapters 17 and 20 for a discussion of tablespaces and resources.

To change a password, use the **alter user** command:

```
alter user Dora identified by psyche;
```

Now Dora has the password "psyche" instead of "avocado." However, Dora cannot log into her account until she first has the CREATE SESSION system privilege:

```
grant CREATE SESSION to Dora;
```

You'll see additional examples of system privilege grants later in this chapter.

Password Management

Passwords can expire, and accounts may be locked due to repeated failed attempts to connect. When you change your password, a password history may be maintained to prevent reuse of previous passwords.

The expiration characteristics of your account's password are determined by the profile assigned to your account. Profiles, which are created by the **create profile** command, are managed by the DBA (database administrator, discussed later in the chapter). See the CREATE PROFILE entry in the Alphabetical Reference for full details on the **create profile** command.

Relative to passwords and account access, profiles can enforce the following:

- The "lifetime" of your password, which determines how frequently you must change it
- The grace period following your password's "expiration date" during which you can change the password
- The number of consecutive failed connect attempts allowed before the account is automatically "locked"
- The number of days the account will remain locked
- The number of days that must pass before you can reuse a password
- The number of password changes that must take place before you can reuse a password

Additional password management features allow the minimum length and complexity of passwords to be enforced.

In addition to the **alter user** command, you can use the **password** command in SQL*Plus to change your password. If you use the **password** command, your new password will not be displayed on the screen as you type. Database administrators can change any user's password via the **password** command; other users can change only their own password.

When you enter the **password** command, you will be prompted for the old and new passwords, as shown in the following listing:

```
connect dora/psyche
password
```

```
Changing password for dora
Old password:
New password:
Retype new password:
```

When the password has been successfully changed, you will receive the feedback:

```
Password changed
```

You can set another user's password from a DBA account. Simply append the username to the **password** command. You will not be asked for the old password:

```
password dora
Changing password for dora
New password:
Retype new password:
```

Enforcing Password Expiration

You can use profiles to manage the expiration, reuse, and complexity of passwords. You can limit the lifetime of a password, and lock an account whose password is too old. You can also force a password to be at least moderately complex, and lock any account that has repeated failed login attempts.

For example, if you set the FAILED_LOGIN_ATTEMPTS resource of the user's profile to 5, then four consecutive failed login attempts will be allowed for the account; the fifth will cause the account to be locked.

NOTE
If the correct password is supplied on the fifth attempt, the "failed login attempt count" is reset to 0, allowing for five more consecutive unsuccessful login attempts before the account is locked.

In the following listing, the LIMITED_PROFILE profile is created for use by the user JANE:

```
create profile LIMITED_PROFILE limit
FAILED_LOGIN_ATTEMPTS 5;

create user JANE identified by EYRE
profile LIMITED_PROFILE;

grant CREATE SESSION to JANE;
```

If there are five consecutive failed connection attempts to the JANE account, the account will be automatically locked by Oracle. When you then use the correct password for the JANE account, you will receive an error.

```
connect jane/eyre
ERROR:
ORA-28000: the account is locked
```

To unlock the account, use the **account unlock** clause of the **alter user** command (from a DBA account), as shown in the following listing:

```
alter user JANE account unlock;
```

Following the unlocking of the account, connections to the JANE account will once again be allowed. You can manually lock an account via the **account lock** clause of the **alter user** command.

```
alter user JANE account lock;
```

NOTE
*You can specify **account lock** as part of the **create user** command.*

If an account becomes locked due to repeated connection failures, it will automatically become unlocked when its profile's PASSWORD_LOCK_TIME value is exceeded. For example, if PASSWORD_LOCK_TIME is set to 1, the JANE account in the previous example would be locked for one day, after which the account would be unlocked again.

You can establish a maximum lifetime for a password via the PASSWORD_LIFE_TIME resource within profiles. For example, you could force users of the LIMITED_PROFILE profile to change their passwords every 30 days:

```
alter profile LIMITED_PROFILE limit
PASSWORD_LIFE_TIME 30;
```

In this example, the **alter profile** command is used to modify the LIMITED_PROFILE profile. The PASSWORD_LIFE_TIME value is set to 30, so each account that uses that profile will have its password expire after 30 days. If your password has expired, you must change it the next time you log in, unless the profile has a specified grace period for expired passwords. The grace period parameter is called PASSWORD_GRACE_TIME. If the password is not changed within the grace period, the account expires.

NOTE
*If you are going to use the PASSWORD_LIFE_TIME parameter,
you need to give the users a way to change their passwords easily.*

An "expired" account is different from a "locked" account. A locked account, as discussed earlier in this section, may be automatically unlocked by the passage of time. An expired account, however, requires manual intervention by the DBA to be reenabled.

NOTE
*If you use the password expiration features, make sure the accounts
that own your applications have different profile settings; otherwise,
the accounts may become locked and the application may become
unusable.*

To reenable an expired account, execute the **alter user** command. In this example, the DBA manually expires JANE's password:

```
alter user jane password expire;

User altered.
```

Next, JANE attempts to connect to her account. When she provides her password, she is immediately prompted for a new password for the account.

```
connect jane/eyre
ERROR:
ORA-28001: the password has expired

Changing password for jane
New password:
Retype new password:
Password changed
Connected.
```

You can also force users to change their passwords when they first access their accounts, via the **password expire** clause of the **create user** command. The **create user** command does not, however, allow you to set an expiration date for the new password set by the user; to do that, you must use the PASSWORD_LIFE_TIME profile parameter shown in the previous examples.

To see the password expiration date of any account, query the Expiry_Date column of the DBA_USERS data dictionary view. Users who want to see the password expiration date for their accounts can query the Expiry_Date column of the USER_USERS data dictionary view (via either SQL*Plus or a client-based query tool).

Enforcing Password Reuse Limitations

To prevent a password from being reused, you can use one of two profile parameters: PASSWORD_REUSE_MAX or PASSWORD_REUSE_TIME. These two parameters are mutually exclusive; if you set a value for one of them, the other must be set to UNLIMITED.

The PASSWORD_REUSE_TIME parameter specifies the number of days that must pass before a password can be reused. For example, if you set PASSWORD_REUSE_TIME to 60, you cannot reuse the same password within 60 days.

The PASSWORD_REUSE_MAX parameter specifies the number of password changes that must occur before a password can be reused. If you attempt to reuse the password before the limit is reached, Oracle will reject your password change.

For example, you can set PASSWORD_REUSE_MAX for the LIMITED_PROFILE profile created earlier in this chapter:

```
alter profile LIMITED_PROFILE limit
PASSWORD_REUSE_MAX 3
PASSWORD_REUSE_TIME UNLIMITED;
```

If the user JANE now attempts to reuse a recent password, the password change attempt will fail. For example, suppose she changes her password, as in the following line:

```
alter user JANE identified by austen;
```

And then she changes it again:

```
alter user JANE identified by whitley;
```

During her next password change, she attempts to reuse a recent password, and the attempt fails:

```
alter user jane identified by austen;
alter user jane identified by austen
*
ERROR at line 1:
ORA-28007: the password cannot be reused
```

She cannot reuse any of her recent passwords; she will need to come up with a new password.

Standard Roles

At the beginning of this chapter, we created a user named Dora. Now that Dora has an account, what can she do in Oracle? At this point, nothing—Dora has no system privileges other than CREATE SESSION. In many cases, application users receive privileges via roles. You can group system privileges and object accesses into roles specific to your application users' needs. You can create your own roles for application access, and you can use Oracle's default roles for some system access requirements. The most important standard roles created during database creation are

CONNECT, RESOURCE, and DBA	Provided for compatibility with previous versions of Oracle database software.
DELETE_CATALOG_ROLE, EXECUTE_CATALOG_ROLE, SELECT_CATALOG_ROLE	These roles are provided for accessing data dictionary views and packages.
EXP_FULL_DATABASE, IMP_FULL_DATABASE	These roles are provided for convenience in using the Import and Export utilities.
AQ_USER_ROLE, AQ_ADMINISTRATOR_ROLE	These roles are needed for Oracle Advanced Queuing.
SNMPAGENT	This role is used by the Enterprise Manager Intelligent Agent.
RECOVERY_CATALOG_OWNER	This role is required for the creation of a recovery catalog schema owner.
SCHEDULER_ADMIN	This role allows the grantee to execute the DBMS_SCHEDULER package's procedures; should be restricted to DBAs.

CONNECT, RESOURCE, and DBA are provided for backward compatibility and should no longer be used. CONNECT gives users the ability to log in and perform basic functions. Users with CONNECT may create tables, views, sequences, clusters, synonyms, and database links. Users with RESOURCE can create their own tables, sequences, procedures, triggers, datatypes,

operators, indextypes, indexes, and clusters. Users with the RESOURCE role also receive the UNLIMITED TABLESPACE system privilege, allowing them to bypass quotas on all tablespaces. Users with the DBA role can perform database administration functions, including creating and altering users, tablespaces, and objects.

In place of CONNECT, RESOURCE, and DBA, you should create your own roles that have privileges to execute specific system privileges. In the following sections you will see how to grant privileges to users and roles.

Format for the grant Command

Here is the format for the **grant** command for system privileges (see the Alphabetical Reference for the full syntax diagram):

```
grant {system privilege | role | all [privileges] }
      [, {system privilege | role | all [privileges] }. . .]
      to {user | role} [, {user | role}]. . .
      [identified by password ]
      [with admin option]
```

You can grant any system privilege or role to another user, to another role, or to **public**. The **with admin option** clause permits the grantee to bestow the privilege or role on other users or roles. The **all** clause grants the user or role all privileges except the SELECT ANY DICTIONARY system privilege.

The grantor can revoke a role from a user as well.

Revoking Privileges

Privileges granted can be taken away. The **revoke** command is similar to the **grant** command:

```
revoke {system privilege | role | all [privileges] }
       [, {system privilege | role | all [privileges] }. . .]
       from {user | role} [, {user | role}]. . .
```

An individual with the DBA role can revoke CONNECT, RESOURCE, DBA, or any other privilege or role from anyone, including another DBA. This, of course, is dangerous, and is why DBA privileges should be given neither lightly nor to more than a tiny minority who really need them.

NOTE
Revoking everything from a given user does not eliminate that user from Oracle, nor does it destroy any tables that user had created; it simply prohibits that user's access to them. Other users with access to the tables will still have exactly the same access they've always had.

To remove a user and all the resources owned by that user, use the **drop user** command, like this:

```
drop user username [cascade];
```

The **cascade** option drops the user along with all the objects owned by the user, including referential integrity constraints. The **cascade** option invalidates views, synonyms, stored procedures, functions, or packages that refer to objects in the dropped user's schema. If you don't use the **cascade** option and there are still objects owned by the user, Oracle does not drop the user and instead returns an error message.

What Users Can Grant

A user can grant privileges on any object he or she owns. The database administrator can grant any system privilege.

Suppose that user Dora owns the COMFORT table and is a database administrator. Create two new users, Bob and Judy, with these privileges:

```
create user Judy identified by sarah;

User created.

grant CREATE SESSION to Judy;

Grant succeeded.

create user Bob identified by carolyn;

User created.

grant CREATE SESSION, CREATE TABLE, CREATE VIEW,
CREATE SYNONYM to bob;

Grant succeeded.

alter user bob
default tablespace users
quota 5m on users;

User altered.
```

This sequence of commands gives both Judy and Bob the ability to connect to Oracle, and gives Bob some extra capabilities. But can either do anything with Dora's tables? Not without explicit access.

To give others access to your tables, use a second form of the **grant** command:

```
grant { object privilege | all [privileges] }
      [(column [, column] . . .)]
      [, { object privilege | all [privileges] }
      [(column [, column] . . .)] ] . . .
      on object to {user | role}
      [with grant option]
      [with hierarchy option];
```

The privileges a user can grant include these:

- On the user's tables, views, and materialized views:

    ```
    FLASHBACK
    INSERT
    UPDATE  (all or specific columns)
    DELETE
    SELECT
    ```

 The INSERT, UPDATE, and DELETE privileges can only be granted on materialized views if they are updateable. See Chapter 24 for details on the creation of materialized views.

- On tables, you can also grant:

    ```
    ALTER  (table—all or specific columns)
    DEBUG
    REFERENCES
    INDEX (columns in a table)
    ON COMMIT REFRESH
    QUERY REWRITE
    ALL  (of the items previously listed)
    ```

- On procedures, functions, packages, abstract datatypes, libraries, indextypes, and operators:

    ```
    EXECUTE
    DEBUG
    ```

- On sequences:

    ```
    SELECT
    ALTER
    ```

- On directories (for BFILE LOB datatypes and external tables):

    ```
    READ
    WRITE
    ```

- On abstract datatypes and views:

    ```
    UNDER  (for the ability to create subviews under a view, or subtypes under a type)
    ```

When you execute another user's procedure or function, it is typically executed using the privileges of its owner. This means you don't need explicit access to the data the procedure or function uses; you see only the result of the execution, not the underlying data. You can also create stored procedures that execute under the privileges of the invoking user instead of the procedure owner; see Chapter 31 for details.

Dora gives Bob SELECT access to the COMFORT table:

```
grant select on COMFORT to Bob;

Grant succeeded.
```

The **with grant option** clause of the **grant** command allows the recipient of that grant to pass along the privileges he or she has received to other users. If the user Dora grants privileges on her

tables to the user Bob using **with grant option**, Bob can make grants on Dora's tables to other users (Bob can only pass along those privileges—such as SELECT—that he has been granted). If you intend to create views based on another user's tables and grant access to those views to other users, you first must be granted access **with grant option** to the base tables.

Moving to Another User with connect

To test the success of her grant, Dora connects to Bob's username with the **connect** command. This command may be used via one of the following methods:

- By entering both the username and password on the same line as the command

- By entering the command alone and then responding to prompts

- By entering the command and username and responding to the prompt for the password

The latter two methods suppress the display of the password and are therefore inherently more secure. The following listing shows a sample connection to the database:

```
connect Bob/carolyn

Connected.
```

Once connected, Dora selects from the table to which Bob has been given SELECT access.

NOTE
Unless a synonym is used, the table name must be preceded by the username of the table's owner. Without this, Oracle will say the table does not exist.

```
select * from Dora.COMFORT;
```

CITY	SAMPLEDAT	NOON	MIDNIGHT	PRECIPITATION
SAN FRANCISCO	21-MAR-03	62.5	42.3	.5
SAN FRANCISCO	22-JUN-03	51.1	71.9	.1
SAN FRANCISCO	23-SEP-03		61.5	.1
SAN FRANCISCO	22-DEC-03	52.6	39.8	2.3
KEENE	21-MAR-03	39.9	-1.2	4.4
KEENE	22-JUN-03	85.1	66.7	1.3
KEENE	23-SEP-03	99.8	82.6	
KEENE	22-DEC-03	-7.2	-1.2	3.9

A view named COMFORT is created, which is simply a straight **select** from the table Dora.COMFORT:

```
create view COMFORT as select * from Dora.COMFORT;

View created.
```

Selecting from this view will produce exactly the same results as selecting from Dora.COMFORT:

```
select * from COMFORT;

CITY          SAMPLEDAT NOON MIDNIGHT PRECIPITATION
------------- --------- ---- -------- -------------
SAN FRANCISCO 21-MAR-03 62.5     42.3           .5
SAN FRANCISCO 22-JUN-03 51.1     71.9           .1
SAN FRANCISCO 23-SEP-03          61.5           .1
SAN FRANCISCO 22-DEC-03 52.6     39.8          2.3
KEENE         21-MAR-03 39.9     -1.2          4.4
KEENE         22-JUN-03 85.1     66.7          1.3
KEENE         23-SEP-03 99.8     82.6
KEENE         22-DEC-03 -7.2     -1.2          3.9
```

Now Dora returns to her own username and creates a view that selects only a part of the COMFORT table:

```
connect Dora/psyche
Connected.

create view SOMECOMFORT as
select * from COMFORT
 where City = 'KEENE';

View created.
```

She then grants both SELECT and UPDATE privileges to Bob *on this view,* and revokes all privileges from Bob (via the **revoke** command) for the whole COMFORT table:

```
grant select, update on SOMECOMFORT to Bob;

Grant succeeded.

revoke all on COMFORT from Bob;

Revoke succeeded.
```

Dora then reconnects to Bob's username to test the effects of this change:

```
connect Bob/carolyn
Connected.

select * from COMFORT;
               *
ERROR at line 1:
ORA-04063: view "BOB.COMFORT" has errors
```

Attempting to select from his COMFORT view fails because the underlying table named in Bob's view was the Dora.COMFORT table. Not surprisingly, attempting to select from Dora.COMFORT

would produce exactly the same message. Next, an attempt to select from Dora.SOMECOMFORT is made:

```
select * from Dora.SOMECOMFORT;

CITY           SAMPLEDAT NOON MIDNIGHT PRECIPITATION
-------------  --------- ---- -------- -------------
KEENE          21-MAR-03 39.9     -1.2           4.4
KEENE          22-JUN-03 85.1     66.7           1.3
KEENE          23-SEP-03 99.8     82.6
KEENE          22-DEC-03 -7.2     -1.2           3.9
```

This works perfectly well, even though direct access to the COMFORT table had been revoked, because Dora gave Bob access to a portion of COMFORT through the SOMECOMFORT view. It is just that portion of the table related to KEENE.

This shows a powerful security feature of Oracle: You can create a view using virtually any restrictions you like or any computations in the columns, and then give access to the view, rather than to the underlying tables, to other users. They will see only the information the view presents. This can even be extended to be user specific. The "Security by User" section later in this chapter gives complete details on this feature.

Now, the view LITTLECOMFORT is created under Bob's username, on top of the view SOMECOMFORT:

```
create view LITTLECOMFORT as select * from Dora.SOMECOMFORT;

View created.
```

And the row for September 23, 2003, is updated:

```
update LITTLECOMFORT set Noon = 88
  where SampleDate = '23-SEP-03';

1 row updated.
```

When the view LITTLECOMFORT is queried, it shows the effect of the **update**:

```
select * from LITTLECOMFORT;

CITY           SAMPLEDAT NOON MIDNIGHT PRECIPITATION
-------------  --------- ---- -------- -------------
KEENE          21-MAR-03 39.9     -1.2           4.4
KEENE          22-JUN-03 85.1     66.7           1.3
KEENE          23-SEP-03   88     82.6
KEENE          22-DEC-03 -7.2     -1.2           3.9
```

A query of Dora.SOMECOMFORT would show the same results, as would a query of COMFORT itself if Dora made it on her own username. The **update** was successful against the underlying table, even though it went through two views (LITTLECOMFORT and SOMECOMFORT) to reach it.

> **NOTE**
> *You need to grant users SELECT access to any table in which they can update or delete records. This is in keeping with the evolving ANSI standard and reflects the fact that a user who only has the UPDATE or DELETE privilege on a table could use the database's feedback comments to discover information about the underlying data.*

create synonym

An alternative method to creating a view that includes an entire table or view from another user is to create a synonym:

```
create synonym BOBCOMFORT for Dora.SOMECOMFORT;
```

This synonym can be treated exactly like a view. See the **create synonym** command in the Alphabetical Reference.

Using Ungranted Privileges

Let's say an attempt is made to delete the row just updated:

```
delete from LITTLECOMFORT where SampleDate = '23-SEP-03';
              *
ERROR at line 1:
ORA-01031: insufficient privileges
```

Bob has not been given DELETE privileges by Dora, so the attempt fails.

Passing Privileges

Bob can grant authority for other users to access his tables, but he cannot bestow on other users access to tables that don't belong to him. Here, he attempts to give INSERT authority to Judy:

```
grant insert on Dora.SOMECOMFORT to Judy;
     *
ERROR at line 1:
ORA-01031: insufficient privileges
```

Because Bob does not have this authority, he fails to give it to Judy. Next, Bob tries to pass on a privilege he does have, SELECT:

```
grant select on Dora.SOMECOMFORT to Judy;
     *
ERROR at line 1:
ORA-01031: insufficient privileges
```

He cannot grant this privilege, either, because the view SOMECOMFORT does not belong to him. If he had been granted access to SOMECOMFORT **with grant option**, then the preceding **grant** command would have succeeded. The view LITTLECOMFORT does belong to him, though, so he can try to pass authority to that view on to Judy:

```
grant select on LITTLECOMFORT to Judy;

ERROR at line 1:
ORA-01720: grant option does not exist for 'DORA.SOMECOMFORT'
```

Because the LITTLECOMFORT view relies on one of Dora's views, and Bob was not granted SELECT **with grant option** on that view, Bob's grant fails.

In addition, a new table, owned by Bob, is created and loaded with the current information from his view LITTLECOMFORT:

```
create table NOCOMFORT as
select * from LITTLECOMFORT;

Table created.
```

The SELECT privilege on the NOCOMFORT table is granted to Judy:

```
grant select on NOCOMFORT to Judy;

Grant succeeded.
```

Queries are made from Judy's account against the table for which Bob granted the SELECT privilege to Judy:

```
connect Judy/sarah
select * from Bob.NOCOMFORT;

CITY          SAMPLEDAT NOON  MIDNIGHT PRECIPITATION
------------- --------- ----- -------- -------------
KEENE         21-MAR-03 39.9  -1.2         4.4
KEENE         22-JUN-03 85.1  66.7         1.3
KEENE         23-SEP-03 88    82.6
KEENE         22-DEC-03 -7.2  -1.2         3.9
```

This grant was successful. The NOCOMFORT table was created, and is owned, by Bob's username. He was able to successfully give access to this table.

If Dora wants Bob to be able to pass on his privileges to others, she can add another clause to the **grant** statement:

```
connect Dora/psyche
grant select, update on SOMECOMFORT to Bob with grant option;

Grant succeeded.
```

The **with grant option** clause enables Bob to pass on access to SOMECOMFORT to Judy through his LITTLECOMFORT view. Note that attempts to access a table to which a user does not have the SELECT privilege always result in the following message:

```
ERROR at line 1:
ORA-00942: table or view does not exist
```

This message appears (rather than a message about not having access privilege) so that a person without permission to query a table doesn't know that it even exists.

Creating a Role

In addition to the default roles shown earlier in this chapter, you can create your own roles within Oracle. The roles you create can comprise table or system privileges or a combination of both. In the following sections, you will see how to create and administer roles.

To create a role, you need to have the CREATE ROLE system privilege. The syntax for role creation is shown in the following listing:

```
create role role_name
[not identified
|identified {by password | using [schema.]package
|externally | globally }];
```

When a role is first created, it has no privileges associated with it. Password options for roles are discussed in "Adding a Password to a Role," later in this chapter.

Two sample **create role** commands are shown in the following example:

```
create role CLERK;
create role MANAGER;
```

The first command creates a role called CLERK, which will be used in the examples in the following sections of this chapter. The second command creates a role called MANAGER, which will also be featured in those examples.

Granting Privileges to a Role

Once a role has been created, you may grant privileges to it. The syntax for the **grant** command is the same for roles as it is for users. When granting privileges to roles, you use the role name in the **to** clause of the **grant** command, as shown in the following listing:

```
grant select on COMFORT to CLERK;
```

As shown in this example, the role name takes the place of the username in the **grant** command. The privilege to select from the COMFORT table will now be available to any user of the CLERK role.

If you are a DBA, or have been granted the GRANT ANY PRIVILEGE system role, you may grant system privileges—such as CREATE SESSION, CREATE SYNONYM, and CREATE VIEW— to roles. These privileges will then be available to any user of your role.

The ability to log into the database is given via the CREATE SESSION system privilege. In the following example, this privilege is granted to the CLERK role. This privilege is also granted to the MANAGER role, along with the CREATE VIEW system privilege.

```
grant CREATE SESSION to CLERK;
grant CREATE SESSION, CREATE VIEW to MANAGER;
```

Granting a Role to Another Role

Roles can be granted to other roles. You can do this via the **grant** command, as shown in the following example:

grant CLERK to MANAGER;

> **NOTE**
> *You can't have circular grants, so you cannot now grant MANAGER to CLERK.*

In this example, the CLERK role is granted to the MANAGER role. Even though you have not directly granted any table privileges to the MANAGER role, it will now inherit any privileges that have been granted to the CLERK role. Organizing roles in this way is a common design for hierarchical organizations.

When granting a role to another role (or to a user, as in the following section), you may grant the role using the **with admin option** clause, as shown in the following listing:

grant CLERK to MANAGER with admin option;

If the **with admin option** clause is used, the grantee has the authority to grant the role to other users or roles. The grantee can also alter or drop the role.

Granting a Role to Users

Roles can be granted to users. When granted to users, roles can be thought of as named sets of privileges. Instead of granting each privilege to each user, you grant the privileges to the role and then grant the role to each user. This greatly simplifies the administrative tasks involved in the management of privileges.

> **NOTE**
> *Privileges that are granted to users via roles cannot be used as the basis for views, procedures, functions, packages, or foreign keys. When creating these types of database objects, you must rely on direct grants of the necessary privileges.*

You can grant a role to a user via the **grant** command, as shown in the following example:

grant CLERK to Bob;

The user Bob in this example will have all the privileges that were granted to the CLERK role (CREATE SESSION and SELECT privileges on COMFORT).

When granting a role to a user, you may grant the role using the **with admin option** clause, as shown in the following listing:

grant MANAGER to Dora with admin option;

Dora now has the authority to grant the MANAGER role to other users or roles, or to alter or drop the role.

Adding a Password to a Role

You can use the **alter role** command for only one purpose: to change the authority needed to enable it. By default, roles do not have passwords associated with them. To enable security for a role, use the **identified** keyword in the **alter role** command. There are two ways to implement this security.

First, you can use the **identified by** clause of the **alter role** command to specify a password, as shown in the following listing:

```
alter role MANAGER identified by cygnusxi;
```

Anytime a user tries to activate that role, the password will be required. If, however, that role is set up as a default role for the user, no password will be required for that role when the user logs in. See the upcoming "Enabling and Disabling Roles" section of this chapter for more details on these topics.

Roles can be tied to operating system privileges as well. If this capability is available on your operating system, you use the **identified externally** clause of the **alter role** command. When the role is enabled, Oracle will check the operating system to verify your access. Altering a role to use this security feature is shown in the following example:

```
alter role MANAGER identified externally;
```

In most UNIX systems, the verification process uses the /etc/group file. To use this file for any operating system, the OS_ROLES database startup parameter in the init.ora file must be set to TRUE.

The following example of this verification process is for a database instance called "Local" on a UNIX system. The server's /etc/group file may contain the following entry:

```
ora_local_manager_d:NONE:1:dora
```

This entry grants the MANAGER role to the account named Dora. The **_d** suffix indicates that this role is to be granted by default when Dora logs in. An **_a** suffix would indicate that this role is to be enabled **with admin option**. If this role were also the user's default role, the suffix would be **_ad**. If more than one user were granted this role, the additional usernames would be appended to the /etc/group entry, as shown in the following listing:

```
ora_local_manager_d:NONE:1:dora,judy
```

If you use this option, roles in the database will be enabled via the operating system.

Removing a Password from a Role

To remove a password from a role, use the **not identified** clause of the **alter role** command, as shown in the following listing. By default, roles do not have passwords.

```
alter role MANAGER not identified;
```

Enabling and Disabling Roles

When a user's account is altered, a list of default roles for that user can be created via the **default role** clause of the **alter user** command. The default action of this command sets all of a user's roles as default roles, enabling all of them every time the user logs in.

NOTE
The maximum number of roles a user can have enabled at any time is set via the MAX_ENABLED_ROLES database initialization parameter.

The syntax for this portion of the **alter user** command is as follows:

```
alter user username
default role {[role1, role2]
[all | all except role1, role2][NONE]};
```

As shown by this syntax, a user can be altered to have, by default, specific roles enabled, all roles enabled, all except specific roles enabled, or no roles enabled. For example, the following **alter user** command will enable the CLERK role whenever Bob logs in:

```
alter user Bob
default role CLERK;
```

To enable a nondefault role, use the **set role** command, as shown in this example:

```
set role CLERK;
```

To see what roles are enabled within your current session, select from the SESSION_ROLES data dictionary view. Query SESSION_PRIVS to see the currently enabled system privileges.
You may also use the **all** and **all except** clauses that were available in the **alter user** command:

```
set role all;
set role all except CLERK;
```

If a role has a password associated with it, that password must be specified via an **identified by** clause:

```
set role MANAGER identified by cygnusxi;
```

To disable a role in your session, use the **set role none** command, as shown in the following listing. This will disable all roles in your current session. Once all the roles have been disabled, reenable the ones you want.

```
set role none;
```

Because you may find it necessary to execute a **set role none** command from time to time, you may want to grant the CREATE SESSION privilege to users directly rather than via roles.

Revoking Privileges from a Role

To revoke a privilege from a role, use the **revoke** command, described earlier in this chapter. Specify the privilege, object name (if it is an object privilege), and role name, as shown in the following example:

```
revoke SELECT on COMFORT from CLERK;
```

Users of the CLERK role will then be unable to query the COMFORT table.

Dropping a Role

To drop a role, use the **drop role** command, as shown in the following example:

```
drop role MANAGER;
drop role CLERK;
```

The roles you specify, and their associated privileges, will be removed from the database entirely. **Grant**s and **revoke**s of system and object privileges take effect immediately. **Grant**s and **revoke**s of roles are only observed when a current user issues a **set role** command or a new user session is started.

Granting UPDATE to Specific Columns

You may want to grant users the SELECT privilege to more columns than you want to grant them the UPDATE privilege. Because SELECT columns can be restricted through a view, to further restrict the columns that can be updated requires a special form of the user's **grant** command. Here is an example for two columns in the COMFORT table:

```
grant update (Noon, Midnight) on COMFORT to Judy;
```

Revoking Object Privileges

If object privileges can be granted, they can also be taken away. This is similar to the **grant** command:

```
revoke { object privilege | all [privileges]}
       [(column [, column]. . . )]
[, { object privilege | all [privileges]}
       [(column [, column]. . . )]]. . .]
on object
from {user | role} [,{user | role}]
[cascade constraints] [force];
```

revoke all removes any of the privileges listed previously, from SELECT through INDEX; revoking individual privileges will leave intact others that had also been granted. The **with grant option** is revoked along with the privilege to which it was attached; the **revoke** then cascades so users who received their access via the **with grant option** user also have their privileges revoked.

If a user defines referential integrity constraints on the object, Oracle drops these constraints if you revoke privileges on the object using the **cascade constraints** option. The **force** option applies

to user-defined datatypes (see Chapter 33). The **force** option revokes the EXECUTE privilege on user-defined datatype objects with table or type dependencies; all dependent objects will be marked as invalid and the data in dependent tables will become inaccessible until the necessary privilege is regranted.

Security by User

Access to tables can be granted specifically, table by table and view by view, to each user or role. There is, however, an additional technique that will simplify this process in some cases. Recall the BOOKSHELF_CHECKOUT records:

```
select Name, SUBSTR(Title,1,30) from BOOKSHELF_CHECKOUT;
```

```
NAME                         SUBSTR(TITLE,1,30)
------------------------     ------------------------------
JED HOPKINS                  INNUMERACY
GERHARDT KENTGEN             WONDERFUL LIFE
DORAH TALBOT                 EITHER/OR
EMILY TALBOT                 ANNE OF GREEN GABLES
PAT LAVAY                    THE SHIPPING NEWS
ROLAND BRANDT                THE SHIPPING NEWS
ROLAND BRANDT                THE DISCOVERERS
ROLAND BRANDT                WEST WITH THE NIGHT
EMILY TALBOT                 MIDNIGHT MAGIC
EMILY TALBOT                 HARRY POTTER AND THE GOBLET OF
PAT LAVAY                    THE MISMEASURE OF MAN
DORAH TALBOT                 POLAR EXPRESS
DORAH TALBOT                 GOOD DOG, CARL
GERHARDT KENTGEN             THE MISMEASURE OF MAN
FRED FULLER                  JOHN ADAMS
FRED FULLER                  TRUMAN
JED HOPKINS                  TO KILL A MOCKINGBIRD
DORAH TALBOT                 MY LEDGER
GERHARDT KENTGEN             MIDNIGHT MAGIC
```

To enable each borrower to access this table, but restrict the access given to a view of only each borrower's own single row, you could create 19 separate views, each with a different name in the **where** clause, and you could make separate grants to each of these views for each borrower. Alternatively, you could create a view whose **where** clause contains User, the pseudo-column, like this:

```
create or replace view MY_CHECKOUT as
select * from BOOKSHELF_CHECKOUT
 where SUBSTR(Name,1,INSTR(Name,' ')-1) = User;
```

The owner of the BOOKSHELF_CHECKOUT table can create this view and grant SELECT on it to users. A user can then query the BOOKSHELF_CHECKOUT table through the MY_CHECKOUT view. The **where** clause will find his or her username in the Name column (see the **where** clause) and return just that user's records.

In the following example, a user name Jed is created and granted access to the MY_CHECKOUT view. Selecting from that view yields just those books checked out by him. This example assumes that the schema owning the BOOKSHELF_CHECKOUT table is named PRACTICE and is a database administrator:

```
create user jed identified by hop;

User created.

grant CREATE SESSION to jed;

Grant succeeded.

grant select on MY_CHECKOUT to jed;

Grant succeeded.

connect jed/hop

Connected.

select * from Practice.MY_CHECKOUT;

NAME
------------------------
TITLE
----------------------------------------------------------
CHECKOUTD RETURNEDD
--------- ---------
JED HOPKINS
INNUMERACY
01-JAN-02 22-JAN-02

JED HOPKINS
TO KILL A MOCKINGBIRD
15-FEB-02 01-MAR-02
```

Whenever MY_CHECKOUT is queried, it will return records depending on the pseudo-column User—the user of SQL*Plus at the moment the view is queried.

Granting Access to the Public

Rather than grant access to every worker, the **grant** command can be generalized to the public:

```
grant select on MY_CHECKOUT to public;
```

This gives everyone access, including users created after this **grant** was made. However, each user will still have to access the table using the owner's username as a prefix. To avoid this, a DBA may create a *public synonym* (which creates a name accessible to all users that stands for Practice.MY_CHECKOUT):

```
create public synonym MY_CHECKOUT for Practice.MY_CHECKOUT;
```

From this point forward, anyone can access MY_CHECKOUT without prefixing it with the schema owner (Practice in this case). This approach gives tremendous flexibility for security. Workers could see only their own salaries, for instance, in a table that contains salaries for everyone. If, however, a user creates a table or view with the same name as a public synonym, any future SQL statements by this user will act on this new table or view, and not on the one by the same name to which the public has access.

> **NOTE**
> *All these accesses—and all attempts at system-level operations, such as logins—may be audited. See AUDIT in the Alphabetical Reference for an introduction to Oracle's security-auditing capabilities.*

Granting Limited Resources

When granting resource quotas in an Oracle database, you use the **quota** parameter of the **create user** or **alter user** command, as shown in the following listing. In this example, Bob is granted a quota of 100MB in the USERS tablespace:

```
alter user Bob
quota 100M on USERS;
```

A user's space quota may be set when the user is created, via the **create user** command. If you want to remove limits on a user's space quota, you can grant that user the UNLIMITED TABLESPACE system privilege. See the **create user** and **alter user** commands in the Alphabetical Reference for further details on these commands.

Profiles can also be used to enforce other resource limits, such as the amount of CPU time or idle time a user's requests to Oracle can take. A profile detailing these resource limits is created and then assigned to one or more users. See the **create profile** and **alter user** command entries in the Alphabetical Reference for full details.

PART
III

Beyond the Basics

CHAPTER 19

Advanced Security—
Virtual Private
Databases

n prior chapters, you have seen how to use views to enhance security by displaying only the rows that meet specified criteria. In this chapter, you will see how to use a Virtual Private Database (VPD) to provide that type of record-level security across your application tables. In VPD, you attach security policies directly to tables, views, and synonyms so there is no way for users to bypass your security settings.

In a VPD, any SQL used to access a table, view, or synonym protected by a VPD policy is dynamically modified to include a limiting condition—a **where** clause or an **and** clause. The modification occurs transparently, and the user sees only the data that passes the limiting condition in the **where** clause. This fine-grained access allows a great deal of control over all accesses of your application tables. VPD policies can be applied to **select**, **insert**, **update**, **index**, and **delete** commands. You can create different security policies for each type of access—one for **select**s, another for **insert**s, and so on.

As of Oracle Database 10g, VPD has been extended to include column-level VPD, in which security policies are applied only when a particular column or columns are accessed. Oracle Database 10g also supports column masking, in which protected columns may be displayed with **NULL** values if their rows are returned. Additionally, auditing has been enhanced so DBAs can perform fine-grained auditing of **select**, **insert**, **update**, and **delete** commands.

NOTE
Implementing VPD requires the use of some advanced features—procedures, triggers, and PL/SQL. These features are covered in Part IV of this book. If you are not already familiar with those features, you may wish to review Part IV before proceeding with the advanced material in this chapter.

Initial Configuration

VPD allows you to customize the ways different users see the same table. To go through the full example shown in this chapter, you will need access to a SYSDBA-privileged account.

VPD requires the use of a package named DBMS_RLS. From the SYSDBA-privileged account, grant EXECUTE privilege on the DBMS_RLS package to all users. Also, create the users that will be used during the examples: PRACTICE (which will own the tables), ADAMS, and BURLINGTON, as shown in the following listing:

```
connect system/password as SYSDBA

grant execute on DBMS_RLS to public;

create user ADAMS identified by john7;
create user BURLINGTON identified by newj2;
grant CREATE SESSION to ADAMS, BURLINGTON;
```

From the SYSDBA-privileged account, create the PRACTICE user (if it does not already exist) and give it the CREATE ANY CONTEXT and CREATE PUBLIC SYNONYM system privileges:

```
grant CREATE ANY CONTEXT, CREATE PUBLIC SYNONYM to PRACTICE;
```

Within the PRACTICE user, you should now create two tables: the STOCK_ACCOUNT table and the STOCK_TRX table. The STOCK_ACCOUNT table contains one row for each account that can perform stock trades. The STOCK_TRX table contains one row for each stock bought or sold by that account holder.

```
connect practice/practice

create table STOCK_ACCOUNT
(Account          NUMBER(10),
AccountLongName  VARCHAR2(50));

insert into STOCK_ACCOUNT values (
1234, 'ADAMS');
insert into STOCK_ACCOUNT values (
7777, 'BURLINGTON');

create table STOCK_TRX (
Account   NUMBER(10),
Symbol    VARCHAR2(20),
Price     NUMBER(6,2),
Quantity  NUMBER(6),
Trx_Flag  VARCHAR2(1));

insert into STOCK_TRX values (
  1234, 'ADSP', 31.75, 100, 'B');
insert into STOCK_TRX values (
  7777, 'ADSP', 31.50, 300, 'S');
insert into STOCK_TRX values (
  1234, 'ADSP', 31.55, 100, 'B');
insert into STOCK_TRX values (
  7777, 'OCKS', 21.75, 1000, 'B');
commit;
```

Once those tables are created, grant the ADAMS and BURLINGTON users access to them:

```
grant SELECT, INSERT on STOCK_TRX to ADAMS, BURLINGTON;
grant SELECT on STOCK_ACCOUNT to ADAMS, BURLINGTON;
```

You now have the application configuration set—the PRACTICE schema owns the data table (STOCK_TRX) and has a table that you can use to map usernames to account numbers (STOCK_ACCOUNT). With this configuration in place, you can create an application context, as described in the next section.

Create an Application Context

The next step in the VPD configuration is to create an application context. The purpose of the context is to define the rules you will use to separate users. The context will be part of each session's characteristics.

First, use the **create context** command to specify the name of the package you will use to set the rules:

```
connect PRACTICE/PRACTICE

create context PRACTICE using PRACTICE.CONTEXT_PACKAGE;
```

Next, create the package with that same name (CONTEXT_PACKAGE). See Chapter 31 for details on the use of packages. The package consists of a single procedure call:

```
create or replace package CONTEXT_PACKAGE AS
  procedure SET_CONTEXT;
end;
/
```

Now that the package header has been created, the package body may be created. The following listing shows the package body that will set the context for each session.

```
create or replace package body CONTEXT_PACKAGE is
    procedure Set_Context IS
      v_user   VARCHAR2(30);
      v_id     NUMBER;
    begin
      DBMS_SESSION.SET_CONTEXT('PRACTICE','SETUP','TRUE');
      v_user := SYS_CONTEXT('USERENV','SESSION_USER');
      begin
        select Account
          into v_id
          from STOCK_ACCOUNT
         where AccountLongName = v_user;
        DBMS_SESSION.SET_CONTEXT('PRACTICE','USER_ID', v_id);
      exception
        WHEN NO_DATA_FOUND then
          DBMS_SESSION.SET_CONTEXT('PRACTICE','USER_ID', 0);
      end;
      DBMS_SESSION.SET_CONTEXT('PRACTICE','SETUP','FALSE');
    end SET_CONTEXT;
end CONTEXT_PACKAGE;
/
```

The core of this package body is a single query:

```
    select Account
      into v_id
      from STOCK_ACCOUNT
     where AccountLongName = v_user;
```

The STOCK_ACCOUNT table will contain a row for each user (Adams, Burlington, and so on). This query takes the name of the user who logged in and compares it to the AccountLongName values in the STOCK_ACCOUNT table. If there is a match, then the Account value is returned.

If there is no match, then another part of the package returns a 0 as the account number. The Account value is set as the *User_ID* variable for the session:

```
DBMS_SESSION.SET_CONTEXT('PRACTICE','USER_ID', v_id);
```

You will be able to reference this context value in your programs, and VPD restrictions will be based on the context setting.

Now that the package has been created, grant public access to it:

```
grant EXECUTE on PRACTICE.CONTEXT_PACKAGE to public;
create public synonym CONTEXT_PACKAGE for PRACTICE.CONTEXT_PACKAGE;
```

The rules for establishing the context for sessions are now ready to be activated, as described in the next section.

Create a Logon Trigger

In order for the context to be set within each user's session, you must create a trigger that will be executed each time a user logs into the database (see Chapter 30 for full details on triggers).

```
rem  NOTE: connect to a SYSDBA account before running this
rem
create or replace trigger PRACTICE.SET_SECURITY_CONTEXT
after logon on database
begin
  PRACTICE.CONTEXT_PACKAGE.SET_CONTEXT;
end;
/
```

Each time a user logs in, Oracle will execute the SET_CONTEXT procedure within the PRACTICE user's CONTEXT_PACKAGE package. That procedure will query the STOCK_ACCOUNT table and see if there is a matching account name; if there is a match, then the session's context will be altered to reflect the Account value.

You should test the context setting before going past this point in the implementation of a VPD. You can use the **SYS_CONTEXT** function to determine whether the configuration is working properly, as shown in the following listing:

```
connect adams/john7

select SYS_CONTEXT('USERENV', 'SESSION_USER') Username,
       SYS_CONTEXT('PRACTICE', 'USER_ID') ID
from DUAL;

USERNAME
-----------------------------------------------------------
ID
-----------------------------------------------------------
ADAMS
1234
```

The **SYS_CONTEXT** function output shows the power of the VPD configuration. For each user who logs in, Oracle will check the STOCK_ACCOUNT table and will use the matching Account value to set a value for the session's *User_ID*. In this case, Oracle looked up the ADAMS user in the STOCK_ACCOUNT table, found its Account value (1234), and set its session's *User_ID* variable to that value. If you have that information, you can restrict access to rows in other tables based on the Account data in the STOCK_ACCOUNT table. VPD allows you to restrict that access automatically with no need to create views. Every time a user attempts to access a table, access can be restricted regardless of the tool used.

If you log in as a user not listed in the STOCK_ACCOUNT table (triggering a NO_DATA_FOUND exception), your *User_ID* value will be 0, as the procedure dictates:

```
    WHEN NO_DATA_FOUND then
        DBMS_SESSION.SET_CONTEXT('PRACTICE','USER_ID', 0);
```

Create a Security Policy

At this point, the context and the logon triggers have been created. For the context package to have an effect on the users' interaction with the database, you need to create a security package that acts on the output of the context package.

First, define the package header. In this example, there are two types of actions supported against the STOCK_TRX table (**insert**s and **select**s), so two functions will be created within the package:

```
connect PRACTICE/PRACTICE

create or replace package SECURITY_PACKAGE as
  function STOCK_TRX_INSERT_SECURITY(Owner VARCHAR2, Objname VARCHAR2)
    return VARCHAR2;
  function STOCK_TRX_SELECT_SECURITY(Owner VARCHAR2, Objname VARCHAR2)
    return VARCHAR2;
end SECURITY_PACKAGE;
/
```

Next, create the package body. Both functions follow the same pattern, geared toward generating a predicate that will be applied every time a user queries the STOCK_TRX table. If the session username is the owner of the table, then the predicate is **NULL**. For all other users, the *User_ID* context variable is evaluated, and is passed as a limiting condition to any query. The object of these functions is to generate a predicate such as **where Account=1234** to be applied each time the table is queried by a user.

```
create or replace package body SECURITY_PACKAGE is
  function STOCK_TRX_SELECT_SECURITY(Owner VARCHAR2, Objname VARCHAR2)
  return VARCHAR2 is
    Predicate VARCHAR2(2000);
  begin
    Predicate := '1=2';
    if (SYS_CONTEXT('USERENV','SESSION_USER') = 'PRACTICE') then
      Predicate := NULL;
```

```
    else
      Predicate := 'ACCOUNT = SYS_CONTEXT(''PRACTICE'',''USER_ID'')';
    end if;
    return Predicate;
  END STOCK_TRX_SELECT_SECURITY;

  function STOCK_TRX_INSERT_SECURITY(Owner VARCHAR2, Objname VARCHAR2)
   return VARCHAR2 is
    Predicate VARCHAR2(2000);
  begin
    Predicate := '1=2';
    if (SYS_CONTEXT('USERENV','SESSION_USER') = 'PRACTICE') then
      Predicate := NULL;
    else
      Predicate := 'ACCOUNT = SYS_CONTEXT(''PRACTICE'',''USER_ID'')';
    end if;
    return Predicate;
  end STOCK_TRX_INSERT_SECURITY;
end SECURITY_PACKAGE;
/
```

Since this package will be executed by all users who access the STOCK_TRX table, grant users the privilege to execute it, and create a public synonym.

```
grant EXECUTE ON PRACTICE.SECURITY_PACKAGE to public;
create public synonym SECURITY_PACKAGE for PRACTICE.SECURITY_PACKAGE;
```

Apply the Security Policy to Tables

Now that the security package exists, you can relate it to tables. To add a policy to a table, use the ADD_POLICY procedure of the DBMS_RLS package, as shown in the following listing:

```
begin
    DBMS_RLS.ADD_POLICY('PRACTICE', 'STOCK_TRX', 'STOCK_TRX_INSERT_POLICY',
                        'PRACTICE', 'SECURITY_PACKAGE.STOCK_TRX_INSERT_SECURITY',
                        'INSERT', TRUE);
    DBMS_RLS.ADD_POLICY('PRACTICE', 'STOCK_TRX', 'STOCK_TRX_SELECT_POLICY',
                        'PRACTICE', 'SECURITY_PACKAGE.STOCK_TRX_SELECT_SECURITY',
                        'SELECT');
end;
/
```

The ADD_POLICY procedure is executed two times. In the first execution, the **STOCK_TRX_ INSERT_SECURITY** function is specified for execution during attempts to insert rows into the STOCK_TRX table. In the second execution, the **STOCK_TRX_SELECT_SECURITY** function is applied to queries of the STOCK_TRX tables. You can have distinct rules for security for different operations against the table. The variables passed to the ADD_POLICY procedure are the schema name, table name, and policy name, the schema name and function name for the security function, and the operation affected.

Test VPD

To see the results of the security policy, query the table. The STOCK_TRX table has four rows, two from the ADAMS account (1234) and two from the BURLINGTON account (7777). Log in as one of those users and query the table:

```
connect adams/john7

select * from PRACTICE.STOCK_TRX;

    ACCOUNT SYMBOL                     PRICE   QUANTITY T
 ---------- -------------------- ---------- ---------- -
       1234 ADSP                      31.75        100 B
       1234 ADSP                      31.55        100 B
```

Although the ADAMS user did not provide a **where** clause in his query, Oracle applied a predicate to his query, limiting the results to rows with the Account value of 1234. What if the BURLINGTON user attempts the same query?

```
connect burlington/newj2

select * from PRACTICE.STOCK_TRX;

    ACCOUNT SYMBOL                     PRICE   QUANTITY T
 ---------- -------------------- ---------- ---------- -
       7777 ADSP                       31.5        300 S
       7777 OCKS                      21.75       1000 B
```

The BURLINGTON user only sees the rows with the Account value of 7777, based on his row in the STOCK_ACCOUNT table.

NOTE
Because the STOCK_ACCOUNT table will be queried for each logon, make sure the query to retrieve the user context data is properly tuned. See Chapter 43 for an overview of tuning.

What about other users? If they are not in the STOCK_ACCOUNT table, they cannot retrieve rows from the STOCK_TRX table:

```
connect system/manager

select * from PRACTICE.STOCK_TRX;

no rows selected
```

In addition to **select**s, **insert**s were limited by the security policy; a user can only insert rows into STOCK_TRX if the Account value matches the user's context settings. Attempts to insert other rows fail:

```
connect PRACTICE/PRACTICE
grant INSERT on STOCK_TRX to ADAMS;

connect adams/john7

insert into PRACTICE.STOCK_TRX
values
(7777, 'ADSP',31.5,100, 'B');

ERROR at line 1:
ORAC-28115: policy with check option violation
```

The ORA-28115 error indicates that the user attempted to insert a row that the user would not be able to select due to the VPD settings.

How to Implement Column-Level VPD

As of Oracle Database 10g, you can implement VPD at the column level. If a column with secure data is referenced by a query, you can use column-level VPD to apply a security policy or display the column with **NULL** values. This approach is different from the row-based VPD shown in the prior examples; in column-level VPD all rows may be displayed, but the columns may be shielded from the user. You can apply column-level VPD to a table or a view.

To use column-level VPD, specify a value for the *sec_relevant_cols* input parameters for the ADD_POLICY procedure of DBMS_RLS. If the STOCK_TRX_SELECT_POLICY did not already exist, you could use the following command:

```
begin
    DBMS_RLS.ADD_POLICY
                (object_schema=>'PRACTICE',
                    object_name=>'STOCK_TRX',
                    policy_name=>'STOCK_TRX_SELECT_POLICY',
            function_schema=>'PRACTICE',
            policy_function=>'SECURITY_PACKAGE.STOCK_TRX_SELECT_SECURITY',
            sec_relevant_cols=>'Price');
end;
/
```

By default, the rows will be returned based on the security policy function when the Price column is referenced by a query. To use the column masking option, tell Oracle to return all rows by setting the *sec_relevant_cols_opt* parameter to DBMS_RLS.ALL_ROWS, following the *sec_relevant_cols* parameter setting.

When this version of the policy is used, all rows will be returned by the query. For the rows that the user would not normally be able to see, the secure column (Price) will display **NULL** values. The Price values will be displayed for rows that the user can normally see.

Column masking applies only to queries, not to DML operations. Note that your applications must support the display of **NULL** values if you use column masking.

How to Disable VPD

To remove a VPD functionality, reverse the steps shown in this chapter: Remove the policy from the table (via the DROP_POLICY procedure of the DBMS_RLS package), drop the logon trigger, and optionally drop the other packages.

Table 19-1 lists the procedures within the DBMS_RLS package.

To drop a policy, execute the DROP_POLICY procedure. Its three input variables are the schema name, the object name, and the policy. The following example drops the STOCK_TRX_INSERT_POLICY:

```
DBMS_RLS.DROP_POLICY('PRACTICE', 'STOCK_TRX', 'STOCK_TRX_INSERT_POLICY');
```

Similarly, you can drop the STOCK_TRX_SELECT_POLICY:

```
DBMS_RLS.DROP_POLICY('PRACTICE', 'STOCK_TRX', 'STOCK_TRX_SELECT_POLICY');
```

Procedure	Purpose
ADD_POLICY	Add a policy to a table, view, or synonym
DROP_POLICY	Drop a policy from a table, view, or synonym
REFRESH_POLICY	Invalidate cursors associated with nonstatic policies
ENABLE_POLICY	Enable (or disable) a policy you previously added to a table, view, or synonym
CREATE_POLICY_GROUP	Create a policy group
ADD_GROUPED_POLICY	Add a policy to the specified policy group
ADD_POLICY_CONTEXT	Add the context for the active application
DELETE_POLICY_GROUP	Drop a policy group
DROP_GROUPED_POLICY	Drop a policy that is a member of the specified group
DROP_POLICY_CONTEXT	Drop the context for the application
ENABLE_GROUPED_POLICY	Enable a policy within a group
DISABLE_GROUPED_POLICY	Disable a policy within a group
REFRESH_GROUPED_POLICY	Reparse the SQL statements associated with a refreshed policy

TABLE 19-1. *DBMS_RLS Procedures*

At this point, the policy will be dropped, but the login trigger will still be executing during each login. Remember to drop the trigger (in this case, PRACTICE.SET_SECURITY_CONTEXT) so the database does not perform unnecessary work. If the VPD restrictions are no longer needed, you can then drop the packages that set the application context.

How to Use Policy Groups

As shown in Table 19-1, a number of the available procedures within DBMS_RLS deal with *policy groups*. You can create policy groups, add policies to a policy group, and enable policies within a group.

You can create groups that integrate policies affecting the same tables. If multiple applications use the same tables, you can use groups to manage the table-level policies that should be enabled during application usage. All policies in a policy group can be applied at application run time.

By default, all policies belong to the SYS_DEFAULT policy group. Policies in the SYS_DEFAULT policy group will always be executed along with the policy group specified by the driving context. You cannot drop the SYS_DEFAULT policy group.

To add a new policy group, use the CREATE_POLICY_GROUP procedure. The syntax is

```
DBMS_RLS.CREATE_POLICY_GROUP (
    object_schema    VARCHAR2,
    object_name      VARCHAR2,
    policy_group     VARCHAR2);
```

You can then add a policy to the group via the ADD_GROUPED_POLICY procedure. Its syntax is

```
DBMS_RLS.ADD_GROUPED_POLICY(
    object_schema    VARCHAR2,
    object_name      VARCHAR2,
    policy_group     VARCHAR2,
    policy_name      VARCHAR2,
    function_schema  VARCHAR2,
    policy_function  VARCHAR2,
    statement_types  VARCHAR2,
    update_check     BOOLEAN,
    enabled          BOOLEAN,
    static_policy    IN BOOLEAN  FALSE,
    policy_type      IN BINARY_INTEGER NULL,
    long_predicate   IN BOOLEAN  FALSE,
    sec_relevant_cols IN VARCHAR2);
```

For example, you can create a policy group named TRXAUDIT, then add the STOCK_TRX_SELECT_POLICY to it:

```
begin
DBMS_RLS.CREATE_POLICY_GROUP('PRACTICE','STOCK_TRX','TRXAUDIT');
DBMS_RLS.ADD_GROUPED_POLICY('PRACTICE','STOCK_TRX','TRXAUDIT',
'STOCK_TRX_SELECT_POLICY','PRACTICE', 'SECURITY_PACKAGE.STOCK_TRX_SELECT_SECURITY');
end;
/
```

When the database is accessed, the application initializes the driving context to specify the policy group to use. In the **create context** command, specify the name of the procedure to use (in the examples in this chapter, the context is set via PRACTICE.CONTEXT_PACKAGE).

```
create context PRACTICE using PRACTICE.CONTEXT_PACKAGE;
```

PRACTICE.CONTEXT_PACKAGE executed the SET_CONTEXT procedure to set the application context:

```
DBMS_SESSION.SET_CONTEXT('PRACTICE','SETUP','TRUE');
```

For policy groups, the third parameter passed to SET_CONTEXT will be the policy group name. For the application to invoke a specific context group, rewrite CONTEXT_PACKAGE to support a third input variable (policy group) and add that to the SET_CONTEXT execution:

```
DBMS_SESSION.SET_CONTEXT('PRACTICE','SETUP', policy_group);
```

Within your application, execute CONTEXT_PACKAGE and set the policy group value to TRXAUDIT. When the user queries the STOCK_TRX table, the VPD restrictions in SYS_DEFAULT and the TRXAUDIT policy group will then be applied.

You can remove a policy from a policy group via DROP_GROUPED_POLICY, disable it via DISABLE_GROUPED_POLICY, or re-enable it via ENABLE_GROUPED_POLICY. Use DELETE_POLICY_GROUP to drop the policy group entirely. See the *Oracle Database Security Guide* for additional information on the procedures available within the DBMS_RLS package.

CHAPTER
20

Working with Tablespaces

In this chapter, you will see an overview of the use of tablespaces, along with the commands needed to create and alter tablespaces. The commands needed to create and maintain tablespaces require you to have database administrator privileges. The creation and maintenance of tablespaces is described in greater detail in Chapter 46. The goals of this chapter are to introduce the concepts, review new features, and provide developers with the information needed to make informed design decisions relative to their usage of tablespaces.

Tablespaces and the Structure of the Database

People who have worked with computers for any period of time are familiar with the concept of a file; it's a place on disk where information is stored, and it has a name. Its size is usually not fixed: If you add information to the file, it can grow larger and take up more disk space, up to the maximum available. This process is managed by the operating system, and often involves distributing the information in the file over several smaller sections of the disk that are not physically near each other. The operating system handles the logical connection of these smaller sections without your being aware of it at all. To you, the file looks like a single whole.

Oracle uses files as a part of its organizational scheme, but its logical structure goes beyond the concept of a file. A *datafile* is an operating system file used to store Oracle data. Each datafile is assigned to a *tablespace*—a logical division within the database. Tablespaces commonly include SYSTEM (for Oracle's internal data dictionary), SYSAUX (for auxiliary internal objects), USERS (for user objects), and others for application tables, indexes, and additional database structures.

The datafiles can have a fixed size or can be allowed to extend themselves automatically when they are filled, up to a defined limit. To add more space to a tablespace, you can manually extend your datafiles or add new datafiles. New rows can then be added to existing tables, and those tables may then have rows in multiple datafiles.

Each table has a single area of disk space, called a *segment,* set aside for it in the tablespace. Each segment, in turn, has an initial area of disk space, called the *initial extent,* set aside for it in the tablespace. Once the segment has used up this space, the *next extent,* another single area of disk space, is set aside for it. When it has used this up as well, yet another next extent is set aside. This process continues with every table until the whole tablespace is full. At that point, someone has to add a new file to the tablespace or extend the tablespace's files before any more growth in the tables can take place.

Every database also contains a SYSTEM tablespace, which contains the data dictionary as well as the names and locations of all the tablespaces, tables, indexes, and clusters for this database. The objects within the SYSTEM tablespace are owned by the SYS and SYSTEM users; no other users should own objects in this tablespace because they may impact the rest of the database.

NOTE
*As of Oracle Database 10g, you can rename a tablespace via the **alter tablespace** command.*

Tablespace Contents

You can query the USER_TABLESPACES data dictionary view to see the tablespaces available in the database. Tablespaces are created by privileged users, via the **create tablespace** command. The simplest syntax is

```
create tablespace tablespace_name
datafile datafile_name filesize;
```

Database administrators specify the tablespace space-allocation method when creating the tablespace. The following example creates a tablespace whose initial space allocation is a single 100MB file, but that file can automatically extend itself as needed:

```
create tablespace USERS_2
datafile '/u01/oradata/users_2_01.dbf'
    size 100M autoextend on;
```

In this chapter, the focus is on the developer's use of tablespaces. Database administrators should see Chapter 46 and the Alphabetical Reference for the detailed commands and options involved in creating tablespaces.

The Contents column of USER_TABLESPACES shows the type of objects supported in each tablespace. The following shows a sample listing from an Oracle Database 10g installation:

```
select Tablespace_Name, Contents from USER_TABLESPACES;

TABLESPACE_NAME                     CONTENTS
------------------------------      ---------
SYSTEM                              PERMANENT
UNDOTBS1                            UNDO
SYSAUX                             PERMANENT
TEMP                               TEMPORARY
USERS                              PERMANENT
```

The SYSTEM, SYSAUX, and USERS tablespaces support permanent objects—tables, indexes, and other user objects. The TEMP tablespace supports only temporary segments—segments created and managed by Oracle to support sorting operations. The UNDOTBS1 tablespace supports undo segment management (see Chapters 27 and 28).

When you create a table without specifying a tablespace, the table will be stored in your default tablespace. You can see that setting via the USER_USERS data dictionary view:

```
select Default_Tablespace, Temporary_Tablespace
    from USER_USERS;

DEFAULT_TABLESPACE              TEMPORARY_TABLESPACE
------------------------------  ------------------------------
USERS                           TEMP
```

In this example, the default tablespace is USERS and the temporary tablespace is TEMP. Those settings can be changed via the **alter user** command.

Although USERS is your default tablespace, you may not have any *quota* on the tablespace. To see how much space you have been granted in a tablespace, query USER_TS_QUOTAS, as shown in the following listing:

```
select * from USER_TS_QUOTAS;

TABLESPACE_NAME          BYTES  MAX_BYTES     BLOCKS MAX_BLOCKS
------------------- ---------- ---------- ---------- ----------
USERS                    131072         -1         16         -1
```

In this case, the MAX_BYTES and MAX_BLOCKS values—the maximum space you can use—are both –1. If the value is negative, you have unlimited quota in that tablespace. In this example, the user has only used 16 database blocks in 131,072 bytes. Because there are 1,024 bytes in a kilobyte, the user has 128KB allocated in the USERS tablespace.

The space in tablespaces can be *locally managed*. As an alternative, the space management can be *dictionary managed* (the space management records are maintained in the data dictionary). In general, locally managed tablespaces are simpler to administer. You can display the extent management setting via the Extent_Management column of USER_TABLESPACES:

```
select Tablespace_Name, Extent_Management from USER_TABLESPACES;

TABLESPACE_NAME                 EXTENT_MAN
------------------------------- ----------
SYSTEM                          LOCAL
UNDOTBS1                        LOCAL
SYSAUX                          LOCAL
TEMP                            LOCAL
USERS                           LOCAL
```

In a locally managed tablespace, the space map for the tablespace is maintained in the headers of the tablespace's datafiles. To see the datafiles allocated to a tablespace, database administrators can query the DBA_DATA_FILES data dictionary view; there is no equivalent view for nonprivileged users.

The default values for storage are operating system specific. You can query USER_TABLESPACES to see the block size and the defaults for the initial extent size, next extent size, minimum number of extents, maximum number of extents, and pctincrease settings for objects:

```
select Tablespace_Name,
       Block_Size,
       Initial_Extent,
       Next_Extent,
       Min_Extents,
       Max_Extents,
       Pct_Increase
  from USER_TABLESPACES;
```

To override the default settings, you can use the **storage** clause when creating a table or index. See the entry for the **storage** clause in the Alphabetical Reference for the full syntax. In general, you should work with the database administrators to establish appropriate defaults for the locally managed tablespaces and then rely on that sizing for your objects. Unless there are objects with extraordinary space requirements, you should avoid setting custom sizes for each of your tables and indexes. If you do not specify a **storage** clause when you create an object, it will use the default for its tablespace. If you do not specify a **tablespace** clause, the object will be stored in your default tablespace.

You can query the free space in a tablespace via the USER_FREE_SPACE data dictionary view. USER_FREE_SPACE will display one row for each contiguous free extent within a tablespace, as well as its exact location and length.

RECYCLEBIN Space in Tablespaces

As of Oracle Database 10g, dropped objects do not release their allocated space unless you specify the **purge** clause when dropping them. By default, the objects maintain their space, allowing you to later recover them via the **flashback table to before drop** command (see Chapter 28).

The space currently used by dropped objects is recorded in each user's RECYCLEBIN view (or, for the DBA, the DBA_RECYCLEBIN view). You can see how many bytes you are presently using in each tablespace, and you can use the **purge** command to purge old entries from the RECYCLEBIN. Here's an example:

```
select Space --number of blocks still allocated
   from RECYCLEBIN
where Ts_Name = 'USERS';
```

See the **purge** command in the Alphabetical Reference and Chapter 28 for further details.

Read-Only Tablespaces

DBAs can alter a tablespace via the **alter tablespace** command. Tablespaces may be altered to be read-only:

```
alter tablespace USERS read only;
```

Or they can be changed from read-only to writable:

```
alter tablespace USERS read write;
```

The data in a read-only tablespace cannot be altered. Although nonprivileged users cannot execute these commands, you should be aware of them because they may alter how you physically store your data. If you can move the unchanging data to its own tablespace, you may be able to designate the entire tablespace as read-only. Using read-only tablespaces may simplify backup and recovery efforts.

NOTE
You can drop objects from read-only tablespaces.

The read-only status for tablespaces is displayed via the Status column of the USER_TABLESPACES data dictionary view, as shown in the following example:

```
alter tablespace USERS read only;

Tablespace altered.

select Status from USER_TABLESPACES
 where Tablespace_Name = 'USERS';

STATUS
---------
READ ONLY

alter tablespace USERS read write;

Tablespace altered.

select Status from USER_TABLESPACES
 where Tablespace_Name = 'USERS';

STATUS
---------
ONLINE
```

nologging Tablespaces

You can disable the creation of redo log entries for specific objects. By default, Oracle generates log entries for all transactions. If you wish to bypass that functionality—for instance, if you are loading data and you can completely re-create all the transactions—you can specify that the loaded object or the tablespace be maintained in **nologging** mode.

You can see the current logging status for tablespaces by querying the Logging column of USER_TABLESPACES.

Temporary Tablespaces

When you execute a command that performs a sorting or grouping operation, Oracle may create a temporary segment to manage the data. The temporary segment is created in a temporary tablespace, and the user executing the command does not have to manage that data. Oracle will dynamically create the temporary segment and will release its space when the instance is shut down and restarted. If there is not enough temporary space available and the temporary tablespace datafiles cannot auto-extend, the command will fail. Each user in the database has an associated temporary tablespace—there may be just one such tablespace for all users to share. A default temporary tablespace is set at the database level so all new users will have the same temporary tablespace unless a different one is specified during the **create user** or **alter user** command.

As of Oracle Database 10g, you can create multiple temporary tablespaces and group them. Assign the temporary tablespaces to tablespace groups via the **tablespace group** clause of the **create temporary tablespace** or **alter tablespace** command. You can then specify the group as a user's default tablespace. Tablespace groups can help to support parallel operations involving sorts.

Tablespaces for System-Managed Undo

You can use *Automatic Undo Management (AUM)* to place all undo data in a single tablespace. When you create an undo tablespace, Oracle manages the storage, retention, and space utilization for your rollback data via *system-managed undo (SMU)*. When a retention time is set (in the database's initialization parameter file), Oracle will make a best effort to retain all committed undo data in the database for the specified number of seconds. With that setting, any query taking less than the retention time should not result in an error as long as the undo tablespace has been sized properly. While the database is running, DBAs can change the UNDO_RETENTION parameter value via the **alter system** command.

As of Oracle Database 10*g*, you can guarantee undo data is retained, even at the expense of current transactions in the database. When you create the undo tablespace, specify **retention guarantee** as part of your **create database** or **create undo tablespace** command. Use care with this setting, because it may force transactions to fail in order to guarantee the retention of old undo data in the undo tablespace.

Supporting Flashback Database

As of Oracle Database 10*g*, you can use the **flashback database** command to revert an entire database to a prior point in time. DBAs can configure tablespaces to be excluded from this option—the **alter tablespace flashback off** command tells Oracle to exclude that tablespace's transaction from the data written to the flashback database area. See Chapter 28 for details on **flashback database** command usage.

Transporting Tablespaces

A *transportable* tablespace is a tablespace that can be "unplugged" from one database and "plugged into" another. To be transportable, a tablespace—or a set of tablespaces—must be self-contained. The tablespace set cannot contain any objects that refer to objects in other tablespaces. Therefore, if you transport a tablespace containing indexes, you must move the tablespace containing the indexes' base tables as part of the same transportable tablespace set. The better you have organized and distributed your objects among tablespaces, the easier it is to generate a self-contained set of tablespaces to transport.

To transport tablespaces, you need to generate a tablespace set, copy or move that tablespace set to the new database, and plug the set into the new database. Because these are privileged operations, you must have database administration privileges to execute them. As a developer, you should be aware of this capability, because it can significantly reduce the time required to migrate self-contained data among databases. For instance, you may create and populate a read-only tablespace of historical data in a test environment and then transport it to a production database, even across platforms. See Chapter 46 for details on transporting tablespaces.

Planning Your Tablespace Usage

With all these options, Oracle can support very complex environments. You can maintain a read-only set of historical data tables alongside active transaction tables. You can place the most actively used tables in datafiles that are located on the fastest disks. You can partition tables (see Chapter 17) and store each partition in a separate tablespace. With all these options available, you should establish a basic set of guidelines for your tablespace architecture. This plan should

be part of your early design efforts so you can take the best advantage of the available features. The following guidelines should be a starting point for your plan.

Separate Active and Static Tables

Tables actively used by transactions have space considerations that differ significantly from static lookup tables. The static tables may never need to be altered or moved; the active tables may need to be actively managed, moved, or reorganized. To simplify the management of the static tables, isolate them in a dedicated tablespace. Within the most active tables, there may be further divisions—some of them may be extremely critical to the performance of the application, and you may decide to move them to yet another tablespace.

Taking this approach a step further, separate the active and static partitions of tables and indexes. Ideally, this separation will allow you to focus your tuning efforts on the objects that have the most direct impact on performance while eliminating the impact of other object usage on the immediate environment.

Separate Indexes and Tables

Indexes may be managed separately from tables—you may create or drop indexes while the base table stays unchanged. Because their space is managed separately, indexes should be stored in dedicated tablespaces. You will then be able to create and rebuild indexes without worrying about the impact of that operation on the space available to your tables.

Separate Large and Small Objects

In general, small tables tend to be fairly static lookup tables—such as a list of countries, for example. Oracle provides tuning options for small tables (such as caching) that are not appropriate for large tables (which have their own set of tuning options). Because the administration of these types of tables may be dissimilar, you should try to keep them separate. In general, separating active and static tables will take care of this objective as well.

Separate Application Tables from Core Objects

The two sets of core objects to be aware of are the Oracle core objects and the enterprise objects. Oracle's core objects are stored in its default tablespaces—SYSTEM, SYSAUX, the temporary tablespace, and the undo tablespace. Do not create any application objects in these tablespaces or under any of the schemas provided by Oracle.

Within your application, you may have some objects that are core to the enterprise and could be reused by multiple applications. Because these objects may need to be indexed and managed to account for the needs of multiple applications, they should be maintained apart from the other objects your application needs.

Grouping the objects in the database according to the categories described here may seem fairly simplistic, but it is a critical part of successfully deploying an enterprise-scale database application. The better you plan the distribution of I/O and space, the easier it will be to implement, tune, and manage the application's database structures. Furthermore, database administrators can manage the tablespace separately—taking them offline, backing them up, or isolating their I/O activity. In later chapters, you will see details on other types of objects (such as materialized views) as well as the commands needed to create and alter tablespaces.

CHAPTER
21

Using SQL*Loader
to Load Data

n the scripts provided for the practice tables, a large number of **insert** commands are executed. In place of those **insert**s, you could create a file containing the data to be loaded and then use Oracle's SQL*Loader utility to load the data. This chapter provides you with an overview of the use of SQL*Loader and its major capabilities. Two additional data-movement utilities, Data Pump Export and Data Pump Import, are covered in Chapter 22. SQL*Loader, Data Pump Export, and Data Pump Import are described in great detail in the *Oracle Database Utilities* provided with the standard Oracle documentation set.

SQL*Loader loads data from external files into tables in the Oracle database. SQL*Loader uses two primary files: the datafile, which contains the information to be loaded, and the control file, which contains information on the format of the data, the records and fields within the file, the order in which they are to be loaded, and even, when needed, the names of the multiple files that will be used for data. You can combine the control file information into the datafile itself, although the two are usually separated to make it easier to reuse the control file.

When executed, SQL*Loader will automatically create a log file and a "bad" file. The log file records the status of the load, such as the number of rows processed and the number of rows committed. The "bad" file will contain all the rows that were rejected during the load due to data errors, such as nonunique values in primary key columns.

Within the control file, you can specify additional commands to govern the load criteria. If these criteria are not met by a row, the row will be written to a "discard" file. The log, bad, and discard files will by default have the extensions .log, .bad, and .dsc, respectively. Control files are typically given the extension .ctl.

SQL*Loader is a powerful utility for loading data, for several reasons:

- It is highly flexible, allowing you to manipulate the data as it is being loaded.

- You can use SQL*Loader to break a single large data set into multiple sets of data during commit processing, significantly reducing the size of the transactions processed by the load.

- You can use its Direct Path loading option to perform loads very quickly.

To start using SQL*Loader, you should first become familiar with the control file, as described in the next section.

The Control File

The control file tells Oracle how to read and load the data. The control file tells SQL*Loader where to find the source data for the load and the tables into which to load the data, along with any other rules that must be applied during the load processing. These rules can include restrictions for discards (similar to **where** clauses for queries) and instructions for combining multiple physical rows in an input file into a single row during an **insert**. SQL*Loader will use the control file to create the **insert** commands executed for the data load.

The control file is created at the operating-system level, using any text editor that enables you to save plain text files. Within the control file, commands do not have to obey any rigid formatting requirements, but standardizing your command syntax will make later maintenance of the control file simpler.

The following listing shows a sample control file for loading data into the BOOKSHELF table:

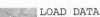

```
LOAD DATA
INFILE 'bookshelf.dat'
INTO TABLE BOOKSHELF
(Title          POSITION(01:100)   CHAR,
 Publisher      POSITION(101:120)  CHAR,
 CategoryName   POSITION(121:140)  CHAR,
 Rating         POSITION(141:142)  CHAR)
```

In this example, data will be loaded from the file bookshelf.dat into the BOOKSHELF table. The bookshelf.dat file will contain the data for all four of the BOOKSHELF columns, with whitespace padding out the unused characters in those fields. Thus, the Publisher column value always begins at space 101 in the file, even if the Title value is less than 100 characters. Although this formatting makes the input file larger, it may simplify the loading process. No length needs to be given for the fields, since the starting and ending positions within the input data stream effectively give the field length.

The **infile** clause names the input file, and the **into table** clause specifies the table into which the data will be loaded. Each of the columns is listed, along with the position where its data resides in each physical record in the file. This format allows you to load data even if the source data's column order does not match the order of columns in your table.

To perform this load, the user executing the load must have INSERT privilege on the BOOKSHELF table.

Loading Variable-Length Data

If the columns in your input file have variable lengths, you can use SQL*Loader commands to tell Oracle how to determine when a value ends. In the following example, commas separate the input values:

```
LOAD DATA
INFILE 'bookshelf.dat'
BADFILE '/user/load/bookshelf.bad'
TRUNCATE
INTO TABLE BOOKSHELF
FIELDS TERMINATED BY ","
(Title, Publisher, CategoryName, Rating)
```

NOTE
Be sure to select a delimiter that is not present within the values being loaded. In this example, a comma is the delimiter, so any comma present within any text string being loaded will be interpreted as an end-of-field character.

The **fields terminated by ","** clause tells SQL*Loader that during the load, each column value will be terminated by a comma. Thus, the input file does not have to be 142 characters wide for each row, as was the case in the first load example. The lengths of the columns are not specified in the control file, since they will be determined during the load.

In this example, the name of the bad file is specified by the **badfile** clause. In general, the name of the bad file is only given when you want to redirect the file to a different directory.

This example also shows the use of the **truncate** clause within a control file. When this control file is executed by SQL*Loader, the BOOKSHELF table will be **truncate**d before the start of the load. Since **truncate** commands cannot be rolled back, you should use care when using this option. In addition to **truncate**, you can use the following options:

- **append** Adds rows to the table.

- **insert** Adds rows to an empty table. If the table is not empty, the load will abort with an error.

- **replace** Empties the table and then adds the new rows. The user must have DELETE privilege on the table.

Starting the Load

To execute the commands in the control file, you need to run SQL*Loader with the appropriate parameters. SQL*Loader is started via the **SQLLDR** command at the operating-system prompt (in UNIX, use **sqlldr**).

NOTE
*The SQL*Loader executable may consist of the name SQLLDR followed by a version number. Consult your platform-specific Oracle documentation for the exact name. For Oracle Database 10g, the executable file should be named SQLLDR.*

When you execute **SQLLDR**, you need to specify the control file, username/password, and other critical load information, as shown in Table 21-1.

Each load must have a control file, since none of the input parameters specify critical information for the load—the input file and the table being loaded.

You can separate the arguments to **SQLLDR** with commas. Enter them with the keywords (such as **userid** or **log**), followed by the parameter value. Keywords are always followed by an equal sign (=) and the appropriate argument.

SQLLDR Keyword	Description
Userid	Username and password for the load, separated by a slash.
Control	Name of the control file.
Log	Name of the log file.
Bad	Name of the bad file.
Discard	Name of the discard file.

TABLE 21-1. *SQL*Loader Options*

SQLLDR Keyword	Description
Discardmax	Maximum number of rows to discard before stopping the load. The default is to allow all discards.
Skip	Number of logical rows in the input file to skip before starting to load data. Usually used during reloads from the same input file following a partial load. The default is 0.
Load	Number of logical rows to load. The default is all.
Errors	Number of errors to allow. The default is 50.
Rows	Number of rows to commit at a time. Use this parameter to break up the transaction size during the load. The default for conventional path loads is 64; the default for Direct Path loads is all rows.
Bindsize	Size of conventional path bind array, in bytes. The default is operating-system–dependent.
Silent	Suppress messages during the load.
Direct	Use Direct Path loading. The default is FALSE.
Parfile	Name of the parameter file that contains additional load parameter specifications.
Parallel	Perform parallel loading. The default is FALSE.
File	File to allocate extents from (for parallel loading).
Skip_Unusable_Indexes	Allows loads into tables that have indexes in unusable states. The default is FALSE.
Skip_Index_Maintenance	Stops index maintenance for Direct Path loads, leaving them in unusable states. The default is FALSE.
Readsize	Size of the read buffer; default is 1MB.
External_table	Use external table for load; default is NOT_USED; other valid values are GENERATE_ONLY and EXECUTE.
Columnarrayrows	Number of rows for Direct Path column array; default is 5,000.
Streamsize	Size in bytes of the Direct Path stream buffer; default is 256,000.
Multithreading	A flag to indicate if multithreading should be used during a direct path load.
Resumable	A TRUE/FALSE flag to enable or disable resumable operations for the current session; default is FALSE.
Resumable_name	Text identifier for the resumable operation.
Resumable_timeout	Wait time for resumable operation; default is 7200 seconds.

TABLE 21-1. *SQL*Loader Options* (continued)

If the **userid** keyword is omitted and no username/password is provided as the first argument, you will be asked for it. If a slash is given after the equal sign, an externally identified account will be used. You also can use an Oracle Net database specification string to log into a remote database and load the data into it. For example, your command may start

```
sqlldr userid=usernm/mypass@dev
```

The **direct** keyword, which invokes the Direct Path load option, is described in "Direct Path Loading" later in this chapter.

The **silent** keyword tells **SQLLDR** to suppress certain informative data:

- HEADER suppresses the SQL*LOADER header.

- FEEDBACK suppresses the feedback at each commit point.

- ERRORS suppresses the logging (in the log file) of each record that caused an Oracle error, although the count is still logged.

- DISCARDS suppresses the logging (in the log file) of each record that was discarded, although the count is still logged.

- PARTITIONS disables the writing of the per-partition statistics to the log file.

- ALL suppresses all of the preceding.

If more than one of these is entered, separate each with a comma and enclose the list in parentheses. For example, you can suppress the **header** and **errors** information via the following keyword setting:

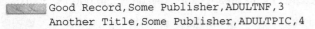
```
silent=(HEADER,ERRORS)
```

NOTE
Commands in the control file override any in the calling command line.

Let's load a sample set of data into the BOOKSHELF table, which has four columns (Title, Publisher, CategoryName, and Rating). Create a plain text file named bookshelf.txt. The data to be loaded should be the only two lines in the file:

```
Good Record,Some Publisher,ADULTNF,3
Another Title,Some Publisher,ADULTPIC,4
```

NOTE
Each line is ended by a carriage return. Even though the first line's last value is not as long as the column it is being loaded into, the row will stop at the carriage return.

The data is separated by commas, and we don't want to delete the data previously loaded into BOOKSHELF, so the control file will look like this:

```
LOAD DATA
INFILE 'bookshelf.txt'
APPEND
INTO TABLE BOOKSHELF
FIELDS TERMINATED BY ","
(Title, Publisher, CategoryName, Rating)
```

Save that file as bookshelf.ctl, in the same directory as the input data file. Next, run **SQLLDR** and tell it to use the control file. This example assumes that the BOOKSHELF table exists under the PRACTICE schema:

```
sqlldr practice/practice control=bookshelf.ctl log=bookshelf.log
```

When the load completes, you should have one successfully loaded record and one failure. The successfully loaded record will be in the BOOKSHELF table:

```
select Title
   from BOOKSHELF
 where Publisher like '%Publisher';

TITLE
----------------------------------------
Good Record
```

A file named bookshelf.bad will be created, and will contain one record:

```
Another Title,Some Publisher,ADULTPIC,4
```

Why was that record rejected? Check the log file, bookshelf.log, which will say, in part:

```
Record 2: Rejected - Error on table BOOKSHELF.
ORA-02291: integrity constraint (PRACTICE.CATFK) violated -
parent key not found

Table BOOKSHELF:
  1 Row successfully loaded.
  1 Row not loaded due to data errors.
```

Row 2, the "Another Title" row, was rejected because the value for the CategoryName column violated the foreign key constraint—ADULTPIC is not listed as a category in the CATEGORY table.

Because the rows that failed are isolated into the bad file, you can use that file as the input for a later load once the data has been corrected.

Logical and Physical Records

In Table 21-1, several of the keywords refer to "logical" rows. A *logical* row is a row that is inserted into the database. Depending on the structure of the input file, multiple physical rows may be combined to make a single logical row.

For example, the input file may look like this:

```
Good Record,Some Publisher,ADULTNF,3
```

in which case there would be a one-to-one relationship between that physical record and the logical record it creates. But the datafile may look like this instead:

```
Good Record,
Some Publisher,
ADULTNF,
3
```

To combine the data, you need to specify continuation rules. In this case, the column values are split one to a line, so there is a set number of physical records for each logical record. To combine them, use the **concatenate** clause within the control file. In this case, you would specify **concatenate 4** to create a single logical row from the four physical rows.

The logic for creating a single logical record from multiple physical records can be much more complex than a simple concatenation. You can use the **continueif** clause to specify the conditions that cause logical records to be continued. You can further manipulate the input data to create multiple logical records from a single physical record (via the use of multiple **into table** clauses). See the control file syntax in the "SQLLDR" entry of the Alphabetical Reference in this book, and the notes in the following section.

You can use SQL*Loader to generate multiple inserts from a single physical row (similar to the multitable insert capability described in Chapter 15). For example, suppose the input data is denormalized, with fields City and Rainfall, while the input data is in the format City, Rainfall1, Rainfall2, Rainfall3. The control file would resemble the following (depending on the actual physical stop and start positions of the data in the file):

```
into table RAINFALL
when City != '     '
(City      POSITION(1:5)      CHAR,
 Rainfall  POSITION(6:10)     INTEGER EXTERNAL)    -- 1st row
--
into table RAINFALL
when City != '     '
(City      POSITION(1:5)      CHAR,
 Rainfall  POSITION(11:16)    INTEGER EXTERNAL)    -- 2nd row
--
into table RAINFALL
when City != '     '
(City      POSITION(1:5)      CHAR,
 Rainfall  POSITION(16:21)    INTEGER EXTERNAL)    -- 3rd row
```

Note that separate **into table** clauses operate on each physical row. In this example, they generate separate rows in the RAINFALL table; they could also be used to insert rows into multiple tables.

Control File Syntax Notes

The full syntax for SQL*Loader control files is shown in the "SQLLDR" entry in the Alphabetical Reference, so it is not repeated here.

Within the **load** clause, you can specify that the load is **recoverable** or **unrecoverable**. The **unrecoverable** clause only applies to Direct Path loading, and is described in "Tuning Data Loads" later in this chapter.

In addition to using the **concatenate** clause, you can use the **continueif** clause to control the manner in which physical records are assembled into logical records. The **this** clause refers to the current physical record, while the **next** clause refers to the next physical record. For example, you could create a two-character continuation character at the start of each physical record. If that record should be concatenated to the preceding record, set that value equal to '******'. You could then use the **continueif next (1:2)= '**'** clause to create a single logical record from the multiple physical records. The '******' continuation character will not be part of the merged record.

The syntax for the **into table** clause includes a **when** clause. The **when** clause, shown in the following listing, serves as a filter applied to rows prior to their insertion into the table. For example, you can specify

```
when Rating>'3'
```

to load only books with ratings greater than 3 into the table. Any row that does not pass the **when** condition will be written to the discard file. Thus, the discard file contains rows that can be used for later loads, but that did not pass the current set of **when** conditions. You can use multiple **when** conditions, connected with **and** clauses.

Use the **trailing nullcols** clause if you are loading variable-length records for which the last column does not always have a value. With this clause in effect, SQL*Loader will generate **NULL** values for those columns.

As shown in an example earlier in this chapter, you can use the **fields terminated by** clause to load variable-length data. Rather than being terminated by a character, the fields can be **terminated by whitespace** or **enclosed by** characters or **optionally enclosed by** other characters.

For example, the following entry loads AuthorName values and sets the values to uppercase during the insert. If the value is blank, a **NULL** is inserted:

```
AuthorName POSITION(10:34)  CHAR  TERMINATED BY WHITESPACE
       NULLIF AuthorName=BLANKS  "UPPER(:AuthorName)"
```

When you load DATE datatype values, you can specify a date mask. For example, if you had a column named ReturnDate and the incoming data is in the format Mon-DD-YYYY in the first 11 places of the record, you could specify the ReturnDate portion of the load as follows:

```
ReturnDate POSITION (1:11) DATE "Mon-DD-YYYY"
```

Within the **into table** clause, you can use the **recnum** keyword to assign a record number to each logical record as it is read from the datafile, and that value will be inserted into the assigned column of the table. The **constant** keyword allows you to assign a constant value to a column during the load. For character columns, enclose the constant value within single quotes. If you use the **sysdate** keyword, the selected column will be populated with the current system date and time.

```
CheckOutDate SYSDATE
```

If you use the **sequence** option, SQL*Loader will maintain a sequence of values during the load. As records are processed, the sequence value will be increased by the increment you specify. If the rows fail during **insert** (and are sent to the bad file), those sequence values will not be reused. If you use the **max** keyword within the sequence option, the sequence values will use the current

maximum value of the column as the starting point for the sequence. The following listing shows the use of the **sequence** option:

```
Seqnum_col  SEQUENCE(MAX,1)
```

You can also specify the starting value and increment for a sequence to use when inserting. The following example inserts values starting with a value of 100, incrementing by 2. If a row is rejected during the **insert**, its sequence value is skipped.

```
Seqnum_col  SEQUENCE(100,2)
```

If you store numbers in VARCHAR2 columns, avoid using the **sequence** option for those columns. For example, if your table already contains the values 1 through 10 in a VARCHAR2 column, then the maximum value within that column is 9—the greatest character string. Using that as the basis for a **sequence** option will cause SQL*Loader to attempt to **insert** a record using 10 as the newly created value—and that may conflict with the existing record. This behavior illustrates why storing numbers in character columns is a poor practice in general.

SQL*Loader control files can support complex logic and business rules. For example, your input data for a column holding monetary values may have an implied decimal; 9990 would be inserted as 99.90. In SQL*Loader, you could insert this by performing the calculation during the data load:

```
money_amount   position (20:28) external decimal(9) ":tax_amount/100"
```

See the "SQL*Loader Case Studies" of the *Oracle Utilities Guide* for additional SQL*Loader examples and sample control files.

Managing Data Loads

Loading large data volumes is a batch operation. Batch operations should not be performed concurrently with the small transactions prevalent in many database applications. If you have many concurrent users executing small transactions against a table, you should schedule your batch operations against that table to occur at a time when very few users are accessing the table.

Oracle maintains *read consistency* for users' queries. If you execute the SQL*Loader job against the table at the same time that other users are querying the table, Oracle will internally maintain undo entries to enable those users to see their data as it existed when they first queried the data. To minimize the amount of work Oracle must perform to maintain read consistency (and to minimize the associated performance degradation caused by this overhead), schedule your long-running data load jobs to be performed when few other actions are occurring in the database. In particular, avoid contention with other accesses of the same table.

Design your data load processing to be easy to maintain and reuse. Establish guidelines for the structure and format of the input datafiles. The more standardized the input data formats are, the simpler it will be to reuse old control files for the data loads. For repeated scheduled loads into the same table, your goal should be to reuse the same control file each time. Following each load, you will need to review and move the log, bad, data, and discard files so they do not accidentally get overwritten.

Within the control file, use comments to indicate any special processing functions being performed. To create a comment within the control file, begin the line with two dashes, as shown in the following example:

```
-- Limit the load to LA employees:
when Location='LA'
```

If you have properly commented your control file, you will increase the chance that it can be reused during future loads. You will also simplify the maintenance of the data load process itself, as described in the next section.

Repeating Data Loads

Data loads do not always work exactly as planned. Many variables are involved in a data load, and not all of them will always be under your control. For example, the owner of the source data may change its data formatting, invalidating part of your control file. Business rules may change, forcing additional changes. Database structures and space availability may change, further affecting your ability to load the data.

In an ideal case, a data load will either fully succeed or fully fail. However, in many cases, a data load will partially succeed, making the recovery process more difficult. If some of the records have been inserted into the table, then attempting to reinsert those records should result in a primary key violation. If you are generating the primary key value during the **insert** (via the **sequence** option), then those rows may not fail the second time—and will be inserted twice.

To determine where a load failed, use the log file. The log file will record the commit points as well as the errors encountered. All of the rejected records should be in either the bad file or the discard file. You can minimize the recovery effort by forcing the load to fail if many errors are encountered. To force the load to abort before a large number of errors is encountered, use the **errors** keyword of the **SQLLDR** command. You can also use the **discardmax** keyword to limit the number of discarded records permitted before the load aborts.

If you set **errors** to 0, the first error will cause the load to fail. What if that load fails after 100 records have been inserted? You will have two options: Identify and delete the inserted records and reapply the whole load, or skip the successfully inserted records. You can use the **skip** keyword of **SQLLDR** to skip the first 100 records during its load processing. The load will then continue with record 101 (which, we hope, has been fixed prior to the reload attempt). If you cannot identify the rows that have just been loaded into the table, you will need to use the **skip** option during the restart process.

The proper settings for **errors** and **discardmax** depend on the load. If you have full control over the data load process, and the data is properly "cleaned" before being extracted to a load file, you may have very little tolerance for errors and discards. On the other hand, if you do not have control over the source for the input datafile, you need to set **errors** and **discardmax** high enough to allow the load to complete. After the load has completed, you need to review the log file, correct the data in the bad file, and reload the data using the original bad file as the new input file. If rows have been incorrectly discarded, you need to do an additional load using the original discard file as the new input file.

After modifying the errant CategoryName value, you can rerun the BOOKSHELF table load example using the original bookshelf.dat file. During the reload, you have two options when using the original input datafile.

■ Skip the first row by specifying **skip=1** in the **SQLLDR** command line.

■ Attempt to load both rows, whereby the first row fails because it has already been loaded (and thus causes a primary key violation).

Alternatively, you can use the bad file as the new input datafile and not worry about errors and skipped rows.

Tuning Data Loads

In addition to running the data load processes at off-peak hours, you can take other steps to improve the load performance. The following steps all impact your overall database environment and must be coordinated with the database administrator. The tuning of a data load should not be allowed to have a negative impact on the database or on the business processes it supports.

First, batch data loads may be timed to occur while the database is in NOARCHIVELOG mode. While in NOARCHIVELOG mode, the database does not keep an archive of its online redo log files prior to overwriting them. Eliminating the archiving process improves the performance of transactions. Since the data is being loaded from a file, you can re-create the loaded data at a later time by reloading the datafile rather than recovering it from an archived redo log file.

However, there are significant potential issues with disabling ARCHIVELOG mode. You will not be able to perform a point-in-time recovery of the database unless archiving is enabled. If non-batch transactions are performed in the database, you will probably need to run the database in ARCHIVELOG mode all the time, including during your loads. Furthermore, switching between ARCHIVELOG and NOARCHIVELOG modes requires you to shut down the instance. If you switch the instance to NOARCHIVELOG mode, perform your data load, and then switch the instance back to ARCHIVELOG mode, you should perform a backup of the database (see Chapter 46) immediately following the restart.

Instead of running the entire database in NOARCHIVELOG mode, you can disable archiving for your data load process by using the **unrecoverable** keyword within SQL*Loader. The **unrecoverable** option disables the writing of redo log entries for the transactions within the data load. You should only use this option if you will be able to re-create the transactions from the input files during a recovery. If you follow this strategy, you must have adequate space to store old input files in case they are needed for future recoveries. The **unrecoverable** option is only available for Direct Path loads, as described in the next section.

Rather than control the redo log activity at the load process level, you can control it at the table or partition level. If you define an object as **nologging**, then block-level inserts performed by SQL*Loader Direct Path loading and the **insert /*+ APPEND */** command will not generate redo log entries. The block-level inserts will require additional space, as they will not reuse existing blocks below the table's high-water mark.

If your operating environment has multiple processors, you can take advantage of the CPUs by parallelizing the data load. The **parallel** option of **SQLLDR**, as described in the next section, uses multiple concurrent data load processes to reduce the overall time required to load the data.

In addition to these approaches, you should work with your database administrator to make sure the database environment and structures are properly tuned for data loads. Tuning efforts should include the following:

■ Preallocate space for the table, to minimize dynamic extensions during the loads.

■ Allocate sufficient memory resources to the shared memory areas.

- Streamline the data-writing process by creating multiple database writer (DBWR) processes for the database.

- Remove any unnecessary triggers during the data loads. If possible, disable or remove the triggers prior to the load, and perform the trigger operations on the loaded data manually after it has been loaded.

- Remove or disable any unnecessary constraints on the table. You can use SQL*Loader to dynamically disable and reenable constraints.

- Remove any indexes on the tables. If the data has been properly cleaned prior to the data load, then uniqueness checks and foreign key validations will not be necessary during the loads. Dropping indexes prior to data loads significantly improves performance.

Direct Path Loading

SQL*Loader generates a large number of **insert** statements. To avoid the overhead associated with using a large number of **insert**s, you may use the Direct Path option in SQL*Loader. The Direct Path option creates preformatted data blocks and inserts those blocks into the table. As a result, the performance of your load can dramatically improve. To use the Direct Path option, you must not be performing any functions on the values being read from the input file.

Any indexes on the table being loaded will be placed into a temporary DIRECT LOAD state (you can query the index status from USER_INDEXES). Oracle will move the old index values to a temporary index it creates and manages. Once the load has completed, the old index values will be merged with the new values to create the new index, and Oracle will drop the temporary index it created. When the index is once again valid, its status will change to VALID. To minimize the amount of space necessary for the temporary index, presort the data by the indexed columns. The name of the index for which the data is presorted should be specified via a **sorted indexes** clause in the control file.

To use the Direct Path option, specify

```
DIRECT=TRUE
```

as a keyword on the **SQLLDR** command line or include this option in the control file.

If you use the Direct Path option, you can use the **unrecoverable** keyword to improve your data load performance. This instructs Oracle not to generate redo log entries for the load. If you need to recover the database at a later point, you will need to reexecute the data load in order to recover the table's data. All conventional path loads are recoverable, and all Direct Path loads are recoverable by default.

Direct Path loads are faster than conventional loads, and **unrecoverable** Direct Path loads are faster still. Since performing **unrecoverable** loads impacts your recovery operations, you need to weigh the costs of that impact against the performance benefit you will realize. If your hardware environment has additional resources available during the load, you can use the **parallel** Direct Path load option to divide the data load work among multiple processes. The parallel Direct Path operations may complete the load job faster than a single Direct Path load.

Instead of using the **parallel** option, you could partition the table being loaded (see Chapter 17). Since SQL*Loader allows you to load a single partition, you could execute multiple concurrent SQL*Loader jobs to populate the separate partitions of a partitioned table. This method requires

more database administration work (to configure and manage the partitions), but it gives you more flexibility in the parallelization and scheduling of the load jobs.

You can take advantage of multithreaded loading functionality for Direct Path loads to convert column arrays to stream buffers and perform stream buffer loading in parallel. Use the **streamsize** parameter and **multithreading** flag to enable this feature.

Direct Path loading may impact the space required for the table's data. Since Direct Path loading inserts blocks of data, it does not follow the usual methods for allocating space within a table. The blocks are inserted at the end of the table, after its *high-water mark*, which is the highest block into which the table's data has ever been written. If you **insert** 100 blocks worth of data into a table and then **delete** all of the rows, the high-water mark for the table will still be set at 100. If you then perform a conventional SQL*Loader data load, the rows will be inserted into the already allocated blocks. If you instead perform a Direct Path load, Oracle will insert new blocks of data following block 100, potentially increasing the space allocation for the table. The only way to lower the high-water mark for a table is to **truncate** it (which deletes all rows and cannot be rolled back) or to drop and re-create it. You should work with your database administrator to identify space issues prior to starting your load.

NOTE
*As shown earlier in this chapter, you can issue a **truncate** command as part of the control file syntax. The table will be truncated prior to the data's being loaded.*

Additional Features

In addition to features noted earlier in this chapter, SQL*Loader features support for Unicode and expanded datatypes. SQL*Loader can load integer and zoned/packed decimal datatypes across platforms with different byte ordering and accept EBCDIC-based zoned or packed decimal data encoded in IBM format. SQL*Loader also offers support for loading XML columns, loading object types with subtypes (see Chapter 33), and Unicode (UTF16 character set). SQL*Loader also provides native support for the date, time, and interval-related datatypes (see Chapter 10).

If a SQL*Loader job fails, you may be able to resume it where it failed using the **resumable**, **resumable_name**, and **resumable_timeout** options. For example, if the segment to which the loader job was writing could not extend, you can disable the load job, fix the space allocation problem, and resume the job. Your ability to perform these actions depends on the configuration of the database; work with your DBA to make sure the resumable features are enabled and that adequate undo history is maintained for your purposes.

You can access external files as if they are tables inside the database. This *external table* feature, described in Chapter 26, allows you to potentially avoid loading large volumes of data into the database. See Chapter 26 for implementation details.

CHAPTER
22

Using Data Pump
Export and Import

ntroduced with Oracle Database 10g, Data Pump provides a server-based data extraction and import utility. Its features include significant architectural and functional enhancements over the original Import and Export utilities. Data Pump allows you to stop and restart jobs, see the status of running jobs, and restrict the data that is exported and imported.

NOTE
Data Pump can use files generated via the original Export utility, but the original Import utility cannot use the files generated from Data Pump Export.

Data Pump runs as a server process, benefiting users in multiple ways. The client process that starts the job can disconnect and later reattach to the job. Performance is enhanced (as compared to Export/Import) because the data no longer has to be processed by a client program. Data Pump extractions and loads can be parallelized, further enhancing performance.

In this chapter, you will see how to use Data Pump, along with descriptions and examples of its major options.

Creating a Directory

Data Pump requires you to create directories for the datafiles and log files it will create and read. Use the **create directory** command to create the directory pointer within Oracle to the external directory you will use. Users who will access the Data Pump files must have the READ and WRITE privileges on the directory.

NOTE
*Before you start, verify that the external directory exists and that the user who will be issuing the **create directory** command has the CREATE ANY DIRECTORY system privilege.*

The following example creates a directory named DTPUMP and grants READ and WRITE access to the PRACTICE schema:

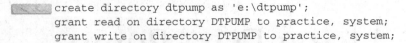

```
create directory dtpump as 'e:\dtpump';
grant read on directory DTPUMP to practice, system;
grant write on directory DTPUMP to practice, system;
```

The PRACTICE and SYSTEM schemas can now use the DTPUMP directory for Data Pump jobs.

Data Pump Export Options

Oracle provides a utility, expdp, that serves as the interface to Data Pump. If you have previous experience with the Export utility, some of the options will be familiar. However, there are significant features available only via Data Pump. Table 22-1 shows the command-line input parameters for expdp when a job is created.

Parameter	Description
ATTACH	Connects a client session to a currently running Data Pump Export job.
CONTENT	Filters what is exported: DATA_ONLY, METADATA_ONLY, or ALL.
DIRECTORY	Specifies the destination directory for the log file and the dump file set.
DUMPFILE	Specifies the names and directories for dump files.
ESTIMATE	Determines the method used to estimate the dump file size (BLOCKS or STATISTICS).
ESTIMATE_ONLY	Y/N flag is used to instruct Data Pump whether the data should be exported or just estimated.
EXCLUDE	Specifies the criteria for excluding objects and data from being exported.
FILESIZE	Specifies the maximum file size of each export dump file.
FLASHBACK_SCN	SCN for the database to flash back to during the export (see Chapter 27).
FLASHBACK_TIME	Timestamp for the database to flash back to during the export (see Chapter 27).
FULL	Tells Data Pump to export all data and metadata in a Full mode export.
HELP	Displays a list of available commands and options.
INCLUDE	Specifies the criteria for which objects and data will be exported.
JOB_NAME	Specifies a name for the job; the default is system generated.
LOGFILE	Name and optional directory name for the export log.
NETWORK_LINK	Specifies the source database link for a Data Pump job exporting a remote database.
NOLOGFILE	Y/N flag is used to suppress log file creation.
PARALLEL	Sets the number of workers for the Data Pump Export job.
PARFILE	Names the parameter file to use, if any.
QUERY	Filters rows from tables during the export.
SCHEMAS	Names the schemas to be exported for a Schema mode export.
STATUS	Displays detailed status of the Data Pump job.
TABLES	Lists the tables and partitions to be exported for a Table mode export.
TABLESPACES	Lists the tablespaces to be exported.
TRANSPORT_FULL_CHECK	Specifies whether the tablespaces being exported should first be verified as a self-contained set.

TABLE 22-1. *Command-Line Input Parameters for expdp*

Parameter	Description
TRANSPORT_ TABLESPACES	Specifies a Transportable Tablespace mode export.
VERSION	Specifies the version of database objects to be created so the dump file set can be compatible with earlier releases of Oracle. Options are COMPATIBLE, LATEST, and database version numbers (not lower than 10.0.0).

TABLE 22-1. *Command-Line Input Parameters for expdp* (continued)

As shown in Table 22-1, five modes of Data Pump exports are supported. *Full* exports extract all the database's data and metadata. *Schema* exports extract the data and metadata for specific user schemas. *Tablespace* exports extract the data and metadata for tablespaces, and *Table* exports extract data and metadata for tables and their partitions. *Transportable Tablespace* exports extract metadata for specific tablespaces.

NOTE
You must have the EXP_FULL_DATABASE system privilege in order to perform a Full export or a Transportable Tablespace export.

When you submit a job, Oracle will give the job a system-generated name. If you specify a name for the job via the JOB_NAME parameter, you must be certain the job name will not conflict with the name of any table or view in your schema. During Data Pump jobs, Oracle will create and maintain a master table for the duration of the job. The master table will have the same name as the Data Pump job, so its name cannot conflict with existing objects.

While a job is running, you can execute the commands listed in Table 22-2 via Data Pump's interface.

Parameter	Description
ADD_FILE	Add dump files
CONTINUE_CLIENT	Exit the interactive mode and enter logging mode
EXIT_CLIENT	Exit the client session, but leave the server Data Pump Export job running
HELP	Display online help for the import
KILL_JOB	Kill the current job and detach related client sessions
PARALLEL	Alter the number of workers for the Data Pump Export job

TABLE 22-2. *Parameters for Interactive Mode Data Pump Export*

Parameter	Description
START_JOB	Restart the attached job
STATUS	Display a detailed status of the Data Pump job
STOP_JOB	Stop the job for later restart

TABLE 22-2. *Parameters for Interactive Mode Data Pump Export* (continued)

As the entries in Table 22-2 imply, you can change many features of a running Data Pump Export job via the interactive command mode. If the dump area runs out of space, you can attach to the job, add files, and restart the job at that point; there is no need to kill the job or reexecute it from the start. You can display the job status at any time, either via the STATUS parameter or via the USER_DATAPUMP_JOBS and DBA_DATAPUMP_JOBS data dictionary views or the V$SESSION_LONGOPS view.

Starting a Data Pump Export Job

You can store your job parameters in a parameter file, referenced via the PARFILE parameter of expdp. For example, you can create a file name dp1.par with the following entries:

```
DIRECTORY=dtpump
DUMPFILE=metadataonly.dmp
CONTENT=METADATA_ONLY
```

You can then start the Data Pump Export job:

```
expdp practice/practice PARFILE=dp1.par
```

Oracle will then pass the dp1.par entries to the Data Pump Export job. A Schema-type Data Pump Export (the default type) will be executed, and the output (the metadata listings, but no data) will be written to a file in the dtpump directory previously defined. When you execute the expdp command, the output will be in the following format (there will be separate lines for each major object type—tables, grants, indexes, and so on):

```
Export: Release 10.1.0.1.0 on Wednesday, 26 May, 2004 17:29
Copyright (c) 2003, Oracle.  All rights reserved.

Connected to: Oracle10i Enterprise Edition Release 10.1.0.1.0
With the Partitioning, OLAP and Data Mining options
FLASHBACK automatically enabled to preserve database integrity.
Starting "PRACTICE"."SYS_EXPORT_SCHEMA_01":  practice/******** parfile=dp1.par
Processing object type SCHEMA_EXPORT/SE_PRE_SCHEMA_PROCOBJECT/PROCACT_SCHEMA
Processing object type SCHEMA_EXPORT/TYPE/TYPE_SPEC
Processing object type SCHEMA_EXPORT/TABLE/TABLE
Processing object type SCHEMA_EXPORT/TABLE/GRANT/OBJECT_GRANT
```

```
Processing object type SCHEMA_EXPORT/TABLE/INDEX/INDEX
Processing object type SCHEMA_EXPORT/TABLE/CONSTRAINT/CONSTRAINT
Processing object type SCHEMA_EXPORT/TABLE/COMMENT
Processing object type SCHEMA_EXPORT/VIEW/VIEW
Processing object type SCHEMA_EXPORT/PACKAGE/PACKAGE_SPEC
Processing object type SCHEMA_EXPORT/PACKAGE/PACKAGE_BODY
Processing object type SCHEMA_EXPORT/PACKAGE/GRANT/OBJECT_GRANT
Processing object type SCHEMA_EXPORT/TABLE/CONSTRAINT/REF_CONSTRAINT
Processing object type SCHEMA_EXPORT/SE_EV_TRIGGER/TRIGGER
Master table "PRACTICE"."SYS_EXPORT_SCHEMA_01" successfully loaded/unloaded
******************************************************************************
Dump file set for PRACTICE.SYS_EXPORT_SCHEMA_01 is:
  E:\DTPUMP\METADATAONLY.DMP
Job "PRACTICE"."SYS_EXPORT_SCHEMA_01" successfully completed at 17:30
```

The output file, as shown in the listing, is named metadataonly.dmp. The output dump file contains XML entries for re-creating the structures for the Practice schema. During the export, Data Pump created and used an external table named SYS_EXPORT_SCHEMA_01.

NOTE
Dump files will not overwrite previously existing dump files in the same directory.

You can use multiple directories and dump files for a single Data Pump Export. Within the DUMPFILE parameter setting, list the directory along with the filename, in this format:

```
DUMPFILE=directory1:file1.dmp,
         directory2:file2.dmp
```

Stopping and Restarting Running Jobs

After you have started a Data Pump Export job, you can close the client window you used to start the job. Because it is server based, the export will continue to run. You can then attach to the job, check its status, and alter it. For example, you can start the job via expdp:

```
expdp practice/practice PARFILE=dp1.par
```

Press CTRL-C to leave the log display, and Data Pump will return you to the Export prompt:

```
Export>
```

Exit to the operating system via the EXIT_CLIENT command:

```
Export> EXIT_CLIENT
```

You can then restart the client and attach to the currently running job under your schema:

```
expdp practice/practice attach
```

NOTE
This sample export finishes quickly, so the job may finish before you reattach to it.

If you gave a name to your Data Pump Export job, specify the name as part of the ATTACH parameter call. For example, if you had named the job PRACTICE_JOB, attach to the job by name:

```
expdp practice/practice attach=PRACTICE_JOB
```

When you attach to a running job, Data Pump will display the status of the job—its basic configuration parameters and its current status. You can then issue the CONTINUE_CLIENT command to see the log entries as they are generated, or you can alter the running job:

```
Export> CONTINUE_CLIENT
```

You can stop a job via the STOP_JOB option:

```
Export> STOP_JOB
```

With the job stopped, you can then add additional dump files in new directories, via the ADD_FILE option. You can then restart the job:

```
Export> START_JOB
```

You can specify a log file location for the export log via the LOGFILE parameter. If you do not specify a LOGFILE value, the log file will be written to the same directory as the dump file.

Exporting from Another Database

You can use the NETWORK_LINK parameter to export data from a different database. If you are logged into the HQ database and you have a database link to a separate database, Data Pump can use that link to connect to the database and extract its data.

NOTE
If the source database is read-only, the user on the source database must have a locally managed tablespace assigned as the temporary tablespace; otherwise, the job will fail.

In your parameter file (or on the expdp command line), set the NETWORK_LINK parameter equal to the name of your database link. The Data Pump Export will write the data from the remote database to the directory defined in your local database.

Using EXCLUDE, INCLUDE, and QUERY

You can exclude or include sets of tables from the Data Pump Export via the EXCLUDE and INCLUDE options. You can exclude objects by type and by name. If an object is excluded, all its dependent objects are also excluded. The format for the EXCLUDE option is

```
EXCLUDE=object_type[:name_clause] [, ...]
```

NOTE
You cannot specify EXCLUDE if you specify CONTENT=DATA_ONLY.

For example, to exclude the PRACTICE schema from a full export, the format for the EXCLUDE option would be

```
EXCLUDE=SCHEMA:"='PRACTICE'"
```

NOTE
You can specify more than one EXCLUDE option within the same Data Pump Export job.

The EXCLUDE option in the preceding listing contains a limiting condition (='PRACTICE') within a set of double quotes. The *object_type* variable can be any Oracle object type, including grant, index, and table. The *name_clause* variable restricts the values returned. For example, to exclude from the export all tables whose names contain begin with 'TEMP', you could specify the following:

```
EXCLUDE=TABLE:"LIKE 'TEMP%'"
```

When you enter this at the command line, you may need to use escape characters so the quotation marks and other special characters are properly passed to Oracle. Your expdp command will be in the format

```
expdp practice/practice EXCLUDE=TABLE:\"LIKE \'TEMP%\'\"
```

NOTE
This example shows part of the syntax, not the full syntax for the command.

If no *name_clause* value is provided, all objects of the specified type are excluded. To exclude all indexes, for example, you would specify the following:

```
expdp practice/practice EXCLUDE=INDEX
```

For a listing of the objects you can filter, query the DATABASE_EXPORT_OBJECTS, SCHEMA_EXPORT_OBJECTS, and TABLE_EXPORT_OBJECTS data dictionary views. If the *object_type* value is CONSTRAINT, NOT NULL constraints will not be excluded. Additionally, constraints needed for a table to be created successfully (such as primary key constraints for index-organized tables) cannot be excluded. If the *object_type* value is USER, the user definitions are excluded, but the objects within the user schemas will still be exported. Use the SCHEMA *object_type*, as shown in the previous example, to exclude a user and all of the user's objects. If the *object_type* value is GRANT, all object grants and system privilege grants are excluded.

A second option, INCLUDE, is also available. When you use INCLUDE, only those objects that pass the criteria are exported; all others are excluded. INCLUDE and EXCLUDE are mutually exclusive. The format for INCLUDE is

```
INCLUDE = object_type[:name_clause] [, ...]
```

> **NOTE**
> *You cannot specify INCLUDE if you specify CONTENT=DATA_ONLY.*

For example, to export two tables and all procedures, your parameter file may include these two lines:

```
INCLUDE=TABLE:"IN ('BOOKSHELF','BOOKSHELF_AUTHOR')"
INCLUDE=PROCEDURE
```

What rows will be exported for the objects that meet the EXCLUDE or INCLUDE criteria? By default, all rows are exported for each table. You can use the QUERY option to limit the rows that are returned. The format for the QUERY option is

```
QUERY = [schema.][table_name:] query_clause
```

If you do not specify values for the *schema* and *table_name* variables, the *query_clause* will be applied to all the exported tables. Because *query_clause* will usually include specific column names, you should be very careful when selecting the tables to include in the export.

You can specify a QUERY value for a single table, as shown in the following listing:

```
QUERY=BOOKSHELF:'"WHERE Rating > 2"'
```

As a result, the dump file will only contain rows that meet the QUERY criteria as well as the INCLUDE or EXCLUDE criteria. You can also apply these restrictions during the subsequent Data Pump Import, as described in the next section of this chapter.

Data Pump Import Options

To import a dump file exported via Data Pump Export, use Data Pump Import. As with the export process, the import process runs as a server-based job you can manage as it executes. You can interact with Data Pump Import via the command-line interface, a parameter file, and an interactive interface. Table 22-3 lists the parameters for the command-line interface.

> **NOTE**
> *The directory for the dump file and log file must already exist; see the prior section on the **create directory** command.*

As with Data Pump Export, five modes are supported: Full, Schema, Table, Tablespace, and Transportable Tablespace. If no mode is specified, Oracle attempts to load the entire dump file.

Parameter	Description
ATTACH	Attaches the client to a server session and places you in interactive mode.
CONTENT	Filters what is imported: ALL, DATA_ONLY, or METADATA_ONLY.
DIRECTORY	Specifies the location of the dump file set and the destination directory for the log and SQL files.
DUMPFILE	Specifies the names and, optionally, the directories for the dump file set.
ESTIMATE	Determines the method used to estimate the dump file size (BLOCKS or STATISTICS).
EXCLUDE	Excludes objects and data from being imported.
FLASHBACK_SCN	SCN for the database to flash back to during the import (see Chapter 27).
FLASHBACK_TIME	Timestamp for the database to flash back to during the import (see Chapter 27).
FULL	Y/N flag is used to specify that you want to import the full dump file.
HELP	Displays online help for the import.
INCLUDE	Specifies the criteria for objects to be imported.
JOB_NAME	Specifies a name for the job; the default is system generated.
LOGFILE	Name and optional directory name for the import log.
NETWORK_LINK	Specifies the source database link for a Data Pump job importing a remote database.
NOLOGFILE	Y/N flag is used to suppress log file creation.
PARALLEL	Sets the number of workers for the Data Pump Import job.
PARFILE	Names the parameter file to use, if any.
QUERY	Filters rows from tables during the import.
REMAP_DATAFILE	Changes the name of the source datafile to the target datafile in **create library**, **create tablespace**, and **create directory** commands during the import.
REMAP_SCHEMA	Imports data exported from the source schema into the target schema.
REMAP_TABLESPACE	Imports data exported from the source tablespace into the target tablespace.
REUSE_DATAFILES	Specifies whether existing datafiles should be reused by **create tablespace** commands during Full mode imports.
SCHEMAS	Names the schemas to be imported for a Schema mode import.

TABLE 22-3. *Data Pump Import Command-Line Parameters*

Parameter	Description
SKIP_UNUSABLE_INDEXES	Y/N flag. If set to Y, the import does not load data into tables whose indexes are set to the Index Unusable state.
SQLFILE	Names the file to which the DDL for the import will be written. The data and metadata will not be loaded into the target database.
STATUS	Displays detailed status of the Data Pump job.
STREAMS_CONFIGURATION	Y/N flag is used to specify whether Streams configuration information should be imported.
TABLE_EXISTS_ACTION	Instructs Import how to proceed if the table being imported already exists. Values include SKIP, APPEND, TRUNCATE, and REPLACE. The default is APPEND if CONTENT=DATA_ONLY; otherwise, the default is SKIP.
TABLES	Lists tables for a Table mode import.
TABLESPACES	Lists tablespaces for a Tablespace mode import.
TRANSFORM	Directs changes to the segment attributes or storage during import.
TRANSPORT_DATAFILES	Lists the datafiles to be imported during a Transportable Tablespace mode import.
TRANSPORT_FULL_CHECK	Specifies whether the tablespaces being imported should first be verified as a self-contained set.
TRANSPORT_TABLESPACES	Lists the tablespaces to be imported during a Transportable Tablespace mode import.
VERSION	Specifies the version of database objects to be created so the dump file set can be compatible with earlier releases of Oracle. Options are COMPATIBLE, LATEST, and database version numbers (not lower than 10.0.0). Only valid for NETWORK_LINK and SQLFILE.

TABLE 22-3. *Data Pump Import Command-Line Parameters* (continued)

Table 22-4 lists the parameters that are valid in the interactive mode of Data Pump Import.

Parameter	Description
CONTINUE_CLIENT	Exit the interactive mode and enter logging mode. The job will be restarted if idle.
EXIT_CLIENT	Exit the client session, but leave the server Data Pump Import job running.
HELP	Display online help for the import.

TABLE 22-4. *Interactive Parameters for Data Pump Import*

Parameter	Description
KILL_JOB	Kill the current job and detach related client sessions.
PARALLEL	Alter the number of workers for the Data Pump Import job.
START_JOB	Restart the attached job.
STATUS	Display detailed status of the Data Pump job.
STOP_JOB	Stop the job for later restart.

TABLE 22-4. *Interactive Parameters for Data Pump Import* (continued)

Many of the Data Pump Import parameters are the same as those available for Data Pump Export. In the following sections, you will see how to start an import job, along with descriptions of the major options unique to Data Pump Import.

Starting a Data Pump Import Job

You can start a Data Pump Import job via the impdp executable provided with Oracle Database 10g. Use the command-line parameters to specify the import mode and the locations for all the files. You can store the parameter values in a parameter file and then reference the file via the PARFILE option.

In the first export example of this chapter, the parameter file named dp1.par contained the following entries:

```
DIRECTORY=dtpump
DUMPFILE=metadataonly.dmp
CONTENT=METADATA_ONLY
```

The import will create the PRACTICE schema's objects in a different schema. The REMAP_SCHEMA option allows you to import objects into a different schema than was used for the export. If you want to change the tablespace assignments for the objects at the same time, use the REMAP_TABLESPACE option. The format for REMAP_SCHEMA is

```
REMAP_SCHEMA=source_schema:target_schema
```

Create a new user account to hold the objects:

```
create user Newpractice identified by newp;
grant CREATE SESSION to Newpractice;
grant CONNECT, RESOURCE to Newpractice;
grant CREATE TABLE to Newpractice;
grant CREATE INDEX to Newpractice;
```

You can now add the REMAP_SCHEMA line to the dp1.par parameter file:

```
DIRECTORY=dtpump
DUMPFILE=metadataonly.dmp
CONTENT=METADATA_ONLY
REMAP_SCHEMA=Practice:Newpractice
```

You can now start the import job. Because you are changing the owning schema for the data, you must have the IMP_FULL_DATABASE system privilege. Data Pump Import jobs are started via the impdp executable. The following listing shows the creation of a Data Pump Import job using the dp1.par parameter file.

```
impdp system/passwd parfile=dp1.par
```

NOTE
All dump files must be specified at the time the job is started.

Oracle will then perform the import and display its progress. Because the NOLOGFILE option was not specified, the log file for the import will be placed in the same directory as the dump file and will be given the name import.log. You can verify the success of the import by logging into the NEWPRACTICE schema. The NEWPRACTICE schema should have a copy of all the valid objects that have previously been created in the PRACTICE schema.

What if a table being imported already existed? In this example, with the CONTENT option set to METADATA_ONLY, the table would be skipped by default. If the CONTENT option was set to DATA_ONLY, the new data would be appended to the existing table data. To alter this behavior, use the TABLE_EXISTS_ACTION option. Valid values for TABLE_EXISTS_OPTION are SKIP, APPEND, TRUNCATE, and REPLACE.

Stopping and Restarting Running Jobs

After you have started a Data Pump Import job, you can close the client window you used to start the job. Because it is server based, the import will continue to run. You can then attach to the job, check its status, and alter it:

```
impdp system/passwd PARFILE=dp1.par
```

Press CTRL-C to leave the log display, and Data Pump will return you to the Import prompt:

```
Import>
```

Exit to the operating system via the EXIT_CLIENT command:

```
Import> EXIT_CLIENT
```

You can then restart the client and attach to the currently running job under your schema:

```
impdp system/passwd attach
```

If you gave a name to your Data Pump Import job, specify the name as part of the ATTACH parameter call. When you attach to a running job, Data Pump will display the status of the

job—its basic configuration parameters and its current status. You can then issue the CONTINUE_CLIENT command to see the log entries as they are generated, or you can alter the running job:

```
Import> CONTINUE_CLIENT
```

You can stop a job via the STOP_JOB option:

```
Import> STOP_JOB
```

While the job is stopped, you can increase its parallelism via the PARALLEL option. You can then restart the job:

```
Import> START_JOB
```

EXCLUDE, INCLUDE, and QUERY

Data Pump Import, like Data Pump Export, allows you to restrict the data processed via the use of the EXCLUDE, INCLUDE, and QUERY options, as described earlier in this chapter. Because you can use these options on both the export and the import, you can be very flexible in your imports. For example, you may choose to export an entire table but only import part of it—the rows that match your QUERY criteria. You could choose to export an entire schema but when recovering the database via import include only the most necessary tables so the application downtime can be minimized. EXCLUDE, INCLUDE, and QUERY provide powerful capabilities to developers and database administrators during both export and import jobs.

Transforming Imported Objects

In addition to changing or selecting schemas, tablespaces, datafiles, and rows during the import, you can change the segment attributes and storage requirements during import via the TRANSFORM option. The format for TRANSFORM is

```
TRANSFORM = transform_name:value[:object_type]
```

The *transform_name* variable can have a value of SEGMENT_ATTRIBUTES or STORAGE. You can use the *value* variable to include or exclude segment attributes (physical attributes, storage attributes, tablespaces, and logging). The *object_type* variable is optional and, if specified, must be either TABLE or INDEX.

For example, object storage requirements may change during an export/import—you may be using the QUERY option to limit the rows imported, or you may be importing only the metadata without the table data. To eliminate the exported storage clauses from the imported tables, add the following to the parameter file:

```
TRANSFORM=STORAGE:n:table
```

To eliminate the exported tablespace and storage clauses from all tables and indexes, use the following:

```
TRANSFORM=SEGMENT_ATTRIBUTES:n
```

When the objects are imported, they will be assigned to the user's default tablespace and will have used that tablespace's default storage parameters.

Generating SQL

Instead of importing the data and objects, you can generate the SQL for the objects (not the data) and store it in a file on your operating system. The file will be written to the directory and file specified via the SQLFILE option. The SQLFILE option format is

```
SQLFILE=[directory_object:]file_name
```

NOTE
If you do not specify a value for the directory_object *variable, the file will be created in the dump file directory.*

The following listing shows a sample parameter file for an import using the SQLFILE option. Note that the CONTENT option is not specified. The output will be written to the dtpump directory.

```
DIRECTORY=dtpump
DUMPFILE=metadataonly.dmp
SQLFILE=sql.txt
```

You can then run the import to populate the sql.txt file:

```
impdp practice/practice parfile=dp1.par
```

In the sql.txt file the import creates, you will see entries for each of the object types within the schema. The format for the output file will be similar to the following listing, although the object IDs and SCNs will be specific to your environment. For brevity, not all entries in the file are shown here.

```
-- CONNECT PRACTICE
-- new object type path is: SCHEMA_EXPORT/
SE_PRE_SCHEMA_PROCOBJACT/PROCACT_SCHEMA

BEGIN
sys.dbms_logrep_imp.instantiate_schema(schema_name=>'PRACTICE',
export_db_name=>'ORCL', inst_scn=>'3377908');
COMMIT;
END;
/

-- new object type path is: SCHEMA_EXPORT/TYPE/TYPE_SPEC
CREATE TYPE "PRACTICE"."ADDRESS_TY"
   OID '48D49FA5EB6D447C8D4C1417D849D63A' as object
(Street   VARCHAR2(50),
 City     VARCHAR2(25),
 State    CHAR(2),
 Zip      NUMBER);
/
```

```
CREATE TYPE "PRACTICE"."CUSTOMER_TY"
   OID '8C429A2DD41042228170643EF24BE75A' as object
(Customer_ID NUMBER,
 Name          VARCHAR2(25),
 Street        VARCHAR2(50),
 City          VARCHAR2(25),
 State         CHAR(2),
 Zip           NUMBER);
/

CREATE TYPE "PRACTICE"."PERSON_TY"
   OID '76270312D764478FAFDD47BF4533A5F8' as object
(Name          VARCHAR2(25),
 Address       ADDRESS_TY);
/

-- new object type path is: SCHEMA_EXPORT/TABLE/TABLE
CREATE TABLE "PRACTICE"."CUSTOMER"
    (  "CUSTOMER_ID" NUMBER,
       "NAME" VARCHAR2(25),
       "STREET" VARCHAR2(50),
       "CITY" VARCHAR2(25),
       "STATE" CHAR(2),
       "ZIP" NUMBER
    ) PCTFREE 10 PCTUSED 40 INITRANS 1 MAXTRANS 255 NOCOMPRESS LOGGING
STORAGE(INITIAL 65536 NEXT 1048576 MINEXTENTS 1 MAXEXTENTS 2147483645
PCTINCREASE 0 FREELISTS 1 FREELIST GROUPS 1 BUFFER_POOL DEFAULT)
 TABLESPACE "USERS" ;

CREATE TABLE "PRACTICE"."CUSTOMER_CALL"
    (  "CUSTOMER_ID" NUMBER,
       "CALL_NUMBER" NUMBER,
       "CALL_DATE" DATE
    ) PCTFREE 10 PCTUSED 40 INITRANS 1 MAXTRANS 255 NOCOMPRESS LOGGING
STORAGE(INITIAL 65536 NEXT 1048576 MINEXTENTS 1 MAXEXTENTS 2147483645
PCTINCREASE 0 FREELISTS 1 FREELIST GROUPS 1 BUFFER_POOL DEFAULT)
  TABLESPACE "USERS" ;

CREATE TABLE "PRACTICE"."STOCK_TRX"
    (  "ACCOUNT" NUMBER(10,0),
       "SYMBOL" VARCHAR2(20),
       "PRICE" NUMBER(6,2),
       "QUANTITY" NUMBER(6,0),
       "TRX_FLAG" VARCHAR2(1)
    ) PCTFREE 10 PCTUSED 40 INITRANS 1 MAXTRANS 255 NOCOMPRESS LOGGING
STORAGE(INITIAL 65536 NEXT 1048576 MINEXTENTS 1 MAXEXTENTS 2147483645
PCTINCREASE 0 FREELISTS 1 FREELIST GROUPS 1 BUFFER_POOL DEFAULT)
  TABLESPACE "USERS" ;

CREATE TABLE "PRACTICE"."STOCK_ACCOUNT"
```

```
(   "ACCOUNT" NUMBER(10,0),
    "ACCOUNTLONGNAME" VARCHAR2(50)
) PCTFREE 10 PCTUSED 40 INITRANS 1 MAXTRANS 255 NOCOMPRESS LOGGING
STORAGE(INITIAL 65536 NEXT 1048576 MINEXTENTS 1 MAXEXTENTS 2147483645
PCTINCREASE 0 FREELISTS 1 FREELIST GROUPS 1 BUFFER_POOL DEFAULT)
  TABLESPACE "USERS" ;

-- new object type path is: SCHEMA_EXPORT/TABLE/GRANT/OBJECT_GRANT
GRANT SELECT ON "PRACTICE"."STOCK_TRX" TO "ADAMS";
GRANT SELECT ON "PRACTICE"."STOCK_TRX" TO "BURLINGTON";
GRANT SELECT ON "PRACTICE"."STOCK_ACCOUNT" TO "ADAMS";
GRANT SELECT ON "PRACTICE"."STOCK_ACCOUNT" TO "BURLINGTON";
GRANT INSERT ON "PRACTICE"."STOCK_TRX" TO "ADAMS";

-- new object type path is: SCHEMA_EXPORT/TABLE/INDEX/INDEX
CREATE UNIQUE INDEX "PRACTICE"."CUSTOMER_PK" ON "PRACTICE"."CUSTOMER"
("CUSTOMER_ID")
  PCTFREE 10 INITRANS 2 MAXTRANS 255
STORAGE(INITIAL 65536 NEXT 1048576 MINEXTENTS 1 MAXEXTENTS 2147483645
PCTINCREASE 0 FREELISTS 1 FREELIST GROUPS 1 BUFFER_POOL DEFAULT)
  TABLESPACE "USERS" PARALLEL 1 ;

ALTER INDEX "PRACTICE"."CUSTOMER_PK" NOPARALLEL;
```

The SQLFILE output is a plain text file, so you can edit the file, use it within SQL*Plus, or keep it as documentation of your application's database structures.

Comparing Data Pump Export/Import to Export/Import

The original Export and Import utilities are still available via the exp and imp executables. As shown in this chapter, there are many ways in which Data Pump Export and Import offer superior capabilities over the original Export and Import utilities. Data Pump's server-based architecture leads to performance gains and improved manageability. However, Data Pump does not support the incremental commit capability offered by the COMMIT and BUFFER parameters in the original Import. Also, Data Pump will not automatically merge multiple extents into a single extent during the Data Pump Export/Import process; the original Export/Import offer this functionality via the COMPRESS parameter. In Data Pump, you can use the TRANSFORM option to suppress the storage attributes during the import—an option that many users of the original Export/Import may prefer over the COMPRESS functionality.

If you are importing data via Data Pump into an existing table using either the APPEND or TRUNCATE settings of the TABLE_EXISTS_ACTION option and a row violates an active constraint, the load is discontinued and no data is loaded. In the original Import, the load would have continued.

CHAPTER
23

Accessing
Remote Data

 s your databases grow in size and number, you will very likely need to share data among them. Sharing data requires a method of locating and accessing the data. In Oracle, remote data accesses such as queries and updates are enabled through the use of database links. As described in this chapter, database links allow users to treat a group of distributed databases as if they were a single, integrated database. In this chapter, you will also find information about direct connections to remote databases, such as those used in client-server applications.

Database Links

Database links tell Oracle how to get from one database to another. You may also specify the access path in an ad hoc fashion (see "Dynamic Links: Using the SQL*Plus copy Command," later in this chapter). If you will frequently use the same connection to a remote database, a database link is appropriate.

How a Database Link Works

A database link requires Oracle Net (previously known as SQL*Net and Net8) to be running on each of the machines (hosts) involved in the remote database access. Oracle Net is usually started by the database administrator (DBA) or the system manager. A sample architecture for a remote access using a database link is shown in Figure 23-1. This figure shows two hosts, each running Oracle Net. There is a database on each of the hosts. A database link establishes a connection from the first database (named LOCAL, on the Branch host) to the second database (named REMOTE, on the Headquarters host). The database link shown in Figure 23-1 is located in the LOCAL database.

Database links specify the following connection information:

■ The communications protocol (such as TCP/IP) to use during the connection

■ The host on which the remote database resides

■ The name of the database on the remote host

■ The name of a valid account in the remote database

■ The password for that account

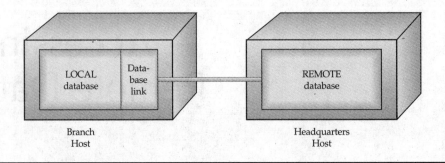

FIGURE 23-1. *Sample architecture for a database link*

When used, a database link actually logs in as a user in the remote database and then logs out when the remote data access is complete. A database link can be *private,* owned by a single user, or *public,* in which case all users in the LOCAL database can use the link.

The syntax for creating a database link is shown in "Syntax for Database Links," later in this chapter.

Using a Database Link for Remote Queries

If you are a user in the LOCAL database shown in Figure 23-1, you can access objects in the REMOTE database via a database link. To do this, simply append the database link name to the name of any table or view that is accessible to the remote account. When appending the database link name to a table or view name, you must precede the database link name with an @ sign.

For local tables, you reference the table name in the **from** clause:

```
select *
  from BOOKSHELF;
```

For remote tables, use a database link named REMOTE_CONNECT. In the **from** clause, reference the table name followed by @REMOTE_CONNECT:

```
select *
  from BOOKSHELF@REMOTE_CONNECT;
```

When the database link in the preceding query is used, Oracle will log into the database specified by the database link, using the username and password provided by the link. It will then query the BOOKSHELF table in that account and return the data to the user who initiated the query. This is shown graphically in Figure 23-2. The REMOTE_CONNECT database link shown in Figure 23-2 is located in the LOCAL database.

As shown in Figure 23-2, logging into the LOCAL database and using the REMOTE_CONNECT database link in your **from** clause returns the same results as logging in directly to the remote database and executing the query without the database link. It makes the remote database seem local.

NOTE
The maximum number of database links that can be used in a single query is set via the OPEN_LINKS parameter in the database's initialization parameter file. This parameter defaults to four.

FIGURE 23-2. *Using a database link for a remote query*

Queries executed using database links do have some restrictions. You should avoid using database links in queries that use the **connect by**, **start with**, and **prior** keywords. Some queries using these keywords will work (for example, if **prior** is not used outside of the **connect by** clause, and **start with** does not use a subquery), but most uses of tree-structured queries will fail when using database links.

Using a Database Link for Synonyms and Views

You may create local synonyms and views that reference remote objects. To do this, reference the database link name, preceded by an @ sign, wherever you refer to a remote table. The following example shows how to do this for synonyms. The **create synonym** command in this example is executed from an account in the LOCAL database.

```
create synonym BOOKSHELF_SYN
   for BOOKSHELF@REMOTE_CONNECT;
```

In this example, a synonym called BOOKSHELF_SYN is created for the BOOKSHELF table accessed via the REMOTE_CONNECT database link. Every time this synonym is used in a **from** clause of a query, the remote database will be queried. This is very similar to the remote queries shown earlier; the only real change is that the database link is now defined as part of a local object (in this case, a synonym).

What if the remote account that is accessed by the database link does not own the table being referenced? In that event, any synonyms available to the remote account (either private or public) can be used. If no such synonyms exist for a table that the remote account has been granted access to, you must specify the table owner's name in the query, as shown in the following example:

```
create synonym BOOKSHELF_SYN
   for Practice.BOOKSHELF@REMOTE_CONNECT;
```

In this example, the remote account used by the database link does not own the BOOKSHELF table, nor does the remote account have a synonym called BOOKSHELF. It does, however, have privileges on the BOOKSHELF table owned by the remote user Practice in the REMOTE database. Therefore, the owner and table name are specified; both are interpreted in the REMOTE database. The syntax for these queries and synonyms is almost the same as if everything were in the local database; the only addition is the database link name.

To use a database link in a view, simply add it as a suffix to table names in the **create view** command. The following example creates a view in the local database of a remote table using the REMOTE_CONNECT database link:

```
create view LOCAL_BOOKSHELF_VIEW
as
select * from BOOKSHELF@REMOTE_CONNECT
 where Title >  'M';
```

The **from** clause in this example refers to BOOKSHELF@REMOTE_CONNECT. Therefore, the base table for this view is not in the same database as the view. Also note that a **where** clause is placed on the query, to limit the number of records returned by it for the view.

This view may now be treated the same as any other view in the local database. Access to this view can be granted to other users, provided those users also have access to the REMOTE_CONNECT database link.

Using a Database Link for Remote Updates

The database link syntax for remote updates is the same as that for remote queries. Append the name of the database link to the name of the table being updated. For example, to change the Rating values for books in a remote BOOKSHELF table, you would execute the **update** command shown in the following listing:

```
update BOOKSHELF@REMOTE_CONNECT
    set Rating = '5'
 where Title = 'INNUMERACY';
```

This **update** command will use the REMOTE_CONNECT database link to log into the remote database. It will then **update** the BOOKSHELF table in that database, based on the **set** and **where** conditions specified.

You can use subqueries in the **set** portion of the **update** command (refer to Chapter 15). The **from** clause of such subqueries can reference either the local database or a remote database. To refer to the remote database in a subquery, append the database link name to the table names in the **from** clause of the subquery. An example of this is shown in the following listing:

```
update BOOKSHELF@REMOTE_CONNECT          /*in remote database*/
    set Rating =
        (select Rating
         from BOOKSHELF@REMOTE_CONNECT  /*in remote database*/
         where Title = 'WONDERFUL LIFE')
where Title = 'INNUMERACY';
```

NOTE
If you do not append the database link name to the table names in the
from *clause of* ***update*** *subqueries, tables in the local database will be*
used. This is true even if the table being updated is in a remote database.

In this example, the remote BOOKSHELF table is updated based on the Rating value on the remote BOOKSHELF table. If the database link is not used in the subquery, as in the following example, then the BOOKSHELF table in the local database will be used instead. If this is unintended, it will cause local data to be mixed into the remote database table. If you're doing this on purpose, be *very* careful.

```
update BOOKSHELF@REMOTE_CONNECT          /*in remote database*/
    set Rating =
        (select Rating
         from BOOKSHELF               /*in local database*/
         where Title = 'WONDERFUL LIFE')
where Title = 'INNUMERACY';
```

Syntax for Database Links

You can create a database link with the following command:

```
create [shared] [public] database link REMOTE_CONNECT
connect to {current_user | username
identified by password [authentication clause]}
using 'connect string';
```

The specific syntax to use when creating a database link depends on two criteria:

- The "public" or "private" status of the database link
- The use of default or explicit logins for the remote database

These criteria and their associated syntax are described in turn in the following sections.

NOTE
To create a database link, you must have the CREATE DATABASE LINK system privilege. The account to which you will be connecting in the remote database must have the CREATE SESSION system privilege. Both of these system privileges are included as part of the CONNECT role in Oracle. The CONNECT role in Oracle Database 10g exists only for backward compatibility with earlier releases.

If the value of the GLOBAL_NAMES initialization parameter is TRUE, the database link must have the same name as the database to which it connects. If the value of GLOBAL_NAMES is FALSE and you have changed the global name of the database, you can specify the global name.

Public vs. Private Database Links

As mentioned earlier, a *public* database link is available to all users in a database. By contrast, a *private* database link is only available to the user who created it. It is not possible for one user to grant access on a private database link to another user. The database link must either be public (available to all users) or private.

To specify a database link as public, use the **public** keyword in the **create database link** command, as shown in the following example:

```
create public database link REMOTE_CONNECT
connect to username identified by password
  using 'connect string';
```

NOTE
To create a public database link, you must have the CREATE PUBLIC DATABASE LINK system privilege. This privilege is included in the DBA role in Oracle. The DBA role in Oracle Database 10g exists only for backward compatibility with earlier releases.

Default vs. Explicit Logins

In place of the **connect to … identified by …** clause, you can use **connect to current_user** when creating a database link. If you use the **current_user** option, then when that link is used, it will attempt to open a session in the remote database that has the same username and password as the local database account. This is called a *default login,* because the username/password combination will default to the combination in use in the local database.

The following listing shows an example of a public database link created with a default login (the use of default logins is described further in "Using the User Pseudo-Column in Views," later in this chapter):

```
create public database link REMOTE_CONNECT
connect to current_user
 using 'HQ';
```

When this database link is used, it will attempt to log into the remote database identified by the 'HQ' service name using the current user's username and password. If the current username is not valid in the remote database, or if the password is different, the login attempt will fail. This failure will cause the SQL statement using the link to fail.

An *explicit* login specifies a username and password that the database link will use while connecting to the remote database. No matter which local account uses the link, the same remote account will be used. The following listing shows the creation of a database link with an explicit login:

```
create public database link REMOTE_CONNECT
connect to WAREHOUSE identified by ACCESS339
   using 'HQ';
```

This example shows a common usage of explicit logins in database links. In the remote database, a user named Warehouse was created and was given the password ACCESS339. The Warehouse account can then be granted SELECT access to specific tables, solely for use by database links. The REMOTE_CONNECT database link then provides access to the remote Warehouse account for all local users.

Connect String Syntax

Oracle Net uses *service names* to identify remote connections. The connection details for these service names are contained in files that are distributed to each host in the network. When a service name is encountered, Oracle checks the local Oracle Net configuration file (called tnsnames.ora) to determine which protocol, host name, and database name to use during the connection. All the connection information is found in external files.

When using Oracle Net, you must know the name of the service that points to the remote database. For example, if the service name HQ specifies the connection parameters for the database you need, then HQ should be used as the connect string in the **create database link** command. The following example shows a private database link, using a default login and an Oracle Net service name:

```
create database link REMOTE_CONNECT
connect to current_user
 using 'HQ';
```

When this link is used, Oracle checks the tnsnames.ora file on the local host to determine which database to connect to. When it attempts to log into that database, it uses the current user's username and password.

The tnsnames.ora files for a network of databases should be coordinated by the DBAs for those databases. A typical entry in the tnsnames.ora file (for a network using the TCP/IP protocol) is shown in the following listing:

```
HQ =(DESCRIPTION=
      (ADDRESS_LIST =
            (ADDRESS = (PROTOCOL=TCP)
            (HOST=host1)
            (PORT=1521))
      )
      (CONNECT DATA=
            (SERVICE_NAME = HQ.host1)
      )
)
```

In this listing, the HQ service name is mapped to a connect descriptor that tells the database which protocol to use (TCP/IP) and which host (host1) and database (HQ) to connect to. The "port" information refers to the port on the host that will be used for the connection; that data is environment specific. Different protocols will have different keywords, but they all must convey the same content.

Using Shared Database Links

If you use the Shared Server option for your database connections and your application will employ many concurrent database link connections, you may benefit from using *shared database links*. A shared database link uses shared server connections to support the database link connections. If you have multiple concurrent database link accesses into a remote database, you can use shared database links to reduce the number of server connections required.

To create a shared database link, use the **shared** keyword of the **create database link** command. As shown in the following listing, you will also need to specify a schema and password for the remote database:

```
create shared database link HR_LINK_SHARED
connect to current_user
authenticated by HR identified by puffin55556d
using 'hq';
```

The HR_LINK_SHARED database link uses the connected user's username and password when accessing the 'hq' database, as specified via the **connect to current_user** clause. In order to prevent unauthorized attempts to use the shared link, shared links require the **authenticated by** clause. In this example, the account used for authentication is an application account, but you can also use an empty schema for authentication. The authentication account must have the CREATE SESSION system privilege. During usage of the HR_LINK_SHARED link, connection attempts will include authentication against the HR link account.

If you change the password on the authentication account, you will need to drop and re-create each database link that references it. To simplify maintenance, create an account that is only used

for the authentication of shared database link connections. The account should have only the CREATE SESSION system privilege and should not have any privileges on any of the application tables.

If your application uses database links infrequently, you should use traditional database links without the **shared** clause. Without the **shared** clause, each database link connection requires a separate connection to the remote database.

Using Synonyms for Location Transparency

Over the lifespan of an application, its data very likely will move from one database to another, or from one host to another. Therefore, it will simplify application maintenance if the exact physical location of a database object is shielded from the user (and the application).

The best way to implement such location transparency is through the use of synonyms. Instead of writing applications (or SQL*Plus reports) that contain queries that specify a table's owner, such as

```
select *
   from Practice.BOOKSHELF;
```

you should create a synonym for that table and then reference the synonym in the query, as shown here:

```
create synonym BOOKSHELF
    for Practice.BOOKSHELF;

select *
   from BOOKSHELF;
```

The logic required to find the data has thus been moved out of your application and into the database. Moving the table location logic to the database will be a benefit anytime you move the table from one schema to another.

In addition to hiding the ownership of tables from an application, you can hide the data's physical location through the use of database links and synonyms. By using local synonyms for remote tables, you move another layer of logic out of the application and into the database. For example, the local synonym BOOKSHELF, as defined in the following listing, refers to a table that is located in a different database, on a different host. If that table ever moves, only the link has to be changed; the application code, which uses the synonym, will not change.

```
create synonym BOOKSHELF
    for BOOKSHELF@REMOTE_CONNECT;
```

If the remote account used by the database link is not the owner of the object being referenced, you have two options. First, you can reference an available synonym in the remote database:

```
create synonym BOOKSHELF
    for BOOKSHELF@REMOTE_CONNECT;
```

Here, BOOKSHELF, in the remote account used by the database link, is a synonym for another user's BOOKSHELF table.

Second, you can include the remote owner's name when creating the local synonym, as shown in the following listing:

```
create synonym BOOKSHELF
    for Practice.BOOKSHELF@REMOTE_CONNECT;
```

These two examples will result in the same functionality for your queries, but there are differences between them. The second example, which includes the owner name, is potentially more difficult to maintain, because you are not using a synonym in the remote database and the remote object may be moved at a later time, thus invalidating your local synonym.

Using the User Pseudo-Column in Views

The User pseudo-column is very useful when you are using remote data access methods. For example, you may not want all remote users to see all records in a table. To solve this problem, you must think of remote users as special users within your database. To enforce the data restriction, you need to create a view that the remote accounts will access. But what can you use in the **where** clause to properly restrict the records? The User pseudo-column, combined with properly selected usernames, allows you to enforce this restriction.

As you may recall from Chapter 18, queries used to define views may also reference *pseudo-columns*. A pseudo-column is a "column" that returns a value when it is selected, but it is not an actual column in a table. The User pseudo-column, when selected, always returns the Oracle username that executed the query. So, if a column in the table contains usernames, those values can be compared against the User pseudo-column to restrict its records, as shown in the following example. In this example, the NAME table is queried. If the value of the first part of the Name column is the same as the name of the user entering the query, records will be returned.

```
create view MY_CHECKOUT as
select * from BOOKSHELF_CHECKOUT
 where SUBSTR(Name,1,INSTR(Name,' ')-1) = User;
```

NOTE
We need to shift our point of view for this discussion. Because the discussion concerns operations on the database that owns the table being queried, that database will be referred to as the "local" database, and the users from other databases will be referred to as "remote" users.

When restricting remote access to the rows of your table, you should first consider which columns would be the best to use for the restriction. There are usually logical divisions to the data within a table, such as Department or Region. For each distinct division, create a separate user account in your local database. For this example, let's add a Region column to the BOOKSHELF table. We will now be able to record the list of books from multiple distributed locations in a single table:

```
alter table BOOKSHELF
add
(Region VARCHAR2(10));
```

Suppose you have four major regions represented in your BOOKSHELF table, and you have created an Oracle account for each region. You could then set up each remote user's database link to use his or her specific user account in your local database. For this example, assume the regions are called NORTH, EAST, SOUTH, and WEST. For each of the regions, a specific database link would be created. For example, the members of the SOUTH department would use the database link shown in the following listing:

```
create database link SOUTH_LINK
connect to SOUTH identified by PAW
   using 'HQ';
```

The database link shown in this example is a private database link with an explicit login to the SOUTH account in the remote database.

When remote users query via their database links (such as SOUTH_LINK from the previous example), they will be logged into the HQ database, with their Department name (such as SOUTH) as their username. Therefore, the value of the User column for any table that the user queries will be SOUTH.

Now create a view of your base table, comparing the User pseudo-column to the value of the Department column in the view's **where** clause:

```
create or replace view RESTRICTED_BOOKSHELF
     as select *
  from BOOKSHELF
 where Region = User;
```

A user who connects via the SOUTH_LINK database link—and thus is logged in as the SOUTH user—would only be able to see the BOOKSHELF records that have a Region value equal to 'SOUTH'. If users are accessing your table from a remote database, their logins are occurring via database links—and you know the local accounts they are using because you set them up.

This type of restriction can also be performed in the remote database rather than in the database where the table resides. Users in the remote database may create views within their databases of the following form:

```
create or replace view SOUTH_BOOKSHELF
     as select *
  from BOOKSHELF@REMOTE_CONNECT
 where Region = 'SOUTH';
```

In this case, the Region restriction is still in force, but it is administered locally, and the Region restriction is coded into the view's query. Choosing between the two restriction options (local or remote) is based on the number of accounts required for the desired restriction to be enforced.

To secure your production database, you should limit the privileges granted to the accounts used by database links. Grant those privileges via roles, and use views (with the **with read only** or **with check option** clause) to further limit the ability of those accounts to be used to make unauthorized changes to the data.

Dynamic Links: Using the SQL*Plus copy Command

The SQL*Plus **copy** command allows data to be copied between databases (or within the same database) via SQL*Plus. Although it allows you to select which columns to copy, it works best when all the columns of a table are being chosen. The greatest benefit from using this command is its ability to **commit** after each array of data has been processed (explained shortly). This in turn generates transactions that are of a manageable size.

NOTE
*The **copy** command is not being enhanced to handle datatypes or features introduced with or after Oracle8i. The **copy** command is likely to be made obsolete in a future release.*

Consider the case of a large table, such as BOOKSHELF_CHECKOUT. What if the BOOKSHELF_CHECKOUT table has 100,000 rows that use a total of 100MB of space, and you need to make a copy of that table into a different database? The easiest option involves creating a database link and then using that link in a **create table ... as select** command, as shown next:

```
create database link REMOTE_CONNECT
connect to PRACTICE identified by PRACTICE
  using 'HQ';

create table BOOKSHELF_CHECKOUT
as
select * from BOOKSHELF_CHECKOUT@REMOTE_CONNECT;
```

The first command creates the database link, and the second creates a new table based on all the data in the remote table.

Unfortunately, this option creates a very large transaction (all 100,000 rows would be inserted into the new table as a single transaction) that places a large burden on internal Oracle structures called *rollback segments*. Rollback segments and system-managed undo (see Chapter 46) store the prior image of data until that data is committed to the database. Because this table is being populated by a single **insert**, a single, large transaction is generated that may exceed the space in the currently available rollback segments. This failure will in turn cause the table creation to fail.

To break the transaction into smaller entries, use the SQL*Plus **copy** command, which has the following syntax:

```
copy from
[remote username/remote password@connect string]
[to username/password@connect string]
{append|create|insert|replace}
table name
using subquery;
```

If the current account is to be the destination of the copied data, the word **to** and the local username, password, and connect string are not necessary. If the current account is to be the source of the copied data, the remote connection information for the data source is not necessary.

To set the transaction entry size, use the SQL*Plus **set** command to set a value for the **arraysize** parameter. This determines the number of records that will be retrieved in each batch. The **copycommit** parameter tells SQL*Plus how many batches should be committed at one time. The following SQL*Plus script accomplishes the same data-copying goal that the **create table as** command met; however, it breaks up the single transaction into multiple transactions. In this example, the data is committed after every 1,000 records. This reduces the transaction's rollback segment entry size needed from 100MB to 1MB.

```
set copycommit 1
set arraysize 1000

copy from PRACTICE/PRACTICE@HQ -
create BOOKSHELF_CHECKOUT -
using -
select * from BOOKSHELF_CHECKOUT
```

NOTE
Except for the last line, each line in the **copy** *command must be terminated with a dash (-) because this is a SQL*Plus command.*

Here are the different data options within the **copy** command:

Option	Description
APPEND	Inserts the rows into the destination table. Automatically creates the table if it does not exist.
CREATE	Creates the table and then inserts the rows.
INSERT	Inserts the rows into the destination table if it exists; otherwise, returns an error. When using INSERT, all columns must be specified in the **using** subquery.
REPLACE	Drops the existing destination table and replaces it with a new table containing the copied data.

The feedback provided by the **copy** command may be confusing at first. After the final commit is complete, the database reports to the user the number of records that were committed in the *last* batch. It does not report the total number of records committed (unless they are all committed in a single batch).

Connecting to a Remote Database

In addition to the interdatabase connections described earlier in this chapter, you may connect directly to a remote database via an Oracle tool. Therefore, instead of typing

```
sqlplus username/password
```

and accessing your local database, you can go directly to a remote database. To do this, enter your username and password along with the Oracle Net connect string for the remote database:

```
sqlplus username/password@HQ
```

This command will log you in directly to the HQ database. The host configuration for this type of login is shown in Figure 23-3; the Branch host has the Oracle tools (such as SQL*Plus) on it and is running Oracle Net, and the REMOTE host is running Oracle Net and has an Oracle database. There may or may not be a database on the Branch host; specifying the Oracle Net connect string to the remote database forces Oracle to ignore any local databases.

As Figure 23-3 shows, there are very few hardware requirements for the Branch host. All it has to support is the front-end tool and Oracle Net—a typical configuration for client-server applications. A client machine, such as the Branch host, is used primarily for presentation of the data via the database access tools. The server side, such as the Headquarters host, is used to maintain the data and process the data access requests from users.

Regardless of the configuration you use and the configuration tools available, you need to tell Oracle Net how to find the remote database. Work with your DBA to make sure the remote server is properly configured to listen for new connection requests and to make sure the client machines are properly configured to issue those requests.

FIGURE 23-3. *Sample architecture for a remote connection*

CHAPTER
24

Using Materialized
Views

o improve the performance of an application, you can make local copies of remote tables that use distributed data, or create summary tables based on **group by** operations. Oracle provides *materialized views* to store copies of data or aggregations. Materialized views can be used to replicate all or part of a single table, or to replicate the result of a query against multiple tables; refreshes of the replicated data can be done automatically by the database at time intervals that you specify. In this chapter, you will see the general usage of materialized views, including their refresh strategies, followed by a description of the optimization strategies available.

Functionality

Materialized views are copies (also known as *replicas*) of data, based upon queries. In its simplest form, a materialized view can be thought of as a table created by a command such as the following:

```
create table LOCAL_BOOKSHELF
as
select * from BOOKSHELF@REMOTE_CONNECT;
```

In this example, a table named LOCAL_BOOKSHELF is created in the local database and is populated with data from a remote database (defined by the database link named REMOTE_CONNECT). Once the LOCAL_BOOKSHELF table is created, though, its data may immediately become out of sync with the master table (BOOKSHELF@REMOTE_CONNECT). Also, LOCAL_BOOKSHELF may be updated by local users, further complicating its synchronization with the master table.

Despite these synchronization problems, there are benefits to replicating data in this way. Creating local copies of remote data may improve the performance of distributed queries, particularly if the master table's data does not change frequently. You may also use the local table creation process to restrict the rows returned, restrict the columns returned, or generate new columns (such as by applying functions to selected values). This is a common strategy for decision-support environments, in which complex queries are used to periodically "roll up" data into summary tables for use during analyses.

Materialized views automate the data replication and refresh processes. When materialized views are created, a *refresh interval* is established to schedule refreshes of replicated data. Local updates can be prevented, and transaction-based refreshes can be used. Transaction-based refreshes, available for many types of materialized views, send from the master database only those rows that have changed for the materialized view. This capability, described later in this chapter, may significantly improve the performance of your refreshes.

Required System Privileges

To create a materialized view, you must have the privileges needed to create the underlying objects it will use. You must have the CREATE MATERIALIZED VIEW privilege, as well as the CREATE TABLE or CREATE ANY TABLE system privileges. In addition, you must have either the UNLIMITED TABLESPACE system privilege or a sufficient specified space quota in a local tablespace. To create a refresh-on-commit materialized view, you must also have the ON COMMIT REFRESH system privilege on any tables you do not own, or the ON COMMIT REFRESH system privilege.

Materialized views of remote tables require queries of remote tables; therefore, you must have privileges to use a database link that accesses the remote database. The link you use can be either public or private. If the database link is private, you need to have the CREATE DATABASE LINK system privilege to create the database link. See Chapter 23 for further information on database links.

If you are creating materialized views to take advantage of the *query rewrite* feature (in which the optimizer dynamically chooses to select data from the materialized view instead of the underlying table), you must have the QUERY REWRITE privilege. If the tables are in another user's schema, you must have the GLOBAL QUERY REWRITE privilege. If the materialized view is created with **on commit refresh** specified, you must have the ON COMMIT REFRESH system privilege or the ON COMMIT REFRESH object privilege on each table outside your schema.

Required Table Privileges

When creating a materialized view, you can reference tables in a remote database via a database link. The account that the database link uses in the remote database must have access to the tables and views used by the database link. You cannot create a materialized view based on objects owned by the user SYS.

Within the local database, you can grant SELECT privilege on a materialized view to other local users. Since most materialized views are read-only (although they can be updatable), no additional grants are necessary. If you create an updatable materialized view, you must grant users UPDATE privilege on both the materialized view and the underlying local table it accesses.

Read-Only vs. Updatable

A *read-only* materialized view cannot pass data changes from itself back to its master table. An *updatable* materialized view can send changes to its master table.

Although that may seem to be a simple distinction, the underlying differences between these two types of materialized views are not simple. A read-only materialized view is implemented as a **create table as select** command. When transactions occur, they occur only within the master table; the transactions are sent to the read-only materialized view. Thus, the method by which the rows in the materialized view change is controlled—the materialized view's rows only change following a change to the materialized view's master table.

In an updatable materialized view, there is less control over the method by which rows in the materialized view are changed. Rows may be changed based on changes in the master table, or rows may be changed directly by users of the materialized view. As a result, you need to send records from the master table to the materialized view, *and* vice versa. Since multiple sources of changes exist, multiple masters exist (referred to as a *multimaster configuration*).

During the transfer of records from the materialized view to master, you need to decide how you will reconcile conflicts. For example, what if the record with ID=1 is deleted at the materialized view site, while at the master site, a record is created in a separate table that references (via a foreign key) the ID=1 record? You cannot delete the ID=1 record from the master site, since that record has a "child" record that relates to it. You cannot insert the child record at the materialized view site, since the parent (ID=1) record has been deleted. How do you plan to resolve such conflicts?

Read-only materialized views let you avoid the need for conflict resolution by forcing all transactions to occur in the controlled master table. This may limit your functionality, but it is an appropriate solution for the vast majority of replication needs. If you need multimaster replication, see the *Advanced Replication Guide* for guidelines and detailed implementation instructions.

create materialized view Syntax

The basic syntax for creating a materialized view is shown in the following listing. See the Alphabetical Reference for the full command syntax. Following the command description, examples are given that illustrate the creation of local replicas of remote data.

```
create materialized view [user.]name
[ organization index iot_clause]
[ { { segment attributes clauses }
  | cluster cluster (column [, column] ...) }
  [ {partitioning clause | parallel clause | build clause } ]
  | on prebuilt table [ {with | without} reduced precision ] ]
[ using index
  [ { physical attributes clauses| tablespace clause }
    [ physical attributes clauses| tablespace clause ]
    | using no index ]
[ refresh clause ]
[ for update ] [{disable | enable} query rewrite]
 as subquery;
```

The **create materialized view** command has four major sections. The first section is the header, in which the materialized view is named (the first line in the listing):

```
create materialized view [user.]name
```

The materialized view will be created in your user account (schema) unless a different username is specified in the header. In the second section, the storage parameters are set:

```
[ organization index iot_clause]
[ { { segment attributes clauses }
  | cluster cluster (column [, column] ...) }
  [ {partitioning clause | parallel clause | build clause } ]
  | on prebuilt table [ {with | without} reduced precision ] ]
[ using index
  [ { physical attributes clauses| tablespace clause }
    [ physical attributes clauses| tablespace clause ]
    | using no index ]
```

The storage parameters will be applied to a table that will be created in the local database. For information about the available storage parameters, see the "Storage" entry in the Alphabetical Reference. If the data has already been replicated to a local table, you can use the **on prebuilt table** clause to tell Oracle to use that table as a materialized view.

NOTE
You can specify the storage parameters to be used for the index that is automatically created on the materialized view.

In the third section, the refresh options are set:

[*refresh clause*]

The syntax for *refresh clause* is

```
{ refresh
  { { fast | complete | force }
  | on { demand | commit }
  | { start with | next } date
  | with { primary key | rowid }
  | using
    { default [ master | local ] rollback segment
    | [ master | local ] rollback segment rollback_segment
    }
    [ default [ master | local ] rollback segment
    | [ master | local ] rollback segment rollback_segment
    ]...
  }
  [ { fast | complete | force }
  | on { demand | commit }
  | { start with | next } date
  | with { primary key | rowid }
  | using
    { default [ master | local ] rollback segment
    | [ master | local ] rollback segment rollback_segment
    }
    [ default [ master | local ] rollback segment
    | [ master | local ] rollback segment rollback_segment
    ]...
  ]...
| never refresh
}
```

The **refresh** option specifies the mechanism Oracle should use when refreshing the materialized view. The three options available are **fast**, **complete**, and **force**. Fast refreshes are only available if Oracle can match rows in the materialized view directly to rows in the base table(s); they use tables called *materialized view logs* to send specific rows from the master table to the materialized view. Complete refreshes truncate the data and reexecute the materialized view's base query to repopulate it. The **force** option for refreshes tells Oracle to use a fast refresh if it is available; otherwise, a complete refresh will be used. If you have created a simple materialized view but want to use complete refreshes, specify **refresh complete** in your **create materialized view** command. The refresh options are further described in "Refreshing Materialized Views," later in this chapter. Within this section of the **create materialized view** command, you also specify the mechanism used to relate values in the materialized view to the master table—whether RowIDs or primary key values should be used. By default, primary keys are used.

If the master query for the materialized view references a join or a single-table aggregate, you can use the **on commit** option to control the replication of changes. If you use **on commit**, changes will be sent from the master to the replica when the changes are committed on the master table. If you specify **on demand**, the refresh will occur when you manually execute a refresh command.

The fourth section of the **create materialized view** command is the query that the materialized view will use:

```
[ for update ] [{disable | enable} query rewrite]
as subquery
```

If you specify **for update**, the materialized view will be updatable; otherwise, it will be read-only. Most materialized views are read-only replicas of the master data. If you use updatable materialized views, you need to be concerned with issues such as two-way replication of changes and the reconciliation of conflicting data changes. Updatable materialized views are an example of multimaster replication; for full details on implementing a multimaster replication environment, see the *Advanced Replication Guide*.

NOTE
The query that forms the basis of the materialized view should not use the User or SysDate pseudo-columns.

The following example creates a read-only materialized view called LOCAL_BOOKSHELF in a local database, based on a remote table named BOOKSHELF that is accessible via the REMOTE_CONNECT database link. The materialized view is placed in the USERS tablespace.

```
create materialized view LOCAL_BOOKSHELF
tablespace USERS
refresh force
start with SysDate next SysDate+7
with primary key
as
select * from BOOKSHELF@REMOTE_CONNECT;
```

Oracle responds with

```
Materialized view created.
```

The command shown in the preceding example will create a read-only materialized view called LOCAL_BOOKSHELF. Its underlying table will be created in a tablespace named USERS. You can place materialized view logs in tablespaces apart from the materialized views they support. The **force** refresh option is specified because no materialized view log exists on the base table for the materialized view; Oracle will try to use a fast refresh but will use a complete refresh until the materialized view log is created. The materialized view's query specifies that the entire BOOKSHELF table, with no modifications, is to be copied to the local database. As soon as the LOCAL_BOOKSHELF materialized view is created, its underlying table will be populated with the BOOKSHELF data. Thereafter, the materialized view will be refreshed every seven days. The storage parameters that are not specified will use the default values for those parameters for the USERS tablespace.

The following example creates a materialized view named LOCAL_CATEGORY_COUNT in a local database, based on a remote table named BOOKSHELF in a database accessed via the REMOTE_CONNECT database link.

```
create materialized view LOCAL_CATEGORY_COUNT
tablespace USERS
refresh force
start with SysDate next SysDate+7
 as
select CategoryName, COUNT(*) CountPerCat
  from BOOKSHELF@REMOTE_CONNECT
 group by CategoryName;
```

The query in the LOCAL_CATEGORY_COUNT materialized view counts the number of books in each category in the remote BOOKSHELF table.

There are a few important points to note about the two examples shown in this section:

- The **group by** query used in the LOCAL_CATEGORY_COUNT materialized view could be performed in SQL*Plus against the LOCAL_BOOKSHELF materialized view. That is, the **group by** operation can be performed outside of the materialized view.

- Since LOCAL_CATEGORY_COUNT uses a **group by** clause, it is a complex materialized view and may only be able to use complete refreshes. LOCAL_BOOKSHELF, as a simple materialized view, can use fast refreshes.

The two materialized views shown in the preceding examples reference the same table. Since one of the materialized views is a simple materialized view that replicates all columns and all rows of the master table, the second materialized view may at first appear to be redundant. However, sometimes the second, complex materialized view is the more useful of the two.

How can this be? First, remember that these materialized views are being used to service the query needs of *local* users. If those users always perform **group by** operations in their queries, and their grouping columns are fixed, then LOCAL_CATEGORY_COUNT may be more useful to them. Second, if the transaction volume on the master BOOKSHELF table is very high, or the master BOOKSHELF table is very small, there may not be a significant difference in the refresh times of the fast and complete refreshes. The most appropriate materialized view is the one that is most productive for your users.

Types of Materialized Views

The materialized views shown in the previous examples illustrated two types of materialized views. In the first, the materialized view created a local copy of remote data, with no aggregations. In the second, an aggregation was performed. Both of the base queries could be extended to include joins of multiple tables. The key distinguishing factor is the use of aggregations in the second example.

A third type of materialized view is a nested materialized view—a materialized view whose definition is based on another materialized view.

The type of materialized view will impact your ability to perform *fast refreshes* of the materialized view. A fast refresh will refresh the materialized view with the rows that have changed in its base table(s) since its last refresh. If you cannot perform a fast refresh, you will have to use a *complete refresh*, which is usually more expensive in terms of time and resources. Fast refreshes require the use of materialized view logs (shown later in this chapter) on all tables referenced in the materialized view's base query.

If the materialized view contains an aggregate, a fast refresh will be possible if the **select** list contains all of the **group by** columns and there must be a **COUNT(*)** and **COUNT(*column_name*)** on any aggregated columns.

If the materialized view contains only joins but no aggregates, fast refresh is available after any **insert**, **update**, or **delete** to the base tables. The RowID columns from each table must be present in the **select** list for the materialized view's base query, and all of the referenced tables must have materialized view logs.

Because they send the incremental changes from the referenced tables to the materialized view, fast refreshes usually represent the fastest way to update the data in your materialized views.

RowID vs. Primary Key–Based Materialized Views

You can base materialized views on primary key values of the master table instead of basing them on the master table's RowIDs. You should decide between these options based on several factors:

- **System stability** If the master site is not stable, then you may need to perform database recoveries involving the master table. When you use Oracle's Data Pump Export and Import utilities to perform recoveries, the RowID values of rows will change. If the system requires frequent exports and imports, you should use primary key–based materialized views.

- **Size of materialized view log table** Oracle allows you to store the changes to master tables in separate tables called *materialized view logs* (described later in this chapter). If the primary key consists of many columns, the materialized view log table for a primary key–based materialized view may be considerably larger than the materialized view log for a comparable RowID-based materialized view.

- **Referential integrity** To use primary key–based materialized views, you must have defined a primary key on the master table. If you cannot define a primary key on the master table, then you must use RowID-based materialized views.

Using Prebuilt Tables

When you create a materialized view, you can specify **build immediate** to populate the materialized view immediately or **build deferred** to populate the materialized view later (via a complete refresh). If you need to carefully manage the transactions that initially populate the materialized view, you can create a table that has the same structure as the materialized view and populate it. When the table is fully loaded and properly indexed, use the **on prebuilt table** clause of the **create materialized view** command. The table and the materialized view must have the same name, and the table must have the same columns and datatypes as the materialized view (you can specify **with reduced precision** to accommodate differences in precision). The table can contain additional, unmanaged columns.

Once the table has been registered as a materialized view, you can maintain it via refreshes, and the optimizer can use it in query rewrite operations. For query rewrite to work properly on a prebuilt table, you must set the QUERY_REWRITE_INTEGRITY initialization parameter to STALE_TOLERATED or TRUSTED.

Indexing Materialized View Tables

When you create a materialized view, Oracle creates a local base table containing the data that satisfies the base query. Because that data has been replicated with a goal in mind (usually to improve performance in the database or the network), it is important to follow through to that goal after the materialized view has been created. Performance improvements for queries are usually gained through the use of indexes. Columns that are frequently used in the **where** clauses of queries should be indexed; if a set of columns is frequently accessed in queries, then a concatenated index on that set of columns can be created. (See Chapter 43 for more information on the Oracle optimizer.)

Oracle does not automatically create indexes for complex materialized views on columns other than the primary key. You need to create these indexes manually. To create indexes on your local base table, use the **create index** command (see the Alphabetical Reference). Do *not* create any constraints on the materialized view's local base table; Oracle will maintain the constraint-based relationships on the master tables.

Since no indexes are created on the columns that users are likely to query from the materialized view, you should create indexes on the materialized view's local base table.

Using Materialized Views to Alter Query Execution Paths

For a large database, a materialized view may offer several performance benefits. You can use materialized views to influence the optimizer to change the execution paths for queries. This feature, called *query rewrite,* enables the optimizer to use a materialized view in place of the table queried by the materialized view, even if the materialized view is not named in the query. For example, if you have a large SALES table, you may create a materialized view that sums the SALES data by region. If a user queries the SALES table for the sum of the SALES data for a region, Oracle can redirect that query to use your materialized view in place of the SALES table. As a result, you can reduce the number of accesses against your largest tables, improving the system performance. Further, since the data in the materialized view is already grouped by region, summarization does not have to be performed at the time the query is issued.

NOTE
*You must specify **enable query rewrite** in the materialized view definition for the view to be used as part of a query rewrite operation.*

To use the query rewrite capability effectively, you should create a dimension that defines the hierarchies within the table's data. To execute the **create dimension** command, you will need to have been granted the CREATE DIMENSION system privilege. You can create a dimension that supports the hierarchy between the COUNTRY and CONTINENT sample tables:

```
create dimension GEOGRAPHY
    level COUNTRY_ID      is COUNTRY.Country
    level CONTINENT_id    is CONTINENT.Continent
```

```
hierarchy COUNTRY_ROLLUP (
    COUNTRY_ID              child of
    CONTINENT_ID
join key COUNTRY.Continent references CONTINENT_id);
```

To enable a materialized view for query rewrite, all of the master tables for the materialized view must be in the materialized view's schema, and you must have the QUERY REWRITE system privilege. If the view and the tables are in separate schemas, you must have the GLOBAL QUERY REWRITE system privilege. In general, you should create materialized views in the same schema as the tables on which they are based; otherwise, you will need to manage the permissions and grants required to create and maintain the materialized view.

NOTE
You can enable or disable query rewrite at the SQL statement level via the REWRITE and NOREWRITE hints. When using the REWRITE hint, you can specify materialized views for the optimizer to consider.

NOTE
Query rewrite decisions are based on the costs of the different execution paths, so your statistics should be kept up to date.

For query rewrite to be possible, you must set the following initialization parameters:

- OPTIMIZER_MODE = ALL_ROWS or FIRST_ROWS

- QUERY_REWRITE_ENABLED = TRUE

- QUERY_REWRITE_INTEGRITY = STALE_TOLERATED, TRUSTED, or ENFORCED

By default, QUERY_REWRITE_INTEGRITY is set to ENFORCED; in this mode all constraints must be validated. The optimizer only uses fresh data from the materialized views and only uses those relationships that are based on ENABLED VALIDATED primary, unique, or foreign key constraints. In TRUSTED mode, the optimizer trusts that the data in the materialized view is fresh and the relationships declared in dimensions and constraints are correct. In STALE_TOLERATED mode, the optimizer uses materialized views that are valid but contain stale data, as well as those that contain fresh data.

If you set QUERY_REWRITE_ENABLED to FORCE, the optimizer will rewrite queries to use materialized views even when the estimated query cost of the original query is lower.

If query rewrite occurs, the explain plan for the query (see Chapter 43) will list the materialized view as one of the objects accessed, along with an operation listed as "MAT_VIEW REWRITE ACCESS". You can use the DBMS_MVIEW.EXPLAIN_REWRITE procedure to see if rewrite is possible for a query, and which materialized views would be involved. If the query cannot be rewritten, the procedure will document the reasons.

EXPLAIN_REWRITE takes three input parameters—the query, a materialized view name, and a statement identifier—and can store its output in a table. Oracle provides the **create table** command for the output table in a script named utlxrw.sql in the /rdbms/admin directory under the Oracle software home directory. The utlxrw.sql script creates a table named REWRITE_TABLE.

You can query the REWRITE_TABLE for the original cost, rewritten cost, and the optimizer's decision. The Message column will display the reasons for the optimizer's decision.

See the *Data Warehousing Guide* for further details and constraints related to query rewrite.

Using DBMS_ADVISOR

As of Oracle Database 10g, you can use the SQL Access Advisor to generate recommendations for the creation and indexing of materialized views. The SQL Access Advisor may recommend specific indexes (and types of indexes) to improve the performance of joins and other queries. The SQL Access Advisor may also generate recommendations for altering a materialized view so it supports query rewrite or fast refreshes. You can execute the SQL Access Advisor from within Oracle Enterprise Manager or via executions of the DBMS_ADVISOR package.

NOTE
For best results from the DBMS_ADVISOR package, you should gather statistics about all tables, indexes, and join columns prior to generating recommendations.

To use the SQL Access Advisor, either from Oracle Enterprise Manager or via DBMS_ADVISOR, you follow four steps:

1. Create a task

2. Define the workload

3. Generate recommendations

4. View and implement recommendations

You can create a task in one of two ways: by executing the DBMS_ADVISOR.CREATE_TASK procedure or by using the DBMS_ADVISOR.QUICK_TUNE procedure (as shown in the next section).

The workload consists of one or more SQL statements plus the statistics and attributes that relate to the statement. The workload may include all SQL statements for an application. The SQL Access Advisor ranks the entries in the workload according to statistics and business importance. The workload is created using the DBMS_ADVISOR.CREATE_SQLWKLD procedure. To associate a workload with a parent Advisor task, use the DBMS_ADVISOR.ADD_SQLWKLD_REF procedure. If a workload is not provided, the SQL Access Advisor can generate and use a hypothetical workload based on the dimensions defined in your schema.

Once a task exists and a workload is associated with the task, you can generate recommendations via the DBMS_ADVISOR.EXECUTE_TASK procedure. The SQL Access Advisor will consider the workload and the system statistics and will attempt to generate recommendations for tuning the application. You can see the recommendations by executing the DBMS_ADVISOR.GET_TASK_SCRIPT function or via data dictionary views. Each recommendation can be viewed via USER_ADVISOR_RECOMMENDATIONS (there are "ALL" and "DBA" versions of this view available, as well). To relate recommendations to a SQL statement, you will need to use the USER_ADVISOR_SQLA_WK_STMTS view and USER_ADVISOR_ACTIONS.

When you execute the GET_TASK_SCRIPT procedure, Oracle generates an executable SQL file that will contain the commands needed to create, alter, or drop the recommended objects. You should review the generated script prior to executing it, particularly noting the tablespace specifications. In the following section you will see how to use the QUICK_TUNE procedure to simplify the tuning advisor process for a single command.

Performing a Quick Tune

To tune a single SQL statement, use the QUICK_TUNE procedure of the DBMS_ADVISOR package. QUICK_TUNE has two input parameters—a task name and a SQL statement. Using QUICK_TUNE shields the user from the steps involved in creating workloads and tasks via DBMS_ADVISOR.

For example, the following procedure call evaluates a query

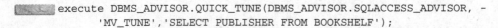

```
execute DBMS_ADVISOR.QUICK_TUNE(DBMS_ADVISOR.SQLACCESS_ADVISOR, -
    'MV_TUNE','SELECT PUBLISHER FROM BOOKSHELF');
```

NOTE
The user executing this command needs the ADVISOR system privilege.

The recommendation generated by QUICK_TUNE can be viewed via USER_ADVISOR_ACTIONS, but it is easier to read if you use the DBMS_ADVISOR procedures to generate a script file. The recommendation is that a materialized view be created to support the query. Since only one SQL statement was provided, this recommendation is given in isolation and does not consider any other aspects of the database or application.

You can use the CREATE_FILE procedure to automate the generation of a file containing the scripts needed to implement the recommendations. First, create a directory object to hold the file:

```
create directory scripts as 'e:\scripts';
grant read on directory scripts to public;
grant write on directory scripts to public;
```

Next, execute the CREATE_FILE procedure. It has three input variables: the script (generated via GET_TASK_SCRIPT, to which you pass the name of the task), the output directory, and the name of the file to be created:

```
execute DBMS_ADVISOR.CREATE_FILE(DBMS_ADVISOR.GET_TASK_SCRIPT('MV_TUNE'),-
'SCRIPTS','MV_TUNE.sql');
```

The MV_TUNE.sql file created by the CREATE_FILE procedure will contain commands similar to those shown in the following listing. Depending on the specific version of Oracle, the recommendations may differ.

```
Rem  Username:        PRACTICE
Rem  Task:            MV_TUNE
Rem

set feedback 1
set linesize 80
```

```
set trimspool on
set tab off
set pagesize 60

whenever sqlerror CONTINUE

CREATE MATERIALIZED VIEW "PRACTICE"."MV$$_021F0001"
    REFRESH FORCE WITH ROWID
    ENABLE QUERY REWRITE
    AS SELECT PRACTICE.BOOKSHELF.ROWID C1,
"PRACTICE"."BOOKSHELF"."PUBLISHER" M1
FROM PRACTICE.BOOKSHELF;

begin
  dbms_stats.gather_table_stats('"PRACTICE"',
'"MV$$_021F0001"',NULL,dbms_stats.auto_sample_size);
end;
/

whenever sqlerror EXIT SQL.SQLCODE

begin
dbms_advisor.mark_recommendation('MV_TUNE',1,'IMPLEMENTED');
end;
/
```

The MARK_RECOMMENDATION procedure allows you to annotate the recommendation so that it can be skipped during subsequent script generations. Valid actions for MARK_RECOMMENDATION include ACCEPT, IGNORE, IMPLEMENTED, and REJECT.

You can use the TUNE_MVIEW procedure of the DBMS_ADVISOR package to generate recommendations for the reconfiguration of your materialized views. TUNE_VIEW generates two sets of output results—for the creation of new materialized views, and for the removal of previously created materialized views. The end result should be a set of materialized views that can be fast refreshed, replacing materialized views that cannot be fast refreshed.

You can view the TUNE_MVIEW output via the USER_TUNE_MVIEW data dictionary view, or you can generate its scripts via the GET_TASK_SCRIPT and CREATE_FILE procedures shown in the previous listings.

Refreshing Materialized Views

The data in a materialized view may be replicated either once (when the view is created) or at intervals. The **create materialized view** command allows you to set the refresh interval, delegating the responsibility for scheduling and performing the refreshes to the database. In the following sections, you will see how to perform both manual and automatic refreshes.

What Kind of Refreshes Can Be Performed?

To see what kind of refresh and rewrite capabilities are possible for your materialized views, you can query the MV_CAPABILITIES_TABLE table. The capabilities may change between versions, so you should reevaluate your refresh capabilities following Oracle software upgrades. To create

this table, execute the utlxmv.sql script located in the /rdbms/admin directory under the Oracle software home directory.

The columns of MV_CAPABILITIES TABLE are

```
desc MV_CAPABILITIES_TABLE

Name                                     Null?    Type
---------------------------------------- -------- ------------------
STATEMENT_ID                                      VARCHAR2(30)
MVOWNER                                           VARCHAR2(30)
MVNAME                                            VARCHAR2(30)
CAPABILITY_NAME                                   VARCHAR2(30)
POSSIBLE                                          CHAR(1)
RELATED_TEXT                                      VARCHAR2(2000)
RELATED_NUM                                       NUMBER
MSGNO                                             NUMBER(38)
MSGTXT                                            VARCHAR2(2000)
SEQ                                               NUMBER
```

To populate the MV_CAPABILITIES_TABLE table, execute the DBMS_MVIEW.EXPLAIN_ MVIEW procedure, using the name of the materialized view as the input value as shown in the following listing:

```
execute DBMS_MVIEW.EXPLAIN_MVIEW('local_category_count');
```

The utlxmv.sql script provides guidance on the interpretation of the column values, as shown in the following listing:

```
CREATE TABLE MV_CAPABILITIES_TABLE
  (STATEMENT_ID      VARCHAR(30),   -- Client-supplied unique statement identifier
  MVOWNER            VARCHAR(30),   -- NULL for SELECT based EXPLAIN_MVIEW
  MVNAME             VARCHAR(30),   -- NULL for SELECT based EXPLAIN_MVIEW
  CAPABILITY_NAME    VARCHAR(30),   -- A descriptive name of the particular
                                    -- capability:
                                    -- REWRITE
                                    --    Can do at least full text match
                                    --    rewrite
                                    -- REWRITE_PARTIAL_TEXT_MATCH
                                    --    Can do at least full and partial
                                    --    text match rewrite
                                    -- REWRITE_GENERAL
                                    --    Can do all forms of rewrite
                                    -- REFRESH
                                    --    Can do at least complete refresh
                                    -- REFRESH_FROM_LOG_AFTER_INSERT
                                    --    Can do fast refresh from an mv log
                                    --    or change capture table at least
                                    --    when update operations are
```

```
                                   --    restricted to INSERT
                              -- REFRESH_FROM_LOG_AFTER_ANY
                              --    can do fast refresh from an mv log
                              --    or change capture table after any
                              --    combination of updates
                              -- PCT
                              --    Can do Enhanced Update Tracking on
                              --    the table named in the RELATED_NAME
                              --    column.  EUT is needed for fast
                              --    refresh after partitioned
                              --    maintenance operations on the table
                              --     named in the RELATED_NAME column
                              --     and to do non-stale tolerated
                              --     rewrite when the mv is partially
                              --     stale with respect to the table
                              --     named in the RELATED_NAME column.
                              --     EUT can also sometimes enable fast
                              --     refresh of updates to the table
                              --     named in the RELATED_NAME column
                              --     when fast refresh from an mv log
                              --     or change capture table is not
                              --     possible.
   POSSIBLE         CHARACTER(1),  -- T = capability is possible
                              -- F = capability is not possible
   RELATED_TEXT     VARCHAR(2000),-- Owner.table.column, alias name, etc.
                              -- related to this message.  The
                              -- specific meaning of this column
                              -- depends on the MSGNO column.  See
                              -- the documentation for
                               -- DBMS_MVIEW.EXPLAIN_MVIEW() for details
   RELATED_NUM      NUMBER,      -- When there is a numeric value
                              -- associated with a row, it goes here.
                              -- The specific meaning of this column
                              -- depends on the MSGNO column.  See
                              -- the documentation for
                              -- DBMS_MVIEW.EXPLAIN_MVIEW() for details
   MSGNO            INTEGER,     -- When available, QSM message #
                              -- explaining why not possible or more
                              -- details when enabled.
   MSGTXT           VARCHAR(2000),-- Text associated with MSGNO.
   SEQ              NUMBER);     -- Useful in ORDER BY clause when
                              -- selecting from this table.
```

Once the EXPLAIN_MVIEW procedure has been executed, you can query MV_CAPABILITIES_ TABLE to determine your options.

```
select Capability_Name, Msgtxt
  from MV_CAPABILITIES_TABLE
 where Msgtxt is not null;
```

For the LOCAL_BOOKSHELF materialized view, the query returns:

```
CAPABILITY_NAME
------------------------------
MSGTXT
----------------------------------------------------------------
PCT_TABLE
relation is not a partitioned table

REFRESH_FAST_AFTER_INSERT
the detail table does not have a materialized view log

REFRESH_FAST_AFTER_ONETAB_DML
see the reason why REFRESH_FAST_AFTER_INSERT is disabled

REFRESH_FAST_AFTER_ANY_DML
see the reason why REFRESH_FAST_AFTER_ONETAB_DML is disabled

REFRESH_FAST_PCT
PCT is not possible on any of the detail tables in the
materialized view

REWRITE_FULL_TEXT_MATCH
query rewrite is disabled on the materialized view

REWRITE_PARTIAL_TEXT_MATCH
query rewrite is disabled on the materialized view

REWRITE_GENERAL
query rewrite is disabled on the materialized view

REWRITE_PCT
general rewrite is not possible or PCT is not possible on
any of the detail tables

PCT_TABLE_REWRITE
relation is not a partitioned table

10 rows selected.
```

Since the **query rewrite** clause was not specified during the creation of the materialized view, the query rewrite capabilities are disabled for LOCAL_BOOKSHELF. Fast refresh capabilities are not supported because the base table does not have a materialized view log. If you change your materialized view or its base table, you should regenerate the data in MV_CAPABILITIES_TABLE to see the new capabilities.

As shown in the preceding listing, the LOCAL_BOOKSHELF materialized view cannot use a fast refresh because its base table does not have a materialized view log. There are other constraints that will limit your ability to use fast refreshes:

■ The materialized view must not contain references to nonrepeating expressions such as SysDate and RowNum.

- The materialized view must not contain references to RAW or LONG RAW datatypes.

- For materialized views based on joins, RowIDs from all tables in the **from** list must be part of the **select** list.

- If there are outer joins, all the joins must be connected by **and**s, the **where** clause must have no selections, and unique constraints must exist on the join columns of the inner join table.

- For materialized views based on aggregates, the materialized view logs must contain all columns from the referenced tables, must specify the **rowid** and **including new values** clauses, and must specify the **sequence** clause.

See the *Data Warehousing Guide* for additional restrictions related to fast refreshes of complex aggregates.

NOTE
*You can specify an **order by** clause in the **create materialized view** command. The **order by** clause will only affect the initial creation of the materialized view; it will not affect any refresh.*

Automatic Refreshes

Consider the LOCAL_BOOKSHELF materialized view described earlier. Its refresh schedule settings, defined by its **create materialized view** command, are shown in bold in the following listing:

```
create materialized view LOCAL_BOOKSHELF
  tablespace USERS
refresh force
start with SysDate next SysDate+7
with primary key
as
select * from BOOKSHELF@REMOTE_CONNECT;
```

The refresh schedule has three components. First, the type of refresh (**fast**, **complete**, **never**, or **force**) is specified. Fast refreshes use *materialized view logs* (described later in this chapter) to send changed rows from the master table to the materialized view. Complete refreshes delete all rows from the materialized view and repopulate it. The **force** option for refreshes tells Oracle to use a fast refresh if it is available; otherwise, a complete refresh will be used.

The **start with** clause tells the database when to perform the first replication from the master table to the local base table. It must evaluate to a future point in time. If you do not specify a **start with** time but specify a **next** value, Oracle will use the **next** clause to determine the start time. To maintain control over your replication schedule, you should specify a value for the **start with** clause.

The **next** clause tells Oracle how long to wait between refreshes. Since it will be applied to a different base time each time the materialized view is refreshed, the **next** clause specifies a date expression instead of a fixed date. In the preceding example, the expression is

```
next SysDate+7
```

Every time the materialized view is refreshed, the next refresh will be scheduled for seven days later. Although the refresh schedule in this example is fairly simple, you can use many of Oracle's date functions to customize a refresh schedule. For example, if you want to refresh every Monday at noon, regardless of the current date, you can set the **next** clause to

```
NEXT_DAY(TRUNC(SysDate),'MONDAY')+12/24
```

This example will find the next Monday after the current system date; the time portion of that date will be truncated, and 12 hours will be added to the date. (For information on date functions in Oracle, see Chapter 10.)

For automatic materialized view refreshes to occur, you must have at least one background snapshot refresh process running in your database. The refresh process periodically "wakes up" and checks whether any materialized views in the database need to be refreshed. The number of processes running in your database is determined by an initialization parameter called JOB_QUEUE_PROCESSES. That parameter must be set (in your initialization parameter file) to a value greater than 0; for most cases, a value of 1 should be sufficient. A coordinator process starts job queue processes as needed.

If the database is not running the job queue processes, you need to use manual refresh methods, described in the next section.

Manual Refreshes

In addition to the database's automatic refreshes, you can perform manual refreshes of materialized views. These override the normally scheduled refreshes; the new **start with** value will be based on the time of your manual refresh.

To refresh a single materialized view, use DBMS_MVIEW.REFRESH. Its two main parameters are the name of the materialized view to be refreshed and the method to use. For this method, you can specify 'c' for a complete refresh, 'f' for fast refresh, 'p' for a fast refresh using Partition Change Tracking (PCT), and '?' for force. For example:

```
execute DBMS_MVIEW.REFRESH('local_bookshelf','c');
```

NOTE
Partition Change Tracking (PCT) occurs when partition maintenance operations have been performed on the tables referenced by the materialized view. In PCT, Oracle performs the refresh by recomputing the rows in the materialized view affected by the changed partitions in the detail tables, avoiding the need for a complete refresh.

If you are refreshing multiple materialized views via a single execution of DBMS_MVIEW .REFRESH, list the names of all the materialized views in the first parameter, and their matching refresh methods in the second parameter, as shown here:

```
execute DBMS_MVIEW.REFRESH('local_bookshelf,local_category_count','?c');
```

In this example, the materialized view named LOCAL_BOOKSHELF will be refreshed via a force refresh, while the second materialized view will use a complete refresh.

You can use a separate procedure in the DBMS_MVIEW package to refresh all of the materialized views that are scheduled to be automatically refreshed. This procedure, named REFRESH_ALL, will refresh each materialized view separately. It does not accept any parameters. The following listing shows an example of its execution:

```
execute DBMS_MVIEW.REFRESH_ALL_MVIEWS;
```

Since the materialized views will be refreshed via REFRESH_ALL consecutively, they are not all refreshed at the same time. Therefore, a database or server failure during the execution of this procedure may cause the local materialized views to be out of sync with each other. If that happens, simply rerun this procedure after the database has been recovered. As an alternative, you can create refresh groups, as described in the next section.

Another procedure within DBMS_MVIEWS, REFRESH_ALL_MVIEWS, refreshes all materialized views that have the following properties:

- The materialized view has not been refreshed since the most recent change to a master table or master materialized view on which materialized view depends.

- The materialized view and all of the master tables or master materialized views on which materialized view depends are local.

- The materialized view is in the view DBA_MVIEWS.

If you create nested materialized views, you can use the DBMS_MVIEW.REFRESH_DEPENDENT procedure to ensure all materialized views within a tree are refreshed.

create materialized view log Syntax

A materialized view log is a table that records changes to the rows in the master table and the materialized views' replication history. The record of changed rows can then be used during refreshes to send out to the materialized views only those rows that have changed in the master table. Multiple materialized views based on the same table can use the same materialized view log.

The full syntax for the **create materialized view log** command is shown in the Alphabetical Reference. The following listing shows part of the syntax; as you may note from its syntax, it has all of the parameters normally associated with tables:

```
create materialized view log on [schema .] table
[{ physical_attributes_clause
 | tablespace tablespace
 | { logging | nologging }
 | { cache | nocache }
 }
 [ physical_attributes_clause
 | tablespace tablespace
 | { logging | nologging }
 | { cache | nocache }
 ]...
]
[parallel_clause] [partitioning_clauses]
```

```
[with
 { object id | primary key | rowid | sequence | ( column [, column]... ) }
 [, { object id | primary key | rowid | sequence | ( column [, column]... ) }]...
]
[{ including | excluding } new values];
```

The **create materialized view log** command is executed in the master table's database, usually by the owner of the master table. Materialized view logs should not be created for tables that are only involved in complex materialized views (since they wouldn't be used). No name is specified for the materialized view log.

A materialized view log for the BOOKSHELF table can be created via the following command, executed from within the account that owns the table:

```
create materialized view log on BOOKSHELF
with sequence,ROWID
(Title, Publisher, CategoryName, Rating)
including new values;
```

The **with sequence** clause is needed to support the replication of mixed-DML operations against multiple base tables.

Because materialized view logs may grow unpredictably over time in production databases, you should consider storing their associated objects in tablespaces that are dedicated to materialized view logs.

Required System Privileges

To create the materialized view log, you must have CREATE TABLE and CREATE TRIGGER system privileges. If you are creating the materialized view log from a user account that does not own the master table, you need to have CREATE ANY TABLE, COMMENT ANY TABLE, and CREATE ANY TRIGGER system privileges as well as SELECT privilege on the materialized view master table.

Altering Materialized Views and Logs

You may alter the storage parameters, refresh option, and refresh schedule for existing materialized views. If you are unsure of the current settings for a snapshot, check the USER_MVIEWS data dictionary view.

The syntax for the **alter materialized view** command is shown in the Alphabetical Reference. The command in the following listing alters the refresh option used by the LOCAL_BOOKSHELF materialized view:

```
alter materialized view LOCAL_BOOKSHELF
refresh complete;
```

All future refreshes of LOCAL_BOOKSHELF will refresh the entire local base table.

To alter a materialized view, you must either own the materialized view or have the ALTER ANY MATERIALIZED VIEW system privilege.

To alter a materialized view log, you must own the table, have ALTER privilege for the table, or have ALTER ANY TABLE system privilege.

If you created the materialized view log without the RowID or the **sequence** clauses, you can add them after the fact via the **alter materialized view** command.

Dropping Materialized Views and Logs

To drop a materialized view, you must have the system privileges required to drop both the materialized view and all of its related objects. You need to have DROP MATERIALIZED VIEW if the object is in your schema, or DROP ANY MATERIALIZED VIEW system privilege if the materialized view is not in your schema.

The following command drops the LOCAL_CATEGORY_COUNT materialized view created earlier in this chapter:

```
drop materialized view LOCAL_CATEGORY_COUNT;
```

NOTE
When you drop a materialized view that was created on a prebuilt table, the table still exists but the materialized view is dropped.

Materialized view logs can be dropped via the **drop materialized view log** command. Once the materialized view log is dropped from a master table, no fast refreshes can be performed for simple materialized views based on that table. A materialized view log should be dropped when no simple materialized views are based on the master table. The following command drops the materialized view log that was created on the BOOKSHELF table earlier in this chapter:

```
drop materialized view log on BOOKSHELF;
```

To drop a materialized view log, you must have the ability to drop both the materialized view log and its related objects. If you own the materialized view log, you must have the DROP TABLE and DROP TRIGGER system privileges. If you do not own the materialized view log, you need the DROP ANY TABLE and DROP ANY TRIGGER system privileges to execute this command.

CHAPTER
25

Using Oracle Text
for Text Searches

s the amount of text in your database increases, so does the complexity of the text queries performed against the database. Instead of just performing string matches, you will need new text-search features—such as weighting the terms in a search of multiple terms, or ranking the results of a text search.

You can use Oracle Text to perform text-based searches. Text-searching capabilities include wildcard searching, "fuzzy matches," relevance ranking, proximity searching, term weighting, and word expansions. In this chapter, you'll see how to configure and use Oracle Text.

Adding Text to the Database

You can add text to a database either by physically storing the text in a table or by storing pointers to external files in the database. That is, for the books on the bookshelf, you can store reviews either in the database or in external files. If you store the reviews in external files, then you store the filenames in the database.

To store the reviews in the database, create the BOOK_REVIEW tables. In this chapter, you will see examples of two types of indexes: CONTEXT and CTXCAT. To support these examples, two separate tables will be created: BOOK_REVIEW_CONTEXT and BOOK_REVIEW_CTXCAT, both loaded with the same data.

```
create table BOOK_REVIEW_CONTEXT
(Title       VARCHAR2(100) primary key,
Reviewer     VARCHAR2(25),
Review_Date  DATE,
Review_Text  VARCHAR2(4000));

insert into BOOK_REVIEW_CONTEXT values
('MY LEDGER', 'EMILY TALBOT', '01-MAY-02',
'A fascinating look into the transactions and finances of G. B. Talbot
and Dora Talbot as they managed a property in New Hampshire around 1900.
The stories come through the purchases - for medicine, doctor visits and
gravesites - for workers during harvests - for gifts at the general store
at Christmas.  A great read. ');

create table BOOK_REVIEW_CTXCAT
(Title       VARCHAR2(100) primary key,
Reviewer     VARCHAR2(25),
Review_Date  DATE,
Review_Text  VARCHAR2(4000));

insert into BOOK_REVIEW_CTXCAT values
('MY LEDGER', 'EMILY TALBOT', '01-MAY-02',
'A fascinating look into the transactions and finances of G. B. Talbot
and Dora Talbot as they managed a property in New Hampshire around 1900.
The stories come through the purchases - for medicine, doctor visits and
gravesites - for workers during harvests - for gifts at the general store
at Christmas.  A great read. ');
```

The Review_Text column of the BOOK_REVIEW tables is defined as having a VARCHAR2(4000) datatype. For longer values, consider the use of CLOB datatypes. See Chapter 35 for details on CLOB datatypes.

You can select the review text from the database:

```
set linesize 74

select Review_Text
  from BOOK_REVIEW_CONTEXT
 where Title = 'MY LEDGER';

REVIEW_TEXT
----------------------------------------------------------------------
A fascinating look into the transactions and finances of G. B. Talbot
and Dora Talbot as they managed a property in New Hampshire around 1900.
The stories come through the purchases - for medicine, doctor visits and
gravesites - for workers during harvests - for gifts at the general store
at Christmas.  A great read.
```

Text Queries and Text Indexes

Querying text is different from querying data because words have shades of meaning, relationships to other words, and opposites. You may want to search for words that are near each other, or words that are related to others. These queries would be extremely difficult if all you had available were the standard relational operators. By extending SQL to include text indexes, Oracle Text permits you to ask very complex questions about the text.

To use Oracle Text, you need to create a text index on the column in which the text is stored. *Text index* is a slightly confusing term—it is actually a collection of tables and indexes that store information about the text stored in the column.

In this chapter, you will see examples of both CONTEXT and CTXCAT text indexes. You can use a third type of type index, CTXRULE, to build a content-based document classification application. See the *Oracle Text Application Developer's Guide* for details on the use of CTXRULE indexes.

NOTE
Before creating a text index on a table, you must create a primary key for the table if one does not already exist.

You can create a text index via a special version of the **create index** command. For a CONTEXT index, specify the Ctxsys.Context index type in the **indextype** clause, as shown in the following listing:

```
create index Review_Context_Index
     on BOOK_REVIEW_CONTEXT(Review_Text)
indextype is ctxsys.context;
```

When the text index is created, Oracle creates a number of indexes and tables in your schema to support your text queries. You can rebuild your text index via the **alter index** command, just as you would for any other index.

You can use a CTXCAT index type in place of the CONTEXT index type:

```
create index Review_CtxCat_Index
    on BOOK_REVIEW_CTXCAT(Review_Text)
indextype is ctxsys.ctxcat;
```

The CTXCAT index type supports the transactional synchronization of data between the base table (BOOK_REVIEW_CTXCAT) and its text index. With CONTEXT indexes, you need to manually tell Oracle to update the values in the text index after data changes in the base table. CTXCAT index types do not generate "score" values during text queries (as CONTEXT indexes do), but the query syntax is largely the same for the two types. The following sections illustrate the types of text queries you can perform via Oracle Text.

Text Queries

Once a text index is created on the Review_Text column of the BOOK_REVIEW_CONTEXT table, text-searching capabilities increase dramatically. You can now look for any book review that contains the word 'property':

```
select Title
   from BOOK_REVIEW_CONTEXT
 where CONTAINS(Review_Text, 'property') >0;
```

NOTE
The matching row will be returned regardless of the case of the word 'property' within the text-indexed column.

The **CONTAINS** function takes two parameters—the column name and the search string—and checks the text index for the Review_Text column. If the word "property" is found in the Review_Text column's text index, then a *score* greater than 0 is returned by the database, and the matching Title value is returned. The score is an evaluation of how well the record being returned matches the criteria specified in the **CONTAINS** function.

If you create a CTXCAT index, use the **CATSEARCH** function in place of **CONTAINS**. **CATSEARCH** takes three parameters: the column name, the search string, and the name of the index set. Index sets are described in the "Index Sets" section, later in this chapter. For this example, there is no index set, so that parameter is set to **NULL**:

```
select Title
   from BOOK_REVIEW_CTXCAT
 where CATSEARCH(Review_Text, 'property', NULL) >0;
```

CATSEARCH does not compute a score but uses the >0 syntax, simplifying your migration from CONTEXT indexes to CTXCAT indexes. CTXCAT indexes support the use of index sets, described later in this chapter.

When a function such as **CONTAINS** or **CATSEARCH** is used in a query, the text portion of the query is processed by Oracle Text. The remainder of the query is processed just like a regular query within the database. The results of the text query processing and the regular query processing are merged to return a single set of records to the user.

Available Text Query Expressions

Oracle Text would be rather limited if it allowed you to search only for exact matches of words. Oracle Text offers a broad array of text-searching capabilities you can use to customize your queries. Most of the text-searching capabilities are enabled via the **CONTAINS** and **CATSEARCH** functions, which can appear only in the **where** clause of a **select** statement or subquery, never in the **where** clauses of **insert**s, **update**s, or **delete**s.

The operators within **CONTAINS** allow you to perform the following text searches:

- Exact matches of a word or phrase
- Exact matches of multiple words, using Boolean logic to combine searches
- Searches based on how close words are to each other in the text
- Searches for words that share the same word "stem"
- "Fuzzy" matches of words
- Searches for words that sound like other words

CATSEARCH supports the exact-match search functions as well as the creation of index sets, described later in this chapter. In the following sections, you will see examples of these types of text searches, along with information about the operators you can use to customize text searches.

Searching for an Exact Match of a Word

The following query of the BOOK_REVIEW tables returns the title for all reviews including the word "property":

```
REM  CONTAINS method for CONTEXT indexes:
select Title
  from BOOK_REVIEW_CONTEXT
 where CONTAINS(Review_Text, 'property')>0;

REM  CATSEARCH method for CTXCAT indexes:
select Title
  from BOOK_REVIEW_CTXCAT
 where CATSEARCH(Review_Text, 'property', NULL)>0;
```

Within the function calls, the > sign is called a *threshold* operator. The preceding text search can be translated to the following:

```
select all the Title column values
from the BOOK_REVIEW_CONTEXT table
where the score for the text search of the Review_Text column
```

```
for an exact match of the word 'property'
exceeds a threshold value of 0.
```

The threshold analysis compares the score—the internal score Oracle calculated when the text search was performed—to the specified threshold value. Score values for individual searches range from 0 to 10 for each occurrence of the search string within the text. For CONTEXT indexes, you can display the score as part of your query.

To show the text-search score, use the **SCORE** function, which has a single parameter—a label you assign to the score within the text search:

```
column Title format a30

select Title, SCORE(10)
  from BOOK_REVIEW_CONTEXT
 where CONTAINS(Review_Text, 'property', 10)>0;

TITLE                             SCORE(10)
------------------------------- ----------
MY LEDGER                                 3
```

In this listing, the **CONTAINS** function's parameters are modified to include a label (10) for the text-search operation performed. The **SCORE** function will display the score of the text search associated with that label. The score is an internal calculation based on how well the indexed text matches the search criteria.

For CONTEXT indexes, you can use the **SCORE** function in the **select** list (as shown in the preceding query) or in a **group by** clause or an **order by** clause.

Searching for an Exact Match of Multiple Words

What if you want to search the text for multiple words? You can use Boolean logic (ANDs and ORs) to combine the results of multiple text searches in a single query. You can also search for multiple terms within the same function calls and let Oracle resolve the search results.

For example, if you wanted to search for reviews that have the words "property" and "harvests" in the review text, you could enter the following query:

```
REM  CONTAINS method for CONTEXT indexes:
select Title
  from BOOK_REVIEW_CONTEXT
 where CONTAINS(Review_Text, 'property AND harvests')>0;

REM  CATSEARCH method for CTXCAT indexes:
select Title
  from BOOK_REVIEW_CTXCAT
 where CATSEARCH(Review_Text, 'property AND harvests', NULL)>0;
```

NOTE
This search does not look for the phrase "property and harvests" but rather for two individual words anywhere in the searched text. You will see the syntax for phrase searches in the next section.

Instead of using AND in the CONTEXT index query, you could have used an ampersand (&). Before using this method in SQL*Plus, you should **set define off** so the & character will not be seen as part of a variable name:

```
set define off

REM  CONTAINS method for CONTEXT indexes:
select Title
  from BOOK_REVIEW_CONTEXT
 where CONTAINS(Review_Text, 'property & harvests')>0;
```

For the CTXCAT index, the word AND can be left out entirely:

```
REM  CATSEARCH method for CTXCAT indexes:
select Title
  from BOOK_REVIEW_CTXCAT
 where CATSEARCH(Review_Text, 'property harvests', NULL)>0;
```

Using either the & character or the word AND denotes an AND operation—so the **CONTAINS** function will return a row only if the review text includes *both* the words "property" and "harvests." Each search must pass the threshold criteria defined for the search scores. If you want to search for more than two terms, just add them to the **CONTAINS** or **CATSEARCH** clause, as shown in the following listing:

```
REM  CONTAINS method for CONTEXT indexes:
select Title
  from BOOK_REVIEW_CONTEXT
 where CONTAINS(Review_Text, 'property AND harvests AND workers')>0;

REM  CATSEARCH method for CTXCAT indexes:
select Title
  from BOOK_REVIEW_CTXCAT
 where CATSEARCH(Review_Text, 'property harvests workers', NULL)>0;
```

The query in this listing returns a row only if its search scores for "property," "harvests," and "workers" are all greater than 0.

In addition to AND, you can use the OR operator—in which case a record is returned if either of the search conditions meets the defined threshold. The symbol for OR in Oracle Text is a vertical line (|), so the following two queries are processed identically:

```
REM  CONTAINS method for CONTEXT indexes:
select Title
  from BOOK_REVIEW_CONTEXT
 where CONTAINS(Review_Text, 'property OR harvests')>0;

select Title
  from BOOK_REVIEW_CONTEXT
 where CONTAINS(Review_Text, 'property | harvests')>0;
```

When these queries are executed, a record is returned if either of the two separate searches (for "property" and "harvests") returns a score greater than 0.

```
REM   CATSEARCH method for CTXCAT indexes:

select Title
   from BOOK_REVIEW_CTXCAT
 where CATSEARCH(Review_Text, 'property OR harvests', NULL)>0;

select Title
   from BOOK_REVIEW_CTXCAT
 where CATSEARCH(Review_Text, 'property | harvests', NULL)>0;
```

The ACCUM (accumulate) operator provides another method for combining searches. ACCUM adds together the scores of the individual searches and compares the accumulated score to the threshold value. The symbol for ACCUM is a comma (,). Therefore, the two queries shown in the following listing are equivalent:

```
REM   CONTAINS method for CONTEXT indexes:
select Title
   from BOOK_REVIEW_CONTEXT
 where CONTAINS(Review_Text, 'property ACCUM harvests')>0;

select Title
   from BOOK_REVIEW_CONTEXT
 where CONTAINS(Review_Text, 'property , harvests')>0;
```

The ACCUM syntax is supported in **CATSEARCH** function calls but should not be used because **CATSEARCH** does not calculate a score to compare to the threshold value.

You can also use Oracle Text to subtract the scores from multiple searches before comparing the result to the threshold score. The MINUS operator in **CONTAINS** subtracts the score of the second term's search from the score of the first term's search. The queries in the following listing will determine the search score for "property" and subtract from it the search score for "house" and then compare the difference to the threshold score.

In this example, the second search term ("house") is not found in the indexed text. If the second term is in the text (for example, "harvests"), then no rows will be returned.

```
REM   CONTAINS method for CONTEXT indexes:
select Title
   from BOOK_REVIEW_CONTEXT
 where CONTAINS(Review_Text, 'property MINUS house')>0;

select Title
   from BOOK_REVIEW_CONTEXT
 where CONTAINS(Review_Text, 'property - house')>0;
```

You can use the symbol – in place of the MINUS operator, as shown in the preceding listing.

For CONTEXT indexes, the – operator reduces the score when comparing the overall search score to the threshold value, but it does not eliminate the row from consideration. To eliminate rows based on search terms in CONTEXT indexes, use the ~ character as the NOT operator.

For CTXCAT indexes, the symbol – has a different meaning than it does with CONTEXT indexes. For CTXCAT indexes, – tells Oracle Text not to return the row if the search term after the – is found (like ~ in CONTEXT indexes). If the second term is found, **CATSEARCH** will not return the row. For **CATSEARCH** queries, you can replace – with the word NOT.

```
REM  CATSEARCH method for CTXCAT indexes:

select Title
  from BOOK_REVIEW_CTXCAT
 where CATSEARCH(Review_Text, 'property - harvests', NULL)>0;

select Title
  from BOOK_REVIEW_CTXCAT
 where CATSEARCH(Review_Text, 'property NOT harvests', NULL)>0;
```

You can use parentheses to clarify the logic within your search criteria. If your search uses both ANDs and ORs, you should use parentheses to clarify the way in which the rows are processed. For example, the following query returns a row if the searched text contains either the word "house" or both the words "workers" and "harvests":

```
REM  CONTAINS method for CONTEXT indexes:
select Title
  from BOOK_REVIEW_CONTEXT
 where CONTAINS(Review_Text, 'house OR (workers AND harvests)')>0;
```

CATSEARCH does not require the word AND between "workers" and "harvests":

```
REM  CATSEARCH method for CTXCAT indexes:
select Title
  from BOOK_REVIEW_CTXCAT
 where CATSEARCH(Review_Text, 'house | (workers harvests)', NULL)>0;
```

If you change the location of the parentheses, you change the logic of the text search. The following query returns a row if the searched text contains either "house" or "workers" and also contains the word "harvests":

```
select Title
  from BOOK_REVIEW_CONTEXT
 where CONTAINS(Review_Text, '(house OR workers) AND harvests')>0;
```

When evaluating the scores of multiple searches against CONTEXT indexes, you can tell Oracle Text to weigh the scores of some searches more heavily than others. For example, if you want the search score for "harvests" to be doubled when compared to the threshold score, you can use the asterisk symbol (*) to indicate the factor by which the search score should be multiplied.

The following query will double the search score for "harvests" when it is evaluated in an OR condition:

```
select Title, SCORE(10)
  from BOOK_REVIEW_CONTEXT
 where CONTAINS(Review_Text, 'harvests*2 OR property*1',10)>5;
```

Through the use of the AND, OR, ACCUM, and MINUS operators, you should be able to search for any combination of word matches.

NOTE
The EQUIV operator treats two search terms as the same during search scoring. EQUIV (which can be replaced with =) may be useful in combination with the operators that compare search scores.

In the next section, you will see how to search for phrases.

Searching for an Exact Match of a Phrase

When searching for an exact match for a phrase, you specify the whole phrase as part of the search string. If your phrase includes a reserved word (such as "and," "or," or "minus"), you need to use the escape characters shown in this section so that the search is executed properly. If the search phrase includes a reserved word within Oracle Text, then you must use curly braces ({}) to enclose the text.

The following query searches for any title whose review entry includes the phrase "doctor visits."

```
REM  CONTAINS method for CONTEXT indexes:
select Title
  from BOOK_REVIEW_CONTEXT
 where CONTAINS(Review_Text, 'doctor visits')>0;

REM  CATSEARCH method for CTXCAT indexes:
select Title
  from BOOK_REVIEW_CTXCAT
 where CATSEARCH(Review_Text, 'doctor visits',NULL)>0;
```

The following query searches for the phrase "transactions and finances." The word "and" is enclosed in braces.

```
REM  CONTAINS method for CONTEXT indexes:
select Title
  from BOOK_REVIEW_CONTEXT
 where CONTAINS(Review_Text, 'transactions {and} finances')>0;

REM  CATSEARCH method for CTXCAT indexes:
select Title
  from BOOK_REVIEW_CTXCAT
 where CATSEARCH(Review_Text, 'transactions {and} finances',NULL)>0;
```

The query of 'transactions {and} finances' is different from a query of 'transactions and finances'. The query of 'transactions {and} finances' returns a record only if the *phrase* "transactions and finances" exists in the searched text. The query of 'transactions and finances' returns a record if the search score for the *word* "transactions" and the search score for the *word* "finances" are both above the threshold score (or in a CTXCAT index, if both are found).

You can enclose the entire phrase within curly braces, in which case any reserved words within the phrase will be treated as part of the search criteria, as shown in the following example:

```
REM  CONTAINS method for CONTEXT indexes:
select Title
  from BOOK_REVIEW_CONTEXT
 where CONTAINS(Review_Text, '{transactions and finances}')>0;
```

Searches for Words That Are Near Each Other

You can use the *proximity search* capability to perform a text search based on how close terms are to each other within the searched document. A proximity search returns a high score for words that are next to each other, and it returns a low score for words that are far apart. If the words are next to each other, the proximity search returns a score of 100.

To use proximity searching against CONTEXT indexes, use the keyword NEAR, as shown in the following example:

```
REM  CONTAINS method for CONTEXT indexes:
select Title
  from BOOK_REVIEW_CONTEXT
 where CONTAINS(Review_Text, 'workers NEAR harvests')>0;
```

You can replace the NEAR operator with its equivalent symbol, the semicolon (;). The revised query is shown in the following listing:

```
REM  CONTAINS method for CONTEXT indexes:
select Title
  from BOOK_REVIEW_CONTEXT
 where CONTAINS(Review_Text, 'workers ; harvests')>0;
```

In CONTEXT index queries, you can specify the maximum number of words between the search terms. For example, for words within ten words of each other, you may use a search string of 'NEAR((workers, harvests),10)'.

You can use the phrase- and word-searching methods shown in this chapter to search for exact matches of words and phrases, as well as to perform proximity searches of exact words and phrases. Thus far, all the searches have used exact matches of the search terms as the basis for the search. In the next four sections, you will see how to expand the search terms via four methods: wildcards, word stems, fuzzy matches, and SOUNDEX searches.

Using Wildcards During Searches

In the previous examples in this chapter, the queries selected text values that exactly match the criteria specified. For example, the search terms included "workers" but not "worker." You can use wildcards to expand the list of valid search terms used during your query.

Just as in regular text-string wildcard processing, two wildcards are available:

Character	Description
%	Percent sign; multiple-character wildcard
_	Underscore; single-character wildcard

The following query will search for all text matches for all words that start with the characters "worker":

```
REM  CONTAINS method for CONTEXT indexes:
select Title
  from BOOK_REVIEW_CONTEXT
 where CONTAINS(Review_Text, 'worker%')>0;
```

The following query limits the expansion of the text string to exactly three characters. In place of the % sign in the preceding query, three underscores (_ _ _) are used. Because the underscore is a single-character wildcard, the text string cannot expand beyond three characters during the search. For example, the word "workers" could be returned by the text search, but the word "workplace" would be too long to be returned.

```
REM  CONTAINS method for CONTEXT indexes:
select Title
  from BOOK_REVIEW_CONTEXT
 where CONTAINS(Review_Text, 'work___')>0;
```

You should use wildcards when you are certain of some of the characters within the search string. If you are uncertain of the search string, you should use one of the methods described in the following sections—word stems, fuzzy matches, or SOUNDEX matches.

Searching for Words That Share the Same Stem

Rather than using wildcards, you can use *stem-expansion* capabilities to expand the list of text strings. Given the "stem" of a word, Oracle will expand the list of words to search for to include all words having the same stem. Sample expansions are shown here:

Stem	Sample Expansions
play	plays, played, playing, playful
works	working, work, worked, workman, workplace
have	had, has, haven't, hasn't
story	stories

Because "works" and "work" have the same stem, a stem-expansion search using the word "works" will return text containing the word "work."

To use stem expansion within a query, you need to use the dollar sign ($) symbol. Within the search string, the $ should immediately precede the word to be expanded.

The following listing shows the result of a query against BOOK_REVIEW_CONTEXT for all reviews that contain a word sharing the stem of the word "manage":

```
REM  CONTAINS method for CONTEXT indexes:
select Title
  from BOOK_REVIEW_CONTEXT
 where CONTAINS(Review_Text, '$manage')>0;
```

When this query is executed, Oracle expands the word "$manage" to include all words with the same stem and then performs the search. If a review contains one of the words with a stem of "manage," the record will be returned to the user.

The expansion of terms via word stems simplifies the querying process for the user. You no longer need to know what form of a verb or noun was used when the text was entered—all forms are used as the basis for the search. You do not need to specify specific text strings, as you do when querying for exact matches or using wildcards. Instead, you specify a word, and Oracle Text dynamically determines all the words that should be searched for, based on the word you specified.

Searching for Fuzzy Matches

A *fuzzy match* expands the specified search term to include words that are spelled similarly but that do not necessarily have the same word stem. Fuzzy matches are most helpful when the text contains misspellings. The misspellings can be either in the searched text or in the search string specified by the user during the query.

For example, "MY LEDGER" will not be returned by this query because its review does not contain the word "hardest":

```
REM  CONTAINS method for CONTEXT indexes:
select Title
   from BOOK_REVIEW_CONTEXT
 where CONTAINS(Review_Text, 'hardest')>0;
```

It does, however, contain the word "harvest." A fuzzy match will return reviews containing the word "harvest," even though "harvest" has a different word stem than the word used as the search term.

To use a fuzzy match, precede the search term with a question mark, with no space between the question mark and the beginning of the search term. The following example illustrates the use of the fuzzy match capability:

```
REM  CONTAINS method for CONTEXT indexes:
select Title
   from BOOK_REVIEW_CONTEXT
 where CONTAINS(Review_Text, '?hardest')>0;
```

Searches for Words That Sound Like Other Words

Stem-expansion searches expand a search term to multiple terms based on the stem of the word. Fuzzy matches expand a search term based on similar words in the text index. A third kind of search-term expansion, SOUNDEX, expands search terms based on how the word sounds. The SOUNDEX expansion method uses the same text-matching logic available via the **SOUNDEX** function in SQL.

To use the SOUNDEX option, you must precede the search term with an exclamation mark (!). During the search, Oracle evaluates the SOUNDEX values of the terms in the text index and searches for all words that have the same SOUNDEX value.

As shown in the following query, you can search for all reviews that include the word "great," using a SOUNDEX match technique:

```
REM  CONTAINS method for CONTEXT indexes:
select Title
```

```
   from BOOK_REVIEW_CONTEXT
 where CONTAINS(Review_Text, '!grate')>0;
```

The "MY LEDGER" review is returned because the words "grate" and "great" have the same SOUNDEX value.

You can also *nest* operators, allowing you to perform stem expansions on the terms returned by a fuzzy match. In the following example, a fuzzy match is performed on the word "stir," and the terms returned from the fuzzy match are expanded using stem expansion:

```
REM  CONTAINS method for CONTEXT indexes:
select Title
   from BOOK_REVIEW_CONTEXT
 where CONTAINS(Review_Text, '$?stir')>0;
```

The major search options for **CONTAINS** are summarized in Table 25-1. For a list of all supported syntax (including thesaurus use, synonym expansion, and XML support), see the

Operator	Description
OR	Returns a record if either search term has a score that exceeds the threshold.
\|	Same as OR.
AND	Returns a record if both search terms have a score that exceeds the threshold.
&	Same as AND.
ACCUM	Returns a record if the sum of the search terms' scores exceeds the threshold.
,	Same as ACCUM.
MINUS	Returns a record if the score of the first search minus the score of the second search exceeds the threshold.
–	Same as MINUS.
*	Assigns different weights to the score of the searches.
NEAR	The score will be based on how near the search terms are to each other in the searched text.
;	Same as NEAR.
NOT	Excludes the row if the term after the NOT is found.
~	Same as NOT.

TABLE 25-1. *Major CONTAINS Options*

Operator	Description
EQUIV	Treats two terms (term1 equiv term2) as the same during search scoring.
=	Same as EQUIV.
{}	Encloses reserved words such as AND if they are part of the search term.
%	Multiple-character wildcard.
_	Single-character wildcard.
$	Performs stem expansion of the search term prior to performing the search.
?	Performs a fuzzy match of the search term prior to performing the search.
!	Performs a SOUNDEX search.
()	Specifies the order in which search criteria are evaluated.

TABLE 25-1. *Major CONTAINS Options* (continued)

Oracle Text Reference guide. The search options for **CATSEARCH** are summarized in Table 25-2. Table 25-2 does not list the deprecated **CONTAINS** features, such as ACCUM, that are not documented as supported features for **CATSEARCH**.

Operator	Description
\|	Returns a record if either search term is found.
AND	Returns a record if both search terms are found. This is the default action, so (a b) is treated as (a AND b).
-	If there are spaces around the hyphen, CATSEARCH returns rows that contain the term preceding the "-" and do not contain the term following it. A hyphen with no space is treated as a regular character.
NOT	Same as -.
" "	Encloses phrases.
()	Specifies the order in which search criteria are evaluated.
*	Wildcard character to match multiple characters. Can be at the end of the term or in the middle of characters.

TABLE 25-2. *CATSEARCH Options*

Using the ABOUT Operator

In Oracle Text, you can search on themes of documents. Thematic searching is integrated with text-term searching. You can use the ABOUT operator to search for terms that have to do with the theme of the document rather than the specific terms within the document. Here's an example:

```
REM  CONTAINS method for CONTEXT indexes:
select Title
  from BOOK_REVIEW_CONTEXT
 where CONTAINS(Review_Text, 'ABOUT(medicine)')>0;

REM  CATSEARCH method for CTXCAT indexes:
select Title
  from BOOK_REVIEW_CTXCAT
 where CATSEARCH(Review_Text, 'ABOUT(medicine)', NULL)>0;
```

Index Synchronization

By default, when using CONTEXT indexes, you will have to manage the text index contents; the text indexes will not be updated when the base table is updated. As soon as a Review_Text value is updated, its text index is out of sync with the base table. To sync the index, execute the SYNC_INDEX procedure of the CTX_DDL package, as shown in the following listing.

NOTE
Grant the PRACTICE user EXECUTE privilege on the CTX_DDL package to support these maintenance activities.

```
execute CTX_DDL.SYNC_INDEX('REVIEW_CONTEXT_INDEX');
```

As of Oracle Database 10g, CONTEXT indexes can be maintained automatically, at commit time, or at specified intervals. As part of the **create index** command for a CONTEXT index, you can use the **sync** clause:

```
[[METADATA] SYNC (MANUAL | EVERY "interval" | ON COMMIT)]
```

Here's an example:

```
drop index Review_Context_Index;

create index Review_Context_Index
    on BOOK_REVIEW_CONTEXT(Review_Text)
indextype is ctxsys.context
parameters ('sync (on commit)');
```

Index Sets

Historically, problems with queries of text indexes have occurred when other criteria are used alongside text searches as part of the **where** clause. For example, are **where** clauses on nontext

columns applied before or after the text searches are completed, and how are the results properly ordered? To improve the "mixed" query capability, you can use index sets. The indexes within the index set may be on structured relational columns or on text columns.

To create an index set, use the CTX_DDL package to create the index set and add indexes to it. When you create a text index, you can then specify the index set it belongs to. To execute this example, you should first drop the REVIEW_CTXCAT_INDEX text index (created earlier in this chapter) on the BOOK_REVIEW_CTXCAT table:

```
drop index REVIEW_CTXCAT_INDEX;
```

To create an index set named Reviews, use the CREATE_INDEX_SET procedure:

```
execute CTX_DDL.CREATE_INDEX_SET('Reviews');
```

You can now add indexes to the index set via the ADD_INDEX procedure. First, add a standard, nontext index:

```
execute CTX_DDL.ADD_INDEX('Reviews', 'Reviewer');
execute CTX_DDL.ADD_INDEX('Reviews', 'Review_Date');
```

Now create a CTXCAT text index. Specify Ctxsys.Ctxcat as the index type, and list the index set in the **parameters** clause:

```
create index REVIEW_CTXCAT_INDEX
    on BOOK_REVIEW_CTXCAT(Review_Text)
  indextype is CTXSYS.CTXCAT
parameters ('index set Reviews');
```

You can now order your results by the result of the combined index set search:

```
select * from BOOK_REVIEW_CTXCAT
  where CATSEARCH(Review_Text, 'great',
               'Reviewer=''EMILY TALBOT''
                order by Review_Date desc')>0;
```

To resolve this query, Oracle Text will use the index set, allowing you to order the results properly. Note that there are two quotes around the string 'EMILY TALBOT' because this is a text string search—it will be converted to a set of single quotes when the query is executed.

Index sets can contain up to 99 indexes on NUMBER, DATE, CHAR, and VARCHAR2 datatypes. No column in an index set index can exceed 30 bytes (so in this example, the Title column cannot be indexed as part of an index set). The indexed columns must not contain **NULL** values.

As of Oracle Database 10*g*, Oracle Text includes a tracing facility to help identify bottlenecks in indexing and querying. Use the ADD_TRACE procedure of the CTX_OUTPUT package to enable the trace. The available traces include the time spent on the different search components, the number of bytes read, and the number of rows processed.

For more details on index sets, text index management, text application development, and tracing, see *Oracle Text Application Developer's Guide* and *Oracle Text Reference,* both provided as part of the standard Oracle documentation set.

CHAPTER
26

Using External Tables

You can use the external table feature to access external files as if they were tables inside the database. When you create an external table, you define its structure and location within Oracle. When you query the table, Oracle reads the external table and returns the results just as if the data had been stored within the database. But because the data is outside the database, you do not have to be concerned about the process for loading it into the database—a potentially significant benefit for data warehouses and large databases.

External tables have limits—you cannot **update** or **delete** their rows from within Oracle, and you cannot index them. Because they are part of the database application, you will have to account for them as part of your backup and recovery processes. Despite these complications, external tables can be a powerful addition to your database architecture plans. As of Oracle Database 10*g*, you can use external tables to unload data from tables to external files via the ORACLE_DATAPUMP access driver.

Accessing the External Data

To access external files from within Oracle, you must first use the **create directory** command to define a directory object pointing to the external files' location. Users who will access the external files must have the READ privilege on the directory.

> **NOTE**
> *Before you start, verify that the external directory exists and that the*
> *user who will be issuing the **create directory** command has the CREATE*
> *ANY DIRECTORY system privilege.*

The following example creates a directory named BOOK_DIR and grants READ and WRITE access to the PRACTICE schema:

```
create directory BOOK_DIR as 'e:\oracle\external';
grant read on directory BOOK_DIR to practice;
grant write on directory BOOK_DIR to practice;
```

The PRACTICE user can now read files in the e:\oracle\external directory as if he or she were inside the database. Because PRACTICE has also been granted WRITE privilege on that directory, the PRACTICE user can create log, discard, and bad files within the directory—just as if that user were executing the SQL*Loader utility (see Chapter 21).

The following listing generates two files for sample data—one from BOOKSHELF and one from BOOKSHELF_AUTHOR. Note that the **spool** command cannot use the directory name created via **create directory**; you need to specify the full operating-system directory name.

```
connect practice/practice
```

```
set pagesize 0 newpage 0 feedback off
select Title||'~'||Publisher||'~'||CategoryName||'~'||Rating||'~'
  from BOOKSHELF
 order by Title
```

```
spool e:\oracle\external\bookshelf_dump.lst
/
spool off

select Title||'~'||AuthorName||'~'
  from BOOKSHELF_AUTHOR
 order by Title

spool e:\oracle\external\book_auth_dump.lst
/
spool off
```

In addition to the data, the output files will contain a single line at the top with "SQL> /" and a final line that reads "SQL> spool off". To simplify the examples, you should manually edit the file at the operating system level to delete these extra lines before proceeding.

If another user is to access the data in the bookshelf_dump.lst and book_auth_dump.lst files, you must grant that user READ privilege on the BOOK_DIR directory:

```
grant read on directory BOOK_DIR to another_user;
```

Also, the files themselves must be readable by the Oracle user at the operating system level.

Creating an External Table

Now that the external data is available and accessible, you can create a table structure that accesses it. To do so, you need to use the **organization external** clause of the **create table** command. Within that clause, you can specify the data structure much as you would for a SQL*Loader control file. The following listing shows the creation of the BOOKSHELF_EXT table, based on the data in the bookshelf.lst spool file created in the prior section:

```
set feedback on heading on newpage 1 pagesize 60

create table BOOKSHELF_EXT
(Title        VARCHAR2(100),
Publisher     VARCHAR2(20),
CategoryName VARCHAR2(20),
Rating        VARCHAR2(2)
)
organization external
(type ORACLE_LOADER
 default directory BOOK_DIR
 access parameters (records delimited by newline
 fields terminated by "~"
                 (Title        CHAR(100),
                  Publisher    CHAR(20),
                  CategoryName CHAR(20),
                  Rating       CHAR(2)
                 ))
 location ('bookshelf_dump.lst')
);
```

Oracle will respond with

```
Table created.
```

although no data will have been created inside the Oracle database.

Similarly, you can create a table based on the book_auth_dump.lst spool file:

```
create table BOOKSHELF_AUTHOR_EXT
(Title        VARCHAR2(100),
AuthorName    VARCHAR2(50)
)
organization external
(type ORACLE_LOADER
 default directory BOOK_DIR
 access parameters (records delimited by newline
                    fields terminated by "~"
                  (Title         CHAR(100),
                   AuthorName    CHAR(50)
                  ))
 location ('book_auth_dump.lst')
);
```

NOTE
Oracle will perform only cursory validation when the external table is created. You will not see most errors until you attempt to query the table. The syntax for the access parameters is very specific, and minor errors in the access definition—including the order of the clauses— may prevent all the rows from being accessed.

You can verify the contents of the external tables by querying from them and comparing them to the source tables, as shown in the following listing:

```
select Title from BOOKSHELF
  where CategoryName = 'CHILDRENPIC';

TITLE
----------------------------------------
GOOD DOG, CARL
POLAR EXPRESS
RUNAWAY BUNNY

3 rows selected.

select Title from BOOKSHELF_EXT
  where CategoryName = 'CHILDRENPIC';
```

```
TITLE
---------------------------------------------
GOOD DOG, CARL
POLAR EXPRESS
RUNAWAY BUNNY

3 rows selected.

select COUNT(*) from BOOKSHELF_AUTHOR;

  COUNT(*)
----------
        37

select COUNT(*) from BOOKSHELF_AUTHOR_EXT;

  COUNT(*)
----------
        37
```

You can join the "internal" table BOOKSHELF_AUTHOR to its external counterpart, BOOKSHELF_AUTHOR_EXT, to verify there are no rows missing or added:

```
select * from BOOKSHELF_AUTHOR BA
where not exists
(select 'x' from BOOKSHELF_AUTHOR_EXT BAE
  where BA.Title = BAE.Title
    and BA.AuthorName = BAE.AuthorName);

no rows selected
```

The BOOKSHELF_AUTHOR_EXT table points to the book_auth_dump.lst file. If you alter the data in the file, the data in BOOKSHELF_AUTHOR_EXT will change. As illustrated here, you can query external tables the same way you query standard tables—in joins, as part of views, and so on. You can perform functions on the external table columns during queries just as you would for standard tables.

You can query the USER_EXTERNAL_TABLES data dictionary view for information about your external tables, including the default directory and access definitions:

```
desc USER_EXTERNAL_TABLES
```

Name	Null?	Type
TABLE_NAME	NOT NULL	VARCHAR2(30)
TYPE_OWNER		CHAR(3)
TYPE_NAME	NOT NULL	VARCHAR2(30)
DEFAULT_DIRECTORY_OWNER		CHAR(3)
DEFAULT_DIRECTORY_NAME	NOT NULL	VARCHAR2(30)

```
REJECT_LIMIT                                    VARCHAR2(40)
ACCESS_TYPE                                      VARCHAR2(7)
ACCESS_PARAMETERS                               VARCHAR2(4000)
PROPERTY                                        VARCHAR2(10)
```

For example, the BOOKSHELF_AUTHOR_EXT table uses BOOK_DIR as its default directory, as shown in the following listing:

```
select Default_Directory_Name,
       Access_Parameters
  from USER_EXTERNAL_TABLES
 where Table_Name = 'BOOKSHELF_AUTHOR_EXT';

DEFAULT_DIRECTORY_NAME
------------------------------
ACCESS_PARAMETERS
--------------------------------------------------
BOOK_DIR
records delimited by newline
                  fields terminated by "~"
                 (Title        CHAR(100),
                  AuthorName   CHAR(50)
                 )
```

USER_EXTERNAL_TABLES does not show the name of the external file (or files) that the table references. To see that information, query USER_EXTERNAL_LOCATIONS:

```
select * from USER_EXTERNAL_LOCATIONS;

TABLE_NAME
------------------------------
LOCATION
----------------------------------------------
DIR DIRECTORY_NAME
--- ------------------------------
BOOKSHELF_EXT
bookshelf_dump.lst
SYS BOOK_DIR

BOOKSHELF_AUTHOR_EXT
book_auth_dump.lst
SYS BOOK_DIR
```

External Table Creation Options

Within the **organization external** clause are four main subclauses: **type**, **default directory**, **access parameters**, and **location**. When you create an external table, you can use these clauses to customize the way Oracle views the external data.

Type and Default Directory

The syntax for the **type** component is

```
( [type access_driver_type] external_data_properties )
[reject limit { integer | unlimited }]
```

For external tables, the access driver is the API used to transform the external data. Use **type ORACLE_LOADER** for your external tables—as shown in the examples earlier in this chapter—or ORACLE_DATAPUMP if you are using Data Pump (see Chapter 22). The ORACLE_DATAPUMP driver lets you unload data into an external table and then reload it into an Oracle database. You must specify the ORACLE_DATAPUMP access driver if you use the **as** *subquery* clause to unload data from one database and then reload it. The **type ORACLE_LOADER** access driver is the default.

NOTE
Because the access driver is part of the Oracle software, only files accessible by the database can be accessed as external tables. Files the Oracle user cannot access cannot be used as external tables.

Following the **type** declaration, you can set a "reject limit" value. By default, no rows can be rejected—any problem with any row will cause the **select** statement to return an error. Let's generate another copy of the BOOKSHELF data to a separate file, and this time leave in the extra lines SQL*Plus inserts during the **spool** operation:

```
set pagesize 0 newpage 0 feedback off
select Title||'~'||Publisher||'~'||CategoryName||'~'||Rating||'~'
  from BOOKSHELF
 order by Title

spool e:\oracle\external\bookshelf_dump_2.lst
/
spool off
```

Now let's create a new table that references this spool file, telling Oracle to skip the first record (**skip 1**) and to allow one other error (**reject limit 1**). That will account for the "/" character in the first line and "SQL> spool off" in the last line:

```
set feedback on heading on newpage 1 pagesize 60

create table BOOKSHELF_EXT_2
```

```
(Title        VARCHAR2(100),
Publisher     VARCHAR2(20),
CategoryName VARCHAR2(20),
Rating        VARCHAR2(2)
)
organization external
(type ORACLE_LOADER
 default directory BOOK_DIR
 access parameters (records delimited by newline
                    skip 1
                    fields terminated by
                    "~"
                    (Title        CHAR(100),
                     Publisher    CHAR(20),
                     CategoryName CHAR(20),
                     Rating       CHAR(2)
                    ) )
 location ('bookshelf_dump_2.lst')
)
reject limit 1
;
```

You can now verify the number of rows in the table:

```
set feedback on heading on newpage 1 pagesize 60
select COUNT(*) from BOOKSHELF_EXT_2;

  COUNT(*)
----------
        31
```

The **default directory** clause specifies the directory object to be used for all datafiles that do not specify another directory. If you use multiple external files located in multiple directories, you can name one of them as the default directory and specify the others by directory name in the **location** clause. You must use directory object names (such as BOOK_DIR) in the **location** clause, not the full directory path name.

Access Parameters

The **access parameters** clause tells Oracle how to map the rows in the file to rows in the table. Its syntax is shown in the following illustration:

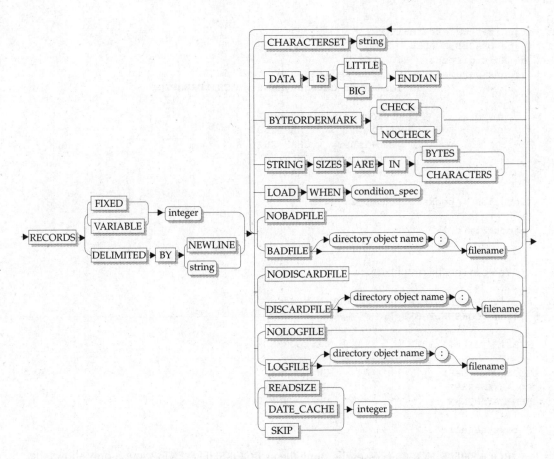

Within the **access parameters** clause, you first tell Oracle how to create a record—whether its length is fixed or variable, and how rows are delimited. In the case of the BOOKSHELF_EXT example, the records are delimited by newlines. If there were multiple rows on a single line, you could use a character string as a separator between rows. Because the external data may come from a non-Oracle database, Oracle supports multiple character sets and string sizes.

As with SQL*Loader, you can specify a **when** clause to limit which rows are selected. In the following listing, the BOOKSHELF_EXT_3 table is created, with a **when** clause (shown in bold) to limit it to only books in the CHILDRENPIC category.

```
create table BOOKSHELF_EXT_3
(Title         VARCHAR2(100),
 Publisher     VARCHAR2(20),
 CategoryName  VARCHAR2(20),
 Rating        VARCHAR2(2)
)
```

```
organization external
(type ORACLE_LOADER
 default directory BOOK_DIR
 access parameters (records delimited by newline
                        load when CategoryName = 'CHILDRENPIC'
                                        skip 1
                        fields terminated by "~"
                        (Title         CHAR(100),
                         Publisher     CHAR(20),
                         CategoryName CHAR(20),
                         Rating        CHAR(2)
                        ) )
 location ('bookshelf_dump_2.lst')
)
reject limit 1
;
```

You can see the result here:

```
select SUBSTR(Title, 1,30), CategoryName
  from BOOKSHELF_EXT_3;

SUBSTR(TITLE,1,30)                CATEGORYNAME
------------------------------    --------------------
GOOD DOG, CARL                    CHILDRENPIC
POLAR EXPRESS                     CHILDRENPIC
RUNAWAY BUNNY                     CHILDRENPIC

3 rows selected.
```

BOOKSHELF_EXT_3 accesses the same file as BOOKSHELF_EXT_2, but it only shows the records for the CHILDRENPIC category due to its **load when** clause.

As with SQL*Loader, you can create a log file, a bad file, and a discard file. Rows that fail the **load when** condition will be written to the discard file. Rows that fail the **access parameters** conditions will be written to the bad file, and the load details will be written to the log file. For all three types of files, you can specify a directory object along with the filename so that you can write the output to a directory other than your input datafile directory. You can specify **nodiscardfile**, **nobadfile**, and **nologfile** to prevent these files from being created. Use directory object names (such as BOOK_DIR in this chapter's examples) when specifying locations for discard files, bad files, and log files. If you don't specify locations for log files, bad files, and discard files, Oracle creates them in the default directory with system-generated names.

Within the **access parameters** clause, you also specify the field definitions and delimiters, such as

```
fields terminated by "~"
(Title         CHAR(100),
 Publisher     CHAR(20),
 CategoryName CHAR(20),
 Rating        CHAR(2))
```

You can use the **missing field values are null** clause to set values for **NULL** column values, but you must exercise caution when using this option. For example, the AUTHOR table has **NULL** values in its Comments column. The external table creation for AUTHOR_EXT is shown in the following listing:

```
set pagesize 0 newpage 0 feedback off
select AuthorName||'~'||Comments||'~'
  from AUTHOR
 order by AuthorName

spool e:\oracle\external\author_dump.lst
/
spool off

set feedback on heading on newpage 1 pagesize 60
create table AUTHOR_EXT
(AuthorName    VARCHAR2(50),
 Comments      VARCHAR2(100)
)
organization external
(type ORACLE_LOADER
 default directory BOOK_DIR
 access parameters (records delimited by newline
                    skip 1
                    fields terminated by "~"
                    missing field values are null
                    (AuthorName    CHAR(50),
                     Comments      CHAR(100)
                    ) )
 location ('author_dump.lst')
)
reject limit 1
;
```

But this is not correct—if you select the AuthorName values from AUTHOR_EXT, you will see that the values include the following:

```
select AuthorName from AUTHOR_EXT
  where AuthorName like 'S%';

AUTHORNAME
----------------------------------------------------
SOREN KIERKEGAARD
STEPHEN AMBROSE
STEPHEN JAY GOULD
SQL> spool off

4 rows selected.
```

Because of the **missing field values are null** clause, the "SQL> spool off" line at the end of the listing was read as an AuthorName value, with a **NULL** Comments value. This highlights the problem with coding exceptions into your loader definitions—you need to make sure you fully understand the source data and the way the loader will treat it. In most cases, your data integrity will be better served by forcing rows to fail (into bad files or discard files) and evaluating the failed rows apart from your general loads.

See the SQL*Loader entry in the Alphabetical Reference for the full syntax available for the **access parameters** clause.

Location

In the **location** clause, you specify the datafiles to use as the source data for the table. You can name multiple files in the **location** clause if they all exist in directory objects the user has READ privilege on. The following example combines two separate BOOKSHELF spool files to illustrate the ability to combine multiple files into a single external table:

```
create table BOOKSHELF_EXT_4
(Title         VARCHAR2(100),
Publisher      VARCHAR2(20),
CategoryName   VARCHAR2(20),
Rating         VARCHAR2(2)
)
organization external
(type ORACLE_LOADER
 default directory BOOK_DIR
 access parameters (records delimited by newline
                    skip 1
                    fields terminated by "~"
                    (Title         CHAR(100),
                     Publisher     CHAR(20),
                     CategoryName  CHAR(20),
                     Rating        CHAR(2)
                    ) )
 location ('bookshelf_dump_2.lst', 'bookshelf_dump.lst')
)
reject limit 1
;
```

The order of the files is important—**skip 1** applies to the first file, not to the second file. The second file, bookshelf_dump.lst, is the file that was previously edited to eliminate the nondata rows in its first and last rows. The result, reflecting the rows in both, is shown in the following listing:

```
select COUNT(*) from BOOKSHELF_EXT_4;

  COUNT(*)
----------
        62
```

Altering External Tables

You can alter external table definitions to change the way Oracle interprets the flat file. The available options are detailed in the following subsections.

Access Parameters

You can change the access parameters without dropping and re-creating the external table definition, thereby preserving grants, file definitions, and so on. For example, here's how to increase the number of records to skip in the BOOKSHELF_EXT_4 table:

```
alter table BOOKSHELF_EXT_4
access parameters (records delimited by newline
                   skip 10
                   fields terminated by "~"
                   (Title        CHAR(100),
                    Publisher     CHAR(20),
                    CategoryName CHAR(20),
                    Rating        CHAR(2)
                   ) );

select COUNT(*) from BOOKSHELF_EXT_4;

  COUNT(*)
----------
        53
```

Add Column

You can use the **add column** clause of the **alter table** command to add a column to the external table, using the same syntax used for standard tables.

Default Directory

You can use the **default directory** clause of the **alter table** command to change the default directory for the external files accessed by the table. The directory must be created via the **create directory** command.

Drop Column

You can use the **drop column** clause of the **alter table** command to drop a column from the external table, using the same syntax used for standard tables. The data in the file remains unchanged.

Location

You can change the files accessed by the external table via the **location** clause of the **alter table** command. You may use this option to add new files to the list or to change the order in which the external table accesses the files.

Modify Column

You can use the **modify column** clause of the **alter table** command to modify a column in the external table, using the same syntax used for standard tables.

Parallel

You can use the **parallel** clause of the **alter table** command to change the degree of parallelism for the external table, using the same syntax used for standard tables.

Project Column

The **project column** clause of the **alter table** command tells the access driver how to validate rows in subsequent queries. If you use the **project column referenced** option, the access driver only processes the columns selected by the query. If you then query a different set of columns from the external table, the results may be inconsistent with the first query's results. If you use the **project column all** option, the access driver processes all columns defined on the external table, resulting in a consistent set of query results. The **project column referenced** option is the default.

Reject Limit

You can use the **reject limit** clause of the **alter table** command to change the allowable number of rejected rows for the external table. Here's an example:

```
alter table BOOKSHELF_EXT_3
reject limit 5;
```

Rename To

You can use the **rename to** clause of the **alter table** command to change the name of the external table, using the same syntax used for standard tables. Here's an example:

```
alter table BOOKSHELF_EXT_3
rename to BE3;
```

Limitations, Benefits, and Potential Uses of External Tables

External tables have limitations that may make them inappropriate for some online transaction-processing applications. You cannot perform any **update** or **delete** operations on external tables. The more dynamic the table is, the less appropriate external files may be. As shown in the examples earlier in this chapter, you can change the files dynamically at the operating system level. If your application generates **insert**s only, you may be able to write those inserted records into an external file instead of a database table.

You cannot index external tables. The lack of indexes on external tables does not have to be a negative factor in application performance. Queries of external tables complete very quickly, even though a full table scan is required with each access. There is I/O involved, but modern I/O systems use caching and RAID techniques to significantly reduce the performance penalty associated with repeated full scans of the same file.

NOTE
To analyze external tables, use the DBMS_STATS package.
*You cannot analyze external tables via the **analyze** command.*

You cannot specify constraints on an external table. Even creating a **NOT NULL** or foreign key constraint fails:

```
alter table BOOKSHELF_EXT add constraint CATFK
foreign key (CategoryName) references CATEGORY(CategoryName);

foreign key (CategoryName) references CATEGORY(CategoryName)
*
ERROR at line 2:
ORA-30657: operation not supported on external organized table
```

Despite these limitations, external tables offer many useful features. You can join external tables (to each other, or to standard tables). You can use hints to force the optimizer to choose different join paths, and you can see the results in the query execution paths (see Chapter 43 for details on hints and the Oracle optimizer).

As an alternative to data loading, external tables offer DBAs and application developers the possibility of accessing data without supporting long-running load programs. Because the files can be edited at the operating system level, you can quickly replace a table's data without worrying about outstanding transactions modifying the table. For example, you could use this capability to create multiple external tables and create a **union all** view across them, creating a partition view across multiple files. You can then manage each table's data separately at the file system level, replacing its contents as needed.

Because the external table can be queried, you can use the external table as the data source for an **insert as select** command. During that operation, Oracle will attempt to load the external files in parallel, potentially improving performance. To further improve performance of the **insert as select** operation, you should use the APPEND hint to force block-level inserts. When you specify the degree of parallelism for the **insert as select** operation, Oracle starts multiple ORACLE_LOADER access drivers to process the data in parallel. To further enhance load performance, avoid using variable-length fields, delimited fields, character set conversion, **NULLIF**, **DEFAULTIF**, and datatype conversion operations. Turning off **badfile** (with **nobadfile**) eliminates the costs associated with the file creation and the maintenance of the original row's context.

During the **insert as select**, you can perform functions on the data as it is processed. You can perform the functions either in the **insert as select** command syntax or in the external table definition. This capability highlights an important benefit of external tables—you can centralize the representation and processing requirements for your data, building translation routines into your table definitions. There is no processing data stored in SQL*Loader control files or PL/SQL routines; all the logic is built into the table definition, accessible via USER_EXTERNAL_TABLES.

During queries, external tables allow you to select specific data sets (via the **load when** clause, as illustrated in this chapter). If you have multiple data sources for a data warehouse load, you can choose which data will be made available even while the data is outside the database. You can

use this feature to maintain application availability during data loads. These loads can occur in parallel if the external file has a FIXED file format.

The limited-access feature also allows you to enforce complex security rules concerning data access. For example, you may keep sensitive data outside the database, in a secure directory. Users with READ access to that directory would be able to use the external table and join it to other tables; users without that access would be limited to the data inserted into the publicly accessible tables. Highly secure data, or lightly accessed dynamic data, need not be inserted into the database until it is needed, if at all.

If you use external tables in your database architecture, you must make sure your backup and recovery plans account for those files as well as the rest of your database. If the external files change more rapidly than the database files, you may need to back them up more frequently in order to take advantage of Oracle's full recovery capabilities.

CHAPTER
27

Using Flashback
Queries

As part of its read consistency model, Oracle displays data that has been committed to the database. As of Oracle9*i*, you can query data as it existed prior to a transaction being committed. If you accidentally **commit** an errant **update** or **delete**, you can use this capability—called a *flashback query*—to see the data as it existed prior to the **commit**. You can use the results of the flashback query to restore the data.

To support flashback queries, your database should use system-managed undo, a feature introduced in Oracle9*i* to automate management of rollback segments; see your DBA to determine if this feature is enabled in your environment. The DBA must create an undo tablespace, enable Automatic Undo Management, and establish an undo retention time window. Flashback queries can be executed against remote databases.

NOTE
See Chapter 46 for details on the DBA activities needed to support flashback queries.

Oracle will attempt to maintain enough undo information in the undo tablespace to support flashback queries during the retention time period. The retention time setting and the amount of space available in the undo tablespace can significantly impact your ability to successfully execute a flashback query.

NOTE
Oracle uses undo to roll back transactions and support flashback queries. Oracle uses redo (captured in the online redo log files) to apply transactions during database recoveries.

Flashback queries are important tools during partial recovery efforts. In general, you should not rely on flashback queries as part of your application design because of their dependence on system elements outside of the application developer's control (such as the number of transactions during a time period and the size of the undo tablespace). Rather, you should treat them as an option during critical periods of testing, support, and data recovery. For example, you could use them to create copies of tables at multiple past points in time for use when reconstructing changed data.

NOTE
To use some features of flashback queries, you must have the EXECUTE privilege on the DBMS_FLASHBACK package. Most users will not need privileges on this package.

Time-Based Flashback Example

The BOOK_ORDER table has six records, as shown in the following listing:

```
column Title format a30
select * from BOOK_ORDER;
```

```
TITLE                          PUBLISHER              CATEGORYNAME
---------------------------    ------------------     -------------
SHOELESS JOE                   MARINER                ADULTFIC
GOSPEL                         PICADOR                ADULTFIC
SOMETHING SO STRONG            PANDORAS               ADULTNF
GALILEO'S DAUGHTER             PENGUIN                ADULTNF
LONGITUDE                      PENGUIN                ADULTNF
ONCE REMOVED                   SANCTUARY PUB          ADULTNF

6 rows selected.
```

A shipment has arrived, and the old BOOK_ORDER records are deleted and then the deletion is committed. Unfortunately, not all the books were in the shipment, so the **delete** is inappropriate:

```
delete from BOOK_ORDER;
commit;
```

How can you reconstruct the unreceived book records from the BOOK_ORDER table, since you only have the received books in hand? You could perform a database recovery by using Data Pump Import (see Chapter 22) to restore the table, or you could perform a physical database recovery to recover the database to a point in time prior to the **delete**. However, with flashback queries, you can avoid the need to perform these recovery operations.

First, let's query the old data from the database. As of Oracle9i Release 2, you can use the **as of timestamp** and **as of scn** clauses of the **select** command to specify how far Oracle should flash back the data.

NOTE
In Oracle9i's first release, 9.0.1, this syntax is not supported; you need to execute procedures within the DBMS_FLASHBACK package and write PL/SQL loops to perform any transactions based on the data.

```
select COUNT(*) from BOOK_ORDER;

  COUNT(*)
----------
         0

select COUNT(*) from BOOK_ORDER
 as of timestamp (SysDate - 5/1440);

  COUNT(*)
----------
         6
```

When you execute a flashback query, only the state of the data is changed. The current system time is used (as you can see by querying the SysDate value), and the current data dictionary is used. If the structure of the table has changed, the query will fail.

Saving the Data

As shown in the BOOK_ORDER example, flashback queries are simple to implement, provided the undo management of the database is properly configured and the undo information is available. But how can you work with the flashback data?

The simplest method involves saving the data to a separate table. There are 1440 minutes in a day, so "SysDate – 5/1440" will direct the database to a point in time five minutes ago. Note that the query may return no rows if more than five minutes have passed since the **commit**.

```
create table BOOK_ORDER_OLD
as select * from BOOK_ORDER
from BOOK_ORDER
 as of timestamp (SysDate - 5/1440);

Table created.

select COUNT(*) from BOOK_ORDER_OLD;

  COUNT(*)
-----------
         6
```

You can verify that the data is correct:

```
column Title format a30

select * from BOOK_ORDER_OLD;

TITLE                          PUBLISHER                 CATEGORYNAME
------------------------------ ------------------------- ------------
SHOELESS JOE                   MARINER                   ADULTFIC
GOSPEL                         PICADOR                   ADULTFIC
SOMETHING SO STRONG            PANDORAS                  ADULTNF
GALILEO'S DAUGHTER             PENGUIN                   ADULTNF
LONGITUDE                      PENGUIN                   ADULTNF
ONCE REMOVED                   SANCTUARY PUB             ADULTNF

6 rows selected.
```

You can then work with that data to restore the missing data, perform selective updates, insert only incorrectly deleted rows, or whatever other operation is needed.

The new table, BOOK_ORDER_OLD, has no indexes on it and no referential integrity constraints. If you need to join it to other tables, you may need to create flashback copies of multiple tables in order to maintain the referential integrity of the data. Also, note that each query is executed at a different point in time—and the relative times used in the **as of timestamp** clause can therefore lead to confusing or inconsistent results.

You can work directly with the old data—however, you are relying on the old data being available for your transaction. It is generally safer to create a table and store the old data temporarily as you work with it.

Limitations of Time-Based Flashbacks

The preceding example showed how to use the system timestamp during your flashback query. As noted, that method provides limited support for multi-table flashbacks. To perform complex flashbacks correctly, you should use the system change number (SCN).

Oracle internally uses the SCN, not the system timestamp, to generate the flashback data, even when you specify the **as of timestamp** clause. The system timestamp is matched to SCN values every five minutes; the table SYS.SMON_SCN_TIME records the last 1440 matches of SCN to the system timestamp. When you flash back to a point in time, Oracle uses the most recent five-minute timestamp preceding the requested time. If SMON_SCN_TIME has a record for 1:00 P.M. and for 1:05 P.M., a request for a flashback to 1:04 P.M. will return the data from 1:00 P.M.

SMON_SCN_TIME only maintains the most recent 1440 entries, so flashback queries that go beyond the most recent five days in an always-open database must use an SCN-based approach, as described in the next section. If you shut down your database periodically (such as for offline backups), the 1440 records in SMON_SCN_TIME will span more than five days.

To see the most recent entries in SYS.SMON_SCN_TIME, execute the following query as SYS, connected as SYSDBA:

```
select TO_CHAR(Time_DP,'DD-MON-YYYY HH24:MI:SS')
  from SYS.SMON_SCN_TIME
 order by Time_DP desc ;
```

SCN-Based Flashback Example

When you perform time-based flashbacks, you are really doing SCN-based flashbacks; you're just relying on Oracle to find an SCN near the time you specified. If you know the exact SCN, you can perform a flashback with a great degree of precision.

To begin an SCN-based flashback, you must first know the SCN of your transaction. To get the latest change number, issue a **commit** and then use the **as of scn** clause of the **select** command. You can find the current SCN by executing the **GET_SYSTEM_CHANGE_NUMBER** function of the DBMS_FLASHBACK package prior to executing your transaction.

NOTE
Prior to executing the following example, you must have been granted the EXECUTE privilege on the DBMS_FLASHBACK package.

The following example shows this process as part of a transaction against the BOOK_ORDER_ OLD table created and populated in the first part in this chapter. First, the current SCN is assigned to a variable named SCN_FLASH and displayed via the SQL*Plus **print** command:

```
commit;

variable SCN_FLASH number;
execute :SCN_FLASH :=DBMS_FLASHBACK.GET_SYSTEM_CHANGE_NUMBER;

PL/SQL procedure successfully completed.
```

```
print SCN_FLASH

 SCN_FLASH
----------
    529732
```

Next, the **delete** command is issued and the result is committed:

```
delete from BOOK_ORDER_OLD;

6 rows deleted.

commit;
```

You can now query the flashback data. Although the SCN value is known, you can continue to use the SCN_FLASH variable value if you are within the same session:

```
select COUNT(*) from BOOK_ORDER_OLD;

  COUNT(*)
----------
         0

select COUNT(*) from BOOK_ORDER_OLD
 as of scn (:scn_flash);

  COUNT(*)
----------
         6
```

You can now use the flashback data in BOOK_ORDER_OLD, accessed by the **as of scn** clause, to populate it with its old values:

```
insert into BOOK_ORDER_OLD
select * from BOOK_ORDER_OLD
 as of scn (:scn_flash);

6 rows created.

commit;
```

NOTE
*DDL operations that alter the structure of a table invalidate the old undo data for the table, and flashback capabilities are limited to the time since the DDL was executed. Space-related changes (such as changing **pctfree**) do not invalidate the old undo data. See Chapter 28 for details on the **flashback table** and **flashback database** commands.*

What If the Flashback Query Fails?

If there is not enough space in the undo tablespace to maintain all the data needed for the flashback query, the query will fail. Even if the DBA created a large undo tablespace, it is possible for a series of large transactions to use all the space available. A portion of each failed query will be written to the database's alert log.

From the perspective of a user attempting to recover old data, you should attempt to recover data that is as correct and timely as possible. Often, you may need to execute multiple flashback queries to determine how far back you can successfully query the data, and then save the oldest data you can access and the data closest to the point at which the problem occurred. Once the oldest data is gone from the undo tablespace, you can no longer use flashback queries to retrieve it.

If it is not possible to flash back to data that is old enough for your needs, you will need to perform some sort of database recovery—either flashing back the entire database or recovering specific tables and tablespaces via traditional DBA methods (see Chapter 46). If this problem happens routinely, the undo retention time should be increased, the space allotted for the undo tablespace should be increased, and the application usage should be examined to determine why questionable transactions are occurring on a persistent basis.

What SCN Is Associated with Each Row?

As of Oracle Database 10g, you can see the most recent SCN associated with each row in the database.

Let's start by repopulating our BOOK_ORDER table with the data that was restored to the BOOK_ORDER_OLD table:

```
delete from BOOK_ORDER;

0 rows deleted.

insert into BOOK_ORDER
select * from BOOK_ORDER_OLD;

6 rows created.

commit;
```

Now, use the ORA_ROWSCN pseudo-column introduced in Oracle Database 10g to see the SCN associated with each row:

```
select Title, ORA_ROWSCN from BOOK_ORDER;

TITLE                             ORA_ROWSCN
-------------------------------- ----------
SHOELESS JOE                          553531
GOSPEL                                553531
SOMETHING SO STRONG                   553531
GALILEO'S DAUGHTER                    553531
LONGITUDE                             553531
ONCE REMOVED                          553531
```

All the rows were part of the same transaction, occurring at SCN 553531 (the SCN in your database will differ from the one in this example). Now, wait for other transactions to occur in the database and then insert a new row:

```
insert into BOOK_ORDER
values ('INNUMERACY','VINTAGE BOOKS','ADULTNF');

1 row created.

commit;
```

Now that a new change has been committed, you can see the SCN associated with it:

```
select Title, ORA_ROWSCN from BOOK_ORDER;

TITLE                         ORA_ROWSCN
----------------------------- ----------
SHOELESS JOE                      553531
GOSPEL                            553531
SOMETHING SO STRONG               553531
GALILEO'S DAUGHTER                553531
LONGITUDE                         553531
ONCE REMOVED                      553531
INNUMERACY                        553853
```

What time does that SCN map to? You can use the **SCN_TO_TIMESTAMP** function to display the date at which the change was made:

```
select SCN_TO_TIMESTAMP(555853) from DUAL;

SCN_TO_TIMESTAMP(555853)
-------------------------------------------------
20-FEB-04 03.11.28.000000000 PM
```

You can integrate the two queries to see the latest transaction times for each row:

```
select Title, SCN_TO_TIMESTAMP(ORA_ROWSCN)
  from BOOK_ORDER;
```

Flashback Version Queries

As of Oracle Database 10g, you can display the different versions of rows that existed during specified intervals. As with the examples shown previously in this chapter, the changes are SCN dependent, so only those that are committed will be displayed.

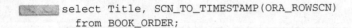

NOTE
Flashback version queries require that the DBA has set a nonzero value for the UNDO_RETENTION initialization parameter. If the UNDO_RETENTION value is too low, you may get an ORA-30052 error.

To prepare for these examples, delete the old rows from BOOK_ORDER:

```
delete from BOOK_ORDER;
```

Next, repopulate BOOK_ORDER:

```
select SysTimeStamp from DUAL;

insert into BOOK_ORDER
select * from BOOK_ORDER_OLD;

select SysTimeStamp from DUAL;
```

Then, wait for a few minutes and update all rows:

```
select SysTimeStamp from DUAL;

update BOOK_ORDER set CategoryName = 'ADULTF';

select SysTimeStamp from DUAL;
```

To execute a flashback version query, use the **versions between** clause of the **select** command. You can specify either the timestamp or the SCN. In this example, the format for the timestamp clause is based on Oracle's standard format (**select SysTimeStamp from DUAL** for the current value):

```
select *
   from BOOK_ORDER
versions between timestamp
   to_timestamp('20—FEB-04 16.00.20','DD-MON-YY HH24.MI.SS')
   and
   to_timestamp('20—FEB-04 16.06.20','DD-MON-YY HH24.MI.SS') ;
```

When you execute the query, Oracle will return one row for each version of each row that occurred between the start and end points you specify in the **versions between** clause. For the rows that are returned, you can query additional pseudo-columns:

Pseudo-Column	Description
VERSIONS_STARTSCN	The SCN when the data first had the values reflected. If **NULL**, then the row was created before the lower bound for the query.
VERSIONS_STARTTIME	The timestamp when the data first had the values reflected. If **NULL**, then the row was created before the lower bound for the query.
VERSIONS_ENDSCN	The SCN when the row version expired. If **NULL**, then the row is current or has been deleted.
VERSIONS_ENDTIME	The timestamp when the row version expired. If **NULL**, then the row is current or has been deleted.
VERSIONS_XID	The identifier of the transaction that created the row version.
VERSIONS_OPERATION	The operation that performed the transaction (I for insert, U for update, D for delete).

The following example shows the use of the flashback version query. The Versions_StartSCN values are **NULL** for the current rows; the old rows have been updated. The timestamps will be different on your platform.

```
select Title, Versions_StartSCN, Versions_Operation
   from BOOK_ORDER
versions between timestamp
   TO_TIMESTAMP('20-FEB-04 16.00.20','DD-MON-YY HH24.MI.SS')
   and
   TO_TIMESTAMP('20-FEB-04 16.06.20','DD-MON-YY HH24.MI.SS') ;

TITLE                            VERSIONS_STARTSCN V
-------------------------------- ----------------- -
ONCE REMOVED                                568127 U
LONGITUDE                                   568127 U
GALILEO'S DAUGHTER                          568127 U
SOMETHING SO STRONG                         568127 U
GOSPEL                                      568127 U
SHOELESS JOE                                568127 U
SHOELESS JOE
GOSPEL
SOMETHING SO STRONG
GALILEO'S DAUGHTER
LONGITUDE
ONCE REMOVED
```

The **versions between** clause can be used in subqueries of DML and DDL commands.

As of Oracle Database 10*g*, you can use the FLASHBACK_TRANSACTION_QUERY data dictionary view to track changes made by a particular transaction. For a given transaction, FLASHBACK_TRANSACTION_QUERY shows the name of the user who executed it, the operation performed, the table to which the transaction was applied, the start and end SCNs and timestamps, and the SQL needed to undo the transaction.

Planning for Flashbacks

For DBAs, flashback queries may offer a means of performing partial recovery operations quickly. If the data can be reconstructed via flashback queries, and if the data volume is not overwhelming, you may be able to save the results of multiple flashback queries in separate tables. You could then compare the data in the tables via the SQL options shown in prior chapters—correlated subqueries, **exists**, **not exists**, **minus**, and so on. If you cannot avoid the need for a recovery operation, you should be able to pinpoint the time period to be used for a time-based recovery operation.

As you will see in the next chapter, Oracle Database 10*g* introduces additional options—the **flashback database** and **flashback table** commands.

For application developers and application administrators, flashback queries provide an important tool for reconstructing data. Flashback queries may be particularly critical during testing and support operations. Rather than making flashback queries part of your production application design, you should use them as a fallback option for those support cases that cannot be resolved before data is affected.

CHAPTER
28

Flashback—Tables
and Databases

 s of Oracle Database 10*g*, you can use the **flashback table** and **flashback database** commands to simplify your data-recovery efforts. The **flashback table** command automates the process of restoring a full table to its prior state. The **flashback database** command flashes back an entire database, and it requires modifications to the database status and its logs. In the following sections, you will see details on implementing these options.

The flashback table Command

The **flashback table** command restores an earlier state of a table in the event of human or application error. Oracle cannot restore a table to an earlier state across any DDL operations that change the structure of the table.

NOTE
The database should be using Automatic Undo Management (AUM) for flashback table to work. The ability to flash back to old data is limited by the amount of undo retained in the undo tablespace and the UNDO_RETENTION initialization parameter setting.

You cannot roll back a **flashback table** statement. However, you can issue another **flashback table** statement and specify a time just prior to the current time.

NOTE
Record the current SCN before issuing a flashback table command.

Privileges Required

You must have either the FLASHBACK object privilege on the table or the FLASHBACK ANY TABLE system privilege. You must also have SELECT, INSERT, DELETE, and ALTER object privileges on the table. Row movement must be enabled for all tables in the flashback list. To flash back a table to before a **drop table** operation, you only need the privileges necessary to drop the table.

Recovering Dropped Tables

Consider the AUTHOR table:

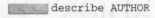
```
describe AUTHOR

Name                  Null?     Type
------------------    --------  ----------------------------
AUTHORNAME            NOT NULL  VARCHAR2(50)
COMMENTS                        VARCHAR2(100)
```

Now, assume that the table is dropped accidentally. This usually happens when a privileged user intends to drop a table in a development/test environment but is pointing to the production database when the command is executed.

```
drop table AUTHOR cascade constraints;
```

```
Table dropped.
```

How can the table be recovered? As of Oracle Database 10g, a dropped table does not fully disappear. Its blocks are still maintained in its tablespace, and it still counts against your space quota. You can see the dropped objects by querying the RECYCLEBIN data dictionary view. Note that the format for the Object_Name column may differ between versions.

```
select * from RECYCLEBIN;
```

OBJECT_NAME		ORIGINAL_NAME		OPERATION
TYPE		TS_NAME		CREATETIME
DROPTIME		DROPSCN PARTITION_NAME		CAN CAN
RELATED BASE_OBJECT	PURGE_OBJECT		SPACE	
RB$$48448$TABLE$0		AUTHOR		DROP
TABLE		USERS		2004-02-23:16:10:58
2004-02-25:14:30:23	720519			YES YES
48448	48448	48448	8	
RB$$48449$INDEX$0		SYS_C004828		DROP
INDEX		USERS		2004-02-23:16:10:58
2004-02-25:14:30:23	720516			NO YES
48448	48448	48449	8	

RECYCLEBIN is a public synonym for the USER_RECYCLEBIN data dictionary view, showing the recycle bin entries for the current user. DBAs can see all dropped objects via the DBA_RECYCLEBIN data dictionary view.

As shown in the preceding listing, Oracle has dropped the AUTHOR table and its associated primary key index. Although they have been dropped, they are still available for flashback. Note that the recycle bin listings show the SCN for the **drop** command used to drop the base object.

You can use the **flashback table to before drop** command to recover the table from the recycle bin:

```
flashback table AUTHOR to before drop;
```

```
Flashback complete.
```

The table has been restored, along with its rows, indexes, and statistics, as shown here:

```
select COUNT(*) from AUTHOR;
```

```
  COUNT(*)
----------
        31
```

What happens if you drop the AUTHOR table, re-create it, then drop it again? The recycle bin will contain both the tables. Each entry in the recycle bin will be identified via its SCN and the timestamp for the drop.

NOTE
*The **flashback table to before drop** command does not recover referential constraints.*

To purge old entries from the recycle bin, use the **purge** command. You can purge all your dropped objects, all dropped objects in the database (if you are a DBA), all objects in a specific tablespace, or all objects for a particular user in a specific tablespace. See the **purge** command in the Alphabetical Reference for the full syntax and command options.

You can use the **rename to** clause of the **flashback table** command to rename the table as you flash it back.

Flashing Back to SCN or Timestamp

As shown in Chapter 27, you can save the results of a flashback query in a separate table while the main table stays unaffected. You can also update the rows of a table based on the results of a flashback query. You can use the **flashback table** command to transform a table into its prior version—wiping out the changes that were made since the specified flashback point.

During a **flashback table** operation, Oracle acquires exclusive DML locks on all the tables specified. The command is executed in a single transaction across all tables; if any of them fails, the entire statement fails. You can flash back a table to a specific SCN or timestamp.

NOTE
flashback table to scn or to timestamp does not preserve RowIDs.

The following **update** command attempts to update the comment for the entry for Clement Hurd. However, the **where** clause is not specified; all rows are updated with the same comment, and the change is committed.

```
update AUTHOR
   set Comments = 'ILLUSTRATOR OF BOOKS FOR CHILDREN';

31 rows updated.

commit;
```

In this case, we know that almost the entire table has incorrect data, and we know the transaction that was executed incorrectly. To recover the correct data, we can flash back the database to a prior time and then apply any new commands needed to bring the data up to date.

First, let's make sure we know the current SCN in case we need to return to this point:

```
commit;

variable SCN_FLASH number;
execute :SCN_FLASH :=DBMS_FLASHBACK.GET_SYSTEM_CHANGE_NUMBER;
```

```
PL/SQL procedure successfully completed.

print SCN_FLASH

 SCN_FLASH
----------
    720880
```

Now, let's flash back the table to a time just prior to the update. First, we must enable row movement for the table:

```
alter table AUTHOR enable row movement;

Table altered.
```

We can then flash back the table:

```
flashback table AUTHOR to timestamp (systimestamp - 5/1440);
```

You can use the **to scn** clause if you wish to specify an SCN instead of a timestamp.

Indexes and Statistics

When a table is flashed back, its statistics are not flashed back. Indexes that exist on the table are reverted and reflect the state of the table at the flashback point. Indexes dropped since the flashback point are not restored. Indexes created since the flashback point will continue to exist and will be updated to reflect the older data.

The flashback database Command

The **flashback database** command returns the database to a past time or SCN, providing a fast alternative to performing incomplete database recovery. Following a **flashback database** operation, in order to have write access to the flashed back database you must reopen it with an **alter database open resetlogs** command. You must have the SYSDBA system privilege in order to use the **flashback database** command.

> **NOTE**
> *The database must have been put in flashback mode with an **alter database flashback on** command. The database must be mounted in exclusive mode but not be open when that command is executed.*

The syntax for the **flashback database** command is as follows:

```
flashback [standby] database [database]
{ to {scn | timestamp} expr
| to before  {scn | timestamp } expr
}
```

You can use either the **to scn** or **to timestamp** clause to set the point to which the entire database should be flashed back. You can flash back **to before** a critical point (such as a transaction that produced an unintended consequence for multiple tables). Use the ORA_ROWSCN pseudo-column to see the SCNs of transactions that most recently acted on rows.

To use **flashback database**, you must first alter the database while it is mounted but not open. If you have not already done so, you will need to shut down your database and enable flashback during the startup process:

```
startup mount exclusive;
alter database archivelog;
alter database flashback on;
alter database open;
```

NOTE
*You must have enabled media recovery via the **alter database archivelog** command prior to executing the **alter database flashback on** command.*

Two initialization parameter settings control how much flashback data is retained in the database. The DB_FLASHBACK_RETENTION_TARGET initialization parameter sets the upper limit (in minutes) for how far in time the database can be flashed back. The DB_RECOVERY_ FILE_DEST initialization parameter sets the size of the flash recovery area. Note that the **flashback table** command uses the undo tablespace, whereas the **flashback database** command relies on flashback logs stored in a flash recovery area.

You can determine how far back you can flash back the database by querying the V$FLASHBACK_DATABASE_LOG view. The amount of flashback data retained in the database is controlled by the initialization parameter and the size of the flash recovery area. The following listing shows the available columns in V$FLASHBACK_DATABASE_LOG and sample contents:

```
desc V$FLASHBACK_DATABASE_LOG

Name                                     Null?    Type
---------------------------------------- -------- -------
OLDEST_FLASHBACK_SCN                              NUMBER
OLDEST_FLASHBACK_TIME                             DATE
RETENTION_TARGET                                  NUMBER
FLASHBACK_SIZE                                    NUMBER
ESTIMATED_FLASHBACK_SIZE                          NUMBER

select * from V$FLASHBACK_DATABASE_LOG;

OLDEST_FLASHBACK_SCN OLDEST_FL RETENTION_TARGET FLASHBACK_SIZE
-------------------- --------- ---------------- --------------
ESTIMATED_FLASHBACK_SIZE
------------------------
              722689 25-FEB-04             1440        8192000
             0
```

You can verify the database's flashback status by querying V$DATABASE; the Flashback_On column will have a value of YES if the flashback has been enabled for the database.

```
select Current_SCN, Flashback_On from V$DATABASE;

CURRENT_SCN      FLA
---------------- ---
        723649 YES
```

With the database open for over an hour, verify that the flashback data is available and then flash it back—you will lose all transactions that occurred during that time:

```
shutdown;
startup mount exclusive;
flashback database to timestamp sysdate-1/24;
```

Note that the **flashback database** command requires that the database be mounted in exclusive mode, which will affect its participation in any RAC clusters (see Chapter 40).

When you execute the **flashback database** command, Oracle checks to make sure all required archived and online redo log files available. If the logs are available, the online datafiles are reverted to the time or SCN specified.

If there is not enough data online in the archive logs and the flashback area, you will need to use traditional database recovery methods to recover the data. For example, you may need to use a file system recovery method followed by rolling the data forward.

Once the flashback has completed, you must open the database using the **resetlogs** option in order to have write access to the database:

```
alter database open resetlogs;
```

To turn off the flashback database option, execute the **alter database flashback off** command when the database is mounted but not open:

```
startup mount exclusive;
alter database flashback off;
alter database open;
```

As shown in this and the preceding chapter, you can use the flashback options to perform an array of actions—recovering old data, reverting a table to its earlier data, maintaining a history of changes on a row basis, and quickly restoring an entire database. All of these actions are greatly simplified if the database has been configured to support Automatic Undo Management. Also, note that the **flashback database** command requires modification of the database status. Although these requirements can present additional burdens to DBAs, the benefits involved in terms of the number of recoveries required and the speed with which those recoveries can be completed may be dramatic.

PART
IV

PL/SQL

CHAPTER
29

An Introduction
to PL/SQL

L/SQL is Oracle's procedural language (PL) superset of the Structured Query Language (SQL). You can use PL/SQL to do such things as codify your business rules through the creation of stored procedures and packages, trigger database events to occur, and add programming logic to the execution of SQL commands.

The steps involved in the creation of triggers, stored procedures, and packages are described in the following chapters in this part of this book. In this chapter, you will see the basic structures and syntax used in PL/SQL.

PL/SQL Overview

PL/SQL code is grouped into structures called *blocks.* If you create a stored procedure or package, you give the block of PL/SQL code a name; if the block of PL/SQL code is not given a name, it is called an *anonymous block.* The examples in this chapter will feature anonymous blocks of PL/SQL code; the following chapters in Part IV illustrate the creation of named blocks.

A block of PL/SQL code contains three sections:

Section	Description
Declarations	Defines and initializes the variables and cursors used in the block
Executable Commands	Uses flow-control commands (such as **if** commands and loops) to execute the commands and assign values to the declared variables
Exception Handling	Provides customized handling of error conditions

Within a PL/SQL block, the first section is the Declarations section. Within the Declarations section, you define the variables and cursors that the block will use. The Declarations section starts with the keyword **declare** and ends when the Executable Commands section starts (as indicated by the keyword **begin**). The Executable Commands section is followed by the Exception Handling section; **exception** keyword signals the start of the Exception Handling section. The PL/SQL block is terminated by the **end** keyword.

The structure of a typical PL/SQL block is shown in the following listing:

```
declare
  <declarations section>
begin
  <executable commands>
 exception
  <exception handling>
end;
```

In the following sections of this chapter, you will see descriptions of each section of the PL/SQL block.

Declarations Section

The Declarations section begins a PL/SQL block. The Declarations section starts with the **declare** keyword, followed by a list of variable and cursor definitions. You can define variables to have

constant values, and variables can inherit datatypes from existing columns and query results, as shown in the following examples.

In the following listing, the area of a circle is calculated. The result is stored in a table named AREAS. The AREAS table has two columns to store radius and area values. The area of the circle is calculated by squaring the value for the circle's radius and multiplying that value by the constant *pi*:

```
declare
    pi       constant NUMBER(9,7) := 3.1415927;
    radius INTEGER(5);
    area    NUMBER(14,2);
begin
    radius := 3;
    area := pi*power(radius,2);
    insert into AREAS values (radius, area);
end;
/
```

The **end;** line signals the end of the PL/SQL block; depending on the tool you use, you may need to add a slash (/) to execute the PL/SQL block. When the PL/SQL block is executed, you will receive the following response from Oracle:

```
PL/SQL procedure successfully completed.
```

To verify that the PL/SQL block completed correctly, you can select from the database the rows that were inserted by the PL/SQL code. The query and results in the following listing show the row the PL/SQL block created in the AREAS table:

```
select *
    from AREAS;

    RADIUS        AREA
---------- ----------
         3      28.27
```

The output shows that a single row was inserted into the AREAS table by the PL/SQL block. Only one row was created because only one Radius value was specified.

In the first section of the PL/SQL block, shown in the following listing, three variables are declared. You must declare the variables that will be used in the Executable Commands section of the PL/SQL block.

```
declare
    pi       constant NUMBER(9,7) := 3.1415927;
    radius INTEGER(5);
    area    NUMBER(14,2);
```

The first variable declared is *pi*, which is set to a constant value via the **constant** keyword. Because it is declared as a **constant**, the value of the variable *pi* cannot be changed in the Executable Commands section. The value is assigned via the **:=** operator:

```
pi       constant NUMBER(9,7) := 3.1415927;
```

You can also assign constant values via the **default** keyword:

```
pi      NUMBER(9,7) DEFAULT 3.1415927;
```

The next two variables are defined but are not given default values:

```
radius INTEGER(5);
 area   NUMBER(14,2);
```

You can assign an initial value to a variable in the Declarations section. To set an initial value for a variable, simply follow its datatype specification with the value assignment, as shown in the following listing:

```
radius INTEGER(5)  := 3;
```

In the example, the datatypes include NUMBER and INTEGER. PL/SQL datatypes include all the valid SQL datatypes as well as complex datatypes based on query structures. Table 29-1 lists the supported PL/SQL datatypes.

Scalar Datatypes

BINARY_DOUBLE*	FLOAT	NUMBER	SMALLINT
BINARY_FLOAT*	INT	NUMERIC	STRING
BINARY_INTEGER	INTEGER	NVARCHAR2	TIMESTAMP
BOOLEAN	INTERVAL DAY TO SECOND	PLS_INTEGER	TIMESTAMP WITH LOCAL TIME ZONE
CHAR	INTERVAL YEAR TO MONTH	POSITIVE	TIMESTAMP WITH TIME ZONE
CHARACTER	LONG	POSITIVEN	UROWID
DATE	LONG RAW	RAW	VARCHAR
DEC	NATURAL	REAL	VARCHAR2
DECIMAL	NATURALN	ROWID	
DOUBLE PRECISION	NCHAR	SIGNTYPE	

*As of Oracle Database 10g, the new datatypes BINARY_FLOAT and BINARY_DOUBLE can improve performance in number-crunching applications, such as processing scientific data.

TABLE 29-1. *PL/SQL Datatypes*

Composite Types

RECORD	TABLE	VARRAY

Reference Types

REF CURSOR	REF *object_type*

LOB Types

BFILE	BLOB	CLOB**	NCLOB**

You can implicitly convert from CLOB to NCLOB or from NCLOB to CLOB. However, because this can be an expensive operation, it might help maintainability to continue using the **TO_CLOB and **TO_NCLOB** functions.

TABLE 29-1. *PL/SQL Datatypes* (continued)

In the following example, a cursor is declared to retrieve a record from the RADIUS_VALS table. RADIUS_VALS is a table with one column, named Radius, that holds radius values to be used in these examples. The cursor is declared in the Declarations section, and a variable named *rad_val* is declared with a datatype based on the cursor's results.

NOTE
For this example, the table RADIUS_VALS contains a single row with a Radius value of 3.

```
declare
    pi      constant NUMBER(9,7) := 3.1415927;
    area    NUMBER(14,2);
    cursor rad_cursor is
        select * from RADIUS_VALS;
    rad_val rad_cursor%ROWTYPE;
begin
    open rad_cursor;
    fetch rad_cursor into rad_val;
        area := pi*power(rad_val.radius,2);
        insert into AREAS values (rad_val.radius, area);
    close rad_cursor;
end;
/
```

In the first part of the Declarations section, the *pi* and *area* variables are defined, as they were in the examples earlier in this chapter. The *radius* variable is not defined; instead, a cursor named *rad_cursor* is defined. The cursor definition consists of a cursor name (*rad_cursor*) and a query (**select * from RADIUS_VALS;**). A cursor holds the results of a query for processing by other commands within the PL/SQL block:

```
declare
    pi      constant NUMBER(9,7) := 3.1415927;
    area    NUMBER(14,2);
    cursor rad_cursor is
        select * from RADIUS_VALS;
```

A final declaration creates a variable whose structure is anchored by the cursor's result set:

```
rad_val rad_cursor%ROWTYPE;
```

The *rad_val* variable will be able to reference each column of the query's result set. In this example, the query only returns a single column, but if the table contained multiple columns, you would be able to reference all of them via the *rad_val* variable.

In addition to the %ROWTYPE declaration, you can use the %TYPE declaration to inherit datatype information. If you use the %ROWTYPE declaration, the variable inherits the column and datatype information for all the columns in the cursor's result set. If you use the %TYPE declaration, the variable only inherits the definition of the column used to define it. You can even base %TYPE definitions on cursors, as shown in the following example:

```
cursor rad_cursor is
        select * from RADIUS_VALS;
 rad_val rad_cursor%ROWTYPE;
 rad_val_radius  rad_val.Radius%TYPE;
```

In the preceding listing, the *rad_val* variable inherits the datatypes of the result set of the *rad_cursor* cursor. The *rad_val_radius* variable inherits the datatype of the Radius column within the *rad_val* variable.

The advantage of datatype anchoring using %ROWTYPE and %TYPE definitions is that it makes the datatype definitions in your PL/SQL code independent of the underlying data structures. If the RADIUS_VALS Radius column is changed from a NUMBER(5) datatype to a NUMBER(4,2) datatype, you do not need to modify your PL/SQL code; the datatype assigned to the associated variables will be determined dynamically at runtime.

Executable Commands Section

In the Executable Commands section, you manipulate the variables and cursors declared in the Declarations section of your PL/SQL block. The Executable Commands section always starts with the keyword **begin**. In the following listing, the first PL/SQL block example from the Declarations section is repeated: The area of a circle is calculated, and the results are inserted into the AREAS table:

```
declare
   pi      constant NUMBER(9,7) := 3.1415927;
   radius INTEGER(5);
   area   NUMBER(14,2);
begin
   radius := 3;
   area := pi*power(radius,2);
   insert into AREAS values (radius, area);
end;
/
```

In the preceding listing, the Executable Commands section is as follows:

```
begin
    radius := 3;
    area := pi*power(radius,2);
    insert into AREAS values (radius, area);
end;
```

Following the **begin** keyword, the PL/SQL block's work begins. First, a value is assigned to the *radius* variable, and the *radius* variable and the *pi* constant value are used to determine the value of the *area* variable. The Radius and Area values are then inserted into the AREAS table.

The Executable Commands section of the PL/SQL block may contain commands that execute the cursors declared in the Declarations section. In the following example (from the "Declarations Section" section of this chapter), the Executable Commands section features several commands that reference the *rad_cursor* cursor:

```
declare
    pi        constant NUMBER(9,7) := 3.1415927;
    area      NUMBER(14,2);
    cursor rad_cursor is
        select * from RADIUS_VALS;
    rad_val rad_cursor%ROWTYPE;
begin
    open rad_cursor;
    fetch rad_cursor into rad_val;
      area := pi*power(rad_val.radius,2);
      insert into AREAS values (rad_val.radius, area);
    close rad_cursor;
end;
/
```

In the first command involving the cursor, the **open** command is used:

```
open rad_cursor;
```

When the *rad_cursor* cursor is **open**ed, the query declared for that cursor is executed and the records to be returned are identified. Next, records are **fetch**ed from the cursor:

```
fetch rad_cursor into rad_val;
```

In the Declarations section, the *rad_val* variable is declared to anchor its datatypes to the *rad_cursor* cursor:

```
cursor rad_cursor is
        select * from RADIUS_VALS;
    rad_val rad_cursor%ROWTYPE;
```

When you **fetch** a record from the cursor into the *rad_val* variable, you can still address each column value selected via the cursor's query. When the cursor's data is no longer needed, you can **close** the cursor, as shown in the following listing:

```
close rad_cursor;
```

The Executable Commands section may contain conditional logic, such as **if** commands and loops. In the following sections, you will see examples of each of the major types of flow-control operations permitted in PL/SQL. You can use the flow-control operations to alter the manner in which the fetched records and executable commands are managed.

Conditional Logic

Within PL/SQL, you can use **if**, **else**, **elsif**, and **case** commands to control the flow of commands within the Executable Commands section. The formats of the **if** clauses are shown in the following listing:

```
if   <some condition>
  then   <some command>
elsif  <some condition>
  then   <some command>
else  <some command>
end if;
```

You can nest **if** conditions within each other, as shown in the following listing:

```
if   <some condition>
  then
    if  <some condition>
      then   <some command>
    end if;
else  <some command>
end if;
```

By nesting **if** conditions, you can quickly develop complex logic flows within your Executable Commands section. When nesting **if** conditions, make sure you are not making the flow control more complex than it needs to be; always check to see whether logical conditions can be combined into simpler orders.

The "area of a circle" example used in the previous section will now be modified to include conditional logic. In the following listing, the Executable Commands section of the PL/SQL block has been modified to include **if** and **then** commands:

```
declare
    pi      constant NUMBER(9,7) := 3.1415927;
    area    NUMBER(14,2);
    cursor rad_cursor is
        select * from RADIUS_VALS;
    rad_val rad_cursor%ROWTYPE;
begin
  open rad_cursor;
  fetch rad_cursor into rad_val;
    area := pi*power(rad_val.radius,2);
    if  area > 30
```

```
      then
          insert into AREAS values (rad_val.radius, area);
      end if;
  close rad_cursor;
end;
/
```

In the preceding listing, an **if** condition is used to control the flow of commands within the Executable Commands section of the PL/SQL block. The flow-control commands are shown in the following listing:

```
if  area > 30
   then
       insert into AREAS values (rad_val.radius, area);
   end if;
```

The flow-control commands in this example begin after the *area* variable's value has been determined. If the value is greater than 30, then a record will be inserted into the AREAS table; if the value is less than 30, then no record will be inserted into the table. You can use this sort of flow control to direct which of several SQL statements are to be executed, based on the conditions in your **if** conditions.

The following listing shows the syntax for flow control involving SQL commands:

```
if  area>30
   then  <some command>
elsif  area<10
   then  <some command>
else  <some command>
end if;
```

Following illustrations of the supported types of loops, you will see the use of **case** commands for flow control.

Loops

You can use loops to process multiple records within a single PL/SQL block. PL/SQL supports three types of loops:

Simple loops	A loop that keeps repeating until an **exit** or **exit when** statement is reached within the loop
FOR loops	A loop that repeats a specified number of times
WHILE loops	A loop that repeats while a condition is met

In the following sections, you will see examples of each type of loop. The loop examples use as their starting point the PL/SQL blocks used previously in this chapter. You can use loops to process multiple records from a cursor.

Simple Loops

In the following listing, a simple loop is used to generate multiple rows in the AREAS table. The loop is started by the **loop** keyword, and the **exit when** clause determines when the loop should be exited. An **end loop** clause identifies the end of the loop.

```
declare
   pi      constant NUMBER(9,7) := 3.1415927;
   radius INTEGER(5);
   area   NUMBER(14,2);
begin
   radius := 3;
   loop
     area := pi*power(radius,2);
       insert into AREAS values (radius, area);
     radius := radius+1;
     exit when area >100;
   end loop;
end;
/
```

The loop section of this example establishes the flow control for the commands in the Executable Commands section of the PL/SQL block. The steps within the loop are described in the following commented version of the **loop** commands:

```
loop
        /* Calculate the area, based on the radius value.   */
     area := pi*power(radius,2);
        /* Insert the current values into the AREAS table.  */
        insert into AREAS values (radius, area);
        /* Increment the radius value by 1.                 */
     radius := radius+1;
        /* Evaluate the last calculated area.  If the value */
        /* exceeds 100, then exit.  Otherwise, repeat the   */
        /* loop using the new radius value.                 */
     exit when area >100;
        /* Signal the end of the loop.                      */
   end loop;
```

The loop should generate multiple entries in the AREAS table. The first record will be the record generated by a Radius value of 3. Once an *area* value exceeds 100, no more records will be inserted into the AREAS table.

Sample output following the execution of the PL/SQL block is shown in the following listing:

```
select *
  from AREAS
 order by Radius;
```

```
    RADIUS      AREA
---------- ----------
         3      28.27
         4      50.27
         5      78.54
         6      113.1
```

Because the *area* value for a Radius value of 6 exceeds 100, no further Radius values are processed and the PL/SQL block completes.

Simple Cursor Loops

You can use the attributes of a cursor—such as whether or not any rows are left to be fetched—as the exit criteria for a loop. In the following example, a cursor is executed until no more rows are returned by the query. To determine the status of the cursor, the cursor's attributes are checked. Cursors have four attributes you can use in your program:

%FOUND A record can be fetched from the cursor.

%NOTFOUND No more records can be fetched from the cursor.

%ISOPEN The cursor has been opened.

%ROWCOUNT The number of rows fetched from the cursor so far.

The %FOUND, %NOTFOUND, and %ISOPEN cursor attributes are Booleans; they are set to either TRUE or FALSE. Because they are Boolean attributes, you can evaluate their settings without explicitly matching them to values of TRUE or FALSE. For example, the following command will cause an exit to occur when rad_cursor%NOTFOUND is TRUE:

```
exit when rad_cursor%NOTFOUND;
```

In the following listing, a simple loop is used to process multiple rows from a cursor:

```
declare
  pi      constant NUMBER(9,7) := 3.1415927;
  area    NUMBER(14,2);
  cursor rad_cursor is
     select * from RADIUS_VALS;
  rad_val rad_cursor%ROWTYPE;
begin
  open rad_cursor;
  loop
    fetch rad_cursor into rad_val;
    exit when rad_cursor%NOTFOUND;
      area := pi*power(rad_val.radius,2);
      insert into AREAS values (rad_val.radius, area);
  end loop;
  close rad_cursor;
end;
/
```

The loop section of the PL/SQL block uses values from the RADIUS_VALS table as its input. Instead of basing the exit criteria on the Area value, the cursor's %NOTFOUND attribute is checked. If no more rows are found in the cursor, then %NOTFOUND will be TRUE—and, therefore, the loop will be exited. The commented version of the loop is shown in the following listing:

```
loop
      /*  Within the loop, fetch a record.          */
   fetch rad_cursor into rad_val;
      /*  If the fetch attempt reveals no more       */
      /*  records in the cursor, then exit the loop. */
   exit when rad_cursor%NOTFOUND;
      /*  If the fetch attempt returned a record,    */
      /*  then process the Radius value and insert   */
      /*  a record into the AREAS table.             */
   area := pi*power(rad_val.radius,2);
   insert into AREAS values (rad_val.radius, area);
      /*  Signal the end of the loop.                */
   end loop;
```

When the preceding PL/SQL block is executed, every record in the RADIUS_VALS table will be processed by the loop. So far, the RADIUS_VALS table only contains one record—a Radius value of 3.

NOTE
Prior to executing the PL/SQL block for this section, add two new Radius values—4 and 10—to the RADIUS_VALS table.

The following listing shows the addition of the new records to the RADIUS_VALS table:

```
insert into RADIUS_VALS values (4);
insert into RADIUS_VALS values (10);
commit;

select *
  from RADIUS_VALS
 order by Radius;

    RADIUS
----------
         3
         4
        10
```

Once the new records have been added to the RADIUS_VALS table, execute the PL/SQL block shown earlier in this section. The output of the PL/SQL block is shown in the following listing:

```
select *
  from AREAS
 order by Radius;
```

```
RADIUS       AREA
----------  ----------
        3     28.27
        4     50.27
       10    314.16
```

The query of the AREAS table shows that every record in the RADIUS_VALS table was fetched from the cursor and processed. When there were no more records to process in the cursor, the loop was exited and the PL/SQL block completed.

FOR Loops

A simple loop executes until an **exit** condition is met, whereas a FOR loop executes a specified number of times. An example of a FOR loop is shown in the following listing. The FOR loop's start is indicated by the keyword **for**, followed by the criteria used to determine when the processing is complete and the loop can be exited. Because the number of times the loop is executed is set when the loop is begun, an **exit** command isn't needed within the loop.

In the following example, the areas of circles are calculated based on Radius values ranging from 1 through 7, inclusive.

```
delete from AREAS;

declare
  pi      constant NUMBER(9,7) := 3.1415927;
  radius INTEGER(5);
  area    NUMBER(14,2);
begin
  for radius in 1..7 loop
    area := pi*power(radius,2);
    insert into AREAS values (radius, area);
  end loop;
end;
/
```

The steps involved in processing the loop are shown in the following commented listing:

```
    /*  Specify the criteria for the number of loop      */
    /*  executions.                                       */
  for radius in 1..7 loop
    /*  Calculate the area using the current Radius       */
    /*  value.                                            */
    area := pi*power(radius,2);
    /*  Insert the area and radius values into the AREAS  */
    /*  table.                                            */
    insert into AREAS values (radius, area);
    /*  Signal the end of the loop.                       */
  end loop;
```

Note that there is no line that says

```
radius := radius+1;
```

in the FOR loop. Because the specification of the loop specifies

```
for radius in 1..7 loop
```

the Radius values are already specified. For each value, all the commands within the loop are executed (these commands can include other conditional logic, such as **if** conditions). Once the loop has completed processing a Radius value, the limits on the **for** clause are checked, and either the next Radius value is used or the loop execution is complete.

Sample output from the FOR loop execution is shown in the following listing:

```
select *
  from AREAS
 order by Radius;

    RADIUS        AREA
---------- ----------
         1        3.14
         2       12.57
         3       28.27
         4       50.27
         5       78.54
         6       113.1
         7      153.94

7 rows selected.
```

Cursor FOR Loops

Whereas a FOR loop executes a specified number of times, a Cursor FOR loop uses the results of a query to dynamically determine the number of times the loop is executed. In a Cursor FOR loop, the opening, fetching, and closing of cursors is performed implicitly; you do not need to explicitly specify these actions.

The following listing shows a Cursor FOR loop that queries the RADIUS_VALS table and inserts records into the AREAS table:

```
delete from AREAS;

declare
  pi      constant NUMBER(9,7) := 3.1415927;
  area    NUMBER(14,2);
  cursor rad_cursor is
      select * from RADIUS_VALS;
begin
  for rad_val in rad_cursor
    loop
      area := pi*power(rad_val.radius,2);
      insert into AREAS values (rad_val.radius, area);
    end loop;
end;
/
```

In a Cursor FOR loop, there is no **open** or **fetch** command. The command

```
for rad_val in rad_cursor
```

implicitly opens the *rad_cursor* cursor and fetches a value into the *rad_val* variable. When no more records are in the cursor, the loop is exited and the cursor is closed. In a Cursor FOR loop, there is no need for a **close** command. Note that *rad_val* is not explicitly declared in the block.

The loop portion of the PL/SQL block is shown in the following listing, with comments to indicate the flow of control. The loop is controlled by the existence of a fetchable record in the *rad_cursor* cursor. There is no need to check the cursor's %NOTFOUND attribute—that is automated via the Cursor FOR loop.

```
   /*  If a record can be fetched from the cursor,    */
   /*  then fetch it into the rad_val variable.  If   */
   /*  no rows can be fetched, then skip the loop.    */
 for rad_val in rad_cursor
   /*  Begin the loop commands.                       */
 loop
    /*  Calculate the area based on the Radius value */
    /*  and insert a record into the AREAS table.    */
   area := pi*power(rad_val.radius,2);
   insert into AREAS values (rad_val.radius, area);
   /*  Signal the end of the loop commands.          */
 end loop;
```

Sample output is shown in the following listing; for this example, the RADIUS_VALS table has three records, with Radius values of 3, 4, and 10:

```
select *
  from RADIUS_VALS
 order by Radius;

    RADIUS
----------
         3
         4
        10
```

The execution of the PL/SQL block with the Cursor FOR loop will generate the following records in the AREAS table:

```
select *
  from AREAS
 order by Radius;

    RADIUS        AREA
---------- ----------
         3       28.27
         4       50.27
        10      314.16
```

WHILE Loops

A WHILE loop is processed until an exit condition is met. Instead of the exit condition being specified via an **exit** command within the loop, the exit condition is specified in the **while** command that initiates the loop.

In the following listing, a WHILE loop is created so that multiple Radius values will be processed. If the current value of the Radius variable meets the **while** condition in the loop's specification, then the loop's commands are processed. Once a Radius value fails the **while** condition in the loop's specification, the loop's execution is terminated:

```
delete from AREAS;

declare
  pi       constant NUMBER(9,7) := 3.1415927;
  radius  INTEGER(5);
  area     NUMBER(14,2);
begin
  radius := 3;
  while radius<=7
    loop
      area := pi*power(radius,2);
      insert into AREAS values (radius, area);
    radius := radius+1;
  end loop;
end;
/
```

The WHILE loop is similar in structure to the simple loop because it terminates based on a variable's value. The following listing shows the steps involved in the loop, with embedded comments:

```
    /*  Set an initial value for the Radius variable.    */
  radius := 3;
    /*  Establish the criteria for the termination of    */
    /*  the loop.  If the condition is met, execute the   */
    /*  commands within the loop.  If the condition is    */
    /*  not met, then terminate the loop.                 */
  while radius<=7
      /*  Begin the commands to be executed.              */
    loop
      /*  Calculate the area based on the current         */
      /*  Radius value and insert a record in the         */
      /*  AREAS table.                                    */
      area := pi*power(radius,2);
      insert into AREAS values (radius, area);
    /*  Set a new value for the Radius variable.  The     */
    /*  new value of Radius will be evaluated against     */
    /*  the termination criteria and the loop commands    */
    /*  will be executed for the new Radius value or      */
    /*  the loop will terminate.                          */
```

```
   radius := radius+1;
    /*  Signal the end of the commands within the loop. */
   end loop;
```

When executed, the PL/SQL block in the previous listing will generate records in the AREAS table. The output of the PL/SQL block is shown in the following listing:

```
select *
  from AREAS
 order by Radius;

    RADIUS        AREA
---------- ----------
         3       28.27
         4       50.27
         5       78.54
         6       113.1
         7      153.94
```

Because of the value assigned to the Radius variable prior to the loop, the loop is forced to execute at least once. You should verify that your variable assignments meet the conditions used to limit the loop executions.

CASE Statements

You can use **case** statements to control the branching logic within your PL/SQL blocks. For example, you can use **case** statements to assign values conditionally or to transform values prior to inserting them. In the following example, **case** expressions use the Radius values to determine which rows to insert into the AREAS table:

```
declare
    pi      constant NUMBER(9,7) := 3.1415927;
    area    NUMBER(14,2);
    cursor rad_cursor is
        select * from RADIUS_VALS;
    rad_val rad_cursor%ROWTYPE;
begin
    open rad_cursor;
    loop
      fetch rad_cursor into rad_val;
      exit when rad_cursor%NOTFOUND;
      area := pi*power(rad_val.radius,2);
      case
        when rad_val.Radius = 3
          then
            insert into AREAS values (rad_val.radius, area);
        when rad_val.Radius = 4
          then
            insert into AREAS values (rad_val.radius, area);
        when rad_val.Radius = 10
```

```
       then
          insert into AREAS values (0, 0);
       else raise CASE_NOT_FOUND;
     end case;
  end loop;
  close rad_cursor;
end;
/
```

This block generates the following output. When the Radius value is 10, the **case** clause inserts a row with the Radius and Area values both set to 0:

```
select * from AREAS;

    RADIUS       AREA
---------- ----------
         3      28.27
         4      50.27
         0          0
```

The keyword **case** begins the clause:

```
     case
        when rad_val.Radius = 3
          then
             insert into AREAS values (rad_val.radius, area);
```

The **when** clauses are evaluated sequentially. The **else** keyword within the **case** clause works similarly to the **else** keyword within an **if-then** clause. If you omit the **else** keyword, PL/SQL adds the following implicit **else** clause:

```
else raise CASE_NOT_FOUND;
```

The **end case** clause ends the **case** clause. The **case** clause is commonly used to translate lists of values to their descriptions, as in the case of the bookshelf category names. The following listing shows how CategoryName values can be translated to other values as part of SQL commands:

```
     case CategoryName
        when  'ADULTFIC' then 'Adult Fiction'
        when  'ADULTNF' then 'Adult Nonfiction'
        when  'ADULTREF' then 'Adult Reference'
        when  'CHILDRENFIC' then 'Children Fiction'
        when  'CHILDRENNF' then 'Children Nonfiction'
        when  'CHILDRENPIC' then 'Children Picturebook'
        else CategoryName
     end
```

See Chapter 16 for examples of the complex uses of **case**.

Exception Handling Section

When user-defined or system-related exceptions (errors) are encountered, the control of the PL/SQL block shifts to the Exception Handling section. Within the Exception Handling section, the **when** clause is used to evaluate which exception is to be "raised"—that is, executed.

If an exception is raised within the Executable Commands section of your PL/SQL block, the flow of commands immediately leaves the Executable Commands section and searches the Exception Handling section for an exception matching the error encountered. PL/SQL provides a set of system-defined exceptions and allows you to add your own exceptions. Examples of user-defined exceptions are shown in Chapters 30 and 31.

The Exception Handling section always begins with the keyword **exception**, and it precedes the **end** command that terminates the Executable Commands section of the PL/SQL block. The placement of the Exception Handling section within the PL/SQL block is shown in the following listing:

```
declare
   <declarations section>
begin
   <executable commands>
 exception
   <exception handling>
end;
```

The Exception Handling section of a PL/SQL block is optional—none of the PL/SQL blocks shown previously in this chapter included an Exception Handling section. However, the examples shown in this chapter have been based on a very small set of known input values with very limited processing performed.

In the following listing, the simple loop for calculating the area of a circle is shown, with two modifications. A new variable named *some_variable* is declared in the Declarations section, and a calculation to determine the variable's value is created in the Executable Commands section.

```
declare
   pi      constant NUMBER(9,7) := 3.1415927;
   radius INTEGER(5);
   area    NUMBER(14,2);
   some_variable   NUMBER(14,2);
begin
   radius := 3;
   loop
     some_variable := 1/(radius-4);
     area := pi*power(radius,2);
       insert into AREAS values (radius, area);
     radius := radius+1;
     exit when area >100;
   end loop;
end;
/
```

Because the calculation for *some_variable* involves division, you may encounter a situation in which the calculation attempts to divide by zero—an error condition. The first time through the loop, the *radius* variable (with an initial value of 3) is processed and a record is inserted into the AREAS table. The second time through the loop, the *radius* variable has a value of 4—and the calculation for *some_variable* encounters an error:

```
declare
*
ERROR at line 1:
ORA-01476: divisor is equal to zero
ORA-06512: at line 9
```

Because an error was encountered, the first row inserted into AREAS is rolled back, and the PL/SQL block terminates.

You can modify the processing of the error condition by adding an Exception Handling section to the PL/SQL block, as shown in the following listing:

```
delete from AREAS;

declare
  pi      constant NUMBER(9,7) := 3.1415927;
  radius INTEGER(5);
  area    NUMBER(14,2);
  some_variable   NUMBER(14,2);
begin
  radius := 3;
  loop
    some_variable := 1/(radius-4);
    area := pi*power(radius,2);
      insert into AREAS values (radius, area);
    radius := radius+1;
    exit when area >100;
  end loop;
exception
  when ZERO_DIVIDE
  then insert into AREAS values (0,0);
end;
/
```

The Exception Handling section of the PL/SQL block is repeated in the following listing:

```
exception
  when ZERO_DIVIDE
  then insert into AREAS values (0,0);
```

When the PL/SQL block encounters an error, it scans the Exception Handling section for the defined exceptions. In this case, it finds the ZERO_DIVIDE exception, which is one of the system-defined exceptions available in PL/SQL. In addition to the system-defined exceptions and user-defined exceptions, you can use the **when others** clause to address all exceptions not defined

within your Exception Handling section. The command within the Exception Handling section for the matching exception is executed and a row is inserted into the AREAS table. The output of the PL/SQL block is shown in the following listing:

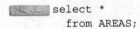

```
select *
  from AREAS;

     RADIUS        AREA
---------- ----------
         3       28.27
         0           0
```

The output shows that the first Radius value (3) was processed and that the exception was encountered on the second pass through the loop.

NOTE
*Once an exception is encountered, you cannot return to your normal flow of command processing within the Executable Commands section. If you need to maintain control within the Executable Commands section, you should use **if** conditions to test for possible exceptions before they are encountered by the program, or create a nested block with its own local exception handling.*

The available system-defined exceptions are listed in the "Exceptions" entry in the Alphabetical Reference. Examples of user-defined exceptions are shown in Chapters 30 and 31.

See Chapter 32 for details on the use of dynamic PL/SQL, which allows for the dynamic creation of the commands executed within the PL/SQL block.

PL/SQL supports complex queries that use the most recent features in Oracle's SQL. For example, flashback version queries (see Chapter 27) and regular expression functions (see Chapter 8) are both supported within PL/SQL as of their introduction in Oracle Database 10*g*. See those chapters for details on the new features; they can be introduced into your PL/SQL and may simplify and enhance your processing capabilities.

CHAPTER
30

Triggers

 trigger defines an action the database should take when some database-related event occurs. Triggers may be used to supplement declarative referential integrity, to enforce complex business rules, or to audit changes to data. The code within a trigger, called the *trigger body,* is made up of PL/SQL blocks (see Chapter 29).

The execution of triggers is transparent to the user. Triggers are executed by the database when specific types of data manipulation commands are performed on specific tables. Such commands may include **insert**s, **update**s, and **delete**s. Updates of specific columns may also be used as triggering events. Triggering events may also include DDL commands and database events such as shutdowns and logins.

Because of their flexibility, triggers may supplement referential integrity; they should not be used to replace it. When enforcing the business rules in an application, you should first rely on the declarative referential integrity available with Oracle; use triggers to enforce rules that cannot be coded through referential integrity.

Required System Privileges

To create a trigger on a table, you must be able to alter that table. Therefore, you must either own the table, or have the ALTER privilege for the table, or have the ALTER ANY TABLE system privilege. In addition, you must have the CREATE TRIGGER system privilege; to create triggers in another user's schema you must have the CREATE ANY TRIGGER system privilege. The CREATE TRIGGER system privilege is part of the RESOURCE role provided with Oracle.

NOTE
*The RESOURCE role is provided in Oracle Database 10g only
for backward compatibility and should not be used regularly.*

To *alter* a trigger, you must either own the trigger or have the ALTER ANY TRIGGER system privilege. You may also enable or disable triggers by altering the tables they are based on, which requires that you have either the ALTER privilege for that table or the ALTER ANY TABLE system privilege. For information on altering triggers, see "Enabling and Disabling Triggers," later in this chapter.

To create a trigger on a database-level event, you must have the ADMINISTER DATABASE TRIGGER system privilege.

Required Table Privileges

Triggers may reference tables other than the one that initiated the triggering event. For example, if you use triggers to audit changes to data in the BOOKSHELF table, then you may insert a record into a different table (say, BOOKSHELF_AUDIT) every time a record is changed in BOOKSHELF. To do this, you need to have privileges to insert into BOOKSHELF_AUDIT (to perform the triggered transaction).

NOTE
*The privileges needed for triggered transactions cannot come from
roles; they must be granted directly to the creator of the trigger.*

Types of Triggers

A trigger's type is defined by the type of triggering transaction and by the level at which the trigger is executed. In the following sections, you will see descriptions of these classifications, along with relevant restrictions.

Row-Level Triggers

Row-level triggers execute once for each row affected by a DML statement. For the BOOKSHELF table auditing example described earlier, each row that is changed in the BOOKSHELF table may be processed by the trigger. Row-level triggers are the most common type of trigger; they are often used in data auditing applications. Row-level triggers are also useful for keeping distributed data in sync. Materialized views, which use internal row-level triggers for this purpose, are described in Chapter 24.

Row-level triggers are created using the **for each row** clause in the **create trigger** command. The syntax for triggers is shown in "Trigger Syntax," later in this chapter.

Statement-Level Triggers

Statement-level triggers execute once for each DML statement. For example, if a single INSERT statement inserts 500 rows into the BOOKSHELF table, a statement-level trigger on that table would only be executed once. Statement-level triggers therefore are not often used for data-related activities; they are normally used to enforce additional security measures on the types of actions that may be performed on a table.

Statement-level triggers are the default type of trigger created via the **create trigger** command. The syntax for triggers is shown in "Trigger Syntax," later in this chapter.

BEFORE and AFTER Triggers

Because triggers are executed by events, they may be set to occur immediately before or after those events. Since the events that execute triggers include database DML statements, triggers can be executed immediately before or after **insert**s, **update**s, and **delete**s. For database-level events, additional restrictions apply; you cannot trigger an event to occur before a login or startup takes place.

Within the trigger, you can reference the old and new values involved in the DML statement. The access required for the old and new data may determine which type of trigger you need. "Old" refers to the data as it existed prior to the DML statement; **update**s and **delete**s usually reference old values. "New" values are the data values that the DML statement creates (such as the columns in an inserted record).

If you need to set a column value in an inserted row via your trigger, then you need to use a BEFORE INSERT trigger to access the "new" values. Using an AFTER INSERT trigger would not allow you to set the inserted value, since the row will already have been inserted into the table.

Row-level AFTER triggers are frequently used in auditing applications, since they do not fire until the row has been modified. The row's successful modification implies that it has passed the referential integrity constraints defined for that table.

INSTEAD OF Triggers

You can use INSTEAD OF triggers to tell Oracle what to do *instead of* performing the actions that invoked the trigger. For example, you could use an INSTEAD OF trigger on a view to redirect **insert**s

into a table or to **update** multiple tables that are part of a view. You can use INSTEAD OF triggers on either object views (see Chapter 33) or relational views.

For example, if a view involves a join of two tables, your ability to use the **update** command on records in the view is limited. However, if you use an INSTEAD OF trigger, you can tell Oracle how to **update**, **delete**, or **insert** records in the view's underlying tables when a user attempts to change values via the view. The code in the INSTEAD OF trigger is executed *in place of* the **insert**, **update**, or **delete** command you enter.

> **NOTE**
> *You can access or change LOB data within BEFORE and INSTEAD OF triggers.*

In this chapter, you will see how to implement basic triggers. INSTEAD OF triggers, which were initially introduced to support object views, are described in Chapter 33.

Schema Triggers

You can create triggers on schema-level operations such as **create table**, **alter table**, **drop table**, **audit**, **rename**, **truncate**, and **revoke**. You can even create a **before ddl** trigger. For the most part, schema-level triggers provide two capabilities: preventing DDL operations and providing additional security monitoring when DDL operations occur.

Database-Level Triggers

You can create triggers to be fired on database events, including errors, logins, logoffs, shutdowns, and startups. You can use this type of trigger to automate database maintenance or auditing actions. Virtual Private Databases, as described in Chapter 19, rely on database-level triggers to establish session-context variable values.

Trigger Syntax

The full syntax for the **create trigger** command is shown in the Alphabetical Reference section of this book. The following listing contains an abbreviated version of the command syntax:

```
create [or replace] trigger [schema .] trigger
{ before | after | instead of }
{ dml_event_clause
| { ddl_event [or ddl_event]...
  | database_event [or database_event]...
  }
  on { [schema .] schema | database }
}
[when ( condition ) ]
{ pl/sql_block | call_procedure_statement }
```

The syntax options available depend on the type of trigger in use. For example, a trigger on a DML event will use the *dml_event_clause*, which follows this syntax:

```
{ delete | insert | update [of column [, column]...] }
[or { delete | insert | update [of column [, column]...] }]...
on { [schema .] table | [nested table nested_table_column of] [schema .] view
}
[referencing_clause] [for each row]
```

Clearly, there is a great deal of flexibility in the design of a trigger. The **before** and **after** keywords indicate whether the trigger should be executed before or after the triggering event. If the **instead of** clause is used, the trigger's code will be executed instead of the event that caused the trigger to be invoked. The **delete**, **insert**, and **update** keywords (the last of which may include a column list) indicate the type of data manipulation that will constitute a triggering event. When referring to the old and new values of columns, you can use the defaults ("old" and "new") or you can use the **referencing** clause to specify other names.

When the **for each row** clause is used, the trigger will be a row-level trigger; otherwise, it will be a statement-level trigger. The **when** clause is used to further restrict when the trigger is executed. The restrictions enforced in the **when** clause may include checks of old and new data values.

For example, suppose we want to track any changes to the Rating value in the BOOKSHELF table whenever rating values are lowered. First, we'll create a table that will store the audit records:

```
drop table BOOKSHELF_AUDIT;
create table BOOKSHELF_AUDIT
(Title         VARCHAR2(100),
Publisher      VARCHAR2(20),
CategoryName   VARCHAR2(20),
Old_Rating     VARCHAR2(2),
New_Rating     VARCHAR2(2),
Audit_Date     DATE);
```

The following row-level BEFORE UPDATE trigger will be executed only if the Rating value is lowered. This example also illustrates the use of the **new** keyword, which refers to the new value of the column, and the **old** keyword, which refers to the old value of the column.

```
create or replace trigger BOOKSHELF_BEF_UPD_ROW
before update on BOOKSHELF
for each row
when (new.Rating < old.Rating)
begin
  insert into BOOKSHELF_AUDIT
    (Title, Publisher, CategoryName,
    Old_Rating, New_Rating, Audit_Date)
  values
    (:old.Title, :old.Publisher, :old.CategoryName,
    :old.Rating, :new.Rating, Sysdate);
end;
/
```

Breaking this **create trigger** command into its components makes it easier to understand. First, the trigger is named:

```
create or replace trigger BOOKSHELF_BEF_UPD_ROW
```

The name of the trigger contains the name of the table it acts upon and the type of trigger it is. (See "Naming Triggers," later in this chapter, for information on naming conventions.)

This trigger applies to the BOOKSHELF table; it will be executed before **update** transactions have been committed to the database:

```
before update on BOOKSHELF
```

Because the **for each row** clause is used, the trigger will apply to each row changed by the **update** statement. If this clause is not used, then the trigger will execute at the statement level.

```
for each row
```

The **when** clause adds further criteria to the triggering condition. The triggering event not only must be an **update** of the BOOKSHELF table, but also must reflect a lowering of the Rating value:

```
when (new.Rating < old.Rating)
```

The PL/SQL code shown in the following listing is the trigger body. The commands shown here are to be executed for every **update** of the BOOKSHELF table that passes the **when** condition. For this to succeed, the BOOKSHELF_AUDIT table must exist, and the owner of the trigger must have been granted privileges (directly, not via roles) on that table. This example **insert**s the old values from the BOOKSHELF record into the BOOKSHELF_AUDIT table before the BOOKSHELF record is updated.

```
begin
    insert into BOOKSHELF_AUDIT
    (Title, Publisher, CategoryName,
     Old_Rating, New_Rating, Audit_Date)
    values
    (:old.Title, :old.Publisher, :old.CategoryName,
     :old.Rating, :new.Rating, Sysdate);
end;
```

NOTE
*When the **new** and **old** keywords are referenced in the PL/SQL block, they are preceded by colons (:).*

This example is typical of auditing triggers. The auditing activity is completely transparent to the user who performs the **update** of the BOOKSHELF table. However, the transaction against the BOOKSHELF table is dependent on the successful execution of the trigger.

Combining DML Trigger Types

Triggers for multiple **insert**, **update**, and **delete** commands on a table can be combined into a single trigger, provided they are all at the same level (row level or statement level). The following

example shows a trigger that is executed whenever an **insert** or an **update** occurs. Several points (shown in bold) should stand out in this example:

- The **update** portion of the trigger occurs only when the Rating column's value is updated.

- An **if** clause is used within the PL/SQL block to determine which of the two commands invoked the trigger.

- The column to be changed is specified in the *dml_event_clause* instead of in the **when** clause, as in prior examples.

```
drop trigger BOOKSHELF_BEF_UPD_ROW;

create or replace trigger BOOKSHELF_BEF_UPD_INS_ROW
before insert or update of Rating on BOOKSHELF
for each row
begin
  if INSERTING then
    insert into BOOKSHELF_AUDIT
      (Title, Publisher, CategoryName,
       New_Rating, Audit_Date)
    values
      (:new.Title, :new.Publisher, :new.CategoryName,
       :new.Rating, Sysdate);
  else -- if not inserting then we are updating the Rating
    insert into BOOKSHELF_AUDIT
      (Title, Publisher, CategoryName,
       Old_Rating, New_Rating, Audit_Date)
    values
      (:old.Title, :old.Publisher, :old.CategoryName,
       :old.Rating, :new.Rating, Sysdate);
  end if;
end;
/
```

Again, look at the trigger's component parts. First, it is named and identified as a BEFORE INSERT and BEFORE UPDATE (of Rating) trigger, executing **for each row**:

```
create or replace trigger BOOKSHELF_BEF_UPD_INS_ROW
before insert or update of Rating on BOOKSHELF
for each row
```

The trigger body then follows. In the first part of the trigger body, shown in the following listing, the type of transaction is checked via an **if** clause. Valid transaction types are INSERTING, DELETING, and UPDATING. In this case, the trigger checks to see if the record is being inserted into the BOOKSHELF table. If it is, then the first part of the trigger body is executed. The INSERTING portion of the trigger body inserts the new values of the record into the BOOKSHELF_AUDIT table.

```
begin
  if INSERTING then
```

```
insert into BOOKSHELF_AUDIT
  (Title, Publisher, CategoryName,
   New_Rating, Audit_Date)
values
  (:new.Title, :new.Publisher, :new.CategoryName,
   :new.Rating, Sysdate);
```

Other transaction types can then be checked. In this example, because the trigger executed, the transaction must be either an **insert** or an **update** of the Rating column. Since the **if** clause in the first half of the trigger body checks for **insert**s, and the trigger is only executed for **insert**s and **update**s, the only conditions that should execute the second half of the trigger body are **update**s of Rating. Therefore, no additional **if** clauses are necessary to determine the DML event type. This portion of the trigger body is the same as in the previous example: Prior to being updated, the old values in the row are written to the BOOKSHELF_AUDIT table.

```
else -- if not inserting then we are updating the Rating
  insert into BOOKSHELF_AUDIT
    (Title, Publisher, CategoryName,
     Old_Rating, New_Rating, Audit_Date)
  values
    (:old.Title, :old.Publisher, :old.CategoryName,
     :old.Rating, :new.Rating, Sysdate);
```

Combining trigger types in this manner may help you to coordinate trigger development among multiple developers, since it consolidates all the database events that depend on a single table.

Setting Inserted Values

You may use triggers to set column values during **insert**s and **update**s. The previous examples in this chapter set the BOOKSHELF_AUDIT.Audit_Date value to the result of the SYSDATE function. You may also use updates to support different application needs, such as storing an uppercase version of a value along with the mixed-case version entered by users. In that case, you may have partially denormalized your table to include a column for the derived data. Storing this data in an uppercase format (for this example, in the column UpperPerson) allows you to display data to the users in its natural format while using the uppercase column during queries.

Since the uppercase version of the value is derived data, it may become out of sync with the user-entered column. Unless your application supplies a value for the uppercase version during **insert**s, that column's value will be **NULL** when a new row is entered.

To avoid this synchronization problem, you can use a table-level trigger. Put a BEFORE INSERT and a BEFORE UPDATE trigger on the table; they will act at the row level. As shown in the following listing, this approach can set a new value for UpperName every time the Name column's value is changed in BOOKSHELF_CHECKOUT:

```
alter table BOOKSHELF_CHECKOUT add (UpperName VARCHAR2(25));

create or replace trigger BOOKSHELF_CHECKOUT_BUI_ROW
before insert or update of Name on BOOKSHELF_CHECKOUT
for each row
begin
```

```
    :new.UpperName := UPPER(:new.Name);
end;
/
```

In this example, the trigger body determines the value for UpperName by using the UPPER function on the Name column. This trigger will be executed every time a row is inserted into BOOKSHELF_ CHECKOUT and every time the Name column is updated. The Name and UpperName columns will thus be kept in sync.

Maintaining Duplicated Data

The method of setting values via triggers, shown in the preceding section, can be combined with the remote data access methods described in Chapter 23. As with materialized views, you may replicate all or some of the rows in a table.

For example, you may want to create and maintain a second copy of your application's audit log. By doing so, you safeguard against a single application's erasing the audit log records created by multiple applications. Duplicate audit logs are frequently used in security monitoring.

Consider the BOOKSHELF_AUDIT table used in the examples in this chapter. A second table, BOOKSHELF_AUDIT_DUP, could be created, possibly in a remote database. For this example, assume that a database link called AUDIT_LINK can be used to connect the user to the database in which BOOKSHELF_AUDIT_DUP resides (refer to Chapter 23 for details on database links).

```
drop table BOOKSHELF_AUDIT_DUP;
create table BOOKSHELF_AUDIT_DUP
(Title          VARCHAR2(100),
Publisher       VARCHAR2(20),
CategoryName VARCHAR2(20),
Old_Rating      VARCHAR2(2),
New_Rating      VARCHAR2(2),
Audit_Date      DATE);
```

To automate populating the BOOKSHELF_AUDIT_DUP table, the following trigger could be placed on the BOOKSHELF_AUDIT table:

```
create or replace trigger BOOKSHELF_AUDIT_AFT_INS_ROW
after insert on BOOKSHELF_AUDIT
for each row
begin
 insert into BOOKSHELF_AUDIT_DUP@AUDIT_LINK
    (Title, Publisher, CategoryName,
    New_Rating, Audit_Date)
   values (:new.Title, :new.Publisher, :new.CategoryName,
    :new.New_Rating, :new.Audit_Date);
end;
/
```

As the trigger header shows, this trigger executes for each row that is inserted into the BOOKSHELF_ AUDIT table. It inserts a single record into the BOOKSHELF_AUDIT_DUP table in the database defined by the AUDIT_LINK database link. AUDIT_LINK may point to a database located on a remote server. If there is any problem with the remote insert initiated via the trigger, the local insert will fail.

For asynchronous replication requirements, consider using materialized views instead (see Chapter 24).

You can see the actions of these triggers by inserting a row into BOOKSHELF:

```
insert into BOOKSHELF
(Title, Publisher, CategoryName, Rating) values
('HARRY POTTER AND THE CHAMBER OF SECRETS',
'SCHOLASTIC','CHILDRENFIC','4');

1 row created.

select Title from BOOKSHELF_AUDIT;

TITLE
--------------------------------------------------
HARRY POTTER AND THE CHAMBER OF SECRETS

select Title from BOOKSHELF_AUDIT_DUP;

TITLE
--------------------------------------------------
HARRY POTTER AND THE CHAMBER OF SECRETS
```

Customizing Error Conditions

Within a single trigger, you may establish different error conditions. For each of the error conditions you define, you may select an error message that appears when the error occurs. The error numbers and messages that are displayed to the user are set via the RAISE_APPLICATION_ERROR procedure, which may be called from within any trigger.

The following example shows a statement-level BEFORE DELETE trigger on the BOOKSHELF table. When a user attempts to **delete** a record from the BOOKSHELF table, this trigger is executed and checks two system conditions: that the day of the week is neither Saturday nor Sunday, and that the Oracle username of the account performing the **delete** begins with the letters "LIB." The trigger's components will be described following the listing.

```
create or replace trigger BOOKSHELF_BEF_DEL
before delete on BOOKSHELF
declare
  weekend_error EXCEPTION;
  not_library_user EXCEPTION;
begin
 if TO_CHAR(SysDate,'DY') = 'SAT' or
    TO_CHAR(SysDate,'DY') = 'SUN' THEN
   RAISE weekend_error;
end if;
if SUBSTR(User,1,3) <> 'LIB' THEN
   RAISE not_library_user;
end if;
```

```
EXCEPTION
  WHEN weekend_error THEN
    RAISE_APPLICATION_ERROR (-20001,
      'Deletions not allowed on weekends');
  WHEN not_library_user THEN
    RAISE_APPLICATION_ERROR (-20002,
      'Deletions only allowed by Library users');
end;
/
```

The header of the trigger defines it as a statement-level BEFORE DELETE trigger:

```
create or replace trigger BOOKSHELF_BEF_DEL
before delete on BOOKSHELF
```

There are no **when** clauses in this trigger, so the trigger body is executed for all **delete**s.

The next portion of the trigger declares the names of the two exceptions that are defined within this trigger:

```
declare
  weekend_error EXCEPTION;
  not_library_user EXCEPTION;
```

The first part of the trigger body contains an **if** clause that uses the TO_CHAR function on the SYSDATE function. If the current day is either Saturday or Sunday, then the WEEKEND_ERROR error condition is raised. This error condition, called an *exception*, must be defined within the trigger body.

```
if TO_CHAR(SysDate,'DY') = 'SAT' or
   TO_CHAR(SysDate,'DY') = 'SUN' THEN
   RAISE weekend_error;
end if;
```

A second **if** clause checks the User pseudo-column to see if its first three letters are "LIB." If the username does not begin with "LIB," then the NOT_LIBRARY_USER exception is raised. In this example, the <> operator is used; this is equivalent to != (meaning "not equals").

```
if SUBSTR(User,1,3) <> 'LIB' THEN
   RAISE not_library_user;
end if;
```

The final portion of the trigger body tells the trigger how to handle the exceptions. It begins with the keyword **exception**, followed by a **when** clause for each of the exceptions. Each of the exceptions in this trigger calls the RAISE_APPLICATION_ERROR procedure, which takes two input parameters: the error number (which must be between –20001 and –20999), and the error message to be displayed. In this example, two different error messages are defined, one for each of the defined exceptions:

```
EXCEPTION
  WHEN weekend_error THEN
    RAISE_APPLICATION_ERROR (-20001,
```

```
        'Deletions not allowed on weekends');
   WHEN not_library_user THEN
     RAISE_APPLICATION_ERROR (-20002,
       'Deletions only allowed by Library users');
```

The use of the RAISE_APPLICATION_ERROR procedure gives you great flexibility in managing the error conditions that may be encountered within your trigger. For a further description of procedures, see Chapter 31.

NOTE
*The exceptions will still be raised even if the **delete** operations find no rows to delete.*

When a non-"LIB" user attempts to delete a row from BOOKSHELF on a weekday, this is the result:

```
delete from BOOKSHELF
where Title = 'MY LEDGER';

delete from BOOKSHELF
             *
ERROR at line 1:
ORA-20002: Deletions only allowed by Library users
ORA-06512: at "PRACTICE.BOOKSHELF_BEF_DEL", line 17
ORA-04088: error during execution of trigger 'PRACTICE.BOOKSHELF_BEF_DEL'
```

If you attempt to delete a row on a Saturday or Sunday, the ORA-20001 error is returned instead. As soon as an exception is encountered, Oracle leaves the main executable commands section of the trigger and processes the exception. You will only see the first exception encountered.

Calling Procedures Within Triggers

Rather than creating a large block of code within a trigger body, you can save the code as a stored procedure and call the procedure from within the trigger, by using the **call** command. For example, if you create an INSERT_BOOKSHELF_AUDIT_DUP procedure that inserts rows into BOOKSHELF_AUDIT_DUP, you can call it from a trigger on the BOOKSHELF_AUDIT table, as shown in the following listing:

```
create or replace trigger BOOKSHELF_AFT_INS_ROW
after insert on BOOKSHELF_AUDIT
for each row
begin
call INSERT_BOOKSHELF_AUDIT_DUP(:new.Title, :new.Publisher,
   :new.CategoryName, :new.Old_Rating, :new.New_Rating,
   :new.Audit_Date);
end;
/
```

Naming Triggers

The name of a trigger should clearly indicate the table it applies to, the DML commands that trigger it, its before/after status, and whether it is a row-level or statement-level trigger. Since a trigger name cannot exceed 30 characters in length, you need to use a standard set of abbreviations when naming. In general, the trigger name should include as much of the table name as possible. Thus, when creating a BEFORE UPDATE, row-level trigger on a table named BOOKSHELF_CHECKOUT, you should not name the trigger BEFORE_UPDATE_ROW_LEVEL_BC. A better name would be BOOKSHELF_CHECKOUT_BEF_UPD_ROW.

Creating DDL Event Triggers

You can create triggers that are executed when a DDL event occurs. If you are planning to use this feature solely for security purposes, you should investigate using the **audit** command instead. For example, you can use a DDL event trigger to execute the trigger code for **create**, **alter**, and **drop** commands performed on a cluster, function, index, package, procedure, role, sequence, synonym, table, tablespace, trigger, type, user, or view. If you use the **on schema** clause, the trigger will execute for any new data dictionary objects created in your schema. The following example will execute a procedure named INSERT_AUDIT_RECORD whenever objects are created within your schema:

```
create or replace trigger CREATE_DB_OBJECT_AUDIT
after create on schema
begin
  call INSERT_AUDIT_RECORD (ora_dict_obj_name);
end;
/
```

As shown in this example, you can reference system attributes such as the object name. The available attributes are listed in Table 30-1.

To protect the objects within a schema, you may want to create a trigger that is executed for each attempted **drop table** command. That trigger will have to be a BEFORE DROP trigger:

```
create or replace trigger PREVENT_DROP
  before drop on Practice.schema
begin
  if ora_dict_obj_owner = 'PRACTICE'
    and ora_dict_obj_name like 'BOO%'
    and ora_dict_obj_type = 'TABLE'
  then
    RAISE_APPLICATION_ERROR (
      -20002, 'Operation not permitted.');
  end if;
end;
/
```

Note that the trigger references the event attributes within its **if** clauses. Attempting to drop a table in the Practice schema whose name starts with BOO results in the following:

```
drop table BOOKSHELF_AUDIT_DUP;
```

```
drop table BOOKSHELF_AUDIT_DUP
*
ERROR at line 1:
ORA-00604: error occurred at recursive SQL level 1
ORA-20002: Operation not permitted.
ORA-06512: at line 6
```

You can use the RAISE_APPLICATION_ERROR procedure to further customize the error message displayed to the user.

Creating Database Event Triggers

Like DML events, database events can execute triggers. When a database event occurs (a shutdown, startup, or error), you can execute a trigger that references the attributes of the event (as with DDL events). You could use a database event trigger to perform system maintenance functions immediately after each database startup.

For example, the following trigger pins packages on each database startup. *Pinning packages* is an effective way of keeping large PL/SQL objects in the shared pool of memory, improving performance, and enhancing database stability. This trigger, PIN_ON_STARTUP, will run each time the database is started. You should create this trigger while connected as a user with ADMINISTER DATABASE TRIGGER privilege.

```
rem  while connected as a user with the
rem  ADMINISTER DATABASE TRIGGER system privilege:

create or replace trigger PIN_ON_STARTUP
after startup on database
begin
    DBMS_SHARED_POOL.KEEP (
        'SYS.STANDARD', 'P');
end;
/
```

This example shows a simple trigger that will be executed immediately after a database startup. You can modify the list of packages in the trigger body to include those most used by your applications.

Startup and shutdown triggers can access the ora_instance_num, ora_database_name, ora_login_user, and ora_sysevent attributes listed in Table 30-1. See the Alphabetical Reference for the full **create trigger** command syntax.

Enabling and Disabling Triggers

Unlike declarative integrity constraints (such as NOT NULL and PRIMARY KEY), triggers do not necessarily affect all rows in a table. They only affect operations of the specified type, and then only while the trigger is enabled. Any data created prior to a trigger's creation will not be affected by the trigger.

By default, a trigger is enabled when it is created. However, there are situations in which you may want to disable a trigger. The two most common reasons involve data loads. During large data loads, you may want to disable triggers that would execute during the load. Disabling the triggers during data loads may dramatically improve the performance of the load. After the data

has been loaded, you need to manually perform the data manipulation that the trigger would have performed had it been enabled during the data load.

The second data load–related reason for disabling a trigger occurs when a data load fails and has to be performed a second time. In such a case, it is likely that the data load partially succeeded— and thus the trigger was executed for a portion of the records loaded. During a subsequent load, the same records would be inserted. Thus, it is possible that the same trigger will be executed twice for the same **insert** operation (when that **insert** operation occurs during both loads). Depending on the nature of the operations and the triggers, this may not be desirable. If the trigger was enabled during the failed load, then it may need to be disabled prior to the start of a second data-load process. After the data has been loaded, you need to manually perform the data manipulation that the trigger would have performed had it been enabled during the data load.

To enable a trigger, use the **alter trigger** command with the **enable** keyword. To use this command, you must either own the table or have the ALTER ANY TRIGGER system privilege. A sample **alter trigger** command is shown in the following listing:

```
alter trigger  BOOKSHELF_BEF_UPD_INS_ROW enable;
```

A second method of enabling triggers uses the **alter table** command, with the **enable all triggers** clause. You may not enable specific triggers with this command; you must use the **alter trigger** command to do that. The following example shows the usage of the **alter table** command:

```
alter table BOOKSHELF enable all triggers;
```

To use the **alter table** command, you must either own the table or have the ALTER ANY TABLE system privilege.

You can disable triggers using the same basic commands (requiring the same privileges) with modifications to their clauses. For the **alter trigger** command, use the **disable** clause:

```
alter trigger BOOKSHELF_BEF_UPD_INS_ROW disable;
```

For the **alter table** command, use the **disable all triggers** clause:

```
alter table BOOKSHELF disable all triggers;
```

You can manually compile triggers. Use the **alter trigger compile** command to manually compile existing triggers that have become invalid. Since triggers have dependencies, they can become invalid if an object the trigger depends on changes. The **alter trigger debug** command allows PL/SQL information to be generated during trigger recompilation.

Replacing Triggers

The status of a trigger is the only portion that can be altered. To alter a trigger's body, the trigger must be re-created or replaced. When replacing a trigger, use the **create or replace trigger** command (refer to "Trigger Syntax" and the examples earlier in the chapter).

Dropping Triggers

Triggers may be dropped via the **drop trigger** command. To drop a trigger, you must either own the trigger or have the DROP ANY TRIGGER system privilege. An example of this command is shown in Table 30-1:

```
drop trigger BOOKSHELF_BEF_UPD_INS_ROW;
```

Attribute	Type	Description	Example		
ora_client_ip_address	VARCHAR2	Returns the IP address of the client in a LOGON event when the underlying protocol is TCP/IP.	```if (ora_sysevent = 'LOGON')``` ``` then addr := ora_client_ip_``` ```address;``` ```end if;```		
ora_database_name	VARCHAR2(50)	Database name.	```Declare``` ``` db_name VARCHAR2(50);``` ```begin``` ``` db_name := ora_database_``` ```name;``` ```end;```		
ora_des_encrypted_password	VARCHAR2	The DES encrypted password of the user being created or altered.	```if (ora_dict_obj_type = 'USER')``` ``` then insert into event_table``` ```(ora_des_encrypted_password);``` ```end if;```		
ora_dict_obj_name	VARCHAR(30)	Name of the dictionary object on which the DDL operation occurred.	```insert into event_table``` ```('Changed object is '		ora_``` ```dict_obj_name');```
ora_dict_obj_name_list (name_list OUT ora_name_list_t)	BINARY_INTEGER	Returns the list of object names of objects being modified in the event.	```if (ora_sysevent = 'ASSOCIATE``` ```STATISTICS')``` ``` then number_modified := ora_``` ```dict_obj_name_list (name_list);``` ```end if;```		
ora_dict_obj_owner	VARCHAR(30)	Owner of the dictionary object on which the DDL operation occurred.	```insert into event_table ('object``` ```owner is'		ora_dict_obj_``` ```owner');```
ora_dict_obj_owner_list(owner_list OUT ora_name_list_t)	BINARY_INTEGER	Returns the list of object owners of objects being modified in the event.	```if (ora_sysevent = 'ASSOCIATE``` ```STATISTICS')``` ``` then number_of_modified_``` ```objects := ora_dict_obj_owner_``` ```list(owner_list);``` ```end if;```		

TABLE 30-1. *System-Defined Event Attributes*

Attribute	Type	Description	Example								
ora_dict_obj_type	VARCHAR(20)	Type of the dictionary object on which the DDL operation occurred.	`insert into event_table ('This object is a '		ora_dict_obj_type);`						
ora_grantee(user_list OUT ora_name_list_t)	BINARY_INTEGER	Returns the grantees of a grant event in the OUT parameter; returns the number of grantees in the return value.	`if (ora_sysevent = 'GRANT') then number_of_users := ora_grantee(user_list); end if;`								
ora_instance_num	NUMBER	Instance number.	`if (ora_instance_num = 1) then insert into event_table ('1'); end if;`								
ora_is_alter_column(column_name IN VARCHAR2)	BOOLEAN	Returns true if the specified column is altered.	`if (ora_sysevent = 'ALTER' and ora_dict_obj_type = 'TABLE') then alter_column := ora_is_alter_column('FOO'); end if;`								
ora_is_creating_nested_table	BOOLEAN	Returns true if the current event is creating a nested table.	`if (ora_sysevent = 'CREATE' and ora_dict_obj_type = 'TABLE' and ora_is_creating_nested_table) then insert into event_tab values ('A nested table is created'); end if;`								
ora_is_drop_column(column_name IN VARCHAR2)	BOOLEAN	Returns true if the specified column is dropped.	`if (ora_sysevent = 'ALTER' and ora_dict_obj_type = 'TABLE') then drop_column := ora_is_drop_column('FOO'); end if;`								
ora_is_servererror	BOOLEAN	Returns true if given error is on error stack, FALSE otherwise.	`if (ora_is_servererror(error_number)) then insert into event_table ('Server error!!'); end if;`								
ora_login_user	VARCHAR2(30)	Login username.	`select ora_login_user from dual;`								
ora_partition_pos	BINARY_INTEGER	In an INSTEAD OF trigger for CREATE TABLE, the position within the SQL text where you could insert a PARTITION clause.	`-- Retrieve ora_sql_txt into -- sql_text variable first.` `n := ora_partition_pos; new_stmt := substr(sql_text, 1, n-1)		' '		my_partition_clause		' '		substr(sql_text, n));`

TABLE 30-1. *System-Defined Event Attributes* (continued)

Attribute	Type	Description	Example		
ora_privilege_list(privilege_list OUT ora_name_ list_t)	BINARY_INTEGER	Returns the list of privileges being granted by the grantee or the list of privileges revoked from the revokees in the OUT parameter; returns the number of privileges in the return value.	`if (ora_sysevent = 'GRANT' or` `ora_sysevent = 'REVOKE')` `then number_of_privileges :=` `ora_privilege_list(priv_list);` `end if;`		
ora_revokee (user_list OUT ora_name_ list_t)	BINARY_INTEGER	Returns the revokees of a revoke event in the OUT parameter; returns the number of revokees in the return value.	`if (ora_sysevent = 'REVOKE')` `then` `number_of_users := ora_` `revokee(user_list);`		
ora_server_error	NUMBER	Given a position (1 for top of stack), it returns the error number at that position on error stack.	`insert into event_table ('top` `stack error '		ora_server_` `error(1));`
ora_server_error_depth	BINARY_INTEGER	Returns the total number of error messages on the error stack.	`n := ora_server_error_depth;` `-- This value is used with` `-- other functions such as` `-- ora_server_error`		
ora_server_error_msg (position in binary_integer)	VARCHAR2	Given a position (1 for top of stack), it returns the error message at that position on error stack.	`insert into event_table ('top` `stack error message'		ora_` `server_error_msg(1));`
ora_server_error_num_params (position in binary_integer)	BINARY_INTEGER	Given a position (1 for top of stack), it returns the number of strings that have been substituted into the error message using a format like "%s".	`n := ora_server_error_num_` `params(1);`		
ora_server_error_param (position in binary_integer, param in binary_integer)	VARCHAR2	Given a position (1 for top of stack) and a parameter number, returns the matching "%s", "%d", and so on substitution value in the error message.	`-- E.g. the 2nd %s in a message` `-- like "Expected %s, found %s"` `param := ora_server_error_` `param(1,2);`		

TABLE 30-1. *System-Defined Event Attributes* (continued)

Attribute	Type	Description	Example								
ora_sql_txt (sql_text out ora_name_list_t)	BINARY_INTEGER	Returns the SQL text of the triggering statement in the OUT parameter. If the statement is long, it is broken up into multiple PL/SQL table elements. The function return value specifies how many elements are in the PL/SQL table.	`sql_text ora_name_list_t;` `stmt VARCHAR2(2000);` `...` `n := ora_sql_txt(sql_text);` `for i in 1..n loop` ` stmt := stmt		sql_text(i);` `end loop;` `insert into event_table ('text` `of triggering statement: '		` `stmt);`				
ora_sysevent	VARCHAR2(20)	System event firing the trigger: Event name is same as that in the syntax.	`insert into event_table (ora_` `sysevent);`								
ora_with_grant_option	BOOLEAN	Returns true if the privileges are granted with grant option.	`if (ora_sysevent = 'GRANT' and` `ora_with_grant_option = TRUE)` ` then insert into event_table` `('with grant option');` `end if;`								
space_error_info(error_number OUT NUMBER, error_type OUT VARCHAR2, object_owner OUT VARCHAR2, table_space_name OUT VARCHAR2, object_name OUT VARCHAR2, sub_object_name OUT VARCHAR2)	BOOLEAN	Returns true if the error is related to an out-of-space condition, and fills in the OUT parameters with information about the object that caused the error.	`if (space_error_info(eno, typ,` `owner, ts, obj, subobj) = TRUE)` `then.put_line('The` `object '		run out of` `space.');` `dbms_outputobj		' owned by '` `		owner		' has` `end if;`

TABLE 30-1. *System-Defined Event Attributes* (continued)

TABLE B30.1. Sales-Related Event Attributes (continued)

CHAPTER

31

Procedures, Functions, and Packages

ophisticated business rules and application logic can be stored as *procedures* within Oracle. Stored procedures—groups of SQL, PL/SQL, and Java statements—enable you to move code that enforces business rules from your application to the database. As a result, the code will be stored once for use by multiple applications. Because Oracle supports stored procedures, the code within your applications can become more consistent and easier to maintain.

NOTE
For details on Java and its use in stored procedures, see Chapters 37, 38, and 39. This chapter will focus on PL/SQL procedures.

You may group procedures and other PL/SQL commands into *packages*. In the following sections, you will see implementation details and recommendations for packages, procedures, and *functions* (procedures that can return values to the user).

You may experience performance gains when using procedures, for two reasons:

■ The processing of complex business rules may be performed within the database—and therefore by the server. In client-server or three-tier applications, shifting complex processing from the application (on the client) to the database (on the server) may dramatically improve performance.

■ Because the procedural code is stored within the database and is fairly static, you may also benefit from the reuse of the same queries within the database. The Shared SQL Area in the System Global Area (SGA) will store the parsed versions of the executed commands. Thus, the second time a procedure is executed, it may be able to take advantage of the parsing that was previously performed, improving the performance of the procedure's execution.

In addition to these advantages, your application development efforts may also benefit. Business rules that are consolidated within the database no longer need to be written into each application, thus saving you time during application creation and simplifying the maintenance process.

Required System Privileges

To create a procedural object, you must have the CREATE PROCEDURE system privilege. If the procedural object will be in another user's schema, then you must have the CREATE ANY PROCEDURE system privilege.

Executing Procedures

Once a procedural object has been created, it may be executed. When a procedural object is executed, it may rely on the table privileges of its owner or may rely on the privileges of the user who is executing it. When the procedure is created using the definer's rights, a user executing the procedure does not need to be granted access to the tables that the procedure accesses. If a procedure relies on the invoker's rights, the user must have access to all of the database objects

accessed by the procedure. Unless stated otherwise, the examples in this chapter assume users are executing procedures under the owner's privileges.

To allow other users to execute your procedural object, **grant** them the EXECUTE privilege on that object, as shown in the following example:

```
grant execute on MY_PROCEDURE to Dora;
```

The user Dora will now be able to execute the procedure named MY_PROCEDURE. If you do not **grant** the EXECUTE privilege to users, they must have the EXECUTE ANY PROCEDURE system privilege in order to execute the procedure.

When executed, procedures usually have variables passed to them. For example, a procedure that interacts with the BOOKSHELF table may accept as input a value for the Title column. In this example, we will assume that the procedure creates a new record in the BOOKSHELF table when a new book is received (from the list of books in the BOOK_ORDER table). This procedure can be called from any application within the database (provided the user calling the procedure has been granted the EXECUTE privilege for it).

The syntax used to execute a procedure depends on the environment from which the procedure is called. From within SQL*Plus, a procedure can be executed by using the **execute** command, followed by the procedure name. Any arguments to be passed to the procedure must be enclosed in parentheses following the procedure name, as shown in the following example (which uses a procedure called NEW_BOOK):

```
execute NEW_BOOK('ONCE REMOVED');
```

The command will execute the NEW_BOOK procedure, passing to it the value ONCE REMOVED.

From within another procedure, function, package, or trigger, the procedure can be called without the **execute** command. If the NEW_BOOK procedure was called from a trigger on the BOOK_ORDER table, the body of that trigger may include the following command:

```
NEW_BOOK(:new.Title);
```

The NEW_BOOK procedure will be executed using the new value of the Title column as its input. (See Chapter 30 for further information on the use of old and new values within triggers.)

To execute a procedure owned by another user, you must either create a synonym for that procedure or reference the owner's name during the execution, as shown in the following listing:

```
execute Practice.NEW_BOOK('ONCE REMOVED');
```

The command will execute the NEW_BOOK procedure in the Practice schema.

Alternatively, a synonym for the procedure could be created by using the following command:

```
create synonym NEW_BOOK for Practice.NEW_BOOK;
```

The owner of that synonym would then no longer need to refer to the procedure's owner to execute the procedure. You could simply enter the command:

```
execute NEW_BOOK('ONCE REMOVED');
```

and the synonym would point to the proper procedure.

When you execute remote procedures, the name of a database link must be specified (see Chapter 23 for information on database links). The name of the database link must immediately follow the procedure's name and precede the variables, as shown in the following example:

```
execute NEW_BOOK@REMOTE_CONNECT('ONCE REMOVED');
```

The command uses the REMOTE_CONNECT database link to access a procedure called NEW_ BOOK in a remote database.

To make the location of the procedure transparent to the user, a synonym may be created for the remote procedure, as shown in the following example:

```
create synonym NEW_BOOK
    for NEW_BOOK@REMOTE_CONNECT;
```

Once this synonym has been created, the user may refer to the remote procedure by using the name of the synonym. Oracle assumes that all remote procedure calls involve updates in the remote database.

Required Table Privileges

Procedural objects may reference tables. For the objects to execute properly, the owner of the procedure, package, or function being executed must have privileges on the tables it uses. Unless you are using invoker rights, the user who is executing the procedural object does not need privileges on its underlying tables.

NOTE
The privileges needed for procedures, packages, and functions cannot come from roles; they must be granted directly to the owner of the procedure, package, or function.

Procedures vs. Functions

Procedures do not have to return a value to the caller. Functions can return a value to the caller, and functions can be directly referenced in queries. This value is returned through the use of the **return** keyword within the function. Examples of functions are shown in "create function Syntax," later in this chapter.

Procedures vs. Packages

Packages are groups of procedures, functions, variables, and SQL statements grouped together into a single unit. To execute a procedure within a package, you must first list the package name, and then list the procedure name, as shown in the following example:

```
execute BOOK_INVENTORY.NEW_BOOK('ONCE REMOVED');
```

Here, the NEW_BOOK procedure within the BOOK_INVENTORY package was executed.

Packages allow multiple procedures to use the same variables and cursors. Procedures within packages may be either available to the public (as is the NEW_BOOK procedure in the prior example) or private, in which case they are only accessible via commands from within the package (such as calls from other procedures). Examples of packages are shown in "create package Syntax," later in this chapter.

Packages may also include commands that are to be executed each time the package is called, regardless of the procedure or function called within the package. Thus, packages not only group procedures but also give you the ability to execute commands that are not procedure specific. See "Initializing Packages," later in this chapter, for an example of code that is executed each time a package is called.

create procedure Syntax

The full syntax for the **create procedure** command is shown in the Alphabetical Reference. The brief syntax is

```
create [or replace] procedure [schema .] procedure
[( argument [ in | out | in out ] [nocopy] datatype
   [, argument [ in | out | in out ] [nocopy] datatype]...
 )]
[authid { current_user | definer }]
{ is | as } { pl/sql_subprogram_body |
   language { java name 'string'| c [name name] library lib_name
}};
```

Both the header and the body of the procedure are created by this command.

The NEW_BOOK procedure is created by the command shown in the following listing:

```
create or replace procedure NEW_BOOK (aTitle IN VARCHAR2,
      aPublisher IN VARCHAR2, aCategoryName IN VARCHAR2)
as
begin
    insert into BOOKSHELF (Title, Publisher, CategoryName, Rating)
      values (aTitle, aPublisher, aCategoryName, NULL);
    delete from BOOK_ORDER
      where Title = aTitle;
end;
/
```

The NEW_BOOK procedure will accept a book's title, publisher, and category as its input. It can be called from any application. It inserts a record into the BOOKSHELF table, with a **NULL** value for the Rating column, and deletes the matching Title from the BOOK_ORDER table.

If a procedure already exists, you may replace it via the **create or replace procedure** command. The benefit of using this command (instead of dropping and re-creating the old procedure) is that the EXECUTE privilege grants previously made on the procedure will remain in place.

The IN qualifier is used for arguments for which values must be specified when calling the procedure. In the NEW_BOOK example, the aTitle, aPublisher, and aCategoryName arguments are declared as IN. The OUT qualifier signifies that the procedure passes a value back to the caller through this argument. The IN OUT qualifier signifies that the argument is both an IN and an

OUT: A value must be specified for this argument when the procedure is called, and the procedure will return a value to the caller via this argument. If no qualifier type is specified, then the default value is IN.

In the **create procedure** syntax, **authid** refers to the type of authentication: definer rights (the default) or invoker rights (the **current_user**). The **nocopy** keyword tells Oracle to pass the variable value back to the user as quickly as possible.

By default, a procedure consists of a block of code written in PL/SQL (*block* refers to the code that the procedure will execute when called). In the NEW_BOOK example, the block is as follows:

```
begin
    insert into BOOKSHELF (Title, Publisher, CategoryName, Rating)
      values (aTitle, aPublisher, aCategoryName, NULL);
    delete from BOOK_ORDER
      where Title = aTitle;
end;
```

The PL/SQL block shown is fairly simple, consisting of a single SQL statement. PL/SQL blocks within procedures can include any DML statement; they cannot be used for DDL statements (such as **create view**).

Alternatively, **language** refers to the language in which the code is written. For Java examples, see Chapter 39.

The following listing shows the execution of the NEW_BOOK procedure, and the resulting changes to the BOOK_ORDER and BOOKSHELF tables.

```
select Title from BOOK_ORDER;

TITLE
----------------------------------------------------------------
GALILEO'S DAUGHTER
GOSPEL
LONGITUDE
ONCE REMOVED
SHOELESS JOE
SOMETHING SO STRONG

execute NEW_BOOK('ONCE REMOVED','SANCTUARY PUB','ADULTNF');

PL/SQL procedure successfully completed.

select Title from BOOK_ORDER;

TITLE
----------------------------------------------------------------
GALILEO'S DAUGHTER
GOSPEL
LONGITUDE
SHOELESS JOE
SOMETHING SO STRONG
```

```
select * from BOOKSHELF
 where Title = 'ONCE REMOVED';

TITLE
-------------------------------------------------------------------
PUBLISHER            CATEGORYNAME         RA
-------------------  -------------------  --
ONCE REMOVED
SANCTUARY PUB        ADULTNF
```

NOTE
You can make external C procedures and Java libraries available within PL/SQL by creating external procedures. You will need to set up an agent (named extproc by default) in the network configuration files. If you need to reference external libraries, work with your database administrator to configure the network environment, the agents that are needed, and the creation of directories and libraries within the database.

create function Syntax

The syntax for the **create function** command is more complicated than the syntax for the **create procedure** command. At a high level, the syntax is

```
create [or replace] function [schema .] function
[( argument [ in | out | in out ] [nocopy] datatype
   [, argument [ in | out | in out ] [nocopy] datatype]...
 )]
return datatype
[{ invoker_rights_clause | deterministic | parallel_enable_clause }
 [ invoker_rights_clause | deterministic | parallel_enable_clause ]...
]
{ { aggregate | pipelined } using [schema .] implementation_type
| [pipelined] { is | as } { pl/sql_function_body | call_spec }};
```

Both the header and the body of the function are created by this command.

The **return** keyword specifies the datatype of the function's return value. This can be any valid PL/SQL datatype (see Chapter 29). Every function must have a **return** clause, since the function must, by definition, return a value to the calling environment.

The following example shows a function named **OVERDUE_CHARGES**, which returns the overdue book charges by person, based on calculations against the BOOKSHELF_CHECKOUT table. The input is the person's name, while the output is the balance for that person.

```
create or replace function OVERDUE_CHARGES (aName IN VARCHAR2)
   return NUMBER
   is
   owed_amount NUMBER(10,2);
begin
     select SUM(((ReturnedDate-CheckoutDate) -14)*0.20)
```

```
        into owed_amount
          from BOOKSHELF_CHECKOUT
        where Name = aName;
     RETURN(owed_amount);
end;
/
```

First, the function is named and the input is specified:

```
create or replace function OVERDUE_CHARGES (aName IN VARCHAR2)
```

Next, we define the characteristics of the value to be returned. The definition of the variable whose value will be returned has three parts: its datatype, its name, and its length. The datatype in this example is set via the **return NUMBER** clause. The variable is then named *owed_amount*, and is defined as a NUMBER(10,2). Thus, all three parts of the variable—its datatype, its name, and its length—have been defined.

```
    return NUMBER
    is
    owed_amount NUMBER(10,2);
```

The PL/SQL block follows. In the SQL statement, the sum of all late charges ($0.20 per day over 14 days) is calculated. The sum is selected into a variable called *owed_amount* (which we previously defined). The **RETURN(owed_amount)** command line then returns the value in the *owed_amount* variable to the calling program.

```
begin
      select SUM(((ReturnedDate-CheckoutDate) -14)*0.20)
      into owed_amount
        from BOOKSHELF_CHECKOUT
       where Name = aName;
    RETURN(owed_amount);
end;
```

If a function already exists, you may replace it via the **create or replace function** command. If you use the **or replace** clause, any EXECUTE grants previously made on the function will remain in place.

If the function is to be created in a different schema, you must have the CREATE ANY PROCEDURE system privilege. If no schema is specified, the function will be created in your schema. To create a function in your schema, you must have been granted the CREATE PROCEDURE system privilege (which is part of the RESOURCE role). Having the privilege to create procedures gives you the privilege to create functions and packages as well.

You can check the function by creating a variable and setting its value equal to the function's returned value:

```
variable owed number;
execute :owed := OVERDUE_CHARGES('FRED FULLER');

PL/SQL procedure successfully completed.
```

You can verify the results by printing the variable's value:

```
print owed

     OWED
----------
     3.8
```

Referencing Remote Tables in Procedures

Remote tables can be accessed by the SQL statements in procedures. A remote table can be queried via a database link in the procedure, as shown in the following example. In this example, the NEW_BOOK procedure inserts a record into the BOOKSHELF table in the database defined by the REMOTE_CONNECT database link while deleting from a local copy of BOOK_ORDER.

```
create or replace procedure NEW_BOOK (aTitle IN VARCHAR2,
    aPublisher IN VARCHAR2, aCategoryName IN VARCHAR2)
as
begin
    insert into BOOKSHELF@REMOTE_CONNECT
      (Title, Publisher, CategoryName, Rating)
      values (aTitle, aPublisher, aCategoryName, NULL);
    delete from BOOK_ORDER
      where Title = aTitle;
end;
/
```

Procedures may also use local synonyms. For example, you may create a local synonym for a remote table, as follows:

```
create synonym BOOKSHELF for BOOKSHELF@REMOTE_CONNECT;
```

You can then rewrite your procedure to remove the database link specifications:

```
create or replace procedure NEW_BOOK (aTitle IN VARCHAR2,
    aPublisher IN VARCHAR2, aCategoryName IN VARCHAR2)
as
begin
    insert into BOOKSHELF
      (Title, Publisher, CategoryName, Rating)
      values (aTitle, aPublisher, aCategoryName, NULL);
    delete from BOOK_ORDER
      where Title = aTitle;
end;
/
```

Removing database link names from procedures allows you to remove the details of the table's physical location from the procedure. If the table changes location, only the synonym will change, while the procedure will still be valid.

Debugging Procedures

The SQL*Plus **show errors** command displays all the errors associated with the most recently created procedural object. This command checks the USER_ERRORS data dictionary view for the errors associated with the most recent compilation attempt for that object. **show errors** displays the line and column number for each error, as well as the text of the error message.

To view errors associated with previously created procedural objects, you may query USER_ERRORS directly, as shown in the following listing. This example queries USER_ERRORS for error messages encountered during the creation of the **OVERDUE_CHARGES** function shown earlier in this chapter. If any errors were encountered, the lines in the code that resulted in the error conditions would be returned by the query.

```
select Line,      /*Line number of the error. */
       Position,  /*Column number of the error.*/
       Text       /*Text of the error message.*/
  from USER_ERRORS
 where Name = 'OVERDUE_CHARGES'
   and Type = 'FUNCTION'
 order by Sequence;
```

Valid values for the Type column are VIEW, PROCEDURE, PACKAGE, FUNCTION, and PACKAGE BODY.

Two other data dictionary view levels—ALL and DBA—may also be used to retrieve information about errors involving procedural objects. For information on these views, see Chapter 42.

Using the DBMS_OUTPUT Package

In addition to the debugging information provided by the **show errors** command, you may use the DBMS_OUTPUT package, one of a set of packages that is automatically installed when you create an Oracle database.

To use DBMS_OUTPUT, you must issue the **set serveroutput on** command before executing the procedural object you will be debugging.

DBMS_OUTPUT allows you to use three debugging functions within your package:

PUT	Puts multiple outputs on the same line
PUT_LINE	Puts each output on a separate line
NEW_LINE	Used with **PUT**; signals the end of the current output line

PUT and **PUT_LINE** are used to generate the debugging information you want to display. For example, if you are debugging a procedure that includes a loop (refer to Chapter 29), you may want to track the changes in a variable with each pass through the loop. To track the variable's value, you may use a command similar to the one shown in the following listing. In this example, the value of the Owed_Amount column is printed, prefixed by the literal string 'Owed:'.

```
DBMS_OUTPUT.PUT_LINE('Owed:'||Owed_Amount);
```

You may also use **PUT** and **PUT_LINE** outside of loops, but such uses may be better accomplished via the use of the **return** command in functions (refer to "create function Syntax," earlier in this chapter).

> **NOTE**
> *For additional debugging capabilities, you can use the DBMS_ DEBUG procedure if you have the DEBUG CONNECT SESSION system privilege. The DEBUG ANY PROCEDURE system privilege is equivalent to having the DEBUG privilege for all objects in the database.*

Creating Your Own Functions

Rather than just calling custom functions via **execute** commands, you may use them within SQL expressions. This enables you to extend the functionality of SQL, customizing it to your needs. Such functions can be used in the same manner as Oracle-provided functions such as **SUBSTR** and **TO_CHAR**. Custom functions cannot be used in CHECK or DEFAULT constraints and cannot manipulate any database values.

You can call either stand-alone functions (created via the **create function** command shown in the previous sections) or functions declared in package specifications (to be covered in "create package Syntax" later in this chapter). Procedures are not directly callable from SQL, but may be called by the functions you create.

For example, consider the **OVERDUE_CHARGES** function shown earlier in this chapter, which calculated the total owed for overdue books. It had a single input variable—the person's name. However, to see the **OVERDUE_CHARGES** results for all of the book borrowers, you would normally need to execute this procedure once for each record in the BOOKSHELF_CHECKOUT table.

You can improve the overdue charges calculation process. Consider the following query:

```
create view BOOK_BORROWERS
 as select distinct Name from BOOKSHELF_CHECKOUT;

select Name,
       OVERDUE_CHARGES(Name)
  from BOOK_BORROWERS;
```

Oracle returns the following output:

```
NAME                        OVERDUE_CHARGES(NAME)
-------------------------   ---------------------
DORAH TALBOT                                  -.8
EMILY TALBOT                                   .2
FRED FULLER                                   3.8
GERHARDT KENTGEN                              2.8
JED HOPKINS                                   1.4
PAT LAVAY                                     2.6
ROLAND BRANDT                                22.6

7 rows selected.
```

This single query uses the custom **OVERDUE_CHARGES** function to calculate the overdue charges for all book borrowers. It's not quite correct—people are getting credit for books they returned early. You can use the **create or replace function** command to add a **where** clause to the function's query:

```
create or replace function OVERDUE_CHARGES (aName IN VARCHAR2)
   return NUMBER
   is
   owed_amount NUMBER(10,2);
begin
    select SUM(((ReturnedDate-CheckoutDate) -14)*0.20)
    into owed_amount
      from BOOKSHELF_CHECKOUT
    where Name = aName
       and ReturnedDate-CheckoutDate > 14;
   RETURN(owed_amount);
end;
/
```

The corrected output is shown in the following listing:

```
select Name,
       OVERDUE_CHARGES(Name)
  from BOOK_BORROWERS;

NAME                         OVERDUE_CHARGES(NAME)
-------------------------    ---------------------
DORAH TALBOT                                    .4
EMILY TALBOT                                    .8
FRED FULLER                                    3.8
GERHARDT KENTGEN                               4.6
JED HOPKINS                                    1.4
PAT LAVAY                                      3.4
ROLAND BRANDT                                 22.6
```

The query selected each name from BOOK_BORROWERS; for each name, it executed the **OVERDUE_CHARGES** function, which selected data from BOOKSHELF_CHECKOUT.

To take advantage of this feature, your functions must follow the same guidelines as Oracle's functions. Most notably, they must not update the database, and must contain only IN parameters.

> **NOTE**
> *Although this technique works, it has performance costs. The more data there is in the table, the bigger the performance penalty will be when comparing this method to a traditional join.*

Customizing Error Conditions

You may establish different error conditions within procedural objects (refer to Chapter 30 for examples of customized error conditions within triggers). For each of the error conditions you

define, you may select an error message that will appear when the error occurs. The error numbers and messages that are displayed to the user are set by you via the RAISE_APPLICATION_ERROR procedure, which may be called from within any procedural object.

You can call RAISE_APPLICATION_ERROR from within procedures, packages, and functions. It requires two inputs: the message number and the message text. You get to assign both the message number and the text that will be displayed to the user. This is a very powerful addition to the standard exceptions that are available in PL/SQL (see "Exception" in the Alphabetical Reference).

The following example shows the **OVERDUE_CHARGES** function defined earlier in this chapter. Now, however, it has an additional section (shown in bold). Titled EXCEPTION, this section tells Oracle how to handle nonstandard processing. In this example, the NO_DATA_FOUND exception's standard message is overridden via the RAISE_APPLICATION_ERROR procedure.

```
create or replace function OVERDUE_CHARGES (aName IN VARCHAR2)
    return NUMBER
    is
    owed_amount NUMBER(10,2);
begin
    select SUM(((ReturnedDate-CheckoutDate) -14)*0.20)
    into owed_amount
        from BOOKSHELF_CHECKOUT
    where Name = aName
        and (ReturnedDate-CheckoutDate) > 14;
    RETURN(owed_amount);
    EXCEPTION
      when NO_DATA_FOUND THEN
        RAISE_APPLICATION_ERROR(-20100,
        'No books borrowed.');
end;
/
```

In the preceding example, the NO_DATA_FOUND exception was used. If you want to define custom exceptions, you need to name the exception in a Declarations section of the procedure, which immediately precedes the **begin** command. As shown in the following listing, this section should include entries for each of the custom exceptions you have defined, listed as type EXCEPTION:

```
declare
some_custom_error EXCEPTION;
```

NOTE
If you are using the exceptions already defined within PL/SQL, you do not need to list them in the Declarations section of the procedural object. See "Exception" in the Alphabetical Reference for a list of the predefined exceptions.

In the **exception** portion of the procedural object's code, you tell the database how to handle the exceptions. It begins with the keyword **exception**, followed by a **when** clause for each exception. Each exception may call the RAISE_ APPLICATION_ERROR procedure, which takes two input

parameters: the error number (which must be between –20001 and –20999) and the error message to be displayed. In the preceding example, only one exception was defined. Multiple exceptions can be defined, as shown in the following listing; you may use the **when others** clause to handle all nonspecified exceptions:

```
EXCEPTION
  when NO_DATA_FOUND THEN
    RAISE_APPLICATION_ERROR(-20100,
    'No books borrowed.');
  when some_custom_error THEN
      RAISE_APPLICATION_ERROR (-20101,
        'Some custom error message.');
```

The use of the RAISE_APPLICATION_ERROR procedure gives you great flexibility in managing the error conditions that may be encountered within procedural objects.

Naming Procedures and Functions

Procedures and functions should be named according to the business function they perform or business rule they enforce. There should be no ambiguity about their purpose.

The NEW_BOOK procedure shown earlier should be renamed. NEW_BOOK performs a business function—inserting records into BOOKSHELF and deleting them from BOOK_ORDER—so its name should reflect that function. A better choice for the name would be RECEIVE_BOOK_ORDER. Since it performs a function, a verb (in this case, "receive") should describe what it does. The name of the procedure should also include the name of the major table(s) it impacts. If the tables are properly named, then the name of the table should be the direct object upon which the verb acts (in this case, BOOK_ORDER or BOOKSHELF). For the sake of consistency, we will continue to refer to the procedure as NEW_BOOK for the remainder of this chapter.

create package Syntax

When creating packages, the package specification and the package body are created separately. Thus, there are two commands to use: **create package** for the package specification, and **create package body** for the package body. Both of these commands require that you have the CREATE PROCEDURE system privilege. If the package is to be created in a schema other than your own, then you must have the CREATE ANY PROCEDURE system privilege.

Here is the syntax for creating package specifications:

```
create [or replace] package [user.] package
[authid {definer | current_user} ]
{is | as}
 package specification;
```

A *package specification* consists of the list of functions, procedures, variables, constants, cursors, and exceptions that will be available to users of the package.

A sample **create package** command is shown in the following listing. In this example, the BOOK_MANAGEMENT package is created. The **OVERDUE_CHARGES** function and NEW_BOOK procedure seen earlier in this chapter are included in the package.

```
create or replace package BOOK_MANAGEMENT
as
   function OVERDUE_CHARGES(aName IN VARCHAR2) return NUMBER;
   procedure NEW_BOOK (aTitle IN VARCHAR2,
      aPublisher IN VARCHAR2, aCategoryName IN VARCHAR2);
end BOOK_MANAGEMENT;
/
```

NOTE
*You may append the name of the procedural object to the **end** clause
to make it easier to coordinate the logic within your code.*

A *package body* contains the blocks and specifications for all of the public objects listed in the package specification. The package body may include objects that are not listed in the package specification; such objects are said to be *private* and are not available to users of the package. Private objects may only be called by other objects within the same package body. A package body may also include code that is run every time the package is invoked, regardless of the part of the package that is executed—see "Initializing Packages," later in this chapter, for an example.

The syntax for creating package bodies is

```
create [or replace] package body [user.] package body
{is | as}
 package body;
```

The name of the package body should be the same as the name of the package specification.

Continuing the BOOK_MANAGEMENT example, its package body can be created via the **create package body** command shown in the following example:

```
create or replace package body BOOK_MANAGEMENT
as
function OVERDUE_CHARGES (aName IN VARCHAR2)
  return NUMBER
  is
  owed_amount NUMBER(10,2);
begin
     select SUM(((ReturnedDate-CheckoutDate) -14)*0.20)
     into owed_amount
        from BOOKSHELF_CHECKOUT
      where Name = aName
          and (ReturnedDate-CheckoutDate) > 14;
   RETURN(owed_amount);
   EXCEPTION
    when NO_DATA_FOUND THEN
      RAISE_APPLICATION_ERROR(-20100,
       'No books borrowed.');
  end OVERDUE_CHARGES;
procedure NEW_BOOK (aTitle IN VARCHAR2,
    aPublisher IN VARCHAR2, aCategoryName IN VARCHAR2)
```

```
is
begin
    insert into BOOKSHELF
     (Title, Publisher, CategoryName, Rating)
      values (aTitle, aPublisher, aCategoryName, NULL);
    delete from BOOK_ORDER
      where Title = aTitle;
end NEW_BOOK;
end BOOK_MANAGEMENT;
/
```

The **create or replace package body** command shown in the preceding example combines the **create function** command for the **OVERDUE_CHARGES** function with the **create procedure** command for the NEW_BOOK procedure. The **end** clauses all have the names of their associated objects appended to them (shown in bold in the prior listing).

Additional functions, procedures, exceptions, variables, cursors, and constants may be defined within the package body, but they will not be available to the public unless they have been declared within the package specification (via the **create package** command). If a user has been granted the EXECUTE privilege on a package, then that user can access any of the public objects that are declared in the package specification.

> **NOTE**
> *You can hide the internals of your application code by using the PL/SQL wrapper. The WRAP executable (found in the /bin directory under the Oracle software home directory) takes an input filename as its input and generates an output file containing the object code. You cannot unwrap a package that has been wrapped.*

Initializing Packages

Packages may include code that is to be run the first time a user executes a function or procedure in the package within each session. In the following example, the BOOK_MANAGEMENT package body is modified to include a SQL statement that records the current user's username and the timestamp for the first time a package component is executed within the session. Two new variables must also be declared in the package body to record these values.

Since the two new variables are declared within the package body, they are not available to the public. Within the package body, they are separated from the procedures and functions. The package initialization code is shown in bold in the following listing:

```
create or replace package body BOOK_MANAGEMENT
as
User_Name VARCHAR2(30);
Entry_Date DATE;
function OVERDUE_CHARGES (aName IN VARCHAR2)
  return NUMBER
```

```
 is
  owed_amount NUMBER(10,2);
begin
     select SUM(((ReturnedDate-CheckoutDate) -14)*0.20)
     into owed_amount
        from BOOKSHELF_CHECKOUT
      where Name = aName
        and (ReturnedDate-CheckoutDate) > 14;
    RETURN(owed_amount);
  EXCEPTION
   when NO_DATA_FOUND THEN
     RAISE_APPLICATION_ERROR(-20100,
     'No books borrowed.');
end OVERDUE_CHARGES;
procedure NEW_BOOK (aTitle IN VARCHAR2,
   aPublisher IN VARCHAR2, aCategoryName IN VARCHAR2)
is
begin
    insert into BOOKSHELF
     (Title, Publisher, CategoryName, Rating)
      values (aTitle, aPublisher, aCategoryName, NULL);
    delete from BOOK_ORDER
      where Title = aTitle;
end NEW_BOOK;
begin
  select User, SysDate
    into User_Name, Entry_Date
    from DUAL;
end BOOK_MANAGEMENT;
/
```

NOTE
*The code that is to be run the first time that a component of the package is executed is stored in its own PL/SQL block at the bottom of the package body. It does not have its own **end** clause; it uses the package body's **end** clause.*

The first time a BOOK_MANAGEMENT package component is executed in the user's session, the *User_Name* and *Entry_Date* variables will be populated by the query shown in the previous listing. These two variables can then be used by the functions and procedures within the package, although in the interest of brevity this example does not use them.

To **execute** a procedure or function that is within a package, specify both the package name and the name of the procedure or function in the **execute** command, as follows:

```
execute BOOK_MANAGEMENT.NEW_BOOK('SOMETHING SO STRONG','PANDORAS','ADULTNF');
```

Viewing Source Code for Procedural Objects

The source code for existing procedures, functions, packages, and package bodies can be queried from the following data dictionary views:

USER_SOURCE	For procedural objects owned by the user
ALL_SOURCE	For procedural objects owned by the user or to which the user has been granted access
DBA_SOURCE	For all procedural objects in the database

Select information from the USER_SOURCE view via a query similar to the one shown in the following listing. In this example, the Text column is selected, ordered by the Line number. The Name of the object and the object Type are used to define which object's source code is to be displayed. The following example uses the NEW_BOOK procedure shown earlier in this chapter:

```
select Text
  from USER_SOURCE
 where Name = 'NEW_BOOK'
   and Type = 'PROCEDURE'
 order by Line;

TEXT
-----------------------------------------------------------------
procedure NEW_BOOK (aTitle IN VARCHAR2,
   aPublisher IN VARCHAR2, aCategoryName IN VARCHAR2)
as
begin
   insert into BOOKSHELF (Title, Publisher, CategoryName, Rating)
     values (aTitle, aPublisher, aCategoryName, NULL);
   delete from BOOK_ORDER
     where Title = aTitle;
end;
```

As shown in this example, the USER_SOURCE view contains one record for each line of the NEW_BOOK procedure. The sequence of the lines is maintained by the Line column; therefore, the Line column should be used in the **order by** clause.

Valid values for the Type column are PROCEDURE, FUNCTION, PACKAGE, PACKAGE BODY, JAVA SOURCE, TYPE, and TYPE BODY.

Compiling Procedures, Functions, and Packages

Oracle compiles procedural objects when they are created. However, procedural objects may become invalid if the database objects they reference change. The next time the procedural objects are executed, they will be recompiled by the database.

You can avoid this run-time compiling—and the performance degradation it may cause—by explicitly recompiling the procedures, functions, and packages. To recompile a procedure, use the **alter procedure** command, as shown in the following listing. The **compile** clause is the only valid option for this command.

```
alter procedure NEW_BOOK compile;
```

To recompile a procedure, you must either own the procedure or have the ALTER ANY PROCEDURE system privilege.

To recompile a function, use the **alter function** command, with the **compile** clause:

```
alter function OVERDUE_CHARGES compile;
```

To recompile a function, you must either own the function or have the ALTER ANY PROCEDURE system privilege.

When recompiling packages, you may either recompile both the package specification and the body or just recompile the package body. By default, both the package specification and the package body are recompiled. You cannot use the **alter function** or **alter procedure** command to recompile functions and procedures stored within a package.

If the source code for the procedures or functions within the package body has changed but the package specification has not, you may want to recompile only the package body. In most cases, it is appropriate to recompile both the specification and the package body.

The following is the syntax for the **alter package** command:

```
alter package [user.] package_name
compile [debug] [package | body | specification];
```

To recompile a package, use the preceding **alter package** command with the **compile** clause, as follows:

```
alter package BOOK_MANAGEMENT compile;
```

To recompile a package, you must either own the package or have the ALTER ANY PROCEDURE system privilege. Since neither PACKAGE nor BODY was specified in the preceding example, the default of PACKAGE was used, resulting in the recompilation of both the package specification and the package body.

Replacing Procedures, Functions, and Packages

Procedures, functions, and packages may be replaced via their respective **create or replace** command. Using the **or replace** clause keeps in place any existing grants that have been made for those objects. If you choose to drop and re-create procedural objects, you have to regrant any EXECUTE privileges that were previously granted.

Dropping Procedures, Functions, and Packages

To drop a procedure, use the **drop procedure** command, as follows:

```
drop procedure NEW_BOOK;
```

To drop a procedure, you must either own the procedure or have the DROP ANY PROCEDURE system privilege.

To drop a function, use the **drop function** command, as follows:

```
drop function OVERDUE_CHARGES;
```

To drop a function, you must either own the function or have the DROP ANY PROCEDURE system privilege.

To drop a package body, use the **drop package** command with the **body** clause, as follows:

```
drop package body BOOK_MANAGEMENT;
```

To drop a package body, you must either own the package or have the DROP ANY PROCEDURE system privilege.

To drop a package (both the specification and the body), use the **drop package** command, as follows:

```
drop package BOOK_MANAGEMENT;
```

To drop a package, you must either own the package or have the DROP ANY PROCEDURE system privilege.

CHAPTER
32

Using Native
Dynamic SQL and
DBMS_SQL

ou can use *native dynamic SQL* to create general-purpose procedures and to execute DDL commands within PL/SQL. You can use dynamic SQL to execute SQL commands that are built at run time rather than at program-creation time. You can use dynamic SQL within your stored procedural objects (such as packages) and in anonymous PL/SQL blocks. For example, you can create procedures that create tables, that take table names as input parameters, or that take **where** clauses as input parameters.

Using EXECUTE IMMEDIATE

The script in the following example creates a procedure called ANYSTRING. The ANYSTRING procedure has a single input variable: a SQL command. When you execute the ANYSTRING procedure, you pass it the SQL command to execute; the SQL command may be either a DML command (such as **select** or **insert**) or a DDL command (such as **create table**).

```
create or replace procedure ANYSTRING(String IN VARCHAR2) AS
BEGIN
    EXECUTE IMMEDIATE (String);
END;
/
```

You can execute the ANYSTRING procedure via the **execute** command, as shown in the upcoming examples of DDL and DML commands. Note that the strings are not terminated with semicolons.

> **NOTE**
> *If you are going to run DDL commands through dynamic SQL, you must have been granted the necessary system privileges explicitly—not via roles. If you do not have the CREATE TABLE system privilege explicitly granted to you, the following command will fail with an "ORA-01031: insufficient privileges" error:*

```
execute ANYSTRING('create table CD (Artist VARCHAR2(25), Title VARCHAR2(25)) ');

execute ANYSTRING('insert into CD values(''NEIL FINN'',''TRY WHISTLING THIS'') ');
```

The first command in the preceding listing executes the following SQL command:

```
create table CD
(Artist VARCHAR2(25),
 Title  VARCHAR2(25));
```

The second command in the listing inserts a record into the CD table:

```
insert into CD values ('NEIL FINN', 'TRY WHISTLING THIS');
```

If the SQL statements passed to ANYSTRING contain quotes, each quote should be replaced with a set of two quotes, as shown in the preceding execution of ANYSTRING for the **insert** command. After each command, you will receive the following response:

```
PL/SQL procedure successfully completed.
```

You can verify that the commands succeeded by querying the new table:

```
select * from CD;

ARTIST                    TITLE
------------------------- -------------------------
NEIL FINN                 TRY WHISTLING THIS
```

You can write native dynamic SQL for which the input parameters will be passed to the SQL commands:

```
declare
    Symbol VARCHAR2(6) := 'WOND';
begin
        EXECUTE IMMEDIATE 'delete from STOCK where Symbol = :symbol'
        USING Symbol;
end;
/
```

The *symbol* variable is set equal to the value 'WOND', and that value is then passed to the **delete** command via the **using** clause.

In the following listing, a procedure named DELETE_ROWS will delete all rows from the table passed in as a variable. If a *where_clause* value is entered when the procedure is executed, it will be dynamically appended to the **delete** command; otherwise, all rows will be deleted.

```
create or replace procedure DELETE_ROWS (
    Table_Name in VARCHAR2,
    Condition in VARCHAR2 default NULL) as
    Where_Clause VARCHAR2(100) := ' where ' || Condition;
begin
    if Condition is NULL then Where_Clause := NULL; end if;
    execute immediate 'delete from ' || Table_Name || Where_Clause;
end;
/
```

You can call the DELETE_ROWS procedure anytime you want to delete rows from a table. You could call it within another procedure or within an application without having to grant anyone access to perform **delete** commands directly within SQL*Plus. The following command will delete all the rows in the DEPT table:

```
execute DELETE_ROWS('STOCK');
```

In addition to calling SQL statements, you can execute procedures and PL/SQL blocks via native dynamic SQL.

Using Bind Variables

One of the benefits of native dynamic SQL is the ability to use bind variables in your code. For example, consider this example from earlier in this chapter:

```
declare
    Symbol VARCHAR2(6) := 'WOND';
begin
    EXECUTE IMMEDIATE 'delete from STOCK where Symbol = :symbol'
    USING Symbol;
end;
/
```

In the preceding listing, *:symbol* is a bind variable. Successive values of *symbol* can be passed in to the EXECUTE IMMEDIATE command. Because a bind variable is used, the command will not have to be parsed repeatedly. If you monitor the database as the application is used, you will see in V$SQL one entry for the command. If you had not used bind variables, you would see a separate entry in V$SQL for each separate execution of the command. That is, instead of seeing

```
delete from STOCK where Symbol = :symbol
```

in the library cache, you would see one entry for each unique deletion, such as

```
delete from STOCK where Symbol = 'WOND'
```

and so on.

Each of these commands would be separately parsed, and each would be taking space in memory. Failing to use bind variables may thus fill your SGA with a large number of very similar commands—a waste of the resources that the database is supposed to be exploiting and a potential cause of performance problems. Database administrators can resolve a portion of this problem by setting the CURSOR_SHARING initialization parameter to SIMILAR, but at its heart this is a problem that should be solved by using a proper development approach.

When the query is run, bind arguments replace their corresponding placeholders in the string. Each of the placeholders must be associated with a bind variable in the **using** clause or a **returning into** clause. Bind variables can be numeric, character, or string literals.

The following example illustrates the use of bind variables within a dynamic **update** statement:

```
declare
    sql_stmt    VARCHAR2(200);
    Symbol      VARCHAR2(6) := 'ADSP';
    CloseToday  NUMBER(6,2);
begin
    sql_stmt := 'update STOCK set CloseToday = 32 WHERE Symbol = :1
        RETURNING CloseToday INTO :2';
    EXECUTE IMMEDIATE sql_stmt USING Symbol RETURNING INTO CloseToday;
```

```
end;
/
```

The **returning into** clause is only used in **insert**, **update**, and **delete** commands that have a **returning** clause. For each value returned by the command, there must be a corresponding variable in the **returning into** clause.

Using DBMS_SQL

Prior to Oracle9*i*, dynamic SQL required the use of the DBMS_SQL package. You can still use the DBMS_SQL method, as shown in this section. Using DBMS_SQL may give you greater control over the processing flow within the dynamic SQL, but it is generally more complicated to write than the native dynamic SQL shown earlier in this chapter.

The script in the following example creates the DBMS_SQL version of the ANYSTRING procedure shown earlier. The ANYSTRING procedure has a single input variable: a SQL command. When you execute the ANYSTRING procedure, you pass it the SQL command to execute; the SQL command may be either a DML command (such as **select** or **insert**) or a DDL command (such as **create table**).

```
create or replace procedure ANYSTRING(String IN VARCHAR2) AS
     Cursor_Name INTEGER;
     Ret INTEGER;
BEGIN
     Cursor_Name := DBMS_SQL.OPEN_CURSOR;
     DBMS_SQL.PARSE(Cursor_Name, String, dbms_sql.Native);
     Ret := DBMS_SQL.EXECUTE(Cursor_Name);
     DBMS_SQL.CLOSE_CURSOR(Cursor_Name);
END;
/
```

As with the earlier version, you can execute the ANYSTRING procedure via the **execute** command, as shown in the following examples of DDL and DML commands:

```
execute ANYSTRING('drop table CD');

execute ANYSTRING('create table CD (Artist VARCHAR2(25), Title VARCHAR2(25))');

execute ANYSTRING('insert into CD values(''NEIL FINN'',''TRY WHISTLING THIS'')');
```

If the SQL statements passed to ANYSTRING contain quotes, each quote should be replaced with a set of two quotes, as shown in the preceding execution of ANYSTRING for the **insert** command. After each command, you will receive the following response:

```
PL/SQL procedure successfully completed.
```

You can verify that the commands succeeded by querying the new table, as shown in the next example.

```
select * from CD;

ARTIST                        TITLE
--------------------------    --------------------------
NEIL FINN                     TRY WHISTLING THIS
```

In the following sections, you will see descriptions of the major functions and procedures used within dynamic SQL statements.

OPEN_CURSOR

The **OPEN_CURSOR** function of the DBMS_SQL package opens a cursor and returns to your program a cursor ID number. Thus, within the ANYSTRING procedure, the *cursor_name* variable is defined as an INTEGER datatype:

```
Cursor_Name INTEGER;
```

Within the Executable Commands section, the *cursor_name* variable is set to the output of the **OPEN_CURSOR** execution:

```
Cursor_Name := DBMS_SQL.OPEN_CURSOR;
```

PARSE

Parsing a statement checks its syntax and associates the statement with the cursor. To parse a statement, use the **PARSE** procedure of the DBMS_SQL package. For example, in the ANYSTRING procedure, the following command parses the SQL command. **PARSE** takes three parameters: the cursor ID, the command being parsed, and a language flag.

```
DBMS_SQL.PARSE(Cursor_Name, String, dbms_sql.Native);
```

The language flag specifies the behavior for the statement. The "Native" setting shown in this example specifies behavior according to the current version of the database.

NOTE
*DDL commands (such as **create table**) are executed when they are parsed.*

BIND_VARIABLE and BIND_ARRAY

If your dynamic SQL procedure performs data manipulation, you will need to use bind variables. Any dynamic SQL command that **insert**s, **update**s, or **delete**s records needs to use either the **BIND_VARIABLE** or **BIND_ARRAY** procedure within DBMS_SQL as part of its processing. You must call one of these procedures to supply the value of a variable in your program to the placeholder. When the SQL statement is then executed, Oracle uses the data that your program has placed in the output and input, or *bind*, variables.

For example, the **PARSE** execution in the following listing parses a SQL command in which one of the values is unknown—the value of the bind variable used in the procedure:

```
DBMS_SQL.PARSE(Cursor_Name, 'delete from CD where Artist > :artist',
                   dbms_sql.Native);
```

Following the **PARSE** execution, you must bind the *:artist* bind variable to the *artist_name* variable passed to the procedure. When a user executes the procedure, a value will be specified for the *artist_name* variable. The **BIND_VARIABLE** procedure shown in the following listing will bind the *artist_name* value to the *:artist* bind variable used by the command string being parsed:

```
DBMS_SQL.BIND_VARIABLE(Cursor_Name, ':artist', artist_name);
```

You can use dynamic SQL to execute a DML statement multiple times—each time with a different bind variable. You can use the **BIND_ARRAY** procedure to bind an array of values, each of which will be used as an input variable once per **EXECUTE**.

EXECUTE

To execute your dynamically created SQL statement, use the **EXECUTE** function of the DBMS_SQL package. The following listing, from the ANYSTRING procedure, shows the use of the **EXECUTE** function:

```
Ret := DBMS_SQL.EXECUTE(Cursor_Name);
```

When you use the **EXECUTE** function, you pass the cursor ID value (in this example, the *cursor_name* variable) as input. The *ret* variable holds the output of the **EXECUTE** function, which will be the number of rows processed (if the executed statement performs DML).

DEFINE_COLUMN

If your cursor performs a query, you must execute the **DEFINE_COLUMN** function once for each column being selected. If the column is defined with a LONG datatype, you must use the **DEFINE_COLUMN_LONG** function in place of **DEFINE_COLUMN**. If you are selecting values into a PL/SQL array, you must use **DEFINE_ARRAY** in place of **DEFINE_COLUMN**.

For example, consider the query parsed in the following command:

```
DBMS_SQL.PARSE(Cursor_Name,'select Artist, Title from CD',
                   dbms_sql.Native);
```

Prior to executing the cursor, you must define the columns by their position in the query, as shown in the following listing:

```
DBMS_SQL.DEFINE_COLUMN(Cursor_Name, 1, Artist, 25);
DBMS_SQL.DEFINE_COLUMN(Cursor_Name, 2, Title, 25);
```

Once you have defined the columns, you can use the **EXECUTE** function to execute the cursor.

FETCH_ROWS, EXECUTE_AND_FETCH, and COLUMN_VALUE

If your dynamic SQL command performs a query, you can call the **FETCH_ROWS** function to retrieve the query's rows. The **EXECUTE_AND_FETCH** function both executes and fetches rows.

For example, suppose there is a table called CD_COPY, with the same column definitions as the CD table created earlier in this chapter. You can use dynamic SQL to **select** records from the CD table and **insert** them into the CD_COPY table. For this example, the Get_CD_Cursor statement will retrieve rows from the CD table, and the Insert_CD_Copy_Cursor statement will insert the retrieved values into the CD_COPY table.

In this example, the Get_CD_Cursor cursor has already been parsed. The sample code executes the **FETCH_ROWS** function. If the number of rows fetched is greater than zero, the record will be processed.

```
if DBMS_SQL.FETCH_ROWS(Get_CD_Cursor)>0 then
```

For the fetched record, the **COLUMN_VALUE** procedure is executed once for each column selected:

```
DBMS_SQL.COLUMN_VALUE(Get_CD_Cursor, 1, Artist);
DBMS_SQL.COLUMN_VALUE(Get_CD_Cursor, 2, Title);
```

Now that the queried values have been bound to variables, you can bind those values into the cursor that **insert**s records into the CD_COPY table:

```
DBMS_SQL.BIND_VARIABLE(Insert_CD_Copy_Cursor, 'artist', Artist);
DBMS_SQL.BIND_VARIABLE(Insert_CD_Copy_Cursor, 'title', Title);
```

You can now execute the cursor that **insert**s values into the CD_COPY table:

```
Ret := DBMS_SQL.EXECUTE(Insert_CD_COPY_Cursor);
```

The *ret* variable will hold the number of rows **insert**ed into the CD_COPY table. If you called a procedure from within an anonymous PL/SQL block, execute the **VARIABLE_VALUE** function to retrieve the values assigned to its output variables.

CLOSE_CURSOR

You can close an open cursor by executing the **CLOSE_CURSOR** procedure of the DBMS_SQL package. The example in the following listing, from the ANYSTRING procedure, shows that the **CLOSE_CURSOR** procedure uses the cursor ID value as its sole input parameter:

```
DBMS_SQL.CLOSE_CURSOR(Cursor_Name);
```

Closing a cursor frees the memory used by the cursor and reduces the number of concurrently open cursors in your session.

Table 32-1 lists the major functions and procedures available in dynamic SQL, along with a brief description of each.

Function or Procedure	Description
BIND_ARRAY	Binds a value to an array.
BIND_VARIABLE	Binds a value to a variable.
CLOSE_CURSOR	Closes a cursor.
COLUMN_VALUE	Returns the value of a cursor element within a cursor's query.
COLUMN_VALUE_LONG	Returns all or a portion of a LONG datatype element within a cursor's query.
DEFINE_ARRAY	Defines an array to be selected from a cursor's query.
DEFINE_COLUMN	Defines a column to be selected from a cursor's query.
DEFINE_COLUMN_LONG	Defines a LONG datatype column to be selected from a cursor's query.
DESCRIBE_COLUMNS	Describes columns for a cursor opened and parsed through DBMS_SQL.
DESCRIBE_COLUMNS2	Alternative to DESCRIBE_COLUMNS.
EXECUTE	Executes a cursor.
EXECUTE_AND_FETCH	Executes a cursor and fetches rows from the cursor.
FETCH_ROWS	Fetches a row from a cursor.
IS_OPEN	Checks to see if a cursor is open; possible return values are TRUE and FALSE.
LAST_ERROR_POSITION	Returns the position in the SQL statement where an error occurred.
LAST_ROW_COUNT	Shows the number of rows fetched.
LAST_ROW_ID	Shows the ROWID value of the last row processed.
LAST_SQL_FUNCTION_CODE	Returns the SQL function code for a statement.
OPEN_CURSOR	Opens a cursor and returns the cursor ID value.
PARSE	Parses a statement. If the statement is a DDL command, it is immediately executed.
VARIABLE_VALUE	Returns the value of a variable in a cursor.

TABLE 32-1. *Procedures and Functions in DBMS_SQL*

PART
V

Object-Relational
Databases

CHAPTER
33

Implementing Types,
Object Views,
and Methods

 n this chapter, you will see details on the use of abstract datatypes. This chapter covers topics such as security administration for abstract datatypes and the indexing of abstract datatype attributes. The creation of methods for abstract datatypes is also shown, along with the use of object views and INSTEAD OF triggers.

To use the information provided in this chapter, you should be familiar with datatypes (see Chapter 4), views (see Chapter 18), the **grant** command (see Chapter 19), indexes (see Chapter 17), and PL/SQL procedures and triggers (see Chapters 29, 30, and 31). Elements of each of these topics play a part in the implementation of an object-relational database.

Working with Abstract Datatypes

You can use abstract datatypes to group related columns into objects. For example, columns that are part of address information can be grouped into an ADDRESS_TY datatype via the **create type** command. For this example, use an account named Dora with CONNECT and RESOURCE roles:

```
rem  while connected as Dora:

create type ADDRESS_TY as object
(Street  VARCHAR2(50),
 City    VARCHAR2(25),
 State   CHAR(2),
 Zip     NUMBER);
/
```

The **create type** command in the preceding listing creates an ADDRESS_TY abstract datatype. You can use ADDRESS_TY when creating additional database objects. For example, the following **create type** command creates the PERSON_TY datatype, using the ADDRESS_TY datatype as the datatype for its Address column:

```
create type PERSON_TY as object
(Name      VARCHAR2(25),
 Address   ADDRESS_TY);
/
```

Because the Address column of the PERSON_TY datatype uses the ADDRESS_TY datatype, it holds not one value but four—the four columns that constitute the ADDRESS_TY datatype.

Security for Abstract Datatypes

The preceding example assumed that the same user owned both the ADDRESS_TY datatype and the PERSON_TY datatype. What if the owner of the PERSON_TY datatype were different from the ADDRESS_TY datatype's owner?

For example, what if the account named Dora owns the ADDRESS_TY datatype, and the user of the account named George tries to create the PERSON_TY datatype? George executes the following command:

```
rem  while connected as George:

create type PERSON_TY as object
(Name     VARCHAR2(25),
 Address  ADDRESS_TY);
/
```

If George does not own the ADDRESS_TY abstract datatype, Oracle will respond to this **create type** command with the following message:

```
Warning: Type created with compilation errors.
```

The compilation errors are caused by problems creating the *constructor method*—a special method created by Oracle when the datatype is created. Oracle cannot resolve the reference to the ADDRESS_TY datatype because George does not own a datatype with that name. George could issue the **create type** command again (using the **or replace** clause) to specifically reference Dora's ADDRESS_TY datatype:

```
create or replace type PERSON_TY as object
(Name     VARCHAR2(25),
 Address  Dora.ADDRESS_TY);
/

Warning: Type created with compilation errors.
```

To see the errors associated with the datatype creation, use the **show errors** command:

```
show errors
Errors for TYPE PERSON_TY:

LINE/COL ERROR
-------- ----------------------------------------------------------
0/0      PL/SQL: Compilation unit analysis terminated
3/11     PLS-00201: identifier 'DORA.ADDRESS_TY' must be declared
```

George will not be able to create the PERSON_TY datatype (which includes the ADDRESS_TY datatype) unless Dora first grants him EXECUTE privilege on her type. The following listing shows this grant:

```
rem  while connected as Dora:

grant EXECUTE on ADDRESS_TY to George;
```

Now that the proper grants are in place, George can create a datatype that is based on Dora's ADDRESS_TY datatype, as shown in the following listing.

```
rem  while connected as George:

create or replace type PERSON_TY as object
(Name     VARCHAR2(25),
 Address  Dora.ADDRESS_TY);
/
```

Using another user's datatypes is not trivial. For example, during **insert** operations, you must specify the owner of each type or use a synonym. George can create a table based on his PERSON_TY datatype (which includes Dora's ADDRESS_TY datatype), as shown in the following listing:

```
create table CUSTOMER
(Customer_ID  NUMBER,
 Person       PERSON_TY);
```

If George owned the PERSON_TY and ADDRESS_TY datatypes, an **insert** into CUSTOMER would use the following format:

```
insert into CUSTOMER values
(1,PERSON_TY('SomeName',
   ADDRESS_TY('StreetValue','CityValue','ST',11111)));
```

Because George does not own the ADDRESS_TY datatype, this command will fail. During the **insert**, the ADDRESS_TY constructor method is used—and Dora owns it. Therefore, the **insert** command must be modified to specify Dora as the owner of ADDRESS_TY. The following example shows the corrected **insert** statement, with the reference to Dora shown in bold:

```
insert into CUSTOMER values
(1,PERSON_TY('SomeName',
   Dora.ADDRESS_TY('StreetValue','CityValue','ST',11111)));
```

George can simplify the SQL by creating a synonym named ADDRESS_TY:

```
create synonym ADDRESS_TY for Dora.ADDRESS_TY;
```

This synonym can be used in queries, DML, and DDL.

You can use a synonym for another user's datatype during queries and inserts. For example, George's insert works now that the ADDRESS_TY synonym exists:

```
insert into CUSTOMER values
(1,PERSON_TY('SomeName',
   ADDRESS_TY('StreetValue','CityValue','ST',11111)));
```

NOTE
When you create a synonym, Oracle does not check the validity of the object for which you are creating a synonym. When you create synonym x for y, Oracle does not check to make sure that y is a valid object name or valid object type. The validity of that object is only checked when the object is accessed via the synonym.

In a relational-cnly implementation of Oracle, you grant the EXECUTE privilege on procedural objects such as procedures and packages. Within the object-relational implementation of Oracle, the EXECUTE privilege is extended to cover abstract datatypes as well. The EXECUTE privilege is appropriate because abstract datatypes can include *methods*—PL/SQL functions and procedures that operate on the datatype. If you grant someone the privilege to use your datatype, you are granting the user the privilege to execute the methods you have defined on the datatype. Although Dora did not yet define any methods on the ADDRESS_TY datatype, Oracle automatically creates constructor methods to access the data. Any object (such as PERSON_TY) that uses the ADDRESS_TY datatype uses the constructor method associated with ADDRESS_TY. Even if you haven't created any methods for your abstract datatype, it still has procedures associated with it.

You can describe CUSTOMER:

```
describe CUSTOMER
```

```
Name                                          Null?     Type
----------------------------------------- --------  ---------
CUSTOMER_ID                                         NUMBER
PERSON                                              PERSON_TY
```

You can use the **set describe depth** command in SQL*Plus to show the datatype attributes for tables that use object-relational features. You can specify depth values from 1 to 50:

```
set describe depth 2
```

```
desc CUSTOMER
```

```
Name                                          Null?     Type
----------------------------------------- --------  ----------------
CUSTOMER_ID                                         NUMBER
PERSON                                              PERSON_TY
   NAME                                             VARCHAR2(25)
   ADDRESS                                          DORA.ADDRESS_TY
```

```
set describe depth 3
```

```
desc customer
```

```
Name                                          Null?     Type
----------------------------------------- --------  ----------------
CUSTOMER_ID                                         NUMBER
PERSON                                              PERSON_TY
   NAME                                             VARCHAR2(25)
   ADDRESS                                          DORA.ADDRESS_TY
      STREET                                        VARCHAR2(50)
      CITY                                          VARCHAR2(25)
      STATE                                         CHAR(2)
      ZIP                                           NUMBER
```

Indexing Abstract Datatype Attributes

As shown in the previous listings, the CUSTOMER table contains a normal column (Customer_ID) and a Person column that is defined by the PERSON_TY abstract datatype.

From the datatype definitions shown in the preceding section of this chapter, you can see that PERSON_TY has one column (Name) followed by an Address column defined by the ADDRESS_TY datatype.

During queries, you fully qualify the datatype attributes when referencing columns within the abstract datatypes by prefacing the attribute name with the column name and by prefacing the column name with a correlation variable. For example, the following query returns the Customer_ID column along with the Name column. The Name column is an attribute of the datatype that defines the Person column, so you refer to the attribute as Person.Name:

```
select Customer_ID, C.Person.Name
   from CUSTOMER C;
```

NOTE
When querying the attributes of an abstract datatype, you must use a correlation variable for the table, as shown in this example.

To set the display attributes for an abstract datatype's attributes in SQL*Plus, use the **column** command, specifying the name of the datatype and the attribute:

```
column Customer_ID format 9999999
column Person.Name format A25
```

You can refer to attributes within the ADDRESS_TY datatype by specifying the full path through the related columns. For example, the Street column is referred to as Person.Address.Street, fully describing its location within the structure of the table. In the following example, the City column is referenced twice—once in the list of columns to select, and once within the **where** clause. In each reference, a correlation variable (in this example, C) is required.

```
select C.Person.Name,
       C.Person.Address.City
  from CUSTOMER C
 where C.Person.Address.City like 'C%';
```

Because the City column is used with a range search in the **where** clause, the Oracle optimizer may be able to use an index when resolving the query. If an index is available on the City column, Oracle can quickly find all the rows that have City values starting with the letter *C*, as requested by the query.

NOTE
See Chapter 43 for guidelines regarding the columns to index.

To create an index on a column that is part of an abstract datatype, you need to specify the full path to the column as part of the **create index** command. To create an index on the City column (which is part of the Address column), you can execute the following command:

```
create index I_CUSTOMER$CITY
on CUSTOMER(Person.Address.City);
```

This command will create an index named I_CUSTOMER$CITY on the Person.Address.City column. Whenever the City column is accessed, the Oracle optimizer will evaluate the SQL used to access the data and determine if the new index can be useful for improving the performance of the query.

NOTE
*In the **create index** command, you do not use correlation variables when referencing the attributes of abstract datatypes.*

When creating tables based on abstract datatypes, you should consider how the columns within the abstract datatypes will be accessed. If, like the City column in the preceding example, certain columns will commonly be used as part of limiting conditions in queries, they should be indexed. In this regard, the representation of multiple columns in a single abstract datatype may hinder your application performance because it may obscure the need to index specific columns within the datatype. When using abstract datatypes, you become accustomed to treating a group of columns as a single entity, such as the Address columns or the Person columns. It is important to remember that the optimizer, when evaluating query access paths, will consider the columns individually. In addition, remember that indexing the City column in one table that uses the ADDRESS_ TY datatype does not affect the City column in a second table that uses the ADDRESS_TY datatype. For example, if there is a second table named BRANCH that uses the ADDRESS_TY datatype, *its* City column will not be indexed unless you create an index for it. The fact that there is an index on the City column in the CUSTOMER table will have no impact on the City column in the BRANCH table.

Therefore, one of the advantages of abstract datatypes—the ability to improve adherence to standards for logical data representation—does not extend to the physical data representation. You need to address each physical implementation separately.

Implementing Object Views

The CUSTOMER table created in the previous section of this chapter assumed that a PERSON_TY datatype already existed. When implementing object-relational database applications, you should first use the relational database design methods described in the first part of this book. After the database design is properly normalized, you should look for groups of columns (or individual columns) that constitute the representation of an abstract datatype. You can then create your tables based on the abstract datatypes, as shown earlier in this chapter.

But what if your tables already exist? What if you have previously created a relational database application and now want to implement object-relational concepts in your application without rebuilding and re-creating the entire application? To do this, you need the ability to overlay object-oriented (OO) structures, such as abstract datatypes, on existing relational tables. Oracle provides *object views* as a means for defining objects used by existing relational tables.

NOTE
Throughout the examples in this book, the names of object views will
always end with the suffix OV.

In the examples earlier in this chapter, the order of operations was as follows:

1. Create the ADDRESS_TY datatype.

2. Create the PERSON_TY datatype, using the ADDRESS_TY datatype.

3. Create the CUSTOMER table, using the PERSON_TY datatype.

If the CUSTOMER table already existed, you could create the ADDRESS_TY and PERSON_TY datatypes and use object views to relate them to the CUSTOMER table. In the following listing, the CUSTOMER table is created as a relational table, using only the built-in datatypes. To keep the examples separated, create these objects under a new schema.

```
rem    connected as a new user:

drop table CUSTOMER;

create table CUSTOMER
(Customer_ID NUMBER    primary key,
 Name         VARCHAR2(25),
 Street       VARCHAR2(50),
 City         VARCHAR2(25),
 State        CHAR(2),
 Zip          NUMBER);
```

If you want to create another table or application that stores information about people and addresses, you may choose to create the ADDRESS_TY and PERSON_TY datatypes. However, for consistency, they should be applied to the CUSTOMER table as well.

With the CUSTOMER table already created (and possibly containing data), you should create the abstract datatypes. First, create ADDRESS_TY:

```
drop type PERSON_TY;
drop type ADDRESS_TY;
create or replace type ADDRESS_TY as object
(Street  VARCHAR2(50),
 City    VARCHAR2(25),
 State   CHAR(2),
 Zip     NUMBER);
/
```

Next, create PERSON_TY, which uses ADDRESS_TY:

```
create or replace type PERSON_TY as object
(Name        VARCHAR2(25),
 Address     ADDRESS_TY);
/
```

Now, create an object view based on the CUSTOMER table using the datatypes you have defined. An object view starts with the **create view** command. Within the **create view** command, you specify the query that will form the basis of the view. You'll use the datatypes you just created. The code for creating the CUSTOMER_OV object view is shown in the following listing:

```
create view CUSTOMER_OV (Customer_ID, Person) as
select Customer_ID,
       PERSON_TY(Name,
       ADDRESS_TY(Street, City, State, Zip))
  from CUSTOMER;
```

Let's look at this command closely. In the first line, the object view is named:

```
create view CUSTOMER_OV (Customer_ID, Person) as
```

The CUSTOMER_OV view will have two columns: the Customer_ID column and the Person column (the latter is defined by the PERSON_TY datatype). Note that you cannot specify "object" as an option within the **create view** command.

In the next section of the **create view** command, you create the query that will form the basis for the view:

```
select Customer_ID,
       PERSON_TY(Name,
       ADDRESS_TY(Street, City, State, Zip))
  from CUSTOMER;
```

This example presents several important syntax issues. When a table is built on existing abstract datatypes, you select column values from the table by referring to the names of the columns (such as Person and Address in earlier examples) instead of their constructor methods. When creating the object view, however, you refer to the names of the constructor methods (PERSON_TY and ADDRESS_TY) instead.

You can use a **where** clause in the query that forms the basis of the object view. In the following example, CUSTOMER_OV is modified to include a **where** clause that limits it to showing the CUSTOMER values for which the State column has a value of 'DE':

```
create or replace view CUSTOMER_OV (Customer_ID, Person) as
select Customer_ID,
       PERSON_TY(Name,
       ADDRESS_TY(Street, City, State, Zip))
  from CUSTOMER
 where State = 'DE';
```

Note that when you create the object view CUSTOMER_OV, the **where** clause of the view's base query does not refer to the abstract datatype. Instead, it refers directly to the CUSTOMER table. The **where** clause refers directly to the State column because the query refers directly to the CUSTOMER table—a relational table that is not based on any abstract datatypes.

To create object views based on relational tables, the order of operations is as follows:

1. Create the CUSTOMER table if it does not already exist.

2. Create the ADDRESS_TY datatype.

3. Create the PERSON_TY datatype, using the ADDRESS_TY datatype.

4. Create the CUSTOMER_OV object view, using the defined datatypes.

There are two main benefits to using object views. First, they allow you to create abstract datatypes that operate against tables that already exist. Because you can use the same abstract datatypes in multiple tables within your application, you can improve your application's adherence to standard representation of data and your ability to reuse existing objects. Because you can define methods for the abstract datatypes, the methods will apply to the data within any new tables you create as well as to your existing tables.

Second, object views provide two different ways to enter data into the base table. The flexibility of data manipulation for object views—being able to treat the base table as either a relational table or an object table—is a significant benefit for application developers. In the next section, you will see the data-manipulation options available for object views.

Manipulating Data via Object Views

You can update the data in the CUSTOMER table via the CUSTOMER_OV object view, or you can update the CUSTOMER table directly. By treating CUSTOMER as just a table, you can insert data into it via a normal SQL **insert** command, as shown in the following example:

```
insert into CUSTOMER values
(123,'SIGMUND','47 HAFFNER RD','LEWISTON','NJ',22222);
```

This **insert** command inserts a single record into the CUSTOMER table. Even though you have created an object view on the table, you can still treat the CUSTOMER table as a regular relational table.

Because the object view has been created on the CUSTOMER table, you can **insert** into CUSTOMER via the constructor methods used by the view. As previously shown in this chapter, when you insert data into an object that uses abstract datatypes, you specify the names of the constructor methods within the **insert** command. The example shown in the following listing inserts a single record into the CUSTOMER_OV object view using the CUSTOMER_TY, PERSON_TY, and ADDRESS_TY constructor methods:

```
insert into CUSTOMER_OV values
    (234,
    PERSON_TY('EVELYN',
    ADDRESS_TY('555 HIGH ST','LOWLANDS PARK','NE',33333)));
```

Because you can use either method to insert values into the CUSTOMER_OV object view, you can standardize the manner in which your application performs data manipulation. If your **insert**s are all based on abstract datatypes, you can use the same kind of code for **insert**s regardless of whether the abstract datatypes were created before or after the table was.

You can query the rows just entered from either CUSTOMER or CUSTOMER_OV; but because the view has a **where** clause, CUSTOMER_OV will only show the rows that pass that limiting condition.

Using INSTEAD OF Triggers

If you create an object view, you can use an INSTEAD OF trigger to tell Oracle how to update the underlying tables that are part of the view. You can use INSTEAD OF triggers on either object views or standard relational views.

For example, if a view involves a join of two tables, your ability to **update** records in the view is limited. However, if you use an INSTEAD OF trigger, you can tell Oracle how to update, delete, or insert records in tables when a user attempts to change values via the view. The code in the INSTEAD OF trigger is executed *in place of* the **insert**, **update**, or **delete** command you enter.

For example, you may have a view that joins the BOOKSHELF table to BOOKSHELF_AUTHOR:

```
create or replace view AUTHOR_PUBLISHER as
select BA.AuthorName, Title, B.Publisher
  from BOOKSHELF_AUTHOR BA inner join BOOKSHELF B
 using (Title);
```

You can select values from this view—and if you use INSTEAD OF triggers, you can also perform data manipulation via this view. Consider these records:

```
select AuthorName, Publisher from AUTHOR_PUBLISHER
  where AuthorName = 'W. P. KINSELLA';

AUTHORNAME                                               PUBLISHER
-------------------------------------------------------- ----------
W. P. KINSELLA                                           MARINER
W. P. KINSELLA                                           BALLANTINE
```

If we attempt to update the Publisher value, the update fails:

```
update AUTHOR_PUBLISHER
   set Publisher = 'MARINER'
 where AuthorName = 'W. P. KINSELLA';

set Publisher = 'MARINER'
    *
ERROR at line 2:
ORA-01779: cannot modify a column which maps to a
           non key-preserved table
```

The problem is that Oracle cannot determine which publisher in which record to update in BOOKSHELF. To perform the update via the view, you will need to use an INSTEAD OF trigger.

In the following listing, an INSTEAD OF trigger for the AUTHOR_PUBLISHER view is created:

```
create or replace trigger AUTHOR_PUBLISHER_UPDATE
instead of UPDATE on AUTHOR_PUBLISHER
for each row
begin
  if :old.Publisher <> :new.Publisher
  then
     update BOOKSHELF
        set Publisher = :new.Publisher
      where Title = :old.Title;
  end if;
  if :old.AuthorName <> :new.AuthorName
  then
     update BOOKSHELF_AUTHOR
        set AuthorName = :new.AuthorName
      where Title = :old.Title;
  end if;
end;
/
```

In the first part of this trigger, the trigger is named and its purpose is described via the **instead of** clause. The trigger has been named to make its function clear: It is used to support **update** commands executed against the AUTHOR_PUBLISHER view. It is a row-level trigger; each changed row will be processed, as shown next:

```
create trigger AUTHOR_PUBLISHER_UPDATE
instead of UPDATE on AUTHOR_PUBLISHER
for each row
```

The next section of the trigger tells Oracle how to process the **update**. In the first check within the trigger body, the Publisher value is checked. If the old Publisher value is equal to the new Publisher value, no changes are made. If the values are not the same, the BOOKSHELF table is updated with the new Publisher value:

```
begin
  if :old.Publisher <> :new.Publisher
  then
     update BOOKSHELF
        set Publisher = :new.Publisher
      where Title = :old.Title;
  end if;
```

In the next section of the trigger, the AuthorName value is evaluated. If the AuthorName value has changed, the BOOKSHELF table is updated to reflect the new AuthorName value:

```
  if :old.AuthorName <> :new.AuthorName
  then
     update BOOKSHELF_AUTHOR
```

```
        set AuthorName = :new.AuthorName
      where Title = :old.Title;
   end if;
```

Thus, the view relies on two tables—BOOKSHELF and BOOKSHELF_AUTHOR—and an **update** of the view can update *either* or *both* of the tables. The INSTEAD OF trigger, introduced to support object views, is a powerful tool for application development.

You can now update the AUTHOR_PUBLISHER view directly and have the trigger update the proper underlying table. For example, the following command will update the BOOKSHELF table:

```
update AUTHOR_PUBLISHER
    set Publisher = 'MARINER'
 where AuthorName = 'W. P. KINSELLA';
```

```
2 rows updated.
```

Verify the **update** by querying the BOOKSHELF table:

```
select Publisher from BOOKSHELF
  where Title in
(select Title from BOOKSHELF_AUTHOR
  where AuthorName = 'W. P. KINSELLA');
```

```
PUBLISHER
-------------------
MARINER
MARINER
```

INSTEAD OF triggers are very powerful. As shown in this example, you can use them to perform operations against different database tables, using the flow-control logic available within PL/SQL. In dealing with object views, you can use INSTEAD OF triggers to redirect DML against the object views to the base tables for the views.

Methods

When you created an object view on the CUSTOMER table, you defined abstract datatypes that the table used. Those datatypes help to standardize the representation of data, but they serve another purpose as well. You can define methods that apply to datatypes, and by applying those datatypes to existing tables, you can apply those methods to the data in those tables.

Consider the CUSTOMER_OV object view:

```
create or replace view CUSTOMER_OV (Customer_ID, Person) as
select Customer_ID,
       PERSON_TY(Name,
       ADDRESS_TY(Street, City, State, Zip))
   from CUSTOMER;
```

This view applies the PERSON_TY and ADDRESS_TY abstract datatypes to the data in the CUSTOMER table. If any methods are associated with those datatypes, they will apply to the data in the table. When you create an abstract datatype, you use the **create type** command. When you create a method, you use the **create type body** command.

Syntax for Creating Methods

Before creating the body for a method, you must name the method within the datatype declaration. For example, let's create a new datatype, ANIMAL_TY. The datatype definition for ANIMAL_TY is shown in the following listing:

```
create or replace type ANIMAL_TY as object
(Breed         VARCHAR2(25),
 Name          VARCHAR2(25),
 BirthDate   DATE,
member function AGE (BirthDate IN DATE) return NUMBER);
/
```

The ANIMAL_TY datatype could be used as part of an object view on the BREEDING table used in Chapter 14. In the BREEDING table, the name of an offspring, its sex, its parents, and its birthdate are recorded.

Within the **create type** command, the line

```
member function AGE (BirthDate IN DATE) return NUMBER)
```

names the function that is a "member" of the ANIMAL_TY datatype. Because AGE will return a value, it is a function (see Chapter 31). To define the AGE function, use the **create type body** command, whose full syntax is shown in the Alphabetical Reference.

Let's create the AGE function as a member function within the ANIMAL_TY datatype. The AGE function will return the age, in days, of the animals:

```
create or replace type body ANIMAL_TY as
member function Age (BirthDate DATE) return NUMBER is
    begin
    RETURN ROUND(SysDate - BirthDate);
    end;
end;
/
```

If you had additional functions or procedures to code, you would specify them within the same **create type body** command, before the final **end** clause.

Now that the AGE function has been created, it is associated with the ANIMAL_TY datatype. If a table uses this datatype, it can use the AGE function.

NOTE
You cannot drop or re-create a type that is in use by a table.

You can use the AGE function within a query. If ANIMAL_TY is used as the datatype for a column named Animal in the table named ANIMAL, the table structure could be as follows:

```
create table ANIMAL
(ID       NUMBER,
 Animal  ANIMAL_TY);

insert into ANIMAL values
(11,ANIMAL_TY('COW','MIMI',TO_DATE('01-JAN-1997','DD-MON-YYYY')));
```

You can now invoke the AGE function, which is part of the ANIMAL_TY datatype. Like the attributes of an abstract datatype, the member methods are referenced using the column names that use the datatypes (in this case, Animal.AGE). Your result will reflect the current system date when you execute the query:

```
select A.Animal.AGE(A.Animal.BirthDate)
   from ANIMAL A;

A.ANIMAL.AGE(A.ANIMAL.BIRTHDATE)
--------------------------------
                            2694
```

The A.Animal.AGE(A.Animal.BirthDate) call executes the AGE method within the ANIMAL_TY datatype. Therefore, you do not have to store variable data such as age within your database. Instead, you can store static data—such as birthdate—in your database and use function and procedure calls to derive the variable data.

NOTE
In this example, you need to use correlation variables in two places—
when calling the AGE method and when passing the name of the
BirthDate column to that method.

Managing Methods

You can add new methods to a datatype by altering the datatype (via the **alter type** command). When altering a datatype, list all its methods, both the old and the new. After altering the datatype, alter the datatype's body, listing all the datatype's methods in a single command.

You do not need to grant EXECUTE privilege on the member functions and procedures of abstract datatypes. If you grant another user EXECUTE privilege on the ANIMAL_TY datatype, that user automatically has EXECUTE privilege on the methods that are part of the datatype. Thus, the grant of access to the datatype includes both the data representation and its data access methods, in accordance with OO concepts.

When creating member functions, you can specify them as being map methods or order methods (or neither, as in the case of the ANIMAL_TY.Age member function). A *map method* returns the relative position of a given record in the ordering of all records within the object. A type body can contain only one map method, which must be a function.

An *order method* is a member function that takes a record in the object as an explicit argument and returns an integer value. If the returned value is negative, zero, or positive, the implicit "self" argument of the function is less than, equal to, or greater than, respectively, that of the explicitly specified record. When multiple rows within an object are compared in an **order by** clause, the order method is automatically executed to order the rows returned. A datatype specification can contain only one order method, which must be a function with the return type INTEGER.

The notion of ordering within the rows of an abstract datatype may have more relevance when you consider the implementation of *collectors*—datatypes that hold multiple values per row. Oracle offers two types of collectors, called *nested tables* and *varying arrays*. In the next chapter, you will see how to implement these collector types.

CHAPTER
34

Collectors
(Nested Tables and
Varying Arrays)

ollectors make use of abstract datatypes. You should be familiar with the creation and implementation of abstract datatypes (see Chapter 33) before attempting to use varying arrays and nested tables.

Varying Arrays

A *varying array* allows you to store repeating attributes of a record in a single row. For example, suppose you want to track which of your tools were borrowed by which of your neighbors. You could model this in a relational database by creating a BORROWER table:

```
create table BORROWER
(Name            VARCHAR2(25),
 Tool            VARCHAR2(25),
constraint BORROWER_PK primary key (Name, Tool));
```

Even though the borrower's Name value does not change, it is repeated in each record because it is part of the primary key. Collectors such as varying arrays allow you to repeat *only* those column values that change, potentially saving storage space. You can use collectors to accurately represent relationships between datatypes in your database objects. In the following sections, you will see how to create and use collectors.

Creating a Varying Array

You can create a varying array based on either an abstract datatype or one of Oracle's standard datatypes (such as NUMBER). For example, you could create a new datatype, TOOL_TY, as shown in the following listing, which has only one column; you should limit varying arrays to one column. If you need to use multiple columns in an array, consider using nested tables (described later in this chapter).

```
create type TOOL_TY as object
(ToolName  VARCHAR2(25));
/
```

You do not have to create the base type—in this case, TOOL_TY—before you can create a varying array (to be named TOOLS_VA). Because the varying array is based on only one column, you can create the TOOLS_VA type in a single step. To create the varying array, use the **as varray()** clause of the **create type** command:

```
create or replace type TOOLS_VA as varray(5) of VARCHAR2(25);
/
```

When this **create type** command is executed, a type named TOOLS_VA is created. The **as varray(5)** clause tells Oracle that a varying array is being created, and it will hold a maximum of five entries per record. The name of the varying array is the pluralized TOOLS (instead of TOOL) to show that this type will be used to hold multiple records. The suffix VA makes it clear that the type is a varying array. You can now use this type as the basis for a column definition, as shown in the following listing:

```
drop table BORROWER;

create table BORROWER
(Name           VARCHAR2(25),
 Tools          TOOLS_VA,
constraint BORROWER_PK primary key (Name));
```

Describing the Varying Array

The BORROWER table will contain one record for each borrower, even if that borrower has multiple tools. The multiple tools will be stored in the Tools column, using the TOOLS_VA varying array. You can describe the BORROWER table as follows:

```
desc BORROWER
```

```
Name                             Null?    Type
-------------------------------  -------- ------------
NAME                             NOT NULL VARCHAR2(25)
TOOLS                                     TOOLS_VA
```

Note that the **set describe depth** command shown in Chapter 33 will not affect this output. You can query similar information from USER_TAB_COLUMNS:

```
column Data_Type format a12

select Column_Name,
       Data_Type
  from USER_TAB_COLUMNS
 where Table_Name = 'BORROWER';
```

```
COLUMN_NAME                      DATA_TYPE
-------------------------------  ------------
NAME                             VARCHAR2
TOOLS                            TOOLS_VA
```

USER_TYPES shows TOOLS_VA is a collection, with no attributes:

```
select TypeCode,
       Attributes
  from USER_TYPES
 where Type_Name = 'TOOLS_VA';
```

```
TYPECODE                         ATTRIBUTES
-------------------------------  ----------
COLLECTION                                0
```

For more details on TOOLS_VA, query the USER_COLL_TYPES data dictionary view, as shown in the following listing:

```
select Coll_Type,
       Elem_Type_Owner,
```

```
        Elem_Type_Name,
        Upper_Bound,
        Length
  from USER_COLL_TYPES
 where Type_Name = 'TOOLS_VA';

COLL_TYPE                           ELEM_TYPE_OWNER
------------------------------      ------------------------------
ELEM_TYPE_NAME                      UPPER_BOUND    LENGTH
------------------------------      -----------    ----------
VARYING ARRAY
VARCHAR2                                      5            25
```

If you base a varying array on an existing abstract datatype, the datatype's owner will be displayed in the Elem_Type_Owner column, and the datatype's name will be displayed in the Elem_Type_Name column. Because TOOLS_VA uses VARCHAR2 instead of an abstract datatype, the Elem_Type_Owner column's value is **NULL**.

Inserting Records into the Varying Array

Because a varying array is an abstract datatype, you need to use constructor methods to insert records into tables that use varying arrays. Furthermore, because the varying array is itself an abstract datatype, you may need to nest calls to multiple constructor methods to insert a record into a table that uses a varying array.

The following command will insert a single record into the BORROWER table. In this example, the record will have a single Name column value and three Tools values.

```
insert into BORROWER values
('JED HOPKINS',
  TOOLS_VA('HAMMER','SLEDGE','AX'));
```

This **insert** command first specifies the value for the Name column. Because the Name column is not part of any abstract datatype, it is populated in the same way you would insert values into any relational column:

```
insert into BORROWER values
('JED HOPKINS',
```

The next part of the **insert** command inserts records into the Tools column. Because the Tools column uses the TOOLS_VA varying array, you need to use the TOOLS_VA constructor method:

```
TOOLS_VA('HAMMER','SLEDGE','AX'));
```

Because this is a varying array, you can pass multiple values to the TOOLS_VA constructor method. As the preceding listing shows, three tools are listed in a single **insert** for the single borrower name. If the varying array had been based on the TOOL_TY datatype, you would have instead nested calls to TOOL_TY within the TOOLS_VA calls:

```
insert into BORROWER values
('JED HOPKINS',
  TOOLS_VA(
    TOOL_TY('HAMMER'),
    TOOL_TY('SLEDGE'),
    TOOL_TY('AX')));
```

Basing the varying array on an Oracle-supplied datatype (and using only a single column) instead of an abstract or user-defined datatype simplifies the **insert** command by eliminating the nested calls to additional constructor methods.

The TOOLS_VA varying array was defined to have up to five values. In this **insert** command, only three values were entered for the row; the other two are uninitialized. If you want to set the uninitialized values to **NULL**, you can specify that in the **insert** command:

```
insert into BORROWER values
('JED HOPKINS',
  TOOLS_VA('HAMMER','SLEDGE','AX',NULL,NULL));
```

If you specify too many values to insert into the varying array, Oracle responds with the following:

```
ORA-22909: exceeded maximum VARRAY limit
```

You cannot insert records into a table that contains a varying array unless you know the structure and datatypes within the array. This example assumes that all the datatypes used by the BORROWER table were within the schema used to create the BORROWER table. If the datatypes are owned by a separate schema, the creator of the BORROWER table will need EXECUTE privilege on those datatypes. See Chapter 33 for examples of using datatypes created under other schemas.

Selecting Data from Varying Arrays

You can query the varying array data directly from the table:

```
select Tools from BORROWER;

TOOLS
--------------------------------------------
TOOLS_VA('HAMMER', 'SLEDGE', 'AX')
```

You can use the **TABLE** function in the **from** clause to display the data from varying arrays on separate lines. Consider the following query and its output:

```
select B.Name, N.*
  from BORROWER B, TABLE(B.Tools) N;

NAME                        COLUMN_VALUE
------------------------    -------------------------
JED HOPKINS                 HAMMER
JED HOPKINS                 SLEDGE
JED HOPKINS                 AX
```

How did that work? The **TABLE** function took as its input the name of the varying array, and its output is given the alias N. The values within N are selected, generating the second column of the output.

To display the varying array data on separate lines, you can also use PL/SQL. You can query the varying array to determine its maximum number of entries per row, called its LIMIT, and the current number of entries per row, called its COUNT. To retrieve the COUNT, LIMIT, and data from a varying array, you can use a set of nested Cursor FOR loops, as shown in the following listing:

NOTE
For an overview of PL/SQL and Cursor FOR loops, see Chapter 29.

```
set serveroutput on
declare
    cursor borrower_cursor is
        select * from BORROWER;
begin
    for borrower_rec in borrower_cursor
    loop
        dbms_output.put_line('Contact Name: '||borrower_rec.Name);
        for i in 1..borrower_rec.Tools.Count
        loop
            dbms_output.put_line(borrower_rec.Tools(i));
        end loop;
    end loop;
end;
/
```

The following is the output of this PL/SQL script:

```
Contact Name: JED HOPKINS
HAMMER
SLEDGE
AX

PL/SQL procedure successfully completed.
```

The script uses several PL/SQL features to retrieve data from the varying array. The data will be displayed via the PUT_LINE procedure of the DBMS_OUTPUT package (see Chapter 31), so you must first enable PL/SQL output to be displayed:

```
set serveroutput on
```

In the Declarations section of the PL/SQL block, a cursor is declared; the cursor's query selects all the values from the BORROWER table:

```
declare
    cursor borrower_cursor is
        select * from BORROWER;
```

The Executable Commands section of the PL/SQL block contains two nested FOR loops. In the first loop, each record from the cursor is evaluated and the Name value is printed via PUT_LINE:

```
begin
    for borrower_rec in borrower_cursor
    loop
      dbms_output.put_line('Contact Name: '||borrower_rec.Name);
```

NOTE
You should only print character data via PUT_LINE. PL/SQL will print numeric values via PUT_LINE, but you cannot concatenate them to expressions before printing. Therefore, you may need to use the **TO_CHAR** *function on numeric data before printing it via PUT_LINE.*

In the next section of the PL/SQL block, the rows are evaluated further to retrieve the data stored in the varying array. A second FOR loop, nested within the first loop, is executed. The inner FOR loop is limited by the number of values in the array, as defined by the **COUNT** method (the maximum number of values in the array is available via the **LIMIT** method).

The values in the Tools array will be printed, one by one, by this loop:

```
    for i in 1..borrower_rec.Tools.Count
      loop
        dbms_output.put_line(borrower_rec.Tools(i));
```

The notation

```
Tools(i)
```

tells Oracle to print the array value that corresponds to the value of *i*. Thus, the first time through the loop, the first value in the array is printed; then the value of *i* is incremented, and the second value in the array is printed.

The last part of the PL/SQL block closes the two nested loops and ends the block:

```
    end loop;
    end loop;
end;
```

Because this method involves nested loops within PL/SQL, selecting data from varying arrays is not trivial.

Note that we may get a different number of tools for each borrower—anywhere from zero to five. For example, the following row would insert a row with just one entry in the varying array:

```
insert into BORROWER values
('FRED FULLER',
  TOOLS_VA('HAMMER'));
```

You can select that data via PL/SQL, via the **TABLE** function, or via SQL:

```
select B.Name, N.*
  from BORROWER B, TABLE(B.Tools) N;
```

```
NAME                         COLUMN_VALUE
------------------------      ------------------------
JED HOPKINS                   HAMMER
JED HOPKINS                   SLEDGE
JED HOPKINS                   AX
FRED FULLER                   HAMMER
```

For greater flexibility in selecting data from collectors, you should consider the use of nested tables, as described in the next section.

NOTE
*You can use the **modify limit** clause of the **alter type** command to change the maximum number of entries allowed in a varying array.*

Following the examples of the use of nested tables, you will see additional functions that can be used against varying arrays and nested tables.

Nested Tables

Whereas varying arrays have a limited number of entries, a second type of collector, called a *nested table*, has no limit on the number of entries per row. A nested table is, as its name implies, a table within a table. In this case, it is a table that is represented as a column within another table. You can have multiple rows in the nested table for each row in the main table.

For example, if you have a table of animal breeders, you may also have data about their animals. Using a nested table, you could store the information about breeders and all of their animals within the same table. Consider the ANIMAL_TY datatype introduced in Chapter 33:

```
create or replace type ANIMAL_TY as object
(Breed      VARCHAR2(25),
 Name       VARCHAR2(25),
 BirthDate  DATE);
/
```

NOTE
To keep this example simple, this version of the ANIMAL_TY datatype does not include any methods. For this example, you should drop the ANIMAL table if it exists in your practice schema.

The ANIMAL_TY datatype contains a record for each animal—its breed, name, and birth date. To use this datatype as the basis for a nested table, you need to create a new datatype:

```
create type ANIMALS_NT as table of ANIMAL_TY;
/
```

The **as table of** clause of this **create type** command tells Oracle that you will be using this type as the basis for a nested table. The name of the type, ANIMALS_NT, has a pluralized root to indicate that it stores multiple rows, and it has the suffix NT to indicate that it will be a nested table.

You can now create a table of breeders, using the ANIMALS_TY datatype:

```
create table BREEDER
(BreederName       VARCHAR2(25),
 Animals           ANIMALS_NT)
 nested table ANIMALS store as ANIMALS_NT_TAB;
```

In this **create table** command, the BREEDER table is created. The first column of the BREEDER table is a BreederName column. The second column is a column named Animals, whose definition is the nested table ANIMALS_NT.

When creating a table that includes a nested table, you must specify the name of the table that will be used to store the nested table's data. That is, the data for the nested table is not stored "inline" with the rest of the table's data. Instead, it is stored apart from the main table. The data in the Animals column will be stored in one table, and the data in the BreederName column will be stored in a separate table. Oracle will maintain pointers between the tables. In this example, the "out-of-line" data for the nested table is stored in a table named ANIMALS_NT_TAB:

```
nested table ANIMALS store as ANIMALS_NT_TAB;
```

This example highlights the importance of naming standards for collectors. If you pluralize the column names ("Animals" instead of "Animal") and consistently use suffixes (TY, NT, and so forth), you can tell what an object is just by its name. Furthermore, because nested tables and varying arrays may be based directly on previously defined datatypes, their names may mirror the names of the datatypes on which they are based. Therefore, a datatype named ANIMAL_TY could be used as the basis for a varying array named ANIMALS_VA or a nested table named ANIMALS_NT. The nested table would have an associated out-of-line table named ANIMALS_NT_TAB. If you know that a table named ANIMALS_NT_TAB exists and you are consistent in your object naming, you automatically know that it stores data based on a datatype named ANIMAL_TY.

Specifying Tablespaces for Nested Tables

When you create the BREEDER table with the ANIMALS nested table, the nested table's storage is created in the same table as the parent table. If you create a nested table within a nested table, the child table is created in the same tablespace as its parent table unless you specify a tablespace.

You can use the **create table** command to specify a tablespace for the nested table, as shown in the following listing. In this example, the BREEDER table will be stored in the user's default tablespace, whereas the ANIMALS nested table will be stored in the USERS tablespace:

```
drop table BREEDER;

create table BREEDER
(BreederName       VARCHAR2(25),
```

```
Animals              ANIMALS_NT)
nested table ANIMALS store as ANIMALS_NT_TAB (tablespace USERS);
```

You can move the nested table via the **move** clause of the **alter table** command. If you execute the **alter table move** command on the BREEDER table, its nested table will not be moved. To move the nested table, use the name of the storage table listed in the **create table** command:

```
alter table ANIMALS_NT_TAB move tablespace PRACTICE;
```

Inserting Records into a Nested Table

You can insert records into a nested table by using the constructor methods for its datatype. For the Animals column, the datatype is ANIMALS_NT; therefore, you will use the ANIMALS_NT constructor method. The ANIMALS_NT type, in turn, uses the ANIMAL_TY datatype. As shown in the following example, inserting a record into the BREEDER table requires you to use both the ANIMALS_NT and ANIMAL_TY constructor methods. In the example, three animals are listed for the breeder named Jane James.

```
insert into BREEDER values
('JANE JAMES',
  ANIMALS_NT(
        ANIMAL_TY('DOG', 'BUTCH', '31-MAR-01'),
        ANIMAL_TY('DOG', 'ROVER', '05-JUN-01'),
        ANIMAL_TY('DOG', 'JULIO', '10-JUN-01')
));
```

This **insert** command first specifies the name of the breeder:

```
insert into BREEDER values
('JANE JAMES',
```

Next, the value for the Animals column is entered. Because the Animals column uses the ANIMALS_NT nested table, the ANIMALS_NT constructor method is called:

```
ANIMALS_NT(
```

The ANIMALS_NT nested table uses the ANIMAL_TY datatype, so the ANIMAL_TY constructor method is called for each value inserted:

```
        ANIMAL_TY('DOG', 'BUTCH', '31-MAR-01'),
        ANIMAL_TY('DOG', 'ROVER', '05-JUN-01'),
        ANIMAL_TY('DOG', 'JULIO', '10-JUN-01')
));
```

You can see the datatypes that constitute the table and its nested table via the **describe** command. Use the **set describe depth** SQL*Plus command to enable the display of the datatype attributes:

```
set describe depth 2

desc breeder
```

Name	Null?	Type
BREEDERNAME		VARCHAR2(25)
ANIMALS		ANIMALS_NT
BREED		VARCHAR2(25)
NAME		VARCHAR2(25)
BIRTHDATE		DATE

You can query this metadata from USER_TAB_COLUMNS, USER_TYPES, USER_COLL_TYPES, and USER_TYPE_ATTRS data dictionary views, as in the examples earlier in this chapter.

Querying Nested Tables

Nested tables support a great variety of queries. A nested table is a column within a table. To support queries of the columns and rows of a nested table, use the **TABLE** function introduced earlier in this chapter.

To see how the **TABLE** function is used, first consider the nested table by itself. If it were a normal column of a relational table, you would be able to query it via a normal **select** command:

```
select BirthDate   /* This won't work.*/
   from ANIMALS_NT
where Name = 'JULIO';
```

ANIMALS_NT is not a normal table; it's a datatype. To select columns (such as BirthDate) from the nested table, you first need to "flatten" the table so it can be queried. First, apply the **TABLE** function to the nested table column (BREEDER.Animals), as shown in the following listing:

```
select BreederName, N.Name, N.BirthDate
   from BREEDER, TABLE(BREEDER.Animals) N;
```

BREEDERNAME	NAME	BIRTHDATE
JANE JAMES	BUTCH	31-MAR-01
JANE JAMES	ROVER	05-JUN-01
JANE JAMES	JULIO	10-JUN-01

With the data in this format, it is simple to retrieve the proper row:

```
select BreederName, N.Name, N.BirthDate
   from BREEDER, TABLE(BREEDER.Animals) N
where N.Name = 'JULIO';
```

BREEDERNAME	NAME	BIRTHDATE
JANE JAMES	JULIO	10-JUN-01

Inserts, Updates, and Deletes with the TABLE Function

You can use the **TABLE** function whenever you need to perform **insert**s or **update**s directly against the nested table. For example, a breeder probably will have more animals as time goes by, so

you need the ability to add new records to the ANIMALS_NT nested table within the BREEDER table. You will have to insert records into the nested table without adding new records into the BREEDER table, and you will need to relate the new Animal records to breeders who are already in the BREEDER table.

The following **insert** statement adds a new record to the nested table in Jane James's BREEDER record:

```
insert into TABLE(select Animals
                  from BREEDER
                  where BreederName = 'JANE JAMES')
values
(ANIMAL_TY('DOG','MARCUS','01-AUG-01'));
```

The **insert** does not provide a value for the BreederName column; we are only inserting into the nested table of a breeder's row. The **TABLE** function is again used to "flatten" the nested table in the Animals column (for Jane's row), and the new values are inserted. Note the use of the **where** clause within the **TABLE** function call to specify the rows to be acted on.

You can also update the dog's birth date. Julio's birth date was originally entered as 10-JUN-01 but has since been discovered to be 01-SEP-01. The following **update** changes the nested table's BirthDate value for Julio. Its syntax and structure are very close to the query examples shown earlier in this chapter.

```
update TABLE(select Animals
             from BREEDER
             where BreederName = 'JANE JAMES') N
   set N.BirthDate = '01-SEP-01'
 where N.Name = 'JULIO';
```

You can verify this change by querying the nested table data:

```
select BreederName, N.Name, N.BirthDate
  from BREEDER, TABLE(BREEDER.Animals) N;
```

BREEDERNAME	NAME	BIRTHDATE
JANE JAMES	BUTCH	31-MAR-01
JANE JAMES	ROVER	05-JUN-01
JANE JAMES	JULIO	01-SEP-01
JANE JAMES	MARCUS	01-AUG-01

You can delete nested table entries as well:

```
delete TABLE(select Animals
             from BREEDER
             where BreederName = 'JANE JAMES') N
 where N.Name = 'JULIO';

1 row deleted.
```

```
select BreederName, N.Name, N.BirthDate
  from BREEDER, TABLE(BREEDER.Animals) N;

BREEDERNAME                     NAME                        BIRTHDATE
----------------------          --------------------        ---------
JANE JAMES                      BUTCH                       31-MAR-01
JANE JAMES                      ROVER                       05-JUN-01
JANE JAMES                      MARCUS                      01-AUG-01
```

Additional Functions for Nested Tables and Varying Arrays

As of Oracle Database 10g, you can use several new functions against nested tables and varying arrays. These functions are discussed in this section.

The **CARDINALITY** function returns the number of elements in a nested table or varying array:

```
select CARDINALITY(Animals) from BREEDER;

CARDINALITY(ANIMALS)
--------------------
                   3
```

The **MULTISET EXCEPT** function takes two nested tables as input and returns the set of records that are in the first nested table but not in the second nested table (similar to a **minus** operator). **MULTISET INTERSECT** returns the rows two nested tables have in common. **MULTISET UNION** performs a union of two nested tables; you can specify **MULTISET UNION ALL** (the default) or **MULTISET UNION DISTINCT**.

The **SET** function converts a nested table into a set while eliminating duplicates, returning a nested table of distinct values:

```
set linesize 60
select SET(Animals) from BREEDER;

SET(ANIMALS)(BREED, NAME, BIRTHDATE)
-------------------------------------------------------------
ANIMALS_NT(ANIMAL_TY('DOG', 'BUTCH', '31-MAR-01'), ANIMAL_TY
('DOG', 'ROVER', '05-JUN-01'), ANIMAL_TY('DOG', 'MARCUS', '0
1-AUG-01'))
```

See the Alphabetical Reference for the syntax for these functions, along with the **COLLECT**, **POWERMULTISET**, and **POWERMULTISET_BY_CARDINALITY** functions.

Management Issues for Nested Tables and Varying Arrays

When storing data that is related to a table, you can choose one of three methods: a varying array, a nested table, or a separate table. If you have a limited number of rows, a varying array

may be appropriate. As the number of rows increases, however, you may begin to encounter performance problems while accessing the varying array. These problems may be caused by a characteristic of varying arrays: They cannot be indexed. Nested tables and standard relational tables, however, can be indexed. As a result, the performance of a **varray** collector may worsen as it grows in size.

Varying arrays are further burdened by the difficulty in querying data from them. If varying arrays are not a good solution for your application, which alternative should you use—a nested table or a separate relational table? It depends. Nested tables and relational tables serve different purposes, so your answer depends on what you are trying to do with the data. Here are the key differences:

- Nested tables are abstract datatypes, created via the **create type** command. Therefore, they can have methods associated with them. If you plan to attach methods to the data, you should use nested tables instead of relational tables. Alternatively, you could consider using object views with methods, as described in Chapter 33.

- Relational tables are easily related to other relational tables. If the data may be related to many other tables, it may be best not to nest the data within one table. Storing it in its own table will give you the greatest flexibility in managing the data relationships.

Variability in Collectors

You can use abstract datatypes to enforce standards within your database. However, you may not be able to realize the same standardization benefits when you are using collectors. Consider the TOOLS_VA varying array shown earlier in this chapter. If another application or table wants to use a TOOLS_VA varying array, that application must use the same definition for the array, including the same maximum number of values. However, the new application may have a different value for the maximum number of tools. Therefore, the array must be altered to support the greatest possible number of values it may contain in any of its implementations. As a result, the usefulness of the array's limiting powers may diminish. To support multiple array limits, you would need to create multiple arrays, thus eliminating any object reuse benefits you may have received from creating the varying arrays. You would then need to manage the different array limits and know what the limit is in each array.

You may also find that multiple nested tables are similar, with a difference in only one or two columns. You may be tempted to create a single, all-inclusive nested table type that is used in multiple tables, but that table would also encounter management problems. You would need to know which columns of the nested table were valid for which implementations. If you cannot use the same column structure, with the same meaning and relevance of the columns in each instance, you should not use a shared nested-table datatype. If you want to use nested tables in that environment, you should create a separate nested-table datatype for each instance in which you will use the nested table, and manage them all separately. Having multiple nested-table datatypes will complicate the management of the database.

Location of the Data

In a varying array, the data in the array is stored with the rest of the data in the table. In nested tables, however, the data may be stored "out of line" (and as shown earlier in this chapter, the data may be stored in a separate tablespace). As a result, the amount of data scanned during

queries that do not involve the collector data may be less for a nested table than for a varying array. That is, during a query, the database will not need to read through the data in the nested table; if a varying array is used, the database may need to read through the varying array's data to find the data it needs. Out-of-line data, as used by nested tables, can improve the performance of queries.

Out-of-line collector data mimics the way the data would be stored in a normal relational database application. For example, in a relational application, you would store related data (such as workers and skills) in separate tables, and the tables would be physically stored apart. Out-of-line nested tables store their data apart from the main table but maintain a relationship with the main table. Out-of-line data may improve the performance of queries by distributing across multiple tables the I/O performed against the main table.

Out-of-line data is also used to store large objects (LOBs) that are stored internally (as opposed to BFILEs, which are pointers to LOBs external to the database). In the next chapter, you will see how to create and manipulate LOB values. The combination of abstract datatypes, object views, collectors, and LOBs provides a strong foundation for the implementation of an object-relational database application.

CHAPTER
35

Using Large Objects

In place of LONG and LONG RAW, you can use the LOB datatypes (BLOB, CLOB, NCLOB, and BFILE) for storage of long data. Although Oracle still allows LONG and LONG RAW columns to be created, Oracle recommends that you create new columns using the LOB datatypes and that you convert existing LONG and LONG RAW columns to CLOB or BLOB columns, respectively. If you use one of these datatypes to store large objects (LOBs), you can take advantage of new capabilities for viewing and manipulating the data. You can also use Oracle Text (see Chapter 25) to perform text searches on CLOB data.

In this chapter, you will see how to use the LOB datatypes and how to manipulate the data—which does not even have to be stored within the database!

Available Datatypes

Four types of LOBs are supported:

LOB Datatype	Description
BLOB	Binary LOB. Binary data stored in the database.
CLOB	Character LOB. Character data stored in the database.
BFILE	Binary File. Read-only binary data stored outside the database, the length of which is limited by the operating system.
NCLOB	A CLOB column that supports a multibyte character set.

You can create multiple LOBs per table. For example, suppose you want to create a PROPOSAL table to track formal proposals you submit. Your proposal records may consist of a series of word processing files and spreadsheets used to document and price the proposed work. The PROPOSAL table will contain VARCHAR2 datatypes (for columns such as the name of the proposal recipient) plus LOB datatypes (containing the word processing and spreadsheet files).

NOTE
You cannot create multiple LONG or LONG RAW columns in a single table.

The **create table** command in the following listing creates the PROPOSAL table:

```
create table PROPOSAL
  (Proposal_ID          NUMBER(10),
   Recipient_Name       VARCHAR2(25),
   Proposal_Name        VARCHAR2(25),
   Short_Description     VARCHAR2(1000),
   Proposal_Text        CLOB,
   Budget               BLOB,
   Cover_Letter         BFILE,
constraint PROPOSAL_PK primary key (Proposal_ID));
```

Because you may submit multiple proposals to the same recipient, assign each proposal a Proposal_ID number. The PROPOSAL table stores the recipient of the proposal, the name of the proposal, and a short description. Then, taking advantage of the LOB datatypes available in Oracle, the PROPOSAL table includes three columns:

Proposal_Text A CLOB containing the text of the proposal

Budget A BLOB containing a spreadsheet showing calculations of the cost and profit for the proposed work

Cover_Letter A binary file (BFILE) stored outside the database that contains your cover letter that accompanies the proposal

Each row in the PROPOSAL table will have up to three LOB values stored. Oracle will use the normal database capabilities to support data integrity and concurrency for the Proposal and Budget entries, but not for the Cover_Letter values. Because the Cover_Letter column uses the BFILE datatype, its data is stored outside the database. Internally, the database stores only a locator value that allows it to find the external file, thus reducing the space and management requirements for the database. Oracle does not guarantee the data integrity of BFILE files stored outside the database. Also, Oracle does not validate that these files exist when you insert a record using a BFILE datatype. Data concurrency and integrity are maintained only for internally stored LOBs.

The data for the LOB columns may be physically apart from the PROPOSAL table. Within the PROPOSAL table, Oracle stores locator values that point to data locations. For BFILE datatypes, the locator points to an external file; for BLOB and CLOB datatypes, the locator points to a separate data location that the database creates to hold the LOB data. The data location for the LOB data may be inline with the rest of the PROPOSAL row or stored out of line. By default, the LOB data is stored inline if its length is less than approximately 4000 bytes.

Storing the data *out of line* allows the database to avoid having to scan the LOB data each time it reads multiple rows from the database. The LOB data will only be read when it is required; otherwise, only its locator values will be read. You can specify the storage parameters (tablespace and sizing) for the area used to hold the LOB data, as described in the next section.

Specifying Storage for LOB Data

When you create a table that includes a LOB column, you can specify the storage parameters for the area used for the LOB data. Thus, for a table that has no LOB columns, you may have a **storage** clause in the **create table** command (see Chapter 17). If the table has at least one LOB column, you also need an additional **lob** clause within your **create table** command.

Consider the PROPOSAL table, this time with a **tablespace** clause:

```
create table PROPOSAL
 (Proposal_ID          NUMBER(10),
  Recipient_Name       VARCHAR2(25),
  Proposal_Name        VARCHAR2(25),
  Short_Description    VARCHAR2(1000),
  Proposal_Text        CLOB,
  Budget               BLOB,
  Cover_Letter         BFILE,
```

```
constraint PROPOSAL_PK primary key (Proposal_ID))
 tablespace PROPOSALS;
```

Because there are three LOB columns, the **create table** command should be modified to include the storage specifications for the out-of-line LOB data (if you plan to store the LOB data out of line). Two of the LOB columns—Proposal_Text and Budget—will store data within the database. The revised version of the **create table** command, with the LOB storage clause specified, is shown in the following listing:

```
create table PROPOSAL
(Proposal_ID        NUMBER(10),
 Recipient_Name     VARCHAR2(25),
 Proposal_Name      VARCHAR2(25),
 Short_Description   VARCHAR2(1000),
 Proposal_Text      CLOB,
 Budget             BLOB,
 Cover_Letter       BFILE,
constraint PROPOSAL_PK primary key (Proposal_ID))
 tablespace PROPOSALS
lob (Proposal_Text, Budget) store as
(tablespace Proposal_Lobs
    storage (initial 100K next 100K pctincrease 0)
             chunk 16K pctversion 10 nocache logging);
```

The last four lines of the **create table** command tell Oracle how to store the out-of-line LOB data. The instructions are as follows:

```
lob (Proposal_Text, Budget) store as
(tablespace Proposal_Lobs
    storage (initial 100K next 100K pctincrease 0)
             chunk 16K pctversion 10 nocache logging);
```

The **lob** clause tells Oracle that the next set of commands deals with the out-of-line storage specifications for the table's LOB columns. The two LOB columns (Proposal_Text and Budget) are explicitly listed. When the two columns' values are stored out of line, they are stored in a segment as specified via the **lob** clause:

```
lob (Proposal_Text, Budget) store as
```

NOTE
*If there were only one LOB column, you could specify a name for the LOB segment. You would name the segment immediately after the **store as** clause in the preceding command.*

The next two lines specify the tablespace and storage parameters for the out-of-line LOB storage. The **tablespace** clause assigns the out-of-line data to the PROPOSAL_LOBS tablespace, and an optional **storage** clause can be used to specify the **initial**, **next**, and **pctincrease** values the out-of-line data storage will use. See the entry for the **storage** clause in the Alphabetical Reference for an explanation of the available storage parameters for segments.

(tablespace Proposal_Lobs

Because the segments are for storing LOB data, several additional parameters are available, and they are specified within the **lob** clause:

chunk 16K pctversion 10

The **chunk** LOB storage parameter tells Oracle how much space to allocate during each LOB value manipulation. The default **chunk** size is 1KB, going up to a maximum value of 32KB.

The **pctversion** parameter is the maximum percentage of overall LOB storage space used for creating new versions of the LOB. By default, older versions of the LOB data will not be overwritten until 10 percent of the available LOB storage space is used.

The last two parameters of the LOB storage space tell Oracle how to handle the LOB data during reads and writes:

nocache logging);

The **nocache** parameter in the **lob** storage clause specifies that the LOB values are not stored in memory for faster access during queries. The default **lob** storage setting is **nocache**; its opposite is **cache**.

The **logging** parameter specifies that all operations against the LOB data will be recorded in the database's redo log files. The opposite of **logging**, **nologging**, keeps operations from being recorded in the redo log files, thereby improving the performance of table-creation operations. You can also specify the **tablespace** and **storage** parameters for a LOB index. See the **create table** command entry in the Alphabetical Reference for the full syntax related to LOB indexes.

If you specify **cache** and omit the **nologging/logging** clause, logging is automatically implemented because you cannot specify **cache nologging**. If **cache** is not specified and the **nologging/logging** clause is omitted, the logging value is obtained from the tablespace in which the LOB value is stored.

Now that the table has been created, you can begin to enter records into it. In the next section, you will see how to insert LOB values into the PROPOSAL table and how to use the DBMS_LOB package to manipulate the values.

Manipulating and Selecting LOB Values

LOB data can be selected or manipulated in several ways. You can use the character string functions you would use on VARCHAR2 columns against LOB datatypes. For large LOB values (100KB or more in length), or for more complex operations against the data, you should manipulate LOB data via the DBMS_LOB package. Other methods for manipulating LOB data include using application programming interface (API) and Oracle Call Interface (OCI) programs. In this section, you will see the use of the string functions plus an overview of the DBMS_LOB package. As these examples demonstrate, LOBs are much more flexible than LONG datatypes in terms of data-manipulation possibilities.

Initializing Values

Consider the PROPOSAL table again. The Proposal_ID column is the primary key column for the PROPOSAL table. The PROPOSAL table contains three LOB columns—one BLOB column, one

CLOB, and one BFILE. For each of the LOB columns, Oracle will store a *locator value* that tells it where to find any out-of-line data stored for the record.

When you insert a record into a table that contains LOBs, you use functions to tell Oracle to create an empty locator value for the internally stored LOB columns. An empty locator value is different from a **NULL** value. If an internally stored LOB column's value is **NULL**, you have to set it to an empty locator value before updating it to a non-**NULL** value.

Suppose you begin to work on a proposal and enter a record in the PROPOSAL table. At this point, you have neither a budget spreadsheet nor a cover letter. The **insert** command is shown in the following listing:

```
insert into PROPOSAL
(Proposal_ID, Recipient_Name, Proposal_Name, Short_Description,
 Proposal_Text,
 Budget, Cover_Letter)
values
(1, 'DOT RODALE', 'MAINTAIN ORGANIC GARDEN', NULL,
 'This is the text of a proposal to maintain an organic garden.',
 EMPTY_BLOB(),NULL);
```

The inserted record has a Proposal_ID value of 1 and a Recipient_Name value of DOT RODALE. The Proposal_Name value is MAINTAIN ORGANIC GARDEN and the Short_Description column is left **NULL** for now. The Proposal_Text column is set equal to a short character string for now. To set the Budget column to an empty locator value, you use the **EMPTY_BLOB** function. If you had wanted to set a CLOB datatype column equal to an empty locator value, you would have used the **EMPTY_CLOB** function. The Cover_Letter column, because it is an externally stored BFILE value, is set to **NULL**.

To set a LOB column to an empty locator value, you have to know its datatype:

BLOB	Use **EMPTY_BLOB()**
CLOB	Use **EMPTY_CLOB()**
NCLOB	Use **EMPTY_CLOB()**
BFILE	Use **BFILENAME**

You use the **BFILENAME** procedure to point to a directory and filename combination. Before entering a value for the directory in the **BFILENAME** function, a user with the DBA role or the CREATE ANY DIRECTORY system privilege must create the directory. To create a directory, use the **create directory** command, as shown in the following example:

```
create directory proposal_dir as '/u01/proposal/letters';
```

When inserting BFILE entries, you refer to the logical directory name—such as proposal_dir—instead of the physical directory name on the operating system. Users with DBA authority can grant READ access to the directory names to users. See the entry for the **create directory** command in the Alphabetical Reference for further details.

You can now enter a second PROPOSAL record; this record will have a Cover_Letter value:

```
insert into PROPOSAL
(Proposal_ID, Recipient_Name, Proposal_Name, Short_Description,
 Proposal_Text, Budget,
Cover_Letter)
values
(2, 'BRAD OHMONT', 'REBUILD FENCE', NULL,
 EMPTY_CLOB(), EMPTY_BLOB(),
 BFILENAME('proposal_dir','P2.DOC'));
```

In this listing, a second proposal—rebuilding a fence—is inserted into the PROPOSAL table. The **EMPTY_CLOB()** and **EMPTY_BLOB()** functions are used to insert empty locator values in the table. The **BFILENAME** function tells Oracle exactly where to find the cover letter—it's in the proposal_dir directory and its name is P2.DOC. Within the **BFILENAME** function, the first parameter is always the directory name, and the second parameter is the name of the file within that directory.

NOTE
The P2.DOC file does not have to exist for this record to be inserted successfully.

When you select the value from a LOB column, Oracle uses the locator value to find the data that is associated with the LOB data. You never need to know or specify the locator values. And, as you'll see in the following sections, you can do things with LOB values that are impossible to do with LONG datatypes.

Using insert with Subqueries

What if you want to duplicate a proposal record? For example, suppose you begin to work on a third proposal, and it is very similar to the first proposal:

```
insert into PROPOSAL
(Proposal_ID, Recipient_Name, Proposal_Name, Short_Description,
 Proposal_Text, Budget, Cover_Letter)
select 3, 'SKIP GATES', 'CLEAR GATES FIELD', NULL,
          Proposal_Text, Budget, Cover_Letter
  from PROPOSAL
 where Proposal_ID = 1;
```

This **insert** command tells Oracle to find the PROPOSAL record with a Proposal_ID value of 1. Take the Proposal_Text, Budget, and Cover_Letter column values and the literal values specified (3, SKIP GATES, and so forth) and insert a new record into the PROPOSAL table. Note that the inserted LOB columns will be set to empty locator values. The ability to perform **insert**s based on queries is a significant advantage of using LOB datatypes—you cannot perform this type of **insert** if a LONG column is part of the query.

NOTE
*If you use **insert as select** to populate LOB values, you may have multiple BFILE values pointing to the same external file. You may need to update the new values to point to the correct external files. Oracle does not maintain data integrity for the external files.*

Updating LOB Values

In the third record that was created, the Proposal_Text value was copied from the first record. To update the Proposal_Text value of the record that has a Proposal_ID of 3, execute the following command:

```
update PROPOSAL
   set Proposal_Text = 'This is the new proposal text.'
 where Proposal_ID = 3;
```

You can also update the Cover_Letter column to point to the correct cover letter. Use the **BFILENAME** function to point to the correct file:

```
update PROPOSAL
   set Cover_Letter = BFILENAME('proposal_dir', 'P3.DOC')
 where Proposal_ID = 3;
```

You can update **NULL** values of BFILE columns without first setting them to empty locator values. If you had inserted a record with a **NULL** value for Budget (a BLOB column), you could not update the Budget column's value unless you first set its value to **EMPTY_BLOB()** via an **update** command. After setting the value to **EMPTY_BLOB()** and establishing an empty locator value, you could then update the Budget column value.

Using String Functions to Manipulate LOB Values

You can use the Oracle-provided string functions against CLOB values. For example, you can use **SUBSTR**, **INSTR**, **LTRIM**, and **INITCAP** to modify the strings. See Chapter 7 for descriptions of the built-in string functions.

In the PROPOSAL table, the Proposal_Text column is defined as a CLOB datatype. Here are the three Proposal_Text values (the second is **NULL**):

```
select Proposal_Text from PROPOSAL;

PROPOSAL_TEXT
-----------------------------------------------------------------
This is the text of a proposal to maintain an organic garden.

This is the new proposal text.
```

Applying **INITCAP** to the third record yields this result:

```
select INITCAP(Proposal_Text) from PROPOSAL
  where Proposal_ID = 3;

INITCAP(PROPOSAL_TEXT)
---------------------------------------------------
This Is The New Proposal Text.
```

Applying **INSTR** to all three rows returns the expected result:

```
select INSTR(Proposal_Text,'new',1,1) from PROPOSAL;

INSTR(PROPOSAL_TEXT,'NEW',1,1)
-----------------------------
                            0
                            0
                           13
```

You can use **SUBSTR** to return the first ten characters of the text:

```
select SUBSTR(Proposal_Text,1,10) from PROPOSAL
  where Proposal_ID = 3;

SUBSTR(PROPOSAL_TEXT,1,10)
------------------------------------
This is th
```

However, you cannot perform **NVL** and **DECODE** on the CLOB columns:

```
select NVL(Proposal_Text, 'Null') from PROPOSAL;
                  *
ERROR at line 1:
ORA-00932: inconsistent datatypes: expected CLOB got CHAR
```

For complex manipulations, you should use the DBMS_LOB package, as described in the following sections.

NOTE
The regular expression functions (see Chapter 8) may be used against LOB datatypes.

Using DBMS_LOB to Manipulate LOB Values

You can use the DBMS_LOB package to change or select LOB values. In the following sections, you will see how to perform SQL functions such as **SUBSTR** and **INSTR** on LOB values, as well as how to append to LOB values, compare LOB values, and read LOB values.

The string comparison and manipulation procedures and functions available within the DBMS_LOB package are listed in Table 35-1.

Subprogram	Description
APPEND procedure	Appends the contents of the source LOB to the destination LOB
CLOSE procedure	Closes a previously opened internal or external LOB
COMPARE function	Compares two entire LOBs or parts of two LOBs
COPY procedure	Copies all, or part, of the source LOB to the destination LOB
CONVERTOCLOB procedure	Reads character data from a source CLOB or NCLOB instance, converts the character data to the specified character, writes the converted data to a destination BLOB instance in binary format, and returns the new offsets
COPY procedure	Copies all, or part, of the source LOB to the destination LOB
CREATETEMPORARY procedure	Creates a temporary BLOB or CLOB and its corresponding index in the user's default temporary tablespace
ERASE procedure	Erases all or part of a LOB
FILECLOSE procedure	Closes the file
FILECLOSEALL procedure	Closes all previously opened files
FILEEXISTS function	Checks whether the file exists on the server
FILEGETNAME procedure	Gets the directory alias and filename
FILEISOPEN function	Checks whether the file was opened using the input BFILE locators
FILEOPEN procedure	Opens a file
FREETEMPORARY procedure	Frees the temporary BLOB or CLOB in the user's default temporary tablespace
GETCHUNKSIZE function	Returns the amount of space used in the LOB chunk to store the LOB value
GETLENGTH function	Gets the length of the LOB value
GET_STORAGE_LIMIT function	Returns the storage limit for LOBs in your database configuration
INSTR function	Returns the matching position of the nth occurrence of the pattern in the LOB
ISOPEN function	Checks to see whether the LOB was already opened using the input locator
ISTEMPORARY function	Checks whether the locator is pointing to a temporary LOB

TABLE 35-1. *DBMS_LOB Functions and Procedures*

Subprogram	Description
LOADFROMFILE procedure	Loads BFILE data into an internal LOB
LOADBLOBFROMFILE procedure	Loads BFILE data into an internal BLOB
LOADCLOBFROMFILE procedure	Loads BFILE data into an internal CLOB
OPEN procedure	Opens a LOB (internal, external, or temporary) in the indicated mode
READ procedure	Reads data from the LOB starting at the specified offset
SUBSTR function	Returns part of the LOB value starting at the specified offset
TRIM procedure	Trims the LOB value to the specified shorter length
WRITE procedure	Writes data to the LOB from a specified offset
WRITEAPPEND procedure	Writes a buffer to the end of a LOB

TABLE 35-1. *DBMS_LOB Functions and Procedures* (continued)

The major procedures and functions available within the DBMS_LOB package are described in the following sections. When using BFILEs, the maximum number of files you can concurrently have open is limited by the setting of the SESSION_MAX_OPEN_FILES parameter in the database's system parameter file. The default maximum number of concurrently open BFILE files is 10; the maximum is either 50 or the value of the MAX_OPEN_FILES parameter, whichever is lower.

In the following examples, the Proposal_Text CLOB column is used to show the impact of the major procedures and functions.

READ
The READ procedure reads a piece of a LOB value. In the PROPOSAL table example, the Proposal_Text for the first row is

```
select Proposal_Text
  from PROPOSAL
 where Proposal_ID = 1;

PROPOSAL_TEXT
------------------------------------------------------------
This is the text of a proposal to maintain an organic garden.
```

This is a fairly short description, so it could have been stored in a VARCHAR2 datatype column. Because it is stored in a CLOB column, though, its maximum length is much greater than it would have been if it had been stored in a VARCHAR2 column—it can expand to 8TB in length. For these examples, we'll use this short string for purposes of demonstration; you can use the same functions and operations against longer CLOB strings, as well.

The READ procedure has four parameters, which must be specified in this order:

1. The LOB locator (for either a BLOB, CLOB, or BFILE)

2. The number of bytes or characters to be read

3. The offset (starting point of the read) from the beginning of the LOB value

4. The output data from the READ procedure

If the end of the LOB value is reached before the specified number of bytes is read, the READ procedure will return an error.

Because the READ procedure requires the LOB locator as input, the READ procedure is executed within PL/SQL blocks. You will need to select the LOB locator value, provide that as input to the READ procedure, and then display the text read via the DBMS_OUTPUT package.

A Word About the DBMS_OUTPUT Package As noted in Chapter 31, you can use the DBMS_OUTPUT package to display the values of variables within a PL/SQL block. The PUT_LINE procedure within DBMS_OUTPUT displays the specified output on a line. Before using the DBMS_OUTPUT package, you should first execute the **set serveroutput on** command. In the next section, you'll see how to create the PL/SQL block that will read the data from a LOB.

A READ Example To use the READ procedure, you need to know the locator value of the LOB you want to read. The locator value must be selected from the table that contains the LOB. Because the locator value must be supplied as input to the READ procedure, you should use PL/SQL variables to hold the locator value. The READ procedure, in turn, will place its output in a PL/SQL variable. You can use the DBMS_OUTPUT package to display the output value. The structure of the PL/SQL block for this example is as follows:

```
declare
    variable to hold locator value
    variable to hold the amount (the number of characters/bytes to read)
    variable to hold the offset
    variable to hold the output
begin
  set value for amount_var;
  set value for offset_var;
  select locator value into locator var from table;
  DBMS_LOB.READ(locator var, amount var, offset var, output var);
  DBMS_OUTPUT.PUT_LINE('Output:' || output var);
end;
```

NOTE
See Chapter 29 for an overview of PL/SQL blocks and their components.

For the PROPOSAL table, selecting the first ten characters from the Proposal_Text column would look like this:

```
declare
     locator_var    CLOB;
     amount_var     INTEGER;
     offset_var     INTEGER;
     output_var     VARCHAR2(10);
begin
  amount_var := 10;
  offset_var := 1;
  select Proposal_Text into locator_var
    from PROPOSAL
   where Proposal_ID = 1;
  DBMS_LOB.READ(locator_var, amount_var, offset_var, output_var);
  DBMS_OUTPUT.PUT_LINE('Start of proposal text: ' || output_var);
end;
/
```

When you execute the preceding PL/SQL block, the output will match the SQL **SUBSTR** example shown earlier:

```
Start of proposal text: This is th
```

```
PL/SQL procedure successfully completed.
```

The output shows the first ten characters of the Proposal_Text value, starting at the first character of the LOB value.

The PL/SQL block in the preceding example first declared the variables to use:

```
declare
     locator_var    CLOB;
     amount_var     INTEGER;
     offset_var     INTEGER;
     output_var     VARCHAR2(10);
```

Next, values were assigned to the variables:

```
begin
  amount_var := 10;
  offset_var := 1;
```

Then the locator value was selected from the table and stored in a variable named *locator_var:*

```
select Proposal_Text into locator_var
     from PROPOSAL
   where Proposal_ID = 1;
```

Next, the READ procedure was called, using the values that had been assigned so far:

```
DBMS_LOB.READ(locator_var, amount_var, offset_var, output_var);
```

As a result of the execution of the READ procedure, the *output_var* variable will be populated with the data that was read. The PUT_LINE procedure displays that data:

```
DBMS_OUTPUT.PUT_LINE('Start of proposal text: ' || output_var);
```

This format for PL/SQL blocks will be used throughout the rest of this chapter. You can optionally set the variable values when they are declared.

If you want to select a different portion of the Proposal_Text CLOB, just change the amount and offset variables. If you change the number of characters read, you need to change the size of the output variable, too. In the following example, 12 characters are read from Proposal_Text, starting from the tenth character:

```
declare
    locator_var    CLOB;
    amount_var     INTEGER;
    offset_var     INTEGER;
    output_var     VARCHAR2(12);
begin
  amount_var := 12;
  offset_var := 10;
  select Proposal_Text into locator_var
    from PROPOSAL
   where Proposal_ID = 1;
  DBMS_LOB.READ(locator_var, amount_var, offset_var, output_var);
  DBMS_OUTPUT.PUT_LINE('Part of proposal text: ' || output_var);
end;
/
```

Output from this PL/SQL block is shown in the following listing:

```
Part of proposal text: he text of a

PL/SQL procedure successfully completed.
```

If Proposal_Text had been created as a VARCHAR2 column, you could have selected this data using the **SUBSTR** function. However, you would have been limited to a maximum column length of 4,000 characters. Also, note that the LOB column can contain binary data (BLOB datatypes), and you can use the READ procedure to select data from BLOBs in the same way you select from CLOBs. For BLOBs, you should declare the output buffer to use the RAW datatype. In PL/SQL, RAW and VARCHAR2 datatypes (used for the output variables for CLOB and BLOB reads) have a maximum length of 32,767 characters.

For the READ procedure, possible exceptions are VALUE_ERROR, INVALID_ARGVAL, NO_DATA_FOUND, UNOPENED_FILE, NOEXIST_DIRECTORY, NOPRIV_DIRECTORY, INVALID_DIRECTORY, and INVALID_OPERATION.

SUBSTR

The SUBSTR function within the DBMS_LOB package performs the SQL **SUBSTR** function on a LOB value. This function has three input parameters, which must be specified in this order:

1. The LOB locator

2. The number of bytes or characters to be read

3. The offset (starting point of the read) from the beginning of the LOB value

Because SUBSTR is a function, there is no output variable value returned directly from SUBSTR as there was with READ. For the READ procedure, you declared an output variable and then populated it within the READ procedure call. The PL/SQL block used for the READ procedure is shown in the following listing, with the lines related to the output variable shown in bold:

```
declare
    locator_var    CLOB;
    amount_var     INTEGER;
    offset_var     INTEGER;
    output_var     VARCHAR2(12);
begin
  amount_var := 12;
  offset_var := 10;
  select Proposal_Text into locator_var
    from PROPOSAL
  where Proposal_ID = 1;
  DBMS_LOB.READ(locator_var, amount_var, offset_var, output_var);
  DBMS_OUTPUT.PUT_LINE('Section of proposal text: ' || output_var);
end;
/
```

Because SUBSTR is a function, you will populate the output variable differently. The format is

```
output_var := DBMS_LOB.SUBSTR(locator_var, amount_var, offset_var);
```

The preceding PL/SQL statement uses the SUBSTR function of the DBMS_LOB package to select 12 characters from the Proposal_Text LOB column, starting at the tenth character. The full PL/SQL block is

```
declare
    locator_var    CLOB;
    amount_var     INTEGER;
    offset_var     INTEGER;
    output_var     VARCHAR2(12);
begin
  amount_var := 12;
  offset_var := 10;
  select Proposal_Text into locator_var
    from PROPOSAL
  where Proposal_ID = 1;
  output_var := DBMS_LOB.SUBSTR(locator_var, amount_var, offset_var);
  DBMS_OUTPUT.PUT_LINE('Section of proposal text: ' || output_var);
end;
/
```

The output is shown in the following listing:

```
Section of proposal text: he text of a
PL/SQL procedure successfully completed.
```

The equivalent SQL function call is

```
select SUBSTR(Proposal_Text,10,12)
  from PROPOSAL
 where Proposal_ID = 1;
```

The SUBSTR example differs from the READ example in only two ways: the name of the function call, and the manner of assigning a value to the output variable. As with the READ procedure example, the PUT_LINE procedure of the DBMS_OUTPUT package is used to display the results.

In general, you should use the SUBSTR function whenever you are interested in selecting only a specific section of the LOB value. The READ function can be used to select only a portion of a text string (as in the previous examples), but it is more often used within a loop. For example, suppose the LOB value is larger than the largest allowed RAW or VARCHAR2 variable in PL/SQL (32,767 characters). In that case, you can use the READ procedure within a loop to read all the data from the LOB value. Refer to Chapter 29 for details on the different loop options available in PL/SQL.

For the SUBSTR function, possible exceptions are UNOPENED_FILE, NOEXIST_DIRECTORY, NOPRIV_DIRECTORY, INVALID_DIRECTORY, and INVALID_OPERATION.

INSTR

The INSTR function within the DBMS_LOB package performs the SQL **INSTR** function on a LOB value.

The INSTR function has four input parameters, which must be specified in this order:

1. The LOB locator
2. The pattern to be tested for (RAW bytes for BLOBs, character strings for CLOBs)
3. The offset (starting point of the read) from the beginning of the LOB value
4. The occurrence of the pattern within the LOB value

The INSTR function within DBMS_LOB searches the LOB for a specific pattern of bytes or characters. The occurrence variable allows you to specify which occurrence of the pattern within the searched value should be returned. The output of the INSTR function is the position of the start of the pattern within the searched string. For example, in SQL,

```
INSTR('ABCABC','A',1,1) = 1
```

means that within the string ABCABC, the pattern A is searched for, starting at the first position of the string, and looking for the first occurrence. The A is found in the first position of the searched string. If you start the search at the second position of the string, the answer will be different:

```
INSTR('ABCABC','A',2,1) = 4
```

Because this **INSTR** starts at the second position, the first *A* is not part of the value that is searched. Instead, the first *A* found is the one in the fourth position.

If you change the last parameter in the SQL **INSTR** to look for the second occurrence of the string *A*, starting at the second position, the pattern is not found:

```
INSTR('ABCABC','A',2,2) = 0
```

If the SQL **INSTR** function cannot find the matching occurrence of the pattern, 0 is returned. The INSTR function of the DBMS_LOB package operates in the same manner.

Because INSTR is a function, you need to assign its output variable in the same manner as the SUBSTR function's output variable was assigned. In the following listing, the Proposal_Text CLOB value is searched for the string 'pr'. The *position_var* variable is declared to hold the output of the INSTR function.

```
declare
    locator_var    CLOB;
    pattern_var    VARCHAR2(2);
    offset_var     INTEGER;
    occur_var      INTEGER;
    position_var   INTEGER;
begin
  pattern_var := 'pr';
  offset_var := 1;
  occur_var := 1;
  select Proposal_Text into locator_var
    from PROPOSAL
   where Proposal_ID = 1;
  position_var := DBMS_LOB.INSTR(locator_var, pattern_var,
offset_var, occur_var);
  DBMS_OUTPUT.PUT_LINE('Found string at position: ' || position_var);
end;
/
```

The output would be

```
Found string at position: 23

PL/SQL procedure successfully completed.
```

The output shows that the search string 'pr' is found within the Proposal_Text, starting at the 23rd character of the LOB value. Because Oracle supports SQL string functions against CLOB columns, this function call is equivalent to the following query:

```
select INSTR(Proposal_Text ,'pr',1,1)
    from PROPOSAL
   where Proposal_ID = 1;
```

For the INSTR function, possible exceptions are UNOPENED_FILE, NOEXIST_DIRECTORY, NOPRIV_DIRECTORY, INVALID_DIRECTORY, and INVALID_OPERATION.

GETLENGTH

The GETLENGTH function of the DBMS_LOB package returns the length of the LOB value. The DBMS_LOB.GETLENGTH function is similar in function to the SQL **LENGTH** function, but it's used only for LOB values.

The GETLENGTH function of the DBMS_LOB package has only one input parameter: the locator value for the LOB. In the following listing, variables are declared to hold the locator value and the output value. The GETLENGTH function is then executed, and the result is reported via the PUT_LINE procedure:

```
declare
    locator_var    CLOB;
    length_var     INTEGER;
begin
  select Proposal_Text into locator_var
    from PROPOSAL
   where Proposal_ID = 1;
  length_var := DBMS_LOB.GETLENGTH(locator_var);
  DBMS_OUTPUT.PUT_LINE('Length of LOB: ' || length_var);
end;
/
```

The following is the GETLENGTH output:

```
Length of LOB: 61

PL/SQL procedure successfully completed.
```

If the LOB value is **NULL**, the GETLENGTH function will return a value of **NULL**.

The equivalent SQL function for CLOB values is

```
select LENGTH(Proposal_Text)
   from PROPOSAL
 where Proposal_ID = 1;
```

COMPARE

The COMPARE function of the DBMS_LOB package compares two LOB values. If the two LOB values are the same, the COMPARE function returns 0; otherwise, it returns a nonzero integer value (usually 1 or –1). To execute the COMPARE function, the DBMS_LOB package essentially performs two READ functions and compares the results. Thus, for each of the LOB values to be compared, you need to supply a locator value and an offset value; the number of characters or bytes to be compared will be the same for both LOB values. You can only compare LOBs of the same datatype.

The COMPARE function has five input parameters, which must be specified in this order:

1. The LOB locator for the first LOB

2. The LOB locator for the second LOB

3. The amount variable (the number of bytes or characters to compare)

4. The offset (starting point of the read) from the beginning of the first LOB value

5. The offset (starting point of the read) from the beginning of the second LOB value

Because the two LOBs being compared can have different offset values, you can compare the first part of one LOB value with the second part of a different LOB value. The example in the following listing compares the first 25 characters of the Proposal_Text values from two entries—the Proposal_ID 1 record and the Proposal_ID 3 record:

```
declare
    first_locator_var      CLOB;
    second_locator_var     CLOB;
    amount_var             INTEGER;
    first_offset_var       INTEGER;
    second_offset_var      INTEGER;
    output_var             INTEGER;
begin
    amount_var        := 25;
    first_offset_var  := 1;
    second_offset_var := 1;
    select Proposal_Text into first_locator_var
      from PROPOSAL
     where Proposal_ID = 1;
    select Proposal_Text into second_locator_var
      from PROPOSAL
     where Proposal_ID = 3;
    output_var :=DBMS_LOB.COMPARE(first_locator_var, second_locator_var,
            amount_var, first_offset_var, second_offset_var);
    DBMS_OUTPUT.PUT_LINE('Comparison value (0 if the same): '||
      output_var);
end;
/
```

The following is the output:

```
Comparison value (0 if the same): 1

PL/SQL procedure successfully completed.
```

If the two strings are the same, the COMPARE function will return 0.

In the following listing, the same two LOBs are compared, but this time only their first five characters are used for the comparison. Because both start with the characters "This ", the COMPARE will return 0:

```
declare
    first_locator_var      CLOB;
    second_locator_var     CLOB;
    amount_var             INTEGER;
    first_offset_var       INTEGER;
    second_offset_var      INTEGER;
```

```
       output_var              INTEGER;
begin
  amount_var         := 5;
  first_offset_var   := 1;
  second_offset_var := 1;
  select Proposal_Text into first_locator_var
    from PROPOSAL
   where Proposal_ID = 1;
  select Proposal_Text into second_locator_var
    from PROPOSAL
   where Proposal_ID = 3;
  output_var :=DBMS_LOB.COMPARE(first_locator_var, second_locator_var,
          amount_var, first_offset_var, second_offset_var);
  DBMS_OUTPUT.PUT_LINE('Comparison value (0 if the same): ' ||
  output_var);
end;
/

Comparison value (0 if the same): 0

PL/SQL procedure successfully completed.
```

The COMPARE function allows you to compare character strings to character strings and compare binary data to binary data. If you are using the COMPARE function on BLOB columns, you should define the locator variables as RAW datatypes.

For the COMPARE function, possible exceptions are UNOPENED_FILE, NOEXIST_DIRECTORY, NOPRIV_DIRECTORY, INVALID_DIRECTORY, and INVALID_OPERATION.

WRITE

The WRITE procedure of the DBMS_LOB package allows you to write data in specific locations of the LOB. For example, you can write binary data into a section of a BLOB, overwriting the existing data there. You can write character data into CLOB fields using the WRITE procedure. This procedure has four input parameters, which must be specified in this order:

1. The LOB locator for the LOB

2. The amount variable (the number of bytes or characters to write)

3. The offset (starting point of the write) from the beginning of the LOB value

4. The buffer variable assigned to the character string or binary data being added

Because the WRITE procedure updates the LOB value, you should first lock the row via a **select for update**, as shown in bold in the following listing. In this example, a record is selected and locked. The text ADD NEW TEXT is then written to the LOB value, overwriting the data starting in position 10 (as defined by the offset variable).

```
declare
    locator_var   CLOB;
    amount_var    INTEGER;
```

```
    offset_var      INTEGER;
    buffer_var      VARCHAR2(12);
begin
  amount_var := 12;
  offset_var := 10;
  buffer_var := 'ADD NEW TEXT';
  select Proposal_Text into locator_var
    from PROPOSAL
  where Proposal_ID = 3
    for update;
  DBMS_LOB.WRITE(locator_var, amount_var, offset_var, buffer_var);
commit;
end;
/
```

Because the WRITE procedure changes the data, a **commit** command is added before the **end** clause of the PL/SQL block.

NOTE
*Test without a **commit** first so you can see the impact of your procedure call before committing the change to the database.*

For the WRITE procedure, no output is provided. To see the changed data, you need to either call the READ procedure (within the same PL/SQL block, if you want) or select the LOB value from the table again:

```
select Proposal_Text
    from PROPOSAL
  where Proposal_ID = 3;

PROPOSAL_TEXT
-----------------------------------------------------------
This is tADD NEW TEXTsal text.
```

The WRITE procedure overwrote 12 characters, starting at the tenth character of Proposal_Text. You can use the WRITEAPPEND procedure to append new data to the end of an existing LOB value.

For CLOB data, you can rewrite this using an **update** statement combined with **SUBSTR** and concatenation functions.

For the WRITE function, possible exceptions are VALUE_ERROR and INVALID_ARGVAL.

APPEND

The APPEND procedure of the DBMS_LOB package appends data from one LOB to a second LOB. Because this amounts to an update of a LOB value, the record being updated should be locked prior to executing the APPEND procedure.

The APPEND procedure takes only two parameters: the locator value for the destination LOB, and the locator value for the source LOB. If either parameter is **NULL**, the APPEND procedure will return an error.

In the following example, two locator variables are defined. The first locator variable is named *dest_locator_var;* this is the locator value for the LOB into which the data is to be appended. The second locator variable, *source_locator_var,* is the locator value for the source data that is to be appended to the destination LOB. The destination LOB, because it is being updated, is locked via a **select for update** command. In this example, the Proposal_Text value for the Proposal_ID 1 record is appended to the Proposal_Text value for the Proposal_ID 3 record:

```
declare
    dest_locator_var    CLOB;
    source_locator_var  CLOB;
begin
  select Proposal_Text into dest_locator_var
    from PROPOSAL
   where Proposal_ID = 3
     for update;
  select Proposal_Text into source_locator_var
    from PROPOSAL
   where Proposal_ID = 1;
  DBMS_LOB.APPEND(dest_locator_var, source_locator_var);
commit;
end;
/
```

To see the changed data, you can select the record from the PROPOSAL table:

```
select Proposal_Text
  from PROPOSAL
 where Proposal_ID = 3;

PROPOSAL_TEXT
----------------------------------------------------------------
This is tADD NEW TEXTsal text.This is the text of a proposal to
maintain an orga
```

What happened to the rest of the text? By default, only 80 characters of LONG and LOB values are displayed during queries. To see the rest of the text, use the **set long** command:

```
set long 1000

select Proposal_Text
  from PROPOSAL
 where Proposal_ID = 3;

PROPOSAL_TEXT
----------------------------------------------------------------
This is tADD NEW TEXTsal text.This is the text of a proposal to
maintain an organic garden.
```

In this example, the first 1,000 characters of the LOB value were displayed. If you need to know how long the LOB is, use the GETLENGTH function, as described earlier in this chapter.

In addition to allowing you to append CLOB values, the APPEND procedure allows you to append BLOB values. When appending BLOB data, you need to be aware of the format of the BLOB data and the impact of appending new data on the end of the BLOB value. For BLOB values, the APPEND function may be most useful for applications in which the BLOB contains only raw data (such as digital data transmissions) rather than formatted binary data (such as spreadsheet files formatted by a program).

For CLOB data, you could rewrite this with an **update** statement, setting the Proposal_Text value equal to the concatenation of multiple values.

For the APPEND procedure, VALUE_ERROR is the only defined exception.

ERASE

You can use the ERASE procedure of the DBMS_LOB package to erase the characters or bytes in any part of a LOB. You can use ERASE to erase the entire LOB value, or you can specify which section of the LOB to erase. ERASE is similar in function to WRITE. If you erase data in a BLOB value, the data is replaced with zero-byte filler. If you erase data in a CLOB value, spaces are inserted into the CLOB.

Because you are updating a LOB value, you should follow the standard procedures for LOB updates: Lock the row and commit when the procedure has completed.

In the following PL/SQL block, a portion of Proposal_Text for the record with Proposal_ID 3 is erased. The erased characters will start at an offset of 10 and continue for 17 characters. The parameters for the ERASE procedure, in order, are

1. The LOB locator for the LOB

2. The amount variable (the number of bytes or characters to erase)

3. The offset (starting point of the erasure) from the beginning of the LOB value

```
declare
    locator_var    CLOB;
    amount_var     INTEGER;
    offset_var     INTEGER;
begin
  amount_var := 17;
  offset_var := 10;
  select Proposal_Text into locator_var
    from PROPOSAL
   where Proposal_ID = 3
     for update;
  DBMS_LOB.ERASE(locator_var, amount_var, offset_var);
commit;
end;
/
```

The change to the record can be seen by querying the Proposal_Text value:

```
select Proposal_Text
  from PROPOSAL
 where Proposal_ID = 3;
```

```
PROPOSAL_TEXT
---------------------------------------------------------------
This is t                    ext.This is the text of a proposal to
maintain an organic garden.
```

NOTE
The space previously held by the erased data is replaced by blanks; the rest of the data in the LOB does not change its position.

For CLOB data, you can rewrite this operation using an **update** statement, setting a new value for Proposal_Text by concatenating **SUBSTR** results and a blank string.

For the ERASE procedure, possible exceptions are VALUE_ERROR and INVALID_ARGVAL.

TRIM

You can use the TRIM procedure of the DBMS_LOB package to reduce the size of a LOB value by trimming characters or bytes from the end of the value (like the SQL **RTRIM** function). When the TRIM procedure is executed, you specify the locator value for the LOB and the LOB's new length.

In the following listing, the Proposal_Text for the Proposal_ID 3 record is trimmed to its first ten characters. Because the TRIM procedure changes the data, a **commit** command is added before the **end** clause of the PL/SQL block.

```
declare
    locator_var     CLOB;
    new_length_var  INTEGER;
begin
  new_length_var   := 10;
  select Proposal_Text into locator_var
    from PROPOSAL
  where Proposal_ID = 3
    for update;
  DBMS_LOB.TRIM(locator_var, new_length_var);
commit;
end;
/
```

For the TRIM procedure, no output is provided. To see the changed data, you need to select the LOB value from the table again:

```
select Proposal_Text
    from PROPOSAL
  where Proposal_ID = 3;

PROPOSAL_TEXT
---------------------------------------------------------------
This is t
```

The sample output shows the results of the TRIM procedure following the ERASE procedure executed in the preceding section. For CLOB data, you could rewrite this as a simple **update**:

```
update PROPOSAL
    set Proposal_Text = SUBSTR(Proposal_Text,1,10)
  where Proposal_ID = 3;
```

For the TRIM procedure, possible exceptions are VALUE_ERROR and INVALID_ARGVAL.

COPY

You can use the COPY procedure of the DBMS_LOB package to copy data from a part of one LOB into a second LOB. Unlike with the APPEND procedure, you do not have to copy the full text of one LOB value into another. During the COPY procedure, you can specify the offset to read from and the offset to write to. The five parameters of the COPY procedure are, in order:

1. The destination LOB locator

2. The source LOB locator

3. The amount (the number of characters or bytes to copy)

4. The offset to start writing to within the destination LOB value

5. The offset to start reading from within the destination LOB value

COPY is a combination of the READ and WRITE capabilities. Like the WRITE operation, the COPY procedure modifies the LOB value. Therefore, the record should first be locked, and the PL/SQL block must contain a **commit** command. In the following example, the first 61 characters of the Proposal_ID 1 record are copied to the Proposal_ID 3 record. Because the destination LOB uses an offset of 1, the copied data will *overwrite* data within the destination LOB.

```
declare
    dest_locator_var     CLOB;
    source_locator_var   CLOB;
    amount_var           INTEGER;
    dest_offset_var      INTEGER;
    source_offset_var    INTEGER;
begin
  amount_var          := 61;
  dest_offset_var     := 1;
  source_offset_var   := 1;
  select Proposal_Text into dest_locator_var
    from PROPOSAL
   where Proposal_ID = 3
     for update;
  select Proposal_Text into source_locator_var
    from PROPOSAL
   where Proposal_ID = 1;
  DBMS_LOB.COPY(dest_locator_var, source_locator_var,
      amount_var, dest_offset_var, source_offset_var);
commit;
end;
/
```

The COPY procedure displays no output. To see the changed data, you need to select the LOB value from the table again:

```
select Proposal_Text
    from PROPOSAL
    where Proposal_ID = 3;

PROPOSAL_TEXT
-------------------------------------------------------------
This is the text of a proposal to maintain an organic garden.
```

For the COPY procedure, possible exceptions are VALUE_ERROR and INVALID_ARGVAL.

Using the BFILE Functions and Procedures

Because BFILE values are stored externally, several functions and procedures are used to manipulate the files prior to executing READ, SUBSTR, INSTR, GETLENGTH, or COMPARE operations on BFILE LOBs. The BFILE-related procedures and functions within DBMS_LOB, shown earlier in Table 35-1, allow you to open files, close files, get the filename, check whether a file exists, and check whether a file is open. The existence-check function is necessary because Oracle does not maintain the data stored in the external file; Oracle only maintains the pointer created via the BFILENAME procedure when the record is inserted or updated. You should use the procedures and functions in Table 35-1 to control the files used by your PL/SQL code. For example, to read the first ten bytes from the Cover_Letter BFILE for the Proposal_ID 2 record, you would open the file and then execute the READ procedure. The PUT_LINE procedure of the DBMS_OUTPUT package can then be called to show the data that was read.

As part of the standard Oracle installation, examples of LOB interactions are created in the /rdbms/demo/logs directories beneath the Oracle software home directory. The subdirectories there contain demonstrations of the use of PL/SQL, Java, OCI, Pro*C, Pro*COBOL, and Visual Basic against LOBs.

For example, the file fpattern.sql in the /rdbms/demo/logs/plsql directory shows how to apply the COMPARE function shown earlier in this chapter to BFILE LOBs. Note that it relies on specific directories as part of its execution; see *Application Developer's Guide—Large Objects* for full details of all demos provided.

```
/* This file is installed in the following path when you install */
/* the database: $ORACLE_HOME/rdbms/demo/lobs/plsql/fpattern.sql */
/* Checking if a pattern exists in a BFILE using instr */
/* Procedure compareBFILEs_proc is not part of DBMS_LOB package: */

CREATE OR REPLACE PROCEDURE compareBFILEs_proc IS
    /* Initialize the BFILE locator: */
    file_loc1    BFILE := BFILENAME('MEDIA_DIR', 'keyboard.jpg');
    file_loc2    BFILE;
    Retval        INTEGER;
BEGIN
    DBMS_OUTPUT.PUT_LINE('------------ LOB COMPARE EXAMPLE ------------');
    /* Select the LOB: */
```

```
    SELECT ad_graphic INTO File_loc2 FROM print_media
        WHERE Product_ID = 3060 AND ad_id = 11001;
    /* Open the BFILEs: */
    DBMS_LOB.OPEN(File_loc1, DBMS_LOB.LOB_READONLY);
    DBMS_LOB.OPEN(File_loc2, DBMS_LOB.LOB_READONLY);
  Retval := DBMS_LOB.COMPARE(File_loc2, File_loc1, DBMS_LOB.LOBMAXSIZE, 1, 1);
    /* Close the BFILEs: */
    DBMS_LOB.CLOSE(File_loc1);
    DBMS_LOB.CLOSE(File_loc2);
END;
/
```

The approach shown in this example mimics that of the COMPARE example shown earlier. Because we are working with BFILEs, there are two additional sections: the DBMS_LOB.OPEN calls to open the files and the DBMS_LOB.CLOSE calls to close the files when the COMPARE has completed.

Reading data from BFILEs follows the steps shown earlier for the READ function, with the addition of the calls to open and close the file. The READ process is illustrated via the fread.sql demo file provided by Oracle in the /rdbms/demo/logs/plsql subdirectory:

```
/* This file is installed in the following path when you install */
/* the database: $ORACLE_HOME/rdbms/demo/lobs/plsql/fread.sql */
/* Reading data from a BFILE. */
/* Procedure readBFILE_proc is not part of DBMS_LOB package: */

CREATE OR REPLACE PROCEDURE readBFILE_proc IS
    file_loc        BFILE;
    Amount          INTEGER := 32767;
    Position        INTEGER := 1;
    Buffer          RAW(32767);
BEGIN
    DBMS_OUTPUT.PUT_LINE('------------ BFILE READ EXAMPLE ------------');
    /* Select the LOB: */
    SELECT ad_graphic INTO File_loc FROM print_media
        WHERE product_id = 3060 AND ad_id = 11001;
    /* Open the BFILE: */
    DBMS_LOB.OPEN(File_loc, DBMS_LOB.LOB_READONLY);
    /* Read data: */
    DBMS_LOB.READ(File_loc, Amount, Position, Buffer);
    /* Close the BFILE: */
    DBMS_LOB.CLOSE(File_loc);
END;
/
```

If you use an Exception Handling section in your PL/SQL block, you need to be sure to include FILECLOSE procedure calls within the declared exceptions. (Refer to Chapter 29 for further details on exception handling within PL/SQL blocks.)

To move data from an external file into a BLOB datatype, you can create a BFILE datatype in a table and use the **BFILENAME** function to create a LOB locator that points to the external file.

The **BFILENAME** function takes two parameters: the directory name and the filename. Here's an example:

```
insert into PROPOSAL (Proposal_ID, Cover_Letter)
values (4, BFILENAME ('proposal_dir','extfile.doc'));
```

You can then open the file and use the LOADFROMFILE, LOADBLOBFROMFILE, or LOADCLOBFROMFILE procedure to load the BLOB datatype with the data from the external file.

If the data is presently in a LONG datatype, you can change it to a CLOB or NCLOB column via the **alter table** command. You can also use **alter table** to change a LONG RAW column to a BLOB datatype column. For **insert as select** operations, you can use the **TO_LOB** SQL function to move the data from the LONG column to a BLOB column.

Deleting LOBS

When you delete LOB values, the locator value is deleted. If the deleted value is an internal LOB (BLOB, CLOB, or NCLOB), both the locator and the LOB value are deleted. If the deleted value is an external LOB (BFILE), only the locator value is deleted; you will need to manually delete the file to which the locator points.

CHAPTER
36

Advanced Object-
Oriented Concepts

I n the preceding chapters, all of the object-oriented programming (OOP) features of Oracle shown shared two characteristics: They are embedded objects, and they are column objects. An *embedded object* is one that is completely contained within another. For example, a nested table is contained within a table, so it is an embedded object. Although a nested table's data is stored apart from the main table, its data can only be accessed via the main table. A *column object* is one that is represented as a column in a table. For example, a varying array is represented as a column in a table, so it is a column object.

To take full advantage of OOP capabilities, a database must also support *row objects*—objects that are represented as rows instead of columns. The row objects are not embedded objects; instead, they are *referenced objects,* accessible via references from other objects. In this chapter, you will see how row objects are created and referenced.

Object-oriented structures may not be appropriate for many applications—you may be limited based on your toolset, interfaces, or existing relationships within the database. In this chapter, you will see how Oracle has implemented row objects and how to use object views to bridge the object-oriented and relational architectures. In addition to row objects, this chapter covers the application of objects to PL/SQL—creating *object PL/SQL.*

Row Objects vs. Column Objects

The distinction between row objects and column objects is critical. First, consider column objects. Column objects are based on extensions of features already in the database. An abstract datatype or a varying array can be embedded as a column within a table. A nested table or a large object (LOB) can be stored in a single column of a table. In each case, the object is represented as a column within a table.

Nested tables and LOBs, however, involve data that is stored out-of-line from the main table. When you use a LOB (see Chapter 35), you specify the storage values for the table that will store the LOB data, and Oracle creates LOB locators that point from the main table to the rows in the LOB table if the LOB data is stored out-of-line. When you create a nested table, you specify the name of the table in which the nested table's records will be stored—and Oracle creates pointers from the main table to the records in the nested tables. Thus, the main table and its embedded nested table are related.

In row objects, the objects are represented as rows, not columns. The data is not embedded within the main table; instead, the main table contains a reference to another table. Nested tables, since they are stored apart from the main table, provide a useful tool for understanding row objects. What if the nested table's data is not embedded within the main table, and each of its rows is a row object? The main table will define references to the related data.

The object-relational features of Oracle described in earlier chapters relied on column objects. In this chapter, the focus is on the advanced OOP capabilities, which are based on row objects. You use row objects to create references between the rows of different tables.

Object Tables and OIDs

In an *object table,* each row is a row object. An object table differs from a normal relational table in several ways. First, each row within the object table has an *OID*—an object identifier value—assigned by Oracle when the row is created. Second, the rows of an object table can be referenced by other objects within the database.

You can create an object table via the **create table** command. Consider the ANIMAL_TY datatype shown in previous chapters. To avoid conflicts with objects created during earlier chapters, create this type in a new schema:

```
create or replace type ANIMAL_TY as object
(Breed        VARCHAR2(25),
 Name         VARCHAR2(25),
 BirthDate    DATE);
/
```

NOTE
To keep this example simple, the ANIMAL_TY datatype is created without any member functions.

To create an object table of the ANIMAL_TY datatype, issue the following **create table** command:

```
create table ANIMAL of ANIMAL_TY;

Table created.
```

Note that the command has an unusual syntax—creating the table **of** an abstract datatype. The resulting table may first appear to be a normal relational table:

```
describe ANIMAL

Name                             Null?     Type
-------------------------------- --------- ------------
BREED                                      VARCHAR2(25)
NAME                                       VARCHAR2(25)
BIRTHDATE                                  DATE
```

The ANIMAL table's columns map to the attributes of the ANIMAL_TY datatype. However, there are significant differences in how you can use the table, since it is an object table. As noted earlier in this section, each row within the object table will have an OID value, and the rows can be referenced as objects.

Inserting Rows into Object Tables

Because ANIMAL is an object table, you can use its datatype's constructor method when **insert**ing data into the table. Since the ANIMAL table is based on the ANIMAL_TY abstract datatype, the ANIMAL_TY constructor method can be used when **insert**ing values into ANIMAL.

NOTE
Refer to Chapter 33 for detailed discussions of constructor methods.

In the following listing, three rows are **insert**ed into the ANIMAL object table. In each command, the ANIMAL_TY constructor method is called.

```
insert into ANIMAL values
       (ANIMAL_TY('MULE','FRANCES', '01-APR-02'));
insert into ANIMAL values
       (ANIMAL_TY('DOG','BENJI', '03-SEP-01'));
insert into ANIMAL values
       (ANIMAL_TY('CROCODILE','LYLE', '14-MAY-00'));
```

If the abstract datatype on which the object table is based is itself based on a second abstract datatype, you may need to nest calls to multiple constructor methods within your **insert** command. (Refer to Chapter 33 for examples of nested abstract datatypes.)

> **NOTE**
> *If an object table is based on a datatype that does not contain any nested datatypes, you can also **insert** records into the object table using the normal **insert** command syntax for relational tables.*

When you **insert** a row into an object table, Oracle assigns an OID to the row. Having an OID allows you to use the row as a referenceable object. OID values are not reused.

Selecting Values from Object Tables

When the ANIMAL table was created, it was based entirely on the ANIMAL_TY datatype:

```
create table ANIMAL of ANIMAL_TY;
```

When you select from a table that contains an abstract datatype, you refer to the abstract datatype's columns as part of the table's columns. That is, if you used the ANIMAL_TY datatype as the basis for a *column* named Animal, then you would select the animal names by selecting Animal.Name from the table.

An object table, though, is based on a datatype—it has no other columns. Therefore, you do not need to reference the datatype when accessing the columns. To select the names from the ANIMAL table, just query the datatype's attributes directly:

```
select Name
   from ANIMAL;

NAME
------------------------
FRANCES
BENJI
LYLE
```

You can refer to the columns within the **where** clause just as if ANIMAL were a relational table:

```
select Name
   from ANIMAL
```

```
where Breed = 'CROCODILE';

NAME
-------------------------
LYLE
```

If the ANIMAL_TY datatype used another abstract datatype for one of its columns, that datatype's column would be referenced during all **select**s, **update**s, and **delete**s.

Updates and Deletes from Object Tables

If the object table is based on an abstract datatype that uses no other abstract datatypes, an **update** or **delete** of an object table uses the same format as you would use for relational tables. The ANIMAL_TY datatype does not use any other abstract datatype for one of its columns, so your **update**s and **delete**s from the ANIMAL object table behave the same as if ANIMAL were a relational table.

In the following command, one of the rows of ANIMAL is **update**d:

```
update ANIMAL
    set BirthDate = '01-MAY-00'
 where Name = 'LYLE';

1 row updated.
```

Note that during the **update**, the columns of the object table are referred to as if ANIMAL were a relational table. During a **delete**, you use the same means to reference the object table's columns in the **where** clause:

```
delete from ANIMAL
  where Name = 'LYLE';

1 row deleted.
```

Keeping a crocodile alongside mules and dogs probably wasn't such a good idea anyway.

The REF Function

The **REF** function allows you to reference existing row objects. For example, the ANIMAL table has (after the deletion of one row, shown in the preceding section) two row objects, each of which has an OID value assigned to it. You can see the OID assigned to each row by using the **REF** function, as shown here:

```
select REF(A)
   from ANIMAL  A
 where Name = 'FRANCES';

REF(A)
------------------------------------------------------------
0000280209F525172CC0F84F8ABABF0F0F46ECB7209A233BD5F
FD34A7E82D8C0C5CFB88FC0010002270000
```

NOTE
*Your **REF(A)** value should be different from the one shown here.
The **REF(A)** value is wrapped over multiple lines in this listing.*

In the preceding listing, the ANIMAL table was given the alias *A*, and that alias was used as input to the **REF** function. The output shows the OID for the row object that met the limiting condition of the query.

NOTE
*The **REF** function takes as its input the alias given to the object table. The other functions shown later in this chapter also take aliases as inputs, so you should be familiar with this syntax.*

Since the **REF** function can only reference row objects, you cannot use it to reference column objects. Column objects include abstract datatypes, LOBs, and collectors.

As you can see, the **REF** function by itself does not give you any useful information. You need to use another function—**DEREF**—that translates the **REF** output into values. You can then use **REF** and **DEREF** to reference row-object values, as described in the next section.

Using the DEREF Function

The **REF** function takes a row object as its argument and returns a reference value. The **DEREF** function does the opposite—it takes a reference value (the OID generated for a reference) and returns the value of the row object.

Earlier in this chapter, the ANIMAL object table was created using the ANIMAL_TY abstract datatype:

```
create table ANIMAL of ANIMAL_TY;
```

To see how **DEREF** and **REF** work together, consider a table that is related to the ANIMAL table. The KEEPER table will track the people who take care of the animals. It will have a column for the name of the keeper (KeeperName) and a reference to the ANIMAL object table (AnimalKept), as shown in the following listing:

```
create table KEEPER
(KeeperName       VARCHAR2(25),
 AnimalKept       REF  ANIMAL_TY);
```

The first part of the **create table** command looks normal:

```
create table KEEPER
(KeeperName       VARCHAR2(25),
```

but the last line shows a new feature:

```
AnimalKept       REF  ANIMAL_TY);
```

The AnimalKept column references data that is stored elsewhere. The **REF** function points the AnimalKept column to a row object of the ANIMAL_TY datatype. Since ANIMAL is an object table of the ANIMAL_TY datatype, the AnimalKept column can point to the row objects within the ANIMAL object table. You can point the REF to any object table of that type.

When you **describe** the KEEPER table, you can see that its AnimalKept column relies on a **REF**:

```
describe KEEPER

Name                                 Null?    Type
------------------------------------ -------- ----
KEEPERNAME                                    VARCHAR2(25)
ANIMALKEPT                                    REF OF ANIMAL_TY
```

To see the full details, use a higher value for the **describe** depth:

```
set describe depth 2

desc KEEPER

Name                                 Null?    Type
------------------------------------ -------- ----------------
KEEPERNAME                                    VARCHAR2(25)
ANIMALKEPT                                    REF OF ANIMAL_TY
  BREED                                       VARCHAR2(25)
  NAME                                        VARCHAR2(25)
  BIRTHDATE                                   DATE
```

Now, **insert** a record into KEEPER. You need to use the **REF** function to store the ANIMAL references in the AnimalKept column.

```
insert into KEEPER
select 'CATHERINE WEILZ',
       REF(A)
  from ANIMAL A
 where Name = 'BENJI';
```

Let's look at this **insert** command closely. First, the KeeperName value is selected as a literal value:

```
insert into KEEPER
select 'CATHERINE WEILZ',
```

Next, the value for the AnimalKept column must be specified. But the datatype of AnimalKept is REF OF ANIMAL_TY, so you must select the reference from the ANIMAL object table to populate the AnimalKept column:

```
       REF(A)
  from ANIMAL A
 where Name = 'BENJI';
```

What's going on here? First, the ANIMAL object table is queried, and the **REF** function returns the OID for the row object selected. The OID is then stored in the KEEPER table as a pointer to that row object in the ANIMAL object table.

Does the KEEPER table contain the animal information? No. KEEPER contains the name of the keeper and a reference to a row object in the ANIMAL table. You can see the reference OID by querying KEEPER:

```
select * from KEEPER;

KEEPERNAME
-------------------------
ANIMALKEPT
----------------------------------------------------
CATHERINE WEILZ
00002202088817DC34109A4A929C632C0FAF1F78EF9A233BD5F
FD34A7E82D8C0C5CFB88FC0
```

NOTE
Your AnimalKept value and text wrapping will differ from those shown here.

The AnimalKept column, as shown in this listing, contains the reference to the row object, not the value of the data stored in the row object.

You can't see the referenced value unless you use the **DEREF** function. When you select from KEEPER, Oracle will use the OID to evaluate the reference (**REF**). The **DEREF** function will take the reference and return a value.

In the following query, the value of the AnimalKept column in KEEPER is the parameter passed to the **DEREF** function. **DEREF** will take the OID from AnimalKept and find the referenced object; the function will evaluate the reference and return the values to the user.

```
select DEREF(K.AnimalKept)
  from KEEPER K
 where KeeperName = 'CATHERINE WEILZ';

DEREF(K.ANIMALKEPT)(BREED, NAME, BIRTHDATE)
----------------------------------------------------
ANIMAL_TY('DOG', 'BENJI', '03-SEP-01')
```

NOTE
*The parameter for the **DEREF** function is the column name of the REF column, not the table name.*

The result shows that the CATHERINE WEILZ record in KEEPER references an ANIMAL record for the animal named BENJI. A few aspects of this query are noteworthy:

■ The query used a reference to a row object to travel from one table (KEEPER) to a second (the ANIMAL object table). Thus, a join is performed in the background, without your specifying the join criteria.

■ The object table itself is not mentioned in the query. The only table listed in the query is KEEPER. You do not need to know the name of the object table to **DEREF** its values.

■ The entire referenced row object was returned, not just part of the row.

These are significant differences that separate object queries from relational queries. Thus, when querying your tables, you need to know the way in which their relationships are established. Are the relationships based on foreign keys and primary keys, or on object tables and **REF** datatypes? If you are planning to use Oracle's object-oriented features, you need to accommodate the changes in SQL and the ways relationships are enforced. To help smooth the transition between relational and object-oriented approaches, Oracle allows you to create object views that contain **REF**s superimposed on existing relational tables. See "Object Views with REFs" later in this chapter.

The VALUE Function
The **DEREF** function was applied to the relational table—the KEEPER table, in this case. The **DEREF** function returns the value of the reference that goes from the relational table to the object table.

What about querying from the object table? Can you select from ANIMAL?

```
select * from ANIMAL;

BREED                          NAME                         BIRTHDATE
------------------------       ------------------------     ---------
MULE                           FRANCES                      01-APR-02
DOG                            BENJI                        03-SEP-01
```

Even though ANIMAL is an object table, you can select from it as if it were a relational table. This is consistent with the examples of **insert**s and **select**s shown earlier in this chapter. However, that is not what was shown via the **DEREF**. The **DEREF** showed the full structure of the abstract datatype used by the ANIMAL object table:

```
select DEREF(K.AnimalKept)
  from KEEPER K
 where KeeperName = 'CATHERINE WEILZ';

DEREF(K.ANIMALKEPT)(BREED, NAME, BIRTHDATE)
------------------------------------------------------
ANIMAL_TY('DOG', 'BENJI', '03-SEP-01')
```

To see the same structures from a query of the ANIMAL object table, use the **VALUE** function. As shown in the following listing, **VALUE** shows you the data in the same format that **DEREF** will use. The parameter for the **VALUE** function is the table alias.

```
select VALUE(A)
  from ANIMAL A
```

```
   where Name = 'BENJI';

VALUE(A)(BREED, NAME, BIRTHDATE)
----------------------------------------
ANIMAL_TY('DOG', 'BENJI', '03-SEP-01')
```

The **VALUE** function is useful when debugging references and within PL/SQL, as shown in "Object PL/SQL," later in this chapter. Since it allows you to query the formatted values directly from the object table, you can select those values without using the **DEREF** query of KEEPER's AnimalKept column.

Invalid References

You can **delete** the object to which a reference points. For example, you can **delete** a row from the ANIMAL object table to which a KEEPER record points:

```
delete from ANIMAL
 where Name = 'BENJI';
```

The record in KEEPER that references this ANIMAL record will now have what is called a *dangling REF.* If you **insert** a new ANIMAL row for the animal named BENJI, it won't be recognized as being part of the same reference established earlier. The reason is that the first time you **insert**ed a BENJI row, Oracle generated an OID for the row object, and that is what the KEEPER column referenced. When you **delete**d the row object, the OID went away—and Oracle does not reuse OID numbers. Therefore, when the new BENJI record is entered, it is given a *new* OID value— and the KEEPER record still points to the old value.

This is a critical difference between relational and OOP systems. In a relational system, the join between two tables is dependent only on the current data. In an OOP system, the join is between objects—and just the fact that two objects have the same data doesn't mean they are the same.

Object Views with REFs

You can use object views to superimpose OOP structures on existing relational tables (refer to Chapter 33). For example, you can create abstract datatypes and use them within the object view of an existing table. Using object views allows you to access the table via either relational command syntax or abstract datatype syntax. As a result, object views provide an important technological bridge from existing relational applications to object-relational applications.

A Quick Review of Object Views

This example from Chapter 33 will serve as part of the basis for the advanced object views in this chapter. First, a CUSTOMER table is created, with the Customer_ID column as its primary key:

```
create table CUSTOMER
(Customer_ID NUMBER constraint CUSTOMER_PK primary key,
 Name        VARCHAR2(25),
 Street      VARCHAR2(50),
 City        VARCHAR2(25),
```

```
State        CHAR(2),
Zip          NUMBER);
```

Next, two abstract datatypes are created. The first, ADDRESS_TY, contains attributes for addresses: Street, City, State, and Zip. The second, PERSON_TY, contains a Name attribute plus an Address attribute that uses the ADDRESS_TY datatype, as shown in the following listing:

```
create or replace type ADDRESS_TY as object
(Street  VARCHAR2(50),
 City    VARCHAR2(25),
 State   CHAR(2),
 Zip     NUMBER);
/

create or replace type PERSON_TY as object
(Name        VARCHAR2(25),
 Address     ADDRESS_TY);
/
```

Since the CUSTOMER table was created without using the ADDRESS_TY and PERSON_TY datatypes, you need to use object views in order to access CUSTOMER data via object-based accesses (such as methods). You can create an object view that specifies the abstract datatypes that apply to the CUSTOMER table. In the following listing, the CUSTOMER_OV object view is created:

```
create view CUSTOMER_OV (Customer_ID, Person) as
select Customer_ID,
       PERSON_TY(Name,
       ADDRESS_TY(Street, City, State, Zip))
  from CUSTOMER;
```

In the creation of the CUSTOMER_OV object view, the constructor methods for the two abstract datatypes (ADDRESS_TY and PERSON_TY) are specified. You can now access the CUSTOMER table directly (as a relational table) or via the constructor methods for the abstract datatypes.

The CUSTOMER table will be used in the next set of examples in this chapter.

Object Views Involving References

If the CUSTOMER table shown in the previous section is related to another table, you can use object views to create a reference between the tables. That is, Oracle will use the existing primary key/ foreign key relationships to simulate OIDs for use by **REF**s between the tables. You will thus be able to access the tables either as relational tables or as objects. When you treat the tables as objects, you will be able to use the **REF**s to automatically perform joins of the tables (refer to "Using the **DEREF** Function," earlier in this chapter, for examples).

The CUSTOMER table has a primary key of Customer_ID. Let's create a small table that will contain a foreign key reference to the Customer_ID column. In the following listing, the CUSTOMER_ CALL table is created. The primary key of the CUSTOMER_CALL table is the combination of Customer_ID and Call_Number. The Customer_ID column of CUSTOMER_CALL is a foreign key

back to CUSTOMER—you cannot record a call for a customer who does not already have a record in CUSTOMER. A single nonkey attribute, Call_Date, is created within the CUSTOMER_CALL table.

```
create table CUSTOMER_CALL
(Customer_ID    NUMBER,
 Call_Number    NUMBER,
 Call_Date      DATE,
 constraint CUSTOMER_CALL_PK
     primary key (Customer_ID, Call_Number),
 constraint CUSTOMER_CALL_FK foreign key (Customer_ID)
   references CUSTOMER(Customer_ID));
```

For example, you could have the following CUSTOMER and CUSTOMER_CALL entries:

```
insert into CUSTOMER values
(123,'SIGMUND','47 HAFFNER RD','LEWISTON','NJ',22222);
insert into CUSTOMER values
(234,'EVELYN','555 HIGH ST','LOWLANDS PARK','NE',33333);

insert into CUSTOMER_CALL values
(123,1,TRUNC(SysDate)-1);
insert into CUSTOMER_CALL values
(123,2,TRUNC(SysDate));
```

The foreign key from CUSTOMER_CALL to CUSTOMER defines the relationship between the tables. From an OOP point of view, the records in CUSTOMER_CALL reference the records in CUSTOMER. Therefore, we must find a way to assign OID values to the records in CUSTOMER and generate references in CUSTOMER_CALL.

How to Generate OIDs
First, use an object view to assign OIDs to the records in CUSTOMER. Remember that OIDs are assigned to records in an object table—and an object table, in turn, is based on an abstract datatype. Therefore, we first need to create an abstract datatype that has the same structure as the CUSTOMER table:

```
create or replace type CUSTOMER_TY as object
(Customer_ID NUMBER,
 Name         VARCHAR2(25),
 Street       VARCHAR2(50),
 City         VARCHAR2(25),
 State        CHAR(2),
 Zip          NUMBER);
/
```

Now, create an object view based on the CUSTOMER_TY type, while assigning OID values to the records in CUSTOMER:

```
create or replace view CUSTOMER_OV of CUSTOMER_TY
with object identifier (Customer_ID) as
```

```
select Customer_ID, Name, Street, City, State, Zip
  from CUSTOMER;
```

The first part of this **create view** command gives the view its name (CUSTOMER_OV) and tells Oracle that the view's structure is based on the CUSTOMER_TY datatype:

```
create or replace view CUSTOMER_OV of CUSTOMER_TY
```

The next part of the **create view** command tells the database how to construct OID values for the rows in CUSTOMER. The **with object identifier** clause is followed by the column to use for the OID—in this case, the Customer_ID value. This will allow you to address the rows within the CUSTOMER table as if they were referenceable row objects within an object table.

```
with object identifier (Customer_ID) as
```

The final part of the **create view** command gives the query on which the view's data access will be based. The columns in the query must match the columns in the view's base datatype.

```
select Customer_ID, Name, Street, City, State, Zip
  from CUSTOMER;
```

The rows of CUSTOMER are now accessible as row objects via the CUSTOMER_OV view. The OID values generated for the CUSTOMER_OV rows are called *pkOID*s, because they are based on CUSTOMER's primary key values. Relational tables can be accessed as row objects if you create object views for them.

How to Generate References

The rows of CUSTOMER_CALL reference rows in CUSTOMER. From a relational perspective, the relationship is determined by the foreign key pointing from the CUSTOMER_CALL.Customer_ID column to the CUSTOMER.Customer_ID column. Now that the CUSTOMER_OV object view has been created, and the rows in CUSTOMER can be accessed via OIDs, you need to create reference values in CUSTOMER_CALL that reference CUSTOMER. Once the **REF**s are in place, you will be able to use the **DEREF** function (shown earlier in this chapter) to access the CUSTOMER data from within CUSTOMER_CALL.

The **create view** command for the object view of CUSTOMER_CALL is shown in the following listing. It uses a new function, **MAKE_REF**, which is described following the listing.

```
create view CUSTOMER_CALL_OV as
select MAKE_REF(CUSTOMER_OV, Customer_ID) Customer_ID,
       Call_Number,
       Call_Date
  from CUSTOMER_CALL;
```

With the exception of the **MAKE_REF** operation, this **create view** command looks like a normal **create view** command. The **MAKE_REF** operation is shown in this line:

```
select MAKE_REF(CUSTOMER_OV, Customer_ID) Customer_ID,
```

The **MAKE_REF** function takes as arguments the name of the object view being referenced and the name of the column (or columns) that form the foreign key in the local table. In this case, the Customer_ID column of the CUSTOMER_CALL table references the column that is used as the basis of OID generation in the CUSTOMER_OV object view. Therefore, two parameters are passed to **MAKE_REF**: CUSTOMER_OV and Customer_ID. The result of the **MAKE_REF** operation is given the column alias Customer_ID. Since this command creates a view, the result of an operation must be given a column alias.

What does **MAKE_REF** do? It creates references (called *pkREFs*, since they are based on primary keys) from the CUSTOMER_CALL_OV view to the CUSTOMER_OV view. You can now query the two views as if CUSTOMER_OV were an object table and CUSTOMER_CALL_OV were a table that contains a REF datatype that references CUSTOMER_OV.

Querying the Object Views

The queries of the object views with REFs mirror the structure of the queries of table REFs. You use the **DEREF** function to select the value of the referenced data, as shown earlier in this chapter. Applied to the object views, the query will be

```
select DEREF(CCOV.Customer_ID)
  from CUSTOMER_CALL_OV CCOV
 where Call_Date = TRUNC(SysDate);

DEREF(CCOV.CUSTOMER_ID)(CUSTOMER_ID, NAME, STREET, CITY, STATE,ZIP)
------------------------------------------------------------------
CUSTOMER_TY(123, 'SIGMUND', '47 HAFFNER RD', 'LEWISTON','NJ',22222)
```

The query found the record in CUSTOMER_CALL for which the Call_Date value was the current system date. It then took the Customer_ID value from that record and evaluated its reference. That Customer_ID value, from the **MAKE_REF** function, pointed to a pkOID value in the CUSTOMER_OV object view. The CUSTOMER_OV object view returned the record whose pkOID matched the referenced value. The **DEREF** function then returned the value of the referenced row. The query thus returned rows from CUSTOMER even though the user only queried CUSTOMER_CALL.

Object views of column objects enable you to work with tables as if they were both relational tables and object-relational tables. When extended to row objects, object views enable you to generate OID values based on established foreign key/primary key relationships. Object views allow you to continue to use the existing constraints and standard **insert**, **update**, **delete**, and **select** commands. They also allow you to use OOP features such as references against the object tables. Object views thus provide an important technological bridge for migrating to an OOP database architecture.

As described earlier in this chapter, Oracle performs joins that resolve the references defined in the database. When the referenced data is retrieved, it brings back the entire row object that was referenced. To reference the data, you need to establish pkOIDs in the table that is the "primary key" table in the relationship, and use **MAKE_REF** to generate references in the table that is the "foreign key" table in the relationship. You can then work with the data as if it were stored in object tables.

Object PL/SQL

PL/SQL programs can use the abstract datatypes you have created. Whereas earlier versions of PL/SQL could only use the Oracle-provided datatypes (such as DATE, NUMBER, and VARCHAR2), you can now use your own user-defined datatypes as well. The result is the merging of SQL, procedural logic, and OOP extensions—a combination referred to as *object PL/SQL*.

The following anonymous PL/SQL block uses object PL/SQL concepts. The CUSTOMER_TY abstract datatype is used as the datatype for the *Cust1* variable, and its value is populated by a query of the CUSTOMER_OV object view.

```
set serveroutput on
declare
    Cust1        CUSTOMER_TY;
begin
    select VALUE(COV)  into Cust1
      from CUSTOMER_OV COV
     where Customer_ID = 123;
   DBMS_OUTPUT.PUT_LINE(Cust1.Name);
   DBMS_OUTPUT.PUT_LINE(Cust1.Street);
end;
/
```

The output of this PL/SQL block is

```
SIGMUND
47 HAFFNER RD
```

In the first part of the PL/SQL block, a variable is declared using the CUSTOMER_TY datatype:

```
declare
     Cust1        CUSTOMER_TY;
```

The *Cust1* variable value is selected from the CUSTOMER_OV object view (created in the preceding section of this chapter). The **VALUE** function is used to retrieve the data in the structure of the abstract datatype. Since the data will be selected in the format of the abstract datatype, you need to use the CUSTOMER_OV object view created on the CUSTOMER table.

```
begin
    select VALUE(COV)  into Cust1
      from CUSTOMER_OV COV
     where Customer_ID = 123;
```

The Cust1.Name and Cust1.Street values are then retrieved from the attributes of the *Cust1* variable and displayed. You cannot pass the entire *Cust1* variable to the PUT_LINE procedure.

```
   DBMS_OUTPUT.PUT_LINE(Cust1.Name);
   DBMS_OUTPUT.PUT_LINE(Cust1.Street);
end;
```

This is a deliberately simple example, but it shows the power of object PL/SQL. You can use object PL/SQL anywhere you use abstract datatypes. Your PL/SQL is thus no longer bound to the Oracle-provided datatypes, and may more accurately reflect the objects in your database. In this example, an object view was queried to illustrate that the queries can access either column objects or row objects. You can then select the attributes of the abstract datatype and manipulate or display them. If you have defined methods for the abstract datatype, you can apply them as well.

For example, you can call the datatype's constructor methods within your PL/SQL blocks. In the following example, a variable named *NewCust* is defined using the CUSTOMER_TY datatype. The *NewCust* variable is then set equal to a set of values using the CUSTOMER_TY constructor method. The *NewCust* variable's set of values is then **insert**ed via the CUSTOMER_OV object view.

```
declare
    NewCust     CUSTOMER_TY;
begin
    NewCust :=
       CUSTOMER_TY(345,'NewCust','StreetVal', 'City','ST',00000);
    insert into CUSTOMER_OV
    values (NewCust);
end;
/
```

You can see the result of the **insert** by querying CUSTOMER_OV:

```
select Customer_ID, Name from CUSTOMER_OV;

CUSTOMER_ID NAME
----------- ------------------------
        123 SIGMUND
        234 EVELYN
        345 NewCust
```

In addition to calling constructor methods, you can call the methods you have created on your abstract datatypes. If you will be comparing the values of variables that use the abstract datatypes, you will need to define map or order methods for the datatypes. This capability allows you to further extend object PL/SQL—you define the datatypes and the functions at the database level, and they are callable within any of your PL/SQL programs. Object PL/SQL represents a significant enhancement over traditional PL/SQL.

Objects in the Database

The features available in Oracle—column objects, row objects, and object extensions to PL/SQL—enable you to implement objects in your database without sacrificing the investment you have already made in analysis and design. You can continue to create systems based on relational design techniques and tune them based on relational access methods. The tools that Oracle provides allow you to create an OOP layer above your relational tables. Once you have that layer in place, you can access the relational data as if it were stored in a fully OOP database.

Having an OOP layer allows you to realize some of the benefits of an OOP system, such as abstraction and encapsulation. You can apply the methods for each abstract datatype across a set

of consistently implemented objects, and benefit from object reuse and standards enforcement. At the same time, you can benefit from Oracle's relational features. The ability to use both relational and object technology within an application lets you use the proper tool for the proper job within the database.

Note that implementing object-relational features may force you to change your approach to data relationships and the tools you use to access the data. If you use row objects, the relationships among tables are among row objects, not their data—possibly resulting in dangling REFs. Additionally, unless you use object views you will need to use new SQL syntax for queries and DML operations.

When implementing the object portion of an object-relational database, start by defining the abstract datatypes that are the core components of your business. Every object-relational feature, whether it relates to column objects or row objects, is based on an abstract datatype. The better you have defined your datatypes and their methods, the better you will be able to implement objects. If necessary, nest objects so that you can have multiple variations of the same core datatype. The result will be a database that is properly designed to take advantage of both relational and object-oriented features.

PART
VI

Java in Oracle

CHAPTER
37

An Introduction
to Java

I n this chapter, you will see an overview of Java as it relates to Oracle database applications. There are numerous uses of Java beyond Oracle applications, and there are many features of the language that will not be used by most Oracle developers. The goal of this chapter is to provide developers who have a background in SQL and PL/SQL with an understanding of the Java language structures. This is not an exhaustive review of Java (numerous books are available that accomplish that goal) but rather a short overview of the Java language components most commonly used by Oracle developers.

Although in many cases PL/SQL and Java correlate well to each other, there are significant differences in terminology and usage. That shouldn't be surprising because the two programming languages were developed independently. Furthermore, PL/SQL's object oriented capabilities were not part of its initial implementation, whereas Java has been object oriented since its inception. To use Java effectively, you need to take a different approach than the one you may have taken in the past with PL/SQL.

Chapter 29 presented an introduction to the PL/SQL language structures and flow control. This chapter mirrors that approach: You will see the structures used by Java and the basic flow-control methods provided. Where applicable, you will also see the matching PL/SQL structures. You should be familiar with PL/SQL (Chapter 29); packages, functions, and procedures (Chapter 31); and abstract datatypes and methods (Chapter 33) before reading this chapter.

Java vs. PL/SQL: An Overview

In comparing PL/SQL to Java, you get no further than the basic PL/SQL structure—a block—before you encounter a significant difference in terminology between the two languages. In PL/SQL, a *block* is a structured piece of code that has a Declarations section, an Executable Commands section, and an Exception Handling section. For a PL/SQL block, the structure may be represented as follows:

```
declare
   <declarations section>
begin
   <executable commands>
 exception
   <exception handling>
end;
```

In Java, the term *block* refers to a much smaller subset of code. In Java, a block is a collection of statements enclosed by curly braces, { and }. For example, the following pseudo-code contains two Java blocks:

```
if (some condition) {
   block of code to process if condition is met
}
else {
   block of code to process if condition is not met
}
```

Within PL/SQL, that entire code section would be merely one part of a larger block; within Java, it contains two separate blocks. Throughout this chapter, all references to "blocks" refer to Java blocks unless otherwise specified.

A PL/SQL procedure is bound by a **begin** and **end**, whereas a Java method is bound by opening and closing braces. These braces are also utilized to isolate individual blocks of scoped code, or as indicators of the opening and closing of conditional segments.

A second major difference between PL/SQL and Java is in the declaration of variables. In a PL/SQL block, you define your variables before you begin the Executable Commands section. In a Java program, you can define variables where they are needed within the program. A Java program has no Declarations section comparable to the one used in PL/SQL blocks.

Throughout this chapter, you will see a number of other differences between PL/SQL and Java. It's important to remember that Java does not replace PL/SQL within your applications—you can continue to use PL/SQL for Oracle applications. For data-retrieval operations, you should test the performance of PL/SQL and Java before deciding on a technical direction to follow.

Getting Started

To use the examples in this section, you need a copy of the Java Development Kit (JDK), which is available for free download from http://java.sun.com/. You need to install the JDK on the server on which you will be running the Java programs. As of the time of this writing, JDK 1.4 is the most recent production release; most development efforts use JDK 1.3.1. At a minimum, you should use JDK 1.2.2.

NOTE
*The JDK is installed as part of the Oracle Database 10g installation.
Be sure to install both the database kernel software and the software
that comes on the Companion CD.*

Declarations

Within Java, you can declare variables as needed. A variable has a name and a datatype, and it's used to store a data value during the program's execution. A variable also has a scope, allowing it to be publicly accessible or private—similar to the manner in which procedures within packages can have private variables.

Here are examples of Java variable declarations:

```
char     aCharVariable = 'J';
boolean aBooleanVariable = false;
```

By convention, Java variables always start with a lowercase letter, as shown in this example, where the datatypes are CHAR and BOOLEAN, and each variable is assigned an initial value. Note that the assignment character in Java is =, as opposed to := or => in PL/SQL. Each declaration is terminated with a semicolon.

The available primitive datatypes in Java are listed in Table 37-1.

In addition to the primitive datatypes listed in Table 37-1, you can use reference datatypes, which are based on the contents of variables. You may note that there is no primitive datatype for variable-length character strings—Java provides a String class for that purpose. Classes are discussed later in this chapter.

Datatype	Description
Byte	Byte-length integer
Short	Short integer
Int	Integer
Long	Long integer
Float	Single-precision floating-point real number
Double	Double-precision floating-point real number
Char	A single Unicode character
Boolean	A Boolean value, true or false

TABLE 37-1. *Primitive Java Datatypes*

Executable Commands

You can assign values to variables via the use of expressions and statements. The arithmetic operators supported by Java include the following:

Operator	Description
*	Multiplication
/	Division
+	Addition
–	Subtraction
%	Modulus

In addition to these operators, you can use Java's unary operators to simplify your coding. For example, you can increment variables via the ++ operator, as shown here:

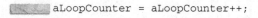

```
aLoopCounter = aLoopCounter++;
```

Or you could simply write this:

```
aLoopCounter++
```

NOTE
*The ++ operator is called a unary operator because it has only one operand. If an operator requires two operands (such as *), it is called a binary operator.*

In PL/SQL, that would have been written as follows:

```
aLoopCounter := aLoopCounter +1;
```

If the ++ operator is placed in front of the variable name, it is a *pre-increment* operator rather than a *post-increment* operator:

```
int anotherCounter = ++aLoopCounter;
```

In this example, the variable *anotherCounter* is set to the incremented value of *aLoopCounter*. By contrast,

```
int anotherCounter = aLoopCounter++;
```

sets *anotherCounter* to the value of *aLoopCounter* before it is incremented. You can decrement a variable's value via the -- unary operator:

```
aLoopCounter = aLoopCounter--;
```

You can also combine the assignment of values with an operation. For example, instead of writing

```
aNumberVariable = aNumberVariable * 2;
```

you can write

```
aNumberVariable *= 2;
```

You can perform similar combinations using /=, %=, +=, and –=.

If you perform multiple arithmetic operations, you should use parentheses to clearly indicate the order in which the operations should be evaluated, as shown in the following example:

```
aNumberVariable = (aNumberVariable*2) +2;
```

Terminating these operations with semicolons makes them *statements*—complete units of execution.

Conditional Logic

You can evaluate variables by using expressions and statements. To do so, you may use one or more of the fundamental classes provided as part of Java. A full listing of those methods is beyond the scope of this book; see Sun's Java documentation site or one of the many Java books available for the functionality currently provided.

NOTE
The number of supplied classes usually changes dramatically with each release of Java.

In the following listing, the Character.isUpperCase method is used to evaluate the *aCharVariable* variable declared earlier:

```
if (Character.isUpperCase(aCharVariable)) {
    some commands to execute
}
```

If the *aCharVariable* value is uppercase, the commands in the following block will be executed; otherwise, flow will continue to the next part of the program.

The following is the general syntax for **if** clauses:

```
if (expression) {
    statement
}
```

Notice the lack of a **then** clause. If the expression being evaluated is true, the following block is automatically executed. Also, note the lack of an **end if** clause. Java blocks are simply terminated by the closing brace of the statement.

You can also have **else** clauses to evaluate different conditions, as shown in the following listing:

```
if (expression) {
    statement
}
else {
    statement
}
```

If you have multiple conditions to check, you can use the **else if** clause to evaluate each in turn, ending with an **else** clause. The following listing illustrates the use of **else if** clauses:

```
if (aCharVariable == 'V') {
    statement
}
else if (aCharVariable == 'J') {
    statement
}
else {
    statement
}
```

NOTE
*PL/SQL supports the use of **elsif** clauses to choose between alternatives. A single **if** clause can have multiple **elsif** clauses.*

In addition to supporting **if** clauses for conditional logic, Java features a **switch** clause. Used in conjunction with its **break** clause and statement labels, the **switch** clause can approximate the functionality of **goto** clauses (which Java does not support). First, let's look at a simple **switch** example. Using the **case** statement, multiple values of the *aMonth* variable are evaluated. Depending

on the *aMonth* value, the text name for the month is displayed, and the processing leaves the
switch block by means of a **break**.

```
int aMonth=2;
switch (aMonth) {
  case 1:
      System.out.println("January");
      break;
  case 2:
      System.out.println("February");
      break;
  case 3:
      System.out.println("March");
      break;
  default:
      System.out.println("Out of range");
      break;
}
```

NOTE
*In Java, the arguments of a **case** statement must be integers.*

This kind of code is much more complex to write than a simple **TO_CHAR**, but it illustrates
the **switch** usage. The **switch** operator takes the *aMonth* variable as its input and then evaluates
its value. If the value matches a **case** value, the System.out.println method is called to print the
month's name, and processing control leaves the **switch** block by means of a **break**. If the value
does not match one of the **case** clauses, the **default** option is executed.

Where does control go? By default, it goes to the next section of the program. However, you
have the option of creating labels for sections of your code and passing the names of those labels
to the **break** clause. The following listing shows an example of a label and a **break** clause:

```
somelabel:
if (aCharVariable == 'V') {
  statement
}
else {
  statement
}
int aMonth=2;
switch (aMonth) {
  case 1:
      System.out.println("January");
      break somelabel;
  case 2:
      System.out.println("February");
      break someotherlabel;
  case 3:
      System.out.println("March");
```

```
        break somethirdlabel;
    default:
        System.out.println("Out of range");
        break;
}
```

In this example, the **if** clause is evaluated, followed by the **switch** clause. Note that the *aMonth* variable is not declared until just before it is needed. For this example, the *aMonth* variable is assigned a value of 2, so the program will display the word "February" and will then branch over to the section of code identified by the someotherlabel label. If the *aMonth* value had been 1, the **if** clause at the beginning of the code listing would have been reexecuted.

Java also supports a *ternary* operator—an operator that takes three operands and whose function is similar to that of **DECODE**. Acting as an inline if-else combination, the ternary operator evaluates an expression. If the expression evaluates to true, the second operand is returned; otherwise, the third is returned. The syntax is as follows:

```
expression ? operand1 : operand2
```

The following listing shows a sample ternary operation:

```
aStatusVariable = (aCharVariable == 'V') ? "OK" :  "Invalid";
```

In this example, the expression

```
(aCharVariable == 'V')
```

is evaluated. If it is true, "OK" is returned; otherwise, "Invalid" is returned.

You can use the ternary operator to simulate the use of a **GREATEST** function:

```
double greatest = (a > b) ? a : b;
```

In this example, the expression (a > b) is evaluated, where *a* and *b* are the names of variables. If that expression is true, *a*'s value is returned; otherwise, *b*'s value is returned.

NOTE
*Java has a "greatest" method for numeric values—the Max method within the java.lang.Math class. The ternary example in the preceding listing can be rewritten as **double greatest = Math.Max(a, b);***

You can combine multiple logic checks via the use of AND and OR operations. In Java, an AND operation is represented by the && operator:

```
if (aCharVariable == 'V' && aMonth == 3) {
  statement
}
```

The OR operation is represented by ||, as shown in the following listing:

```
if (aCharVariable == 'V' || aMonth == 3) {
    statement
}
```

For performance reasons, the && and || operations are carried out only if required; the second expression is not evaluated if the first expression determines the result. In the case of the AND operator, if the first value is false, the evaluation ends at that point and the Boolean value false is returned. In the case of the OR operator, if the first expression is false, the second expression will still be evaluated because only one of the test conditions needs to be true for the Boolean value true to be returned. If the first value of the OR operator were true, subsequent expressions would not need to be evaluated and true would be returned.

The & and | operators are bitwise AND and OR; they are not short-circuited as && and || are. All expressions will always be evaluated. This functionality can be important if you are testing the return values of method calls and you need to make sure the methods are executed.

Loops

Java supports three main types of loops: WHILE loops, DO-WHILE loops, and FOR loops. In this section, you will see examples of each type of loop. Because Java is not written as an extension of SQL, it does not support Cursor FOR loops as PL/SQL does.

WHILE Loops and DO-WHILE Loops

A **while** clause evaluates a condition; if the condition is true, the associated block of statements is executed. The syntax for a WHILE loop is of the following form:

```
while (expression) {
    statement
    statement
}
```

The WHILE loop executes the block of statements (the section within the { and } braces) repeatedly until the *expression* is no longer true:

```
int aNumberVariable = 3;
while (aNumberVariable < 7) {
    some_processing_statement
    aNumberVariable++;
}
```

In this example, a counter variable *(aNumberVariable)* is created and initialized. The variable's value is then evaluated via the **while** clause. If the value is less than 7, the associated statement block is executed. As part of that block, the variable is incremented. When the block completes, the variable is again evaluated and the loop continues.

NOTE
For examples of WHILE loop processing, see "Classes" later in this chapter.

You could also write this as a DO-WHILE loop:

```
int aNumberVariable = 3;
do {
  some_processing_statement
  aNumberVariable++;
} while (aNumberVariable < 7);
```

In a DO-WHILE loop, the expression's value is not evaluated until the block has been processed at least one time.

FOR Loops

You can use a FOR loop to repeatedly execute a block of code. In a FOR loop, you specify an initial value, a termination value, and an increment for the loop counter. The loop counter will be incremented each time through the loop, by the increment you specify, until the termination value is reached. The following is the syntax for a FOR loop:

```
for (initialization; termination; increment) {
  statement;
}
```

The prior section's WHILE example can be rewritten with a **for** clause, as shown in the following listing:

```
for (int aNumberVariable=3; aNumberVariable<7; aNumberVariable++)  {
  some_processing_statement
}
```

The **for** clause version for this example is much shorter than the **while** version. In this example, the *aNumberVariable* variable is declared and initialized within the FOR loop. As long as the variable's value does not exceed 7, the block will be executed. For each pass through the loop, the variable's value is incremented by 1 via the ++ unary operator.

Within a loop, you can use the **continue** clause to jump to another statement within the loop. If you just use the **continue** clause by itself, the process flow will jump to the end of the loop body and evaluate the loop's termination test. If you use **continue** with a label (as shown previously in the section on the **switch** clause), processing will continue at the next iteration of the labeled loop.

Cursors and Loops

Within PL/SQL, you can use Cursor FOR loops to iterate through the results of a query. You can use Java's WHILE and FOR loops to simulate the functionality of a PL/SQL Cursor FOR loop. The examples provided with Oracle show how this can be accomplished. Oracle provides sample files on the Companion disc that accompanies the Oracle software installation. The Companion disc uses the Oracle Universal Installer to load software drivers and demonstration files, including those supporting JDBC development. Following installation of the Companion disc, the JDBC examples will be in a file named demo.zip in the /jdbc/demo subdirectory under the Oracle software home directory; when unzipped, the files referred to in this chapter will be located in the /jdbc/demo/samples/generic subdirectory. The SelectEmployee.java demo issues the following commands:

```
Statement stmt  conn.createStatement();
ResultSet rset = stmt.executeQuery ("select FIRST_NAME, "
                                    + "LAST_NAME from EMPLOYEES");

// Iterate through the result and print the employee names
    while (rset.next ())
      System.out.println (rset.getString (1) + " " + rset.getString (2));
```

This example assumes that a connection to the database has already been established. The first line of the example creates a variable called *stmt,* based on a connection variable called *conn* (not shown in this partial listing). The second line of the example creates a variable called *rset,* based on the result set that the query *stmt* will return. Following a comment (prefixed by //), a **while** clause fetches each row in the result set. If the fetch retrieves a row from the result set, the ENAME from that EMP row is printed; otherwise, the loop will end.

From a programming perspective, you should be specific in the data returned (as in the preceding example), specifying the column names to be returned.

The JDBC (Java Database Connectivity; see Chapter 38) demos provided by Oracle show examples of queries involving procedure calls, LOBs, and DML. In most cases, your Java code will be performing in a similar manner to the previous example: Write the process flow-control language in Java and pass it a statement to execute. Based on the outcome of that statement, you can direct different actions to occur via the use of **while**, **for**, **if**, **break**, **continue**, and **switch** clauses, as shown earlier in this chapter.

Exception Handling

In a PL/SQL procedure, you have a single EXCEPTION block; in Java, you can have as many try/ catch blocks as you desire. Java provides a robust set of error-handling routines and enables you to create complex error-handling procedures. In PL/SQL, you **raise** an exception; in Java, you **throw** exceptions. If an exception is thrown, you need to use the Java **catch** clause to capture and properly process the exception.

Java's exception-handling syntax is based on three blocks: **try**, **catch**, and **finally**. The **try** block includes the statements that might throw an exception. The **catch** block immediately following the **try** block associates exception handlers with the exceptions that may be thrown by the **try** block. The **finally** block cleans up any system resources not properly cleaned up during the **catch** block processing. The general structure is as follows:

```
try {
  statements
}
catch ( ) {
  statements
}
catch ( ) {
  statements
}
finally {
  statements
}
```

For example, consider the following Java code:

```
try {
    Statement stmt = conn.createStatement ();

    stmt.execute ("drop table plsqltest");
}
catch (SQLException e) {
}
```

In this example, a variable named *stmt* is created to execute a **drop table** command. If the execution fails—for example, if the table does not exist—how will that error be processed? The **catch** clause tells Java to handle it via an exception object called SQLException, a standard part of Java's SQL implementation. As shown in the example, the **catch** clause takes two parameters (an exception object and a variable name) and is optionally followed by a block of statements to execute.

The **try** block can contain multiple statements, or you can create separate **try** blocks for each statement. In general, it is easier to manage exception handling if you consolidate your **catch** blocks, so consolidating your **try** blocks will help you manage your code as it changes and grows. The **when others** clause in PL/SQL is essentially **catch (Throwable th)** in Java.

The **finally** block cleans up the state of the current code section before passing control to any subsequent parts of the program. At run time, the contents of the **finally** block are always executed, regardless of the outcome of the **try** block. For example, you could use the **finally** block to close a database connection.

Reserved Words

The reserved words in Java are listed in Table 37-2. You cannot use these words as the names of classes, methods, or variables.

abstract	else	interface	super
boolean	extends	long	switch
break	false	native	synchronized
byte	final	new	this
case	finally	null	throw
catch	float	package	throws
char	for	private	transient
class	goto	protected	true
const	if	public	try

TABLE 37-2. *Reserved Words in Java*

continue	implements	return	void
default	import	short	volatile
do	instanceof	static	while
double	int	strictfp	

TABLE 37-2. *Reserved Words in Java* (continued)

Classes

In the prior sections of this chapter, you saw the basic syntax structures for Java. In this section, you will see how to use that syntax to create and use objects. A simple program for printing the word "Oracle" is shown in the following listing:

```
public class HelloOracle {
   public static void main (String[] args) {
      System.out.println("Oracle");
   }
}
```

This example creates a *class* called HelloOracle. Within the HelloOracle class, a public method called *main* is created. The main method prints the word "Oracle." This is significantly more complex than

```
select 'Oracle' from dual;
```

but the Java version has features lacking in the SQL version. HelloOracle is a class, and as such its methods can be called from within other classes. HelloOracle could have multiple methods; in this example, it has only the main method.

The main method's declaration (**public static void main**) has a number of keywords that you should become familiar with:

public Defining the class as **public** allows all classes to call this method.

static Declares that this is a class method; you use **static** to declare class methods. An additional option is the keyword **final** for methods and variables whose values cannot change (similar to PL/SQL's **constant** option).

void Specifies the return value's datatype from the procedure. Because this procedure does not return values, its type is **void**.

In this example, the method is given the name *main* because that will simplify running the class's method. Now that the class has been created, you can compile and load it.

NOTE
To compile and execute a Java class, you must have the JDK on your server. The following examples assume that the binaries that are part of that kit are located in a directory that is automatically searched via the PATH environment variable and that the directory containing your class files is included in the CLASSPATH environment variable. The programs referenced here (javac and java) are located in the /bin subdirectory of the JDK software directory.

First, save the program as a plain text file called HelloOracle.java. Next, compile it:

```
javac HelloOracle.java
```

A new file, called HelloOracle.class, will be created on your server. You can then run the class:

```
java HelloOracle
```

Then the output will be displayed:

```
Oracle
```

As shown in the HelloOracle example, the class is first given a name, along with other optional attributes related to its inheritance of other classes' attributes. In the class body, all the class variables and methods are defined. As with abstract datatypes in Oracle, Java classes have methods associated with them for the manipulation of their related data.

Let's consider a more complex example. The following listing is a Java program that computes the area of a circle, given a radius value as input (see Chapter 29 for the PL/SQL version):

```
//  AreaOfCircle.java
//
public class AreaOfCircle {
  public static void main(String[] args) {
    try {
        int input = Integer.parseInt(args[0]);
        double result=area(input);
        System.out.println(result);
    }
    catch (ArrayIndexOutOfBoundsException oob) {
        System.out.println("You did not provide the radius of the circle.");
        System.out.println("Usage: java AreaOfCircle 10");
    }
    catch (NumberFormatException nfe) {
        System.out.println("Enter a valid number for the radius.");
        System.out.println("Usage: java AreaOfCircle 10");
    }
} /// main

  public static double area (int rad) {
    double pi=3.1415927;
```

```
        double areacircle=pi*rad*rad;
        return areacircle;
    } /// area
} ///AreaOfCircle
```

NOTE
*Be sure to include a closing brace, }, for each block. In the examples
shown in this chapter, the closing braces are always on lines by
themselves to simplify debugging and processing flow-control errors .
that may arise.*

First, note that the class and the name of the file must be the same. In this case, the class is
named AreaOfCircle, so this text is stored in a file called AreaOfCircle.java. The class has two
methods, called main and area. When you execute the class, the main method is automatically
executed. The main method takes the string provided as input and parses it as an integer into the
input variable:

```
int input=Integer.parseInt(args[0]);
```

There are at least two possible exceptions that could be thrown when running this code. The
first exception handled, ArrayIndexOutOfBoundsException, occurs when you try to reference a
position in an array that doesn't exist. Because the code explicitly references the first position of
the array named args (args[0]), an exception will be thrown if no data was passed to the program.
The other possible error, NumberFormatException, would occur if a nonnumeric value was
passed in. For example, if you ran the program by entering "java AreaOfCircle XYZ" instead of
"java AreaOfCircle 123", the NumberFormatException would be thrown because XYZ isn't a
valid number. Both of these exceptions are handled by the two **catch** statements that provide the
user with useful feedback regarding the cause of the error:

```
catch (ArrayIndexOutOfBoundsException oob) {
    System.out.println("You did not provide the radius of the circle.");
    System.out.println("Usage: java AreaOfCircle 10");
}
catch (NumberFormatException nfe) {
    System.out.println("Enter a valid number for the radius.");
    System.out.println("Usage: java AreaOfCircle 10");
}
```

Next, a variable named *result* is declared and is set equal to the value returned by the call to
area(input):

```
double result=area(input);
```

To process that directive, the area method is executed using the *input* variable's value as its
input. That method is as follows:

```
public static double area (int rad) {
    double pi=3.1415927;
```

```
   double areacircle=pi*rad*rad;
   return areacircle;
}
```

In its definition, the area method specifies that it will accept one variable, an integer type named rad. That variable's value (passed from the input variable in the main method) is then processed, and a variable named *areacircle* is calculated and returned to main. In main, that value is then printed:

```
   double result=area(input);
   System.out.println(result);
```

Testing the program is straightforward:

```
javac AreaOfCircle.java
java AreaOfCircle 10
```

The following is the output:

```
314.15927
```

Let's extend this example to include WHILE loop processing. In this example, the area method will be called repeatedly until the resulting input value exceeds a given value:

```
// AreaOfCircleWhile.java
//
public class AreaOfCircleWhile {
   public static void main(String[] args) {
      try {
        int input=Integer.parseInt(args[0]);
        while (input < 7) {
          double result=area(input);
          System.out.println(result);
          input++;
        }
      }
      catch (ArrayIndexOutOfBoundsException oob) {
         System.out.println("You did not provide the radius of the circle.");
         System.out.println("Usage: java AreaOfCircle 10");
      }
      catch (NumberFormatException nfe) {
         System.out.println("Enter a valid number for the radius.");
         System.out.println("Usage: java AreaOfCircle 10");
      }
   } /// main
   public static double area (int rad) {
      double pi=3.1415927;
      double areacircle=pi*rad*rad;
      return areacircle;
   } /// area
} /// AreaOfCircleWhile
```

In this listing, the area method and the exception-handling blocks are unchanged from the prior example. The change is in the main method:

```
int input=Integer.parseInt(args[0]);
while (input < 7) {
    double result=area(input);
    System.out.println(result);
    input++;
}
```

While the input value is less than 7, the input value will be processed. After the area for that radius value has been calculated and printed, the input value is incremented:

```
input++;
```

Then the loop is evaluated again. Sample output is shown in the following listing:

```
javac AreaOfCircleWhile.java
java AreaOfCircleWhile 4

50.2654832
78.5398175
113.0973372
```

The output shows the area calculations for input radius values of 4, 5, and 6.

This example is not as complete as a finished program—you may need additional exception handling to handle nonintegers, for example—but the structure is the important lesson to learn from this example. In addition to the methods shown in this example, you could create a constructor for the AreaOfCircleWhile class. All Java classes have constructors (see Chapter 31) to initialize new objects based on the class. The constructor's name is the same as the name of the class. If you create a class with no constructor, Java will create a default constructor at run time. Like a method, the constructor body can contain local variable declarations, loops, and statement blocks. The constructor initializes these variables for the class.

In the following chapters, you will see how to implement Java within Oracle—within stored procedures and via JDBC. Those chapters assume that you have the basic knowledge of Java provided in this chapter. For additional information about the Java language, see the Sun Microsystems Web site and the variety of books devoted to Java.

CHAPTER
38

JDBC Programming

ava Database Connectivity (JDBC) builds on the Java and programming basics described earlier in this book. The discussions and examples in this chapter assume you are familiar with the Java syntax and structures described in Chapter 37. This chapter does not cover every aspect of JDBC but focuses on its basic configuration and usage.

You can use JDBC to execute dynamic SQL statements in Java programs. Oracle provides sample files on the Companion disc that accompanies the Oracle software installation. The Companion disc uses the Oracle Universal Installer to load software drivers and demonstration files, including those supporting JDBC development. Following installation of the Companion disc, the JDBC examples will be in a file named demo.zip in the /jdbc/demo subdirectory under the Oracle software home directory; when unzipped, the files referred to in this chapter will be located in the /jdbc/demo/samples/generic directory.

The following listing is from the SelectExample.java demo file. The SelectExample.java demo issues the following commands after establishing a database connection:

```
// Create a Statement
Statement stmt = conn.createStatement ();

// Select first_name and last_name column from the employees table
ResultSet rset = stmt.executeQuery ("select FIRST_NAME, "
                          + "LAST_NAME from EMPLOYEES");

// Iterate through the result and print the employee names
while (rset.next ())
   System.out.println (rset.getString (1) + " " + rset.getString (2));
```

When you execute a SQL statement via JDBC—in this case, **select First_Name, Last_Name from EMPLOYEES**—the SQL statement is not checked for errors until it is run. The JDBC program that contains the SQL command will compile even if the SQL statement is invalid.

Getting Started

To use the examples in this section, you need a copy of the Java Development Kit (JDK), which is installed during the Oracle Database Companion CD installation process.

Additional Steps for Windows Users

If you will be accessing Oracle via JDBC, you must set the CLASSPATH environment variable to find the classes12.zip file provided by Oracle. The file is located in the /jdbc/lib directory beneath your Oracle home directory, or it's available for download from http://technet.oracle.com. You must also check the setting of your PATH environment variable.

NOTE
Setting the CLASSPATH environment variable is not performed by the standard Oracle installation, so you need to do it manually. If the system variables are not properly set, you will not be able to compile Java classes that use Oracle's JDBC classes. The system variable setting procedure differs by operating system version. In Windows 2000, use the System icon under the Control Panel to add and edit environment variable settings.

Create an environment variable named CLASSPATH if it doesn't already exist (it won't for an initial Java setup). This variable must have two entries, separated by a semicolon. The first entry must be a period, which denotes the current directory. The second entry must be the directory for the classes12.zip file:

```
.;E:\oracle\ora10\jdbc\lib\classes12.zip
```

If CLASSPATH is not set correctly, you will get a NoClassDefFoundError error when you run a compiled class.

NOTE
Be sure to use a version of the JDK that is compatible with the Oracle release you are using. If you use a new release of the JDK with an older release of Oracle's drivers, you may encounter "access violation" errors when executing your programs.

The PATH environment variable should already be set; append the following entry to its value:

```
;E:\oracle\ora10\jdbc\lib\classes12.zip
```

Replace "E:\oracle\ora10" with your Oracle software home directory.

Testing Your Connection

Oracle provides a sample program called JdbcCheckup.java that you can use to verify your JDBC configuration. This file may be in a zip file (demo.zip on the /jdbc/demo directory) or in /jdbc/demo/samples/generic if you have unzipped it. You will need to extract it before running the program. Go to the directory where the sample file is, then compile and execute the JdbcCheckup.java class:

```
javac JdbcCheckup.java
java JdbcCheckup
```

NOTE
Java commands are case sensitive. When you execute JdbcCheckup, you are prompted for a username, password, and connect string for a database. That connection information will be used to attempt a connection; if successful, that attempt will return the following output:

```
Connecting to the database...Connecting...
connected.
Hello World.
Your JDBC installation is correct.
```

If you don't receive feedback telling you that your installation is correct, you need to check your configuration. Common problems include incorrectly set environment variables (PATH and CLASSPATH) and mismatched versions of database connection drivers. If you change the environment variable values, you need to shut down and restart the command windows for the changes to take effect.

Using the JDBC Classes

JDBC is implemented in Oracle via a set of Oracle-provided classes whose names begin with oracle.sql, whereas the standard JDBC classes provided with the JDK begin with java.sql. The JdbcCheckup.java class, shown in the following listing, provides a good roadmap for beginning JDBC programmers. The JdbcCheckup.java class assumes you are using Oracle Net to connect to the database.

NOTE
The following code is provided by Oracle. Your programming standards may implement these commands differently, such as by calling System.out.println in place of System.out.print, or by placing the brackets in different places.

```
/*
 * This sample can be used to check the JDBC installation.
 * Just run it and provide the connect information.  It will select
 * "Hello World" from the database.
 *
 * note: jdk1.2 or later version is recommended.
 */

// You need to import the java.sql package to use JDBC
import java.sql.*;

// We import java.io to be able to read from the command line
import java.io.*;

import oracle.jdbc.pool.OracleDataSource;

class JdbcCheckup
{
  public static void main (String args [])
       throws SQLException, IOException
  {
    // Prompt the user for connect information
    System.out.println ("Please enter information to test connection to the
database");
    String user;
    String password;
    String database;

    user = readEntry ("user: ");
    int slash_index = user.indexOf ('/');
    if (slash_index != -1)
    {
      password = user.substring (slash_index + 1);
      user = user.substring (0, slash_index);
    }
```

```
else
  password = readEntry ("password: ");
database = readEntry ("database (a TNSNAME entry, name-value pairs): ");

// Create an OracleDataSource and set URL
OracleDataSource ods = new OracleDataSource();
ods.setURL("jdbc:oracle:oci8:" + user + "/" + password + "@" + database);

System.out.print ("Connecting to the database...");
System.out.flush ();

// Connect to the database
// You can put a database name after the @ sign in the connection URL.

System.out.println ("Connecting...");
Connection conn = ods.getConnection();

System.out.println ("connected.");

// Create a statement
Statement stmt = conn.createStatement ();

// Do the SQL "Hello World" thing
ResultSet rset = stmt.executeQuery ("select 'Hello World' from dual");

while (rset.next ())
  System.out.println (rset.getString (1));

System.out.println ("Your JDBC installation is correct.");

// close the resultSet
rset.close();

// Close the statement
stmt.close();

// Close the connection
conn.close();
}

// Utility function to read a line from standard input
static String readEntry (String prompt)
{
  try
  {
    StringBuffer buffer = new StringBuffer ();
    System.out.print (prompt);
    System.out.flush ();
    int c = System.in.read ();
    while (c != '\n' && c != -1)
```

```
    {
      buffer.append ((char)c);
      c = System.in.read ();
    }
    return buffer.toString ().trim ();
  }
  catch (IOException e)
  {
    return "";
  }
 }
}
```

NOTE
Production applications would be expected to include many more exception-handling sections than shown in this brief example. See Chapter 37 for an example of exception handling.

Starting at the top, this script first imports the java.sql classes provided by Sun Microsystems:

```
import java.sql.*;
```

The Oracle-provided data source driver is then imported:

```
import oracle.jdbc.pool.OracleDataSource;
```

When you are prompted for information, the *user* variable is populated via a call to the readEntry function:

```
    user = readEntry ("user: ");
```

The readEntry function is defined later in the class, in the section beginning

```
    // Utility function to read a line from standard input
    static String readEntry (String prompt)
```

Once the connection data has been input, a *connection object* is created to maintain the state of the database session, based on the OracleDataSource definition. The getConnection call in the following listing starts the connection:

```
    Connection conn = ods.getConnection();
```

If you receive an error during the connection, this step is usually the cause. An incorrect username/password combination, a mismatched set of drivers, or failure to install and configure Oracle Net will cause this step to fail.

By default, a connection object is created with **autocommit** turned on—every transaction is automatically committed. To change that setting, you can use the following command (assuming you name the connection object conn, as shown in the example):

```
conn.setAutoCommit(false);
```

The class then creates a statement, executes a hard-coded query, and prints the output:

```
    // Create a statement
    Statement stmt = conn.createStatement ();

    // Do the SQL "Hello World" thing
    ResultSet rset = stmt.executeQuery ("select 'Hello World' from dual");

    while (rset.next ())
      System.out.println (rset.getString (1));
```

The result set, statement, and connection are then closed and the program completes. Note that there are two steps in executing the statement: First, it's created via the call to the createStatement method. Second, it's executed via the executeQuery method. In place of executeQuery, you can use execute or, if you're running an **insert**, **update**, or **delete** SQL statement, executeUpdate. If you select a column value (instead of just a text string), you should specify that column value in the print command, as shown in the following listing:

```
  ResultSet rset =stmt.executeQuery("select User from dual");
 while (rset.next ()) {
    System.out.println (rset.getString ("USER"));
```

Using JDBC for Data Manipulation

Let's combine the pieces that have been described so far—the basic connection syntax from this chapter with the Java classes from Chapter 37. The example in this section will query the RADIUS_VALS table, calculate an area for each value, and insert those values into the AREAS table. Therefore, it requires the use of the Java equivalent of a Cursor FOR loop, along with support for executable commands and **insert**s.

For the example, put three records into the RADIUS_VALS table and delete any rows in the AREAS table:

```
delete from RADIUS_VALS;
insert into RADIUS_VALS(Radius) values (3);
insert into RADIUS_VALS(Radius) values (4);
insert into RADIUS_VALS(Radius) values (10);
delete from AREAS;
commit;
```

The following listing, JdbcCircle.java, contains the connection components from JdbcCheckup .java. The executable commands for the circle area start in the section called RetrieveRadius, shown in bold in the listing.

```
// You need to import the java.sql package to use JDBC
import java.sql.*;
// We import java.io to be able to read from the command line
import java.io.*;
```

```java
import oracle.jdbc.pool.OracleDataSource;

class JdbcCircle {

  public static void main (String args [])
        throws SQLException, IOException {

    // Prompt the user for connect information
    System.out.println ("Please enter information for connection");
    String user;
    String password;
    String database;

    user = readEntry ("user: ");
    int slash_index = user.indexOf ('/');
    if (slash_index != -1) {

      password = user.substring (slash_index + 1);
      user = user.substring (0, slash_index);
    }
    else {
      password = readEntry ("password: ");
    }
    database = readEntry ("database (a TNSNAME entry): ");
    System.out.println ("Connecting to the database...");

    // Create an OracleDataSource and set URL
    OracleDataSource ods = new OracleDataSource();
    ods.setURL("jdbc:oracle:oci8:" + user + "/" + password + "@" + database);
    System.out.flush ();

    // Connect to the database
    // You can put a database name after the @ sign in the connection URL.

    Connection conn = ods.getConnection();

    System.out.println ("connected.");

    // Create a statement
    Statement stmt = conn.createStatement ();

    // RetrieveRadius
    ResultSet rset =stmt.executeQuery("select Radius from RADIUS_VALS");

    while (rset.next ())  {
      // if you wish to print the values:
      // System.out.println (rset.getInt ("RADIUS"));
      int radInput =  rset.getInt ("RADIUS");
```

```
      // Retrieve Radius value, calculate area:
      double result = area(radInput);

      // insert the value into AREAS
      String sql = "insert into AREAS values ("+radInput+","+result+ ")";
      // If you want to print the SQL statement:
      // System.out.println(sql);

      // Create a statement for the insert:
      Statement insArea = conn.createStatement();
      // Execute the insert:
      boolean insertResult = insArea.execute(sql);
    }

    // close the resultSet
    rset.close();
    // Close the statement
    stmt.close();
    // Close the connection
    conn.close();
  }

// Utility function to calculate the area
public static double area (int rad) {
   double pi=3.1415927;
   double areacircle=pi*rad*rad;
   return areacircle;
}

// Utility function to read a line from standard input
static String readEntry (String prompt) {

   try {
     StringBuffer buffer = new StringBuffer ();
     System.out.print (prompt);
     System.out.flush ();
     int c = System.in.read ();
     while (c != '\n' && c != -1) {

       buffer.append ((char)c);
       c = System.in.read ();
     }
     return buffer.toString ().trim ();
   }
   catch (IOException e) {
     return "";
   }
 }
}
```

In the RetrieveRadius section, the query to be executed is passed to the executeQuery method. The result of the query is stored in a variable named *rset*.

```
// RetrieveRadius
    ResultSet rset =stmt.executeQuery("select Radius from RADIUS_VALS");
```

As noted in Chapter 37, you can use a WHILE loop in Java to approximate the functionality of a PL/SQL Cursor FOR loop. The following part of the RetrieveRadius section uses the getInt method to retrieve the integer Radius value from the result set. If the value had been a string, the getString method would have been used instead.

```
    while (rset.next ())  {
    // if you wish to print the values:
    // System.out.println (rset.getInt ("RADIUS"));
    int radInput =  rset.getInt ("RADIUS");
```

The *radInput* variable, assigned in the preceding listing, can now be used as input to the area calculation. The area calculation is performed via a utility function (see the full JdbcCircle listing) based on the code examples presented in Chapter 37.

```
// Retrieve Radius value, calculate area:
    double result = area(radInput);
```

We now have the radius value (the *radInput* variable) and the area value (the *result* variable) to use when populating the AREAS table. Let's build the **insert** statement to perform the insert. First, use the string concatenation functions in Java to concatenate text with the variable values. Make sure not to include a semicolon at the end of the generated command string.

```
    // insert the value into AREAS
    String sql = "insert into AREAS values ("+radInput+","+result+ ")";
    // If you want to print the SQL statement:
    // System.out.println(sql);
```

Next, create a statement and execute the **insert** command (via a call to the *sql* variable that contains the command text):

```
    // Create a statement for the insert:
    Statement insArea = conn.createStatement();
    // Execute the insert:
    boolean insertResult = insArea.execute(sql);
```

Did it work? Compile and execute the JdbcCircle.java file:

```
javac JdbcCircle.java
java JdbcCircle
```

When prompted, provide a username and password for the owner of the RADIUS_VALS and AREAS tables. After the program completes, check the AREAS table:

```
select * from AREAS
  order by Radius;

    RADIUS       AREA
--------- ---------
        3      28.27
        4      50.27
       10     314.16
```

This example is based on a simple calculation—the area of a circle—but it illustrates the key concepts in JDBC development: connecting to the database, retrieving data, implementing a Cursor FOR loop, assigning variables, generating a dynamic SQL statement, and executing DML.

JDBC supports extensive programming features, including statement caching, connection caching, connection failover, distributed transactions, support for LOBs, and more. See the *Oracle Database JDBC Developer's Guide and Reference* for further details on the use of JDBC.

CHAPTER
39

Java Stored
Procedures

ou can write stored procedures, triggers, object type methods, and functions that call Java classes. In this chapter, you will see a sample set of Java procedures, along with the commands required to execute a procedure. To get the most from this chapter, you should already be familiar with Java structures (refer to Chapter 37) and the uses of Java classes and JDBC (Chapter 38). You should also be familiar with the basic syntax and usage of stored procedures (refer to Chapter 31).

To focus on the database access operations of the Java classes, the example in this chapter is brief. The following class, called BookshelfDML, contains methods to insert and delete records from the BOOKSHELF table. In this example, the calculation of the area is not performed; rather, all required values are supplied during the **insert**. The following listing shows the BookshelfDML.java file:

```java
import java.sql.*;
import java.io.*;
import oracle.jdbc.*;

public class BookshelfDML {
  public static void insertBookshelf (String title, String publisher,
    String categoryname, String rating) throws SQLException {
    String sql = "INSERT INTO BOOKSHELF VALUES (?,?,?,?)";
    try {
      Connection conn =
        DriverManager.getConnection("jdbc:default:connection:");
      PreparedStatement pstmt = conn.prepareStatement(sql);
      pstmt.setString(1, title);
      pstmt.setString(2, publisher);
      pstmt.setString(3, categoryname);
      pstmt.setString(4, rating);
      pstmt.executeUpdate();
      pstmt.close();
    } catch (SQLException e) {System.err.println(e.getMessage());}
  }

  public static void updateBookshelf (String rating,
    String title) throws SQLException {
    String sql = "UPDATE BOOKSHELF SET Rating = ? " +
      "WHERE Title = ? ";
    try {
      Connection conn =
        DriverManager.getConnection("jdbc:default:connection:");
      PreparedStatement pstmt = conn.prepareStatement(sql);
      pstmt.setString(1, rating);
      pstmt.setString(2, title);
      pstmt.executeUpdate();
      pstmt.close();
    } catch (SQLException e) {System.err.println(e.getMessage());}
  }
```

```
public static void deleteBookshelf (String title) throws SQLException {
    String sql = "DELETE FROM BOOKSHELF WHERE TITLE = ?";
    try {
      Connection conn =
        DriverManager.getConnection("jdbc:default:connection:");
      PreparedStatement pstmt = conn.prepareStatement(sql);
      pstmt.setString(1, title);
      pstmt.executeUpdate();
      pstmt.close();
    } catch (SQLException e) {System.err.println(e.getMessage());}
  }
}
```

The BookshelfDML.java file defines the BookshelfDML class. Within the BookshelfDML class, there are separate methods for processing **insert**s, **update**s, and **delete**s. In each of the method specifications, the datatypes for the BOOKSHELF table's related columns are specified (in this example, they are all VARCHAR2 datatypes).

These parameters use the datatypes provided as part of Oracle's class libraries. If you use the standard Java datatypes, you may encounter datatype-related problems during the class execution.

The next part of the insert method inserts the values into the BOOKSHELF table:

```
String sql = "INSERT INTO BOOKSHELF VALUES (?,?,?,?)";
```

The four variables are defined via setString (setInt would have been used for integers):

```
pstmt.setString(1, title);
pstmt.setString(2, publisher);
pstmt.setString(3, categoryname);
pstmt.setString(4, rating);
```

Note that the variable names are case sensitive—they must exactly match the names declared earlier.

The delete method is very similar in structure. Its SQL statement is

```
String sql = "DELETE FROM BOOKSHELF WHERE TITLE = ?";
```

Note that no part of the class creates a connection to the database, in contrast with the examples in Chapter 38. The connection used to invoke this class will provide the connection context for the class's methods.

You can verify that the class compiles properly by processing it via the Java compiler. Note that this step will not validate your SQL:

```
javac BookshelfDML.java
```

This step should complete successfully. If you encounter errors during this compilation step, check your environment configuration (see Chapter 38) and your class file.

Loading the Class into the Database

You can use the loadjava utility to load the class into the database. The syntax for the loadjava utility is as follows:

```
loadjava {-user | -u} username/password[@database]
    [-option_name -option_name ...] filename filename ...
```

The options available for the loadjava utility are shown in Table 39-1.

Option	Description
<filenames>	Any number and combination of .java, .class, .sqlj, .ser, .jar, .zip, and resource filename arguments, in any order.
andresolve	Compiles source files and resolves each class file as it is loaded.
debug	Generates debugging information.
definer	Specifies that the methods of uploaded classes will execute with the privileges of their definer, not their invoker. By default, methods execute with the privileges of their invoker.
encoding	Sets (or resets) the option *-encoding* in the database table JAVA$OPTIONS to the specified value.
fileout	Prints messages to an output file.
force	Forces the loading of Java class files regardless of whether they have been loaded before. By default, previously loaded class files are rejected.
grant	Grants EXECUTE privilege on uploaded classes to the listed users and roles.
help	Prints loadjava help text.
javaresource	Directs loadjava to load a JAR file without unpacking it.
nousage	Suppresses the usage message given if either no option is specified or the *-help* option is specified.
noserverside	Changes the behavior of the server-side loadjava tool to use a JDBC driver to access objects.
noverify	Causes the classes to be loaded without bytecode verification. You must be granted oracle.aurora.security.JServerPermission(Verifier) to execute this option. In addition, this option must be used in conjunction with *-r*.
oci8	Directs loadjava to communicate with the database using the OCI JDBC driver. This option (the default) and *-thin* are mutually exclusive.
resolve	Resolves all external references in the loaded and compiled classes. If this option is not specified, files are loaded but not compiled or resolved until run time.

TABLE 39-1. *Loadjava Options*

Option	Description
resolver	Binds newly created class schema objects to a user-defined resolver spec.
schema	Specifies the schema for newly created objects.
stdout	Causes the output to be directed to stdout, rather than to stderr.
synonym	Automatically creates a public synonym for the uploaded classes.
tableschema	Creates the loadjava internal tables within this specified schema, rather than in the Java file destination schema.
thin	Directs loadjava to communicate with the database using the thin JDBC driver. This option and -oci8 are mutually exclusive.
time	Prints a timestamp on every message.
unresolvedok	When combined with -resolve, this option ignores unresolved errors.
user	Specifies a user, password, and database connect string for the load.
verbose	Enables the display of progress messages during loadjava execution.

TABLE 39-1. *Loadjava Options* (continued)

For example, to load the BookshelfDML.java file into the Practice schema in an instance named "orcl," you can use the following command:

```
loadjava -u Practice/practice@orcl.world -verbose BookshelfDML.java
```

You should see a series of comments related to the loading of the class into the database. If any errors are reported, the load will not complete.

NOTE
The name of the class should not match the name of any of the existing objects in your schema.

The AreasDML class is now loaded into the database. During the load, Oracle will create multiple tables and Java objects within your schema.

NOTE
*You can load Java files manually from local BFILE or LOB columns via the **create java [source | class | resource]** commands.*

If you are running your database on a standalone server and you have not defined a service name for the database, you will need to specify a full connection specification for the loadjava program call. The format will be

```
loadjava -u practice/practice@localhost:1521:orcl -v BookshelfDML.java
```

How to Access the Class

Now that the BookshelfDML class has been loaded into the database, you must create a procedure to call each of the methods. The **create procedure** command in the following listing creates a procedure called InsertBookshelfViaJava:

```
create or replace procedure InsertBookshelfViaJava
(Title VARCHAR2, Publisher VARCHAR2,
 CategoryName VARCHAR2, Rating VARCHAR2 )
as
language java
name 'BookshelfDML.insertBookshelf(java.lang.String, java.lang.String,
java.lang.String, java.lang.String)';
/
```

This brief procedure has four parameters—the four columns of the BOOKSHELF table. Its **language java** clause tells Oracle that the procedure is calling a Java method. The name of the method is specified in the **name** clause (be sure to be consistent with your use of capital letters). The formats for the Java method call are then specified.

A separate procedure will delete the BOOKSHELF table's records via a method call:

```
create or replace procedure DeleteBookshelfViaJava
(Title VARCHAR2 )
as
language java
name 'BookshelfDML.deleteBookshelf(java.lang.String)';
/
```

A third procedure will update the Rating value based on Title:

```
create or replace procedure UpdateBookshelfViaJava
(Rating VARCHAR2, Title VARCHAR2 )
as
language java
name 'BookshelfDML.updateBookshelf(java.lang.String, java.lang.String)';
/
```

Now, go into SQL*Plus and use the **call** command to execute the Java classes:

```
call InsertBookshelfViaJava('TEST','TESTPub','ADULTNF','2');
```

You will see this response:

```
Call completed.
```

Instead of using **call**, you can execute the procedure within a PL/SQL block:

```
begin
   InsertBookshelfViaJava('TEST','TESTPub','ADULTNF','2');
end;
/
```

The **call** command will pass the column values as parameters to the InsertBookshelfViaJava stored procedure. It will format them according to the specifications in the **name** clause and will pass them to the BookshelfDML.insertBookshelf method. That method will use your current connection to execute its commands, and the row will be inserted. Most of these libraries and classes will not have been loaded yet within the database. That's a lot of steps to go through, so performance will be affected the first time you run the Java stored procedure, but subsequent executions will be much faster. You can verify its success by querying the BOOKSHELF table:

```
column Title format a10
select * from BOOKSHELF where Title like 'TEST';
```

TITLE	PUBLISHER	CATEGORYNAME	RA
TEST	TESTPub	ADULTNF	2

You can update the rating via UpdateBookshelfViaJava:

```
begin
   UpdateBookshelfViaJava('3','TEST');
end;
/

select * from BOOKSHELF where Title like 'TEST';
```

TITLE	PUBLISHER	CATEGORYNAME	RA
TEST	TESTPub	ADULTNF	3

And you can delete that record via a call to DeleteBookshelfViaJava:

```
begin
   DeleteBookshelfViaJava('TEST');
end;
/

select * from BOOKSHELF where Title like 'TEST';

no rows selected
```

The call to DeleteBookshelfViaJava will complete much faster than the call to InsertBookshelfViaJava, because your Java libraries will have been loaded the first time you executed InsertBookshelfViaJava.

If your insert is not acceptable—for example, if you attempt to insert a character string into a NUMBER datatype column—Oracle will display an error. When debugging Java stored procedures, you can call System.err.println from within your Java code, as shown in the BookshelfDML.java listing earlier in this chapter. To display the output within your SQL*Plus session, you must first execute the following commands:

```
set serveroutput on
call DBMS_JAVA.SET_OUTPUT(10000);
```

Calling DBMS_JAVA.SET_OUTPUT will redirect the output of System.out.println to DBMS_OUTPUT.PUT_LINE.

Calling Java Stored Procedures Directly

As of Oracle Database 10g, Oracle provides an application programming interface (API) to support direct invocation of static Java stored procedures. The classes for this method are found in the oracle.jpub.reflect package, so you must import this package into your client-side code. The Java interface for the API is

```
public class Client
{
    public static String getSignature(Class[]);
    public static Object invoke(Connection, String, String,
                                String, Object[]);
    public static Object invoke(Connection, String, String,
                                Class[], Object[]);
}
```

When accessed via this API, the procedures' arguments cannot be OUT or IN OUT. Returned values must all be part of the function result. Note that the method invocation will use invoker's rights. See the Java developer's guides that accompany the Oracle software installation for further details on the API.

Where to Perform Commands

The BookshelfDML example is intended to provide an overview of the implementation of Java stored procedures. Suppose you now want to make the procedures more complex, involving additional tables and calculations. As shown in Chapters 29, 37, and 38, you can perform those calculations either in Java or in PL/SQL.

Your choice of a platform and language for your data processing will impact your performance. In general, you will pay a performance penalty the first time you execute a Java stored procedure (as the classes are loaded), but subsequent executions will not pay the same penalty. If you repeatedly execute the same commands, the performance impact of the first execution will be minimal.

Logging out and logging back in impacts your performance, but not nearly as much as the first execution of the procedure. When you use Java stored procedures, you must be aware of the way in which the application interacts with Oracle. If your users frequently log out and log back in, they will pay a performance penalty the first time they execute the procedure following each login. Furthermore, the first execution of the procedure following a database startup will pay the most severe performance penalty. The performance impact of these actions must be taken into account during the design stage of your application development.

Here are some tips to reduce the performance penalties associated with the Java stored procedure calls:

- Execute each Java stored procedure following database startup. In the case of the BookshelfDML example, this may involve inserting and deleting a test record following each startup.

- Reduce the number of short-term database connections (for example, by connection pooling).

- Perform most of your direct database manipulation via standard SQL and PL/SQL.

Java is an appropriate technology to use for many computational processes and for display manipulation. In general, SQL and PL/SQL are slightly more efficient than Java for database connections and data manipulation. However, the performance of Java within Oracle makes it a strong alternative to PL/SQL; the primary source of the performance penalty for Java stored procedures is the time required to go through the PL/SQL wrapper. When designing applications that integrate Java, SQL, and PL/SQL, focus on using each language for the functions that it performs best.

If your code involves many loops and manipulations of data, Java may outperform PL/SQL. The costs of using Java—for Java object creation and the PL/SQL header interaction—may be offset by the improved performance Java yields during the actual work. Note that the compiled native PL/SQL available in Oracle Database 10g should provide a strong alternative to Java from a performance perspective.

In general, actions that involve selecting data from the database and manipulating it are best handled by PL/SQL and SQL. Computations on the selected data may be processed faster by Java. In your application design, be sure to use the proper tool for the proper function, and avoid unnecessary performance penalties.

PART
VII

Clustered Oracle—
The Grid

CHAPTER
40

Oracle Real
Application Clusters

n an Oracle Real Application Clusters (RAC) environment, multiple instances access a single database. The instances are commonly created on separate servers that are connected via a high-speed interconnect with access to a shared disk area. The database files reside on a shared set of disks, and each instance has its own control files and online redo log files that are also stored on the shared disks.

A user can be directed to connect to the database through one of the instances attached to it; if an instance goes down, the connection may be dynamically reconnected to the database via another instance in the cluster. RAC thus provides a high-availability solution (accounting for server and instance failure) and a scalable high-performance solution (by increasing the memory and processors available to the connecting processes).

In this chapter, you will see an overview of the installation and management of RAC. Many of the details are operating-system–specific, but the configuration process flow will be the same across platforms. The focus of this chapter will be the common processes and the features introduced in Oracle Database 10g to enhance RAC management and implementation.

Preinstallation Steps

Before starting the Oracle RAC installation, you need to verify that your environment and cluster are properly configured to support it. The servers that will host the instances are referred to as nodes in the cluster. Each of the nodes should have external shared disks. Each node should have redundant switches to support failover requirements. Each node should have one private Internet Protocol (IP) address for private connections and one public IP address for client connections and connection failovers from other nodes. Oracle Database 10g provides a tool called VIPCA (Virtual IP Configuration Assistant) to support the configuration of your IP addresses.

Each node must support TCP/IP (Transmission Control Protocol/Internet Protocol) and a supported interconnect software protocol.

NOTE
You must choose an interconnect that is supported by Oracle. See the Metalink site (http://metalink.oracle.com) for the latest certification matrix.

Oracle provides clusterware, simplifying the installation and configuration process. Installation steps related to the clusterware configuration are described in Chapter 41. For the shared disk area, Oracle recommends the use of its Automatic Storage Management feature (see Chapter 46).

NOTE
Be sure to install all required patches on the operating system prior to starting the installation process. As part of your standard Oracle software installation procedures, you should review all required operating system patch levels.

Installing RAC

The installation of RAC in Oracle Database 10g is a two-step process. In the first step, use the Oracle Universal Installer (OUI) to install CRS (Cluster Ready Services). CRS, available as of Oracle

Database 10*g*, provides an integrated set of solutions for cluster management. You can use CRS to manage cluster membership, group services, group resource management, and high-availability configuration. You can use CRS to define services that support distributing workload across servers. The Automatic Workload Repository (AWR) collects statistics on the services; see Chapter 46 for further details on AWR.

NOTE
RAC works with vendor-supported clusterware as well as Oracle's clusterware. While users of earlier versions of RAC may already have a third-party solution in place, this chapter focuses on Oracle's offering.

NOTE
*RAC is available with both the Standard Edition and the Enterprise Edition of Oracle Database 10*g.

Both steps of the installation process use the OUI; see Chapter 2 for details on OUI. After completing the first step (installation of the CRS), you can begin the second step of the installation: installing the Oracle Database 10*g* software with RAC in a different Oracle home directory than you used in the first step. You should also use the installer to create and configure services for your RAC environment. After your software installation completes, OUI will start the Database Configuration Assistant to complete environment configuration and create the RAC database.

NOTE
*If you have installed a previous Oracle clustered database version, the Database Upgrade Assistant (DBUA) will upgrade your database to the Release 10*g *version of RAC.*

Storage

As of Oracle Database 10*g*, you can use Automatic Storage Management (ASM) to create disk groups and simplify their management. As described in Chapter 46, database administrators can add new disks to disk groups; Oracle will manage the contents and the distribution of the files among the disks involved.

You can use ASM to provide redundancy from within Oracle if there is no hardware redundancy available. When you define the disk group, you can specify a failure group; Oracle will use the failure group as a redundant version of the primary group of disks in the disk group. Oracle's installation programs refer to the software-based redundancy as "normal" redundancy. You can specify multiple failure groups for additional redundant protection (at the cost of additional space). If hardware mirroring is available, you can use external (file-system–based) redundancy.

Many RAC environments use a combination of raw devices and logical volume management software. Logical volume management (LVM) provides a file-system management interface to raw devices.

You can use ASM disk groups to further reduce the management complexity of the RAC database—Oracle manages the files and the file systems. You can administer the files and disk groups manually or via Oracle Enterprise Manager (OEM)'s Grid Control options (see Chapter 41).

Initialization Parameters

As part of configuring the instances, you must set values for the database initialization parameters maintained in the server parameter file. RAC installations should use the server parameter file to manage the set of parameters shared by the instances.

The initialization parameters listed in Table 40-1 must have the same value for all instances in the RAC cluster, along with their descriptions from Oracle.

Parameter	Description
ACTIVE_INSTANCE_COUNT	Enables you to designate one instance in a two-instance cluster as the primary instance and the other instance as the secondary instance. This parameter has no functionality in a cluster with more than two instances. When you set this parameter to 1, the first instance you start up becomes the primary instance and accepts client connections. The second instance starts up as a secondary instance and can accept client connections only if the first instance fails. In such an event, the secondary instance becomes the primary instance.
CLUSTER_DATABASE	True/false flag that specifies whether or not Real Application Clusters is enabled. Set to TRUE.
CONTROL_FILES	Specifies one or more names of control files, separated by commas.
DB_BLOCK_SIZE	Specifies (in bytes) the size of Oracle database blocks.
DB_DOMAIN	Specifies the logical location of the database within the network structure. The value consists of the extension components of a global database name, consisting of valid identifiers, separated by periods.
DB_FILES	Specifies the maximum number of database files that can be opened for this database. The maximum valid value is the maximum number of files, subject to operating-system constraint, that will ever be specified for the database, including files to be added by **add datafile** commands. If you increase the value of DB_FILES, then you must shut down and restart all instances accessing the database before the new value can take effect. If you have a primary and standby database, then they should have the same value for this parameter.
DB_NAME	Specifies a database identifier of up to eight characters. This parameter must be specified and must correspond to the name specified in the **create database** command.
DB_RECOVERY_FILE_DEST	Specifies the default location for the flash recovery area. The flash recovery area contains multiplexed copies of current control files and online redo logs, as well as archived redo logs, flashback logs, and RMAN backups. Specifying this parameter without also specifying the DB_RECOVERY_FILE_DEST_SIZE initialization parameter is not allowed.

TABLE 40-1. *Initialization Parameters with the Same Values Across RAC Instances*

Parameter	Description
DB_RECOVERY_FILE_DEST_SIZE	Specifies (in bytes) the hard limit on the total space to be used by target database recovery files created in the flash recovery area.
DB_UNIQUE_NAME	Specifies a globally unique name for the database. Every database's DB_UNIQUE_NAME must be unique within the enterprise.
MAX_COMMIT_PROPAGATION_DELAY	This initialization parameter should not be changed except under a limited set of circumstances specific to the cluster database. This parameter specifies the maximum amount of time allowed before the system change number (SCN) held in the SGA of an instance is refreshed by the log writer process (LGWR). It determines whether the local SCN should be refreshed from the lock value when getting the snapshot SCN for a query. Units are in hundredths of seconds. Under very unusual circumstances involving rapid updates and queries of the same data from different instances, the SCN might not be refreshed in a timely manner. Setting the parameter to zero causes the SCN to be refreshed immediately after a commit. The default value (700 hundredths of a second, or seven seconds) is an upper bound that allows the preferred existing high-performance mechanism to remain in place.
SPFILE	Names the current server parameter file (SPFILE) in use. This parameter can be defined in a client-side PFILE to indicate the name of the server parameter file to use. When the default server parameter file is used by the server, the value of SPFILE is internally set by the server.
TRACE_ENABLED	True/false flag that ontrols tracing of the execution history, or code path, of Oracle. When this parameter is set to TRUE, Oracle records information in log files when errors occur. Oracle records this information for all instances, even if only one instance terminates.
UNDO_MANAGEMENT	Specifies which undo space management mode the system should use. When set to AUTO, the instance starts in automatic undo management mode. In manual undo management mode, undo space is allocated externally as rollback segments.

TABLE 40-1. *Initialization Parameters with the Same Values Across RAC Instances* (continued)

NOTE
The setting for DML_LOCKS must be identical for all instances only if set to 0.

Table 40-2 lists the initialization parameters that must have unique values for each instance in the RAC cluster, along with their descriptions from Oracle.

Parameter	Description
INSTANCE_NUMBER	Specifies a unique number that maps the instance to one free list group for each database object created with storage parameter FREELIST GROUPS.
ROLLBACK_SEGMENTS	Allocates one or more rollback segments by name to this instance. When UNDO_MANAGEMENT is set to AUTO, ROLLBACK_SEGMENTS is ignored.
THREAD	If specified, this parameter must have unique values on all instances. The THREAD parameter specifies the number of the redo thread to be used by an instance. You can specify any available redo thread number as long as that thread number is enabled and is not used.
UNDO_TABLESPACE	Specifies the undo tablespace to be used when an instance starts up. If this parameter is specified when the instance is in manual undo management mode, then an error will occur and startup will fail.

TABLE 40-2. *Initialization Parameters with Distinct Values Across RAC Instances*

NOTE
Within an instance, set INSTANCE_NUMBER and THREAD to the same value.

In addition to the parameters shown in the preceding tables, you should specify values for the following initialization parameters:

Parameter	Description
CLUSTER_DATABASE_INSTANCES	Sets the number of instances in the RAC environment.
DISPATCHERS	Sets DISPATCHERS to enable a shared server configuration (in which multiple user processes connect to a dispatcher).

Starting and Stopping RAC Instances

You can use Grid Control to manage all of the instances associated with a RAC database. You can stop, start, and monitor databases, instances, and their listeners via Grid Control. As with any non-RAC database, you can use SQL*Plus to issue **shutdown** and **startup** commands. For RAC databases you can also use the SRVCTL utility, as shown in the examples in this section.

Regardless of the tool used to shut down or start the instance, the following rules apply to RAC clusters:

- Shutting down an instance does not affect the operation of other running instances.
- Shutting down a database mounted in shared mode requires that you shut down every instance in the RAC cluster.

- After a **shutdown normal** or a **shutdown immediate**, no instance recovery is needed. If you use **shutdown abort** on a RAC instance, a still-running instance performs instance recovery for the shutdown instance. If the aborted instance was the last one running, the next instance to start will perform the recovery.

- If you use **shutdown transactional** with the **local** option, all transactions in the instance will have to be either committed or rolled back prior to the shutdown. Transactions on other instances do not impact the local **shutdown transactional**. If you do not specify the **local** clause, then the **shutdown transactional** will wait for all transactions on all instances that started prior to the **shutdown** command to complete.

You can use SQL*Plus commands to shut down and start up RAC databases one at a time until the whole environment has started. See Chapter 46 for details on **startup** and **shutdown** commands. You can start up an instance on your local node via the **startup mount** command.

You can use the SRVCTL utility to manage multiple instances in a single command. The syntax to start instances is

```
srvctl start instance -d <db_name> -i <inst_name_list>
                [-o <start_options>] [-c <connect_str> | -q]
```

The keyword following **srvctl start** specifies the service being started—instance, database, service, nodeapps, or asm. Note that multiple instances can be passed as part of the *inst_name_list* parameter value (via a comma-separated list). The *start_options* are **open**, **mount**, and **nomount**. The *connect_str* parameter allows you to pass a connect string when connecting to the database. The *q* parameter, if specified, tells SRVCTL to prompt for user connection information when SRVCTL is run; by default SRVCTL will connect to the local database as SYSDBA.

The following command will start and open a local database named MYDB:

```
srvctl start -database -d mydb -o open
```

The following command will start two instances for the MYDB database:

```
srvctl start instance -d mydb -i mydb1,mydb2
```

For ASM instances, specify the node name (-n), the instance name (-i), and the startup options (-o), as in the following example:

```
srvctl start asm -n mynode1 -i asm1 -o open
```

NOTE
*To see the instances that are part of your cluster, you can either use OEM or SQL*Plus. From within SQL*Plus, query the V$ACTIVE_INSTANCES view. The view will display one row for each instance—showing the instance number, the host name, and the instance name.*

You can use the

```
srvctl stop {database | instance | service | nodeapps | asm }
```

command to stop databases, instances, and other services.

SRVCTL Command	Description
srvctl add {database\|instance\|service\|nodeapps\|asm}	Adds a configuration to your cluster database configuration. **srvctl add service** adds services to a database and assigns them to instances. You can use the **srvctl add service** command to configure the Transparent Application Failover (TAF) policy for a service.
srvctl config {database\|service\|nodeapps\|asm}	Displays the configuration information stored in the Oracle Cluster Registry.
srvctl disable {database\|instance\|service\|asm}	Disables the named object and prevents it from being started automatically.
srvctl enable {database\|instance\|service\|asm}	Enables the named object to be started automatically.
srvctl getenv {database\|instance\|service\|nodeapps}	Displays environment status.
srvctl modify {database\|instance\|service\|nodeapps}	Modifies the object configuration without removing and adding the CRS resources.
srvctl relocate service	Relocates the named service names from one named instance to another named instance.
srvctl remove {database\|instance\|service\|nodeapps\|asm}	Removes the named object from the cluster environment.
srvctl setenv {database\|instance\|service\|nodeapps}	Sets environment values in the configuration file.
srvctl start {database\|instance\|service\|nodeapps\|asm}	Starts CRS-enabled, nonrunning applications for the database, all or named instances, all or named service names, or node-level applications.
srvctl status {database\|instance\|service\|nodeapps\|asm}	Displays the current state of the named object.
srvctl stop {database\|instance\|service\|nodeapps\|asm}	Stops the CRS applications for the database, all or named instances, all or named service names, or node level applications.
srvctl unsetenv {database\|instance\|service\|nodeapps}	Unsets environment values in the configuration file.

TABLE 40-3. *SRVCTL Command Options*

Other available SRVCTL commands are listed in Table 40-3.

Transparent Application Failover

RAC provides support for transparent application failover (TAF) in the event of an instance failure. To guard against hardware failure, the database file storage must be failure tolerant (usually through the use of RAID arrays, mirroring, or ASM-enforced software mirroring). When a user connects to the database through an instance, any transactions executed by the user are recorded in the redo log thread for that instance.

If an instance fails (or is shut down via a **shutdown abort**), one of the surviving instances will perform the needed recoveries. With TAF, the user's connection will be reestablished via another instance in the same cluster, connecting to the same database.

When you install and configure the RAC environment, Oracle configures the network services for you. For example, if you create a service called db.us.acme.com, the service name entry in the tnsnames.ora file may resemble this:

```
db.us.acme.com=
(description= (load_balance=on) (failover=on)
(address_list=
  (address=(protocol=tcp)(host=db1-server)(port=1521))
  (address=(protocol=tcp)(host=db2-server)(port=1521)))
(connect_data= (service_name=db.us.acme.com)))
```

The user can connect to the instance via the db.us.acme.com service name (for example, via a remote SQL*Plus session) and execute queries. While the user is connected, you can shut down the db1-server host. If the user—still in the same session—attempts to execute another query, the session will be transparently reestablished via the db2-server host and the query will be executed.

The listener.ora file entry for the database will contain entries similar to the following listing:

```
listeners_db.us.acme.com=
(address=(protocol=tcp)(host=db1-server)(port=1521)) (address=(protocol=
tcp)(host=db2-server)(port=1521))
```

If the user has changed environment variables within the session (via **alter session**), or has set session-specific variables, those values may need to be reestablished in the newly connected session.

Services

As described earlier in this chapter, you can create and manage services within your RAC cluster. You can assign services to run on one or more instances; services integrate cluster database resources to simplify cluster manageability.

As shown in Table 40-2, you can use SVRCTL to create and add services. You can assign services to instances for preferred (normal) and available (recovery) processing. You can identify other instances that are available to support the service levels change or for planned outages.

NOTE
You can use the DBCA to manage service assignments and service preferences.

Adding Nodes and Instances to the Cluster

You can add nodes to an existing cluster and you can add instances to an existing RAC environment. The nodes must meet the criteria listed earlier in this chapter—they must be configured with the proper networking protocol configurations and they must support high-speed data transmissions with the other nodes in the cluster. It is generally simplest to make the operating system on the new node a copy of one of the existing nodes in the cluster. As described in Chapter 41, the nodes must be able to execute remote commands via equivalence files.

The specific installation steps for the new node vary by operating system. In general, a UNIX cluster administrator will add the new node to the clusterware configuration (based on directions from its vendor). You can then start the Oracle Universal Installer (OUI) in addNode mode (in UNIX, via <CRS_HOME>/OUI/bin/addNode.sh and in Windows via <CRS_HOME>\oui\bin\addNode.bat). OUI will then present you with a series of prompts to add the new node to the cluster as it verifies the configuration.

OUI will then begin the installation process, instantiating root scripts if needed, copying the CRS files to the new nodes if needed, and then prompting you to run several scripts at the operating

system level. OUI then saves the cluster inventory. You can then execute the CRSSETUP utility to add CRS information for the new nodes. You can then run one final utility, RACGONS, to configure the Oracle Notification Services port for the new server. See the Oracle documentation for the syntax of the CRSSETUP and RACGONS utilities, as they involve detailed configuration of node names, node numbers, and ports.

Once the node has been added to the cluster, you can add an instance. Start the Database Configuration Assistant (see Chapter 2) and choose "Real Application Clusters database". You can then select "Add Instance" and the name of the database the instance will access. Enter the instance parameters where prompted and accept the summary information to initiate the instance creation. Oracle will create the instance and its network services.

To remove an existing instance from a RAC cluster, start the DBCA on a node other than the node hosting the instance that will be removed. The DBCA will display a list of the current instances in the configuration; select the one to be removed from the list. DBCA will display a list of services assigned to that instance so you can relocate them to other instances in the cluster. The selected instance will be deregistered from the RAC cluster.

Managing the Cluster Registry and Services

The Oracle Cluster Registry (OCR) contains configuration details for the database, services, and other cluster components. As shown in Table 40-2, you can use the **srvctl config** command to display the configuration details stored in the OCR. You should make copies of the registry on a regular basis to support any recovery needs you may have later.

One of the CRS-registered instances in the cluster will automatically back up the OCR every four hours, retaining three backup copies. Additional backups are taken once per day and once per week. You cannot modify the backup frequency or the number of backups retained. You can take additional backups via the ocrconfig tool, allowing you to make backups before and after significant changes to the cluster database environment. The OCRCONFIG options are shown in Table 40-4.

Option	Purpose
-export	To export the contents of the OCR into a target file.
-import	To import OCR contents from a previously *exported* OCR file.
-restore	To restore the OCR from an automatically created OCR backup file.
-backuploc	To change OCR backup file location. For this entry, use a full path that is accessible by all nodes.
-showbackup	To display the location, timestamp, and the node name of origin for the last three automatically created backup files.
-upgrade	To upgrade the OCR to a later version.
-downgrade	To downgrade the OCR to an earlier version.
-help	To display help for the ocrconfig commands.

TABLE 40-4. *OCRCONFIG Options*

CHAPTER
41

Grid Architecture
and Management

he *g* in Oracle Database 10*g* stands for "grid." Grid computing supports the ability to treat the computing infrastructure as a shared service whose composition is managed outside the view of the client applications. In this sense, the computing service can be analogous to an electrical utility in which the systems that provide the service are not directly seen by the end users. The source of the electrical power and the systems used to manage it are unseen by the user.

In a grid architecture, you can manage resources to support end-user needs dynamically. The grid architecture helps improve application availability and also supports resource provisioning to handle changing workloads. Grid resources include servers, disks, and instances. In prior releases, Oracle provided capabilities for some grid-related features—most notably Oracle9*i* Real Application Clusters (RAC). Oracle Database 10*g* introduces additional tools that facilitate grid management of your applications, providing a full set of options supporting grid computing. Features supporting grid computing include:

- **Real Application Clusters** You can create multiple instances that access the same database, allowing you to distribute the memory workload across multiple servers. You can add new instances to the cluster as needed.

- **Automated Storage Management** You can create diskgroups (see Chapter 46) of available disks and assign datafiles to the diskgroups. Oracle will then manage the I/O accesses to the diskgroups and redistribute the files as necessary.

- **Replication technology** Fast replication of data among databases supports the use of databases as part of a grid of available data sources. Replication technology includes transportable tablespaces (see Chapter 46), materialized views (see Chapter 24), Oracle Streams (log-based replication), and distributed transactions (see Chapter 23).

- **Security technology** You can support shared use of databases by different applications or business processes. In a shared database, you may need to create virtual databases that prevent unauthorized access of data belonging to other business areas or applications. See Chapter 19 for details on Virtual Private Databases.

- **Resource scheduling via Oracle Enterprise Manager (OEM)** You can use procedures within the DBMS_SCHEDULER package to create programs in Oracle that support the execution of shell scripts at the operating system level in addition to jobs that execute with the database. You can create programs via the CREATE_PROGRAM procedure, schedule them via CREATE_SCHEDULE, and submit the job via CREATE_JOB.

In this chapter, you will see an overview of grid features and how they fit into the grid computing architecture. The implementation of the grid requires that the infrastructure be configured to support the distributed and flexible architecture required. In the next section, you will see the critical configuration elements for the hardware and operating systems components.

Hardware and Operating System Configuration Issues

To support a grid architecture with multiple instances, you must be able to support instances on separate servers. If the instances are part of an RAC environment, the environment must have a

shared disk area that is accessible via a high-speed network. Oracle runs on all major operating systems, so its grid capabilities will not be hindered by restrictions to one particular operating system. Note that RAC is not supported across operating systems in the grid environment.

Blade servers commonly are used in RAC and grid environments. A "blade" is a computing system that includes processors and memory on a single board in the server, while other server features are shared among a set of blades. You can install a new blade into a server, and the blade will take advantage of the power, network access, storage, and infrastructure capabilities already installed. Blade servers can be modified to support expanded processing requirements without significantly impacting the area required to support the server.

The servers themselves must be accessed virtually—that is, a user application should be able to connect to an IP address that in turn can connect to one of many servers in a set. If one of the servers becomes unavailable, other servers in the set will be able to fulfill the request without interrupting the application. Users who are already connected to the application will have their connections redirected to an instance on a separate server. The servers should have external shared disks, a private IP address, a public IP address, and redundant switches.

The storage architecture must also support the grid concept—multiple servers accessing a shared disk service. The server architecture and operating system must support a storage technology that supports concurrent access to the shared disk services. Oracle's grid architecture supports Storage Area Networks (SANs), Network Attached Storage (NAS), and iSCSI (a block-mode form of NAS). When used in the grid, SANs and iSCSI require either a cluster file system or raw volumes. NAS volumes can be shared among servers without the need for a cluster file system.

The shared storage will be used for the critical files in the database—the datafiles, control files, online redo log files, and system parameter file—plus additional files used to manage the cluster of instances. The files must all be accessible by all servers in the cluster. The Oracle software may also be stored in the shared area.

Traditional file systems do not support the access requirements of grid architectures, so you need to use a file system that supports the concurrent access requirements. The most common options are raw devices and cluster file systems. Raw devices have been used for years to support Oracle RAC environments because they support concurrent access by multiple processes. However, their administration has traditionally been more complex than comparable file system administration. Both raw devices and cluster file systems require block-mode storage such as SANs and iSCSI.

In general, file systems are simpler to manage than raw devices—they can be easily resized, moved, and renamed. In general, the access speeds for raw devices and cluster file systems are comparable. Unless you have a specific reason for using raw devices in your environment, you should favor the use of cluster file systems in your grid. Oracle provides its own cluster file system, the Oracle Cluster File System (OCFS) to support shared file access.

Oracle Cluster File System

Oracle Cluster File System (OCFS) is designed to support concurrent access to a shared set of database files. To download and install OCFS, go to Oracle's Metalink site (http://metalink.oracle.com). Enter the following search terms within Metalink:

```
download oracle cluster file system
```

A list of related technical documents will be displayed. Choose the Metalink document that matches your operating system and follow the instructions to find the download locations. For example, for Linux, the downloads are available via http://oss.oracle.com, which in turn points to

http://oss.oracle.com/projects/ocfs/. The download site also includes links to best-practices documents, user guides, and design documentation.

In general, the OCFS installation process follows these steps:

1. Download the OCFS software for your environment.

2. Download the related installation documentation. Note that the installation process and software is specific to the operating system and version.

3. Perform the installation.

4. Copy the OCFS utilities into a shared directory (in UNIX, /usr/sbin).

5. Use the ocfstool utility to create the configuration files (such as /etc/ocf.conf).

6. Make sure the load_ocfs command is automatically run at startup (in Oracle Database 10g, this should be performed during the installation).

7. Use the fdisk utility to create the appropriate partitions that will be formatted with the Oracle Cluster File System. Use ocfstool to format the partitions.

8. Create mount points for the OCFS file systems (/u01, /u02, and so on) and mount each file system.

9. Create entries in the /etc/fstab file for each OCFS file system.

As with network-attached storage, it is useful to reboot one or more RAC nodes following the installation to verify that the correct number of OCFS volumes remounted.

NOTE
See your operating system–specific documentation for additional installation steps, the version certification matrix, and other requirements.

Accessing the Other Servers

In a RAC-ready environment, you should be able to run commands on all other servers in the cluster without providing a password. For example, in UNIX you should be able to use the rsh and rcp commands across the servers. You should work with your network managers and system administrators to determine the proper technical solution for your environment. Your choices for this requirement may be limited by your environment's security policies and practices.

For example, you may be able to use /home/oracle/rhosts files to permit host equivalences for the Oracle user. You can specify the hosts from which connections are permitted via the rhosts access method. See Chapter 40 for additional details on RAC implementation details, including recommended kernel configurations.

Oracle Cluster Manager

The Oracle Cluster Manager (OCM) is installed via the Oracle Universal Installer. OCM requires that the public and private host names for each server in the cluster be entered in two separate

screens. Make sure those names exactly correspond (the first public server entered must be the first private server entered) to avoid problems in later installation steps.

OCM features an agent that monitors the servers to determine if they are all still available. Depending on the version of Oracle RAC you are using, this agent may be called watchdogd or hangcheck-timer.

Create log directories (such as $ORACLE_HOME/oracm/log) for Oracle to use prior to starting the OCM.

You can now start OCM and install the Oracle RAC software.

Adding Servers to the Grid

When a server is to be made available ("provisioned") to an RAC database, the systems administrator must perform several steps:

1. Bring the server into the same network as the other nodes in the cluster.

2. Enable the new server to access the shared storage.

3. Enable the new server to access the other servers in the cluster.

4. Install the clustering software on the server. The new server should be recognized as part of the same cluster as the other servers, and it should have the proper access to the shared storage. Ensure that the new server uses the same clustering software as the other servers in the cluster.

5. Install the Oracle software on the server. Use the Oracle Universal Installer to install the Oracle software and add the new server to the Oracle RAC database via the Database Creation Assistant (DBCA). During the installation (which requires the Enterprise Edition), select a Software Only installation, which does not create a database. Run the configuration file (on UNIX, it's root.sh) to complete the installation.

Adding Instances to the Grid

To create an instance on the new server, make sure the Global Services Daemon (GSD) is running on all the servers. To start GSD on UNIX, enter the following command:

```
gsdctl start
```

Once GSD is running, start the OUI and choose the "Cluster database" options. You should be taken to an Instance Management page from which you can choose to add instances to the existing cluster. You will be prompted for information similar to that displayed during database installation—redo log group details, tablespace information, and instance name. When you accept the settings, the DBCA will start and will create the instance you requested.

To drop an instance from the grid, go through OUI to the Instance Management page. Select "Delete Instance," along with the name of the instance to remove from the cluster, and the DBCA will delete the instance.

Sharing Data Across the Grid

To this point, the focus of this chapter has been on RAC databases—shared datafiles accessed by multiple instances located within a cluster. The grid is bigger than just RAC. You may have multiple RAC databases, or multiple single-instance databases, which you dynamically manage via grid technologies.

To support multiple-database configurations, Oracle offers an array of technologies. Replication technologies include:

- **Database links** You can establish links between accounts in separate databases, for use in replicating read-only or updateable copies of tables. See Chapter 23 for details on remote access.

- **Procedures and triggers** To maintain replicated data synchronously, you can create a trigger that creates a transaction in a remote database when a transaction is committed in a local database. If the transaction in the remote database fails, the local transaction fails and the two databases stay synchronized. See Chapters 30 and 31.

- **Materialized views** You can create materialized views based on remote objects. Materialize views can be refreshed with data from the source system at commit time or on a predetermined schedule. Through the use of materialized view logs, you can use fast refreshes to send incremental changes from the source system to the materialized view. See Chapter 24.

- **Transportable tablespaces** You can move large volumes of data from one database to another via transportable tablespaces. For example, you can "unplug" a tablespace from a test environment and then rapidly plug it into multiple different databases. As of Oracle Database 10g, the source and target databases can be on differing platforms. See Chapter 46.

- **External tables** You can treat files outside the database as if they were tables, querying them as if the lines in the files were rows in a table. The files can be located on shared disks. See Chapter 26.

- **Oracle Streams** Oracle Streams uses the redo log entries to generate the SQL needed to replicate transactions across databases.

- **Data Pump Export and Import** You can use Data Pump Export and Import to create server-side jobs that extract and load data from your databases. See Chapter 22.

You can use all these technologies to make your data available across your grid. In the next section, you will see further details on the management capabilities introduced to support the grid architecture.

Managing the Grid

In Oracle Database 10g, Oracle Enterprise Manager (OEM) introduces or enhances a number of components designed to support management of the grid. These components include the following:

- **Grid Control Console** An OEM interface that allows you to easily manage all hosts, databases, listeners, and application servers in your computing environment.

- **Oracle Management Agent** A process deployed on each monitored host. It's responsible for monitoring all targets on the host, for communicating that information to the middle-tier Management Service, and for managing and maintaining the host and its targets. The agent requires at least 360MB of initial disk space and 20MB of memory.

- **Oracle Management Service** A J2EE application that displays the Grid Control Console, works with all Management Agents to process monitoring and jobs information, and uses the Management Repository as its data store. The Oracle Management Service is installed with and deployed on the Oracle application server. The application server instance Oracle creates to support the Oracle Management Service should not be used for any other purpose. The service requires at least 240MB of disk space and 1GB of memory. The application server requires 500MB of disk space and at least 512MB of memory.

- **Oracle Management Repository** Two tablespaces in an Oracle database that store information about the targets and applications managed within OEM. The Oracle Management Agents collect the data and use the Oracle Management Service to load data into the Oracle Management Repository. The Oracle Management Repository can be accessed by multiple administrators in the grid. The recommended size for the repository is 1GB of disk space and 2GB of memory.

When you install Oracle Enterprise Manager 10g Grid Control, you can use a new database or an existing database for the repository. If you use an existing database, the database can be local or remote to the server on which you are performing the installation. The repository must be installed in a database for which fine-grained access control is enabled (check V$OPTION to verify this setting).

NOTE
The Enterprise Manager Repository Configuration Assistant will fail if the SYSMAN user already exists in the database you specify for the repository, or if the repository already exists in that database.

NOTE
If you use an existing database, you may need to apply patches for the repository to function properly.

To install the Oracle Management Agent, run the OUI on each server in the environment. During the installation, choose Additional Management Agent as the installation type. Silent installation options are also available; see the "Oracle 10g Grid Control Configuration and Installation" document for silent installation guidelines. Oracle provides standard response files to use for silent installations.

Following the installation, run the root.sh command file as the root user to complete the post-installation process.

Enabling Patch Searches and Downloads

You can use OEM to access Oracle Metalink to search for patches and downloads for your environment. If you did not specify your connection information during installation, you can go to the Grid Control page of OEM and access the Setup | Patching Setup page. On that page you can enter your Metalink username and password and the Metalink patch search site:

 http://oracle.com/support/metalink/index.html

You can use this configuration to search for and download patches from within your OEM interface.

NOTE
If your network configuration prevents you from accessing the Metalink site, you must set the proxy settings for OEM to access Metalink. The proxy settings are in the /sysman/config/ emoms.properties file.

Setting Credentials for the Job System

In Windows-based systems (NT 4, Windows 2000, Windows 2003, and Windows XP), you must set the proper credentials for the Jobs system to work properly in OEM. When submitting a job, the user must have the "Log on as a batch job" privilege enabled. By default, the Management Agent is installed as a LocalSystem user.

To enable this setting in Windows 2000 and Windows XP, start the Local Security Policy tool located in the Control Panel. Choose Local Policies | User Rights Assignment. Double-click the "Log on as a batch job" entry and add the name of the user. Restart the server for the change to take effect.

In Windows NT 4, choose the User Manager tool within the Programs | Administrative Tools option on the Start menu. Select Policies | User Rights and then click Show Advanced User Rights. Select "Log on as a batch job" from the drop-down menu and add the name of the user who will be submitting an OEM job.

Configuring Databases for Monitoring

To enable a database to be monitored, you must allow its DBSNMP account to be accessed. Because this account may be locked in your environment, check that the account is accessible (you may need to use the **alter user dbsnmp account unlock** command). You can then go to the Configure Database | Properties page of the OEM Grid Control Console and configure the database for monitoring. On that page, enter the password for the DBSNMP user in the targeted database.

For ASM monitoring targets, navigate to Targets | All Targets from the OEM Grid Control Console. When you configure the target, you will be prompted for the SYS password to use in ASM monitoring.

Launching OEM

OEM is a graphical interface to the administration of the grid components. Its interface is largely intuitive, but there are some things to be particularly aware of within OEM:

- If you have configured a Management Agent on a server, supported targets on the same server will be detected and will be monitored via OEM.

- You can configure automatic e-mail notifications from OEM by default. You can configure additional notification methods as needed.

- You can group targets, create roles, and create administrators within OEM.

OEM relies on the Oracle Management Repository, Oracle Management Agent, and Oracle Management Service to function properly.

Because the repository is a database, you can stop and start it via the **shutdown** and **startup** commands in SQL*Plus. The Oracle Management Service, however, requires the use of the EMCTL utility installed with Oracle. To start the Oracle Management Service, use the following command in UNIX:

```
emctl start oms
```

And here's how to stop the service:

```
emctl stop oms
```

You can verify its status via **emctl status oms**. Here's how to start all components of the Application Server, including the Management Service:

```
opmnctl startall
```

To stop all components, use **opmnctl stopall**.

Oracle Management Agents on Windows are managed via the Services control panel. To start agents on UNIX platforms, use the **emctl start agent** command. You can stop an agent via **emctl stop agent** and check its status via **emctl status agent**.

Once all the components have been started, you can access the OEM Grid Control Console via the proper URL, which is generally in the following format:

```
http://mgmtserver_hostname.domain:port/em
```

Initialization Parameters for the Repository

Table 41-1 shows the minimum required database-initialization parameters for the database in which the Oracle Management Repository is stored.

NOTE
Do not set a value for RESOURCE_MANAGER_PLAN.

Table 41-2 lists the additional recommended parameter settings for the Oracle Management Repository.

Parameter	Minimum Value
job_queue_processes	10
db_block_size	8192
remote_login_passwordfile	EXCLUSIVE
timed_statistics	TRUE
open_cursors	300
shared_pool_size	67108864
dispatchers	NULL or not present in the file
aq_tm_processes	1 or greater
compatible	9.0.1.3 or greater

TABLE 41-1. *Required Minimum Values for the Oracle Management Repository*

Parameter	Value
db_cache_size	134217728
session_cached_cursors	200
large_pool_size	0
processes	150
fast_start_mttr_target	300
hash_area_size	1048576
sort_area_size	1048576
pga_aggregate_target	33554432
undo_management	AUTO
undo_retention	10800
undo_tablespace	UNDOTBS

TABLE 41-2. *Recommended Parameters for the Oracle Management Repository Database*

PART
VIII

Hitchhiker's Guides

CHAPTER
42

The Hitchhiker's Guide to the Oracle Data Dictionary

Oracle's data dictionary stores all the information that is used to manage the objects in the database. Although the data dictionary is usually the domain of database administrators (DBAs), it also is a source of valuable information for developers and end users.

In this chapter, you will see the data dictionary—Oracle's internal directory—from the perspective of an end user; the data dictionary tables and views are not listed alphabetically, but rather are grouped by function (tables, security, and so on). This organization is designed to let you quickly find your way to the information you need. The most-used data dictionary views are all shown here, along with examples of their usage.

Depending on which Oracle configuration options you are using, some of the groups will not apply to your database. The most commonly used views are listed first. The groupings used in this chapter are, in order:

- New Views Introduced in Oracle Database 10*g*
- New Columns Introduced in Oracle Database 10*g*
- The Road Maps: DICTIONARY (DICT) and DICT_COLUMNS
- Things You Select From: Tables (and Columns), Views, Synonyms, and Sequences
- Constraints and Comments
- Indexes and Clusters
- Abstract Datatypes, ORDBMS-Related Structures, and LOBs
- Database Links and Materialized Views
- Triggers, Procedures, Functions, and Packages
- Dimensions
- Space Allocation and Usage, Including Partitions and Subpartitions
- Users and Privileges
- Roles
- Auditing
- Miscellaneous
- Monitoring: The V$ Dynamic Performance Tables

NOTE
As new features are added, it is expected that the data dictionary will be modified with each future release of Oracle.

A Note about Nomenclature

With some exceptions, the names of the objects in the Oracle data dictionary begin with one of three prefixes: "USER," "ALL," or "DBA." Records in the "USER" views usually show information

about objects owned by the account performing the query. Records in the "ALL" views include the "USER" records plus information about objects on which privileges have been granted to PUBLIC or to the user. "DBA" views encompass all of the database objects, regardless of owner. For most database objects, "USER," "ALL," and "DBA" views are available.

In keeping with the user focus of this guide, the emphasis will be on the "USER" views or those that are accessible to all users. The "ALL" and "DBA" views will be described when they are applicable.

New Views Introduced in Oracle Database 10*g*

For users familiar with the data dictionary in Oracle9*i*, Table 42-1 lists the views that are introduced in Oracle Database 10*g*.

ALL_ Views	DBA_ Views	USER_ Views
	DBA_ADVISOR_ACTIONS	USER_ADVISOR_ACTIONS
	DBA_ADVISOR_COMMANDS	
	DBA_ADVISOR_DEFINITIONS	
	DBA_ADVISOR_FINDINGS	USER_ADVISOR_FINDINGS
	DBA_ADVISOR_JOURNAL	USER_ADVISOR_JOURNAL
	DBA_ADVISOR_LOG	USER_ADVISOR_LOG
	DBA_ADVISOR_OBJECT_TYPES	
	DBA_ADVISOR_OBJECTS	USER_ADVISOR_OBJECTS
	DBA_ADVISOR_PARAMETERS	USER_ADVISOR_PARAMETERS
	DBA_ADVISOR_RATIONALE	USER_ADVISOR_RATIONALE
	DBA_ADVISOR_RECOMMENDATIONS	USER_ADVISOR_RECOMMENDATIONS
	DBA_ADVISOR_SQLA_REC_SUM	USER_ADVISOR_SQLA_REC_SUM
	DBA_ADVISOR_SQLA_WK_MAP	USER_ADVISOR_SQLA_WK_MAP
	DBA_ADVISOR_SQLA_WK_STMTS	USER_ADVISOR_SQLA_WK_STMTS
	DBA_ADVISOR_SQLW_JOURNAL	USER_ADVISOR_SQLW_JOURNAL
	DBA_ADVISOR_SQLW_PARAMETERS	USER_ADVISOR_SQLW_PARAMETERS
	DBA_ADVISOR_SQLW_STMTS	USER_ADVISOR_SQLW_STMTS
	DBA_ADVISOR_SQLW_SUM	USER_ADVISOR_SQLW_SUM
	DBA_ADVISOR_SQLW_TABLES	USER_ADVISOR_SQLW_TABLES
	DBA_ADVISOR_SQLW_TEMPLATES	USER_ADVISOR_SQLW_TEMPLATES
	DBA_ADVISOR_TASKS	USER_ADVISOR_TASKS
	DBA_ADVISOR_TEMPLATES	USER_ADVISOR_TEMPLATES
	DBA_ADVISOR_USAGE	

TABLE 42-1. *New Data Dictionary Views in Oracle Database 10g*

ALL_ Views	DBA_ Views	USER_ Views
	DBA_ALERT_HISTORY	
ALL_APPLY_ENQUEUE	DBA_APPLY_ENQUEUE	
ALL_APPLY_EXECUTE	DBA_APPLY_EXECUTE	
	DBA_APPLY_INSTANTIATED_GLOBAL	
	DBA_APPLY_INSTANTIATED_SCHEMAS	
ALL_APPLY_TABLE_COLUMNS	DBA_APPLY_TABLE_COLUMNS	
ALL_AUDIT_POLICY_COLUMNS	DBA_AUDIT_POLICY_COLUMNS	USER_AUDIT_POLICY_COLUMNS
ALL_AW_PS		
ALL_AWS		
ALL_CAPTURE_EXTRA_ATTRIBUTES	DBA_CAPTURE_EXTRA_ATTRIBUTES	
	DBA_COMMON_AUDIT_TRAIL	
	DBA_DATAPUMP_JOBS	USER_DATAPUMP_JOBS
	DBA_DATAPUMP_SESSIONS	
	DBA_ENABLED_AGGREGATIONS	
	DBA_ENABLED_TRACES	
	DBA_FEATURE_USAGE_STATISTICS	
	DBA_HIGH_WATER_MARK_STATISTICS	
	DBA_HIST_ACTIVE_SESS_HISTORY	
	DBA_HIST_BASELINE	
	DBA_HIST_BG_EVENT_SUMMARY	
	DBA_HIST_BUFFER_POOL_STAT	
	DBA_HIST_CR_BLOCK_SERVER	
	DBA_HIST_CURRENT_BLOCK_SERVER	
	DBA_HIST_DATABASE_INSTANCE	
	DBA_HIST_DATAFILE	
	DBA_HIST_DB_CACHE_ADVICE	
	DBA_HIST_DLM_MISC	
	DBA_HIST_ENQUEUE_STAT	
	DBA_HIST_EVENT_NAME	
	DBA_HIST_FILEMETRIC_HISTORY	
	DBA_HIST_FILESTATXS	
	DBA_HIST_INSTANCE_RECOVERY	
	DBA_HIST_JAVA_POOL_ADVICE	
	DBA_HIST_LATCH	
	DBA_HIST_LATCH_CHILDREN	

TABLE 42-1. *New Data Dictionary Views in Oracle Database 10g (continued)*

ALL_ Views	DBA_ Views	USER_ Views
	DBA_HIST_LATCH_MISSES_SUMMARY	
	DBA_HIST_LATCH_NAME	
	DBA_HIST_LATCH_PARENT	
	DBA_HIST_LIBRARYCACHE	
	DBA_HIST_LOG	
	DBA_HIST_METRIC_NAME	
	DBA_HIST_MTTR_TARGET_ADVICE	
	DBA_HIST_OPTIMIZER_ENV	
	DBA_HIST_OSSTAT	
	DBA_HIST_OSSTAT_NAME	
	DBA_HIST_PARAMETER	
	DBA_HIST_PARAMETER_NAME	
	DBA_HIST_PGA_TARGET_ADVICE	
	DBA_HIST_PGASTAT	
	DBA_HIST_RESOURCE_LIMIT	
	DBA_HIST_ROLLSTAT	
	DBA_HIST_ROWCACHE_SUMMARY	
	DBA_HIST_SEG_STAT	
	DBA_HIST_SEG_STAT_OBJ	
	DBA_HIST_SERVICE_NAME	
	DBA_HIST_SERVICE_STAT	
	DBA_HIST_SERVICE_WAIT_CLASS	
	DBA_HIST_SESSMETRIC_HISTORY	
	DBA_HIST_SGA	
	DBA_HIST_SGASTAT	
	DBA_HIST_SHARED_POOL_ADVICE	
	DBA_HIST_SNAP_ERROR	
	DBA_HIST_SNAPSHOT	
	DBA_HIST_SQL_PLAN	
	DBA_HIST_SQL_SUMMARY	
	DBA_HIST_SQL_WORKAREA_HSTGRM	
	DBA_HIST_SQLBIND	
	DBA_HIST_SQLSTAT	
	DBA_HIST_SQLTEXT	
	DBA_HIST_STAT_NAME	

TABLE 42-1. *New Data Dictionary Views in Oracle Database 10*g (continued)

ALL_ Views	DBA_ Views	USER_ Views
	DBA_HIST_SYS_TIME_MODEL	
	DBA_HIST_SYSMETRIC_HISTORY	
	DBA_HIST_SYSMETRIC_SUMMARY	
	DBA_HIST_SYSSTAT	
	DBA_HIST_SYSTEM_EVENT	
	DBA_HIST_TABLESPACE_STAT	
	DBA_HIST_TBSPC_SPACE_USAGE	
	DBA_HIST_TEMPFILE	
	DBA_HIST_TEMPSTATXS	
	DBA_HIST_THREAD	
	DBA_HIST_UNDOSTAT	
	DBA_HIST_WAITCLASSMET_HISTORY	
	DBA_HIST_WAITSTAT	
	DBA_HIST_WR_CONTROL	
ALL_IND_STATISTICS	DBA_IND_STATISTICS	USER_IND_STATISTICS
ALL_INDEXTYPE_ARRAYTYPES	DBA_INDEXTYPE_ARRAYTYPES	USER_INDEXTYPE_ARRAYTYPES
	DBA_LOGMNR_LOG	
	DBA_LOGMNR_PURGED_LOG	
	DBA_LOGMNR_SESSION	
ALL_MVIEW_COMMENTS	DBA_MVIEW_COMMENTS	USER_MVIEW_COMMENTS
ALL_NESTED_TABLE_COLS	DBA_NESTED_TABLE_COLS	USER_NESTED_TABLE_COLS
	DBA_OUTSTANDING_ALERTS	
ALL_PLSQL_OBJECT_SETTINGS	DBA_PLSQL_OBJECT_SETTINGS	USER_PLSQL_OBJECT_SETTINGS
	DBA_RECYCLEBIN	USER_RECYCLEBIN
	DBA_REDEFINITION_ERRORS	
	DBA_REDEFINITION_OBJECTS	
	DBA_REGISTERED_ARCHIVED_LOG	
ALL_REWRITE_EQUIVALENCES	DBA_REWRITE_EQUIVALENCES	USER_REWRITE_EQUIVALENCES
	DBA_RSRC_GROUP_MAPPINGS	
	DBA_RSRC_MAPPING_PRIORITY	
ALL_SCHEDULER_JOB_ARGS	DBA_SCHEDULER_JOB_ARGS	USER_SCHEDULER_JOB_ARGS
ALL_SCHEDULER_JOB_CLASSES	DBA_SCHEDULER_JOB_CLASSES	
ALL_SCHEDULER_JOB_LOG	DBA_SCHEDULER_JOB_LOG	USER_SCHEDULER_JOB_LOG
ALL_SCHEDULER_JOB_RUN_DETAILS	DBA_SCHEDULER_JOB_RUN_DETAILS	USER_SCHEDULER_JOB_RUN_DETAILS

TABLE 42-1. *New Data Dictionary Views in Oracle Database 10*g *(continued)*

ALL_ Views	**DBA_ Views**	**USER_ Views**
ALL_SCHEDULER_JOBS	DBA_SCHEDULER_JOBS	USER_SCHEDULER_JOBS
ALL_SCHEDULER_PROGRAM_ARGS	DBA_SCHEDULER_PROGRAM_ARGS	USER_SCHEDULER_PROGRAM_ARGS
ALL_SCHEDULER_PROGRAMS	DBA_SCHEDULER_PROGRAMS	USER_SCHEDULER_PROGRAMS
ALL_SCHEDULER_RUNNING_JOBS	DBA_SCHEDULER_RUNNING_JOBS	USER_SCHEDULER_RUNNING_JOBS
ALL_SCHEDULER_SCHEDULES	DBA_SCHEDULER_SCHEDULES	USER_SCHEDULER_SCHEDULES
ALL_SCHEDULER_WINDOW_DETAILS	DBA_SCHEDULER_WINDOW_DETAILS	
ALL_SCHEDULER_WINDOW_GROUPS	DBA_SCHEDULER_WINDOW_GROUPS	
ALL_SCHEDULER_WINDOW_LOG	DBA_SCHEDULER_WINDOW_LOG	
ALL_SCHEDULER_WINDOWS	DBA_SCHEDULER_WINDOWS	
ALL_SCHEDULER_WINGROUP_MEMBERS	DBA_SCHEDULER_WINGROUP_MEMBERS	
ALL_SEC_RELEVANT_COLS	DBA_SEC_RELEVANT_COLS	USER_SEC_RELEVANT_COLS
	DBA_SERVER_REGISTRY	
ALL_SERVICES	DBA_SERVICES	
	DBA_SQL_PROFILES	
	DBA_SQLSET	USER_SQLSET
	DBA_SQLSET_BINDS	USER_SQLSET_BINDS
	DBA_SQLSET_REFERENCES	USER_SQLSET_REFERENCES
	DBA_SQLSET_STATEMENTS	USER_SQLSET_STATEMENTS
	DBA_SQLTUNE_BINDS	USER_SQLTUNE_BINDS
	DBA_SQLTUNE_PLANS	USER_SQLTUNE_PLANS
	DBA_SQLTUNE_RATIONALE_PLAN	USER_SQLTUNE_RATIONALE_PLAN
	DBA_SQLTUNE_STATISTICS	USER_SQLTUNE_STATISTICS
	DBA_STREAMS_ADMINISTRATOR	
ALL_STREAMS_MESSAGE_CONSUMERS	DBA_STREAMS_MESSAGE_CONSUMERS	
ALL_STREAMS_MESSAGE_RULES	DBA_STREAMS_MESSAGE_RULES	
ALL_STREAMS_NEWLY_SUPPORTED	DBA_STREAMS_NEWLY_SUPPORTED	
ALL_STREAMS_RULES	DBA_STREAMS_RULES	
ALL_STREAMS_TRANSFORM_FUNCTION	DBA_STREAMS_TRANSFORM_FUNCTION	
ALL_STREAMS_UNSUPPORTED	DBA_STREAMS_UNSUPPORTED	
ALL_TAB_STATISTICS	DBA_TAB_STATISTICS	USER_TAB_STATISTICS
	DBA_TABLESPACE_GROUPS	
	DBA_THRESHOLDS	
	DBA_TUNE_MVIEW	USER_TUNE_MVIEW
ALL_WARNING_SETTINGS	DBA_WARNING_SETTINGS	USER_WARNING_SETTINGS

TABLE 42-1. *New Data Dictionary Views in Oracle Database 10*g (continued)

Some of the views introduced with Oracle Database 10*g* reflect dramatic functionality additions. For example, USER_RECYCLEBIN (accessible via the RECYCLEBIN public synonym) supports the re-creation of dropped objects. See Chapter 28 for examples of the **flashback table** command. Other features supported by the new views include the enhanced advisor capabilities.

New Columns Introduced in Oracle Database 10*g*

For users familiar with the data dictionary in Oracle9*i*, Table 42-2 lists the columns that are introduced to previously existing data dictionary views in Oracle Database 10*g*.

Static Data Dictionary View	New Columns
ALL_ALL_TABLES	DROPPED
ALL_APPLY	PRECOMMIT_HANDLER
	MAX_APPLIED_MESSAGE_NUMBER
	NEGATIVE_RULE_SET_NAME
	NEGATIVE_RULE_SET_OWNER
	STATUS_CHANGE_TIME
	ERROR_NUMBER
	ERROR_MESSAGE
ALL_APPLY_DML_HANDLERS	APPLY_NAME
ALL_APPLY_PROGRESS	SOURCE_DATABASE
ALL_AUDIT_POLICIES	SEL
	INS
	UPD
	DEL
	AUDIT_TRAIL
	POLICY_COLUMN_OPTIONS
ALL_CAPTURE	CAPTURE_USER
	CAPTURED_SCN
	APPLIED_SCN
	USE_DATABASE_LINK
	FIRST_SCN
	SOURCE_DATABASE
	SOURCE_DBID
	SOURCE_RESETLOGS_SCN
	SOURCE_RESETLOGS_TIME
	LOGMINER_ID
	NEGATIVE_RULE_SET_NAME
	NEGATIVE_RULE_SET_OWNER
	MAX_CHECKPOINT_SCN
	REQUIRED_CHECKPOINT_SCN
	LOGFILE_ASSIGNMENT
	STATUS_CHANGE_TIME
	ERROR_NUMBER
	ERROR_MESSAGE
	VERSION
	CAPTURE_TYPE
ALL_DEF_AUDIT_OPTS	FBK
ALL_DIM_ATTRIBUTES	ATTRIBUTE_NAME

TABLE 42-2. *New Data Dictionary Columns in Oracle Database 10*g

Static Data Dictionary View	New Columns
ALL_ERRORS	ATTRIBUTE MESSAGE_NUMBER
ALL_EXTERNAL_TABLES	PROPERTY
ALL_INDEXES	IOT_REDUNDANT_PKEY_ELIM DROPPED
ALL_INDEXTYPES	ARRAY_DML
ALL_LOBS	TABLESPACE_NAME FORMAT PARTITIONED
ALL_LOG_GROUP_COLUMNS	LOGGING_PROPERTY
ALL_LOG_GROUPS	LOG_GROUP_TYPE GENERATED
ALL_MVIEWS	UNKNOWN_TRUSTED_FD STALE_SINCE
ALL_OBJECT_TABLES	DROPPED
ALL_OUTLINES	COMPATIBLE ENABLED FORMAT
ALL_PART_COL_STATISTICS	HISTOGRAM
ALL_POLICIES	IDX POLICY_TYPE LONG_PREDICATE
ALL_PROPAGATION	NEGATIVE_RULE_SET_OWNER NEGATIVE_RULE_SET_NAME
ALL_SUBPART_COL_STATISTICS	HISTOGRAM
ALL_SUBSCRIBED_COLUMNS	SUBSCRIPTION_NAME
ALL_SUBSCRIBED_TABLES	SUBSCRIPTION_NAME
ALL_SUBSCRIPTIONS	SUBSCRIPTION_NAME
ALL_TAB_COL_STATISTICS	HISTOGRAM
ALL_TAB_COLS	HISTOGRAM QUALIFIED_COL_NAME
ALL_TAB_COLUMNS	HISTOGRAM
ALL_TAB_MODIFICATIONS	DROP_SEGMENTS
ALL_TABLES	DROPPED
DBA_ALL_TABLES	DROPPED
DBA_APPLY	PRECOMMIT_HANDLER MAX_APPLIED_MESSAGE_NUMBER NEGATIVE_RULE_SET_NAME NEGATIVE_RULE_SET_OWNER STATUS_CHANGE_TIME ERROR_NUMBER ERROR_MESSAGE

TABLE 42-2. *New Data Dictionary Columns in Oracle Database 10*g (continued)

Static Data Dictionary View	New Columns
DBA_APPLY_DML_HANDLERS	APPLY_NAME
DBA_APPLY_PROGRESS	SOURCE_DATABASE
DBA_AUDIT_EXISTS	EXTENDED_TIMESTAMP PROXY_SESSIONID GLOBAL_UID INSTANCE_NUMBER OS_PROCESS TRANSACTIONID SCN SQL_BIND SQL_TEXT
DBA_AUDIT_OBJECT	EXTENDED_TIMESTAMP PROXY_SESSIONID GLOBAL_UID INSTANCE_NUMBER OS_PROCESS TRANSACTIONID SCN SQL_BIND SQL_TEXT
DBA_AUDIT_POLICIES	SEL INS UPD DEL AUDIT_TRAIL POLICY_COLUMN_OPTIONS
DBA_AUDIT_SESSION	EXTENDED_TIMESTAMP PROXY_SESSIONID GLOBAL_UID INSTANCE_NUMBER OS_PROCESS
DBA_AUDIT_STATEMENT	EXTENDED_TIMESTAMP PROXY_SESSIONID GLOBAL_UID INSTANCE_NUMBER OS_PROCESS TRANSACTIONID SCN SQL_BIND SQL_TEXT
DBA_AUDIT_TRAIL	EXTENDED_TIMESTAMP PROXY_SESSIONID GLOBAL_UID INSTANCE_NUMBER OS_PROCESS TRANSACTIONID SCN SQL_BIND SQL_TEXT

TABLE 42-2. *New Data Dictionary Columns in Oracle Database 10*g (continued)

Static Data Dictionary View	New Columns
DBA_AW_PS	MAXPAGES
DBA_CAPTURE	CAPTURE_USER
	USE_DATABASE_LINK
	FIRST_SCN
	SOURCE_DATABASE
	SOURCE_DBID
	SOURCE_RESETLOGS_SCN
	SOURCE_RESETLOGS_TIME
	LOGMINER_ID
	NEGATIVE_RULE_SET_NAME
	NEGATIVE_RULE_SET_OWNER
	MAX_CHECKPOINT_SCN
	REQUIRED_CHECKPOINT_SCN
	LOGFILE_ASSIGNMENT
	STATUS_CHANGE_TIME
	ERROR_NUMBER
	ERROR_MESSAGE
	VERSION
	CAPTURE_TYPE
DBA_DIM_ATTRIBUTES	ATTRIBUTE_NAME
DBA_ERRORS	ATTRIBUTE
	MESSAGE_NUMBER
DBA_EXTERNAL_TABLES	PROPERTY
DBA_FGA_AUDIT_TRAIL	STATEMENT_TYPE
	EXTENDED_TIMESTAMP
	PROXY_SESSIONID
	GLOBAL_UID
	INSTANCE_NUMBER
	OS_PROCESS
	TRANSACTIONID
	STATEMENTID
	ENTRYID
DBA_INDEXES	IOT_REDUNDANT_PKEY_ELIM
	DROPPED
DBA_INDEXTYPES	ARRAY_DML
DBA_LOBS	TABLESPACE_NAME
	FORMAT
	PARTITIONED
DBA_LOG_GROUP_COLUMNS	LOGGING_PROPERTY
DBA_LOG_GROUPS	LOG_GROUP_TYPE
	GENERATED
DBA_LOGSTDBY_LOG	APPLIED
DBA_LOGSTDBY_PROGRESS	APPLIED_THREAD#
	APPLIED_SEQUENCE#
	READ_THREAD#
	READ_SEQUENCE#
	NEWEST_THREAD#
	NEWEST_SEQUENCE#

TABLE 42-2. *New Data Dictionary Columns in Oracle Database 10g (continued)*

Static Data Dictionary View	New Columns
DBA_LOGSTDBY_SKIP	USE_LIKE ESC
DBA_LOGSTDBY_UNSUPPORTED	ATTRIBUTES TPROP SEGSPARE1 TFLAGS
DBA_MVIEWS	UNKNOWN_TRUSTED_FD STALE_SINCE
DBA_OBJ_AUDIT_OPTS	FBK
DBA_OBJECT_TABLES	DROPPED
DBA_OUTLINES	COMPATIBLE ENABLED FORMAT
DBA_PART_COL_STATISTICS	HISTOGRAM
DBA_POLICIES	IDX POLICY_TYPE LONG_PREDICATE
DBA_PROPAGATION	NEGATIVE_RULE_SET_OWNER NEGATIVE_RULE_SET_NAME
DBA_PROXIES	AUTHENTICATION
DBA_REGISTRY	NAMESPACE
DBA_REGISTRY_HIERARCHY	NAMESPACE
DBA_RSRC_PLAN_DIRECTIVES	MAX_IDLE_TIME MAX_IDLE_BLOCKER_TIME SWITCH_TIME_IN_CALL
DBA_SUBPART_COL_STATISTICS	HISTOGRAM
DBA_SUBSCRIBED_COLUMNS	SUBSCRIPTION_NAME
DBA_SUBSCRIBED_TABLES	SUBSCRIPTION_NAME
DBA_SUBSCRIPTIONS	SUBSCRIPTION_NAME
DBA_TAB_COL_STATISTICS	HISTOGRAM
DBA_TAB_COLS	HISTOGRAM QUALIFIED_COL_NAME
DBA_TAB_COLUMNS	HISTOGRAM
DBA_TAB_MODIFICATIONS	DROP_SEGMENTS
DBA_TABLES	DROPPED
DBA_TABLESPACES	RETENTION BIGFILE
USER_ALL_TABLES	DROPPED

TABLE 42-2. *New Data Dictionary Columns in Oracle Database 10*g (continued)

Static Data Dictionary View	New Columns
USER_AUDIT_OBJECT	EXTENDED_TIMESTAMP PROXY_SESSIONID GLOBAL_UID INSTANCE_NUMBER OS_PROCESS TRANSACTIONID SCN SQL_BIND SQL_TEXT
USER_AUDIT_POLICIES	SEL INS UPD DEL AUDIT_TRAIL POLICY_COLUMN_OPTIONS
USER_AUDIT_SESSION	EXTENDED_TIMESTAMP PROXY_SESSIONID GLOBAL_UID INSTANCE_NUMBER OS_PROCESS
USER_AUDIT_STATEMENT	EXTENDED_TIMESTAMP PROXY_SESSIONID GLOBAL_UID INSTANCE_NUMBER OS_PROCESS TRANSACTIONID SCN SQL_BIND SQL_TEXT
USER_AUDIT_TRAIL	EXTENDED_TIMESTAMP PROXY_SESSIONID GLOBAL_UID INSTANCE_NUMBER OS_PROCESS TRANSACTIONID SCN SQL_BIND SQL_TEXT
USER_AW_PS	MAXPAGES
USER_DIM_ATTRIBUTES	ATTRIBUTE_NAME
USER_ERRORS	ATTRIBUTE MESSAGE_NUMBER
USER_EXTERNAL_TABLES	PROPERTY
USER_INDEXES	IOT_REDUNDANT_PKEY_ELIM DROPPED

TABLE 42-2. *New Data Dictionary Columns in Oracle Database 10*g *(continued)*

Static Data Dictionary View	New Columns
USER_INDEXTYPES	ARRAY_DML
USER_LOBS	TABLESPACE_NAME FORMAT PARTITIONED
USER_LOG_GROUP_COLUMNS	LOGGING_PROPERTY
USER_LOG_GROUPS	LOG_GROUP_TYPE GENERATED
USER_MVIEWS	UNKNOWN_TRUSTED_FD STALE_SINCE
USER_OBJ_AUDIT_OPTS	FBK
USER_OBJECT_TABLES	DROPPED
USER_OUTLINES	COMPATIBLE ENABLED FORMAT
USER_PART_COL_STATISTICS	HISTOGRAM
USER_POLICIES	IDX POLICY_TYPE LONG_PREDICATE
USER_PROXIES	AUTHENTICATION
USER_PUBLISHED_COLUMNS	CHANGE_SET_NAME PUB_ID
USER_REGISTRY	NAMESPACE
USER_SUBPART_COL_STATISTICS	HISTOGRAM
USER_SUBSCRIBED_COLUMNS	SUBSCRIPTION_NAME
USER_SUBSCRIBED_TABLES	SUBSCRIPTION_NAME
USER_SUBSCRIPTIONS	SUBSCRIPTION_NAME
USER_TAB_COL_STATISTICS	HISTOGRAM
USER_TAB_COLS	HISTOGRAM QUALIFIED_COL_NAME
USER_TAB_COLUMNS	HISTOGRAM
USER_TAB_MODIFICATIONS	DROP_SEGMENTS
USER_TABLES	DROPPED
USER_TABLESPACES	RETENTION BIGFILE

TABLE 42-2. *New Data Dictionary Columns in Oracle Database 10*g (continued)

The Road Maps: DICTIONARY (DICT) and DICT_COLUMNS

Descriptions for the objects that make up the Oracle data dictionary are accessible via a view named DICTIONARY. This view, also accessible via the public synonym DICT, queries the database to determine which data dictionary views you can see. It also searches for public synonyms for those views.

The following example queries DICT for the names of all data dictionary views whose names include the string 'VIEWS'. Selecting from DICT via a non-DBA account, as shown in the following listing, returns the object name and comments for each data dictionary object that matches your search criteria. There are only two columns in this view: Table_Name and the table's associated Comments.

```
column Comments format a35 word_wrapped
column Table_Name format a25

select Table_Name, Comments
  from DICT
 where Table_Name like '%VIEWS%'
 order by Table_Name;

TABLE_NAME                COMMENTS
------------------------- -----------------------------------
ALL_BASE_TABLE_MVIEWS     All materialized views with log(s)
                          in the database that the user can
                          see
ALL_MVIEWS                All materialized views in the
                          database
ALL_REGISTERED_MVIEWS     Remote materialized views of local
                          tables that the user can see
ALL_VIEWS                 Description of views accessible to
                          the user
ALL_XML_VIEWS             Description of all XMLType
                          views that the user has privileges
                          on
USER_BASE_TABLE_MVIEWS    All materialized views with log(s)
                          owned by the user in the database
USER_MVIEWS               All materialized views in the
                          database
USER_REGISTERED_MVIEWS    Remote materialized views of local
                          tables currently using logs owned
                          by the user
USER_VIEWS                Description of the user's own views
USER_XML_VIEWS            Description of the user's own
                          XMLType views
```

You can query the columns of the dictionary views via the DICT_COLUMNS view. Like the DICTIONARY view, DICT_COLUMNS displays the comments that have been entered into the database for the data dictionary views. DICT_COLUMNS has three columns: Table_Name, Column_Name, and Comments. Querying DICT_COLUMNS lets you determine which data dictionary views would be most useful for your needs.

For example, if you want to view space allocation and usage information for your database objects but are not sure which data dictionary views store that information, you can query DICT_COLUMNS, as shown in the following example, which looks for all the dictionary tables that have a column named Blocks:

```
select Table_Name
   from DICT_COLUMNS
 where Column_Name = 'BLOCKS'
   and Table_Name like 'USER%'
 order by Table_Name;

TABLE_NAME
--------------------
USER_ALL_TABLES
USER_EXTENTS
USER_FREE_SPACE
USER_OBJECT_TABLES
USER_SEGMENTS
USER_TABLES
USER_TAB_PARTITIONS
USER_TAB_STATISTICS
USER_TAB_SUBPARTITIONS
USER_TS_QUOTAS
```

To list all of the available column names that you could have used in the last example, query DICT_COLUMNS:

```
select distinct Column_Name
   from DICT_COLUMNS
 order by Column_Name;
```

Whenever you're unsure about where to find the data you want, just check DICTIONARY and DICT_COLUMNS. If it appears that a large number of views could be useful, query DICTIONARY (as in the first example) to see the comments on each view.

Things You Select From: Tables (and Columns), Views, Synonyms, and Sequences

A user's catalog lists all of those objects that the user can **select** records from; that is, any object that can be listed in the **from** clause of a query. Although sequences are not referenced directly in **from** clauses, Oracle includes them in the catalog. In this section, you will see how to retrieve information about tables, columns, views, synonyms, sequences, and the user catalog.

Catalog: USER_CATALOG (CAT)

Querying USER_CATALOG will display all tables, views, synonyms, and sequences the user owns. The Table_Name column shows the name of the object (even if it is not a table), and the Table_Type column shows the type of object:

```
select Table_Name, Table_Type
  from USER_CATALOG
 where Table_Name like 'T%';
```

USER_CATALOG may also be referred to by the public synonym CAT.

Two additional catalogs are available. ALL_CATALOG lists everything in your USER_CATALOG view plus any objects that you or PUBLIC have been granted access to. DBA_CATALOG is a DBA-level version of the catalog showing all tables, views, sequences, and synonyms in the database. In addition to the Table_Name and Table_Type columns shown in the USER_CATALOG query, ALL_CATALOG and DBA_CATALOG include an Owner column.

Objects: USER_OBJECTS (OBJ)

USER_CATALOG only displays information for tables, views, sequences, and synonyms. To retrieve information on all types of objects, query USER_OBJECTS. You can use this view to find out about many types of objects, including clusters, database links, directories, functions, indexes, libraries, packages, package bodies, Java classes, abstract datatypes, resource plans, sequences, synonyms, tables, triggers, materialized views, LOBs, and views. USER_OBJECTS' columns are listed in Table 42-3.

Column Name	Description
Object_Name	The name of the object
SubObject_Name	The name of the subobject, such as a partition name
Object_ID	A unique, Oracle-assigned ID for the object
Data_Object_ID	The object number of the segment that contains the object's data
Object_Type	The object type ('TABLE', 'INDEX', 'TABLE PARTITION', and so on)
Created	The timestamp for the object's creation (a DATE column)
Last_DDL_Time	The timestamp for the last DDL command used on the object, including **alter**, **grant**, and **revoke**
Timestamp	The timestamp for the object's creation (same as Created, but stored as a character column)
Status	The status of the object ('VALID' or 'INVALID')
Temporary	A flag to indicate whether the object is a temporary table
Generated	A flag to indicate whether the object's name was system generated
Secondary	A flag to indicate whether the object is a secondary index created by a domain index

TABLE 42-3. *Columns in USER_OBJECTS*

USER_OBJECTS (also known by its public synonym OBJ) contains several vital pieces of information that are not found in other data dictionary views. It records the creation date of objects (the Created column) and the last time an object was altered (the Last_DDL_Time column). These columns are very useful when trying to reconcile different sets of objects in the same application.

NOTE
If you re-create objects in any way, such as via the Import utility, their Created values will change to the last time they were created.

Two additional object listings are available. ALL_OBJECTS lists everything in your USER_OBJECTS view plus any objects for which access has been granted to you or PUBLIC. DBA_OBJECTS is a DBA-level version of the object listing, showing all of the objects in the database. In addition to the columns shown in the USER_OBJECTS view, ALL_OBJECTS and DBA_OBJECTS include an Owner column.

Tables: USER_TABLES (TABS)

Although all of a user's objects are shown in USER_OBJECTS, few attributes of those objects are shown there. To get more information about an object, you need to look at the view that is specific to that type of object. For tables, that view is USER_TABLES. It can also be referenced via the public synonym TABS.

NOTE
Earlier versions of Oracle included a view called TAB. That view, which is similar in function to TABS, is still supported because of Oracle products that reference it. However, TAB does not contain the columns that TABS contains. Use TABS in your data dictionary queries.

The columns in USER_TABLES can be divided into four major categories (Identification, Space-Related, Statistics-Related, and Other), as shown in Table 42-4.

The table's name is shown in the Table_Name column. The Backed_Up column shows whether or not the table has been backed up since its last modification. The Partitioned column will have a value of 'YES' if the table has been partitioned (data dictionary views related to partitions are described in the "Space Allocation and Usage, Including Partitions and Subpartitions" section of this chapter).

The Space-Related columns, such as Pct_Free, Initial_Extent, Max_Extents, and Pct_Increase, are described in the "Storage" entry of the Alphabetical Reference. The Statistics-Related columns, such as Num_Rows, Blocks, Empty_Blocks, Avg_Row_Len, and Last_Analyzed, are populated when the table is analyzed.

NOTE
As of Oracle Database 10g, you can use the USER_TAB_STATISTICS view to access the statistics for your tables.

Identification	Space-Related	Statistics-Related	Other
Table_Name	Tablespace_Name	Num_Rows	Degree
Backed_Up	Cluster_Name	Blocks	Instances
Partitioned	Pct_Free	Empty_Blocks	Cache
IOT_Name	Pct_Used	Avg_Space	Table_Lock
Logging	Ini_Trans	Chain_Cnt	Buffer_Pool
IOT_Type	Max_Trans	Avg_Row_Len	Row_Movement
Temporary	Initial_Extent	Sample_Size	Duration
Nested	Next_Extent	Last_Analyzed	Skip_Corrupt
Secondary	Min_Extents	Avg_Space_Freelist_Blocks	Monitoring
	Max_Extents	Num_Freelist_Blocks	Cluster_Owner
	Pct_Increase	Global_Stats	Dependencies
	Freelists	User_Stats	Dropped
	Freelist_Groups		Compression

TABLE 42-4. *Column in USER_TABLES.*

Querying the Table_Name column from USER_TABLES will display the names of all of the tables in the current account. The following query lists all of the tables whose names begin with the letter *L*:

```
select Table_Name from USER_TABLES
 where Table_Name like 'L%';
```

The ALL_TABLES view shows all of the tables owned by the user as well as any to which the user has been granted access (either directly or via grants to PUBLIC). Most third-party reporting tools that list available tables for queries obtain that list by querying ALL_TABLES. Since ALL_TABLES can contain entries for multiple users, it contains an Owner column in addition to the columns in USER_TABLES. DBA_TABLES, which lists all tables in the database, has the same column definitions as ALL_TABLES.

The Degree and Instances columns in USER_TABLES relate to how the table is queried during parallel queries. For information on Degree, Instances, and the other table parameters, see **CREATE TABLE** in the Alphabetical Reference.

NOTE
*For external tables, see USER_EXTERNAL_TABLES
and USER_EXTERNAL_LOCATIONS.*

As of Oracle Database 10g, USER_TABLES and other data dictionary views contain a new column named Dropped. That column will have a value of 'YES' or 'NO'; see the section on the recycle bin for information on descriptions of drop objects.

Columns: USER_TAB_COLUMNS (COLS)

Although users do not query from columns, the data dictionary view that shows columns is closely tied to the data dictionary view of tables. This view, called USER_TAB_COLUMNS, lists information specific to columns. USER_TAB_COLUMNS can also be queried via the public synonym COLS.

The columns you can query from USER_TAB_COLUMNS can be separated into three major categories:

- Identification, such as Table_Name, Column_Name, and Column_ID

- Definition-Related, such as Data_Type, Data_Length, Data_Precision, Data_Scale, Nullable, and Default_Length

- Statistics-Related, such as Num_Distinct Low_Value, High_Value, Density, Num_Nulls, and others

The Table_Name and Column_Name columns contain the names of your tables and columns. The usage of the Definition-Related columns is described in the "Datatypes" entry in the Alphabetical Reference. The Statistics-Related columns are populated when the table is analyzed. Statistics for columns are also provided in the USER_TAB_COL_STATISTICS view (described shortly).

To see the column definitions for a table, query USER_TAB_COLUMNS, specifying the Table_Name in the **where** clause:

```
select Column_Name, Data_Type
  from USER_TAB_COLUMNS
 where Table_Name = 'NEWSPAPER';

COLUMN_NAME    DATA_TYPE
-------------- ---------
FEATURE        VARCHAR2
SECTION        CHAR
PAGE           NUMBER
```

The information in this example is also obtainable via the SQL*Plus **describe** command; however, **describe** does not give you the option of seeing the column defaults and statistics. The ALL_TAB_COLUMNS view shows the columns for all of the tables and views owned by the user as well as any to which the user has been granted access (either via direct grants or via grants to PUBLIC). Since ALL_TAB_COLUMNS can contain entries for multiple users, it contains an Owner column in addition to the columns in USER_TAB_COLUMNS. DBA_TAB_COLUMNS, which lists the column definitions for all tables and views in the database, has the same column definitions as ALL_TAB_COLUMNS.

Column Statistics

Most of the column statistics are available in both USER_TAB_COLUMNS (their former home) and USER_TAB_COL_STATISTICS. The columns available in USER_TAB_COL_STATISTICS are

the Statistics-Related columns of USER_TAB_COLUMNS plus the Table_Name and Column_ Name columns.

USER_TAB_COL_STATISTICS contains statistics columns that are also provided via USER_TAB_ COLUMNS for backward compatibility. You should access them via USER_TAB_COL_STATISTICS.

Column Value Histograms

You can use histograms to improve the analysis used by the cost-based optimizer. The USER_ TAB_HISTOGRAMS view contains information about each column's histogram: the Table_Name, Column_Name, Endpoint_Number, Endpoint_Value, and Endpoint_Actual_Value. The values in USER_TAB_HISTOGRAMS are used by the optimizer to determine the distribution of the column values within the table. "ALL" and "DBA" versions of USER_TAB_HISTOGRAMS are available.

Updatable Columns

You can update records in views that contain joins in their view queries, provided the join meets certain criteria. The USER_UPDATABLE_COLUMNS view lists all columns you can update. You can query the Owner, Table_Name, and Column_Name for the column; the Updatable column will have a value of 'YES' if the column can be updated, and a value of 'NO' if the column cannot be updated. You can also query to determine whether you can insert or delete records from the view via the Insertable and Deletable columns.

Views: USER_VIEWS

The base query of a view is accessible via the USER_VIEWS data dictionary view, which contains ten columns; the three main columns are as follows:

View_Name	The name of the view
Text_Length	The length of the view's base query, in characters
Text	The query that the view uses

The other columns, described later in this section, are related to object views.

NOTE
This section only applies to traditional views. For materialized views, see "Database Links and Materialized Views" later in the chapter.

The Text column is a LONG datatype. This may cause a problem when querying USER_VIEWS via SQL*Plus, because SQL*Plus truncates LONGs. The point at which truncation occurs, however, can be changed via the **set long** command. USER_VIEWS provides a mechanism for determining the proper setting for the LONG truncation point, as you'll see in the following example.

The Text_Length column shows the length of the view's query. Therefore, the SQL*Plus LONG truncation point must be set to a value equal to or greater than the view's Text_Length value. For example, the following listing shows a view whose View_Name is AGING and whose Text_ Length is 355:

```
select View_Name, Text_Length
  from USER_VIEWS
 where View_Name = 'AGING';
```

```
View_Name           Text_Length
----------------    ------------
AGING               355
```

Since the length of the view's text is 355 characters, use the **set long** command to increase the LONG truncation point to at least 355 (the default is 80) to see the full text of the view's query:

```
set long 355
```

You can then query USER_VIEWS for the view's Text, using the query shown in the following listing:

```
select Text
  from USER_VIEWS
 where View_Name = 'AGING';
```

If you had not used the **set long** command, then the output would have been truncated at 80 characters, with no message telling you why the truncation occurred. Before querying other views, you will need to recheck their Text_Length values.

NOTE
You can query the column definitions for views from USER_TAB_COLUMNS, the same view you query for tables.

If you use column aliases in your views, and your column aliases are part of the view's query, then your data dictionary queries for information about views will be simplified. Since the entire text of the view's query is displayed in USER_VIEWS, the column aliases will be displayed as well.

You can create views using this format:

```
create view NEWSPAPER_VIEW (SomeFeature, SomeSection)
    as select Feature, Section
  from NEWSPAPER;
```

Listing the column names in the header of the **create view** command removes the column aliases from the query and thus prevents you from seeing them via USER_VIEWS. The only way to see the view's column names would be to query USER_TAB_COLUMNS. If the column names are in the query, then you only need to query one data dictionary view (USER_VIEWS) for both the query and the column names.

For example, given the NEWSPAPER_VIEW view created in the last example, if you were to query USER_VIEWS, you would see

```
select Text
  from USER_VIEWS
 where View_Name ='NEWSPAPER_VIEW';

TEXT
----------------------------------------
select Feature, Section from NEWSPAPER
```

This query does *not* show you the new column names you assigned, since you did not make those column names part of the view's query. To make those column names show up in USER_VIEWS, add them as column aliases in the view's query:

```
create view NEWSPAPER_VIEW
    as select Feature SomeFeature, Section SomeSection
  from NEWSPAPER;
```

Now when you query USER_VIEWS, the column aliases will be displayed as part of the view's query text:

```
select Text
  from USER_VIEWS
where View_Name ='NEWSPAPER_VIEW';

TEXT
-------------------------------------------------
select Feature SomeFeature, Section SomeSection
  from NEWSPAPER
```

To support object views, USER_VIEWS contains the following columns:

Type_Text	Type clause of the typed view
Type_Text_Length	Length of the type clause of the typed view
OID_Text	WITH OID clause of the typed view
OID_Text_Length	Length of the WITH OID clause of the typed view
View_Type_Owner	Owner of the view's type for typed views
View_Type	Type of the view

See Chapters 33 and 36 for information on object views and types.

The ALL_VIEWS view lists all of the views owned by the user as well as any views to which the user has been granted access, either via direct grants or via grants to PUBLIC. Since ALL_VIEWS can contain entries for multiple users, it contains an Owner column in addition to the columns listed earlier in this section. DBA_VIEWS, which lists all views in the database, has the same column definitions as ALL_VIEWS.

Synonyms: USER_SYNONYMS (SYN)

USER_SYNONYMS lists all of the synonyms that a user owns. The columns are as follows:

Synonym_Name	The name of the synonym
Table_Owner	The owner of the table that the synonym refers to
Table_Name	The name of the table that the synonym refers to
DB_Link	The name of the database link used in the synonym

USER_SYNONYMS is useful when debugging programs or resolving problems with users' access to objects within applications. USER_SYNONYMS is also known by the public synonym SYN.

The DB_Link column will be **NULL** if the synonym does not use a database link. Therefore, if you want to see a list of the database links currently in use by the synonyms owned by your account, execute this query:

```
select distinct DB_Link
  from USER_SYNONYMS
 where DB_Link is not null;
```

The ALL_SYNONYMS view lists all of the synonyms owned by the user, public synonyms, and all synonyms to which the user has been granted access. Since ALL_SYNONYMS can contain entries for multiple users, it contains an Owner column in addition to the columns listed earlier in this section. DBA_SYNONYMS, which lists all synonyms in the database, has the same column definitions as ALL_SYNONYMS.

Sequences: USER_SEQUENCES (SEQ)

To display the attributes of sequences, you can query the USER_SEQUENCES data dictionary view. This view can also be queried using the public synonym SEQ. The columns of USER_SEQUENCES are as follows:

Column Name	Description
Sequence_Name	Name of the sequence
Min_Value	Minimum value of the sequence
Max_Value	Maximum value of the sequence
Increment_By	Increment between sequence values
Cycle_Flag	A flag to indicate whether the value should cycle back to the Min_Value once the Max_Value is reached
Order_Flag	A flag to indicate whether sequence numbers are generated in order
Cache_Size	The number of sequence entries cached in memory
Last_Number	The last sequence number written to disk or cached

The Last_Number column is not updated during normal database operation; it is used during database restart/recovery operations.

ALL_SEQUENCES lists all of the sequences owned by the user or to which the user or PUBLIC has been granted access. Since ALL_SEQUENCES can contain entries for multiple users, it contains a Sequence_Owner column in addition to the columns listed. DBA_SEQUENCES, which lists all sequences in the database, has the same column definitions as ALL_SEQUENCES.

Recycle Bin—USER_RECYCLEBIN and DBA_RECYCLEBIN

As of Oracle Database 10g you can use the **flashback table** command to recover tables and dependent objects that have been dropped. To see the objects presently in your recycle bin, query USER_RECYCLEBIN. The public synonym RECYCLEBIN can be used in place of USER_RECYCLEBIN in your queries. You will see the original object name, whether it can be recovered (the Can_Undrop column), and whether it was dropped because it was related to a base object that was dropped (the Base_Object column value).

Objects stay in the recycle bin until they are purged. Objects can be removed from the recycle bin automatically if there is no longer any free space in the tablespace they were dropped from. DBAs can see all objects in all users' recycle bins via the DBA_RECYCLEBIN view. There is no "ALL" version of this view. See the entry for the **purge** command for details on removing objects from the recycle bin.

Constraints and Comments

Constraints and comments help you to understand how tables and columns relate to each other. Comments are strictly informational; they do not enforce any conditions on the data stored in the objects they describe. Constraints, on the other hand, define the conditions under which that data is valid. Typical constraints include NOT NULL, UNIQUE, PRIMARY KEY, and FOREIGN KEY. In the following sections, you will see how to retrieve data about constraints and comments from the data dictionary.

Constraints: USER_CONSTRAINTS

Constraint information is accessible via the USER_CONSTRAINTS view. This information is very useful when trying to alter data constraints or resolve problems with an application's data. The columns of this view are listed in Table 42-5.

Column Name	Description
Owner	The owner of the constraint.
Constraint_Name	The name of the constraint.
Constraint_Type	The type of constraint: 'C' CHECK constraint; includes NOT NULLs 'P' PRIMARY KEY constraint 'R' FOREIGN KEY (reference) constraint 'U' UNIQUE constraint 'V' WITH CHECK OPTION constraint (for views) 'O' WITH READ ONLY constraint (for views)
Table_Name	The name of the table associated with the constraint.

TABLE 42-5. *Columns in USER_CONSTRAINTS*

Column Name	Description
Search_Condition	The search condition used (for CHECK constraints).
R_Owner	The owner of the table referenced by a FOREIGN KEY constraint.
R_Constraint_Name	The name of the constraint referenced by a FOREIGN KEY constraint.
Delete_Rule	The action to take on the FOREIGN KEY tables when a PRIMARY KEY record is deleted (CASCADE or NO ACTION).
Status	The status of the constraint (ENABLED or DISABLED).
Deferrable	A flag to indicate whether the constraint can be deferred.
Deferred	A flag to indicate whether the constraint was initially deferred.
Validated	A flag (VALIDATED or NOT VALIDATED) to indicate whether all data obeys the constraint.
Generated	A flag to indicate whether the constraint name has been generated by the database.
Bad	A flag to indicate whether a date was used in the constraint creation without specifying a century value for CHECK constraints, resulting in ambiguous two-digit years; applies only to constraints in databases upgraded from prior versions of Oracle. Such constraints may result in ORA-02436 errors if not dropped and re-created properly.
Rely	A flag to indicate if the constraint is enforced or unenforced.
Last_Change	The date the constraint was last enabled or disabled.
Index_Owner	Owner of the related index.
Index_Name	Name of the related index.
Invalid	Valid/invalid flag.
View_Related	Yes/No flag to record if the constraint is view related.

TABLE 42-5. *Columns in USER_CONSTRAINTS* (continued)

Although this is a "USER" view, it contains an Owner column. In this view, Owner refers to the owner of the constraint, not the owner of the table (which is the user).

Valid values for the Constraint_Type column are shown in Table 42-5. Understanding the constraint types is crucial when you are trying to get useful information about your constraints.

FOREIGN KEY constraints will always have values for the R_Owner and R_Constraint_Name columns. These two columns will tell you which constraint the FOREIGN KEY references. A FOREIGN KEY references another *constraint,* not another column. NOT NULL constraints on columns are stored as CHECK constraints, so they have a Constraint_Type of 'C'.

Querying USER_CONSTRAINTS will give you the names of all the constraints on a table. This is important when trying to interpret error messages that only provide the name of the constraint that was violated.

Once you know the name and type of a constraint, you can check the columns associated with it via the USER_CONS_COLUMNS view, described in the next section.

If you do not assign constraint names when creating them, Oracle will generate unique constraint names. See "Integrity Constraint" in the Alphabetical Reference for further details. If a constraint name has been system-generated, that fact will be indicated via the Generated column.

If you defer a constraint (as indicated by the Deferred column), the constraint will not be enforced for the duration of a transaction. For example, if you were performing bulk **update**s on related tables and could not guarantee the order of transactions, you may decide to defer constraint checking on the tables until all of the **update**s have completed.

ALL_CONSTRAINTS lists the constraints on all of the tables that the user or PUBLIC can access. DBA_CONSTRAINTS lists all of the constraints in the database. Each of these views has the same set of columns as USER_CONSTRAINTS (since they all include the Owner column).

Constraint Columns: USER_CONS_COLUMNS

You can view the columns associated with constraints via the USER_CONS_COLUMNS data dictionary view. If you have already queried USER_CONSTRAINTS to obtain the types and names of the constraints involved, you can use USER_CONS_COLUMNS to determine which columns are involved in the constraint. The columns in this view are the following:

Owner	The owner of the constraint
Constraint_Name	The name of the constraint
Table_Name	The name of the table associated with the constraint
Column_Name	The name of the column associated with the constraint
Position	The order of the column within the constraint definition

There are only two columns in USER_CONS_COLUMNS that are not in USER_CONSTRAINTS: Column_Name and Position. A sample query of this table is shown in the following listing:

```
select Column_Name, Position
  from USER_CONS_COLUMNS
 where Constraint_Name = 'SYS_C0008791';

COLUMN_NAME   POSITION
------------  --------
FIRSTNAME            1
LASTNAME             2
```

As shown in the preceding listing, the combination of FirstName and LastName forms the constraint (in this case, a primary key).

The Position column is significant. When you create a UNIQUE or PRIMARY KEY constraint, Oracle automatically creates a unique index on the set of columns you specify. The index is created based on the column order you specify. The column order, in turn, affects the performance of the index. An index comprising multiple columns may be used most efficiently if the leading column

of that index (Position=1) is used in the query's **where** clause. See Chapter 43 for further details on the optimizer.

The ALL_CONS_COLUMNS and DBA_CONS_COLUMNS views have the same column definitions as USER_CONS_COLUMNS. ALL_CONS_COLUMNS can be used to display column information about constraints on all tables that the user can access regardless of owner. DBA_CONS_COLUMNS lists the column-level constraint information for the entire database.

Constraint Exceptions: EXCEPTIONS

When enabling constraints on tables that already contain data, you may encounter constraint violations within the data. For example, you may attempt to create a PRIMARY KEY constraint on a column that contains the same value for multiple records, but such an attempt would fail due to uniqueness constraint violations.

You can capture information about the rows that cause constraint creations to fail. First, create a table called EXCEPTIONS in your schema; the SQL script that should be used to create this table is named utlexcpt.sql, and is usually located in the /rdbms/admin directory under the Oracle home directory.

The EXCEPTIONS table contains four columns: Row_ID (the ROWID of each row that violated the constraint), Owner (the owner of the violated constraint), Table_Name (the table on which the violated constraint was created), and Constraint (the constraint violated by the row). After creating the EXCEPTIONS table, attempt to enable a PRIMARY KEY constraint:

```
alter table NEWSPAPER enable PRIMARY KEY
exceptions into EXCEPTIONS;

ORA-02437: cannot enable (NEWSPAPER.SYS_C00516) - primary key violated
```

The constraint creation fails, and a reference to all rows that violate the constraint is placed in the EXCEPTIONS table. For example, if the PRIMARY KEY constraint in the last example generated exceptions, then you could query the EXCEPTIONS table as shown in the following listing:

```
select Owner, Table_Name, Constraint from EXCEPTIONS;

OWNER      TABLE_NAME CONSTRAINT
---------- ---------- ----------
PRACTICE   NEWSPAPER  SYS_C00516
PRACTICE   NEWSPAPER  SYS_C00516
```

Two rows violated the constraint named SYS_C00516 (which, in this example, is the constraint name given to the PRIMARY KEY constraint for the NEWSPAPER table). You can determine which rows of the NEWSPAPER table correspond to these exceptions by joining the Row_ID column of the EXCEPTIONS table to the ROWID pseudo-column of the table on which the constraint was being placed (in this example, the NEWSPAPER table):

```
select *
  from NEWSPAPER
 where RowID in
       (select Row_ID from EXCEPTIONS);
```

The rows that caused the constraint violations will then be displayed.

NOTE
Row_ID is an actual column in the EXCEPTIONS table, with a datatype of ROWID. It is joined to the ROWID pseudo-column in the table from which the exceptions were generated.

NOTE
Flashback and recovery operations may change the ROWIDs for rows previously inserted into tables.

Table Comments: USER_TAB_COMMENTS

You can add a comment to a table, view, or column after it has been created. Comments on the data dictionary views are the basis for the records displayed via the DICTIONARY and DICT_COLUMNS views. To display comments about your own tables, use the USER_TAB_COMMENTS view.

USER_TAB_COMMENTS contains three columns:

Table_Name	The name of the table or view
Table_Type	The object type (table, object table, or view)
Comments	Comments that have been entered for the object

To add a comment to a table, use the **comment** command, as shown in the following listing:

```
comment on table BIRTHDAY is 'Birthday list for Blacksburg
    employees';
```

Query USER_TAB_COMMENTS by specifying the Table_Name you want to see the comments for, as shown in the following listing:

```
select Comments
  from USER_TAB_COMMENTS
 where Table_Name = 'BIRTHDAY';

COMMENTS
----------------------------------------
Birthday list for Blacksburg
    employees
```

To remove a comment, set the comment to two single quotes with no space between them:

```
comment on table BIRTHDAY is '';
```

You can view the comments on all of the tables you can access via the ALL_TAB_COMMENTS view. ALL_TAB_COMMENTS has an additional column, Owner, which specifies the owner of the table. DBA_TAB_COMMENTS lists all of the tables in the database, and it has an Owner column as well.

Column Comments: USER_COL_COMMENTS

USER_COL_COMMENTS displays the comments that have been entered for columns within your tables. These comments are added to the database via the **comment** command. USER_COL_COMMENTS contains three columns:

Table_Name	The name of the table or view
Column_Name	The name of the column
Comments	Comments that have been entered for the column

To add a comment to a column, use the **comment** command, as shown in the following listing:

```
comment on column BIRTHDAY.AGE is 'Age in years';
```

Query USER_COL_COMMENTS by specifying the Table_Name and Column_Name you want to see the comments for.

```
select Comments
   from USER_COL_COMMENTS
 where Table_Name = 'BIRTHDAY'
   and Column_Name = 'AGE';
```

To remove a comment, set the comment to two single quotes with no space between them:

```
comment on column BIRTHDAY.AGE is '';
```

You can view the column comments on all of the tables you can access via the ALL_COL_COMMENTS view. ALL_COL_COMMENTS has an additional column, Owner, which specifies the owner of the table. DBA_COL_COMMENTS lists all of the columns in all of the tables in the database, and it has an Owner column as well.

Indexes and Clusters

Indexes and clusters do not change the data that is stored in tables; however, they do change the way that data is accessed and stored. In the following sections, you will see data dictionary views that describe indexes and clusters. You will see descriptions of the data dictionary views related to partitioned indexes in "Space Allocation and Usage, Including Partitions and Subpartitions" in this chapter.

Indexes: USER_INDEXES (IND)

In Oracle, indexes are very closely related to constraints. The PRIMARY KEY and UNIQUE constraints always have associated unique indexes. As with constraints, two data dictionary views are used to query information about indexes: USER_INDEXES and USER_IND_COLUMNS. USER_INDEXES is also known by its public synonym, IND.

The columns in USER_INDEXES can be grouped into four categories, as shown in Table 42-6.

The name of the index is shown in the Index_Name column. The owner and name for the table being indexed are in the Table_Owner and Table_Name columns. The Uniqueness column will

Identification	Space-Related	Statistics-Related	Other
Index_Name	Tablespace_Name	Blevel	Degree
Table_Owner	Ini_Trans	Leaf_Blocks	Instances
Table_Name	Max_Trans	Distinct_Keys	Include_Column
Table_Type	Initial_Extent	Avg_Leaf_Blocks_Per_Key	Buffer_Pool
Uniqueness	Next_Extent	Avg_Data_Blocks_Per_Key	Duration
Status	Min_Extents	Clustering_Factor	Pct_Direct_Access
Partitioned	Max_Extents	Num_Rows	Parameters
Index_Type	Pct_Increase	Sample_Size	Domidx_Status
Temporary	Pct_Free	Last_Analyzed	Domidx_Opstatus
Generated	Freelists	User_Stats	Funcidx_Status
Logging	Freelist_Groups	Global_Stats	Join_Index
Compression	Pct_Threshold		IOT_Redundant_Pkey_Elim
Prefix_Length			Dropped
Secondary			
Ityp_Owner			
Ityp_Name			

TABLE 42-6. *Columns in USER_INDEXES*

be set to UNIQUE for unique indexes and set to NONUNIQUE for nonunique indexes. Table_Type records whether the index is on a 'TABLE' or a 'CLUSTER'. The Dropped column, available as of Oracle Database 10*g*, identifies indexes that are in the recycle bin.

The Space-Related columns are described in the "Storage" entry in the Alphabetical Reference.

The Statistics-Related columns are populated when the table is analyzed (see the **analyze** command in the Alphabetical Reference). The Degree and Instances columns refer to the degree of parallelism used when the index is created.

NOTE
*As of Oracle Database 10g, you can use the USER_IND_STATISTICS view to access the statistics for your indexes.To see all of the indexes on a table, query USER_INDEXES using the Table_Owner and Table_ Name columns in the **where** clause, as shown in the following listing:*

```
select Index_Name, Uniqueness
  from USER_INDEXES
 where Table_Owner = 'PRACTICE'
   and Table_Name = 'BIRTHDAY';

INDEX_NAME        UNIQUENES
---------------- ---------
PK_BIRTHDAY       UNIQUE
```

The Clustering_Factor column is not directly related to clusters, but rather represents the degree to which the rows in the table are ordered. The more ordered those rows are, the more efficient range queries will be (*range queries* are those in which a range of values is given for a column, such as **where LastName like 'A%'**).

To discover which columns are part of the index, and their order within the index, you need to query the USER_IND_COLUMNS view, which is described in the next section.

ALL_INDEXES shows all of the indexes owned by the user as well as any created on tables to which the user or PUBLIC has been granted access. Since ALL_INDEXES can contain entries for multiple users, it contains an Owner column in addition to the columns shown in Table 42-6. DBA_INDEXES, which lists all indexes in the database, has the same column definitions as ALL_INDEXES.

NOTE
For function-based indexes, see USER_IND_EXPRESSIONS.

Indexed Columns: USER_IND_COLUMNS

You can determine which columns are in an index by querying USER_IND_COLUMNS. The columns available via this view are as follows:

Index_Name	The name of the index
Table_Name	The name of the indexed table
Column_Name	The name of a column within the index
Column_Position	The column's position within the index
Column_Length	The indexed length of the column
Char_Length	Maximum code point length of the column (Unicode)
Descend	A Y/N flag to indicate whether or not the column is sorted in descending order

Five columns in this view are not in USER_INDEXES: Column_Name, Column_Position, Column_Length, Char_Length, and Descend. Column_Length, like the Statistics-Related columns in USER_INDEXES, is populated when the index's base table is analyzed. A sample query of this table, using the Index_Name from the USER_INDEXES example, is shown in the following listing (in this example, the Column_Position column is given the alias Pos):

```
select Column_Name, Column_Position Pos
  from USER_IND_COLUMNS
 where Index_Name = 'PK_BIRTHDAY';

COLUMN_NAME   POS
------------  ---
FIRSTNAME      1
LASTNAME       2
```

As you can see from this query, the PK_BIRTHDAY index consists of two columns: FirstName and LastName, in that order. See Chapter 43 for details on how the optimizer uses multicolumn indexes.

ALL_IND_COLUMNS can be used to display column information about indexes on all tables that the user can access regardless of owner. DBA_IND_COLUMNS lists the column-level index information for the entire database.

Bitmap Join Index Columns: USER_JOIN_IND_COLUMNS

If you create a bitmap join index (introduced in Oracle9*i*), you can query USER_JOIN_IND_ COLUMNS for the join details. USER_JOIN_IND_COLUMNS records the names of the tables involved in the join, the inner and outer join columns, and the dimension and fact tables involved.

Clusters: USER_CLUSTERS (CLU)

The storage and statistics parameters associated with clusters are accessible via USER_CLUSTERS (also known by the public synonym CLU). The columns in this data dictionary view are shown in Table 42-7, separated by type.

The Cluster_Name column contains the name of the cluster. Cluster_Type specifies whether the cluster uses a standard B*-tree index or a hashing function for the cluster.

The usage of the Space-Related columns is described in the "Storage" entry in the Alphabetical Reference. The Statistics-Related columns are populated when the table is analyzed.

ALL_CLUSTERS and DBA_CLUSTERS have an additional column, Owner, since they list clusters in multiple schemas.

Identification	Space-Related	Statistics-Related	Other
Cluster_Name	Tablespace_Name	Avg_Blocks_Per_Key	Degree
Cluster_Type	Pct_Free	Hashkeys	Instances
Function	Pct_Used		Cache
	Key_Size		Buffer_Pool
	Ini_Trans		Single_Table
	Max_Trans		Dependencies
	Initial_Extent		
	Next_Extent		
	Min_Extents		
	Max_Extents		
	Pct_Increase		
	Freelists		
	Freelist_Groups		

TABLE 42-7. *Columns in USER_CLUSTERS*

Cluster Columns: USER_CLU_COLUMNS

To see the mapping of table columns to cluster columns, query USER_CLU_COLUMNS, whose columns are the following:

Cluster_Name	The name of the cluster
Clu_Column_Name	The name of the key column in the cluster
Table_Name	The name of a table within the cluster
Tab_Column_Name	The name of the key column in the table

Since a single cluster can store data from multiple tables, USER_CLU_COLUMNS is useful for determining which columns of which tables map to the cluster's columns.

There is no "ALL" version of this view. There are only USER_CLU_COLUMNS for the user's cluster columns, and DBA_CLU_COLUMNS, which shows the column mappings for all clusters in the database.

Abstract Datatypes, ORDBMS-Related Structures, and LOBs

In the following sections, you will see the data dictionary views associated with object-relational structures such as abstract datatypes, methods, and large objects (LOBs). "ALL" and "DBA" versions of all of these data dictionary views are available. Because they contain records for multiple owners, the "ALL" and "DBA" versions of these views contain Owner columns as well as the columns listed in this section.

Abstract Datatypes: USER_TYPES

Abstract datatypes created within your schema are listed in USER_TYPES, which includes columns for the Type_Name, number of attributes (Attributes), and number of methods (Methods) defined for the datatype.

For example, the ANIMAL_TY datatype has three attributes and one method (methods are defined via the **create type body** command), as shown in the following listing:

```
select Type_Name,
       Attributes,
       Methods
  from USER_TYPES
 where Type_Name = 'ANIMAL_TY';

TYPE_NAME                       ATTRIBUTES    METHODS
------------------------------- ----------- -----------
ANIMAL_TY                                 3           1
```

Datatype Attributes: USER_TYPE_ATTRS

To see the attributes of a datatype, you need to query the USER_TYPE_ATTRS view. The columns in USER_TYPE_ATTRS are shown in Table 42-8.

Column Name	Description
Type_Name	Name of the type
Attr_Name	Name of the attribute
Attr_Type_Mod	The type modifier of the attribute
Attr_Type_Owner	Owner of the attribute's type, if the attribute is based on another datatype
Attr_Type_Name	Name of the type of the attribute
Length	Length of the attribute
Precision	Precision of the attribute
Scale	Scale of the attribute
Character_Set_Name	Character set of the attribute
Attr_No	Ordinal position of the attribute within the type definition
Inherited	Yes/No flag to indicate if the attribute is inherited from a supertype

TABLE 42-8. *Columns in USER_TYPE_ATTRS*

You can query USER_TYPE_ATTRS to see the relationships between nested abstract datatypes. For example, the PERSON_TY datatype uses the ADDRESS_TY datatype, as shown in the following listing:

```
select Attr_Name,
       Length,
       Attr_Type_Name
  from USER_TYPE_ATTRS
 where Type_Name = 'PERSON_TY';

ATTR_NAME                          LENGTH ATTR_TYPE_NAME
------------------------------ ---------- ------------------
NAME                                   25 VARCHAR2
ADDRESS                                   ADDRESS_TY
```

Datatype Methods: USER_TYPE_METHODS and USER_METHOD_PARAMS

If a type has methods defined for it, then you query USER_TYPE_METHODS to determine the methods' names. USER_TYPE_METHODS contains columns showing the type name (Type_Name), method name (Method_Name), method number (Method_No, used for overloaded methods), and type of method (Method_Type). USER_TYPE_METHODS also includes columns that show the number of parameters (Parameters) and results (Results) returned by the method.

For example, the ANIMAL_TY datatype has one method, a member function named AGE. The AGE method has one input parameter (Birthdate) and one output result (the age, in days).

Querying USER_TYPE_METHODS shows that *two* parameters are defined for AGE, not one as expected:

```
select Parameters,
       Results
  from USER_TYPE_METHODS
 where Type_Name = 'ANIMAL_TY'
   and Method_Name = 'AGE';

PARAMETERS    RESULTS
----------  ----------
         2           1
```

Why does AGE have two parameters if it only has one input parameter defined? To find out, you can query USER_METHOD_PARAMS, which describes the parameters for your methods:

```
select Param_Name, Param_No, Param_Type_Name
  from USER_METHOD_PARAMS
 order by Param_No;

PARAM_NAME                         PARAM_NO PARAM_TYPE_NAME
--------------------------------  ---------- -----------------
SELF                                      1 ANIMAL_TY
BIRTHDATE                                 2 DATE
```

USER_METHOD_PARAMS shows that for each method, Oracle creates an implicit SELF parameter. The results of your methods are shown in USER_METHOD_RESULTS:

```
select Method_Name,
       Result_Type_Name
  from USER_METHOD_RESULTS
 where Type_Name = 'ANIMAL_TY';

METHOD_NAME                       RESULT_TYPE_NAME
--------------------------------  ----------------------------
AGE                               NUMBER
```

Other Datatypes: USER_REFS, USER_COLL_TYPES, and USER_NESTED_TABLES

If you use REFs (see Chapter 36), you can query the USER_REFS data dictionary view to display the REFs you have defined. USER_REFS will show the name of the table containing the REF column (Table_Name) and the column name of the object column (Column_Name). The attributes of the REF—such as whether or not it is stored with the ROWID—are also accessible via USER_REFS.

Collector types (nested tables and varying arrays) are described via the USER_COLL_TYPES data dictionary view. The columns of USER_COLL_TYPES include Type_Name, Upper_Bound (for varying arrays), and the Length and Precision of the elements. You can use USER_COLL_TYPES in conjunction with the abstract datatype data dictionary views shown earlier in this section to determine the type structure of a collector. You can also query USER_NESTED_TABLES and USER_VARRAYS to see details for your collections.

LOBs: USER_LOBS

As described in Chapter 35, you can store large objects inside the database. The USER_LOBS view provides information on the LOBs defined in your tables; a sample listing is shown here:

```
column column_name format A30

select Table_Name,
       Column_Name
  from USER_LOBS;

TABLE_NAME                               COLUMN_NAME
-------------------------------          -------------------------------
PROPOSAL                                 PROPOSAL_TEXT
PROPOSAL                                 BUDGET
```

USER_LOBS also shows the names of the segments used to hold the LOB data when it grows large; however, it does not show the datatypes of the LOB columns. To see the LOB datatypes, you can either **describe** the table that includes the LOBs or query USER_TAB_COLUMNS (as shown earlier in this chapter).

To use BFILE datatypes for LOBs, you have to create directories (see the entry for the **create directory** command in the Alphabetical Reference). The ALL_DIRECTORIES data dictionary shows the Owner, Directory_Name, and Directory_Path columns for each directory to which you have been granted access. A "DBA" version of this view is also available. No "USER" version of this view is available.

Database Links and Materialized Views

Database links and materialized views are used to manage access to remote data. Depending on the type of materialized view you use, you may be able to use materialized view logs. In the following sections, you will see descriptions of the data dictionary views you can use to display information about database links and materialized views. For further information on database links, see Chapter 23. For further information on materialized views, see Chapter 24.

Database Links: USER_DB_LINKS

To see the database links created under your account, query USER_DB_LINKS. The columns of this view, including the link name (DB_Link), username to connect to (Username), the account password (Password), and the connection string (Host), show the information about the remote connection that the link will be used to establish. The Username and Password values will be used to log in to the remote database defined by the Host value.

The Host column stores the Oracle Net service names. This column stores the exact character string you specify during the **create database link** command, and does not alter its case. Therefore, you should be careful with the case you use when creating database links. Otherwise, your queries against USER_DB_LINKS will have to take into account inconsistencies in the case of the Host column. For example, looking for a database link that uses the 'HQ' service descriptor would require you to enter

```
Select * from USER_DB_LINKS
  where UPPER(Host) = 'HQ';
```

since it is possible that there are entries with a Host value of 'hq' instead of 'HQ'.

NOTE
If you are using default logins to the remote database,
*then Password will be **NULL**.*

The ALL_DB_LINKS view lists all of the database links that either are owned by the user or are PUBLIC database links. DBA_DB_LINKS lists all database links in the database. ALL_DB_LINKS and DBA_DB_LINKS share most of the same column definitions as USER_DB_LINKS; they have an Owner column rather than the Password column.

See Chapter 23 for further information on the uses of database links.

Materialized Views

You can query USER_MVIEWS to display information about the materialized views owned by your account. This view, whose columns are listed in Table 42-9, shows the structural information about the materialized view as well as its refresh schedule.

NOTE
See Chapter 24 for details on materialized views.

The name of the materialized view is found in the Mview_Name column of USER_MVIEWS. The local base table for the view is the Container_Name column. New USER_MVIEWS columns are available as of Oracle Database 10g, including Stale_Since (when the materialized view became stale).To determine which database links are being used by your materialized views, query the Master_Link column, as shown in the following example:

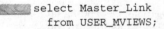
```
select Master_Link
   from USER_MVIEWS;
```

The names of the database links returned by this query can be used as input for queries against USER_DB_LINKS. This query will display all of the database link information available for database links used in your materialized views:

```
select *
   from USER_DB_LINKS
  where DB_Link in
       (select Master_Link
           from USER_MVIEWS);
```

Additional queries that are useful in the management of materialized views are provided in Chapter 24.

The ALL_MVIEWS and DBA_MVIEWS views have the same column definitions as USER_ MVIEWS. You can use ALL_MVIEWS to display information about all materialized views that the user can access regardless of owner. DBA_MVIEWS lists materialized view information for all users in the database.

Two related views—USER_REFRESH and USER_REFRESH_CHILDREN—display information about refresh groups. USER_MVIEW_REFRESH_TIMES shows the last time each materialized view

was refreshed. As of Oracle Database 10g, you can access comments on the materialized views via USER_MVIEW_COMMENTS, and query rewrite details via USER_REWRITE_EQUIVALENCES.

Column Name	Description
Owner	The account that owns the materialized view
Mview_Name	The name of the materialized view
Container_Name	The base table (in the local database) for the materialized view's data
Query	The query that defines the materialized view
Query_Len	The length of the materialized view's base query
Updatable	A flag to indicate whether the snapshot can be updated
Update_Log	The name of the table that logs changes made to an updatable snapshot
Master_Rollback_Seg	The rollback segment to use during snapshot population and refresh operations
Master_Link	The database link used to access the master database
Rewrite_Enabled	A Yes/No flag to indicate if query rewrite is enabled for the view
Rewrite_Capability	Rules and restrictions for query rewrites
Refresh_Mode	DEMAND, COMMIT, or NEVER, depending on the refresh mode for the view
Refresh_Method	Values used to drive a fast refresh of the view (Complete, Fast, Never, or Force)
Build_Mode	IMMEDIATE, DEFERRED, or PREBUILT instantiation of the materialized view data during its creation
Fast_Refreshable	Methods available for fast refresh of the materialized view
Last_Refresh_Type	The most recent refresh type used
Last_Refresh_Date	A timestamp to record the last time the snapshot's data was refreshed
Staleness	The status of the materialized view's data relative to its master tables
After_Fast_Refresh	Staleness status following a fast refresh
Compile_State	Validity of the materialized view
Use_No_Index	Yes/No flag to indicate if the materialized view was created with the USING NO INDEX clause
Unknown_Trusted_FD	Indicates if the materialized view used trusted constraints for the refresh.
Stale_Since	Time the materialized view became stale

TABLE 42-9. *Columns in USER_MVIEWS*

Additional Materialized View Capabilities

You can query USER_MVIEW_ANALYSIS to see the materialized views that support query rewrite. If a materialized view contains references to a remote table, it will not be listed in this view. You can query the owner of the materialized view, its name (Mview_Name), and the owner of the base table (Mview_Table_Owner). Many of the columns in this view are flags, such as Summary ('Y' if the view contains an aggregation), Known_Stale ('Y' if the view's data is inconsistent with the base table), and Contains_Views ('Y' if the materialized view references a view).

If the materialized view contains aggregations, you can query USER_MVIEW_AGGREGATES for details on the aggregations. Columns in this view are as follows:

Owner	Owner of the materialized view
Mview_Name	Name of the materialized view
Position_in_Select	Position within the query
Container_Column	Name of the column
Agg_Function	Aggregate function
DistinctFlag	'Y' if the aggregation uses the DISTINCT function
Measure	The SQL text of the measure, excluding the aggregate function

You can query details of the relations within materialized views from the USER_MVIEW_DETAIL_RELATIONS and USER_MVIEW_KEYS data dictionary views. If the materialized view is based on joins, see USER_MVIEW_JOINS for the join details. In general, USER_MVIEW_ANALYSIS will be the most commonly used data dictionary view related to materialized views.

Materialized View Logs: USER_MVIEW_LOGS

Materialized view logs can be used by many materialized views to determine which records in the master table need to be refreshed in the materialized view of that table. You can query USER_MVIEW_LOGS for information about a user's logs, including the name of the master table (Master), the table holding the log records (Log_Table), and whether the materialized view is based on the primary key or the ROWID (the Primary_Key and ROWIDs columns). USER_MVIEW_LOGS is usually queried for maintenance purposes, such as to determine the name of the trigger used to create the materialized view log records.

DBA_MVIEW_LOGS has the same column definitions as USER_MVIEW_LOGS, and shows all materialized view logs in the database. You can query USER_BASE_TABLE_MVIEWS for a listing of the materialized view master tables using materialized view logs.

Triggers, Procedures, Functions, and Packages

You can use procedures, packages, and triggers—blocks of PL/SQL code stored in the database— to enforce business rules or to perform complicated processing. Triggers are described in Chapter 30. Procedures, functions, and packages are described in Chapter 31. In the following sections, you will see how to query the data dictionary for information about triggers, procedures, packages, and functions.

Triggers: USER_TRIGGERS

USER_TRIGGERS contains information about the triggers owned by your account. This view, whose columns are listed in Table 42-10, shows the trigger type and body.

The ALL_TRIGGERS view lists the triggers for all tables to which you have access. DBA_TRIGGERS lists all of the triggers in the database. Both of these views contain an additional column, Owner, which records the owner of the trigger.

A second trigger-related data dictionary view, USER_TRIGGER_COLS, shows how columns are used by a trigger. It lists the name of each column affected by a trigger, as well as how the trigger is used. Like USER_TRIGGERS, "ALL" and "DBA" versions of this data dictionary view are available.

Procedures, Functions, and Packages: USER_SOURCE

The source code for existing procedures, functions, packages, and package bodies can be queried from the USER_SOURCE data dictionary view. The Type column in USER_SOURCE identifies the procedural object as a 'PROCEDURE', 'FUNCTION', 'PACKAGE', 'PACKAGE BODY', 'TRIGGER', 'TYPE', 'TYPE BODY', or 'JAVA SOURCE'. Each line of code is stored in a separate record in USER_SOURCE.

Column Name	Description
Trigger_Name	Name of the trigger
Trigger_Type	The type of trigger (BEFORE STATEMENT, BEFORE EACH ROW, and so on)
Triggering_Event	The command that executes the trigger (INSERT, UPDATE, or DELETE)
Table_Owner	The owner of the table that the trigger is defined for
Base_Object_Type	The type of object on which the trigger is based (TABLE, VIEW, SCHEMA, or DATABASE)
Table_Name	The name of the table or view that the trigger is defined for
Column_Name	For nested table triggers, the name of the nested table column
Referencing_Names	Names used for referencing OLD and NEW values in the trigger
When_Clause	The **when** clause used for the trigger
Status	Whether the trigger is ENABLED or DISABLED
Description	The description for the trigger
Action_Type	Action type for the trigger body (CALL or PL/SQL)
Trigger_Body	The trigger text

TABLE 42-10. *Columns in USER_TRIGGERS*

You can select information from USER_SOURCE via a query similar to the one shown in the following listing. In this example, the Text column is selected and ordered by Line number. The Name of the object and the object Type are used to specify which object's source code to display.

```
select Text
   from USER_SOURCE
 where Name = '&procedure_name'
   and Type = 'PROCEDURE'
 order by Line;
```

> **NOTE**
> *The sequence of the lines is maintained by the Line column; therefore, the Line column should be used in the **order by** clause.*

The ALL_SOURCE and DBA_SOURCE views have all of the columns found in USER_SOURCE plus an additional Owner column (the owner of the object). ALL_SOURCE can be used to display the source code for all procedural objects that the user can access regardless of owner. DBA_SOURCE lists the source code for all users in the database.

> **NOTE**
> *To see the persistent parameter settings for PL/SQL units, query USER_STORED_SETTINGS.*

Code Errors: USER_ERRORS

The **show errors** command in SQL*Plus checks the USER_ERRORS data dictionary view for the errors associated with the most recent compilation attempt for a procedural object. **show errors** will display the line and column number for each error, as well as the text of the error message.

To view errors associated with previously created procedural objects, you may query USER_ERRORS directly. You may need to do this when viewing errors associated with package bodies, since a package compilation that results in an error may not display the package body's error when you execute the **show error** command. You may also need to query USER_ERRORS when you encounter compilation errors with multiple procedural objects.

The following are the columns available in USER_ERRORS:

Name	The name of the procedural object
Type	The object type ('PROCEDURE', 'FUNCTION', 'PACKAGE', 'PACKAGE BODY', 'TRIGGER', 'TYPE', 'TYPE BODY', 'VIEW', 'JAVA CLASS', or 'JAVA SOURCE')
Sequence	The line sequence number, for use in the query's **order by** clause
Line	The line number within the source code at which the error occurs
Position	The position within the Line at which the error occurs
Text	The text of the error message
Attribute	Flag to indicate whether the selected row is an error ('ERROR') or a warning ('WARNING')
Message_Number	Numerical error number, without prefix

Queries against this view should always include the Sequence column in the **order by** clause. "ALL" and "DBA" versions of this view are also available; they feature an additional column, Owner, which records the owner of the object.

Code Size: USER_OBJECT_SIZE

You can query the amount of space used in the SYSTEM tablespace for a procedural object from the USER_OBJECT_SIZE data dictionary view. As shown in the following listing, the four separate size areas can be added together to determine the total space used in the SYSTEM data dictionary tables to store the object. The four Size columns, along with the Name and Type columns, constitute all of the columns in this view.

```
select Source_Size+Code_Size+Parsed_Size+Error_Size Total
   from USER_OBJECT_SIZE
 where Name = '&procedure_name'
   and Type = 'PROCEDURE';
```

There is also a "DBA" version of this view available: DBA_OBJECT_SIZE lists the sizes for all objects in the database.

Dimensions

You can create and maintain dimensions and hierarchies.

You can query the Dimension_Name column of the USER_DIMENSIONS view to see the names of your dimensions. USER_DIMENSIONS also contains columns for the dimension owner (Owner), status (the Invalid column, set to 'Y' or 'N'), and revision level (the Revision column). The attributes of a dimension are accessed via additional data dictionary views.

To see the hierarchies within a dimension, query USER_DIM_HIERARCHIES. This view has only three columns: Owner, Dimension_Name, and Hierarchy_Name. Querying USER_DIM_HIERARCHIES for the GEOGRAPHY dimension returns the name of its hierarchies:

```
select Hierarchy_Name
   from USER_DIM_HIERARCHIES;

HIERARCHY_NAME
-------------------------------
COUNTRY_ROLLUP
```

You can see the hierarchy details for COUNTRY_ROLLUP by querying USER_DIM_CHILD_OF, as shown in the following listing. The first command creates a dimension named GEOGRAPHY that records the hierarchies of countries and continents.

```
create dimension GEOGRAPHY
    level COUNTRY_ID       is COUNTRY.Country
    level CONTINENT_ID     is CONTINENT.Continent
    hierarchy COUNTRY_ROLLUP (
       COUNTRY_ID             child of
       CONTINENT_ID
    join key COUNTRY.Continent references CONTINENT_id);
```

```
column join_key_id format a4

select Child_Level_Name,
       Parent_Level_Name,
       Position, Join_Key_Id
  from USER_DIM_CHILD_OF
where Hierarchy_Name = 'COUNTRY_ROLLUP';

CHILD_LEVEL_NAME         PARENT_LEVEL_NAME                      POSITION JOIN
--------------------     ------------------------------------  -------- ----
COUNTRY_ID               CONTINENT_ID                                 1 1
```

To see the join key for a hierarchy, query USER_DIM_JOIN_KEY:

```
select Level_name, Child_Join_Column
  from USER_DIM_JOIN_KEY
 where Dimension_Name = 'GEOGRAPHY'
   and Hierarchy_Name = 'COUNTRY_ROLLUP';

LEVEL_NAME                      CHILD_JOIN_COLUMN
------------------------------  -------------------------------
CONTINENT_ID                    CONTINENT
```

You can see the levels of a dimension by querying the USER_DIM_LEVELS data dictionary view, and see the key columns for the levels via USER_DIM_LEVEL_KEY. Attribute information for dimensions is accessible via USER_DIM_ATTRIBUTES.

There are "ALL" and "DBA" views of all of the data dictionary views related to dimensions. Because the "USER" views for dimensions contain an Owner column, there are no additional columns found in the corresponding "ALL" and "DBA" views.

Space Allocation and Usage, Including Partitions and Subpartitions

You can query the data dictionary to determine the space that is available and allocated for database objects. In the following sections, you will see how to determine the default storage parameters for objects, your space usage quota, available free space, and the way in which objects are physically stored. For information on Oracle's methods of storing data, see Chapters 20 and 46.

Tablespaces: USER_TABLESPACES

You can query the USER_TABLESPACES data dictionary view to determine which tablespaces you have been granted access to and the default storage parameters in each. A tablespace's default storage parameters will be used for each object stored within that tablespace unless the **create** or **alter** command for that object specifies its own storage parameters. The Storage-Related columns in USER_TABLESPACES, listed in Table 42-11, are very similar to the Storage-Related columns in USER_TABLES. See the "Storage" entry of the Alphabetical Reference for further details.

There is no "ALL" version of this view. DBA_TABLESPACES shows the storage parameters for all tablespaces.

Column Name	Description
Tablespace_Name	The name of the tablespace.
Block_Size	Database block size in use for this tablespace.
Initial_Extent	The default INITIAL parameter for objects in the tablespace.
Next_Extent	The default NEXT parameter for objects in the tablespace.
Min_Extents	The default MINEXTENTS parameter for objects in the tablespace.
Max_Extents	The default MAXEXTENTS parameter for objects in the tablespace.
Pct_Increase	The default PCTINCREASE parameter for objects in the tablespace.
Min_Extlen	The minimum extent size for objects in the tablespace.
Status	The tablespace's status ('ONLINE', 'OFFLINE', 'INVALID', 'READ ONLY'). An "invalid" tablespace is one that has been dropped; its record is still visible via this view.
Contents	A flag to indicate whether the tablespace is used to store permanent objects ('PERMANENT') or only temporary segments ('TEMPORARY').
Logging	A flag to indicate the default LOGGING/NOLOGGING parameter value for objects in the tablespace.
Extent_Management	Where extent management is performed for the tablespace ('DICTIONARY' or 'LOCAL').
Allocation_Type	Type of extent allocation in effect.
Segment_Space_Management	Flag to indicate if free space is managed via free lists ('MANUAL') or bitmaps ('AUTO').
Retention	Undo tablespace retention ('GUARANTEE','NO GUARANTEE', or 'NOT APPLY').
Bigfile	Indicates if the tablespace is a bigfile tablespace ('YES') or a smallfile tablespace ('NO').
Force_Logging	Yes/No flag to indicate if tablespace is in force logging mode.

TABLE 42-11. *Columns in USER_TABLESPACES*

Space Quotas: USER_TS_QUOTAS

USER_TS_QUOTAS is a very useful view for determining the amount of space you have currently allocated and the maximum amount of space available to you by tablespace. A sample query of USER_TS_QUOTAS is shown in the following listing:

```
select * from USER_TS_QUOTAS;

TABLESPACE_NAME    BYTES  MAX_BYTES    BLOCKS MAX_BLOCKS
--------------- ---------- ---------- ---------- ----------
USERS              67584          0         33          0
```

USER_TS_QUOTAS contains one record for each Tablespace_Name. The Bytes column reflects the number of bytes allocated to objects owned by the user. Max_Bytes is the maximum number of bytes the user can own in that tablespace; if there is no quota for that tablespace, then Max_Bytes will display a value of 0. The Bytes and Max_Bytes columns are translated into Oracle blocks in the Blocks and Max_Blocks columns, respectively.

There is no "ALL" version of this view. DBA_TS_QUOTAS shows the storage quotas for all users for all tablespaces and is a very effective way to list space usage across the entire database.

Segments and Extents: USER_SEGMENTS and USER_EXTENTS

As described in Chapter 20, space is allocated to objects (such as tables, clusters, and indexes) in *segments*, the physical counterparts to the logical objects created in the database. You can query USER_SEGMENTS to see the current storage parameters and space usage in effect for your segments. USER_SEGMENTS is very useful when you are in danger of exceeding one of the storage limits; its columns are listed in Table 42-12.

Column Name	Description
Segment_Name	The name of the segment
Partition_Name	**NULL** if the object is not partitioned; otherwise, the segment's partition name
Segment_Type	The type of segment ('TABLE', 'CLUSTER', 'INDEX', 'ROLLBACK', and so on)
Tablespace_Name	The name of the tablespace in which the segment is stored
Bytes	The number of bytes allocated to the segment
Blocks	The number of Oracle blocks allocated to the segment
Extents	The number of extents in the segment
Initial_Extent	The size of thse initial extent in the segment
Next_Extent	The value of the NEXT parameter for the segment
Min_Extents	The minimum number of extents in the segment
Max_Extents	The value of the MAXEXTENTS parameter for the segment
Pct_Increase	The value of the PCTINCREASE parameter for the segment
Freelists	The number of process freelists (lists of data blocks in the segment that can be used during inserts) allocated to the segment; if a segment has multiple freelists, then contention for free blocks during concurrent **inserts** will be lessened
Freelist_Groups	The number of freelist groups allocated to the segment
Buffer_Pool	Buffer pool into which the segment will be read ('DEFAULT', 'KEEP', or 'RECYCLE') if you have defined multiple buffer pools

TABLE 42-12. *Columns in USER_SEGMENTS*

Segments consist of contiguous sections called *extents.* The extents that constitute segments are described in USER_EXTENTS. In USER_EXTENTS, you will see the actual size of each extent within the segment; this is very useful for tracking the impact of changes to the **next** and **pctincrease** settings. In addition to the Segment_Name, Segment_Type, and Tablespace_Name columns, USER_EXTENTS has three new columns: Extent_ID (to identify the extent within the segment), Bytes (the size of the extent, in bytes), and Blocks (the size of the extent, in Oracle blocks).

Both USER_SEGMENTS and USER_EXTENTS have "DBA" versions, which are useful for listing the space usage of objects across owners. Both DBA_SEGMENTS and DBA_EXTENTS have an additional Owner column. If you want to list all of the owners who own segments in a tablespace, you can query based on the Tablespace_Name column in DBA_SEGMENTS, and list all of the owners of segments in that tablespace. There are no "ALL" versions of these views.

Partitions and Subpartitions

A single table's data can be stored across multiple partitions. See Chapter 17 for examples of partitions and descriptions of the indexing options available. To see how a table is partitioned, you should query the USER_PART_TABLES data dictionary view, whose columns are listed, by category, in Table 42-13.

Most of the columns of USER_PART_TABLES define the default storage parameters for the table partitions. When a partition is added to the table, it will by default use the storage parameters shown in USER_PART_TABLES. USER_PART_TABLES also shows the number of partitions in the table (Partition_Count), the number of columns in the partition key (Partitioning_Key_Count), and the type of partitioning (Partitioning_Type).

Identification	Storage-Related
Table_Name	Def_Tablespace_Name
Partitioning_Type	Def_Pct_Free
Subpartitioning_Type	Def_Pct_Used
Partition_Count	Def_Ini_Trans
Def_Subpartition_Count	Def_Max_Trans
Partitioning_Key_Count	Def_Initial_Extent
Subpartitioning_Key_Count	Def_Next_Extent
Def_Logging	Def_Min_Extents
Def_Buffer_Pool	Def_Max_Extents
	Def_Pct_Increase
	Def_Freelists
	Def_Freelist_Groups
	Def_Compression

TABLE 42-13. *Columns in USER_PART_TABLES*

Identification	Storage-Related	Statistics-Related
Table_Name	Tablespace_Name	Num_Rows
Composite	Pct_Free	Blocks
Partition_Name	Pct_Used	Empty_Blocks
Subpartition_Count	Ini_Trans	Avg_Space
High_Value	Max_Trans	Chain_Cnt
High_Value_Length	Initial_Extent	Avg_Row_Len
Partition_Position	Next_Extent	Sample_Size
Logging	Min_Extent	Last_Analyzed
Buffer_Pool	Max_Extent	Global_Stats
	Pct_Increase	User_Stats
	Freelists	
	Freelist_Groups	
	Compression	

TABLE 42-14. *Columns in USER_TAB_PARTITIONS*

USER_PART_TABLES stores a single row for each table that has been partitioned. To see information about each of the individual partitions that belong to the table, you can query USER_TAB_PARTITIONS. In USER_TAB_PARTITIONS, you will see one row for each of the table's partitions. The columns of USER_TAB_PARTITIONS are shown, by category, in Table 42-14.

USER_TAB_PARTITIONS contains columns that identify the table to which the partition belongs and shows the partition's storage parameters and the statistics for the partition. The Statistics-Related columns are populated when the table is analyzed. The Identification columns show the high value for the range used to define the partition (High_Value) and the position of the partition within the table (Partition_Position).

The columns used for the partition key are accessible via the USER_PART_KEY_COLUMNS data dictionary view. USER_PART_KEY_COLUMNS contains only four columns:

Name	The name of the partitioned table or index
Object_Type	Object type (TABLE or INDEX)
Column_Name	The name of the column that is part of the partition key
Column_Position	The position of the column within the partition key

Statistics for the partition columns are accessible via the USER_PART_COL_STATISTICS data dictionary view. The columns in USER_PART_COL_STATISTICS closely mirror those in USER_TAB_COL_STATISTICS.

Data histogram information for partitions is accessible via the USER_PART_HISTOGRAMS data dictionary view. The columns of this view display the endpoint values for each of the buckets in the histogram. The columns are Table_Name, Partition_Name, Column_Name, Bucket_Number, Endpoint_Value, and Endpoint_Actual_Value.

Since indexes may be partitioned, there is a USER_IND_PARTITIONS data dictionary view available. The columns in USER_IND_PARTITIONS can be grouped into three categories, as shown in Table 42-15.

The columns in USER_IND_PARTITIONS parallel those in USER_INDEXES, with a few modifications to the Identification columns. The Identification columns for partitioned indexes include the name of the partition, the high value for the partition, and the position of the partition within the table. The Statistics-Related columns are populated when the partition is analyzed. The Space-Related columns describe the space allocation for the index; see the "Storage" entry in the Alphabetical Reference for information on storage parameters.

If a partition has subpartitions, you can see the details for the subpartitions via data dictionary views. USER_IND_SUBPARTITIONS contains the Space-Related and Statistics-Related columns of USER_IND_PARTITIONS, along with columns to identify the subpartition (Subpartition_Name and Subpartition_Position). Similarly, USER_TAB_SUBPARTITIONS contains the Space-Related and Statistics-Related columns of USER_TAB_PARTITIONS, along with Subpartition_Name and Subpartition_Position columns. Thus, you can determine the space definitions of each of your partitions and subpartitions.

As shown earlier in this section, you can query the USER_PART_COL_STATISTICS and USER_PART_HISTOGRAMS data dictionary views for statistical information regarding partitions. For

Identification	Space-Related	Statistics-Related
Index_Name	Tablespace_Name	Blevel
Composite	Ini_Trans	Leaf_Blocks
Partition_Name	Max_Trans	Distinct_Keys
Subpartition_Count	Initial_Extent	Avg_Leaf_Blocks_Per_Key
High_Value	Next_Extent	Avg_Data_Blocks_Per_Key
High_Value_Length	Min_Extent	Clustering_Factor
Partition_Position	Max_Extent	Num_Rows
Status	Pct_Increase	Sample_Size
Logging	Pct_Free	Last_Analyzed
Buffer_Pool	Freelists	User_Stats
Compression	Freelist_Groups	Pct_Direct_Access
Domidx_Opstatus		Global_Stats
Parameters		

TABLE 42-15. *Columns in USER_IND_PARTITIONS*

subpartitions, you can query USER_SUBPART_COL_STATISTICS and USER_SUBPART_HISTOGRAMS, whose structures mirror that of the partition statistics views. To see the subpartition key columns, you can query USER_SUBPART_KEY_COLUMNS, whose column structure is identical to that of USER_PART_KEY_COLUMNS.

Free Space: USER_FREE_SPACE

In addition to viewing the space you have used, you can also query the data dictionary to see how much space is currently marked as "free" space. USER_FREE_SPACE lists the free extents in all tablespaces accessible to the user. It lists by Tablespace_Name the File_ID, Block_ID, and relative file number of the starting point of the free extent. The size of the free extent is listed in both bytes and blocks. DBA_FREE_SPACE is frequently used by DBAs to monitor the amount of free space available and the degree to which it has become fragmented.

Users and Privileges

Users and their privileges are recorded within the data dictionary. In the following sections, you will see how to query the data dictionary for information about user accounts, resource limits, and user privileges.

Users: USER_USERS

You can query USER_USERS to list information about your account. The USER_USERS view includes your Username, User_ID (a number assigned by the database), Default_Tablespace, Temporary_Tablespace, and Created date (when your account was created). The Account_Status column in USER_USERS displays the status of your account, whether it is locked, unlocked ('OPEN'), or expired. If the account is locked, the Lock_Date column will display the date the account was locked and the Expiry_Date column will display the date of expiration. You can also query information about the resource consumer group (Initial_Rsrc_Consumer_Group) assigned to you by the DBA, and your External_Name value.

ALL_USERS contains only the Username, User_ID, and Created columns from USER_USERS, but it lists that information for all accounts in the database. ALL_USERS is useful when you need to know the usernames that are available (for example, during **grant** commands). DBA_USERS contains all of the columns in USER_USERS, plus two additional columns: Password (the encrypted password for the account) and Profile (the user's resource profile). DBA_USERS lists this information for all users in the database.

Resource Limits: USER_RESOURCE_LIMITS

In Oracle, *profiles* can be used to place limits on the amount of system and database resources available to a user. If no profiles are created in a database, the default profile, which specifies unlimited resources for all users, will be used. The resources that can be limited are described in the **create profile** entry of the Alphabetical Reference. Profiles enforce additional security measures, such as expiration dates on accounts and the minimum length of passwords.

To view the limits that are in place for your current session, you can query USER_RESOURCE_LIMITS. Its columns are the following:

Resource_Name The name of the resource (for example, SESSIONS_PER_USER)

Limit The limit placed on this resource

USER_PASSWORD_LIMITS describes the password profile parameters for the user. It has the same columns as USER_RESOURCE_LIMITS.

There is no "ALL" or "DBA" version of this view; it is limited to the user's current session. To see the cost associated with each available resource, you can query the RESOURCE_COST view. DBAs can access the DBA_PROFILES view to see the resource limits for all profiles. The Resource_ Type column of DBA_PROFILES indicates whether the resource profile is a 'PASSWORD' or 'KERNEL' profile.

Table Privileges: USER_TAB_PRIVS

To view grants for which you are the grantee, the grantor, or the object owner, query USER_TAB_ PRIVS (user table privileges). In addition to its Grantee, Grantor, and Owner columns, this view contains columns for the Table_Name, Hierarchy, Privilege, and a flag (set to 'YES' or 'NO') to indicate whether the privilege was granted **with admin option** (Grantable).

USER_TAB_PRIVS_MADE displays the USER_TAB_PRIVS records for which the user is the owner (it therefore lacks an Owner column). USER_TAB_PRIVS_RECD (user table privileges received) displays the USER_TAB_PRIVS records for which the user is the grantee (it therefore lacks a Grantee column). Since both USER_TAB_PRIVS_MADE and USER_TAB_PRIVS_RECD are simply subsets of USER_TAB_PRIVS, you can duplicate their functionality simply by querying against USER_TAB_ PRIVS with an appropriate **where** clause to view the subset you want.

There are "ALL" versions available for USER_TAB_PRIVS, USER_TAB_PRIVS_MADE, and USER_ TAB_PRIVS_RECD. The "ALL" versions list those objects for which either the user or PUBLIC is the grantee or grantor. There is a "DBA" version of USER_TAB_PRIVS named DBA_TAB_PRIVS that lists all object privileges granted to all users in the database. DBA_TAB_PRIVS has the same column definitions as USER_TAB_PRIVS. Instead of an Owner column, ALL_TAB_PRIVS has a Table_Schema column that displays the schema of the object.

Column Privileges: USER_COL_PRIVS

In addition to granting privileges on tables, you can also grant privileges at the column level. For example, you can grant users the ability to **update** only certain columns in a table. See Chapter 18 and the **grant** command in the Alphabetical Reference for further details.

The data dictionary views used to display column privileges are almost identical in design to the table privileges views described in the previous section. There is an additional Column_Name column in each of the COL views, and the Hierarchy column is not found there. USER_COL_PRIVS is analogous to USER_TAB_PRIVS, USER_COL_PRIVS_MADE is analogous to USER_TAB_PRIVS_ MADE, and USER_COL_PRIVS_RECD is analogous to USER_TAB_PRIVS_RECD.

"ALL" versions are available for all of the column privileges views. DBA_COL_PRIVS lists all column privileges that have been granted to users in the database (just as DBA_TAB_PRIVS lists all table privileges granted to users).

System Privileges: USER_SYS_PRIVS

USER_SYS_PRIVS lists the system privileges that have been granted to the user. Its columns are Username, Privilege, and Admin_Option (a flag set to 'YES' or 'NO' to indicate whether the privilege

was granted **with admin option**). All system privileges directly granted to a user are displayed via this view. System privileges granted to a user via a role are not displayed here. The following query shows sample output for the PRACTICE account:

```
select Username, Privilege * from USER_SYS_PRIVS;

USERNAME                        PRIVILEGE
------------------------------  ------------------------
PRACTICE                        CREATE DIMENSION
PRACTICE                        UNLIMITED TABLESPACE
```

There is no "ALL" version of this view. To see the system privileges granted to all users in the database, query DBA_SYS_PRIVS, which has nearly the same column definitions as USER_SYS_PRIVS (the DBA version has a Grantee column, while the USER version has a Username column).

Roles

In addition to privileges granted directly to users, sets of privileges may be grouped into roles. Roles may be granted to users or to other roles, and may consist of both object and system privileges. For information on the use and management of roles, see Chapter 18.

To see which roles have been granted to you, query the USER_ROLE_PRIVS data dictionary view. Any roles that have been granted to PUBLIC will also be listed here. The available columns for USER_ROLE_PRIVS are as follows:

Username	The username (may be 'PUBLIC')
Granted_Role	The name of the role granted to the user
Admin_Option	A flag to indicate whether the role was granted **with admin option** ('YES' or 'NO')
Default_Role	A flag to indicate whether the role is the user's default role ('YES' or 'NO')
OS_Granted	A flag to indicate whether the operating system is being used to manage roles ('YES' or 'NO')

To list all of the roles available in the database, you need to have DBA authority; you can then query DBA_ROLES to list all roles. DBA_ROLE_PRIVS lists the assignment of those roles to all of the users in the database.

Roles may receive three different types of grants, and each has a corresponding data dictionary view:

Table/column grants	ROLE_TAB_PRIVS. Similar to USER_TAB_PRIVS and USER_COL_PRIVS, except that it has a Role column instead of a Grantee column and does not have a Grantor column.
System privileges	ROLE_SYS_PRIVS. Similar to USER_SYS_PRIVS, except that it has a Role column instead of a Username column.
Role grants	ROLE_ROLE_PRIVS. Lists all roles that have been granted to other roles.

NOTE
*If you are not a DBA, these data dictionary views list only those roles
that have been granted to you.*

In addition to these views, there are two views, each with a single column, that list the
privileges and roles enabled for the current session:

SESSION_PRIVS	The Privilege column lists all system privileges available to the session, whether granted directly or via roles.
SESSION_ROLES	The Role column lists all roles that are currently enabled for the session.

SESSION_PRIVS and SESSION_ROLES are available to all users.

NOTE
*See Chapter 18 for information on enabling and disabling roles
and the setting of default roles.*

Auditing

As a non-DBA user within an Oracle database, you cannot enable the database's auditing features.
If auditing has been enabled, there are data dictionary views that anyone can use to view the audit
trail.

Many different audit trail data dictionary views are available. Most of these views are based
on a single audit trail table in the database (SYS.AUD$). The most generic of the audit trail views
available is named USER_AUDIT_TRAIL. Its columns are described in Table 42-16. Since this view

Column Name	Description
OS_Username	The audited user's operating system account
Username	The Oracle username of the audited user
UserHost	A numeric ID for the instance used by the audited user
Terminal	The user's operating-system terminal identifier
TimeStamp	The date and time the audit record was created
Owner	The owner of the object affected by an action (for action audits)
Obj_Name	The name of the object affected by an action (for action audits)
Action	The numeric code for the audited action
Action_Name	The name of the audited action
New_Owner	The owner of the object named in the New_Name column

TABLE 42-16. *Columns in USER_AUDIT_TRAIL*

Column Name	Description
New_Name	The new name of an object that has been **renamed**
Obj_Privilege	The object privilege that has been **granted** or **revoked**
Sys_Privilege	The system privilege that has been **granted** or **revoked**
Admin_Option	A flag to indicate whether the role or system privilege was **granted with admin option** ('Y' or 'N')
Grantee	The username specified in a **grant** or **revoke** command
Audit_Option	The auditing options set via an **audit** command
Ses_Actions	A string of characters serving as a session summary, recording success and failure for different actions
Logoff_Time	The date and time the user logged off
Logoff_LRead	The number of logical reads performed during the session
Logoff_PRead	The number of physical reads performed during the session
Logoff_LWrite	The number of logical writes performed during the session
Logoff_DLock	The number of deadlocks detected during the session
Comment_Text	A text comment on the audit trail entry
SessionID	The numeric ID for the session
EntryID	A numeric ID for the audit trail entry
StatementID	The numeric ID for each command that was executed
ReturnCode	The return code for each command that was executed; if the command was successful, then the ReturnCode will be 0
Priv_Used	The system privilege used to execute the action
Client_ID	Client ID
Session_CPU	Session CPU used
Extended_Timestamp	Timestamp of the creation of the audit trail entry in session's time zone
Proxy_SessionID	Proxy session serial number, if enterprise user has logged through a proxy mechanism
Global_UID	Global user identifier for the user, if the user had logged in as an enterprise user
Instance_Number	Instance number as specified in the initialization parameter file
OS_Process	Operating-system process identifier of the Oracle server process
TransactionID	Transaction identifier of the transaction in which the object is accessed or modified
SCN	SCN of the query
SQL_Bind	Bind variable data of the query
SQL_Text	SQL text of the query

TABLE 42-16. *Columns in USER_AUDIT_TRAIL (continued)*

shows the audit records for many different types of actions, many of the columns may be inapplicable for any given row. The "DBA" version of this view, DBA_AUDIT_TRAIL, lists all entries from the audit trail table; USER_AUDIT_TRAIL lists only those that are relevant to the user.

As of Oracle Database 10*g*, a number of new columns are available in USER_AUDIT_TRAIL, including SQL_Text, SQL_Bind, OS_Process, and SCN. See the chapters related to flashback query usage for details on the uses of SCN (System Change Number) values.

As shown in Table 42-16, a vast array of auditing capabilities is available (see the **audit** command in the Alphabetical Reference for a complete listing). Each type of audit can be accessed via its own data dictionary view. The following are the available views:

USER_AUDIT_OBJECT	For statements concerning objects
USER_AUDIT_SESSION	For connections and disconnections
USER_AUDIT_STATEMENT	For **grant**, **revoke**, **audit**, **noaudit**, and **alter system** commands issued by the user

There are "DBA" versions available for each of the "USER" views in the previous list; the "DBA" versions show all of the audit trail records that fit into the view's category.

You can view the auditing options that are currently in effect for your objects by querying USER_OBJ_AUDIT_OPTS. For each object listed in USER_OBJ_AUDIT_OPTS, the audit options for each command that may be performed on that object (identified by the Object_Name and Object_Type columns) are listed in USER_OBJ_AUDIT_OPTS. The column names of USER_OBJ_AUDIT_OPTS correspond to the first three letters of the command (for example, Alt for **alter**, Upd for **update**, and so on). Each column will record whether that command is audited for that object when the command is successful ('S'), unsuccessful ('U'), or both. The default auditing options in effect for any new objects in the database can be displayed via the ALL_DEF_AUDIT_OPTS view, which has the same column naming conventions as USER_OBJ_AUDIT_OPTS. USER_OBJ_AUDIT_OPTS includes Object_Name and Object_Type columns.

The commands that can be audited are stored in a reference table named AUDIT_ACTIONS, which has two columns: Action (the numeric code for the action) and Name (the name of the action/command). Action and Name correspond to the Action and Action_Name columns of USER_AUDIT_TRAIL.

DBAs can use several additional auditing views that do not have "USER" counterparts, including DBA_AUDIT_EXISTS, DBA_PRIV_AUDIT_OPTS, DBA_STMT_AUDIT_OPTS, and STMT_AUDIT_OPTION_MAP. See the *Oracle Database Reference* for details on these DBA-only views.

Miscellaneous

In addition to the data dictionary views described earlier in this chapter, several miscellaneous views and tables may be available within your data dictionary. These views and tables include DBA-only views and the table used when the **explain plan** command is executed. In the following sections, you will see brief descriptions for each of the miscellaneous view types.

Monitoring: The V$ Dynamic Performance Tables

The views that monitor the database environment performance are called the *dynamic performance views*. The dynamic performance views are commonly referred to as the *V$* (pronounced "Vee-Dollar") tables, because they all begin with the letter *V* followed by the dollar sign ($).

The definitions and usage of columns within the monitoring views are subject to change with each version of the database that is released. Correctly interpreting the results of ad hoc queries against views usually requires referring to the *Oracle Database Administrator's Guide*. The V$ tables are normally used only by the DBA. Consult the *Oracle Database Reference* and the *Oracle DBA Handbook* for details on the use of the V$ views.

CHAINED_ROWS

The **analyze** command can be used to generate a listing of the chained or migrated rows within a table. This listing of chained rows can be stored in a table called CHAINED_ROWS. To create the CHAINED_ROWS table in your schema, run the utlchain.sql script (usually found in the /rdbms/ admin subdirectory under the Oracle home directory).

To populate the CHAINED_ROWS table, use the **list chained rows into** clause of the **analyze** command, as shown in the following listing:

```
analyze TABLE BIRTHDAY list chained rows into CHAINED_ROWS;
```

The CHAINED_ROWS table lists the Owner_Name, Table_Name, Cluster_Name (if the table is in a cluster), Partition_Name (if the table is partitioned), Subpartition_Name (if the table contains subpartitions), Head_RowID (the ROWID for the row), and an Analyze_TimeStamp column that shows the last time the table or cluster was analyzed. You can query the table based on the Head_ RowID values in CHAINED_ROWS, as shown in the following example:

```
select * from BIRTHDAY
  where RowID in
        (select Head_RowID
           from CHAINED_ROWS
          where Table_Name = 'BIRTHDAY');
```

If the chained row is short in length, then it may be possible to eliminate the chaining by deleting and reinserting the row.

PLAN_TABLE

When tuning SQL statements, you may want to determine the steps that the optimizer will take to execute your query. To view the query path, you must first create a table in your schema named PLAN_TABLE. The script used to create this table is called utlxplan.sql, and is usually stored in the /rdbms/admin subdirectory of the Oracle software home directory.

After you have created the PLAN_TABLE table in your schema, you can use the **explain plan** command, which will generate records in your PLAN_TABLE, tagged with the Statement_ID value you specify for the query you want to have explained. See Chapter 43 for details on the generation of the explain plan listings.

The ID and Parent_ID columns in PLAN_TABLE establish the hierarchy of steps (Operations) that the optimizer will follow when executing the query. See Chapter 43 for details on the Oracle optimizer and the interpretation of PLAN_TABLE records.

Interdependencies: USER_DEPENDENCIES and IDEPTREE

Objects within Oracle databases can depend upon each other. For example, a stored procedure may depend upon a table, or a package may depend upon a package body. When an object within the database changes, any procedural object that depends upon it will have to be recompiled. This recompilation can take place either automatically at run time (with a consequential performance penalty) or manually (see Chapter 31 for details on compiling procedural objects).

Two sets of data dictionary views are available to help you track dependencies. The first is USER_DEPENDENCIES, which lists all *direct* dependencies of objects. However, this only goes one level down the dependency tree. To fully evaluate dependencies, you must create the recursive dependency-tracking objects in your schema. To create these objects, run the utldtree.sql script (usually located in the /rdbms/admin subdirectory of the Oracle home directory). This script creates two objects you can query: DEPTREE and IDEPTREE. They contain identical information (although their column definitions differ), but IDEPTREE is indented based on the pseudo-column Level, and is thus easier to read and interpret.

DBA-Only Views

Since this chapter is intended for use by developers and end users, the data dictionary views available only to DBAs are not covered here. The DBA-only views are used to provide information about distributed transactions, lock contention, rollback segments, and other internal database functions. For information on the use of the DBA-only views, see the *Oracle Database Administrator's Guide*.

Oracle Label Security

Users of Oracle Label Security can view additional data dictionary views, including ALL_SA_GROUPS, ALL_SA_POLICIES, ALL_SA_USERS, and ALL_SA_USER_PRIVS. For details on the usage of these views, see the *Oracle Label Security Administrator's Guide*.

SQL*Loader Direct Load Views

To manage the direct load option within SQL*Loader, Oracle maintains a number of data dictionary views. These generally are only queried for debugging purposes, upon request from Oracle Customer Support. The SQL*Loader direct load option is described under the "SQLLDR" entry in the Alphabetical Reference; its supporting data dictionary views are listed here:

- LOADER_COL_INFO
- LOADER_CONSTRAINT_INFO
- LOADER_FILE_TS
- LOADER_PARAM_INFO
- LOADER_PART_INFO
- LOADER_REF_INFO
- LOADER_TAB_INFO
- LOADER_TRIGGER_INFO

For details on the use of these views, see the catldr.sql script, usually located in the /rdbms/ admin subdirectory of the Oracle home directory.

Globalization Support Views

Three data dictionary views are used to display information about the Globalization Support parameters currently in effect in the database. Nonstandard values for the NLS parameters (such as NLS_DATE_FORMAT and NLS_SORT) can be set via the database's parameter file or via the **alter session** command. (See the **alter session** command in the Alphabetical Reference for further information on NLS settings.) To see the current NLS settings for your session, instance, and database, query NLS_SESSION_PARAMETERS, NLS_INSTANCE_PARAMETERS, and NLS_DATABASE_ PARAMETERS, respectively.

Libraries

Your PL/SQL routines (see Chapter 31) can call external C programs. To see which external C program libraries are owned by you, you can query USER_LIBRARIES, which displays the name of the library (Library_Name), the associated file (File_Spec), whether or not the library is dynamically loadable (Dynamic), and the library's status (Status). ALL_LIBRARIES and DBA_LIBRARIES are also available; they include an additional Owner column to indicate the owner of the library. For further information on libraries, see the entry for the **create library** command in the Alphabetical Reference.

Heterogeneous Services

To support the management of heterogeneous services, Oracle provides a number of data dictionary views. All of the views in this category begin with the letters "HS" instead of "DBA." In general, these views are used primarily by DBAs. For details on the "HS" views, see the *Oracle Database Reference*.

Indextypes and Operators

Operators and indextypes are closely related. You can use the **create operator** command to create a new operator and define its bindings. You can reference operators in indextypes and in SQL statements. The operators, in turn, reference functions, packages, types, and other user-defined objects.

You can query the USER_OPERATORS view to see each operator's Owner, Operator_Name, and Number_of_Binds values. Ancillary information for operators is accessible via USER_OPANCILLARY, and you can query USER_OPARGUMENTS to see the operator arguments. You can query USER_ OPBINDINGS to see the operator bindings.

USER_INDEXTYPE_OPERATORS lists the operators supported by indextypes. Indextypes, in turn, are displayed via USER_INDEXTYPES. There are "ALL" and "DBA" views of all the operator and indextype views. As of Oracle Database 10*g*, you can see the indextype arraytypes via the USER_INDEXTYPE_ARRAYTYPES view.

Outlines

When you use stored outlines, you can retrieve the names of, and details for, the outlines via the USER_OUTLINES data dictionary views. To see the hints that make up the outlines, query USER_ OUTLINE_HINTS. There are "ALL" and "DBA" versions of USER_OUTLINES and USER_OUTLINE_ HINTS.

Advisors

As of Oracle Database 10g, users can access data dictionary views related to tuning recommendations. These views begin with "USER_ADVISOR_" and there is a matching set of views at the "DBA_" level, and there are DBA-only advisor views as well (such as DBA_ADVISOR_DEFINITIONS).

For example, USER_ADVISOR_ACTIONS contains data about the actions associated with all recommendations in the database. Each action is specified in the Command column, with six related attribute columns. USER_ADVISOR_LOG displays information about the current state of all the tasks, as well as execution-specific data such as progress monitoring and completion status. Parameters for the advisors are accessible via USER_ADVISOR_PARAMETERS; you can see the rationale for recommendations via the USER_ADVISOR_RATIONALE view.

For the results of an analysis of all recommendations in the database, see the USER_ADVISOR_ RECOMMENDATIONS view. A recommendation can have multiple actions associated with it (see USER_ADVISOR_ACTIONS) based on the rationales used.

Schedulers

As of Oracle Database 10g, you can access a set of views related to Scheduler jobs in the database. These include USER_SCHEDULER_JOBS (all Scheduler jobs owned by the user), USER_SCHEDULER_ PROGRAMS (the scheduler programs), and USER_SCHEDULER_PROGRAM_ARGS (the arguments for the scheduler programs). You can see the execution details for the jobs via the USER_SCHEDULER_ JOB_LOG, USER_SCHEDULER_JOB_RUN_DETAILS, and USER_SCHEDULER_RUNNING_JOBS views. You can see the schedules via USER_SCHEDULER_SCHEDULES.

CHAPTER
43

The Hitchhiker's Guide to Tuning Applications and SQL

ith each new release of its products, Oracle adds features to enhance the performance of your applications. These features may include new options that you must manually implement (such as partitioning) or under-the-cover changes that provide a performance benefit without your making any changes to your application.

Do not approach tuning as something done after an application goes into production, or after a system test has been performed. As you will see, planning for the performance of an application must be part of the design process.

In this chapter, you will see a description of the major new tuning changes introduced with Oracle Database 10g. A set of guidelines and best practices related to tuning Oracle applications is also provided. The final section of the chapter is dedicated to integrating those features with the recommended best practices. You will also see guidelines for generating and interpreting explain plans and stored outlines.

New Tuning Features in Oracle Database 10g

Oracle Database 10g introduces a number of new features aimed at simplifying and automating the tuning process. DBAs and developers who previously had to perform manual steps related to tuning will now find that the database performs some of these steps with no intervention. Note that the database cannot redesign your application; it can only make the commands it receives complete as quickly as possible. Please see the "Tuning—Best Practices" section for the principles of sound performance design. As this book is intended for all users, the DBA-specific tools are not the focus here; rather, the focus is on designing and developing systems whose performance can be easily administered.

The following performance-related features are new as of Oracle Database 10g. For further details on all tuning-related features, see the *Performance Tuning Guide* that comes as part of the Oracle documentation set.

Automatic Tools

Oracle Database 10g introduces a number of tools designed to automate performance management. These features include Automatic Statistics Collection, Automatic Database Diagnostic Monitoring (ADDM), and Automatic SQL Tuning. To support these tools, the Automatic Workload Repository collects, processes, and maintains performance statistics for problem detection and self-tuning purposes.

ADDM reduces the amount of effort that is required to diagnose and tune Oracle systems. The SQL Tuning Advisor feature provides a quick and efficient technique for optimizing SQL statements. See the Oracle Enterprise Manager toolset and related documentation regarding the use of these tools.

The Automatic Statistics Collection feature automates the collection of optimizer statistics for objects. Objects with stale or no statistics are automatically analyzed, so administrators no longer need to keep track of what does and what does not need to be analyzed, nor to perform analysis by hand. The GATHER_STATS_JOB job is automatically scheduled to gather statistics for objects whose statistics are either missing or stale.

As of Oracle9i, you can alter the sizes of some of the caches and pools in the SGA while the database is running. In Oracle Database 10g, those changes can be made automatically by Oracle without your intervention. To enable Automatic Shared Memory Management, set the SGA_TARGET initialization parameter to a nonzero value and set the STATISTICS_LEVEL parameter to 'TYPICAL' or 'ALL'.

End-to-End Tracing

Application end-to-end tracing identifies the source of an excessive workload, such as an expensive SQL statement, by client identifier, service, module, or action. Workload problems can be identified by client identifier, service (a group of applications with common attributes), application module, or action. Service names are set via DBMS_SERVICE.CREATE_SERVICE or the SERVICE_NAMES initialization parameter. Set the module and action names via the SET MODULE and SET ACTION procedures of DBMS_APPLICATION_INFO.

The trcsess Utility

The trcsess command-line utility consolidates trace information from selected trace files based on specified criteria (Session ID, Client ID, Service name, Action name, or Module name). Trcsess merges the trace information into a single output file, which can then be processed via TKPROF.

Optimizer Modifications

Within the optimizer, the major changes in Oracle Database 10*g* include:

- Obsolescence of the rule-based optimizer.

- Changed parameters for the OPTIMIZER_MODE initialization parameter. CHOOSE and RULE are no longer valid; ALL_ROWS is the default.

- Dynamic sampling set via OPTIMIZER_DYNAMIC_SAMPLING now defaults to 2.

- CPU Costing has been added to the cost calculations. The cost unit is time.

- New hints available for queries include SPREAD_MIN_ANALYSIS, USE_NL_WITH_INDEX, QB_NAME, NO_QUERY_TRANSFORMATION, NO_USE_NL, NO_USE_MERGE, NO_USE_HASH, NO_INDEX_FFS, NO_INDEX_SS, NO_STAR_TRANSFORMATION, INDEX_SS, INDEX_SS_ASC, and INDEX_SS_DESC.

- Hints that have been renamed include NO_PARALLEL (formerly NOPARALLEL), NO_PARALLEL_INDEX (formerly NOPARALLEL_INDEX), and NO_REWRITE (formerly NOREWRITE).

- The AND_EQUAL, HASH_AJ, MERGE_AJ, NL_AJ, HASH_SJ, MERGE_SJ, NL_SJ, ORDERED_ PREDICATES, ROWID, and STAR hints have been deprecated and should not be used.

- Hash-partitioned global indexes can improve performance of indexes where a small number of leaf blocks in the index have high contention in multiuser OLTP environments.

- Obsolescence of Oracle Trace; use TKPROF or SQL Trace instead.

- Additional V$ views are available, such as V$OSSTAT for operating-system statistics and the views related to the metrics, thresholds, and advisors related to the advisors available via Oracle Enterprise Manager.

Regardless of the tuning options you use for the database or individual SQL statements, the performance of your application may be determined in large part by the extent to which you comply with best practices related to the design of the application. In the following section you will see common design pitfalls and solutions.

Tuning—Best Practices

At least 50% of the time—conservatively—performance problems are designed into an application. During the design of the application and the related database structures, the application architects may not know all the ways in which the business will use the application data over time. As a result, there may always be some components whose performance is poor during the initial release, while other problems will appear later as the business usage of the application changes.

In some cases, the fix will be relatively straightforward—changing an initialization parameter, adding an index, or rescheduling large operations. In other cases, the problem cannot be fixed without altering the application architecture. For example, an application may be designed to heavily reuse functions for all data access—so that functions call other functions, which call additional functions even to perform the simplest database actions. As a result, a single database call may result in tens of thousands of function calls and database accesses. Such an application will usually not scale well; as more users are added to the system, the burden of the number of executions per user will slow the performance for the individual users. Tuning the individual SQL statements executed as part of that application may yield little performance benefit; the statements themselves may be well tuned already. Rather, it is the sheer number of executions that leads to the performance problem.

The following best practices may seem overly simplistic—but they are violated over and over in database applications, and those violations directly result in performance problems. There are always exceptions to the rules—the next change to your software or environment may allow you to violate the rules without affecting your performance. In general, though, following these rules will allow you to meet performance requirements as the application usage increases.

Do as Little as Possible

End users do not care, in general, if the underlying database structures are fully normalized to Third Normal Form or if they are laid out in compliance with object-oriented standards. Users want to perform a business process, and the database application should be a tool that helps that business process complete as quickly as possible. The focus of your design should not be the achievement of theoretical design perfection; it should always be on the end user's ability to do his or her job. Simplify the processes involved at every step in the application.

In Your Application Design, Strive to Eliminate Logical Reads

In the past, there was a heavy focus on eliminating physical reads—and while this is still a good idea, no physical reads occur unless logical reads require them.

Let's take a simple example. Select the current time from DUAL. If you select down to the second level, the value will change 86,400 times per day. Yet there are application designers who repeatedly perform this query, executing it millions of times per day. Such a query likely performs few physical reads throughout the day—so if you are focused solely on tuning the physical I/O, you would likely disregard it. However, it can significantly impact the performance of the application. How? By using the CPU resources available. Each execution of the query will force Oracle to perform work, using processing power to find and return the correct data. As more and more users execute the command repeatedly, you may find that the number of logical reads used by the query exceeds all other queries. In some cases, multiple processors on the server are dedicated to servicing repeated small queries of this sort. What business benefit do they generate? Little to none.

Consider the following real-world example. A programmer wanted to implement a pause in a program, forcing it to wait 30 seconds between the completion of two steps. Since the performance

of the environment would not be consistent over time, the programmer coded the routine in the following format (shown in pseudo-code):

```
perform Step 1
select SysDate from DUAL into a StartTime variable
begin loop
    select SysDate from DUAL in a CurrentTime variable;
    Compare CurrentTime with the StartTime variable value.
    If 30 seconds have passed, exit the loop;
        Otherwise repeat the loop, calculating SysDate again.
end loop
perform Step 2.
```

Is that a reasonable approach? Absolutely not! It will do what the developer wanted, but at a significant cost to the application and there is nothing a database administrator can do to improve its performance. In this case the cost will not be due to I/O activity—the DUAL table will stay in the instance's memory area—but rather in CPU activity. Every time this program is run, by every user, the database will spend 30 seconds consuming as many CPU resources as the system can support. In this particular case the **select SysDate from DUAL** query accounted for over 40% of all of the CPU time used by the application. All of that CPU time was wasted. Tuning the individual SQL statement will not help; the application design must be revised to eliminate the needless execution of commands.

For those who favor tuning based on the buffer cache hit ratio, this database had a hit ratio of almost 100% due to the high number of completely unnecessary logical reads without related physical reads. The buffer cache hit ratio compares the number of logical reads to the number of physical reads; if 10% of the logical reads require physical reads, the buffer cache hit ratio is 100 less 10, or 90%. Low hit ratios identify databases that perform a high number of physical reads; extremely high hit ratios such as found in this example may identify databases that perform an excessive number of logical reads.

In Your Application Design, Strive to Avoid Trips to the Database
Remember that you are tuning an application, not a query. You may need to combine multiple queries into a single procedure so that the database can be visited once rather than multiple times for each screen. This bundled-query approach is particularly relevant for "thin-client" applications that rely on multiple application tiers. Look for queries that are interrelated based on the values they return, and see if there are opportunities to transform them into single blocks of code. The goal is not to make a monolithic query that will never complete; the goal is to avoid doing work that does not need to be done. In this case, the constant back-and-forth communication between the database server, the application server, and the end user's computer is targeted for tuning.

This problem is commonly seen on complex data-entry forms in which each field displayed on the screen is populated via a separate query. Each of those queries is a separate trip to the database. As with the example in the previous section, the database is forced to execute large numbers of related queries. Even if each of those queries is tuned, the burden of the number of commands— multiplied by the number of users—will consume the CPU resources available on the server. Such a design may also impact the network usage, but the network is seldom the problem—the issue is the number of times the database is accessed.

Within your packages and procedures, you should strive to eliminate unnecessary database accesses. Store commonly needed values in local variables instead of repeatedly querying the

database. If you don't need to make a trip to the database for information, don't make it. That sounds simple, but you would be amazed at how often applications fail to consider this advice.

There is no initialization parameter that can make this change take effect. It is a design issue and requires the active involvement of developers, designers, DBAs, and application users in the application performance planning and tuning process.

For Reporting Systems, Store the Data the Way the Users Will Query It

If you know the queries that will be executed—such as via parameterized reports—you should strive to store the data so that Oracle will do as little work as possible to transform the format of the data in your tables into the format presented to the user. This may require the creation and maintenance of materialized views or reporting tables. That maintenance is of course extra work for the database to perform—but it is performed in batch mode and does not directly affect the end user. The end user, on the other hand, benefits from the ability to perform the query faster. The database as a whole will perform fewer logical and physical reads because the accesses to the base tables to populate and refresh the materialized views are performed infrequently when compared to the end-user queries against the views.

Avoid Repeated Connections to the Database

Opening a database connection is one of the slowest operations you can perform. If you need to connect to the database, keep the connection open and reuse the connection. At the application level, you may be able to use connection pooling to support this need. Within the database you may be able to use stored procedures, packages, and other methods to maintain connections while you are performing your processing.

Another real-life example: An application designer wanted to verify that the database was running prior to executing a report. The solution was to open a session and execute the following query: **select count(*) from DUAL**. If the query came back with the proper result (1), then the database was running, a new connection would be opened, and the report query would be executed. What is wrong with that approach? In small systems you may be able to survive such a design decision. In OLTP systems with a high number of concurrent users, you will encounter significant performance problems as the database spends most of its time opening and closing connections. Within the database, the **select count(*) from DUAL** query will be executed millions of times per day—Oracle will spend the bulk of the resources available to the application opening and closing connections and returning the database status to the application. The query performs little I/O but its impact is seen in its CPU usage and the constant opening of connections.

Why is such a step even needed? If you properly handle the errors from the report queries themselves, it would be obvious that the database connection is not functioning properly in the event of a failure. The unnecessary database availability check is made worse by the failure to reuse the same connection. No DBA action can correct this; the application must be designed from the start to reuse connections properly.

Use the Right Indexes

In an effort to eliminate physical reads, some application developers create many indexes on every table. Aside from their impact on data load times (discussed in the "Test Correctly" section later in this chapter), it is possible that many of the indexes will never be needed. In OLTP applications, you should not use bitmap indexes; if a column has few distinct values, you should consider leaving it unindexed. As of Oracle9*i*, the optimizer supports skip-scan index accesses, so you may use

an index on a set of columns even if the leading column of the index is not a limiting condition for the query.

Do It as Simply as Possible

Now that you have eliminated the performance costs of unnecessary logical reads, unneeded database trips, unmanaged connections, and inappropriate indexes, take a look at the commands that remain.

Go Atomic

You can use SQL to combine many steps into one large query. In some cases, this may benefit your application—you can create stored procedures and reuse the code and reduce the number of database trips performed. However, you can take this too far, creating large queries that fail to complete quickly enough. These queries commonly include multiple sets of grouping operations, inline views, and complex multi-row calculations against millions of rows.

If you are performing batch operations, you may be able to break such a query into its atomic components, creating temporary tables to store the data from each step. If you have an operation that takes hours to complete, you almost always can find a way to break it into smaller component parts. Divide and conquer the performance problem.

For example, a batch operation may combine data from multiple tables, perform joins and sorts, and then insert the result into a table. On a small scale this may perform satisfactorily. On a large scale, you may have to divide this operation into multiple steps:

1. Create a work table. Insert rows into it from one of the source tables for the query, selecting only those rows and columns that you care about later in the process.

2. Create a second work table for the columns and rows from the second table.

3. Create any needed indexes on the work tables. Note that all of the steps to this point can be parallelized—the inserts, the queries of the source tables, and the creation of the indexes.

4. Perform the join, again parallelized. The join output may go into another work table.

5. Perform any sorts needed. Sort as little data as possible.

6. Insert the data into the target table.

Why go through all of those steps? Because you can tune them individually, you may be able to tune them to complete much faster individually than Oracle can complete them as a single command. For batch operations, you should consider making the steps as simple as possible. You will need to manage the space allocated for the work tables, but this approach can generate significant benefits to your batch-processing performance.

Eliminate Unnecessary Sorts

As part of the example in the preceding section, the sort operation was performed last. In general, sort operations are inappropriate for OLTP applications. Sort operations do not return any rows to the user until the entire set of rows is sorted. Row operations, on the other hand, return rows to the user as soon as those rows are available.

Consider the following simple test: Perform a full table scan of a large table. As soon as the query starts to execute, the first rows are displayed. Now, perform the same full table scan but

add an **order by** clause on an unindexed column. No rows will be displayed until all of the rows have been sorted. Why does this happen? Because for the second query Oracle performs a SORT ORDER BY operation on the results of the full table scan. As it is a set operation, the set must be completed before the next operation is performed.

Now, imagine an application in which there are many queries executed within a procedure. Each of the queries has an **order by** clause. This turns into a series of nested sorts—no operation can start until the one before it completes.

Note that **union** operations perform sorts. If it is appropriate for the business logic, use a **union all** operation in place of a **union**, as a **union all** does not perform a sort (because it does not eliminate duplicates).

During index creations, you may be able to eliminate subsequent sorts by using the **compute statistics** clause of the **create index** command and gathering the statistics as the index is created.

Eliminate the Need to Query Undo Segments

When performing a query, Oracle will need to maintain a read-consistent image of the rows queried. If a row is modified by another user, the database will need to query the undo segment to see the row as it existed at the time your query began. Application designs that call for queries to frequently access data that others may be changing at the same time force the database to do more work—it has to look in multiple locations for one piece of data. Again, this is a design issue. DBAs may be able to configure the undo segment areas to reduce the possibility of queries encountering errors, but correcting the fundamental problem requires a change to the application design.

Tell the Database What It Needs to Know

Oracle's optimizer relies on statistics when it evaluates the thousands of possible paths to take during the execution of a query. How you manage those statistics can significantly impact the performance of your queries.

Keep Your Statistics Updated

How often should you gather statistics? With each major change to the data in your tables, you should reanalyze the tables. If you have partitioned the tables, you can analyze them on a partition-by-partition basis. As of Oracle Database 10g, you can use the Automatic Statistics Gathering feature to automate the collection of statistics. By default, that process gathers statistics during a maintenance window from 10 P.M. to 6 A.M. each night and all day on weekends.

Since the analysis job is usually a batch operation performed after hours, you can tune it by improving sort and full table scan performance at the session level. If you are performing the analysis manually, use the **alter session** command to dramatically increase the settings for the DB_FILE_MULTIBLOCK_READ_COUNT and SORT_AREA_SIZE parameters prior to gathering the statistics. The result will be greatly enhanced performance for the sorts and full table scans the analysis performs.

Hint Where Needed

In most cases, the cost-based optimizer (CBO) selects the most efficient execution path for queries. However, you may have information about a better path. For example, you may be querying tables in remote databases, in which case you would want to avoid constantly connecting to the remote account. You may give Oracle a hint to influence the join operations, the overall query goal, the specific indexes used, or the parallelism of the query. See the "Related Hints" sections later in this chapter for an overview of the major hints.

Maximize the Throughput in the Environment

In an ideal environment, there is never a need to query information outside the database; all of the data stays in memory all of the time. Unless you are working with a very small database, however, this is not a realistic approach. In this section, you will see guidelines for maximizing the throughput of the environment.

Use Disk Caching

If Oracle cannot find the data it needs in the database, it performs a physical read. But how many of the physical reads actually reach the disk? If you use disk caching, you may be able to prevent as much as 90% of the access requests for the most-needed blocks. If the database buffer cache hit ratio is 90%, you are accessing the disks 10% of the time—and if the disk cache prevents 90% of those requests from reaching the disk, your effective hit ratio is 99%. Oracle's internal statistics do not reflect this improvement; you will need to work with your disk administrators to configure and monitor the disk cache.

Use a Larger Database Block Size

There is only one reason not to use the largest block size available in your environment for a new database: if you cannot support a greater number of users performing updates and inserts against a single block. Other than that, increasing the database block size should improve the performance of almost everything in your application. Larger database block sizes help keep indexes from splitting levels and help keep more data in memory longer. To support many concurrent inserts and updates, increase the settings for the **freelists** and **pctfree** parameters at the object level.

Store Data Efficiently at the Block Level

Oracle stores blocks of data in memory. It is in your best interest to make sure those blocks are as densely packed with data as possible. If your data storage is inefficient at the block level, you will not gain as much benefit as you can from the caches available in the database.

If the rows in your application are not going to be updated, set the **pctfree** as low as possible. For partitioned tables, set the **pctfree** value for each partition to maximize the row storage within blocks. Set a low **pctfree** value for indexes.

By default, the **pctused** parameter is set to 40 for all database blocks, and **pctfree** is set to 10. If you use the defaults, then as rows are added to the table, rows will be added to a block until the block is 90% full; at that point the block will be removed from the "free list" and all new inserts will use other blocks in the table. Updates of the rows in the block will use the space reserved by the **pctfree** setting. Rows may then be deleted from the block, but the block will not be added back to the free list until the space usage within the block drops below the **pctused** setting. This means that in applications that feature many **delete**s and **insert**s of rows, it is common to find many blocks using just slightly above the **pctused** value of each block. In that case, each block is just over 40% used, so each block in the buffer cache is only that full—resulting in a significant increase in the number of blocks requested to complete each command. If your application performs many **delete**s and **insert**s, you should consider increasing **pctused** so the block will be readded to the free list as quickly as possible.

If the **pctfree** setting is too low, updates may force Oracle to move the row (called a *migrated row*). In some cases row chaining is inevitable, such as when your row length is greater than your database block size. When row chaining and migration occur, each access of a row will require accessing multiple blocks, impacting the number of logical reads required for each command. You can detect row chaining by analyzing the table and then checking its statistics via USER_TABLES.

Designing to Throughput, Not Disk Space

Take an application that is running on eight 9GB disks and move it to a single 72GB disk. Will the application run faster or slower? In general, it will run slower, since the throughput of the single disk is unlikely to be equal to the combined throughput of the eight separate disks. Rather than designing your disk layout based on the space available (a common method), design it based on the throughput of the disks available. You may decide to use only part of each disk. The remaining space on the disk will not be used by the production application unless the throughput available for that disk improves.

Avoid the Use of the Temporary Segments

Whenever possible, perform all sorts in memory. Any operation that writes to the temporary segments is potentially wasting resources. Oracle uses temporary segments when the SORT_AREA_SIZE parameter does not allocate enough memory to support the sorting requirements of operations. Sorting operations include index creations, **order by** clauses, statistics gathering, **group by** operations, and some joins. As noted earlier in this chapter, you should strive to sort as few rows as possible. When performing the sorts that remain, perform them in memory. Note that you can alter the SORT_AREA_SIZE setting for your session via the **alter session** command.

Favor Fewer, Faster Processors

Given the choice, use a small number of fast processors in place of a larger number of slower processors. The operating system will have fewer processing queues to manage and will generally perform better.

Divide and Conquer Your Data

If you cannot avoid performing expensive operations on your database, you can attempt to split the work into more manageable chunks. Often you can severely limit the number of rows acted on by your operations, substantially improving performance.

Use Partitions

Partitions can benefit end users, DBAs, and application support personnel. For end users there are two potential benefits: improved query performance and improved availability for the database. Query performance may improve because of *partition elimination*. The optimizer knows what partitions may contain the data requested by a query. As a result, the partitions that will not participate are eliminated from the query process. Since fewer logical and physical reads are needed, the query should complete faster.

The availability improves because of the benefits partitions generate for DBAs and application support personnel. Many administrative functions can be performed on single partitions, allowing the rest of the table to be unaffected. For example, you can **truncate** a single partition of a table. You can split a partition, move it to a different tablespace, or switch it with an existing table (so that the previously independent table is then considered a partition). You can gather statistics on one partition at a time. All of these capabilities narrow the scope of administrative functions, reducing their impact on the availability of the database as a whole.

Use Materialized Views

You can use materialized views to divide the types of operations users perform against your tables. When you create a materialized view, you can direct users to query the materialized view directly or you can rely on Oracle's query rewrite capability to redirect queries to the materialized view.

As a result, you will have two copies of the data—one that services the input of new transactional data, and a second, the materialized view, that services queries. As a result, you can take one of them offline for maintenance without affecting the availability of the other. Also note that you can index the base table and the materialized view differently, with each having the structures needed for the specific data access types it is intended for.

See Chapter 24 for details on the implementation of materialized views.

Use Parallelism

Almost every major operation can be parallelized—including queries, inserts, object creations, and data loads. The parallel options allow you to involve multiple processors in the execution of a single command, effectively dividing the command into multiple smaller coordinated commands. As a result, the command may perform better. You can specify a degree of parallelism at the object level and can override it via hints in your queries.

Test Correctly

In most development methodologies, application testing has multiple phases, including module testing, full system testing, and performance stress testing. Many times, the full system test and performance stress test are not performed adequately due to time constraints as the application nears its delivery deadline. The result is that applications are released into production without any way to guarantee that the functionality and performance of the application as a whole will meet the needs of the users. This is a serious and significant flaw and should not be tolerated by any user of the application. Users do not need just one component of the application to function properly; they need the entire application to work properly in support of a business process. If they cannot do a day's worth of business in a day, the application fails.

This is a key tenet regarding identifying the need for tuning: *If the application slows the speed of the business process, it should be tuned.* The tests you perform must be able to determine if the application will hinder the speed of the business process under the expected production load.

Test with Large Volumes of Data

As described earlier in this chapter, objects within the database function differently after they have been used for some time. For example, the **pctfree** and **pctused** settings may make it likely that blocks will be only half-used or rows will be chained. Each of these causes performance problems that will only be seen after the application has been used for some time.

A further problem with data volume concerns indexes. As B*-tree indexes grow in size, they may split internally—the level of entries within the index increases. As a result, you can picture the new level as being an index within the index. The additional level in the index increases the effect of the index on data load rates. You will not see this impact until *after* the index is split. Applications that work acceptably for the first week or two in production, only to suddenly falter after the data volume reaches critical levels, do not support the business needs. In testing, there is no substitute for production data loaded at production rates while the tables already contain a substantial amount of data.

Test with Many Concurrent Users

Testing with a single user does not reflect the expected production usage of most database applications. You must be able to determine if concurrent users will encounter deadlocks, data consistency issues, or performance problems. For example, suppose an application module uses a work table during its processing. Rows are inserted into the table, manipulated, and then queried.

A separate application module does similar processing—and uses the same table. When executed at the same time, the two processes attempt to use each other's data. Unless you are testing with multiple users executing multiple application functions simultaneously, you may not discover this problem and the business data errors it will generate.

Testing with many concurrent users will also help to identify areas in the application in which users frequently use undo segments to complete their queries, impacting performance.

Test the Impact of Indexes on Your Load Times

Every **insert**, **update**, or **delete** of an indexed column may be about three times slower than the same transaction against an unindexed table. There are some exceptions—sorted data has much less of an impact, for example—but the rule is generally true. If you can load three thousand rows per second into an unindexed table in your environment, adding a single index to the table should slow your insert speed to around a thousand rows per second. The impact is dependent on your operating environment, the data structures involved, and the degree to which the data is sorted.

How many rows per second can you insert in your environment? Perform a series of simple tests. Create a table with no indexes and insert a large number of rows into it. Repeat the tests to reduce the impact of physical reads on the timing results. Calculate the number of rows inserted per second. In most environments you can insert tens of thousands of rows per second into the database. Perform the same test in your other database environments so you can identify any that are significantly different than the others.

Now consider your application. Are you able to insert rows into your tables via your application at anywhere near the rate you just calculated? Many applications run at less than 5% of the rate the environment will support. They are bogged down by unneeded indexes or the type of code design issues described earlier in this chapter. If their load rate decreases—say from 40 rows per second to 20 rows per second—the tuning focus should not be solely on how that decrease occurred but also on how the application managed to get only 40 rows per second inserted in an environment that supports thousands of rows inserted per second.

Make All Tests Repeatable

Most regulated industries have standards for tests. Their standards are so reasonable that *all* testing efforts should follow them. Among the standards is that all tests must be repeatable. To be compliant with the standards, you must be able to re-create the data set used, the exact action performed, the exact result expected, and the exact result seen and recorded. Preproduction tests for validation of the application must be performed on the production hardware. Moving the application to different hardware requires retesting the application. The tester and the business users must sign off on all tests.

Most people, on hearing those restrictions, would agree that they are good steps to take in any testing process. Indeed, your business users may be expecting that the people developing the application are following such standards even if they are not required by the industry. But are they followed, and if not, then why not? There are two commonly cited reasons for not following such standards: time and cost. Such tests require planning, personnel resources, business user involvement, and time for execution and documentation. Testing on production-caliber hardware may require the purchase of additional servers. Those are the most evident costs—but what is the business cost of failing to perform such tests? The testing requirements for validated systems in the U.S. pharmaceutical industry were implemented because those systems directly impact the integrity of critical products such as the safety of the blood supply. If your business has critical components served by your application (and if it does not, then why are you building the application?), you must consider the costs of insufficient, rushed testing and communicate those potential costs to the

business users. The evaluation of the risks of incorrect data or unacceptably slow performance must involve the business users. In turn, that may lead to an extended deadline to support proper testing.

In many cases, the rushed testing cycle occurs because there was not a testing standard in place at the start of the project. If there is a consistent, thorough, and well-documented testing standard in place at the enterprise level when the project starts, then the testing cycle will be shorter when it is finally executed. Testers will have known long in advance that repeatable data sets will be needed. Templates for tests will be available. If there is an issue with any test result, or if the application needs to be retested following a change, the test can be repeated. And the application users will know that the testing is robust enough to simulate the production usage of the application. If the system fails the tests for performance reasons, the problem may be a design issue (as described in the previous sections) or a problem with an individual query. In the following sections you will see how to display the execution path for a SQL statement, the major operations involved, and the related hints you can employ when tuning SQL.

Generating and Reading Explain Plans

You can display the execution path for a query in either of two ways:

- The **set autotrace on** command
- The **explain plan** command

In the following sections, both commands are explained; for the remainder of the chapter, the **set autotrace on** command will be used to illustrate execution paths as reported by the optimizer.

Using set autotrace on

You can have the execution path automatically displayed for every transaction you execute within SQL*Plus. The **set autotrace on** command will cause each query, after being executed, to display both its execution path and high-level trace information about the processing involved in resolving the query.

To use the **set autotrace on** command, you must have first created a PLAN_TABLE table within your account. The PLAN_TABLE structure may change with each release of Oracle, so you should drop and re-create your copy of PLAN_TABLE with each Oracle upgrade. The commands shown in the following listing will drop any existing PLAN_TABLE and replace it with the current version.

NOTE
*In order for you to use **set autotrace on**, your DBA must have first created the PLUSTRACE role in the database and granted that role to your account. The PLUSTRACE role gives you access to the underlying performance-related views in the Oracle data dictionary. The script to create the PLUSTRACE role is called plustrce.sql, usually found in the /sqlplus/admin directory under the Oracle software home directory.*

The file that creates the PLAN_TABLE table is located in the /rdbms/admin subdirectory under the Oracle software home directory.

```
drop table PLAN_TABLE;
@$ORACLE_HOME/rdbms/admin/utlxplan.sql
```

When you use **set autotrace on**, records are inserted into your copy of the PLAN_TABLE to show the order of operations executed. After the query completes, the selected data is displayed. After the query's data is displayed, the order of operations is shown followed by statistical information about the query processing. The following explanation of **set autotrace on** focuses on the section of the output that displays the order of operations.

NOTE
To show the explain plan output without running the query,
*use the **set autotrace on trace explain** command.*

If you use the **set autotrace on** command with its default options, you will not see the explain plan for your queries until *after* they complete. The **explain plan** command (described next) shows the execution paths without running the queries first. Therefore, if the performance of a query is unknown, you may choose to use the **explain plan** command before running it. If you are fairly certain that the performance of a query is acceptable, use **set autotrace on** to verify its execution path.

NOTE
*When you use the **set autotrace on** command, Oracle will automatically*
delete the records it inserts into PLAN_TABLE once the execution path
has been displayed.

If you use the parallel query options or query remote databases, an additional section of the **set autotrace on** output will show the text of the queries executed by the parallel query server processes or the query executed within the remote database.

To disable the autotrace feature, use the **set autotrace off** command.

In order to use **set autotrace**, you must be able to access the database via SQL*Plus. If you have SQL access but not SQL*Plus access, you can use **explain plan** instead, as described in the next section.

In the following example, a full table scan of the BOOKSHELF table is executed. The rows of output are not displayed in this output, for the sake of brevity. The order of operations is displayed below the query.

```
select *
  from BOOKSHELF;

Execution Plan
----------------------------------------------------------
   0      SELECT STATEMENT Optimizer=ALL_ROWS (Cost=1 Card=31 Bytes=12
          40)
   1    0   TABLE ACCESS (FULL) OF 'BOOKSHELF' (TABLE) (Cost=4 Card=31
          Bytes=1240)
```

The "Execution Plan" shows the steps the optimizer will use to execute the query. Each step is assigned an ID value (starting with 0). The second number shows the "parent" operation of the

current operation. Thus, for the preceding example, the second operation—the TABLE ACCESS (FULL) OF 'BOOKSHELF'—has a parent operation (the **select** statement itself). Each step displays a cumulative cost for that step plus all of its child steps.

You can generate the order of operations for DML commands, too. In the following example, a **delete** statement's execution path is shown:

```
delete
    from BOOKSHELF_AUTHOR;

Execution Plan
-------------------------------------------------------------
   0        DELETE STATEMENT Optimizer=ALL_ROWS (Cost=4 Card=37 Bytes=12
            58)
   1    0    DELETE OF 'BOOKSHELF_AUTHOR'
   2    1      TABLE ACCESS (FULL) OF 'BOOKSHELF_AUTHOR' (TABLE) (Cost=
            4 Card=37 Bytes=1258)
```

The **delete** command, as expected, involves a full table scan. If you have analyzed your tables, the Execution Plan column's output shows the number of rows from each table, the relative cost of each step, and the overall cost of the operation. The costs shown at the steps are cumulative; they are the costs of that step plus all of its child steps. You could use that information to pinpoint the operations that are the most costly during the processing of the query.

In the following example, a slightly more complex query is executed. An index-based query is made against the BOOKSHELF table, using its primary key index.

```
select /*+ INDEX(bookshelf) */ *
    from BOOKSHELF
 where Title like 'M%';

Execution Plan
-------------------------------------------------------------
   0        SELECT STATEMENT Optimizer=ALL_ROWS (Cost=3 Card=2 Bytes=80)
   1    0    TABLE ACCESS (BY INDEX ROWID) OF 'BOOKSHELF' (TABLE) (Cost
            =3 Card=2 Bytes=80)
   2    1      INDEX (RANGE SCAN) OF 'SYS_C004834' (INDEX (UNIQUE)) (Co
            st=1 Card=2)
```

This listing includes three operations. Operation #2, the INDEX RANGE SCAN of the BOOKSHELF primary key index (its name was system-generated) provides data to operation #1, the TABLE ACCESS BY INDEX ROWID operation. The data returned from the TABLE ACCESS BY INDEX ROWID is used to satisfy the query (operation #0).

The preceding output also shows that the optimizer is automatically indenting each successive step within the execution plan. In general, you should read the list of operations from the inside out and from top to bottom. Thus, if two operations are listed, the one that is the most indented will usually be executed first. If the two operations are at the same level of indentation, then the one that is listed first (with the lowest operation number) will be executed first.

In the following example, BOOKSHELF and BOOKSHELF_AUTHOR are joined without the benefit of indexes. Oracle will use a join operation called a merge join, in which each table is separately sorted prior to the two sorted row sets being joined:

```
select /*+ USE_MERGE (bookshelf, bookshelf_author)*/
       BOOKSHELF_AUTHOR.AuthorName
  from BOOKSHELF, BOOKSHELF_AUTHOR
 where BOOKSHELF.Title = BOOKSHELF_AUTHOR.Title;

Execution Plan
----------------------------------------------------------
   0        SELECT STATEMENT Optimizer=ALL_ROWS (Cost=7 Card=5 Bytes=320)
   1    0    MERGE JOIN (Cost=7 Card=5 Bytes=320)
   2    1     INDEX (FULL SCAN) OF 'SYS_C004834' (INDEX (UNIQUE)) (Cos
             t=1 Card=31)
   3    1     SORT (JOIN) (Cost=5 Card=37 Bytes=1258)
   4    3      TABLE ACCESS (FULL) OF 'BOOKSHELF_AUTHOR' (TABLE) (Cos
             t=1 Card=37 Bytes=1258)
```

The indentation here may seem confusing at first, but the operational parentage information provided by the operation numbers clarifies the order of operations. The innermost operations are performed first—the TABLE ACCESS FULL and INDEX FULL SCAN operations. Next, the full table scan's data is processed via a SORT JOIN operation (in operation #4), while the output from the index scan (which is sorted already) is used as the basis for a TABLE ACCESS BY INDEX ROWID (step 2). Both step 2 and step 4 have operation #1, the MERGE JOIN, as their parent operations. The MERGE JOIN operation provides data back to the user via the **select** statement.

If the same query were run as a NESTED LOOPS join, a different execution path would be generated. As shown in the following listing, the NESTED LOOPS join would be able to take advantage of the primary key index on the Title column of the BOOKSHELF table.

NOTE
Based on the size of the tables and the available statistics, Oracle may choose to perform a different type of join, called a hash join, instead of a NESTED LOOPS join.

```
select /*+ INDEX(bookshelf) */
       BOOKSHELF_AUTHOR.AuthorName
  from BOOKSHELF, BOOKSHELF_AUTHOR
 where BOOKSHELF.Title = BOOKSHELF_AUTHOR.Title

Execution Plan
----------------------------------------------------------
   0        SELECT STATEMENT Optimizer=ALL_ROWS (Cost=4 Card=37 Bytes=19
             24)
   1    0    NESTED LOOPS (Cost=4 Card=37 Bytes=1924)
   2    1     TABLE ACCESS (FULL) OF 'BOOKSHELF_AUTHOR' (TABLE) (Cost=
             4 Card=37 Bytes=1258)
   3    1     INDEX (UNIQUE SCAN) OF 'SYS_C004834' (INDEX (UNIQUE)) (C
             ost=1 Card=1 Bytes=18)
```

NESTED LOOPS joins are among the few execution paths that do not follow the "read from the inside out" rule of indented execution paths. To read the NESTED LOOPS execution path correctly, examine the order of the operations that directly provide data to the NESTED LOOPS operation (in this case, operations #2 and #3). Of those two operations, the operation with the lowest number (#2, in this example) is executed first. Thus, the TABLE ACCESS FULL of the BOOKSHELF_AUTHOR table is executed first (BOOKSHELF_AUTHOR is the driving table for the query).

Once you have established the driving table for the query, the rest of the execution path can be read from the inside out and from top to bottom. The second operation performed is the INDEX UNIQUE SCAN of the BOOKSHELF primary key index. The NESTED LOOPS operation is then able to return rows to the user.

If a hash join had been selected instead of a NESTED LOOPS join, the execution path would have been

```
select /*+ USE_HASH (bookshelf) */
       BOOKSHELF_AUTHOR.AuthorName
  from BOOKSHELF, BOOKSHELF_AUTHOR
 where BOOKSHELF.Title = BOOKSHELF_AUTHOR.Title;

Execution Plan
-----------------------------------------------------------
   0      SELECT STATEMENT Optimizer=ALL_ROWS (Cost=6 Card=37 Bytes=19
          24)
   1    0   HASH JOIN (Cost=6 Card=37 Bytes=1924)
   2    1     INDEX (FULL SCAN) OF 'SYS_C004834' (INDEX (UNIQUE)) (Cos
          t=2 Card=31 Bytes=558)
   3    1     TABLE ACCESS (FULL) OF 'BOOKSHELF_AUTHOR' (TABLE) (Cost=
          1 Card=37 Bytes=1258)
```

The hash join execution path shows that two separate scans are performed. Since the two operations are listed at the same level of indentation, the BOOKSHELF table's primary key index is scanned first (since it has the lower operation number).

Using explain plan

You can use the **explain plan** command to generate the execution path for a query without first running the query. To use the **explain plan** command, you must first create a PLAN_TABLE table in your schema (see the previous instructions on creating the table). To determine the execution path of a query, prefix the query with the following SQL:

```
explain plan
for
```

An example of the execution of the **explain plan** command is shown in the following listing:

```
explain plan
for
select /*+ USE_HASH (bookshelf) */
       BOOKSHELF_AUTHOR.AuthorName
  from BOOKSHELF, BOOKSHELF_AUTHOR
 where BOOKSHELF.Title = BOOKSHELF_AUTHOR.Title;
```

When the **explain plan** command is executed, records will be inserted into PLAN_TABLE. You can query PLAN_TABLE directly or you can use the DBMS_XPLAN package to format the results for you. The use of the DBMS_XPLAN package is shown in the following listing:

```
select * from table(DBMS_XPLAN.Display);
```

The result is a formatted explain plan listing:

```
PLAN_TABLE_OUTPUT
--------------------------------------------------------------------------------
--------------------------------------------------------------------------------
| Id  | Operation            | Name             | Rows  | Bytes | Cost (%CPU)| Time     |
--------------------------------------------------------------------------------
|   0 | SELECT STATEMENT     |                  |    37 |  1924 |    4  (25)| 00:00:01 |
|*  1 |  HASH JOIN           |                  |    37 |  1924 |    4  (25)| 00:00:01 |
|   2 |   INDEX FULL SCAN    | SYS_C004834      |    32 |   608 |    1 (100)| 00:00:01 |
|   3 |   TABLE ACCESS FULL| BOOKSHELF_AUTHOR |    37 |  1258 |    4  (25)| 00:00:01 |

Predicate Information (identified by operation id):
---------------------------------------------------
   1 - access("BOOKSHELF"."TITLE"="BOOKSHELF_AUTHOR"."TITLE")
```

The output includes the Cost column, which displays the relative "cost" of each step and its child steps. It also includes the ID values, indenting to show the relationships between steps, and an additional section listing the limiting conditions applied at each step.

When tuning a query, you should watch for steps that scan many rows but only return a small number of rows. For example, you should avoid performing a full table scan on a multimillion row table in order to return three rows. You can use the explain plan output to identify those steps that deal with the greatest number of rows.

Major Operations Within Explain Plans

As illustrated in the preceding listings, the explain plan for a query provides insight into the methods Oracle uses to retrieve and process rows. In the following sections you will see descriptions of the most commonly used operations.

TABLE ACCESS FULL

A full table scan sequentially reads each row of a table. The optimizer calls the operation used during a full table scan a TABLE ACCESS FULL. To optimize the performance of a full table scan, Oracle reads multiple blocks during each database read.

A full table scan may be used whenever there is no **where** clause on a query. For example, the following query selects all of the rows from the BOOKSHELF table:

```
select *
   from BOOKSHELF;
```

To resolve the preceding query, Oracle will perform a full table scan of the BOOKSHELF table. If the BOOKSHELF table is small, a full table scan of BOOKSHELF may be fairly quick, incurring little performance cost. However, as BOOKSHELF grows in size, the cost of performing a full table

scan grows. If you have multiple users performing full table scans of BOOKSHELF, then the cost associated with the full table scans grows even faster.

With proper planning, full table scans need not be performance problems. You should work with your database administrators to make sure the database has been configured to take advantage of features such as Parallel Query and multiblock reads. Unless you have properly configured your environment for full table scans, you should carefully monitor their use.

NOTE
Depending on the data being selected, the optimizer may choose to use a full scan of an index in place of a full table scan.

TABLE ACCESS BY INDEX ROWID

To improve the performance of table accesses, you can use Oracle operations that access rows by their ROWID values. The ROWID records the physical location where the row is stored. Oracle uses indexes to correlate data values with ROWID values—and thus with physical locations of the data. Given the ROWID of a row, Oracle can use the TABLE ACCESS BY INDEX ROWID operation to retrieve the row.

When you know the ROWID, you know exactly where the row is physically located. You can use indexes to access the ROWID information, as described in the next major section, "Operations That Use Indexes." Because indexes provide quick access to ROWID values, they help to improve the performance of queries that make use of indexed columns.

Related Hints

Within a query, you can specify hints that direct the CBO in its processing of the query. To specify a hint, use the syntax shown in the following example. Immediately after the **select** keyword, enter the following string:

```
/*+
```

Next, add the hint, such as

```
FULL(bookshelf)
```

Close the hint with the following string:

```
*/
```

Hints use Oracle's syntax for comments within queries, with the addition of the + sign at the start of the hint. Throughout this chapter, the hints relevant to each operation will be described. For table accesses, the FULL hint tells Oracle to perform a full table scan (the TABLE ACCESS FULL operation) on the listed table, as shown in the following listing:

```
select /*+ FULL(bookshelf) */ *
  from BOOKSHELF
 where Title like 'T%';
```

If you did not use the FULL hint, Oracle would normally plan to use the primary key index on the Title column to resolve this query. Since the table is presently small, the full table scan is not costly. As the table grows, you would probably favor the use of a ROWID-based access for this query.

Operations That Use Indexes

Within Oracle are two major types of indexes: *unique indexes,* in which each row of the indexed table contains a unique value for the indexed column(s), and *nonunique indexes,* in which the rows' indexed values can repeat. The operations used to read data from the indexes depend on the type of index in use and the way in which you write the query that accesses the index.

Consider the BOOKSHELF table:

```
create table BOOKSHELF
(Title        VARCHAR2(100) primary key,
Publisher     VARCHAR2(20),
CategoryName VARCHAR2(20),
Rating        VARCHAR2(2),
constraint CATFK foreign key (CategoryName)
references CATEGORY(CategoryName));
```

The Title column is the primary key for the BOOKSHELF table—that is, it uniquely identifies each row, and each attribute is dependent on the Title value.

Whenever a PRIMARY KEY or UNIQUE constraint is created, Oracle creates a unique index to enforce uniqueness of the values in the column. As defined by the **create table** command, a PRIMARY KEY constraint will be created on the BOOKSHELF table. The index that supports the primary key will be given a system-generated name, since the constraint was not explicitly named.

You can create indexes on other columns of the BOOKSHELF table manually. For example, you could create a nonunique index on the CategoryName column via the **create index** command:

```
create index I_BOOKSHELF_CATEGORY
    on BOOKSHELF(CategoryName)
tablespace INDEXES
compute statistics;
```

The BOOKSHELF table now has two indexes on it: a unique index on the Title column, and a nonunique index on the CategoryName column. One or more of the indexes could be used during the resolution of a query, depending on how the query is written and executed. As part of the index creation, its statistics were gathered via the **compute statistics** clause. Since the table is already populated with rows, you do not need to execute a separate command to analyze the index.

INDEX UNIQUE SCAN

To use an index during a query, your query must be written to allow the use of an index. In most cases, you allow the optimizer to use an index via the **where** clause of the query. For example, the following query could use the unique index on the Title column:

```
select *
   from BOOKSHELF
 where Title = 'INNUMERACY';
```

Internally, the execution of the preceding query will be divided into two steps. First, the Title column index will be accessed via an INDEX UNIQUE SCAN operation. The ROWID value that

matches the title 'INNUMERACY' will be returned from the index; that ROWID value will then be used to query BOOKSHELF via a TABLE ACCESS BY INDEX ROWID operation.

If all of the columns selected by the query had been contained within the index, then Oracle would not have needed to use the TABLE ACCESS BY INDEX ROWID operation; since the data would be in the index, the index would be all that is needed to satisfy the query. Because the query selected all columns from the BOOKSHELF table, and the index did not contain all of the columns of the BOOKSHELF table, the TABLE ACCESS BY INDEX ROWID operation was necessary.

INDEX RANGE SCAN

If you query the database based on a range of values, or if you query using a nonunique index, then an INDEX RANGE SCAN operation is used to query the index.

Consider the BOOKSHELF table again, with a unique index on its Title column. A query of the form

```
select Title
  from BOOKSHELF
 where Title like 'M%';
```

would return all Title values beginning with 'M'. Since the **where** clause uses the Title column, the primary key index on the Title column can be used while resolving the query. However, a unique value is not specified in the **where** clause; a range of values is specified. Therefore, the unique primary key index will be accessed via an INDEX RANGE SCAN operation. Because INDEX RANGE SCAN operations require reading multiple values from the index, they are less efficient than INDEX UNIQUE SCAN operations.

In the preceding example, only the Title column was selected by the query. Since the values for the Title column are stored in the primary key index—which is being scanned—there is no need for the database to access the BOOKSHELF table directly during the query execution. The INDEX RANGE SCAN of the primary key index is the only operation required to resolve the query.

The CategoryName column of the BOOKSHELF table has a nonunique index on its values. If you specify a limiting condition for CategoryName values in your query's **where** clause, an INDEX RANGE SCAN of the CategoryName index may be performed. Since the BOOKSHELF$CATEGORY index is a nonunique index, the database cannot perform an INDEX UNIQUE SCAN on BOOKSHELF$CATEGORY, even if CategoryName is equated to a single value in your query.

When Indexes Are Used

Since indexes have a great impact on the performance of queries, you should be aware of the conditions under which an index will be used to resolve a query. The following sections describe the conditions that can cause an index to be used while resolving a query.

If You Set an Indexed Column Equal to a Value

In the BOOKSHELF table, the CategoryName column has a nonunique index named BOOKSHELF$CATEGORY. A query that compares the CategoryName column to a value will be able to use the BOOKSHELF$CATEGORY index.

The following query compares the CategoryName column to the value 'ADULTNF':

```
select Title
  from BOOKSHELF
 where CategoryName = 'ADULTNF';
```

Since the BOOKSHELF$CATEGORY index is a nonunique index, this query may return multiple rows, and an INDEX RANGE SCAN operation may be used when reading data from it. Depending on the table's statistics, Oracle may choose to perform a full table scan instead.

If it uses the index, the execution of the preceding query may include two operations: an INDEX RANGE SCAN of BOOKSHELF$CATEGORY (to get the ROWID values for all of the rows with 'ADULTNF' values in the CategoryName column), followed by a TABLE ACCESS BY INDEX ROWID of the BOOKSHELF table (to retrieve the Title column values).

If a column has a unique index created on it, and the column is compared to a value with an = sign, then an INDEX UNIQUE SCAN will be used instead of an INDEX RANGE SCAN.

If You Specify a Range of Values for an Indexed Column

You do not need to specify explicit values in order for an index to be used. The INDEX RANGE SCAN operation can scan an index for ranges of values. In the following query, the Title column of the BOOKSHELF table is queried for a range of values (those that start with *M*):

```
select Title
   from BOOKSHELF
 where Title like 'M%';
```

A range scan can also be performed when using the > or < operators:

```
select Title
   from BOOKSHELF
 where Title > 'M';
```

When specifying a range of values for a column, an index will not be used to resolve the query if the first character specified is a wildcard. The following query will *not* perform an INDEX RANGE SCAN on the available indexes:

```
select Publisher
   from BOOKSHELF
 where Title like '%M%';
```

Since the first character of the string used for value comparisons is a wildcard, the index cannot be used to find the associated data quickly. Therefore, a full table scan (TABLE ACCESS FULL operation) will be performed instead. Depending on the statistics for the table and the index, Oracle may choose to perform a full scan of the index instead. In this example, if the selected column is the Title column, the optimizer may choose to perform a full scan of the primary key index rather than a full scan of the BOOKSHELF table.

If No Functions Are Performed on the Column in the where Clause

Consider the following query, which will use the BOOKSHELF$CATEGORY index:

```
select COUNT(*)
   from BOOKSHELF
 where CategoryName = 'ADULTNF';
```

What if you did not know whether the values in the CategoryName column were stored as uppercase, mixed case, or lowercase values? In that event, you may write the query as follows:

```
select COUNT(*)
  from BOOKSHELF
 where UPPER(CategoryName) = 'ADULTNF';
```

The **UPPER** function changes the Manager values to uppercase before comparing them to the value 'ADULTNF'. However, using the function on the column may prevent the optimizer from using an index on that column. The preceding query (using the **UPPER** function) will perform a TABLE ACCESS FULL of the BOOKSHELF table unless you have created a function-based index on UPPER(CategoryName); see Chapter 17 for details on function-based indexes.

If you concatenate two columns together or a string to a column, then indexes on those columns will not be used. The index stores the real value for the column, and any change to that value will prevent the optimizer from using the index.

If No IS NULL or IS NOT NULL Checks Are Used for the Indexed Column

NULL values are not stored in indexes. Therefore, the following query will not use an index; there is no way the index could help to resolve the query:

```
select Title
  from BOOKSHELF
 where CategoryName is null;
```

Since CategoryName is the only column with a limiting condition in the query, and the limiting condition is a **NULL** check, the BOOKSHELF$CATEGORY index will not be used and a TABLE ACCESS FULL operation will be used to resolve the query.

What if an **IS NOT NULL** check is performed on the column? All of the non-**NULL** values for the column are stored in the index; however, the index search would not be efficient. To resolve the query, the optimizer would need to read every value from the index and access the table for each row returned from the index. In most cases, it would be more efficient to perform a full table scan than to perform an index scan (with associated TABLE ACCESS BY INDEX ROWID operations) for all of the values returned from the index. Therefore, the following query may not use an index:

```
select Title
  from BOOKSHELF
 where CategoryName is not null;
```

If the selected columns are in an index, the optimizer may choose to perform a full index scan in place of the full table scan.

If Equivalence Conditions Are Used

In the examples in the prior sections, the Title value was compared to a value with an = sign, as in this query:

```
select *
  from BOOKSHELF
 where Title = 'INNUMERACY';
```

What if you wanted to select all of the records that did not have a Title of 'INNUMERACY'? The **=** would be replaced with **!=**, and the query would now be

```
select *
  from BOOKSHELF
 where Title != 'INNUMERACY';
```

When resolving the revised query, the optimizer may not use an index. Indexes are used when values are compared exactly to another value—when the limiting conditions are equalities, not inequalities. The optimizer would only choose an index in this example if it decided the full index scan (plus the TABLE ACCESS BY INDEX ROWID operations to get all the columns) would be faster than a full table scan.

Another example of an inequality is the **not in** clause, when used with a subquery. The following query selects values from the BOOKSHELF table for books that aren't written by Stephen Jay Gould:

```
select *
  from BOOKSHELF
 where Title NOT IN
(select Title
   from BOOKSHELF_AUTHOR
  where AuthorName = 'STEPHEN JAY GOULD');
```

In some cases, the query in the preceding listing would not be able to use an index on the Title column of the BOOKSHELF table, since it is not set equal to any value. Instead, the BOOKSHELF.Title value is used with a **not in** clause to eliminate the rows that match those returned by the subquery. To use an index, you should set the indexed column equal to a value. In many cases, Oracle will internally rewrite the **not in** as a **not exists** clause, allowing the query to use an index. The following query, which uses an **in** clause, could use an index on the BOOKSHELF.Title column or could perform a nonindexed join between the tables; the optimizer will choose the path with the lowest cost based on the available statistics:

```
select *
  from BOOKSHELF
 where Title IN
(select Title
   from BOOKSHELF_AUTHOR
  where AuthorName = 'STEPHEN JAY GOULD');
```

If the Leading Column of a Multicolumn Index Is Set Equal to a Value

An index can be created on a single column or on multiple columns. If the index is created on multiple columns, the index will be used if the leading column of the index is used in a limiting condition of the query.

If your query specifies values for only the nonleading columns of the index, the index can be used via the index skip-scan feature introduced in Oracle9*i*. Skip-scan index access enables the optimizer to potentially use a concatenated index even if its leading column is not listed in the **where** clause. You may need to use the INDEX hint (described in the next section) to tell the optimizer to use the index for a skip-scan access. As of Oracle Database 10*g*, you can use the INDEX_SS hint to suggest a skip-scan index access.

If the MAX or MIN Function Is Used

If you select the **MAX** or **MIN** value of an indexed column, the optimizer may use the index to quickly find the maximum or minimum value for the column.

If the Index Is Selective

All of the previous rules for determining whether an index will be used consider the syntax of the query being performed and the structure of the index available. The optimizer can use the selectivity of the index to judge whether using the index will lower the cost of executing the query.

In a highly selective index, a small number of records are associated with each distinct column value. For example, if there are 100 records in a table and 80 distinct values for a column in that table, the selectivity of an index on that column is 80 / 100 = 0.80. The higher the selectivity, the fewer the number of rows returned for each distinct value in the column.

The number of rows returned per distinct value is important during range scans. If an index has a low selectivity, then the many INDEX RANGE SCAN operations and TABLE ACCESS BY INDEX ROWID operations used to retrieve the data may involve more work than a TABLE ACCESS FULL of the table.

The selectivity of an index is not considered by the optimizer unless you have analyzed the index. The optimizer can use histograms to make judgments about the distribution of data within a table. For example, if the data values are heavily skewed so that most of the values are in a very small data range, the optimizer may avoid using the index for values in that range while using the index for values outside the range.

Related Hints

Several hints are available to direct the optimizer in its use of indexes. The INDEX hint is the most commonly used index-related hint. The INDEX hint tells the optimizer to use an index-based scan on the specified table. You do not need to mention the index name when using the INDEX hint, although you can list specific indexes if you choose.

For example, the following query uses the INDEX hint to suggest the use of an index on the BOOKSHELF table during the resolution of the query:

```
select /*+ index(bookshelf bookshelf$category) */ Title
   from BOOKSHELF
 where CategoryName = 'ADULTNF';
```

According to the rules provided earlier in this section, the preceding query should use the index without the hint being needed. However, if the index is nonselective or the table is small, the optimizer may choose to ignore the index. If you know that the index is selective for the data values given, you can use the INDEX hint to force an index-based data access path to be used.

In the hint syntax, name the table (or its alias, if you give the table an alias) and, optionally, the name of the suggested index. The optimizer may choose to disregard any hints you provide.

If you do not list a specific index in the INDEX hint, and multiple indexes are available for the table, the optimizer evaluates the available indexes and chooses the index whose scan is likely to have the lowest cost. The optimizer could also choose to scan several indexes and merge them via the AND-EQUAL operation described in the previous section.

A second hint, INDEX_ASC, functions the same as the INDEX hint: It suggests an ascending index scan for resolving queries against specific tables. A third index-based hint, INDEX_DESC, tells the optimizer to scan the index in descending order (from its highest value to its lowest).

To suggest an index fast full scan, use the INDEX_FFS hint. The ROWID hint is similar to the INDEX hint, suggesting the use of the TABLE ACCESS BY INDEX ROWID method for the specified table. The AND_EQUAL hint suggests the optimizer merge the results of multiple index scans.

Additional Tuning Issues for Indexes

When you're creating indexes on a table, two issues commonly arise: Should you use multiple indexes or a single concatenated index, and if you use a concatenated index, which column should be the leading column of the index?

In general, it is faster for the optimizer to scan a single concatenated index than to scan and merge two separate indexes. The more rows returned from the scan, the more likely the concatenated index scan will outperform the merge of the two index scans. As you add more columns to the concatenated index, it becomes less efficient for range scans.

For the concatenated index, which column should be the leading column of the index? The leading column should be very frequently used as a limiting condition against the table, and it should be highly selective. In a concatenated index, the optimizer will base its estimates of the index's selectivity (and thus its likelihood of being used) on the selectivity of the leading column of the index. Of these two criteria—being used in limiting conditions and being the most selective column—the first is more important.

A highly selective index based on a column that is never used in limiting conditions will never be used. A poorly selective index on a column that is frequently used in limiting conditions will not benefit your performance greatly. If you cannot achieve the goal of creating an index that is both highly selective and frequently used, then you should consider creating separate indexes for the columns to be indexed.

Many applications emphasize online transaction processing over batch processing; there may be many concurrent online users but a small number of concurrent batch users. In general, index-based scans allow online users to access data more quickly than if a full table scan had been performed. When creating your application, you should be aware of the kinds of queries executed within the application and the limiting conditions in those queries. If you are familiar with the queries executed against the database, you may be able to index the tables so that the online users can quickly retrieve the data they need. When the database performance directly impacts the online business process, the application should perform as few database accesses as possible.

Operations That Manipulate Data Sets

Once the data has been returned from the table or index, it can be manipulated. You can group the records, sort them, count them, lock them, or merge the results of the query with the results of other queries (via the **union**, **minus**, and **intersect** operators). In the following sections, you will see how the data manipulation operations are used.

Most of the operations that manipulate sets of records do not return records to the users until the entire operation is completed. For example, sorting records while eliminating duplicates (known as a SORT UNIQUE NOSORT operation) cannot return records to the user until all of the records have been evaluated for uniqueness. On the other hand, index scan operations and table access operations can return records to the user as soon as a record is found.

When an INDEX RANGE SCAN operation is performed, the first row returned from the query passes the criteria of the limiting conditions set by the query—there is no need to evaluate the next record returned prior to displaying the first record. If a set operation—such as a sorting operation—is performed, then the records will not be immediately displayed. During set operations, the user will have to wait for all rows to be processed by the operation. Therefore, you should limit the

number of set operations performed by queries used by online users (to limit the perceived response time of the application). Sorting and grouping operations are most common in large reports and batch transactions.

Ordering Rows

Three of Oracle's internal operations sort rows without grouping the rows. The first is the SORT ORDER BY operation, which is used when an **order by** clause is used in a query. For example, the BOOKSHELF table is queried and sorted by Publisher:

```
select Title from BOOKSHELF
 order by Publisher;
```

When the preceding query is executed, the optimizer will retrieve the data from the BOOKSHELF table via a TABLE ACCESS FULL operation (since there are no limiting conditions for the query, all rows will be returned). The retrieved records will not be immediately displayed to the user; a SORT ORDER BY operation will sort the records before the user sees any results.

Occasionally, a sorting operation may be required to eliminate duplicates as it sorts records. For example, what if you only want to see the distinct Publisher values in the BOOKSHELF table? The query would be as follows:

```
select DISTINCT Publisher from BOOKSHELF;
```

As with the prior query, this query has no limiting conditions, so a TABLE ACCESS FULL operation will be used to retrieve the records from the BOOKSHELF table. However, the **distinct** keyword tells the optimizer to only return the distinct values for the Publisher column.

To resolve the query, the optimizer takes the records returned by the TABLE ACCESS FULL operation and sorts them via a SORT UNIQUE NOSORT operation. No records will be displayed to the user until all of the records have been processed.

In addition to being used by the **distinct** keyword, the SORT UNIQUE NOSORT operation is invoked when the **minus**, **intersect**, and **union** (but not **union all**) functions are used.

A third sorting operation, SORT JOIN, is always used as part of a MERGE JOIN operation and is never used on its own. The implications of SORT JOIN on the performance of joins are described in "Operations That Perform Joins," later in this chapter.

Grouping Rows

Two of Oracle's internal operations sort rows while grouping like records together. The two operations—SORT AGGREGATE and SORT GROUP BY—are used in conjunction with grouping functions (such as **MIN**, **MAX**, and **COUNT**). The syntax of the query determines which operation is used.

In the following query, the maximum Publisher value, alphabetically, is selected from the BOOKSHELF table:

```
select MAX(Publisher)
  from BOOKSHELF;
```

To resolve the query, the optimizer will perform two separate operations. First, a TABLE ACCESS FULL operation will select the Publisher values from the table. Second, the rows will be analyzed via a SORT AGGREGATE operation, which will return the maximum Publisher value to the user.

If the Publisher column were indexed, the index could be used to resolve queries of the maximum or minimum value for the index (as described in "Operations That Use Indexes," earlier in this chapter). Since the Publisher column is not indexed, a sorting operation is required. The maximum Publisher value will not be returned by this query until all of the records have been read and the SORT AGGREGATE operation has completed.

The SORT AGGREGATE operation was used in the preceding example because there is no **group by** clause in the query. Queries that use the **group by** clause use an internal operation named SORT GROUP BY.

What if you want to know the number of titles from each publisher? The following query selects the count of each Publisher value from the BOOKSHELF table using a **group by** clause:

```
select Publisher, COUNT(*)
   from BOOKSHELF
 group by Publisher;
```

This query returns one record for each distinct Publisher value. For each Publisher value, the number of its occurrences in the BOOKSHELF table will be calculated and displayed in the COUNT(*) column.

To resolve this query, Oracle will first perform a full table scan (there are no limiting conditions for the query). Since a **group by** clause is used, the rows returned from the TABLE ACCESS FULL operation will be processed by a SORT GROUP BY operation. Once all the rows have been sorted into groups and the count for each group has been calculated, the records will be returned to the user. As with the other sorting operations, no records are returned to the user until all of the records have been processed.

The operations to this point have involved simple examples—full table scans, index scans, and sorting operations. Most queries that access a single table use the operations described in the previous sections. When tuning a query for an online user, avoid using the sorting and grouping operations that force users to wait for records to be processed. When possible, write queries that allow application users to receive records quickly as the query is resolved. The fewer sorting and grouping operations you perform, the faster the first record will be returned to the user. In a batch transaction, the performance of the query is measured by its overall time to complete, not the time to return the first row. As a result, batch transactions may use sorting and grouping operations without impacting the perceived performance of the application.

If your application does not require all of the rows to be sorted prior to presenting query output, consider using the FIRST_ROWS hint. FIRST_ROWS tells the optimizer to favor execution paths that do not perform set operations.

UNION, MINUS, and INTERSECT

The **union**, **minus**, and **intersect** clauses allow the results of multiple queries to be processed and compared. Each of the functions has an associated operation—the names of the operations are UNION, MINUS, and INTERSECTION.

The following query selects all of the Title values from the BOOKSHELF table and from the BOOK_ORDER table:

```
select Title
   from BOOKSHELF
 UNION
select Title
   from BOOK_ORDER;
```

When the preceding query is executed, the optimizer will execute each of the queries separately, and then combine the results. The first query is

```
select Title
   from BOOKSHELF
```

There are no limiting conditions in the query, and the Title column is indexed, so the primary key index on the BOOKSHELF table will be scanned.
 The second query is

```
select Title
   from BOOK_ORDER
```

There are no limiting conditions in the query, and the Title column is indexed, so the primary key index on the BOOK_ORDER table will be scanned.
 Since the query performs a **union** of the results of the two queries, the two result sets will then be merged via a UNION-ALL operation. Using the **union** operator forces Oracle to eliminate duplicate records, so the result set is processed by a SORT UNIQUE NOSORT operation before the records are returned to the user. If the query had used a **union all** clause in place of **union**, the SORT UNIQUE NOSORT operation would not have been necessary. The query would be

```
select Title
   from BOOKSHELF
 UNION ALL
select Title
   from BOOK_ORDER;
```

 When processing the revised query, the optimizer would perform the scans required by the two queries, followed by a UNION-ALL operation. No SORT UNIQUE NOSORT operation would be required, since a **union all** clause does not eliminate duplicate records.
 When processing the **union** query, the optimizer addresses each of the **union**ed queries separately. Although the examples shown in the preceding listings all involved simple queries with full table scans, the **union**ed queries can be very complex, with correspondingly complex execution paths. The results are not returned to the user until all of the records have been processed.

NOTE
*UNION ALL is a row operation. UNION, which includes
a SORT UNIQUE NOSORT, is a set operation.*

 When a **minus** clause is used, the query is processed in a manner very similar to the execution path used for the **union** example. In the following query, the Title values from the BOOKSHELF and BOOK_ORDER tables are compared. If a Title value exists in BOOK_ORDER but does not exist in BOOKSHELF, then that value will be returned by the query. In other words, we want to see all of the Titles on order that we don't already have.

```
select Title
   from BOOK_ORDER
```

```
   MINUS
select Title
  from BOOKSHELF;
```

When the query is executed, the two **minus**ed queries will be executed separately. The first of the queries,

```
select Title
  from BOOK_ORDER
```

requires an index scan based on the BOOK_ORDER primary key. The second query,

```
select Title
  from BOOKSHELF
```

requires a full index scan of the BOOKSHELF primary key index.

To execute the **minus** clause, each of the sets of records returned by the full table scans is sorted via a SORT UNIQUE NOSORT operation (in which rows are sorted and duplicates are eliminated). The sorted sets of rows are then processed by the MINUS operation. The MINUS operation is not performed until each set of records returned by the queries is sorted. Neither of the sorting operations returns records until the sorting operation completes, so the MINUS operation cannot begin until both of the SORT UNIQUE NOSORT operations have completed. Like the **union** query example, the example query shown for the MINUS operation will perform poorly for online users who measure performance by the speed with which the first row is returned by the query.

The **intersect** clause compares the results of two queries and determines the rows they have in common. The following query determines the Title values that are found in both the BOOKSHELF and BOOK_ORDER tables:

```
select Title
  from BOOK_ORDER
INTERSECT
select Title
  from BOOKSHELF;
```

To process the **INTERSECT** query, the optimizer starts by evaluating each of the queries separately. The first query,

```
select Title
  from BOOK_ORDER
```

requires a full scan against the BOOK_ORDER primary key index. The second query,

```
select Title
  from BOOKSHELF
```

requires a full scan of the BOOKSHELF primary key index. The results of the two table scans are each processed separately by SORT UNIQUE NOSORT operations. That is, the rows from BOOK_ORDER are sorted, and the rows from BOOKSHELF are sorted. The results of the two sorts are compared by the INTERSECTION operation, and the Title values returned from both sorts are returned by the **intersect** clause.

The execution path of a query that uses an **intersect** clause requires SORT UNIQUE NOSORT operations to be used. Since SORT UNIQUE NOSORT operations do not return records to the user until the entire set of rows has been sorted, queries using the **intersect** clause will have to wait for both sorts to complete before the INTERSECTION operation can be performed. Because of the reliance on sort operations, queries using the **intersect** clause will not return any records to the user until the sorts complete.

The **union**, **minus**, and **intersect** clauses all involve processing sets of rows prior to returning any rows to the user. Online users of an application may perceive that queries using these functions perform poorly, even if the table accesses involved are tuned; the reliance on sorting operations will affect the speed with which the first row is returned to the user.

Selecting from Views

When you create a view, Oracle stores the query that the view is based on. For example, the following view is based on the BOOKSHELF table:

```
create or replace view ADULTFIC as
select Title, Publisher
  from BOOKSHELF
 where CategoryName = 'ADULTFIC';
```

When you select from the ADULTFIC view, the optimizer will take the criteria from your query and combine them with the query text of the view. If you specify limiting conditions in your query of the view, those limiting conditions will—if possible—be applied to the view's query text. For example, if you execute the query

```
select Title, Publisher
  from ADULTFIC
 where Title like 'T%';
```

the optimizer will combine your limiting condition

```
where Title like 'T%';
```

with the view's query text, and it will execute the query

```
select Title, Publisher
  from BOOKSHELF
 where CategoryName = 'ADULTFIC'
   and Title like 'T%';
```

In this example, the view will have no impact on the performance of the query. When the view's text is merged with your query's limiting conditions, the options available to the optimizer increase; it can choose among more indexes and more data access paths.

The way that a view is processed depends on the query on which the view is based. If the view's query text cannot be merged with the query that uses the view, the view will be resolved first before the rest of the conditions are applied. Consider the following view:

```
create or replace view PUBLISHER_COUNT as
select Publisher, COUNT(*) Count_Pub
```

```
     from BOOKSHELF
group by Publisher;
```

The PUBLISHER_COUNT view will display one row for each distinct Publisher value in the BOOKSHELF table along with the number of records that have that value. The Count_Pub column of the PUBLISHER_COUNT view records the count per distinct Publisher value.

How will the optimizer process the following query of the PUBLISHER_COUNT view?

```
select *
  from PUBLISHER_COUNT
 where Count_Pub > 1;
```

The query refers to the view's Count_Pub column. However, the query's **where** clause cannot be combined with the view's query text, since Count_Pub is created via a grouping operation. The **where** clause cannot be applied until *after* the result set from the PUBLISHER_COUNT view has been completely resolved.

Views that contain grouping operations are resolved before the rest of the query's criteria are applied. Like the sorting operations, views with grouping operations do not return any records until the entire result set has been processed. If the view does not contain grouping operations, the query text may be merged with the limiting conditions of the query that selects from the view. As a result, views with grouping operations limit the number of choices available to the optimizer and do not return records until all of the rows are processed—and such views may perform poorly when queried by online users.

When the query is processed, the optimizer will first resolve the view. Since the view's query is

```
select Publisher, COUNT(*) Count_Pub
  from BOOKSHELF
 group by Publisher;
```

the optimizer will read the data from the BOOKSHELF table via a TABLE ACCESS FULL operation. Since a **group by** clause is used, the rows from the TABLE ACCESS FULL operation will be processed by a SORT GROUP BY operation. An additional operation—FILTER—will then process the data. The FILTER operation is used to eliminate rows based on the criteria in the query:

```
where Count_Pub > 1
```

If you use a view that has a **group by** clause, rows will not be returned from the view until all of the rows have been processed by the view. As a result, it may take a long time for the first row to be returned by the query, and the perceived performance of the view by online users may be unacceptable. If you can remove the sorting and grouping operations from your views, you increase the likelihood that the view text can be merged with the text of the query that calls the view—and as a result, the performance may improve (although the query may use other set operations that negatively impact the performance).

When the query text is merged with the view text, the options available to the optimizer increase. For example, the combination of the query's limiting conditions with the view's limiting conditions may allow a previously unusable index to be used during the execution of the query.

The automatic merging of the query text and view text can be disabled via the NO_MERGE hint. The PUSH_PRED hint forces a join predicate into a view; PUSH_SUBQ causes nonmerged subqueries to be evaluated as early as possible in the execution path.

Selecting from Subqueries

Whenever possible, the optimizer will combine the text from a subquery with the rest of the query. For example, consider the following query:

```
select Title
   from BOOKSHELF
 where Title in
(select Title from BOOK_ORDER);
```

The optimizer, in evaluating the preceding query, will determine that the query is functionally equivalent to the following join of the BOOKSHELF and BOOK_ORDER tables:

```
select BOOKSHELF.Title
   from BOOKSHELF, BOOK_ORDER
 where BOOKSHELF.Title = BOOK_ORDER.Title;
```

With the query now written as a join, the optimizer has a number of operations available to process the data (as described in the following section, "Operations That Perform Joins").

If the subquery cannot be resolved as a join, it will be resolved before the rest of the query text is processed against the data—similar in function to the manner in which the FILTER operation is used for views. As a matter of fact, the FILTER operation is used for subqueries if the subqueries cannot be merged with the rest of the query!

Subqueries that rely on grouping operations have the same tuning issues as views that contain grouping operations. The rows from such subqueries must be fully processed before the rest of the query's limiting conditions can be applied.

Operations That Perform Joins

Often, a single query will need to select columns from multiple tables. To select the data from multiple tables, the tables are joined in the SQL statement—the tables are listed in the **from** clause, and the join conditions are listed in the **where** clause. In the following example, the BOOKSHELF and BOOK_ORDER tables are joined, based on their common Title column values:

```
select BOOKSHELF.Title
   from BOOKSHELF, BOOK_ORDER
 where BOOKSHELF.Title = BOOK_ORDER.Title;
```

which can be rewritten as:

```
select Title
   from BOOKSHELF inner join BOOK_ORDER
 using (Title);
```

or:

```
select Title
   from BOOKSHELF natural inner join BOOK_ORDER;
```

The join conditions can function as limiting conditions for the join. Since the BOOKSHELF.Title column is equated to a value in the **where** clause in the first listing, the optimizer may be able to use

an index on the BOOKSHELF.Title column during the execution of the query. If an index is available on the BOOK_ORDER.Title column, that index would be considered for use by the optimizer as well.

Oracle has three main methods for processing joins: MERGE JOIN operations, NESTED LOOPS operations, and HASH JOIN operations. Based on the conditions in your query, the available indexes, and the available statistics, the optimizer will choose which join operation to use. Depending on the nature of your application and queries, you may want to force the optimizer to use a method different from its first choice of join methods. In the following sections, you will see the characteristics of the different join methods and the conditions under which each is most useful.

How Oracle Handles Joins of More than Two Tables

If a query joins more than two tables, the optimizer treats the query as a set of multiple joins. For example, if your query joined three tables, then the optimizer would execute the joins by joining two of the tables together, and then joining the result set of that join to the third table. The size of the result set from the initial join impacts the performance of the rest of the joins. If the size of the result set from the initial join is large, then many rows will be processed by the second join.

If your query joins three tables of varying size—such as a small table named SMALL, a medium-sized table named MEDIUM, and a large table named LARGE—you need to be aware of the order in which the tables will be joined. If the join of MEDIUM to LARGE will return many rows, then the join of the result set of that join with the SMALL table may perform a great deal of work. Alternatively, if SMALL and MEDIUM were joined first, then the join between the result set of the SMALL-MEDIUM join and the LARGE table may minimize the amount of work performed by the query.

MERGE JOIN

In a MERGE JOIN operation, the two inputs to the join are processed separately, sorted, and joined. MERGE JOIN operations are commonly used when there are no indexes available for the limiting conditions of the query.

In the following query, the BOOKSHELF and BOOKSHELF_AUTHOR tables are joined. If neither table has an index on its Title column, then there are no indexes that can be used during the query (since there are no other limiting conditions in the query). The example uses a hint to force a merge join to be used:

```
select /*+ USE_MERGE (bookshelf, bookshelf_author)*/
       BOOKSHELF_AUTHOR.AuthorName
  from BOOKSHELF, BOOKSHELF_AUTHOR
 where BOOKSHELF.Title = BOOKSHELF_AUTHOR.Title
   and BOOKSHELF.Publisher > 'T%';
```

or

```
select /*+ USE_MERGE (bookshelf, bookshelf_author)*/
       BOOKSHELF_AUTHOR.AuthorName
  from BOOKSHELF inner join BOOKSHELF_AUTHOR
    on BOOKSHELF.Title = BOOKSHELF_AUTHOR.Title
 where BOOKSHELF.Publisher > 'T%';
```

To resolve the query, the optimizer may choose to perform a MERGE JOIN of the tables. To perform the MERGE JOIN, each of the tables is read individually (usually by a TABLE ACCESS FULL operation or a full index scan). The set of rows returned from the table scan of the BOOKSHELF_

AUTHOR table is sorted by a SORT JOIN operation. The set of rows returned from the INDEX FULL SCAN and TABLE ACCESS BY INDEX ROWID of the BOOKSHELF table is already sorted (in the index), so no additional SORT JOIN operation is needed for that part of the execution path. The data from the SORT JOIN operations is then merged via a MERGE JOIN operation.

When a MERGE JOIN operation is used to join two sets of records, each set of records is processed separately before being joined. The MERGE JOIN operation cannot begin until it has received data from both of the SORT JOIN operations that provide input to it. The SORT JOIN operations, in turn, will not provide data to the MERGE JOIN operation until all of the rows have been sorted. If indexes are used as data sources, the SORT JOIN operations may be bypassed.

If the MERGE JOIN operation has to wait for two separate SORT JOIN operations to complete, a join that uses the MERGE JOIN operation will typically perform poorly for online users. The perceived poor performance is due to the delay in returning the first row of the join to the users. As the tables increase in size, the time required for the sorts to be completed increases dramatically. If the tables are of greatly unequal size, then the sorting operation performed on the larger table will negatively impact the performance of the overall query.

Since MERGE JOIN operations involve full scanning and sorting of the tables involved, you should only use MERGE JOIN operations if both tables are very small or if both tables are very large. If both tables are very small, then the process of scanning and sorting the tables will complete quickly. If both tables are very large, then the sorting and scanning operations required by MERGE JOIN operations can take advantage of Oracle's parallel options.

Oracle can parallelize operations, allowing multiple processors to participate in the execution of a single command. Among the operations that can be parallelized are the TABLE ACCESS FULL and sorting operations. Since a MERGE JOIN uses the TABLE ACCESS FULL and sorting operations, it can take full advantage of Oracle's parallel options. Parallelizing queries involving MERGE JOIN operations frequently improves the performance of the queries (provided there are adequate system resources available to support the parallel operations).

NESTED LOOPS

NESTED LOOPS operations join two tables via a looping method: The records from one table are retrieved, and for each record retrieved, an access is performed of the second table. The access of the second table is performed via an index-based access.

A form of the query from the preceding MERGE JOIN section is shown in the following listing. A hint is used to recommend an index-based access of the BOOKSHELF table:

```
select /*+ INDEX(bookshelf) */
       BOOKSHELF_AUTHOR.AuthorName
  from BOOKSHELF, BOOKSHELF_AUTHOR
 where BOOKSHELF.Title = BOOKSHELF_AUTHOR.Title;
```

Since the Title column of the BOOKSHELF table is used as part of the join condition in the query, the primary key index can resolve the join. When the query is executed, a NESTED LOOPS operation can be used to execute the join.

To execute a NESTED LOOPS join, the optimizer must first select a *driving table* for the join, which is the table that will be read first (usually via a TABLE ACCESS FULL operation, although index scans are commonly seen). For each record in the driving table, the second table in the join will be queried. The example query joins BOOKSHELF and BOOKSHELF_AUTHOR, based on values of the Title column. During the NESTED LOOPS execution, an operation will select all of the records from the BOOKSHELF_AUTHOR table. The primary key index of the BOOKSHELF

table will be probed to determine whether it contains an entry for the value in the current record from the BOOKSHELF_AUTHOR table. If a match is found, then the Title value will be returned from the BOOKSHELF primary key index. If other columns were needed from BOOKSHELF, the row would be selected from the BOOKSHELF table via a TABLE ACCESS BY INDEX ROWID operation.

At least two data access operations are involved in the NESTED LOOPS join: an access of the driving table and an access, usually index-based, of the driven table. The data access methods most commonly used—TABLE ACCESS FULL, TABLE ACCESS BY INDEX ROWID, and index scans—return records to successive operations as soon as a record is found; they do not wait for the whole set of records to be selected. Because these operations can provide the first matching rows quickly to users, NESTED LOOPS joins are commonly used for joins that are frequently executed by online users.

When implementing NESTED LOOPS joins, you need to consider the size of the driving table. If the driving table is large and is read via a full table scan, then the TABLE ACCESS FULL operation performed on it may negatively affect the performance of the query. If indexes are available on both sides of the join, Oracle will select a driving table for the query. The optimizer will check the statistics for the size of the tables and the selectivity of the indexes and will choose the path with the lowest overall cost.

When joining three tables together, Oracle performs two separate joins: a join of two tables to generate a set of records, and then a join between that set of records and the third table. If NESTED LOOPS joins are used, then the order in which the tables are joined is critical. The output from the first join generates a set of records, and that set of records is used as the driving table for the second join.

The size of the set of records returned by the first join impacts the performance of the second join—and thus may have a significant impact on the performance of the overall query. You should attempt to join the most selective tables first so that the impact of those joins on future joins will be negligible. If large tables are joined in the first join of a multijoin query, then the size of the tables will impact each successive join and will negatively impact the overall performance of the query. The optimizer should select the proper join path; you can confirm the costs and join path by generating the explain plan.

NESTED LOOPS joins are useful when the tables in the join are of unequal size—you can use the smaller table as the driving table and select from the larger table via an index-based access. The more selective the index is, the faster the query will complete.

HASH JOIN

The optimizer may dynamically choose to perform joins using the HASH JOIN operation in place of either MERGE JOIN or NESTED LOOPS. The HASH JOIN operation compares two tables in memory. During a hash join, the first table is scanned and the database applies "hashing" functions to the data to prepare the table for the join. The values from the second table are then read (typically via a TABLE ACCESS FULL operation), and the hashing function compares the second table with the first table. The rows that result in matches are returned to the user.

The optimizer may choose to perform hash joins even if indexes are available. In the sample query shown in the following listing, the BOOKSHELF and BOOKSHELF_AUTHOR tables are joined on the Title column:

```
select /*+ USE_HASH (bookshelf) */
       BOOKSHELF_AUTHOR.AuthorName
  from BOOKSHELF, BOOKSHELF_AUTHOR
 where BOOKSHELF.Title = BOOKSHELF_AUTHOR.Title;
```

The BOOKSHELF table has a unique index on its Title column. Since the index is available and can be used to evaluate the join conditions, the optimizer may choose to perform a NESTED LOOPS join of the two tables as shown in the previous section. If a hash join is performed, then each table will be read via a separate operation. The data from the table and index scans will serve as input to a HASH JOIN operation. The hash join does not rely on operations that process sets of rows. The operations involved in hash joins return records quickly to users. Hash joins are appropriate for queries executed by online users if the tables are small and can be scanned quickly.

Processing Outer Joins

When processing an outer join, the optimizer will use one of the three methods described in the previous sections. For example, if the sample query were performing an outer join between BOOK_ORDER and CATEGORY (to see which categories had no books on order), a NESTED LOOPS OUTER operation may be used instead of a NESTED LOOPS operation. In a NESTED LOOPS OUTER operation, the table that is the "outer" table for the outer join is typically used as the driving table for the query; as the records of the inner table are scanned for matching records, **NULL** values are returned for rows with no matches.

Related Hints

You can use hints to override the optimizer's selection of a join method. Hints allow you to specify the type of join method to use or the goal of the join method.

In addition to the hints described in this section, you can use the FULL and INDEX hints, described earlier, to influence the way in which joins are processed. For example, if you use a hint to force a NESTED LOOPS join to be used, then you may also use an INDEX hint to specify which index should be used during the NESTED LOOPS join and which table should be accessed via a full table scan.

Hints About Goals

You can specify a hint that directs the optimizer to execute a query with a specific goal in mind. The available goals related to joins are the following:

- **ALL_ROWS** Execute the query so that all of the rows are returned as quickly as possible.

- **FIRST_ROWS** Execute the query so that the first row will be returned as quickly as possible.

By default, the optimizer will execute a query using an execution path that is selected to minimize the total time needed to resolve the query. Thus, the default is to use ALL_ROWS as the goal. If the optimizer is only concerned about the total time needed to return all rows for the query, then set-based operations such as sorts and MERGE JOIN can be used. However, the ALL_ROWS goal may not always be appropriate. For example, online users tend to judge the performance of a system based on the time it takes for a query to return the first row of data. The users thus have FIRST_ROWS as their primary goal, with the time it takes to return all of the rows as a secondary goal.

The available hints mimic the goals: the ALL_ROWS hint allows the optimizer to choose from all available operations to minimize the overall processing time for the query, and the FIRST_ROWS hint tells the optimizer to select an execution path that minimizes the time required to return the first row to the user.

If you use the FIRST_ROWS hint, the optimizer will be less likely to use MERGE JOIN and more likely to use NESTED LOOPS.

Hints About Methods

In addition to specifying the goals the optimizer should use when evaluating join method alternatives, you can list the specific operations to use and the tables to use them on. If a query involves only two tables, you do not need to specify the tables to join when providing a hint for a join method to use.

The USE_NL hint tells the optimizer to use a NESTED LOOPS operation to join tables. In the following example, the USE_NL hint is specified for the join query example. Within the hint, the BOOKSHELF table is listed as the inner table for the join.

```
select /*+ USE_NL(bookshelf) */
       BOOKSHELF_AUTHOR.AuthorName
  from BOOKSHELF, BOOKSHELF_AUTHOR
 where BOOKSHELF.Title = BOOKSHELF_AUTHOR.Title;
```

If you want all of the joins in a many-table query to use NESTED LOOPS operations, you could just specify the USE_NL hint with no table references. In general, you should specify table names whenever you use a hint to specify a join method, because you do not know how the query may be used in the future. You may not even know how the database objects are currently set up—for example, one of the objects in your **from** clause may be a view that has been tuned to use MERGE JOIN operations.

If you specify a table in a hint, you should refer to the table alias or the unqualified table name. That is, if your **from** clause refers to a table as

```
from FRED.HIS_TABLE, ME.MY_TABLE
```

then you should *not* specify a hint such as

```
/*+ USE_NL(ME.MY_TABLE) */
```

Instead, you should refer to the table by its name, without the owner:

```
/*+ USE_NL(my_table) */
```

If multiple tables have the same name, then you should assign table aliases to the tables and refer to the aliases in the hint. For example, if you join a table to itself, then the **from** clause may include the text shown in the following listing:

```
from BOOKSHELF B1, BOOKSHELF B2
```

A hint forcing the BOOKSHELF-BOOKSHELF join to use NESTED LOOPS would be written to use the table aliases, as shown in the following listing:

```
/*+ USE_NL(b2) */
```

The optimizer will ignore any hint that isn't written with the proper syntax. Any hint with improper syntax will be treated as a comment (since it is enclosed within the /* and */ characters).

If you are using NESTED LOOPS joins, then you need to be concerned about the order in which the tables are joined. The ORDERED hint, when used with NESTED LOOPS joins, influences the order in which tables are joined.

When you use the ORDERED hint, the tables will be joined in the order in which they are listed in the **from** clause of the query. If the **from** clause contains three tables, such as

```
from BOOK_ORDER, BOOKSHELF, BOOKSHELF_AUTHOR
```

then the first two tables will be joined by the first join, and the result of that join will be joined to the third table.

Since the order of joins is critical to the performance of NESTED LOOPS joins, the ORDERED hint is often used in conjunction with the USE_NL hint. If you use hints to specify the join order, you need to be certain that the relative distribution of values within the joined tables will not change dramatically over time; otherwise, the specified join order may cause performance problems in the future.

You can use the USE_MERGE hint to tell the optimizer to perform a MERGE JOIN between specified tables. In the following listing, the hint instructs the optimizer to perform a MERGE JOIN operation between BOOKSHELF and BOOKSHELF_AUTHOR:

```
select /*+ USE_MERGE (bookshelf, bookshelf_author)*/
       BOOKSHELF_AUTHOR.AuthorName
  from BOOKSHELF, BOOKSHELF_AUTHOR
 where BOOKSHELF.Title = BOOKSHELF_AUTHOR.Title
   and BOOKSHELF.Publisher > 'T%';
```

You can use the USE_HASH hint to tell the optimizer to consider using a HASH JOIN method. If no tables are specified, then the optimizer will select the first table to be scanned into memory based on the available statistics.

```
select /*+ USE_HASH (bookshelf) */
       BOOKSHELF_AUTHOR.AuthorName
  from BOOKSHELF, BOOKSHELF_AUTHOR
 where BOOKSHELF.Title = BOOKSHELF_AUTHOR.Title;
```

Additional Tuning Issues

As noted in the discussions of NESTED LOOPS and MERGE JOIN operations, operations differ in the time they take to return the first row from a query. Since MERGE JOIN relies on set-based operations, it will not return records to the user until all of the rows have been processed. NESTED LOOPS, on the other hand, can return rows to the user as soon as rows are available.

Because NESTED LOOPS joins are capable of returning rows to users quickly, they are often used for queries that are frequently executed by online users. Their efficiency at returning the first

row, however, is often impacted by set-based operations applied to the rows that have been selected. For example, adding an **order by** clause to a query adds a SORT ORDER BY operation to the end of the query processing—and no rows will be displayed to the user until all of the rows have been sorted.

As described in "Operations That Use Indexes," earlier in this chapter, using functions on a column prevents the database from using an index on that column during data searches unless you have created a function-based index.

Some techniques that were used in previous versions of Oracle to disable indexes no longer are available. For example, some developers would append a null string to each column involved in a join in an effort to suppress index usage:

```
select BOOKSHELF_AUTHOR.AuthorName
  from BOOKSHELF, BOOKSHELF_AUTHOR
 where BOOKSHELF.Title||'' = BOOKSHELF_AUTHOR.Title||'';
```

In Oracle Database 10g, the optimizer does not allow the null strings to block the index usage— the query uses the index on the BOOKSHELF.Title column as part of a HASH JOIN execution.

As noted during the discussion of the NESTED LOOPS operation, the order of joins is as important as the join method selected. If a large or nonselective join is the first join in a series, the large data set returned will negatively impact the performance of the subsequent joins in the query as well as the performance of the query as a whole.

Depending on the hints, optimizer goal, and statistics, the optimizer may choose to use a variety of join methods within the same query. For example, the optimizer may evaluate a three-table query as a NESTED LOOPS join of two tables, followed by a MERGE JOIN of the NESTED LOOPS output with the third table. Such combinations of join types are usually found when the ALL_ROWS optimizer goal is in effect.

To see the order of operations, you can use the **set autotrace on** command to see the execution path, as described earlier in this chapter.

Parallelism and Cache Issues

In addition to the operations and hints listed in the previous sections, you can use two other sets of hints to influence the query processing. The additional hints allow you to control the parallelism of queries and the caching of data within the data buffer cache.

If your server has multiple processors, and the data being queried is distributed across multiple devices, then you may be able to improve the processing of your queries by parallelizing the data access and sorting operations. When a query is parallelized, multiple processes are run in parallel, each of which accesses or sorts data. A query coordinator process distributes the workload and assembles the query results for the user.

The *degree of parallelism*—the number of scanning or sorting processes started for a query— can be set at the table level (see the **create table** command in the Alphabetical Reference). The optimizer will detect the table-level settings for the degree of parallelism and will determine the number of query server processes to be used during the query. The optimizer will dynamically check the number of processors and devices involved in the query and will base its parallelism decisions on the available resources.

You can influence the parallelism of your queries via the PARALLEL hint. In the following example, a degree of parallelism of 4 is set for a query of the BOOKSHELF table:

```
select /*+ PARALLEL (bookshelf,4) */ *
   from BOOKSHELF;
```

If you are using the Real Application Clusters option, you can specify an "instances" parameter in the PARALLEL hint. In the following query, the full table scan process will be parallelized, with a proposed degree of parallelism of 4 across two instances:

```
select /*+ PARALLEL(bookshelf,4,2) */ *
   from BOOKSHELF
 order by Publisher;
```

In the preceding query, a second operation—the SORT ORDER BY operation for the **order by Publisher** clause—was added. Because the sorting operation can also be parallelized, the query may use nine query server processes instead of five (four for the table scan, four for the sort, and one for the query coordinator). The optimizer will dynamically determine the degree of parallelism to use based on the table's settings, the database layout, and the available system resources.

If you want to disable parallelism for a query, you can use the NO_PARALLEL hint (called NOPARALLEL in versions prior to Oracle Database 10g). The NO_PARALLEL hint may be used if you want to serially execute a query against a table whose queries are typically executed in a parallelized fashion.

If a small, frequently accessed table is read via a full table scan, that table's data can be kept in the SGA for as long as possible. You can mark the table as belonging to the "Keep" pool, using the **buffer_pool** clause of the **create table** or **alter table** command. If the table has been designated for storage in the Keep pool, its blocks in memory are kept apart from the main cache. If the Keep pool is sized adequately, the blocks will remain in memory until the database is shut down.

If a table is commonly used by many queries or users, and there is no appropriate indexing scheme available for the query, then you should use the Keep pool to improve the performance of accesses to that table. This approach is most useful for static tables.

Implementing Stored Outlines

As you migrate from one database to another, the execution paths for your queries may change. Your execution paths may change for several reasons:

- You may be using a different optimizer in different databases (cost-based in one, rule-based in another).

- You may have enabled different optimizer features in the different databases.

- The statistics for the queried tables may differ in the databases.

- The frequency with which statistics are gathered may differ among the databases.

- The databases may be running different versions of the Oracle kernel.

The effects of these differences on your execution paths can be dramatic and can have a significant negative impact on your query performance as you migrate or upgrade your application. To minimize the impact of these differences on your query performance, Oracle introduced a feature called a *stored outline* in Oracle8i.

A stored outline stores a set of hints for a query. Those hints will be used every time the query is executed. Using the stored hints will increase the likelihood that the query will use the same execution path each time. Hints do not mandate an execution path (they're hints, not commands) but do decrease the impact of database moves on your query performance.

To start creating hints for all queries, set the CREATE_STORED_OUTLINES initialization parameter to TRUE; thereafter, all the outlines will be saved under the DEFAULT category. As an alternative, you can create custom categories of outlines and use the category name as a value in the initialization parameter file, as shown in the following listing:

```
CREATE_STORED_OUTLINES = development
```

In this example, stored outlines will be stored for queries within the DEVELOPMENT category.

You must have the CREATE ANY OUTLINE system privilege in order to create an outline. Use the **create outline** command to create an outline for a query, as shown in the following listing:

```
create outline REORDERS
    for category DEVELOPMENT
     on
select BOOKSHELF.Title
  from BOOKSHELF, BOOK_ORDER
 where BOOKSHELF.Title = BOOK_ORDER.Title;
```

NOTE
If you do not specify a name for your outline, the outline will be given a system-generated name.

If you have set CREATE_STORED_OUTLINES to TRUE in your initialization parameter file, the RDBMS will create stored outlines for your queries; using the **create outline** command gives you more control over the outlines that are created.

NOTE
*You can create outlines for DML commands and for **create table as select** commands.*

Once an outline has been created, you can alter it. For example, you may need to alter the outline to reflect significant changes in data volumes and distribution. You can use the **rebuild** clause of the **alter outline** command to regenerate the hints used during query execution:

```
alter outline REORDERS rebuild;
```

NOTE
You need the ALTER ANY OUTLINE system privilege to use this command.

You can also rename an outline via the **rename** clause of the **alter outline** command:

```
alter outline REORDERS rename to BOOK_REORDERS;
```

You can change the category of an outline via the **change category** clause of the **alter outline** command.

You can enable the usage of stored outlines by setting the USE_STORED_OUTLINES parameter to TRUE within your session (via **alter session**) or within your database (via **alter system**).

To manage stored outlines, use the OUTLN_PKG package, which gives you three capabilities:

■ Drop outlines that have never been used

■ Drop outlines within a specific category

■ Move outlines from one category to another

Each of these three capabilities has a corresponding procedure within OUTLN_PKG. To drop outlines that have never been used, execute the DROP_UNUSED procedure, as shown in the following listing:

```
execute OUTLN_PKG.DROP_UNUSED;
```

To drop all of the outlines within a category, execute the DROP_BY_CAT procedure, which has the name of the category as its only input parameter. The following example drops all of the outlines within the DEVELOPMENT category:

```
execute OUTLN_PKG.DROP_BY_CAT -
  (cat => 'DEVELOPMENT');
```

To reassign outlines from an old category to a new category, use the UPDATE_BY_CAT procedure, as shown in the following example.

```
execute OUTLN_PKG.UPDATE_BY_CAT -
  (old_cat => 'DEVELOPMENT', -
  new_cat => 'TEST');
```

To drop a specific outline, use the **drop outline** command.

Review

The preceding sections have shown the methods used by the optimizer to access and manipulate data. When tuning queries, you need to keep in mind several factors:

■ **The goal of the user** Do you want rows to be quickly returned, or do you care more about the total throughput time for the query?

■ **The application design** How does this query fit within the overall design of the application? How is it executed? Are there external factors that affect its performance?

- **The type of joins used** Are the tables properly indexed?

- **The size of the tables** How large are the tables that are being queried? If there are multiple joins, how large is the set of data returned from each join?

- **The selectivity of the data** How selective are the indexes in use?

- **The sorting operations** How many sorting operations are performed? Are nested sorting operations being performed?

If you can carefully manage the issues related to performance, then the number of "problem" queries within your database should diminish. If a query appears to be taking more resources than it should, then you should use the **set autotrace on** or **explain plan** command to determine the order of operations used for the query. You can use the tips and discussions provided throughout this chapter to then tune the operations or the set of operations.

CHAPTER
44

Case Studies
in Tuning

s described in Chapter 43, performance tuning begins with design. In many cases, the core performance problem in a database application has been designed into the system. You may be able to identify the most resource-intensive parts of the application, focusing future tuning efforts on specific database parameters or SQL statements. In this chapter, you will see case studies related to different performance problems and their resolutions. The case studies present three common problem areas—environmental issues, problem queries, and application architecture—from an application tuner's perspective.

Case Study 1: Waits, Waits, and More Waits

A large online transaction-processing system experienced significant performance problems as the number of concurrent users increased. At times of intense batch activity, such as month-end closing processes, the system performance was unacceptable for the online users. Is the problem with the environment, the application, or the implementation of the application in the environment? To identify the core problems and develop a path toward improved performance, the database statistics were reviewed. The system was complex, but the core problems from Oracle's perspective were similar to those described in Chapter 43—the database was being asked to execute a large number of slow commands.

The first step in tuning the database involved looking at the dynamic performance statistics during times when the application was performing acceptably and then again when the performance was unacceptable. The Statspack utility was used to gather the statistics. For these intervals, the following statistics were examined in detail:

- Number of executions per second

- Number of logical reads per second

- Number of waits per physical reads

- Number of waits during data writes

- Number of waits for undo segment headers and blocks

- Number of physical reads per second

- Number of sorts performed on disk and in memory

Capturing these statistics is important, both to identify problem areas and to measure the impact on performance as the database environment and application SQL are changed during the tuning process. Each of these statistics—or components of it—is reported via Statspack. You can select the statistics for the database because it was last started from the dynamic performance views, such as V$SYSSTAT and V$WAITSTAT, but those statistics will be skewed by other activity in the database unassociated with your application. The following table shows the initial statistics gathered over a three-hour test. The results are shown here in the format provided at the start of a Statspack report:

Statistic	Value
Test duration	10,800 seconds (3 hours)
Executions per second	1,700
Logical reads per second	67,000
Physical reads per second	6,300
DB writer waits	600,000
Undo header waits	300
Sorts in memory	800,000
Sorts on disk	200
Physical read waits that occurred: Db file sequential read (1 block reads) Db file scattered read (multiblock reads)	 32,700,000 4,500,000
Transactions per second	10
Physical writes per second	100

Given this information, what is the first area to focus on? The system was very active—1,700 executions per second and 67,000 logical reads per second were evidence of a large number of database requests executed constantly over a three-hour period. To properly analyze the statistics, you should start by transforming them into a consistent set of units. In this example, let's consider all the activity on a per-second basis. Divide the statistics that were previously presented at the interval level by 10,800 to see their per-second values:

Statistic	Value (per Second)
Executions	1,700
Logical reads	67,000
Physical reads	6,300
DB writer waits	55
Undo header waits	0.03
Sorts in memory	74
Sorts on disk	0.02
Physical read waits that occurred: Db file sequential read (1 block reads) Db file scattered read (multiblock reads)	 3,028 416
Transactions	10
Physical writes	100

With all the statistics presented in the same units, you can quickly develop an overview of what an average second looks like in the database. The total number of physical read waits occurring during a typical second was 3,028 + 416 = 3,444. Those waits were incurred when the database attempts to resolve a request for a physical read—and in a typical second, there are 6,300 such requests. Therefore, a physical read event had to wait, on average, almost 55 percent of the time (3,444 / 6,300). Only about 45 percent of the read requests were completed without a wait occurring.

At the same time, writes were also waiting. There were 55 data block waits per second as the database attempted to perform 100 physical writes—again, a 55 percent wait ratio. A review of the datafile I/O statistics (available via Statspack and via queries against V$FILESTAT) showed that the database I/O was distributed evenly across the most active tablespaces. If the I/O were not evenly distributed, it is likely that a single disk or set of disks encountering problems would be the main source of the I/O waits.

How could you reduce the number of physical waits? If you only considered the queries that are performing full table scans as possible causes of performance problems, you would very likely have little impact on this application. Full table scans led to the scattered read waits shown in the prior table—and they account for only 12 percent (416 / 3,444) of the physical read waits that occurred. If you completely removed all the waits generated by full table scans, you probably would not have a significant impact on the performance of the application.

Given this scenario, the following hypotheses can be developed:

- The application requirements exceeded the I/O capacity of the system as it is configured.

- The application generated a large number of SQL command executions.

- Most of the SQL commands executed do not generate physical reads. The data block buffer cache hit ratio is over 90 percent (1 – 6,300 / 67,000, in this case).

- The application may be consuming large amounts of CPU resources as well, because it is executing many commands and very actively managing the I/O queue.

Given those hypotheses, where should the tuning effort start? The application profile was of a read-intensive application (there are 6,300 physical reads per second to go with only 100 physical writes). The queries themselves appeared to be fairly well tuned (as judged by the overall hit ratio; there were likely to be individual queries that were not properly tuned). Both reads and waits were reporting the same problem—they could not access the disks fast enough to avoid waits. As a result, the focus should first be on stabilizing the I/O environment. Is it performing well? If there is no problem found with the I/O system and the application SQL cannot be changed, the environment might have to be upgraded or enhanced to support the loads generated by the application.

In most modern enterprise-scale configurations, a buffer area is available for the disk environment. As a result, most physical read requests do not reach the disk; the buffer services the read requests. In this study, around 10 percent of logical reads generated physical read requests. The I/O environment was intended to handle 90 percent of those physical read requests via its buffer. Because the buffer in this environment was not properly configured to support this volume activity, most physical read requests were reaching the disk. Improving the use of the buffer improved all I/O in the environment and eliminated many of the disk accesses.

As a side effect of the I/O improvement, the CPU requirements of the application may be reduced. The CPU requirements may be lowered because the system does not have to spend so much time managing I/O queues—and those resources are now available to user processes instead.

It is possible that some other process on the system may now be free to take more of the available resources, illustrating the need to continue monitoring the system even after the tuning effort has been completed.

To further reduce the system load, operations that could be performed in batch mode were removed from the online processing portion of the application. For comparison, the following table shows the statistics following the tuning of the I/O environment and the modification of the application:

Statistic	Value (per Second)
Logical reads	67,000
Physical reads	3,830 (was 6,300)
DB writer waits	25 (was 55)
Physical read waits that occurred:	
Db file sequential read (1-block reads)	466 (was 3,028)
Db file scattered read (multiblock reads)	173 (was 416)
Transactions	10
Physical writes	115

In the revised environment, the number of physical reads was reduced by 40 percent, but the number of waits was reduced by over 80 percent. The database was able to support the same number of logical reads, transactions, and physical writes (with fewer waits during writes)—and the end-user performance is now acceptable.

This is not the end of the story—there are still waits occurring, the database will grow over time, users will develop new queries, and application modules will be added over time. During those changes, you should track the critical statistics over time so you can isolate the impact of changes on the environment, identify problem areas, and forecast future performance.

Case Study 2: Application-Killing Queries

Almost every database will eventually support a query that consumes many more resources than it should. The query may be performing multiple full table scans (in the event that indexes are missing). The query may be generating Cartesian products (when multiple tables are listed in the **from** clause but their join syntax is not specified). The query may be performing multiple nested sorts of millions of rows.

In general, when tuning SQL you should strive to work with as few rows as possible. If you only need ten rows out of a ten-million-row table, try to use an index that returns as few rows as possible for your **where** clause criteria, and then filter through those rows for the ten rows you want.

Although this approach may seem straightforward, it is repeatedly violated. When developing an application, you should consider how each of the SQL statements you write will be executed—its frequency, its performance requirements for each execution, its dependencies on other commands, the indexes it will use, and so on. The goal is to support the business process as efficiently as possible. If you fail to consider how the code will be used, the application may suffer and the speed of the application may drive the speed of the business process—an unacceptable condition.

In a large online processing application, queries of the following format were the most frequently executed commands (based on the statistics in the Executions column of V$SQL). Because the query performs a full table scan, the cumulative number of physical reads (the Disk_Reads column) approaches the cumulative number of logical reads (the Buffer_Gets column) in its V$SQL entry:

```
select T35.C1
from T35
where (lower(T35.C4) like '%tom clark%');
```

There are at least three things wrong with this query if it is to be used in a production application. If you were to run this query one time, the performance might be acceptable—you'll be performing a full table scan of the T35 table because of the reasons listed in the next paragraph. But what happens when many users concurrently execute similar queries, and the T35 table contains millions of rows? What if you make this kind of query available to a world of users via a Web interface? The application performance suffers and adversely impacts the very process the application is supposed to support.

The problems with the query include the following:

■ *There's no use of bind variables.* Every execution of the query will be parsed separately unless the database administrator has set the CURSOR_SHARING initialization parameter to FORCE or SIMILAR (the preferred setting). If CURSOR_SHARING is set to EXACT, the shared SQL area will be filled with thousands of almost identical commands, separately parsed and differing only in the literal value passed in as the search string.

■ *No function-based index was defined on the C4 column, but the query is performing a* ***LOWER*** *function on the column.* If there is only a standard index available, Oracle may not be able to use the index to support this query.

■ *The search string begins with a percent wildcard.* As a result, you would expect Oracle to perform a full table scan in order to find values that meet the criteria.

NOTE
You should generate the explain plan for any queries that are targeted for tuning.

Let's consider one possible solution to the third problem—the content of the search string. In this application, the user typed in the name ("tom clark" in this case) and the application code put wildcards in front and behind the name, trying to maximize the number of potential matches that would be found. The application developer presented the user with all the potential values that could possibly match the exact search string.

From the database administration side, you can make sure CURSOR_SHARING is properly configured, and you can create a function-based index on the C4 column so index scans may be chosen instead of table scans. But the core problem remains—how can the query be rewritten to select as few rows as possible in order to generate its result set?

The answer lies in the use of Oracle Text. As described in Chapter 25, you can create text indexes on columns to support searches for strings, wildcards, text expansions, and more. In this

case, you will pass the name as the search string, and the text index will search its indexed values for matches—taking into account the wildcards. The application developer will have to change the query to use the Oracle Text syntax, and the database administrator will need to create and maintain the text index objects. However, the performance benefits are significant—the full text scans on the large table are eliminated.

NOTE
If you use indexes to index names, you need to create an empty stoplist. Otherwise, Oracle will skip common words (such as 'AN') that may be real names.

In this particular case, the use of text indexes for this query dramatically reduced the search times for the Web-based users. The number of physical and logical reads against the search table was cut significantly and remained low as the application grew. The database administrator and application maintenance team had additional text index objects to manage as a trade-off for the performance benefit gained.

Text indexes are not the solution to every problem. In most situations, a standard index containing multiple columns will be the solution. The important step is to identify the most resource-intensive queries (by querying V$SQL or using Statspack) and reviewing them from an application architecture perspective. For each query, ask what it is used for and why it is doing what it is doing. Consider a simple query such as the following:

```
select COUNT(*) from COUNTRIES;
```

Individually, each execution of this query will complete very quickly—there are only several hundred countries, and the table can be cached in the data block buffer cache. But if this query is executed several million times a day, it may perform more logical reads than any other query in the database. Those logical reads translate into CPU resources allocated for repeated queries of static data that could be spent on more useful queries of dynamic data. When looking for problem queries, be sure to check for queries that are executed many times in addition to those that are expensive for each execution.

Case Study 3: Long-Running Batch Jobs

A company was planning to move a large volume of data on a repeated basis from a transactional system to a reporting system. The transactional system was outside of their control, so there was no opportunity to use database links, materialized views, or other replication methods directly interacting with the source system. Instead, the data source was a single large file sent each day from the transactional system.

Attempting to load the large file into the reporting system repeatedly caused availability problems—the time needed to load the data through conventional inserts exceeded the available time window for the operation. Any failures during the loading process created even greater problems because the partially loaded data was deleted and reloaded. As a result, the performance of the load job affected the availability of the entire reporting application. Based on the current and anticipated data volumes, the amount of data loaded daily is expected to triple within 12 months.

Assuming the database is properly configured so there are no I/O or memory issues to resolve, several approaches are available to resolve this type of problem:

- Even though the source system provides the data in one set, you may not have to insert it all at once. Instead of loading data into the reporting system once each day, consider sending incremental loads throughout the day. If the loading process does not impact the queries (for example, by invalidating indexes during the load or causing irregularities in the reported data), these small loads may be able to work alongside user queries.

- Don't load the data; use external tables instead. This approach is ideal for situations in which a small number of well-defined queries report against the data a small number of times.

- Parallelize all operations. Use all the available resources on the server. Although this may help the current performance problems, it may affect the application's ability to scale well with increased data volumes.

- Load the data into temporary work tables; then treat them as partitions of existing tables.

Each of these options involves at least a minor design change, and you cannot select the proper solution and make the change without understanding how the end users use the data. Is the data loaded into a single table or into multiple tables? Do the end users directly access the tables the data is loaded into? How stale can the data in the tables be?

Let's first consider the worst-case scenario: The users need all the data available at once, so no incremental feed is available. The loaded data is inserted into multiple related tables. Further, the load should have minimal impact on the availability of the rest of the data in the database. Lastly, the end users query the loaded tables directly.

In such a scenario, you should consider partitioning the table being loaded. For each day's data load, create a new table whose structure is the same as the table the users will be querying. Load the data into the table, index it, analyze it, and perform whatever transforms are necessary to properly format the data for the user. When the data is ready for presentation to the user, execute the **alter table exchange partition** command, telling Oracle to treat the table you have created as a partition of the table the users will query. Because you only touch the application's tables when you add the new partition, the downtime for the application is minimal—particularly if you are able to use only local indexes on the partitioned table.

The **exchange partition** approach effectively divides the two operations being performed on the table—its loading by you and its querying by the users. Once you are able to separate those two operations, your design and maintenance capabilities increase dramatically.

Consider a slightly better scenario: The users need all the data available at once, but they do not directly query the table being loaded. The users query materialized views based on the table. You should tune the materialized views to make the materialized views fast-refreshable, allowing changes to the loaded table to be incrementally applied to the objects the users will be querying. Again, separating the bulk load operation from the queries of the same objects significantly enhances your maintenance options. See Chapter 24 for details on the configuration of materialized view refresh options.

If the users always query materialized views that aggregate the data, you should consider not loading the data at all. Instead, use external tables (see Chapter 26) to reference the data file during an **insert as select** operation into a summary table. External tables cannot be indexed and

will therefore result in a full scan of the file—but because you are not loading the raw data, the **insert as select** of the summary may complete faster than if you had loaded the data and then aggregated it. As a side benefit, you only have to store the raw data once (at the file system level) rather than twice.

Regardless of which of these options you choose, you should investigate the use of options that exploit the available system resources—including parallel query, parallel DML, parallel loading, partitioning, and bulk processing. In terms of improving the performance of the load itself, there are many features available: using **nologging** during loads, using SQL*Loader Direct Path loads, and starting parallel Data Pump jobs. Note that many of these options can be applied on a partition-by-partition level.

Tuning batch loads requires you to make an educated judgment about the degree to which set processing will be used. You can configure the application to process one row at a time. For example, you can insert one row into a master table and then insert all its children rows into other tables before inserting a second row into the master table and repeating the process. That row-based approach will suffer as the volume of rows increases. The row-based approach guarantees read consistency across the loaded tables, but if the job is executed during off hours (or the **exchange partition** method is used), that benefit may not be realized by the users.

By comparison, you can create set operations that process huge volumes of rows at once. It is likely that at some point the number of rows processed in a set will impact the performance of the load, particularly if complex sorts are involved. In such a case, you may need to break the large batch process into smaller steps and process smaller groups. For example, the operation flow may be

1. Select 100,000 rows from the input tables.

2. Perform the aggregations and transforms on those rows.

3. Store the results of those aggregations and transforms in a temporary work table.

4. Select the next 100,000 rows from the input tables.

5. Repeat until all the rows have been processed and inserted into the temporary work table.

6. Properly index and analyze the temporary work table.

7. Perform additional operations on the data in the temporary work table (such as generating grand totals or new columns or performing joins with other tables).

8. Insert rows from the temporary work table into the production table.

9. Drop or truncate the temporary work table.

Such a sequence of operations attempts to gain the benefits of both approaches—a procedural approach that operates on sets of rows. How large should each set of rows be? That depends on your operating environment, the operations performed, and the data itself. You should properly test the process to make sure the more procedural approach completes faster than the single batch operation. You should take into consideration the greater number of potential points of failure in the procedural approach, and handle exceptions accordingly.

In this example, the original daily load job took 12 hours to complete. By breaking it into smaller pieces, the total time was reduced to three hours—long enough to run the job multiple times within the load window if required.

Those design decisions require you to know your data, how it is used, and how it affects the business process. Regardless of your architecture, you need to be able to test the application while simulating a real-life workload under repeatable conditions. During the tests and during production usage, you must be able to monitor the environment and the application for performance problems as the data volumes grow.

During the tuning process, you may have to make trade-offs. For example, in the batch-process tuning effort, you may allocate more disk space to the database (for the temporary work table) in order to improve overall performance. Each part of the application should be considered as a critical part of the whole application, and developed and planned accordingly. When the application performance affects the business process performance, you should identify the problem areas—such as the environment, particular queries, or the data-flow architecture—and implement a design more in tune with the application's needs.

CHAPTER
45

The Hitchhiker's
Guide to Oracle
Application Server 10g

eveloping applications for the Web is a complex process. The number of programming languages, APIs, frameworks, and development platforms continues to grow at a lightning pace. IT departments wanting to maintain their competitive advantage are asked to evaluate and embrace new technologies faster than ever before, leading to shorter development times for projects and less time for developers to absorb new technologies. These factors—coupled with the fact that developers are increasingly called upon to have a working knowledge of and provide input on things such as database design, networking, development methodologies, code-generating tools, Java frameworks, and source code management—have led to a crisis in the development world: Developers don't have enough hours in the day to learn all the aspects of the tasks they need to be productive members of their IT departments. Luckily for Oracle developers, Oracle has provided a series of products that allow you to create and test applications quickly, interface with the Oracle database seamlessly, and deploy those applications to the Web securely and with minimal effort. Oracle's development and Application Server products have the added advantage of maturity: They are stable, proven technologies, used in a wide range of production environments throughout the world.

At the core of your development efforts is the Application Server, sometimes incorrectly referred to as a *Web server* (Web servers are a subcomponent of an Application Server). The Application Server takes requests from a client application (most likely a Web browser), processes these requests, and returns the results. The Application Server, depending on the type of request it receives, can call other programs or speak to databases to satisfy the client's request. Application Servers use TCP/IP, the protocol defining the rules for establishing connections between computers, and HTTP (Hypertext Transfer Protocol) to control the communication between a Web browser and a Web Server.

Oracle Application Server 10*g* is a product designed to meet all the challenges your organization faces when putting your applications on the Web. Although the details of installation and administration of the Application Server are beyond the scope of this chapter, all Oracle developers can benefit from an understanding of the basic framework of Web development and Oracle's solutions for each of these framework pieces. In the language used in Oracle's documentation, the implementations of these solutions are called *services,* and they are integrated into the Oracle Application Server 10*g* product stack.

NOTE
For more information regarding the installation and administration of Oracle Application Server 10g, see the Oracle Application Server 10g Administration Handbook *by John Garmany and Donald K. Burleson (Oracle Press, 2004).*

The number of tools and services provided by Oracle Application Server 10*g* can seem overwhelming. You are certainly not required to implement every service provided by Oracle Application Server 10*g*. Services that are installed and configured but not used waste resources, so choose your installation options carefully. Organizations can pick and choose those services they wish to exploit. Even if a particular service is not selected during installation, you can go back and add that functionality to Oracle Application Server 10*g* at a later date without affecting your current production setup.

A good example of this would be the Forms Server that is part of Oracle Application Server 10*g*. Forms Server allows you to take existing Oracle Forms and serve them up over the Web. Perhaps

your organization has begun by using Oracle Portal to quickly develop some forms and reports that are published over the Web to the employees. This initial project has proven to be so popular that the decision has been made to move Oracle Forms, Oracle Reports, and Oracle Discoverer Worksheets (which have richer feature sets than their equivalent components in Oracle Portal) to the Web and to integrate some of those components with Oracle Portal. An administrator can reconfigure the Application Server to add the necessary functionality without affecting any of the work performed up to this point.

Your organization can thus move to a Web-based model without losing the time and effort already invested in Oracle Forms, Oracle Reports, or Oracle Discoverer development. As your needs grow, you can augment your development efforts with PL/SQL server pages (PSPs) or a tool such as JDeveloper to implement technologies such as JavaServer pages (JSPs), Enterprise JavaBeans (EJBs), Struts, or Java applets. As the site traffic grows, you can increase performance by implementing the Web Cache service to cache the most heavily used pages. Power users can create their own ad hoc reports using Discoverer. You can expand your portal to integrate content, Web-based components (such as forms, reports, or XML-based portlets), and content from external sites with a minimal investment in development and design time. The feature set of Oracle Application Server 10*g* can tackle virtually any development challenge organizations face today.

The architecture of Oracle Application Server 10*g* allows you to scale by adding more Application Servers (called *mid-tiers* in Oracle's documentation) and more Web Cache servers. You can even allow others to incorporate your content through the use of XML and Enterprise JavaBeans. All of this is managed through a single Web interface—the Enterprise Manager Web Site Application Server Control.

One could argue that it is not necessary for developers to understand the architecture of Oracle Application Server 10*g*. However, I strongly urge you to make the effort to understand the fundamentals of how the Application Server does its basic functions. The administrative details of Oracle Application Server 10*g* will probably be handled by a systems administrator or a DBA, but there are many steps that fall upon the developer's shoulders.

What Is Oracle Application Server 10*g*?

Oracle Application Server 10*g* is an Application Server designed to support all major Web development languages and frameworks. It is a collection of services designed together to integrate seamlessly with Oracle databases and deliver content dynamically over the Web. Here's a list of some of its features:

- **Oracle HTTP Server** Oracle Application Server 10*g* includes an HTTP server based on the Apache HTTP Server, version 1.3.28. The Apache server is the most popular Web server in use today. It is highly customizable, and its architecture fully supports enhancements via modules.

- **Oracle Portal** A complete, Web-based development environment that allows you to develop and implement production-quality applications quickly and easily.

- **Oracle Wireless** Offers complete support for enabling your applications on a multitude of wireless devices.

- **Oracle Identity Management** Security features that can be applied across all types of applications served up by Oracle Application Server 10*g*.

- ■ **PL/SQL Integration** The ability to call PL/SQL stored procedures directly from your HTML-based applications via the PL/SQL Web Toolkit and the mod_plsql module included with Apache.

- ■ **Forms, Reports, and Discoverer Servers** Give you the ability to serve Oracle Forms, Oracle Reports, and Oracle Discoverer Workbooks and Worksheets over the Web and integrate those components with Oracle Portal.

On top of all these features, Oracle Application Server 10*g* also supports the full Java 2 Enterprise Edition technology stack, including the following:

- ■ **Enterprise JavaBeans (EJBs)** EJBs enable applications to use entity, session, and message-driven beans. EJB comes with an EJB container that provides services for you. Services include transaction, persistence, and lifecycle management.

- ■ **Servlets** **Servlets** can generate dynamic responses to Web requests.

- ■ **JavaServer Pages (JSPs)** JSPs enable you to mix Java and HTML to author Web applications easily. JSPs also enable you to generate dynamic responses to Web requests. Servlets and JSPs run within a "Web container," which also provides services similar to those provided by the EJB container.

- ■ **Java Authentication and Authorization Service (JAAS)** JAAS enables you to authenticate users (ensuring that users are who they claim to be) and authorizes users (checking that the users have access to an object before executing or returning the object).

- ■ **Java Message Service (JMS)** JMS enables you to send and receive data and events asynchronously.

- ■ **Java Transaction API (JTA)** JTA enables your applications to participate in distributed transactions and access transaction services from other components.

- ■ **J2EE Connector Architecture** The J2EE Connector Architecture enables you to connect and perform operations on enterprise information systems.

Out of the box, Oracle Application Server 10*g* includes programs and Web pages for the administration of this complex environment. The Enterprise Manager Web Site Application Server Control provides numerous pages for monitoring the various services in Oracle Application Server 10*g* and gives administrators the ability to edit configuration files and review log files via a Web browser. This is invaluable for remote administration of Application Server instances when it is difficult to provide direct access to a server, and it simplifies the administrator's job by not having to make him or her remember the filenames and directory paths of the many log and configuration files used by Oracle Application Server 10*g*. Certain configuration editor pages even have syntax-checking functionality built into them, allowing administrators to verify their changes before attempting to implement modifications to components on the server. Most of the tasks that can be performed on these pages are administrative and are of little interest to the developer, but there are pages devoted to the creation and maintenance of containers, which give developers the ability to deploy their applications quickly and easily through a graphical interface.

The power of Oracle Application Server 10*g* lies in its seamless integration with various Internet and programmatic standards and the Oracle database. It has evolved into a product that enables

you and your organization to benefit from the true power of the Internet by providing a reliable, scalable, and secure deployment platform. Figure 45-1 provides a visual representation of the Oracle Application Server 10*g* product.

Communication Services	Business Logic Services	Presentation Services	Business Intelligence Services
Oracle HTTP Server (Apache)	Oracle BC4J/EJB	Apache JServ	Oracle Reports 10*g*
mod_plsql	Oracle 8*i*/9*i*/10*g* JVM	Oracle OC4J	Oracle Discoverer Plus/Viewer
mod_jserv mod_oc4j mod_ose	Oracle 8*i*/9*i*/10*g* PL/SQL	Oracle JSP/PSP	
mod_dms mod_onsint mod_oprocmgr	Oracle Forms 10*g*		
mod_oradav	Content Management Services	Portal Services	Caching Services
mod_ossl mod_osso	Content Management SDK	Oracle Portal 10*g*	Oracle Web Cache 10*g*

Developer's Toolkits
XML Toolkit
Content Management Toolkit
MapViewer Toolkit
Wireless Toolkit
Portal Development Toolkit

System Services	
Oracle Enterprise Manager	Oracle Identity Management

FIGURE 45-1. *Oracle Application Server 10g architecture*

The boxes at the top of each section represent the different categories of services. The ovals represent Oracle's implementation of those services. This chapter discusses, at a high level, the various services that Oracle Application Server 10g provides and why you, as a developer, are interested in them. The architecture of Oracle Application Server 10g may seem overly complex, but this is necessary because it reflects Oracle's commitment to the numerous open standards and frameworks that constitute modern Web development. The architecture also gives Oracle Application Server 10g a level of scalability and reliability not seen in most application servers.

The two major pieces of Oracle Application Server 10g are the middle tier, which provides components for deploying and running applications over the Web, and the infrastructure, which maintains security and clustering information. In a one-to-many relationship, a single infrastructure can maintain security and clustering information for one or many middle tiers. When you install Oracle Application Server 10g, you must decide if you'll need an infrastructure, because that piece needs to be installed first. The different types of middle-tier installations—and whether they are dependant on an infrastructure—are discussed next.

What are an infrastructure and middle tier composed of? Each piece is composed of a series of programs that provide various services to the Apache server. As an analogy, think of the services that run on a Windows machine—they are programs that provide various services to the operating system. In the same way, the programs that constitute the infrastructure and middle tiers provide services to the Application Server instance. The middle tier has three different versions that you can install, depending on your needs and licensing:

- J2EE and Web Cache
- Portal and Wireless
- Business Intelligence and Forms

Table 45-1 lists the different middle-tier components of Oracle Application Server 10g configured with each type of installation.

Component	J2EE and Web Cache	Portal and Wireless	Business Intelligence and Forms
Oracle HTTP Server	X	X	X
OC4J	X	X	X
OracleAS Web Cache	X	X	X
Oracle Enterprise Manager Web Site	X	X	X
OracleAS TopLink	X	X	X
OracleAS Portal		X	X
OracleAS Wireless		X	X
OracleAS Personalization			X
OracleAS Discoverer			X
OracleAS Reports Services			X
OracleAS Forms Services			X

TABLE 45-1. *Middle-Tier Components by Installation Type*

Based on this table, if you plan to serve Oracle Forms, Oracle Reports, and/or Oracle Discoverer Workbooks and Worksheets over the Web, you should install the Business Intelligence and Forms option. If you want to use Oracle Portal and/or develop applications to be used with wireless (hand-held) devices, select the Portal and Wireless option. If you only need a Web server to deploy J2EE applications, select the J2EE and Web Cache option. When you install the middle tier, you are creating an OracleAS "instance."

NOTE
The meaning of the word "instance" in this context is different from the more general use of "instance," which is commonly used to refer to an Oracle database instance.

Figure 45-2 shows the administration page with all the services for a middle tier installed with the Business Intelligence and Forms option.

As of 8.1.7, the Oracle database includes an HTTP server as part of its installation. It provides only the first two components in Table 45-1: an HTTP server and OC4J containers.

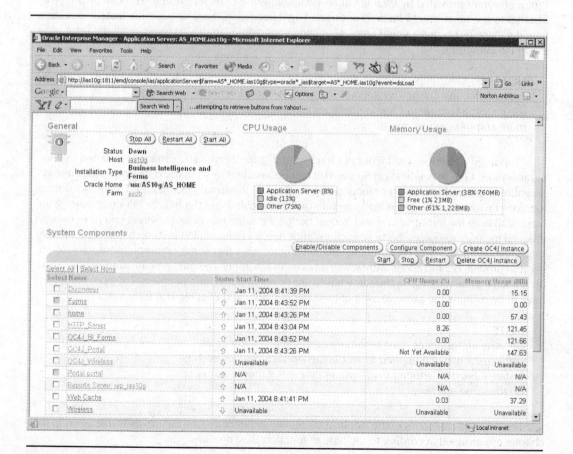

FIGURE 45-2. *Middle tier administration screen*

The second major piece of Oracle Application Server 10*g* is called the *infrastructure*. The infrastructure is an instance of Oracle Application Server 10*g* that maintains security and clustering information. In Oracle's documentation, the different types of security components provided by Oracle are called "Identity Management." The Identity Management components provide directory, security, and user management functionality. The Identity Management components are as follows:

- Oracle Internet Directory
- OracleAS Single Sign-On
- Oracle Delegated Administration Services
- Oracle Directory Integration and Provisioning
- OracleAS Certificate Authority

For both the Business Intelligence and Forms option and the Portal and Wireless option, an infrastructure is required. The infrastructure, by default, uses an Oracle 9*i* database to store Identity Management information, but an Oracle9*i* or Oracle10*g* database can be manually specified. The Identity Management information is referenced through an LDAP (Lightweight Directory Access Protocol) server provided by Oracle called *Oracle Internet Directory (OID)*. You can instruct the installer to use an existing Oracle9*i* or Oracle10*g* database instance or have the installer create a new database instance for you. Figure 45-3 shows the administration page with all the services for an infrastructure.

NOTE
Technically, the Forms and Reports Servers can be configured to not use an infrastructure in Oracle Application Server 10g, but it is far more common to use one.

"Topology" describes the layout of Oracle Application Server 10*g* instances installed in your organization. Oracle Application Server 10*g* can be installed in so many different ways, there is an entire chapter, titled "Recommended Topologies," in the installation guide. The most common topology involves installing the infrastructure on one machine and the middle tier on another. You can install both the infrastructure and middle tier on the same machine, provided you have enough disk and memory resources (because each instance needs to be installed in its own ORACLE_HOME) or numerous middle tiers on numerous servers. Figure 45-4 lists some common topologies. In an effort to provide organizations with a high amount of flexibility, the infrastructure and middle tiers do not have to be running on the same hardware or operating system platform. They do, however, have to be running the same version of the Oracle Application Server 10*g* software.

NOTE
Because all instances must be running the same version of the software, any patch applied to an Oracle Application Server 10g instance must be applied to all instances, even if they're running on the same machine.

The different categories of the Application Server architecture (see Figure 45-1) discussed in this chapter are grouped according to the type of function they provide:

- **Communication services** Handle requests to and from the Web
- **Business Logic services** The development tools and languages for building applications
- **Presentation services** Development tools and languages for building dynamic Web pages
- **Caching services** Tools for improving Web site performance
- **Content Management services** Tools for managing documents in the database
- **Portal services** Provide publishing features for content and portlets
- **Business Intelligence services** Provide reports and ad hoc queries
- **Database services** The Oracle database for storing application data
- **Persistence Layer services** Provide an object-relational framework
- **Developer's toolkits** Application programming interfaces (APIs) to aid in the creation of applications

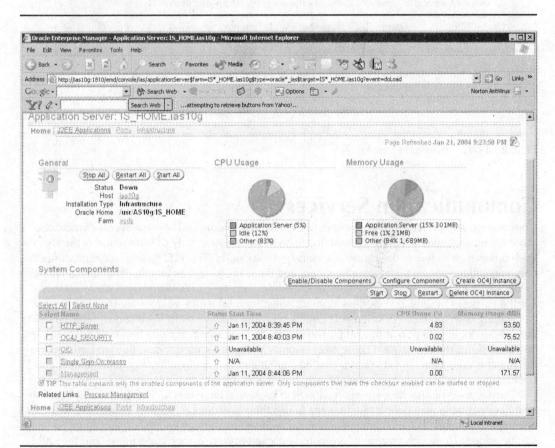

FIGURE 45-3. *Administration screen for the infrastructure*

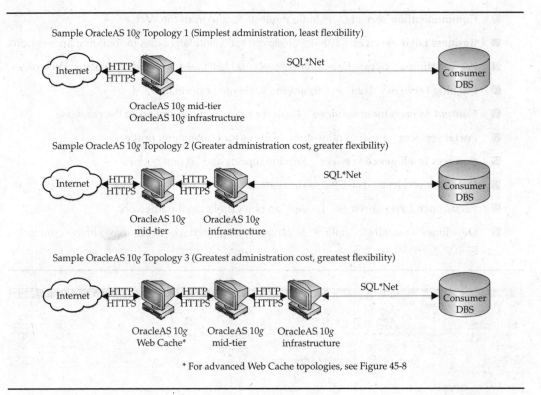

FIGURE 45-4. *Common topologies*

Communication Services

Communication services provide connectivity between clients and servers over the Internet or, more accurately, over a TCP/IP connection. The most common way of interaction is through a Web browser, which uses the Hypertext Transfer Protocol (HTTP). HTTP can handle multimedia communication services such as audio, video, and data. Tools such as Oracle Portal take advantage of these features to seamlessly store and retrieve almost any type of data from an Oracle database. For the purposes of Oracle Web development, the communication services are the Web Server.

Starting with Oracle9*i*AS Release 1, Oracle has used Apache as its Web server, referred to in the Oracle documentation as the *HTTP Server.* Apache has a large base of knowledge available for its administration because it is the most popular Web server used today. By standardizing on the Apache Web server, Oracle has provided a great amount of flexibility to administrators and organizations that wish to move their Oracle-based applications to the Web.

The designers of Apache were smart enough to know that there was no way they could anticipate every conceivable way people might want to use their Web server, so they designed it with an open-ended interface that incorporates a modular architecture through which additional functionality can be added. These enhancements are commonly referred to as *mods* (modules), and they all begin with the prefix "mod_". Modules may be linked statically to the Web server or may be loaded

dynamically at run time using Dynamic Shared Object (DSO) support on UNIX or dynamically linked libraries (DLLs) on Windows. The API for these modular components is based on the C programming language. Table 45-2 lists the mods that come with the Apache server provided with Oracle Application Server 10*g*.

For more information about Apache, go to http://www.apache.org.

Module	Functionality Provided to the Apache Server	Provided by Oracle?	Supported by Oracle?
mod_access	The directives provided by mod_access are used in <Directory>, <Files>, and <Location> sections as well as .htaccess files to control access to particular parts of the server.	No	Yes
mod_actions	The Action directive lets you run CGI scripts whenever a file of a certain type is requested. The Script directive lets you run CGI scripts whenever a particular method is used in a request.	No	Yes
mod_alias	The directives contained in this module allow for manipulation and control of URLs as requests arrive at the server. The Alias and ScriptAlias directives are used to map between URLs and file system paths.	No	Yes
mod_asis	This module provides the handler send-as-is, which causes Apache to send the document without adding most of the usual HTTP headers.	No	Yes
mod_auth	This module allows the use of HTTP Basic Authentication to restrict access by looking up users in plain-text password and group files.	No	Yes
mod_auth_anon	This module does access control in a manner similar to anonymous-ftp sites; that is, have a "magic" user ID of "anonymous" and the e-mail address as a password.	No	Yes
mod_auth_db	This module provides an alternative to DBM files for those systems that support DB and not DBM.	No	No
mod_auth_dbm	This module provides for HTTP Basic Authentication, where the usernames and passwords are stored in DBM-type database files.	No	No
mod_auth_digest	This is an updated version of mod_digest using MD5 authentication (experimental).	No	No
mod_autoindex	This module provides for automatic directory indexing.	No	Yes
mod_cern_meta	This module emulates the CERN HTTPD metafile semantics. Metafiles are HTTP headers that can be output in addition to the normal range of headers for each file accessed.	No	No

TABLE 45-2. *Apache Modules Provided in Oracle Application Server 10*g

Module	Functionality Provided to the Apache Server	Provided by Oracle?	Supported by Oracle?
mod_cern_headers	This module allows reverse proxies that terminate SSL connections in front of Oracle HTTP Server to transfer information regarding an SSL connection to Oracle HTTP Server.	No	Yes
mod_cgi	Any file that has the MIME type application /x-httpd-cgi or handler cgi-script is treated as a CGI script, and run by the server, with its output being returned to the client.	No	Yes
mod_define	Provides support for Distributed Authoring and Versioning.	No	Yes (UNIX only)
mod_digest	This module implements an older version of the MD5 Digest Authentication.	No	Yes
mod_dir	The DirectoryIndex directive sets the name of a file written by the user, typically called index.html, used as the index of a directory.	No	Yes
mod_dms	Enables you to monitor the performance of site components with Oracle's Dynamic Monitoring Service (DMS).	Yes	Yes
mod_env	This module allows for control of the environment that will be provided to CGI scripts and SSI pages.	No	Yes
mod_example	The files in the src/modules/example directory under the Apache distribution directory tree are provided as an example to those who wish to write modules that use the Apache API.	No	No
mod_expires	This module provides for the generation of Expires HTTP headers (an instruction to the client about the document's validity and persistence) according to user-specified criteria.	No	Yes
mod_fastcgi	Routes requests to fastcgi modules.	No	Yes
mod_headers	This module provides for the customization of HTTP response headers.	No	Yes
mod_imap	This module processes .map files, thereby replacing the functionality of the imagemap CGI program.	No	No
mod_include	This module provides a handler that will process files before they are sent to the client.	No	Yes
mod_info	This module provides a comprehensive overview of the server configuration, including all installed modules and directives in the configuration files.	No	Yes
mod_isapi	This module implements the Internet Server extension API. It allows Internet Server extensions (for example, ISAPI DLL modules) to be served by Apache for Windows.	No	No

TABLE 45-2. *Apache Modules Provided in Oracle Application Server 10g* (continued)

Module	Functionality Provided to the Apache Server	Provided by Oracle?	Supported by Oracle?
mod_jserv	Converts HTTP requests to servlet requests, returning HTTP responses to the client. This is disabled by default in the Oracle HTTP Server distribution; use mod_oc4j instead.	No	Yes
mod_log_config	This module provides for logging of the requests made to the server, using the Common Log Format or a user-specified format.	No	Yes
mod_mime	This module is used to determine various bits of "meta information" about documents. The directives AddCharset, AddEncoding, AddHandler, AddLanguage, and AddType are all used to map file extensions onto the meta-information for that file.	No	Yes
mod_mime_magic	This module provides for determining the MIME type of a file by looking at a few bytes of its contents. It is intended as a "second line of defense" for cases that mod_mime can't resolve.	No	Yes
mod_mmap_static	This module maps a list of statically configured files into memory. This is an experimental module and should be used with care.	No	No
mod_negotiation	This module provides for content selection; it's defined as the selection of a document that best matches the client's capabilities.	No	Yes
mod_oc4j	Routes requests to the OC4J instances.	Yes	Yes
mod_onsint	Provides integration support with Oracle Notification Service (ONS) and Oracle Process Manager and Notification Server (OPMN).	Yes	Yes
mod_oprocmgr	Provides process management and load-balancing services to JServ processes. It is provided for legacy users of JServ. JServ is disabled by default in the Oracle HTTP Server configuration. Oracle recommends using OC4J and mod_oc4j (which are both enabled by default).	Yes	Yes
mod_oradav	Enhancement to mod_dav to allow Oracle DB as a backing store.	Yes	Yes
mod_ossl	Enables strong cryptography for Oracle HTTP Server. It is very similar to mod_ssl; mod_ossl is based on the Oracle implementation of SSL, which supports SSL, version 3.	Yes	Yes
mod_osso	Supports single sign-on across sites and across applications.	Yes	Yes
mod_perl	Runs Perl programs.	No	Yes

TABLE 45-2. *Apache Modules Provided in Oracle Application Server 10g* (continued)

Module	Functionality Provided to the Apache Server	Provided by Oracle?	Supported by Oracle?
mod_plsql	Routes requests to PL/SQL programs in a database and enables making requests to database stored procedures from the browser.	Yes	Yes
mod_proxy	This module implements proxying capabilities for FTP, CONNECT (for SSL), HTTP/0.9, HTTP/1.0, and (as of Apache 1.3.23) HTTP/1.1.	No	Yes
mod_rewrite	This module uses a rule-based rewriting engine (based on a regular-expression parser) to rewrite requested URLs on the fly.	No	Yes
mod_setenvif	This module allows you to set environment variables according to whether different aspects of the request match regular expressions you specify.	No	Yes
mod_so	On selected operating systems, this module can be used to load modules into Apache at run time via the Dynamic Shared Object (DSO) mechanism, rather than requiring a recompilation (experimental).	No	Yes
mod_speling	This module attempts to correct misspellings of URLs that users might have entered, by ignoring capitalization and by allowing up to one misspelling.	No	Yes
mod_status	This module allows a server administrator to find out how well his or her server is performing. An HTML page is presented that gives the current server statistics in an easily readable form.	No	Yes
mod_unique_id	This module provides a magic token for each request, which is guaranteed to be unique across "all" requests under very specific conditions. The unique identifier is even unique across multiple machines in a properly configured cluster of machines.	No	Yes
mod_userdir	This module provides for user-specific directories. The UserDir directive sets the real directory in a user's home directory to use when a request for a document for a user is received.	No	Yes
mod_usertrack	This module uses cookies to provide for a clickstream log of user activity on a site. Oracle Application Server 10g contains a service called Clickstream Intelligence that enhances this functionality.	No	Yes
mod_vhost_alias	This module creates dynamically configured virtual hosts by allowing the IP address and/or the Host: header of the HTTP request to be used as part of the pathname to determine what files to serve.	No	Yes

TABLE 45-2. *Apache Modules Provided in Oracle Application Server 10*g *(continued)*

Content Management Services

All organizations have different types of data they use on a regular basis in the course of their activities. Some of this data is in spreadsheets, some in Oracle databases, some in non-Oracle databases, some in picture and sound files—the list goes on and on. *Content management* refers to the process of capturing, storing, sorting, codifying, integrating, updating, and protecting any and all of an organization's information. Oracle Application Server 10*g* provides content management services that allow organizations to store, manage, and retrieve all different types of data in a central place—namely, an Oracle database.

Storing disparate data is not the only objective, however. For any content management service to be truly useful, it must also take into account such factors as connecting to other people's information, approval and publication processes, indexing, search and retrieval capabilities, security, collaboration, accessibility, reuse, and digital rights management. In Oracle9*i*AS Release 1, Oracle introduced the Oracle Internet File System (iFS), which stores files in an Oracle8*i* or 9*i* database. iFS, in effect, made all content available in a file hierarchy that could be accessed through a Web browser, Windows networking, or FTP (File Transfer Protocol), independent of platform (except for Windows networking, of course). Oracle Application Server 10*g* has added many new features to its content management capabilities and renamed it the *Oracle Content Management Software Development Kit.* The Content Manager SDK has support for all major content-management services listed previously.

Oracle Ultra Search can be used to search across corporate Web servers, databases, mail servers, file servers, and Oracle10*g* Portal instances. Ultra Search is based on Oracle10*g* Text technology and is an out-of-the box solution that requires no SQL coding. It uses a crawler to index documents (the documents stay in their own repositories), and the crawled information is used to build an index that stays within your firewall in an Oracle database.

Business Logic Services

Not every technology is appropriate for every circumstance, and no one tool is the "right" one to go with. Some of the technologies are good for displaying (or *presenting*) data and are generally classified under the category "presentation services." Other technologies are better for holding application logic and are generally classified under "business logic services." That's not to say these technologies are mutually exclusive—you could put your business logic into a technology designed for presenting data (such as a JSP application) if you wanted to—but the presentation and business logic services were designed with the idea of separating the code that drives the business from the code that controls how the end user interacts with data, with the intent of making applications easier to maintain and enhance, particularly in a collaborative environment where numerous programmers with different skills sets will be working on a single project.

Traditionally, the technology used for Web-based business logic services was Enterprise JavaBeans. The Enterprise JavaBeans (EJB) technology is the server-side component architecture for the Java 2 Enterprise Edition (J2EE) platform. EJB technology enables development of distributed, transactional, secure, and portable applications based on Java technology. The EJB specification is one of the several Java APIs in the J2EE platform. The specification details how an Application Server provides server-side objects with

- Web Services
- Persistence

- Transactions
- Concurrency control
- Events using Java Messaging Service (JMS)
- Naming and Directory Services
- Security
- Deployment of components in an Application Server

Search for a definition of "persistence" on the Internet and you'll find so many different variations that you'll probably be more confused after searching than you were before. The one that most closely matches my idea of persistence comes from the unlikely source www.posc.org:

"That quality of an instance of data related to its existence beyond and outside of the life of its creating process or the lives of other processes that use it. In this context, *persistence* is normally used in describing the life of objects relative to sessions, i.e., whether or not they live beyond sessions."

See the discussion of TopLink later in this chapter under the section "Persistence Layer Services" for more information regarding Oracle's strategic direction regarding persistence implementation for OC4J.

Additionally, the Enterprise JavaBean specification defines the roles played by the EJB container and the EJBs as well as how to deploy the EJBs in a container.

Central to the understanding of EJBs is the concept of patterns. Sun defines a pattern as follows:

"A recurring solution to a problem in a context. A *context* is the environment, surroundings, situation, or interrelated conditions within which something exists. A *problem* is an unsettled question, something that needs to be investigated and solved. A problem can be specified by a set of causes and effects. Typically, the problem is constrained by the context in which it occurs. Finally, the *solution* refers to the answer to the problem in a context that helps resolve the issues."

A solution to a problem is not considered a pattern unless there is some way to show that the solution can be applied to recurring types of problems in the solution's definition. Patterns are described by five main characteristics: context, problem, solution, forces, and consequences.

EJBs, however, are notoriously difficult to program and maintain. In response to this, Oracle created a business logic service framework called Business Components for Java (BC4J), which seeks to remove much of the complexity of EJB while continuing to provide all its functionality. With BC4J, developers can author and test object-oriented business logic in components that automatically integrate with relational databases, reuse business logic through multiple views of data, and access and update those views from servlets or JSPs.

You may be asking yourself why it is even necessary to store business logic in the middle tier. After all, don't most Oracle-based applications store their business logic in database packages, procedures, functions, and triggers? There are several reasons for implementing business logic via BC4J:

- You do not want to mix object-oriented and relational paradigms in your application.

- You will be accessing the database only through clients using BC4J.

- Your programming staff is skilled in Java, and not in PL/SQL.

- You will be accessing both Oracle and non-Oracle databases.

Some companies may not want to be "locked into Oracle." In other words, they want to have database vendor freedom. This is generally a bad practice—you won't maximize the performance of your Oracle application.

Designing, authoring, debugging, documenting, delivering, and maintaining a J2EE design patterns framework takes a significant amount of time and effort. BC4J implements patterns for developers, giving them a significant advantage in getting their J2EE applications built, deployed, and enhanced more quickly.

It is not a requirement, of course, to store your business logic in the middle tier. Traditionally, Oracle developers have stored their business logic inside the Oracle database in the form of packages, procedures, functions, triggers, and constraints. To assist in the development of Web-based applications, Oracle provides an Apache module called mod_plsql that allows you to make requests to stored procedures in the database directly from the browser. As of Oracle 8.1.7, a group of packages called the PL/SQL Web Toolkit has been included as part of the built-in packages in the database. By using the toolkit, you can generate Web pages; query, retrieve, and display data from an Oracle database; dynamically calculate the contents of Web pages; and much more.

You can also store business logic within an Oracle Form. Oracle Application Server 10*g*, when installed with the Business Intelligence and Forms option, can serve Oracle Forms over the Web to a client's Web browser, where the form is displayed as a Java applet containing the user interface for the form's run-time engine. When you submit a URL to launch an Oracle Forms–based application, the Web listener accepts the request and downloads the Oracle Forms applet to your browser. The Oracle Forms applet then establishes a persistent connection to an Oracle Forms run-time engine. All processing takes place between the Oracle Forms applet and the Oracle Forms Services run-time engine, which seamlessly handles any queries or commits to the database. The Oracle Forms Server can be configured to use Oracle Application Server 10*g*'s Single Sign-On (SSO) and Oracle Internet Directory (OID) capabilities to secure access. Oracle Forms can also be integrated into Oracle Portal to use its publishing capabilities.

Presentation Services

As discussed in prior sections, technologies such as BC4J and Oracle Forms are good for writing, testing, and maintaining your business logic. Other technologies, however, are better suited for displaying your applications. Presentation Services deliver dynamic content to client browsers, supporting servlets, business intelligence, PL/SQL Server Pages, JavaServer Pages, Perl/CGI scripts, and PHP. You can use Presentation Services to build your presentation layer for your Web applications. Although Oracle puts these services into a separate group, you can think of them grouped with the Business Logic Services, in that your application logic can reside within these components. I recommend, however, that you break your business logic into executable components, which can then be called or invoked by these services.

Apache JServ (mod_jserv) is a module for the Apache Web server that implements Sun's Java Servlet API for running server-side Java code. Java servlets must be executed from within a Java Virtual Machine (JVM), and hence any servlet execution environment must include a JVM. The complexity of adding a JVM to the Apache server would degrade the Apache architecture, so the solution adopted for Apache JServ was to separate the JVM from the Apache server. This separation provides several benefits:

■ It allows the use of any compatible JVM from any vendor. No modifications need be made to the Web server when a change is made to the JVM (such as by an upgrade).

■ It improves stability by separating the processes, allowing process-level protections by the operating system. If the JVM should crash or be misconfigured, the Web server will still operate normally.

■ It allows for advanced functionality, including automatic startup, separate JVMs for different configurations, and the ability to support load balancing on high-traffic sites.

Although the Apache module for handling servlet requests (mod_jserv) is still available in Oracle Application Server 10*g*, it is provided for backward compatibility only. Oracle recommends converting your legacy applications to use Oracle Application Server Containers for J2EE (OC4J).

OC4J is the core J2EE run-time component of Oracle Application Server 10*g* implemented as a module (mod_oc4j) in the Apache Web server. OC4J is J2EE 1.3 compatible and runs on standard J2SE distributions, making it easy to use and highly productive for developers, while at the same time offering outstanding performance and scalability for production environments. OC4J provides complete support for the technologies listed in Table 45-3.

JavaServer Pages is a server-side technology that is an extension to the Java servlet technology. JSPs have a dynamic scripting capability that works in tandem with HTML code, separating the

Java Technology	Version of Specification Supported in Oracle Application Server 10*g* Release 1
JSPs	1.2
Servlets	2.3
EJBs	2.0
JMS	1.0.2b
JDBC	2.0
SOAP	1.1
WSDL	1.1
UDDI	2.0

TABLE 45-3. *Java Technologies Supported by OC4J*

user interface from content generation, enabling designers to change the overall page layout without altering the underlying dynamic content. Developers can benefit by using JSP technology without having to learn the Java language. They can also extend the JSP language through the use of simple tag handlers and easily maintain pages through the use of the JSP Standard Tag Library (JSTL).

PL/SQL Server Pages (PSPs) is a technology provided by Oracle. It works on the same principles as JSPs, except that it uses PL/SQL as its scripting language. This can be beneficial for shops with minimal Java expertise. PSPs are compiled components executed as Oracle Stored Procedures. The Oracle PSP service includes the PSP Compiler and the PL/SQL Web Toolkit. Existing Web pages can be made dynamic by embedding PL/SQL tags to perform database operations and display the results. Because PSPs are executed as stored procedures, it is important to note that the processing of PSPs occurs on the Database Server; the other technologies discussed in this chapter execute on the Application Server.

Business Intelligence Services

Business Intelligence Services can help you gain insight into internal business operations, customers, and suppliers. The basic business intelligence requirements usually include data quality, data analysis, and information access. The ultimate goal of Business Intelligence Services is to provide up-to-the-second business insight, most commonly provided with reporting tools. Oracle provides two enterprise-quality reporting tools: Oracle Reports and Oracle Discoverer. The choice of which tool to implement (or the decision to implement both) will be based on the needs and skill level of the employees in your organization. Both of these tools, in conjunction with Oracle Application Server 10*g*, provide the ability to easily make reports available over the Web.

Similar to the Forms Server discussed earlier, the Reports Server allows you to publish Oracle Reports on an internal company intranet, an external company extranet, or over the Web. In addition, the Reports Server can interface with a mail server to automatically deliver reports to the mailbox of selected users or groups. The Reports Server consists of the server component, run-time engines, and the servlet runner. When a client submits a request for a report, the Oracle HTTP Server Web listener routes that request to the Oracle Reports Services server component. The server then routes the request to the Oracle Reports Services run-time engine, which runs the report. The report output is then sent back to the client through the Oracle HTTP Server Web listener. Reports can be formatted as HTML, XML, .pdfs (Adobe Acrobat), or as plain text for the user. Developers can also easily customize the report for import into Microsoft Excel or any other commonly supported document Multipurpose Internet Mail Extensions (MIME) types. The Oracle Reports Server can be configured to use Oracle Application Server 10*g*'s Single Sign-On (SSO) and Oracle Internet Directory (OID) capabilities to secure access. Reports can also be integrated easily with Oracle Portal so that they can take advantage of Portal's publishing, security, and visual template features.

Oracle Discoverer is a reporting tool that gives ad hoc query capabilities to your end users. Targeted at power users, Discoverer enables you to access information from the database and create dynamic reports that accept parameters and have drill-down or data-pivoting capabilities, all without the need to learn SQL. Invoking a Discoverer Workbook or Worksheet over the Web can be made as simple as clicking a URL that invokes the Discoverer Web component called Discoverer Viewer. This link can be constructed to invoke a particular Workbook query automatically, giving the user the results in a Web browser with the ability to interact with the query results to

drill up or down, enter values into optional parameters, or to follow links to other Workbooks or applications. Figure 45-5 shows an Oracle Discoverer Workbook displayed in Discoverer Plus.

There is no environment in Oracle Application Server 10*g* to develop Oracle Forms and Reports. The Forms Server and Reports Server components exist solely to take Oracle Forms and Oracle Reports and serve them up on the Web. Oracle Discoverer Server has the ability to serve Discoverer Workbooks and Worksheets over the Web, but it also has the ability to develop Workbooks and Worksheets using a Web browser as its interface. This piece of the Discoverer Server, called *Discoverer Plus,* can be used as a replacement to the Oracle Discoverer Desktop. By using the Discoverer Plus Web interface, you will no longer have to install the Discoverer Desktop software on every client that needs to create and manage Workbooks and Worksheets. The Discoverer Administrator program, which is used to administer End-User Layers (EULs) and Discoverer privileges, is still required. Figure 45-6 shows an Oracle Discoverer Worksheet displayed over the Web in the Discoverer Plus environment.

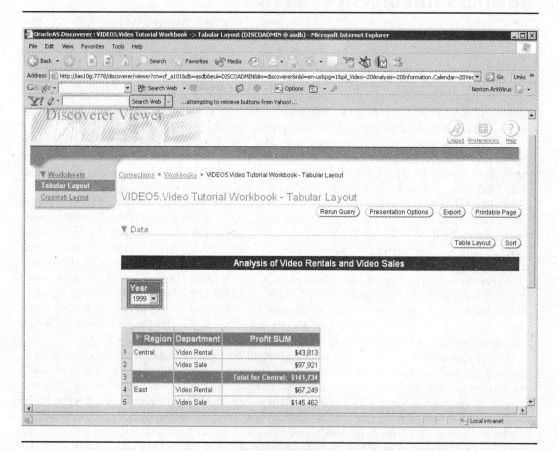

FIGURE 45-5. *An Oracle Discoverer Workbook viewed through a Web browser*

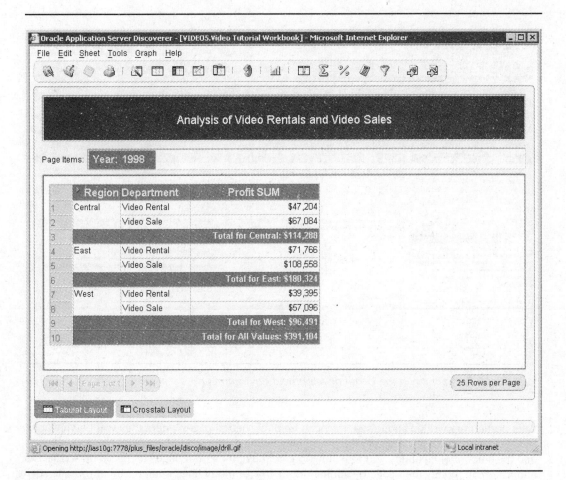

FIGURE 45-6. *The Discoverer Plus development environment*

Portal Services

An *enterprise portal* is an application that enables organizations to unlock internally and externally stored information and provide users a single gateway to personalized information needed to make informed business decisions. By providing end users with relevant data from across multiple data sources and presenting that information in a context that is meaningful to the user, portals offer the promise of providing competitive advantage through new business processes, increasing productivity by putting more power into the hands of business users and increasing effectiveness through knowledge sharing and reduced search time.

Oracle Portal can handle and display virtually any type of data, giving you the ability to create portals that give users access to Web applications, business documents, business intelligence reports, charts, and links to other forms of data that can exist both inside and outside your corporate intranet. Portal pages contain regions, which can hold items of content such as spreadsheet or word processor files, or portlets, which provide access to Web resources such as applications or other Web pages.

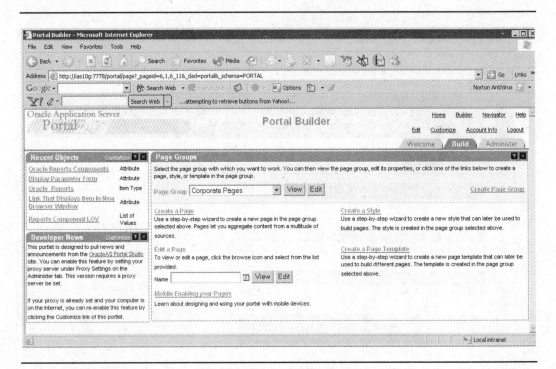

FIGURE 45-7. *Screen of the Portal development environment*

After portlets are written and tested, they can be published to pages where they will be viewable by those users who have access to the pages. Depending on the level of expertise of your end users and the amount of flexibility you're willing to give them, the Portal page can be set up so that the end users can modify their page by adding, removing, or modifying content, similar to a site such as http://my.yahoo.com. Oracle Portal is unique in the sense that its development environment is itself a Portal application. Once your developers and administrators become comfortable with the Portal environment, it will be easy for them to understand the mechanics of Portal development. Combined with the wizard-based approach to developing Portal applications, your developers can be productive in a very short period of time. Figure 45-7 shows a Portal development screen.

Web Services

Web Services are Web-based applications that dynamically interact with other Web applications using open standards that include XML (eXtensible Markup Language), SOAP (Simple Object Access Protocol), and UDDI (Universal Description, Discovery, and Integration). Such applications typically run behind the scenes, with one program "talking to" another (server to server). Using the UDDI discovery system, the goal of Web Services is to register a service on the Internet, allow an application to search for and find the service, and then to seamlessly exchange data with it. Web Services are either "request-and-response" or "one-way" style, and they can use either synchronous or asynchronous communication. The fundamental unit of exchange between Web Services clients and Web Services, of either style or type of communication, is a message.

Web Services enable software components to interact around the world. Because Web Services use open, XML-based protocols that are lightweight and simple, their acceptance and use have gained a tremendous amount of support in recent years. A Web Service does the following things:

- **Exposes and describes itself** A Web Service defines its functionality and attributes so that other applications can understand it. By providing a WSDL file, a Web Service makes its functionality available to other applications.

- **Allows other services to locate it on the Web** A Web Service can be registered in a UDDI Registry so that applications can locate it.

- **Can be invoked** Once a Web Service has been located and examined, the remote application can invoke the service using an Internet standard protocol (such as HTTP or SMTP).

Developer Toolkits

To support application development and deployment, Oracle provides several toolkits containing libraries and tools. OracleAS Developer Kits 10*g* provide APIs (application programming interfaces) that enable you to develop OracleAS Portal, OracleAS Wireless, XML, and LDAP applications. Developer kits are used in development environments, not in staging or production environments. The code in a developer kit is deployed in production. It is possible to develop your own developer kits.

XML Toolkit

Oracle XML Developer's Kit 10*g* (XDK) is a set of components, tools, and utilities in Java, C, and C++ (available in Oracle Database 10*g* and Oracle Application Server 10*g*) that eases the task of building and deploying XML-enabled applications. The production Oracle XDK is fully supported and comes with a commercial redistribution license. Oracle XDK consists of the following components:

- **XML parsers** Create and parse XML using the DOM (Document Object Model), SAX (Simple API for XML), and JAXP (Java API for XML Processing) interfaces. Directly access XMLType in Oracle Database 10*g* with unified C DOM interfaces. DOM support includes the 3.0 specification.

- **XSLT (eXtensible Stylesheet Language Transformation) processors** Transform or render XML (now with XSLT 2.0 Java support).

- **XSLT VM and compiler** Provide a high-performance C XSLT transformation engine using compiled stylesheets.

- **XML schema processors** Support XML schema validation. Now include validator interfaces for stream-based processing.

- **XML JavaBeans** Parse, transform, diff, retrieve, and compress XML documents via Java components.

- **XML class generator** Now supporting JAXP, the XML class generator automatically generates classes from DTDs (Document Type Definitions) and XML schemas to send XML from Web forms or applications.

- **XML SQL utility** Generates XML documents, DTDs, and XML schemas from SQL queries in Java and inserts XML documents into Oracle databases.

- **XSQL servlet** Combines XML, SQL, and XSLT in the server to deliver dynamic Web content and build sophisticated database-backed Web sites and services.

- **XML pipeline processor** Invokes Java processes through XML control files.

- **TransX utility** Makes it easier to load globalized seed data and messages into Oracle databases.

Content Management Toolkit

The Oracle Content Management SDK provides a set of Java APIs for folders, versioning, check-in/check-out, security, searching, extensible metadata, and other standard operations for the development of content-oriented applications. You can access your content with your choice of tools through the following protocols:

- **FTP** The File Transfer Protocol allows the transfer of one or more files from one machine to another across the Internet.

- **SMB** Server Message Block is a protocol for sharing files, printers, serial ports, and communications abstractions such as named pipes and mail slots between computers.

- **WebDAV** Web Distributed Authoring and Versioning is a mechanism that supports the collaborative development of Web pages.

- **NFS** The Network File System is a protocol suite developed and licensed by Sun Microsystems that allows different makes of computers running different operating systems to share files and disk storage.

- **AFP** The Apple Filing Protocol is Apple's network protocol for providing file server/client access in an AppleShare network.

- **IMAP4** Internet Messaging Access Protocol 4 is a network standard that allows users to manage e-mail messages and folders from multiple locations and systems. Users can choose to store their messages on their own local computer (or *client)* or on a server.

- **SMTP** The Simple Mail Transfer Protocol is a protocol used to send e-mail on the Internet. SMTP is a set of rules regarding the interaction between a program sending e-mail and a program receiving e-mail.

Developers can also create custom/proprietary protocol servers. The Oracle Content Management SDK is fully integrated with Oracle Text, Oracle Workflow, Oracle interMedia, Oracle Advanced Queuing, and other Oracle API products. It is also integrated with Oracle platform infrastructure products such as Oracle Internet Directory. It was formerly known as *Oracle Internet File System.*

Oracle Application Server MapViewer Toolkit

Both geographic and location data are managed in a native type within Oracle Database 10*g.* Oracle provides the following technologies to make use of geographic information:

- **Oracle Locator** Provides core location functionality to support a variety of Location-Based Services (LBS) and third-party GIS solutions.

- **Oracle Spatial** A database option for Oracle9*i* and Oracle10*g* Enterprise Edition that provides advanced spatial features to support high-end GIS and LBS solutions.

- **Oracle MapViewer** An Oracle Application Server Java component and JDeveloper extension used for map rendering and viewing geospatial data managed by Oracle Spatial or Locator.

Wireless Toolkit

Oracle Application Server Wireless (OracleAS Wireless) is a comprehensive and flexible wireless and voice platform. Enterprises can deploy wireless browser-based applications, voice applications, notifications, Java 2 Micro Edition (J2ME), and two-way messaging applications. OracleAS Wireless helps enterprises and service providers efficiently build, manage, and maintain wireless and voice applications. Some of the main features of OracleAS Wireless include the following:

- **Multi-Channel Server** Enables applications to be accessed through multiple delivery methods such as SMS, voice access, WAP, Pocket PCs, and so on. Developers can focus on creating mobile applications for any channel in one future-proof, open-standards language.

- **J2ME support** Java 2 Micro Edition provides a lightweight run-time environment for mobile devices, enabling client-side development based on industry standards instead of proprietary device interfaces.

- **J2ME Developer's Kit** Offers the ability to extend Web Services to J2ME devices.

- **J2ME Provisioning System** This Web-based application manager allows users to upload J2ME applications to the database repository for efficient management and secure storage.

- **Notifications and Multi-Media Messaging** This feature enhances intelligent messaging with new functionality for actionable alerts, message adaptation, and failover delivery control.

- **Web Clipping** Allows clipping and scraping of existing Web content to create wireless applications that reuse existing PC browser-based applications.

- **Location Services** Give access to the full Location-Based Service (LBS) functionality, such as user positioning, geo-coding, mapping, driving directions, and business directory lookup.

To develop mobile applications, Oracle has created the Wireless Developer's Kit, a download that provides developers with documentation, samples, code templates, and wizards for common mobile user interface constructs. The Wireless Development Kit can be used on any PC or laptop—connected or disconnected—to build and test wireless and voice applications. Developers can use any IDE to develop their mobile application, including Oracle JDeveloper. The JDeveloper Wireless Extension includes built-in simulators that allow developers to preview the mobile application, code templates, wizards, code insight, and automatic deployment to Oracle Application Servers.

Wireless applications can be deployed in the following ways:

- **Hosted Services** Oracle provides a hosting service that maintains logins and allows access to a secure repository. This is the fastest way to implement your wireless development.

- **In-house deployment** Corporations deploy and maintain their own firewall-based security infrastructure.

- **In-house with hosted Web Services** Corporations install the Oracle9*i*AS Wireless infrastructure within their own premises while using the desired features as a Web Service.

Security is provided through a number of different protocols, depending on the type of wireless application:

- **Browser-based applications** Secured via the IEEE 802.11 protocol: HTTPS, WAP 1.2, WAP 2.0.

- **SMS (Short Message Service)** Secured via GPRS (General Packet Radio Service) protocol security; applications can use Symmetric Shared Encryption Keys.

- **E-mail** Security is usually guaranteed in the domain if the e-mail server and application server are located at the mobile operator. If the servers reside at the enterprise, a secure channel (Secure Sockets Layer [SSL] or Transport Layer Security [TLS]) needs to be used.

- **Voice** HTTPS can secure the channel between the voice gateway and the application server.

OracleAS Wireless supports the following messaging capabilities:

- **Push messaging** Messages are sent to mobile users using the notifications engine or a custom application.

- **Mobile-initiated pull messaging** Mobile users send a message to invoke a server-side application, which replies by sending a message to the mobile user.

- **Server-initiated pull messaging** The server sends a message to which the mobile user can respond.

Out of the box, the following channels and protocols are supported in OracleAS Wireless:

- **SMS, EMS, and SmartMessages** SMPP (Logica, CMG, Comverse), UCP (CMG), CIMD (Nokia), Nokia GSM Phone Modems with data cable, Mobileway V-SMSC, and Vodafone VVSP

- **MMS** SMTP (Ericsson, LogicaCMG), EAIF (Nokia), and MM7 (Ericsson, LogicaCMG)

- **E-mail** IMAP, POP3, and SMTP

- **Fax** Captaris RightFax

- **Voice notifications** VoiceGenie Voice Gateway

- **Pagers** WCTP

- **Instant messaging (IM)** Jabber (also as a gateway to AOL, MSN, Yahoo!, ICQ, and so on)

Portal Development Kit

The wizard-based approach to developing Portal components allows developers to create and deploy Web-based components and applications extremely quickly. There are, however, serious limitations to any type of wizard-based development environment. The ability to customize and extend the functionality of components generated through a wizard-based development environment is arduous at best—and impossible in many cases.

The Portal Development Kit (PDK) provides developers with tools and articles providing advanced techniques for extending the functionality of Portal components beyond what is available through the component wizards in Portal. The PDK is a framework that enables the development of portlets for seamless integration with OracleAS Portal. Using the PDK, developers can create portlets either as PL/SQL stored procedures (Database Providers) or in any other Web language, including Java, Web Services, XML, ASP, Perl, and so on (Web Providers). The PDK includes the following:

- **JPDK** Provides APIs for creating Java-based and Web Services–based portlets.

- **Java Portlet Container** Provides a run-time environment for portlets coded to the JPDK Portlet API.

- **OmniPortlet** Provides wizards that enable Portal page designers to publish SQL, XML, Web Services, spreadsheet, and existing Web page data directly to a Portal page.

- **Web Clipping Portlet** Enables page designers to collect existing Web content into centralized Portal pages as a means of content consolidation. Page designers can clip page content from an existing Web site and deliver it as a portlet to a Portal page.

- **PL/SQL Development Kit** Provides APIs for developing Database Providers.

- **Utilities** Used to simplify the development and testing of portlets.

- **Java Portlet Wizard** A JDeveloper add-in that provides a wizard-based utility for creating JPDK-based portlets.

- **PL/SQL Generator** A hosted utility that simplifies the creation of PL/SQL-based portlets.

- **Test Suite** Includes the Provider Test and Test Harness utilities for testing Web Providers without having an installation of the OracleAS Portal.

- **Samples** Various code samples highlighting development solutions.

- **Articles** Development white papers explaining development issues in depth.

Go to http://portalstudio.oracle.com for more information about downloading and installing the Portal Development Kit.

Persistence Layer Services

When you're developing Java applications that interface with Oracle, the integration between Java's object-oriented features, such as object references, business rules, complex relationships, and inheritance, and Oracle's relational database features, such as stored procedures, tables, rows, columns, and foreign keys (referred to as *object-relational [O-R] mapping*) requires an effort that is commonly underestimated by both developers and project managers. The problem of bridging object-oriented and relational technologies is referred to as *object-relational impedance mismatch*, and the fundamental differences in modeling, design, and skill sets can prolong development work. This can lead to deployed applications that are at best difficult to maintain and, at worst, unreliable and impossible to enhance. In addition to these issues, developers also need the ability to translate object-oriented data into relational data, referred to as *object-relational mapping*. A product that easily enables the integration of relational database and Java technologies, while allowing database designers and Java developers to maintain database and application design principles, would be invaluable. Oracle recognized the developer's need for these features and has created a product that not only addresses all the complex issues mentioned previously, but also adds features such as the following:

- A query framework that allows developers to define queries using various technologies

- A transaction framework that provides object-level transaction support

- Performance enhancements that include a fully configurable cache that ensures object identity

OracleAS TopLink integrates the object and relational worlds. It allows applications and application developers to manage Java objects using relational databases. OracleAS TopLink is robust enough to work with any Java-supporting database and any Application Server that supports Java and J2EE containers. Here are some of the major features of OracleAS TopLink:

- **The OracleAS Mapping Workbench** A visual tool that creates and maps metadata describing the relationship between Java classes and relational tables.

- **Advanced mapping support** This includes support for the following mappings:

 - Direct-to-Field

 - One-to-One

 - Variable One-to-One

 - One-to-Many

 - Many-to-Many

 - Aggregate Object

 - Aggregate-Collection

 - Transformation

 - Object Type

- Type Conversion

- Serialized Object

- Direct Collection

- Nested Tables

- VArrays and OREFs

- Multi-Table

- Inheritance

- **Object caching** Stores data returned as objects from the database for future use, minimizing database and network access. The following cache types are supported:

 - **Soft** Objects are maintained through garbage collection sweeps until memory is at a premium.

 - **Hard** Objects are not garbage collected.

 - **Weak** Objects exist in the cache as long as they are being used.

 - **Full** All objects are cached and not removed.

- **Query flexibility** Developers can define queries using the following items:

 - An object-oriented expression framework

 - Query By Example (QBE)

 - Enterprise JavaBeans Query Language (EJB QL)

 - SQL

 - Stored procedures

- **Object-level transaction support** Transactions are supported through the "Unit of Work," a Java-based transaction. During a Unit of Work, the application modifies business objects; when the Unit of Work is committed, OracleAS TopLink updates the database, based on what has changed, thereby executing the minimally required SQL.

OracleAS TopLink consists of three main components:

- **Development tools** Consist of the OracleAS Mapping Workbench, which creates and manages the mapping metadata that describes the relationship between Java classes and relational tables, and the OracleAS Sessions Editor, which describes how TopLink communicates with the data source at run time by creating the session.xml file.

- **Run-time tools** Consist of the Web client, an interface that interacts with any OracleAS TopLink ServerSession, and the Performance Profiler, which provides performance-tuning and run-time diagnostics.

- **Class libraries** Consist of the TopLink API, which is called at run time to retrieve and store Java objects.

Caching Services

Web caching is the process of keeping frequently used pages in memory so that the HTTP Server can display them quickly instead of repeatedly processing requests for those URLs. By implementing caching, you allow your clients to experience faster page retrievals, and you greatly reduce the load on the Web Server. It is one of the most effective ways to scale your application without the need for recoding or purchasing new hardware.

Oracle Application Server 10*g* contains a component called the Web Cache. It is a content-aware service that improves the performance, scalability, and availability of Web sites. OracleAS Web Cache 10*g* uses caching and compression technologies to optimize application performance and more efficiently utilize low-cost, existing hardware resources. Built-in workload management features ensure application reliability and help maintain quality of service under heavy loads. And new in this release, end-user performance-monitoring features provide unparalleled insight into end-user service levels. The real power of OracleAS Web Cache is its ability to cache both static and dynamically generated pages.

The Web Cache can be configured to run on its own server or on the middle-tier server (see Figure 45-8). In either configuration, the Web Cache is placed in front of the Web Server to cache pages and provide content to those browsers that request it. If the Web Cache, acting as a virtual server or virtual request router, can satisfy these requests, it will provide content to the clients. If the requested content is not cached by the Web Cache or has been marked invalid for any reason, the content is retrieved from the Web Server and cached in the Web Cache. OracleAS Web Cache allows you to define invalidation rules, which can be used to control the amount and types of cached content in your server. Some of the key benefits of OracleAS Web Cache can be measured by dramatic improvements in the following areas:

- **Resource usage** Higher throughput and scalability.

- **User experience** Faster response times without sacrificing personalization.

- **Availability** Intelligent workload management.

- **Productivity** No need to roll your own cache means faster time-to-market.

- **Bottom line** Reduced infrastructure load translates into cost savings.

- **Intelligence** Better visibility into end-user service levels.

Some of the key features of OracleAS Web Cache include

- Efficient use of low-cost hardware

- Fine-grained cache control

- Workload management and reliability

- End-user experience management

- Advanced networking

- Single-vendor manageability and integration

- Flexible deployments

Sample Web Cache Topology 1 (Simplest administration, least flexibility)

Sample Web Cache Topology 2 (Higher cost of administration, greater flexibility)

Sample Web Cache Topology 3 (Highest cost of administration, greatest flexibility)

FIGURE 45-8. *Possible Web Cache topologies*

The new features of OracleAS Web Cache include enhancements in the following categories:

■ **End-user performance management** This is the most significant new Web Cache feature. Administrators can configure OracleAS Web Cache to measure end-user response times for individual URLs, sets of URLs, or even entire Web-based applications, regardless of whether the URLs are cached. The Analyze functionality lets you view detailed reports in context by group, URL, domain, visitor, or application, as well as in a daily, weekly, or monthly context. Further drill-downs provide you with response time and load distribution information to help balance Web server resources.

■ **Security** Web Cache now supports applications that require client-side SSL certificates for PKI-based authentication. Oracle Application Server now supports nCipher's BHAPI-compliant hardware for deployment on servers running Web Cache and/or Oracle HTTP Server.

■ **Caching** Previously, administrators could either cache one version of a page for all browsers or cache one version for each browser type and version. Now, administrators can customize the caching rules to define groups of browsers that will share a cached version of a page.

■ **Invalidation** The 9.0.4 release of Web Cache introduces an inline invalidation mechanism as an additional means of managing content freshness. Inline invalidation provides a useful way for origin servers to "piggyback" invalidation messages on transactional responses sent to Web Cache. In previous releases of Web Cache, the URL-based cache key was the unique identifier for a cached document. Invalidation requests needed to specify either exact URLs or a set of URLs and headers matching a regular expression in order to invalidate cached objects. Because it can be difficult for applications to map URLs to the underlying data used to generate those URLs, Web Cache invalidation has been extended in 9.0.4 to support search keys. Cached objects can now be associated with multiple application-specified search keys, with the URL-based key being the primary key.

■ **Compression** The Web Cache compression engine now supports self-describing compression policies and more compressible content by compressing documents containing session-encoded URLs, ESI tags, or the <!--WEBCACHETAG--> and <!--WEBCACHEEND--> tags.

■ **Load balancing and request routing** Support for session binding in a cache cluster allows Web Cache to bind a user session to a particular origin Web server. This feature is used to consecutively route requests for a unique session to the same origin server, allowing stateful load balancing.

■ **HTTP protocol support** OracleAS Web Cache now supports chunked transfer encoding. HTTP 1.0 (with connection keep-alive) was used in prior releases of Web Cache, which caused problems for servers that generated dynamic content with unknown content length. OracleAS's support for HTTP 1.1 allows for a persistent connection to the Web Cache, even when content length is undetermined.

■ **Usability and manageability** OracleAS Web Cache now includes improved access logging, event logging and diagnostics, reporting on popular cache misses, integration with Oracle Process Management and Notification (OPMN), and dynamic configuration for select parameters.

Figure 45-9 shows the administration screen for the Web Cache Server. The Database Cache, introduced in Oracle9*i*AS Release 1, has been discontinued.

System Services

Oracle provides numerous system services to help make your interaction with Oracle Application Server 10*g* easier. Most of the system services made available through the Enterprise Manager Application Server Control Web pages are of interest mainly to administrators, but developers will benefit from an understanding of the Application Server Control pages when the deployment of applications is discussed.

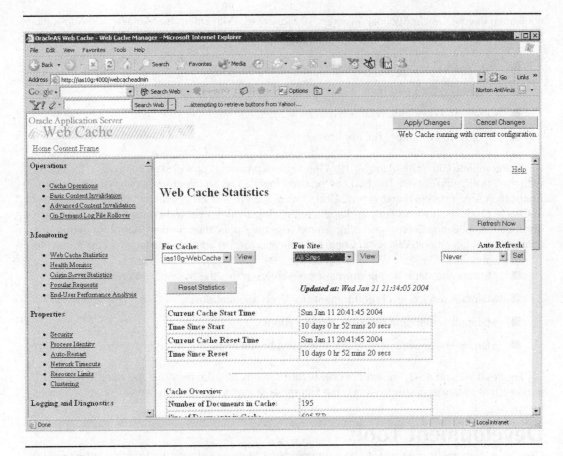

FIGURE 45-9. *The Web Cache administration screen*

Enterprise Manager 10g Grid Control

Oracle Application Server 10g is supported by a Web-based management system—Oracle Enterprise Manager 10g. Enterprise Manager provides both a simple, out-of-box application server administration interface and a comprehensive system for managing and monitoring large-scale Oracle systems.

The Application Server administration interface, known as *Application Server Control,* is automatically installed with Oracle Application Server 10g. It is designed to help you manage your individual Application Server instances, Application Server farms (an Application Server grouped with its corresponding infrastructure), and Oracle Application Server clusters. From the Application Server Control, you can monitor the entire Oracle Application Server platform (including J2EE, Portal, Wireless, and Business Intelligence components) and perform administrative tasks, such as configuration changes to your application server components and real-time monitoring of all services

configured in your Oracle Application Server 10*g* instances. With Enterprise Manager 10*g* Application Server Control, administrators can do the following:

- Manage and configure Application Server components.
- Monitor server performance and Application Server logs.
- Create and configure J2EE services.
- Deploy and monitor J2EE applications.

The complete Enterprise Manager 10*g* Grid Control product is provided as an optional installation with the Application Server. The two can be used together as an integrated system for complete Application Server system management. Grid Control is a Web-based system for central management of Oracle products, host systems, and applications. It provides a central console for monitoring distributed Application Servers and is integrated with the Application Server Control for performing administration operations. With Grid Control, Application Server administrators can do the following:

- Monitor the status and performance of servers across the business enterprise.
- Maintain service-level requirements for Web applications.
- Maintain system and software configurations.
- Manage the entire system stack employed by the application server system.

Figures 45-2 and 45-3, shown previously, are screens for administering the middle tier and infrastructure instances, respectively, via the Enterprise Manager Application Server Control Web site.

Development Tools

Does your Web application have to be written in Java? Many developers believe that to be true, but as you will see, you have many options available to you as an Oracle developer. Oracle provides numerous tools that allow you to leverage existing (or legacy) code into applications that can be deployed over the Web with minimal effort. In general, there are two types of Web applications:

- **HTML-based** Application code (residing on the server or in an Oracle database) that produces a series of HTML pages. There is no limitation as to what language is used to generate these pages.
- **Applet-based** Java code downloaded to the client's browser and executed there. Applets give the developer full control of the interface, but at a price—the time needed to download the applet may be prohibitive for all but the most trivial of applications.

Except for Discoverer Plus and Portal, there is no development environment provided with Oracle Application Server 10*g*. You will have to make a decision as to what technology to use when beginning your development. No "one" tool is perfect for solving all your development needs, and virtually all organizations use a combination of different tools and technologies. The most valuable developers in modern IT shops are those who are fluent in numerous technologies.

Choosing the right development tool is not an easy task, and it is not a decision to be made lightly. Human nature being what it is, people tend to gravitate to things they know and feel comfortable with. Some hard questions need to be answered before deciding on a technology— or a combination of technologies.

How Will Your Application Be Accessed?

It is not enough to deploy an application over the Web and then not worry about how users will access it, although this was the original promise of browser-based applications. There are three basic ways of delivering your application, and each one of these will affect the development decisions you will need to make:

- **Intranet** In this environment, users access the application over a network inside a company or organization, which uses software like that used on the Internet but is for internal use only and not accessible to the public. This option gives you the most flexibility in your development decisions because there is some likelihood that users of your application will have fast network connections and a single browser.

- **Extranet** In this environment, users access the application over a private network that uses the Internet protocols and the public telecommunications system to share a business's information, data, or operations with external suppliers, vendors, or customers. An extranet can be viewed as the external part of a company's intranet. Here, your development options begin to decrease because there will be questions regarding browser types and firewall issues, which may block certain types of communications between the clients and the server.

- **Internet** In this environment, users can access the application from anywhere in the world. This option has the least amount of flexibility in terms of your development decisions, because the application will have to be "generic" enough to support all types of browsers and all types of access (dial-up, broadband, and so on). It will be almost impossible to deliver any applet-based application via this method.

How Complex Is the User Interface?

Applets give the developer the greatest control over the look and feel of the user interface. As mentioned before, this comes at a great price—namely, the time required to download the applet to the browser. In an intranet or extranet setting, this may be acceptable, but it will be virtually impossible to serve applets over the Internet. If it is decided to go with an HTML-based application, it must be determined whether users can be productive with a standard interface, or if sophisticated HTML tools (such as Dreamweaver) will need to be utilized to create something more complex.

What Types of Users Will Be Using Your Application?

In general, users can be broken into three categories:

- **Casual users** For these users, speed is the most important factor. Casual users will probably demand that an application start with minimal load time and provide data access immediately. These users will usually be satisfied with HTML-based applications.

■ **"Heads-down" users** These users work with an application for an extended period of time, and a startup period of a minute will probably be acceptable in a trade-off to the productivity gains realized throughout the day. These users may benefit from an Applet-based application.

■ **Power users** These users demand applications they can customize—either the interface of the application or the types of queries and data used in the application. For these users, flexibility and interaction are the most important features, which will probably require an Applet-based application.

Oracle Forms

Oracle Forms is one of Oracle's oldest and most mature development products. It has been traditionally used to create client/server applications. It is similar in design and philosophy to Microsoft's Visual Basic development environment. Countless Forms-based applications are still in production environments around the world today.

As development efforts started moving toward Web- and browser-based deployments, the demand to create an environment that still supports Forms-based development (preserving legacy code and knowledge) and introduces Web deployment (eliminating the high cost of maintaining clients with multiple operating systems, nonstandard configurations, and so on) began to grow.

Oracle Application Server 10*g* includes a service called the *Forms Server* that is installed with the Business Intelligence and Forms option. It handles serving Oracle Forms over the Web, gathering metrics to assist in administration and tuning, and integrating with Oracle's Identity Management features. There are numerous configuration parameters to modify virtually every aspect of the Forms environment on the Web.

Starting with Oracle Forms 9*i* (the current version is Oracle Forms 10*g*), Oracle no longer provides the Forms run-time environment to deploy Forms in a traditional client-server environment. The only way to test an Oracle Form you have developed is to run it as a Web form through a Forms Server provided with the Oracle Forms 10*g* development environment.

Oracle Reports

Much of what has been said about Oracle Forms also applies to Oracle Reports. It is a mature and stable product that allows developers to create reports quickly and easily. It also suffers from the high administration costs of deployment because Reports run-time libraries need to be installed and maintained on every machine that needs to run an Oracle Report.

The Reports Server can be configured to integrate with Oracle's Identity Management features for security. Like Oracle Forms 9*i*, every version of Oracle Reports since 9*i* (the current version is Oracle Reports 10*g*) no longer provides the Reports run-time environment to run Oracle Reports in a traditional client-server environment. The only way to test a report you have developed is to run it as a Web report through a Reports Server provided with the Oracle Reports 10*g* development environment.

Multiple Reports Servers can be defined for each middle tier in Oracle Application Server 10*g*. This gives another layer of scalability for your environment. If you wish to integrate Reports with Oracle Portal, you can create calendars in Portal to limit the access times for certain reports, Report Servers, and printers. You can also use the Portal security model to limit access to any of these components.

Oracle Discoverer

As mentioned earlier in this chapter, Oracle Discoverer Server contains a component to view and interact with Discoverer Worksheets over the Web (Discoverer Viewer) and a component to create and modify Worksheets (Discoverer Plus). The ad hoc capabilities of Oracle Discoverer can allow your development staff to offload reports design and generation to power users. By putting the full capabilities of the Discoverer desktop onto the Web, Oracle makes the implementation of Discoverer a simple experience for most organizations.

Discoverer also integrates seamlessly with Oracle Portal via an internal portlet provided by Oracle called the *Discoverer portlet*. This portlet allows you define the Workbook and Worksheet you wish to display, any parameters to be passed to the Worksheet, and a Refresh Options setting that allows you to specify the length of time a particular report will be cached (in Portal's Cache, not the Web Cache). The Discoverer Worksheet becomes a portlet and can have any of Portal's security and display properties applied to it.

Java Tools

In an integrated development environment (IDE), the tools have been integrated to collaborate with each other (for example, the output of one tool can be used as the input for another tool). Attempting to build Java applications without an IDE using the free Java compiler provided in the Java Software Development Kit from Sun is possible, but it's a less-than-optimal environment. Oracle's Java IDE, JDeveloper, has so many essential tools, only the hardiest of Java programmers would ever attempt to build production-quality Java applications without it. Here's a quick list of JDeveloper's most prominent features:

- **Three profiling modes** These modes enable you to create a statistical analysis of the performance of your application with respect to its functionality, both at compile time and run time; its use of memory in the Java heap; and the occurrence and duration of various events.

- **A public Extension SDK** This enables the development environment to be extended and customized.

- **Native support for SQL, PL/SQL, and XML** This support includes syntax highlighting and code insight, as well as PL/SQL development, PL/SQL debugging, and SQL tuning. Additionally, JDeveloper provides direct access to the database, allowing you to create, view, modify, and delete tables, views, triggers, indexes, sequences, and more.

- **Robust debugging support for both Java and PL/SQL** Debugging in these two environments is seamlessly integrated when an Oracle9*i* or later database is used, giving you the ability to step from Java code directly into PL/SQL code within the same debugging session.

- **Class diagrams** The goal of class modeling is to visualize classes or components—and the relationships between them—that compose all or part of a system design. Classes and components modeled on a class diagram are synchronized to ensure that changes made to modeled elements are reflected in their implementation files and that changes to the implementation files are visualized on the diagram.

■ **Activity diagrams** Processes performed in a business or system can be visualized using modeled activities, flows, and states on activity diagrams. An activity can represent a single process, or it can represent a subactivity model (that is, the activity can be broken down into a set of subactivities, which themselves form an activity model).

■ **All aspects of EJB development, from conception to implementation** EJB support includes modeling and wizard-based development of EJB sessions; entity and message-driven beans; the ability to add, edit, and delete EJBs and EJB properties using the EJB Module Editor; reverse-engineering of database tables and foreign key relationships as CMP (Container-Managed Persistence) entity beans and CMRs (Container Managed Relationships); the ability to test EJBs locally in the IDE; and the ability to check EJBs for deployment errors and inconsistencies using the EJB Verifier.

■ **J2EE deployment** Allows developers to package and assemble J2EE modules into standard archives such as EJBs, JARs, WARs, and EARs. These archives can be deployed with a single click to Oracle Application Server Containers for J2EE (OC4J).

■ **Built-in J2EE Applications Framework** Oracle Business Components for Java (BC4J) is a standards-based, server-side framework for creating scalable, high-performance J2EE applications. The framework provides design-time facilities and run-time services to simplify the task of building, debugging, customizing, and reusing business components.

■ **Application Development Framework (ADF)** This is the most exciting new feature of JDeveloper for developers. The ADF is Oracle's solution to the ever-increasing complexity of the J2EE platform. Based on the Model-View-Controller (MVC) architecture, Oracle ADF lets application developers focus on the business domain rather than on the underlying technologies. By using visual, declarative, and guided-coding techniques, the framework allows application developers who are not J2EE experts to quickly become productive. The framework is based on industry standards, allowing applications built with ADF to be deployed on any J2EE server and connect to any SQL database.

■ **Integration of the TopLink Mapping Workbench** Oracle JDeveloper 10*g* seamlessly integrates with the Mapping Workbench, giving developers the ability to do the following:

 ■ Automatically map descriptors

 ■ Generate database schemas from object models

 ■ Generate object models from database schemas

 ■ Generate both CMP (Container-Managed Persistence) and BMP (Bean-Managed Persistence) entity beans

 ■ Import an object model from any IDE or UML modeling tool

 ■ Connect and interact with any relational database with a JDBC-compliant driver

HTML DB

HTML DB occupies a unique space in the world of Oracle Web development. It is a Web development tool, but it is not part of the Oracle Application Server 10*g* product stack. The Oracle HTML DB engine is stored in the database, and is accessible via the HTTP Server that comes

standard with the Oracle10*g* database. It is intended primarily for simple Web-based applications that do not require the sophisticated features provided with Oracle Application Server 10*g*. HTML DB is composed of three main pieces:

- **Application Builder** Helps you assemble an HTML user interface on top of database objects. The Oracle HTML DB engine takes care of presenting your application using templates and UI elements.

- **SQL Workshop** Enables you to interact with the database through a Web browser. With it, you can view or create database objects, run SQL commands, and query by example.

- **Data Workshop** Helps you import plain-text and spreadsheet data into database tables and export data from database tables.

All HTML DB applications are displayed in your browser from data queried from the database, called *application definitions.* This metadata provides information about your application to the HTML DB engine, and therefore no code is generated (or needed). The Oracle HTML DB rendering engine reads the application definition and displays the application accordingly.

CHAPTER
46

The Hitchhiker's Guide to Database Administration

n this chapter, you will see the basic steps involved in administering an Oracle Database 10*g* database. There are many components to the database administrator (DBA) job, and there are books written specifically for DBAs. This chapter will provide an overview of the tasks of a DBA, along with guidance on the usage of standard DBA tools. This chapter does not provide a full, detailed description of every DBA task.

In earlier chapters, you have already seen many of the functions of a DBA, such as creating tables, indexes, views, users, synonyms, database links, and packages. The DBA topics described in this chapter will therefore focus on the production-control functions of the DBA role:

- Creating a database

- Starting and stopping the database

- Sizing and managing the memory areas for the database

- Allocating and managing space for the objects

- Creating and managing undo

- Performing backups

For each of these topics, many options are available to developers and DBAs. The following sections of this chapter should provide you with enough information to get started, and to learn what questions to ask of your DBAs and system administrators. For further details on all of these topics, see *Oracle DBA Handbook*.

Creating a Database

The simplest way to generate a **create database** script is via the Oracle Universal Installer (OUI). When you install Oracle, OUI gives you the option to create a database. If you use that option, OUI will create a small database that is useful for practice or as the basis for application development. The **create database** scripts provided by Oracle give you a solid template for your standard **create database** scripts. A sample **create database** script is shown in Chapter 2. See the **create database** entry in the Alphabetical Reference for the full command syntax.

The **create database** command is issued from within SQL*Plus, via an account with the SYSDBA system privilege:

```
connect system/manager as sysdba
startup nomount
create database...
```

To issue **connect as SYSDBA** successfully, you must have the proper authorization at the operating-system and database levels. See your operating-system–specific Oracle documentation for information on the operating-system rights needed.

Using the Oracle Enterprise Manager

Oracle Enterprise Manager (OEM), a graphical user interface (GUI) tool, is supplied as part of the standard Oracle toolset to enable DBAs to manage databases from a personal computer.

The OEM toolset provides a robust interface for remote database administration. All DBAs can use the same central OEM repository (a set of tables created in a database) to perform their work. In addition to those changes, OEM includes task scheduling and assignment features to enable around-the-clock database coverage.

You must make several key decisions before installing and configuring OEM. You need to decide where the OEM repository is to be created and how and when you are going to perform backups to protect this repository. Since you can use OEM as an interface to Oracle Recovery Manager (RMAN), recovery information can be stored in the OEM repository. You may want to create a small, separate database in which to store the OEM repository. You should ensure that this database is backed up frequently so that recovery of the repository itself is assured.

If you are the only DBA working with the OEM toolset, you will not have to consider who will handle administration of specific databases in your environment. If there are several DBAs at the site, you will need to determine task definitions, database responsibilities, and schedules. With OEM, you can grant levels of access and privilege to each DBA in the group on a task-by-task basis. You can configure OEM to enable you to send e-mail requests and assignments to other DBAs or take control of a problem to speed resolution.

If you have a previous version of OEM installed, migrate that repository to the newest version to take advantage of the new features. If you have more than one repository on your system, you will need to take precautions to ensure that you migrate each version of the repository without damaging currently stored information.

Oracle supports the Simple Network Messaging Protocol (SNMP). By supporting SNMP, Oracle products can be easily integrated into monitoring tools for systems and networks.

Although you do not have to use OEM, it provides a common GUI for managing your databases. As your enterprise grows in size (and in number of databases and DBAs), the consistency of the DBA interface will support consistent implementation of your change-control and production-control processes.

OEM enables you to manage Real Application Clusters (RAC) environments and Grid environments. By providing a graphical interface to the administration or the database, OEM simplifies the learning curve for new DBAs and allows very complex functions to be performed easily.

Starting and Stopping the Database

To start a database, issue the **startup** command from within SQL*Plus, as shown in the following listing. In the examples in this chapter, the name of the database is MYDB.

```
connect system/manager as sysdba;
startup open MYDB;
```

Alternatively, you can mount the database:

```
connect system/manager as sysdba;
startup mount MYDB;
```

When the database is mounted but not open, you can manage its files. For example, if you moved some of the database's files while the database was shut down, you need to let Oracle know where to find them before it will restart. To give the new locations of the files, you can mount the

database (as shown in the preceding listing) and then use the **alter database** command to rename the old files to their new locations. Once you have finished telling Oracle the new locations for the files, you can open the database via the **alter database open** command.

Four primary options are available for shutting down the database. In a normal shutdown (the default), Oracle waits for all users to log out of the database before shutting down. In a transactional shutdown, Oracle waits for active transactions to complete before shutting down. In an immediate shutdown, Oracle rolls back all existing uncommitted transactions and logs out any users currently logged in. In an abort shutdown, the database immediately shuts down, and all uncommitted transactions are lost.

NOTE
While the database is in the process of shutting down or starting up, no new logins are permitted.

To perform a normal shutdown, use the **shutdown** command. For a transactional shutdown, use **shutdown transactional**. An immediate shutdown, as shown in the following listing, uses the **shutdown immediate** version of the **shutdown** command. To abort the database, use **shutdown abort**.

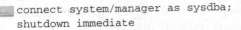

```
connect system/manager as sysdba;
shutdown immediate
```

If you use **shutdown abort**, Oracle will automatically perform recovery operations during the next database startup. A **shutdown abort** may also be useful in situations where the database needs to be stopped in the shortest possible time, for example, for an impending power failure. During the subsequent startup, Oracle will perform any necessary recovery operations.

You may also use OEM to start up and shut down the instance, via the General tab on the Instance Manager/Configuration screen.

Sizing and Managing Memory Areas

When you start a database, Oracle allocates a memory area (the System Global Area, or SGA) shared by all of the database users. The two largest areas of the SGA are usually the *database buffer cache* and the *shared pool*; their size will directly impact the memory requirements for the database and the performance of database operations. Their sizes are controlled by parameters in the database's initialization file.

The database buffer cache is an area in the SGA used to hold the data blocks that are read from the data segments in the database, such as tables and indexes. The size of the database buffer cache is determined by the DB_CACHE_SIZE parameter (expressed in terms of number of bytes) in the initialization parameter file for the database. The default size for the database blocks is set via the DB_BLOCK_SIZE parameter specified in the parameter file during database creation. Managing the size of the database buffer cache is an important part of managing and tuning the database.

The database has a default block size, but you can establish cache areas for different database block sizes and then create tablespaces to use those caches. For example, you can create a 4KB block size database with some tablespaces set to 8KB. The size of the 8KB cache would be set via the

DB_8K_CACHE_SIZE parameter. To create tablespaces to use that cache, specify **blocksize 8K** as part of the **create tablespace** command. If the default block size for the database is 4KB, you would not set a value for DB_4K_CACHE_SIZE; the size specified for DB_CACHE_SIZE would be used for the 4KB cache.

NOTE
The cache for the block size must exist before you create a tablespace that uses that block size.

The different cache areas can be resized while the database is running. The caches must be increased or decreased in *granules*. For a database with an SGA less than 128M, the granule size is 4M—so DB_8K_CACHE_SIZE can be 4M, 8M, 12M, and so on. If you attempt to use any other setting, Oracle will round it up to the next granule size. The following listing shows the setting of the DB_8K_CACHE_SIZE parameter.

```
alter system set DB_8K_CACHE_SIZE = 8m;
```

If you create a tablespace that uses a non-default database block size, you must be sure that the related cache size parameter (such as DB_8K_CACHE_SIZE) is updated in your database parameter file. If you are using an init.ora file, you must update it with the new value. If you are using a system parameter file (the preferred method), it will be automatically updated when you execute the **alter system** command with the **scope=both** clause.

NOTE
You cannot alter the SGA_MAX_SIZE or JAVA_POOL_SIZE parameter values while the database is open.

Oracle will manage the space in the buffer caches by using an algorithm that keeps the most actively used blocks in memory for as long as possible. When free space is needed in the cache, the new data blocks will either use the space occupied by infrequently accessed blocks or the space occupied by a modified block once it has been written out to disk.

If the SGA is not large enough to hold the most frequently used data, different objects will contend for space within the data block buffer cache. Contention is particularly likely when multiple applications use the same database and thus share the same SGA. In that case, the most recently used tables and indexes from each application constantly contend for space in the SGA with the most recently used objects from other applications. As a result, requests for data from the data block buffer cache will result in a lower ratio of "hits" to "misses." Data block buffer cache misses result in physical I/Os for data reads, resulting in performance degradation.

The shared pool stores the data dictionary cache (information about the database structures) and the *library cache* (information about statements that are run against the database). While the data block buffer and dictionary cache enable sharing of structural and data information among users in the database, the library cache allows the sharing of commonly used SQL statements.

The shared pool contains the execution plan and parse tree for SQL statements run against the database. The second time that an identical SQL statement is run (by any user), Oracle is able to take advantage of the parse information available in the shared pool to expedite the statement's

execution. Like the data block buffer cache, the shared pool is managed via an LRU algorithm. As the shared pool fills, less recently used execution paths and parse trees will be removed from the library cache to make room for new entries. If the shared pool is too small, statements will be continually reloaded into the library cache, affecting performance.

The size (in bytes) of the shared pool is set via the SHARED_POOL_SIZE initialization parameter. Like the other caches, the shared pool size can be altered while the database is open.

As of Oracle Database 10g, you can use Automatic Shared Memory Management (ASMM). To activate ASMM, set a nonzero value for the SGA_TARGET database initialization parameter. After you set SGA_TARGET to the size of the SGA you want (that is, all of the caches added together), you then set the other cache-related parameters (DB_CACHE_SIZE, SHARED_POOL_SIZE, JAVA_POOL_SIZE, and LARGE_POOL_SIZE) each to 0. Shut down and restart the database for those changes to take effect; the database will then begin actively managing the sizes of the different caches. You can monitor the sizes of the caches at any time via the V$SGASTAT dynamic performance view.

NOTE
While the database is running, you can alter the SGA_TARGET parameter value and Oracle will automatically alter the sizes of the related caches.

As the workload in the database changes, the database will alter the cache sizes to reflect the needs of the application. For example, if there is a heavy batch-processing load at night and a more intensive online transaction load during the day, the database may alter the cache sizes as the load changes. These changes occur automatically, without DBA intervention. If you specify a value for a pool in your initialization parameter file, then Oracle will use that as the minimum value for that pool.

NOTE
DBAs can create KEEP and RECYCLE pools in the buffer cache. KEEP and RECYCLE pools are not affected by the dynamic cache resizing.

From within OEM, you can see if dynamic memory management is enabled by clicking on the Memory Parameters option; the Automatic Shared Memory Management button can be set to Enabled or Disabled.

The Initialization Parameter File

The characteristics of the database instance—such as the size of the SGA and the number of background processes—are specified during startup. These parameters are stored in a binary file called the system parameter file. To generate the system parameter file for an open database, use the **create spfile** command. You can generate a readable version of the system parameter file via the **create pfile from spfile** command. See the Alphabetical Reference for the command syntax for these commands. The "pfile" version of the parameter file, formerly known as the init.ora file, usually contains the database name as part of the filename. For example, a database named MYDB may have a pfile file named initmydb.ora. In general, you should use the server parameter file option for managing your parameter settings because it supports dynamic changes to the parameters while the database is running.

Allocating and Managing Space for the Objects

When a database is created, it is divided into multiple logical sections called *tablespaces*. The SYSTEM tablespace is the first tablespace created, and the SYSAUX tablespace is created as part of every Oracle Database 10*g* database. You can then create additional tablespaces to hold different types of data (such as tables, indexes, and undo segments). As of Oracle Database 10*g*, tablespaces can be renamed via the **rename to** clause of the **alter tablespace** command.

When a tablespace is created, *datafiles* are created to hold its data. These files immediately allocate the space specified during their creation. Each datafile can support only one tablespace. Datafiles can be set to automatically extend when they run out of space; you can set the increment by which they extend and their maximum size. Each user's schema is a collection of logical database objects, such as tables and indexes, that refer to physical data structures that are stored in tablespaces. Objects from a user's schema may be stored in multiple tablespaces, and a single tablespace can contain objects from multiple schemas.

When a database object (such as a table or index) is created, it is assigned to a tablespace via user defaults or specific instructions. A *segment* is created in that tablespace to hold the data associated with that object.

A segment is made up of sections called *extents*—contiguous sets of Oracle blocks. Once the existing extents can no longer hold new data, the segment will obtain another extent. If a segment is composed of multiple extents, there is no guarantee that those extents will be contiguous.

Tablespaces can be created as locally managed (the default) or dictionary managed. In a dictionary-managed tablespace, the extent location information is stored in the data dictionary. In a locally managed tablespace, that data is stored in the datafile headers. Oracle encourages the use of locally managed tablespaces. To review, databases have one or more tablespaces, and tablespaces consist of one or more datafiles. Within those tablespaces, Oracle stores segments for database objects. Each segment can have multiple extents.

Managing the space used by tablespaces, datafiles, segments, and database objects is one of the basic functions of the DBA. The intent of this overview is to aid you in the planning of their physical storage. As you will see, Oracle Database 10*g* adds new features that simplify space planning and management.

Implications of the storage Clause

The amount of space used by a segment is determined by its storage parameters. These parameters are determined by the database at segment-creation time; if no specific storage parameters are given in the **create table**, **create index**, or **create cluster** command, then the database will use the default storage parameters for the tablespace in which the segment is to be stored.

NOTE
*You can assign default tablespaces to users, and assign space quotas within those tablespaces, via the **create user**, **alter user**, and **grant** commands. See the Alphabetical Reference for the command syntax.*

When you create a table, index, or other segment, you can use the default values for a locally managed tablespace (the recommended option) or specify a **storage** clause as part of the **create**

command. You can also specify a **tablespace** clause, enabling you to direct Oracle to store the data in a particular tablespace. For example, a **create table** command in a dictionary-managed tablespace may include the following clauses:

```
tablespace USERS
storage (initial 1M next 1M pctincrease 0
minextents 1 maxextents 200)
```

If no **storage** clause is specified, the tablespace's default storage parameters will be used. For a locally managed USERS tablespace, the **create table** command would only need to include

```
tablespace USERS
```

The storage parameters specify the **initial** extent size, the **next** extent size, the **pctincrease** (a factor by which each successive extent will geometrically grow), the **maxextents** (maximum number of extents), and the **minextents** (minimum number of extents). After the segment has been created, the **initial** and **minextents** values cannot be altered unless you perform a reorganization of the object. The default values for the storage parameters for each tablespace are available in the DBA_TABLESPACES and USER_TABLESPACES views.

When you create a tablespace, you specify its default storage parameters. The following command creates a locally managed tablespace and specifies its default storage parameters. See the syntax for **create tablespace** in the Alphabetical Reference.

```
create tablespace CODES_TABLES
datafile '/u01/oracle/VLDB/codes_tables.dbf' size 10M
extent management local uniform size 256K;
```

When a segment is created, it will acquire at least one extent. The initial extent will be used to store data until it no longer has any free space available (the **pctfree** clause can be used to reserve a percentage of space within each block in the segment to remain available for updates of existing rows). If you create a dictionary-managed tablespace, the extent sizes may not be uniform; the segment will extend by obtaining a second extent of the size specified by the **next** parameter. By default, tablespaces will be created with local extent management.

Assuming that the block size for the database in which this tablespace is created is 4KB in this example, the tablespace is created with the extent management declared as **local** and with a uniform size of 256KB. Each bit in the bitmap describes 64 blocks (256/4). If the **uniform size** clause is omitted, the default is **autoallocate**. The default **size** for **uniform** is 1MB.

NOTE
*If you specify **local** in a **create tablespace** command, you cannot specify a **default storage** clause, **minextents**, or **temporary**.*

Locally managed tablespaces can take over some of the space management tasks performed by DBAs in dictionary-managed tablespaces. Because of their architecture, they are less likely to be fragmented, and their objects are less likely to have space-related problems.

NOTE
As of Oracle9i Release 2 (version 9.2), you can create a locally managed SYSTEM tablespace.

You can create a set of locally managed tablespaces with a small number of storage parameters and resolve most of the space requests in your database. For example, you could create three DATA tablespaces as shown here:

```
create tablespace DATA_SMALL
datafile '/u01/oracle/VLDB/data_small.dbf'
size 10M
extent management local uniform size 1M;

create tablespace DATA_MEDIUM
datafile '/u01/oracle/VLDB/data_medium.dbf'
size 100M
extent management local uniform size 4M;

create tablespace DATA_LARGE
datafile '/u01/oracle/VLDB/data_large.dbf'
size 1000M
extent management local uniform size 16M;
```

In this example, the DATA_SMALL tablespace creates objects with extent sizes that are each 1MB; DATA_MEDIUM uses 4MB extent sizes, and DATA_LARGE uses 16MB extent sizes. If you have a small table, simply place it in the DATA_SMALL tablespace. If it grows significantly in size, you can move it to the DATA_MEDIUM or DATA_LARGE tablespace.

Within each of these example tablespaces, all objects will have the same storage parameters, simplifying any future maintenance you perform. Using consistent extent sizes also improves the reuse of space once an object has been dropped from the tablespace or moved.

The following sections describe space management of each major object type. Note that if you use locally managed tablespaces, many of the **storage** clause issues do not apply; you rely on the tablespace to manage the space based on the parameters defined at the tablespace level. Although this may result in some overallocation of space, it will greatly simplify the space management operations in your database.

Table Segments

Table segments, also called *data segments*, store the rows of data associated with tables or clusters. Each data segment contains a header block that serves as a space directory for the segment.

Once a data segment acquires an extent, it keeps that extent until the segment is either dropped, **truncate**d, or compressed via the Oracle Database 10g options. Deleting rows from a table via the **delete** command has no impact on the amount of space that has been allocated to that table. The number of extents will increase until either (1) the **maxextents** value is reached (if one is set), (2) the user's quota in the tablespace is reached, or (3) the tablespace runs out of space (if the datafiles cannot autoextend).

To minimize the amount of wasted space in a data block, tune the **pctfree** parameter. The **pctfree** parameter specifies the amount of space that will be kept free within each datablock. The free space can then be used when **NULL**-valued columns are updated to have values, or when updates to other values in the row force the total length of the row to increase. The proper setting of **pctfree** is application-specific since it is dependent on the nature of the updates that are being performed.

You can use the **alter table** command to alter most storage parameters for an existing table. You can use the **move** option of the **alter table** command to change the tablespace assignment for a table.

Index Segments

Like table segments, *index segments* hold the space that has been allocated to them until they are dropped; however, they can also be indirectly dropped if the table or cluster they index is dropped. To minimize contention, indexes should be stored in a tablespace that is different from the tablespace that holds their associated tables.

Index segments in dictionary-managed tablespaces have **storage** clauses that specify their **initial**, **next**, **minextents**, **maxextents**, and **pctincrease** values, and they are as likely to be fragmented as their tables are.

You can use the **rebuild** option of the **alter index** command to alter the **storage** and **tablespace** settings for an index. In the following listing, the JOB_PK index is rebuilt in the INDEXES tablespace.

```
alter index JOB_PK rebuild
tablespace INDEXES;
```

During the index **rebuild** process, both the old and the new indexes will temporarily coexist in the database. Therefore, you must have enough space available to store both indexes prior to executing the **alter index rebuild** command.

While the index is being built, the optimizer can gather statistics about the index's contents. Use the **compute statistics** clause of the **create index** and **alter index rebuild** commands to generate the statistics while the index is being built; the combined operation will be faster than separate creation and statistics-gathering commands.

Rollback Segments and System-Managed Undo

Rollback segments can dynamically shrink to a specified size, or they can be manually shrunk to a size of your choosing. The **optimal** clause, which allows rollback segments to shrink to an **optimal** size after extending, helps to provide interim support to systems that have not been properly implemented for the way they are being used. For system-managed undo (SMU), Oracle automatically allocates and deallocates undo segments as processing requires.

You can use *Automatic Undo Management* to place all undo data in a single tablespace. When you create an undo tablespace, Oracle manages the storage, retention, and space utilization for your rollback data via SMU.

To start using SMU, you must first create an undo tablespace using the following command:

```
create undo tablespace undo_tablespace datafile 'filespec' size n;
```

Next, set the UNDO_MANAGEMENT initialization parameter in your system parameter file or init.ora file to AUTO. Specify your undo tablespace via the UNDO_TABLESPACE initialization parameter. You will not need to create or manage any rollback segments within the undo tablespace.

Setting Undo Retention

You can explicitly manage how long Oracle retains undo data in the undo tablespace via the UNDO_RETENTION initialization parameter. Retaining undo serves two purposes: it supports the retention of inactive, in-use data for long-running queries, and it supports queries that show the prior state of current data (see Chapter 27).

For example, if you set

```
UNDO_RETENTION=600
```

then Oracle will make a best effort to retain all committed undo data in the database for 600 seconds. With that setting, any query taking less than 10 minutes should not result in an ORA-1555 ("Snapshot too old") error. While the database is running, you can change the UNDO_RETENTION parameter value via the **alter system** command. As of Oracle Database 10g, you can use the **create tablespace** and **alter tablespace** commands to force Oracle to guarantee that the requested undo retention is maintained even at the expense of current transactions.

Creating an Undo Tablespace

You can create an undo tablespace during the database creation process, as shown in the following listing:

```
create database UNDODB
undo tablespace UNDO_TBS
...
```

In an existing database, you can use the **create tablespace** command to create an undo tablespace:

```
create undo tablespace UNDO_TBS
datafile '/u01/oracle/undodb/undo_tbs_1.dbf'
size 100m;
```

See the Alphabetical Reference for the full syntax of the **create tablespace** command.

Once you have created an undo tablespace, you can manage it via the **alter tablespace** command. For example, you can add datafiles to the undo tablespace or rename existing datafiles the same as you would for any other tablespace. To stop using a tablespace as your undo tablespace, use the **alter system** command to set a new value for the UNDO_TABLESPACE initialization parameter, or change that parameter during a database shutdown/startup.

Temporary Segments

Temporary segments store temporary data during sorting operations (such as large queries, index creations, and **union**s). Each user has a temporary tablespace specified when the account is created via **create user**, or altered via **alter user**. The user's temporary tablespace must be a tablespace that has been designated as a temporary tablespace; as of Oracle9i, permanent tablespaces cannot be used for this purpose.

When you create a database, you can specify a default temporary tablespace for all users. For an existing database, you can change the default tablespace via the **alter database** command, as shown in the following listing:

```
alter database default temporary tablespace TEMP;
```

When you alter the database's default temporary tablespace assignment, users who had been assigned the old default temporary tablespace will be redirected to the new default temporary tablespace. To see the current default temporary tablespace, execute the following query:

```
select Property_Value
   from DATABASE_PROPERTIES
  where Property_Name = 'DEFAULT_TEMP_TABLESPACE';
```

You can specify a tablespace as a "temporary" tablespace via the **create temporary tablespace** command. A temporary tablespace cannot be used to hold any permanent segments, only temporary segments created during operations. The first sort to use the temporary tablespace allocates a temporary segment within the temporary tablespace; when the query completes, the space used by the temporary segment is not dropped. Instead, the space used by the temporary segment is available for use by other queries, allowing the sorting operation to avoid the costs of allocating and releasing space for temporary segments. If your application frequently uses temporary segments for sorting operations, the sorting process should perform better if a dedicated temporary tablespace is used.

As of Oracle Database 10g, you can create multiple temporary tablespaces and group them. Assign the temporary tablespaces to tablespace groups via the **tablespace group** clause of the **create temporary tablespace** or **alter tablespace** command. You can then specify the group as a user's default tablespace. Tablespace groups can help to support parallel operations involving sorts.To dedicate an existing tablespace for temporary segments, specify the **temporary** clause of the **create tablespace** or **alter tablespace** command, as shown in the following listing:

```
alter tablespace TEMP temporary;
```

NOTE
If there are any permanent segments (tables or indexes, for example) stored in TEMP, the command shown in the preceding listing will fail.

To enable the TEMP tablespace to store permanent (nontemporary) objects, use the **permanent** clause of the **create tablespace** or **alter tablespace** command, as shown in the following listing:

```
alter tablespace TEMP permanent;
```

The Contents column in the DBA_TABLESPACES data dictionary view displays the status of the tablespace as either "TEMPORARY" or "PERMANENT."

Free Space

A *free extent* in a tablespace is a collection of contiguous free blocks in the tablespace. A tablespace may contain multiple data extents and free extents. When a segment is dropped, its extents are not, by default, deallocated and marked as free. As of Oracle Database 10g, the default behavior is for the space to be retained while the object moves to the user's recycle bin. You can recover the object from the recycle bin via the **flashback table to before drop** command (see Chapter 28). Space can be freed from the recycle bin via the **purge** command (see the Alphabetical Reference).

In dictionary-managed tablespaces, free extents are not always recombined with neighboring free extents; the barriers between these free extents may be maintained. The SMON (System Monitor) background process periodically coalesces neighboring free extents, provided the default **pctincrease** for the tablespace is nonzero.

NOTE
The SMON background process only coalesces tablespaces whose default ***pctincrease*** *value is nonzero. A* ***pctincrease*** *of any non-zero value will force SMON to coalesce the adjacent free space in a tablespace but will only coalesce eight areas of adjoining extents at a time. Each of the eight coalesces will join two or more extents together to create one larger extent. For best space management, use locally managed tablespaces so that you never have to worry about coalescing. If you must use dictionary-managed tablespaces, maintain a* ***pctincrease*** *of 0 and periodically coalesce any dropped extents manually.*

To force the tablespace to coalesce its free space, use the **coalesce** clause of the **alter tablespace** clause, as shown in the following listing:

```
alter tablespace DATA coalesce;
```

The preceding command will force the neighboring free extents in the DATA tablespace to be coalesced into larger free extents. The command will coalesce up to eight separate areas, just like SMON.

NOTE
The ***alter tablespace*** *command will not coalesce free extents that are separated by data extents.*

Locally managed tablespaces do not require the same degree of free space management. Since locally managed tablespaces can be configured to have consistent extent sizes for all segments, dropped extents are easily reused.

When allocating a new extent, Oracle will not merge contiguous free extents unless there is no alternative. In dictionary-managed tables, this can result in the large free extent at the rear of the tablespace being used while the smaller free extents toward the front of the tablespace are relatively unused. The small free extents become "speed bumps" in the tablespace because they are not, by themselves, of adequate size to be of use. As this usage pattern progresses, the amount of space wasted in the tablespace increases.

In an ideal database, all objects are created at their appropriate size, and all free space is always stored together, a resource pool waiting to be used. If you can avoid dynamic space allocation during application usage, you remove both a performance impact and a source of potential application failure.

Sizing Database Objects

Choosing the proper space allocation parameters for database objects is critical. Developers should begin estimating space requirements before the first database objects are created. Afterward, the space requirements can be refined based on actual usage statistics. The following sections discuss the space estimation methods for tables, indexes, and clusters.

Why Size Objects?

You should size your database objects for three reasons:

- To preallocate space in the database, thereby minimizing the amount of future work required to manage object space requirements

- To reduce the amount of space wasted due to overallocation of space

- To improve the likelihood of a dropped free extent being reused by another segment

You can accomplish all of these goals by following the sizing methodology shown in the following sections. This methodology is based on Oracle's internal methods for allocating space to database objects. Rather than rely on detailed calculations, the methodology relies on approximations that will dramatically simplify the sizing process while simplifying the long-term maintainability of the database.

The Golden Rule for Space Calculations

Keep your space calculations simple, generic, and consistent across databases. There are far more productive ways to spend your work time than performing extremely detailed space calculations that Oracle may ignore anyway. Even if you follow the most rigorous sizing calculations, you cannot be sure how Oracle will load the data into the table or index.

Consider an index on a table with 100,000 rows. During tests, loading the data into the table in sorted order required 920 blocks for the index. The table and index were then truncated and the data was reloaded in a nonsorted order; the index now required 1,370 blocks. The 49 percent increase in space required by the index was due to Oracle's internal index management processes. If you can't reliably be within 49 percent of the correct answer, why spend a lot of time on sizing exercises?

In the following section, you'll see how to simplify the space estimation process, freeing you to perform much more useful DBA functions. These processes should be followed whether you are generating the default storage values for a dictionary-managed tablespace or the extent sizes for locally managed tablespaces.

The Ground Rules for Space Calculations

Oracle follows a set of internal rules when allocating space:

- Oracle only allocates whole blocks, not parts of blocks.

- Oracle allocates sets of blocks.

- Oracle may allocate larger or smaller sets of blocks depending on the available free space in the tablespace.

The first two rules can serve as the basis for fairly exact space estimates, but the third overrides the first two. Even if you try to allocate exactly 20 blocks for a table, Oracle may find a free extent that is 22 blocks and use it rather than leave a 2-block free extent.

Your goal should be to work with Oracle's space allocation methods instead of against them. If you use consistent extent sizes, you can largely delegate the space allocation to Oracle.

The Impact of Extent Size on Performance

No direct performance benefit is gained by reducing the number of extents in a table. In some situations (such as in parallel query environments), having multiple extents in a table can reduce I/O contention and enhance your performance. To simplify management, the extents need to be properly sized.

Oracle reads data from tables in two ways: by RowID (usually immediately following an index access) and via full table scans. If the data is read via RowID, then the number of extents in the table is not a factor in the read performance. Oracle will read each row from its physical location (as specified in the RowID) and retrieve the data.

To avoid paying any possible performance penalties for your extent sizes, you must choose between one of the following strategies:

1. Create extents that are significantly larger than the I/O buffer size for your operating system. If the extents are very large, then very few additional reads will be necessary even if the extent size is not a multiple of the I/O buffer size.

2. Set DB_FILE_MULTIBLOCK_READ_COUNT to take full advantage of the I/O buffer size for your operating system. Note that setting it too high may make the optimizer think that full table scans are more efficient than they actually are, resulting in changes to existing execution plans.

3. If you must create small extents, choose extent sizes that are a multiple of the I/O buffer size for your operating system.

To maximize the reuse of dropped free extents in dictionary-managed tablespaces, use a pool of extent sizes that meets the following criterion: *every extent size will hold an integral multiple of every smaller extent size.* The simplest implementation of this rule is to create extent sizes that increase by doubling: 1MB, 2MB, 4MB, 8MB, 16MB, 32MB. To reduce the number of extent sizes to manage, you can quadruple the values instead of doubling: 1MB, 4MB, 16MB, and so on. Using those values for extent sizes will eliminate I/O problems and will enhance the likelihood that dropped extents will be reused.

Sizing the Objects

To effectively manage your space, all you need to do is select a set of space values that meet the criteria described in the preceding sections. Once the space allocations are finalized, separate them by tablespace. For example:

```
create tablespace DATA_1M
datafile '/u01/oracle/VLDB/data_1m.dbf'
size 100M
extent management local uniform size 1M;
```

```
create tablespace DATA_4M
datafile '/u02/oracle/VLDB/data_4m.dbf'
size 400M
extent management local uniform size 4M;

create tablespace DATA_16M
datafile '/u03/oracle/VLDB/data_16m.dbf'
size 16000M
extent management local uniform size 16M;
```

In this example, three separate DATA tablespaces are created, with extent sizes of 1MB, 4MB, and 16MB. If you need to create a table 3MB in size, you can either create it with three 1MB extents in DATA_1M or with one 4MB extent in DATA_4M. A table that will grow to 10MB can be placed in DATA_16M.

As your tables grow in size, your default storage clauses will grow in a consistent fashion, following the space rules and your standards for extent sizes. DATA_64M would be next, followed by DATA_256M and DATA_1G. Use the same extent sizes across your databases to ease space management of your entire database environment.

As the extent sizes grow, the distribution of extent sizes across tablespaces will usually result in a separation of table types—small static tables will be isolated in the tablespaces with small extent sizes. Large transaction processing tables (or their partitions) will be segregated to the large extent size tables, simplifying later management and tuning activities.

NOTE
As of Oracle9i, the database block size may change at the tablespace level. Be sure the extent sizes you choose account for the largest block size in use in the database. Limiting the usage of nonstandard block sizes in the database will simplify cross-database maintenance and your sizing procedures.

Monitoring an Undo Tablespace

As described in Chapter 27, you can use system-managed undo (SMU) to simplify transaction management. Specify values for the UNDO_TABLESPACE, UNDO_RETENTION, and UNDO_MANAGEMENT initialization parameters.

NOTE
If you are using rollback segments instead of SMU, see the entries for **create rollback segment**, **alter rollback segment**, *and* **set transaction** *in the Alphabetical Reference.*

The primary view for gathering statistics on the undo tablespace usage is V$UNDOSTAT. The V$UNDOSTAT view provides a histogram of the retained data usage. In ten-minute intervals, Oracle records the total number of undo blocks consumed in the UndoBlks column of V$UNDOSTAT, and the number of transactions supported in the TxnCount column. You can use the data from V$UNDOSTAT to determine if the undo tablespace is properly sized for the transaction volume of the application. Oracle maintains 144 rows in V$UNDOSTAT, reflecting the past day's statistics.

Other columns of interest in V$UNDOSTAT include MaxQuerylen, which records the duration in seconds of the longest query executed; the undo retention must be greater than this value. If the NoSpaceErrCnt column of V$UNDOSTAT has a nonzero value, you should add space to the undo tablespace to avoid future space-related errors. Another column, SsOlderRcnt, records the number of times an ORA-01555 ("snapshot too old") error occurred. Increasing the UNDO_RETENTION value can reduce the occurrence of this error.

Automating Storage Management

As of Oracle Database 10g, you can use automatic storage management (ASM) to enhance and simplify your storage management efforts. ASM offers a number of significant advantages, including:

- You can easily add new disks to the set of disks available to the database; Oracle will decide how to best use the disks to distribute the I/O workload.

- The I/O workload will be dynamically distributed among the available disks, without DBA intervention.

- The I/O stripe width can be maintained at different levels for different types of files, all maintained by the database.

- Software mirroring can be enabled if hardware mirroring is not.

Configuring ASM

To use ASM, you must configure an ASM instance. First, specify 'ASM' as the value for the INSTANCE_TYPE initialization parameter (default value is 'RDBMS'):

```
INSTANCE_TYPE = ASM
```

You can then use the **create diskgroup** command with the available disks. For example, you may have four disks available to you:

```
create diskgroup DISKGROUP1
external redundancy
disk '/u01', '/u02', '/u03', '/u04';
```

NOTE
You can use wildcards in the disk names.

The **external redundancy** clause means that the disk group is relying on hardware mirroring. To use software mirroring, use the **normal redundancy** clause and specify the disks that make up the mirror set via the **failgroup** clause. In software mirroring, Oracle uses the mirror set as a set of disks, not as a one-to-one mirror of the diskgroup disks.

To see the disks that constitute a disk group, query the V$ASM_DISK dynamic view.

Now that the disk group is available, create a tablespace that uses the disk group as shown in the following example:

```
create tablespace USERS2 datafile '+diskgroup1/users2_01'
size 500m;
```

Oracle will create the datafile for the USERS2 tablespace in the specified disk group and will manage its I/O requirements across the available disks. If you need to add more disks to the disk group, use the **alter diskgroup** command:

```
alter diskgroup DISKGROUP1 add disk '/u05';
```

Diskgroups may be dropped via the **drop diskgroup** command.

Segment Space Management

In addition to automating the management of storage at the diskgroup level, Oracle Database 10g introduces capabilities for managing the space within segments. You can use these options to reclaim unused space within segments, estimate future space needs, and reorganize tables online.

If your application frequently deletes rows from a table, that table's blocks may be only partially filled with rows. You can manually compress the space within the table via the **alter table** command. First, enable row movement within the table:

```
alter table BOOKSHELF_CHECKOUT enable row movement;
```

Next, have Oracle move rows within the table to compress the allocation of rows within blocks:

```
alter table BOOKSHELF_CHECKOUT shrink space compact;
```

The **shrink space compact** operation will reorganize the rows of the table so they are stored more compactly. However, the high-water mark for the table—the highest block number to which rows have ever been written—is unaffected. Since all full table scans will read all blocks up to the high-water mark, you should adjust that value. Prior to Oracle Database 10g, you can only change the high-water mark by rebuilding or truncating a table. As of Oracle Database 10g, you can adjust the high-water mark via the **shrink space** clause of the **alter table** command. For example:

```
alter table BOOKSHELF_CHECKOUT shrink space;
```

You can cascade the effects of this change to the table's indexes via the **shrink space cascade** option.

To predict space usage, you can use the OBJECT_GROWTH_TREND function of the DBMS_ SPACE package. As parameters, pass the schema name, object name, and object type, as shown in the following listing. You should run this as a SYSDBA-privileged user.

```
select * from
table(DBMS_SPACE.OBJECT_GROWTH_TREND
('PRACTICE','BOOKSHELF_CHECKOUT','TABLE'));
```

The output will show the past space usage for the object along with projected space requirements for the object. The results are based on statistics gathered via the Automated Workload Repository (AWR), an Oracle Database 10g feature. Using a new background process, MMON, AWR collects and stores database statistics that support administration and tuning on an hourly basis. The information gathered via AWR allows Oracle to project your future space usage as well as identify tuning opportunities.

Transporting Tablespaces

A transportable tablespace is a tablespace that can be "unplugged" from one database and "plugged into" another. To be transportable, a tablespace—or a set of tablespaces—must be self-contained. The tablespace set cannot contain any objects that refer to objects in other tablespaces. Thus, if you transport a tablespace containing indexes, you must move the tablespace containing the indexes' base tables as part of the same transportable tablespace set. The better you have organized and distributed your objects among tablespaces, the easier it is to generate a self-contained set of tablespaces to transport.

To transport tablespaces, you need to generate a tablespace set, copy or move that tablespace set to the new database, and plug the set into the new database. The databases must be on the same operating system, with the same version of Oracle and character set.

Generating a Transportable Tablespace Set

A transportable tablespace set contains all of the datafiles for the tablespaces being moved, along with an export of the metadata for those tablespaces. You can optionally choose whether to include referential integrity constraints as part of the transportable tablespace set. If you choose to use referential integrity constraints, the transportable tablespace set will increase to include the tables required to maintain the key relationships. Referential integrity is optional because you may have the same code tables in multiple databases. For example, you may be planning to move a tablespace from your test database to your production database. If you have a COUNTRY table in the test database, then you may already have an identical COUNTRY table in the production database. Since the codes tables are identical in the two databases, you do not need to transport that portion of the referential integrity constraints. You could transport the tablespace and then re-enable the referential integrity in the target database once the tablespace has been moved, simplifying the creation of the transportable tablespace set.

To determine if a tablespace set is self-contained, execute the TRANSPORT_SET_CHECK procedure of the DBMS_TTS package. This procedure takes two input parameters: the set of tablespaces and a Boolean flag set to TRUE if you want referential integrity constraints to be considered. In the following example, referential integrity constraints are not considered for the combination of the AGG_DATA and AGG_INDEXES tablespaces:

```
execute DBMS_TTS.TRANSPORT_SET_CHECK('AGG_DATA,AGG_INDEXES',FALSE);
```

NOTE
You cannot transport the SYSTEM, SYSAUX, or temporary tablespaces.

If there are any self-containment violations in the specified set, Oracle will populate the TRANSPORT_SET_VIOLATIONS data dictionary view. If there are no violations, the view will be empty.

Once you have selected a self-contained set of tablespaces, make the tablespaces read-only, as shown here:

```
alter tablespace AGG_DATA read only;
alter tablespace AGG_INDEXES read only;
```

Next, export the metadata for the tablespaces, using the TRANSPORT_TABLESPACES and TABLESPACES Export parameters:

```
exp TRANSPORT_TABLESPACE=Y TABLESPACES=(AGG_DATA,AGG_INDEXES) CONSTRAINTS=N
GRANTS=Y TRIGGERS=N
```

As shown in the example, you can specify whether triggers, constraints, and grants are exported along with the tablespace metadata. You should also note the names of the accounts that own objects in the transportable tablespace set. You can now copy the tablespaces' datafiles to a separate area. If needed, you can put the tablespaces back into read-write mode in their current database. After you have generated the transportable tablespace set, you can move its files (including the export) to an area that the target database can access.

Plugging in the Transportable Tablespace Set

Once the transportable tablespace set has been moved to an area accessible to the target database, you can plug the set into the target database. First, use Import to import the exported metadata:

```
imp TRANSPORT_TABLESPACE=Y DATAFILES=(agg_data.dbf, agg_indexes.dbf)
```

In the import, you specify the datafiles that are part of the transportable tablespace set. You can optionally specify the tablespaces (via the TABLESPACES parameter) and the object owners (via the OWNERS parameter).

After the import completes, all tablespaces in the transportable tablespace set are left in read-only mode. You can issue the **alter tablespace read write** command in the target database to place the new tablespaces in read-write mode.

```
alter tablespace AGG_DATA read write;
alter tablespace AGG_INDEXES read write;
```

Note that you cannot change the ownership of the objects being transported.

Transportable tablespaces support very fast movement of large datasets. In a data warehouse, you could use transportable tablespaces to publish aggregations from core warehouse to data mart, or from the data marts to a global data warehouse. Any read-only data can be quickly distributed to multiple databases—instead of sending SQL scripts, you can send datafiles and exported metadata. This modified data movement process may greatly simplify your procedures for managing remote databases, remote data marts, and large data-movement operations.

NOTE
*As of Oracle Database 10g, the source and target operating systems can be different; endian conversion is supported during this process. The datafiles must be converted via RMAN's **convert tablespace...to platform** command.*

Performing Backups

Like the rest of the material in this chapter, this section provides an overview. Backup and recovery is a complex topic, and all backup and recovery methods should be thoroughly tested and practiced

before being implemented in a production environment. The purpose of this section is to give developers an understanding of Oracle's capabilities, along with the impact of the backup decisions on recovery efforts and availability. Before using backup and recovery methods in a production environment, you should refer to books that are dedicated to that topic, including Oracle's documentation.

The backup methods provided by Oracle can be categorized as follows:

- Logical backups using Data Pump Export and Import

- Logical backups using Export (and its companion utility, Import)

- Physical file system backups: offline backups and online backups

- Incremental physical file system backups via Recovery Manager (RMAN)

The following sections describe each of these methods and their capabilities.

Export and Import vs. Data Pump Export and Import

As of Oracle Database 10g, you can use Data Pump Export and Import in place of the Export and Import utilities provided with prior versions of Oracle. There is only one situation in which you should continue to use the old versions of Export and Import: when performing indirect migrations of databases across versions of Oracle. For regular maintenance operations, you should use the Data Pump versions of these utilities as they offer significant benefits over their predecessors. See Chapter 22 for a detailed description of the Data Pump utilities.

Since Data Pump Export and Data Pump Import are covered elsewhere in this book, the following sections will focus on the use of the earlier versions of Import and Export. See Chapter 3 for details on their use in indirect database upgrades.

NOTE
For the remainder of this chapter, the terms Export and Import refer to the prior versions of those utilities, not the Data Pump versions.

Export and Import

Oracle's Export utility queries the database, including the data dictionary, and writes the output to a binary file called an *export dump file*. You can export the full database, specific users, or specific tables. During exports, you may choose whether or not to export the data dictionary information associated with tables, such as the grants, indexes, and constraints associated with them. The file written by Export will contain the commands necessary to completely re-create all of the chosen objects and data.

You can perform tablespace-level exports to export all of the objects contained in a tablespace. Any indexes defined on the exported tables would also be exported. Tablespace-level exports use the **tablespaces** clause of the Export utility, as described later in this chapter.

Once data has been exported, it may be imported via Oracle's Import utility. The Import utility reads the binary export dump file created by Export and executes the commands found there. For example, these commands may include a **create table** command, followed by an **insert** command to load data into the table.

The data that has been exported does not have to be imported into the same database, or the same schema, as was used to generate the export dump file. You may use the export dump file to create a duplicate set of the exported objects under a different schema or in a separate database.

You can import either all or part of the exported data. If you import the entire export dump file from a Full export, then all of the database objects—including tablespaces, datafiles, and users—will be created during the import. However, it is often useful to pre-create tablespaces and users in order to specify the physical distribution of objects in the database.

If you are only going to import part of the data from the export dump file, then the tablespaces, datafiles, and users that will own and store that data should be set up prior to the import.

Exported data may be imported into an Oracle database created under the next higher version of the Oracle software. See Chapter 3 for the versions of Export to use when upgrading and downgrading Oracle software versions. The README.doc files that accompany Oracle releases detail the requirements for using Export and Import across specific versions.

Export

The Export utility has four levels of functionality: Full mode, Tablespace mode, User mode, and Table mode. You can export partitions via a modified version of Table mode exports.

In Full mode, the full database is exported. The entire data dictionary is read, and the DDL needed to re-create the full database is written to the export dump file. This file includes creation commands for all tablespaces, all users, and all of the objects, data, and privileges in their schemas.

In Tablespace mode, all of the objects contained in the specified tablespace(s) will be exported, including the definition of indexes on the contained objects, even if they are in another tablespace.

In User mode, a user's objects are exported, as well as the data within them. All grants and indexes created by the user on the user's objects are also exported. Grants and indexes created by users other than the owner are not exported.

In Table mode, a specified table is exported. The table's structure, indexes, and grants are exported along with or without its data. Table mode can also export the full set of tables owned by a user (by specifying the schema owner but no table names). You can also specify partitions of a table to export.

Export can be run interactively, through Oracle Enterprise Manager, or via command files. The run-time options that can be specified for Export are listed in Table 46-1, along with their default values in Oracle Database 10g.

A number of the parameters conflict with each other or may result in inconsistent instructions for Export. For example, setting **full**=Y and **owner**=HR would fail, since the **full** parameter calls for a Full export, while the **owner** parameter specifies a User export.

NOTE
The default values and available parameters may change with each release of Oracle.

You can display the Export parameters online via the following command:

```
exp help=Y
```

Keyword	Description
userid	Username/password of the account running the export. **userid** must be the first parameter on the command line.
buffer	Size of the buffer used to fetch data rows. The default is system dependent; this value is usually set to a high value (> 64,000).
file	Name of the export dump file; default is expdat.dmp.
compress	A Y/N flag to indicate whether export should compress fragmented segments into single extents. This affects the **storage** clauses that will be stored in the export file for those objects. Default is Y. Having objects in one large extent is not always the best choice. For large tables, you should use **compress**=N.
grants	A Y/N flag to indicate whether **grant**s on database objects will be exported. Default is Y.
indexes	A Y/N flag to indicate whether indexes on tables will be exported. Default is Y.
direct	A Y/N flag to indicate if a direct export should be performed. A direct export bypasses the buffer cache during the export, generating significant performance gains for the export process. Default is N.
log	The name of a file to which the log of the export will be written.
rows	A Y/N flag to indicate whether rows should be exported. If this is set to N, then only the DDL for the database objects will be created in the export file. Default is Y.
consistent	A Y/N flag to indicate whether a read-consistent version of all exported objects should be maintained. This is needed when tables that are related to each other are being modified by users during the export process.
object_ consistent	A Y/N flag to indicate whether consistent versions of the exported objects should be maintained at the object level, even across partitions. Default is N.
full	If set to Y, then a Full database export is performed. Default is N.
owner	A list of database accounts to be exported; User exports of those accounts may then be performed.
tables	A list of tables to be exported; Table exports of those tables may then be performed. As of Oracle9*i*, this parameter supports the use of the % and _ wildcards for pattern matching.
recordlength	The length, in bytes, of the export dump file record. Usually not specified unless you are going to transfer the export file between different operating systems.
triggers	A Y/N flag to indicate if triggers should be exported. Default is Y.

TABLE 46-1. *Run-Time Options for Export*

Keyword	Description
statistics	A parameter to indicate whether **analyze** commands for the exported objects should be written to the export dump file. Valid values are COMPUTE, ESTIMATE (the default), and N. In earlier versions of Oracle, this parameter was called **analyze**.
parfile	The name of a parameter file to be passed to Export. This file may contain entries for all of the parameters listed here.
constraints	A Y/N flag to indicate whether constraints on tables are exported. Default is Y.
feedback	The number of rows after which to display progress during Table exports. The default value is 0, so no feedback is displayed until a table is completely exported.
filesize	The maximum size for an export dump file. If multiple files are listed in the **file** entry, the export will be directed to those files based on the **filesize** setting.
flashback_scn	Specifies the SCN Export will use to enable flashback. The export is performed with data consistent as of this SCN.
flashback_time	Time used to get the SCN closest to the specified time. The export is performed with data consistent as of this SCN.
query	A **where** clause that will be applied to each table during the export.
resumable	A Y/N flag to indicate if the session is resumable following errors. Default is N.
resumable_name	The specified value is inserted into the DBA_RESUMABLE view to help identify the resumable statement.
resumable_timeout	The wait time for resumable statements.
tts_full_check	Perform full or partial dependency check for transportable tablespaces.
volsize	Number of bytes to write to each tape volume.
tablespaces	The tablespaces whose tables should be exported, including all tables that have a partition located in the specified tablespaces.
transport_tablespace	Set to Y if you are using the transportable tablespace option. Use in conjunction with the **tablespaces** keyword. Default is N.

TABLE 46-1. *Run-Time Options for Export* (continued)

The **compress=Y** option alters the **initial** parameter of the **storage** clause for segments that have multiple extents. During a subsequent import, the total allocated space for that segment will be compressed into a single extent. There are two important points to note concerning this functionality:

■ First, it is the *allocated,* not the *used,* space that is compressed. An empty table with 300MB allocated to it in three 100MB extents will be compressed into a single empty 300MB extent. No space will be reclaimed.

■ Second, if the tablespace has multiple datafiles, a segment may allocate space that is greater than the size of the largest datafile. In that case, using **compress**=Y would change the **storage** clause to have an **initial** extent size that is greater than any datafile size. If the datafile cannot extend itself, the object creation will fail during import.

In the following example, the **compress**=Y option is used, as the HR and THUMPER owners are exported:

```
exp system/manager file=expdat.dmp compress=Y owner=(HR,THUMPER)
```

Consistent Exports

During the process of writing the database's data to the export dump file, Export reads one table at a time. Thus, although Export started at a specific point in time, each table is read at a different time. The data as it exists in each table at the moment Export starts to read *that table* is what will be exported. Since most tables are related to other tables, this may result in inconsistent data being exported if users are modifying data during the export. The export dump file may contain inconsistent data, such as foreign key records from one table without matching primary key records from a related table.

To avoid inconsistency in your exports, there are two options:

■ First, you should schedule exports to occur when no one is making modifications to tables. If feasible, you can use the **startup restrict** option to make sure only DBAs are logged in while the export is occurring.

■ Second, you can use the **consistent** parameter. This parameter is only available for complete exports. During a consistent export, Oracle will try to create a read-consistent version of the exported data as of the time the export started. You will get "snapshot too old" errors if Oracle cannot re-create the read-consistent version of the tables. To guarantee you will not encounter "snapshot too old" errors, you must create large rollback segments or a large undo tablespace, because Oracle will overwrite old rollback segment entries without regard to your **consistent**=Y setting.

■ Third, you could quiesce the database, which restricts logins to SYSDBA-privileged users. While the database is quiesced, all ongoing transactions and queries appear to hang, and no new user logins are permitted.

Whenever possible, guarantee the consistency of exported data by running exports while the database is not being used or is opened in restricted mode. If you are unable to do this, restrict the database usage during the export and perform a **consistent**=Y export.

Another alternative is to create two parameter files (**parfile**). One file will contain the names of the majority of tables within your database or schema. You can use this file for your first export with the default of **consistent**=N. The second file, containing the names of the tables whose consistency must be maintained, is used to perform an export with **consistent**=Y. Using this approach, the size of your rollback segments will not need to be as large, and the performance of your system will not suffer as much.

Exporting Tablespaces

The better you have distributed your application schema owners and their objects across tablespaces, the easier it will be to export them. For example, if you want to export all of the objects in the AP_ DATA schema, you can execute a User export if only a single user owns objects in that tablespace. If multiple users own objects in the DATA tablespace, you can export all of the objects within the tablespace using one command regardless of which schema owns the object:

```
exp demo/demo tablespaces=DATA
```

If any table has a partition in the specified tablespace, the entire table will be exported. If you set **indexes**=Y, the tables' associated indexes will be exported regardless of their tablespace location.

Exporting Partitions

You can reference partitions and subpartitions within tables when you perform Table exports. For example, if the SALES table in the THUMPER schema is partitioned into PART1, PART2, and PART3, then you can export the entire table or its partitions.

To export the entire table, use the **tables** parameter of Export:

```
exp system/manager FILE=expdat.dmp TABLES=(Thumper.SALES)
```

To export a specific partition or subpartition, list the partition or subpartition name following the table name. The table name and the partition name should be separated by a colon (:). In the following listing, the PART1 partition is exported:

```
exp system/manager FILE=expdat.dmp TABLES=(Thumper.SALES:Part1)
```

If you export a partition, all of its subpartitions will be exported.

Import

The Import utility reads the export dump file and runs the commands stored there. Import may be used to selectively bring back objects or users from the export dump file.

You can run Import either interactively or via command files. The run-time options that can be specified for Import and their default values are listed in Table 46-2.

Keyword	Description
userid	Username/password of the account running the import; this must be the first parameter, and the "**userid=**" text is optional.
buffer	Size of the buffer used to fetch data rows. The default is system dependent; this value is usually set to a high value (>100,000).

TABLE 46-2. *Import Run-Time Options*

Keyword	Description
file	Name of the export dump file to be imported.
show	A Y/N flag to specify whether the file contents should be displayed rather than executed. Default is N.
ignore	A Y/N flag to indicate whether the import should ignore errors encountered when issuing **create** commands. This flag is used if the objects being imported already exist. Default is N.
grants	A Y/N flag to indicate whether grants on database objects will be imported. Default is Y.
indexes	A Y/N flag to indicate whether indexes on tables will be imported. Default is Y.
rows	A Y/N flag to indicate whether rows should be imported. If this is set to N, then only the DDL for the database objects will be executed. Default is Y.
log	The name of a file to which the log of the import will be written.
full	A Y/N flag; if set to Y, then the Full export dump file is imported. Default is N.
fromuser	A list of database accounts whose objects should be read from the export dump file (when FULL=N).
touser	A list of database accounts into which objects in the export dump file will be imported. **fromuser** and **touser** do not have to be set to the same value.
tables	A list of tables to be imported. As of Oracle9*i*, the % and _ wildcards are supported for table names.
recordlength	The length, in bytes, of the export dump file record. Usually left at the default value unless you are going to transfer the export file between different operating systems.
commit	A Y/N flag to indicate whether Import should **commit** after each array (whose size is set by **buffer**). If this is set to N (the default), then Import will **commit** after every table is imported. For large tables, **commit**=N requires equally large undo segments.
parfile	The name of a parameter file to be passed to Import. This file may contain entries for all of the parameters listed here.
constraints	A Y/N flag to indicate whether constraints on tables will be imported. Default is Y.
destroy	A Y/N flag to indicate whether the **create tablespace** commands found in dump files from Full exports will be executed (thereby destroying the datafiles in the database being imported into). Default is N.

TABLE 46-2. *Import Run-Time Options* (continued)

Keyword	Description
indexfile	This option writes all of the **create table**, **create cluster**, and **create index** commands to a file, rather than running them. All but the **create index** commands will be commented out. If **constraints**=Y, then constraints will be written to the file as well. This file can then be run (with slight modifications) after importing with **indexes**=N. It is useful for separating tables and indexes into separate tablespaces.
skip_unusable_ indexes	A Y/N flag that indicates if Import should skip partition indexes marked as "unusable." You may want to skip the indexes during import and manually create them later to improve index creation performance. Default is N.
feedback	The number of rows after which to display progress during table imports. The default value is 0, so no feedback is displayed until a table is completely imported.
toid_novalidate	Enables Import to skip validation of specified object types.
filesize	The maximum dump size that was specified on export if the parameter **filesize** was used on export.
statistics	A flag to indicate if precomputed statistics should be imported. Default is ALWAYS; other values are NONE, SAFE (for nonquestionable statistics), and RECALCULATE (recalculate during the import).
resumable	A Y/N flag to indicate if the session is resumable following errors. Default is N.
resumable_ name	The specified value is inserted into the DBA_RESUMABLE view to help identify the resumable statement.
resumable_ timeout	The wait time for resumable statements.
streams_ configuration	A Y/N flag to indicate if Oracle Streams configuration data found in the export dump file should be imported. Default is Y.
streams_ instantiation	A Y/N flag to indicate if Oracle Streams instantiation metadata should be imported if present in the export dump file. Default is N.
compile	A Y/N flag to indicate if procedures, functions, and packages should be recompiled during import. Default is Y.
volsize	Maximum number of bytes in a file on each volume of tape.
transport_ tablespace	A Y/N flag to indicate that transportable tablespace metadata is to be imported into the database. Default is N.
tablespaces	The name or list of names of tablespaces to be transported into the database.
datafiles	The list of datafiles to be transported into the database.
tts_owners	The name or list of names of owners of data in the transportable tablespace.

TABLE 46-2. *Import Run-Time Options* (continued)

A number of the Import parameters conflict with each other or may result in inconsistent instructions for Import. For example, setting **full**=Y and **fromuser**=HR would fail, since the **full** parameter calls for a Full import, while the **fromuser** parameter specifies a User import.

Undo Space Requirements

By default, the database will issue a **commit** after every table is completely imported. To reduce the sizes of the undo entries, specify **commit**=Y along with a value for **buffer**. A **commit** will then be executed after every **buffer**'s worth of data, as shown in the following example. In the first **import** command shown, a **commit** is executed after every table is loaded. In the second command shown, a **commit** is executed after every 64,000 bytes of data are inserted.

```
imp system/manager file=expdat.dmp
imp system/manager file=expdat.dmp buffer=64000 commit=Y
```

How large should **buffer** be? **buffer** should be large enough to handle the largest single row to be imported. If you do not know the longest row length that was exported, start with a reasonable value (such as 50,000) and run the import. If an IMP-00020 error is returned, then the **buffer** size is not large enough. Increase it and try the import again.

When using **commit**=Y, remember that a **commit** is being performed for each **buffer** array. This implies that if the import of a table fails, it is possible that some of the rows in that table may have already been imported and **commit**ted. The partial load may then be either used or **delete**d prior to running the import again.

In tables with BFILE, LONG, LOB, REF, ROWID, and UROWID columns, rows are inserted individually. The **buffer** value does not have to accommodate the LONG and LOB portions of the row; Import will attempt to allocate additional buffer areas as needed for those portions.

Importing into Different Accounts

To move objects from one user to another user via Export/Import, perform a User export of the owner of the objects. During the import, specify the owner as the **fromuser** and the account that is to own the objects as the **touser**.

For example, to copy THUMPER's objects into the FLOWER account, you could execute the following commands. The first command exports the THUMPER owner, and the second command imports the THUMPER objects into the FLOWER account.

```
exp system/manager file=thumper.dat owner=thumper grants=N
  indexes=Y rows=Y

imp system/manager file=thumper.dat FROMUSER=thumper TOUSER=flower
    rows=Y indexes=Y
```

See the *Oracle Database Utilities 10g Release 1* for further details on Export and Import, along with data recovery examples.

Offline Backups

An offline backup (sometimes called a cold backup) is a physical backup of the database files, made after the database has been shut down via either a **shutdown normal** or a **shutdown immediate** or a **shutdown transactional**. While the database is shut down, each of the files that is actively

used by the database is backed up. These files provide a complete image of the database as it existed at the moment it was shut down.

The following files should be backed up during cold backups:

- All datafiles
- All control files
- All online redo logs

You may optionally choose to back up the database initialization parameter file, particularly if the backup will serve as the basis for a disaster recovery process.

Having all of these files backed up *while the database is closed* provides a complete image of the database as it existed at the time it was closed. The full set of these files could be retrieved from the backups at a later date and the database would be able to function. It is *not* valid to perform a file system backup of the database while it is open unless an online backup is being performed (as discussed later in this chapter).

Ideally, all of the datafiles are located in directories at the same level on each device. For example, all database files may be stored in an instance-specific subdirectory under an /oracle directory for each device (such as /db01/oracle/MYDB). Directories such as these should contain all of the datafiles, redo log files, and control files for a database. The only file you may optionally add to the offline backup that will not be in this location is the production initialization parameter file, which should be in either the /app/oracle/admin/*INSTANCE_NAME*/pfile subdirectory under the Oracle software base directory, or the /database directory under the Oracle software home directory.

If you use the directory structure in the prior example, your backup commands are greatly simplified, since you will be able to use wildcards in the filenames. After shutting down the database, back up the files to the backup destination area (either a tape or a separate disk area).

Since offline backups involve changes to the database's availability, they are usually scheduled to occur at night.

Offline backups are very reliable. To reduce their impact on the database's availability, you may use online backups. As described in the following section, online backups use Oracle's ARCHIVELOG mode to allow consistent file system backups during database usage.

Online Backups

You can use online backups for any database that is running in ARCHIVELOG mode. In this mode, the online redo logs are archived, creating a full log of all transactions within the database.

Oracle writes to the online redo log files in a cyclical fashion; after filling the first log file, it begins writing to the second log until that one fills, and then begins writing to the third. Once the last online redo log file is filled, the LGWR (Log Writer) background process begins to overwrite the contents of the first redo log file.

When Oracle is run in ARCHIVELOG mode, the ARC0-ARC9 (Archiver) background processes make a copy of each redo log file before overwriting it. These archived redo log files are usually written to a disk device. The archived redo log files may also be written directly to a tape device, but this tends to be very operator-intensive.

You can perform file system backups of a database while that database is open, provided the database is running in ARCHIVELOG mode. An online backup involves setting each tablespace

(or the entire database) into a backup state, backing up the related datafiles, and then restoring the tablespaces to their normal state.

NOTE
When using the Oracle-supplied RMAN utility, you do not have to place each tablespace into a backup state. The utility will put the tablespace into and take it out of the backup state automatically.

The database can be fully recovered from an online backup, and can, via the archived redo logs, be rolled forward to any point in time. When the database is then opened, any committed transactions that were in the database at that time will have been restored and any uncommitted transactions will have been rolled back.

While the database is open, the following files are backed up:

- All datafiles
- All archived redo log files
- One control file, via the **alter database** command

Online backup procedures are very powerful for two reasons. First, they provide full point-in-time recovery. Databases that are not running in ARCHIVELOG mode can only be recovered to the point in time when the backup occurred. Second, they allow the database to remain open during the file system backup. Thus, even databases that cannot be shut down due to user requirements can still have file system backups.

Getting Started

To make use of the ARCHIVELOG capability, the database must first be placed in ARCHIVELOG mode. The following listing shows the steps needed to place a database in ARCHIVELOG mode. Run SQL*Plus and mount the database (providing its name in place of "mydb" in these examples), then alter it as shown here:

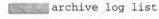

```
connect system/manager as sysdba
startup mount mydb;
alter database archivelog;
alter database open;
```

The following command will display the current ARCHIVELOG status of the database from within SQL*Plus:

```
archive log list
```

NOTE
To see the currently active online redo log and its sequence number, query the V$LOG dynamic view.

To change a database back to NOARCHIVELOG mode, use the following set of commands after shutting down the database:

```
connect system/manager as sysdba
startup mount mydb;
alter database noarchivelog;
alter database open;
```

A database that has been placed in ARCHIVELOG mode will remain in that mode until it is placed in NOARCHIVELOG mode. The location of the archived redo log files is determined by the settings in the database's parameter file. The parameters to note are as follows (with sample values):

```
log_archive_dest_1        = /db01/oracle/arch/CC1/arch
log_archive_dest_state_1  = ENABLE
log_archive_format = arch%s.arc
```

In this example, the archived redo log files are being written to the directory /db01/oracle/arch/CC1. The archived redo log files will all begin with the letters "arch," followed by a sequence number. For example, the archived redo log file directory may contain the following files:

```
arch_170.arc
arch_171.arc
arch_172.arc
```

Each of these files contains the data from a single online redo log. They are numbered sequentially, in the order in which they were created. The size of the archived redo log files varies, but does not exceed the size of the online redo log files. Within the LOG_ARCHIVE_FORMAT setting, the available variables are

Variable	Description
%s	Log sequence number
%S	Log sequence number, zero filled
%t	Thread number
%T	Thread number, zero filled
%a	Activation ID
%d	Database ID
%r	Resetlogs ID that ensures unique names are constructed for the archived log files across multiple incarnations of the database

If the destination directory of the archived redo log files runs out of space, then ARCH will stop processing the online redo log data and the database will temporarily hang. This situation can be resolved by adding more space to the archived redo log file destination disk or by backing up the archived redo log files and then removing them from this directory.

NOTE
*Never delete archived redo log files until you have backed them
up and verified that you can restore them successfully.*

Although the initialization parameter LOG_ARCHIVE_START parameter may be set to TRUE,
the database will *not* be in ARCHIVELOG mode unless you have executed the **alter database
archivelog** command shown earlier in this section. Once the database is in ARCHIVELOG mode,
it will remain in that mode through subsequent database shutdowns and startups until you explicitly
place it in NOARCHIVELOG mode via the **alter database noarchivelog** command.

NOTE
*The archivelog destination area is different from the flash recovery
area. As described in Chapter 28, the flash recovery area supports
the **flashback database** command. See Chapter 28 for details of
this command and the associated parameters.*

Performing Online Database Backups

Once a database is running in ARCHIVELOG mode, you can back it up while it is open and
available to users. This capability allows round-the-clock database availability to be achieved
while still guaranteeing the recoverability of the database.

Although online backups can be performed during normal working hours, they should be
scheduled for the times of the least user activity for several reasons. First, the online backups will
use operating-system commands to back up the physical files, and these commands will use the
available I/O resources in the system (impacting the system performance for interactive users).
Second, while the tablespaces are being backed up, the manner in which transactions are written
to the archived redo log files changes. When you put a tablespace in "backup" mode, the DBWR
process writes all of the blocks in the buffer cache that belong to any file that is part of the tablespace
back to disk. When the blocks are read back into memory and then changed, they will be copied
to the log buffer the first time that a change is made to them. As long as they stay in the buffer
cache, they will not be recopied to the online redo log file. This will use a great deal more space
in the archived redo log file destination directory.

The command file for a hot backup has three parts:

1. A backup of the datafiles, which in turn consists of

 a. Setting the tablespaces into backup state

 b. Backing up the tablespace's datafiles

 c. Restoring the tablespace to its normal state

2. Backup of the archived redo log files, which consists of

 a. Recording which files are in the archived redo log destination directory

 b. Backing up the archived redo log files, then (optionally) deleting or compressing them

3. Backup of the control file via the **alter database backup controlfile** command

NOTE
The online backup process is automated via the RMAN utility.

You can create a script to perform the backups, but the use of RMAN is preferred.

When the datafiles are being backed up, you may back them up directly to tape or to disk. If you have enough disk space available, choose the latter option, since it will greatly reduce the time necessary for the backup procedures to complete.

Recovery Manager

A Recovery Manager utility called RMAN is provided with the Oracle database to enable you to back up and recover your databases in an automated manner using either a command-line mode or the Recovery Manager from within the Oracle Enterprise Manager. You can use either approach to back up, restore, and recover database files.

Recovery Manager keeps track of backups either through a Recovery Catalog or by placing the required information into the control file for the database being backed up. Recovery Manager adds new backup capabilities that are unavailable in the other Oracle backup utilities. There are four components within the Recovery Manager: the RMAN executable, one or more target databases, the recovery catalog database, and the media management software. The only components that you must have are the RMAN executable and a target database.

Recovery Manager allows you to perform incremental physical backups of datafiles. During a full (called a *level 0*) datafile backup, all of the blocks ever used in the datafile are backed up. During a cumulative (*level 1*) datafile backup, all of the blocks used since the last full datafile backup are backed up. An incremental (*level 2*) datafile backup backs up only those blocks that have changed since the most recent cumulative or full backup. You can define the levels used for incremental backups.

The ability to perform incremental and cumulative backups of datafiles may greatly improve the performance of backups. The greatest performance improvements will be realized by very large databases in which only a small subset of a large tablespace changes. Using the traditional backup methods, you would need to back up all of the datafiles in the tablespace. Using Recovery Manager, you only back up the blocks that have changed since the last backup.

During database recovery using Recovery Manager, you need to know which files are current, which are restored, and the backup method you plan to use. If you use the recovery catalog, Recovery Manager stores its catalog of information in an Oracle database—and you need to back up that database or else you may lose your entire backup and recovery catalog of information.

Recovery Manager is only used by DBAs, who need to make the decisions regarding the Recovery Manager architecture for your environment (for example, deciding on the location of the recovery catalog). You should work with your DBA to understand the recovery options in use and their implications for database availability and recovery time.

Enhancements to RMAN in Oracle Database 10g

The version of RMAN that is provided with Oracle Database 10g resolves performance and functionality issues with earlier releases while adding new capabilities. The features introduced with Oracle Database 10g include:

■ The ability to *span resetlogs operations* during recoveries. In Oracle Database 10g you can use all archived redo log files, before and after an **alter database resetlogs** operation, to perform a recovery.

■ *Recovery previews.* You can use the **restore database preview** command within RMAN to preview the backups needed for a recovery. You can use the **restore tablespace … preview** command to perform the same analysis at the tablespace level.

■ *Faster incremental backups.* Although they supported incremental backups, previous versions of RMAN detected changed blocks by scanning all of the possible blocks—creating a performance issue within the backup. As of Oracle Database 10g, you can create a file that will track the blocks that have changed. Use the **alter database** command to create a change log file:

```
alter database enable block change tracking
using file 'filename';
```

Oracle will then create a binary file to use for change tracking. You can disable block-level change tracking via the **alter database disable block change tracking** command. Query V$BLOCK_CHANGE_TRACKING to see the current status.

■ *Merged backups.* Instead of maintaining multiple levels of backups across multiple days, you can have your incremental backups dynamically merged with prior backups. Thus, if you take a full backup on one day and an incremental backup on the next day, your recovery efforts will be simplified if you use the new merging capabilities, since you would only need one (merged) backup for your recovery effort. The merge occurs as part of the **backup** command within RMAN—it will make a copy of the prior backup and merge that with your new incremental changes.

■ *Compressed backups.* RMAN can compress the backup files as they are written, significantly lowering your disk space requirements for disk-based backups.

Where to Go from Here

In this chapter, you've seen a high-level overview of the topics that production DBAs deal with every day. In addition to the topics discussed here, DBAs monitor databases, tune databases, install software, maintain database connectivity, and many other tasks. If you are interested in learning more about those tasks, see your Oracle documentation set or the *Oracle DBA Handbook*. The more developers understand about database administration, the more likely they are to build applications that take advantage of the database's inherent capabilities.

CHAPTER
47

The Hitchhiker's Guide to XML in Oracle

ML (eXtensible Markup Language) is a standardized syntax for describing hierarchical data. Rather than being a programming language, XML is a universal format for structured documents and data. Its tag-based syntax will be familiar to those familiar with HTML (Hypertext Markup Language) and gives it the flexibility to handle complex data. Whereas HTML tells a Web browser how to present data, XML tells applications what the data means.

XML is well suited to solving data-interchange problems among heterogeneous systems; database-resident data is easily accessed, converted, and stored. In this chapter, you will see an overview of the XML access methods available in Oracle Database 10g. XML and its toolsets are evolving; see http://www.w3.org for the most current information.[1]

Document Type Definitions, Elements, and Attributes

In XML, application-specific tags or "elements" wrap around the data they describe. The syntax for these tags is defined in a special kind of XML document called a *Document Type Definition (DTD)*. The DTD defines the structure for a valid XML document. The structure is strictly hierarchical.

Each XML document is an instantiation of an *infoset*—the abstract data model consisting of a document and its information items. Information items are mostly elements, attributes, and content. For example, an XML infoset may contain the following:

```
<book>
   <title>MY LEDGER</title>
   <chapter num="1">
      <title>Beginning</title>
      <text>&chapter1;</text>
   </chapter>
</book>
```

In this example, the tags <book> and </book> define the starting and ending points of the infoset. The XML document describes a book named "MY LEDGER." That book has chapters, and the first chapter's title is "Beginning." The text of the chapter is not stored inside the XML document; instead, a pointer is created to an external file.

In addition to being a tag in the file, "title" is an element. It has content (in this example, "MY LEDGER"). As shown in this example, you can set the content of elements by providing values between tags (for the title) or within the tag (as in the chapter number setting). Elements can contain content, child elements, or both, or they may be empty. For data interchange, you should avoid creating elements that contain both content and child elements. To create an empty element, its tag would be in this format:

```
<name/>
```

[1] For further reading, we suggest *Oracle Database 10g XML & SQL: Design, Build & Manage XML Applications in Java, C, C++ & PL/SQL*, by Scardina, Chang, and Wang (McGraw-Hill/Osborne, 2004).

NOTE
Element names are case sensitive.

Each element has exactly one parent, and a parent can have any number of children. The strict hierarchical nature of XML means that if an element starts within another element (such as "chapter" within "book"), its ending tag must precede the ending tag for the parent element.

As shown in the book example, elements have attributes. For example, the chapter element has an attribute named *num.* The attribute value is enclosed in double quotes:

```
<chapter num="1">
```

NOTE
Like element names, attribute names are case sensitive.

In general, applications use element attributes for specific items (such as the chapter number) and element content for the bulk of the data (in this case, the chapter text).

An XML document is said to be "well-formed" if the following conditions are met:

- Every start tag has a matching end tag.

- Elements do not overlap.

- There is one root element.

- Attribute values are always within quotes.

- An element does not have two attributes within the same name.

- Comments and processing instructions do not appear inside tags.

- There are no "unescaped" < or & signs in an element's or attribute's character data.

These are the basic syntax rules. If an XML document conforms to these rules, it may still not be valid. To be valid, the XML document must conform to the rules of a Document Type Definition (DTD). The DTD is a formal way of describing what elements and entities may appear in an XML document, and what each element's contents and attributes are.

For example, consider the following XML document:

```
<?xml version="1.0" encoding="UTF-8"?>
<!DOCTYPE CustomerList SYSTEM "Example1.dtd">
<CustomerList>
    <Customer preferredCustomer="">
        <ID>12345</ID>
        <Address>
            <Name>TUSC</Name>
            <Street>377 E BUTTERFIELD RD</Street>
            <City>LOMBARD</City>
            <State>IL</State>
```

```
        <Country>USA</Country>
        <ZIP_CODE>60148</ZIP_CODE>
        <PHONE>630-960-2909</PHONE>
      </Address>
      <CreditRating>EXCELLENT</CreditRating>
      <SalesRepID></SalesRepID>
      <RegionID>5</RegionID>
      <Comments>THIS IS A TEST XML DOCUMENT</Comments>
      <ShippingMethod>M</ShippingMethod>
    </Customer>
</CustomerList>
```

The first line is an XML declaration, which starts with "<?" and ends with "?>":

```
<?xml version="1.0" encoding="UTF-8"?>
```

The *version* attribute should be set to 1.0 for now. The *encoding* attribute is optional; its default value is UTF-8. You can also set a third attribute, *standalone*. In this case, the XML document is not a standalone document; it has a related DTD, as specified in the second line:

```
<!DOCTYPE CustomerList SYSTEM "Example1.dtd">
```

The related DTD file Example1.dtd for this example is shown in the following listing:

```
<?xml version="1.0" encoding="UTF-8"?>
<!ELEMENT CustomerList (Customer*)>
<!ELEMENT Customer (ID, Address, CreditRating*, SalesRepID*,
                    RegionID, Comments*, ShippingMethod)>
<!ATTLIST Customer preferredCustomer CDATA #IMPLIED>
<!ELEMENT ID (#PCDATA)>
<!ELEMENT Address (Name, Street*, City, County,
                   State, Country, ZIP_CODE, PHONE)>
<!ELEMENT Name (#PCDATA)>
<!ELEMENT Street (#PCDATA)>
<!ELEMENT City (#PCDATA)>
<!ELEMENT County (#PCDATA)>
<!ELEMENT State (#PCDATA)>
<!ELEMENT Country (#PCDATA)>
<!ELEMENT ZIP_CODE (#PCDATA)>
<!ELEMENT PHONE (#PCDATA)>
<!ELEMENT CreditRating (#PCDATA)>
<!ELEMENT SalesRepID (#PCDATA)>
<!ELEMENT RegionID (#PCDATA)>
<!ELEMENT Comments (#PCDATA)>
<!ELEMENT ShippingMethod (#PCDATA)>
```

The DTD is analogous to the control file specifications for external tables. It tells applications what they will find in the XML document—the element names and the hierarchy of elements. An XML document can have only one DTD.

The syntax for the element declarations is

```
<!ELEMENT element_name (content_model)>
```

where *content_model* specifies what children an element can or must have and the order they are in. The simplest content model is #PCDATA, which says that the element can contain only parsed character data. Here's an example:

```
<!ELEMENT Name (#PCDATA)>
```

In this example, the CustomerList element contains zero or more "Customer" elements, as indicated by the * suffix:

```
<!ELEMENT CustomerList (Customer*)>
```

The allowable suffixes are as follows:

* Permits zero or more occurrences

+ Permits one or more occurrences

? Permits zero or one occurrences

As shown in the Address element specification, you can specify a sequence of multiple elements by separating them with commas:

```
<!ELEMENT Address (Name, Street*, City, County,
                   State, Country, ZIP_CODE, PHONE)>
```

You can provide multiple options within the specification, separated by the vertical bar (|) character. For example, a point on a two-dimensional graph may be specified via its horizontal and vertical measurements or its distance and angle from the center:

```
<!ELEMENT Point ((x,y) | (distance, angle))>
```

For real-world applications, DTDs can quickly become very complex. You can have attribute lists, external references, entity attributes, IDs, conditional inclusions, and other structures within your DTD. Refer to XML documentation for a thorough review of DTD structures and options.

NOTE
Before creating a DTD for a standard business operation, see if one is already available for your purpose. Web sites such as http://www.xml.org/xml/registry.jsp provide many examples of DTDs. These registries provide a valuable resource for the documentation of industry-standard DTDs and their components.

XML Schema

The XML Schema specification is an alternative to DTDs. It includes datatyping, which is particularly helpful when working with relational databases. Whereas DTDs are not extensible (they're just control files), XML Schema is extensible in the following ways:

- Parts of schemas can be reused in other schemas.

- Complex structures can be reused in other schemas.

- Derived datatypes can be created based on existing datatypes.

- A single document instance can reference multiple schemas.

Within XML Schema, elements are declared using xsd:element, as shown in the following listing:

```
<xsd:element name="Date">
```

The element's datatype can be declared via the *type* attribute:

```
<xsd:element name="Date" type="date">
```

You can specify the minimum and maximum number of occurrences for the element via the *minOccurs* and *maxOccurs* attributes:

```
<xsd:element name="Date" type="date" minOccurs="0" maxOccurs="1">
```

Built-in XML Schema types include primitive types (such as string, Boolean, number, float, date, time, and datetime) and derived types (such as normalizedString, integer, token, and language). The full list of types can be found at http://www.w3.org/TR/xmlschema-2/.

You can create and name complex types, just as you can create abstract datatypes in Oracle. The following code creates the "Address" type:

```
<xsd:complexType name="Address">
    <xsd:sequence>
        <xsd:element name="Street1"/>
        <xsd:element name="Street2"/>
        <xsd:element name="City"/>
        <xsd:element name="State"/>
        <xsd:element name="Zip"/>
    </xsd:sequence>
</xsd:complexType>
```

You can then refer to the "Address" complex type when defining your elements:

```
<xsd:element name="mailingAddress" type="Address"/>
<xsd:element name="billingAddress" type="Address"/>
```

If you are declaring a content model for a single element, use an anonymous type, as shown in the following listing:

```
<xsd:element name="Name">
    <xsd:complexType>
        <xsd:sequence>
            <xsd:element name="First"/>
            <xsd:element name="MiddleInitial"/>
            <xsd:element name="Last"/>
        </xsd:sequence>
    </xsd:complexType
</xsd:element>
```

Attributes are declared using xsd:attribute, as shown in the following example:

```
<xsd:attribute name="paid" type="boolean"/>
```

You can create attributes within a complex type:

```
<xsd:element name="Invoice">
    <xsd:complexType>
        <xsd:attribute name="paid" use="optional" default="True"/>
    </xsd:complexType>
</xsd:element>
```

In addition to creating attributes, you can create attribute groups and model groups. Model groups are groups or element definitions, named for reuse. The "group" element must be a top-level schema component (a child of the "schema" element). For example, the following listing shows the creation of a MealOptions group, referenced by the "FlightDinner" element:

```
<xsd:element name="FlightDinner">
    <xsd:sequence>
        <xsd:element ref="Name"/>
        <xsd:group ref="MealOptions"/>
    </xsd:sequence>
</xsd:element>

<xsd:group name="MealOptions">
    <xsd:choice>
        <xsd:element name="Fish" type="Meal"/>
        <xsd:element name="Meat" type="Meal"/>
        <xsd:element name="Vegetarian" type="Meal"/>
    </xsd:choice>
</xsd:group>
```

Attributes are commonly grouped together if elements often use the same set of attributes. This is similar to the approach described in Part V of this book, in which common attributes were combined to form new datatypes. For example, the following definition for a "Product" element uses an attribute group named *productDetails*. Other elements can reuse this same attribute group, improving your ability to enforce a standardized representation of this data.

```
<xsd:element name="Product">
    <xsd:complexType>
```

```
        <xsd:attributeGroup ref="productDetails"/>
    </xsd:complexType>
</xsd:element>

<xsd:attributeGroup name="productDetails">
    <xsd:attribute name="productID" use="required" type="xsd:ID"/>
    <xsd:attribute name="name" use="required" type="xsd:string"/>
    <xsd:attribute name="description" use="required" type="xsd:string"/>
    <xsd:attribute name="unit" type="xsd:positiveInteger"/>
    <xsd:attribute name="price" use="required" type="xsd:decimal"/>
    <xsd:attribute name="stock" type="xsd:integer"/>
</xsd:attributeGroup>
```

You can enforce uniqueness within a document instance by using xsd:unique:

```
<xsd:unique name="uniqueProductID">
    <xsd:selector xpath="tc:Product/"/>
    <xsd:field xpath="tc:@productID"/>
</xsd:unique>
```

Uniqueness is declared at the same level as the complex type definition for the "Product" element. The *tc:* namespace is for the schema you are creating and is declared in the xsd:schema element. The xsd:selector value specifies the elements to constrain (the "Product" elements), and xsd:field specifies the attribute to constrain (productID).

You can use xsd:key and xsd:keyref to create references between elements. For example, you can create a "Customer" element and then reference it from multiple "Invoice" elements:

```
<xsd:key name="customerID">
    <xsd:selector xpath="tc:SalesData/"/>
    <xsd:field xpath="tc:Customer/@CustID"/>
</xsd:key>

<xsd:keyref name="item" refer="customerID">
    <xsd:selector xpath="tc:SalesData/"/>
    <xsd:field xpath="tc:Invoice/@CustID"/>
</xsd:keyref>
```

To allow an element to be **NULL**, use the *nillable* attribute:

```
<xsd:element name="FlightDinner" nillable="true"/>
```

Using XSU to Select, Insert, Update, and Delete XML Values

You can use Oracle's XML-SQL Utility (XSU) to convert the result of a SQL query to XML. XSU supports dynamic generation of DTDs and the insertion of XML into database tables. You can also use XSU to update or delete rows from database objects.

You can access XSU via Java and PL/SQL APIs (application programming interfaces). The XSU Java classes are part of the Oracle kernel software. The PL/SQL API is a wrapper that publishes the Java classes to PL/SQL (see Chapter 39). Because the XSU classes are stored in the database, you can write new stored procedures to directly access XSU's Java classes. Because a PL/SQL API is available, XSU's functionality can be accessed directly through SQL.

For example, you can generate the XML version of the RATING table via the XSU PL/SQL procedures. The following listing creates a procedure named PRINTCLOBOUT that will be called as part of the data-output process. The data will be read in as a CLOB.

```
create or replace procedure PRINTCLOBOUT(result IN OUT NOCOPY CLOB)
 is
xmlstr varchar2(32767);
line varchar2(2000);
begin
  xmlstr := dbms_lob.SUBSTR(result,32767);
  loop
    exit when xmlstr is null;
    line := substr(xmlstr,1,instr(xmlstr,chr(10))-1);
    dbms_output.put_line('| '||line);
    xmlstr := substr(xmlstr,instr(xmlstr,chr(10))+1);
  end loop;
end;
/
```

Now that the PRINTCLOBOUT procedure exists, run the following anonymous PL/SQL block. This block queries the RATING table, so that table must be accessible from your schema (see the accompanying CD-ROM).

NOTE
*You must **set serveroutput on** prior to executing this PL/SQL block.*

```
declare
  queryCtx DBMS_XMLquery.ctxType;
  result CLOB;
begin
  -- set up the query context...
  queryCtx := DBMS_XMLQuery.newContext('select * from rating');
   -- get the result..
  result := DBMS_XMLQuery.getXML(queryCtx);
  -- Now you can use the result to put it in tables/send as messages..
  printClobOut(result);
  DBMS_XMLQuery.closeContext(queryCtx);  -- you must close the query..
end;
/
```

The result is the RATING table, formatted with XML tags:

```
<?xml version = '1.0'?>
<ROWSET>
   <ROW num="1">
      <RATING>1</RATING>
      <RATINGDESCRIPTION>ENTERTAINMENT</RATINGDESCRIPTION>
   </ROW>
   <ROW num="2">
      <RATING>2</RATING>
      <RATINGDESCRIPTION>BACKGROUND INFORMATION</RATINGDESCRIPTION>
   </ROW>
   <ROW num="3">
      <RATING>3</RATING>
      <RATINGDESCRIPTION>RECOMMENDED</RATINGDESCRIPTION>
   </ROW>
   <ROW num="4">
      <RATING>4</RATING>
      <RATINGDESCRIPTION>STRONGLY RECOMMENDED</RATINGDESCRIPTION>
   </ROW>
   <ROW num="5">
      <RATING>5</RATING>
      <RATINGDESCRIPTION>REQUIRED READING</RATINGDESCRIPTION>
   </ROW>
</ROWSET>
```

PL/SQL procedure successfully completed.

Insert, Update, and Delete Processing with XSU

To insert a document into a table or view, use the DBMS_XMLSave package. XSU will parse the document and create an **insert** statement that inserts the values into all the columns of the table or view. An absent element is treated as a **NULL** value.

```
create or replace procedure INSPROC(xmlDoc IN CLOB,
tableName IN VARCHAR2) is
   insCtx DBMS_XMLSave.ctxType;
   rows number;
begin
   insCtx := DBMS_XMLSave.newContext(tableName); -- get the context
   rows := DBMS_XMLSave.insertXML(insCtx,xmlDoc); -- insert the doc
   DBMS_XMLSave.closeContext(insCtx);            -- close the handle
end;
/
```

You can now pass in XML documents as CLOB input values to the INSPROC procedure, along with the table name. INSPROC will take the XML document and insert its values into the table. Updates can be executed via calls to a separate procedure, UPDATEPROC, shown in the following listing:

```
create or replace procedure UPDATEPROC ( xmlDoc IN clob) is
   updCtx DBMS_XMLSave.ctxType;
   rows number;
begin
   updCtx := DBMS_XMLSave.newContext('RATING');   -- get context
   DBMS_XMLSave.clearUpdateColumnList(updCtx); -- clear settings
   DBMS_XMLSave.setKeyColumn(updCtx,'RATING'); -- set RATING as key
   rows := DBMS_XMLSave.updateXML(updCtx,xmlDoc);   -- update
   DBMS_XMLSave.closeContext(updCtx);                -- close context
end;
/
```

In this example, the Rating column is the key column used for the update's **where** clause:

```
DBMS_XMLSave.setKeyColumn(updCtx,'RATING'); -- set RATING as key
```

The new values are passed in as an XML document in CLOB format, and the RATING table values are updated based on the contents of the XML document.

Delete operations function in much the same way. The following procedure takes an XML document as its input, establishes the Rating column as the key for the RATING table, and performs the **delete** based on the key values in the input document. Note that newContext takes the table name RATING as its input value, whereas setKeyColumn takes the key column name (which in this case happens to also be Rating).

```
create or replace procedure DELETEPROC(xmlDoc IN clob) is
   delCtx DBMS_XMLSave.ctxType;
   rows number;
begin
   delCtx  := DBMS_XMLSave.newContext('RATING');
   DBMS_XMLSave.setKeyColumn(delCtx,'RATING');
   rows := DBMS_XMLSave.deleteXML(delCtx,xmlDoc);
   DBMS_XMLSave.closeContext(delCtx);
end;
/
```

XSU and Java

If you prefer, you can perform the XSU DML operations via calls to Java classes instead of the PL/SQL procedures. In place of the DBMS_XMLQuery package, you should execute the oracle.xml.sql .query.OracleXMLQuery class. In place of the DBMS_XMLSave package, use oracle.xml.sql.dml .OracleXMLSave.

For example, the Oracle-provided sample Java program for XML queries is customized slightly in the following listing. It relies on connection management in a fashion very similar to that shown in the JDBC examples (see Chapter 38). The program imports the oracle.xml.sql.query.OracleXMLQuery class, enabling it to get the XML string; Java's System.out.println method is then called to display the output.

```
import oracle.xml.sql.query.OracleXMLQuery;
import java.lang.*;
```

```java
import java.sql.*;

// class to test the String generation!
class testXMLSQL {

    public static void main(String[] argv)
    {

        try{
            // create the connection
            Connection conn  = getConnection("practice","practice");

            // Create the query class.
            OracleXMLQuery qry = new OracleXMLQuery(conn, "select * from rating");

            // Get the XML string
            String str = qry.getXMLString();

            // Print the XML output
            System.out.println(" The XML output is:\n"+str);
            // Always close the query to get rid of any resources..
            qry.close();
        }catch(SQLException e){
            System.out.println(e.toString());
        }
    }

    // Get the connection given the user name and password..!
    private static Connection getConnection(String username,
    String password)
        throws SQLException
    {
        // register the JDBC driver..
        DriverManager.registerDriver(new oracle.jdbc.OracleDriver());

        // Create the connection using the OCI8 driver
        Connection conn =
        DriverManager.getConnection("jdbc:oracle:oci8:@or90",username,password);

        return conn;
    }
}
```

For details on connection management and Java, see Part VI of this book.

Customizing the Query Process

You can create your own procedures to simplify the interaction with the DBMS_XMLQuery and DBMS_XMLSave packages. For example, the following listing creates a function named GET_XML, which will select the rows from the table and display them in XML format.

```
create function GET_XML (in_SQL varchar2)
    return CLOB
is queryCtx DBMS_XMLQuery.ctxType;
    result CLOB;
begin   queryCtx := DBMS_XMLQuery.newContext(in_SQL);
    result := DBMS_XMLQuery.getXML(queryCtx);
    DBMS_XMLQuery.closeContext(queryCtx);
    return result;
end;
/
```

The data will be returned in CLOB format, so you can use the **set long** command to set the maximum display length (the default is 80 characters). You can call GET_XML from within SQL queries, as shown in the following listing:

```
set pagesize 100 long 2000

select GET_XML('select * from category') from DUAL;

GET_XML('SELECT*FROMCATEGORY')
--------------------------------------------------
<?xml version = '1.0'?>
<ROWSET>
    <ROW num="1">
        <CATEGORYNAME>ADULTREF</CATEGORYNAME>
        <PARENTCATEGORY>ADULT</PARENTCATEGORY>
        <SUBCATEGORY>REFERENCE</SUBCATEGORY>
    </ROW>
    <ROW num="2">
        <CATEGORYNAME>ADULTFIC</CATEGORYNAME>
        <PARENTCATEGORY>ADULT</PARENTCATEGORY>
        <SUBCATEGORY>FICTION</SUBCATEGORY>
    </ROW>
    <ROW num="3">
        <CATEGORYNAME>ADULTNF</CATEGORYNAME>
        <PARENTCATEGORY>ADULT</PARENTCATEGORY>
        <SUBCATEGORY>NONFICTION</SUBCATEGORY>
    </ROW>
    <ROW num="4">
        <CATEGORYNAME>CHILDRENPIC</CATEGORYNAME>
        <PARENTCATEGORY>CHILDREN</PARENTCATEGORY>
        <SUBCATEGORY>PICTURE BOOK</SUBCATEGORY>
    </ROW>
    <ROW num="5">
        <CATEGORYNAME>CHILDRENFIC</CATEGORYNAME>
        <PARENTCATEGORY>CHILDREN</PARENTCATEGORY>
        <SUBCATEGORY>FICTION</SUBCATEGORY>
    </ROW>
    <ROW num="6">
        <CATEGORYNAME>CHILDRENNF</CATEGORYNAME>
        <PARENTCATEGORY>CHILDREN</PARENTCATEGORY>
```

```
      <SUBCATEGORY>NONFICTION</SUBCATEGORY>
   </ROW>
</ROWSET>
```

Using XMLType

You can use XMLType as a datatype in your tables. XML.Type can be used to store and query XML data in the database. As a type, XMLType has member functions (see Chapter 33) to access, extract, and query XML data using a class of operations known as Xpath expressions. The SYS_XMLGEN, SYS_XMLAGG, and DBMS_XMLGEN packages create XMLType values from existing object-relational data. When you designate a column as using the XMLType datatype, Oracle will store the data internally in a CLOB datatype.

The following listing shows the creation of a table using the XMLType datatype:

```
create table MY_XML_TABLE
(Key1       NUMBER,
Xml_Column  SYS.XMLTYPE);
```

If you describe the table, you will see its columns:

```
desc MY_XML_TABLE
```

Name	Null?	Type
KEY1		NUMBER
XML_COLUMN		SYS.XMLTYPE

If you increase the describe depth, you will see the member functions for the XMLType column as well. The following listing shows the first few of the many functions and methods available:

```
set describe depth 5
desc MY_XML_TABLE
```

Name	Null?	Type
KEY1		NUMBER
XML_COLUMN		SYS.XMLTYPE

```
METHOD
------
STATIC FUNCTION CREATEXML RETURNS XMLTYPE
```

Argument Name	Type	In/Out	Default?
XMLDATA	CLOB	IN	

```
METHOD
------
MEMBER FUNCTION EXTRACT RETURNS XMLTYPE
```

Argument Name	Type	In/Out	Default?
XPATH	VARCHAR2	IN	

```
METHOD
------
 MEMBER FUNCTION EXISTSNODE RETURNS NUMBER
 Argument Name                      Type                      In/Out Default?
 -----------------------------      ----------------------    ------ --------
 XPATH                              VARCHAR2                   IN

METHOD
------
 MEMBER FUNCTION ISFRAGMENT RETURNS NUMBER

METHOD
------
 MEMBER FUNCTION GETCLOBVAL RETURNS CLOB

METHOD
------
 MEMBER FUNCTION GETSTRINGVAL RETURNS VARCHAR2

METHOD
------
 MEMBER FUNCTION GETNUMBERVAL RETURNS NUMBER
```

You can now insert values into MY_XML_TABLE by calling XMLType's CREATEXML method:

```
insert into MY_XML_TABLE (Key1, Xml_Column)
values (1, SYS.XMLTYPE.CREATEXML
 ('<book>
  <title>MY LEDGER</title>
  <chapter num= "1 ">
     <title>Beginning</title>
     <text>This is the ledger of G.B. Talbot</text>
  </chapter>
</book>'));
```

You can query the data by calling the GETCLOBVAL method. For example, the query

```
select M.Xml_Column.GETCLOBVAL() as XML_Data
  from MY_XML_TABLE M
 where Key1 = 1;
```

returns this data:

```
XML_DATA
-------------------------------------------------------
<book>
  <title>MY LEDGER</title>
  <chapter num="1">
     <title>Beginning</title>
     <text>This is the ledger of G.B. Talbot</text>
  </chapter>
|</book>
```

NOTE
You can create functional indexes on columns created with the
XMLType datatype to improve the performance of queries.

Other Features

This chapter has shown a very high-level view of the interaction of XML data with the Oracle
database. There are many other possibilities, including the use of style sheets for data formatting,
and creating XSQL pages. You can even create text indexes on XMLType columns:

```
create index XML_INDEX on MY_XML_TABLE (Xml_Column)
  indextype is ctxsys.context;
```

NOTE
See Chapter 25 for further details on text indexes.

Oracle provides the following packages to interact with XML data:

DBMS_XMLGEN Converts the results of SQL queries to canonical XML format, returning
them as a CLOB. DBMS_XMLGEN is implemented in C and compiled
in the database kernel. DBMS_XMLGEN is similar in functionality to the
DBMS_XMLQuery package.

SYS_XMLGEN Generates XML within SQL queries. DBMS_XMLGEN and other packages
operate at a query level, giving aggregated results for the *entire* query. SYS_
XMLGEN operates on a *single* argument inside a SQL query and converts
the result to XML.
SYS_XMLGEN takes in a scalar value, object type, or an XMLType
instance to be converted to an XML document. It also takes an optional
XMLGenFormatType object to specify formatting options for the result.
SYS_XMLGEN returns an XMLType.

SYS_XMLAGG Aggregates over a set of XMLTypes. SYS_XMLAGG aggregates all the
input XML documents/fragments and produces a single XML document
by concatenating XML fragments and adding a top-level tag that defaults
to ROWSET.

Oracle provides utilities to support additional uses, such as oraxml (a command-line interface
to parse an XML document) and oraxsl (a command-line interface used to apply a style sheet on
multiple XML documents). A full discussion of every utility and data-access method is beyond the
scope of this book; see the XML documentation provided with Oracle Database 10*g* for additional
options and sample programs. See the Alphabetical Reference for descriptions of functions that
act on XMLType instances, including EXTRACT, EXTRACTVALUE, SYS_XMLAGG, SYS_XMLGEN,
UPDATEXML, XMLAGG, XMLCONCAT, and XMLELEMENT.

PART

IX

Alphabetical Reference

his chapter contains references for most major Oracle commands, keywords, features, and functions, with cross-referencing of topics. The reference is intended for use by both developers and users of Oracle, but assumes some familiarity with the products. Reading the introduction to this reference will help you make the most productive use of the entries.

What This Alphabetical Reference Includes

This alphabetical reference contains entries for virtually every Oracle command in SQL, PL/SQL, and SQL*Plus, as well as definitions of all relevant terms used in Oracle Database 10g and SQL. Each command is listed with its correct format or syntax, an explanation of its purpose and use, the product or products in which it is used, and important details, restrictions, and hints about it, along with examples to illustrate proper usage. Topics are in alphabetical order and are cross-referenced, both within the alphabetical reference and to preceding chapters in the book.

What This Alphabetical Reference Does Not Include

This is not a tutorial; it does not explain the screen-oriented development and administration tools. Additionally, there are a few areas where usage is likely to be so specialized or infrequent that inclusion here did not seem of much benefit. In these instances, the text refers you to the Oracle manual in which you can find the needed information.

General Format of Entries

Entries in this reference are typically either definitions of terms or descriptions of functions, commands, and keywords. These are usually structured in seven sections: the keyword, its type, the products in which it is used, a SEE ALSO cross-reference, the format in which the keyword appears, a description of its components, and an example of its use. A typical entry looks like the following:

RPAD
SEE ALSO CHARACTER FUNCTIONS, **LPAD, LTRIM, RTRIM, TRIM**, Chapter 7
FORMAT RPAD(*string,length* [,'*set*'])
DESCRIPTION Right **PAD**. **RPAD** makes a string a certain length by adding a certain set of characters to the right. If *set* is not specified, the default pad character is a space.
EXAMPLE

```
select RPAD('HELLO ',24,'WORLD') from DUAL;
```

produces this:

```
HELLO WORLDWORLDWORLDWOR
```

The Sections of Each Entry

The KEYWORD usually appears on a line by itself. In some cases a brief definition follows. If a keyword has more than one definition, either in different Oracle tools or in different Oracle versions, the keyword is followed by a brief qualifier to indicate that more than one listing exists for this keyword.

SEE ALSO suggests other topics that are closely related to the keyword, or gives the chapter or chapters in the book that give detailed descriptions of how the keyword is used in practice. Occasionally you will be referred to an Oracle manual or other reference book that contains detail beyond the scope of this reference.

FORMAT generally follows the notation of Oracle manuals, with all SQL and other keywords in uppercase. In actual use, these must be entered exactly as they are shown (except that case is irrelevant). Variables and variable parameters are shown in lowercase *italic*. This indicates that some appropriate value should be substituted. When parentheses are shown, they must be entered where they appear, as must words shown in uppercase.

Standard Usages for Variables

Some standard usages for variables follow:

This Variable	Indicates
column	The name of a column
database	The name of a database
link	The name of a link in Oracle Net
password	A password
segment	The name of a segment
table	The name of a table
tablespace	The name of a tablespace
user	The name of a user or owner
view	The name of a view

Other Formatting Guidelines

Some other guidelines for formatting follow:

- ■ **character** means the value must be a single character.

- ■ **string** typically represents a character column or an expression or column that can be treated like a CHAR or VARCHAR2 column after automatic data conversion.

- ■ **value** usually represents a NUMBER column or an expression or column that can be treated like a NUMBER column after automatic data conversion.

- ■ **date** usually represents a DATE column or an expression or column that can be treated like a DATE column after automatic data conversion.

- ■ **datetime** usually represents a TIMESTAMP column or an expression or column that can be treated like a TIMESTAMP column after automatic data conversion.

- ■ **integer** must be a whole number, such as –3, 0, or 12.

- ■ **expression** means any form of a column. This could be a literal, a variable, a mathematical computation, a function, or virtually any combination of functions and columns whose final result is a single value, such as a string, a number, or a date.

- ■ Occasionally other notation is used as well, such as **condition** or **query**. This is explained or is apparent in context.

- Optional items are enclosed in square brackets, as in [*user.*], meaning that *user* is not necessarily required.

- Alternative items in a list are separated by a single broken vertical bar, as in OFF | ON, which should be read "OFF or ON." On some systems, this vertical bar is displayed as a solid vertical bar.

- Required options, where one item of a list of items is required, are surrounded by curly braces, as in {OFF | ON}.

- The default item in a list, if there is one, will be listed first.

- Three periods (an ellipsis) indicate that the preceding expression can be repeated any number of times, as in **column [,column]. . .,** which means that **,column** may be any number of additional columns separated by commas.

- In rare instances, normal notation is either insufficient or inappropriate for what is being shown. In these cases, the **DESCRIPTION** section spells out more fully what is intended in the **FORMAT** section.

Other Elements of a Listing

A few commands have a return type, which indicates the datatype of the value returned by a function.

DESCRIPTION is an explanation of the command and its parts. **Boldface** words within the description usually refer to either commands or variables shown in the FORMAT section.

EXAMPLE shows either the results of a function or how a keyword is used in a real command. The style of the examples is not the same as the style of the FORMAT section. Instead, it follows the style of the first part of this book (described in Chapter 3), since that style is more typical of real coding practice.

The Order of the Keywords

This reference is in alphabetical order, with all entries that begin with symbols coming before the first entry beginning with the letter *A*.

Words that are hyphenated or that have an underscore character in them are alphabetized as if the hyphen or underscore were a space.

Symbols

The symbols are listed in order of appearance with a short definition or name.

_	**underline (also called underscore, underbar)**
!	**exclamation mark**
"	**double quotation mark**
#	**pound sign**
$	**dollar sign**
?	**question mark**
%	**percent sign**
&	**ampersand**
&&	**double ampersand**

'	single quotation mark or apostrophe		
()	parentheses		
*	asterisk or multiplication		
**	exponentiation in PL/SQL		
+	plus		
-	subtraction or hyphen		
- -	double hyphen, SQL comment minus or hyphen		
.	period or dot, a name or variable separator		
..	to		
/	division or slash		
/*	slash asterisk, SQL comment divided by or slash		
:	colon		
:=	is set equal to in PL/SQL		
;	semicolon		
<< >>	label name delimiter in PL/SQL		
<	less than		
<=	less than or equal to		
< >	not equal		
!=	not equal		
=	equal		
>	greater than		
>=	greater than or equal to		
@	at sign		
@@	double at sign		
[]	square brackets		
^	caret		
^=	not equal		
{}	curly braces		
¦	broken vertical bar		
			concatenation

_ (Underscore)

The underscore represents a single position with the **LIKE** operator. *See* **LIKE**.

_EDITOR

See **EDIT**.

! (Exclamation Mark)

SEE ALSO $, =, **CONTAINS**, **SOUNDEX**, Chapter 25

FORMAT Within SQL, **!** is used as part of the "not equal" expression, **!=**. For example, you can select all the city values that are not in the continent of Asia:

```
select City
  from LOCATION
 where Continent != 'ASIA';
```

For CONTEXT text indexes, **!** signals the text engine to perform a **SOUNDEX** search. The terms to search for will be expanded to include terms that sound like the search term, using the text's **SOUNDEX** value to determine possible matches.

```
select Title
   from BOOK_REVIEW_CONTEXT
 where CONTAINS(Review_Text, '!grate')>0;
```

" (Double Quotation Mark)

SEE ALSO **ALIAS**, **TO_CHAR**, Chapters 7 and 10

DESCRIPTION " surrounds a table or column alias that contains special characters or a space, or surrounds literal text in a date format clause of **TO_CHAR**.

EXAMPLE Here " is used as an alias:

```
select NEXT_DAY(CycleDate,'FRIDAY') "Pay Day!"
   from PAYDAY;
```

And here it is used as a formatting portion of **TO_CHAR**:

```
select FirstName, Birthdate, TO_CHAR(BirthDate,
        '"Baby Girl on" fmMonth ddth, YYYY, "at" HH:MI "in the Morning"')
        "Formatted"
   from BIRTHDAY
 where FirstName = 'VICTORIA';
```

```
FIRSTNAME        BIRTHDATE Formatted
---------------  --------- ------------------------------
VICTORIA         20-MAY-49 Baby Girl on May 20th, 1949,
                           at 3:27 in the Morning
```

(Pound Sign)

SEE ALSO **REMARK**, /* */, Chapter 6

DESCRIPTION # completes a block of documentation in a SQL*Plus start file where the block is begun by the word DOCUMENT. SQL*Plus ignores all lines from the line where it sees the word DOCUMENT until the line after the #.

$ (Dollar Sign)

SEE ALSO @, @@, **HOST**, **START**, **CONTAINS**, Chapter 25

FORMAT For SQL*Plus:

```
$ host_command
```

In UNIX environments, the **$** symbol can be replaced with **!** when executing host commands.
 For CONTEXT text indexes:

```
select column
  from table
 where CONTAINS(text_column, '$search_term') >0;
```

DESCRIPTION **$** passes any host command back to the operating system for execution without exiting SQL*Plus. **$** is shorthand for **HOST**. This doesn't work on all hardware or operating systems.
 For a CONTEXT text index, **$** instructs the search engine to perform a stem expansion on the search term. A stem expansion includes in the search those words that have the same word stem. For example, a stem expansion of the word 'sing' would include 'singing', 'sang', and 'sung'.

? (Question Mark)
SEE ALSO **CONTAINS**, Chapter 25
FORMAT

```
select column
  from table
 where CONTAINS(text_column, '?term')>0;
```

DESCRIPTION For CONTEXT text indexes, **?** instructs the text engine to perform a fuzzy match search. The terms to search for will be expanded to include terms that are spelled similarly to the search term, using the text index as the source for possible matches.

% (Percent)
% is a wildcard used to represent any number of positions and characters with the **LIKE** operator. *See* **LIKE**.

%FOUND
SEE ALSO **%ISOPEN**, **%NOTFOUND**, **%ROWCOUNT**, **CURSOR**, **SQL CURSOR**, Chapter 29
FORMAT

```
cursor%FOUND
```

or

```
SQL%FOUND
```

DESCRIPTION **%FOUND** is a success flag for **select**, **insert**, **update**, and **delete**. *cursor* is the name of an explicit cursor declared in a PL/SQL block, or the implicit cursor named **SQL**. **%FOUND** can be attached to a cursor name as a suffix. The two together are a success flag for the execution of **SELECT**, **INSERT**, **UPDATE**, and **DELETE** statements in PL/SQL blocks.
 PL/SQL temporarily sets aside a section of memory as a scratchpad for the execution of SQL statements, and for storing certain kinds of information (or *attributes*) about the state of that execution. If the SQL statement is a **select**, this area will contain one row of data.
 %FOUND is one of those attributes. **%FOUND** is typically tested (via **IF/THEN** logic) after an explicit **fetch** has been performed from the cursor. It will be TRUE if the **fetch** retrieved a row, and FALSE otherwise. It always evaluates to TRUE, FALSE, or **NULL**. **%NOTFOUND** is the logical opposite. It is FALSE when **%FOUND** is TRUE, TRUE when **%FOUND** is FALSE, and **NULL** when **%FOUND** is **NULL**.

Testing **%FOUND** for the condition of an explicit cursor before it is **OPEN**ed raises an EXCEPTION (error code ORA-01001, INVALID CURSOR).

%ISOPEN

SEE ALSO SQL CURSOR, Chapter 29
FORMAT

```
cursor%ISOPEN
```

DESCRIPTION *cursor* must be either the name of an explicitly declared cursor or the implicit cursor named **SQL**. **%ISOPEN** evaluates to TRUE if the named cursor is open, and to FALSE if it is not. **SQL%ISOPEN** will *always* evaluate to FALSE, because the SQL cursor is opened and closed automatically when a SQL statement not explicitly declared is executed (*see* **SQL CURSOR**). **%ISOPEN** is used in PL/SQL logic; it cannot be a part of a SQL statement.

%NOTFOUND

See %FOUND.

%ROWCOUNT

SEE ALSO CLOSE, DECLARE, DELETE, FETCH, INSERT, OPEN, SELECT, UPDATE, Chapter 29
FORMAT

```
cursor%ROWCOUNT
```

DESCRIPTION *cursor* must be either the name of an explicitly declared cursor or the implicit cursor named **SQL**. *cursor***%ROWCOUNT** contains the cumulative total number of rows that have been **fetch**ed from the active set in this cursor. **%ROWCOUNT** can be used to intentionally process only a fixed number of rows, but is more commonly used as an exception handler for **select**s that are intended to return just one row (for example, **select. . . into**). In these cases, **%ROWCOUNT** is set to 0 if no rows are returned (**%NOTFOUND** can make this test as well), and to 2 if more than one row is returned, regardless of the actual number.

%ROWCOUNT is used in PL/SQL logic; it cannot be a part of a SQL statement. If **SQL%ROWCOUNT** is used, it can only refer to the most recently opened implicit cursor. If no implicit cursor has been opened, **SQL%ROWCOUNT** returns **NULL**.

%ROWTYPE

SEE ALSO FETCH, Chapter 29
FORMAT

```
{[user.]table | cursor}%ROWTYPE
```

DESCRIPTION **%ROWTYPE** declares a record variable to have the same structure as an entire row in a table (or view), or as a row retrieved by the named cursor. **%ROWTYPE** is used as part of a variable declaration and assures that the variable will contain the appropriate fields and datatypes to handle all of the columns being fetched. If [*user.*]*table* is used, the table (or view) must exist in the database.

To create a variable that will contain corresponding fields, use **declare**, a variable name, and **%ROWTYPE** with the table name, and then select a row into the record. Because the variable has the same structure as the table, you can reference the fields as *variable.field*, using notation similar to

table.column used in SQL statements. **select. . .into** and **fetch. . .into** are the only methods for loading an entire record variable. Individual fields within the record can be loaded using :=, as shown here:

```
BOOKSHELF_RECORD.Publisher := 'PANDORAS';
```

If a cursor is used as the prefix for **%ROWTYPE**, then it can contain a **select** statement with only as many columns as are needed. However, if a column that is **fetch**ed from a named cursor is an expression, rather than a simple column name, the expression must be given an alias in the **select** statement before it can be referenced using this technique.

%TYPE

SEE ALSO %ROWTYPE, Chapter 29
FORMAT

```
{[user.]table.column | variable}%TYPE
```

DESCRIPTION **%TYPE** is used to declare a variable to be of the same type as a previously declared variable, or as a particular column in a table that exists in the database you're connected to.

EXAMPLE In this example a new variable, Writer, is declared to be the same type as the AuthorName column in the AUTHOR table. Since Writer now exists, it can be used to declare yet another new variable, Coauthor.

```
Writer    AUTHOR.AuthorName%TYPE;
Coauthor  Writer%TYPE;
```

& or && (Ampersand or Double Ampersand)

SEE ALSO :, ACCEPT, DEFINE, START, CONTAINS, Chapter 25
FORMAT For SQL*Plus:

```
&integer
&variable
&&variable
```

For CONTEXT indexes:

```
select Title
  from BOOK_REVIEW_CONTEXT
 where CONTAINS(Review_Text, 'property & harvests')>0;
```

DESCRIPTION & and && can be used in several ways (&& applies only to the second definition):

- ■ As a prefix for parameters in a SQL*Plus start file. Values are substituted for &1, &2, etc. *See* **START**.

- ■ As a prefix for a substitution variable in a SQL command in SQL*Plus. SQL*Plus will prompt for a value if an undefined & or && variable is found. && will define the variable and thereby preserve its value; & will not define or preserve the value, but only substitute what is entered one time. *See* **ACCEPT** and **DEFINE**.

- ■ When using CONTEXT indexes, & is used to signal an AND condition for text searches involving multiple search terms. If any of the search terms is not found, the text will not be returned by the search.

' (Single Quotation Mark)

SEE ALSO " (Double Quotation Mark), Chapter 7

FORMAT

```
'string'
```

DESCRIPTION ' surrounds a literal, such as a character string or date constant. To use one quotation mark or an apostrophe in a string constant, use two ' marks (not a double quotation mark). Avoid the use of apostrophes in data (and elsewhere) whenever possible.

EXAMPLE

```
select 'William' from DUAL;
```

produces this:

```
William
```

whereas

```
select 'William''s brother' from DUAL;
```

produces this:

```
William's brother
```

() (Parentheses)

SEE ALSO PRECEDENCE, SUBQUERY, UPDATE, Chapters 13 and 15

DESCRIPTION Parentheses enclose subqueries or lists of columns, or control precedence within expressions.

* (Multiplication)

SEE ALSO +, -, /, Chapters 9 and 25

FORMAT

```
value1 * value2
```

DESCRIPTION *value1* * *value2* means *value1* multiplied by *value2*. For CONTEXT indexes, * is used to weight the individual search terms differently.

** (Exponentiation)

SEE ALSO POWER

FORMAT

```
x ** y
```

DESCRIPTION x is raised to the power y. x and y may be constants, variables, columns, or expressions. Both must be numeric.

EXAMPLE $4**4 = 256$

+ (Addition)

SEE ALSO -, *, /, Chapter 8

FORMAT

```
value1 + value2
```

DESCRIPTION *value1 + value2* means *value1* plus *value2*.

– (Subtraction [Form 1])
SEE ALSO +, *, /, Chapter 8, **CONTAINS**, **MINUS**, Chapter 25
FORMAT

```
value1 - value2
```

DESCRIPTION *value1 – value2* means *value1* minus *value2*. For CONTEXT indexes, a – tells the text search of two terms to subtract the score of the second term's search from the score of the first term's search before comparing the result to the threshold score. For CTXCAT indexes, a – tells the text search engine to exclude the row from the result set if the term following the – is found.

- (Hyphen [Form 2])
SEE ALSO Chapter 6
FORMAT

```
command text -
        text -
        text
```

DESCRIPTION SQL*Plus command continuation; a - continues a command on the following line.
EXAMPLE

```
ttitle left 'Current Portfolio' -
right 'November 1st, 1999'        skip 1 -
center 'Industry Listings   '  skip 4;
```

-- (Comment)
SEE ALSO /* */, **REMARK**, Chapter 6
FORMAT

```
-- any text
```

DESCRIPTION -- tells Oracle a comment has begun. Everything from that point to the end of the line is treated as a comment. These delimiters are used only within SQL itself or in PL/SQL and must appear before the **SQLTERMINATOR**.
EXAMPLE

```
select Feature, Section, Page
-- this is just a comment
  from NEWSPAPER    -- this is another comment
 where Section = 'F';
```

. (Period or Dot [Form 1]) (SQL*Plus)
FORMAT

```
&variable.suffix
```

DESCRIPTION The . is a variable separator, which is used in SQL*Plus to separate the variable name from a suffix so that the suffix is not considered a part of the variable name.

EXAMPLE Here, the suffix "st" is effectively concatenated to the contents of the variable &Avenue:

```
define Avenue = 21
select '100 &Avenue.st Street' from DUAL;
```

produces this:

```
100 21st Street
```

This same technique might also be used in a **WHERE** clause.

. (Period or Dot [Form 2])
SEE ALSO SYNTAX OPERATORS, Chapter 21
FORMAT

```
[user.][table.]column
```

DESCRIPTION The . is a name separator, used to specify the complete name of a column, including (optionally) its table or user. The . is also used to address columns within abstract datatypes during **select**s, **update**s, and **delete**s.

EXAMPLE

```
select Practice.BOOKSHELF.Title
  from Practice.BOOKSHELF, Practice.BOOKSHELF_AUTHOR
 where Practice.BOOKSHELF.Title = Practice.BOOKSHELF_AUTHOR.Title;
```

If the table contains columns based on an abstract datatype, the datatype's attributes may be accessed via the . notation.

```
select C.Person.Address.City
  from Company C
 where C.Person.Address.State = 'FL';
```

See Chapter 33 for further examples.

.. (To)
See **LOOP**.

/ (Division [Form 1])
SEE ALSO +, –, *, Chapter 9
FORMAT

```
value1 / value2
```

DESCRIPTION *value1 / value2* means *value1* divided by *value2*.

/ (Slash [Form 2]) (SQL*Plus)
SEE ALSO ;, BUFFER, EDIT, GET, RUN, SET, SQLTERMINATOR

DESCRIPTION / executes the SQL in the SQL buffer without displaying it, unlike **RUN**, which displays it first.

/* */ (Comment)
SEE ALSO REMARK, Chapter 6
FORMAT

```
/* any text */
```

DESCRIPTION /* tells Oracle a comment has begun. Everything Oracle sees from that point forward, even for many words and lines, it regards as a comment until it sees the ending */, which ends the comment. Comments cannot be embedded within comments; that is, a /* is terminated by the first following */, even if there is an intervening /*.

EXAMPLE

```
select Feature, Section, Page
    /* this is a multi-line comment
        used to extensively document the code */
  from NEWSPAPER
 where Section = 'F';
```

: (Colon, Host Variable Prefix)
SEE ALSO INDICATOR VARIABLE
FORMAT

```
:name
```

DESCRIPTION name is the name of a host variable. When PL/SQL is embedded in a host language through an Oracle precompiler, host variables can be referenced from within the PL/SQL blocks by prefixing their host language names with a colon. In effect, this is the host variable. If PL/SQL changes its value through an assignment (:=), the value of the host variable is changed. Host variables may be used anywhere a PL/SQL variable can be used. The one exception is in assigning the value **NULL** to a host variable, which is not supported directly, but requires the use of an indicator variable.

EXAMPLE

```
int   BookCount;
...
    select COUNT(*) into :BookCount from BOOKSHELF;
```

:= (Set Equal To)
SEE ALSO DECLARE, FETCH, SELECT INTO, Chapter 29
FORMAT

```
variable := expression
```

DESCRIPTION The PL/SQL variable is set equal to the expression, which may be a constant, **NULL**, or a calculation with other variables, literals, and PL/SQL functions.

EXAMPLE

```
Extension := Quantity * Price;
Title := 'BARBERS WHO SHAVE THEMSELVES';
Name := NULL;
```

; (Semicolon)

SEE ALSO **/** (Slash), **BUFFER**, **EDIT**, **GET**, **RUN**, **SQLTERMINATOR**, **CONTAINS**, **NEAR**, Chapter 25

DESCRIPTION **;** executes the SQL or the command that precedes it. For CONTEXT indexes, **;** indicates that a proximity search should be executed for the specified text strings. If the search terms are 'summer' and 'lease', then a proximity search for the two terms could be

```
select Text
  from SONNET
 where CONTAINS(Text,'summer;lease') >0;
```

When evaluating the text search results, text with the words 'summer' and 'lease' near to each other in the text will have higher scores than text with the words 'summer' and 'lease' farther apart.

< < > > (PL/SQL Label Name Delimiter)

See **BEGIN**, BLOCK STRUCTURE, **END**, **GOTO**, **LOOP**, Chapter 29.

@ ("At" Sign [Form 1]) (SQL*Plus)

SEE ALSO **@@**, **START**

FORMAT

```
@file
```

DESCRIPTION **@** starts the SQL*Plus start file named *file*. **@** is similar to **START**, but does not allow command-line arguments.

@ ("At" Sign [Form 2])

SEE ALSO **CONNECT**, **COPY**, DATABASE LINK, Chapter 23

FORMAT

```
CON[NECT] user[/password] [@database];
COPY [FROM user/password@database]
     [TO user/password@database]
     {APPEND | CREATE | INSERT | REPLACE}
     table [ (column, [column]...) ]
     USING query;
SELECT...   FROM [user.]table[link]   [, [user.]table[@link] ]...
```

DESCRIPTION **@** prefixes a database name in a **CONNECT** or **COPY** command, or a link name in a **FROM** clause.

@@ (Double "At" Sign) (SQL*Plus)

SEE ALSO **@** (Form 1), **START**

FORMAT

```
@@file
```

DESCRIPTION @@ starts a nested SQL*Plus start file named *file*. @@ is similar to @, but differs in that @@, when used in a command file, will search for a start file in the same directory as the command file that called it (rather than in the directory you are in when you execute the command file).

{} (Curly Braces)

SEE ALSO **CONTAINS**, Chapter 25, Chapter 37

FORMAT For text searches, {} indicate that the enclosed text should be considered part of the search string even if it is a reserved word. For example, if the search term is 'in and out', and you want to search for the entire phrase, then you must enclose the word 'and' within braces:

```
REM  CONTAINS method for CONTEXT indexes:
select Title
   from BOOK_REVIEW_CONTEXT
 where CONTAINS(Review_Text, 'transactions {and} finances')>0;
```

Within Java, {} indicate the beginning and ending of a block. See Chapter 37 for examples of Java blocks.

| (Vertical Bar)

SEE ALSO **BTITLE, HEADSEP, TTITLE**, Chapter 6, Chapter 25

FORMAT

```
text|text
```

DESCRIPTION When used in a SQL*Plus **COLUMN**, **TTITLE**, or **BTITLE** command, | is the default **HEADSEP** character, and is used to denote the splitting of a line onto a second line. (When used in listings in this Reference, | denotes a break between alternative choices: *variable | literal* would be read "variable or literal." On some machines this shows as a solid vertical bar.) Within text queries, | signals an OR condition for searches involving two search terms. If either of the search terms is found, and its search score exceeds the specified threshold value, the text will be returned by the search.

EXAMPLE Here's how | is used as a **HEADSEP** character.

```
TTITLE 'This is the First Line|and This is the Second'
```

produces this:

```
This is the First Line
and This is the Second
```

Here's how | is used as an **OR** clause in a text search query:

```
REM  CONTAINS method for CONTEXT indexes:
select Title
   from BOOK_REVIEW_CONTEXT
 where CONTAINS(Review_Text, 'property | harvests')>0;
REM  CATSEARCH method for CTXCAT indexes:
select Title
   from BOOK_REVIEW_CTXCAT
 where CATSEARCH(Review_Text, 'property | harvests', NULL)>0;
```

|| (Concatenation)

SEE ALSO . (Period or Dot [Form 1]), **CONCAT**, **SUBSTR**, Chapter 7
FORMAT

```
expression1 || expression2
```

DESCRIPTION || concatenates two strings together.

EXAMPLE Use || to display a column of cities, followed by a comma, a space, and the country:

```
select City||', '||Country from LOCATION;
```

ABS (Absolute Value)

SEE ALSO NUMBER FUNCTIONS, Chapter 9
FORMAT

```
ABS(value)
```

value must be a number, whether a literal number, the name of a number column, a literal character string containing a valid number, or a character column containing only a valid number.

DESCRIPTION Absolute value is the measure of the magnitude of something, and is always a positive number.

EXAMPLES

```
ABS(146) = 146
ABS(-30) =  30
ABS('-27.88') = 27.88
```

ABSTRACT DATATYPES

Abstract datatypes are datatypes that consist of one or more attributes. Rather than being constrained to the standard datatypes of NUMBER, DATE, and VARCHAR2, abstract datatypes can consist of multiple attributes and/or other, previously defined abstract datatypes. Abstract datatypes are also known as *user-defined types (UDTs)*. See Chapter 33 for examples, and **CREATE TYPE** for creation syntax.

ACCEPT

SEE ALSO &, &&, DEFINE
FORMAT

```
ACC[EPT] variable [NUM[BER]|CHAR|DATE|BINARY_FLOAT|BINARY_DOUBLE] [FOR[MAT]
format]   [DEF[AULT] default] [PROMPT text | NOPR[OMPT]] [HIDE]
```

DESCRIPTION **ACCEPT** takes input from a user's keyboard and puts it in the named variable with the specified datatype. If the variable has not been previously **DEFINE**d, it is created. FORMAT specifies the input format for the reply (such as A20). DEFAULT sets the default value if a reply is not given. PROMPT displays the text to the user before accepting the input. NOPROMPT skips a line and waits for input without displaying any prompt. Using neither PROMPT nor NOPROMPT causes **ACCEPT** to invent a prompt asking for the value of the variable. HIDE suppresses the user's entry, and is valuable for passwords and the like.

EXAMPLE The following prompts the user with "How hot?" and puts the user's entry in a number variable named Temperature:

```
ACCEPT Temperature NUMBER PROMPT 'How hot? '
```

ACCUMULATE
See CONTAINS.

ACOS
SEE ALSO ASIN, ATAN, ATAN2, COS, COSH, EXP, LN, LOG, SIN, SINH, TAN, TANH
FORMAT

```
ACOS(value)
```

DESCRIPTION ACOS returns the arc cosine of a value. Input values range from −1 to 1; outputs are expressed in radians.

ADD_MONTHS
SEE ALSO DATE FUNCTIONS, Chapter 10
FORMAT

```
ADD_MONTHS(date,integer)
```

DESCRIPTION ADD_MONTHS adds a number of months to *date*, and returns the date that is that many months in the future. *date* must be a legitimate Oracle date. *integer* must be an integer; a noninteger value will be truncated to the next smallest integer. A negative value for *integer* will return a date in the past.

EXAMPLE ADD_MONTHS adds 1 month and 0.3 month to April 22, 2001:

```
select ADD_MONTHS(TO_DATE('22-APR-01'),1),
       ADD_MONTHS(TO_DATE('22-APR-01'),.3) from DUAL;

ADD_MONTH ADD_MONTH
--------- ---------
22-MAY-01 22-APR-01
```

AGGREGATE FUNCTIONS
SEE ALSO Chapter 9
DESCRIPTION An aggregate function computes a single summary value (such as sum or average) from the individual number values in a group of values. This is an alphabetical list of all current group functions in the Oracle version of SQL. Each of these is listed elsewhere in this reference under its own name, with its proper format and use. Aggregate functions are useful in select lists and **ORDER BY** and **HAVING** clauses.

FUNCTION NAME AND USE

 AVG gives the average of the values for a group of rows.

 COLLECT takes the input *column* value and creates a nested table of the input type out of the rows selected.

 CORR returns the coefficient of correlation of a set of number pairs.

 CORR_* supports nonparametric or rank correlation (**CORR_K** and **CORR_S**).

 COUNT gives the count of rows for a column, or for a table (with *).

 COVAR_POP returns the population covariance of a set of number pairs.

COVAR_SAMP returns the sample covariance of a set of number pairs.

CUME_DIST calculates the cumulative distribution of a value in a group of values.

DENSE_RANK computes the rank of a row in an ordered group of rows.

FIRST operates on a set of values from a set of rows that ranks as the first with respect to a given sorting specification.

GROUP_ID distinguishes duplicate groups resulting from a GROUP BY specification.

GROUPING distinguishes superaggregate rows from regular grouped rows.

GROUPING_ID returns a number corresponding to the GROUPING bit vector associated with a row.

LAST operates on a set of values from a set of rows that ranks as the last with respect to a given sorting specification.

MAX gives the maximum of all values for a group of rows.

MEDIAN gives the median value for a group of rows, ignoring **NULL**s.

MIN gives the minimum of all values for a group of rows.

PERCENT_RANK performs a percent ranking calculation.

PERCENTILE_CONT is a percentile calculation function that assumes a continuous distribution model.

PERCENTILE_DISC is a percentile calculation function that assumes a discrete distribution model.

RANK calculates the rank of a value in a group of values.

REGR functions perform linear regression analysis on a group of values.

STATS_BINOMIAL_TEST tests the difference between a sample proportion and a given proportion.

STATS_CROSSTAB analyzes two nominal values.

STATS_F_TEST tests whether two variables are significantly different.

STATS_KS_TEST tests whether two variables are from the same population.

STATS_MODE returns the value that occurs with the greatest frequency in a group.

STATS_MW_TEST tests two independent samples against a null hypothesis.

STATS_ONE_WAY_ANOVA is a one-way analysis of variance.

STATS_T_TEST_* functions measure the significance of a difference of means.

STATS_WSR_TEST determines whether the differences between samples are significantly different from zero.

STDDEV gives the standard deviation of all values for a group of rows.

STDDEV_POP computes the population standard deviation and returns the square root of the population variance.

STDDEV_SAMP computes the cumulative sample standard deviation and returns the square root of the sample variance.

SUM gives the sum of all values for a group of rows.

VAR_POP returns the population variance of a set of numbers after discarding the **NULL**s in this set.

VAR_SAMP returns the sample variance of a set of numbers after discarding the **NULL**s in this set.

VARIANCE gives the variance of all values for a group of rows.

ALIAS

An alias is a temporary name assigned to a table or a column within a SQL statement and is used to refer to it elsewhere in the same statement (if a table) or in a SQL*Plus command (if a column). You can use the AS keyword to separate the column definition from its alias. *See* " (Double Quotation Mark), **AS**, and **SELECT**. When used for a table, the alias is referred to as a *correlation name*.

ALL

SEE ALSO ANY, **BETWEEN**, **EXISTS**, **IN**, LOGICAL OPERATORS, Chapter 13

FORMAT

```
operator ALL list
```

DESCRIPTION != **ALL** is the equivalent of **NOT IN**. *operator* can be any one of =, >, >=, <, <=, or !=, and *list* can be a series of literal strings (such as 'Talbot', 'Jones', 'Hild'), a series of literal numbers (such as 2, 43, 76, 32.06, 444), or a column from a subquery, where each row of the subquery becomes a member of the list, such as this:

```
LOCATION.City != ALL (select City from WEATHER)
```

The *list* value can be a series of columns in the **WHERE** clause of the main query, as shown here:

```
Prospect != ALL (Vendor, Client)
```

RESTRICTIONS *list* cannot be a series of columns in a subquery, such as this:

```
Prospect != ALL (select Vendor, Client from . . .)
```

Many people find this operator and the **ANY** operator very difficult to remember, because the logic for some of their cases is not immediately intuitive. As a result, some form of **EXISTS** is usually substituted. The combination of an operator with **ALL** and a list can be illustrated with the following explanations:

Page = ALL (4,2,7)	Page is equal to every item in the list—no number qualifies. A subquery *could* return a list where all the items were identical, and a value of Page could be equal to every one of them, but this would be very rare.
Page > ALL (4,2,7)	Page is greater than the greatest item in the list (4,2,7)—anything larger than 7 qualifies.
Page >= ALL (4,2,7)	Page is greater than or equal to the greatest item in the list (4,2,7)—anything equal to or larger than 7 qualifies.
Page < ALL (4,2,7)	Page is less than the lowest item in the list (4,2,7)—anything below 2 qualifies.
Page <= ALL (4,2,7)	Page is less than or equal to the lowest item in the list (4,2,7)—anything equal to or lower than 2 qualifies.
Page != ALL (4,2,7)	Page is not equal to any item in the list—any number qualifies except 4, 2, and 7.

ALLOCATE (Embedded SQL)

SEE ALSO **DECLARE CURSOR**, *Programmer's Guide to the Oracle Precompilers*

FORMAT

```
EXEC SQL [AT   db_name | :host_variable }]
 ALLOCATE { :cursor_variable | :host_ptr }
 [[INDICATOR] :ind_ptr]
```

DESCRIPTION The **ALLOCATE** clause allocates a cursor variable that will be referenced in a PL/SQL block. See the *Programmer's Guide to the Oracle Precompilers* for details on **ALLOCATE** and related clauses such as the host pointer.

ALTER CLUSTER

SEE ALSO **CREATE CLUSTER**, **CREATE TABLE**, **STORAGE**, Chapter 17

FORMAT

alter_cluster::=

physical_attributes_clause::=

allocate_extent_clause::=

deallocate_unused_clause::=

size_clause::=

parallel_clause::=

DESCRIPTION Descriptions of the parameters can be found under **CREATE TABLE**. They have the same purpose and effect, except that here they are used to alter a cluster. Size is described under **CREATE CLUSTER**. In order to alter a cluster, you must either own the cluster or have ALTER ANY CLUSTER system privilege.

All tables in a cluster use the values for **PCTFREE**, **PCTUSED**, **INITRANS**, **TABLESPACE**, and **STORAGE** set by **CREATE CLUSTER**. **ALTER CLUSTER** changes these values for future cluster blocks, but does not affect those that already exist. **ALTER CLUSTER** does not allow changing the **extent** parameters in **STORAGE**. The **DEALLOCATE UNUSED** clause allows the cluster to shrink in size, freeing unused space.

EXAMPLE

```
alter cluster BOOKandAUTHOR size 1024;
```

ALTER DATABASE

SEE ALSO **ALTER ROLLBACK SEGMENT**, **CREATE DATABASE**, **RECOVER**, **STARTUP**, **SHUTDOWN**, Chapter 46

FORMAT
alter_database::=

startup_clauses::=

recovery_clauses::=

general_recovery::=

full_database_recovery::=

partial_database_recovery::=

parallel_clause::=

managed_standby_recovery::=

recover_clause::=

cancel_clause::=

finish_clause::=

database_file_clauses::=

create_datafile_clause::=

alter_datafile_clause::=

size_clause::=

alter_tempfile_clause::=

autoextend_clause::=

maxsize_clause::=

logfile_clauses::=

add_logfile_clauses::=

drop_logfile_clauses::=

supplemental_db_logging::=

supplemental_id_key_clause::=

logfile_descriptor::=

controlfile_clauses::=

trace_file_clause::=

standby_database_clauses::=

activate_standy_db_clause::=

maximize_standby_db_clause::=

register_logfile_clause::=

commit_switchover_clause::=

start_standby_clause::=

stop_standby_clause::=

default_settings_clauses::=

set_time_zone_clause::=

flashback_mode_clause::=

redo_thread_clauses::=

security_clause::=

DESCRIPTION To alter a database, you must have the ALTER DATABASE system privilege. *database* is the database name, and must be eight or fewer characters long.

When a database is first created, it is **MOUNT**ed in **EXCLUSIVE** mode, meaning no one but its creator has access to it. To allow multiple instances to access the database, use **MOUNT PARALLEL** if you have installed the Oracle Real Application Clusters option.

After mounting a database, you **OPEN** it. **RESETLOGS** resets the redo log, cleaning out any redo entries. You use this option to restore a database after a partial recovery from a media failure. The **NORESETLOGS** option leaves everything the same when you **OPEN** the database.

You can recover the database with a **RECOVER** clause. This command performs media recovery for a lost database. You can use multiple recovery processes to apply redo entries to datafiles for each instance. *See* **RECOVER**. You can **BACKUP** a **CONTROLFILE** to the specified file or to a trace file.

STANDBY databases provide a mechanism for automated failover in the event of a database failure. See the *Oracle Database Administrator's Guide* for details on the creation and management of standby databases.

RENAME changes the name of an existing database or redo log file. DBAs can also **CREATE DATAFILE**s and **CREATE TEMPFILE**s and manage the increments by which datafiles autoextend. The **AUTOEXTEND** clause can be used to dynamically extend datafiles as needed, in increments of **NEXT** size, to a maximum of **MAXSIZE** (or **UNLIMITED**). You can use the **RESIZE** clause to increase or decrease the size of an existing datafile. You can bring a file **ONLINE** or take it **OFFLINE** with the **DATAFILE** clause. You can **CREATE** a new **DATAFILE** to replace an old one to re-create a datafile lost without backup.

ARCHIVELOG and **NOARCHIVELOG** define the way redo log files are used. **NOARCHIVELOG** is the default, and using it means that redo log files will be reused without saving their contents elsewhere. This provides instance recovery except from a media failure, such as a disk crash. **ARCHIVELOG** forces redo log files to be archived (usually to another disk or a tape), so that you can recover from a media failure. This mode also supports instance recovery.

ADD LOGFILE adds a redo log file or files to the database. *redo_logfile_spec* specifies the redo log file names and sizes. **SIZE** is the number of bytes set aside for this file. Suffixing this with **K** multiplies the value by 1024; using **M** multiplies it by 1048576. **REUSE** (without **SIZE**) means destroy the contents of any file by this name and give the name to this database. **SIZE** with **REUSE** creates the file if it doesn't exist, and checks its size if it does. **SIZE** alone creates the file if it doesn't exist, but returns an error if it does exist. The redo log file is assigned to a thread, either explicitly with the **THREAD** clause or to the thread assigned to the current instance of Oracle. A **GROUP** is a collection of redo log files. You can add a **GROUP** of redo log files by listing them, and you can name the group with an integer.

ADD LOGFILE MEMBER adds new files to an existing redo log file group, either by specifying the **GROUP** integer or by listing all the redo log files in the group.

DROP LOGFILE drops an existing redo log file group. **DROP LOGFILE MEMBER** drops one or more members of a redo log file group.

You can **RENAME GLOBAL_NAME** to change the name of the database. If you specify a domain, tell Oracle where the database is on the network. You must change references to the database from remote databases as well.

You can use the **RESET COMPATIBILITY** option, in conjunction with the **COMPATIBLE** parameter in the initialization parameter file, to revert from compatibility with one version of Oracle to a previous version.

You can **ENABLE** or **DISABLE** a **THREAD**. **PUBLIC** makes the thread available to any instance not requesting a specific thread.

As of Oracle Database 10g, you can perform the following actions via **ALTER DATABASE**:

- Specify multiple temporary tablespaces (a *tablespace group*) as the database default temporary tablespace (using the **DEFAULT TEMPORARY TABLESPACE** clause) .

- Assign or reassign a tablespace as the database default permanent tablespace (using the **DEFAULT TABLESPACE** clause)

- Reset the target recovery incarnation for the database from the current incarnation to the prior incarnation

- Begin backup of all the datafiles in the database

- Enable block change tracking for incremental backups of the database

- Update both global and local partitioned indexes as part of table partition maintenance operations

- Revert the entire database, or some tablespaces of the database, to an earlier version

- Control the relationship between primary databases and logical and physical standby databases (via the clauses related to standby management)

- Assign or reassign a tablespace as the default permanent tablespace for the database (via the **DEFAULT SETTINGS** clause)

- Add a redo log file or enable a redo log thread by specifying an instance name rather than a thread number

- Instruct Oracle Database 10g to compress archivelog files prior to transmission to a remote site or storage to disk

ALTER DIMENSION

SEE ALSO **CREATE DIMENSION**, **DROP DIMENSION**, Chapter 24

FORMAT

alter_dimension::=

level_clause::=

hierarchy_clause::=

dimension_join_clause::=

attribute_clause::=

extended_attribute_clause::=

DESCRIPTION **ALTER DIMENSION** modifies the attributes, hierarchy, and levels of an existing dimension. *See* **CREATE DIMENSION**.

EXAMPLE

```
alter dimension TIME drop hierarchy MONTH_TO_DATE;
```

ALTER DISKGROUP

SEE ALSO **CREATE DISKGROUP**, **DROP DISKGROUP**, Chapter 46

FORMAT

alter_diskgroup::=

disk_clauses::=

diskgroup_clauses::=

add_disk_clause::=

qualified_disk_clause::=

size_clause::=

drop_disk_clauses::=

resize_disk_clauses::=

undrop_disk_clause::=

rebalance_diskgroup_clause::=

check_diskgroup_clauses::=

diskgroup_template_clauses::=

qualified_template_clause::=

diskgroup_directory_clauses::=

diskgroup_alias_clauses::=

drop_diskgroup_file_clause::=

diskgroup_availability::=

DESCRIPTION **ALTER DISKGROUP** lets you perform a number of operations on a disk group or on the disks in a disk group.

The **DISK_CLAUSES** options include adding, dropping, and resizing disks within a group. Within the **DISKGROUP_CLAUSES** option, you can rebalance and check disk groups.

The **ALTER DISKGROUP** command is only valid if you have installed Automated Storage Management (ASM) and have started an ASM instance.

For example, to drop a disk from an existing disk group:

```
alter diskgroup DGROUP_01 drop disk DGROUP_01_0001;
```

ALTER FUNCTION
SEE ALSO **CREATE FUNCTION**, **DROP FUNCTION**, Chapter 31
FORMAT
alter_function::=

compiler_parameters_clause::=

alter_index::=

DESCRIPTION Use the **ALTER FUNCTION** command to recompile an invalid stand-alone stored function. Explicit recompilation eliminates the need for implicit run-time recompilation. Use the **DEBUG** option to generate and store the code for use by the PL/SQL debugger.

EXAMPLE

```
alter function OVERDUE_CHARGES compile;
```

ALTER INDEX

SEE ALSO **CREATE INDEX**, **DROP INDEX**, **STORAGE**, Chapters 17 and 43

FORMAT

deallocate_unused_clause::=

allocate_extent_clause::=

size_clause::=

shrink_clause::=

parallel_clause::=

physical_attributes_clause::=

logging_clause::=

rebuild_clause::=

key_compression::=

alter_index_partitioning::=

modify_index_default_attrs::=

add_hash_index_partition::=

coalesce_index_partition::=

COALESCE → PARTITION → parallel_clause

modify_index_partition::=

rename_index_partition::=

drop_index_partition::=

split_index_partition::=

index_partition_description::=

segment_attributes_clause::=

modify_index_subpartition::=

DESCRIPTION *user* is the user who owns the index you wish to alter (if you are not that user, you must have DBA privileges). *index* is the name of an existing index. *See* **CREATE TABLE** for a description of **INITRANS**. The default for **INITRANS** for indexes is 2. **STORAGE** contains subclauses that are described under **STORAGE**. You must have INDEX privilege on the table in order to create an index, and you must also either own the index or have the ALTER ANY INDEX system privilege.

You can use the **REBUILD** clause of the **ALTER INDEX** command to change the storage characteristics of an existing index. **REBUILD** uses the existing index as the basis for the new index. All index storage commands are supported, such as **STORAGE** (for extent allocation), **TABLESPACE** (to move the index to a new tablespace), and **INITRANS** (to change the initial number of entries).

You can modify, rename, drop, split, or rebuild index partitions.

COMPRESS enables key compression, eliminating repeated occurrence of key column values for nonunique indexes. *integer* specifies the prefix length (number of prefix columns to compress). By default, indexes are not compressed. You cannot compress a bitmapped index.

COMPUTE STATISTICS generates statistics for the cost based optimizer at the time the index is rebuilt.

ALTER INDEXTYPE
SEE ALSO CREATE INDEXTYPE, DROP INDEXTYPE
FORMAT
alter_indextype::=

using_type_clause::=

array_DML_clause::=

DESCRIPTION Use **ALTER INDEXTYPE** to add or drop an operator of the indextype, to modify the implementation type, or to change the properties of the indextype.

ALTER JAVA

SEE ALSO **CREATE JAVA**, **DROP JAVA**, Chapter 37
FORMAT
alter_java::=

invoker_rights_clause::=

DESCRIPTION **ALTER JAVA** recompiles a Java source schema object. You can also use this command to change the authorization enforced (definer or current user). To alter Java source schema objects, you must either own the source or class or have the ALTER ANY PROCEDURE system privilege.

ALTER MATERIALIZED VIEW

SEE ALSO CREATE MATERIALIZED VIEW, DROP MATERIALIZED VIEW, MATERIALIZED VIEW, Chapter 24

FORMAT

alter_materialized_view::=

physical_attributes_clause::=

table_compression::=

LOB_storage_clause::=

LOB_parameters::=

modify_LOB_storage_clause::=

modify_LOB_parameters::=

parallel_clause::=

logging_clause::=

allocate_extent_clause::=

deallocate_unused_clause::=

size_clause::=

shrink_clause::=

alter_iot_clauses::=

index_org_table_clause::=

index_org_overflow_clause::=

alter_overflow_clause::=

add_overflow_clause::=

scoped_table_ref_constraint::=

alter_mv_refresh::=

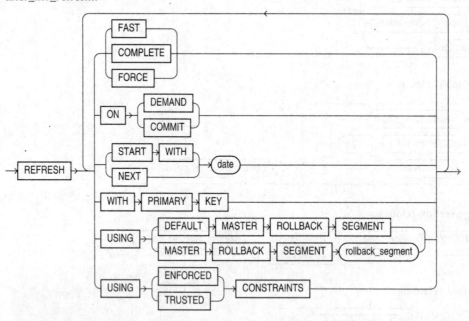

DESCRIPTION The keyword **SNAPSHOT** is supported as a replacement for **MATERIALIZED VIEW** for backward compatibility.

ALTER MATERIALIZED VIEW lets you change the storage characteristics or refresh mode and times of a materialized view. You can also enable or disable query rewrite for the materialized view. To alter

a materialized view, you must own the materialized view or have ALTER ANY SNAPSHOT or ALTER ANY MATERIALIZED VIEW system privilege. *See* **CREATE MATERIALIZED VIEW** and Chapter 24 for details.

EXAMPLE

```
alter materialized view MONTHLY_SALES
    enable query rewrite;
```

ALTER MATERIALIZED VIEW LOG

SEE ALSO **CREATE MATERIALIZED VIEW, CREATE MATERIALIZED VIEW LOG, DROP MATERIALIZED VIEW LOG**, Chapter 24

FORMAT

alter_materialized_view_log::=

new_values_clause::=

physical_attributes_clause::=

allocate_extent_clause::=

size_clause::=

shrink_clause::=

parallel_clause::=

DESCRIPTION The keyword **SNAPSHOT** is supported as a replacement for **MATERIALIZED VIEW** for backward compatibility.

 ALTER MATERIALIZED VIEW LOG lets you change the storage characteristics of a materialized view log. To alter the log, you must either have the ALTER privilege on the log table or have the ALTER ANY TABLE system privilege. *See* **CREATE MATERIALIZED VIEW LOG** and Chapter 24.

As of Oracle Database 10g, you can use the **FORCE** clause to specify the addition of attributes that the materialized view log already has, without causing Oracle to return an error. Also, you can use the new **SEQUENCE** clause to instruct Oracle to record a sequence value in the materialized view log.

ALTER OPERATOR

SEE ALSO **CREATE OPERATOR, DROP OPERATOR**
FORMAT
alter_operator::=

add_binding_clause::=

implementation_clause::=

context_clause::=

using_function_clause::=

drop_binding_clause::=

DESCRIPTION You can use **ALTER OPERATOR** to add bindings to, drop bindings from, or compile an existing operator.

ALTER OUTLINE
SEE ALSO **CREATE OUTLINE, DROP OUTLINE**, Chapter 43
FORMAT
alter_outline::=

DESCRIPTION You can use **ALTER OUTLINE** to rename a stored outline or to assign it to a different category. Stored outlines maintain sets of hints for previously executed queries. *See* Chapter 43.

ALTER PACKAGE
SEE ALSO **CREATE PACKAGE, DROP PACKAGE**, Chapter 31
FORMAT
alter_package::=

compiler_parameters_clause::=

DESCRIPTION **ALTER PACKAGE** recompiles a package specification and/or body. If you recompile the specification using **PACKAGE**, you recompile both the specification and the body. Recompiling the specification will cause referencing procedures to be recompiled. You can recompile the **BODY** without affecting the specification. To alter a package, you must either be the owner of the package or have ALTER ANY PROCEDURE system privilege.

ALTER PROCEDURE

SEE ALSO **CREATE PROCEDURE**, **DROP PROCEDURE**, Chapter 31

FORMAT

alter_procedure::=

compiler_parameters_clause::=

DESCRIPTION **ALTER PROCEDURE** recompiles a PL/SQL procedure. You can avoid run-time overhead and error messages by explicitly compiling a procedure in advance. To alter a procedure, you must either own the procedure or have ALTER ANY PROCEDURE system privilege.

ALTER PROFILE

SEE ALSO **CREATE PROFILE**, **DROP PROFILE**, Chapter 18

FORMAT

alter_profile::=

resource_parameters::=

password_parameters::=

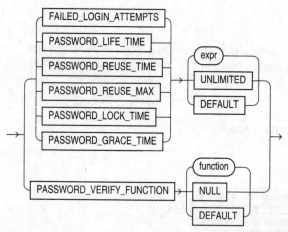

DESCRIPTION **ALTER PROFILE** lets you modify a particular profile setting. *See* **CREATE PROFILE** for details.

ALTER RESOURCE COST

SEE ALSO **CREATE PROFILE**
FORMAT
alter_resource_cost::=

DESCRIPTION The resource cost formula calculates the total cost of resources used in an Oracle session. **ALTER RESOURCE COST** lets you assign a weight to several resources. CPU_PER_SESSION is the amount of CPU used in a session in hundredths of a second. CONNECT_TIME is the elapsed time of the session in minutes. LOGICAL_READS_PER_SESSION is the number of data blocks read from both memory and disk during a session. PRIVATE_SGA is the number of bytes in a private System Global Area (SGA), which is only relevant if you are using the shared server architecture. By assigning weights, you change the formula used to calculate total resource cost.

ALTER ROLE

SEE ALSO **CREATE ROLE**, **DROP ROLE**, Chapter 18
FORMAT
alter_role::=

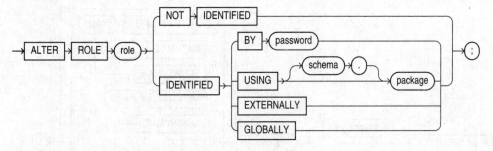

DESCRIPTION **ALTER ROLE** lets you modify a role.

ALTER ROLLBACK SEGMENT

SEE ALSO **CREATE DATABASE, CREATE ROLLBACK SEGMENT, CREATE TABLESPACE, DROP ROLLBACK SEGMENT, STORAGE**, Chapter 46

FORMAT
alter_rollback_segment::=

DESCRIPTION *rollback_segment* is a name assigned to this rollback segment. **STORAGE** contains subclauses that are described under **STORAGE**. The **INITIAL** and **MINEXTENTS** options are not applicable. A rollback segment can be taken **ONLINE** or **OFFLINE** while the database is open. You can **SHRINK** it to a specified size (the default is its **OPTIMAL** size).

You should use System-Managed Undo so that the database will automatically create and drop rollback segments as needed.

ALTER SEQUENCE

SEE ALSO **AUDIT**, **CREATE SEQUENCE**, **DROP SEQUENCE**, **GRANT**, **REVOKE**, **NEXTVAL** and **CURRVAL** under PSEUDO-COLUMNS, Chapter 17

FORMAT
alter_sequence::=

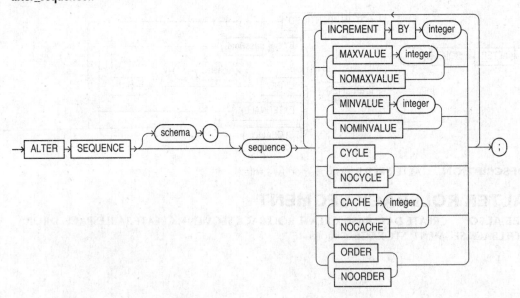

DESCRIPTION All of these options affect the future use of an existing sequence with the name *sequence*. (Note that **start with** is not available. To change the value with which a sequence starts, you must **DROP** the sequence and **CREATE** it again.)

A new **MAXVALUE** cannot be specified that is lower than the existing **CURRVAL** on an ascending sequence (one that has a positive number as its **INCREMENT BY**). A similar rule applies for **MINVALUE** on a descending sequence (which has a negative **INCREMENT BY**).

To alter a sequence, you must either have the ALTER privilege on the sequence or have the ALTER ANY SEQUENCE system privilege.

All other features of **ALTER SEQUENCE** work as they do in **CREATE SEQUENCE**, except that they apply to an existing sequence. *See* **CREATE SEQUENCE** for details.

ALTER SESSION
SEE ALSO ALTER SYSTEM
FORMAT
alter_session::=

alter_session_set_clause::=

DESCRIPTION The **ALTER SESSION** command alters settings in effect for the current user session. To generate performance statistics for SQL statement processing by Oracle, set SQL_TRACE to TRUE. To turn them off, set it to FALSE. The initialization parameter SQL_TRACE sets the initial value for this trace.

 ADVISE allows you to send transaction handling advice to remote databases involved in distributed transactions. You can **CLOSE** a **DATABASE LINK** to eliminate the session's link to a remote database.

 You can specify whether procedures can **COMMIT** or not, the degree to which DML operations are parallelized, and whether resumable operations are enabled. If you enable parallel DML or DDL for your session, you still must specify the PARALLEL hint for the operations to be executed in parallel.

 To enable or disable resumable space allocation, you must have the RESUMABLE system privilege.

ALTER SYSTEM
SEE ALSO ALTER SESSION, ARCHIVE_LOG, CREATE PROFILE
FORMAT
alter_system::=

archive_log_clause::=

checkpoint_clause::=

check_datafiles_clause::=

distributed_recov_clauses::=

restricted_session_clauses::=

end_session_clauses::=

quiesce_clauses::=

shutdown_dispatcher_clause::=

alter_system_set_clause::=

alter_system_reset_clause::=

DESCRIPTION **ALTER SYSTEM** lets you configure your Oracle instance in many ways. Via the **SET** options, you can change many of the initialization parameter values while the database is running. If you are using a system parameter file, the changes are saved and will be in effect the next time the database is started. If you are using an initialization parameter file (such as init.ora), you need to modify that file so the change is in effect during subsequent database startups.

You can also use the **ALTER SYSTEM** command to **SWITCH LOGFILE**, forcing Oracle to change redo log file groups.

CHECKPOINT performs a checkpoint for (**GLOBAL**) all instances or (**LOCAL**) your instance of Oracle. **CHECK DATAFILES** verifies that every instance (**GLOBAL**) or your instance (**LOCAL**) of Oracle can access all online datafiles.

ENABLE or **DISABLE RESTRICTED SESSION** turns on or off a restricted session, accessible only to users with that system privilege.

ENABLE or **DISABLE DISTRIBUTED RECOVERY** turns this option on or off, respectively.

FLUSH SHARED_POOL clears all data from the SGA shared pool.

FLUSH BUFFER_CACHE, available as of Oracle Database 10g, clears the buffer cache of the SGA.

SUSPEND suspends database activity; **RESUME** re-enables the database.

QUIESCE RESTRICTED places the database into a consistent state during which only SYS and SYSTEM, connected as SYSDBA, can perform operations. **UNQUIESCE** returns the database to its normal mode.

ARCHIVE LOG manually archives the redo log files or enables automatic archiving.

KILL SESSION ends a session with both the SID column and the SERIAL# column of the V$SESSION table identifying the session. **DISCONNECT SESSION**, unlike **KILL SESSION**, gives you the option of forcing the session's outstanding transactions to be posted prior to the termination of the session.

ALTER TABLE
SEE ALSO **CREATE TABLE**, **DISABLE**, **DROP**, **ENABLE**, Chapters 17 and 46
FORMAT
alter_table::=

alter_table_properties::=

physical_attributes_clause::=

logging_clause::=

table_compression::=

supplemental_table_logging::=

supplemental_log_grp_clause::=

supplemental_id_key_clause::=

allocate_extent_clause::=

deallocate_unused_clause::=

size_clause::=

shrink_clause::=

upgrade_table_clause::=

records_per_block_clause::=

parallel_clause::=

row_movement_clause::=

alter_iot_clauses::=

index_org_table_clause::=

mapping_table_clauses::=

key_compression::=

index_org_overflow_clause::=

segment_attributes_clause::=

alter_overflow_clause::=

add_overflow_clause::=

alter_mapping_table_clauses::=

column_clauses::=

add_column_clause::=

modify_column_clauses::=

modify_col_properties::=

modify_col_substitutable::=

drop_column_clause::=

rename_column_clause::=

modify_collection_retrieval::=

constraint_clauses::=

drop_contraint_clause::=

column_properties::=

object_type_col_properties::=

substitutable_column_clause::=

nested_table_col_properties::=

object_properties::=

supplemental_logging_props::=

physical_properties::=

varray_col_properties::=

LOB_storage_clause::=

LOB_parameters::=

modify_LOB_storage_clause::=

modify_LOB_parameters::=

alter_varray_col_properties::=

LOB_partition_storage::=

XMLType_column_properties::=

XMLType_storage::=

XMLSchema_spec::=

alter_external_table_clauses::=

external_data_properties::=

alter_table_partitioning::=

modify_table_default_attrs::=

set_subpartition_template::=

modify_table_partition::=

modify_range_partition::=

modify_hash_partition::=

modify_list_partition::=

modify_table_subpartition::=

move_table_partition::=

move_table_subpartition::=

add_table_partition::=

add_range_partition_clause::=

add_harsh_partition_clause::=

add_list_partition_clause::=

coalesce_table_partition::=

drop_table_partition::=

drop_table_subpartition::=

rename_partition_subpart::=

truncate_partition_subpart::=

split_table_partition::=

split_table_subpartition::=

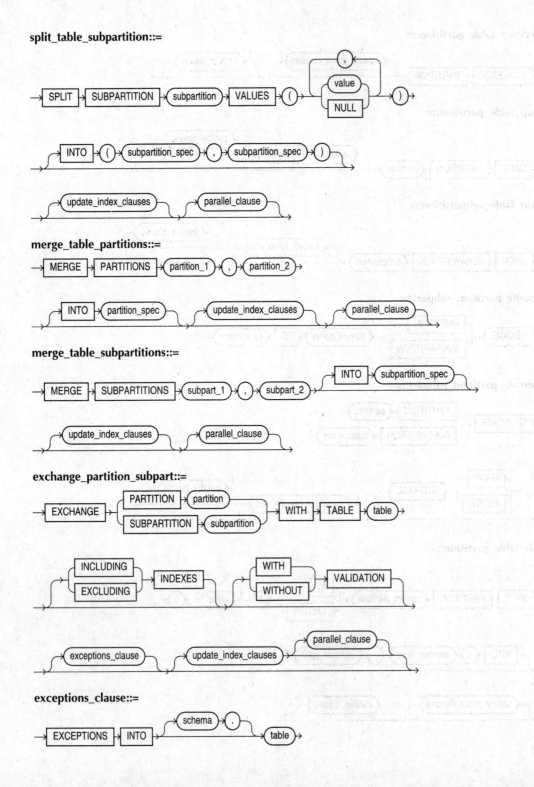

merge_table_partitions::=

merge_table_subpartitions::=

exchange_partition_subpart::=

exceptions_clause::=

list_values_clause::=

range_values_clause::=

partitioning_storage_clause::=

partition_attributes::=

add_hash_subpartition::=

add_list_subpartition::=

modify_hash_subpartition::=

modify_list_subpartition::=

table_partition_description::=

partition_level_subpartition::=

partition_spec::=

subpartition_spec::=

update_index_clauses::=

update_global_index_clause::=

update_all_indexes_clause::=

update_index_partition::=

update_index_subpartition::=

index_partition_description::=

index_subpartition_clause::=

parallel_clause::=

move_table_clause::=

enable_disable_clause::=

using_index_clause::=

index_properties::=

index_attributes::=

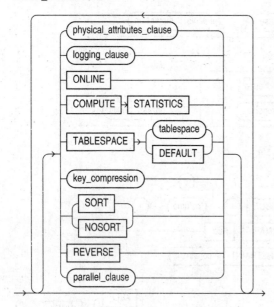

DESCRIPTION **ALTER TABLE** changes the definition of an existing table. **ADD** allows you to add a new column to the end of an existing table, or add a constraint to the table's definition. These follow the same format used in **CREATE TABLE**.

MODIFY changes an existing column, with some restrictions:

- You may change the type of column or decrease its size only if the column is **NULL** in every row of the table.

- A **NOT NULL** column may be added only to a table with no rows.

- An existing column can be modified to **NOT NULL** only if it has a non-**NULL** value in every row or if a default value is specified during the alteration.

- Increasing the length of a **NOT NULL** column without specifying **NULL** will leave it **NOT NULL**.

You can use the **SET UNUSED** clause to mark columns as unused. When you use the **DROP UNUSED COLUMNS** clause, the table will be reorganized and all unused columns will be dropped.

ALLOCATE EXTENT lets you allocate a new extent explicitly. **ENABLE** and **DISABLE** enable and disable constraints. All other features of **ALTER TABLE** work as they do in **CREATE TABLE**, except that they apply to an existing table. *See* **CREATE TABLE** for details.

In order to alter a table, you must either have the ALTER privilege for that table or have the ALTER ANY TABLE system privilege.

CACHE specifies that the blocks for this table, when read, are to be marked as "most recently used" and kept in the data block buffer cache for as long as possible. This option is useful if the tables are small and fairly static. **NOCACHE** (the default) reverts the table back to the normal Last Recently Used (LRU) list behavior.

PARALLEL, along with **DEGREE** and **INSTANCES**, specifies the parallel characteristics of the table (for databases using the Real Application Clusters option). **DEGREE** specifies the number of query servers

to use; **INSTANCES** specifies how the table is to be split among instances of Real Application Clusters for parallel query processing. An integer *n* specifies that the table is to be split among the specified number of available instances.

You can use **ALTER TABLE** to **ADD**, **DROP**, **EXCHANGE**, **MODIFY**, **MOVE**, **SPLIT**, or **TRUNCATE** partitions. *See* Chapter 17 and **CREATE TABLE**.

The LOB storage clauses specify the storage area to be used for LOB data that will not be stored in the table itself (out-of-line).

The **MOVE ONLINE** option allows you to access a table for DML operations during an online table reorganization. The **MOVE** and **MOVE ONLINE** options are only available for nonpartitioned index-organized tables. During a **MOVE ONLINE** operation, parallel DML operations against the table are not supported.

As of Oracle Database 10g, you can use the **COMPRESS** keyword to instruct Oracle to compress data segments to reduce disk and memory use for tables that are loaded with direct-path **INSERT**s.

ALTER TABLESPACE

SEE ALSO **CREATE TABLESPACE**, **DROP TABLESPACE**, **STORAGE**, Chapters 20 and 46
FORMAT
alter_tablespace::=

size_clause::=

datafile_tempfile_clauses::=

tablespace_logging_clauses::=

tablespace_group_clause::=

tablespace_state_clauses::=

autoextend_clause::=

maxsize_clause::=

flashback_mode_clause::=

tablespace_retention_clause::=

DESCRIPTION *tablespace* is the name of an existing tablespace. **ADD DATAFILE** adds to the tablespace a file or series of files described according to a *file_specification*, which defines the database filenames and sizes.

The filename format is operating system specific. **SIZE** is the number of bytes set aside for this file. Suffixing this with **K** multiplies the value by 1024; using **M** multiplies it by 1048576. **REUSE** (without **SIZE**) means destroy the contents of any file by this name and assign it for use by this tablespace. **REUSE** with **SIZE** creates the file if it doesn't exist, and checks its size if it does. **SIZE** alone creates the file if it doesn't exist, but returns an error if it does exist.

You can use the **AUTOEXTEND** clause to dynamically resize your datafiles as needed, in increments of **NEXT** size, to a maximum of **MAXSIZE** (or UNLIMITED).

NOLOGGING specifies the default action for the writing of redo log entries for certain types of transactions in the tablespace. You can override this setting at the object level. **RENAME DATAFILE** changes the name of an existing tablespace file. The tablespace should be offline while the renaming takes place. Note that **RENAME** does not actually rename the files; it only associates their new names with this tablespace. Actually renaming operating system files must be done with the operating system itself. To properly rename files, first **ALTER TABLESPACE OFFLINE**, rename the files in the operating system, **RENAME** them with **ALTER TABLESPACE**, and then **ALTER TABLESPACE ONLINE**.

DEFAULT STORAGE defines the default storage for all future objects created in this tablespace, unless those defaults are overridden, such as by **CREATE TABLE**. **ONLINE** brings the tablespace back online. **OFFLINE** takes it offline, either without waiting for its users to log off (**IMMEDIATE**) or after they've all stopped using it (**NORMAL**).

MINIMUM EXTENT sets the minimum size for any extent created in the tablespace. **COALESCE** combines neighboring free extents in the tablespace into fewer, larger free extents.

READ ONLY tablespaces are never updated by Oracle, and can be placed on read-only media. Read-only tablespaces do not need repeated backups. All tablespaces are created read-write. To change a read-only tablespace back to read-write status, use the **READ WRITE** clause.

BEGIN BACKUP can be executed at any time. It puts the tablespace in a state such that an online backup can occur while users are accessing the tablespace. **END BACKUP** indicates the system backup is finished. If the tablespace is online, any system backup must also back up archive redo logs. If it is offline, this is unnecessary.

TEMPORARY tablespaces cannot contain any permanent objects (such as tables or indexes); they can only hold the temporary segments used by Oracle during the processing of sorting operations and index creations. A **PERMANENT** tablespace can hold every type of Oracle segment.

NOTE
*For bigfile tablespaces, you can use **ALTER TABLESPACE** for commands (such as **RESIZE**) that would only work at the datafile level for smallfile tablespaces.*

As of Oracle Database 10g, you can rename a tablespace (the **RENAME** clause). You can also guarantee that unexpired undo data will be preserved, even at the expense of ongoing transactions that require undo space (via **RETENTION GUARANTEE**).

ALTER TRIGGER
SEE ALSO CREATE TRIGGER, DROP TRIGGER, ENABLE, TRIGGER, Chapter 30

FORMAT
alter_trigger::=

compiler_parameters_clause::=

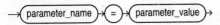

DESCRIPTION **ALTER TRIGGER** enables, disables, renames, or recompiles a PL/SQL trigger. To use the **ALTER TRIGGER** command, you must either own the trigger or have ALTER ANY TRIGGER system privilege.

You can use the **COMPILE** clause to manually recompile an invalid trigger object. Since triggers have dependencies, they can become invalid if an object the trigger depends on changes. The **DEBUG** clause allows PL/SQL information to be generated during trigger recompilation.

ALTER TYPE
SEE ALSO **CREATE TYPE**, **CREATE TYPE BODY**, Chapter 33
FORMAT
alter_type::=

compile_type_clause::=

compiler_parameters_clause::=

replace_type_clause::=

invoker_rights_clause::=

element_spec::=

inheritance_clauses::=

subprogram_spec::=

procedure_spec::=

function_spec::=

constructor_spec::=

map_order_function_spec::=

pragma_clause::=

alter_method_spec::=

alter_attribute_definition::=

alter_collection_clauses::=

dependent_handling_clause::=

exceptions_clause::=

DESCRIPTION **ALTER TYPE** allows you to modify existing abstract datatypes. When you create a method that acts on the abstract datatype, you use the **CREATE TYPE BODY** command (see entry in this appendix). Each method defined in the type body must first be listed in the type.

As of Oracle Database 10g, you can modify varying arrays and nested tables of scalar types.

ALTER USER

SEE ALSO **CREATE TABLESPACE, GRANT, CREATE PROFILE, CREATE USER**, Chapter 18
FORMAT
alter_user::=

proxy_clause::=

proxy_authentication::=

DESCRIPTION You use **ALTER USER** to change a user's password, or the **DEFAULT** tablespace (for objects the user owns) or **TEMPORARY** tablespace (for temporary segments used by the user). Without **ALTER USER**, the defaults for both of these are set by the defaults of the first tablespace (both for objects and temporary segments) to which the user is **GRANT**ed resources and the default temporary tablespace defined at the database level. **ALTER USER** can also change the quota, the resource profile, or the default role (*see* **CREATE USER**). You can use the **PASSWORD EXPIRE** clause to force a user's password to expire, in which case the user must change his or her password during the next login. The **ACCOUNT UNLOCK** clause allows you to unlock an account that has exceeded its maximum number of consecutive failed login attempts. *See* **CREATE PROFILE** for details on password control. To alter a user, you must have the ALTER USER system privilege.

You can use the **PROXY** clause to connect as the specified user and to activate all, some, or none of the user's roles. **PROXY** is typically used in three-tier applications involving application servers.

ALTER VIEW

SEE ALSO **CREATE VIEW**, **DROP VIEW**, Chapter 17
FORMAT
alter_view::=

DESCRIPTION ALTER VIEW recompiles a view or alters its constraints. To alter a view, you must either own the view or have ALTER ANY TABLE system privilege.

ANALYTIC FUNCTIONS

Analytic functions compute an aggregate value based on a group of rows they return multiple rows for each group. Many of the analytic functions are listed under the AGGREGATE FUNCTIONS entry; when used as analytic functions, they can only be used within the **ORDER BY** clause.

In the following alphabetical list of analytic functions (see the individual entries for syntax descriptions), the functions followed by an asterisk allow for the use of a windowing clause: **AVG***, **CORR***, **COVAR_POP***, **COVAR_SAMP***, **COUNT***, **CUME_DIST**, **DENSE_RANK**, **FIRST**, **FIRST_VALUE***, **LAG**, **LAST**, **LAST_VALUE***, **LEAD**, **MAX***, **MIN***, **NTILE**, **PERCENT_RANK**, **PERCENTILE_CONT**, **PERCENTILE_DISC**, **RANK**, **RATIO_TO_REPORT**, **REGR_***, **ROW_NUMBER**, **STDDEV***, **STDDEV_POP**, **STDDEV_SAMP**, **SUM***, **VAR_POP***, **VAR_SAMP***, **VARIANCE***.

ANALYZE

SEE ALSO Chapter 43
FORMAT
analyze::=

validation_clauses::=

for_clause::=

into_clause::=

compute_statistics_clause::=

estimate_statistics_clause::=

DESCRIPTION Oracle recommends that you use the DBMS_STATS package in place of the **ANALYZE** command. **ANALYZE** lets you collect statistics about a table, cluster, partition, or index for the optimizer, and stores them in the data dictionary; it lets you delete these statistics; it validates the structure of an object; and it identifies migrated and chained rows of a table or cluster with a listing in a local table. You use the **VALIDATE STRUCTURE** clause to test an object for possible data corruption. To analyze a table, you must either own the table or have the ANALYZE ANY system privilege.

The **LIST CHAINED ROWS** clause records information about row chaining in a table you specify.

AND
See LOGICAL OPERATORS, PRECEDENCE, **CONTAINS**.

ANSI
The American National Standards Institute sets standards for the SQL language and its many elements.

ANY
SEE ALSO ALL, **BETWEEN**, **EXISTS**, **IN**, LOGICAL OPERATORS, Chapter 13
FORMAT

```
operator ANY list
```

DESCRIPTION = ANY is the equivalent of **IN**. *operator* can be any one of =, >, >=, <, <=, or !=, and *list* can be a series of literal strings (such as 'Talbot', 'Jones', or 'Hild'), a series of literal numbers (such as 2, 43, 76, 32.06, or 444), or a column from a subquery, where each row of the subquery becomes a member of the list, as shown here:

```
LOCATION.City = ANY (select City from WEATHER)
```

The *list* variable also can be a series of columns in the **WHERE** clause of the main query, as shown here:

```
Prospect = ANY (Vendor, Client)
```

RESTRICTIONS *list* cannot be a series of columns in a subquery, like this:

```
Prospect = ANY (select Vendor, Client from . . .)
```

Many people find this operator and the **ALL** operator very difficult to remember, because the logic for some of their cases is not immediately intuitive. As a result, some form of **EXISTS** is usually substituted. The combination of an operator with **ANY** and a list can be illustrated with these explanations:

Page = ANY (4,2,7)	Page is in the list (4,2,7)—2, 4, and 7 all qualify.
Page > ANY (4,2,7)	Page is greater than any single item in the list (4,2,7)—even 3 qualifies, because it is greater than 2.
Page >= ANY (4,2,7)	Page is greater than or equal to any single item in the list (4,2,7)—even 2 qualifies, because it is equal to 2.
Page < ANY (4,2,7)	Page is less than any single item in the list (4,2,7)—even 6 qualifies, because it is less than 7.
Page <= ANY (4,2,7)	Page is less than or equal to any single item in the list (4,2,7)—even 7 qualifies.
Page != ANY (4,2,7)	Page is not equal to any single item in the list (4,2,7)—any number qualifies so long as the list has more than one value. With only one value, != **ANY** is the equivalent of !=.

APPEND (SQL*Plus)

SEE ALSO CHANGE, DEL, EDIT, LIST, Chapter 6

FORMAT

```
A[PPEND] text
```

DESCRIPTION **APPEND** is a feature of the SQL*Plus command-line editor. **APPEND** places the text at the end of the current line in the current buffer, with no intervening spaces. If you want a space between the end of the current line and *text*, put two spaces between **APPEND** and *text*. If you want to append a semicolon at the end of a line, put two of them together (one of them will be regarded as a command terminator and discarded). **APPEND** is not available in iSQL*Plus.

EXAMPLE

```
APPEND ;;
```

ARCH PROCESS

One of the background processes used by Oracle, ARCH performs automatic archiving of redo log files when the database is used in **ARCHIVELOG** mode. *See* BACKGROUND PROCESS.

ARCHIVE

In a general sense, archiving means to save data for possible later use. In a specific sense, it means to save the data found in the online redo logs, in the event that the logs are needed to restore the database due to a media failure.

ARCHIVE LOG

SEE ALSO **ALTER DATABASE**, **RECOVER**, Chapter 46
FORMAT

```
ARCHIVE LOG {LIST|STOP}|{START|NEXT|ALL|integer} [TO destination]
```

DESCRIPTION **ARCHIVE LOG** starts or stops automatic archiving of online redo log files, manually archives specific redo log files, or displays information about redo log files. **START** enables automatic archiving; **STOP** disables it. **LIST** shows the archive status for the online redo logs. **NEXT** manually archives the next online redo log file group that has been filled but not yet archived. **ALL** manually archives all filled but not yet archived redo log file groups. You can specify the online redo log group number and the destination area for the archived files.

EXAMPLE

```
ARCHIVE LOG ALL
ARCHIVE LOG LIST
```

ARRAYSIZE (SQL*Plus)

See **SET**.

AS

SEE ALSO **ALIAS**, **TO_CHAR**, Chapters 7 and 10
DESCRIPTION **AS** is used to separate column formulas from column aliases.
EXAMPLE Here **AS** separates the column alias PayDay from its column formula:

```
select NEXT_DAY(CycleDate,'FRIDAY') AS PayDay
from PAYDAY;
```

ASCII

SEE ALSO CHARACTER FUNCTIONS, **ASCIISTR**, **CHR**
FORMAT

```
ASCII(string)
```

DESCRIPTION ASCII is an acronym for American Standard Code for Information Interchange. It is a convention for using digital data to represent printable characters.
 The **ASCII** function will return the ASCII value of the first (leftmost) character in the string. The ASCII value of a character is an integer between 0 and 255. Those between 0 and 127 are well defined. Those above 127 ("extended ASCII set") tend to differ by country, application, and computer manufacturer. The letter *A*, for instance, is equal to the ASCII number 65, *B* is 66, *C* is 67, and so on. The decimal point is 46. A minus sign is 45. The number 0 is 48, 1 is 49, 2 is 50, and so on.

EXAMPLE

```
select ASCII('.'), ASCII(.5),
       ASCII('E'), ASCII('EMILY')
   from DUAL;

ASCII('.') ASCII(.5) ASCII('E') ASCII('EMILY')
---------- --------- ---------- --------------
        46        46         69             69
```

ASCIISTR

SEE ALSO CHARACTER FUNCTIONS, **ASCII**, **CHR**
FORMAT

ASCIISTR(*string*)

DESCRIPTION The **ASCII** function takes a string and returns its ASCII equivalent in the database character set.
EXAMPLE

```
select ASCIISTR('E'), ASCIISTR('EMILY')
  from DUAL;

A ASCII
- -----
E EMILY
```

ASIN

SEE ALSO ACOS, ATAN, ATAN2, COS, COSH, EXP, LN, **LOG**, SIN, SINH, TAN, TANH
FORMAT

ASIN(*value*)

DESCRIPTION ASIN returns the arc sine of a value. Input values range from –1 to 1; outputs are expressed in radians.

ASSOCIATE STATISTICS

SEE ALSO ANALYZE
FORMAT
associate_statistics::=

column_association::=

function_association::=

using_statistics_type::=

default_cost_clause::=

default_selectivity_clause::=

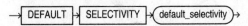

DESCRIPTION **ASSOCIATE STATISTICS** associates a set of statistics functions with one or more columns, stand-alone functions, packages, types, or indexes. You must have the required privileges to **ALTER** the object being modified.

You can view associations in USER_USTATS after you analyze the object with which you are associating your statistics functions.

ATAN

SEE ALSO ACOS, ASIN, ATAN2, COS, COSH, EXP, LN, LOG, SIN, SINH, TAN, TANH

FORMAT

```
ATAN(value)
```

DESCRIPTION ATAN returns the arc tangent of a value. Input values are unbounded; outputs are expressed in radians.

ATAN2

SEE ALSO ACOS, ASIN, ATAN, COS, COSH, EXP, LN, LOG, SIN, SINH, TAN, TANH

FORMAT

```
ATAN2(value1, value2)
```

DESCRIPTION ATAN2 returns the arc tangent of two values. Input values are unbounded; outputs are expressed in radians.

ATTRIBUTE (SQL*Plus)

SEE ALSO COLUMN, Chapter 33

FORMAT

```
ATTRIBUTE [type_name.attribute_name [option ...]]
```

option can be one of the following:

```
ALI[AS] alias
CLE[AR]
FOR[MAT] format
LIKE {type_name.attribute_name|alias}
ON|OFF
```

DESCRIPTION ATTRIBUTE sets the display attributes for attributes of a user-defined type column in SQL*Plus.

EXAMPLE

```
ATTRIBUTE ADDRESS_TY.Street FORMAT A50
```

AUDIT

SEE ALSO CREATE DATABASE LINK, DATA DICTIONARY, **NOAUDIT**, PRIVILEGE

FORMAT

audit::=

sql_statement_clause::=

auditing_by_clause::=

schema_object_clause::=

auditing_on_clause::=

DESCRIPTION You can **AUDIT** statements executed by users and statements that access specific objects.

The *statement options* are as follows:

Option	Audits
CLUSTER	Create, alter, drop, or truncate cluster
CONTEXT	Create or drop context
DATABASE LINK	Create or drop database link
DIMENSION	Create, alter, or drop dimension

Option	Audits	
DIRECTORY	Create or drop directory	
INDEX	Create, alter, or drop index	
MATERIALIZED VIEW	Create, alter, or drop materialized view	
NOT EXISTS	SQL statements that fail because an object does not exist	
PROCEDURE	Create or drop procedure, function, library, or package; create package body	
PROFILE	Create, alter, or drop profile	
PUBLIC DATABASE LINK	Create or drop public database link	
PUBLIC SYNONYM	Create or drop public synonym	
ROLE	Create, alter, drop, or set role	
ROLLBACK SEGMENT	Create, alter, or drop rollback segment	
SEQUENCE	Create or drop sequence	
SESSION	Logon attempts	
SYNONYM	Create or drop synonym	
SYSTEM AUDIT	Audit or noaudit of SQL statements	
SYSTEM GRANT	Grant or revoke system privileges and roles	
TABLE	Create, drop, or truncate table	
TABLESPACE	Create, alter, or drop tablespace	
TRIGGER	Create, alter, or drop trigger; alter table with ENABLE	DISABLE ALL TRIGGERS
TYPE	Create, alter, or drop type or type body	
USER	Create, alter, or drop user	
VIEW	Create or drop view	

The following are additional statement-level options that are available:

Option	Commands Audited
ALTER SEQUENCE	ALTER SEQUENCE
ALTER TABLE	ALTER TABLE
COMMENT TABLE	COMMENT ON TABLE *table, view, materialized view* COMMENT ON COLUMN *table.column, view.column,* *materialized view.column*
DELETE TABLE	DELETE FROM *table, view*
EXECUTE PROCEDURE	CALL Execution of any procedure or function or access to any variable, library, or cursor inside a package
GRANT DIRECTORY	GRANT privilege ON directory REVOKE privilege ON directory
GRANT PROCEDURE	GRANT privilege ON procedure, function, package REVOKE privilege ON procedure, function, package

Option	Commands Audited
GRANT SEQUENCE	GRANT privilege ON sequence REVOKE privilege ON sequence
GRANT TABLE	GRANT privilege ON table, view, materialized view REVOKE privilege ON table, view, materialized view
GRANT TYPE	GRANT privilege ON TYPE REVOKE privilege ON TYPE
INSERT TABLE	INSERT INTO table, view
LOCK TABLE	LOCK TABLE table, view
SELECT SEQUENCE	Any statement containing sequence.CURRVAL or sequence.NEXTVAL
SELECT TABLE	SELECT FROM table, view, materialized view
UPDATE TABLE	UPDATE table, view

BY *user* audits only SQL statements issued by particular users. The default is to audit all users.

WHENEVER [NOT] SUCCESSFUL writes a row to an audit table only when an attempted access to an audited table or system facility is (or is **NOT**) successful. Omitting this optional clause causes a row to be written whether an access is successful or not.

Auditing information is written to a table named SYS.AUD$ and accessed via data dictionary views.

EXAMPLE This audits all updates by a user named CLERK_USER:

```
audit UPDATE TABLE by clerk_user;
```

AUTOCOMMIT (SQL*Plus)

AUTOCOMMIT is a SQL*Plus setting used to automatically commit changes to the database following any SQL command that **insert**s, **update**s, or **delete**s data in the database. *See* **SET**.

AUTORECOVERY (SQL*Plus)

See **SET**.

AVG

SEE ALSO **COMPUTE**, AGGREGATE FUNCTIONS, Chapter 9

FORMAT

```
AVG ( [ DISTINCT | ALL ] expr ) [OVER ( analytic_clause )]
```

DESCRIPTION **AVG** is the average of *expr* for a group of rows. **DISTINCT** forces only unique values to be averaged. **NULL** rows are ignored by this function, which may affect results.

B*-TREE

B*-TREE is a high-performance indexing structure used by Oracle to create and store indexes.

BACKGROUND PROCESS

A background process is one of the processes used by an instance of Oracle to perform and coordinate tasks on behalf of concurrent users of a database.

BEGIN

SEE ALSO BLOCK STRUCTURE, **DECLARE**, **END**, **EXCEPTION**, **TERMINATOR**, Chapter 29

FORMAT

```
[<<block label>>]
[DECLARE]
BEGIN
      ... block logic ...
END [block label];
```

DESCRIPTION **BEGIN** is the opening statement of a PL/SQL block's executable section. It can be followed with any legal PL/SQL logic, and an exception handler, and is closed with the **END** statement. At least one executable statement is required between **BEGIN** and **END**. *See* BLOCK STRUCTURE.

 block label is a name given to a PL/SQL block that starts with the word **BEGIN** and finishes with the word **END**. The word **END** is followed by a terminator, usually a semicolon (*see* **TERMINATOR** for exceptions). *block label* follows normal naming conventions for objects, and must be bracketed by << and >>. These symbols tell PL/SQL that this is a label. **BEGIN** may optionally be preceded by a section called **DECLARE** (which follows the *block label*) and may optionally contain a section called **EXCEPTION**.

BETWEEN

See LOGICAL OPERATORS.

BFILE

BFILE is a datatype (*see* DATATYPES) used for binary LOB data stored outside the database. Oracle does not maintain read consistency or data integrity for the externally stored data. Within the database, a LOB locator value is stored to point to the external file. Before creating a BFILE entry, you must first create a directory. *See* **CREATE DIRECTORY**.

BFILENAME

SEE ALSO BFILE, **CREATE DIRECTORY**, Chapter 35

FORMAT

```
BFILENAME ( 'directory' , 'filename' )
```

DESCRIPTION **BFILENAME** returns a BFILE locator associated with the specified filename and directory object.

BINARY_DOUBLE

See DATATYPES.

BINARY_FLOAT

See DATATYPES.

BIN_TO_NUM

SEE ALSO NUMBER FUNCTIONS, Chapter 9

FORMAT

```
BIN_TO_NUM ( expr [, expr]... )
```

DESCRIPTION BIN_TO_NUM converts a bit vector to its equivalent number.
EXAMPLE

```
select BIN_TO_NUM(1,0,0,1) from DUAL;

BIN_TO_NUM(1,0,0,1)
-------------------
9
```

BIND VARIABLE

A bind variable is a variable in a SQL statement that must be replaced with a valid value or address of a value in order for the statement to successfully execute.

BITAND

SEE ALSO DECODE, Chapter 16
FORMAT

```
BITAND ( argument1, argument2 )
```

DESCRIPTION BITAND computes an **AND** operation on the bits of *argument1* and *argument2*, both of which must resolve to nonnegative integers, and returns an integer. This function is commonly used with the **DECODE** function.

BITMAP INDEX

A bitmap index is a type of index best suited for columns with few distinct values (and thus, poor selectivity). If there are few distinct values for a column, and it is frequently used as a limiting condition in queries, you should consider using a bitmap index for the column. *See* Chapter 17 for further details on bitmap indexes. For full syntax information, *see* **CREATE INDEX**.

BLOB

A BLOB is a binary large object, stored inside the database. *See* Chapter 35.

BLOCK

A block is the basic unit of storage (physical and logical) for all Oracle data. The Oracle block size varies by operating system and may differ from the block size of the host operating system. Common block sizes are 4K, 8K, and 16K. For the size of a block on your specific operating system, refer to your *Installation and User's Guide*. Database block sizes can differ at the tablespace level.

BLOCK STRUCTURE

A block structure is a structure of block sections in PL/SQL.

SEE ALSO **BEGIN, DECLARE, END, EXCEPTION, GOTO**, Chapter 29

DESCRIPTION PL/SQL blocks can be embedded in SQL*Plus and any of several programming languages, through the use of the Oracle precompilers. PL/SQL blocks are structured like this:

```
[<<block label>>]
[DECLARE
.. declarations (CURSOR, VARIABLE and EXCEPTION)...]

BEGIN

... block logic (executable code)...

[EXCEPTION

... exception handling logic (for fatal errors)...]

END [block label];
```

As the brackets show, both the **DECLARE** and **EXCEPTION** sections are optional. A block may optionally be labeled by a block name, which must be bracketed by << and >>.

The sections of a block must be in this order, although blocks may nest inside of other blocks in either the block logic or exception-handling logic sections. *blocks* may be used for branching using a **GOTO**, or as a prefix in referencing a variable in another block (*see* **DECLARE** for details on this). If a variable will be referenced in a cursor declaration, it must be declared before the cursor is declared.

EXAMPLE

```
<<calc_areas>>
DECLARE
    pi        constant NUMBER(9,7) := 3.14159;
    area    NUMBER(14,2);
    cursor rad_cursor is
            select * from RADIUS_VALS;
    rad_val rad_cursor%ROWTYPE;
BEGIN
    open rad_cursor;
     loop
      fetch rad_cursor into rad_val;
        exit when rad_cursor%NOTFOUND;
        area := pi*power(rad_val.radius,2);
        insert into AREAS values (rad_val.radius, area);
     end loop;
    close rad_cursor;
END calc_areas;
```

BREAK (SQL*Plus)

SEE ALSO **CLEAR, COMPUTE**, Chapter 6

FORMAT

```
BRE[AK]  [ON report_element [action [action]]] ...
```

where *report_element* is

{*column*|*expr*|ROW|REPORT}

and *action* is

[SKI[P]*n*][SKI[P] PAGE][NODUP[LICATES]|DUP[LICATES]]

DESCRIPTION A break occurs when SQL*Plus detects a specified change, such as the end of a page or a change in the value of an expression. A break will cause SQL*Plus to perform some action you've specified in the **BREAK** command, such as **SKIP**, and to print some result from a **COMPUTE** command, such as averages or totals for a column. Only one **BREAK** command may be in effect at a time. A new **BREAK** command may specify changes, and their associated actions, that are to cause a break.

A **BREAK ON REPORT** causes a break at the end of a report or query.

A change in the value of an expression may occur at any time prior to the **REPORT** break, and there may be several **ON** expression clauses in a single **BREAK** statement; however, their order in the **BREAK** command should be the same as in the **order by** of the **select** statement. That is, each expression that appears in the **BREAK** command also should be placed in the **order by** clause of **select**, in identical sequence, or the result will be meaningless. In addition, their order should be from the largest grouping to the smallest (for example, ON Corporation, ON Division, ON Project).

ON ROW causes a break for every row selected.

ON PAGE causes a break at the end of each page, and is independent of breaks caused by *expression*, **ON ROW**, or **ON REPORT**.

SKIP skips a number of lines, and **PAGE** or **SKIP PAGE** skips to a new page, before printing the result of the associated **COMPUTE** for the break.

NODUPLICATES suppresses the printing of the values in the expression or column in the **BREAK** for every row except the first one after the **BREAK** occurs.

BREAK by itself will display the current break settings.

CLEAR BREAKS will remove any existing **BREAK**s.

BTITLE (SQL*Plus)
SEE ALSO ACCEPT, DEFINE, PARAMETERS, **REPFOOTER**, **REPHEADER**, **SET HEADSEP**, **TTITLE**
FORMAT

BTI[TLE] [*printspec* [*text*|*variable*]... | OFF | ON]

DESCRIPTION **BTITLE** puts *text* (may be multiline) at the bottom of each page of a report. **OFF** and **ON** suppress and restore the display of the *text* without changing its contents. **BTITLE** by itself displays the current **btitle** options and text or variable. *text* is a bottom title you wish to give this report, and *variable* is a user-defined variable or a system-maintained variable, including SQL.LNO, the current line number, SQL.PNO, the current page number, SQL.RELEASE, the current Oracle release number, SQL.SQLCODE, the current error code, and SQL.USER, the username.

printspec options are as follows:

- **COL** *n* skips directly to position *n* (from the left margin) of the current line.
- **S[KIP]** *n* prints *n* blank lines. If no *n* is specified, one blank line is printed. If *n* is 0, no blank lines are printed and the current position for printing becomes position 1 of the current line (leftmost on the page).
- **TAB** *n* skips forward *n* positions (backward if *n* is negative).
- **BOLD** prints the output data in bold print.

- **LE[FT]**, **CE[NTER]**, and **R[IGHT]** left-justify, center, and right-justify data, respectively, on the current line. Any text or variables following these commands are justified as a group, up to the end of the command, or a **LEFT**, **CENTER**, **RIGHT**, or **COL**. **CENTER** and **RIGHT** use the value set by the **SET LINESIZE** command to determine where to place the text or variable.

- **FORMAT** *string* specifies the format model that will control the format of following text or variables, and follows the same syntax as **FORMAT** in a **COLUMN** command, such as **FORMAT** A12 or **FORMAT** $999,999.99. Each time a **FORMAT** appears, it supersedes the previous one that was in effect. If no **FORMAT** model has been specified, the one set by **SET NUMFORMAT** is used. If **NUMFORMAT** has not been set, the default for SQL*Plus is used.

Data values are printed according to the default format unless a variable has been loaded with a date reformatted by **TO_CHAR**.

Any number of options, text, and variables may be used in a single **BTITLE**. Each is printed in the order specified, and each is positioned and formatted as specified by the clauses that precede it.

BUFFER

Generally speaking, a buffer is a scratchpad, usually in the computer's memory, where commands are staged for editing and execution.

In SQL*Plus, a buffer is an area in memory for editing SQL commands. *See* **EDIT** and **SET**.

BUFFERS (DATABASE)

Buffers are temporary storage places for database blocks that are currently being accessed and changed by database users.

BUFFERS (REDO LOG)

Buffers are temporary storage places for redo log entries that are created by transactions within the database.

CACHES

Caches are temporary holding places for either database data that is currently being accessed or changed by users or data that Oracle requires to support users.

CALL

SEE ALSO **EXECUTE**, Chapter 39

FORMAT

call::=

routine_clause::=

object_access_expression::=

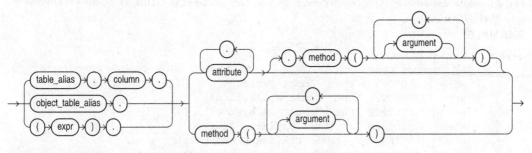

DESCRIPTION You can use **CALL** to execute a stored procedure or function from within SQL. You must have EXECUTE privilege on the procedure or function, or on the package in which the procedure or function exists.

CARDINALITY

SEE ALSO COLLECTION FUNCTIONS
FORMAT

```
CARDINALITY ( nested_table )
```

DESCRIPTION **CARDINALITY** returns the number of elements in a nested table. If the nested table is empty, or is a null collection, then **CARDINALITY** returns **NULL**.

CASE

SEE ALSO OTHER FUNCTIONS, **DECODE**, **TRANSLATE**, Chapter 16
FORMAT
case_expression::=

simple_case_expression::=

searched_case_expression::=

else_clause::=

DESCRIPTION **CASE** supports if-then-else logic within SQL statements. Use **WHEN/THEN** clauses to tell the database what to do for each condition. You can use an **ELSE** clause to handle exceptions to your **WHEN** clauses.

EXAMPLE

```
select distinct
        CASE CategoryName
          when   'ADULTFIC' then 'Adult Fiction'
          when   'ADULTNF' then 'Adult Nonfiction'
          when   'ADULTREF' then 'Adult Reference'
          when   'CHILDRENFIC' then 'Children Fiction'
          when   'CHILDRENNF' then 'Children Nonfiction'
          when   'CHILDRENPIC' then 'Children Picturebook'
          else CategoryName
        end
    from BOOKSHELF;
```

CAST
SEE ALSO NESTED TABLE, Chapter 34
FORMAT

```
CAST ( { expr | ( subquery ) | MULTISET ( subquery ) } AS type_name )
```

DESCRIPTION You can use **CAST** to convert one datatype to another. **CAST** is most commonly used when working with collectors such as nested tables.

CATSEARCH

CATSEARCH is used for text searches against CTXCAT text indexes created within Oracle Text. See Chapter 25 for index creation and text search examples. Supported text search operators include the following:

Operator	Description
\|	Returns a record if either search term has a score that exceeds the threshold.
AND	Returns a record if both search terms have a score that exceeds the threshold. This is the default action.

Operator	Description
-	Returns rows that contain the term preceding the - that do not contain the term following it.
NOT	Same as -.
()	Specifies the order in which search criteria are evaluated.
" "	Encloses phrases.

CEIL
SEE ALSO FLOOR, NUMBER FUNCTIONS
FORMAT
```
CEIL(value)
```

DESCRIPTION CEIL is the smallest integer higher than or equal to *value*.
EXAMPLE
```
CEIL(1.3)  =  2
CEIL(-2.3) = -2
```

CHAINED ROW
A chained row is a row that is stored in more than one database block, and therefore has several row pieces. Long rows (or inline LOBs) whose data is greater than the size of a block always have multiple row pieces. The **ANALYZE** command can identify chained rows and can also provide statistics on the number of chained rows. *See* **ANALYZE**.

CHANGE (SQL*Plus)
SEE ALSO **APPEND, DEL, EDIT, LIST**, Chapter 6
FORMAT
```
C[HANGE] /old text/new text/
```

DESCRIPTION CHANGE is a feature of the SQL*Plus command-line editor. It changes *old text* to *new text* in the current line of the current buffer (the line marked with an * in the LIST). **CHANGE** is not available in iSQL*Plus.

CHANGE ignores case in searching for old text. Three dots are a wildcard. If *old text* is prefixed with '. . .', everything up to and including the first occurrence of *old text* is replaced by *new text*. If *old text* is suffixed with '. . .', everything including and after the first occurrence of *old text* is replaced by *new text*. If *old text* has . . . embedded in it, everything from the part of *old text* before the dots, through the part of *old text* after the dots, is replaced by *new text*.

The space between the **CHANGE** and the first / may be omitted; the final delimiter is unnecessary if no trailing spaces need to be inserted. A delimiter other than / may be used. Any character following the word **CHANGE** (other than a space) is assumed to be the delimiter.

EXAMPLES If this is the current line of the current buffer,
```
where CategoryName = 'ADULTFN'
```
then
```
C /ADULTFN/ADULTNF
```

would change the line to this:

```
where CategoryName = 'ADULTNF'
```

CHAR DATATYPE

See DATATYPES.

CHARACTER FUNCTIONS

SEE ALSO CONVERSION FUNCTIONS, NUMBER FUNCTIONS, OTHER FUNCTIONS, Chapter 7
DESCRIPTION This is an alphabetical list of all current character functions in the Oracle version of SQL. Each of these is listed elsewhere in this reference under its own name, with its proper format and use.

Function Name and Use

```
string || string
```

|| concatenates two strings. The | symbol is called a broken vertical bar, although on some computers it may be a solid bar.

```
ASCII(string)
```

ASCII gives the ASCII value of the first character of a string.

```
CHR(integer)
```

CHR gives the character with an ASCII value equal to a given positive integer.

```
CONCAT(string1,string2)
```

CONCAT concatenates two strings. It is equivalent to ||.

```
INITCAP(string)
```

This stands for **INIT**ial **CAP**ital. It changes the first letter of a word or series of words into uppercase.

```
INSTR(string, set [, start [ ,occurrence ] ])
```

INSTR finds the location of the beginning of a set of characters **IN** a **STR**ing.

```
LENGTH(string)
```

This tells the **LENGTH** of a string.

```
LOWER(string)
```

LOWER converts every letter in a string to lowercase.

```
LPAD(string,length [,'set'])
```

LPAD stands for Left **PAD**. It makes a string a specific length by adding a specified set of characters to the left.

```
LTRIM(string [,'set'])
```

LTRIM stands for Left **TRIM**. It trims all the occurrences of any one of a set of characters off of the left side of a string.

NLS_INITCAP(*string*[, 'NLS_SORT=*sort*'])

NLS_INITCAP stands for **N**ational **L**anguage **S**upport **INIT**ial **CAP**ital. This version of **INITCAP** uses the collating sequence *sort* to do the case conversion.

NLS_LOWER(*string*[, 'NLS_SORT=*sort*'])

NLS_LOWER stands for **N**ational **L**anguage **S**upport **LOWER**case. This version of **LOWER** uses the collating sequence *sort* to do the case conversion.

NLS_UPPER(*string*[, 'NLS_SORT=*sort*'])

NLS_UPPER stands for **N**ational **L**anguage **S**upport **UPPER**case. This version of **UPPER** uses the collating sequence *sort* to do the case conversion.

NLSSORT(*string*[, 'NLS_SORT=*sort*'])

Oracle uses **N**ational **L**anguage **S**upport **SORT**. This gives the collating sequence value of the given string based on the collating sequence *sort* or, if omitted, the National Language Support option chosen for the site.

REGEXP_INSTR(*source_string*, *pattern*
[,*position*,*occurrence*,*return_option*,*match_parameter*])

REGEXP_INSTR returns an integer indicating the start of the search pattern. **REGEXP_INSTR** extends the capabilities of **INSTR** by permitting searches of regular expression patterns.

REGEXP_REPLACE(*source_string*, *pattern*
[,*replace_string*,*position*,*occurrence*,*match_parameter*])

REGEXP_REPLACE returns *source_string* with every occurrence of *pattern* replaced with *replace_string* (zero or more characters). **REGEXP_REPLACE** extends the capabilities of **REPLACE** by permitting searches of regular expression patterns.

REGEXP_SUBSTR(*source_string*, *pattern*
[,*position*,*occurrence*,*match_parameter*])

REGEXP_SUBSTR returns a subset of *source_string* based on the results of a regular expression search. **REGEXP_SUBSTR** extends the capabilities of **SUBSTR** by permitting searches of regular expression patterns.

REPLACE(*string*, *if* [,*then*])

REPLACE returns *string* with every occurrence of *if* replaced with *then* (zero or more characters). If no *then* string is specified, then all occurrences of *if* are removed. See **TRANSLATE**.

RPAD(*string*,*length* [,'*set*'])

RPAD stands for **R**ight **PAD**. It makes a string a specific length by adding a specified set of characters to the right.

RTRIM(*string* [,'*set*'])

RTRIM stands for **R**ight **TRIM**. It trims all the occurrences of any one of a set of characters off of the right side of a string.

SOUNDEX(*string*)

SOUNDEX converts a string to a code value. Names with similar sounds tend to have the same code value. You can use **SOUNDEX** to compare names that might have small spelling differences but are still the same.

SUBSTR(*string, start* [,*count*])

SUBSTRing clips out a piece of a string beginning at *start* position and counting for *count* characters from *start*.

TRANSLATE(*string,if,then*)

This **TRANSLATE**s a string, character by character, based on a positional matching of characters in the *if* string with characters in the *then* string. *See* **REPLACE**.

TREAT(*expr* AS [REF] [*user.*]*type*)

TREAT changes the declared type of an expression.

```
TRIM
( [{ { LEADING | TRAILING | BOTH } [trim_character])
  | trim_character
  }   FROM   ]   trim_source )
```

TRIM removes all the occurrences of any one of a set of characters off of the right side, left side, or both sides of a string.

UPPER(*string*)

UPPER converts every letter in a string into uppercase.

USERENV(*option*)

USERENV returns information about the **USER ENV**ironment, usually for an audit trail. Options include 'ENTRYID', 'SESSIONID', and 'TERMINAL'. **USERENV** is still supported but has been replaced by SYS_CONTEXT's UserEnv namespace.

VSIZE(*string*)

VSIZE gives the storage size of *string* in Oracle.

CHARTOROWID

SEE ALSO CONVERSION FUNCTIONS, **ROWIDTOCHAR**
FORMAT

CHARTOROWID(*string*)

DESCRIPTION This stands for **CHAR**acter **TO ROW ID**entifier. It changes a character string to act like an internal Oracle row identifier, or **ROWID**.

CHR

SEE ALSO **ASCII**, CHARACTER FUNCTIONS
FORMAT

CHR(*integer*)

DESCRIPTION **CHR** will return the character with the ASCII value of *integer*. (*integer* means an integer between 0 and 255, since the ASCII value of a character is an integer between 0 and 255.) Those between 0 and 127 are well defined. Those above 127 (called the extended ASCII set) tend to differ by country, application, and computer manufacturer. The letter *A*, for instance, is equal to the ASCII number 65, *B* is 66, *C* is 67, and so on. The decimal point is 46. A minus sign is 45. The number 0 is 48, 1 is 49, 2 is 50, and so on.

EXAMPLE

```
select CHR(77), CHR(46), CHR(56) from DUAL;

C C C
- - -
M . 8
```

CLAUSE

A clause is a major section of a SQL statement and begins with a keyword such as **select**, **insert**, **update**, **delete**, **from**, **where**, **order by**, **group by**, or **having**.

CLEAR (SQL*Plus)

SEE ALSO BREAK, COLUMN, COMPUTE

FORMAT

```
CL[EAR] option
```

DESCRIPTION **CLEAR** clears the option.

 BRE[AKS] clears breaks set by the **BREAK** command.
 BUFF[ER] clears the current buffer.
 COL[UMNS] clears options set by the **COLUMN** command.
 COMP[UTES] clears options set by the **COMPUTE** command.
 SCR[EEN] clears the screen.
 SQL clears the SQL buffer.
 TIMI[NG] deletes all timing areas created by the **TIMING** command.

EXAMPLES To clear computes, use this:

```
clear computes
```

 To clear column definitions, use this:

```
clear columns
```

CLOB

CLOB is a datatype that supports character large objects. *See* Chapter 35.

CLOSE

SEE ALSO DECLARE, FETCH, FOR, OPEN, Chapter 29

FORMAT

```
CLOSE cursor;
```

DESCRIPTION **CLOSE** closes the named cursor and releases its resources to Oracle for use elsewhere. *cursor* must be the name of a currently open cursor.

Even though a cursor has been closed, its definition has not been lost. You can issue **OPEN** *cursor* again, so long as the cursor was explicitly declared. A FOR loop will also implicitly **OPEN** a declared cursor. *See* CURSOR FOR LOOP.

CLOSED DATABASE

A closed database is a database that is associated with an instance (the database is mounted) but not open. Databases must be closed for some database maintenance functions. This can be accomplished via the SQL statements **ALTER DATABASE** or **SHUTDOWN**.

CLUSTER

A cluster is a means of storing together data from multiple tables, when the data in those tables contains common information and is likely to be accessed concurrently. You can also cluster an individual table. *See* **CREATE CLUSTER**.

CLUSTER INDEX

A cluster index is an index that is manually created after a cluster has been created and before any DML (**select**, **insert**, **update**, or **delete**) statements can operate on the cluster. This index is created on the cluster key columns with the SQL statement **CREATE INDEX**. In Oracle, you can define a hash cluster to index on the primary key. *See* HASH CLUSTER.

CLUSTER KEY

A cluster key is the column or columns that clustered tables have in common, and which is chosen as the storage/access key. For example, two tables, BOOKSHELF and BOOKSHELF_AUTHOR, might be clustered on the column Title. A cluster key is the same thing as a CLUSTER COLUMN.

CMDSEP (SQL*Plus)

See **SET**.

COALESCE

SEE ALSO DECODE, Chapter 16
FORMAT

```
COALESCE(value1, value2, ...)
```

DESCRIPTION **COALESCE** will return the first non-**NULL** value encountered in the list of values provided.

COLLATION

SEE ALSO GROUP BY, INDEX, ORDER BY, Chapter 12

DESCRIPTION The collation or collating sequence is the order in which characters, numbers, and symbols will be sorted because of an **order by** or **group by** clause. These sequences differ based on the collation sequence of the computer's operating system or the national language. EBCDIC (usually IBM and compatible mainframes) and ASCII (most other computers) sequences differ significantly. In spite of these differences, the following rules always apply:

- A number with a larger value is considered "greater" than a smaller one. All negative numbers are smaller than all positive numbers. Thus, −10 is smaller than 10; −100 is smaller than −10.
- A later date is considered greater than an earlier date.

Character strings are compared position by position, starting at the leftmost end of the string, up to the first character that is different. Whichever string has the greater character in that position is considered the greater string. One character is considered greater than another if it appears after the other in the computer's collation sequence. Usually this means that a *B* is greater than an *A*, but the value of *A* compared to *a*, or compared to the number 1, will differ by operating system.

The collation comparison varies slightly depending on whether you are using CHAR or VARCHAR2 strings.

If two VARCHAR2 strings are identical up to the end of the shorter one, the longer string is considered greater. If two strings are identical and the same length, they are considered equal.

With CHAR strings, the shorter string is padded with blanks out to the length of the longer string. If the strings are not identical after this padding, the comparison treats the padded blanks as less than any other character, resulting in the same truth value as the VARCHAR2 comparison. If the strings are identical after, but not before, the padding, the CHAR comparison would treat them as equal, whereas the VARCHAR2 comparison would not.

In SQL it is important that literal numbers be typed without enclosing single quotes. '10' would be considered smaller than '6', since the quotes will cause these to be regarded as character strings rather than numbers, and the '6' will be seen as greater than the '1' in the first position of '10'.

COLLECT

SEE ALSO COLLECTION FUNCTIONS, **CAST**

FORMAT

```
COLLECT(column)
```

DESCRIPTION **COLLECT** takes the input *column* value and creates a nested table of the input type out of the rows selected. To get the results of this function, you must use it within a **CAST** function.

COLLECTION FUNCTIONS

Collection functions operate on nested tables and varying arrays; see Chapter 34 for details. Collection functions available include **CARDINALITY**, **COLLECT**, **POWERMULTISET**, **POWERMULTISET_BY_CARDINALITY**, and **SET**.

COLSEP (SQL*Plus)

See **SET**.

COLUMN (Form 1—Definition)

A column is a subdivision of a table with a column name and a specific datatype. For example, in a table of workers, all of the workers' ages would constitute one column. *See* **ROW**.

COLUMN (Form 2—SQL*Plus)

SEE ALSO **ALIAS**, Chapter 6

FORMAT

```
COL[UMN]    {column | expression}
   [ ALI[AS] alias ]
   [ CLE[AR] | DEF[AULT] ]
   [ ENTMAP {ON|OFF} ]
   [ FOLD_A[FTER] ]
   [ FOLD_B[EFORE] ]
   [ FOR[MAT] format ]
   [ HEA[DING] text
      [ JUS[TIFY] {L[EFT]|C[ENTER]| R[IGHT]} ] ]
   [ LIKE {expression | alias} ]
   [ NEWL[INE] ]
   [ NEW_V[ALUE] variable ]
   [ NOPRI[NT]|PRI[NT] ]
   [ NUL[L] text ]
   [ OLD_V[ALUE] variable ]
   [ ON | OFF ]
   [ WRA[PPED]|WOR[D_WRAPPED]|TRU[NCATED] ]...
```

DESCRIPTION **COLUMN** controls column and column heading formatting. The options are all cumulative, and may be entered either simultaneously on a single line, or on separate lines at any time; the only requirement is that the word **COLUMN** and the column or expression must appear on each separate line. If one of the options is repeated, the most recent specified will be in effect. **COLUMN** by itself displays all the current definitions for all columns. **COLUMN** with only a column or expression will show that column's current definition.

column or *expression* refers to a column or expression used in the **select**. If an expression is used, the expression must be entered exactly the same way that it is in the **select** statement. If the expression in the **select** is **Amount * Rate**, then entering **Rate * Amount** in a **COLUMN** command will not work. If a column or expression is given an alias in the **select** statement, that alias must be used here.

If you **select** columns with the same name from different tables (in sequential selects), a **COLUMN** command for that column name will apply to both. Avoid this by assigning the columns different aliases in the **select** (not with the **COLUMN** command's **ALIAS** clause), and entering a **COLUMN** command for each column's alias.

ALIAS gives this column a new name, which then may be used to reference the column in **BREAK** and **COLUMN** commands.

CLEAR drops the column definition.

DEFAULT leaves the column defined and **ON**, but drops any other options.

ENTMAP allows entity mapping to be turned on or off for selected columns in HTML output.

FOLD_A[FTER] and **FOLD_B[EFORE]** instruct Oracle to fold a single row of output across multiple rows when printed. You can choose to fold the row either before or after the column.

FORMAT specifies the display format of the column. The format must be a literal like A25 or 990.99. Without **FORMAT** specified, the column width is the length as defined in the table.

A LONG column's width defaults to the value of the **SET LONG**. Both regular CHAR and LONG fields can have their width set by a format like **FORMAT A***n*, where *n* is an integer that is the column's new width.

A NUMBER column's width defaults to the value of **SET NUMWIDTH**, but is changed by the width in a **FORMAT** clause such as FORMAT 999,999.99. These options work with both **SET NUMFORMAT** and the **COLUMN FORMAT** commands:

Format	Result
,	Displays a comma.
.	Displays a period.
$99999	A dollar sign is placed in front of every number.
999990	Displays trailing zeroes, and a zero if the value is zero.
099999	Displays leading zeroes.
9999990	The count of nines and zeros determines the maximum digits that can be displayed.
999,999,999.99	Commas and decimals will be placed in the pattern shown.
B99999	The display will be blank if the value is zero.
C999	Displays the ISO currency symbol in this position.
99D99	Displays the decimal in the position indicated.
9.999EEEE	The display will be in scientific notation (4 E's are required).
9G999	Displays the group separator in the position shown.
L999	Displays the local currency symbol.
99999MI	If the number is negative, a minus sign follows the number. The default is for the negative sign to be on the left.
99999PR	Negative numbers are displayed within < and >.
RN or rn	Displays uppercase or lowercase Roman numerals. Values are 1 to 3999.
S9999 or 9999S	Returns leading or trailing + for positive values, – for negative values.
TM	Displays the data in the smallest number of decimal characters possible.
U999	Displays the Euro or other dual currency symbol in the specified position.
999V99	Multiplies number by 10n, where n is the number of digits to the right of V.
X	Displays the hexadecimal value for the rounded value of the specified number of digits.

HEADING relabels a column heading. The default is the column name or the expression. If text has blanks or punctuation characters, it must be in single quotes. The **HEADSEP** character (usually |) in text makes SQL*Plus begin a new line. The **COLUMN** command will remember the current **HEADSEP** character when the column is defined, and continue to use it for this column unless the column is redefined, even if the **HEADSEP** character is changed.

JUSTIFY aligns the heading over the column. By default, this is RIGHT for number columns and LEFT for anything else.

LIKE replicates the column definitions of a previously defined column for the current one, where either the expression or label was used in the other column definition. Only those features of the other column that have not been explicitly defined in the current column command are copied.

NEWLINE starts a new line before printing the column value.

NEW_VALUE names a variable to hold the column's value for use in the **TTITLE** command. *See* Chapter 6 for usage information.

NOPRINT and **PRINT** turn the column's display off or on.

NULL sets text to be displayed if the column has a **NULL** value. The default for this is a string of blanks as wide as the column is defined.

OFF or **ON** turns all these options for a column off or on without affecting its contents.

OLD_VALUE names a variable to hold the column's value for use in the **BTITLE** command.
WRAPPED, **WORD_WRAPPED**, and **TRUNCATED** control how SQL*Plus displays a heading or string value too wide to fit the column. **WRAP** folds the value to the next line. **WORD_WRAP** folds similarly, but breaks on words. **TRUNCATED** truncates the value to the width of the column definition.

COLUMN CONSTRAINT

A column constraint is an integrity constraint placed on a specific column of a table. *See* INTEGRITY CONSTRAINT.

COMMENT

SEE ALSO DATA DICTIONARY VIEWS, Chapter 42
FORMAT

```
COMMENT ON
{ TABLE [schema .] { table | view | materialized view }
| COLUMN [schema .] { table . | view . | materialized view . } column
| OPERATOR [schema .] operator
| INDEXTYPE [schema .] indextype
}
IS 'text';
```

DESCRIPTION **COMMENT** inserts the comment text about an object or column into the data dictionary.

You drop a comment from the database by setting it to an empty string (set *text* to ' ').

COMMIT

To commit means to make changes to data (**insert**s, **update**s, and **delete**s) permanent. Before changes are stored, both the old and new data exist so that changes can be made, or so that the data can be restored to its prior state ("rolled back"). When a user enters the Oracle SQL command **COMMIT**, all changes from that transaction are made permanent.

COMMIT (Form I—Embedded SQL)

SEE ALSO ROLLBACK, SAVEPOINT, SET TRANSACTION, *Programmer's Guide to the Oracle Precompilers*
FORMAT

```
EXEC SQL [AT { database| :host variable}] COMMIT [WORK]
[ [COMMENT 'text' ]. [RELEASE]
| FORCE 'text' [, integer ]]
```

DESCRIPTION You use **COMMIT** to commit work at various stages within a program. Without the explicit use of **COMMIT**, an entire program's work will be considered one transaction, and will not be committed until the program terminates. Any locks obtained will be held until that time, blocking other users from access. **COMMIT** should be used as often as logically feasible.

WORK is optional and has no effect on usage; it is provided for ANSI compatibility. **AT** references a remote database accessed by the **DECLARE DATABASE** command. **RELEASE** disconnects you from the database, whether remote or local. **FORCE** manually commits an in-doubt distributed transaction.

COMMIT (Form 2—PL/SQL Statement)

SEE ALSO ROLLBACK, SAVEPOINT
FORMAT

```
COMMIT [WORK] [ COMMENT 'text' | FORCE 'text' [, integer] ];
```

DESCRIPTION **COMMIT** commits any changes made to the database since the last **COMMIT** was executed implicitly or explicitly. **WORK** is optional and has no effect on usage.

COMMENT associates a text comment with the transaction. The comment can be viewed via the data dictionary view DBA_2PC_PENDING in the event a distributed transaction fails to complete. **FORCE** manually commits an in-doubt distributed transaction.

COMPOSE

SEE ALSO CONVERSION FUNCTIONS, Chapter 11
FORMAT

```
COMPOSE(string)
```

DESCRIPTION **COMPOSE** takes as its argument a string in any datatype, and returns a Unicode string in its fully normalized form in the same character set as the input.

EXAMPLE To display an *o* with an umlaut:

```
select COMPOSE ( 'o' || UNISTR('\0308') ) from DUAL;
```

```
C
-
ö
```

COMPOSITE KEY

A composite key is a primary or foreign key composed of two or more columns.

COMPOSITE PARTITION

A composite partition involves the use of multiple partition methods, such as a range-partitioned table in which the range partitions are then hash-partitioned. *See* Chapter 17.

COMPRESSED INDEX

A compressed index is an index for which only enough index information is stored to identify unique index entries; information that an index stores with the previous or following key is "compressed" (truncated) and not stored to reduce the storage overhead required by an index. *See also* NONCOMPRESSED INDEX.

COMPUTE (SQL*Plus)

SEE ALSO BREAK, AGGREGATE FUNCTIONS
FORMAT

```
COMP[UTE][AVG|COU[NT]|MAX[IMUM]|MIN[IMUM]|NUM[BER]|STD|SUM|VAR[IANCE]]...
    [function LABEL label_name
    OF {expression | column | alias} ...
    ON {expression | column | alias | REPORT | ROW}...]
```

DESCRIPTION *expression* is a column or expression. **COMPUTE** performs computations on columns or expressions selected from a table. It works only with the **BREAK** command.

By default, Oracle will use the function name (**SUM, AVG**, etc.) as the label for the result in the query output. **LABEL** allows you to specify a *label_name* that overrides the default value.

OF names the column or expression whose value is to be computed. These columns also must be in the **select** clause, or the **COMPUTE** will be ignored.

ON coordinates the **COMPUTE** with the **BREAK** command. **COMPUTE** prints the computed value and restarts the computation when the **ON** *expression*'s value changes, or when a specified ROW or REPORT break occurs. *See* **BREAK** for coordination details.

COMPUTE by itself displays the computes in effect.

AVG, MAXIMUM, MINIMUM, STD, SUM, and **VARIANCE** all work on expressions that are numbers. **MAXIMUM** and **MINIMUM** also work on character expressions, but not DATEs. **COUNT** and **NUMBER** work on any expression type.

All of these computes, except **NUMBER**, ignore rows with **NULL** values:

AVG	Gives average value
COUNT	Gives count of non-**NULL** values
MAXIMUM	Gives maximum value
MINIMUM	Gives minimum value
NUMBER	Gives count of all rows returned
STD	Gives standard deviation
SUM	Gives sum of non-**NULL** values
VARIANCE	Gives variance

Successive computes are simply put in order without commas, as in this case:

```
compute sum avg max of Amount Rate on report
```

This will compute the sum, average, and maximum of both Amount and Rate for the entire report.

EXAMPLE To calculate for each Item classification and for the entire report, enter this:

```
break on Report on Industry skip 1
compute sum of Volume on Industry Report
```

CONCAT
See **SET**, ||.

CONCATENATED INDEX (or KEY)
A concatenated index is an index that is created on more than one column of a table. It can be used to guarantee that those columns are unique for every row in the table and to speed access to rows via those columns. *See* COMPOSITE KEY.

CONCURRENCY
Concurrency is a general term that means the access of the same data by multiple users. In database software, concurrency requires complex software programming to ensure that all users see correct data and that all changes are made in the proper order.

CONDITION

A condition is an expression whose value evaluates to either TRUE or FALSE, such as Age > 65.

CONNECT (Form I—SQL*Plus))

SEE ALSO **COMMIT**, **DISCONNECT**, Chapter 23
FORMAT

```
CON[NECT] [{user[/password] [@connect_identifier] |/} [AS SYSOPER|SYSDBA}]];
```

DESCRIPTION You must be in SQL*Plus to use this command, although you don't need to be logged onto Oracle (*see* **DISCONNECT**). **CONNECT** commits any pending changes, logs you off of Oracle, and logs on as the specified *user*. If the *password* is absent, you are prompted for it. It is not displayed when you type it in response to a prompt.

@connect_identifier connects to the named database. It may be on your host, or on another computer connected via Oracle Net.

CONNECT (Form 2—Embedded SQL)

SEE ALSO **COMMIT**, **DECLARE DATABASE**, Chapter 23
FORMAT

```
EXEC SQL CONNECT
  { :user IDENTIFIED BY :password | :user_password }
        [AT { database | :host_variable}]
        [USING :connect_string]
        [ALTER AUTHORIZATION :new_password
        | IN {SYSDBA | SYSOPER } MODE ]
```

DESCRIPTION **CONNECT** connects a host program to a local or remote database. It may be used more than once to connect to multiple databases. *:user_password* is a host variable that contains the Oracle username and password separated by a slash (/). Alternatively, *:user* and *:password* can be entered separately by using the second format.

AT is used to name a database other than the default for this user. It is a required clause to reach any databases other than the user's default database. This name can be used later in other SQL statements with **AT**. This database must be first identified with **DECLARE DATABASE**. **USING** specifies an optional Oracle Net string (such as a service name) used during the **CONNECT** operation. Without the **USING** string, you will be connected to the user's default database, regardless of the database named in the **AT** line.

CONNECT BY

SEE ALSO Chapter 14
FORMAT

```
SELECT expression [,expression]...
  FROM [user.]table
 WHERE condition
CONNECT BY [PRIOR] expression = [PRIOR] expression
 START WITH expression = expression
 ORDER BY expression
```

DESCRIPTION **CONNECT BY** is an operator used in a **SELECT** statement to create reports on inheritance in tree-structured data, such as company organization, family trees, and so on. **START WITH** tells where in the tree to begin. These are the rules:

- The position of **PRIOR** with respect to the **CONNECT BY** expressions determines which expression identifies the root and which identifies the branches of the tree.
- A **WHERE** clause will eliminate individuals from the tree, but not their descendants (or ancestors, depending on the location of **PRIOR**).
- A qualification in the **CONNECT BY** (particularly a not equal sign instead of the equal sign) will eliminate both an individual and all of its descendants.
- **CONNECT BY** cannot be used with a table join in the **WHERE** clause.

EXAMPLE

```
select Cow, Bull, LPAD(' ',6*(Level-1))||Offspring AS Offspring,
       Sex, Birthdate
  from BREEDING
connect by Offspring = PRIOR Cow
 start with Offspring = 'DELLA'
 order by Birthdate;
```

In this example, the following clause:

```
connect by Offspring = PRIOR Cow
```

means the offspring is the cow **PRIOR** to this one.

CONSTRAINT

A constraint is a rule or restriction concerning a piece of data (such as a **NOT NULL** restriction on a column) that is enforced at the data level rather than at the object or application level. *See* INTEGRITY CONSTRAINT.

CONSTRAINTS

SEE ALSO **CREATE TABLE**, INTEGRITY CONSTRAINT, Chapter 17

FORMAT

constraint::=

inline_constraint::=

out_of_line_constraint::=

inline_ref_constraint::=

out_of_line_ref_constraint

references_clause::=

constraint_state::=

using_index_clause::=

index_properties::=

index_attributes::=

exceptions_clause::=

DESCRIPTION Constraints are defined with the **RELATIONAL_PROPERTIES** clause of the **CREATE TABLE** and **ALTER TABLE** commands. You use the constraints clauses to create a constraint or to alter an existing constraint. You can enable and disable constraints. If you disable a constraint and then try to re-enable it, Oracle will check the data. If the constraint cannot be re-enabled, Oracle can write the exceptions out to a separate table for review.

For PRIMARY KEY and UNIQUE constraints, Oracle creates indexes. As part of the constraint clause for those constraints, you can use the **USING INDEX** clause to specify the tablespace and storage for the index.

CONTAINS

CONTAINS is used to evaluate text searches that use CONTEXT indexes within Oracle Text. *See* Chapter 25. Supported text search operators for **CONTAINS** are shown in the following table:

Operator	Description
OR	Returns a record if either search term has a score that exceeds the threshold.
\|	Same as OR.
AND	Returns a record if both search terms have a score that exceeds the threshold.
&	Same as AND.
ACCUM	Returns a record if the sum of the search terms' scores exceeds the threshold.
,	Same as ACCUM.

Operator	Description
MINUS	Returns a record if the score of the first search minus the score of the second search exceeds the threshold.
-	Same as MINUS.
*	Assigns different weights to the score of the searches.
NEAR	The score will be based on how near the search terms are to each other in the searched text.
;	Same as NEAR.
{}	Encloses reserved words such as AND if they are part of the search term.
%	Multiple-character wildcard.
_	Single-character wildcard.
$	Performs stem expansion of the search term prior to performing the search.
?	Performs a fuzzy match (allowing for misspellings) of the search term prior to performing the search.
!	Performs a **SOUNDEX** (phonetic) search.
()	Specifies the order in which search criteria are evaluated.

CONTEXT AREA

A context area is work area in memory where Oracle stores the current SQL statement and, if the statement is a query, one row of the result. The context area holds the state of a cursor.

CONTEXT INDEX

Oracle Text supports three types of text indexes: CONTEXT indexes, CTXCAT indexes, and CTXRULE indexes. CONTEXT indexes use the **CONTAINS** operator and support a wider array of text search capabilities. CTXCAT indexes support a narrower set of search operators but support the creation of index sets. CTXRULE indexes are indexes on columns that contain a set of text queries. *See* Chapter 25 for details.

CONTROL FILE (DATABASE)

A control file is a small administrative file that is required by every database to enable the database to start and run a database system. Multiple identical control files are created for redundancy.

CONTROL FILE (SQL*LOADER)

A SQL*Loader control file tells the SQL*Loader executable where to find the data to be loaded, and how to process the data during the load. Every SQL*Loader session has an associated control file. For control file syntax, see **SQLLDR**. For details on the use of SQL*Loader, see Chapter 21.

CONVERSION FUNCTIONS

SEE ALSO CHARACTER FUNCTIONS, NUMBER FUNCTIONS, AGGREGATE FUNCTIONS, Chapter 11

DESCRIPTION The following is an alphabetical list of all current conversion and transformation functions in Oracle version of SQL.

Function Name	Definition
ASCIISTR	Translates a string in any character set and returns an ASCII string in the database character set.
BIN_TO_NUM	Converts a binary value to its numerical equivalent.
CAST	CASTs one built-in or collection type to another; commonly used with nested tables and varying arrays.
CHARTOROWID	Changes a character string to act like an internal Oracle row identifier, or ROWID.
COMPOSE	Translates a string in any datatype to a Unicode string in its fully normalized form in the same character set as the input.
CONVERT	CONVERTs a character string from one national language character set to another.
DECOMPOSE	Translates a string in any datatype to a Unicode string after canonical decomposition in the same character set as the input.
HEXTORAW	Changes a character string of hex numbers into binary.
NUMTODSINTERVAL	Converts a NUMBER to an INTERVAL DAY TO SECOND literal.
NUMTOYMINTERVAL	Converts a NUMBER to an INTERVAL YEAR TO MONTH literal.
RAWTOHEX	Changes a string of binary numbers to a character string of hex numbers.
RAWTONHEX	Converts RAW to an NVARCHAR2 character value containing its hexadecimal equivalent.
ROWIDTOCHAR	Changes an internal Oracle row identifier, or ROWID, to a character string.
ROWIDTONCHAR	Converts a ROWID value to an NVARCHAR2 datatype.
SCN_TO_TIMESTAMP	Converts a system change number to an approximate timestamp.
TIMESTAMP_TO_SCN	Converts a timestamp to an approximate system change number.
TO_BINARY_DOUBLE	Returns a double-precision floating-point number.
TO_BINARY_FLOAT	Returns a single-precision floating-point number.
TO_CHAR	Converts a NUMBER or DATE to a character string.
TO_CLOB	Converts NCLOB values in a LOB column or other character strings to CLOB values.
TO_DATE	Converts a NUMBER, CHAR, or VARCHAR2 to a DATE (an Oracle datatype).
TO_DSINTERVAL	Converts a character string of CHAR, VARCHAR2, NCHAR, or NVARCHAR2 datatype to an INTERVAL DAY TO SECOND type.
TO_LOB	Converts a LONG to a LOB as part of an **INSERT AS SELECT**.
TO_MULTI_BYTE	Converts the single-byte characters in a character string to multibyte characters.
TO_NCHAR	Converts a character string, NUMBER, or DATE from the database character set to the national character set.
TO_NCLOB	Converts CLOB values in a LOB column or other character strings to NCLOB values.
TO_NUMBER	Converts a CHAR or VARCHAR2 to a number.
TO_SINGLE_BYTE	Converts the multibyte characters in a CHAR or VARCHAR2 to single bytes.
TO_TIMESTAMP	Converts a character string to a value of TIMESTAMP datatype.

Function Name	Definition
TO_TIMESTAMP_TZ	Converts a character string to a value of TIMESTAMP WITH TIME ZONE datatype.
TO_YMINTERVAL	Converts a character string of CHAR, VARCHAR2, NCHAR, or NVARCHAR2 datatype to an INTERVAL YEAR TO MONTH type.
TRANSLATE...USING	**TRANSLATE**s characters in a string into different characters.
UNISTR	Converts a string into Unicode in the database Unicode character set.

CONVERT

SEE ALSO CONVERSION FUNCTIONS

FORMAT

```
CONVERT(string,[destination_set,[source_set]])
```

DESCRIPTION **CONVERT** is used to convert the characters in *string* from one standard bit representation to another, such as from US7ASCII (the default if either set isn't entered) to WE8DEC. This is typically done when data entered into a column on one computer contains characters that can't be properly displayed or printed on another computer. **CONVERT** allows a reasonable translation of one standard to the other in most cases. The most common sets include:

F7DEC	DEC's 7-bit ASCII set for France
US7ASCII	Standard U.S. 7-bit ASCII set
WE8DEC	DEC's 8-bit ASCII set for Western Europe
WE8HP	HP's 8-bit ASCII set for Western Europe
WE8ISO8859P1	ISO 8859-1 Western Europe 8-bit character set
WE8EBCDIC500	IBM West European EBCDIC Code Page 500
WE8PC850	IBM PC Code Page 850

COPY (SQL*Plus)

NOTE
*The SQL*Plus **COPY** command is not being enhanced to handle datatypes or features introduced with, or after, Oracle8i. The **COPY** command is likely to be made obsolete in a future release.*

SEE ALSO **CREATE DATABASE LINK**, Chapter 23

FORMAT

```
COPY [FROM user/password@database]
     [TO user/password@database]
     {APPEND | CREATE | INSERT | REPLACE}
     table [ (column [,column]...) ]
     USING query
```

DESCRIPTION **COPY** copies **FROM** a table **TO** a table in another computer using Oracle Net. **FROM** is the username, password, and database of the source table, and **TO** is the destination table. Either **FROM** or **TO** may be omitted, in which case the user's default database will be used for the missing clause. The source and destination databases must not be the same, so only one of the **FROM** and **TO** clauses may be absent.

 APPEND adds to the destination table; if the table does not exist, it is created. **CREATE** requires that the destination table be created; if it already exists, a 'table already exists' error occurs. **INSERT** adds to the destination table; if the table does not exist, a 'table does not exist' error occurs. **REPLACE** drops the data in the destination table and replaces it with the data from the source table; if the table does not exist, it is created.

 table is the name of the destination table. *column* is the name(s) of the column(s) in the destination table. If named, the number of columns must be the same as in the query. If no columns are named, the copied columns will have the same names in the destination table as they had in the source table. *query* identifies the source table and determines which rows and columns will be copied from it.

 SET LONG (*see* **SET**) determines the length of a long field that can be copied. LONG columns with data longer than the value of LONG will be truncated. **SET COPYCOMMIT** determines how many sets of rows get copied before a commit. **SET ARRAYSIZE** determines how many rows are in a set.

EXAMPLE This example copies BOOKSHELF_CHECKOUT from the EDMESTON database to the database the local SQL*Plus user is connected to. The table LOCAL_CHECKOUT is created by the copy. The columns may be renamed at the destination. Note the use of the dash (-) at the end of each line. This is required. The command does not end with a semicolon (since it is a SQL*Plus command, not a SQL command). *See* the **SET** command for options related to the **COPY** command.

```
copy from PRACTICE/PRACTICE@EDMESTON -
create LOCAL_CHECKOUT (Borrower, Title) -
 using select Name, Title -
        from BOOKSHELF_CHECKOUT
```

COPYCOMMIT (SQL*Plus)

See **SET** and **COPY**.

COPYTYPECHECK (SQL*Plus)

See **SET** and **COPY**.

CORR

SEE ALSO AGGREGATE FUNCTIONS

FORMAT

```
CORR ( expr1 , expr2 ) [OVER ( analytic_clause )]
```

DESCRIPTION **CORR** returns the coefficient of correlation of a set of number pairs. Both *expr1* and *expr2* are number expressions. Oracle applies the function to the set of (*expr1*, *expr2*) after eliminating the pairs for which either *expr1* or *expr2* is **NULL**. Then Oracle makes the following computation:

```
COVAR_POP(expr1, expr2) / (STDDEV_POP(expr1) * STDDEV_POP(expr2))
```

 The function returns a value of type NUMBER. If the function is applied to an empty set, it returns **NULL**.

CORR

SEE ALSO **CORR_K** and **CORR_S**

FORMAT

```
CORR (expr1, expr2 ) OVER (analytic clause)
```

DESCRIPTION **CORR** returns the coefficient of correlation on a set of number pairs. **CORR** can be used as an aggregate or analytic function.

CORR_K and CORR_S

SEE ALSO **CORR**

FORMAT

```
{CORR_K | CORR_S }
  (expr1, expr2 [, { COEFFICIENT |ONE_SIDED_SIG|TWO_SIDED_SIG}])
```

DESCRIPTION The **CORR_K** and **CORR_S** functions support nonparametric or rank correlations. Correlation coefficients take a value ranging from 1 to –1 where 1 indicates a perfect relationship and –1 a perfect inverse relationship. The arguments must either be numeric or implicitly converted to a numeric datatype. **ONE_SIDED_SIG** is for one-tailed significance of the correlation, **TWO_SIDED_SIG** is for two-tailed significance.

CORRELATED QUERY

A correlated query is a subquery that is executed repeatedly, once for each value of a candidate row selected by the main query. The outcome of each execution of the subquery depends on the values of one or more fields in the candidate row; that is, the subquery is correlated with the main query. *See* Chapter 13.

COS

SEE ALSO ACOS, ASIN, ATAN, ATAN2, **COSH**, EXP, LN, LOG, SIN, SINH, TAN, TANH

FORMAT

```
COS(value)
```

DESCRIPTION **COS** returns the cosine of a value, an angle expressed in radians. You can convert a degree angle into radians by multiplying it by pi/180.

COSH

SEE ALSO ACOS, ASIN, ATAN, ATAN2, **COS**, EXP, LN, LOG, SIN, SINH, TAN, TANH

FORMAT

```
COSH(value)
```

DESCRIPTION **COSH** returns the hyperbolic cosine of a *value*.

COUNT

SEE ALSO AGGREGATE FUNCTIONS, Chapters 9 and 12

FORMAT

```
COUNT ( { * | [ DISTINCT | ALL ] expr } ) [OVER ( analytic_clause )]
```

DESCRIPTION **COUNT** counts the number of rows in which *expression* is non-**NULL**, which is then returned by the query. With **DISTINCT**, **COUNT** counts only the distinct non-**NULL** rows. With *****, **COUNT** counts all rows, whether **NULL** or not.

COVAR_POP

SEE ALSO AGGREGATE FUNCTIONS

FORMAT

```
COVAR_POP ( expr1 , expr2 ) [OVER ( analytic_clause )]
```

DESCRIPTION **COVAR_POP** returns the population covariance of a set of number pairs. You can use it as an aggregate or analytic function.

Both *expr1* and *expr2* are number expressions. Oracle applies the function to the set of (*expr1, expr2*) pairs after eliminating all pairs for which either *expr1* or *expr2* is **NULL**. Then Oracle makes the following computation:

```
(SUM(expr1 * expr2) - SUM(expr2) * SUM(expr1) / n) / n
```

where *n* is the number of (*expr1, expr2*) pairs where neither *expr1* nor *expr2* is **NULL**.

COVAR_SAMP

SEE ALSO AGGREGATE FUNCTIONS

FORMAT

```
COVAR_POP ( expr1 , expr2 ) [OVER ( analytic_clause )]
```

DESCRIPTION **COVAR_SAMP** returns the sample covariance of a set of number pairs. You can use it as an aggregate or analytic function.

Both *expr1* and *expr2* are number expressions. Oracle applies the function to the set of (*expr1, expr2*) pairs after eliminating all pairs for which either *expr1* or *expr2* is **NULL**. Then Oracle makes the following computation:

```
(SUM(expr1 * expr2) - SUM(expr1) * SUM(expr2) / n) / (n-1)
```

where *n* is the number of (*expr1, expr2*) pairs where neither *expr1* nor *expr2* is **NULL**.

CREATE CLUSTER

SEE ALSO **CREATE INDEX, CREATE TABLE**, Chapter 17

FORMAT

create_cluster::=

physical_attributes_clause::=

size_clause::=

parallel_clause::=

DESCRIPTION **CREATE CLUSTER** creates a cluster for one or more tables. Tables are added to the cluster using **CREATE TABLE** with the **CLUSTER** clause. **CREATE CLUSTER** requires at least one cluster column from each of the tables. These must have the same datatype and size, but are not required to have the same name. For the tables in a cluster, rows with the same cluster column values are kept together on disk in the same area, the same logical block(s). This can improve performance when the cluster columns are the columns by which the tables are usually joined.

Each distinct value in each cluster column is stored only once, regardless of whether it occurs once or many times in the tables and rows. This typically can reduce the amount of disk space needed to store the tables, but each table continues to appear as if it contains all of its own data. Tables with LONG columns cannot be clustered.

cluster is the name created for the cluster. *column* and *datatype* follow the method of **CREATE TABLE**, except that **NULL** and **NOT NULL** cannot be specified. However, in the actual **CREATE TABLE** statement, at least one cluster column in a cluster must be **NOT NULL**. **SIZE** sets the size in bytes for a logical block (not a physical block). **SPACE** is the cluster's initial disk allocation, as used in **CREATE TABLE**.

SIZE should be the average amount of space needed to store all the rows from all the clustered tables that are associated with a single cluster key. A small **SIZE** value may increase the time needed to access tables in the cluster, but can reduce disk space usage. **SIZE** should be a proper divisor of the physical block size. If not, Oracle will use the next larger divisor. If **SIZE** exceeds the physical block size, Oracle will use the physical block size instead.

By default, the cluster is indexed, and you must create an index on the cluster key before putting any data in the cluster. If you specify the hash cluster form, however, you don't need to (and can't) create an index on the cluster key. Instead, Oracle uses a hash function to store the rows of the table.

You can create your own hash value as a column of the table and use that for hashing with the **HASH IS** clause to tell Oracle to use that column as the hash value. Otherwise, Oracle uses an internal hash function based on the columns of the cluster key. The **HASHKEYS** clause actually creates the hash cluster and specifies the number of hash values, rounded to the nearest prime number. The minimum value is 2.

See **STORAGE** for details on the common storage clause parameters.

CREATE CONTEXT

SEE ALSO ALTER CONTEXT

FORMAT

```
CREATE [OR REPLACE] CONTEXT namespace USING [schema .] package
[ INITIALIZED { EXTERNALLY | GLOBALLY }
| ACCESSED GLOBALLY ] ;
```

DESCRIPTION A context is a set of attributes used to secure an application. **CREATE CONTEXT** creates a namespace for a context and associates the namespace with the externally created package that sets the context. To create a context namespace, you must have the CREATE ANY CONTEXT system privilege.

CREATE CONTROLFILE

SEE ALSO ALTER DATABASE, CREATE DATABASE

FORMAT
create_controlfile::=

logfile_clause::=

character_set_clause::=

CHARACTER → SET → character_set →

DESCRIPTION You can use the **CREATE CONTROLFILE** command to re-create a control file if you have lost your current control file to media failure, if you want to change the name of your database, or if you want to change one of the options for the redo log file or a datafile. In general, this command should be used only by experienced database administrators.

NOTE
Perform a full offline backup of all of your database files before using this command.

The **REUSE** option lets existing control files be reused. If you specify the name of an existing control file but do not use the **REUSE** option, the command will return an error. The **SET** option changes the name of the database, specified by the **DATABASE** clause. The **LOGFILE** clause specifies the redo log file groups, all of which must exist. The **RESETLOGS** versus **NORESETLOGS** clause tells Oracle to reset the current logs or not. The **DATAFILE** line specifies the datafiles for the database, all of which must exist.

The **MAXLOGFILES** option specifies the maximum number of redo log file groups that can be created. The **MAXLOGMEMBERS** option specifies the number of copies for a redo log group. The **MAXLOGHISTORY** option specifies the number of archived redo log file groups for Real Application Clusters. The **MAXDATAFILES** option specifies the maximum number of datafiles that can ever be created for the database. The **MAXINSTANCES** option gives the maximum number of Oracle instances that can mount and open the database. The **ARCHIVELOG** and **NOARCHIVELOG** options turn archiving of the redo log files on and off, respectively.

The **CREATE CONTROLFILE** command needed for an existing database can be generated via the **ALTER DATABASE BACKUP CONTROLFILE TO TRACE** command.

As of Oracle Database 10*g*, you can specify Automatic Storage Management files as well as file system files.

CREATE DATABASE

SEE ALSO **ALTER DATABASE, CREATE CONTROLFILE, CREATE ROLLBACK SEGMENT, CREATE TABLESPACE, SHUTDOWN, STARTUP,** Chapters 2 and 46

FORMAT

create_database::=

database_logging_clauses::=

tablespace_clauses::=

default_tablespace::=

default_temp_tablespace::=

extent_management_clause::=

size_clause::=

undo_tablespace::=

set_time_zone_clause::=

DESCRIPTION *database* is the database name, and must have eight characters or fewer. DB_NAME in init.ora contains the default database name. In general, this command should be used only by experienced database administrators.

NOTE
Using this command in an existing database will erase the specified datafiles.

file_definition defines the redo log file and datafile names and sizes.

```
'file' [SIZE integer [K | M] [REUSE]
```

SIZE is the number of bytes set aside for this file. Suffixing this with **K** multiplies the value by 1024; **M** multiplies it by 1048576 (G and T are also supported). **REUSE** (without **SIZE**) means destroy the contents

of any file by this name and associate the name with this database. **REUSE** with **SIZE** creates the file if it doesn't exist, and checks its size if it does exist. **CONTROLFILE REUSE** overwrites the existing control files defined by the CONTROL_FILES parameter in the initialization parameter file.

LOGFILE names the files to be used as redo log files. If this parameter is not used, Oracle creates two by default. **MAXLOGFILES** overrides the LOG_FILES initialization parameter, and defines the maximum number of redo log files that can ever be created for this database. This number cannot be increased later except by re-creating the control file. The minimum number for files is two. A high number only makes a somewhat larger control file.

DATAFILE names the files to be used for the database itself. **MAXDATAFILES** sets the absolute upper limit for files that can be created for this database, and overrides the DB_FILES initialization parameter. A high number only makes a somewhat larger control file.

As of Oracle Database 10g, you can specify Automatic Storage Management files as well as file system files. When the **AUTOEXTEND** option is turned ON for a datafile, the datafile will dynamically extend as needed in increments of **NEXT** size, to a maximum of **MAXSIZE** (or **UNLIMITED**).

MAXINSTANCES overrides the INSTANCES parameter in init.ora and sets the maximum number of simultaneous instances that can mount and open this database.

ARCHIVELOG and **NOARCHIVELOG** define the way redo log files are used when the database is first created. **NOARCHIVELOG** is the default, and means that redo log files will get reused without saving their contents elsewhere. This provides instance recovery but will not recover from a media failure, such as a disk crash. **ARCHIVELOG** forces redo log files to be archived (usually to another disk or a tape), so that you can recover from a media failure. This mode also supports instance recovery. This parameter can be reset by **ALTER DATABASE**.

The **MAXLOGMEMBERS** option specifies the maximum number of copies of a redo log file group. The **MAXLOGHISTORY** option specifies the maximum number of archived redo log files, useful only for the Real Application Clusters when you are archiving redo log files. The **CHARACTER SET** option specifies the character set used to store data, which depends on the operating system.

For more automated handling of undo (rollback) segments, you can specify the **UNDO TABLESPACE** clause to allocate a tablespace specifically to hold undo data. The database must be started in Automatic Undo Management (AUM) mode.

You can use the **DEFAULT TEMPORARY TABLESPACE** clause to designate a non-SYSTEM tablespace as the default temporary tablespace for all new users created in the database.

As of Oracle Database 10g, you can use the **CREATE DATABASE** command to do the following:

- Create a default permanent tablespace for the database
- Specify datafiles for the SYSAUX tablespace
- Specify a bigfile tablespace as the default for the database
- Override the default for the undo and default temporary tablespaces

CREATE DATABASE LINK

SEE ALSO **CREATE SYNONYM, SELECT,** Chapter 23

FORMAT

```
CREATE [SHARED] [PUBLIC] DATABASE LINK dblink
[ CONNECT TO { CURRENT_USER | user IDENTIFIED BY password
[AUTHENTICATED BY user IDENTIFIED BY password] }
| AUTHENTICATED BY user IDENTIFIED BY password]
[USING 'connect_string'];
```

DESCRIPTION *dblink* is the name given to the link. *connect_string* is the definition of the remote database that can be accessed through Oracle Net and defines the link between a local database and a username on a remote database. **PUBLIC** links can be created only by a user with the CREATE PUBLIC DATABASE LINK system privilege, but are then available to all users except those who have created a private link with the same name. If **PUBLIC** isn't specified, the link is only available to the user who executed the **CREATE DATABASE LINK** statement. *connect_string* is the Oracle Net service name for the remote database.

Remote tables can be accessed just like local tables, except that the table name must be suffixed by *@link* in the **FROM** clause of the **SELECT** statement. Most systems set the maximum number of simultaneous links to four. The DBA can increase this number with the OPEN_LINKS parameter in init.ora.

Tree-structured queries are limited. They may not use the **PRIOR** operator except in the **CONNECT BY** clause. **START WITH** cannot contain a subquery. **CONNECT BY** and **START WITH** cannot use the function **USERENV**('ENTRYID'), or the pseudo-column RowNum.

To create a database link, you must have CREATE DATABASE LINK privilege in the local database, and the CREATE SESSION privilege in a remote database. To create a public database link, you must have the CREATE PUBLIC DATABASE LINK system privilege.

If you use the **CONNECT TO CURRENT_USER** clause, the link will attempt to open a connection in the remote database by using your current username and password. You therefore need to coordinate any password changes you make between the local database and the remote database, or else database links may stop working.

If you use the shared server architecture, you can create **SHARED** database links that eliminate the need for many separate dedicated connections via links. When you create a **SHARED** link, you must supply a valid username and password in the remote database to use as an authentication for the connection.

EXAMPLES The following defines a link named EDMESTON_BOOKS that connects to the Practice username in the EDMESTON database:

```
create database link EDMESTON_BOOKS
connect to Practice identified by Practice
  using 'EDMESTON';
```

You now can query Practice's tables like this:

```
select Title, Publisher
  from BOOKSHELF@EDMESTON_BOOKS;
```

A synonym could also be created to hide the remoteness of the tables:

```
create synonym BOOKSHELF for BOOKSHELF@EDMESTON_BOOKS;
```

CREATE DIMENSION
SEE ALSO **ALTER DIMENSION**, **DROP DIMENSION**, Chapter 24
FORMAT
create_dimension::=

level_clause::=

hierarchy_clause::=

dimension_join_clause::=

attribute_clause::=

extended_attribute_clause::=

DESCRIPTION **CREATE DIMENSION** creates hierarchies among related columns in tables, for use by the optimizer. The optimizer uses dimension values when determining whether a materialized view will return the same data as its base table. To create a dimension, you must have CREATE DIMENSION privilege; to create a dimension in another user's schema, you must have the CREATE ANY DIMENSION privilege.

LEVEL defines the level within the dimension. **HIERARCHY** defines the relationships among the levels. **ATTRIBUTE** assigns specific attributes to levels within the dimension. **JOIN_KEY** defines the join clauses between the levels.

As of Oracle Database 10g, you can assign a name to a dimension attribute that is different from the level name.

EXAMPLES Consider a geography dimension. Continents are divided into countries, so there is a hierarchy between country data and continent data. For a table named COUNTRY, with columns Country and Continent, and a second table named CONTINENT, with a column named Continent:

```
create table CONTINENT (
 Continent     VARCHAR2(30));

create table COUNTRY (
Country      VARCHAR2(30) not null,
Continent    VARCHAR2(30));

create dimension GEOGRAPHY
   level COUNTRY_ID      is COUNTRY.Country
   level CONTINENT_ID    is CONTINENT.Continent
   hierarchy COUNTRY_ROLLUP (
      COUNTRY_ID            child of
      CONTINENT_ID
   join key COUNTRY.Continent references CONTINENT_ID);
```

CREATE DIRECTORY
SEE ALSO BFILE, Chapters 22, 26, and 35
FORMAT

```
CREATE [OR REPLACE] DIRECTORY directory AS 'path_name';
```

DESCRIPTION Within Oracle, a "directory" is an alias for an operating system directory. You must create a directory prior to accessing BFILE datatype values or external tables. *See* Chapter 26 for details on the creation and management of external tables.

CREATE DISKGROUP
SEE ALSO **ALTER DISKGROUP**, **DROP DISKGROUP**, Chapter 46
FORMAT
create_diskgroup::=

qualified_disk_clause::=

size_clause::=

DESCRIPTION

NOTE
CREATE DISKGROUP is valid only if you are using Automatic Storage Management (ASM) and you have started an ASM instance.

CREATE DISKGROUP creates a collection of disks. Oracle manages a disk group as a logical unit and evenly spreads each file across the disks to balance I/O. Oracle automatically distributes database files across the available disks in disk groups and rebalances the storage when the storage configuration changes. **CREATE DISKGROUP** creates a disk group, assigns disks to the disk group, and mounts the disk group for the first time.

CREATE FUNCTION

SEE ALSO ALTER FUNCTION, BLOCK STRUCTURE, **CREATE LIBRARY**, **CREATE PACKAGE**, **CREATE PROCEDURE**, DATATYPES, **DROP FUNCTION**, Chapter 31
FORMAT
create_function::=

invoker_rights_clause::=

parallel_enable_clause::=

streaming_clause::=

call_spec::=

Java_declaration::=

C_declaration::=

DESCRIPTION *function* is the name of the function being defined. A function may have parameters and named arguments of a certain datatype, and every function returns a value of a certain datatype as

specified by the **RETURN** clause. The PL/SQL block defines the behavior of the function as a series of declarations, PL/SQL program statements, and exceptions.

The **IN** qualifier means that you have to specify a value for the parameter when you call the function, but since you always have to do this for a function, the syntax is optional. In a procedure, you can have other kinds of parameters. The difference between a function and a procedure is that a function returns a value to the calling environment.

In order to create a function, you must have the CREATE PROCEDURE system privilege. To create a function in another user's account, you must have the CREATE ANY PROCEDURE system privilege.

Your function can use C libraries that are stored outside of the database (see **CREATE LIBRARY**). If you use Java within your function, you can provide a Java declaration within the **LANGUAGE** clause. The **INVOKER_RIGHTS** clause lets you specify whether the function executes with the privileges of the function owner (the definer) or the current user (the invoker).

CREATE INDEX

SEE ALSO ANALYZE, **ALTER INDEX**, **DROP INDEX**, INTEGRITY CONSTRAINT, **STORAGE**, Chapters 17 and 43

FORMAT

create_index::=

cluster_index_clause::=

table_index_clause::=

bitmap_join_index_clause::=

index_expr::=

index_properties::=

index_attributes::=

physical_attributes_clause::=

logging_clause::=

key_compression::=

domain_index_clause::=

global_partitioned_index::=

individual_hash_partitions::=

partitioning_storage_clause::=

hash_partitions_by_quantity::=

index_partitioning_clause::=

local_partitioned_index::=

on_range_partitioned_table::=

on_list_partitioned_table::=

segment_attributes_clause::=

on_hash_partitioned_table::=

on_comp_partitioned_table::=

index_subpartition_clause::=

parallel_clause::=

DESCRIPTION *index* is a name you assign to this index. It's usually a good idea to make it reflect the table and columns being indexed. *table* and *column(s)* are the table and column(s) for which the index is to be created. A unique index guarantees that each indexed row is unique on the values of the index columns. You can use the UNIQUE constraint on the columns to automatically create unique indexes. Specifying multiple columns will create a composite index. **ASC** and **DESC** mean ascending and descending. **CLUSTER** is the name of the cluster key that is indexed for a cluster. Clusters must have their keys indexed for their associated tables to be accessed. **PCTFREE** is the percentage of space to leave free in the index for new entries and updates. The minimum is zero.

TABLESPACE is the name of the tablespace to which this index is assigned. The physical attributes section contains subclauses that are described under **STORAGE**. **NOSORT** is an option whose primary value is in reducing the time to create an index if, and only if, the values in the column being indexed are already in ascending order. It doesn't harm anything if they later fall out of ascending order, but **NOSORT** works only if they are in order when the index is created. If the rows are not in order, **CREATE INDEX** will return an error message, will not damage anything, and will allow you to rerun it without the **NOSORT** option.

PARALLEL, along with **DEGREE** and **INSTANCES**, specifies the parallel characteristics of the index. **DEGREE** specifies the number of query servers to use to create the index; **INSTANCES** specifies how the index is to be split among instances of Real Application Clusters for parallel query processing. An integer *n* specifies that the index is to be split among the specified number of available instances.

In order to create an index, you must own the indexed table, have INDEX privilege on the table, or have the CREATE ANY INDEX system privilege. To create a function-based index, you must have the QUERY REWRITE privilege.

BITMAP creates a bitmap index, which can be useful for columns with few distinct values. The PARTITION clauses create indexes on partitioned tables. Bitmap join indexes store index key values for multiple tables in a single index (usually for data warehouse applications). Bitmap join indexes use the **FROM** and **WHERE** clauses to specify the tables involved and the join conditions.

REVERSE stores the bytes of the indexed value in reverse order. You cannot reverse a bitmap index.

COMPRESS saves storage space by compressing nonunique, nonpartitioned indexes. During data retrieval, the data will be displayed as if it were uncompressed. You can turn off index compression; re-create the index using the clause **NOCOMPRESS**.

COMPUTE STATISTICS analyzes the index data as the index is created.

As of Oracle Database 10g, you can create global hash-partitioned indexes.

CREATE INDEXTYPE

FORMAT

create_indextype::=

using_type_clause::=

array_DML_clause::=

DESCRIPTION **CREATE INDEXTYPE** specifies the routines used by a domain index. To create an indextype, you must have the CREATE INDEXTYPE system privilege. To create an indextype in another user's schema, you must have the CREATE ANY INDEXTYPE system privilege.

As of Oracle Database 10g, **CREATE INDEXTYPE** supports array inserts using the ODCIIndexInsert method.

CREATE JAVA

SEE ALSO **ALTER JAVA**, **DROP JAVA**, Chapters 37, 38, and 39

FORMAT
create_java::=

invoker_rights_clause::=

DESCRIPTION **CREATE JAVA** creates a Java source, class, or resource. You must have the CREATE PROCEDURE system privilege or (to create the object in another user's schema) the CREATE ANY PROCEDURE system privilege. To replace such a schema object in another user's schema, you must have the ALTER ANY PROCEDURE system privilege.

The **JAVA SOURCE**, **JAVA CLASS**, and **JAVA RESOURCE** clauses load sources, classes, and resources, respectively.

The **AUTHID** lets you specify whether the function executes with the privileges of the function owner or the current user.

EXAMPLE The following command creates a Java source:

```
create java source named "Hello" as
   public class Hello (
      public static String hello() (
         return "Hello World";   ) );
```

CREATE LIBRARY

SEE ALSO **CREATE FUNCTION**, **CREATE PACKAGE BODY**, **CREATE PROCEDURE**, Chapter 31
FORMAT

```
CREATE [OR REPLACE] LIBRARY [schema .] libname
{ IS | AS } 'filespec' [AGENT 'agent_dblink'];
```

DESCRIPTION **CREATE LIBRARY** creates a library object, allowing you to reference an operating-system shared library, from which SQL and PL/SQL can call external 3GL functions and procedures. To use the procedures and functions stored in the library, you must have been granted EXECUTE privilege on the library. Specify the **AGENT** clause if you want external procedures to be run from a database link other than the server. Oracle will use the database link specified by *agent_dblink* to run external procedures. If you omit this clause, the default agent on the server (extproc) will run external procedures.

CREATE MATERIALIZED VIEW

SEE ALSO **ALTER MATERIALIZED VIEW**, **CREATE MATERIALIZED VIEW LOG**, **DROP MATERIALIZED VIEW**, **STORAGE**, Chapter 24
FORMAT
create_materialized_view::=

physical_properties::=

materialized_view_props::=

scoped_table_ref_constraint::=

index_org_table_clause::=

key_compression::=

index_org_overflow-clause::=

create_mv_refresh:=

segment_attributes_clause::=

physical_attributes_clause::=

logging_clause::=

table_compression::=

column_properties::=

object_type_col_properties::=

substitutable_column_clause::=

nested_table_col_properties::=

varray_col_properties::=

LOB_storage_clause::=

LOB_parameters::=

LOB_partition_storage::=

parallel_clause::=

build_clause::=

DESCRIPTION The keyword **SNAPSHOT** is supported in place of **MATERIALIZED VIEW** for backward compatibility.

CREATE MATERIALIZED VIEW creates a materialized view, a table that holds the results of a query, usually on one or more tables, called master tables. The master tables may be in a local database or in a remote database. You can have the data refreshed at intervals by using the **REFRESH** clause.

To enable a materialized view for query rewrite, you must have the QUERY REWRITE system privilege. If the materialized view is based on objects in other schemas, you must have the GLOBAL QUERY REWRITE privilege.

Materialized views cannot contain LONG columns or reference any objects owned by SYS.

A **FAST** refresh uses the materialized view log associated with the master table(s) to refresh the materialized view. A **COMPLETE** refresh reexecutes the query. A **FORCE** refresh lets Oracle make the choice between a **FAST** or a **COMPLETE** refresh. Oracle first refreshes the materialized view on the **START WITH** *date*. If you give a **NEXT** *date*, Oracle refreshes the materialized view at intervals specified by the difference between the **START WITH** and **NEXT** dates.

A simple materialized view selects data from a single master table using a simple query. A complex materialized view selects data using a **GROUP BY**, **CONNECT BY**, subquery, join, or set operation in the query. Oracle can do a **FAST** refresh only on simple materialized views that have materialized view logs.

To create a materialized view in your schema, you must have the CREATE MATERIALIZED VIEW system privilege. To create a materialized view in another user's schema, you must have the CREATE ANY MATERIALIZED VIEW system privilege.

As of Oracle Database 10*g*, the refresh operations are enhanced. *See* Chapter 24 for details on refresh options.

EXAMPLE

```
create materialized view LOCAL_BOOKSHELF
storage (initial 100K next 100K pctincrease 0)
tablespace USERS
refresh force
start with SysDate next SysDate+7
with primary key
as
select * from BOOKSHELF@REMOTE_CONNECT;
```

CREATE MATERIALIZED VIEW LOG

SEE ALSO ALTER MATERIALIZED VIEW LOG, CREATE MATERIALIZED VIEW, DROP MATERIALIZED VIEW LOG, STORAGE, Chapter 24

FORMAT
create_materialized_vw_log::=

physical_attributes_clause::=

logging_clause::=

parallel_clause::=

new_values_clause::=

DESCRIPTION The keyword **SNAPSHOT** is supported in place of **MATERIALIZED VIEW** for backward compatibility.

CREATE MATERIALIZED VIEW LOG creates a table associated with the master table of a materialized view that tracks changes to the master table's data. Oracle uses the materialized view log to **FAST** refresh the materialized views of a master table. The storage options specify the storage of the table. Oracle logs database changes only if there is a simple materialized view based on the master table.

You can have only one log for a given master table, and the log is stored in the same schema as the master table. To create a materialized view log on your own master table, you must have the CREATE TABLE system privilege. If the master table is in another user's schema, you must have the CREATE ANY TABLE and COMMENT ANY TABLE system privileges as well as the SELECT privilege on the master table.

As of Oracle Database 10g, you can use the **SEQUENCE** clause to record a sequence value in the materialized view log.

CREATE OPERATOR

FORMAT
create_operator::=

binding_clause::=

implementation_clause::=

context_clause::=

using_function_clause::=

DESCRIPTION **CREATE OPERATOR** creates a new operator and defines its bindings. You can reference operators in indextypes and in SQL statements. The operators, in turn, reference functions, packages, types, and other user-defined objects.

To create an operator, you must have EXECUTE privilege on the functions and operators referenced by the operator, and the CREATE OPERATOR system privilege. If the operator is created in another user's schema, you must have the CREATE ANY OPERATOR system privilege.

As of Oracle Database 10*g*, you can pass column information to the functional implementation of the operator.

CREATE OUTLINE

SEE ALSO Chapter 43
FORMAT

```
CREATE [OR REPLACE] [ PUBLIC | PRIVATE ] OUTLINE [outline]
[FROM [ PUBLIC | PRIVATE ] source_outline]
[FOR CATEGORY category]
[ON statement];
```

DESCRIPTION **CREATE OUTLINE** creates a stored outline, which is a set of hints used to create the execution plan of the associated query. Later executions of the query will use the same set of hints. You can group stored outlines into categories.

To create an operator, you must have the CREATE ANY OUTLINE system privilege.

EXAMPLE

```
create outline TEST
    for category DEVELOPMENT
    on select AuthorName, COUNT(AuthorName) from BOOKSHELF_AUTHOR group by AuthorName;
```

CREATE PACKAGE

SEE ALSO **ALTER PACKAGE**, **CREATE FUNCTION**, **CREATE PACKAGE BODY**, **CREATE PROCEDURE**, CURSOR, **DROP PACKAGE**, EXCEPTION, RECORD, TABLE, VARIABLE DECLARATION, Chapter 31

FORMAT

```
CREATE [OR REPLACE] PACKAGE [schema .] package
[AUTHID { CURRENT_USER | DEFINER }]
{ IS | AS } pl/sql_package_spec;
```

DESCRIPTION **CREATE PACKAGE** sets up the specification for a PL/SQL package, a group of public procedures, functions, exceptions, variables, constants, and cursors. Adding **OR REPLACE** replaces the package specification if it already exists, which invalidates the package and initiates a recompilation of the package body and any objects that depend on the package specification.

Packaging your procedures and functions lets them share data through variables, constants, and cursors. It enables you to grant the whole collection at once as part of a role. Oracle accesses all the elements of a package more efficiently than it would if they were separate. If you change the package body, which Oracle stores separately from the package specification, you do not have to recompile anything that uses the package.

To create a package, you must have the CREATE PROCEDURE system privilege; to create a package in another user's account, you must have the CREATE ANY PROCEDURE system privilege.

The **AUTHID** clause lets you specify whether the package code executes with the privileges of the package owner or the user who runs the package's code.

CREATE PACKAGE BODY

SEE ALSO **ALTER PACKAGE**, **CREATE FUNCTION**, **CREATE LIBRARY**, **CREATE PACKAGE**, **CREATE PROCEDURE**, CURSOR, **DROP PACKAGE**, EXCEPTION, RECORD, TABLE, VARIABLE DECLARATION, Chapter 31

FORMAT

```
CREATE [OR REPLACE] PACKAGE BODY [schema .] package
{ IS | AS } pl/sql_package_body;
```

DESCRIPTION **CREATE PACKAGE BODY** builds the body of a previously specified package created with **CREATE PACKAGE**. Adding **OR REPLACE** replaces the package body if it already exists. You must have the CREATE PROCEDURE system privilege to create a package body; to create a package body in another user's account, you must have the CREATE ANY PROCEDURE system privilege.

CREATE PFILE

SEE ALSO **CREATE SPFILE**, init.ora

FORMAT

```
CREATE PFILE [= 'pfile_name'] FROM SPFILE [= 'spfile_name'];
```

DESCRIPTION **CREATE PFILE** exports a binary server parameter file into a text-initialization parameter file (init.ora). Creating a text parameter file is a convenient way to get a listing of the current parameter settings being used by the database, and it lets you edit the file easily in a text editor and then convert it back into a server parameter file using the **CREATE SPFILE** statement. You can specify the name of both the source binary server parameter file and the target text parameter file.

EXAMPLE

```
create pfile from spfile;
```

CREATE PROCEDURE

SEE ALSO **ALTER PROCEDURE**, BLOCK STRUCTURE, **CREATE LIBRARY**, **CREATE FUNCTION**, **CREATE PACKAGE**, DATATYPES, **DROP PROCEDURE**, Chapters 31 and 39

FORMAT

create_procedure::=

invoker_rights_clause::=

call_spec::=

Java_declaration::=

C_declaration::=

DESCRIPTION **CREATE PROCEDURE** creates the specification and body of a procedure. A procedure may have parameters, named arguments of a certain datatype. The PL/SQL block defines the behavior of the procedure as a series of declarations, PL/SQL program statements, and exceptions.

The **IN** qualifier means that you have to specify a value for the argument when you call the procedure. The **OUT** qualifier means that the procedure passes a value back to the caller through this argument. The **IN OUT** qualifier combines the meaning of both **IN** and **OUT**—you specify a value, and the procedure replaces it with a value. If you don't have any qualifier, the argument defaults to **IN**. The difference between a function and a procedure is that a function returns a value to the calling environment in addition to any arguments that are **OUT** arguments.

The PL/SQL block can refer to programs in an external C library or to a Java call specification. The *invoker_rights* (**AUTHID**) clause lets you specify whether the procedure executes with the privileges of the function owner or the privileges of the user who is calling the function.

CREATE PROFILE
SEE ALSO **ALTER PROFILE, ALTER RESOURCE COST, ALTER SYSTEM, ALTER USER, CREATE USER, DROP PROFILE**, Chapter 18
FORMAT
create_profile::=

resource_parameters::=

password_parameters::=

DESCRIPTION **CREATE PROFILE** creates a set of limits on the use of database resources. When you associate the profile with a user with **CREATE USER** or **ALTER USER**, you can control what the user does via those limits. To use **CREATE PROFILE**, you must enable resource limits through the initialization parameter RESOURCE_LIMIT or through the **ALTER SYSTEM** command.

SESSIONS_PER_USER limits the user to *integer* concurrent SQL sessions. CPU_PER_SESSION limits the CPU time in hundredths of seconds. CPU_PER_CALL limits the CPU time for a parse, execute, or fetch call in hundredths of seconds. CONNECT_TIME limits elapsed time of a session in minutes. IDLE_ TIME disconnects a user after this number of minutes; this does not apply while a query is running. LOGICAL_READS_PER_SESSION limits the number of blocks read per session; LOGICAL_READS_PER_ CALL does the same thing for parse, execute, or fetch calls. PRIVATE_SGA limits the amount of space you can allocate in the SGA as private; the **K** and **M** options apply only to this limit. COMPOSITE_LIMIT limits the total resource cost for a session in service units based on a weighted sum of CPU, connect time, logical reads, and private SGA resources.

UNLIMITED means there is no limit on a particular resource. DEFAULT picks up the limit from the DEFAULT profile, which you can change through the **ALTER PROFILE** command.

If a user exceeds a limit, Oracle aborts and rolls back the transaction, then ends the session. You must have the CREATE PROFILE system privilege to create a profile. You associate a profile to a user with the **ALTER USER** command.

CREATE ROLE

SEE ALSO **ALTER ROLE, ALTER USER, CREATE USER, DROP ROLE, GRANT, REVOKE,** ROLE, **SET ROLE,** Chapter 18

FORMAT

```
CREATE ROLE role
[ NOT IDENTIFIED
| IDENTIFIED { BY password |
  USING [schema .] package | EXTERNALLY | GLOBALLY }];
```

DESCRIPTION With **CREATE ROLE**, you can create a named role or set of privileges. When you grant the role to a user, you grant him or her all the privileges of that role. You first create the role with **CREATE ROLE**, then grant privileges to the role using the **GRANT** command. When a user wants to access something that the role allows, he or she enables the role with **SET ROLE**. Alternatively, the role can be set as the user's DEFAULT role via the **ALTER USER** or **CREATE USER** command.

If you put password protection on the role, the user who wants to use the privileges must supply the password in the **SET ROLE** command to enable the role. The **USING** *package* clause lets you create an application role, which is a role that can be enabled only by applications using an authorized package. If you do not specify *schema*, Oracle assumes the package is in your own schema.

CREATE ROLLBACK SEGMENT

SEE ALSO **ALTER ROLLBACK SEGMENT, CREATE DATABASE, CREATE TABLESPACE, DROP ROLLBACK SEGMENT, STORAGE**, Chapter 46

FORMAT

```
CREATE [PUBLIC] ROLLBACK SEGMENT rollback_segment
[{ TABLESPACE tablespace | storage_clause }
[ TABLESPACE tablespace | storage_clause ]...];
```

DESCRIPTION *rollback_segment* is a name assigned to this rollback segment. *tablespace* is the name of the tablespace to which this rollback segment is assigned. One tablespace may have multiple rollback segments.

 storage_clause contains subclauses that are described under **STORAGE**. If **PUBLIC** is used, this rollback segment can be used by any instance that requests it; otherwise it is available only to instances that named it in their initialization parameter files. *See* Chapter 46 for details concerning the use and management of rollback segments.

 As of Oracle9*i*, you can use system-managed undo to manage transactions. In system-managed undo environments, the database dynamically creates and drops rollback segments as needed. As of Oracle Database 10*g*, rollback segments exist only in the SYSTEM tablespace.

CREATE SCHEMA

SEE ALSO **CREATE TABLE, CREATE VIEW, GRANT**

FORMAT

```
CREATE SCHEMA AUTHORIZATION schema
{ create_table_statement | create_view_statement | grant_statement }
[ create_table_statement | create_view_statement | grant_statement ]...;
```

DESCRIPTION The **CREATE SCHEMA** command creates a collection of tables, views, and privilege grants as a single transaction. The schema name is the same as your Oracle username. The **CREATE TABLE, CREATE VIEW**, and **GRANT** commands are the standard commands, and the order in which the commands appear is not important, even if there are internal dependencies.

CREATE SEQUENCE

SEE ALSO **ALTER SEQUENCE, AUDIT, DROP SEQUENCE, GRANT, REVOKE, NEXTVAL** and **CURRVAL** under PSEUDO-COLUMNS, Chapter 17

FORMAT

```
CREATE SEQUENCE [schema .] sequence
[{ { INCREMENT BY | START WITH } integer
 | { MAXVALUE integer | NOMAXVALUE }
 | { MINVALUE integer | NOMINVALUE }
 | { CYCLE | NOCYCLE }
 | { CACHE integer | NOCACHE }
 | { ORDER | NOORDER }
 }
```

```
[ { INCREMENT BY | START WITH } integer
| { MAXVALUE integer | NOMAXVALUE }
| { MINVALUE integer | NOMINVALUE }
| { CYCLE | NOCYCLE }
| { CACHE integer | NOCACHE }
| { ORDER | NOORDER } ]... ];
```

DESCRIPTION *sequence* is the name given to the sequence. The default **INCREMENT BY** is 1.
A positive number will increment the sequence number in an interval equal to the integer. A negative
number will decrement (decrease the value of) the sequence in the same way. **START WITH** is the number
with which the sequence will begin. The default **START WITH** is **MAXVALUE** for descending sequences
and **MINVALUE** for ascending; use **START WITH** to override this default.

MINVALUE is the lowest number the sequence will generate. The default is 1 for ascending sequences.
MAXVALUE is the highest number the sequence will generate. For descending sequences, the default
is –1. To allow sequences to progress without limitation, specify only **MINVALUE** for ascending sequences
and **MAXVALUE** for descending sequences. To stop creating sequence numbers and force an error
when an attempt is made to get a new one, specify a **MAXVALUE** on an ascending sequence, or a
MINVALUE on a descending sequence, plus **NOCYCLE**. To restart either type of sequence where its
MAXVALUE or **MINVALUE** made it begin, specify **CYCLE**.

CACHE allows a preallocated set of sequence numbers to be kept in memory. The default is 20.
The value set must be less than **MAXVALUE** minus **MINVALUE**.

ORDER guarantees that sequence numbers will be assigned to instances requesting them in the
order the requests are received. This is required only in applications using Real Application Clusters.

To create a sequence in your own schema, you must have the CREATE SEQUENCE system privilege;
to create a sequence in another user's schema, you must have the CREATE ANY SEQUENCE system
privilege.

CREATE SPFILE
SEE ALSO **CREATE PFILE**, init.ora
FORMAT

```
CREATE SPFILE [= 'spfile_name'] FROM PFILE [= 'pfile_name'];
```

DESCRIPTION **CREATE SPFILE** creates a server parameter file from a client-side text-based
initialization parameter file. Server parameter files are binary files that exist only on the server and are
called from client locations to start up the database. Server parameter files let you make persistent
changes to individual parameters; parameter changes made via **ALTER SYSTEM** commands are retained
across database shutdowns and startups even if no external parameter file is manually updated.

CREATE SYNONYM
SEE ALSO **CREATE DATABASE LINK**, **CREATE TABLE**, **CREATE VIEW**, Chapters 17 and 23
FORMAT

```
CREATE [PUBLIC] SYNONYM [schema .] synonym
  FOR [schema .] object [@ dblink];
```

DESCRIPTION **CREATE SYNONYM** creates a synonym for a table, view, sequence, stored procedure,
function, package, materialized view, Java class object, or synonym, including those on a remote database.
PUBLIC makes the synonym available to all users, but the synonym can be created only by a DBA or
a user with the CREATE PUBLIC DATABASE LINK system privilege. Without **PUBLIC**, users must prefix

the synonym with their username. *synonym* is the synonym name. *schema.object* is the name of the table, view, or synonym to which the synonym refers. You can have a synonym of synonym. *@database_link* is a database link to a remote database. The synonym refers to a table in the remote database as specified by the database link.

EXAMPLE

```
create synonym LOCAL_BOOKSHELF for BOOKSHELF@REMOTE_CONNECT;
```

CREATE TABLE

SEE ALSO **ALTER TABLE**, **CREATE CLUSTER**, **CREATE INDEX**, **CREATE TABLESPACE**, **CREATE TYPE**, DATATYPES, **DROP TABLE**, INTEGRITY CONSTRAINT, OBJECT NAMES, **STORAGE**, Chapters 3, 17, 26, 33, 34, and 36

FORMAT

create_table::=

relational_table::=

object_table::=

XMLType_table::=

relational_properties::=

object_table_substitution::=

object_properties::=

oid_clause::=

oid_index_clause::=

physical_properties::=

segment_attributes_clause::=

physical_attributes_clause::=

table_compression::=

table_properties::=

column_properties::=

object_type_col_properties::=

substitutable_column_clause::=

nested_table_col_properties::=

varray_col_properties::=

LOB_storage_clause::=

LOB_parameters::=

logging_clause::=

LOB_partition_storage::=

XMLType_column_properties::=

XMLType_storage::=

XMLSchema_spec::=

row_movement_clause::=

index_org_table_clause::=

mapping_table_clauses::=

key_compression::=

index_org_overflow_clause::=

supplemental_logging_props::=

supplemental_log_grp_clause::=

supplemental_id_key_clause::=

external_table_clause::=

external_data_properties::=

table_partitioning_clauses::=

range_partitioning::=

hash_partitioning::=

list_partitioning::=

composite_partitioning::=

subpartition_by_hash::=

individual_hash_partitions::=

hash_partitions_by_quantity::=

subpartition_by_list::=

subpartition_template::=

range_values_clause::=

list_values_clause::=

table_partition_description::=

partition_level_subpartition::=

subpartition_spec::=

partitioning_storage_clause::=

parallel_clause::=

enable_disable_clause::=

using_index_clause::=

index_properties::=

index_attributes::=

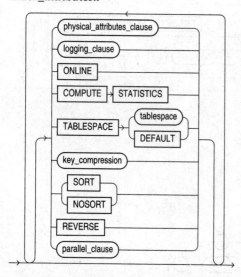

DESCRIPTION *user* is the table owner. If the table owner is absent, *user* defaults to the user issuing this command. *table* is the table name, and follows Oracle naming conventions.

column is the name of a column, and *datatype* is one of the Oracle-supplied datatypes (*see* DATATYPES) or a user-defined type (*see* **CREATE TYPE**). **DEFAULT** specifies a value to be assigned to the column if a row is inserted without a value for this column. The value can be a simple literal or the result of an expression. The expression, however, cannot include a reference to a column, to Level, or to RowNum.

For an existing abstract datatype, you can create an object table. The following example creates an object table called ANIMAL, based on the ANIMAL_TY datatype:

```
create table ANIMAL of ANIMAL_TY;
```

See Part V of this book for details on the usage of object tables.

See INTEGRITY CONSTRAINT for a full description of the column and table constraints.

CLUSTER includes this table in the named cluster. The table columns listed must correspond in order and datatype to the cluster's cluster columns. The names need not be the same as the corresponding cluster's columns, although matching names can help the user to understand what is being done.

INITRANS specifies the initial number of transactions that can update a data block concurrently (**select**s are not counted). **INITRANS** ranges from 1 to 255. 1 is the default. Every transaction takes space (23 bytes in most systems) in the data block itself until the transaction is completed. When more than the **INITRANS** number of transactions are created for the block, space is automatically allocated

for them. Transactions queuing up for execution will occupy more and more free space in the block, although usually there is more free space than is needed for all concurrent transactions.

Whenever Oracle inserts a row into a table, it first looks to see how much space is available in the current block (the size of a block is operating system dependent—see the *Oracle Installation and User's Guide* for your system). If the size of the row will leave less than **PCTFREE** percent in the block, Oracle puts the row in a newly allocated block instead. The default is 10; 0 is the minimum.

PCTUSED defaults to 40. This is the minimum percentage of available space in a block that will make it a candidate for insertion of new rows. Oracle tracks how much space in a block has been made available by deletions. If it falls below **PCTUSED**, Oracle makes the block available for insertions.

STORAGE contains subclauses that are described under **STORAGE**. **TABLESPACE** is the name of the tablespace to which this table is assigned.

The **ENABLE** and **DISABLE** clauses enable and disable constraints, respectively.

PARALLEL, along with **DEGREE** and **INSTANCES**, specifies the parallel characteristics of the table. **DEGREE** specifies the number of query servers to use; **INSTANCES** specifies how the table is to be split among instances of Real Application Clusters for parallel query processing. An integer *n* specifies that the table is to be split among the specified number of available instances.

The **PARTITION** clauses control how the table's data is partitioned—by range, by hash, or by a composite of multiple partition methods. *See* Chapter 17 for details on partitioning.

A temporary table contains data that is visible only to the session that creates it. If a temporary table is defined as **GLOBAL**, its definition may be seen by all users. Temporary tables may not be partitioned and cannot support many standard table features (such as varying array datatypes, LOB datatypes, and index organization). For example, the following command creates a table whose rows will be deleted at the end of the current session:

```
create global temporary table WORK_SCHEDULE (
    StartDate DATE,
    EndDate   DATE,
    PayRate   NUMBER)
    on commit preserve rows;
```

The **AS** clause creates the rows of the new table through the returned query rows. The columns and types of the query must match those defined in the **CREATE TABLE** statement. The query used in the **AS** clause may not contain any LONG datatype columns. You can turn off logging during the **create table ... as select** operation via the **NOLOGGING** keyword. This option disables the redo log entries that would normally be written during the population of the new table, thus improving performance while impacting your ability to recover that data if an instance failure occurs prior to the next backup.

The **LOB** clause specifies the out-of-line data storage used for internally stored LOB (BLOB, CLOB, and NCLOB) data. *See* Chapter 35 for details on LOB management.

The object table definition section applies to object tables, in which each row has an object ID (OID). *See* Chapter 36.

CREATE TABLESPACE

SEE ALSO **ALTER TABLESPACE**, **DROP TABLESPACE**, Chapters 20 and 46
FORMAT
create_tablespace::=

permanent_tablespace_clause::=

logging_clause::=

table_compression::=

extent_management_clause::=

size_clause::=

segment_management_clause::=

flashback_mode_clause::=

temporary_tablespace_clause::=

tablespace_group_clause::=

undo_tablespace_clause::=

tablespace_retention_clause::=

DESCRIPTION *tablespace* is the name of the tablespace, and follows Oracle naming conventions. The DATAFILE is a file or series of files described according to a *file_specification*, which defines the file names and sizes:

```
'file' [SIZE integer [K | M | G | T] [REUSE]
```

The file format is operating system specific. **SIZE** is the number of bytes set aside for this file, in kilobytes (**K**), megabytes (**M**), gigabytes (**G**), or terabytes (**T**). **DEFAULT STORAGE** defines the default storage for all objects created in this tablespace, unless those defaults are overridden in the **CREATE TABLE** command itself. **ONLINE**, the default, indicates that this tablespace will become available to users as soon as it is created. **OFFLINE** prevents access to the tablespace until **ALTER TABLESPACE** changes it to **ONLINE**. DBA_TABLESPACES gives the status of all the tablespaces.

SIZE and **REUSE** together tell Oracle to reuse the file if it already exists (anything it contains will be wiped out) or create it if it doesn't already exist. **SIZE** without **REUSE** creates a file that does not exist, but returns an error if it does. Without **SIZE**, the file must already exist.

The **MINIMUM EXTENT** size parameter specifies the minimum size for extents within the tablespace. The default is operating system specific and database block size specific.

When turned ON, the **AUTOEXTEND** option dynamically extends a datafile as needed in increments of **NEXT** size, to a maximum of **MAXSIZE** (or **UNLIMITED**). If a tablespace will be used only for temporary segments created during query processing, you can create it as a **TEMPORARY** tablespace. If the tablespace will contain permanent objects (such as tables), then you should use the default setting of **PERMANENT**.

EXTENT MANAGEMENT controls the manner in which the extent management data for a tablespace is recorded. By default, extent usage is **LOCAL**—the extent location information is stored in a bitmap within the tablespace's datafiles.

As of Oracle Database 10g, you can use the **BIGFILE** clause to create a bigfile tablespace. Also, you can assign a temporary tablespace to a temporary tablespace group (via the **TABLESPACE GROUP** clause). For undo tablespaces, you can guarantee that unexpired data will be preserved even at the expense of ongoing transactions requiring undo segment space (via **RETENTION GUARANTEE**).

CREATE TRIGGER
SEE ALSO **ALTER TABLE, ALTER TRIGGER**, BLOCK STRUCTURE, **DROP TRIGGER**, Chapters 30 and 33

FORMAT
create_trigger::=

DML_event_clause::=

referencing_clause::=

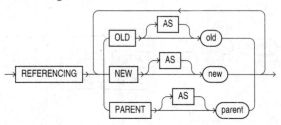

DESCRIPTION **CREATE TRIGGER** creates and enables a database trigger, a stored procedure block associated with a table, specified in the **ON** clause, that Oracle automatically executes when the specified SQL statement executes against the table. You can use triggers to enforce complex constraints and to propagate changes throughout the database instead of in your applications. That way, you implement the triggered code just once, instead of having to implement it in every application.

The main clause of the **CREATE TRIGGER** command specifies the SQL operation that triggers the block (such as **DELETE**, **INSERT**, or **UPDATE**) and when the trigger fires (**BEFORE**, **AFTER**, or **INSTEAD OF** executing the triggering operation). If you specify an **OF** clause on an **UPDATE** trigger, the trigger fires only when you update one or more of the specified columns. Note that you can also create triggers that fire when DDL events occur (including **CREATE**, **ALTER**, and **DROP**) and when specific database events occur (logons, logoffs, database startups, shutdowns, and server errors).

The **REFERENCING** clause specifies a correlation name for the table for the OLD and NEW versions of the table. This lets you use the name when referring to columns, to avoid confusion, particularly when the table name is OLD or NEW. The default names are OLD and NEW.

The **FOR EACH ROW** clause specifies the trigger to be a row trigger, a trigger fired once for each row affected by the triggering operation. The **WHEN** clause restricts the execution of the trigger to happen only when the *condition* is met. This condition is a SQL condition, not a PL/SQL condition.

You can disable and enable triggers through the **ALTER TRIGGER** and **ALTER TABLE** commands. If a trigger is disabled, Oracle does not fire the trigger when a potentially triggering operation occurs. The **CREATE TRIGGER** command automatically enables the trigger.

To create a trigger on a table you own, you must have the CREATE TRIGGER system privilege. To create a trigger on another user's table, you must have the CREATE ANY TRIGGER system privilege. The user must have been directly granted all privileges necessary to execute the stored procedure.

CREATE TYPE

SEE ALSO **CREATE TABLE**, **CREATE TYPE BODY**, Chapters 33 and 34
FORMAT
create_type::=

create_incomplete_type::=

create_object_type::=

invoker_rights_clause::=

sqlj_object_type::=

sqlj_object_type_attr::=

element_spec::=

inheritance_clauses::=

subprogram_spec::=

procedure_spec::=

function_spec::=

constructor_spec::=

map_order_function_spec::=

return_clause::=

sqlj_object_type_sig::=

pragma_clause::=

call_spec::=

Java_declaration::=

C_declaration::=

create_varray_type::=

create_nested_table_type::=

DESCRIPTION **CREATE TYPE** creates an abstract datatype, named varying array (**VARRAY**), nested table type, or an incomplete object type. To create or replace a type, you must have the CREATE TYPE privilege. To create a type in another user's schema, you must have the CREATE ANY TYPE system privilege.

When creating an abstract datatype, you can base it on Oracle's provided datatypes (such as DATE and NUMBER) and on previously defined abstract datatypes.

An "incomplete" type has a name but no attributes or methods. However, it can be referenced by other object types, and so can be used to define object types that refer to each other. If you have two types that refer to each other, you must create one as an incomplete type, then create the second, then re-create the first with its proper definition.

If you plan to create methods for the type, you need to declare the method names in the type specification.

EXAMPLES This example creates a type that will have associated methods:

```
create or replace type ANIMAL_TY as object
(Breed        VARCHAR2(25),
 Name         VARCHAR2(25),
 BirthDate    DATE,
member function AGE (BirthDate IN DATE) return NUMBER,
PRAGMA RESTRICT_REFERENCES(AGE, WNDS));
```

This example creates a varying array:

```
create or replace type TOOLS_VA as varray(5) of VARCHAR2(25);
```

This example creates a type with no methods:

```
create type ADDRESS_TY as object
(Street   VARCHAR2(50),
 City     VARCHAR2(25),
 State    CHAR(2),
 Zip      NUMBER);
```

This example creates a type that uses another type:

```
create type PERSON_TY as object
(Name      VARCHAR2(25),
 Address   ADDRESS_TY);
```

CREATE TYPE BODY

SEE ALSO **CREATE FUNCTION**, **CREATE PROCEDURE**, **CREATE TYPE**, Chapters 31, 33, 34, and 36

FORMAT

create_type_body::=

subprogram_declaration::=

procedure_declaration::=

function_declaration::=

constructor_declaration::=

map_order_func_declaration::=

call_spec::=

Java_declaration::=

C_declaration::=

DESCRIPTION **CREATE TYPE BODY** specifies the methods to be applied to types created via **CREATE TYPE**. You must have the CREATE TYPE privilege to create type bodies. To create a type body in another user's schema, you must have the CREATE ANY TYPE privilege.

EXAMPLE

```
create or replace type body ANIMAL_TY as
member function Age (BirthDate DATE) return NUMBER is
   begin
      RETURN ROUND(SysDate - BirthDate);
   end;
end;
```

CREATE USER

SEE ALSO **ALTER USER, CREATE PROFILE, CREATE ROLE, CREATE TABLESPACE, GRANT,**
Chapter 18

FORMAT
create_user::=

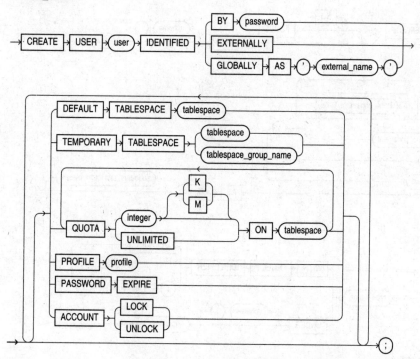

DESCRIPTION **CREATE USER** creates a user account that lets you log into the database with a certain set of privileges and storage settings. If you specify a password, you must supply that password to log on; if you specify the **EXTERNALLY** option, access is verified through operating system security. External verification uses the OS_AUTHENT_PREFIX initialization parameter to prefix the operating system user ID, so the username you specify in **CREATE USER** should contain that prefix (usually OPS$).

The **DEFAULT TABLESPACE** is the tablespace in which the user creates objects. The **TEMPORARY TABLESPACE** is the tablespace in which temporary objects are created for the user's operations.

You can put a **QUOTA** on either of these tablespaces that limits the amount of space, in bytes (kilobytes or megabytes for **K** or **M** options, respectively), that a user can allocate. The **PROFILE** clause assigns a named profile to the user to limit usage of database resources. Oracle assigns the DEFAULT profile to the user if you don't specify a profile.

When you first create a user, the user has no privileges. You must use the **GRANT** command to grant roles and privileges to the user. You should usually grant CREATE SESSION as a minimal privilege.

For information on password expirations and account locking, *see* **CREATE PROFILE** and Chapter 18.

As of Oracle Database 10g, you can assign a user a temporary tablespace group as the designated temporary tablespace, thereby effectively assigning multiple temporary tablespaces to the user.

CREATE VIEW
SEE ALSO **CREATE SYNONYM**, **CREATE TABLE**, **DROP VIEW**, **RENAME**, INTEGRITY CONSTRAINT, Chapters 17 and 33

FORMAT
create_view::=

object_view_clause::=

XMLType_view_clause::=

XMLSchema_spec::=

subquery_restriction_clause::=

DESCRIPTION **CREATE VIEW** defines a view named *view*. *user* is the name of the user for whom the view is created. The **OR REPLACE** option re-creates the view if it already exists. The **FORCE** option creates the view regardless of whether the tables to which the view refers exist or whether the user has privileges on them. The user still can't execute the view, but he or she can create it. The **NO FORCE** option creates the view only if the base tables exist and the user has privileges on them.

If an alias is specified, the view uses the alias as the name of the corresponding column in the query. If an alias is not specified, the view inherits the column name from the query; in this case each column in a query must have a unique name, one that follows normal Oracle naming conventions. It cannot be an expression. An alias in the query itself also can serve to rename the column.

AS *query* identifies the columns of tables and other views that are to appear in this view. Its **WHERE** clause will determine which rows are to be retrieved.

WITH CHECK OPTION restricts **INSERT**s and **UPDATE**s performed through the view to prevent them from creating rows that the view cannot itself select, based on the **WHERE** clause of the **CREATE VIEW** statement. **WITH CHECK OPTION** may be used in a view that is based on another view; however, if the underlying view also has a **WITH CHECK OPTION**, it is ignored.

constraint is a name given to the **CHECK OPTION**. *constraint* is an optional name assigned to this constraint. Without it, Oracle will assign a name in the form **SYS_C*n***, where *n* is an integer. An Oracle-assigned name will usually change during an import, while a user-assigned name will not change.

UPDATE and **DELETE** will work on rows in a view if the view is based on a single table and its query does not contain the **GROUP BY** clause, the **DISTINCT** clause, group functions, or references to the pseudo-column RowNum. You may **UPDATE** views containing other pseudo-columns or expressions, as long as they are not referenced in the **UPDATE**.

You may **insert** rows through a view if the view is based on a single table and if its query does not contain the **GROUP BY** clause, the **DISTINCT** clause, group functions, references to any pseudo-columns, or any expressions; rows may also be inserted through a view with more than one table by using INSTEAD OF triggers. If the view is created **WITH READ ONLY**, then only **SELECT**s are allowed against the view; no data manipulation is allowed.

You can create object views to superimpose abstract datatypes on existing relational tables. *See* Chapter 33.

To create a view, you must have the CREATE VIEW system privilege. To create a view in another user's schema, you must have the CREATE ANY VIEW system privilege.

CREATING A DATABASE

Creating a database is the process of making a database ready for initial use. It includes clearing the database files and loading initial database tables required by the RDBMS. This is accomplished via the SQL statement **CREATE DATABASE**.

CROSS JOIN

The **CROSS** keyword, used as part of the join syntax in a **FROM** clause of a query, lets you specify an inner or cross join. A cross join produces the cross-product of two relations and is essentially the same as the comma-delimited notation for tables in the **FROM** clause.

CTXCAT INDEX

A CTXCAT text index, available in Oracle Text, supports text queries executed with the **CATSEARCH** operator. *See* Chapter 25 for information on Oracle Text.

CUBE

SEE ALSO **GROUPING**, **ROLLUP**, Chapter 12

FORMAT

```
GROUP BY CUBE (column1, column2)
```

DESCRIPTION **CUBE** groups rows based on the values of all possible combinations of expressions for each row, and returns a single row of summary information for each group. You can use the **CUBE** operation to produce crosstab reports. *See* Chapter 12.

CUME_DIST

SEE ALSO AGGREGATE FUNCTIONS

FORMAT For aggregates:

```
CUME_DIST ( expr [, expr]... ) WITHIN GROUP
( ORDER BY
    expr [ DESC | ASC ] [ NULLS { FIRST | LAST }]
    [, expr [ DESC | ASC ] [ NULLS { FIRST | LAST }]]...)
```

For analytics:

```
CUME_DIST ( ) OVER ( [query_partition_clause] order_by_clause )
```

DESCRIPTION **CUME_DIST** calculates the cumulative distribution of a value in a group of values. The range of values returned by **CUME_DIST** is >0 to <=1. Tie values always evaluate to the same cumulative distribution value.

CURRENT_DATE

SEE ALSO DATE FUNCTIONS

FORMAT

```
CURRENT_DATE
```

DESCRIPTION **CURRENT_DATE** returns the current date in the session time zone, in a value in the Gregorian calendar of datatype DATE.

EXAMPLE

```
SELECT CURRENT_DATE FROM DUAL;
```

CURRENT_TIMESTAMP

SEE ALSO DATE FUNCTIONS

FORMAT

```
CURRENT_TIMESTAMP [ ( precision ) ]
```

DESCRIPTION **CURRENT_TIMESTAMP** returns the current date and time in the session time zone, in a value of datatype TIMESTAMP WITH TIME ZONE. The time zone displacement reflects the current local time of the SQL session. If you omit precision, the default is 6. The difference between this function and **LOCALTIMESTAMP** is that **CURRENT_TIMESTAMP** returns a TIMESTAMP WITH TIME ZONE value while **LOCALTIMESTAMP** returns a TIMESTAMP value. *precision* specifies the fractional second precision of the time value returned.

EXAMPLE

```
select CURRENT_TIMESTAMP from DUAL;
```

CURRVAL
See PSEUDO-COLUMNS.

CURSOR
Cursor is also a synonym for context area—a work area in memory where Oracle stores the current SQL statement. For a query, the area in memory also includes column headings and one row retrieved by the query.

CURSOR (PL/SQL)
SEE ALSO **CREATE PACKAGE**, **CREATE PACKAGE BODY**, Chapter 29
FORMAT

```
CURSOR cursor [(parameter datatype[,parameter datatype]...)]
   [IS query]
```

DESCRIPTION You can specify a cursor in a PL/SQL package and declare its body. The specification contains only the list of parameters with their corresponding datatypes, not the **IS** clause, while the body contains both. The parameters may appear anywhere in the query that a constant could appear. You can specify the cursor as a part of the public declarations of the package specification, and then the cursor body as part of the hidden package body.

CURSOR FOR LOOP
In FOR loops, the loop executes a specified number of times. In a cursor FOR loop, the results of a query are used to dynamically determine the number of times the loop is executed. In a cursor FOR loop, the opening, fetching, and closing of cursors is performed implicitly; you do not need to explicitly code these actions.

The following listing shows a cursor FOR loop that queries the RADIUS_VALS table and inserts records into the AREAS table:

```
declare
   pi      constant NUMBER(9,7) := 3.1415927;
   area    NUMBER(14,2);
   cursor rad_cursor is
      select * from RADIUS_VALS;
begin
   for rad_val in rad_cursor
     loop
       area := pi*power(rad_val.radius,2);
       insert into AREAS values (rad_val.radius, area);
     end loop;
end;
```

In a cursor FOR loop, there is no **OPEN** or **FETCH** command. The

```
for rad_val in rad_cursor
```

command implicitly opens the *rad_cursor* cursor and fetches a value into the *rad_val* variable. Note that the *rad_val* variable is not explicitly declared when you use a cursor FOR loop. When there are no more records in the cursor, the loop is exited and the cursor is closed. In a cursor FOR loop, there is no need for a **CLOSE** command. *See* Chapter 29 for further information on cursor management within PL/SQL.

CV

FORMAT

```
CV([dimension_column])
```

DESCRIPTION **CV** can be used only in the **MODEL** clause of a **SELECT** statement. It returns the current value of a dimension column carried from the left side to the right side of a rule to provide relative indexing with respect to the dimension column.

DATA CONTROL LANGUAGE (DCL) STATEMENTS

DCL statements are one category of SQL statements. DCL statements, such as **GRANT**, **GRANT SELECT**, **GRANT UPDATE**, and **REVOKE ALL**, control access to the data and to the database. The other categories are data definition language (DDL) and data manipulation language (DML) statements.

DATA DEFINITION LANGUAGE (DDL) STATEMENTS

DDL statements are one category of SQL statements. DDL statements define (create) or delete (drop) database objects. Examples are **CREATE VIEW**, **CREATE TABLE**, **CREATE INDEX**, **DROP TABLE**, **CREATE FUNCTION**, and **RENAME TABLE**. Executing any DDL command commits any pending changes to the database. The other categories of SQL statements are data control language (DCL) and data manipulation language (DML) statements.

DATA DEFINITION LOCKS

Data definition locks are locks placed on the data dictionary during changes to the structures (definitions) of database objects (such as tables, indexes, views, and clusters) so that those changes occur with no negative impact on the database data. There are three kinds of locks: dictionary operation locks, dictionary definition locks, and table definition locks.

DATA DICTIONARY

The data dictionary is a comprehensive set of tables and views owned by the DBA users SYS and SYSTEM. The data dictionary activates when Oracle is initially installed, and is a central source of information for the Oracle RDBMS itself and for all users of Oracle. The tables are automatically maintained by Oracle, and hold a set of views and tables containing information about database objects, users, privileges, events, and use. *See* Chapter 42.

DATA DICTIONARY VIEWS

SEE ALSO Chapter 42

DESCRIPTION The Oracle data dictionary views are described in Chapter 42.
 For details on the use of the DBA views in the data dictionary, see the *Oracle DBA Handbook*.

DATA INDEPENDENCE

Data independence is the property of well-defined tables that allows the physical and logical structure of a table to change without affecting applications that access the table.

DATA MANIPULATION LANGUAGE (DML) STATEMENTS

DML statements are one category of SQL statements. DML statements, such as **select**, **insert**, **delete**, and **update**, query and update the actual data. The other categories are data control language (DCL) and data definition language (DDL) statements.

DATABASE

Database has two definitions:

- A set of dictionary tables and user tables that are treated as a unit.
- One or more operating system files in which Oracle stores tables, views, and other objects; also, the set of database objects used by a given application.

DATABASE ADMINISTRATOR (DBA)

A DBA is an Oracle user authorized to **GRANT** and **REVOKE** other users' access to the system, modify Oracle options that affect all users, and perform other administrative functions. *See* Chapter 46.

DATABASE LINK

A database link is an object stored in the local database that identifies a remote database, a communication path to the remote database, and, optionally, a username and password for it. Once defined, the database link is used to perform queries on tables in the remote database. *See* Chapter 23.

DATABASE NAME

A database name is a unique identifier used to name a database. It is assigned in the **CREATE DATABASE** command or in the initialization parameter file.

DATABASE OBJECT

A database object is something created and stored in a database. Tables, views, synonyms, indexes, sequences, clusters, and columns are all types of database objects.

DATAFILE

A datafile is any file used to store data in a database. A database is made up of one or more tablespaces, which in turn are made up of one or more datafiles.

DATATYPES

SEE ALSO CHARACTER FUNCTIONS, CONVERSION FUNCTIONS, DATE FUNCTIONS, LIST FUNCTIONS, NUMBER FUNCTIONS, OTHER FUNCTIONS

DESCRIPTION When a table is created and the columns in it are defined, they must each have a datatype specified. Oracle's primary datatypes are VARCHAR2, CHAR, DATE, LONG, LONG RAW, NUMBER, RAW, and ROWID, but for compatibility with other SQL databases, its **CREATE TABLE** statements will accept several versions of these. The following table summarizes the built-in Oracle datatypes:

Datatype	Definition
VARCHAR2(*size*)	Variable-length character string having a maximum of *size* bytes (up to 4000).
NVARCHAR2(*size*)	Variable-length character string having a maximum of *size* bytes (up to 4000) or characters, depending on the choice of national character set.

Datatype	Definition
NUMBER(*precision, scale*)	For NUMBER column of specified *precision* with *scale* digits after the decimal point. *precision* can range from 1 to 38; *scale* can range from –84 to 127.
LONG	Character data of variable size up to 2GB in length.
DATE	Valid dates range from January 1, 4712 B.C. to December 31, 9999 A.D.
BINARY_FLOAT	32-bit floating-point number.
BINARY_DOUBLE	64-bit floating-point number.
TIMESTAMP (*precision*)	Date plus time, where *precision* is the number of digits in the fractional part of the Seconds field (values range from 0 to 9, default is 6).
TIMESTAMP (*precision*) WITH TIME ZONE	TIMESTAMP plus time zone displacement value. *precision* is the number of digits in the fractional part of the Seconds field (values range from 0 to 9, default is 6).
TIMESTAMP (*precision*) WITH LOCAL TIME ZONE	TIMESTAMP, normalized to local time zone.
INTERVAL YEAR (*precision*) TO MONTH	Period of time in years and months, where *precision* is the number of digits in the YEAR datetime field (values range from 0 to 9, default is 2).
INTERVAL DAY (*day_precision*) TO SECOND (*second_precision*)	Period of time in days, hours, minutes, and seconds, where *day_precision* is the number of digits in the DAY datetime field (values range from 0 to 9, default is 2) and *second_precision* is the number of digits in the fractional part of the Seconds field (values range from 0 to 9, default is 6).
RAW(*size*)	Raw binary data, *size* bytes long. Maximum size is 2000 bytes.
LONG RAW	Raw binary data; otherwise the same as LONG.
ROWID	Base 64 string representing the unique address of a row in its table.
UROWID (*size*)	Base 64 string for the logical address of a row in an index-organized table; maximum *size* is 4000 bytes.
CHAR(*size*)	Fixed-length character data, *size* characters long. Maximum size is 2000. Default is 1 byte. Padded on the right with blanks to full length of size.
NCHAR(*size*)	Multibyte character set version of CHAR.
CLOB	Character large object, up to 4GB in length.
NCLOB	Same as CLOB, but containing Unicode characters.
BLOB	Binary large object, up to 4GB in length.
BFILE	Pointer to a binary operating system file.

DATE

DATE is a standard Oracle datatype to store date and time data. Standard date format is 22-APR-04. A DATE column may contain a date and time between January 1, 4712 B.C. and December 31, 9999 A.D.

DATE FORMATS

SEE ALSO DATE FUNCTIONS, Chapter 10

DESCRIPTION Date format models are used in conversion functions. Date model components are listed in the following table:

/,-:.;	Punctuation to be incorporated in display for **TO_CHAR** or ignored in format for **TO_DATE**
A.D. or AD	AD indicator, with or without periods
A.M. or AM	Displays A.M. or P.M., depending upon time of day, with or without periods
B.C. or BC	Same as A.D. or AD
CC	Century: (e.g., 21 for 2004)
SCC	Century, with BC dates prefixed with -
D	Number of days in week: 1 to 7
DAY	Day fully spelled out, padded to 9 characters
DD	Number of days in month: 1 to 31
DDD	Number of days in year, since Jan 1: 1 to 366
DL	Date in local long format; in U.S. format, this is equivalent to fmDay, Month dd, yyyy
DS	Date in local short format; in U.S. format, this is equivalent to MM/DD/RRRR
DY	Three-letter abbreviation of day: FRI
E	Abbreviated era name (Japanese Imperial, ROC Official, and Thai Buddha calendars)
EE	Full era name version of E format
FF [1..9]	Fractional seconds; the number following FF specifies the number of digits in the fractional seconds portion displayed
FM	Suppresses leading and trailing blanks; without FM, all months and days are displayed at same width
FX	Format Exact: specifies exact format matching for the character argument and the date format model
HH	Hour of day: always 1 to 12
HH12	Same as HH
HH24	Hour of day, 24-hour clock: 0 to 23
I	One-digit year from ISO standard
IW	Weeks in year from ISO standard: 1 to 53
IY	Two-digit year from ISO standard
IYY	Three-digit year from ISO standard
IYYY	Four-digit year from ISO standard
J	Julian; days since December 31, 4712 B.C.
MI	Minutes of hour: 0 to 59
MM	Month of year (01 to 12)
MON	Three-letter abbreviation of month: e.g., AUG
MONTH	Month fully spelled out: e.g., AUGUST
P.M.	Same effect as A.M.
Q	Quarter of year: 1 to 4
RM	Roman numeral month

RR	Last two digits of year relative to current date
RRRR	Rounded year, accepting either two- or four-digit input
SS	Seconds of minute: 1 to 60
SSSSS	Seconds since midnight: always 0 to 86399
TS	Short time format, for use with DL or DS
TZD	Daylight savings time information
TZH	Time zone hour
TZM	Time zone minute
TZR	Time zone region
W	Number of weeks in month, where week 1 starts on the first day of the month
WW	Number of weeks in year, where week 1 starts on the first day of the year
X	Local radix character
YEAR or SYEAR	Year spelled out; S marks BC dates with a leading minus sign
YYYY or SYYYY	Full four-digit year; S marks BC dates with a leading minus sign
Y,YYY	Year, with comma
Y	Last one digit of year
YY	Last two digits of year
YYY	Last three digits of year

Date formats that work only with **TO_CHAR** but not **TO_DATE** include:

"string"	*string* is incorporated in display for **TO_CHAR**.
TH	Suffix to a number: ddTH or DDTH produces 24th or 24TH. Capitalization comes from the case of the number—dd or DD—not from the case of the TH. Works with any number in a date: YYYY, DD, MM, HH, MI, SS, and so on.
SP	Suffix to a number that forces number to be spelled out: DDSP, DdSP, or ddSP produces THREE, Three, or three. Capitalization comes from case of number—dd or DD—not from the case of SP. Works with any number in a date: YYYY, DD, MM, HH, MI, SS, and so on.
SPTH	Suffix combination of TH and SP that forces number to be both spelled out and given an ordinal suffix: Ddspth produces Third. Capitalization comes from case of number—dd or DD—not from the case of SP. Works with any number in a date: YYYY, DD, MM, HH, MI, SS, and so on.
THSP	Same as SPTH.

DATE FUNCTIONS

SEE ALSO DATE FORMATS, Chapter 10

DESCRIPTION This is an alphabetical list of all current date functions in Oracle version of SQL. Each of these is listed elsewhere in this reference under its own name, with its proper format and use.

- ■ **ADD_MONTHS**(*date,count*) Adds *count* months to *date*.
- ■ **CURRENT_DATE** Returns the current date in the session's time zone.
- ■ **CURRENT_TIMESTAMP** Returns the current timestamp with the active time zone information.

■ **DBTIMEZONE** Returns the current database timezone, in UTC format.

■ **EXTRACT**(*datetime*) Extracts a portion of a date from a date value, such as extracting the month value from a date column's values.

■ **FROM_TZ** Converts a timestamp value to a timestamp with timezone value.

■ **LAST_DAY**(*date*) Gives date of last day of month that *date* is in.

■ **LOCALTIMESTAMP** Returns the local timestamp in the active time zone, with no time zone information shown.

■ **MONTHS_BETWEEN**(*date2,date1*) Gives *date2–date1* in months (can be fractional months).

■ **NEW_TIME**(*date*, '*this*', '*other*') Gives the *date* (and time) in *this* time zone. *this* will be replaced by a three-letter abbreviation for the current time zone. *other* will be replaced by a three-letter abbreviation for the other time zone for which you'd like to know the time and date.

Time zones are as follows:

AST/ADT	Atlantic standard/daylight time
BST/BDT	Bering standard/daylight time
CST/CDT	Central standard/daylight time
EST/EDT	Eastern standard/daylight time
GMT	Greenwich mean time
HST/HDT	Alaska-Hawaii standard/daylight time
MST/MDT	Mountain standard/daylight time
NST	Newfoundland standard time
PST/PDT	Pacific standard/daylight time
YST/YDT	Yukon standard/daylight time

■ **NEXT_DAY**(*date*,'*day*') Gives date of next day after *date*, where '*day*' is 'Monday', 'Tuesday', and so on.

■ **NUMTODSINTERVAL**(*n*,'*value*') Converts a number or expression *n* to an INTERVAL DAY TO SECOND literal where *value* is the unit of *n*: 'DAY', 'HOUR', 'MINUTE', 'SECOND'.

■ **NUMTOYMINTERVAL**(*n*,'*value*') Converts a number or expression *n* to an INTERVAL YEAR TO MONTH literal where *value* is the unit of *n*: 'YEAR', 'MONTH'.

■ **ROUND**(*date*,'*format*') Without *format* specified, rounds a *date* to 12 A.M. (midnight, the beginning of that day) if time of *date* is before noon; otherwise, rounds up to next day. For use of *format* for rounding, *see* **ROUND**.

■ **SESSIONTIMEZONE** Returns the value of the current session's timezone.

■ **SYS_EXTRACT_UTC**(*datetime_with_timezone*) Extracts the Coordinated Universal Time (UTC) from a datetime field with time zone displacement.

■ **SYSDATE** Returns the current date and time.

■ **SYSTIMESTAMP** Returns the system date, including fractional seconds and time zone of the database.

■ **TO_CHAR**(*date*,'*format*') Reformats *date* according to *format*.

- **TO_DATE**(*string*,'*format*') Converts a *string* in a given '*format*' into an Oracle date. Will also accept a *number* instead of a *string*, with certain limits. '*format*' is restricted.
- **TO_DSINTERVAL**('*value*') Converts *value* of CHAR, VARCHAR2, NCHAR, or NVARCHAR2 datatype to an INTERVAL DAY TO SECOND type.
- **TO_TIMESTAMP**('*value*') Converts *value* of CHAR, VARCHAR2, NCHAR, or NVARCHAR2 datatype to a value of TIMESTAMP datatype.
- **TO_TIMESTAMP_TZ**('*value*') Converts *value* of CHAR, VARCHAR2, NCHAR, or NVARCHAR2 datatype to a value of TIMESTAMP WITH TIMEZONE datatype.
- **TO_YMINTERVAL**('*value*') Converts *value* of CHAR, VARCHAR2, NCHAR, or NVARCHAR2 datatype to a value of INTERVAL YEAR TO MONTH datatype.
- **TRUNC**(*date*,'*format*') Without *format* specified, sets a *date* to 12 A.M. (midnight, the beginning of that day). For use of *format* for truncating, *see* **TRUNC**.
- **TZ_OFFSET**('*value*') Returns the time zone offset corresponding to the value entered based on the date the statement is executed.

DBA
See DATABASE ADMINISTRATOR (DBA).

DBTIMEZONE
SEE ALSO DATE FUNCTIONS
FORMAT

```
DBTIMEZONE
```

DESCRIPTION **DBTIMEZONE** returns the value of the database time zone.
EXAMPLE

```
select DBTIMEZONE from DUAL;
```

DBWR PROCESS
One of the background processes used by Oracle. The **D**ata**b**ase **Wr**iter process writes new data to the database. Also referred to as DBWn.

DCL
See DATA CONTROL LANGUAGE (DCL) STATEMENTS.

DDL
See DATA DEFINITION LANGUAGE (DDL) STATEMENTS.

DDL LOCK
When a user executes a DDL command, Oracle locks the objects referred to in the command with DDL locks. A DDL lock locks objects in the data dictionary.

DEADLOCK
A deadlock is a rare situation in which two or more user processes of a database cannot complete their transactions, because each process is holding a resource that the other process requires (such as a row

in a table) in order to complete. Although these situations occur rarely, Oracle detects and resolves deadlocks by rolling back the work of one of the processes.

DECLARE

The **DECLARE** command allows you to declare cursors, variables, and exceptions for use within PL/SQL blocks. *See* Chapter 29.

DECLARE CURSOR (Form I—Embedded SQL)

SEE ALSO **CLOSE, DECLARE DATABASE, DECLARE STATEMENT, FETCH, OPEN, PREPARE, SELECT, SELECT** (Embedded SQL), *Programmer's Guide to the Oracle Precompilers*

FORMAT

```
EXEC SQL [AT {database | :host_variable}]
DECLARE cursor CURSOR
    FOR {SELECT command | statement}
```

DESCRIPTION The **DECLARE CURSOR** statement must appear before any SQL that references this cursor, and must be compiled in the same source as procedures that reference it. Its name must be unique to the source.

database is the name of a database already declared in a **DECLARE DATABASE** statement and used in a **CONNECT**; *host_variable* is a variable with such a name as its value. *cursor* is the name you assign to this cursor. **SELECT** *command* is a query with no **INTO** clause. Alternatively, a SQL statement or a PL/SQL block already declared in a SQL **DECLARE STATEMENT** statement can be used.

When the **FOR UPDATE OF** clause is included in the **SELECT** statement, an **UPDATE** can reference the cursor with **WHERE CURRENT OF cursor**, although the cursor must still be open, and a row must be present from a **FETCH**.

DECLARE CURSOR (Form 2—PL/SQL)

SEE ALSO **CLOSE, FETCH, OPEN, SELECT. . .INTO**, Chapter 29

FORMAT

```
DECLARE
CURSOR cursor (parameter datatype [,parameter datatype]...)
    IS select_statement
    [FOR UPDATE OF column [,column]...];
```

DESCRIPTION A cursor is a work area that Oracle uses to control the row currently being processed. **DECLARE CURSOR** names a cursor and declares that it **IS** (the result of) a certain *select_statement*. The *select_statement* is required, and may not contain an **INTO** clause. The cursor must be declared. It can then be **OPEN**ed, and rows can then be **FETCH**ed into it. Finally, it can be **CLOSE**d.

Variables cannot be used directly in the **WHERE** clause of the *select_statement* unless they've first been identified as parameters, in a list that precedes the select. Note that **DECLARE CURSOR** does not execute the **SELECT** statement, and the parameters have no values until they are assigned in an **OPEN** statement. Parameters have standard object names, and datatypes including VARCHAR2, CHAR, NUMBER, DATE, and BOOLEAN, all without size or scale, however.

FOR UPDATE OF is required if you wish to affect the current row in the cursor using either **UPDATE** or **DELETE** commands with the **CURRENT OF** clause.

DECLARE DATABASE (Embedded SQL)

SEE ALSO **COMMIT RELEASE** (Embedded SQL), **CONNECT** (Embedded SQL), *Programmer's Guide to the Oracle Precompilers*
FORMAT

```
EXEC SQL DECLARE database DATABASE
```

DESCRIPTION **DECLARE DATABASE** declares the name of a remote database for use in later **AT** clauses of SQL statements, including **COMMIT**, **DECLARE CURSOR**, **DELETE**, **INSERT**, **ROLLBACK**, **SELECT**, and **UPDATE**.

DECLARE STATEMENT (Embedded SQL)

SEE ALSO **CLOSE**, **FETCH**, **OPEN**, **PREPARE**, *Programmer's Guide to the Oracle Precompilers*
FORMAT

```
EXEC SQL [AT {database | :host_variable}]
DECLARE STATEMENT {statement | block_name} STATEMENT
```

DESCRIPTION *statement* is the name of the statement in a **DECLARE CURSOR** statement, and must be identical to the statement name here. *database* is the name of a database previously declared with **DECLARE DATABASE**; *host_variable* may contain such a name as its value. This command is only needed if **DECLARE CURSOR** will come before a **PREPARE** command. When it is used, it should come prior to **DECLARE**, **DESCRIBE**, **OPEN**, or **PREPARE**, and must be compiled in the same source as procedures that reference it.

DECLARE TABLE

SEE ALSO **CREATE TABLE**, *Programmer's Guide to the Oracle Precompilers*
FORMAT

```
EXEC SQL DECLARE table TABLE
(column datatype [NULL|NOT NULL],
    ...);
```

DESCRIPTION *table* is the name of the table being declared. *column* is a column name, and *datatype* is its datatype. This structure is nearly identical to that of **CREATE TABLE**, including the use of **NULL** and **NOT NULL**.

You use **DECLARE TABLE** to tell precompilers to ignore actual Oracle database table definitions when running with SQLCHECK=FULL. The precompilers will regard the table description here as relevant to the program and ignore the table definitions in the database. Use this when table definitions will change, or when a table has not yet been created. If SQLCHECK is not equal to FULL (which means tables and columns will not be checked against the database anyway), this command is ignored by the precompiler and becomes simply documentation.

EXAMPLE

```
EXEC SQL DECLARE COMFORT TABLE (
            City          VARCHAR2(13) NOT NULL,
            SampleDate    DATE NOT NULL,
            Noon          NUMBER(3,1),
            Midnight      NUMBER(3,1),
            Precipitation NUMBER
            );
```

DECODE

SEE ALSO OTHER FUNCTIONS, **CASE**, **TRANSLATE**, Chapter 16

FORMAT

```
DECODE(value,if1,then1[,if2,then2,]... ,else)
```

DESCRIPTION *value* represents any column in a table, regardless of datatype, or any result of a computation, such as one date minus another, a **SUBSTR** of a character column, one number times another, and so on. For each row, *value* is tested. If it equals *if1*, then the result of the **DECODE** is *then1*; if *value* equals *if2*, then the result of the **DECODE** is *then2*, and so on, for virtually as many if/then pairs as you can construct. If *value* equals none of the *if*s, then the result of the **DECODE** is *else*. Each of the *if*s, *then*s, and the *else* also can be a column or the result of a function or computation. Chapter 16 is devoted entirely to **DECODE**.

EXAMPLE

```
select DISTINCT City,
       DECODE(City, 'SAN FRANCISCO', 'CITY BY THE BAY', City)
  from COMFORT;

CITY            DECODE(CITY,'SA
-------------   ---------------
KEENE           KEENE
SAN FRANCISCO   CITY BY THE BAY
```

DECOMPOSE

SEE ALSO CONVERSION FUNCTIONS

FORMAT

```
DECOMPOSE ('string')
```

DESCRIPTION **DECOMPOSE** translates a string in any datatype to a Unicode string after canonical decomposition in the same character set as the input.

DEFAULT

Default is a clause or option value that is used if no alternative is specified. You can specify the default value for a column in a table via a DEFAULT column constraint.

DEFAULT VALUE

The default value is a value that is used unless a different one is specified or entered.

DEFINE (SQL*Plus)

SEE ALSO SET, EDIT

FORMAT

```
DEF[INE] [variable] | [variable = text]
```

DESCRIPTION *variable* is a user or predefined variable whose value you wish to assign or list. *text* is the new value for the variable; it must be a CHAR value and should be enclosed within single quotes if it contains punctuation or blanks. **DEFINE** without a variable will list all variables.

The following variables are predefined by Oracle for each session:

Variable	Description
_CONNECT_IDENTIFIER	Connection identifier used to make current connection
_DATE	Current date, or a user-defined fixed string
_EDITOR	Specifies the editor to be used via the **EDIT** command
_O_RELEASE	Full release number of the database
_O_VERSION	Current version of the database
_PRIVILEGE	Privilege level of the current connection (for example, AS SYSDBA)
_SQLPLUS_RELEASE	Full release number of the SQL*Plus version in use
_USER	Username for current connection

DEL (SQL*Plus)
SEE ALSO APPEND, CHANGE, EDIT, INPUT, LIST, Chapter 6
FORMAT

```
DEL [n | n m | n* | n LAST | * | *n | * LAST | LAST]
```

DESCRIPTION **DEL** deletes the current line of the current buffer. You can delete multiple lines with a single **DEL** command. **DEL** is not available in iSQL*Plus.
EXAMPLE

```
del
```

deletes the current line in the SQL*Plus buffer.

To delete a range of lines with one command, specify the line numbers of the beginning and ending of the range in the **DEL** command. The following command would delete lines 2 through 8 in the current buffer:

```
del 2 8
```

To delete from line 4 to the end, use the * character:

```
del 4*
```

DELETE (Form I—PL/SQL)
SEE ALSO DECLARE CURSOR, UPDATE, Chapter 29
DESCRIPTION In PL/SQL, **DELETE** follows the normal SQL command rules, with these added features:

- A PL/SQL function and/or variable can be used in the **WHERE** clause just as a literal could be.
- **DELETE...WHERE CURRENT OF cursor** can be used in conjunction with a **SELECT FOR UPDATE** to delete the last row **FETCH**ed. The **FETCH** can either be explicit or implicit from a FOR loop.
- Like **UPDATE** and **INSERT**, the **DELETE** command executes only within the SQL cursor. The SQL cursor's attributes can be checked for the success of the **DELETE**. SQL%ROWCOUNT will contain the number of rows deleted. If this is 0, none were **DELETE**d. (Also, SQL%FOUND will be FALSE if none were **DELETE**d.)

DELETE (Form 2—SQL Command)

SEE ALSO DROP TABLE, **FROM**, **INSERT**, **SELECT**, **UPDATE**, **WHERE**, Chapter 15
FORMAT
delete::=

DML_table_expression_clause::=

subquery_restriction_clause::=

table_collection_expression::=

where_clause::=

returning_clause::=

DESCRIPTION **DELETE** deletes from *table* all rows that satisfy *condition*. The *condition* may include a correlated query and use the alias for correlation. If the table is remote, a database link has to be defined. *@link* specifies the link. If *link* is entered, but *user* is not, the query seeks a table owned by the same user on the remote database.

When using the **DELETE** command, you may specify a partition or subpartition. To delete rows from a table, you must have DELETE privileges on the table. If the SQL92_SECURITY initialization parameter is set to TRUE, then you must also have SELECT privileges if the **DELETE** refers to columns in the table itself.

EXAMPLE This example deletes all rows for the city of Keene from the COMFORT table:

```
delete from COMFORT
 where City = 'KEENE';
```

DELETE (Form 3—Embedded SQL)
FORMAT

```
EXEC SQL [AT {db_name | :host_variable} ] [FOR :host_integer | integer]
 DELETE [FROM]
 [ (subquery)
 | [user.] {table / view } [@dblink |PARTITION (partition_name)] ]
[alias] [WHERE {condition | CURRENT OF cursor} ]
[{ RETURN | RETURNING } expr [, expr]... INTO
 :host_variable [[INDICATOR] :ind_variable]
 [, :host_variable [[INDICATOR] :ind_variable]]...]
```

DESCRIPTION This form of the **DELETE** command allows you to delete rows (from a table, view, or index-only table) from within a precompiler program.

DENSE_RANK
SEE ALSO AGGREGATE FUNCTIONS, Chapter 12
FORMAT

```
DENSE_RANK ( expr [, expr]... ) WITHIN GROUP
( ORDER BY
 expr [ DESC | ASC ] [NULLS { FIRST | LAST }]
 [, expr [ DESC | ASC ] [NULLS { FIRST | LAST }]]...)
```

For analytics:

```
DENSE_RANK ( ) OVER ( [query_partition_clause] order_by_clause )
```

DESCRIPTION **DENSE_RANK** computes the rank of a row in an ordered group of rows. *See* Chapter 12 for related examples.

DEPTH
FORMAT

```
DEPTH(integer)
```

DESCRIPTION **DEPTH** is an ancillary function used only with the **UNDER_PATH** and **EQUALS_PATH** conditions. It returns the number of levels in the path specified by the **UNDER_PATH** condition with the same correlation variable. The *integer* value can be any NUMBER integer.

DEREF

The **DEREF** operator returns the value of a referenced object. *See* Chapter 36.

DESCRIBE (Form 1—SQL*Plus)

SEE ALSO CREATE TABLE

FORMAT

```
DESC[RIBE] {[user.]object[@connect_identifier]}
```

DESCRIPTION **DESCRIBE** displays a specified object's definition. If *user* is omitted, SQL*Plus displays the table owned by you. The definition includes the table and its columns, with each column's name, **NULL** or **NOT NULL** status, datatype, and width or precision. **DESCRIBE** can also be used on views, synonyms, and function and procedure specifications.

EXAMPLE

```
describe COMFORT
```

```
Name                             Null?    Type
-------------------------------- -------- ------------
CITY                             NOT NULL VARCHAR2(13)
SAMPLEDATE                       NOT NULL DATE
NOON                                      NUMBER(3,1)
MIDNIGHT                                  NUMBER(3,1)
PRECIPITATION                             NUMBER
```

DESCRIBE (Form 2—Embedded SQL)

SEE ALSO PREPARE

FORMAT

```
EXEC SQL DESCRIBE [ BIND VARIABLES FOR
                  | SELECT LIST FOR]
        statement_name INTO descriptor
```

DESCRIPTION The **DESCRIBE** command initializes a descriptor to hold descriptions of host variables for a dynamic SQL statement or PL/SQL block. The **DESCRIBE** command follows the **PREPARE** command.

DICTIONARY CACHE

The dictionary cache stores data dictionary information in the SGA. Caching dictionary information improves performance because the dictionary information is used frequently. The dictionary cache is part of the Shared SQL Pool.

DICTIONARY LOCKS

A dictionary lock is a shared lock owned by users parsing DML statements, or an exclusive lock owned by users doing DDL commands, to prevent a table from being altered while the dictionaries are queried. There may be many such locks concurrently.

DIMENSION

A dimension is a named set of hierarchies among columns of tables. For example, in the geography dimension, countries are parts of continents, and states are parts of countries. When you define the dimension

relationships, Oracle can use that information when evaluating optimizer choices. If there are materialized views that contain aggregated data, the optimizer can use the dimension definitions to determine if the materialized view can be accessed instead of the base table. *See* **CREATE DIMENSION**.

DIRECTORY

A logical name that points to a physical directory, used by BFILE LOBs and external tables. *See* **CREATE DIRECTORY** and Chapter 26.

DISASSOCIATE STATISTICS

SEE ALSO ASSOCIATE STATISTICS

FORMAT

disassociate_statistics::=

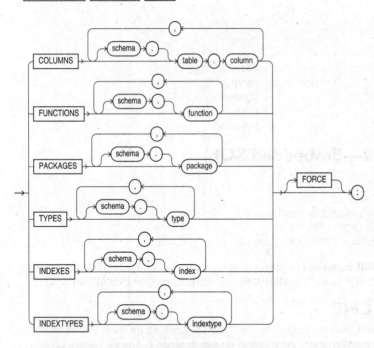

DESCRIPTION **ASSOCIATE STATISTICS** associates a set of statistics functions with one or more columns, stand-alone functions, packages, types, or indexes. **DISASSOCIATE STATISTICS** revokes the associations. You must have ALTER privilege on the base object.

DISCONNECT (SQL*Plus)

SEE ALSO CONNECT, EXIT, QUIT

FORMAT

DISC[ONNECT]

DESCRIPTION **DISCONNECT** commits pending changes to the database and logs you off of Oracle. Your SQL*Plus session remains active and the features of SQL*Plus continue to function, but without any connection to the database. You can edit buffers, use your own editor, spool and stop spooling, or connect to Oracle again, but until a connection is established, no SQL can be executed.

EXIT or **QUIT** will return you to your host's operating system. If you are still connected when you **EXIT** or **QUIT**, you will be automatically disconnected and logged off of Oracle.

DISTINCT

Distinct means unique. It is used as a part of **SELECT** statements and group functions. *See* AGGREGATE FUNCTIONS, **SELECT**.

DISTRIBUTED DATABASE

A distributed database is a collection of databases that can be operated and managed separately and also share information.

DISTRIBUTED PROCESSING

Distributed processing means to perform computation on multiple CPUs to achieve a single result.

DISTRIBUTED QUERY

A distributed query is one that selects data from multiple databases, usually across multiple nodes of a network.

DML

See DATA MANIPULATION LANGUAGE (DML) STATEMENTS.

DML LOCK

When a user executes a SQL statement, the data to which the statement refers is locked in one of several lock modes. The user can also lock data explicitly with a **LOCK** statement.

DROP CLUSTER

SEE ALSO CREATE CLUSTER, DROP TABLE, Chapter 17
FORMAT

```
DROP CLUSTER [schema .] cluster
[INCLUDING TABLES [CASCADE CONSTRAINTS]];
```

DESCRIPTION **DROP CLUSTER** deletes a cluster from the database. You must have DROP ANY CLUSTER privilege if the cluster is not in your own schema. You cannot drop a cluster that contains tables. The tables must be dropped first. The **INCLUDING TABLES** clause drops all the clustered tables automatically. The **CASCADE CONSTRAINTS** option drops all referential integrity constraints from tables outside the cluster that refer to keys in the clustered tables.

Individual tables cannot be removed from a cluster. To accomplish the same effect, copy the table under a new name (use **CREATE TABLE** with AS SELECT), drop the old one (this will remove it from the cluster), **RENAME** the copy to the name of the table you dropped, and then issue the appropriate **GRANT**s, and create the needed indexes.

DROP CONTEXT

SEE ALSO CREATE CONTEXT

FORMAT

```
DROP CONTEXT namespace;
```

DESCRIPTION **DROP CONTEXT** deletes a context namespace from the database. You must have the DROP ANY CONTEXT system privilege.

DROP DATABASE

SEE ALSO CREATE DATABASE, Chapter 46

FORMAT

```
DROP DATABASE ;
```

DESCRIPTION **DROP DATABASE** drops the current database (which must be mounted and closed) and deletes all control files and datafiles listed in the control file. Any related spfile is also deleted. Archived logs and backups are not removed. If the database is on raw disks, **DROP DATABASE** does not delete the actual raw disk special files.

DROP DATABASE LINK

SEE ALSO CREATE DATABASE LINK, Chapter 23

FORMAT

```
DROP [PUBLIC] DATABASE LINK link;
```

DESCRIPTION **DROP DATABASE LINK** drops a database link you own. For a public link, the optional **PUBLIC** keyword must be used, and you must be a DBA to use it. **PUBLIC** cannot be used when dropping a private link. *link* is the name of the link being dropped. You must have the DROP PUBLIC DATABASE LINK system privilege to drop a public database link. You may drop private database links in your account.

EXAMPLE The following will drop a database link named ADAH_AT_HOME:

```
drop database link ADAH_AT_HOME;
```

DROP DIMENSION

SEE ALSO CREATE DIMENSION, Chapter 24

FORMAT

```
DROP DIMENSION [schema .] dimension;
```

DESCRIPTION **DROP DIMENSION** drops a dimension that you own. You must have the DROP ANY DIMENSION system privilege.

EXAMPLE The following will drop the GEOGRAPHY dimension:

```
drop dimension GEOGRAPHY;
```

DROP DIRECTORY

SEE ALSO CREATE DIRECTORY, Chapters 22, 26, and 35

FORMAT

```
DROP DIRECTORY directory_name;
```

DESCRIPTION　**DROP DIRECTORY** drops an existing directory. You must have the DROP ANY DIRECTORY privilege to drop a directory.

NOTE
Do not drop a directory while its files are in use.

EXAMPLE　The following will drop a directory called REVIEWS:

```
drop directory REVIEWS;
```

DROP DISKGROUP

SEE ALSO　**ALTER DISKGROUP, CREATE DISKGROUP**, Chapter 46
FORMAT

```
DROP DISKGROUP diskgroup_name [ {INCLUDING | EXCLUDING} CONTENTS ];
```

DESCRIPTION　For databases using Automated Storage Management (ASM), **DROP DISKGROUP** drops an ASM disk group along with all the files in the disk group. ASM first ensures that no files in the disk group are open; if a file is open, the disk group is not dropped.

DROP FUNCTION

SEE ALSO　**ALTER FUNCTION, CREATE FUNCTION**, Chapter 31
FORMAT

```
DROP FUNCTION [schema.] function_name;
```

DESCRIPTION　**DROP FUNCTION** drops the specified function. Oracle invalidates any objects that depend on or call the function. You must have the DROP ANY PROCEDURE system privilege to drop a function that you do not own.

DROP INDEX

SEE ALSO　**ALTER INDEX, CREATE INDEX, CREATE TABLE**, Chapters 17 and 46
FORMAT

```
DROP INDEX [schema.] index [FORCE];
```

DESCRIPTION　**DROP INDEX** drops the specified index. You must either own the index or have the DROP ANY INDEX system privilege. **FORCE** applies only to domain indexes. This clause drops the domain index even if the indextype routine invocation returns an error or the index is marked **IN PROGRESS**.

DROP INDEXTYPE

SEE ALSO　**CREATE INDEXTYPE**
FORMAT

```
DROP INDEXTYPE [schema.] indextype [FORCE];
```

DESCRIPTION DROP INDEXTYPE drops the specified indextype and any association with statistics types. You must have the DROP ANY INDEXTYPE system privilege.

DROP JAVA
SEE ALSO **CREATE JAVA**, Chapter 37
FORMAT

```
DROP JAVA { SOURCE | CLASS | RESOURCE } [schema.] object_name;
```

DESCRIPTION DROP JAVA drops the specified Java class, source, or resource. You must have the DROP PROCEDURE system privilege. If the object is in another user's schema, you must have the DROP ANY PROCEDURE system privilege.

DROP LIBRARY
SEE ALSO **CREATE LIBRARY**, Chapter 31
FORMAT

```
DROP LIBRARY library_name;
```

DESCRIPTION DROP LIBRARY drops the specified library. You must have the DROP ANY LIBRARY system privilege.

DROP MATERIALIZED VIEW
SEE ALSO **ALTER MATERIALIZED VIEW**, **CREATE MATERIALIZED VIEW**, Chapter 24
FORMAT

```
DROP MATERIALIZED VIEW [schema.] materialized_view [PRESERVE TABLE];
```

DESCRIPTION DROP MATERIALIZED VIEW drops the indicated materialized view. You must either own the materialized view or have the DROP ANY SNAPSHOT or DROP ANY MATERIALIZED VIEW system privilege.

The keyword **SNAPSHOT** is supported in place of **MATERIALIZED VIEW** for backward compatibility.

PRESERVE TABLE lets you retain the materialized view container table and its contents after the materialized view object is dropped. The resulting table has the same name as the dropped materialized view. The metadata associated with the materialized view is dropped but the indexes, nested table columns, and storage tables for those columns are preserved along with their metadata.

If you drop a materialized view that was created on a prebuilt table, the database drops the materialized view and the prebuilt table reverts to its identity as a table.

DROP MATERIALIZED VIEW LOG
SEE ALSO **ALTER MATERIALIZED VIEW LOG**, **CREATE MATERIALIZED VIEW LOG**, Chapter 24
FORMAT

```
DROP MATERIALIZED VIEW LOG ON [schema.] table;
```

DESCRIPTION DROP MATERIALIZED VIEW LOG drops the indicated log table. To drop a materialized view log, you must have the privileges to drop a table. After dropping the log, any materialized views on the master table will get **COMPLETE** refreshes, not **FAST** refreshes.

The keyword **SNAPSHOT** is supported in place of **MATERIALIZED VIEW** for backward compatibility.

DROP OPERATOR

SEE ALSO ALTER OPERATOR
FORMAT

```
DROP OPERATOR [schema.] operator [FORCE];
```

DESCRIPTION **DROP OPERATOR** drops a user-defined operator. You must either own the operator or have the DROP ANY OPERATOR system privilege. Specify **FORCE** to drop the operator even if it is currently being referenced by one or more schema objects (indextypes, packages, functions, procedures, and so on), and mark those dependent objects **INVALID**.

DROP OUTLINE

SEE ALSO CREATE OUTLINE
FORMAT

```
DROP OUTLINE outline;
```

DESCRIPTION **DROP OUTLINE** drops a stored outline from the database. You must have the DROP ANY OUTLINE system privilege. Subsequent executions of SQL statements that used the outline will have their execution paths evaluated at run time.

DROP PACKAGE

SEE ALSO ALTER PACKAGE, **CREATE PACKAGE**, Chapter 31
FORMAT

```
DROP PACKAGE [BODY] [schema.] package;
```

DESCRIPTION **DROP PACKAGE** drops the specified package. Using the optional **BODY** clause drops only the body without dropping the package specification. Oracle invalidates any objects that depend on the package if you drop the package specification, but not if you just drop the body. You must either own the package or have the DROP ANY PROCEDURE system privilege.

DROP PROCEDURE

SEE ALSO ALTER PROCEDURE, **CREATE PROCEDURE**, Chapter 31
FORMAT

```
DROP PROCEDURE [schema.] procedure;
```

DESCRIPTION **DROP PROCEDURE** drops the specified procedure. Oracle invalidates any objects that depend on or call the procedure. You must either own the procedure or have the DROP ANY PROCEDURE system privilege.

DROP PROFILE

SEE ALSO ALTER PROFILE, **CREATE PROFILE**, Chapter 18
FORMAT

```
DROP PROFILE profile [CASCADE];
```

DESCRIPTION **DROP PROFILE** drops the specified profile. You must have the DROP PROFILE system privilege. **CASCADE** deassigns the profile from any users to whom it has been assigned; they

are automatically assigned the DEFAULT profile in its place. You must use **CASCADE** if the profile being dropped is currently assigned to users.

DROP ROLE

SEE ALSO ALTER ROLE, CREATE ROLE, Chapter 18
FORMAT

```
DROP ROLE role;
```

DESCRIPTION DROP ROLE drops the specified role. You must either have been granted the role WITH ADMIN OPTION or have the DROP ANY ROLE system privilege.

DROP ROLLBACK SEGMENT

SEE ALSO ALTER ROLLBACK SEGMENT, CREATE ROLLBACK SEGMENT, CREATE TABLESPACE, SHUTDOWN, STARTUP, Chapter 46
FORMAT

```
DROP ROLLBACK SEGMENT rollback_segment;
```

DESCRIPTION *rollback_segment* is the name of an existing rollback segment to be dropped. The segment must not be in use when this statement is executed. **PUBLIC** is required for dropping public rollback segments.

The Status column of the data dictionary view DBA_ROLLBACK_SEGS can reveal which rollback segments are in use. If the segment is in use, you can either wait until it no longer is in use, or **SHUTDOWN** the database using **IMMEDIATE**, and then bring it up in **EXCLUSIVE** mode using **STARTUP**. You must have the DROP ROLLBACK SEGMENT system privilege to drop a rollback segment.

DROP SEQUENCE

SEE ALSO ALTER SEQUENCE, CREATE SEQUENCE, Chapter 17
FORMAT

```
DROP SEQUENCE [schema.] sequence_name;
```

DESCRIPTION *sequence_name* is the name of the sequence being dropped. To drop a sequence, you must either own the sequence or have the DROP ANY SEQUENCE system privilege.

DROP SYNONYM

SEE ALSO CREATE SYNONYM, Chapter 23
FORMAT

```
DROP [PUBLIC] SYNONYM [schema.] synonym [FORCE];
```

DESCRIPTION DROP SYNONYM drops the specified synonym. To drop a public synonym, you must have the DROP ANY PUBLIC SYNONYM system privilege. To drop a private synonym, you must own the synonym or have the DROP ANY SYNONYM system privilege. You must specify **FORCE** if the synonym has dependent tables or user-defined types.

DROP TABLE

SEE ALSO ALTER TABLE, CREATE INDEX, CREATE TABLE, DROP CLUSTER, Chapter 17

FORMAT

```
DROP TABLE [schema.] table [CASCADE CONSTRAINTS] [PURGE] ;
```

DESCRIPTION **DROP TABLE** drops the specified table. To drop a table, you must either own the table or have the DROP ANY TABLE system privilege. Dropping a table also drops indexes and grants associated with it. Objects built on dropped tables are marked invalid and cease to work.

The **CASCADE CONSTRAINTS** option drops all referential integrity constraints referring to keys in the dropped table.

You can drop a cluster and all of its tables by using the **INCLUDING TABLES** clause on **DROP CLUSTER**.

As of Oracle Database 10*g*, using the **DROP TABLE** statement moves a table or object table to the recycle bin or removes the table and all its data from the database entirely. Unless you specify the **PURGE** clause, the **DROP TABLE** statement does not result in space being released back to the tablespace for use by other objects, and the space continues to count toward the user's space quota. Objects may be automatically purged from the recycle bin if the tablespace runs out of space for new objects.

DROP TABLESPACE

SEE ALSO **ALTER TABLESPACE**, **CREATE DATABASE**, **CREATE TABLESPACE**, Chapter 46
FORMAT

```
DROP TABLESPACE tablespace
[INCLUDING CONTENTS [AND DATAFILES] [CASCADE CONSTRAINTS]];
```

DESCRIPTION *tablespace* is the name of the tablespace being dropped. The **INCLUDING CONTENTS** option allows you to drop a tablespace that contains data. Without **INCLUDING CONTENTS**, only an empty tablespace can be dropped. Tablespaces should be offline (*see* **ALTER TABLESPACE**) before dropping, or the drop operation will be prevented if any users are accessing data, index, rollback, or temporary segments in the tablespace. You must have the DROP TABLESPACE system privilege to use this command.

DROP TRIGGER

SEE ALSO **ALTER TRIGGER**, **CREATE TRIGGER**, Chapters 30 and 33
FORMAT

```
DROP TRIGGER [schema.] trigger;
```

DESCRIPTION **DROP TRIGGER** drops the specified trigger. You must either own the trigger or have the DROP ANY TRIGGER system privilege.

DROP TYPE

SEE ALSO **CREATE TYPE**, Chapter 33
FORMAT

```
DROP TYPE [schema.] type_name [ FORCE | VALIDATE ];
```

DESCRIPTION **DROP TYPE** drops the specification and body of an abstract datatype. You must either own the type or have the DROP ANY TYPE system privilege. Unless you use **FORCE**, you cannot drop a type if a table or other object references it.

DROP TYPE BODY

SEE ALSO CREATE TYPE, CREATE TYPE BODY, DROP TYPE, Chapter 33

FORMAT

```
DROP TYPE BODY [schema.] type_name;
```

DESCRIPTION **DROP TYPE BODY** drops the body of the specified type. You must either own the type or have the DROP ANY TYPE system privilege.

DROP USER

SEE ALSO ALTER USER, CREATE USER, Chapter 18

FORMAT

```
DROP USER user [CASCADE];
```

DESCRIPTION **DROP USER** drops the specified user. You must have the DROP USER system privilege. The **CASCADE** option drops all the objects in the user's schema before dropping the user, and you *must* specify **CASCADE** if the user has any objects in the schema.

DROP VIEW

SEE ALSO CREATE SYNONYM, CREATE TABLE, CREATE VIEW, Chapter 17

FORMAT

```
DROP VIEW [schema.] view [CASCADE CONSTRAINTS];
```

DESCRIPTION **DROP VIEW** drops the specified view. To drop a view, either the view must be in your schema or you must have the DROP ANY VIEW system privilege.

DROPJAVA

DROPJAVA is a utility for removing Java classes from the database. *See* LOADJAVA.

DUAL

SEE ALSO FROM, SELECT, Chapter 10

DESCRIPTION DUAL is a table with only one row and one column in it. Since Oracle's many functions work on both columns and literals, it is possible to demonstrate some of its functionality by using just literals or pseudo-columns. When doing this, the **SELECT** statement doesn't care which columns are in the table, and a single row is more than sufficient to demonstrate a point.

EXAMPLE The following shows the current User and SysDate:

```
select User, SysDate from DUAL;
```

DUMP

SEE ALSO RAWTOHEX

FORMAT

```
DUMP( string [,format [,start [,length] ] ] )
```

DESCRIPTION DUMP displays the value of *string* in internal data format, in ASCII, octal, decimal, hex, or character format. *format* defaults to ASCII or EBCDIC, depending upon your machine; 8 produces

octal, 10 decimal, 16 hex, and 17 character (the same as ASCII or EBCDIC). *start* is the beginning position in the string, and *length* is the number of characters to display. *string* can be a literal or an expression.

EXAMPLE The following shows how characters 1 through 8 are represented in hex for just the City in the first row of the COMFORT table:

```
select City, DUMP(City,16,1,8) from COMFORT where rownum < 2;

CITY           DUMP(CITY,16,1,8)
------------- --------------------------------------
SAN FRANCISCO Typ=1 Len= 13: 53,41,4e,20,46,52,41,4e
```

ECHO (SQL*Plus)

See **SET**.

EDIT (SQL*Plus)

SEE ALSO **DEFINE**, **SET**, Chapter 6

FORMAT

```
ED[IT] [file[.ext]]
```

DESCRIPTION **EDIT** calls an external standard text editor and passes to it the name of the file. If *.ext* is omitted, the extension .sql is appended. If *file* and *.ext* are both omitted, the editor is called and passed the name of a file (constructed by SQL*Plus) that contains the contents of the current buffer. The local user variable _EDITOR determines which text editor is used by **EDIT**. _EDITOR can be changed with **DEFINE**, and this is usually best done in the login.sql file, which is read whenever SQL*Plus is invoked.

EDIT will fail if the current buffer is empty and **EDIT** is called without a filename. You can use the **SET EDITFILE** command to set the default name of the file created by the **EDIT** command.

EMBEDDED (SQL*Plus)

See **SET**.

EMPTY_BLOB

SEE ALSO Chapter 35

FORMAT

```
EMPTY_BLOB()
```

DESCRIPTION **EMPTY_BLOB** returns an empty LOB locator that can be used to initialize a LOB variable or, in an **INSERT** or **UPDATE** statement, to initialize a LOB column or attribute to EMPTY. EMPTY means that the LOB is initialized, but not populated with data.

EXAMPLE

```
UPDATE BOOK_TEXT set BlobCol = EMPTY_BLOB();
```

EMPTY_CLOB

SEE ALSO Chapter 35

FORMAT

```
EMPTY_CLOB()
```

DESCRIPTION EMPTY_CLOB returns an empty LOB locator that can be used to initialize a LOB variable or, in an **INSERT** or **UPDATE** statement, to initialize a LOB column or attribute to EMPTY. EMPTY means that the LOB is initialized, but not populated with data.

EXAMPLE

```
UPDATE BOOK_TEXT set ClobCol = EMPTY_CLOB();
```

END

SEE ALSO **BEGIN**, BLOCK STRUCTURE, Chapter 29

FORMAT

```
END [block label] ;
```

DESCRIPTION **END** is unrelated to the **END IF** and **END LOOP** statements. *See* **IF** and LOOP for details on either of them.

END is the closing statement of a PL/SQL block's executable section (and the entire block). If the block is named at the **BEGIN**, the name must also follow the word **END**. At least one executable statement is required between **BEGIN** and **END**. *See* BLOCK STRUCTURE and Chapters 29 and 31 for more details.

ENQUEUE

Enqueue is the lock on a given resource. Those waiting for a given resource have not yet gotten the enqueue. Enqueues exist for many database resources.

ENTITY

An entity is a person, place, or thing represented by a table. In a table, each row represents an occurrence of that entity.

ENTITY-RELATIONSHIP MODEL

An entity-relationship model is a framework used to model systems for a database. It divides all elements of a system into two categories: entities or relationships.

EQUI-JOIN

An equi-join is a join in which the join comparison operator is an equality, such as

```
where BOOKSHELF.Title = BOOKSHELF_CHECKOUT.Title
```

ESCAPE (SQL*Plus)

See **SET**.

EXCEPTION

SEE ALSO BLOCK STRUCTURE, **DECLARE EXCEPTION**, **RAISE**, Chapter 29

FORMAT

```
EXCEPTION
    {WHEN {OTHERS | exception [OR exception]...}
        THEN statement; [statement;]...}
  [ WHEN {OTHER | exception [OR exception]...}
        THEN statement; [statement;]...]...
```

DESCRIPTION The EXCEPTION section of a PL/SQL block is where program control is transferred whenever an exception flag is raised. Exception flags are either user-defined or system exceptions raised automatically by PL/SQL. *See* **RAISE** for details on user-defined exception flags. The system exception flags are all, in effect, BOOLEAN variables that are either TRUE or FALSE. The **WHEN** clause is used to test these. For example, the NOT_LOGGED_ON flag is raised if you attempt to issue a command to Oracle without being logged on. You do not need to have **DECLARE**d an exception, or **RAISE**d this flag yourself. PL/SQL will do it for you.

When any exception flag is raised, the program immediately halts whatever it was doing and jumps to the EXCEPTION section of the current block. This section, however, doesn't know automatically which exception flag was raised, nor what to do. Therefore, you must code the EXCEPTION section first to check all of the exception flags that are likely to have occurred, and then give action instructions for each. This is what the **WHEN...THEN** logic does. You can use **WHEN** OTHERS as a catch-all to handle unanticipated errors for which you have not declared exceptions.

EXAMPLE Here, one exception flag is tested in the EXCEPTION section. The ZERO_DIVIDE flag is raised when any calculation attempts to divide by zero.

```
declare
  pi      constant NUMBER(9,7) := 3.1415927;
  radius INTEGER(5);
  area    NUMBER(14,2);
  some_variable   NUMBER(14,2);
begin
  radius := 3;
  loop
    some_variable := 1/(radius-4);
    area := pi*power(radius,2);
      insert into AREAS values (radius, area);
    radius := radius+1;
    exit when area > 100;
  end loop;
exception
  when ZERO_DIVIDE
    then insert into AREAS values (0,0);
end;
```

The system-raised exception flags are as follows:

ACCESS_INTO_NULL	Your program attempts to assign values to the attributes of an uninitialized (atomically null) object.
CASE_NOT_FOUND	None of the choices in the **WHEN** clauses of a **CASE** statement is selected, and there is no **ELSE** clause.
COLLECTION_IS_NULL	Your program attempts to apply collection methods other than **EXISTS** to an uninitialized (atomically null) nested table or varying array, or the program attempts to assign values to the elements of an uninitialized nested table or varying array.
CURSOR_ALREADY_OPEN	Your program attempts to open an already open cursor. A cursor must be closed before it can be reopened. A CURSOR FOR LOOP automatically opens the cursor to which it refers. So, your program cannot open that cursor inside the loop.

DUP_VAL_ON_INDEX	Your program attempts to store duplicate values in a database column that is constrained by a unique index.
INVALID_CURSOR	Your program attempts an illegal cursor operation such as closing an unopened cursor.
INVALID_NUMBER	In a SQL statement, the conversion of a character string into a number fails because the string does not represent a valid number. (In procedural statements, VALUE_ERROR is raised.) This exception is also raised when the **LIMIT**-clause expression in a bulk **FETCH** statement does not evaluate to a positive number.
LOGIN_DENIED	Your program attempts to log on to Oracle with an invalid username and/or password.
NO_DATA_FOUND	A **SELECT INTO** statement returns no rows, or your program references a deleted element in a nested table or an uninitialized element in an index-by table. SQL aggregate functions such as **AVG** and **SUM** always return a value or a null. So, a **SELECT INTO** statement that calls an aggregate function never raises NO_DATA_FOUND. The **FETCH** statement is expected to return no rows eventually, so when that happens, no exception is raised.
NOT_LOGGED_ON	Your program issues a database call without being connected to Oracle.
PROGRAM_ERROR	PL/SQL has an internal problem.
ROWTYPE_MISMATCH	The host cursor variable and PL/SQL cursor variable involved in an assignment have incompatible return types. For example, when an open host cursor variable is passed to a stored subprogram, the return types of the actual and formal parameters must be compatible.
SELF_IS_NULL	Your program attempts to call a MEMBER method on a null instance. That is, the built-in parameter SELF (which is always the first parameter passed to a MEMBER method) is null.
STORAGE_ERROR	PL/SQL runs out of memory or memory has been corrupted.
SUBSCRIPT_BEYOND_COUNT	Your program references a nested table or varying array element using an index number larger than the number of elements in the collection.
SUBSCRIPT_OUTSIDE_LIMIT	Your program references a nested table or varying array element using an index number (–1 for example) that is outside the legal range.
SYS_INVALID_ROWID	The conversion of a character string into a universal ROWID fails because the character string does not represent a valid ROWID.
TIMEOUT_ON_RESOURCE	A time-out occurs while Oracle is waiting for a resource.
TOO_MANY_ROWS	A **SELECT INTO** statement returns more than one row.
VALUE_ERROR	An arithmetic, conversion, truncation, or size-constraint error occurs. For example, when your program selects a column value into a character variable, if the value is longer than the declared length of the variable, PL/SQL aborts the assignment and raises VALUE_ERROR. In procedural statements, VALUE_ERROR is raised if the conversion of a character string into a number fails. (In SQL statements, INVALID_NUMBER is raised.)
ZERO_DIVIDE	Your program attempts to divide a number by zero.

The associated Oracle error numbers and SQLCode values are as follows:

Exception	Oracle Error #	SQLCode
ACCESS_INTO_NULL	ORA-06530	-6530
CASE_NOT_FOUND	ORA-06592	-6592
COLLECTION_IS_NULL	ORA-06531	-6531
CURSOR_ALREADY_OPEN	ORA-06511	-6511
DUP_VAL_ON_INDEX	ORA-00001	-1
INVALID_CURSOR	ORA-01001	-1001
INVALID_NUMBER	ORA-01722	-1722
LOGIN_DENIED	ORA-01017	-1017
NO_DATA_FOUND	ORA-01403	+100
NOT_LOGGED_ON	ORA-01012	-1012
PROGRAM_ERROR	ORA-06501	-6501
ROWTYPE_MISMATCH	ORA-06504	-6504
SELF_IS_NULL	ORA-30625	-30625
STORAGE_ERROR	ORA-06500	-6500
SUBSCRIPT_BEYOND_COUNT	ORA-06533	-6533
SUBSCRIPT_OUTSIDE_LIMIT	ORA-06532	-6532
SYS_INVALID_ROWID	ORA-01410	-1410
TIMEOUT_ON_RESOURCE	ORA-00051	-51
TOO_MANY_ROWS	ORA-01422	-1422
VALUE_ERROR	ORA-06502	-6502
ZERO_DIVIDE	ORA-01476	-1476

OTHERS is the catch-all for any exception flags you did not check for in your EXCEPTION section. It must always be the last **WHEN** statement, and must stand alone. It cannot be included with any other exceptions.

Exception handling, particularly as it relates to exceptions you declare, should really be reserved for errors that are fatal—that means normal processing should stop.

If an exception flag is raised that is not tested for in the current block, the program will branch to the EXCEPTION block in the enclosing block, and so on, until either the exception raised is found or control falls through to the host program.

EXCEPTION sections can reference variables in the same manner that the execution block can. That is, they can reference local variables directly, or variables from other blocks by prefixing them with the other block's name.

Use caution in testing for certain kinds of exceptions. For instance, if the EXCEPTION section takes the error message and inserts it into a database table, a NOT_LOGGED_ON exception would put the EXCEPTION section into an infinite loop. Design the statements that follow **THEN** not to duplicate the error that got the program there in the first place. You also may use **RAISE** without an exception name.

This will automatically pass control to the next outer EXCEPTION block, or the main program. *See* **RAISE** for further details.

EXCEPTION_INIT

SEE ALSO **DECLARE CURSOR**, EXCEPTION, **SQLCODE**, *Programmer's Guide to the Oracle Precompilers*

FORMAT

```
PRAGMA EXCEPTION_INIT(exception,integer);
```

DESCRIPTION The standard system exceptions, such as ZERO_DIVIDE, which are referenced by name, are actually no more than the association of a name with the internal Oracle error number. There are hundreds of these error numbers, and only the most common have been given names. Any that are not named will still raise an exception flag and transfer control to the EXCEPTION block, but they will all be caught by OTHERS, rather than by name.

You can change this by assigning your own names to other Oracle error numbers. **EXCEPTION_INIT** allows you to do this. *exception* is the one-word name you assign to the integer error number (*see* Oracle's *Error Messages and Codes Manual* for a complete list). *integer* should be negative if the error code is negative (true for fatal errors), and *exception* must follow normal object naming rules.

Note that the format of this command requires the word **PRAGMA** before **EXCEPTION_INIT**. A pragma is an instruction to the PL/SQL compiler, rather than executable code. The pragma must be in the DECLARE section of a PL/SQL block, and must be preceded by an exception declaration.

EXAMPLE

```
DECLARE
      some_bad_error           exception;
      pragma                   exception_init(some_bad_error, -660);
BEGIN
   ...
   EXCEPTION
      when some_bad_error
            then ...
END;
```

EXCLUSIVE LOCK

An exclusive lock is one that permits other users to query data, but not change it. It differs from a SHARE lock because it does not permit another user to place any type of lock on the same data; several users may place SHARE locks on the same data at the same time.

EXECUTE

SEE ALSO CALL, CREATE FUNCTION, CREATE PACKAGE, CREATE PACKAGE BODY, CREATE PROCEDURE, GRANT, Chapter 31

FORMAT

```
EXECUTE procedural_object_name [arguments];
```

DESCRIPTION **EXECUTE** executes a procedure, package, or function. To execute a procedure within a package, specify both the package name and the procedure name in the **EXECUTE** command, as shown

in the following example. This example executes a procedure named NEW_BOOK, in a package named BOOKSHELF_PACKAGE; the value 'TALE OF TWO CITIES' is passed as input to the procedure.

```
execute BOOKSHELF_PACKAGE.NEW_BOOK('TALE OF TWO CITIES');
```

To execute a procedural object, you must have been granted the EXECUTE privilege on that object. *See* **GRANT**.

EXECUTE (Dynamic Embedded SQL)

SEE ALSO **EXECUTE IMMEDIATE**, **PREPARE**, *Programmer's Guide to the Oracle Precompilers*
FORMAT

```
EXEC SQL [FOR { integer | :array_size }]
 EXECUTE statement_id
 [USING
 { DESCRIPTOR SQLDA_descriptor
 | :host_variable [[INDICATOR] :indicator_variable]
 [, :host_variable [[INDICATOR] :indicator_variable]]... } ]
```

DESCRIPTION *integer* is a host variable used to limit the number of iterations when the **WHERE** clause uses arrays. *statement_id* is the identifier for a prepared **INSERT**, **DELETE**, or **UPDATE** statement to be executed (**SELECT** is not allowed). **USING** introduces a list of substitutions into the host variables of the previously prepared statement.

NOTE
See the Programmer's Guide to the Oracle Precompilers *for a full list of all commands. This reference does not contain all of the possible precompiler commands.*

EXECUTE IMMEDIATE (Dynamic Embedded SQL)

SEE ALSO **EXECUTE**, **PREPARE**, *Programmer's Guide to the Oracle Precompilers*
FORMAT

```
EXEC SQL [AT {database | :host_variable}]
 EXECUTE IMMEDIATE {:string | literal}
```

DESCRIPTION *database* is the name of a database connection other than the default; *host_variable* may contain such a name as its value. *string* is a host variable string containing a SQL statement. *literal* is a character string containing a SQL statement. The **EXECUTE IMMEDIATE** statement cannot contain host variable references other than an executable SQL statement in *string*. The SQL statement is parsed, put into executable form, and executed, and the executable form is destroyed. It is intended only for statements to be executed just once. Statements that require multiple executions should use **PREPARE** and **EXECUTE**, as this eliminates the overhead of parsing for each execution.

NOTE
See the Programmer's Guide to the Oracle Precompilers *for a full list of all commands. This reference does not contain all of the possible precompiler commands.*

EXISTS

SEE ALSO ALL, ANY, IN, NOT EXISTS, Chapter 13

FORMAT

```
select ...
 where EXISTS (select...)
```

DESCRIPTION **EXISTS** returns TRUE in a **WHERE** clause if the subquery that follows it returns at least one row. The **SELECT** clause in the subquery can be a column, a literal, or an asterisk—it doesn't matter. (Convention suggests an asterisk or an x.)

Many people prefer **EXISTS** over **ANY** and **ALL** because it is easier to remember and understand, and most formulations of **ANY** and **ALL** can be reconstructed using **EXISTS**.

EXAMPLE The query shown in the following example uses **EXISTS** to list from the BOOKSHELF table all Publishers that have had books checked out:

```
select Publisher
   from BOOKSHELF B
 where EXISTS
        (select 'x' from BOOKSHELF_CHECKOUT
         where BOOKSHELF_CHECKOUT.Title = B.Title);
```

EXISTSNODE

SEE ALSO Chapter 47

FORMAT

```
EXISTSNODE ( XMLType_instance , Xpath_string )
```

DESCRIPTION **EXISTSNODE** determines whether traversal of the document using the path results in any nodes. It takes as arguments the XMLType instance containing an XML document and a VARCHAR2 string designating a path.

The return value is NUMBER: 0 if no nodes remain after applying the XPath traversal on the document, >0 if any nodes remain.

EXIT (Form 1—PL/SQL)

SEE ALSO END, LOOP, Chapter 29

FORMAT

```
EXIT [loop] [WHEN condition];
```

DESCRIPTION Without any of its options, **EXIT** simply takes you out of the current loop, and branches control to the next statement following the loop. If you are in a nested loop, you can exit from any enclosing loop simply by specifying the loop name. If you specify a condition, you will exit when the condition evaluates to TRUE. Any cursor within a loop is automatically closed when you **EXIT**.

EXIT (Form 2—SQL*Plus)

SEE ALSO COMMIT, DISCONNECT, QUIT, START

FORMAT

```
{EXIT | QUIT} [SUCCESS|FAILURE|WARNING|integer|variable|:BindVariable]
[COMMIT|ROLLBACK]
```

DESCRIPTION EXIT ends a SQL*Plus session and returns the user to the operating system, calling program, or menu. Unless ROLLBACK is specified, **EXIT** commits pending changes to the database. A return code is also returned. SUCCESS, FAILURE, and WARNING have values that are operating system specific; FAILURE and WARNING may be the same on some operating systems.

integer is a value that you can pass back explicitly as the return code; *variable* allows you to set this value dynamically. This can be a user-defined variable, or a system variable, such as SQL.SQLCODE, which always contains the SQLCODE of the last SQL statement executed, either in SQL*Plus or an embedded PL/SQL block.

EXP

SEE ALSO LN, NUMBER FUNCTIONS, Chapter 9

FORMAT

EXP(n)

DESCRIPTION EXP returns *e* raised to the *n*th power; e = 2.718281828....

EXPLAIN PLAN

SEE ALSO Chapter 43

FORMAT

```
EXPLAIN PLAN [SET STATEMENT_ID = 'name']
[INTO [schema.] table [@ dblink]]
FOR statement;
```

DESCRIPTION *name* identifies this plan explanation for this *statement* when it appears in the output table, and follows normal object-naming conventions. If *name* is not specified, the STATEMENT_ID column in the table will be **NULL**. *table* is the name of the output table into which the plan explanation will go. It must be previously created before this procedure can be executed. The start file utlxplan.sql contains the format and can be used to create the default table, named PLAN_TABLE. If *table* is not specified, **EXPLAIN PLAN** will use PLAN_TABLE. *statement* is the simple text of any **SELECT**, **INSERT**, **UPDATE**, or **DELETE** statement you wish to have analyzed for Oracle's execution plan for it.

EXPORT

To *export* is to use one of Oracle's utilities to write selected table data to a file for later retrieval via an import utility. There are two export utilities available: Export, and Data Pump Export. Data Pump Export is available as of Oracle Database 10*g; see* Chapter 22 for details. The Export utility is available for all Oracle versions. For details on the Export utility, *see* Chapter 46. Both utilities are described in the *Oracle Database Utilities 10g Release 1* documentation provided with the Oracle software.

EXPRESSION

An expression is any form of a column. This could be a literal, a variable, a mathematical computation, a function, or virtually any combination of functions and columns whose final result is a single value, such as a string, a number, or a date.

EXTERNAL TABLE

An external table is a file outside the database that is accessible via SQL commands. *See* Chapter 26 for details on the creation and use of external tables.

EXTRACT (datetime)

SEE ALSO DATE FUNCTIONS, Chapter 10

FORMAT

```
EXTRACT
( { { YEAR
    | MONTH
    | DAY
    | HOUR
    | MINUTE
    | SECOND      }
  | { TIMEZONE_HOUR
    | TIMEZONE_MINUTE     }
  | { TIMEZONE_REGION
    | TIMEZONE_ABBR
  } }
  FROM { datetime_value_expression | interval_value_expression } )
```

DESCRIPTION **EXTRACT** extracts and returns the value of a specified datetime field from a datetime or interval value expression.

EXAMPLE

```
select BirthDate,
       EXTRACT(Month from BirthDate) AS Month
  from BIRTHDAY
 where FirstName = 'VICTORIA';

BIRTHDATE       MONTH
--------- ----------
20-MAY-49           5
```

EXTRACT (XML)

SEE ALSO Chapter 47

FORMAT

```
EXTRACT ( XMLType_instance , Xpath_string )
```

DESCRIPTION **EXTRACT** is similar to the **EXISTSNODE** function. It applies a VARCHAR2 XPath string and returns an XMLType instance containing an XML fragment.

EXTRACTVALUE

SEE ALSO XMLType

FORMAT

```
EXTRACTVALUE(XMLType_instance, Xpath_string [,namespace_string])
```

DESCRIPTION **EXTRACTVALUE** takes as arguments an XMLType instance and an XPath expression and returns a scalar value of the resultant node. The result must be a single node and must be a text node, an attribute, or an element. By comparison, the **EXTRACT** function returns an XML fragment; **EXTRACTVALUE** returns the scalar value of the XML fragment.

FEEDBACK (SQL*Plus)

See **SET**.

FETCH

One phase of query execution is the fetch phase, where actual rows of data meeting all search criteria are retrieved from the database.

FETCH (Form I—Embedded SQL)

SEE ALSO **CLOSE**, **DECLARE CURSOR**, **DESCRIBE**, INDICATOR VARIABLE, **OPEN**, **PREPARE**, *Programmer's Guide to the Oracle Precompilers*

FORMAT

```
EXEC SQL [FOR { integer | :array_size }]
 FETCH { cursor | :cursor_variable }
 { USING DESCRIPTOR SQLDA_descriptor
 | INTO :host_variable [[INDICATOR] :indicator_variable]
   [, :host_variable [[INDICATOR] :indicator_variable]]... }
```

DESCRIPTION *integer* is a host variable that sets the maximum number of rows to fetch into the output variables. *cursor* is the name of a cursor previously set up by **DECLARE CURSOR**. :*host_variable* is one or more host variables into which fetched data will be placed. If any of the host variables is an array, then all of them (in the **INTO** list) must be arrays. The **INDICATOR** keyword is optional.

> **NOTE**
> See the Programmer's Guide to the Oracle Precompilers *for a full list of all commands. This reference does not contain all of the possible precompiler commands.*

FETCH (Form 2—PL/SQL)

SEE ALSO %FOUND, %ROWTYPE, CLOSE, DECLARE CURSOR, LOOP, OPEN, SELECT ... INTO, Chapter 29

FORMAT

```
FETCH cursor INTO {record | variable [,variable]...};
```

DESCRIPTION **FETCH** gets a row of data. The named cursor's **SELECT** statement determines which columns are retrieved, and its **WHERE** statement determines which (and how many) rows can be retrieved. This is called the "active set," but it is not available to you for processing until you fetch it, row by row, using the **FETCH** statement. The **FETCH** gets a row from the active set and drops the row's values into the record (or string of variables), which has been defined in the **DECLARE**.

If you use the variable-list method, each column in the select list of the cursor must have a corresponding variable, and each of them must have been declared in the DECLARE section. The datatypes must be the same or compatible.

If you use the record method, the record is **DECLARE**d using the **%ROWTYPE** attribute, which declares the structure of the record to be the same (with the same datatypes) as the column list in the **SELECT**. Each variable within this record can then be accessed individually using the record name as a prefix, and a variable name that is the same as the column name.

EXAMPLE

```
declare
    pi      constant NUMBER(9,7) := 3.1415927;
    area    NUMBER(14,2);
    cursor rad_cursor is
            select * from RADIUS_VALS;
    rad_val rad_cursor%ROWTYPE;
begin
    open rad_cursor;
    loop
        fetch rad_cursor into rad_val;
        exit when rad_cursor%NOTFOUND;
            area := pi*power(rad_val.radius,2);
            insert into AREAS values (rad_val.radius, area);
        end loop;
    close rad_cursor;
end;
```

FIELD

In a table, a field is the information stored at the intersection of a row and a column. *Field* is generally synonymous with *column*, but also can mean an actual column value.

FILE TYPES

Files usually have a name and an extension, for example comfort.tab, where comfort is the filename and .tab is the extension, or file "type." In SQL*Plus, start files that are created using **EDIT** are given the default extension .sql if no extension is specified. In other words,

```
edit misty
```

will create or edit a file named misty.sql, while

```
start misty
```

will attempt to start a file named misty.sql because no extension was specified. Similarly,

```
spool bellwood
```

will create an output file named bellwood.lst, because .lst is the default extension for spooled files. Of course, if either edit or spool is followed by both a filename and extension, the given extension will be used, not the default.

file_specification

SEE ALSO **ALTER TABLESPACE, CREATE CONTROLFILE, CREATE DATABASE, CREATE LIBRARY, CREATE TABLESPACE**

FORMAT

file_specification::=

datafile_tempfile_spec::=

redo_log_file_spec::=

size_clause::=

ASM_filename::=

fully_qualified_file_name::=

numeric_file_name::=

incomplete_file_name::=

alias_file_name::=

autoextend_clause::=

maxsize_clause::=

DESCRIPTION *file_specification* defines the name, location, and size of a file used by the database. For example, when you create a tablespace, you must specify at least one datafile for the tablespace to use. *file_specification* provides the format for the datafile portion of the **CREATE TABLESPACE** command.

As of Oracle Database 10*g*, the file specification subclauses *datafile_tempfile_spec* and *redo_log_file_spec* let you specify Automatic Storage Management files in addition to file system files.

FIRST

SEE ALSO DENSE_RANK, LAST

FORMAT

```
aggregate_function KEEP
( DENSE_RANK FIRST ORDER BY
   expr [ DESC | ASC ] [ NULLS { FIRST | LAST }]
   [, expr [ DESC | ASC ] [ NULLS { FIRST | LAST }]]...
) [OVER query_partitioning_clause]
```

DESCRIPTION **FIRST** is both an aggregate and analytic function that operates on a set of values from a set of rows that rank as the first with respect to a given sorting specification. *aggregate_function* is one of the standard numeric grouping functions (such as **MIN**, **MAX**, **AVG**, and **STDDEV**).

FIRST_VALUE

SEE ALSO LAST_VALUE

FORMAT

```
FIRST_VALUE ( expr ) [IGNORE NULLS] OVER ( analytic_clause )
```

DESCRIPTION **FIRST_VALUE** is an analytic function. It returns the first value in an ordered set of values. If the first value in the set is null, then **FIRST_VALUE** returns **NULL** unless you specify **IGNORE NULLS**.

FLASHBACK DATABASE

SEE ALSO **FLASHBACK TABLE**, Chapter 28
FORMAT
flashback_database::=

DESCRIPTION **FLASHBACK DATABASE** returns the database to a past time or system change number (SCN). This command provides a fast alternative to performing incomplete database recovery. Following a **FLASHBACK DATABASE** operation, in order to have write access to the flashed-back database, you must reopen it with an **ALTER DATABASE OPEN RESETLOGS** command.

NOTE
*The database must have been put in **FLASHBACK** mode with an
ALTER DATABASE FLASHBACK ON command. The database must
be mounted in **EXCLUSIVE** mode but not open.*

You can determine how far back you can flash back the database by querying the V$FLASHBACK_DATABASE_LOG view. The amount of flashback data retained in the database is controlled by the DB_FLASHBACK_RETENTION_TARGET initialization parameter and the size of the flash recovery area. *See* Chapter 28 for further restrictions and examples.

EXAMPLE

```
STARTUP MOUNT EXCLUSIVE;
ALTER DATABASE FLASHBACK ON;
ALTER DATABASE OPEN;
```

With the database open for over an hour, flash it back:

```
SHUTDOWN DATABASE;
STARTUP MOUNT EXCLUSIVE;
FLASHBACK DATABASE TO TIMESTAMP SYSDATE-1/24;
```

FLASHBACK TABLE

SEE ALSO **FLASHBACK DATABASE**, Chapter 28

FORMAT
flashback_table::=

DESCRIPTION **FLASHBACK TABLE** restores an earlier state of a table in the event of human or application error. Oracle cannot restore a table to an earlier state across any DDL operations that change the structure of the table.

NOTE
The database must be using Automatic Undo Management for ***FLASHBACK TABLE*** *to work. The ability to flash back to old data is limited by the amount of undo retained in the undo tablespace and the UNDO_RETENTION initialization parameter setting.*

You cannot roll back a **FLASHBACK TABLE** statement. However, you can issue another **FLASHBACK TABLE** statement and specify a time just prior to the current time.

NOTE
Record the current SCN before you issue a ***FLASHBACK TABLE*** *command.*

You must have either the FLASHBACK object privilege on the table or the FLASHBACK ANY TABLE system privilege. You must also have SELECT, INSERT, DELETE, and ALTER object privileges on the table. Row movement must be enabled for all tables in the flashback list. To flash back a table to before a **DROP TABLE** operation, you only need the privileges necessary to drop the table.

During a **FLASHBACK TABLE** operation, Oracle acquires exclusive DML locks on all tables specified. The command is executed in a single transaction across all tables; if any of them fails, then the entire statement fails.

NOTE
FLASHBACK TABLE TO SCN *or* ***TO TIMESTAMP*** *does not preserve ROWIDs.* ***FLASHBACK TABLE TO BEFORE DROP*** *does not recover referential constraints.*

When a table is flashed back, its statistics are not flashed back. Indexes that exist on the table are reverted and reflect the state of the table at the flashback point. Indexes dropped since the flashback point are not restored. Indexes created since the flashback point continue to exist and will be updated to reflect the older data.

To see the contents of your recycle bin, query USER_RECYCLEBIN.

See Chapter 28 for additional restrictions and examples.

EXAMPLE

```
FLASHBACK TABLE emp TO BEFORE DROP;
```

FLASHBACK QUERY

A flashback query shows data as it existed prior to a **COMMIT**. *See* Chapter 27 for examples and restrictions related to flashback queries.

FLOOR

SEE ALSO **CEIL**, NUMBER FUNCTIONS, Chapter 9

FORMAT

```
FLOOR(value)
```

DESCRIPTION **FLOOR** is the largest integer smaller than or equal to *value*.

EXAMPLE

```
FLOOR(2)   = 2
FLOOR(-2.3) = -3
```

FLUSH (SQL*Plus)

See **SET**.

FOR

See LOOP and CURSOR FOR LOOP.

FOREIGN KEY

A foreign key is one or more columns whose values are based on the primary or candidate key values from another table.

FORMAT

See **BTITLE**, CHAR FORMAT, **COLUMN**, DATE FORMAT, **TO_CHAR**, **TO_DATE**, **TTITLE**.

FORMAT MODEL

A format model is a clause that controls the appearance of numbers, dates, and character strings. Format models for DATE columns are used in date conversion functions such as **TO_CHAR** and **TO_DATE**.

FREE EXTENTS

Free extents are extents of database blocks that have not been allocated to any table or index segment. *Free extents* is another term for free space.

FROM

SEE ALSO DELETE, SELECT, Chapter 5
FORMAT

```
DELETE FROM [user.]table[@link] [alias]
 WHERE condition
```

```
SELECT... FROM [user.]table[@link] [, [user.]table[@link] ]...
```

DESCRIPTION *table* is the name of the table used by **DELETE** or **SELECT**. *link* is the link to a remote database. Both **DELETE** and **SELECT** commands require a **FROM** clause to define the tables from which rows will be deleted or selected. If the table is owned by another user, its name must be prefixed by the owner's username.

If the table is remote, a database link has to be defined. *@link* specifies the link. If *link* is entered but *user* is not, the query seeks a table owned by the user on the remote database. The *condition* may include a correlated query and use the *alias* for correlation.

FROM_TZ

SEE ALSO TIMESTAMP WITH TIME ZONE, Chapter 10
FORMAT

```
FROM_TZ ( timestamp_value , time_zone_value )
```

DESCRIPTION FROM_TZ converts a timestamp value at a time zone to a TIMESTAMP WITH TIME ZONE value. *time_zone_value* is a character string in the format 'TZH:TZM' or a character expression that returns a string in TZR with optional TZD format.

FULL OUTER JOIN

A full outer join performs an outer join in which both tables are used as the "outer" table in the join. Thus, A FULL OUTER JOIN B returns all rows in common between A and B, all rows from A not matched in B matched to **NULL** values, and all rows in B not matched in A matched to **NULL** values.

FULL TABLE SCAN

A full table scan is a method of data retrieval in which Oracle directly searches in a sequential manner all the database blocks for a table (rather than using an index) when looking for the specified data. *See* Chapter 43.

FUNCTION

A function is a predefined operation, such as "convert to uppercase," that may be performed by placing the function's name and arguments in a SQL statement. *See* CHARACTER FUNCTIONS, CONVERSION FUNCTIONS, DATE FUNCTIONS, AGGREGATE FUNCTIONS, ANALYTIC FUNCTIONS, OTHER FUNCTIONS, NUMBER FUNCTIONS, and individual functions.

FUZZY MATCH

A fuzzy match is a type of text search that allows for misspellings or variant spellings. *See* **CONTAINS** and Chapter 25.

GET (SQL*Plus)

SEE ALSO EDIT, SAVE

FORMAT

```
GET file[.ext] [LIS[T] | NOL[IST]]
```

DESCRIPTION **GET** loads a host system file named *file* into the current buffer (whether the SQL buffer or a named buffer). If the file type is not included, **GET** assumes a file type of SQL. **LIST** makes SQL*Plus list the lines being loaded into the buffer. This is the default. **NOLIST** gets the file without listing its contents. If you do not specify a filename extension, .sql is the default value. To change the default filename extension, use the **SET SUFFIX** command; see **SET**.

EXAMPLE This example gets a file called work.sql:

```
get work
```

GLOBAL INDEX

When a table is partitioned, its data is stored in separate segments. When an index is created on the partitioned table, the index can be partitioned so that each of the table partitions has a matching index partition. If the index partitions do not match the table partitions, then the index is a global index. *See* Chapter 17.

GOTO

SEE ALSO BLOCK STRUCTURE, Chapter 29

FORMAT

```
GOTO label;
```

DESCRIPTION **GOTO** transfers control to a section of code preceded by the named *label*. Such a label can be used to precede any legitimate statement within an execution block, or within an EXCEPTION section. There are certain restrictions:

- A **GOTO** cannot transfer control to a block enclosed in the current block, or inside of a **FOR** loop or an **IF** statement.

- A **GOTO** cannot transfer to a label outside of its own block unless it is to a block that encloses its block.

EXAMPLE Here's an informal loop built from a **GOTO** that, without actually knowing ahead of time what the top number will be, **INSERT**s a geometric progression from 1 to about 10,000 into a table:

```
DECLARE
  ...
BEGIN
  x := 0;
  y := 1;
 <<alpha>>
  x := x + 1;
  y := x*y;
  insert ...
  if y > 10000
      then goto beta;
```

```
   goto alpha;
<<beta>>
   exit;
```

GRANT

SEE ALSO **ALTER USER**, **CREATE USER**, PRIVILEGE, **REVOKE**, ROLE, Chapter 18
FORMAT
grant::=

grant_system_privileges::=

grant_object_privileges::=

on_object_clause::=

grantee_clause::=

DESCRIPTION The first form of **GRANT** extends one or more system privileges to users and roles. A system privilege is an authorization to perform one of the various data definition or control commands, such as **ALTER SYSTEM**, **CREATE ROLE**, or **GRANT** itself. *See* PRIVILEGE for details of these privileges. A user is created by **CREATE USER** and is then granted system privileges to enable logging into the database and other operations. A user without grants is unable to do anything at all in Oracle. A *role* is a collection of privileges created by **CREATE ROLE**. As with a user, a role has no privileges when created, but gets them through one or more **GRANT**s. One can grant one role to another role to create a nested network of roles, which gives the database administrator a great deal of flexibility in managing the security of the system.

The **WITH ADMIN OPTION** option lets the granted user or role (the grantee) grant the system privilege or role to other grantees. The grantee can also alter or drop a role granted **WITH ADMIN OPTION**.

The second form of the **GRANT** command grants *object privileges,* privileges that affect specific kinds of objects in Oracle databases, to any user or role. *object* can be a table, view, sequence, procedure, function, package, materialized view, or a synonym for one of these objects. **GRANT**s on a synonym actually become grants on the underlying object that the synonym references. *See* PRIVILEGE for a complete list of object privileges and a discussion of which can be granted for the various objects.

If you are granting INSERT, REFERENCES, or UPDATE privileges on a table or view, **GRANT** can also specify a list of columns of the table or view to which the **GRANT** applies. The **GRANT** applies only to those columns. If **GRANT** has no list of columns, the **GRANT** applies to all columns in the table or view.

PUBLIC grants the privileges to all users present and future.

The **WITH GRANT OPTION** passes along the right to grant the granted privileges to another user or role.

GREATEST
SEE ALSO COLLATION, **LEAST**, LIST FUNCTIONS, **MAX**, Chapters 9 and 10
FORMAT

```
GREATEST(value1, value2, ...)
```

DESCRIPTION **GREATEST** chooses the greatest of a list of values. These can be columns, literals, or expressions, and CHAR, VARCHAR2, NUMBER, or DATE datatypes. A number with a larger value is considered greater than a number with a smaller value. All negative numbers are smaller than all positive numbers. Thus, –10 is smaller than 10; –100 is smaller than –10. A later date is considered greater than an earlier date.

Character strings are compared position by position, starting at the leftmost end of the string, up to the first character that is different. Whichever string has the greater character in that position is considered the greater string. One character is considered greater than another if it appears after the other in the computer's collation sequence. Usually this means that a *B* is greater than an *A*, but the value of *A* compared to *a*, or compared to the number 1, will differ by computer.

If two strings are identical through to the end of the shorter one, the longer string is considered greater. If two strings are identical and the same length, they are considered equal. In SQL, it is important that literal numbers be typed without enclosing single quotes, as '10' would be considered smaller than '6', since the quotes will cause these to be regarded as character strings rather than numbers, and the '6' will be seen as greater than the 1 in the first position of '10'.

Unlike many other Oracle functions and logical operators, the **GREATEST** and **LEAST** functions will not evaluate literal strings that are in date format as dates. In order for **LEAST** and **GREATEST** to work properly, the **TO_DATE** function must be applied to the literal strings.

GROUP BY

SEE ALSO CUBE, HAVING, ORDER BY, ROLLUP, WHERE, Chapter 12

FORMAT

```
SELECT expression [,expression]...
 GROUP BY expression [,expression]...
HAVING condition
   ...
```

DESCRIPTION **GROUP BY** causes a **SELECT** to produce one summary row for all selected rows that have identical values in one or more specified columns or expressions. Each expression in the **SELECT** clause must be one of these things:

- A constant
- A function without parameters (SysDate, User)
- A group function such as **SUM**, **AVG**, **MIN**, **MAX**, or **COUNT**
- Matched identically to an expression in the **GROUP BY** clause

Columns referenced in the **GROUP BY** clause need not be in the **SELECT** clause, though they must be in the table.

You use **HAVING** to determine which groups the **GROUP BY** is to include. A **WHERE** clause, on the other hand, determines which rows are to be included in groups.

GROUP BY and **HAVING** follow **WHERE**, **CONNECT BY**, and **START WITH**. The **ORDER BY** clause is executed after the **WHERE**, **GROUP BY**, and **HAVING** clauses (which execute in that order). It can employ group functions or columns from the **GROUP BY** clause, or a combination. If it uses a group function, that function operates on the groups, and then the **ORDER BY** sorts the *results* of the function in order. If the **ORDER BY** clause uses a column from the **GROUP BY** clause, it sorts the rows that are returned based on that column. Group functions and single columns can be combined in the **ORDER BY** clause (so long as the column is in the **GROUP BY** clause).

In the **ORDER BY** clause, you can specify a group function and the column it affects even though they have nothing at all to do with the group functions or columns in the **SELECT**, **GROUP BY**, or **HAVING** clause. On the other hand, if you specify a column in the **ORDER BY** clause that is not part of a group function, it must be in the **GROUP BY** clause.

EXAMPLE

```
select Title, COUNT(*)
  from BOOKSHELF_AUTHOR
 group by Title
having COUNT(*) > 1;
```

GROUP_ID

SEE ALSO AGGREGATE FUNCTIONS, **GROUP BY**, **GROUPING_ID**, Chapter 12
FORMAT

```
GROUP_ID ( )
```

DESCRIPTION **GROUP_ID** distinguishes duplicate groups resulting from a **GROUP BY** specification.

GROUPING

GROUPING is a function used in conjunction with the **ROLLUP** and **CUBE** functions to detect **NULL**s. *See* **ROLLUP**.

GROUPING_ID

GROUPING_ID returns a number corresponding to the **GROUPING** bit vector associated with a row. *See* **ROLLUP**, **CUBE**, and Chapter 12.

HASH CLUSTER

A hash cluster is a cluster stored by a hash key instead of by an index key. A hash key is a value computed from the key values that represents the location on disk. An index key requires Oracle to look up the location in the index, while a hash key lets Oracle calculate the location.

HASH JOIN

A hash join is a method of performing a join of two tables. A hash join uses hash algorithms (similar to those used for hash clusters) to evaluate rows that meet the join criteria. Although they use similar algorithms, there is no direct relation between hash joins and hash clusters.

HASH PARTITION

In a hash partition, data to be partitioned is processed by a hash algorithm rather than simply being partitioned by range. Hash partitioning therefore spreads small sets of sequential data over more partitions than does range partitioning. *See* **CREATE TABLE**.

HAVING

See GROUP BY.

HEADING (SQL*Plus)

See SET.

HEADSEP (SQL*Plus)

See SET.

HELP (SQL*Plus)

FORMAT

```
HELP | ? [topic]
```

DESCRIPTION The **HELP** command accesses the SQL*Plus help system. **HELP INDEX** displays a list of topics.

HEXTORAW
SEE ALSO RAWTOHEX
FORMAT

```
HEXTORAW(hex_string)
```

DESCRIPTION **HEXTORAW** (**HEX**adecimal **TO RAW**) changes a character string of hex numbers into binary.

HINT

Within a query, you can specify hints that direct the cost-based optimizer in its processing of the query. To specify a hint, use the following syntax. Immediately after the **SELECT** keyword, enter the string

```
/*+
```

Next, add the hint, such as

```
FULL(bookshelf)
```

Close the hint with the following string:

```
*/
```

See Chapter 43 for a description of the available hints and their impact on query processing.

HISTOGRAM

A histogram shows the distribution of data values for a column. The Oracle optimizer can use histograms to determine the efficiency of indexes for specific data value ranges. *See* **ANALYZE**.

HOST (SQL*Plus)
SEE ALSO $, !, @, @@, START
FORMAT

```
HO[ST] command
```

DESCRIPTION A host is a computer on which the Oracle RDBMS is running. The **HOST** command in SQL*Plus passes any **HOST** command back to the operating system for execution without exiting SQL*Plus. SQL*Plus permits embedding local or PL/SQL variables in the **HOST** command string. This doesn't work on all hardware or operating systems. **HOST** is not available within iSQL*Plus.

IF
SEE ALSO LOOP, Chapter 29
FORMAT

```
IF condition
    THEN statement; [statement;]...
  [ELSIF condition THEN statement; [statement;]...
  [ELSIF condition THEN statement; [statement;]...]...]
```

```
[ELSE statement; [statement;]...]
END IF;
```

DESCRIPTION The **IF** statement will execute one or more *statements* if *condition* evaluates to TRUE, after which the program branches to **END IF**. If the *condition* is FALSE, then any number of a series of optional **ELSIF** conditions are tested. If any one is TRUE, the associated *statements* (following **THEN**) are executed, and then the program branches to **END IF**. If none of the **ELSIF** conditions is TRUE (and the original IF condition was not TRUE), then the statements following the optional **ELSE** are executed. Note that the final **ELSE** does not have a condition.

EXAMPLE

```
declare
    pi      constant NUMBER(9,7) := 3.1415927;
    area    NUMBER(14,2);
    cursor rad_cursor is
      select * from RADIUS_VALS;
    rad_val rad_cursor%ROWTYPE;
begin
    open rad_cursor;
    fetch rad_cursor into rad_val;
    area := pi*power(rad_val.radius,2);
      if  area > 30
        then
            insert into AREAS values (rad_val.radius, area);
      end if;
    close rad_cursor;
end;
```

IMPORT

To *import* is to use one of Oracle's utilities to read data from an export dump file and insert it into a database via an import utility. There are two import utilities available: Import and Data Pump Import. Data Pump Import is available as of Oracle Database 10*g*; *see* Chapter 22 for details. The Import utility is available for all Oracle versions. For details on the Import utility, *see* Chapter 46. Both utilities are described in the *Oracle Database Utilities 10g Release 1* documentation provided with the Oracle software.

IN

SEE ALSO **ALL**, **ANY**, LOGICAL OPERATORS, **WHERE**, Chapter 5

FORMAT

```
WHERE expression IN ({'string' [,'string']... | select...})
```

DESCRIPTION **IN** is equivalent to **=ANY**. In the first option, **IN** means the expression is equal to any member of the following list of literal *strings*. In the second option, it means the expression is equal to any value in any row selected from the subquery. The two are logically equivalent, with the first giving a list made of literal strings, and the second building a list from a query.

INDEX

Index is a general term for an Oracle/SQL feature used primarily to speed execution and impose uniqueness upon certain data. In general, indexes provide a faster access method to table data than

doing a full table scan. There are several types of indexes; *see* CONCATENATED INDEX, COMPRESSED INDEX, and UNIQUE INDEX. An index has an entry for each value found in the table's indexed field(s) (except those with a **NULL** value) and pointer(s) to the row(s) having that value.

INDEX SEGMENT

The index segment is the storage that is allocated for an index, as compared to storage allocated to the data in a table.

INDEX-ORGANIZED TABLE

An index-organized table keeps its data sorted according to the primary key column values for the table. An index-organized table allows you to store the entire table's data in an index. A normal index stores only the indexed columns in the index; an index-organized table stores all of the table's columns in the index.

To create an index-organized table, use the **ORGANIZATION INDEX** clause of the **CREATE TABLE** command, as shown in the following example:

```
create table TROUBLE (
City            VARCHAR2(13),
SampleDate      DATE,
Noon            NUMBER(4,1),
Midnight        NUMBER(4,1),
Precipitation NUMBER,
constraint TROUBLE_PK PRIMARY KEY (City, SampleDate))
organization index;
```

To create TROUBLE as an index-organized table, you must create a PRIMARY KEY constraint on it.

In general, index-organized tables are appropriate for associative tables in many-to-many relationships. Ideally, an index-organized table will have few (or no) columns that are not part of its primary key.

See Chapter 17 and **CREATE TABLE**.

INDICATOR VARIABLE

SEE ALSO : (colon, the host variable prefix), *Programmer's Guide to the Oracle Precompilers*

FORMAT

```
:name [INDICATOR] :indicator
```

DESCRIPTION An indicator variable—used when both name and indicator are host language variable names—is a data field whose value indicates whether a host variable should be regarded as **NULL**. (The **INDICATOR** keyword is for readability and has no effect.)

name may be any legitimate host variable data name used in the host program and included in the precompiler's DECLARE section. *indicator* is defined in the precompiler's DECLARE section as a two-byte integer.

Few procedural languages directly support the idea of a variable with a **NULL** or unknown value, although Oracle and SQL do so easily. To extend languages for which Oracle has developed precompilers to support the **NULL** concept, an indicator variable is associated with the host variable, almost like a flag, to indicate whether it is **NULL**. The host variable and its indicator variable may be referenced and set separately in the host language code, but are always concatenated in SQL or PL/SQL.

EXAMPLE

```
BEGIN
    select Title, AuthorName into :Title, :AuthorName:AuthorNameInd
```

```
    from BOOKSHELF_AUTHOR;

  IF :AuthorName:AuthorNameInd IS NULL
    THEN :AuthorName:AuthorNameInd := 'No Auth'
  END IF;
END;
```

Note that both the test to see whether the variable is **NULL** and, if it is, the assignment of 'No Auth' to it are done with the concatenated variable name. PL/SQL knows enough to check the indicator in the first case and set the variable value in the second case. The two variables together are treated just like a single Oracle column. These important points must be noted:

■ Within any single PL/SQL block, a host variable must either always stand alone or always be concatenated with its indicator variable.

■ An indicator variable cannot be referenced alone within PL/SQL, although it can be in the host program.

When setting host variables within the host program, but outside of PL/SQL, note these points:

■ Setting the indicator variable equal to –1 will force the concatenated variable to be regarded within PL/SQL as **NULL**, both in logic tests and for **INSERT**s or **UPDATE**s.

■ Setting the indicator variable greater than or equal to 0 will force the concatenated variable to be regarded as equal to the value in the host variable, and **NOT NULL**.

■ PL/SQL tests the value of all indicator variables on entering a block, and sets them on exiting the block.

When loading concatenated host variables within PL/SQL, via a SQL statement with an **INTO** clause, the following rules apply when checking the indicator variable within the host program, but outside of PL/SQL:

■ The indicator variable will be equal to –1 if the value loaded from the database was **NULL**. The value of the host variable is uncertain, and should be treated as such.

■ The indicator variable will be equal to 0 if the value from the database is loaded completely and correctly into the host variable.

■ The indicator variable will be greater than 0 and equal to the actual length of the data in the database column if only a portion of it could fit in the host variable. The host variable will contain a truncated version of what was in the database column.

init.ora

The init.ora file is a database system parameter file that contains settings and filenames used when a system is started using the **CREATE DATABASE**, **STARTUP**, or **SHUTDOWN** command. You can either use an init.ora file or create a system parameter file via the **CREATE SPFILE** command. *See* **CREATE PFILE** and **CREATE SPFILE**.

INITCAP

SEE ALSO CHARACTER FUNCTIONS, **LOWER**, **UPPER**, Chapter 7

FORMAT

```
INITCAP(string)
```

DESCRIPTION INITCAP (**INIT**ial **CAP**ital) changes the first letter of a word or series of words into uppercase. It also notes the presence of symbols, and will **INITCAP** any letter that follows a space or a symbol, such as a comma, period, colon, semicolon, !, @, #, $, and so on.

EXAMPLE

```
INITCAP('this.is,an-example of!how@initcap#works')
```

produces this:

```
This.Is,An-Example Of!How@Initcap#Works
```

INNER JOIN

Inner joins return rows based on the key values two tables have in common. They support both the **ON** and **USING** clauses. For example, the following query joins BOOK_ORDER to BOOKSHELF based on their Title column values:

```
select BO.Title
   from BOOK_ORDER BO inner join BOOKSHELF B
     on BO.Title = B.Title;
```

That query can be rewritten as:

```
select Title
   from BOOK_ORDER BO inner join BOOKSHELF B
 using (Title);
```

INPUT (SQL*Plus)

SEE ALSO **APPEND, CHANGE, DEL, EDIT**, Chapter 6

FORMAT

```
I[NPUT] [text]
```

DESCRIPTION **INPUT** adds a new line of text after the current line in the current buffer. Using **INPUT** by itself allows multiple lines to be keyed in after the current line, which stops when the system encounters ENTER with nothing else on the line. The space between **INPUT** and *text* will not be added to the line but any additional spaces will be. *See* **DEL** for a discussion of current line. **INPUT** is not available in iSQL*Plus.

INSERT (Form 1—Embedded SQL)

SEE ALSO **EXECUTE, FOR**, *Programmer's Guide to the Oracle Precompilers*

FORMAT

```
EXEC SQL [AT { db_name | :host_variable }]
  [FOR { :host_integer | integer }]
  INSERT INTO
  [ [schema.] { table | view }
    [ @db_link | PARTITION (part_name) ] ]
  [(column) [, (column)]...]
  { VALUES (expr [, expr]...) | subquery }
[{ RETURN | RETURNING } expr [, expr]... INTO
  :host_variable [[INDICATOR] :ind_variable]
  [, :host_variable [[INDICATOR] :ind_variable]]...]
```

DESCRIPTION *db_name* is a database other than the user's default, and *host_variable* contains the name of the database. *:host_integer* is a host value that limits the number of times the **INSERT** will be processed (*see* FOR). *table* is any existing table, view, or synonym, and *db_link* is the name of a remote database where the table is stored. (*See* the **INSERT** Form 3 definition for a discussion of the **VALUES** clause, columns, and query.) *expression* here can be an expression or a host variable in the form *:variable*[*:indicator*].

NOTE
See the Programmer's Guide to the Oracle Precompilers *for a full list of all commands. This reference does not contain all of the possible precompiler commands.*

INSERT (Form 2—PL/SQL)

SEE ALSO SQL CURSOR, Chapter 29
FORMAT

```
INSERT INTO [user.]table[@db_link] [(column [,column]...)]
    VALUES (expression [,expression]...) | query...);
```

DESCRIPTION PL/SQL's use of **INSERT** is identical to its general form (Form 3 in the following section), with these exceptions:

- You may use a PL/SQL variable in an expression for the value in the VALUES list.
- Each variable will be treated in the same way that a constant, with the value of the variable, would be treated.
- If you use the *query...* version of the **INSERT**, you cannot use the **INTO** clause of the **SELECT**.

INSERT (Form 3—SQL Command)

SEE ALSO **CREATE TABLE**, Chapters 5, 15, 33, and 34
FORMAT
insert::=

single_table_insert::=

insert_into_clause::=::=

values_clause::=

returning_clause::=

multi_table_insert::=

conditional_insert_clause::=

DML_table_expression_clause::=

subquery_restriction_clause::=

table_collection_expression::=

DESCRIPTION **INSERT** adds one or more new rows to the table or view. The optional *schema* must be a user to whose table you have been granted insert authority. *table* is the table into which rows are to be inserted. If a list of columns is given, an expression (SQL expression) must be matched for each of those columns. Any columns not in the list receive the value **NULL**, and none of them can be defined **NOT NULL** or the **INSERT** will fail. If a list of columns is not given, values must be given for all columns in the table.

INSERT with a subquery adds as many rows as the query returns, with each query column being matched, position for position, with columns in the column list. If no column list is given, the tables must have the same number and type of columns. The USER_TAB_COLUMNS data dictionary view shows these, as does **DESCRIBE** in SQL*Plus.

EXAMPLE The following inserts a row into the COMFORT table:

```
insert into COMFORT values ('KEENE','23-SEP-03',99.8,82.6,NULL);
```

The following inserts City, SampleDate (both **NOT NULL** columns), and Precipitation into COMFORT:

```
insert into COMFORT (City, SampleDate, Precipitation) values
                ('KEENE','22-DEC-03',3.9);
```

To copy just the data for the city of KEENE into a new table named NEW_HAMPSHIRE, use this:

```
insert into NEW_HAMPSHIRE
select * from COMFORT
 where City = 'KEENE';
```

See Chapter 33 for information on inserting rows into tables that use abstract datatypes. *See* Chapter 34 for details on inserting rows into nested tables and varying arrays.

INSTANCE

An instance is everything required for Oracle to run: background processes (programs), memory, and so on. An instance is the means of accessing a database.

INSTANCE IDENTIFIER

An instance identifier is a means of distinguishing one instance from another when multiple instances exist on one host.

INSTANCE RECOVERY

Instance recovery is recovery in the event of software or hardware failure. This occurs if the software aborted abnormally due to a severe bug, deadlock, or destructive interaction between programs. *See also* MEDIA RECOVERY.

INSTEAD OF TRIGGER

An INSTEAD OF trigger executes a block of PL/SQL code in place of the transaction that causes the trigger to be executed. INSTEAD OF triggers are commonly used to redirect transactions against views. *See* **CREATE TRIGGER** and Chapters 30 and 33.

INSTR

SEE ALSO CHARACTER FUNCTIONS, **SUBSTR**, Chapter 7

FORMAT

```
INSTR(string,set[,start[,occurrence]])
```

DESCRIPTION **INSTR** finds the location of a *set* of characters in a *string*, starting at position *start* in the string, and looking for the first, second, third, and so on *occurrence* of the *set*. This function will also work with NUMBER and DATE datatypes. *start* also can be negative, meaning the search begins with the characters at the end of the string and searches backward.

EXAMPLE To find the third occurrence of 'PI' in this string, use this:

```
INSTR('PETER PIPER PICKED A PECK OF PICKLED PEPPERS','PI',1,3)
```

The result of this function is 30, the location of the third occurrence of 'PI'.

INTEGRITY CONSTRAINT

An integrity constraint is a rule that restricts the range of valid values for a column. It is placed on a column when the table is created. For the syntax, see CONSTRAINTS.

If you do not name a constraint, Oracle assigns a name in the form SYS_C*n*, where *n* is an integer. An Oracle-assigned name will usually change during an import, while a user-assigned name will not change.

NULL permits **NULL** values. **NOT NULL** specifies that every row must have a non-**NULL** value for this column.

UNIQUE forces column values to be unique. There can be only one PRIMARY KEY constraint on a table. If a column is UNIQUE it cannot also be declared the PRIMARY KEY (PRIMARY KEY also enforces uniqueness). An index enforces the UNIQUE or PRIMARY KEY, and the **USING INDEX** clause and its options specify the storage characteristics of that index. *See* **CREATE INDEX** for more information on the options.

REFERENCES identifies this column as a foreign key from [*user.*]*table* [*(column)*]. Omitting *column* implies that the name in the *user.table* is the same as the name in this table. Note that when REFERENCES is used in a *table_constraint* (described shortly), it must be preceded by FOREIGN KEY. This is not used here, as only this column is referenced; *table_constraint* can reference several columns for FOREIGN KEY. ON DELETE CASCADE instructs Oracle to maintain referential integrity automatically by removing foreign key rows in the dependent tables if you remove the primary key row in this table.

CHECK assures that the value for this column passes a condition such as this:

```
Amount number(12,2) CHECK (Amount >= 0)
```

condition may be any valid expression that tests TRUE or FALSE. It can contain functions, any columns from this table, and literals.

The **EXCEPTIONS INTO** clause specifies a table into which Oracle puts information about rows that violate an enabled integrity constraint. This table must be local.

The **DISABLE** option lets you disable the integrity constraint when you create it. When the constraint is disabled, Oracle does not automatically enforce it. You can later enable the constraint with the **ENABLE** clause in **ALTER TABLE**.

You can also create constraints at the table level. Table constraints are identical to column constraints except that a single constraint can reference multiple columns—for example, in declaring a set of three columns as a primary or foreign key.

INTERSECT

SEE ALSO MINUS, QUERY OPERATORS, **UNION**, Chapter 13

FORMAT

```
select...
INTERSECT
select...
```

DESCRIPTION **INTERSECT** combines two queries and returns only those rows from the first **SELECT** statement that are identical to at least one row from the second **SELECT** statement. The number of columns and datatypes must be identical between **SELECT** statements, although the names of the columns do not need to be. The data, however, must be identical in the rows produced for the **INTERSECT**ion to pass them.

INTERVAL DAY TO SECOND

The INTERVAL DAY (*day_precision*) TO SECOND (*second_precision*) datatype stores the period of time in days, hours, minutes, and seconds. You can specify a *day_precision* as the number of digits in the DAY datetime field (default is 2) and a *second_precision* as the number of digits in the fractional part of the Seconds field (default is 6).

INTERVAL YEAR TO MONTH

The INTERVAL YEAR (*precision*) TO MONTH datatype stores the period of time in years and months, where *precision* is the number of digits in the YEAR datetime field (default is 2).

IS A SET

SEE ALSO **IS EMPTY**, Chapter 34

FORMAT

```
nested_table IS [NOT] A SET
```

DESCRIPTION Use an **IS A SET** condition to test whether a specified nested table is composed of unique elements. The condition returns TRUE is the nested table is a set, even if it is a nested table of length zero, and returns FALSE otherwise. It returns **NULL** if the nested table is empty.

IS ANY

SEE ALSO SELECT

FORMAT

```
dimension_column IS ANY
```

DESCRIPTION The **IS ANY** clause is relevant only for interrow calculations, and can be used only in the **MODEL** clause of a **SELECT** statement. Use this condition to qualify all values of a dimension column, including **NULL**. The condition always returns a Boolean value of TRUE to qualify all values of the column.

IS EMPTY

SEE ALSO **IS A SET**, Chapter 34

FORMAT

```
nested table IS [NOT] EMPTY
```

DESCRIPTION Use the **IS [NOT] EMPTY** conditions to test whether a specified nested table is empty, regardless of whether any elements of the collection are **NULL**. The condition returns a Boolean value: TRUE for an **IS EMPTY** condition if the condition is empty, TRUE for an **IS NOT EMPTY** condition if the condition is not empty. If you specify **NULL** for the nested table or array, the result is **NULL**.

IS NULL

SEE ALSO LOGICAL OPERATORS, Chapters 5 and 9

FORMAT

```
WHERE column IS [NOT] NULL
```

DESCRIPTION **IS NULL** tests a column (or an expression) for the absence of any data. A **NULL** test is distinctly different from a test for equality, because **NULL** means that the value is unknown or irrelevant, and it therefore cannot be said to be equal to anything, including another **NULL**.

IS OF type

SEE ALSO VALUE, Chapter 33

FORMAT
is_of_type_conditions::=

DESCRIPTION Use the **IS OF** *type* condition to test object instances based on their specific type information. The condition evaluates to **NULL** if *expr* is **NULL**. If *expr* is not null, then the condition evaluates to TRUE (or FALSE if you specify the **NOT** keyword) under either of these circumstances:

- The most specific type of *expr* is the subtype of one of the types specified in the *type* list and you have not specified **ONLY** for the type.
- The most specific type of *expr* is explicitly specified in the *type* list.

The *expr* frequently takes the form of the **VALUE** function with a correlation variable.

IS PRESENT

SEE ALSO SELECT

FORMAT

```
cell_reference IS PRESENT
```

DESCRIPTION The **IS PRESENT** condition is relevant only for interrow calculations, and can be used only in the **MODEL** clause of a **SELECT** statement. Use this condition to test whether the cell referenced is present prior to the execution of the **MODEL** clause. The condition returns TRUE if the cell exists prior to the execution of the **MODEL** clause, and returns FALSE if it does not.

ITERATION_NUMBER

SEE ALSO SELECT

FORMAT

```
ITERATION_NUMBER
```

DESCRIPTION The **ITERATION_NUMBER** function is relevant only for interrow calculations. It can be used only in the **MODEL** clause of the **SELECT** statement and then only when ITERATE(*number*) is specified in the **MODEL RULES** clause. It returns an integer representing the completed iteration through the model rules. The **ITERATION_NUMBER** function returns 0 during the first iteration. For each subsequent iteration, the **ITERATION_NUMBER** function returns the equivalent of *iteration_number* plus one.

JAVA

Java is a programming language originally developed by Sun Microsystems. You can write stored procedural objects in either PL/SQL or Java. *See* Chapter 37.

JDBC

JDBC is an industry standard application programming interface to databases. Oracle supports JDBC connections. *See* Chapter 38.

JOIN

SEE ALSO SELECT, Chapter 5

FORMAT

```
WHERE TableA.column = TableB.column
```

or

```
FROM TableA INNER JOIN TableB
   on TableA.Column = TableB.Column
```

or

```
FROM TableA INNER JOIN TableB
using(Column)
```

or

```
FROM TableA NATURAL JOIN TableB
```

DESCRIPTION A join combines columns and data from two or more tables (and, in rare cases, of one table with itself). The tables are all listed in the **FROM** clause of the **SELECT** statement, and the relationship between the two tables may specified in the **WHERE** clause, usually by a simple equality, such as this:

```
where BOOK_ORDER.Title = BOOKSHELF.Title
```

This is often called an *equi-join* because it uses the equal sign in the **WHERE** clause. You could join tables using other forms of equality, such as >=, <, and so on, but the results are seldom meaningful. There also are cases in which one or both sides of the equal sign contain an expression, perhaps a **SUBSTR** or a combination of columns, which is used for equality with the other side. This is a fairly common usage.

Joining two tables together without a join clause—either in the **FROM** clause or in the **WHERE** clause—produces a Cartesian product, which combines every row in one table with every row in the other table. An 80-row table combined with a 100-row table would produce an 8000-row result (which is usually quite meaningless).

An *outer join* is a method for intentionally retrieving selected rows from one table that don't match rows in the other table. As of Oracle9*i*, you can use the ANSI standard outer join syntax options (CROSS JOIN, NATURAL JOIN, LEFT OUTER JOIN, RIGHT OUTER JOIN, and FULL OUTER JOIN). *See* Chapter 13 for examples of the syntax for outer joins.

JOIN COLUMN

A join column is a column used to join one table to another. You identify a join column by using it in a **WHERE** clause, **USING** clause, or **ON** clause that specifies the relationship between the two tables.

JULIAN DATE

Julian dates are a means of converting date data so that every date can be expressed as a unique integer. Julian dates can be obtained by using the format mask 'J' with functions on date data. *See* DATE FORMATS.

KEY

A key is a column or columns used to identify rows; it is not the same as an index, although indexes are often used with such columns. *See* FOREIGN KEY, PRIMARY KEY, and UNIQUE KEY.

LABEL (PL/SQL)

A label is a word associated with an executable statement, usually for the purpose of being the target of a **GOTO** statement.

LAG

SEE ALSO **LEAD**

FORMAT

```
LAG ( value_expr [, offset] [, default] )
   OVER ( [query_partition_clause] order_by_clause )
```

DESCRIPTION **LAG** provides access to more than one row of a table at the same time without a self-join. Given a series of rows returned from a query and a position of the cursor, **LAG** provides access to a row at a given physical offset prior to that position.

LAST

SEE ALSO **DENSE_RANK, FIRST**

FORMAT

```
aggregate_function KEEP
( DENSE_RANK LAST ORDER BY
  expr [ DESC | ASC ] [ NULLS { FIRST | LAST }]
  [, expr [ DESC | ASC ] [ NULLS { FIRST | LAST }]]...
) [OVER query_partition_clause]
```

DESCRIPTION **LAST** is both an aggregate and analytic function that operates on a set of values from a set of rows that rank as the last with respect to a given sorting specification. *aggregate_function* is one of the standard numeric grouping functions (such as **MIN**, **MAX**, **AVG**, and **STDDEV**).

LAST_DAY

SEE ALSO **ADD_MONTHS**, DATE FUNCTIONS, **NEXT_DAY**, Chapter 10

FORMAT

```
LAST_DAY (date)
```

DESCRIPTION **LAST_DAY** gives the date of the last day of the month that *date* is in.

EXAMPLE

```
LAST_DAY ('05-NOV-04')
```

produces a result of 30-NOV-04.

LAST_VALUE

SEE ALSO FIRST_VALUE

FORMAT

```
LAST_VALUE ( expr [IGNORE NULLS]) OVER ( analytic_clause )
```

DESCRIPTION **LAST_VALUE** is an analytic function. It returns the last value in an ordered set of values. If the last value in the set is null, then the function returns **NULL** unless you specify **IGNORE NULLS**.

LEAD

SEE ALSO LAG

FORMAT

```
LEAD ( value_expr [, offset] [, default] )
   OVER ( [query_partition_clause] order_by_clause )
```

DESCRIPTION **LEAD** provides access to more than one row of a table at the same time without a self-join. Given a series of rows returned from a query and a position of the cursor, **LEAD** provides access to a row at a given physical offset beyond that position.

LEAST

SEE ALSO **GREATEST**, LIST FUNCTIONS, Chapter 10

FORMAT

```
LEAST(value1, value2, ...)
```

DESCRIPTION **LEAST** is the value of a list of columns, expressions, or values. Values may be VARCHAR2, CHAR, DATE, or NUMBER datatypes, although **LEAST** will not properly evaluate literal dates (such as '20-MAY-04') without the **TO_DATE** function. *See* **GREATEST** for a discussion of evaluating relative values.

LENGTH

SEE ALSO CHARACTER FUNCTIONS, **VSIZE**, Chapter 7

FORMAT

```
LENGTH(string)
```

DESCRIPTION **LENGTH** tells the length of a string, number, date, or expression. The *string* can be CHAR (returned length will include all trailing blanks), VARCHAR2, NCHAR, NVARCHAR2, CLOB, or NCLOB. There are several **LENGTH** functions, all following the same format:

- **LENGTH** calculates the length using characters as defined by the input character set.
- **LENGTHB** uses bytes instead of characters.
- **LENGTHC** uses Unicode complete characters.
- **LENGTH2** uses UCS2 code points.
- **LENGTH4** uses UCS4 code points.

LEVEL

SEE ALSO **CONNECT BY**, PSEUDO-COLUMNS, Chapter 14

FORMAT

```
LEVEL
```

DESCRIPTION Level is a pseudo-column, used with **CONNECT BY**, that is equal to 1 for a root node, 2 for a child of a root, 3 for a child of a child of a root, and so on. Level tells basically how far down a tree you've traveled.

LGWR

LGWR (**Lo**G **WR**iter process) writes redo log entries from the System Global Area to the online redo logs. *See* BACKGROUND PROCESS.

LIBRARY

PL/SQL blocks can reference external subprograms, stored in libraries. *See* **CREATE LIBRARY**.

LIKE

SEE ALSO LOGICAL OPERATORS, Chapter 3

FORMAT

```
WHERE string LIKE string
```

DESCRIPTION **LIKE** performs pattern matching. An underline represents exactly one space. A percent sign represents any number of spaces or characters, including zero. If **LIKE** uses either the _ or % in the first position of a comparison (as in the second and third examples following), any index on the column is ignored.

EXAMPLES

```
Feature LIKE 'MO%'    "Feature begins with the letters MO."
Feature LIKE '_ _I%'  "Feature has an I in the third position."
Feature LIKE '%0%0%'  "Feature has at least two 0's in it."
```

LINESIZE (SQL*Plus)
See **SET**.

LIST (SQL*Plus)
SEE ALSO APPEND, CHANGE, EDIT, INPUT, RUN, Chapter 6
FORMAT

```
L[IST] [n |n m|n* |n LAST|*|*n|*LAST|LAST]
```

DESCRIPTION **LIST** lists lines of the current buffer starting at *n* and ending at *m*, both of which are integers. The end line becomes the current line of the buffer, and is flagged with an asterisk. **LIST** without *n* or *m* lists all lines. **LIST** with a single number will display just that line. The space between **LIST** and *n* is not necessary but it does help readability. **LIST *n*** lists all lines from *n* to the end of the buffer. **LIST *n** lists all lines from the beginning to the specified line.
EXAMPLE Use this to list the current SQL buffer:

```
LIST
```

An asterisk will designate the current line. To list just the second line, use this:

```
LIST 2
```

This also makes 2 the current line in the current buffer.

LIST FUNCTIONS
SEE ALSO All other functions, Chapter 10
DESCRIPTION The following is an alphabetical list of all current list functions in the Oracle version of SQL. Each of these is listed elsewhere in this reference under its own name, with its proper format and use.
This gives the first non-**NULL** value in the set:

```
COALESCE(value1, value2, ...)
```

This gives the greatest value of a list:

```
GREATEST(value1, value2, ...)
```

This gives the least value of a list:

```
LEAST(value1, value2, ...)
```

LN
SEE ALSO NUMBER FUNCTIONS, Chapter 9
FORMAT

```
LN(number)
```

DESCRIPTION LN is the "natural," or base *e*, logarithm of a *number*. If *number* is BINARY_FLOAT, then the function returns BINARY_DOUBLE.

LNNVL

SEE ALSO SELECT

FORMAT

LNNVL (*condition*)

DESCRIPTION LNNVL provides a way to evaluate a condition when one or both operands of the condition may be null. The function can be used only in the **WHERE** clause of a query. It takes as an argument a condition and returns TRUE if the condition is FALSE or UNKNOWN and returns FALSE if the condition is TRUE. **LNNVL** can be used anywhere a scalar expression can appear, even in contexts where the **IS [NOT] NULL**, **AND**, or **OR** conditions are not valid but would otherwise be required to account for potential nulls. **LNNVL** may show up in explain plans when Oracle internally requires **NOT IN** conditions as **NOT EXISTS** conditions.

EXAMPLES If you want to retrieve all rows for which a column is greater than a given value, the standard format would be

where *column* > *value*

To also return the rows for which *column* is **NULL**, use **LNNVL**:

where LNNVL(*column* > *value*)

LOADJAVA

LOADJAVA is a utility for loading Java classes, resources, and sources into the database. You must load your Java classes into the database if you plan to use them in stored procedures. To remove the Java classes from the database, use the DROPJAVA utility. *See* Chapter 39.

LOB

A LOB is a large object. Oracle supports several large object datatypes, including BLOBs (binary large objects), CLOBs (character large objects), and BFILEs (binary files, stored outside the database). *See* Chapter 35 and the **LOB** clause of **CREATE TABLE**.

LOBOFFSET (SQL*Plus)

See **SET**.

LOCAL DATABASE

The local database is usually a database on your host computer. *See* REMOTE DATABASE.

LOCAL INDEX

When a table is partitioned, its data is stored in separate tables. When an index is created on the partitioned table, the index can be partitioned so that each of the table partitions has a matching index partition. The matching index partitions are called *local indexes*. *See* Chapter 17.

LOCALTIMESTAMP

SEE ALSO DATE FUNCTIONS, Chapter 10

FORMAT

```
LOCALTIMESTAMP [( timestamp_precision )]
```

DESCRIPTION **LOCALTIMESTAMP** returns the current date and time in the session time zone as a value of datatype TIMESTAMP.

EXAMPLE

```
SELECT LOCALTIMESTAMP FROM DUAL;
```

LOCALLY MANAGED TABLESPACE

A locally managed tablespace maintains its extent usage information in bitmaps within the tablespace's datafiles. *See* **CREATE TABLESPACE**.

LOCK

To lock data is to temporarily restrict other users' access to data. The restriction that is placed on such data is called "a lock." Lock modes are SHARE, SHARE UPDATE, EXCLUSIVE, SHARE EXCLUSIVE, ROW SHARE, and ROW EXCLUSIVE. Not all locks can be acquired in all modes.

LOCK TABLE

SEE ALSO **COMMIT, DELETE, INSERT, ROLLBACK, SAVEPOINT, UPDATE**

FORMAT

```
LOCK TABLE
[schema.] { table | view }
[ { PARTITION ( partition ) | SUBPARTITION ( subpartition ) }
| @ dblink ]
[, [schema.] { table | view }
 [ { PARTITION ( partition ) | SUBPARTITION ( subpartition ) }
 | @ dblink ] ]...
IN lockmode MODE [NOWAIT];
```

DESCRIPTION **LOCK TABLE** locks a table in one of several specified modes, allowing it to be shared, but without loss of data integrity. Using **LOCK TABLE** allows you to give other users continued but restricted access to the table. Regardless of which option you choose, the table will remain in that lock mode until you **COMMIT** or **ROLLBACK** your transactions.

Lock modes include ROW SHARE, ROW EXCLUSIVE, SHARE UPDATE, SHARE, SHARE ROW EXCLUSIVE, and EXCLUSIVE.

EXCLUSIVE locks permit users to query the locked table but not to do anything else. No other user may lock the table. SHARED locks permit concurrent queries but no updates to the locked table.

With a ROW SHARE or SHARE UPDATE lock, no user can lock the whole table for exclusive access, allowing concurrent access for all users to the table. The two types of lock are synonymous, and SHARE UPDATE exists for compatibility with previous versions of Oracle.

ROW EXCLUSIVE locks are similar to ROW SHARE but they prohibit shared locking, so only one user may access the table at a time.

If a **LOCK TABLE** command cannot be completed (usually because someone else has executed a prior and competing **LOCK TABLE** of some sort), then your **LOCK TABLE** will wait until it can complete. If you wish to avoid this, and simply have control returned to you, use the **NOWAIT** option. Note that you can lock specific partitions and subpartitions.

LOG

SEE ALSO NUMBER FUNCTIONS, Chapter 9

FORMAT

```
LOG(base, number)
```

DESCRIPTION **LOG** gives the logarithm of a *number* for a specified *base*.

EXAMPLE

```
LOG(EXP(1),3) = 1.098612   -- log(e) of 3
LOG(10,100)   = 2          -- log(10) of 100
```

LOGICAL EXPRESSION

A logical expression is one whose value evaluates to either TRUE or FALSE. It is a synonym for CONDITION.

LOGICAL OPERATORS

SEE ALSO PRECEDENCE

FORMAT The following lists all current logical operators in the Oracle version of SQL. Most of these are listed elsewhere in this reference under their own names with their proper format and use. All of these operators work with columns or literals.

Logical Operators that Test a Single Value

```
=    expression    is equal to expression
>    expression    is greater than expression
>=   expression    is greater than or equal to expression
<    expression    is less than expression
<=   expression    is less than or equal to expression
!=   expression    is not equal to expression
^=   expression    is not equal to expression
<>   expression    is not equal to expression

EXISTS (query)
NOT EXISTS (query)

LIKE expression
NOT LIKE expression

expression IS NULL
expression IS NOT NULL
```

Logical Operators that Test More than a Single Value

```
ANY (expression [,expression]... | query)
ALL (expression [,expression]... | query)
```

ANY and **ALL** require an equality operator as a prefix, such as >**ANY**, =**ALL**, and so on.

```
IN (expression [,expression]... | query)
NOT IN (expression [,expression]... | query)
```

```
BETWEEN expression AND expression
NOT BETWEEN expression AND expression
```

Other Logical Operators

+	Addition
–	Subtraction
*	Multiplication
/	Division
**	Exponentiation
\|\|	Concatenation
()	Overrides normal precedence rules, or encloses a subquery
NOT	Reverses logical expression
AND	Combines logical expressions
OR	Combines logical expressions
UNION	Combines results of queries
UNION ALL	Combines results of queries without eliminating duplicates
INTERSECT	Combines results of queries
MINUS	Combines results of queries

LOGIN ACCOUNT

A login account is a username and password combination that allows people to use the Oracle RDBMS. This account is usually separate from your operating system account.

LOBSOURCE (SQL*Plus)

See **SET**.

LONG (SQL*Plus)

See **SET**.

LONG DATATYPE

See DATATYPES.

LONG RAW DATATYPE

A LONG RAW column contains raw binary data, but is otherwise the same as a LONG column. Values entered into LONG RAW columns must be in hex notation.

LOOP

You can use loops to process multiple records within a single PL/SQL block. PL/SQL supports three types of loops:

Simple loops	A loop that keeps repeating until an **EXIT** or **EXIT WHEN** statement is reached within the loop
FOR loops	A loop that repeats a specified number of times
WHILE loops	A loop that repeats until a condition is met

You can use loops to process multiple records from a cursor. The most common cursor loop is a cursor FOR loop. *See* CURSOR FOR LOOP and Chapter 29 for details on using loops for both simple and cursor-based processing logic.

LOWER

SEE ALSO CHARACTER FUNCTIONS, **INITCAP**, **UPPER**, Chapter 7

FORMAT

```
LOWER(string)
```

DESCRIPTION LOWER converts every letter in a string to lowercase.

EXAMPLE

```
LOWER('PeninSula') = peninsula
```

LPAD

SEE ALSO CHARACTER FUNCTIONS, **LTRIM**, **RPAD**, **RTRIM**, Chapter 7

FORMAT

```
LPAD(string,length [,'set'])
```

DESCRIPTION Left PAD makes a *string* a certain *length* by adding a certain *set* of characters to the left of the string. If *set* is not specified, the default pad character is a space.

EXAMPLE

```
LPAD('>',11,'- ')
```

produces

```
- - - - - >
```

LTRIM

SEE ALSO CHARACTER FUNCTIONS, **LPAD**, **RPAD**, **RTRIM**, Chapter 7

FORMAT

```
LTRIM(string [,'set'])
```

DESCRIPTION Left **TRIM** trims all the occurrences of any one of a *set* of characters off of the left side of a *string*.

EXAMPLE

```
LTRIM('NANCY','AN')
```

produces this:

```
CY
```

MAKE_REF

SEE ALSO Chapter 36

FORMAT

```
MAKE_REF ( table | view , key [,key] )
```

DESCRIPTION **MAKE_REF** constructs a **REF** (reference) from the foreign key of a table that references the base table of an object view. **MAKE_REF** allows you to construct references superimposed on existing foreign key relationships. *See* Chapter 36 for examples.

MATERIALIZED VIEW

You can use materialized views to pre-aggregate data and improve query performance. When you create a materialized view, Oracle creates a physical table to hold data that would usually be read via a view. When you create a materialized view, you specify the view's base query as well as a schedule for the refreshes of its data. You can then index the materialized view to enhance the performance of queries against it. As a result, you can provide data to your users in the format they need, indexed appropriately. *See* **CREATE MATERIALIZED VIEW** and Chapter 24.

MATERIALIZED VIEW LOG

When you refresh a materialized view, you can perform a full or incremental refresh. An incremental refresh, called a "fast" refresh, sends only the DML changes from the master table to the materialized view. To track changes to the master table for the materialized view, you must create a materialized view log. The materialized view log must be in the same schema as the master table for the materialized view. Fast refreshes are not available for complex materialized views. *See* **CREATE MATERIALIZED VIEW LOG** and Chapter 24.

MAX

SEE ALSO AGGREGATE FUNCTIONS, **COMPUTE**, **MIN**, Chapter 9
FORMAT

```
MAX([DISTINCT | ALL] value) [OVER analytic_clause]
```

DESCRIPTION **MAX** is the maximum of all *values* for a group of rows. **MAX** ignores **NULL** values. The **DISTINCT** option is not meaningful, since the maximum of all values is identical to the maximum of the distinct values.

MEDIA RECOVERY

Media recovery is recovery in the event of hardware failure that would prevent reading or writing of data and thus operation of the database. *See also* INSTANCE RECOVERY.

MEDIAN

SEE ALSO AVG, COUNT
FORMAT

```
MEDIAN ( expr ) [OVER (query_partition_clause)]
```

DESCRIPTION **MEDIAN** takes a numeric or datetime value and returns the middle value or an interpolated value that would be the middle value once the values are sorted. **NULL**s are ignored.

MERGE

SEE ALSO INSERT, **UPDATE**, Chapter 15

FORMAT
merge::=

merge_update_clause::=

merge_insert_clause::=

where_clause::=

→ WHERE → condition →

DESCRIPTION **MERGE** performs updates and inserts of a target table in a single command, based on a selected set of rows. You specify the conditions to determine whether an insert or update is performed on a row-by-row basis. *See* Chapter 15 for detailed examples.

NOTE
*Since **MERGE** performs queries, you can use hints.*

As of Oracle Database 10g, you can specify either the **UPDATE** or the **INSERT** operation, or both. Also, you can delete rows from the target table during the **UPDATE** operation.

METHOD

A method is a block of code. In reference to user-defined datatypes, a method is a block of PL/SQL code used to encapsulate the data access method for an object. Methods are specified as part of the datatype specification (*see* **CREATE TYPE**) and their body is specified as part of the **CREATE TYPE BODY** command. Users can execute methods on the datatypes for which the methods are defined. The constructor method created for each user-defined datatype is an example of a method. *See* Chapter 33 for examples of methods.

In Java, a method is a member of a class. You can call a class method and pass parameters to it for it to use when executing its commands. *See* Chapter 33 for examples.

MIN

SEE ALSO AGGREGATE FUNCTIONS, **COMPUTE**, **MAX**, Chapter 9

FORMAT

```
MIN([DISTINCT | ALL] value) [OVER (analytic_clause)]
```

DESCRIPTION **MIN** is the minimum of all *values* for a group of rows. **MIN** ignores **NULL** values. The **DISTINCT** option is not meaningful, since the minimum of all values is identical to the minimum of the distinct values.

MINUS

SEE ALSO **INTERSECT**, QUERY OPERATORS, TEXT SEARCH OPERATORS, **UNION**, Chapters 13 and 25

FORMAT

```
select
MINUS
select
```

within Oracle Text queries against CONTEXT indexes:

```
select column
  from TABLE
 where CONTAINS(Text,'text MINUS text') >0;
```

DESCRIPTION **MINUS** combines two queries. It returns only those rows from the first **SELECT** statement that are not produced by the second **SELECT** statement (the first **SELECT MINUS** the second **SELECT**). The number of columns and datatypes must be identical between **SELECT** statements, although the names of the columns do not need to be. The data, however, must be identical in the rows produced for the **MINUS** to reject them. *See* Chapter 13 for a discussion of the important differences and effects of **INTERSECT**, **MINUS**, and **UNION**.

Within text searches against CONTEXT indexes, **MINUS** tells the text search of two terms to subtract the score of the second term's search from the score of the first term's search before comparing the result to the threshold score.

MOD

SEE ALSO NUMBER FUNCTIONS, Chapter 9

FORMAT

```
MOD(value, divisor)
```

DESCRIPTION MOD divides a *value* by a *divisor*, and gives the remainder. **MOD**(23,6) = 5 means divide 23 by 6. The answer is 3 with 5 left over, so 5 is the result of the modulus. *value* and *divisor* can both be any real number, except that *divisor* cannot be 0.

EXAMPLES

```
MOD(100,10)    =  0
MOD(22,23)     = 22
MOD(10,3)      =  1
MOD(-30.23,7)  = -2.23
MOD(4.1,.3)    =  .2
```

The second example shows what **MOD** does whenever the divisor is larger than the dividend (the number being divided). It produces the dividend as a result. Also note this important case:

```
MOD(value,1)    = 0
```

if *value* is an integer. This is a good test to see if a number is an integer.

MODEL FUNCTIONS

Model functions are relevant only for interrow calculations and can be used only in the **MODEL** clause of the **SELECT** statement. They are nonrecursive. The model functions are **CV**, **ITERATION_NUMBER**, **PRESENTNNV**, **PRESENTV**, and **PREVIOUS**.

MONTHS_BETWEEN

SEE ALSO ADD_MONTHS, DATE FUNCTIONS, Chapter 10

FORMAT

```
MONTHS_BETWEEN(date2,date1)
```

DESCRIPTION MONTHS_BETWEEN gives *date2* minus *date1* in months. The result is usually not an integer.

MOUNT A DATABASE

To mount a database is to make it available to the database administrator.

MOUNT AND OPEN A DATABASE

To mount and open a database is to make it available to users.

MULTITHREADED SERVER

See SHARED SERVER.

NANVL

SEE ALSO LNNVL

FORMAT

```
NANVL ( m, n )
```

DESCRIPTION NANVL is useful only for floating-point numbers of type BINARY_FLOAT or BINARY_DOUBLE. Oracle will return an alternative value *n* if the input value *m* is not a number; otherwise it returns *m*.

NATURAL JOIN

A natural join joins two tables based on the key columns they have in common. The syntax is

```
FROM TableA NATURAL JOIN TableB
```

which is equivalent to

```
FROM TableA, TableB
WHERE TableA.KeyColumn = TableB.KeyColumn
```

See Chapter 13 for examples of different types of join syntax.

NCHAR

NCHAR is a multibyte version of the CHAR datatype. It stores fixed-length character data up to 2000 bytes in length. *See* DATATYPES.

NCHR

SEE ALSO CHR

FORMAT

```
NCHR(number)
```

DESCRIPTION NCHR returns the character having the binary equivalent to *number* in the national character set.

NCLOB

The NCLOB datatype is the multibyte version of the CLOB datatype. NCLOB stores character large objects containing Unicode characters, up to a maximum length of 4GB. *See* DATATYPES.

NEAR

SEE ALSO CONTAINS, Chapter 25

DESCRIPTION Within CONTEXT indexes, **NEAR** indicates that a proximity search should be executed for the specified text strings. If the search terms are 'summer' and 'lease', then a proximity search for the two terms could be

```
select Text
  from SONNET
 where CONTAINS(Text,'summer NEAR lease') >0;
```

When evaluating the text search results, text with the words 'summer' and 'lease' near each other in the text will have higher scores than text with the words 'summer' and 'lease' farther apart.

NESTED TABLE

A nested table is a table within a table. In this case, it is a table that is represented as a column within another table. You can have multiple rows in the nested table for each row in the main table. There is no limit to the number of entries per row. *See* Chapter 34 for details on creating, using, and querying nested tables.

NEWPAGE (SQL*Plus)

See SET.

NEW_TIME
See DATE FUNCTIONS.

NEXT_DAY
See DATE FUNCTIONS.

NEXTVAL
See PSEUDO-COLUMNS.

NLS_CHARSET_DECL_LEN
SEE ALSO NCHAR
FORMAT

```
NLS_CHARSET_DECL_LEN ( byte_count , char_set_id )
```

DESCRIPTION NLS_CHARSET_DECL_LEN returns the declaration width (in number of characters) of an NCHAR column.

NLS_CHARSET_ID
SEE ALSO NLS_CHARSET_NAME
FORMAT

```
NLS_CHARSET_ID ( text )
```

DESCRIPTION NLS_CHARSET_ID returns the character set ID number corresponding to the character set name *text*.

NLS_CHARSET_NAME
SEE ALSO NLS_CHARSET_ID
FORMAT

```
NLS_CHARSET_NAME ( number )
```

DESCRIPTION NLS_CHARSET_NAME returns the name of the character set corresponding to ID number *number*.

NLS_INITCAP
SEE ALSO CHARACTER FUNCTIONS, **INITCAP**, Chapter 7
FORMAT

```
NLS_INITCAP(number[, nls_parameters])
```

DESCRIPTION NLS_INITCAP is like the **INITCAP** function except with the addition of a parameter string. The *nls_parameters* string, enclosed in single quotation marks, gives a sort sequence for capitalizing special linguistic sequences. You would usually use **INITCAP** with the default sort sequence for the session, but this function lets you specify the exact sort sequence to use.

NLS_LOWER

SEE ALSO CHARACTER FUNCTIONS, **LOWER**, Chapter 7
FORMAT

```
NLS_LOWER(number[, nls_parameters])
```

DESCRIPTION NLS_LOWER is like the **LOWER** function except with the addition of a parameter string. The *nls_parameters* string, enclosed in single quotation marks, gives a sort sequence for lowercasing special linguistic sequences. You would usually use **LOWER** with the default sort sequence for the session, but this function lets you specify the exact sort sequence to use.

NLS_UPPER

SEE ALSO CHARACTER FUNCTIONS, **UPPER**, Chapter 7
FORMAT

```
NLS_UPPER(number[, nls_parameters])
```

DESCRIPTION NLS_UPPER is like the **UPPER** function except with the addition of a parameter string. The *nls_parameters* string, enclosed in single quotation marks, gives a sort sequence for capitalizing special linguistic sequences. You would usually use **UPPER** with the default sort sequence for the session, but this function lets you specify the exact sort sequence to use.

NLSSORT

SEE ALSO CREATE DATABASE
FORMAT

```
NLSSORT(character[, nls_parameters])
```

DESCRIPTION NLSSORT (National Language Support **SORT**) gives the collating sequence value (an integer) of the given *character* based on the National Language Support option chosen for the site. The *nls_parameters* string, enclosed in single quotation marks, gives a sort sequence for special linguistic sequences if you do not want to use the session or database default.

NOAUDIT

SEE ALSO AUDIT, PRIVILEGE
FORMAT
noaudit::=

sql_statement_clause::=

auditing_by_clause::=

schema_object_clause::=

auditing_on_clause::=

DESCRIPTION **NOAUDIT** stops auditing of SQL statements being audited as a result of the **AUDIT** command. It stops auditing either a statement (*see* **AUDIT**) or a statement authorized by a system privilege (*see* PRIVILEGE). If there is a **BY** clause with a list of users, the command stops the auditing of statements issued by these users. If there is no **BY** clause, Oracle stops auditing the statements for all users. The **WHENEVER SUCCESSFUL** option stops auditing only for those statements that successfully complete; **WHENEVER NOT SUCCESSFUL** stops only for those statements that result in an error.

 NOAUDIT also stops the audit for an option of the use of a table, view, or synonym. To stop the audit of any table, view, or synonym, you must either own them or have DBA authority. *option* refers to the options described shortly. *user* is the username of the object owner. *object* is a table, view, or synonym. *option* specifies what commands the audit should be stopped for. **ON** *object* names the object being audited, and includes a table, view, or synonym of a table, view, or sequence. **ALL** stops the audits of all commands on the object.

 See Chapter 42 for details on the auditing views in the data dictionary.

EXAMPLES The following stops auditing of all attempts at **UPDATE** or **DELETE** on the BOOKSHELF table:

```
noaudit update, delete on BOOKSHELF;
```

This stops auditing of all unsuccessful access to BOOKSHELF:

```
noaudit all on BOOKSHELF whenever not successful;
```

NODE

Node can be either of two definitions:

- In a tree-structured table, a node is one row.
- In a network, a node is the location in the network where a computer is attached.

NOLOGGING

The **NOLOGGING** clause for object creation (tables, LOBs, indexes, partitions, etc.) specifies that the creation of the object will not be logged in the online redo log files, and thus will not be recoverable following a media failure. The object creation is not logged, and neither are certain types of transactions against the object. *See* Chapters 21 and 46.

NON-EQUI-JOIN

A non-equi-join is a join condition other than "equals" (=). *See* EQUI-JOIN.

NOT

SEE ALSO LOGICAL OPERATORS, Chapter 5

DESCRIPTION **NOT** comes before and reverses the effect of any of these logical operators: **BETWEEN**, **IN**, **LIKE**, and **EXISTS**. **NOT** can also come before **NULL**, as in **IS NOT NULL**.

NOT EXISTS

SEE ALSO ALL, ANY, EXISTS, IN, Chapter 13

FORMAT

```
select ...
where NOT EXISTS (select...);
```

DESCRIPTION **NOT EXISTS** returns false in a **WHERE** clause if the subquery that follows it returns one or more rows. The **SELECT** clause in the subquery can be a column, a literal, or an asterisk—it doesn't matter. The only part that matters is whether the **WHERE** clause in the subquery will return a row.

EXAMPLE **NOT EXISTS** is frequently used to determine which records in one table do not have matching records in another table. *See* Chapter 13 for examples of the use of **NOT EXISTS**.

NTILE

SEE ALSO WIDTH_BUCKET

FORMAT

```
NTILE ( expr ) OVER ( [query_partition_clause] order_by_clause )
```

DESCRIPTION **NTILE** is an analytic function. It divides an ordered dataset into a number of buckets indicated by an expression and assigns the appropriate bucket number to each row. The buckets are numbered and the expression must resolve to a positive constant for each partition.

NULL (Form 1—PL/SQL)

SEE ALSO BLOCK STRUCTURE

FORMAT

```
NULL;
```

DESCRIPTION The **NULL** statement has nothing to do with **NULL** values. Its main purpose is to make a section of code more readable by saying, in effect, "do nothing." It also provides a means of having a null block (since PL/SQL requires at least one executable statement between **BEGIN** and **END**). It is usually used as the statement following one (usually the last) of a series of condition tests.

EXAMPLE

```
IF Age > 65 THEN
   ...
ELSEIF AGE BETWEEN 21 and 65 THEN
   ...
ELSE
 NULL;
ENDIF;
```

NULL (Form 2—SQL Column Value)

SEE ALSO AGGREGATE FUNCTIONS, **CREATE TABLE**, INDICATOR VARIABLE, **NVL**, Chapter 5

DESCRIPTION A **NULL** value is one that is unknown, irrelevant, or not meaningful. Any Oracle datatype can be **NULL**. That is, any Oracle column in a given row can be without a value (unless the table was created with **NOT NULL** for that column). **NULL** in a NUMBER datatype is not the same as zero.

Few procedural languages directly support the idea of a variable with a **NULL** or unknown value, although Oracle and SQL do so easily. In order to extend languages for which Oracle has developed precompilers to support the **NULL** concept, an INDICATOR VARIABLE is associated with the host variable, almost like a flag, to indicate whether it is **NULL**. The host variable and its indicator variable may be referenced and set separately in the host language code, but are always concatenated in SQL or PL/SQL.

You use the **NVL** function to detect the absence of a value for a column, and convert the **NULL** value into a real value of the datatype of the column. For instance, **NVL**(Name,'NOT KNOWN') converts a **NULL** value in the column Name into the words NOT KNOWN. For a non-**NULL** value (that is, where a name is present), the **NVL** function simply returns the name. **NVL** works similarly with NUMBERs and DATEs.

Except for **COUNT**(*) and **COMPUTE NUMBER**, aggregate functions ignore **NULL** values. Other functions return a **NULL** value when a **NULL** is present in the value or values they are evaluating:

```
NULL + 1066 is NULL.
LEAST(NULL,'A','Z') is NULL.
```

Since **NULL** represents an unknown value, two columns that are each **NULL** are not equal to each other. Therefore, the equal sign and other logical operators (except for **IS NULL** and **IS NOT NULL**) do not work with **NULL**. For example,

```
where Name = NULL
```

is not a valid **WHERE** clause. **NULL** requires the word **IS**:

```
where Name IS NULL
```

During **ORDER BY** sorts, **NULL** values always come first when the order is ascending, and last when it is descending.

When **NULL** values are stored in the database, they are represented with a single byte if they fall between two columns that have real values, and no bytes if they fall at the end of the row (last in the column definition in the **CREATE TABLE**). If some of the columns in a table are likely to often contain **NULL** values, those columns can be usefully grouped near the end of the **CREATE TABLE** column list; this will save a minor amount of disk space.

NULL values do not appear in indexes, except in the single case where all the values in a cluster key are **NULL**.

NULLIF

SEE ALSO **COALESCE**, **DECODE**, **NULL**, Chapter 16

FORMAT

```
NULLIF ( expr1 , expr2 )
```

DESCRIPTION **NULLIF** compares *expr1* and *expr2*. If they are equal, the function returns **NULL**. If they are not equal, the function returns *expr1*. You cannot specify the literal **NULL** for *expr1*.

The **NULLIF** function is logically equivalent to the following **CASE** expression:

```
CASE WHEN expr1 = expr2 THEN NULL
ELSE expr1 END
```

NUMBER DATATYPE

A NUMBER datatype is a standard Oracle datatype that may contain a number, with or without a decimal point and a sign. Valid values are 0, and positive and negative numbers. NUMBER datatypes are defined as having precision and scale. Precision can range from 1 to 38; scale can range from –84 to 127.

NUMBER FORMATS

SEE ALSO **COLUMN**, Chapter 9

DESCRIPTION These options work with both the **SET NUMFORMAT** and **COLUMN FORMAT** commands:

9999990	The count of nines and zeros determines the maximum digits that can be displayed.
999,999,999.99	Commas and decimals will be placed in the pattern shown.
999990	Displays trailing zeroes.
099999	Displays leading zeroes.
$99999	A dollar sign is placed in front of every number.
B99999	Displays a blank for the integer portion of a fixed-point number when the integer is zero.
99999MI	If the number is negative, a minus sign follows the number. The default is for the negative sign to be on left.

S9999	Returns leading + for positive values, – for negative values.
9999S	Returns trailing + for positive values, – for negative values.
99999PR	Negative numbers are displayed within < and >.
99D99	Displays the decimal in the position indicated.
9G999	Displays the group separator in the position shown.
C9999	Displays the ISO currency symbol in this position.
L999	Displays the local currency symbol in the position specified.
,	Displays a comma.
.	Displays a period.
9.999EEEE	The display will be in scientific notation (4 E's are required).
999V99	Multiplies number by 10n, where n is the number of digits to the right of V. 999V99 turns 1234 into 123400.
9999RN	Displays Roman numeral values, for integer values between 1 and 3999.
TM	Returns the smallest number of characters possible (text minimum).
U999	Returns the Euro or other dual currency symbol in the specified position.
X	Returns the hexadecimal value of the specified number of digits.

NUMBER FUNCTIONS

The following is an ordered list of all current single-value number functions in the Oracle version of SQL. Each of these is listed elsewhere in this reference under its own name, with its proper format and use. Each can be used as a regular SQL function as well as a PL/SQL function. *See* AGGREGATE FUNCTIONS and LIST FUNCTIONS.

Function	Definition
value1 + *value2*	Addition
value1 – *value2*	Subtraction
value1 * *value2*	Multiplication
value1 / *value2*	Division
ABS(*value*)	ABSolute *value*
ACOS(*value*)	Arc COSine of *value*, in radians
ASIN(*value*)	Arc SINe of *value*, in radians
ATAN(*value*)	Arc TANgent of *value*, in radians
ATAN2(*value1, value2*)	Arc TANgent of *value1* and *value2*, in radians
BITAND (*value1, value2*)	BITwise AND of *value1* and *value2*, both of which must resolve to nonnegative integers, and returns an integer
CEIL(*value*)	Numeric CEILing: the smallest integer larger than or equal to *value*
COS(*value*)	COSine of *value*
COSH(*value*)	Hyperbolic COSine of *value*
EXP(*value*)	*e* raised to *value* EXPonent

Function	Definition
FLOOR(*value*)	Largest integer smaller than or equal to *value*
LN(*value*)	Natural Logarithm of *value*
LOG(*value*)	Base 10 LOGarithm of *value*
MOD(*value, divisor*)	MODulus
NANVL(*value1,value2*)	For BINARY_FLOAT and BINARY_DOUBLE numbers, returns *value2* if *value1* is not a number
POWER(*value, exponent*)	*value* raised to an *exponent* POWER
REMAINDER(*value1,value2*)	Remainder of *value1* divided by *value2*
ROUND(*value, precision*)	ROUNDing of *value* to *precision*
SIGN(*value*)	1 if *value* is positive, –1 if negative, 0 if zero
SIN(*value*)	SINe of *value*
SINH(*value*)	Hyperbolic SINe of *value*
SQRT(*value*)	SQuare RooT of *value*
TAN(*value*)	TANgent of *value*
TANH(*value*)	Hyperbolic TANgent of *value*
TRUNC(*value, precision*)	*value* TRUNCated to *precision*
WIDTH_BUCKET(*expr,min,max,num*)	Constructs equal-width histograms

NUMTODSINTERVAL

SEE ALSO DATATYPES, Chapter 11
FORMAT

```
NUMTODSINTERVAL ( n , 'char_expr' )
```

DESCRIPTION **NUMTODSINTERVAL** converts *n* to an INTERVAL DAY TO SECOND literal. *n* can be a number or an expression resolving to a number. *char_expr* can be of CHAR, VARCHAR2, NCHAR, or NVARCHAR2 datatype. The value for *char_expr* specifies the unit of *n* and must resolve to one of the following string values: 'DAY', 'HOUR', 'MINUTE', or 'SECOND'.

NUMTOYMINTERVAL

SEE ALSO DATATYPES, Chapter 11
FORMAT

```
NUMTOYMINTERVAL ( n , 'char_expr' )
```

DESCRIPTION **NUMTOYMINTERVAL** converts number *n* to an INTERVAL YEAR TO MONTH literal. *n* can be a number or an expression resolving to a number. *char_expr* can be of CHAR, VARCHAR2, NCHAR, or NVARCHAR2 datatype. The value for *char_expr* specifies the unit of *n*, and must resolve to either 'YEAR' or 'MONTH'.

NUMWIDTH (SQL*Plus)

See **SET**.

NVARCHAR2

NVARCHAR2 is the multibyte equivalent of the VARCHAR2 datatype. Its maximum length is 4000 bytes. *See* DATATYPES.

NVL

SEE ALSO AGGREGATE FUNCTIONS, **NULL**, OTHER FUNCTIONS, Chapter 9
FORMAT

```
NVL(value, substitute)
```

DESCRIPTION If *value* is **NULL**, this function returns *substitute*. If *value* is not **NULL**, this function returns *value*. *value* can be any Oracle datatype. *substitute* can be a literal, another column, or an expression, but must be the same datatype as *value*.

NVL2

SEE ALSO AGGREGATE FUNCTIONS, **NULL**, OTHER FUNCTIONS, Chapter 9
FORMAT

```
NVL2 ( expr1 , expr2 , expr3 )
```

DESCRIPTION **NVL2** is an extended form of **NVL**. In **NVL2**, *expr1* can never be returned; either *expr2* or *expr3* will be returned. If *expr1* is not **NULL**, **NVL2** returns *expr2*. If *expr1* is **NULL**, **NVL2** returns *expr3*. The argument *expr1* can have any datatype. The arguments *expr2* and *expr3* can have any datatypes except LONG.

OBJECT NAMES

These database objects may be given names: tables, views, synonyms, aliases, columns, indexes, users, sequences, tablespaces, and so on. The following rules govern naming objects:

- The name of an object can be from 1 to 30 characters long, except for database names, which are up to eight characters, and host filenames, whose length is operating-system dependent.
- A name may not contain a quotation mark.
- A name must:
 Begin with a letter
 Contain only the characters A–Z, 0–9, $, #, and _
 Not be an Oracle reserved word (*see* RESERVED WORDS)
 Not duplicate the name of another database object owned by the same user

Object names are not case sensitive. Object names should follow a sensible naming convention.

OBJECT REFERENCE FUNCTIONS

Object reference functions manipulate REFs, which are references to objects of specified object types. The object reference functions are described under their individual entries in this reference. The functions are **DEREF**, **MAKE_REF**, **REF**, **REFTOHEX**, and **VALUE**.

OBJECT TABLE

An object table is a table in which each of its rows is a row object. *See* Chapter 36 and **CREATE TABLE**.

OBJECT VIEW

An object view superimposes abstract datatypes on existing relational tables. Object views allow you to access the relational table's data either via normal SQL commands or via its abstract datatype structures. Object views provide a technological bridge between relational and object-relational databases. *See* Chapters 33 and 36 for examples of object views.

OBJECT-RELATIONAL DATABASE MANAGEMENT SYSTEM

An object-relational database management system (ORDBMS) supports both relational database features (such as primary keys and foreign keys) and object-oriented features (such as inheritance and encapsulation). *See* Part I and Part V of this book for a description of Oracle's implementation of an ORDBMS.

OFFLINE BACKUP

An offline backup is a physical backup of the database files while the database is shut down.

OID

An OID is an object identifier, assigned by Oracle to each object in a database. For example, each row object within an object table has an OID value assigned to it; the OID is used to resolve references to the row objects. Oracle does not reuse OID values after an object is dropped. *See* Chapter 36.

ONLINE BACKUP

Online backup is the ability of Oracle to archive data while the database is still running. The DBA does not need to shut down the database to archive data. Even data currently being accessed can be archived.

ONLINE REDO LOG

Online redo logs are redo log files that are not yet archived. They may be available to the instance for recording activity, or have previously been written but are awaiting archiving.

OPEN

SEE ALSO CLOSE, DECLARE CURSOR, FETCH, LOOP, Chapter 29
FORMAT

```
OPEN cursor [(parameter[,parameter]...]
```

DESCRIPTION OPEN works in conjunction with **DECLARE CURSOR** and **FETCH**. **DECLARE CURSOR** sets up a **SELECT** statement to be executed, and establishes a list of parameters (PL/SQL variables) that are to be used in its **WHERE** clause, but it does not execute the query.

OPEN *cursor*, in effect, executes the query in the named cursor and keeps its results in a staging area, where they can be called in, a row at a time, with **FETCH**, and their column values put into local variables with the **INTO** clause of the **FETCH**. If the cursor **SELECT** statement used parameters, then their actual values are passed to the **SELECT** statement in the parameter list of the **OPEN** statement. They must match in number and position and have compatible datatypes.

There is also an alternative method of associating the values in the **OPEN** statement with those in the **SELECT** list:

```
DECLARE
    cursor mycur(Title, Publisher) is select ...
```

```
BEGIN
    open my_cur(new_book => Title, 'PANDORAS' => Publisher);
```

Here, *new_book*, a PL/SQL variable, loaded perhaps from a data entry screen, is pointed to Title, and therefore loads it with whatever is currently in the variable *new_book*. Publisher is loaded with the value 'PANDORAS', and these then become the parameters of the cursor *my_cur*. (*See* **DECLARE CURSOR** for more details on parameters in cursors.)

You also may combine pointed associations with positional ones, but the positional ones must appear first in the **OPEN** statement's list.

You cannot reopen an open cursor, though you can **CLOSE** it and re**OPEN** it, and you cannot use a cursor for which you have a current **OPEN** statement in a CURSOR FOR LOOP.

OPEN CURSOR (Embedded SQL)

SEE ALSO CLOSE, DECLARE CURSOR, FETCH, PREPARE, *Programmer's Guide to the Oracle Precompilers*

FORMAT

```
EXEC SQL  [FOR { integer | :array_size }]
OPEN cursor
  [USING
   {DESCRIPTOR SQLDBA_descriptor
   | :variable[[ INDICATOR ]:indicator_variable
   [,:variable[ INDICATOR ]:indicator_variable]]... }]
```

DESCRIPTION *cursor* is the name of a cursor previously named in a **DECLARE CURSOR** statement. The optional **USING** references either the host variable list of variables that are to be substituted in the statement in the **DECLARE CURSOR**, based on position (the number and type of variables must be the same), or a descriptor name that references the result of a previous **DESCRIBE**.

OPEN *cursor* allocates a cursor, defines the active set of rows (the host variables are substituted when the cursor is opened), and positions the cursor just before the first row of the set. No rows are retrieved until a **FETCH** is executed. Host variables do not change once they've been substituted. To change them, you must reopen the cursor (you don't have to **CLOSE** it first).

NOTE
See the Programmer's Guide to the Oracle Precompilers *for a full list of all commands. This reference does not contain all of the possible precompiler commands.*

OPERATOR

An operator is a character or reserved word used in an expression to perform an operation, such as addition or comparison, on the elements of the expression. Some examples of operators are * (multiplication), > (greater than comparison), and **ANY** (compares a value to each value returned by a subquery).

OPS$ LOGINS

OPS$ LOGINS are a type of Oracle username in which OPS$ is prefixed to the user's operating system account ID, to simplify logging into Oracle from that ID.

OPTIMIZER

An optimizer is the part of an Oracle kernel that chooses the best way to use the tables and indexes to complete the request made by a SQL statement. *See* Chapter 43.

OR

SEE ALSO AND, **CONTAINS**, Chapters 5 and 25

DESCRIPTION **OR** combines logical expressions so that the result is TRUE if either logical expression is true.

EXAMPLE The following will produce data for both KEENE and SAN FRANCISCO:

```
select * from COMFORT
 where City = 'KEENE' OR City = 'SAN FRANCISCO'
```

Within CONTEXT queries, an **OR** operator can be used for searches involving multiple search terms. If either of the search terms is found, and its search score exceeds the specified threshold value, the text will be returned by the search. *See* Chapter 25.

ORACLE ENTERPRISE MANAGER

Oracle Enterprise Manager (OEM) is a product from Oracle Corporation. OEM provides a graphical interface for common DBA tasks, including features for performance tuning and data management functions. OEM provides a web-based interface to all of the grid components, including the ASM diskgroups.

ORACLE REAL APPLICATION CLUSTERS

In an Oracle Real Application Clusters (RAC) environment, multiple instances (usually on a cluster of servers) access a single set of datafiles. RAC provides server failover capability in a high-availability environment, since users can be directed to multiple servers to access the same data.

ORACLE APPLICATION SERVER 10*g*

Oracle Application Server 10*g* allows developers to access Oracle databases from Web-based applications. The developers call procedures from within the database. The procedures, in turn, retrieve or manipulate data and return results to the developers. *See* Chapter 45.

ORA_HASH

FORMAT

```
ORA_HASH ( expr [, max_bucket [,seed_value] ])
```

DESCRIPTION ORA_HASH computes a hash value for a given expression. This function is useful for operations such as analyzing a subset of data and generating a random sample. *expr* is the data for which Oracle will compute a hash value (usually a column name). *max_bucket* determines the maximum bucket value (0 to 4294967295). The *seed_value* argument (0 to 4294967295) enables Oracle to produce different results with the same *expr*.

ORDBMS

See OBJECT-RELATIONAL DATABASE MANAGEMENT SYSTEM.

ORDER BY

SEE ALSO COLLATION, **FROM**, **GROUP BY**, **HAVING**, **SELECT**, **WHERE**, Chapter 5

FORMAT

```
ORDER BY { expression [,expression]... |
           position [,position]... }
           alias [,alias]... }
[ ASC | DESC ]
```

DESCRIPTION The **ORDER BY** clause causes Oracle to sort the results of a query before they are displayed. This can be done either by *expression*, which can be a simple column name or a complex set of functions, an *alias* (*see* Note below), or a column *position* in the **SELECT** clause (*see* Note below). Rows are ordered first by the first expression or position, then by the second, and so on, based on the collating sequence of the host. If **ORDER BY** is not specified, the order in which rows are selected from a table is indeterminate, and may change from one query to the next.

NOTE
*Oracle still supports the use of column positions in **ORDER BY** clauses, but this feature is no longer part of the SQL standard and is not guaranteed to be supported in future releases. Use column aliases instead.*

ASC or **DESC** specifies ascending or descending order, and may follow each expression, position, or alias in the **ORDER BY** clause. **NULL** values precede ascending and follow descending rows in Oracle.
 ORDER BY follows any other clauses except **FOR UPDATE OF**.
 If **ORDER BY** and **DISTINCT** are both specified, the **ORDER BY** clause may refer only to columns or expressions that are in the **SELECT** clause.
 When the **UNION**, **INTERSECT**, or **MINUS** operator is used, the names of the columns in the first **SELECT** may differ from the names in subsequent **SELECT**s. **ORDER BY** must use the column name from the first **SELECT**.
 Only CHAR, VARCHAR2, NUMBER, and DATE datatypes—and the special datatype ROWID—can appear in an **ORDER BY** clause.
EXAMPLE

```
select Title, Publisher from BOOKSHELF
  order by Title;
```

OTHER FUNCTIONS

This is an alphabetical list of all current functions in the Oracle version of SQL that do not readily fall into any other function category. Each of these is listed elsewhere in this reference under its own name, with its proper format and use.
 BFILENAME, COALESCE, CV, DECODE, DEPTH, DUMP, EMPTY_BLOB, EMPTY_CLOB, EXISTSNODE, EXTRACT, EXTRACTVALUE, GREATEST, LEAST, LNNVL, NLS_CHARSET_DECL_LEN, NLS_CHARSET_ID, NLS_CHARSET_NAME, NULLIF, NVL, NVL2, ORA_HASH, PATH, PRESENTNNV, PRESENTV, PREVIOUS, SYS_CONNECT_BY_PATH, SYS_CONTEXT, SYS_DBURIGEN, SYS_EXTRACT_UTC, SYS_GUID, SYS_TYPEID, SYS_XMLAGG, SYS_XMLGEN, UID, UPDATEXML, USER, USERENV, VSIZE, XMLAGG, XMLCOLATTVAL, XMLCONCAT, XMLFOREST, XMLSEQUENCE, XMLTRANSFORM

OUTER JOIN

See JOIN for a detailed explanation. As of Oracle9*i*, you can use the ANSI standard outer join syntax options (LEFT OUTER JOIN, RIGHT OUTER JOIN, and FULL OUTER JOIN). *See* Chapter 13 for details and examples.

PACKAGE

A package is a PL/SQL object that groups PL/SQL types, variables, SQL cursors, exceptions, procedures, and functions. Each package has a specification and a body. The specification shows the objects you can access when you use the package. The body fully defines all the objects and can contain additional objects used only for the internal workings. You can change the body (for example, by adding procedures to the package) without invalidating any object that uses the package.

See **CREATE PACKAGE**, **CREATE PACKAGE BODY**, CURSOR, EXCEPTION, FUNCTION, TABLE (PL/SQL), RECORD (PL/SQL), PROCEDURE, and Chapter 31.

PAGESIZE (SQL*Plus)

See **SET**.

PARAMETER

A parameter is a value, a column name, or an expression, usually following a function or module name, specifying additional functions or controls that should be observed by the function or module. See PARAMETERS for an example.

PARAMETERS

SEE ALSO &, &&, ACCEPT, DEFINE

DESCRIPTION Parameters allow the execution of a start file with values passed on the SQL*Plus command line. These are simply spaced apart following the name of the start file. Within the file, parameters are referenced by the order in which they appeared on the command line. &1 is the first, &2 the second, and so on. Aside from this rule, the rules for use are the same as for variables loaded using **DEFINE** or **ACCEPT**, and they may be used in SQL statements in the same way.

There is one limitation, however. There is no way to pass a multiple-word argument to a single variable. Each variable can take only one word, date, or number. Attempting to solve this by putting the parameters in quotes on the command line results in the words being concatenated.

EXAMPLE Suppose you have a start file named fred.sql that contains this SQL:

```
select Title, Publisher
  from BOOKSHELF
 where Title > &1;
```

Starting it with this command line:

```
start fred.sql M
```

produces a report of all titles that start with a character > 'M'.

PARENT

In tree-structured data, a parent is a node that has another node as a descendent, or child.

PARENT QUERY

The parent query is the outermost query (the one that displays a result) in a main query containing a subquery.

PARENTHESES

See LOGICAL OPERATORS and RESERVED WORDS.

PARSE

Parsing is the mapping of a SQL statement to a cursor. At parse time, several validation checks are made, such as whether all referenced objects exist, whether grants are proper, and whether statement syntax is correct. Also, decisions regarding execution and optimization are made, such as which indexes will be used.

PASSWORD (SQL*Plus)

SEE ALSO **ALTER USER**, Chapter 18

FORMAT

```
PASSW[ORD] [username]
```

DESCRIPTION You can use the **PASSWORD** command in SQL*Plus to change the password on your account or another account (if you have ALTER ANY USER privilege). If you use the **PASSWORD** command, your new password will not be displayed on the screen as you type. Users with DBA authority can change any user's password via the **PASSWORD** command; other users can change only their own password.

When you enter the **PASSWORD** command, you will be prompted for the old and new passwords.

EXAMPLE

```
password
Changing password for dora
Old password:
New password:
Retype new password:
```

When the password has been successfully changed, you will receive the feedback:

```
Password changed
```

PARALLEL QUERY OPTION

The Parallel Query Option (PQO) splits a single database task into multiple coordinated tasks, enabling the task to use multiple processors. For example, a full table scan or a large sort may be parallelized, enabling multiple processors to take part in the completion of the operation. If there are adequate resources available on the server, then the parallelized operation may complete faster than if it were to run as a single task.

The number of parallel query server processes used to execute an operation is called the *degree of parallelism*, and is set via the **DEGREE** parameter of hints. *See* Chapter 43.

PARTITION

To partition a table is to systematically divide its rows among multiple tables, each with the same structure. You can direct the database to automatically partition a table and its indexes. *See* Chapter 17.

PARTITIONED TABLE

A partitioned table is a table whose rows have been partitioned across multiple smaller tables.

PATH

SEE ALSO DEPTH

FORMAT

 PATH (*correlation_integer*)

DESCRIPTION **PATH** is an ancillary function used only with the **UNDER_PATH** and **EQUALS_PATH** conditions. It returns the relative path that leads to the resource specified in the parent condition. The *correlation_integer* value can be any NUMBER integer. Values less than 1 are treated as 1.

PAUSE (Form 1—SQL*Plus)

See **SET**.

PAUSE (Form 2—SQL*Plus)

SEE ALSO **ACCEPT**, **PROMPT**, Chapter 6

FORMAT

PAU[SE] [*text*];

DESCRIPTION **PAUSE** is similar to **PROMPT**, except **PAUSE** first displays an empty line, then a line containing *text*, then waits for the user to press RETURN. If *text* is not entered, **PAUSE** displays two empty lines, then waits for user to press RETURN.

> **NOTE**
> *PAUSE waits for a* RETURN *from the terminal even if the source of command input has been redirected to be from a file, which means a start file with SET TERMOUT OFF could hang, waiting for a* RETURN, *with no message as to why it was waiting (or that it was waiting). Use* **PAUSE** *with caution.*

EXAMPLE

```
prompt Report Complete.
pause Press RETURN to continue.
```

PCTFREE

PCTFREE is a portion of the data block that is not filled by rows as they are inserted into a table, but is reserved for later updates made to the rows in that block.

PCTUSED

PCTUSED is the percentage of space in a data block that Oracle attempts to keep filled. If the percent used falls below **PCTUSED**, then a block is added to the list of free blocks in the segment. **PCTUSED** may be set on a table-by-table basis.

PERCENT_RANK

SEE ALSO AGGREGATE FUNCTIONS, Chapter 12

FORMAT For aggregates:

```
PERCENT_RANK ( expr [, expr]... ) WITHIN GROUP
( ORDER BY
  expr [ DESC | ASC ] [NULLS { FIRST | LAST }]
  [, expr [ DESC | ASC ] [NULLS { FIRST | LAST }]]...)
```

For analytics:

```
PERCENT_RANK ( ) OVER ( [query_partition_clause] order_by_clause )
```

DESCRIPTION As an aggregate function, **PERCENT_RANK** calculates, for a hypothetical row R identified by the arguments of the function and a corresponding sort specification, the rank of row R minus 1 divided by the number of rows in the aggregate group. This calculation is made as if the hypothetical row R were inserted into the group of rows over which Oracle is to aggregate. The arguments of the function identify a single hypothetical row within each aggregate group. Therefore, they must all evaluate to constant expressions within each aggregate group. The constant argument expressions and the expressions in the **ORDER BY** clause of the aggregate match by position. Therefore, the number of arguments must be the same and their types must be compatible.

The range of values returned by **PERCENT_RANK** is 0 to 1, inclusive. The first row in any set has a **PERCENT_RANK** of 0.

As an analytic function, for a row R, **PERCENT_RANK** calculates the rank of R minus 1, divided by 1 less than the number of rows being evaluated (the entire query result set or a partition).

See Chapter 12 for an example of the use of **PERCENT_RANK**.

PERCENTILE_CONT

SEE ALSO AGGREGATE FUNCTIONS, **PERCENTILE_DISC**, Chapter 12

FORMAT

```
PERCENTILE_CONT ( expr ) WITHIN GROUP ( ORDER BY expr [ DESC | ASC ] )
[OVER ( query_partition_clause )]
```

DESCRIPTION **PERCENTILE_CONT** is an inverse distribution function that assumes a continuous distribution model. It takes a percentile value and a sort specification, and returns an interpolated value that would fall into that percentile value with respect to the sort specification. Nulls are ignored in the calculation.

The first *expr* must evaluate to a numeric value between 0 and 1, because it is a percentile value. This *expr* must be constant within each aggregation group. The **ORDER BY** clause takes a single expression that must be a numeric or datetime value, as these are the types over which Oracle can perform interpolation.

PERCENTILE_DISC

SEE ALSO AGGREGATE FUNCTIONS, **PERCENTILE_CONT**, Chapter 12

FORMAT

```
PERCENTILE_DISC ( expr ) WITHIN GROUP ( ORDER BY expr [ DESC | ASC ] )
[OVER ( query_partition_clause )]
```

DESCRIPTION **PERCENTILE_DISC** is an inverse distribution function that assumes a discrete distribution model. It takes a percentile value and a sort specification and returns an element from the set. Nulls are ignored in the calculation.

The first *expr* must evaluate to a numeric value between 0 and 1, because it is a percentile value. This expression must be constant within each aggregate group. The **ORDER BY** clause takes a single expression that can be of any type that can be sorted.

For a given percentile value P, **PERCENTILE_DISC** function sorts the values of the expression in the **ORDER BY** clause, and returns the one with the smallest **CUME_DIST** value (with respect to the same sort specification) that is greater than or equal to P.

PMON PROCESS

The Process Monitor (PMON) is a background process used for recovery when a process accessing a database fails. *See* BACKGROUND PROCESS.

POWER

SEE ALSO **SQRT**, Chapter 9

FORMAT

```
POWER(value,exponent)
```

DESCRIPTION **POWER** is *value* raised to an *exponent*.

POWERMULTISET

SEE ALSO Chapter 34

FORMAT

```
POWERMULTISET ( expr )
```

DESCRIPTION **POWERMULTISET** takes as input a nested table and returns a nested table of nested tables containing all nonempty subsets (called submultisets) of the input nested table. *expr* can be any expression that evaluates to a nested table; if that nested table is empty, an error is returned.

POWERMULTISET_BY_CARDINALITY

SEE ALSO **POWERMULTISET**

FORMAT

```
POWERMULTISET ( expr, cardinality )
```

DESCRIPTION **POWERMULTISET_BY_CARDINALITY** takes as input a nested table and returns a nested table of nested tables containing all nonempty subsets (called submultisets) of the input nested table of the specified cardinality. *expr* can be any expression that evaluates to a nested table, and *cardinality* can be any positive integer; if that nested table is empty, an error is returned.

PRAGMA

A pragma statement is a directive to the compiler, rather than a piece of executable code. Even though a pragma statement looks like executable code and appears in a program (such as a PL/SQL block), it is not actually executable and doesn't appear as a part of the execution code of that block. Rather, it gives instructions to the compiler. *See* **EXCEPTION_INIT**.

PRECEDENCE

SEE ALSO LOGICAL OPERATORS, QUERY OPERATORS, Chapter 13

DESCRIPTION The following operators are listed in descending order of precedence. Operators with equal precedence are on the same line. Operators of equal precedence are evaluated in succession from left to right. All **AND**s are evaluated before any **OR**. Each of these is listed and described separately under its own symbol or name in this Alphabetical Reference.

Operator	Function
-	SQL*Plus command continuation. Continues a command on the following line.
&	Prefix for parameters in a SQL*Plus start file. Words are substituted for &1, &2, and so on. *See* **START**.
& &&	Prefix for a substitution in a SQL command in SQL*Plus. SQL*Plus will prompt for a value if an undefined & or && variable is found. && also defines the variable and saves the value; & does not. *See* **&** and **&&**, **DEFINE**, and **ACCEPT**.
:	Prefix for a host variable in PL/SQL.
.	Variable separator, used in SQL*Plus to separate the variable name from a suffix, so that the suffix is not considered a part of the variable name.
()	Surrounds subqueries or lists of columns.
'	Surrounds a literal, such as a character string or date constant. To use a ' in a string constant, use two ' marks (not a double quotation mark).
"	Surrounds a table or column alias that contains special characters or a space.
"	Surrounds literal text in a date format clause of **TO_CHAR**.
@	Precedes a database name in a **COPY**, or a link name in a **FROM** clause.
()	Overrides normal operator precedence.
+ -	Prefix sign (positive or negative) for a number or number expression.
* /	Multiplication and division.
+ -	Addition and subtraction.
‖	Char value concatenation.
NOT	Reverses result of an expression.
AND	Returns TRUE if both conditions are true.
OR	Returns TRUE if either condition is true.
UNION	Returns all distinct rows from both of two queries.
INTERSECT	Returns all matching distinct rows from two queries.
MINUS	Returns all distinct rows in the first query that are not in the second.

PRECOMPILER

A precompiler program reads specially structured source code, and writes a modified (precompiled) source program file that a normal compiler can read.

PREDICATE

The predicate is the **WHERE** clause and, more explicitly, a selection criteria clause based on one of the operators (=, !=, **IS**, **IS NOT**, >, >=) and containing no **AND**, **OR**, or **NOT**.

PREPARE (Embedded SQL)

SEE ALSO **CLOSE**, CURSOR, **DECLARE**, **FETCH**, **OPEN**, *Programmer's Guide to the Oracle Precompilers*

FORMAT

```
EXEC SQL [AT { db_name | :host_variable }] PREPARE statement_id
  FROM { :host_string | 'text' | select_command }
```

DESCRIPTION **PREPARE** parses SQL in the host variable *:host_string* or the literal *text*. It assigns a *statement_id* as a reference to the SQL. If the *statement_id* has been used previously, this reference replaces it. The SQL is a **SELECT** statement, and may include a **FOR UPDATE OF** clause. *:host_string* is not the actual name of the host variable used, but a placeholder. **OPEN CURSOR** assigns input host variables in its **USING** clause, and **FETCH** assigns output host variables in its **INTO** clause, based on position. A statement needs to be **PREPARE**d only once. It can then be executed multiple times.

NOTE
See the Programmer's Guide to the Oracle Precompilers *for a full list of all commands. This reference does not contain all of the possible precompiler commands.*

EXAMPLE

```
query_string : string(1..100)
get(query_string);
EXEC SQL prepare FRED from :query_string;
EXEC SQL execute FRED;
```

PRESENTNNV

SEE ALSO PRESENTV

FORMAT

```
PRESENTNNV ( cell_reference, expr1, expr2 )
```

DESCRIPTION **PRESENTNNV** is relevant only for interrow calculations. It can be used only in the **MODEL** clause of the **SELECT** statement and then only on the right side of a model rule. It returns *expr1* when, prior to the execution of the **MODEL** clause, *cell_reference* exists and is not null. Otherwise it returns *expr2*.

PRESENTV

SEE ALSO PRESENTNNV

FORMAT

```
PRESENTV ( cell_reference, expr1, expr2 )
```

DESCRIPTION **PRESENTV** is relevant only for interrow calculations. It can be used only in the **MODEL** clause of the **SELECT** statement and then only on the right side of a model rule. It returns *expr1* when, prior to the execution of the **MODEL** clause, *cell_reference* exists (but may be null). Otherwise it returns *expr2*.

PREVIOUS

SEE ALSO ITERATION_NUMBER

FORMAT

```
PREVIOUS ( cell_reference )
```

DESCRIPTION **PREVIOUS** is relevant only for interrow calculations. It can be used only in the **MODEL** clause of the **SELECT** statement and then only in the **ITERATE ... [UNTIL]** clause of the **MODEL RULES** clause. It returns the value of *cell_reference* at the beginning of each iteration.

PRIMARY KEY

The primary key is the column(s) used to uniquely identify each row of a table.

PRINT

SEE ALSO BIND VARIABLE, **VARIABLE**, Chapter 29

FORMAT

```
PRI[NT] [variable...]
```

DESCRIPTION **PRINT** displays the current value of the specified variable (which is created via the **VARIABLE** command). You can print the current values of multiple variables in a single command.

PRIOR

See CONNECT BY.

PRIVILEGE

A privilege is a permission granted to an Oracle user to execute some action. In Oracle, no user can execute any action without having the privilege to do so.

There are two kinds of privileges: system privileges and object privileges. System privileges extend permission to execute various data definition and data control commands, such as **CREATE TABLE** and **ALTER USER**, or even to log onto the database. Object privileges extend permission to operate on a particular named database object.

System privileges in Oracle include CREATE, ALTER, and DROP privileges for the various **CREATE**, **ALTER**, and **DROP** commands. Privileges with the keyword **ANY** in them mean that the user can exercise the privilege on any schema for which the privilege has been granted, not just his or her own schema. The standard privileges in the list following just give permission to execute the indicated command, and don't require further explanation. Some of the privileges aren't intuitively clear; these are explained here. System privileges include:

Privilege	Permission to
TUNING	
ADVISOR	Access the advisor framework through PL/SQL packages including DBMS_ADVISOR and DBMS_SQLTUNE.
ADMINISTER SQL TUNING SET	Create, drop, select, load, and delete a SQL tuning set owned by the grantee through the DBMS_SQLTUNE package.
ADMINISTER ANY SQL TUNING SET	Create, drop, select, load, and delete a SQL tuning set owned by any user through the DBMS_SQLTUNE package.

Privilege	Permission to
CREATE ANY SQL PROFILE	Accept a SQL profile recommended by the tuning advisor.
DROP ANY SQL PROFILE	Drop an existing SQL profile.
ALTER ANY SQL PROFILE	Alter the attributes of an existing SQL profile.
CLUSTERS	
CREATE CLUSTER	Create clusters in grantee's schema.
CREATE ANY CLUSTER	Create a cluster in any schema. Behaves similarly to **CREATE ANY TABLE**.
ALTER ANY CLUSTER	Alter clusters in any schema.
DROP ANY CLUSTER	Drop clusters in any schema.
CONTEXTS	
CREATE ANY CONTEXT	Create any context namespace.
DROP ANY CONTEXT	Drop any context namespace.
DATABASE	
ALTER DATABASE	Alter the database.
ALTER SYSTEM	Issue **ALTER SYSTEM** statements.
AUDIT SYSTEM	Issue **AUDIT** statements.
DATABASE LINKS	
CREATE DATABASE LINK	Create private database links in grantee's schema.
CREATE PUBLIC DATABASE LINK	Create public database links.
DROP PUBLIC DATABASE LINK	Drop public database links.
DEBUGGING	
DEBUG CONNECT SESSION	Connect the current session to a debugger.
DEBUG ANY PROCEDURE	Debug all PL/SQL and Java code in any database object. Display information on all SQL statements executed by the application.
DIMENSIONS	
CREATE DIMENSION	Create dimensions in the grantee's schema.
CREATE ANY DIMENSION	Create dimensions in any schema.
ALTER ANY DIMENSION	Alter dimensions in any schema.
DROP ANY DIMENSION	Drop dimensions in any schema.
DIRECTORIES	
CREATE ANY DIRECTORY	Create directory database objects.
DROP ANY DIRECTORY	Drop directory database objects.
INDEXTYPES	
CREATE INDEXTYPE	Create an indextype in the grantee's schema.
CREATE ANY INDEXTYPE	Create an indextype in any schema.

Privilege	Permission to
ALTER ANY INDEXTYPE	Modify indextypes in any schema.
DROP ANY INDEXTYPE	Drop an indextype in any schema.
EXECUTE ANY INDEXTYPE	Reference an indextype in any schema.
INDEXES	
CREATE ANY INDEX	Create in any schema a domain index or an index on any table in any schema.
ALTER ANY INDEX	Alter indexes in any schema.
DROP ANY INDEX	Drop indexes in any schema.
JOB SCHEDULER OBJECTS	
CREATE JOB	Create jobs, schedulers, or programs in the grantee's schema (using DBMS_SCHEDULER).
CREATE ANY JOB	Create, alter, or drop jobs, schedules, or programs in any schema.
EXECUTE ANY PROGRAM	Use any program in a job in the grantee's schema.
EXECUTE ANY CLASS	Specify any job class in a job in the grantee's schema.
MANAGE SCHEDULER	Create, alter, or drop any job class, window, or window group.
LIBRARIES	
CREATE LIBRARY	Create external procedure/function libraries in grantee's schema.
CREATE ANY LIBRARY	Create external procedure/function libraries in any schema.
DROP ANY LIBRARY	Drop external procedure/function libraries in any schema.
MATERIALIZED VIEWS	
CREATE MATERIALIZED VIEW	Create a materialized view in the grantee's schema.
CREATE ANY MATERIALIZED VIEW	Create materialized views in any schema.
ALTER ANY MATERIALIZED VIEW	Alter materialized views in any schema.
DROP ANY MATERIALIZED VIEW	Drop materialized views in any schema.
QUERY REWRITE	This privilege has been deprecated.
GLOBAL QUERY REWRITE	Enable rewrite using a materialized view when that materialized view references tables or views in any schema.
ON COMMIT REFRESH	Create a refresh-on-commit materialized view on any table in the database. Alter a refresh-on-demand materialized view on any table in the database to refresh-on-commit.
FLASHBACK ANY TABLE	Issue a FLASHBACK QUERY on any table, view, or materialized view in any schema.
OPERATORS	
CREATE OPERATOR	Create an operator and its bindings in the grantee's schema.
CREATE ANY OPERATOR	Create an operator and its bindings in any schema.
ALTER ANY OPERATOR	Modify an operator in any schema.

Privilege	Permission to
DROP ANY OPERATOR	Drop an operator in any schema.
EXECUTE ANY OPERATOR	Reference an operator in any schema.

OUTLINES

CREATE ANY OUTLINE	Create public outlines that can be used in any schema that uses outlines.
ALTER ANY OUTLINE	Modify outlines.
DROP ANY OUTLINE	Drop outlines.

PROCEDURES

CREATE PROCEDURE	Create stored procedures, functions, and packages in grantee's schema.
CREATE ANY PROCEDURE	Create stored procedures, functions, and packages in any schema.
ALTER ANY PROCEDURE	Alter stored procedures, functions, or packages in any schema.
DROP ANY PROCEDURE	Drop stored procedures, functions, or packages in any schema.
EXECUTE ANY PROCEDURE	Execute procedures or functions (stand-alone or packaged). Reference public package variables in any schema.

PROFILES

CREATE PROFILE	Create profiles.
ALTER PROFILE	Alter profiles.
DROP PROFILE	Drop profiles.

ROLES

CREATE ROLE	Create roles.
ALTER ANY ROLE	Alter any role in the database.
DROP ANY ROLE	Drop roles.
GRANT ANY ROLE	Grant any role in the database.

ROLLBACK SEGMENTS

CREATE ROLLBACK SEGMENT	Create rollback segments.
ALTER ROLLBACK SEGMENT	Alter rollback segments.
DROP ROLLBACK SEGMENT	Drop rollback segments.

SEQUENCES

CREATE SEQUENCE	Create sequences in grantee's schema.
CREATE ANY SEQUENCE	Create sequences in any schema.
ALTER ANY SEQUENCE	Alter any sequence in the database.
DROP ANY SEQUENCE	Drop sequences in any schema.
SELECT ANY SEQUENCE	Reference sequences in any schema.

SESSIONS

CREATE SESSION	Connect to the database.

Privilege	Permission to
ALTER RESOURCE COST	Set costs for session resources.
ALTER SESSION	Issue **ALTER SESSION** statements.
RESTRICTED SESSION	Log on after the instance is started using the SQL*Plus **STARTUP RESTRICT** statement.

SYNONYMS

Privilege	Permission to
CREATE SYNONYM	Create synonyms in grantee's schema.
CREATE ANY SYNONYM	Create private synonyms in any schema.
CREATE PUBLIC SYNONYM	Create public synonyms.
DROP ANY SYNONYM	Drop private synonyms in any schema.
DROP PUBLIC SYNONYM	Drop public synonyms.

TABLES

Privilege	Permission to
CREATE TABLE	Create tables in grantee's schema.
CREATE ANY TABLE	Create tables in any schema. The owner of the schema containing the table must have space quota on the tablespace to contain the table.
ALTER ANY TABLE	Alter any table or view in any schema.
BACKUP ANY TABLE	Use the Export utility to incrementally export objects from the schema of other users.
DELETE ANY TABLE	Delete rows from tables, table partitions, or views in any schema.
DROP ANY TABLE	Drop or truncate tables or table partitions in any schema.
INSERT ANY TABLE	Insert rows into tables and views in any schema.
LOCK ANY TABLE	Lock tables and views in any schema.
SELECT ANY TABLE	Query tables, views, or materialized views in any schema.
FLASHBACK ANY TABLE	Issue a flashback query on any table, view, or materialized view in any schema.
UPDATE ANY TABLE	Update rows in tables and views in any schema.

TABLESPACES

Privilege	Permission to
CREATE TABLESPACE	Create tablespaces.
ALTER TABLESPACE	Alter tablespaces.
DROP TABLESPACE	Drop tablespaces.
MANAGE TABLESPACE	Take tablespaces offline and online and begin and end tablespace backups.
UNLIMITED TABLESPACE	Use an unlimited amount of any tablespace. This privilege overrides any specific quotas assigned. If you revoke this privilege from a user, the user's schema objects remain but further tablespace allocation is denied unless authorized by specific tablespace quotas. You cannot grant this system privilege to roles.

Privilege	Permission to
TRIGGERS	
CREATE TRIGGER	Create a database trigger in grantee's schema.
CREATE ANY TRIGGER	Create database triggers in any schema.
ALTER ANY TRIGGER	Enable, disable, or compile database triggers in any schema.
DROP ANY TRIGGER	Drop database triggers in any schema.
ADMINISTER DATABASE TRIGGER	Create a trigger on DATABASE. (You must also have the CREATE TRIGGER or CREATE ANY TRIGGER privilege.)
TYPES	
CREATE TYPE	Create object types and object type bodies in grantee's schema.
CREATE ANY TYPE	Create object types and object type bodies in any schema.
ALTER ANY TYPE	Alter object types in any schema.
DROP ANY TYPE	Drop object types and object type bodies in any schema.
EXECUTE ANY TYPE	Use and reference object types and collection types in any schema, and invoke methods of an object type in any schema if you make the grant to a specific user. If you grant EXECUTE ANY TYPE to a role, users holding the enabled role will not be able to invoke methods of an object type in any schema.
UNDER ANY TYPE	Create subtypes under any nonfinal object types.
USERS	
CREATE USER	Create users. This privilege also allows the creator to: Assign quotas on any tablespace. Set default and temporary tablespaces. Assign a profile as part of a **CREATE USER** statement.
ALTER USER	Alter any user. This privilege authorizes the grantee to: Change another user's password or authentication method. Assign quotas on any tablespace. Set default and temporary tablespaces. Assign a profile and default roles.
DROP USER	Drop users.
VIEWS	
CREATE VIEW	Create views in grantee's schema.
CREATE ANY VIEW	Create views in any schema.
DROP ANY VIEW	Drop views in any schema.
UNDER ANY VIEW	Create subviews under any object views.
MISCELLANEOUS	
ANALYZE ANY	Analyze any table, cluster, or index in any schema.
AUDIT ANY	Audit any object in any schema using **AUDIT** *schema_objects* statements.
COMMENT ANY TABLE	Comment on any table, view, or column in any schema.

Privilege	Permission to
EXEMPT ACCESS POLICY	Bypass fine-grained access control. This is a very powerful system privilege, as it lets the grantee bypass application-driven security policies. Database administrators should use caution when granting this privilege.
FORCE ANY TRANSACTION	Force the commit or rollback of any in-doubt distributed transaction in the local database. Induce the failure of a distributed transaction.
FORCE TRANSACTION	Force the commit or rollback of grantee's in-doubt distributed transactions in the local database.
GRANT ANY OBJECT PRIVILEGE	Grant any object privilege.
GRANT ANY PRIVILEGE	Grant any system privilege.
RESUMABLE	Enable resumable space allocation.
SELECT ANY DICTIONARY	Query any data dictionary object in the SYS schema. This privilege lets you selectively override the default FALSE setting of the O7_DICTIONARY_ACCESSIBILITY initialization parameter.
SYSDBA	Perform **STARTUP** and **SHUTDOWN** operations. **ALTER DATABASE**: open, mount, back up, or change character set. **CREATE DATABASE**. **ARCHIVELOG** and **RECOVER**. **CREATE SPFILE**. Includes the RESTRICTED SESSION privilege
SYSOPER	Perform **STARTUP** and **SHUTDOWN** operations. **ALTER DATABASE OPEN \| MOUNT \| BACKUP**. **ARCHIVELOG** and **RECOVER**. **CREATE SPFILE**. Includes the RESTRICTED SESSION privilege.

System Roles	Use
CONNECT, RESOURCE, and DBA	Provided for compatibility with previous versions of Oracle Database software.
DELETE_CATALOG_ROLE, EXECUTE_CATALOG_ROLE, SELECT_CATALOG_ROLE	These roles are provided for accessing data dictionary views and packages.
EXP_FULL_DATABASE, IMP_FULL_DATABASE	These roles are provided for convenience in using the Import and Export utilities.
AQ_USER_ROLE, AQ_ADMINISTRATOR_ROLE	These roles are needed for Oracle Advanced Queueing.
SNMPAGENT	This role is used by the Enterprise Manager Intelligent Agent.
RECOVERY_CATALOG_OWNER	This role is required for the creation of a recovery catalog schema owner.
HS_ADMIN_ROLE	Needed for support of Heterogeneous Services.
SCHEDULER_ADMIN	This role allows the grantee to execute the DBMS_SCHEDULER package's procedures.

NOTE
For external tables, the only valid privileges are CREATE ANY TABLE, ALTER ANY TABLE, DROP ANY TABLE, and SELECT ANY TABLE.

Object privileges apply only to certain kinds of objects. The following table shows the relationships and the grantable object privileges.

Object Privilege	Table	View	Sequence	Procedures, Functions, Packages[a]	Materialized View	Directory	Library	User-defined Type	Operator	Index-type
ALTER	X		X							
DELETE	X	X			X[b]					
EXECUTE				X[c]			X[c]	X[c]	X[c]	X[c]
DEBUG	X	X		X				X		
FLASHBACK	X	X			X					
INDEX	X									
INSERT	X	X			X[b]					
ON COMMIT REFRESH	X									
QUERY REWRITE	X									
READ						X				
REFERENCES	X	X								
SELECT	X	X	X		X					
UNDER		X						X		
UPDATE	X	X			X[b]					
WRITE						X				

[a] Oracle treats a Java class, source, or resource as if it were a procedure for purposes of granting object privileges.

[b] The DELETE, INSERT, and UPDATE privileges can be granted only to updatable materialized views.

[c] Job scheduler objects are created using the DBMS_SCHEDULER package. Once these objects are created, you can grant the EXECUTE object privilege on job scheduler classes and programs. You can grant the ALTER privilege on job scheduler jobs, programs, and schedules.

PRO*C

PRO*C is an extension to C that lets you develop user exits and other programs that access the Oracle database. A precompiler converts PRO*C code into normal C code, which can then be compiled. *See the Pro*C/C++ Precompiler Programmer's Guide.*

PROCEDURE

A procedure is a set of instructions (usually combining SQL and PL/SQL commands) saved for calling and repeated execution. *See* **CREATE PROCEDURE**.

PRODUCT_USER_PROFILE

A PRODUCT_USER_PROFILE is a SYSTEM table in Oracle that is used to restrict use of individual Oracle products, by disabling one or more commands available in the product. *See SQL*Plus User's Guide and Reference.*

PROFILE

A profile is a collection of settings in Oracle that limits database resources. *See* **CREATE PROFILE** and Chapter 18.

PROMPT (SQL*Plus)

SEE ALSO ACCEPT

FORMAT

```
PRO[MPT] [text]
```

DESCRIPTION **PROMPT** displays the *text* to the user's screen. If no *text* is specified, then a blank line will be displayed. To display a variable, *see* **PRINT**.

PSEUDO-COLUMNS

DESCRIPTION A pseudo-column is a "column" that yields a value when selected but is not an actual column of the table. Here are the current Oracle pseudo-columns:

Pseudo-Column	Value Returned
CONNECT_BY_ISCYCLE	Equal to 1 if the current row has a child that is also its ancestor, otherwise 0.
CONNECT_BY_ISLEAF	Equal to 1 if the current row is a leaf of the tree defined by the CONNECT BY condition, otherwise 0.
Level	Equal to 1 for a root node, 2 for a child of a root, and so on. Tells basically how far down a tree you've traveled.
sequence.CURRVAL	Current value for this sequence name.
sequence.NEXTVAL	Next value for this sequence name. Also increments the sequence.
VERSIONS_STARTTIME	For flashback version queries, returns the timestamp of the first version of the rows returned by the query.
VERSIONS_STARTSCN	For flashback version queries, returns the SCN of the first version of the rows returned by the query.
VERSIONS_ENDTIME	For flashback version queries, returns the timestamp of the last version of the rows returned by the query.
VERSIONS_ENDSCN	For flashback version queries, returns the SCN of the last version of the rows returned by the query.
VERSIONS_XID	For flashback version queries, for each version of each row, returns the transaction ID of the transaction that created that row version.
VERSIONS_OPERATION	For flashback version queries, for each version of each row, returns a single character for the operation that caused the row version: I (insert), U (update), or D (delete).
OBJECT_ID	Returns the object identifier of a column of an object table or view.

Pseudo-Column	Value Returned
OBJECT_VALUE	Returns system-generated names for the columns of an object table, XMLType table, object view, or XMLType view.
ORA_ROWSCN	Returns the conservative upper-bound SCN of the most recent change to the row, showing approximately when the row was last updated (row-level dependencies should be created for more fine-grained auditing).
ROWID	Returns the row identifier for a row. Use the ROWID in the **UPDATE ... WHERE** and **SELECT ... FOR UPDATE**. This guarantees that only a certain row is updated, and no others.
ROWNUM	Returns the sequence number in which a row was returned when selected from a table. The first row ROWNUM is 1, the second is 2, and so on.
XMLDATA	Lets you access the underlying XMLType LOB data or object relational column.

PUBLIC

Public can have either of two definitions:

- Something public can be visible or available to all users. Synonyms and database links can be public. In Oracle, a user must have CREATE PUBLIC SYNONYM or CREATE PUBLIC DATABASE LINK privilege. Users may GRANT PUBLIC access to their own objects.
- A group to which every database user belongs—the name of that group.

PUBLIC SYNONYM

A public synonym is a synonym for a database object that a user with CREATE PUBLIC SYNONYM privilege has created for use by all Oracle users.

PURGE

SEE ALSO Chapter 46, RECYCLE BIN
FORMAT
purge::=

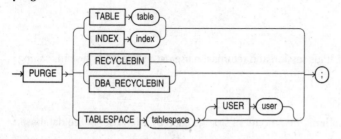

DESCRIPTION **PURGE** removes a table or index from your recycle bin and releases all of the space associated with the object, or removes the entire recycle bin, or removes part or all of a dropped tablespace from the recycle bin.

NOTE
*You cannot roll back a **PURGE** command. You cannot recover an object after it is purged.*

To see the contents of your recycle bin, query the RECYCLEBIN data dictionary view.

You can use the **TABLE** or **INDEX** keywords to specify the name of the object you wish to purge. Specifying **RECYCLEBIN** purges all objects in the user's recycle bin. **DBA_RECYCLEBIN** purges all users' recycle bins. **TABLESPACE** purges all objects residing in the specified tablespace from the recycle bin. **USER** *user* purges space within a tablespace for a particular user.

EXAMPLE To purge an individual table:

```
PURGE TABLE bookshelf;
```

To purge the current user's recycle bin:

```
PURGE RECYCLEBIN;
```

QUERY

A query is a SQL instruction to retrieve data from one or more tables or views. Queries begin with the SQL keyword **SELECT**.

QUERY OPERATORS

The following is an alphabetical list of all current query operators in the Oracle version of SQL. Each of these is listed elsewhere in this reference under its own name, with its proper format and use. *See also* Chapter 13.

Operator	Purpose
INTERSECT	Returns all matching distinct rows from two queries
MINUS	Returns all distinct rows in first query that are not in the second
UNION	Returns all distinct rows from both of two queries
UNION ALL	Returns all rows from both of two queries

QUIT

SEE ALSO **COMMIT, DISCONNECT, EXIT, SET AUTOCOMMIT, START**

FORMAT

```
QUIT
```

DESCRIPTION QUIT ends a SQL*Plus session and returns the user to an operating system, calling program, or menu.

QUOTA

A quota is a resource limit. Quotas can limit the amount of storage used by each user of the database. *See* **CREATE USER** and **ALTER USER**.

RAISE

SEE ALSO **DECLARE EXCEPTION**, EXCEPTION, **EXCEPTION_INIT**

FORMAT

```
RAISE [exception]
```

DESCRIPTION **RAISE** names the exception flag you want to raise, based on a condition that is being tested. The exception must be either one you've explicitly **DECLARE**d, or an internal system exception such as DIVIDE_BY_ZERO (*see* EXCEPTION for a complete list).

A **RAISE** statement causes control to be transferred to the EXCEPTION section of the current block, where you must test to see which exception was raised. If no EXCEPTION section is present, control is passed to the nearest EXCEPTION section of an enclosing block (basically backward through the nesting of the blocks). If no logic is found to handle the exception, control is passed from the PL/SQL to the calling program or environment with an unhandled exception error. (The use of OTHERS can avoid this. *See* EXCEPTION.)

RAISE without an explicitly named exception can be used only in one circumstance: within an EXCEPTION section, to force the current exception to be handled by an enclosing block's EXCEPTION section, rather than the current one. If, for instance, a NOT_LOGGED_ON error had occurred, and your local EXCEPTION section says this:

```
when not_logged_on
   then raise;
```

it would pass control back to the EXCEPTION section of the next enclosing block that had one, or to the program if none was found. That EXCEPTION block could also test for NOT_LOGGED_ON. The benefit here is that for a certain class of errors, particularly where the recovery, tracing, or error-logging steps you want to take may be extensive, you can set every nested block's EXCEPTION section to simply hand the EXCEPTION backward to a single spot for disposition.

RANK

SEE ALSO ANALYTIC FUNCTIONS
FORMAT
rank_aggregate::=

rank_analytic::=

DESCRIPTION **RANK** calculates the rank of a value in a group of values. The return type is NUMBER. Rows with equal values for the ranking criteria receive the same rank.

RATIO_TO_REPORT

SEE ALSO AGGREGATE FUNCTIONS

FORMAT

```
RATIO_TO_REPORT ( expr ) OVER ( [query_partition_clause] )
```

DESCRIPTION **RATIO_TO_REPORT** is an analytic function. It computes the ratio of a value to the sum of a set of values. If *expr* evaluates to **NULL**, the ratio-to-report value also evaluates to **NULL**.

RAW DATATYPE

A RAW column contains binary data in whatever form the host computer stores it. RAW columns are useful for storing binary (noncharacter) data.

RAWTOHEX

SEE ALSO HEXTORAW

FORMAT

```
RAWTOHEX(binary_string)
```

DESCRIPTION **RAWTOHEX** changes a string of binary numbers to a character string of hexadecimal numbers.

RAWTONHEX

SEE ALSO RAWTOHEX

FORMAT

```
RAWTONHEX ( raw )
```

DESCRIPTION **RAWTONHEX** converts *raw* to an NVARCHAR2 character value containing its hexadecimal equivalent.

READ CONSISTENCY

Read consistency is a state that guarantees that all data encountered by a statement/transaction is a consistent set throughout the duration of the statement/transaction. *See* **SET TRANSACTION**.

RECORD (PL/SQL)

SEE ALSO TABLE (PL/SQL), DATATYPES

FORMAT

```
TYPE new_type IS RECORD
 (field {type | table.column%TYPE}[NOT NULL]
 [,field {type | table.column%TYPE}[NOT NULL]...]);
```

DESCRIPTION A RECORD declaration declares a new type that can then be used to declare variables of that type. The individual components of the record are fields, and each has its own datatype. That datatype can be either one of the standard PL/SQL datatypes (including another RECORD but not a TABLE), or a reference to the type of a particular column in a specific table. Each field also may have a **NOT NULL** qualifier that specifies that the field must always have a non-**NULL** value.

You can refer to the individual fields in a record by using dot notation.

RECOVER

RECOVER is a clause within the **ALTER DATABASE** command.

SEE ALSO ALTER DATABASE, Chapter 46
FORMAT

```
RECOVER {general | managed | BEGIN BACKUP | END BACKUP}
```

where the **GENERAL** clause has the following syntax:

```
[AUTOMATIC] [FROM location]
{ {full_database_recovery | partial_database_recovery |LOGFILE filename}
[ {TEST | ALLOW integer CORRUPTION | parallel_clause }
[TEST | ALLOW integer CORRUPTION | parallel_clause]...]
|CONTINUE [DEFAULT]|CANCEL}
```

where the **FULL DATABASE RECOVERY** clause has the following syntax:

```
[STANDBY] DATABASE
[ {UNTIL {CANCEL | TIME date | CHANGE integer} | USING BACKUP CONTROLFILE}
[UNTIL {CANCEL | TIME date | CHANGE integer} | USING BACKUP CONTROLFILE]...]
```

where the **PARTIAL DATABASE RECOVERY** clause has the following syntax:

```
{TABLESPACE tablespace [, tablespace]... | DATAFILE datafilename [, datafilenumber]...
| STANDBY
{TABLESPACE tablespace [, tablespace]... | DATAFILE datafilename [, datafilenumber]...}
UNTIL [CONSISTENT WITH] CONTROLFILE }
```

and the **PARALLEL** clause has the following syntax:

```
{NOPARALLEL | PARALLEL [integer]}
```

and the **MANAGED** clause has the following syntax:

```
MANAGED STANDBY DATABASE recover_clause | cancel_clause | finish_clause
```

and the **RECOVER** clause has the following syntax:

```
{{DISCONNECT [FROM SESSION]|{TIMEOUT integer | NOTIMEOUT}}
 |{NODELAY | DEFAULT DELAY | DELAY integer} | NEXT integer
 |{EXPIRE integer | NO EXPIRE} | parallel_clause
 | USING CURRENT LOGFILE | UNTIL CHANGE integer
 | THROUGH {[THREAD integer] SEQUENCE integer
     | ALL ARCHIVELOG | {ALL|LAST|NEXT} SWITCHOVER}}
[DISCONNECT [FROM SESSION] | {TIMEOUT integer | NOTIMEOUT}
 | {NODELAY|DEFAULT DELAY|DELAY integer}| NEXT integer
 | {EXPIRE integer | NO EXPIRE}| parallel_clause
 | USING CURRENT LOGFILE | UNTIL CHANGE integer
 | THROUGH {[THREAD integer]SEQUENCE integer
     | ALL ARCHIVELOG | {ALL|LAST|NEXT} SWITCHOVER}}
```

and the **CANCEL** clause has the following syntax:

```
CANCEL [IMMEDIATE] [WAIT | NOWAIT]
```

and the **FINISH** clause has the following syntax:

```
[DISCONNECT [FROM SESSION]][parallel_clause]
FINISH [SKIP [STANDBY LOGFILE]][WAIT|NOWAIT]
```

DESCRIPTION The **RECOVER** command, like the **RECOVER** clause of the **ALTER DATABASE** command, recovers a database using various options. **AUTOMATIC** recovery generates the redo log filenames automatically during recovery. The **FROM** clause specifies the location of the archived redo log file group and must be a fully qualified filename. The default is set by the initialization parameter LOG_ARCHIVE_DEST (or LOG_ARCHIVE_DEST_1).

 The **DATABASE** option recovers the entire database and is the default. The **UNTIL CANCEL** alternative recovers the database until you cancel the recovery with the **CANCEL** option. The **UNTIL TIME** alternative recovers up to a specified date and time (in the format YYYY-MM-DD:HH24:MI:SS). The **UNTIL CHANGE** alternative recovers up to a *system change number* (SCN, a unique number assigned to each transaction) specified by an integer. The **USING BACKUP CONTROLFILE** alternative recovers by applying the redo log in a backup control file.

 You can perform trial recoveries via the **TEST** option, and **CONTINUE** a multi-instance recovery even after it has been interrupted. The **DELAY** parameters relate to the application of logs to standby databases during recovery; by default they are delayed as defined via the LOG_ARCHIVE_DEST_*n* parameter values.

RECSEP (SQL*Plus)
See **SET**.

RECSEPCHAR (SQL*Plus)
See **SET**.

RECURSIVE CALL

A recursive call is a nested invocation of the RDBMS; for example, auditing information is recorded in system tables using a recursive call. That is, during a normal database operation, such as an **UPDATE**, another database operation is executed to write log, auditing, or other vital information *about* the normal database operation underway.

RECYCLE BIN

As of Oracle Database 10*g*, dropped objects go into a recycle bin by default rather than being immediately dropped. The recycle bin allows for dropped objects to be restored without the need for a full database recovery. You can purge specific objects from the recycle bin via the **PURGE** command. *See* **PURGE**.

 To see the objects presently in your recycle bin, query the RECYCLEBIN data dictionary view or use the **SHOW RECYCLEBIN** command.

REDO LOG

A redo log is an Oracle-maintained sequential log of actions in the database. The log always consists of at least two files; one is optionally being archived while the other is being written. When the one currently being written fills, the next one is reused.

REDO LOG SEQUENCE NUMBER

The redo log sequence number is a number used to identify a redo log, used when applying the redo log file for recovery.

REF

SEE ALSO Chapter 36
FORMAT

REF (*correlation_variable*)

DESCRIPTION **REF** is a reference function used with object tables; the input correlation variable is a table alias. **REF** returns the object instance for that variable. *See* Chapter 36 for detailed examples.

REFERENTIAL INTEGRITY

Referential integrity is the property that guarantees that values from one column depend on values from another column. This property is enforced through integrity constraints. *See* INTEGRITY CONSTRAINT.

REFTOHEX

SEE ALSO Chapter 36
FORMAT

REFTOHEX (*expr*)

DESCRIPTION **REFTOHEX** converts argument *expr* to a character value containing its hexadecimal equivalent. *expr* must return a REF.

REGEXP_INSTR

SEE ALSO **INSTR**, Chapter 8
FORMAT
regexp_instr::=

DESCRIPTION **REGEXP_INSTR** extends the functionality of the **INSTR** function by letting you search a string for a regular expression pattern. The function evaluates strings using characters as defined by the input character set. It returns an integer indicating the beginning or ending position of the matched substring, depending on the value of the *return_option* argument. If no match is found, the function returns 0.

 See Chapter 8 for examples of the **REGEXP** functions.

REGEXP_LIKE

SEE ALSO **LIKE**, Chapter 8
FORMAT

REGEXP_LIKE(*source_string*, *pattern* [*match_parameter*])

DESCRIPTION REGEXP_LIKE extends the functionality of the **LIKE** operator by letting you search a string for a regular expression pattern. The function evaluates strings using characters as defined by the input character set.

 See Chapter 8 for examples of the **REGEXP** functions.

REGEXP_REPLACE

SEE ALSO **REPLACE**, Chapter 8
FORMAT
regexp_replace::=

DESCRIPTION **REGEXP_REPLACE** extends the functionality of the **REPLACE** function by letting you search a string for a regular expression pattern. By default, the function returns the *source_string* with every occurrence of the regular expression pattern replaced with *replace_string*. The string returned is in the same character set as *source_string*. The function returns VARCHAR2 if the first argument is not a LOB and returns CLOB if the first argument is a LOB.

See Chapter 8 for examples of the **REGEXP** functions.

REGEXP_SUBSTR

SEE ALSO SUBSTR, Chapter 8
FORMAT
regexp_substr::=

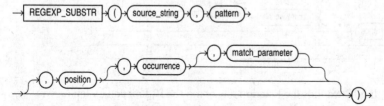

DESCRIPTION **REGEXP_SUBSTR** extends the functionality of the **SUBSTR** function by letting you search a string for a regular expression pattern. It is similar to **REGEXP_INSTR** but instead of returning the position of the substring it returns the substring itself. The function returns the string as VARCHAR2 or CLOB data in the same character set as *source_string*.

See Chapter 8 for examples of the **REGEXP** functions.

REGR_ (LINEAR REGRESSION) FUNCTIONS

SEE ALSO AGGREGATE FUNCTIONS

FORMAT
linear_regr::=

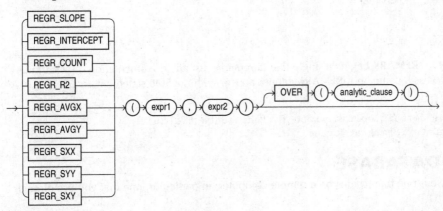

DESCRIPTION The linear regression functions fit an ordinary-least-squares regression line to a set of number pairs. You can use them as both aggregate and analytic functions. **REGR_SLOPE** returns the slope of the line. **REGR_INTERCEPT** returns the y-intercept of the regression line. **REGR_COUNT** returns an integer that is the number of non-**NULL** number pairs used to fit the regression line. **REGR_R2** returns the coefficient of determination for the regression. **REGR_AVGX** evaluates the average of the independent variable (*expr2*) of the regression line. **REGR_AVGY** evaluates the average of the dependent variable (*expr1*) of the regression line. **REGR_SXY**, **REGR_SXX**, and **REGR_SYY** are auxiliary functions used to compute various diagnostic statistics.

RELATIONAL DATABASE MANAGEMENT SYSTEM (RDBMS)

An RDBMS is a computer program for general-purpose data storage and retrieval that organizes data into tables consisting of one or more units of information (rows), each containing the same set of data items (columns). Oracle is a relational database management system.

RELATIONAL OPERATOR

A relational operator is a symbol used in search criteria to indicate a comparison between two values, such as the equal sign in the following **WHERE** clause:

```
where Amount = .10
```

Only those rows are returned (fetched) for which the comparison results in TRUE.

REMAINDER

SEE ALSO NUMBER FUNCTIONS
FORMAT

```
REMAINDER (m, n)
```

DESCRIPTION Available as of Oracle Database 10*g*, **REMAINDER** returns the remainder of *m* divided by *n*.

REMARK (SQL*Plus)

SEE ALSO /* */, - -, Chapter 6

FORMAT

```
REM[ARK] text
```

DESCRIPTION **REMARK** begins a single line of remarks, usually documentation, in a start file. It is not interpreted as a command. **REMARK** cannot appear within a SQL statement.

EXAMPLE

```
REM Reduce the default column width for this data field:
column ActionDate format a6 trunc
```

REMOTE DATABASE

A remote database is one that resides on a remote computer; in particular, one that you use through a database link.

RENAME

SEE ALSO COPY, **CREATE SEQUENCE**, **CREATE SYNONYM**, **CREATE TABLE**, **CREATE VIEW**

FORMAT

```
RENAME old TO new;
```

DESCRIPTION **RENAME** changes the name of a table, view, sequence, or synonym from its old name to a new one. No quotes are used around the names, and the new name must be neither a reserved word nor the name of an existing object for the user.

EXAMPLE The following changes the BOOKSHELF table to the BOOK table:

```
rename BOOKSHELF to BOOK;
```

REPFOOTER (SQL*Plus)

SEE ALSO ACCEPT, BTITLE, DEFINE, PARAMETERS, **REPHEADER**

FORMAT

```
REPF[OOTER] [PAGE][option [text|variable]... | OFF|ON]
```

DESCRIPTION **REPFOOTER** (**REP**ort **FOOTER**) puts a footer (may be multiline) on the last page of a report. OFF and ON suppress and restore, respectively, the display of the text without changing its contents. **REPFOOTER** by itself displays the current **REPFOOTER** options and *text* or *variable*. **PAGE** begins a new page before printing the specified report footer.

text is a footer you wish to give this report, and *variable* is a user-defined variable or a system-maintained variable, including SQL.LNO, the current line number; SQL.PNO, the current page number; SQL.RELEASE, the current Oracle release number; SQL.SQLCODE, the current error code; and SQL.USER, the username.

Valid values for *option* are

- **COL** *n* skips directly to position *n* from the left margin of the current line.
- **S[KIP]** *n* prints *n* blank lines. If no *n* is specified, one blank line is printed. If *n* is 0, no blank lines are printed and the current position for printing becomes position 1 of the current line (leftmost on the page).

- **TAB** *n* skips forward *n* positions (backward if *n* is negative).

- **LE[FT]**, **CE[NTER]**, and **R[IGHT]** left-justify, center, and right-justify data on the current line. Any text or variables following these commands are justified as a group, up to the end of the command, or a LEFT, CENTER, RIGHT, or COL. CENTER and RIGHT use the value set by the **SET LINESIZE** command to determine where to place the text or variable.

- **BOLD** prints data in bold print. SQL*Plus represents bold print on your terminal by repeating the data on three consecutive lines.

- **FORMAT** *string* specifies the format model that will control the format of subsequent text or variables, and follows the same syntax as FORMAT in a **COLUMN** command, such as FORMAT A12 or FORMAT $999,990.99. Each time a FORMAT appears, it supersedes the previous one that was in effect. If no format model has been specified, the one set by **SET NUMFORMAT** is used. If NUMFORMAT has not been set, the default for SQL*Plus is used.

Date values are printed according to the default format unless a variable has been loaded with a date reformatted by **TO_CHAR**.

REPHEADER (SQL*Plus)

SEE ALSO ACCEPT, **BTITLE**, **DEFINE**, PARAMETERS, **REPFOOTER**
FORMAT

REPH[EADER] [PAGE] [*option* [*text*|*variable*]... | OFF|ON]

DESCRIPTION REPHEADER (**REP**ort **HEADER**) puts a header (may be multiline) on the first page of a report. OFF and ON suppress and restore, respectively, the display of the text without changing its contents. **REPHEADER** by itself displays the current **REPHEADER** options and *text* or *variable*. **PAGE** begins a new page after printing the report header.

text is a header you wish to give this report, and *variable* is a user-defined variable or a system-maintained variable, including SQL.LNO, the current line number; SQL.PNO, the current page number; SQL.RELEASE, the current Oracle release number; SQL.SQLCODE, the current error code; and SQL.USER, the username.

Valid values for option are

- **COL** *n* skips directly to position *n* from the left margin of the current line.

- **S[KIP]** *n* prints *n* blank lines. If no *n* is specified, one blank line is printed. If *n* is 0, no blank lines are printed and the current position for printing becomes position 1 of the current line (leftmost on the page).

- **TAB** *n* skips forward *n* positions (backward if *n* is negative).

- **LE[FT]**, **CE[NTER]**, and **R[IGHT]** left-justify, center, and right-justify data on the current line. Any text or variables following these commands are justified as a group, up to the end of the command, or a LEFT, CENTER, RIGHT, or COL. CENTER and RIGHT use the value set by the **SET LINESIZE** command to determine where to place the text or variable.

- **BOLD** prints data in bold print. SQL*Plus represents bold print on your terminal by repeating the data on three consecutive lines.

- **FORMAT** *string* specifies the FORMAT MODEL that will control the format of subsequent text or variables, and follows the same syntax as FORMAT in a **COLUMN** command, such as FORMAT A12 or FORMAT $999,990.99. Each time a FORMAT appears, it supersedes the previous one that was in effect. If no FORMAT MODEL has been specified, the one set by **SET NUMFORMAT** is used. If NUMFORMAT has not been set, the default for SQL*Plus is used.

Date values are printed according to the default format unless a variable has been loaded with a date reformatted by **TO_CHAR**.

REPLACE

SEE ALSO CHARACTER FUNCTIONS, **TRANSLATE**, Chapter 7

FORMAT

```
REPLACE(string,if,then)
```

DESCRIPTION **REPLACE** replaces a character or characters in a string with zero or more characters. *if* is a character or characters. Every time *if* appears in *string*, it is replaced by the contents of *then*.

EXAMPLE

```
REPLACE('GEORGE','GE',null) = OR
REPLACE('BOB','BO','TA') = TAB
```

REPLICATION

Replication is the process of copying data from one database to another. The target to which the replicated data is copied is called the *replica*. To manage replication, you need to determine

- The location, structure, and ownership of the source data
- The update frequency of the source data
- The timeliness requirements for the replica data
- The volatility of the source data
- The intended uses of the replica

If the replica will also be able to make changes, and those changes must be propagated back to the original source database, then you have a *multimaster* configuration and you have to manage conflict resolution and error handling for the environment. In general, single-site ownership of data with multiple read-only replicas is simpler to manage than a multimaster configuration.

See **CREATE MATERIALIZED VIEW, CREATE DATABASE LINK**.

RESERVED WORDS

SEE ALSO OBJECT NAMES

DESCRIPTION A reserved word is one that has a special meaning to SQL, and therefore may not be used as the name of an object. Contrast this to a keyword, which may be used as an object name, but may become a reserved word in the future. Not every word is reserved in all products, so this list is structured to show which products reserve which words. In the following table, the entries with an * are reserved in SQL and in PL/SQL. The entries without an * are reserved only in PL/SQL.

ACCESS	ADD	ALL*	ALTER*	AND*
ANY*	ARRAY	AS*	ASC*	AT
AUDIT	AUTHID	AVG	BEGIN	BETWEEN*
BINARY_INTEGER	BODY	BOOLEAN	BULK	BY*
CASE	CHAR*	CHAR_BASE	CHECK*	CLOSE
CLUSTER*	COALESCE	COLLECT	COLUMN	COMMENT*
COMMIT	COMPRESS*	CONNECT*	CONSTANT	CREATE*

CURRENT*	CURRVAL	CURSOR	DATE*	DAY
DECLARE	DECIMAL*	DEFAULT*	DELETE*	DESC*
DISTINCT*	DO	DROP*	ELSE*	ELSIF
END	EXCEPTION	EXCLUSIVE*	EXECUTE	EXISTS*
EXIT	EXTENDS	EXTRACT	FALSE	FETCH
FILE	FLOAT*	FOR*	FORALL	FROM*
FUNCTION	GOTO	GRANT	GROUP*	HAVING*
HEAP	HOUR	IDENTIFIED	IF	IMMEDIATE*
IN*	INCREMENT	INDEX*	INDICATOR	INITIAL
INSERT*	INTEGER*	INTERFACE	INTERSECT*	INTERVAL
INTO*	IS*	ISOLATION	JAVA	LEVEL*
LIKE*	LIMITED	LOCK*	LONG*	LOOP
MAX	MAXEXTENTS	MIN	MINUS*	MINUTE
MLSLABEL*	MOD	MODE*	MODIFY	MONTH
NATURAL	NATURALN	NEW	NEXTVAL	NOAUDIT
NOCOMPRESS	NOCOPY	NOT*	NOWAIT*	NULL*
NULLIF	NUMBER*	NUMBER_BASE	OCIROWID	OF*
OFFLINE	ON*	ONLINE	OPAQUE	OPEN
OPERATOR	OPTION*	OR*	ORDER*	ORGANIZATION
OTHERS	OUT	PACKAGE	PARTITION	PCTFREE*
PLS_INTEGER	POSITIVE	POSITIVEN	PRAGMA	PRIOR*
PRIVATE	PROCEDURE	PUBLIC*	RAISE	RANGE
RAW*	REAL	RECORD	REF	RELEASE
RENAME	RESOURCE	RETURN	REVERSE	REVOKE
ROLLBACK	ROW*	ROWID*	ROWNUM*	ROWS
ROWTYPE	SAVEPOINT	SECOND	SELECT*	SEPARATE
SET*	SHARE*	SIZE	SMALLINT*	SPACE
SQL	SQLCODE	SQLERRM	START*	STDDEV
SUBTYPE	SUCCESSFUL*	SUM	SYNONYM*	SYSDATE*
TABLE*	THEN*	TIME	TIMESTAMP	TIMEZONE_REGION
TIMEZONE_ABBR	TIMEZONE_MINUTE	TIMEZONE_HOUR	TO*	TRIGGER*
TRUE	TYPE	UID*	UNION*	UNIQUE*
UPDATE	USE	USER*	VALIDATE*	VALUES*
VARCHAR*	VARCHAR2*	VARIANCE	VIEW*	WHEN
WHENEVER*	WHERE*	WHILE	WITH*	WORK
WRITE	YEAR	ZONE		

RESOURCE

Resource is a general term for a logical database object or physical structure that may be locked. Resources that users can directly lock are rows and tables; resources that the RDBMS can lock are numerous and include data dictionary tables, caches, and files.

RESOURCE is also the name of a deprecated role in Oracle. *See* ROLE.

REVERSE-KEY INDEX

In a reverse-key index, the bytes of the indexed value are reversed prior to being stored in the index. Thus, values 1234 and 1235 are indexed as if they were 4321 and 5321. As a result of this reversal, those two values will be stored farther apart. If you are frequently querying the column for an exact match (*column=1234*), then a reverse-key index may reduce block contention within your index. If you are frequently performing range queries (*column>1234* or *column like '123%'*), then traditional indexes should be more appropriate for your needs. *See* **CREATE INDEX**.

REVOKE

SEE ALSO **DISABLE**, **ENABLE**, **GRANT**, PRIVILEGE, Chapter 18
FORMAT
revoke::=

revoke_system_privileges::=

revoke_object_privileges::=

grantee_clause::=

on_object_clause::=

DESCRIPTION The **REVOKE** command takes privileges and roles away from users, or privileges away from roles. Any system privilege may be revoked; *see* PRIVILEGE.

If you revoke a privilege from a user, the user can no longer execute the operations allowed by the privilege. If you revoke a privilege from a role, no user granted the role can execute the allowed operations, unless they are permitted by another role or directly as a user. If you revoke a privilege from PUBLIC, no user granted the privilege through PUBLIC can execute the operations allowed by the privilege.

If you revoke a role from a user, the user can no longer enable the role (*see* **ENABLE**) but may continue exercising the privilege in a current session. If you revoke a role from a role, users granted the role can no longer enable the role but may continue using the privilege during the current session. If you revoke a role from PUBLIC, users granted the role through PUBLIC can no longer enable the role.

For object access, the **REVOKE** command takes away object privileges on a specific object from a user or role. If a user's privileges are revoked, the user may not execute the operations allowed by the privilege on the object. If a role's privileges are revoked, no user granted the role may execute those operations unless they are granted through another role or directly to the user. If the PUBLIC's privileges are revoked, no user granted the privilege through PUBLIC may execute those operations.

The **CASCADE CONSTRAINTS** clause drops any referential integrity constraints defined by the user or by users granted the role. This applies to a REFERENCES privilege.

ROLE

A role is a set of privileges that a user can grant to another user. Oracle has many system-supplied roles, including CONNECT, RESOURCE, and DBA. You can verify the privileges assigned to the roles via the ROLE_SYS_PRIVS and DBA_SYS_PRIVS data dictionary views. You should not rely on the system-provided roles in your application development, since the names and privileges for these roles may change with future releases of Oracle. *See* **CREATE ROLE** for role creation syntax.

See Chapter 18 for examples of creating and using roles.

ROLL FORWARD

To roll forward is to reapply changes to the database. You sometimes need roll forward for media recovery and sometimes for instance recovery. The REDO LOG contains the redo entries used for roll forward.

ROLLBACK

A rollback discards part or all of the work you have done in the current transaction, since the last **COMMIT** or **SAVEPOINT**.

ROLLBACK (Form 1—SQL)

SEE ALSO **COMMIT**, **SET AUTOCOMMIT**, Chapter 15
FORMAT

```
ROLLBACK [WORK] [ TO [SAVEPOINT] savepoint | FORCE 'text' ];
```

DESCRIPTION **ROLLBACK** reverses all changes made to tables in the database since changes were last committed or rolled back and releases any locks on the tables. An automatic rollback occurs whenever a transaction is interrupted, such as by an execution error, a power failure, and so on. **ROLLBACK** affects not just the last **INSERT**, **UPDATE**, or **DELETE** statement but any that have occurred since the last **COMMIT**. This allows you to treat blocks of work as a whole and only **COMMIT** when all of the changes you want are completed.

With **SAVEPOINT**, **ROLLBACK** goes to a specific, named place in the sequence of transactions being processed, the **SAVEPOINT**. It erases any interim **SAVEPOINT**s and releases any table or row locks that occurred after the **SAVEPOINT** was made.

With **FORCE**, **ROLLBACK** manually rolls back an in-doubt transaction identified by the literal text, which is a local or global transaction ID from the data dictionary view DBA_2PC_PENDING.

NOTE
*If **SET AUTOCOMMIT** is ON, every **INSERT**, **UPDATE**, or **DELETE**
immediately and automatically commits the changes to the database.
Typing the word **ROLLBACK** will produce a 'ROLLBACK COMPLETE'
message, but this message won't mean anything since **ROLLBACK**
only rolls back to the last **COMMIT**.*

NOTE
*All DDL commands cause a **COMMIT**.*

ROLLBACK (Form 2—Embedded SQL)

SEE ALSO **COMMIT**, **SAVEPOINT**, **SET TRANSACTION**, *Programmer's Guide to the Oracle Precompilers*
FORMAT

```
EXEC SQL [AT {database | :variable }]
ROLLBACK [WORK]
[TO [SAVEPOINT] savepoint] | [FORCE text] | [RELEASE] ]
```

DESCRIPTION **ROLLBACK** ends the current transaction, reverses any changes resulting from the current transaction, and releases any locks being held, but does not affect host variables or program flow. *database* indicates the name of the database where the **ROLLBACK** should take effect. Its absence indicates the default database for the user. **SAVEPOINT** allows a rollback to a named *savepoint* that has been previously declared. (*See* **SAVEPOINT**.)

FORCE manually rolls back an in-doubt transaction specified by a literal text containing the transaction ID from the DBA_2PC_PENDING data dictionary view. **WORK** is entirely optional and is for readability only.

Both **ROLLBACK** and **COMMIT** have **RELEASE** options. **RELEASE** should be specified by one of them after the last transaction; otherwise locks put on during the program will block other users. **ROLLBACK** occurs automatically (with a **RELEASE**) if the program abnormally terminates.

NOTE
See the Programmer's Guide to the Oracle Precompilers *for a full list of all commands. This reference does not contain all of the possible precompiler commands.*

ROLLBACK SEGMENT

A rollback segment is a storage space within a tablespace that holds transaction information that is used to guarantee data integrity during a rollback and to provide read consistency across multiple transactions. *See* Chapter 46. As of Oracle Database 10g, you should use Automatic Undo Management, in which Oracle dynamically manages undo segments.

ROLLUP

SEE ALSO **GROUPING**, **CUBE**, Chapter 12
FORMAT

```
GROUP BY ROLLUP(column1, column2)
```

DESCRIPTION **ROLLUP** generates subtotals for groups of rows within a query. *See* Chapter 12.

ROUND (Form I—for Dates)

SEE ALSO DATE FUNCTIONS, **ROUND** (NUMBER), **TRUNC**, Chapter 10
FORMAT

```
ROUND (date, 'format')
```

DESCRIPTION **ROUND** rounds *date* according to *format*. Without *format, date* is rounded to the next day if the time is 12:00:00 P.M. (exactly noon) or later, or to today's date if before noon; in other words, it is rounded to the nearest day. The resulting date has its time set to 12 A.M., the very first instant of the day.

FORMATS AVAILABLE FOR ROUNDING

Format	Meaning
CC,SCC	Century (rounds up to January 1 of next century, as of midnight exactly on the morning of January 1 of 1950, 2050, and so on)
SYEAR,SYYYY,Y,YY,YYY, YYYY and YEAR	Year (rounds up to January 1 of the next year as of midnight exactly on the morning of July 1)
IYYY, IYY, IY, I	ISO year
Q	Quarter (rounds up in the second month of the quarter as of midnight exactly on the morning of the 16th, regardless of the number of days in the month)

Format	Meaning
MONTH,MON,MM, RM	Month (rounds up as of midnight exactly on the morning of the 16th regardless of the number of days in the month)
WW	Same day of the week as the first day of the year
IW	Same day of the week as the first day of the ISO year
W	Same day of the week as the first day of the month
DDD,DD,J	Rounds up to the next day as of noon exactly; the same as **ROUND** with no format
DAY,DY,D	Starting day of week
HH,HH12,HH24	Hour
MI	Minute

When **WW** and **W** round, the time of the date being rounded is compared to a date that is set to 12 A.M., the very beginning of the day. The result of **ROUND** is a new date, which is also set to 12 A.M.

ROUND (Form 2—for Numbers)

SEE ALSO CEIL, **FLOOR**, NUMBER FUNCTIONS, **ROUND** (DATE), **TRUNC**, Chapter 9

FORMAT

```
ROUND(value,precision)
```

DESCRIPTION **ROUND** rounds *value* to *precision*, which is an integer and may be positive, negative, or zero. A negative integer rounds to the given number of places to the left of the decimal point; a positive integer rounds to the given number of places to the right of the decimal point.

EXAMPLES

```
ROUND(123.456,0)  = 123
ROUND(123.456,-2) = 100
ROUND(-123.456,2) = -123.46
```

ROW

Row can have either of two definitions:

- One set of fields in a table; for example, the fields representing one book in the table BOOKSHELF.
- One set of fields in the output of a query. RECORD is a synonym.

ROW HEADER

A row header is the portion of each row that contains information about the row other than row data, such as the number of row pieces, columns, and so on.

ROW-LEVEL LOCKING

Row-level locking is a type of locking in which **UPDATE**s to data occur through locking rows in a table and not the entire page.

ROW SEQUENCE NUMBER

A row sequence number is a number assigned to a row as it is inserted into a data block for a table. This number is also stored as row overhead and forms a part of the ROWID.

ROW_NUMBER

SEE ALSO ROWNUM
FORMAT

```
ROW_NUMBER ( ) OVER ( [query_partition_clause] order_by_clause )
```

DESCRIPTION **ROW_NUMBER** is an analytic function. It assigns a unique number to each row to which it is applied (either each row in the partition or each row returned by the query), in the ordered sequence of rows specified in the **ORDER BY** clause, beginning with 1.

ROWID

ROWID is the logical address of a row, and it is unique within the database.

ROWID can be **SELECT**ed, or used in a **WHERE** clause, but cannot be changed by an **INSERT**, **UPDATE**, or **DELETE**. It is not actually a data column, but merely a logical address, made of the database address information. ROWID is useful when used in a **WHERE** clause for rapid **UPDATE**s or **DELETE**s of rows. However, it can change if the table it is in is exported and imported.

The ROWID datatype is a hexadecimal string representing the unique address of a row in a table. This datatype is primarily used for values returned by the ROWID pseudo-column.

ROWIDTOCHAR

SEE ALSO **CHARTOROWID**, CONVERSION FUNCTIONS
FORMAT

```
ROWIDTOCHAR (RowId)
```

DESCRIPTION **ROWIDTOCHAR** (**ROW ID**entifier **TO CHAR**acter) changes an internal Oracle row identifier, or ROWID, to act like a character string. However, Oracle will do this kind of conversion automatically, so this function isn't really needed. It seems to be a debugging tool that has made its way into general availability.

ROWIDTONCHAR

SEE ALSO **CHARTOROWID**, **ROWIDTOCHAR**, CONVERSION FUNCTIONS
FORMAT

```
ROWIDTONCHAR (RowId)
```

DESCRIPTION **ROWIDTONCHAR** (**ROW ID**entifier **TO NCHAR**acter) changes an internal Oracle row identifier, or ROWID, to an NVARCHAR2 datatype.

ROWNUM

SEE ALSO PSEUDO-COLUMNS
FORMAT

```
ROWNUM
```

DESCRIPTION ROWNUM returns the sequence number in which a row was returned when first selected from a table. The first row has a ROWNUM of 1, the second has a ROWNUM of 2, and so on. Note, however, that even a simple **ORDER BY** in the **SELECT** statement may *disorder* the ROWNUMs, which are assigned to the rows before any ordering takes place.

RPAD

SEE ALSO CHARACTER FUNCTIONS, **LPAD**, **LTRIM**, **RTRIM**, **TRIM**, Chapter 7

FORMAT

```
RPAD(string, length [,'set'])
```

DESCRIPTION RPAD (**R**ight **PAD**) makes a string a certain length by adding a certain *set* of characters to the right. If *set* is not specified, the default pad character is a space.

EXAMPLE

```
select RPAD('HELLO ',24,'WORLD') from DUAL;
```

produces this:

```
HELLO WORLDWORLDWORLDWOR
```

RTRIM

SEE ALSO CHARACTER FUNCTIONS, **LPAD**, **LTRIM**, **RPAD**, **TRIM**, Chapter 7

FORMAT

```
RTRIM(string [,'set'])
```

DESCRIPTION RTRIM (**R**ight **TRIM**) trims all the occurrences of any one of a *set* of characters off of the right side of a string.

EXAMPLE

```
RTRIM('GEORGE','OGRE')
```

produces *nothing*, an empty string with zero length! On the other hand,

```
RTRIM('EDYTHE','HET')
```

produces this:

```
EDY
```

RUN

SEE ALSO /, @, @@, **EDIT**, **START**

FORMAT

```
R[UN]
```

DESCRIPTION RUN displays the SQL command in the SQL buffer, and then executes it. **RUN** is similar to the / command, except that / doesn't display the SQL first.

SAVE (SQL*Plus)

SEE ALSO **EDIT**, **GET**, Chapter 6

FORMAT

```
SAV[E] file[.ext] [ CRE[ATE] | REP[LACE] | APP[END] ]
```

DESCRIPTION **SAVE** saves the contents of the current buffer into a host file with the name *file*. If no file type (extension) is specified, the file type .sql is added to the filename. This default extension can be changed with **SET SUFFIX**. **SAVE** commits pending work to the database.

If the file already exists, the **CREATE** option forces **SAVE** to abort and produces an error message. The **REPLACE** option replaces any existing file, or creates a new one if none exists.

The **APPEND** option adds this file to the end of any existing file, or creates a new one if none exists.

EXAMPLE The following saves the contents of the current buffer into a file named lowcost.sql:

```
save lowcost
```

SAVEPOINT

SEE ALSO COMMIT, ROLLBACK, SET TRANSACTION

FORMAT

```
SAVEPOINT savepoint;
```

DESCRIPTION A savepoint is a point within a transaction to which you may roll back. Savepoints allow you to **ROLLBACK** portions of your current transaction. *See* **ROLLBACK**.

The first version shown here is typical of SQL*Plus. The purpose of **SAVEPOINT** is to be able to assign a name to the beginning of a group of SQL statements and later, if necessary, roll back to that name, thus undoing the results of *just that group.* Savepoints can be nested or sequenced, allowing great control over recovery from errors. The idea here is to collect together a series of SQL statements that make up one logical transaction, and hold the **COMMIT** until all the steps within it have been completed successfully. An attempted step may fail, but you'll want to be able to try it again without having to undo everything else prior to it. Here is an example:

```
insert into COMFORT
values ('WALPOLE', '22-APR-04',50.1, 24.8, 0);

savepoint A;

insert into COMFORT
values ('WALPOLE', '27-MAY-04',63.7, 33.8, 0);

savepoint B;

insert into COMFORT
values ('WALPOLE', '07-AUG-04',83.0, 43.8, 0);
```

You can roll back just the last **INSERT** by returning to savepoint B:

```
rollback to savepoint B;
```

This shows that SQL statements, or groups of them, can be collected together and undone in sets or singly. In a host program, or using PL/SQL or SQL*Plus, you may want to set up savepoints that you can roll back to, based on the results of your most recent SQL statement or condition test. **ROLLBACK** allows you to return to a specific step where you named a savepoint.

If a function, a section of logic, or an attempted SQL statement fails, you can return the data in the database back to the state it was in before the local step began. You can then try it again.

SAVEPOINT names must be unique to a transaction (defined by where it ends, with either a **COMMIT** or an unconditional **ROLLBACK**) but do not have to be unique to all of your database objects. You can give a **SAVEPOINT** the same name as a table, for instance (this might even result in more understandable code if the **SAVEPOINT** had the name of the table being updated). Names for **SAVEPOINT**s follow object naming conventions.

If you give a new **SAVEPOINT** the same name as a previous one, the new one replaces the earlier one. The earlier one is lost, and you can no longer roll back to it.

Once a **COMMIT** or an unconditional **ROLLBACK** (not to a savepoint) is issued, all previous **SAVEPOINT**s are erased. Recall that all DDL statements (such as **DISCONNECT**, **CREATE TABLE**, **CREATE INDEX**, and so on) automatically issue an implicit **COMMIT**, and any severe failure (if the program terminates abnormally or the computer goes down) will result in an automatic **ROLLBACK**.

SCAN (SQL*Plus)

See **SET**.

SCN_TO_TIMESTAMP

SEE ALSO ORA_ROWSCN, FLASHBACK QUERY

FORMAT

```
SCN_TO_TIMESTAMP ( number )
```

DESCRIPTION SCN_TO_TIMESTAMP takes as an argument a number that evaluates to a system change number (SCN) and returns the approximate timestamp associated with that SCN. The returned value is of the TIMESTAMP datatype. This function is useful anytime you want to know the timestamp associated with an SCN. For example, it can be used in conjunction with the ORA_ROWSCN pseudo-column to associate a timestamp with the most recent change to a row.

SCORE

The **SCORE** function is used by CONTEXT indexes in Oracle Text to evaluate how well a text string met the specified search criteria. You can display the score of an individual search; more often, the score is compared to a threshold value. *See* Chapter 25.

SEGMENT

A segment is the physical storage for the space allocated to a table, index, or cluster. A table has one segment that consists of all of its extents. Every index has one segment similarly defined. A cluster has at least two segments, one for its data and one for its cluster key index.

SEGMENT HEADER BLOCK

The segment header block is the first block in the first extent of a segment.

SELECT (Form 1—SQL)

SEE ALSO COLLATION, **CONNECT BY**, **DELETE**, **DUAL**, **FROM**, **GROUP BY**, **HAVING**, **INSERT**, **JOIN**, LOGICAL OPERATORS, **ORDER BY**, QUERY OPERATORS, SUBQUERY, SYNTAX OPERATORS, **UPDATE**, **WHERE**

FORMAT
select::=

subquery::=

subquery_factoring_clause::=

select_list::=

table_reference::=

flashback_query_clause::=

query_table_expression::=

sample_clause::=

subquery_restriction_clause::=

table_collection_expression::=

join_clause::=

inner_cross_join_clause::=

outer_join_clause::=

query_partition_clause::=

outer_join_type::=

where_clause::=

hierarchical_query_clause::=

group_by_clause::=

rollup_cube_clause::=

grouping_sets_clause::=

grouping_expression_list::=

expression_list::=

model_clause::=

cell_reference_options::=

returns_rows_clause::=

reference_model::=

main_model::=

model_column_clauses::=

model_column::=

model_rules_clause::=

cell_assignment::=

single_column_for_loop::=

multi_column_for_loop::=

order_by_clause::=

for_update_clause::=

DESCRIPTION **SELECT** retrieves rows from one or more tables or views, either as a command, or as a subquery in another SQL command (within limitations), including **SELECT**, **INSERT**, **UPDATE**, and **DELETE**. **ALL** means that all rows that satisfy the conditions will be returned (this is the default). **DISTINCT** means that only rows that are unique will be returned; any duplicates will be weeded out first.

An * (asterisk) by itself results in all columns from all tables in the **FROM** clause being displayed. *table*.* means that all columns from this table will be displayed. An asterisk by itself cannot be combined with any other columns, but a *table*.* can be followed by column names and expressions, including ROWID.

select_list can include any form of a column. This could be a column name, a literal, a mathematical computation, a function, or several functions combined. The most common version is a simple column name, or a column name prefixed by a table name or table alias. *c_alias* is a renaming of the column or expression. The column alias can be preceded by the word AS. The column alias will become the column heading in the display, and may be referenced by the **COLUMN**, **TTITLE**, and **BTITLE** commands in SQL*Plus. The column alias may be used in the **ORDER BY** clause. If it is more than one word, or will contain characters that are neither numbers nor letters, it must be enclosed in double quotation marks.

schema, *table*, and *dblink* denote the table or view from which the rows will be drawn. *schema* and *dblink* are optional, and their absence makes Oracle default to the current user. However, specifying the user in a query may reduce Oracle's overhead and make the query run more quickly. A subquery can be specified in the **FROM** clause. Oracle will execute the subquery and the resulting rows will be treated as if they came from a view.

A table *t_alias* here will rename the table for this query. This alias, unlike the expression alias, can be referenced elsewhere within the **SELECT** statement itself, for instance as a prefix to any column name coming from that table. In fact, if a table has an alias, the alias *must* be used whenever a column from that table has a table name prefix. Tables are typically aliased when two tables with long names are

joined in a query, and many of their columns have the same name, requiring them to be unambiguously named in the **SELECT** clause. Aliases are also commonly used in correlated subqueries, and when a table is being joined to itself.

condition may be any valid expression that tests true or false. It can contain functions, columns (from these tables), and literals. *position* allows the **ORDER BY** clause to identify the expressions based on their relative position in the **SELECT** clause, rather than on their names. This is valuable for complicated expressions. You should discontinue the use of ordinal positions in **ORDER BY** clauses; column aliases may be used in their place. The current SQL standard does not include support for ordinal positions in **ORDER BY** clauses, and Oracle may not support them in the future. **ASC** and **DESC** specify whether it is an ascending or descending sequence for each expression in the **ORDER BY** clause. *See* COLLATION for a discussion of what these sequences are.

column is a column in a table listed in the **FROM** clause. This cannot be an expression, but must be a real column name. **NOWAIT** means that a **SELECT ... FOR UPDATE** attempt that encounters a locked row will terminate and return immediately to the user, rather than wait and attempt to update the row again in a few moments.

The **FOR UPDATE OF** clause puts locks on the rows that have been selected. **SELECT ... FOR UPDATE OF** should be followed immediately by an **UPDATE ... WHERE** command, or, if you decide not to update anything, by a **COMMIT** or **ROLLBACK**. The **FOR UPDATE OF** clause also includes the actions of **INSERT** and **DELETE**. Once you have locked a row, other users cannot update it until you free it with a **COMMIT** command (or **AUTOCOMMIT**) or **ROLLBACK**. **SELECT ... FOR UPDATE OF** cannot include **DISTINCT**, **GROUP BY**, **UNION**, **INTERSECT**, **MINUS**, or any group function such as **MIN**, **MAX**, **AVG**, or **COUNT**. The columns named have no effect and are present for compatibility with other dialects of SQL. Oracle will lock only the tables that appear in the **FOR UPDATE** clause. If you don't have an **OF** clause listing any tables, Oracle will lock all the tables in the **FROM** clause for update. All the tables must be on the same database, and if there are references to a LONG column or a sequence in the **SELECT**, the tables must be on the same database as the LONG or the sequence.

If you are querying from a partitioned table, you can list the name of the partition you are querying as part of the **FROM** clause of the query. *See* Chapter 17.

The other individual clauses in the **SELECT** statement are all described under their own names elsewhere in this reference. The **AS OF {TIMESTAMP | SCN}** clause for flashback queries was introduced in Oracle9*i* Release 2. The **VERSIONS BETWEEN** clause for flashback version queries is available as of Oracle Database 10*g*.

OTHER NOTES Clauses must be placed in the order shown, except for these:

- **CONNECT BY**, **START WITH**, **GROUP BY**, and **HAVING**, which may be in any order in relation to each other.

- **ORDER BY** and **FOR UPDATE OF**, which may be in any order in relation to each other.

SELECT (Form 2—Embedded SQL)

SEE ALSO **CONNECT, DECLARE CURSOR, DECLARE DATABASE, EXECUTE, FETCH, FOR, PREPARE, UPDATE** (Form 1), **WHENEVER**, *Programmer's Guide to the Oracle Precompilers*

FORMAT

```
EXEC SQL [AT { db_name | :host_variable }]
 SELECT select_list INTO
 :host_variable [[INDICATOR] :indicator_variable]
 [, :host_variable [[INDICATOR] :indicator_variable]]...
 FROM table_list [WHERE condition]
 { [START WITH condition] CONNECT BY condition
 | CONNECT BY condition [START WITH condition]
```

```
| GROUP BY expr [, expr]... [HAVING condition] }
[ [START WITH condition] CONNECT BY condition
| CONNECT BY condition [START WITH condition]
| GROUP BY expr [, expr]... [HAVING condition] ]...
[ WITH READ ONLY | WITH CHECK OPTION ]
[{ UNION | UNION ALL | INTERSECT | MINUS } SELECT command]
[ ORDER BY
    { expr | position } [ ASC | DESC ]
    [, { expr | position } [ ASC | DESC ]]...
| FOR UPDATE
    [OF [[schema.] { table. | view. | materialized view. }] column
    [, OF [[schema.] { table. | view. | materialized view. }] column]...  ]   [NOWAIT] ]
[ ORDER BY
    { expr | position } [ ASC | DESC ]
    [, { expr | position } [ ASC | DESC ]]...
| FOR UPDATE
    [OF [[schema.] { table. | view. | materialized view. }] column
    [, OF [[schema.] { table. | view. | materialized view. }] column]...  ]
    [NOWAIT] ]...
```

DESCRIPTION See the description of the various clauses in **SELECT** (Form 1). The following are the elements unique to embedded SQL:

- **AT** *database* optionally names a database from a previous **CONNECT** statement, for a database name from a previous **DECLARE DATABASE** statement.

- **INTO** :*host_variable* [,:*host_variable*] is the list of host variables into which the results of the **SELECT** statement will be loaded. If any variable in this list is an array, all of the variables in the list must be arrays, though they need not all be the same size arrays.

- The **WHERE** clause may reference nonarray host variables.

- The **SELECT** clause may reference host variables anywhere a constant would have been used.

You can use the embedded **SQL SELECT** with variable arrays to return multiple rows with a single **FETCH**. You also can use it to either **DECLARE CURSOR** or **PREPARE** statements for use with a later **FETCH**, and may include the **FOR UPDATE OF** clause. The later **UPDATE** statement can then reference the columns named in the **FOR UPDATE OF** clause using its own **CURRENT OF** clause. *See* **DECLARE CURSOR** and **UPDATE** (Form 2).

If the embedded **SELECT** returns no rows, SQLCODE is set to +100, and the host variables are left unchanged. In that case, **WHENEVER** lets you change the program flow.

All rows that meet the **SELECT** criteria are locked at the **OPEN**. **COMMIT** releases the locks, and no further **FETCH**ing is permitted. This means you must **FETCH** and process all of the rows you wish to update before you issue a **COMMIT**.

NOTE
See the Programmer's Guide to the Oracle Precompilers *for a full list of all commands. This reference does not contain all of the possible precompiler commands.*

SELECT ... INTO
SEE ALSO %ROWTYPE, %TYPE, DECLARE VARIABLE, FETCH

FORMAT

```
SELECT expression [,expression]...
  INTO {variable [,variable]... | record}
  FROM [user.]table [,[user.]table]...
[where...][group by... [having...]] [order by...];
```

DESCRIPTION This is not the form of the **SELECT** statement used in **DECLARE CURSOR**. This form utilizes the implicit cursor named SQL, executes within an execution section of a block (between **BEGIN** and **END**), and copies the values from a single row being returned into either a string of named variables or a record whose structure is declared by **%ROWTYPE** to be just like the columns being selected. If the form that uses variables is used, they must each be **DECLARE**d and have compatible datatypes with those being retrieved. The order in which they appear in the **INTO** clause must correspond to the order of the associated columns in the **SELECT** clause.

This **SELECT** may be used in a loop with PL/SQL variables appearing in the **WHERE** clause (or even acting like constants in the **SELECT** clause), but each time the **SELECT** executes, it must return only one row. If it produces more than one row, the TOO_MANY_ROWS exception will be **RAISE**d, and SQL%ROWCOUNT will be set to 2 (*see* EXCEPTION for details). SQL%FOUND will be TRUE.

If it produces no rows, the NO_DATA_FOUND exception is **RAISE**d, and SQL%ROWCOUNT will be set to 0. SQL%FOUND will be FALSE.

SEQUENCE

A sequence is a database object used to generate unique integers for use as primary keys. *See* **CREATE SEQUENCE**.

SERVICE NAME

A service name, found in the tnsnames.ora file, is an alias for a database accessed by Oracle Net. Within the tnsnames.ora file, the service name is mapped to a host, port, and instance. You can therefore change the service name for a database without changing the database name, and you can move a database to a different host without changing its service name.

SESSIONTIMEZONE

SEE ALSO Chapter 10

FORMAT

```
SESSIONTIMEZONE
```

DESCRIPTION **SESSIONTIMEZONE** returns the value of the current session's time zone.

EXAMPLE

```
select SESSIONTIMEZONE from DUAL;
```

SET (SQL*Plus)

SEE ALSO **SET TRANSACTION**, **SHOW**, Chapter 6

FORMAT

```
SET feature value
```

where *feature* and *value* are from the following list. The default values are underlined.

- **APPI[NFO]{ON | OFF | *text*}** enables the registering of command files via the DBMS_APPLICATION_ INFO package. The registered name appears in the Module column of the V$SESSION dynamic performance table.

- **ARRAY[SIZE] {15 | *n*}** sets the size of the batch of rows that SQL*Plus will fetch at one time. The range is 1 to 5000. Larger values improve the efficiency of queries and subqueries where many rows will be fetched but use more memory. Values above 100 generally do not produce much improvement. **ARRAYSIZE** has no other effect on the workings of SQL*Plus.

- **AUTO[COMMIT]{ON | OFF | IMM[EDIATE] | *n*}** makes SQL immediately commit any pending changes to the database upon the completion of every SQL command. *n* allows you to specify the number of commands after which a commit will occur. **OFF** stops automatic committing, and you must instead commit changes intentionally with the **COMMIT** command. Many commands, such as **QUIT**, **EXIT**, **CONNECT**, and all DDL commands will cause a **COMMIT** of any pending changes.

- **AUTOP[RINT] {ON | OFF}** sets whether SQL*Plus automatically displays bind variables used in a PL/SQL block or **EXECUTE**d procedure.

- **AUTORECOVERY [ON | OFF]** tells the **RECOVER** command to automatically apply the default filenames of archived redo log files needed during recovery.

- **AUTOT[RACE] {ON | OFF | TRACE[ONLY]} [EXP[LAIN]] [STAT[ISTICS]]** allows you to see the execution path for a query after the query has completed. To see the execution path, you first must have the PLAN_TABLE table created in your schema (it can be created by running the utlxplan.sql file in the /rdbms/admin directory under your Oracle software directory).

- **BLO[CKTERMINATOR] {. | *c* | ON | OFF}** sets the symbol used to denote the end of a PL/SQL block. This cannot be a letter or a number. To execute the block, use **RUN** or **/** (slash).

- **CMDS[EP] {; | *c* | ON | OFF}** sets the character used to separate multiple SQL*Plus commands entered on a line. **ON** and **OFF** control whether or not multiple commands may be entered on a line.

- **COLSEP {_ | *text*}** sets a value to be printed between columns.

- **COM[PATIBILITY]{V7 | V8 | NATIVE}** specifies the version of Oracle to which you are currently connected.

- **CON[CAT] {. | *c* | ON | OFF}** sets a symbol that may be used to terminate or delimit a user variable that is followed by a symbol, character, or word that would otherwise be interpreted as a part of the user variable name. Setting **CONCAT ON** resets its value to a period (.).

- **COPYC[OMMIT] {0 | *n*}** commits rows to the destination database on a cycle of *n* batches of rows (the number of rows in a batch is **SET** by **ARRAYSIZE**). Valid values are 0 to 5000. If value is 0, a commit will occur only at the end of a **COPY** operation.

- **COPYTYPECHECK {ON | OFF}** enables the suppression of datatype checks when using the **COPY** command.

- **DEF[INE] {& | *c* | ON | OFF}** determines whether SQL*Plus will look for and substitute commands for substitution variables and load them with their **DEFINE**d values.

- **DESCRIBE [DEPTH {1 | *n* | ALL}][LINENUM {ON | OFF}][INDENT {ON | OFF}]** sets the depth of the level to which you can recursively describe an object. The valid range of the **DEPTH** clause is from 1 to 50.

- **ECHO {ON | OFF}** SQL*Plus echoes (displays) commands to the screen as they execute from a start file. **OFF** makes SQL*Plus execute them without displaying them. The results of the commands, on the other hand, are controlled by **TERMOUT**.

- **EDITF[ILE]** *file_name[.ext]* sets the default filename created by the **EDIT** command.

- **EMB[EDDED]** {ON | **OFF**} allows a new report in a series of reports to begin anywhere on a page, just after the previous one ended. **OFF** forces the new report to start at the top of a new page.

- **ESC[APE]** {\ | *c* | ON | **OFF**} defines the character you enter as the escape character. **OFF** undefines the escape character. **ON** enables the escape character. **ON** changes the value of *c* back to the default, \. You can use the escape character before the substitution character (set through **SET DEFINE**) to indicate that SQL*Plus should treat the substitution character as an ordinary character rather than as a request for variable substitution.

- **FEED[BACK]** {**6** | *n* | **ON** | **OFF**} makes SQL*Plus show "records selected" after a query if at least *n* records are selected. **ON** and **OFF** turn this display on and off, respectively. **SET FEEDBACK** to 0 is the same as **OFF**.

- **FLAGGER** {**OFF** | **ENTRY** | **INTERMED[IATE]** | **FULL**} sets the FIPS level for SQL92 compliance.

- **FLU[SH]** {**ON** | **OFF**} is used when a start file can be run without needing any display or interaction until it has completed. **OFF** lets the operating system avoid sending output to the display. **ON** restores output to the user's display. **OFF** may improve performance.

- **HEA[DING]** {**ON** | **OFF**} suppresses the headings, both text and underlines, that normally appear above columns. **ON** allows them to be displayed.

- **HEADS[EP]** { | | *c* | **ON** | **OFF**} defines the character you enter as the heading separator character. **ON** and **OFF** turn heading separation on and off, respectively.

- **INSTANCE** [*instance_path* | **LOCAL**] changes the default instance for your session to the specified instance path. Using the **SET INSTANCE** command does not connect to a database. The default instance is used for commands when no instance is specified.

- **LIN[ESIZE]** {**80** | *n*} sets the line width, the total number of characters on a line that can be displayed before wrapping down to the next line. This number is also used when SQL*Plus calculates the proper position for centered or right-aligned titles. The maximum value of *n* is 999. In iSQL*Plus, the default is 150.

- **LOBOF[FSET]** {*n* | **1**} sets the starting position from which CLOB and NCLOB data is retrieved and displayed.

- **LOGSOURCE** [*pathname*] specifies the location from which archive logs are retrieved during recovery. The default value is set by the LOG_ARCHIVE_DEST initialization parameter in the Oracle initialization file. Using the **SET LOGSOURCE** command without a pathname restores the default location.

- **LONG** {**80** | *n*} is the maximum width for displaying or copying (spooling) LONG, CLOB, and NCLOB values. *n* may range from 1 to 2GB.

- **LONGC[HUNKSIZE]** {**80** | *n*} sets the size, in characters, of the increments in which SQL*Plus retrieves a LONG, CLOB, or NCLOB value.

- **MARK[UP]** HTML [ON | **OFF**] [HEAD *text*] [BODY *text*] [TABLE *text*] [ENTMAP {**ON** | OFF}] [SPOOL {ON | **OFF**}] [PRE[FORMAT] {ON | **OFF**}] outputs HTML marked-up text. **SET MARKUP** only specifies that SQL*Plus output will be HTML encoded. You must use **SET MARKUP HTML ON SPOOL ON** and the SQL*Plus **SPOOL** commands to create and name a spool file, and to begin writing HTML output to it. **SET MARKUP** has the same options and behavior as **SQLPLUS -MARKUP**.

- **NEWP[AGE]** {**1** | *n* | **NONE**} sets the number of blank lines to be printed between the bottom of one page and the top title of the next. A 0 (zero) sends a form feed at the top of each page. If the output is being displayed, this will usually clear the screen.

■ **NULL** *text* sets the text that will be substituted when SQL*Plus discovers a null value. **NULL** without text displays blanks.

■ **NUMF[ORMAT]** *format* sets the default number format for displaying number data items. *See* NUMBER FORMATS for details.

■ **NUM[WIDTH]** {**10** | *n*} sets the default width for number displays.

■ **PAGES[IZE]** {**14** | *n*} sets the number of lines per page.

■ **PAU[SE]** {**ON** | **OFF** | *text*} makes SQL*Plus wait for you to press RETURN after it displays each page of output. **OFF** means no pause occurs between pages of display. *text* is the message SQL*Plus will display at the bottom of the screen as it waits for you to press the RETURN key. **PAUSE** will wait before the very first page is displayed; you'll have to press RETURN to see it.

■ **RECSEP** {**WR[APPED]** | **EA[CH]** | **OFF**} specifies the row wrapping rules for query results. Each row SQL*Plus brings back can be separated from other rows by a character, defined by **RECSEPCHAR**. By default, the character is a space, and this only happens for records (and therefore columns) that wrap.

■ **RECSEPCHAR** works with **RECSEP**. The default is a space, but you can set it to another symbol if you wish.

■ **SERVEROUT[PUT]** {**ON** | **OFF**} [**SIZE** *n*] [**FOR[MAT]** {**WRA[PPED]** | **WOR[D_WRAPPED]** | **TRU[NCATED]**}] allows you to display the output of PL/SQL procedures (from the DBMS_ OUTPUT package—*see* the *Application Developer's Guide*). **WRAPPED**, **WORD_WRAPPED**, **TRUNCATED**, and **FORMAT** determine the formatting of the output text.

■ **SHIFT[INOUT]** {**VIS[IBLE]** | **INV[ISIBLE]**} allows correct alignment for terminals that display shift characters. Use **VISIBLE** for terminals that display shift characters as a visible character (for example, a space or a colon). **INVISIBLE** is the opposite and does not display any shift characters.

■ **SHOW[MODE]** {**ON** | **OFF**} makes SQL*Plus display the old and new settings of a **SET** feature and its value when it is changed. **OFF** stops the display of both of these.

■ **SQLBL[ANKLINES]** {**ON** | **OFF**} controls whether SQL*Plus allows blank lines within a SQL command or script. **ON** interprets blank lines and new lines as part of a SQL command or script. **OFF**, the default value, does not allow blank lines or new lines in a SQL command or script.

■ **SQLC[ASE]** {**MIX[ED]** | **LO[WER]** | **UP[PER]**} converts all the text, including literals and identifiers, in either SQL or PL/SQL blocks, before it is executed by Oracle. **MIXED** leaves case just as it is typed. **LOWER** converts everything to lowercase; **UPPER** converts it all to uppercase.

■ **SQLCO[NTINUE]** {**>** | *text*} sets the character sequence to be displayed as a prompt for a long line that must continue on the next line. When you enter a **-** (hyphen) at the end of a SQL*Plus command line, the **SQLCONTINUE** symbols or text will prompt you from the left of the next screen line.

■ **SQLN[UMBER]** {**ON** | **OFF**} tells SQL*Plus that lines of SQL beyond the first one you enter will have line numbers as prompts. If this is **OFF**, the SQLPROMPT will appear only on additional lines.

■ **SQLPLUSCOMPAT[IBILITY]** {*x.y*[*.z*]} sets the behavior or output format of VARIABLE to that of the release or version specified by *x.y*[*.z*], where *x* is the *version* number, *y* is the *release* number, and *z* is the *update* number. In later releases, **SQLPLUSCOMPATIBILITY** may affect features other than VARIABLE. Setting the value of **SQLPLUSCOMPATIBILITY** to a version less than 9.0.0 will result in the VARIABLE definition of NCHAR or NVARCHAR2 datatypes reverting to Oracle8*i* behavior, whereby the size of the variable is in bytes or characters depending on the chosen national character set.

- **SQLPRE[FIX]** {**#** | c} sets the SQL*Plus prefix character. While you are entering a SQL command or PL/SQL block, you can enter a SQL*Plus command on a separate line, prefixed by the SQL*Plus prefix character. SQL*Plus will execute the command immediately without affecting the SQL command or PL/SQL block that you are entering. The prefix character must be a nonalphanumeric character.

- **SQLP[ROMPT]** {**SQL>** | text} sets the SQL*Plus command prompt.

- **SQLT[ERMINATOR]** {**;** | c | **ON** | **OFF**} sets the character used to end and execute SQL commands to c.

- **SUF[FIX]** {**SQL** | text} sets the default file extension that SQL*Plus uses in commands that refer to command files. **SUFFIX** does not control extensions for spool files.

- **TAB** {**ON** | **OFF**} determines how SQL*Plus formats white space in terminal output. **OFF** uses spaces to format white space in the output. **ON** uses the tab character. Tab settings are every eight characters.

- **TERM[OUT]** {**ON** | **OFF**}enables or suppresses the display so that you can spool output from a command file without seeing the output on the screen. **ON** displays the output.

- **TI[ME]** {**ON** | **OFF**} displays the current time before each command prompt. **OFF** suppresses the time display.

- **TIMI[NG]** {**ON** | **OFF**} displays timing statistics on each SQL command or PL/SQL block run. **OFF** suppresses timing of each command.

- **TRIM[OUT]** {**ON** | **OFF**} removes blanks at the end of each line, improving performance especially when you access SQL*Plus from a slow communications device. **OFF** allows SQL*Plus to display trailing blanks.

- **TRIMS[POOL]** {**ON** | **OFF**} removes blanks at the end of each line. **OFF** allows SQL*Plus to include trailing blanks.

- **UND[ERLINE]** {**-** | c | **ON** | **OFF**} sets the character used to underline column headings in SQL*Plus reports.

- **VER[IFY]** {**ON** | **OFF**} controls whether SQL*Plus lists the text of a SQL statement or PL/SQL command before and after SQL*Plus replaces substitution variables with values. **ON** lists the text; **OFF** suppresses the listing.

- **WRA[P]** {**ON** | **OFF**} controls whether SQL*Plus truncates the display of a **SELECT**ed row if it is too long for the current line width. **OFF** truncates the **SELECT**ed row; **ON** allows the **SELECT**ed row to wrap to the next line.

DESCRIPTION SET turns a SQL*Plus feature ON or OFF or to a certain value. All of these features are changed with the **SET** command and displayed with the **SHOW** command. **SHOW** will display a particular command if its name follows the word **SHOW**, or all commands if **SHOW** is entered by itself.

SET (function)
SEE ALSO IS A SET, Chapter 34
FORMAT

```
SET (nested_table)
```

DESCRIPTION SET converts a nested table into a set by eliminating duplicates. The function returns a nested table whose elements are distinct from one another. The returned nested table is of the same type as the input nested table.

SET CONDITION

A set condition is a logical expression containing a query; for example, "Name IN (select. . .)." The name derives from the idea that the query condition will produce a set of records.

SET CONSTRAINTS

SEE ALSO INTEGRITY CONSTRAINT
FORMAT

```
SET { CONSTRAINT | CONSTRAINTS }
{ constraint [, constraint]... | ALL }
{ IMMEDIATE | DEFERRED };
```

DESCRIPTION **SET CONSTRAINTS DEFERRED** tells Oracle not to check the validity of a constraint until the transaction is committed. This allows you to temporarily defer integrity checking of data. Deferred constraints are usually used when performing DML against multiple related tables when you cannot guarantee the order of the transactions. You must either own the table modified by the constraint or have SELECT privilege on the table.

The default setting is **SET CONSTRAINTS IMMEDIATE**, in which case the constraints are checked as soon as a record is inserted into the table.

SET OPERATOR

The set operator is either **UNION**, **INTERSECT**, or **MINUS**. *See also* QUERY OPERATORS.

SET ROLE

SEE ALSO **ALTER USER**, **CREATE ROLE**, Chapter 18
FORMAT

```
SET ROLE
{ role [IDENTIFIED BY password] [, role [IDENTIFIED BY password]]...
| ALL [EXCEPT role [, role]...]
| NONE    };
```

DESCRIPTION **SET ROLE** enables or disables roles granted to a user for the current SQL session. The first option lets the user enable specific roles, optionally giving a password if the role has one (*see* **CREATE ROLE**). The second option lets the user enable **ALL** roles **EXCEPT** for specific ones; these roles must be directly granted to the user, not roles granted through other roles. The **ALL** option does not enable roles with passwords. The third option, **NONE**, disables all roles for the current session.

SET TRANSACTION

SEE ALSO **COMMIT**, **ROLLBACK**, **SAVEPOINT**, TRANSACTION, Chapter 46
FORMAT

```
SET TRANSACTION
{ { READ { ONLY | WRITE }
  | ISOLATION LEVEL { SERIALIZABLE | READ COMMITTED }
  | USE ROLLBACK SEGMENT rollback_segment    }
  [NAME 'test']
| NAME 'test' } ;
```

DESCRIPTION **SET TRANSACTION** starts a transaction. The standard SQL transaction guarantees statement-level read consistency, making sure that the data from a query is consistent while the statement is executing. But some transactions need a stronger guarantee that a series of **SELECT** statements, accessing one or more tables, will see a consistent snapshot of all the data in one instant in time. **SET TRANSACTION READ ONLY** specifies this stronger read consistency. No changes to the queried data by other users will affect the transaction's view of the data. In a read-only transaction, you can use only the **SELECT**, **LOCK TABLE**, **SET ROLE**, **ALTER SESSION**, and **ALTER SYSTEM** commands.

For transactions that include **INSERT**, **UPDATE**, or **DELETE** commands, Oracle assigns a rollback segment to the transaction. **SET TRANSACTION USE ROLLBACK SEGMENT** specifies that the current transaction will use a specific rollback segment.

SET TRANSACTION must be the first SQL statement in a transaction. Placing a **COMMIT** just before **SET TRANSACTION** assures that this is true. The **COMMIT** at the end releases the snapshot of the data. This is important because the database needs to release the resources it has set aside to maintain consistency.

SGA

See SYSTEM GLOBAL AREA (SGA).

SHARED POOL

A shared pool is an area in the Oracle SGA that contains both the dictionary cache and a shared area for the parsed versions of all SQL commands within the database. Its size is determined by the SHARED_POOL_SIZE parameter in the database's initialization parameter file.

SHARED SERVER

Oracle Shared Server, formerly known as the multithreaded server (MTS), supports connections to Oracle via dispatcher processes and shared server processes. Dispatcher processes accept connection requests from users, and shared server processes communicate with the database. Shared Server allows many users to share a small number of shared server processes, potentially reducing the amount of memory required to support the database's users. Shared Server is most effective when there are many users initiating connections, and when the application users frequently interrupt their data input activity.

SHOW (SQL*Plus)

SEE ALSO SET

FORMAT

```
SHO[W] { option }
```

option may be any parameter set via the **SET** command or the following:

```
system_variable
ALL
BTI[TLE]
ERR[ORS] [ { FUNCTION | PROCEDURE | PACKAGE | PACKAGE BODY |
      TRIGGER| VIEW | TYPE | TYPE BODY | DIMENSION | JAVA CLASS } [schema.]name]
LNO
PARAMETERS [parameter_name]
PNO
RECYC[LEBIN] [original_name]
REL[EASE]
REPF[OOTER]
```

```
REPH[EADER]
SGA
SPOO[L]
SQLCODE
TTI[TLE]
USER
```

DESCRIPTION **SHOW** displays the value of a feature of **SET**, or **ALL** features of **SET**, or of the other SQL*Plus items. More than one of these (including more than one **SET** feature) can follow the word **SHOW**, and each will be displayed on a separate line. The rows returned will be ordered alphabetically. The features that can be shown are:

- *system_variable* is any variable set with the **SET** command.
- **BTI[TLE]** displays the current **BTITLE** definition.
- **ERR[ORS]** shows the latest errors encountered with the compilation of a stored object.
- **LNO** shows the current line number (the line in the current page being displayed).
- **PARAMETERS** shows the setting of a specific parameter, or all if none is specified.
- **PNO** displays the page number.
- **RECYC[LEBIN]** shows the names of objects in the recycle bin that can be reverted with the **FLASHBACK TABLE BEFORE DROP** command.
- **REL[EASE]** gives the release number of this version of Oracle.
- **REPF[OOTER]** shows the report footer.
- **REPH[EADER]** shows the report header.
- **SGA** shows the current memory allocations for the SGA.
- **SPOO[L]** tells whether output is being spooled (ON or OFF). *See* **SPOOL**.
- **SQLCODE** shows the error message number of the most recent Oracle error.
- **TTI[TLE]** displays the current **TTITLE** definition.
- **USER** shows the user's ID.

SHOWMODE (SQL*Plus)
See **SET**.

SHUTDOWN
SEE ALSO **STARTUP**, **RECOVER**, Chapter 46
FORMAT

```
SHUTDOWN [ABORT|IMMEDIATE|NORMAL|TRANSACTIONAL [LOCAL]]
```

DESCRIPTION **SHUTDOWN** shuts down an instance, optionally closing and dismounting it. If **ABORT** is used, uncommitted transactions are not rolled back. **NORMAL** (the default) prohibits further connections but waits for all current users to disconnect from the database. **IMMEDIATE** does not wait for current calls to complete or users to disconnect. **TRANSACTIONAL** performs a shutdown while allowing active transactions to complete. **TRANSACTIONAL LOCAL** specifies a transactional shutdown in the local instance only.
You must be connected AS SYSDBA or AS SYSOPER to use **SHUTDOWN**.

SIGN

SEE ALSO +, PRECEDENCE, Chapter 9

FORMAT

```
SIGN(value)
```

DESCRIPTION **SIGN** equals 1 if *value* is positive, –1 if negative, 0 if zero.

EXAMPLE

```
SIGN(33)  =  1
SIGN(-.6) = -1
SIGN(0)   =  0
```

SIN

SEE ALSO ACOS, ASIN, ATAN, ATAN2, **COS**, **COSH**, NUMBER FUNCTIONS, **SINH**, **TAN**, Chapter 9

FORMAT

```
SIN(value)
```

DESCRIPTION **SIN** returns the sine of an angle *value* expressed in radians.

EXAMPLE

```
select SIN(30*3.141593/180) Sine -- sine of 30 degrees in radians
from DUAL;
```

SINH

SEE ALSO ACOS, ASIN, ATAN, ATAN2, **COS**, NUMBER FUNCTIONS, **SIN**, **TAN**, Chapter 9

FORMAT

```
SINH(value)
```

DESCRIPTION **SINH** returns the hyperbolic sine of an angle *value*.

SMON

The **S**ystem **Mon**itor Process is one of the Oracle background processes used to perform recovery and to clean up unused temporary segments. *See* BACKGROUND PROCESS.

SOUNDEX

SEE ALSO LIKE, Chapters 7 and 25

FORMAT

```
SOUNDEX(string)
```

DESCRIPTION **SOUNDEX** finds words that **SOUND** like an **EX**ample *string*. **SOUNDEX** makes certain assumptions about how letters and combinations of letters are usually pronounced. The two words being compared must begin with the same letter. You can perform **SOUNDEX** searches of individual words within text strings in CONTEXT indexes.

EXAMPLE

```
select LastName, FirstName, Phone from ADDRESS
where SOUNDEX(LastName) = SOUNDEX('SEPP');
```

LASTNAME	FIRSTNAME	PHONE
SZEP	FELICIA	214-555-8383
SEP	FELICIA	214-555-8383

SPACE (SQL*Plus)

See **SET**.

SPOOL (SQL*Plus)

SEE ALSO **SET**, Chapter 6

FORMAT

```
SPO[OL] [file[.ext][CRE[ATE]|REP[LACE]|APP[END]]]|OFF|OUT]
```

DESCRIPTION **SPOOL** starts or stops spooling (copying) of SQL*Plus output to a host system file or the system printer. **SPOOL** *file* makes SQL*Plus spool all output to the named file. If the file type is not specified, **SPOOL** adds a default, similar to what **SAVE** does, usually .lst, but with some variation by host. OFF stops spooling. OUT stops spooling and sends the file to the printer. **REPLACE** replaces the contents of an existing file with the same name. To spool output to a file without displaying it, **SET TERMOUT OFF** in the start file prior to the SQL statement, but before the **SPOOL** command. **SPOOL** by itself shows the name of the current (or most recent) spool file.

SQL

SQL (Structured Query Language) is the ANSI industry-standard language, used to manipulate information in a relational database such as Oracle. SQL is formally pronounced "sequel," although common usage also pronounces it "S.Q.L."

SQL CURSOR

SEE ALSO **%FOUND**, **%ISOPEN**, **%NOTFOUND**, **%ROWCOUNT**, Chapter 29

DESCRIPTION *SQL* is the name of the cursor opened implicitly anytime the SQL statement being processed is not part of an explicitly named and opened cursor (*see* **DECLARE**). There is only one of these cursors at any time. The cursor attributes **%FOUND** and **%NOTFOUND** can be tested by checking SQL%FOUND and SQL%NOTFOUND before or after an **INSERT**, **UPDATE**, or **DELETE** (which are never associated with an explicit cursor) or a single-row **SELECT** that happened to be executed without an explicit cursor.

See **%FOUND** for details on these tests. *See* **%ROWCOUNT** for details on the values this attribute has under different conditions. **SQL%ISOPEN** always evaluates to FALSE because Oracle closes the SQL cursor automatically after executing the SQL statement.

SQL*LOADER

SQL*LOADER is a utility for loading data into an Oracle database. *See* **SQLLDR** and Chapter 21.

SQL*Plus

See SQLPLUS.

SQLCASE (SQL*Plus)

See **SET**.

SQLCODE

SEE ALSO EXCEPTION, SQLERRM

FORMAT

```
variable := SQLCODE
```

DESCRIPTION SQLCODE is an error function that returns the latest error number, but outside of an exception handler (*see* EXCEPTION) always returns 0. This is because the occurrence of an exception (that is, when SQLCODE would be nonzero) is expected to immediately transfer control to the EXCEPTION part of the PL/SQL block. Once there, SQLCODE can be tested for its value, or used to assign a value to a variable.

SQLCODE cannot be used as a part of a SQL statement (such as to insert the value of the error code into an error table). However, you can set a variable equal to SQLCODE, and then use the variable in a SQL statement:

```
sql_error := sqlcode;
insert into PROBLEMLOG values (sql_error);
```

SQLCONTINUE (SQL*Plus)

See **SET**.

SQLERRM

SEE ALSO EXCEPTION, **EXCEPTION_INIT**, PRAGMA, SQLCODE

FORMAT

```
SQLERRM[(integer)]
```

DESCRIPTION Without *integer* supplied, SQLERRM returns the error message related to the current SQLCODE. With an integer supplied, it returns the error message related to that integer value. Like SQLCODE, this function cannot be used directly in a SQL statement, but can be used in an assignment:

```
error_message := sqlerrm;
```

or to retrieve the error message associated with the error code 1403:

```
error_message := sqlerrm(1403);
```

Outside of an exception handler (*see* SQLCODE), this function without an integer argument will always return "normal, successful completion." In an exception handler, you will get one of these messages:

- The message associated with an Oracle error
- The words "User-defined exception" for an explicitly raised user exception where you did not assign a message text
- A user-defined message text, loaded using the PRAGMA **EXCEPTION_INIT**

SQLLDR

SEE ALSO Chapter 21

FORMAT The following are the command-line parameters for the **SQLLDR** command:

Userid	Username and password for the load, separated by a slash.
Control	Name of the control file.
Log	Name of the redo log file.
Bad	Name of the bad file.
Data	Name of the datafile.
Discard	Name of the discard file.
Discardmax	Maximum number of rows to discard prior to stopping the load. Default is to allow all discards.
Skip	Number of logical rows in the input file to skip prior to starting to load data. Usually used during reloads from the same input file following a partial load. Default is 0.
Load	Number of logical rows to load. Default is all rows.
Errors	Number of errors to allow. Default is 50.
Rows	Number of rows to commit at a time. Use this parameter to break up the transaction size during the load. Default for conventional path loads is 64, and for Direct Path loads is all rows.
Bindsize	Size of conventional path bind array, in bytes. Default is operating system dependent.
Silent	Y/N flag to suppress messages during the load.
Direct	Uses Direct Path loading. Default is FALSE.
Parfile	Name of the parameter file that contains additional load parameter specifications.
Parallel	Performs parallel loading. Default is FALSE.
File	File to allocate extents from (for parallel loading).
Skip_Unusable_Indexes	Allows loads into tables that have indexes in unusable states. Default is FALSE.
Skip_Index_Maintenance	Stops index maintenance for Direct Path loads, leaving them in unusable states. Default is FALSE.
Commit_Discontinued	Commits loaded rows when load is discontinued. Default is FALSE.
Readsize	Size of the Read buffer, in bytes; default is 1048576.
External_Table	Uses external table for load. Default is NOT_USED; other values are GENERATE_ONLY and EXECUTE.
ColumnArrayRows	Number of rows for Direct Path column array. Default is 5000.
StreamSize	Size of Direct Path stream buffer, in bytes. Default is 256000.
Multithreading	Uses multithreading in Direct Path.
Resumable	Enables or disables Resumable for current session; default is FALSE.
Resumable_Name	Text string used to identify resumable statements.
Resumable_Timeout	Wait time, in seconds, for Resumable. Default is 7200.
Date_Cache	Size (in entries) of data conversion cache. Default is 1000.

DESCRIPTION **SQLLDR** loads data from external files into tables in the Oracle database. *See* Chapter 21 for examples. The syntax for the control file is as follows:

Options clause

Load statement

infile_clause

concatenate_clause

into_table_clause

field_condition

delim_spec

full_fieldname

termination_spec

enclosure_spec

oid_spec

sid_spec

field_list

dgen_fld_spec

ref_spec

init_spec

bfile_spec

filler_fld_spec

scalar_fld_spec

lobfile_spec

pos_spec

datatype_spec

datatype_spec_cont

col_obj_fld_spec

collection_fld_spec

nested_table_spec

varray_spec

sdf_spec

count_spec

SQLNUMBER (SQL*Plus)
See SET.

SQLPLUS
SEE ALSO　　Chapter 6
FORMAT

```
SQLPLUS [user[/password][@database] [@file] ] [-SILENT] |
[/NOLOG] [-SILENT] | [-?]
```

DESCRIPTION　　**SQLPLUS** starts up SQL*Plus. Entering both your username and password will log you onto your default database. Entering just your username will cause SQL*Plus to prompt you for your password, which will not be displayed as you enter it. Entering *@database* will connect you to the named database instead of your default. The *@database* can be anywhere, so long as the computer you are logging onto is connected to it through Oracle Net. There must be no space between *password* and *@database*. For more information about Oracle Net, *see* Chapter 23. *@file* will run the start file immediately after SQL*Plus is loaded. There must be a space before *@file*. If the username and password are not entered on the command line with **SQLPLUS**, they must be the first line in the file. If they are in the file, and you enter them on the command line, you'll get an error message but the start file will run correctly anyway. To put *user* and *password* at the top of the file, separate them with a slash (/):

```
GEORGE/MISTY
```

/NOLOG makes SQL*Plus start, but does not log you onto the Oracle database. You must then use **CONNECT** to attach to Oracle. (*See* **CONNECT**.)

-SILENT suppresses all of SQL*Plus's screen displays, including the command prompts and even the SQL*Plus logon and copyright information. It makes the use of SQL*Plus by another program invisible to the program's user.

-? displays the current version and level number for SQL*Plus without actually starting it up.

EXAMPLE Normal startup of SQL*Plus follows:

```
sqlplus george/misty
```

To start up on the database EDMESTON, use this:

```
sqlplus george/misty@EDMESTON
```

To start the report file REPORT6, which includes the name and password as its first line, use this:

```
sqlplus @report6
```

To start the report file REPORT6, which includes the name and password as its first line, on the database EDMESTON, use this:

```
sqlplus george/misty@EDMESTON @report6
```

SQLPREFIX (SQL*Plus)
See **SET**.

SQLPROMPT (SQL*Plus)
See **SET**.

SQLTERMINATOR (SQL*Plus)
See **SET**.

SQRT
SEE ALSO POWER
FORMAT

```
SQRT(value)
```

DESCRIPTION **SQRT** finds the square root of *value*.
EXAMPLES

```
SQRT(64) = 8
```

The square root of negative numbers is not available in Oracle.

START (SQL*Plus)
SEE ALSO @, @@, ACCEPT, DEFINE, SPOOL, Chapter 6
FORMAT

```
STA[RT] {url|file[.ext]} [parameter] [parameter]...
```

DESCRIPTION **START** executes the contents of the specified start file (so called because it is started by this command). The file may contain any SQL*Plus commands. If no file type is specified, **START** assumes it is .sql. Any parameters following the filename are substituted into variables in the start file; the variables must be named &1, &2, &3, and so on, and will receive the parameters in order, from left to right. Every occurrence in the start file of &1 will get the first parameter. Parameters consisting of more than one word may be enclosed in single quotes (' '); otherwise, parameters are limited to a single word or number each.

EXAMPLE

```
start checkout INNUMERACY
```

where the file checkout.sql contains a variable named &1, into which the string 'INNUMERACY' will be substituted.

STARTUP

SEE ALSO **SHUTDOWN**, **RECOVER**, Chapter 46

FORMAT

```
STARTUP options | upgrade_options
```

where *options* has the following syntax:

```
[FORCE][RESTRICT][PFILE=filename][QUIET][MOUNT[dbname]|
[OPEN [open_options][dbname]]|NOMOUNT]
```

where *open_options* has the following syntax:

```
READ {ONLY | WRITE [RECOVER]} | RECOVER
```

and *upgrade_options* has the following syntax:

```
[PFILE=filename]{UPGRADE|DOWNGRADE} [QUIET]
```

DESCRIPTION **STARTUP** starts an instance. **FORCE** shuts down a running instance with **SHUTDOWN ABORT** prior to starting it. **RESTRICT** allows only privileged users to log in. The **PFILE** option allows you to specify an init.ora file to use during startup (in place of the standard spfile). **STARTUP RECOVER** has the same effect as executing **RECOVER DATABASE** and starting an instance. **UPGRADE** starts the database in **OPEN UPGRADE** mode and should be used only when a database is first started with a new version of the Oracle software.

STATS_BINOMIAL_TEST

FORMAT
stats_binomial_test::=

DESCRIPTION STATS_BINOMIAL_TEST is an exact probability test used for dichotomous variables, where only two possible values exist. It tests the difference between a sample proportion and a given proportion.

STATS_CROSSTAB

FORMAT

stats_crosstab::=

DESCRIPTION STATS_CROSSTAB takes three arguments: two expressions and a return value of type VARCHAR2. *expr1* and *expr2* are the two nominal variables being analyzed. The function returns one number, determined by the value of the third argument. Values for the third argument are CHISQ_OBS, CHISQ_SIG, CHISQ_DF, PHI_COEFFICIENT, CRAMERS_V, CONT_COEFFICIENT, and COHENS_K.

STATS_F_TEST

FORMAT

stats_f_test::=

DESCRIPTION STATS_F_TEST tests whether two variances are significantly different. The observed value of *f* is the ratio of one variance to the other, so values very different from 1 usually indicate significant differences.

STATS_KS_TEST
FORMAT
stats_ks_test::=

DESCRIPTION **STATS_KS_TEST** is a Kolmogorov-Smirnov function that compares two samples to test whether they are from the same population or from populations that have the same distribution. It does not assume that the population from which the samples were taken is normally distributed.

STATS_MODE
FORMAT
STATS_MODE (*expr*)

DESCRIPTION **STATS_MODE** takes as its argument a set of values and returns the value that occurs with the greatest frequency. If more than one mode exists, Oracle chooses one and returns only that one value.

STATS_MW_TEST
FORMAT
stats_mw_test::=

DESCRIPTION A Mann-Whitney test compares two independent samples to test the null hypothesis that two populations have the same distribution function against the alternative hypothesis that the two distribution functions are different.

STATS_ONE_WAY_ANOVA
FORMAT
stats_one_way_anova::=

DESCRIPTION **STATS_ONE_WAY_ANOVA** is a one-way analysis of variance function. It tests differences in means for statistical significance by comparing two different estimates of variance (mean square error and mean squares between). The function returns one number, determined by the value of the third argument (default is SIG, for significance).

STATS_T_TEST_* FUNCTIONS
FORMAT
stats_t_test::=

DESCRIPTION The *t*-test measures the significance of a difference of means. You can use it to compare the means of two groups or the means of one group with a constant. The **STATS_T_TEST_*** functions take three arguments: two expressions and a return value of type VARCHAR2. The functions return one number, determined by the value of the third argument (default is TWO_SIDED_SIG).
 The tests are as follows:

- **STATS_T_TEST_ONE** A one-sample *t*-test
- **STATS_T_TEST_PAIRED** A two-sample, paired *t*-test
- **STATS_T_TEST_INDEP** A *t*-test of two independent groups with the same variance
- **STATS_T_TEST_INDEPU** A *t*-test of two independent groups with unequal variance

The values for the third argument are as follows:

- **STATISTIC** The observed value of *t*
- **DF** Degree of freedom
- **ONE_SIDED_SIG** One-tailed significance of *t*
- **TWO_SIDED_SIG** Two-tailed significance of *t*

STATS_WSR_TEST

FORMAT
stats_wsr_test::=

DESCRIPTION **STATS_WSR_TEST** is a Wilcoxon Signed Ranks test of paired samples to determine whether the median of the differences between the samples is significantly different from zero. If you do not specify the third argument, it defaults to TWO_SIDED_SIG.

STDDEV

SEE ALSO AGGREGATE FUNCTIONS, **VARIANCE**, Chapter 9
FORMAT

```
STDDEV( [ DISTINCT | ALL ] value) [OVER ( analytic_clause )]
```

DESCRIPTION **STDDEV** gives the standard deviation from the norm of values in a group of rows. It ignores **NULL** values in its calculation.

STDDEV_POP

SEE ALSO AGGREGATE FUNCTIONS, **STTDEV**, **STDDEV_SAMP**
FORMAT

```
STDDEV_POP ( expr ) [OVER ( analytic_clause )]
```

DESCRIPTION **STDDEV_POP** computes the population standard deviation and returns the square root of the population variance.

STDDEV_SAMP

SEE ALSO AGGREGATE FUNCTIONS, **STTDEV**, **STDDEV_POP**
FORMAT

```
STDDEV_SAMP ( expr ) [OVER ( analytic_clause )]
```

DESCRIPTION **STDDEV_SAMP** computes the cumulative sample standard deviation and returns the square root of the sample variance.

STORAGE

SEE ALSO BLOCK, CREATE CLUSTER, CREATE INDEX, CREATE ROLLBACK SEGMENT, CREATE MATERIALIZED VIEW, CREATE MATERIALIZED VIEW LOG, CREATE TABLE, CREATE TABLESPACE, as well as the **ALTER** statement for each of these

FORMAT
storage_clause::=

DESCRIPTION The **STORAGE** clause is optional in any of the **CREATE** and **ALTER** statements listed under the preceding SEE ALSO section. **STORAGE** is not a SQL statement, and cannot stand alone. In the following paragraphs, a *block* is a database block (*see* **BLOCK**) with a size depending on the operating system and the database initialization parameters.

INITIAL allocates the first extent of space to the object. If **INITIAL** is not specified, it defaults to five data blocks. The smallest initial extent you can allocate is two data blocks, and the largest depends on your operating system. You can express these numbers either as a simple integer or as an integer followed by **K** or **M** to indicate kilobytes or megabytes, respectively.

NEXT is the size of the extent allocated after the initial extent has been filled. If not specified, it defaults to five data blocks. The smallest next extent you can allocate is one data block, and the largest depends on the operating system. You can use **K** and **M** for kilobytes and megabytes.

PCTINCREASE controls the rate of growth of extents beyond the second. If set to 0, every additional extent will be the same size as the second extent, specified by **NEXT**. If **PCTINCREASE** is a positive integer, each succeeding extent will be that percentage larger than the preceding one. For example, if **PCTINCREASE** is 50 (the default, if it is not specified), each additional extent will be 50 percent larger than the previous one. **PCTINCREASE** cannot be negative. The minimum **PCTINCREASE** is 0, and the maximum depends on the operating system. Oracle rounds the extent size up to the next multiple of the operating system block size.

MINEXTENTS defaults to 1 (or 2 for a rollback segment) if it is not specified, meaning that when the object is created, only the initial extent is allocated. A number larger than 1 will create that many total extents (which don't need to be contiguous on disk, as each extent itself does), and the size of each of them will be determined by the values set with **INITIAL**, **NEXT**, and **PCTINCREASE**. All of these will be allocated when the object is created.

MAXEXTENTS sets the limit on the total number of extents that can be allocated. The minimum limit is 1, with the default and maximum depending on the operating system. You can specify a **MAXEXTENTS** value of **UNLIMITED**.

OPTIMAL sets an optimal size in bytes for a rollback segment. Oracle will dynamically deallocate extents in the rollback segment to maintain the optimal size. **NULL** means that Oracle never deallocates the rollback segment extents, and this is the default behavior. You must supply a size greater than or equal to the initial space allocated for the rollback segment by the **MINEXTENTS**, **INITIAL**, **NEXT**, and **PCTINCREASE** parameters. As of Oracle9*i*, you should use Automatic Undo Management instead of rollback segments.

FREELIST GROUPS gives the number of groups of free lists, with a default value of 1. This setting applies to the Real Application Clusters option of Oracle for tables, clusters, or indexes.

FREELISTS sets the number of free lists for each free list group.

BUFFER_POOL sets the buffer pool into which the table's blocks will be read. By default, all blocks are read into the **DEFAULT** pool. You can create separate pools for blocks you want to keep in memory longer (the **KEEP** pool) or for those you wish to age out of memory quickly (the **RECYCLE** pool).

For most applications, you should use Oracle's space management automation features, including locally managed tablespaces. In a locally managed tablespace, you define the storage parameters once and Oracle manages the space for the objects created within the tablespace.

STORE (SQL*Plus)

SEE ALSO SAVE, START, Chapter 6

FORMAT

```
STORE SET file[.ext] [ CRE[ATE] | REP[LACE] | APP[END] ]
```

DESCRIPTION **STORE** saves all of your SQL*Plus environment settings to a file.

EXAMPLE The following command saves the current SQL*Plus environment settings to a file named settings.sql:

```
store settings.sql
```

SUBPARTITION

A subpartition is a partition of a partition. Typically, a range partition is hash partitioned, creating multiple hash subpartitions for each of the range partitions. *See* Chapter 17.

SUBQUERY

A query (that is, a **SELECT** statement) may be used as a part of another SQL statement (called the parent, or outer statement), including **CREATE TABLE**, **DELETE**, **INSERT**, **SELECT**, and **UPDATE**, or in the SQL*Plus **COPY** command, in order to define the rows or columns that the parent will use in its execution. The results of the child query (also called a subquery) are not themselves displayed, but are passed to the parent SQL statement for its use. The following rules apply:

■ In an **UPDATE** or **CREATE TABLE** command, the subquery must return one value for each column to be inserted or updated. The value or values are then used by the parent SQL statement to **INSERT** or **UPDATE** the rows.

■ A subquery cannot contain **ORDER BY** and **FOR UPDATE OF** clauses.

■ A "correlated" subquery is used in the **WHERE** clause of a **SELECT** statement, and references an alias for the table used by the parent **SELECT** command. It is tested once for each row evaluated for selection by the parent **SELECT** statement (a standard subquery evaluated just once for the parent query). *See* Chapter 13 for further details.

Other than these restrictions, normal rules for a **SELECT** statement apply.

SUBSTITUTION

See **&**, **&&**, **ACCEPT**, and **DEFINE**.

SUBSTR

SEE ALSO 11, CHARACTER FUNCTIONS, **INSTR**, Chapter 7
FORMAT
substr::=

DESCRIPTION **SUBSTR** clips out a piece of a string beginning at *start* and going for *count* characters. If *count* is not specified, the string is clipped from *start* and goes to the end of the string.

There are multiple **SUBSTR** functions: **SUBSTR** calculates length using characters as defined by the input character set. **SUBSTRB** uses bytes instead of characters. **SUBSTRC** uses Unicode complete sets. **SUBSTR2** uses UCS2 code points. **SUBSTR4** uses UCS4 code points.

EXAMPLE

```
SUBSTR('NEWSPAPER',5)
```

produces this:

```
PAPER
```

SUFFIX (SQL*Plus)

See **SET**.

SUM

SEE ALSO **COMPUTE**, AGGREGATE FUNCTIONS, Chapter 9
FORMAT

```
SUM([DISTINCT | ALL] value) [OVER (analytic_clause)]
```

DESCRIPTION **SUM** is the sum of all *values* for a group of rows. **DISTINCT** makes **SUM** add each unique value to the total only once; this is usually not very meaningful.

SYNONYM

A synonym is a name assigned to a table, view, or sequence that may thereafter be used to refer to it. If you have access to another user's table, you may create a synonym for it and refer to it by the synonym alone, without entering the user's name as a qualifier. *See* Chapter 23 and Chapter 42.

SYNTAX

Syntax is a set of rules that determines how to construct a valid statement in a computer language such as SQL.

SYNTAX OPERATORS

SEE ALSO LOGICAL OPERATORS, PRECEDENCE
DESCRIPTION Syntax operators have the highest precedence of all operators, and may appear anywhere in a SQL statement. Here they are listed in descending order of precedence. Operators of equal precedence are evaluated from left to right. Most of these are listed and described separately under their own symbols.

Operator	Function
-	SQL*Plus command continuation. Continues a command on the following line.
&	Prefix for parameters in a SQL*Plus start file. Words are substituted for &1, &2, and so on. *See* **START**.
& &&	Prefix for a substitution variable in a SQL command in SQL*Plus. SQL*Plus will prompt for a value if an undefined **&** or **&&** variable is found. **&&** also defines the variable and saves the value; **&** does not. *See* **&** and **&&**, **DEFINE**, and **ACCEPT**.
:	Prefix for a variable in SQL*FORMS and for a host variable in PL/SQL.
.	Variable separator, used in SQL*Plus to separate the variable name from a suffix so that the suffix is not considered a part of the variable name, and used in SQL between user, table, and column names.
()	Surrounds subqueries and lists of columns, or controls precedence.
'	Surrounds a literal, such as a character string or date constant. To use a ' in a string constant, use two ' marks (not a double quotation mark).
"	Surrounds a table or column alias that contains special characters or a space.
"	Surrounds literal text in a date format clause of **TO_CHAR**.
@	Precedes a database name in a **COPY**, or a link name in a **FROM** clause.

SYS (ORACLE USER)

SYS is one of the DBA users that is created when a database system is installed and initialized (the other is SYSTEM). SYS owns most of the data dictionary tables, while SYSTEM owns the views created on those base tables.

SYSAUX (TABLESPACE)

As of Oracle Database 10g, the SYSAUX tablespace is created via the **CREATE DATABASE** command. SYSAUX contains system-related tables (such as the statistics repository) that are not part of the core data dictionary.

SYS_CONNECT_BY_PATH

SEE ALSO **CONNECT BY**, Chapter 14

FORMAT

```
SYS_CONNECT_BY_PATH (column, char)
```

DESCRIPTION SYS_CONNECT_BY_PATH is valid only in hierarchical queries. It returns the path of a column value from root to node, with column values separated by *char* for each row returned by the **CONNECT BY** condition.

SYS_CONTEXT

SEE ALSO **CREATE CONTEXT**

FORMAT

```
SYS_CONTEXT ( namespace , parameter [, length] )
```

DESCRIPTION SYS_CONTEXT returns the value of *parameter* associated with the context *namespace*.

SYS_DBURIGEN

SEE ALSO Chapter 47

FORMAT

```
SYS_DBURIGEN
( { column | attribute } [rowid]
  [, { column | attribute } [rowid]]...
  [, 'text( )'] )
```

DESCRIPTION SYS_DBURIGEN takes as its argument one or more columns or attributes, and optionally a ROWID, and generates a URL of datatype DBUriType to a particular column or row object. You can then use the URL to retrieve an XML document from the database.

All columns or attributes referenced must reside in the same table. They must perform the function of a primary key. That is, they need not actually match the primary keys of the table, but they must reference a unique value. If you specify multiple columns, all but the final column identify the row in the database, and the last column specified identifies the column within the row.

By default the URL points to a formatted XML document. If you want the URL to point only to the text of the document, specify the optional 'text()'. (In this XML context, the lowercase 'text' is a keyword, not a syntactic placeholder.)

SYS_EXTRACT_UTC

SEE ALSO Chapter 10

FORMAT

```
SYS_EXTRACT_UTC ( datetime_with_timezone )
```

DESCRIPTION **SYS_EXTRACT_UTC** extracts the UTC (Coordinated Universal Time) from a datetime with time zone displacement.

SYS_GUID

FORMAT

```
SYS_GUID ( )
```

DESCRIPTION **SYS_GUID** generates and returns a globally unique identifier (RAW value) made up of 16 bytes. On most platforms, the generated identifier consists of a host identifier and a process or thread identifier of the process or thread invoking the function, and a nonrepeating value (sequence of bytes) for that process or thread.

SYS_TYPEID

SEE ALSO Chapter 36

FORMAT

```
SYS_TYPEID ( object_type_value )
```

DESCRIPTION **SYS_TYPEID** returns the type ID of the most specific type of the operand. This value is used primarily to identify the type-discriminant column underlying a substitutable column. For example, you can use the value returned by **SYS_TYPEID** to build an index on the type-discriminant column.

SYS_XMLAGG

SEE ALSO SYS_XMLGEN, Chapter 47

FORMAT

```
SYS_XMLAGG ( expr [fmt] )
```

DESCRIPTION **SYS_XMLAGG** aggregates all of the XML documents or fragments represented by *expr* and produces a single XML document. It adds a new enclosing element with a default name ROWSET. If you want to format the XML document differently, specify *fmt*, which is an instance of the SYS.XMLGenFormatType object.

SYS_XMLGEN

SEE ALSO SYS_XMLAGG, Chapter 47

FORMAT

```
SYS_XMLGEN ( expr [fmt] )
```

DESCRIPTION **SYS_XMLGEN** takes an expression that evaluates to a particular row and column of the database, and returns an instance of type SYS.XMLType containing an XML document. The *expr* can be a scalar value, a user-defined type, or an XMLType instance.

If *expr* is a scalar value, the function returns an XML element containing the scalar value. If *expr* is a type, the function maps the user-defined type attributes to XML elements. If *expr* is an XMLType instance, then the function encloses the document in an XML element whose default tag name is ROW.

By default the elements of the XML document match the elements of *expr*. For example, if *expr* resolves to a column name, the enclosing XML element will be the same column name. If you want to format the XML document differently, specify *fmt*, which is an instance of the SYS.XMLGenFormatType object.

SYSDATE

SEE ALSO Chapter 10

FORMAT

```
SYSDATE
```

DESCRIPTION SYSDATE returns the current date and time.

EXAMPLE

```
select SYSDATE from DUAL;
```

SYSTEM (ORACLE TABLESPACE)

SYSTEM is the name given to the first tablespace in a database. It contains the data dictionary.

SYSTEM (ORACLE USER)

SYSTEM is one of the DBA users that is created when a database system is installed and initialized (the other is SYS). SYS owns most of the data dictionary tables; SYSTEM owns the views created on those base tables.

SYSTEM GLOBAL AREA (SGA)

The SGA is a shared storage area in memory that is the center of Oracle activity while the database is running. The size of the SGA (and performance of the system) depends on the values of the variable initialization parameters. The SGA provides communication between the user and the background processes.

SYSTIMESTAMP

SEE ALSO Chapter 10

FORMAT

```
SYSTIMESTAMP
```

DESCRIPTION SYSTIMESTAMP returns the current date and time.

EXAMPLE

```
select SYSTIMESTAMP from DUAL;
```

TABLE

A table is the basic data storage structure in a relational database management system. A table consists of one or more units of information (rows), each of which contains the same kinds of values (columns). *See* **CREATE TABLE**.

TABLE (PL/SQL)

SEE ALSO DATATYPES, RECORD (PL/SQL)

FORMAT

```
TYPE new_type IS TABLE OF
{type | table.column%TYPE}[NOT NULL]
INDEX BY BINARY_INTEGER;
```

DESCRIPTION A TABLE declaration declares a new type that can then be used to declare variables of that type. A PL/SQL table has one column and an integer key and can have any number of rows. The datatype of the column can be either one of the standard PL/SQL datatypes (including another RECORD but not a TABLE) or a reference to the type of a particular column in a specific database table. Each field may also have a **NOT NULL** qualifier that specifies that the field must always have a non-**NULL** value.

The **INDEX BY BINARY_INTEGER** clause is required and reminds you that the index is an integer. You can refer to any row of the table with the index in parentheses.

If you refer to an index to which you have not assigned any data, PL/SQL raises the NO_DATA_ FOUND exception.

TABLE ALIAS

A table alias is a temporary substitute for a table name, defined in the **FROM** clause of a **SELECT** statement. *See* **AS** and Chapter 13.

TABLE CONSTRAINT

A table constraint is an integrity constraint that applies to multiple columns of the same table. *See* INTEGRITY CONSTRAINT.

TABLESPACE

A tablespace is a file or set of files that is used to store Oracle data. An Oracle database is composed of the SYSTEM tablespace and most likely other tablespaces. *See* Chapters 20 and 46.

TAN

SEE ALSO ACOS, ASIN, ATAN, ATAN2, COS, COSH, NUMBER FUNCTIONS, **SIN**, **TANH**, Chapter 9

FORMAT

```
TAN(value)
```

DESCRIPTION **TAN** returns the tangent of an angle *value* expressed in radians.

EXAMPLE

```
select TAN(135*3.141593/180) Tan -- tangent of 135 degrees in radians
from DUAL;
```

TANH

SEE ALSO ACOS, ASIN, ATAN, ATAN2, COS, COSH, NUMBER FUNCTIONS, **SIN**, **TAN**, Chapter 9

FORMAT

TANH(*value*)

DESCRIPTION TANH returns the hyperbolic tangent of an angle *value*.

TEMPORARY SEGMENT

A temporary segment is a storage space, within a tablespace, that is used to hold intermediate results of a SQL statement. For example, temporary segments are used when sorting large tables. Temporary segments are usually stored in tablespaces dedicated to them; *see* **CREATE TABLESPACE**.

TERMOUT (SQL*Plus)

See **SET**.

TEXT INDEX

A text index is a set of tables and indexes used by text search programs. Like the index in a book, a text index contains tables of text entries and their locations. *See* Chapter 25.

THEME

A theme is a category of a text document. Text entries may contain themes that do not appear as words within the document. For example, a document about mortgages could have "banking" as one of its themes even if the word "banking" does not appear in the document. *See* Chapter 25.

THROW

In Java, programs throw exceptions via the **TRY** clause, and process exceptions via the **CATCH** and **FINALLY** clauses. *See* Chapter 37.

TIME (SQL*Plus)

See **SET**.

TIMESTAMP

The TIMESTAMP (*fractional_seconds_precision*) datatype records year, month, and day values of date, as well as hour, minute, and second values of time, where *fractional_seconds_precision* is the number of digits in the fractional part of the SECOND datetime field. Accepted values of *fractional_seconds_precision* are 0 to 9. The default is 6. *See* DATATYPES and Chapter 9.

TIMESTAMP WITH TIME ZONE

The TIMESTAMP (*fractional_seconds_precision*) WITH TIME ZONE datatype records year, month, and day values of date, as well as hour, minute, and second values of time, where *fractional_seconds_precision* is the number of digits in the fractional part of the SECOND datetime field. Accepted values of *fractional_seconds_precision* are 0 to 9. The default is 6.

TIMESTAMP WITH LOCAL TIME ZONE

The TIMESTAMP (*fractional_seconds_precision*) WITH LOCAL TIME ZONE datatype records the TIMESTAMP WITH TIME ZONE values, normalized to the database time zone when the data is stored. When the data is retrieved, users see the data in the session time zone.

TIMING (SQL*Plus)

SEE ALSO CLEAR, SET

FORMAT

```
TIMI[NG] [ START area | STOP | SHOW ];
```

DESCRIPTION TIMING keeps track of elapsed time from **START** to **STOP** by area name. **START** opens a timing area and makes *area* its title. *area* must be a single word. Several areas may exist at once. The most recently created one is the current timing area until it is deleted, when the previously created one becomes current. Timing areas are, in effect, nested. The most recently created will always show the least amount of time, because the elapsed time of those before it will be, by definition, longer. Total time for any timing area is its own net time plus those of all the timing areas that followed it.

SHOW gives the current timing area's name and elapsed time.

STOP gives the current timing area's name and elapsed time, deletes the area, and makes the one previous to it (if there was one) the current timing area. *See* the *SQL*Plus User's Guide and Reference* for your host operating system for details on the precise meaning of time on your machine.

EXAMPLE To create a timing area named 1, you enter this:

```
timing start 1
```

To see the current timing area's name and time, but allow it to continue running, enter the following:

```
timing show
```

To see the current timing area's name and accumulated time, stop it, and make the previous one current, use this:

```
timing stop
```

TO_BINARY_DOUBLE

SEE ALSO TO_BINARY_FLOAT

FORMAT

```
TO_BINARY_DOUBLE (expr [, fmt  [, 'nlsparam']] )
```

DESCRIPTION TO_BINARY_DOUBLE returns a double-precision floating-point number. *expr* can be a character string or a numeric value of type NUMBER.

TO_BINARY_FLOAT

SEE ALSO TO_BINARY_DOUBLE

FORMAT

```
TO_BINARY_FLOAT (expr [, fmt  [, 'nlsparam']] )
```

DESCRIPTION TO_BINARY_FLOAT returns a single-precision floating-point number. *expr* can be a character string or a numeric value of type NUMBER.

TO_CHAR (character formats)

SEE ALSO **TO_CHAR (date and number formats)**

FORMAT

```
TO_CHAR ( nchar | clob | nclob )
```

DESCRIPTION The **TO_CHAR** (*character*) function converts NCHAR, NVARCHAR2, CLOB, or NCLOB data to the database character set.

EXAMPLE

```
SELECT TO_CHAR(Title) FROM BOOKSHELF;
```

TO_CHAR (date and number formats)

SEE ALSO DATE FORMATS, DATE FUNCTIONS, NUMBER FORMATS, **TO_DATE**, Chapter 10

FORMAT

```
TO_CHAR(date|interval,'format'[,'nlsparam'])
TO_CHAR(number,'format'[,'nlsparam'])
```

DESCRIPTION **TO_CHAR** reformats *number* or *date* according to *format*. *date* must be a column defined as an Oracle DATE datatype. It cannot be a string even if it is in the default date format of DD-MON-YY. The only way to use a string in which *date* appears in the **TO_CHAR** function is to enclose it within a **TO_DATE** function. The formats possible for this function are numerous. They are listed under NUMBER FORMATS and DATE FORMATS.

EXAMPLE Note the format in the following example. This is necessary in SQL*Plus to avoid the current default date width produced by **TO_CHAR**, which is about 100 characters wide:

```
column Formatted format a30 word_wrapped heading 'Formatted'

select BirthDate, TO_CHAR(BirthDate,'MM/DD/YY') Formatted
  from BIRTHDAY
 where FirstName = 'VICTORIA';

BIRTHDATE Formatted
--------- ------------------------------
20-MAY-49 05/20/49
```

TO_CLOB

SEE ALSO Chapter 35

FORMAT

```
TO_CLOB ( lob_column | char )
```

DESCRIPTION **TO_CLOB** converts NCLOB values in a LOB column or other character strings to CLOB values. *char* can be any of the datatypes CHAR, VARCHAR2, NCHAR, NVARCHAR2, CLOB, or NCLOB. Oracle executes this function by converting the underlying LOB data from the national character set to the database character set. Note that LONG values can be converted directly to CLOB columns via **ALTER TABLE**.

TO_DATE

SEE ALSO DATE FORMATS, DATE FUNCTIONS, **TO_CHAR**, Chapter 10

FORMAT

```
TO_DATE(string,'format'[,'nlsparam'])
```

DESCRIPTION **TO_DATE** converts a *string* in a given format into an Oracle date. It also will accept a number instead of a string, with certain limits. *string* is a literal string, a literal number, or a database column containing a string or a number. In every case but one, the format must correspond to that which is described by *format*. Only if a string is in the format 'DD-MON-YY' can the format be omitted. Note that *format* is restricted. *See* DATE FORMATS for a list of acceptable formats for **TO_DATE**.

EXAMPLE

```
select TO_DATE('02/22/04','MM/DD/YY') from DUAL;

TO_DATE('
---------
22-FEB-04
```

TO_DSINTERVAL

SEE ALSO DATATYPES

FORMAT

```
TO_DSINTERVAL ( char ['nlsparam'] )
```

DESCRIPTION **TO_DSINTERVAL** converts a character string of CHAR, VARCHAR2, NCHAR, or NVARCHAR2 datatype to an INTERVAL DAY TO SECOND type. *char* is the character string to be converted. The only valid NLS parameter you can specify in this function is NLS_NUMERIC_ CHARACTERS. This argument can have the form NLS_NUMERIC_CHARACTERS = "*dg*" where *d* and *g* represent the decimal character and group separator, respectively.

TO_LOB

SEE ALSO INSERT, Chapter 35

FORMAT

```
TO_LOB(long_column)
```

DESCRIPTION **TO_LOB** converts LONG values in *long_column* to LOB values. You can apply this function only to a LONG column, and only in the **SELECT** list of a subquery in an **INSERT** command.

TO_MULTI_BYTE

SEE ALSO CONVERSION FUNCTIONS, Chapter 10

FORMAT

```
TO_MULTI_BYTE(string)
```

DESCRIPTION **TO_MULTI_BYTE** converts the single-byte characters in a character *string* to their multibyte equivalents. If a character has no multibyte equivalent, the function returns the character unconverted.

TO_NCHAR (character)

SEE ALSO CONVERSION FUNCTIONS, **TRANSLATE ... USING**

FORMAT

```
TO_NCHAR ( {char | clob | nclob} [, fmt [, 'nlsparam']] )
```

DESCRIPTION TO_NCHAR (*character*) converts a character string, CLOB, or NCLOB from the database character set to the national character set. This function is equivalent to the **TRANSLATE ... USING** function with a **USING** clause in the national character set.

TO_NCHAR (datetime)

SEE ALSO CONVERSION FUNCTIONS

FORMAT

```
TO_NCHAR ( { datetime | interval } [, fmt [, 'nlsparam']] )
```

DESCRIPTION TO_NCHAR (*datetime*) converts a character string of DATE, TIMESTAMP, TIMESTAMP WITH TIME ZONE, TIMESTAMP WITH LOCAL TIME ZONE, INTERVAL MONTH TO YEAR, or INTERVAL DAY TO SECOND datatype from the database character set to the national character set.

TO_NCHAR (number)

SEE ALSO CONVERSION FUNCTIONS

FORMAT

```
TO_NCHAR ( n [, fmt [, 'nlsparam']] )
```

DESCRIPTION TO_NCHAR (*number*) converts a number to a string in the NVARCHAR2 character set. The optional *fmt* and *nlsparam* corresponding to *n* can be of DATE, TIMESTAMP, TIMESTAMP WITH TIME ZONE, TIMESTAMP WITH LOCAL TIME ZONE, INTERVAL MONTH TO YEAR, or INTERVAL DAY TO SECOND datatype.

TO_NCLOB

SEE ALSO CONVERSION FUNCTIONS, Chapter 35

FORMAT

```
TO_NCLOB ( lob_column | char )
```

DESCRIPTION TO_NCLOB converts CLOB values in a LOB column or other character strings to NCLOB values. *char* can be any of the datatypes CHAR, VARCHAR2, NCHAR, NVARCHAR2, CLOB, or NCLOB. Oracle implements this function by converting the character set of the LOB column from the database character set to the national character set.

TO_NUMBER

SEE ALSO CONVERSION FUNCTIONS, Chapter 9

FORMAT

```
TO_NUMBER(string [, fmt [, 'nlsparam']] )
```

DESCRIPTION TO_NUMBER converts a character *string* to a NUMBER datatype. It requires that the characters in the string be a properly formatted number with only the characters 0–9, –, +, and . included. This function is largely unnecessary due to automatic data conversion done by Oracle, except when used for a character column containing numbers in an **ORDER BY** or a comparison.

EXAMPLE

```
TO_NUMBER('333.46')
```

TO_SINGLE_BYTE

SEE ALSO CONVERSION FUNCTIONS, Chapter 11

FORMAT

```
TO_SINGLE_BYTE(string)
```

DESCRIPTION **TO_SINGLE_BYTE** converts the multibyte characters in a character *string* to their single-byte equivalents. If a multibyte character has no single-byte equivalent, the function returns the character unconverted.

TO_TIMESTAMP

SEE ALSO CONVERSION FUNCTIONS, **TO_CHAR**, TIMESTAMP, **TO_TIMESTAMP_TZ**

FORMAT

```
TO_TIMESTAMP ( char [ , fmt ['nlsparam']] )
```

DESCRIPTION **TO_TIMESTAMP** converts *char* of CHAR, VARCHAR2, NCHAR, or NVARCHAR2 datatype to a value of TIMESTAMP datatype, using a *fmt* format if *char* is not in the default format of the TIMESTAMP datatype. The optional *nlsparam* has the same purpose in this function as in the **TO_CHAR** function for date conversion.

TO_TIMESTAMP_TZ

SEE ALSO CONVERSION FUNCTIONS, **TO_TIMESTAMP**, TIMESTAMP WITH TIME ZONE

FORMAT

```
TO_TIMESTAMP_TZ ( char [ , fmt ['nlsparam']] )
```

DESCRIPTION **TO_TIMESTAMP_TZ** converts *char* of CHAR, VARCHAR2, NCHAR, or NVARCHAR2 datatype to a value of TIMESTAMP WITH TIME ZONE datatype.

TO_YMINTERVAL

SEE ALSO CONVERSION FUNCTIONS, INTERVAL YEAR TO MONTH

FORMAT

```
TO_YMINTERVAL ( char )
```

DESCRIPTION **TO_YMINTERVAL** converts a character string of CHAR, VARCHAR2, NCHAR, or NVARCHAR2 datatype to an INTERVAL YEAR TO MONTH type, where *char* is the character string to be converted.

TRANSACTION

A transaction is a sequence of SQL statements that Oracle treats as a single unit. The set of changes is made permanent with the **COMMIT** statement. Part or all of a transaction can be undone with the **ROLLBACK** statement.

Oracle manages transactions both with locking (*see* LOCK) and a *multiversion consistency model,* which essentially behaves as though each transaction has its own copy of the database—that is, that

there are multiple, overlapping versions of the database in existence at any given time. A transaction starts with the execution of the first SQL statement in the transaction and ends with either the **COMMIT** or **ROLLBACK** statement. By default, Oracle guarantees that a transaction has *statement-level read consistency,* which means that when you execute a query, the data stays the same while Oracle is gathering and returning it. But if a transaction has multiple queries, each query is internally consistent but is not consistent with successive queries. If you want to be able to maintain a consistent view of the data throughout such a transaction, the transaction needs to have *transaction-level read consistency,* which guarantees that the transaction will not see the effects of the committing of other transactions. This read-only transaction, started with **SET TRANSACTION READ ONLY**, can only execute queries and certain control commands (*see* **SET TRANSACTION**).

TRANSACTION PROCESSING

Transaction processing is a form of processing oriented toward logical units of work, rather than separate and individual changes, in order to keep the database consistent.

TRANSLATE

SEE ALSO **REPLACE**, Chapter 11

FORMAT

```
TRANSLATE(string, from, to)
```

DESCRIPTION **TRANSLATE** looks at each character in *string*, and then checks *from* to see if that character is there. If it is, **TRANSLATE** notes the position in *from* where it found the character, and then looks at the same position in *to*. Whatever character it finds there, it substitutes for the character in *string*.

EXAMPLE

```
select TRANSLATE('I LOVE MY OLD THESAURUS','AEIOUY','123456')
from DUAL;

TRANSLATE('ILOVEMYOLDTH
-----------------------
3 L4V2 M6 4LD TH2S15R5S
```

TRANSLATE ... USING

SEE ALSO CONVERSION FUNCTIONS, **CONVERT, TO_NCHAR, UNISTR**

FORMAT

```
TRANSLATE ( text USING { CHAR_CS | NCHAR_CS } )
```

DESCRIPTION **TRANSLATE ... USING** converts *text* into the character set specified for conversions between the database character set and the national character set. The *text* argument is the expression to be converted.

Specifying the **USING CHAR_CS** argument converts *text* into the database character set. The output datatype is VARCHAR2.

Specifying the **USING NCHAR_CS** argument converts *text* into the national character set. The output datatype is NVARCHAR2.

This function is similar to the Oracle **CONVERT** function, but must be used instead of **CONVERT** if either the input or the output datatype is being used as NCHAR or NVARCHAR2. If the input contains UCS2 code points or backslash characters (\), use the **UNISTR** function.

TRANSPORTABLE TABLESPACE

A transportable tablespace is a tablespace that can be "unplugged" from one database and "plugged into" another. To be transportable, a tablespace—or a set of tablespaces—must be self-contained. The tablespace set cannot contain any objects that refer to objects in other tablespaces. Thus, if you transport a tablespace containing indexes, you must move the tablespace containing the indexes' base tables as part of the same transportable tablespace set. The better you have organized and distributed your objects among tablespaces, the easier it is to generate a self-contained set of tablespaces to transport.

To transport tablespaces, you need to generate a tablespace set, copy or move that tablespace set to the new database, and plug the set into the new database. As of Oracle Database 10*g*, tablespaces can be transported across platforms.

See Chapter 46 for details.

TREAT

SEE ALSO **DEREF**, **REF**, Chapter 36
FORMAT

```
TREAT ( expr AS [REF] [schema.] type )
```

DESCRIPTION **TREAT** changes the declared type of an expression.

If the declared type of *expr* is *source_type*, then *type* must be some supertype or subtype of *source_type*. If the most specific type of *expr* is *type* (or some subtype of *type*), then **TREAT** returns *expr*. If the most specific type of *expr* is not *type* (or some subtype of *type*), then **TREAT** returns **NULL**.

If the declared type of *expr* is **REF** *source_type*, then *type* must be some subtype or supertype of *source_type*. If the most specific type of **DEREF**(*expr*) is *type* (or a subtype of *type*), **TREAT** returns *expr*. If the most specific type of **DEREF**(*expr*) is not *type* (or a subtype of *type*), then **TREAT** returns **NULL**.

TREE-STRUCTURED QUERY

A tree-structured query is one whose result shows hierarchical relationships among rows in a table. *See* **CONNECT BY**.

TRIGGER

A database trigger is a stored procedure associated with a table that Oracle automatically executes on one or more specified events (**BEFORE**, **AFTER**, or **INSTEAD OF** an **INSERT**, **UPDATE**, or **DELETE**) affecting the table. Triggers can execute for the table as a whole or for each affected row in the table. *See* Chapter 30 for a full discussion of triggers and examples, and **CREATE TRIGGER** for syntax.

TRIM

SEE ALSO **LTRIM**, **RTRIM**, Chapter 7
FORMAT

```
TRIM
( [{ { LEADING | TRAILING | BOTH } [trim_character])
  | trim_character
  }    FROM   ] trim_source )
```

DESCRIPTION **TRIM** enables you to trim leading or trailing characters (or both) from a character string. If *trim_character* or *trim_source* is a character literal, you must enclose it in single quotes.

If you specify **LEADING**, Oracle removes any leading characters equal to *trim_character*. If you specify **TRAILING**, Oracle removes any trailing characters equal to *trim_character*. If you specify **BOTH** or none of the three, Oracle removes leading and trailing characters equal to *trim_character*.

If you specify only *trim_source*, Oracle removes leading and trailing blank spaces. If either *trim_source* or *trim_character* is a **NULL** value, then the **TRIM** function returns a **NULL**.

EXAMPLE

```
select TRIM('"' from Title) from MAGAZINE;
select TRIM(leading '"' from Title) from MAGAZINE;
select TRIM(trailing '"' from Title) from MAGAZINE;
```

TRIMOUT (SQL*Plus)

See **SET**.

TRUNC (Form 1—for Dates)

SEE ALSO COLUMN, DATE FUNCTIONS, **TRUNC** (Form 2), Chapter 10
FORMAT

```
TRUNC(date,'format')
```

DESCRIPTION **TRUNC** truncates *date* according to *format*. Without a *format*, *date* is truncated to 12 A.M. (midnight), with the first moment of the new day, today's date, for any time up to and including 11:59:59 P.M. (just before midnight). *See* **ROUND** (Form 1) for valid date *format* values.

The result of **TRUNC** is always a date with its time set to 12 A.M., the first moment of the day.

TRUNC (Form 2—for Numbers)

SEE ALSO COLUMN, NUMBER FUNCTIONS, **TRUNC** (Form 1), Chapter 9
FORMAT

```
TRUNC(value,precision)
```

DESCRIPTION **TRUNC** is *value* truncated to *precision*.

EXAMPLES

```
TRUNC(123.45,0)  = 123
TRUNC(123.45,-1) = 120
TRUNC(123.45,-2) = 100
```

TRUNCATE

SEE ALSO CREATE CLUSTER, **DELETE**, **DROP TABLE**, TRIGGER, Chapter 17
FORMAT

```
TRUNCATE
{ TABLE [schema.] table [{ PRESERVE | PURGE } MATERIALIZED VIEW LOG]
| CLUSTER [schema.] cluster }
[{ DROP | REUSE } STORAGE];
```

DESCRIPTION **TRUNCATE** removes all the rows from a table or cluster. You can truncate only an indexed cluster, not a hash cluster (*see* **CREATE CLUSTER**). If you add the **DROP STORAGE** option, **TRUNCATE** will deallocate the space from the deleted rows; if you add the **REUSE STORAGE**

option, **TRUNCATE** will leave the space allocated for new rows in the table. **DROP STORAGE** is the default.

The **TRUNCATE** command is faster than a **DELETE** command because it generates no rollback information, does not fire any **DELETE** triggers (and therefore must be used with caution), and does not record any information in a materialized view log. In addition, using **TRUNCATE** does not invalidate the objects depending on the deleted rows, or the privileges on the table.

> **NOTE**
> *You cannot roll back a **TRUNCATE** statement.*

TTITLE (SQL*Plus)

SEE ALSO **ACCEPT**, **BTITLE**, **DEFINE**, PARAMETERS, **REPFOOTER**, **REPHEADER**
FORMAT

```
TTI[TLE] [option [text|variable]... | OFF | ON]
```

DESCRIPTION **TTITLE** (Top **TITLE**) puts a title (may be multiline) at the top of each page of a report. OFF and ON suppress and restore the display of the text without changing its contents. **TTITLE** by itself displays the current **TTITLE** options and *text* or *variable*.

text is a title you wish to give this report, and *variable* is a user-defined variable or a system-maintained variable, including SQL.LNO, the current line number; SQL.PNO, the current page number; SQL.RELEASE, the current Oracle release number; SQL.SQLCODE, the current error code; and SQL.USER, the username.

SQL*Plus uses **TTITLE** in the new form if the first word after **TTITLE** is a valid option. The valid options are

- **COL** *n* skips directly to position *n* from the left margin of the current line.

- **S[KIP]** *n* prints *n* blank lines. If no *n* is specified, one blank line is printed. If *n* is 0, no blank lines are printed and the current position for printing becomes position 1 of the current line (leftmost on the page).

- **TAB** *n* skips forward *n* positions (backward if *n* is negative).

- **BOLD** prints the output data in bold print.

- **LE[FT]**, **CE[NTER]**, and **R[IGHT]** left-justify, center, and right-justify data on the current line. Any text or variables following these commands are justified as a group, up to the end of the command, or a LEFT, CENTER, RIGHT, or COL. CENTER and RIGHT use the value set by the **SET LINESIZE** command to determine where to place the text or variable.

- **FORMAT** *string* specifies the FORMAT MODEL that will control the format of subsequent text or variables, and follows the same syntax as FORMAT in a **COLUMN** command, such as FORMAT A12 or FORMAT $999,990.99. Each time a FORMAT appears, it supersedes the previous one that was in effect. If no FORMAT MODEL has been specified, the one set by **SET NUMFORMAT** is used. If NUMFORMAT has not been set, the default for SQL*Plus is used.

Date values are printed according to the default format unless a variable has been loaded with a date reformatted by **TO_CHAR**.

Any number of options, pieces of text, and variables may be used in a single **TTITLE**. Each is printed in the order specified, and each is positioned and formatted as specified by the clauses that precede it.

TUPLE

Tuple is a synonym for *row*. It rhymes with "couple."

TWO-PHASE COMMIT

Oracle manages distributed transactions with a special feature called *two-phase commit*. Two-phase commit guarantees that a transaction is valid at all sites by the time it commits or rolls back. All sites either commit or roll back together, no matter what errors occur in the network or on the machines tied together by the network. You don't need to do anything special to have your applications use a two-phase commit.

TYPE

See ABSTRACT DATATYPE and **CREATE TYPE**.

TYPE (Embedded SQL)

SEE ALSO *Programmer's Guide to the Oracle Precompilers*
FORMAT

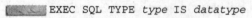

```
EXEC SQL TYPE type IS datatype
```

DESCRIPTION PL/SQL lets you assign an Oracle external datatype to a user-defined datatype. The datatype may include a length, precision, or scale. This external datatype is equivalenced to the user-defined type and assigned to all host variables assigned to the type. For a list of external datatypes, see the *Programmer's Guide to the Oracle Precompilers*.

NOTE
See the Programmer's Guide to the Oracle Precompilers *for a full list of all commands. This reference does not contain all of the possible precompiler commands.*

TYPE BODY

See ABSTRACT DATATYPE, **CREATE TYPE**, and METHOD.

TZ_OFFSET

SEE ALSO **SESSIONTIMEZONE, DBTIMEZONE**
FORMAT

```
TZ_OFFSET
( { 'time_zone_name'
  | '{ + | - } hh : mi'
  | SESSIONTIMEZONE
  | DBTMEZONE
  })
```

DESCRIPTION **TZ_OFFSET** returns the time zone offset corresponding to the value entered based on the date the statement is executed. You can enter a valid time zone name, a time zone offset from UTC (which simply returns itself), or the keyword **SESSIONTIMEZONE** or **DBTIMEZONE**. For a listing of valid values, query the TZNAME column of the V$TIMEZONE_NAMES dynamic performance view.

UID
FORMAT

UID

DESCRIPTION UID returns an integer that uniquely identifies the session user (the user who logged on).

UNDEFINE (SQL*Plus)
SEE ALSO **ACCEPT**, **DEFINE**, PARAMETERS, Chapter 15
FORMAT

UNDEF[INE] *variable*

DESCRIPTION **UNDEFINE** deletes the definition of a user variable that has been defined by **ACCEPT**, **DEFINE**, or as a parameter to the **START** command. You can **UNDEFINE** the current values of multiple variables in a single command. The format is shown in the following listing:

undefine *variable1 variable2 ...*

EXAMPLE To **UNDEFINE** a variable named Total, use this:

undefine Total

UNDERLINE (SQL*Plus)
See **SET**.

UNDO SEGMENT
As of Oracle9*i*, you can use Automatic Undo Management to provide read consistency in place of rollback segments. If you use this option, Oracle will maintain undo segments to track changes and provide rollback capabilities. *See* ROLLBACK SEGMENT and Chapter 46.

UNION
SEE ALSO **INTERSECT**, **MINUS**, QUERY OPERATORS, Chapter 13
FORMAT

select...
 UNION [ALL]
select...

DESCRIPTION **UNION** combines two queries. It returns all distinct rows for both **SELECT** statements or, when **ALL** is specified, all rows regardless of duplication. The number of columns and datatypes must be identical between **SELECT** statements, although the names of the columns do not need to be. *See* Chapter 13 for a discussion of the important differences and effects of **INTERSECT**, **UNION**, and **MINUS**, and the role that precedence plays in the results.

UNIQUE INDEX
A unique index is an index that imposes uniqueness on each value it indexes. The index may be one single column or concatenated (multiple columns). *See* INTEGRITY CONSTRAINT.

UNIQUE KEY

A unique key is one or more columns that must be unique for each row of the table. *See* KEY, PRIMARY KEY, and INTEGRITY CONSTRAINT.

UNISTR

SEE ALSO CONVERSION FUNCTIONS, **CONVERT**, **TRANSLATE … USING**

FORMAT

```
UNISTR ( 'string' )
```

DESCRIPTION UNISTR takes as its argument a string in any character set and returns it in Unicode in the database Unicode character set. To include UCS2 codepoint characters in the string, use the escape backslash (\) followed by the next number. To include the backslash itself, precede it with another backslash (\\).

This function is similar to the **TRANSLATE … USING** function, except that **UNISTR** offers the escape character for UCS2 codepoints and backslash characters.

UNIT OF WORK

In Oracle, a transaction is equivalent to a logical unit of work, which includes all SQL statements since you logged on, last committed, or last rolled back your work. Thus, a transaction can encompass numerous SQL statements, or only one.

UPDATE (Form 1—Embedded SQL)

SEE ALSO **EXECUTE IMMEDIATE**, **FOR**, **PREPARE**, **SELECT** (Form 2), *Programmer's Guide to the Oracle Precompilers*

FORMAT

```
EXEC SQL [AT { dbname | :host_variable }]
 [FOR { :host_integer | integer }]
 UPDATE
 [ (subquery)
 | [schema.] { table | view } [ @db_link | PARTITION (part_name) ] ]
 SET
 { column = { expr | (subquery_2) }
 | (column [, column]...) = (subquery_1) }
 [, { column = { expr | (subquery_2) }
    | (column [, column]...) = (subquery_1)      } ]...
 [WHERE { condition | CURRENT OF cursor }]
 [{ RETURN | RETURNING } expr [, expr]... INTO
 :host_variable [[INDICATOR] :ind_variable]
 [, :host_variable [[INDICATOR] :ind_variable]]...]
```

DESCRIPTION *See* the description of the various clauses in **UPDATE** (Form 3). The elements unique to Embedded SQL follow:

■ **AT** *dbname* optionally names a database from a previous **CONNECT** statement for a database name from a previous **DECLARE DATABASE** statement.

- **FOR** :*host_integer* sets the maximum number of rows that can be fetched. *integer* is a named host variable.

- *expr* may include a host :*variable*[:*indicator*].

- The **WHERE** clause may include host variables or arrays.

- **CURRENT OF** updates the last row fetched for the named *cursor*. However, the cursor must be open and positioned on the row. If it isn't, the **CURRENT OF** clause, which is a part of the **WHERE** clause, causes the **WHERE** to find no rows, and none will be updated. The cursor must have previously been named in a **DECLARE CURSOR** statement with a **SELECT ... FOR UPDATE OF**.

If any host variable in either the **SET** or **WHERE** is an array, then all host variables in both must be arrays, though they do not all need to be the same size arrays. If they are arrays, **UPDATE** is executed once for each set of components in the array, and may update zero or more rows. The maximum number depends on either the size of the smallest array or the integer value in the **FOR** clause, if one is specified. *See* **FOR** for additional details.

NOTE
See the Programmer's Guide to the Oracle Precompilers *for a full list of all commands. This reference does not contain all of the possible precompiler commands.*

UPDATE (Form 2—PL/SQL)
SEE ALSO **DECLARE CURSOR**, SUBQUERY
FORMAT

```
UPDATE [user.]table[@dblink]
SET { column = expression | column = (select expression...)
 [ [,column = expression]... |
 [,column = (select
expression...)]... ] |
 (column [,column]...) = (subquery)}
 [WHERE {condition | CURRENT OF cursor}];
```

DESCRIPTION **UPDATE** in PL/SQL works identically to the normal SQL **UPDATE** statement, with the exception of the alternative **WHERE** clause, **WHERE CURRENT OF** cursor. In this instance, the **UPDATE** statement affects just the single row currently in the cursor as a result of the last **FETCH**. The cursor **SELECT** statement must have included the words **FOR UPDATE**.

Like **INSERT**, **DELETE**, and **SELECT ... INTO**, the **UPDATE** statement always uses the implicit cursor named SQL. This is never declared (although the **SELECT ... FOR UPDATE** statement must be **DECLARE**d in a cursor for the **WHERE CURRENT OF** cursor to be used). Its attributes are set as follows:

- **SQL%ISOPEN** is irrelevant.

- **SQL%FOUND** is TRUE if one or more rows are updated, FALSE if no rows are updated. **SQL%NOTFOUND** is the opposite of SQL%FOUND.

- **SQL%ROWCOUNT** is the number of rows updated.

UPDATE (Form 3—SQL Command)

SEE ALSO DELETE, **INSERT**, **SELECT**, SUBQUERY, **WHERE**, Chapter 15

FORMAT

update::=

DML_table_expression_clause::=

subquery_restriction_clause::=

table_collection_expression::=

update_set_clause::=

where_clause::=

returning_clause::=

DESCRIPTION **UPDATE** changes the values in the listed columns in the specified table. The **WHERE** clause may contain a correlated subquery. A subquery may select from the table that is being updated, although it must return just one row. Without a **WHERE** clause, all rows will be updated. With a **WHERE** clause, only those rows it selects will be updated. The expressions are evaluated as the command is executed, and their results replace the current values for the columns in the row(s).

A subquery must select the same number of columns (with compatible datatypes) as are in parentheses on the left side of the **SET** clause. Columns that are set to equal an expression may precede columns in parentheses set equal to a subquery, all within a single **UPDATE** statement.

EXAMPLE To set **NULL** all Publisher values:

```
update BOOKSHELF set Publisher = NULL ;
```

The following will update the city of Walpole in the COMFORT table, setting the precipitation for all Walpole rows to **NULL**, the noon temperature equal to that in Manchester, and the midnight temperature equal to the noon temperature minus 10 degrees:

```
update COMFORT set Precipitation = NULL,
            (Noon, Midnight) =
        (select Temperature, Temperature - 10
           from WEATHER
          where City = 'MANCHESTER')
 where City = 'WALPOLE';
```

UPDATEXML

SEE ALSO Chapter 47

FORMAT

```
UPDATEXML (XMLType_instance,
[Xpath_string , value_expr [,Xpath_string , value_expr …]
[, namespace_string ] )
```

DESCRIPTION **UPDATEXML** takes as arguments an XMLType instance and an XPath value pair and returns an XMLType instance with the updated value. If *Xpath_string* is an XML element, then the corresponding *value_expr* must be an XMLType instance. If *Xpath_string* is an attribute or text node, then the *value_expr* can be any scalar datatype. The datatypes of the target of each *Xpath_string* and its corresponding *value_expr* must match. The optional *namespace_string* must resolve to a VARCHAR2 value that specifies a default mapping or namespace mapping for prefixes, which Oracle uses when evaluating the XPath expressions.

UPPER

SEE ALSO LOWER, Chapter 7

FORMAT

```
UPPER(string)
```

DESCRIPTION **UPPER** converts every letter in *string* into uppercase.

EXAMPLE

```
upper('Look what you''ve done!')
```

produces this:

```
LOOK WHAT YOU'VE DONE!
```

UROWID

UROWID (Universal RowID) is the datatype for index-organized tables' primary keys. The maximum and default size is 4000 bytes. *See* DATATYPES and **CREATE TABLE**.

USED EXTENTS

Used extents are those that either have been allocated to a data (table) segment—and thus have data in them—or have been reserved for data.

USER

SEE ALSO UID

FORMAT

```
USER
```

DESCRIPTION **USER** is the name by which the current user is known to Oracle. **USER** is a function, and as such can be queried in any **SELECT** statement.

EXAMPLE

```
select USER from DUAL;
```

USER VARIABLES

See **ACCEPT**, **DEFINE**, PARAMETERS.

USERENV

SEE ALSO CHARACTER FUNCTIONS

FORMAT

USERENV(*option*)

DESCRIPTION **USERENV** is a legacy function, replaced by SYS_CONTEXT's UserEnv namespace. The options and their return values are as follows:

'CLIENT_INFO'	Returns up to 64 bytes of user session information that can be stored by an application using the DBMS_APPLICATION_INFO package.
'ENTRYID'	Returns available auditing entry identifier. You cannot use this attribute in distributed SQL statements. To use this keyword in USERENV, the initialization parameter AUDIT_TRAIL must be set to TRUE.
'ISDBA'	Returns 'TRUE' if the user has been authenticated as having DBA privileges through either the operating system or a password file.
'LANG'	Returns the ISO abbreviation for the language name, a shorter form than the existing 'LANGUAGE' parameter.
'LANGUAGE'	Returns the language and territory currently used by your session along with the database character set in this form: language_territory.characterset
'SESSIONID'	Returns your auditing session identifier. You cannot use this attribute in distributed SQL statements.
'TERMINAL'	Returns the operating system identifier for your current session's terminal. In distributed SQL statements, this attribute returns the identifier for your local session. In a distributed environment, this is supported only for remote **SELECT** statements, not for remote **INSERT**, **UPDATE**, or **DELETE** operations.

USERNAME

Username is a word that identifies you as an authorized user of your host computer's operating system or of Oracle. A password is associated with each username.

VALUE

SEE ALSO **DEREF**, **REF**, Chapter 36

FORMAT

VALUE (*correlation_variable*)

DESCRIPTION In a SQL statement, **VALUE** takes as its argument a correlation variable (table alias) associated with a row of an object table and returns object instances stored in the object table. The type of the object instances is the same type as the object table. *See* Chapter 36.

VAR (Embedded SQL)

SEE ALSO **SELECT** (Form 2), VARIABLE DECLARATION, *Programmer's Guide to the Oracle Precompilers*

FORMAT

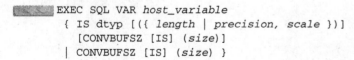
```
EXEC SQL VAR host_variable
  { IS dtyp [({ length | precision, scale })]
    [CONVBUFSZ [IS] (size)]
  | CONVBUFSZ [IS] (size) }
```

DESCRIPTION PL/SQL lets you override the default datatype assignment of a variable via the **VAR** command. Once a variable has been declared, it uses the datatype assigned to it in the **DECLARE** command. **VAR** allows you to change the datatype of a declared variable within a PL/SQL block.

NOTE
See the Programmer's Guide to the Oracle Precompilers *for a full list of all commands. This reference does not contain all of the possible precompiler commands.*

VAR_POP

SEE ALSO GROUPING FUNCTIONS, **VAR_SAMP**, **VARIANCE**

FORMAT

```
VAR_POP ( expr ) [OVER ( analytic_clause )]
```

DESCRIPTION VAR_POP returns the population variance of a set of numbers after discarding the NULLs in this set.

VAR_SAMP

SEE ALSO GROUPING FUNCTIONS, **VAR_POP**, **VARIANCE**

FORMAT

```
VAR_SAMP ( expr ) [OVER ( analytic_clause )]
```

DESCRIPTION VAR_SAMP returns the sample variance of a set of numbers after discarding the NULLs in this set.

VARCHAR2

See DATATYPES.

VARIABLE

SEE ALSO PRINT

FORMAT

```
VAR[IABLE] [variable_name [NUMBER|CHAR|CHAR (n{CHAR|BYTE})|NCHAR|NCHAR(n)
  |VARCHAR2 (n[CHAR|BYTE]) | NVARCHAR2(n) | CLOB | NCLOB | REFCURSOR
  |BINARY_FLOAT | BINARY_DOUBLE
```

DESCRIPTION **VARIABLE** declares a bind variable that can be referenced in PL/SQL. Each variable is assigned a *variable_name* and a type (NUMBER or CHAR). For CHAR variables, a maximum length (*n*) can be specified. **VARIABLE** followed by a variable name lists that variable.

EXAMPLES In the following example, a variable named *bal* is created and is set equal to the result of a function:

```
variable bal NUMBER
begin
  :bal := LATE_FEE('DORAH TALBOT');
end;
```

VARIABLE DECLARATION (PL/SQL)
FORMAT

```
variable [CONSTANT]
{type | identifier%TYPE | [user.]table%ROWTYPE}
  [NOT NULL]
  [{DEFAULT | :=} expression];
```

DESCRIPTION PL/SQL lets you declare variables in a PL/SQL block. If you declare the variable to be CONSTANT, you must initialize the variable with a value in the declaration and you cannot assign a new value to the variable.

The type of the variable can be a PL/SQL type (*see* DATATYPES), the type of another PL/SQL variable or database column given by an identifier, or a ROWTYPE (*see* **%ROWTYPE**) that lets you refer to a record corresponding to a database table.

If you add **NOT NULL** to the declaration, you cannot assign a **NULL** to the variable and you must initialize the variable. The initialization (following a DEFAULT or assignment :=) expression is any valid PL/SQL expression that results in a value of the type declared.

VARIANCE
SEE ALSO ACCEPT, AGGREGATE FUNCTIONS, **COMPUTE**, **DEFINE**, PARAMETERS, **STDDEV**, **VAR_POP**, **VAR_SAMP**, Chapter 9
FORMAT

```
VARIANCE ( [ DISTINCT | ALL ] expr ) [OVER ( analytic_clause )]
```

DESCRIPTION **VARIANCE** gives the variance of all *values* for a group of rows. Like other group functions, **VARIANCE** ignores **NULL** values.

VARRAY
VARRAY is a clause within the **CREATE TYPE** command that tells the database the limit to the number of entries within the varying array. *See* Chapter 34 for detailed examples of varying arrays. *See* **CREATE TYPE** for syntax information.

VARYING ARRAY
A varying array is a collector—for a single row in a table, it can contain multiple entries. The maximum number of varying array entries per row is set when the varying array is created (via **CREATE TYPE**). *See* Chapter 34.

VERIFY (SQL*Plus)

See **SET**.

VERSION NUMBER

The version number is the primary identifying number of Oracle software (9, 10, etc.).

VIEW

A view is a database object that is a logical representation of a table. It is derived from a table but has no storage of its own and often may be used in the same manner as a table. *See* **CREATE VIEW** and Chapter 17.

VIRTUAL COLUMN

A virtual column is a column in a query result whose value is calculated from the value(s) of other column(s).

VSIZE

SEE ALSO CHARACTER FUNCTIONS, **LENGTH**, NUMBER FUNCTIONS, Chapter 9
FORMAT

```
VSIZE(value)
```

DESCRIPTION **VSIZE** is the storage size of *value* in Oracle. For numbers it is usually smaller than the apparent length, because less space is required to store numbers in the database.
EXAMPLES

```
VSIZE(12.345) = 4
```

WHENEVER

SEE ALSO EXECUTE, FETCH
FORMAT

```
EXEC SQL WHENEVER {NOT FOUND | SQLERROR | SQL WARNING}
    {CONTINUE |
    GOTO label |
    STOP |
    DO routine |
    DO BREAK |
    DO CONTINUE}
```

DESCRIPTION **WHENEVER** is not an executable SQL statement, but rather an instruction to the Oracle language processor to embed an IF *condition* THEN GOTO *label* statement after every SQL statement to follow. As each SQL statement executes, its results are tested to see if they meet the *condition*. If they do, the program branches to the *label*.

 WHENEVER may be used with **CONTINUE** or a different label for each of the three possible conditions. Each of these will be in effect for all subsequent SQL statements. A new **WHENEVER** with one of these conditions will completely replace its predecessor for all subsequent SQL statements.

 The **NOT FOUND** condition is raised any time SQLCODE is 100, meaning, for instance, that a **FETCH** failed to return any rows (this includes subqueries in **INSERT** statements).

SQLERROR occurs whenever SQLCODE is less than 0. These are typically fatal errors and require serious error handling.

SQLWARNING occurs when a nonfatal "error" occurs. These include truncation of character strings being loaded into host variables, a select list of columns that doesn't match the INTO list of host variables, and **DELETE** or **UPDATE** statements without **WHERE** clauses.

Usually, initial branching, continuation, stopping, or routine execution is set up at the very beginning of a program, before any executable SQL statements. However, within particular blocks of logic in the body of the program, any or all of these could be replaced depending upon local needs. Note that **WHENEVER** knows nothing about the host language's scoping rules, calls, or branching. From the moment a **WHENEVER** is asserted, its rules remain in effect until another **WHENEVER** (with the same condition) replaces it. On the other hand, your program must obey language scoping rules with regard to the **GOTO** and label.

The **STOP** option stops program execution; the **DO** option calls a host language routine of some kind, the syntax of which depends on your host language. **DO BREAK** performs a break from a loop; **DO CONTINUE** performs a continue statement from a loop when the condition is met.

Lastly, in an error-handling routine, particularly one that may contain SQL statements, **WHENEVER SQLERROR** should probably contain **CONTINUE** or **STOP** or should call an exit routine in order to avoid an infinite loop back into the same error-handling routine.

WHENEVER OSERROR (SQL*Plus)

SEE ALSO WHENEVER SQLERROR

FORMAT

```
WHENEVER OSERROR
{EXIT [SUCCESS|FAILURE|n|variable|:BindVariable] [COMMIT|ROLLBACK]
|CONTINUE [COMMIT|ROLLBACK|NONE]}
```

DESCRIPTION **WHENEVER OSERROR** handles processing logic within SQL*Plus if an operating system error occurs. **EXIT** directs SQL*Plus to exit, and **CONTINUE** turns off **EXIT**. **COMMIT** tells SQL*Plus to issue a **COMMIT** prior to exiting, and **ROLLBACK** tells it to issue a **ROLLBACK** before exiting. The default behavior is **NONE**.

WHENEVER SQLERROR (SQL*Plus)

SEE ALSO WHENEVER OSERROR

FORMAT

```
WHENEVER SQLERROR
{EXIT [SUCCESS|FAILURE|WARNING|n|variable|:BindVariable]
[COMMIT|ROLLBACK]|CONTINUE [COMMIT|ROLLBACK|NONE]}
```

DESCRIPTION **WHENEVER SQLERROR** handles processing logic within SQL*Plus if a SQL command or a PL/SQL block encounters an error. **EXIT** directs SQL*Plus to exit, and **CONTINUE** turns off **EXIT**. **COMMIT** tells SQL*Plus to issue a **COMMIT** prior to exiting, and **ROLLBACK** tells it to issue a **ROLLBACK** before exiting. The default behavior is **NONE**.

NOTE
*SQL and PL/SQL errors initiate **WHENEVER SQLERROR** processing.*
*SQL*Plus errors do not.*

You may place WHENEVER SQLERROR in a start file in front of as many SQL statements as you wish. Each **WHENEVER SQLERROR** will supersede the one before, and will remain in effect until it is itself superseded.

EXAMPLE When the **CREATE TABLE** command in the following example fails because the literal KEENE is not enclosed in single quotation marks, the subsequent **UPDATE** and **SELECT** will never even execute. The **WHENEVER SQLERROR** will exit SQL*Plus immediately, and pass the SQL.SQLCODE back to the host:

```
WHENEVER SQLERROR EXIT SQL.SQLCODE;

create table KEENE as
select * from COMFORT
 where City = KEENE;

update KEENE set Noon = 75;

select * from KEENE;
```

WHERE

SEE ALSO DELETE, LOGICAL OPERATORS, PRECEDENCE, **SELECT**, SYNTAX OPERATORS, **UPDATE**

FORMAT

```
DELETE FROM [user.]table ...
   [ WHERE condition ]
SELECT ...
   [ WHERE condition ]
UPDATE [user.]table [alias] ...
   [WHERE condition ]
```

DESCRIPTION **WHERE** defines those logical conditions that will control which rows a **SELECT** statement will return, a **DELETE** statement will delete, or an **UPDATE** statement will update.

A condition may be defined in one of several ways:

- A comparison between expressions (=, >, !=, and so on)
- A comparison between an expression and a query
- A comparison between a list of expressions and a list of expressions from a query
- A comparison between an expression and **ANY** or **ALL** members of a list or between an expression and the values brought back from a query
- A test to see if an expression is **IN** or **NOT IN** a list, or the results of a query
- A test for being **BETWEEN** or **NOT BETWEEN** one value and another
- A test to see if an expression **IS NULL** or **IS NOT NULL**
- A test to see if there **EXISTS** (or **NOT EXISTS**) any results for a query
- A combination of any of the above, using the conjunctions **AND** and **OR**

EXAMPLES

```
where Section >ANY ('A','C','D');
where City !=ALL (select City from LOCATION);
where Section IN ('A','C','D');
```

```
where City NOT IN (select City from LOCATION);
where Page BETWEEN 4 and 7;
where Skill IS NULL;
where EXISTS (select * from WORKER where Age > 90);
where Section = 'A' or Section = 'B' and Page = 1;
```

WHILE (PL/SQL)

See **LOOP**, Chapter 29

WIDTH_BUCKET

SEE ALSO NTILE

FORMAT

```
WIDTH_BUCKET ( expr , min_value , max_value , num_buckets )
```

DESCRIPTION **WIDTH_BUCKET** constructs equiwidth histograms, in which the histogram range is divided into intervals that have identical size. (Compare this function with **NTILE**, which creates equiheight histograms.) Ideally, each bucket is a "closed-open" interval of the real number line. For a given expression, **WIDTH_BUCKET** returns the bucket number into which the value of this expression would fall after being evaluated. *expr* is the expression (a number or datetime value) for which the histogram is being created. If *expr* evaluates to **NULL**, the expression returns **NULL**. *min_value* and *max_value* are expressions that resolve to the end points of the acceptable range for *expr*. Both of these expressions must also evaluate to number or datetime values, and neither can evaluate to **NULL**. *num_buckets* is an expression that resolves to a constant that indicates the number of buckets. This expression must evaluate to a positive integer.

WRAP (SQL*Plus)

See **SET**.

WRAPPING

Wrapping is to move the end of a heading or title, or the contents of a column, down to a new line when it is too long to fit on one line. (Contrast with **TRUNCATE**.) *See* **COLUMN**.

XML

XML (eXtensible Markup Language) is a standardized syntax for describing hierarchical data. XML provides a universal format for structured documents and data. Its tag-based syntax gives it the flexibility to handle complex data. Whereas HTML tells a Web browser how to present data, XML tells applications what the data means. *See* Chapter 47 for examples.

XMLAGG

SEE ALSO SYS_XMLAGG

FORMAT

```
XMLAGG ( XMLType_instance [order_by_clause] )
```

DESCRIPTION **XMLAGG** is an aggregate function. It takes a collection of XML fragments and returns an aggregated XML document. Any arguments that return **NULL** are dropped from the result.

XMLAGG is similar to **SYS_XMLAGG** except that **XMLAGG** returns a collection of nodes. **XMLAGG** does not accept formatting using the XMLFORMAT object. Also, **XMLAGG** does not enclose the output in an element tag as **SYS_XMLAGG** does.

XMLCOLATTVAL

SEE ALSO Chapter 47
FORMAT

XMLCOLATTVAL (*value_expr* [AS *c_alias*] [, *value_expr* [AS *c_alias*]])

DESCRIPTION **XMLCOLATTVAL** creates an XML fragment and then expands the resulting XML so that each XML fragment has the name *column* with the attribute *name*. You can use the **AS** *c_alias* clause to change the value of the *name* attribute to something other than the column name.
You must specify a value for *value_expr*. If *value_expr* is **NULL**, no element is returned.

XMLCONCAT

SEE ALSO XMLSEQUENCE
FORMAT

XMLCONCAT (*XMLType_instance* [, *XMLType_instance*])

DESCRIPTION **XMLCONCAT** takes as input a series of XMLType instances, concatenates the series of elements for each row, and returns the concatenated series. **XMLCONCAT** is the inverse of **XMLSEQUENCE**.

XMLELEMENT

SEE ALSO SYS_XMLGEN
FORMAT
XMLElement::=

XML_attributes_clause::=

DESCRIPTION **XMLELEMENT** takes an element name for *identifier*, an optional collection of attributes for the element, and arguments that make up the content of the element. It returns an instance of XMLType. **XMLELEMENT** is similar to **SYS_XMLGEN** except that **XMLELEMENT** can include attributes in the XML returned. **XMLELEMENT** does not accept formatting using the XMLFORMAT object.

XMLFOREST

SEE ALSO XMLCONCAT

FORMAT

XMLFOREST (*value_expr* [AS *c_alias*] [, *value_expr* [AS *c_alias*]])

DESCRIPTION **XMLFOREST** converts each of its argument parameters to XML, then returns an XML fragment that is the concatenation of these converted arguments.

XMLSEQUENCE

SEE ALSO XMLCONCAT

FORMAT

XMLSEQUENCE ({ *XMLType_instance* | *sys_refcursor_instance* [, *fmt*] })

DESCRIPTION **XMLSEQUENCE** has two forms:

- The first form takes as input an XMLType instance and returns a varying array of the top-level nodes in the XMLType.
- The second form takes as input a REFCURSOR instance, with an optional instance of the XMLFORMAT object, and returns as an **XMLSEQUENCE** type an XML document for each row of the cursor.

XMLTRANSFORM

SEE ALSO Chapter 47

FORMAT

XMLTRANSFORM (*XMLType_instance* , *XMLType_instance*)

DESCRIPTION **XMLTRANSFORM** takes as arguments an XMLType instance and an XSL style sheet, which itself is a form of XMLType instance. It applies the style sheet to the instance and returns an XMLType.

XMLType

XMLType is a datatype available to store and query XML data in the database. As a type, XMLType has member functions to access, extract, and query XML data using a class of operations known as XPath expressions. The SYS_XMLGEN, SYS_XMLAGG, and DBMS_XMLGEN packages create XMLType values from existing object-relational data. When you designate a column as using the XMLType datatype, Oracle will internally store the data in a CLOB datatype.

The following listing shows the creation of a table using the XMLType datatype:

```
create table MY_XML_TABLE
(Key1      NUMBER,
Xml_Column  SYS.XMLTYPE);

insert into MY_XML_TABLE (Key1, Xml_Column)
```

```
values (1, SYS.XMLTYPE.CREATEXML
 ('<book>
  <title>Complete Reference</title>
  <chapter num= "48">
     <title>Ending</title>
     <text>This is the end of the book.</text>
  </chapter>
</book>'));

select M.Xml_Column.GETCLOBVAL() as XML_Data
   from MY_XML_TABLE M
 where Key1 = 1;
```

See Chapter 47 for additional details on XMLType and its related methods.

Index

Symbols

-- (comment), 101, 113, 947
- (hyphen), 466, 947
' (single quotation marks). *See* single
 quotation marks (')
- (subtraction), 466, 947
! (exclamation mark), 473, 942
& or && (ampersand/double ampersand),
 465, 674–675, 945
" (double quotation marks), 205–207, 942
(pound sign), 942
$ operator, 152, 473, 942–943
% (percent) wildcard, 83, 86, 943
%FOUND, 523, 943–944
%ISOPEN, 523, 944
%NOT FOUND, 523–524
%NOTFOUND, 944
%ROWCOUNT, 523, 944
%ROWTYPE, 518, 944–945
%TYPE, 518, 945
() parentheses. *See* parentheses ()
* (multiplication). *See* multiplication (*)
** (exponentiation), 946
. (period or dot), 947–948
.. (to). *See* loops
/ (division), 168–169, 948
/ (forward slash), 948
/* */ (comment), 103, 113, 949
: (colon), 80, 949
:= (set equal to), 515–522, 949–950

; (semicolon), 472, 950
? (question mark), 152, 473, 943
@ ("at" sign), 425, 426, 950
@@ (double "at" sign), SQL*Plus, 950–951
[] (brackets), 126, 152–153
[...] operator, 152–153
[: :] operator, 152–153
[==] operator, 152–153
\ (backslash operator), 152
\n operator, 152–153
_ (underscore character). *See* underscore (_)
{} (curly braces), 473, 668, 951
{m, n} operator, 152
{m,} operator, 152
{m} operator, 152
| (vertical bar). *See* vertical bar (|)
|| (concatenation), 127–128, 674–675, 952
+ (plus) operator, 152, 946–947
++ (plus, plus) operator, 670–671
<<>> (PL/SQL label name delimiter), 950
= sign, 813–814
> sign (threshold operator), 463

A

abbreviations, 49, 56
ABOUT operator, 474
ABS (absolute value), 171, 175, 952
abstract datatypes, 764–766, 588–593, 952
ACCEPT, 952

H

I

O

X

Z

➡ **New Titles**

Prices are subject to change without notice

ARTIFICIAL INTELLIGENCE

	053153-6	**NARASIMHAN**	AI and the Study of Agentive Behavior	295.00

ASP & ASP .NET

	049917-9	**BUCZEK**	ASP.NET: Developer's Guide	450.00
	049554-8	**BUCZEK**	ASP.NET: Tips and Techniques	295.00
	463525-5	**BUCZEK**	ASP: Developer's Guide (With CD)	395.00
	043621-5	**BUCZEK**	Instant ASP Scripts, 2/e (With CD)	425.00
	052920-5	**BUCZEK**	Instant ASP.NET Applications (With CD)	525.00
	058251-3	**ESPOSITO**	Programming Microsoft ASP.NET	795.00
	043574-X	**FERGUSON**	DeBugging ASP: Troubleshooting for Programmers	295.00
	058489-3	**GIBBS**	Microsoft ASP .NET Coding Strategies with the Microsoft ASP .NET Team	495.00
	053307-5	**KOTHARI**	Developing Microsoft ASP.Net Server Controls an Components	595.00
	049536-X	**MacDonald**	ASP.NET: The Complete Referenc	495.00
	043623-1	**MERCER**	ASP 3.0: A Beginner's Guid	295.00
	049534-3	**MERCER**	ASP.NET: A Beginner's Guide	295.00
	054056-X	**MICROSOFT CORPORATIO**	Building Secure Microsoft ASP.NET Applications	595.00
	054063-2	**POPE**	Microsoft ASP.NET Web Matrix Starter Kit With C	495.00

AUTOCAD

	463563-8	**COHN**	AutoCad 14: The Complete Reference (With CD)	495.00
	463966-8	**COHN**	AutoCad 2000: The Complete Reference	595.00

BUSINESS INTELLIGENCE

	058312-9	**HARPER**	Crystal Reports 9 on Oracle	395.00
	054064-0	**HOWSON**	Business Objects: The Complete Reference	525.00
	053254-0	**PECK**	Crystal Reports 9: The Complete Reference	595.00
➡	058664-0	**PECK**	Crystal Reports: Professional Results	350.00

C, C++ & C# PROGRAMMING

	054059-4	**GRIMES**	Programming with Managed Extensions for Microsoft Visual C++ .Net Version 200	495.00
➡	058866-X	**KENT**	C++ Demystified: A Self-Teaching Guid	295.00
	044779-9	**MICHAELIS**	C# Developer's Headstart	195.00
	463729-0	**MUELLER**	Visual C++ 6 From the Ground Up, 2/e	345.00
	049898-9	**MUELLER**	Visual C++.Net Developer's Guide (With CD)	425.00
	041239-1	**PAPPAS**	DeBugging C++: Troubleshooting for Programmers	375.00
	463810-6	**PAPPAS**	Visual C++ 6: The Complete Referenc	395.00
	049532-7	**PAPPAS**	Visual C++.Net: The Complete Reference	450.00
	058316-1	**PETZOLD**	Programming in the Key of C#	495.00
	044720-9	**SCHILDT**	Borland C++ Builder: The Complete Referenc	485.00
	047384-6	**SCHILDT**	C#: A Beginner's Guide	375.00

	048675-1	**SCHILDT**	C#: The Complete Reference	495.00
	041183-2	**SCHILDT**	C: The Complete Reference, 4/e	425.00
	053416-0	**SCHILDT**	C++ from the Ground Up, 3/e	325.00
	048673-5	**SCHILDT**	C++: A Beginner's Guid	295.00
	053246-X	**SCHILDT**	C++: The Complete Reference, 4/e	395.00
	463870-X	**SCHILDT**	Teach Yourself C++	295.00
➡	058863-5	**SCHILDT**	The Art of C++	395.00
	053049-1	**SMILEY**	Learn to Program with C#	295.00
	053085-8	**SMILEY**	Learn to Program with C+	275.00
	049920-9	**WRIGHT**	C#: Tips and Techniques	375.00

CERTIFICATION GUIDES

	052896-9	**BIRD**	Linux+ Certification Study Guide (With CD)	495.00
	058401-X	**CWSP**	CWSP Certified Wireless Security Professional Official Study Guide (Exam PWO-200)	495.00
	044735-7	**HUTNIK**	All-in-One Cisco CCIE Lab Study Guide, 2/e (With CD)	695.00
	049912-8	**WATTERS**	All-in-One Sun Certified Solaris 8: System Administrator Exam Guide (With CD)	450.00

CISCO NETWORKING

	041299-5	**AMMAN**	CISCO Router Internetworking	425.00
	058300-5	**DEAL**	CCNA CISCO Certified Network Associate Study Guide (Exam 640-801) With C	595.00
	041193-X	**HELD**	CISCO IOS IP: Field Guide	275.00
	041192-1	**HELD**	CISCO Router Performance: Field Guide	275.00
	052889-6	**HILL**	CISCO: The Complete Reference	595.00
	042142-0	**LEWIS**	CISCO TCP/IP Routing Professional Reference, 3/e	350.00
	463844-0	**ROSSI**	CISCO and IP Addressing	295.00
	044494-3	**SACKETT**	CISCO Router Handbook, 2/e	550.00
	044511-7	**SATTERLEE**	CISCO: CCIE Lab Practice Kit (With CD)	495.00
	043900-1	**THOMAS**	ICND: Interconnecting Cisco Network Devices (With CD)	595.00
	463964-1	**VELTE**	CISCO Internetworking with Windows NT & 200	395.00
➡	058973-9	**VELTE**	CISCO: A Beginner's Guide, 3/e	495.00

COLD FUSION

	047286-6	**HOUSER**	Instant Cold Fusion 5 (With CD)	650.00

COMPUTER DICTIONARIES

➡	--	**McGRAW-HILL**	McGraw-Hill Dictionary of Computing an Communications	In Pre

COMPUTER GRAPHICS

	053043-2	**TRIPPE**	SVG for Designers: Using Scalable Vector Graphics in Next Generatio	350.00

COMPUTER ORGANIZATION & ARCHITECTURE

	053236-2	**GOVINDARAJALU**	Computer Architecture and Organization: Design Principles and Applications	295.00

COMPUTER SCIENCE - ADVANCED

	043551-0	**AGRAWAL**	Advances in Data Management 2000 (COMAD 2000): Proceedings of the Tenth International Conference on Management of Dat	395.00

	050245-5	ARORA, SINHA, PUROHIT, DIXIT & RAN	Initiatives in High Performance Computing	495.00
	048387-6	CHAKRAVARTHY	Harnessing and Managing Knowledge (CSI 2002)	395.00
	047424-9	FREEDMAN	Computer Desktop Encyclopedia, 9/e (With CD)	850.00
	058410-9	GUEST	Microsoft .Net and J2EE Interoperability Toolkit (With CD)	550.00
	047277-7	HAIG	Object Oriented Analysis & Design	265.00
	047410-9	IYENGAR & SINHA	ADCOM 2001: Recent Trends in Computing and Communication	645.00
	050273-0	IYER & NAIK	CIT 2002: Proceedings of the 5th International Conference on Information Technology	645.00
	049992-6	JENKINS & IYENGAR	HPC Asia 2002, Vol. I	695.00
	050241-2	JENKINS & IYENGAR	HPC Asia 2002, Vol. II	650.00
	047370-6	KEEN	The Freedom Economy	295.00
	058298-X	MICROSOFT CORPORATIO	Microsoft Application Architecture for .NET: Designing Applications and Services	295.00
	058413-3	MS PRESS	Enterprise Solution Patterns Using Microsoft .Net Version 2.0 Patterns & Practices	395.00
➡	058688-8	PELTZER	.Net & J2EE Interoperability	395.00
	043580-4	RAMASWAMY	The Art and Technology of Software Engineerin	295.00
	043548-0	SINHA	ADCOM 2000: 8th International Conference on Advanced Computing & Communications (December 14-16, 2000)	575.00

COMPUTER SCIENCE - INTRODUCTORY

	043746-7	BEAR	Get Your IT Degree & Get Ahead	325.00
	044496-X	KEYS	How to Be a Successful Technical Trainer	295.00

COMPUTERS AND SOCIETY

	463671-5	JAMBHEKAR	Internet for Libraries and Information Centres (Book Floppy)	350.00
	040311-2	OBEROI	e-Security and You: IT Act 2000 and Its Impact , Digita Authentication and Information Systems Security	195.00

CUSTOMER RELATIONSHIP MANAGEMENT (CRM)

	040273-6	BERSON	Building Data Mining Applications for CRM	375.00
	053250-8	GREENBERG	CRM at the Speed of Light, 2/e	395.00

DATA WAREHOUSING/KNOWLEDGE MANAGEMENT

	463740-1	MATTISON	Web Warehousing & Knowledge Management	350.00

DATABASE MANAGEMENT SYSTEMS (DBMS)

	058743-4	ALLEN	Introduction to Relational Databases and SQL Programming (With 3 CDs)	425.00
	044724-1	ANDERSEN	Access 2002: The Complete Reference (With CD)	675.00
	044710-1	ANDERSEN	How to Do Everything with Access 200	425.00
	463511-5	ANDERSON	Access 2000: The Complete Reference (Book + CD)	525.00
	044507-9	BUCZEK	Instant Access Databases (With CD)	475.00
	462343-5	JONES	FoxPro 2.5 for Windows : Inside and Out	210.00
	049569-6	MELNYK	DB2: The Complete Reference	595.00

DREAMWEAVER

	047249-1	FULLER	Dreamweaver 4 Virtual Classroom (With CD)	495.00
	053129-3	WEST	Dreamweaver MX: A Beginner's Guide	450.00
	053035-1	WEST	Dreamweaver MX: The Complete Reference	525.00

e-BUSINESS

463540-9	**BAJAJ & NAG**	Electronic Commerce: The Cutting Edge of Business	385.00
044474-9	**ELSENPETER**	e-Business: A Beginner's Guide	325.00

ENTERPRISE RESOURCE PLANNING

042130-7	**GHOSH**	SAP Project Management (With CD)	650.00
058686-1	**HERNANDEZ**	SAP R/3 Handbook, 2/e	595.00
042050-5	**HESTER**	J D Edwards OneWorld: A Developer's Guide	650.00
463170-5	**HOFFMAN**	Writing SAP ABAP/4 Programs (Book & CD)	345.00
463169-1	**HOFFMAN** (Pl. see page 16)	Writing SAP ABAP/4 Programs (Book Only) [Exclusively distributed by Book Promoters & Suppliers	245.00
058750-7	**KASTURI**	SAP R/3 ALE & EDI Technologies (With CD)	395.00
040201-9	**MILLER**	Peoplesoft Integration Tools	295.00
463737-1	**MILLER**	SAP R/3 Certification Exam Guide (With CD)	495.00
463944-7	**WILLIAMS**	Implementing SAP R/3 Sales & Distribution	385.00

FLASH

044582-6	**BLAKE**	How to Do Everything With Macromedia Flash 5	295.00
044504-4	**SAHLIN**	FLASH 5: Virtual Classroom (With CD)	425.00
053240-0	**SANDERS**	Macromedia Flash MX Actionscript: The Complete Reference	450.00
049537-8	**UNDERDAHL**	Macromedia Flash MX: The Complete Reference (With CD)	495.00
044741-1	**WOODS**	Macromedia Flash 5 Developer's Guide (With CD)	495.00
049938-1	**WOODS**	Macromedia Flash MX Developer's Guid	495.00

FRONTPAGE

047270-X	**CHINNATHAMBI**	FrontPage 2002: A Beginner's Guide	325.00
044788-8	**JENNETT**	FrontPage 2002 Developer's Guide (With CD)	495.00
044729-2	**MATTHEWS**	Front Page 2002: The Complete Reference (With CD)	595.00
058402-8	**MATTHEWS**	Microsoft Office Frontpage 2003: The Complete Referenc	550.00

HARDWARE MAINTENANCE

043617-7	**BIGELOW**	Bigelow's Virus Troubleshooting Pocket Referenc	225.00
463779-7	**BIGELOW**	Printer Troubleshooting Pocket Reference	195.00
047367-6	**BIGELOW**	Troubleshooting, Maintaining & Repairing PCs, 5/e (With CD)	695.00
053284-2	**CAPUTO**	Build Your Own Server	450.00
044736-5	**GILSTE**	PC Hardware: A Beginner's Guid	350.00
048311-6	**GOVINDARAJALU**	IBM PC and Clones: Hardware, Troubleshooting an Maintenance, 2/e (Book + CD)	595.00
048286-1	**GOVINDARAJALU**	IBM PC and Clones: Hardware, Troubleshooting an Maintenance, 2/e (Book Only)	450.00
053304-0	**JARRETT & SU**	Building Tablet PC Applications	695.00
058242-4	**KELLY**	A+ PC Technician's Pocket Referenc	225.00
058668-3	**MEYERS**	A+ Certification Exam Guide, 5/e (With CD	595.00
053455-1	**MEYERS**	Introduction to PC Hardware and Troubleshooting	395.00
059506-2	**MEYERS**	Mike Meyer's A+ Guide to Managing and Troubleshooting PCs (With CD	650.00
059489-9	**MEYERS**	Mike Meyer's A+ Guide to PC Hardware (With CD)	495.00
049896-2	**ROSENTHAL**	Build Your Own PC, 3/e	225.00

	053255-9	**SIMMONS**	A+ Technicians on the Job Guide to Networking	325.00
	053277-X	**SIMMONS**	A+ Technician's on-the-Job Guide to Windows XP	350.00
	043606-1	**ZACKER**	PC Hardware: The Complete Reference (With CD)	495.00

HTML

	049921-7	**JAMSA**	HTML & Web Design: Tips & Techniques	375.00
	044730-6	**PENCE**	How to Do Everyhting with HTML	375.00
	463794-0	**PETROVSKY**	Dynamic HTML in Action	375.00
	058281-5	**POWELL**	HTML & XHTML: The Complete Reference, 4/e	465.00
	044486-2	**POWELL**	HTML: Programmer's Reference, 2/e	295.00
	044487-0	**WILLARD**	HTML: A Beginner's Guid	275.00

INTEGRATION

	042056-4	**MICHAELIS**	COM+ Programming from the Ground Up	350.00
	054060-8	**TEMPLEMAN**	COM Programming with Microsoft.Net	550.00

INTERNET AND WEB DIRECTORIE

	053069-6	**HAHN**	Internet Yellow Pages 2003 Edition: 10th Anniversary Editio	595.00
	463162-4	**HAHN**	The Internet Complete Reference	395.00
	043718-1	**JONES**	How to Do Everything With the Internet	325.00
	053306-7	**MICROSOFT ACE TEAM**	Performance Testing Microsoft .Net Web Applications (With CD)	395.00
	048699-9	**YOUNG**	Internet: The Complete Reference	395.00
	463981-1	**YOUNG**	Internet: The Complete Reference: Millenium Edition	395.00

JAVA

	047389-7	**BOLLINGER**	JSP: A Beginner's Guid	395.00
	463612-X	**FRENTZEN**	JAVA SCRIPT: Annotated Archives (Book + CD)	475.00
	053141-2	**HANNA**	JSP 2.0: The Complete Reference	450.00
	053251-6	**JONES & FREEMAN**	C# for Java Developers	395.00
	052912-4	**KEOG**	J2EE: The Complete Reference	495.00
	053415-2	**KEOG**	J2ME: The Complete Reference	450.00
➡	058687-X	**KURNIAWAN**	JavaServer Faces Programmin	425.00
	047388-9	**MacAULEY**	JavaScript: Programmer's Reference	325.00
	049916-0	**MOSS**	JAVA Servlets: Developer's Guid	395.00
	463290-6	**NAUGHTON**	JAVA Handbook	300.00
	463774-6	**NELSON**	JAVA Foundation Classes (With CD)	495.00
	463786-X	**O'NEIL**	JAVA Beans From the Ground Up	360.00
	463789-4	**O'NEIL**	Teach Yourself JAVA	325.00
	044579-6	**POLLOCK**	JAVA Script: A Beginner's Guid	375.00
➡	059027-3	**POWELL**	JavaScript: The Complete Reference, 2/e	595.00
	053128-5	**SCHILDT**	JAVA 2: A Beginner's Guide, 2/e	275.00
	049543-2	**SCHILDT**	JAVA 2: The Complete Reference, 5/	395.00
	058270-X	**SCHILDT**	The Art of JAVA	295.00
	463867-X	**SIPLE**	The Complete Guide to JAVA : Database Programmin (With CD)	435.00
	053065-3	**SMILEY**	Learn to Program with JAVA	295.00
	044472-2	**TREMBLETT**	Instant Enterprise JavaBeans (With CD)	395.00
	041188-3	**TREMBLETT**	Instant Java Server Pages (With CD)	395.00
	463975-7	**VENNERS**	Inside the JAVA 2 Virtual Machine	395.00

	044524-9	**WEBB**	Instant Java Script (With CD)	495.00

MICROPROCESSORS AND MICROCOMPUTERS

	048284-5	**IYER & GUPTA**	Embedded Realtime Systems Programming	295.00
	042140-4	**PREDKO**	Programming & Customizing the 8051 Microcontroller (With CD)	315.00

MULTIMEDI

	048343-4	**ARORA**	Indo-European Conference on Multilingua Communication Technologies (IEMCT) - June 24-25, 2002	395.00
➤	058715-9	**FOX**	3DS Max 6 Animation: CG Filmmaking from Concept t Completion (With CD)	595.00
➤	059029-X	**MEADE**	Maya 6: The Complete Referenc	595.00
	047276-9	**VAUGHAN**	Multimedia: Making it Work, 5/e (With CD)	375.00
➤	059695-6	**VAUGHAN**	Multimedia: Making it Work, 6/e (With CD)	375.00

NETWORK & LAN & DATA COMMUNICATIONS

	463675-8	**AMMAN**	Managing Dynamic IP Networks	350.00
➤	058671-3	**BRAGG**	Network Security: The Complete Referenc	495.00
	463780-0	**BROWN**	Implementing Virtual Private Networks	395.00
	047262-9	**BULBROOK**	WAP: A Beginner's Guide	195.00
	052911-6	**CARTY**	Broadband Networking	350.00
	049913-6	**CLARK**	Network Cabling Handbook	495.00
	044576-1	**EDWARDS**	Nortel Networks: A Beginner's Guide	325.00
	044745-4	**FARLEY**	Building Storage Networks, 2/e	395.00
	047239-4	**GORALSKI**	Optical Networking & WDM	350.00
	058235-1	**HALLBERG**	Networking: A Beginner's Guide, 3/e	295.00
	044493-5	**HELD**	Data Over Wireless Networks: Bluetooth, WAP & Wireless LANs	250.00
	044744-6	**HELD**	Voice and Data Internetworking, 3/e	375.00
	053293-1	**HENRICKSON**	IIS 6: The Complete Reference	525.00
	049915-2	**HULL**	Content Delivery Networks: Web Switching for Security, Availability and Spee	395.00
	053242-7	**JAMALEDDINE**	IBM Websphere Application Server Programmin	450.00
	044509-5	**KIMMEL**	Building Delphi 6 Applications (With CD)	525.00
	044478-1	**KNAPP**	Nortel Networks: The Complete Reference (With CD)	750.00
	044523-0	**LONG**	IP Network Desig	295.00
	043719-X	**MAHALINGAM**	Nortel Networks Troubleshooting & Optimization	395.00
	049895-4	**MAIRS**	VPNs: A Beginners Guide	395.00
	058241-6	**MAIWALD**	Network Security: A Beginner's Guide, 2/e	375.00
	054061-6	**McLEAN**	Microsoft .Net Remotin	495.00
	053454-3	**McMAHON**	Introduction to Networkin	350.00
	043948-6	**MILLER**	Analyzing Broadband Networks, 3/e (With CD)	475.00
➤	058864-3	**NOONA**	Hardening Network Infrastructure	495.00
	463804-1	**PARNELL**	Building High-Speed Networks	275.00
	463852-1	**REED**	Implementing Directory Services	375.00
	053143-9	**REID**	802.11 (Wi - Fi) Networking Handbook	325.00
	044742-X	**SHELDON**	Encyclopedia of Networking and Telecommunications (With CD)	795.00
	053292-3	**SPALDING**	Storage Networks: The Complete Reference	550.00
	053041-6	**SPOH**	Data Network Design, 3/e	525.00

	040234-5	**TAYLOR**	Networking Handbook (With CD)	575.00
	044585-0	**VACCA**	Wireless Broadband Networks Handbook: 3G, LMDS & Wireless Internet	495.00
	054058-6	**WIGLEY**	Microsoft.Net Compact Framework (Core Reference)	695.00
	047416-8	**ZACKER**	Networking: The Complete Referenc	595.00
	041267-7	**ZACKER**	Upgrading & Troubleshooting Networks: The Complete Reference	525.00

OPERATING SYSTEMS

➡	058865-1	**BRAGG**	Hardening Windows Systems	495.00
	044738-1	**GARDINIER**	Windows 2000 Performance Tuning and Optimization (With CD)	495.00
	053322-9	**HART-DAVIS**	Windows XP Professional: The Complete Reference	485.00
	053241-9	**HOLCOMBE**	Survey of Operating Systems	295.00
	040204-3	**IVENS**	Windows 2000: The Complete Referenc	395.00
	054081-0	**IVENS**	Windows Server 2003: The Complete Reference	550.00
	463222-1	**KADNIER**	Windows NT 4 : The Complete Referenc	475.00
	044482-X	**LEVIN**	Windows Millennium Edition: The Complete Reference (With CD)	625.00
	053066-1	**LEVIN**	Windows XP Home Edition: The Complete Reference	475.00
	047423-0	**LEVIN**	Windows XP: The Complete Reference (With CD)	650.00
	042044-0	**MATTHEWS**	Windows 2000: A Beginners Guide	350.00
	054068-3	**MATTHEWS**	Windows Server 2003: A Beginner's Guide	375.00
	053127-7	**MATTHEWS**	Windows XP Professional: A Beginner's Guide	295.00
➡	059449-X	**MEYERS**	Mike Meyer's A+ Guide to Operating Systems (With CD)	465.00
	058249-1	**MICROSOF**	Operating.Net Framework-Based Applications (With CD)	495.00
	463754-1	**MORIMOTO**	Windows 2000: Design & Migration	395.00
	463755-X	**SCHILDT**	Windows 2000: Programming from the Ground Up	450.00
	053289-3	**SHIMONSKI**	Windows Server 2003 Clustering and Load Balancing	425.00
	053278-8	**SMITH**	FREEBSD: The Complete Reference, (With CD)	695.00
	049928-4	**WATTERS**	Solaris 9 Administration: A Beginner's Guide	395.00
	049509-2	**WATTERS**	Solaris 9: The Complete Reference	450.00

ORACLE

	048693-X	**ABBEY**	Oracle 9i: A Beginner's Guide	350.00
➡	058793-0	**ABRAMSON**	Oracle Database 10g: A Beginner's Guide	395.00
	049587-4	**ADKOLI**	Oracle 9i for Windows Handbook	375.00
	047417-6	**ALLEN**	Oracle: OCP Building Internet Applications I & II Exam Guide (With CD)	425.00
	041169-7	**ALLEN/THOMAS**	Oracle Certified Professional Financial Applications Consultant Exam Guide	650.00
	048687-5	**BENJAMIN**	OCP Oracle 9i Database: New Features fo Administrators Exam Guide	325.00
	043575-8	**BOBROWSKI**	Oracle 8i for Linux Starter Kit (With CD)	395.00
	048683-2	**BROWN**	Oracle 9i Web Development	495.00
	049572-6	**BURLESON**	Oracle 9i: UNIX Administration Handbook	395.00
	058518-0	**BURLESON**	Oracle High Performance SQL Tuning	395.00
	044719-5	**BURLESON**	Oracle High Performance Tuning with Statspack	395.00
	047386-2	**CHANG**	Oracle 9i: XML Handbook (With CD)	425.00
	044479-X	**COREY**	Oracle 8i: Data Warehousing	425.00
	048682-4	**COUCHMAN**	OCP Oracle 9i Database: Fundamental I Exam Guid	395.00

	047259-9	**COUCHMAN**	Oracle 8i: Certified Professional SQL & PL/SQL Exam Guide (With CD)	395.00
	463556-5	**COUCHMAN**	Oracle Certified Professional DBA Certification Exa Guide (With CD)	525.00
	047420-6	**COUCHMAN**	Oracle OCP Introduction to Oracle 9i: SQL Exam Guid 1ZO-007	395.00
	049893-8	**COUCHMAN**	Oracle: OCA Oracle 9i Associate DBA Certification Exam Guide (With CD)	495.00
	463590-5	**DEVRAJ**	Oracle 24x7 Tips and Techniques	475.00
	048681-6	**FREEMAN**	Oracle 9i New Features	295.00
	053087-4	**FREEMAN**	Oracle 9i: RMAN Backup & Recovery	395.00
➤	058777-9	**FREEMAN**	Oracle Database 10g New Features	395.00
➤	058776-0	**GARMANY**	Oracle Application Server 10g Administration Handbook	450.00
	049531-9	**GERALD**	Oracle: E-Business Suite Manufacturing & Supply Chai Management	450.00
➤	058862-7	**HART**	Oracle Database 10g High Availability with RAC, Flashback & Data Guar	450.00
	058659-4	**IYER**	Oracle E-Business Suite Financials Administration	395.00
	058660-8	**JAMES**	Oracle E-Business Suite Financials Handbook	550.00
	463668-5	**JAMES**	Oracle Financials Handbook	395.00
	049574-2	**JESSE**	Oracle 9i for Windows 2000: Tips & Techniques	395.00
	048636-0	**KAGEYAMA**	CICS Handbook	375.00
	462184-X	**KISHORE & NAIK**	SQL for Professionals	175.00
➤	058972-0	**KNOX**	Effective Oracle Database 10g Security by Design	450.00
	053139-0	**KOLETZKE**	Oracle 9i JDeveloper Handbook	495.00
	463778-9	**KOLETZKE**	Oracle Developer Advanced Forms & Reports	475.00
	058280-7	**KYTE**	Effective Oracle by Design	495.00
	463708-8	**LEON**	SQL: A Complete Reference (With Diskette)	375.00
	047419-2	**LONEY**	Oracle 9i Instant PL/SQL Scripts (With CD)	425.00
	048674-3	**LONEY**	Oracle 9i: DBA Handbook	395.00
	049902-0	**LONEY**	Oracle 9i: The Complete Reference (With CD)	495.00
	043622-3	**MORISSEAU-LEROY**	Oracle 8i: Java Component Programming with EJB, CORBA & JSP	375.00
	053076-9	**MORISSEAU-LEROY**	Oracle 9i: As Building J2EE Applications	395.00
	047261-0	**MORISSEAU-LEROY**	Oracle 9i: SQLJ Programming (With CD)	395.00
	463274-4	**MULLER**	Oracle Developer 2000 Handbook, 2/e	350.00
	042048-3	**MULLER**	Oracle Developer Starter Kit (With CD)	495.00
	054065-9	**NIEMIC**	Oracle 9i Performance Tuning: Tips & Techniques	525.00
	463775-4	**NIEMIC**	Oracle: Performance Tuning: Tips and Techniques	450.00
	048698-0	**O'HEARN**	Oracle OCP Developer PL/SQL Program Units Exam Guide (With CD)	395.00
	049535-1	**PACK**	Oracle: OCP Oracle 9i Database: Performance Tuning Exam Guide	425.00
	058307-2	**PRICE**	Oracle 9i: JDBC Programmin	425.00
➤	058755-8	**PRICE**	Oracle Database 10g SQ	450.00
	041184-0	**SARIN**	Oracle DBA: Tips and Techniques	425.00
➤	059026-5	**SCARDINA**	Oracle Database 10g XML & SQL: Design, Build & Manage XML Applications in Java, C, C++ & PL/SQ	450.00
➤	059028-1	**SHEE**	Oracle Wait Interface: A Practical Guide to Diagnostics & Tuning	495.00
	049892-X	**SMITH**	Oracle Backup and Recovery 10	295.00

	463970-6	**SRIDHARAN**	Oracle Forms 5.0: Includes Developer 2000 Release 2.1	350.00
	049578-5	**THERIAULT**	Oracle 9i DBA 101	395.00
	043576-6	**TREMAYNE**	Oracle: Applications Performance Tuning Handbook (With CD)	495.00
	041181-6	**URMAN**	Oracle 8i: Advanced PL/SQL Programming (with CD)	485.00
	048680-8	**URMAN**	Oracle 9i PL/SQL Programming with C	395.00
	047241-6	**VAIDYANATHA**	Oracle Performance Tuning 10	295.00
	049592-0	**VANDIVIER**	Oracle 9i Application Server Portal Handbook (With 3 CDs)	575.00
	049573-4	**VANTING**	Oracle Enterprise Manager 101	395.00
	044485-4	**VELPURI**	Oracle 8i: Back Up and Recovery Handbook	395.00
	049506-8	**VELPURI**	Oracle OCP Oracle 9i Database: Fundamentals II Exam Guide (With CD)	395.00
	044721-7	**VESTERLI**	Oracle Web Applications 101	395.00
	049568-8	**YEUNG**	Oracle 9i Mobile: Build Wireless, Offline, Push and Voic Applicatio	425.00

OTHER LANGUAGES

	043949-4	**MULLER**	Bluetooth Demystified	375.00
	041180-8	**MYKLAND**	PALM OS Programming from the Ground Up (With CD)	425.00
	053252-4	**SHARP**	Microsoft Visual J# .Net	595.00

PERL PROGRAMMING

	047447-8	**BAL**	Perl Programming for Bioinformatics	595.00
	043745-9	**BROWN**	Active Perl Developer's Guide (With CD)	575.00
	044480-3	**BROWN**	PERL: The Complete Reference, 2/e	625.00
	042131-5	**PESCHKO**	Perl Developer's Guide (With CD)	495.00
	044490-0	**WYKE**	PERL: A Beginner's Guide	300.00

PHOTOSHOP

	044584-2	**GREENBERG**	Photoshop 6: The Complete Reference (With CD)	595.00
	053038-6	**MILBURN**	Photoshop Elements 2: The Complete Reference	595.00
	053067-X	**PLOTKIN**	How To Do Everything With Photoshop Elements 2	450.00

PROGRAMMING TOPICS/PROGRAMMING LANGUAGES

➤	058861-9	**HOLMES**	Struts: The Complete Reference	450.00
	058412-5	**JONES**	Network Programming for the Microsoft .Net Framework	495.00
	048306-X	**KHANNA**	C++ Power Packed: Tips and Techniques for Practicing Programmers	250.00
	463992-7	**SCHILDT**	MFC Programming from the Ground Up, 2/	365.00
	048341-8	**SHANKAR**	The Oracle Companion to J2EE	425.00

PROJECT MANAGEMENT

➤	059048-6	**KEMP**	Project Management Demystifie	325.00
	049929-2	**PHILLIPS**	IT Project Management: On Track from Start to Finish (With CD)	395.00
➤	058685-3	**PHILLIPS**	PMP: Project Management Professional Study Guid (With CD)	595.00

SECURITY

	044616-4	**BURNETT**	RSA Security's Official Guide to Cryptography (With CD)	475.00
	049899-7	**CAVANAUGH**	Fireworks MX: A Beginner's Guide	375.00
	044706-3	**DAVIS**	IP Sec Securing VPNs	395.00

	047369-2	**ERBSCHLOE**	Information Warfare: How to Survive Cyber Attacks	395.00
	463972-2	**GONCALVES**	Firewalls: A Complete Guide	435.00
➡	059047-8	**HERSHEY**	Cryptography Demystified	325.00
	053280-X	**HORTON**	Hacknotes Network Security Portable Reference	295.00
	047272-6	**KING**	Security Architecture Design, Deployment & Operations	395.00
	049555-6	**MAIWALD**	Security Planning & Disaster Recovery	295.00
	047250-5	**MANDIA**	Incident Response: Investigating Computer Crime	395.00
➡	059696-4	**McCLURE & SCAMBRAY**	Hacking Exposed: Network Security Secrets and Solutions, 4/e (With DVD)	595.00
	043953-2	**MOO**	Firebrands: Building Brand Loyalty in the Internet Age	375.00
	044615-6	**NASH**	PKI Implementing and Managing E-Security	395.00
	053286-9	**O'DEA**	Hacknotes Windows Security Portable Referenc	295.00
	053256-7	**O'NEILL**	Web Services Security	295.00
	049937-3	**RAINA**	mCommerce Security: A Beginner's Guide	325.00
	049900-4	**SCAMBRAY**	Hacking Exposed Web Applications	395.00
➡	058725-6	**SCAMBRAY**	Hacking Exposed Windows Server 2003	450.00
	053145-5	**SCHIFFMAN**	Hacker's Challenge 2: Test Your Network Security & Forensic Skills	295.00
➡	058689-6	**SHEMA**	Anti-Hacker Tool Kit, 2/e (With CD)	650.00
	053287-7	**SHEMA**	Hacknotes Web Security Portable Reference	295.00
	058311-0	**STRASSBERG**	Firewalls: The Complete Reference	595.00
	053040-8	**TAYLOR**	Hacking Exposed J2EE & JAVA: Developing Secure Applications with Java	395.00
➡	059490-2	**WOLFE**	Anti-Spam Toolkit (With CD	495.00

SOFTWARE ENGINEERING

	040312-0	**KISHORE & NAIK**	Software Requirements and Estimatio	375.00
	049571-8	**MARINI**	The Document Object Model: Processing Structured Document	350.00
	048340-X	**RADICE**	Software Inspections: How to cut costs, improve quality and shorten time cycles of software projects	395.00
➡	058352-8	**RENU & PRADEEP**	Software Testing: Methodologies, Tools and Processes	350.00

SOFTWARE PACKAGES

	463519-0	**APTECH**	Firewalls and Encryption	195.00
	463518-2	**APTECH**	Net.Commerce	225.00
	463516-6	**APTECH**	VisualAge for Java Programming	195.00
	463192-6	**CRISHNA**	Windows 98	195.00
	044526-5	**ENGLISH**	Exchange 2000 Server Administration: A Beginner's Guid	325.00
	058299-8	**KETTELL**	Microsoft Office 2003: The Complete Reference	575.00
	463267-1	**MANSFIELD**	Working in Microsoft Offic	395.00
	040206-X	**NEIBAUER**	Office 2000 Made Easy: The Basics and Beyond	275.00
	463768-1	**NELSON**	OFFICE 2000: The Complete Reference with C	495.00
	044723-3	**NELSON**	Office XP: The Complete Reference (With CD)	595.00
	053283-4	**OTEY**	ADO.NET: The Complete Reference	625.00
	044748-9	**SCHNOLL**	Exchange 2000 Server: The Complete Reference	475.00

SPREADSHEETING MANUALS

	044707-1	**IVENS**	Excel 2002: The Complete Referenc	395.00

SQL, SYBASE, INGRES, UNIFY AND OTHER RDBMS

	044746-2	**BUCZEK**	Instant SQL Server 2000 Applications (With CD)	575.00
	463560-3	**COFFMAN**	SQL Server 7: The Complete Reference	395.00
	052850-0	**GROFF**	SQL: The Complete Reference, 2/e (With CD)	495.00
➡	058974-7	**HORN**	MySQL Essential Skills: A Beginner's Guide	395.00
	047383-8	**HOULETTE**	Troubleshooting SQL	295.00
➡	058867-8	**LARSON**	Microsoft SQL Server 2000 Reporting Services	525.00
	463803-3	**PETCOVIC**	SQL Server 7: A Beginner's Guid	275.00
	463809-2	**PYEFINCH**	SQL From the Ground Up	275.00
	043720-3	**SUNDERIC**	SQL Server 2000 Stored Procedure Programming	375.00
➡	058684-5	**VASWANI**	MYSQL: The Complete Reference	495.00

UML

	053140-4	**ROFF**	UML: A Beginner's Guide	295.00

UNIX & LINUX

	053285-0	**DHANJANI**	Hacknotes Linux & Unix Security Portable Referenc	295.00
	054069-1	**HATCH**	Hacking Linux Exposed: Linus Security Secrets & Solutions, 2/e	475.00
	049894-6	**MAXWELL**	UNIX System Administration: A Beginner's Guide	395.00
	044473-0	**MILLER**	LINUX for Windows Addicts	325.00
	053144-7	**MUSTER**	Introduction to Unix and Linux (With 2 CDs)	475.00
	049510-6	**MUSTER**	UNIX: Made Easy, 3/e	395.00
	043567-7	**PETERSEN**	LINUX: Programmer's Reference, 2/e	275.00
	052849-7	**PETERSEN**	LINUX: The Complete Reference, 5/e (With CD)	595.00
➡	058709-4	**PETERSEN**	Red Hat Enterprise Linux & Fedora Edition (With DVD)	695.00
	058262-9	**PETERSEN**	Red Hat Linux: Pocket Administrator	295.00
	463760-6	**ROSEN**	UNIX: The Complete Reference	475.00
	044495-1	**SHAH**	LINUX Administration: A Beginner's Guide, 2/e (With CD)	495.00

VISUAL BASIC MANUALS

	052909-4	**BRADLEY**	Programming in Visual Basic.Net, 4/e (With CD)	395.00
	058154-1	**CAMPBELL**	101 Microsoft Visual Basic.Net Applications	525.00
	058411-7	**CONNELL**	Developing Microsoft .Net Controls with Microsoft Visua Basic .Net	495.00
	463557-3	**CORNELL**	Visual Basic 6: From the Ground Up	325.00
	052919-1	**JAMSA**	Visual Basic.Net: Tips & Techniques	395.00
	463666-9	**JERKE**	Visual Basic 6: The Complete Reference (With CD)	395.00
	048679-4	**KANT**	Visual Basic.Net: A Beginner's Guide	275.00
	058248-3	**MacDONALD**	Microsoft Visual Basic.Net Programmer's Cookbook	595.00
	053303-2	**OLIVER**	Designing Enterprise Applications With Microsoft Visua Basic .Net	395.00
	053305-9	**PETZOLD**	Programming Microsoft Windows with Microsoft Visua Basic .Net	695.00
	053308-3	**RICHTER**	Applied Microsoft .Net Framework Programming in Microsoft Visual Basic.Net	650.00
	054079-9	**ROBINSON**	Security for Microsoft Visual Basic.Net	525.00
	047418-4	**SHAPIRO**	Visual Basic.Net: Developer's Headstart	250.00
	049511-4	**SHAPIRO**	Visual Basic.Net: The Complete Reference	450.00
	048678-6	**SMILEY**	Learn to Program with Visual Basic.Net	295.00

	053311-3	SPENCER, EBERHARD & ALEXANDER	OOP: Building Reusable Components with Microsoft Visual Basic .Net	395.00
	463961-7	WARNER	Teach Yourself Visual Basic 6	235.00

VISUAL STUDIO

	054057-8	JOHNSON	Inside Microsoft Visual Studio.Net Version 2003	525.00

WEB PUBLISHING (WEB DESIGN, ASP)

	041238-3	BEN-NATAN	IBM: Websphere Starter Kit (With CD	495.00
	052888-8	EDDY	Adobe Illustrator 10: The Complete Reference	595.00
	058252-1	POWELL	Web Design: The Complete Reference, 2/e	450.00
	049570-X	SAHLIN	Fireworks MX: The Complete Reference	475.00
	047244-0	ULRICH	Web Design Virtual Classroom (With CD)	425.00
	049918-7	VON SEE	XSLT: Developer's Guide	350.00
	044789-6	WILLARD	Web Design: A Beginner's Guide	375.00

WML

	047265-3	JAMSA	WML & WML Script: A Beginner's Guid	295.00

WORD PROCESSING

	044709-8	WEVERKA	Word 2002: The Complete Referenc	425.00

XML

	044484-6	ARCINIEGAS	XML Developer's Guide (With CD)	475.00
	049936-5	DOURNAEE	XML Security	395.00
	053310-5	ESPOSITO	Applied XML Programming for Microsoft.Net	625.00
	463759-2	FINKELSTEIN	Building Corporate Portals with XML	375.00
	058301-3	FOGGO	Programming Microsoft .Net XML Web Services	695.00
	053309-1	FREEMAN	Microsoft .Net XML Web Services Step by Step	395.00
	049897-0	HILLBORG	Wireless XML Developer's Guide	325.00
	054062-4	MACDONALD	Microsoft .Net Distributed Applications: Integrating XM Web Services and .Net Remoting	595.00
	044740-3	MERCER	XML: A Beginner's Guid	315.00
➡	-	PEARLMA	Programming the Web using XM	In Pre
	054055-1	SHELDON	SQL: A Beginner's Guide, 2/e	375.00
	044725-X	WILLIAMSON	XML: The Complete Reference	550.00

LIBRARY SCIENCE : ADVANCED

	463206-X	JAIN	Marketing Information Products & Services : A Primer	350.00

About the CD

How to Use the *Oracle Database 10g: The Complete Reference* CD-ROM

The CD that accompanies this book contains a special electronic Adobe Acrobat pdf-format edition of *Oracle Database 10g: The Complete Reference*. With this electronic version, you can easily transport all of the valuable information contained in the book onto your PC while the printed version of the book remains in your office or home.

> **Note**: *To view the electronic edition of the book on this CD, you will need the Adobe Acrobat Reader program. If you do not already have it pre-installed on your system, you may locate and launch **rp505enu.exe** from your CD to install.*

Viewing and Navigating the Book

You can easily view and navigate specific areas of interest within the book using the hyperlinked Table of Contents provided.

Viewing

1. Insert the CD-ROM into the CD drive of your computer (if you have not already done so).
2. Locate and launch the file **Book.pdf** from your CD drive. This displays the book's Table of Contents at left of screen and actual book pages at right.

Navigating

1. To view a chapter, click the plus sign to the left of the Part in which the chapter resides. This displays all chapters in selected Part.
2. Click the name of the chapter you want to view (displays first page of chapter at right).
3. To view a section within a chapter, click the plus sign to the left of the chapter name (displays sections of chapter below chapter name), and click the name of the section you want to view.

Searching

1. Choose the Search | Query option from the Edit menu.
2. In the Adobe Acrobat Search dialog box, click Indexes.
3. In the Index Selection dialog box, make sure the box next to "Oracle Database 10g: The Complete Reference" is checked.
4. Click Add.
5. In the Add Index dialog box, highlight "Index.pdx." Click Open.
6. In the Index Selection dialog box, click OK.
7. In the Adobe Acrobat Search dialog box, type in the text for which you want to search.
8. Click Search (initiates the search).
9. In the Search Results dialog box, click the View button. This takes you to the first instance of found text matching the search criteria. Alternatively, you can double-click each occurrence of found text in the Results field to be taken to a specific match.

Using the Code

The tables used in this book are available for you to access and use without retyping! You can use these to easily work your way through the examples and experiment with the many techniques illustrated in this book. Simply locate and open **Tables.txt**. You can freely select, copy, and paste the desired text from this file.

NO TECHNICAL SUPPORT IS PROVIDED WITH THIS CD-ROM.